7/94

COLOR AND CULTURE

Practice and Meaning from Antiquity to Abstraction

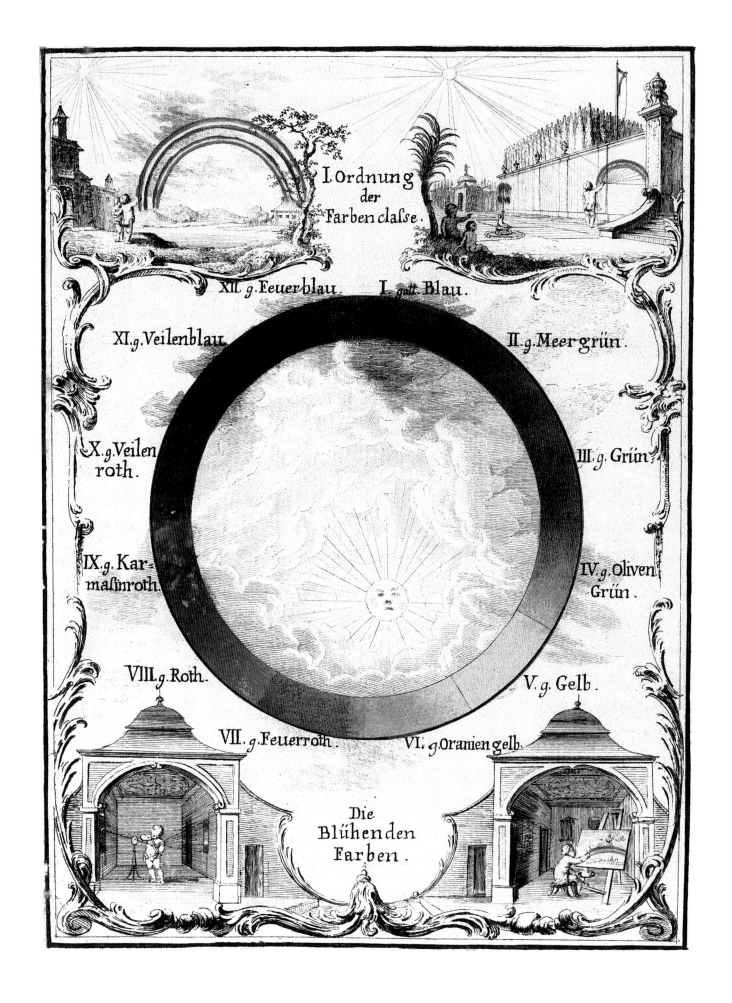

I. Ordnung der Farbenclaſſe.

XII. g. Feuerblau.　I. gatt. Blau.

XI. g. Veilenblau.　II. g. Meergrün.

X. g. Veilenroth.　III. g. Grün.

IX. g. Karmaſinroth.　IV. g. Oliven Grün.

VIII. g. Roth.　V. g. Gelb.

VII. g. Feuerroth.　VI. g. Oranien gelb.

Die Blühenden Farben.

JOHN GAGE

COLOR AND CULTURE

Practice and Meaning
from Antiquity to Abstraction

A Bulfinch Press Book
Little, Brown and Company
Boston · Toronto · London

For Nick and Eva, recalling those Florentine days

FRONTISPIECE

Ignaz Schiffermüller, *The Bright Colors*, from *Versuch eines Farbensystems*,
Vienna 1772. A decorative twelve-part color-circle by an entomologist
who specialized in butterflies, this suggests a "natural" order of colors which
may be experienced both indoors and out. It is one of the first of such circles
to place complementary colors opposite each other: blue (I) opposite
orange (VII/VI), yellow (V) opposite violet (XI), and
red (VIII) opposite sea-green (II).

First North American Edition

ISBN 0-8212-2043-8

Library of Congress Catalog Card Number 93-77614

*Bulfinch Press is an imprint and trademark of
Little, Brown and Company (Inc.)*

*Published simultaneously in Canada by
Little, Brown & Company (Canada) Limited*

PRINTED IN SINGAPORE

CONTENTS

INTRODUCTION

For all its baggage of scholarly apparatus, this is not an academic book. Nor could it be, for its theme – the way in which the societies of Europe and the United States have shaped and developed their experience of colour – falls between too many academic stools. Colour is almost everybody's business but it has rarely been treated in a unified way: thus my book opens and closes with instances of how a failure to look at colour comprehensively has led to absurdities of theory, if not of practice. I begin with the attempt of some nineteenth-century Classical philologists (led by the Liberal statesman Mr Gladstone) to define the nature of the Ancient Greek experience of colour – without consulting Classical archaeologists, so they were led to believe that Greek colour-vision in the fifth century BC was anomalous, even defective, and that our modern visual system had evolved in only a few thousand years. I conclude with an even more astonishing episode in 1960s American art, where a number of fine colourists were able to persuade themselves, their critics and perhaps even some of their public that they had finally released colour from form. This opinion is the more surprising that it was promoted by an artist, Josef Albers, who had had direct experience of the study of the interrelationships between form and colour in the psychologically oriented German art-world of his youth. In other areas of colour-study, there are still some psychologists who believe, for example, that brown is simply a darkened yellow and black no more than an absence of light, beliefs which would have to be modified after a few conversations with practising artists or even after a careful examination of paintings. So, although there are a number of academic areas in which colour is an important topic of investigation and debate, notably the psycho-physics of colour-vision and colorimetry, and linguistics, it is not a subject that has hitherto played much part in the study of Western cultures as a whole – not least perhaps because it has not lent itself easily to academic treatment.

Nor is this book an interdisciplinary study, using one or other of the ways which modern scholars in the humanities have developed to revive their own subjects, in my case the history of art. This is an historical study in the sense that it deals with one thing after another, looks for the origins of the methods and concepts of visual art and treats art as the most vivid surviving manifestation of general attitudes towards colour expressed in visual form. As an historian I am wary of assuming that today's theoretical positions (I am thinking particularly of the notions of experimental psychologists which have filtered into general culture) are likely to survive any longer than those of the past. I see my task as to provide more material for readers to chew on as they think about colour in the context of history and perhaps their own experience of it too. More than other formal characteristics, colour has seemed to most of us to speak directly and unambiguously (a good deal of capital has been made from this assumption, not least in the marketing of goods). I hope my book will make this assumption seem more problematic, but even if it does not, I want my reader to be left not simply with some beautiful images, but also with some stimulating ideas about the visual character of a wide range of societies in the West.

Yet I have not written this study to suggest that if we pool ideas from the various areas of enquiry into colour we shall be able to present a more adequate picture of the role it has played, and can play, in Western societies. I am even less concerned to propose a new academic subject which might draw together the strands of what has hitherto been so dispersed. What interests me is precisely how this fragmentation has come about; what has prevented intelligent and sensitive investigators from coming to a clear understanding of their subject; why so much of what has been written and is still being written about colour cannot be believed. The subject may best be approached from the perspective of history, although the very notion of a history of colour may at first sight seem paradoxical. Why I have ventured into this confusing area, perhaps some autobiography will explain.

As a schoolboy painter I was very much attracted to colour – John Piper was my idol – and when I came to look at the history of art I was puzzled by the neglect of colour in describing and accounting for the styles of historical periods. When I began to read aesthetics, first Berenson and then Ruskin, I was even more astonished by the apparent renunciation of colour in writers to whom it clearly meant so much. Berenson's wonderful account, in *Sketch for a Self-Portrait* (1949), of the first encounter with the 'atmosphere of disembodied colour' in the Upper Church of San Francesco at Assisi showed me that his feeling for colour was not confined to the natural landscape, where he enjoyed it so abundantly, but that he also felt it in art. Yet he did not allow these instincts to override his aesthetic belief that the proper material of visual art was 'tactile values' and 'ideated sensations': hence his preference for Florentine art, especially Florentine drawing.[1] I did not discover until much later how deeply rooted these perceptual prejudices were in the classicizing tradition where representation has been seen as the artist's primary function. Berenson's idealism, his crucial distinction between 'ideated sensations' and 'sensations like those experienced in the workaday world' could only make him hostile to colour. For he saw colour as belonging essentially to this humdrum world, as identifying the artefact as an object among other objects, focusing the attention on its materiality; and he had a very condescending attitude to materials and

46

techniques.[2] It seems to me that it is precisely the continuity between the experience of colour in nature and that experience in art which makes it so important to us, and not only to those who concern themselves with painting.

A more sophisticated thinker than Berenson, Ruskin turned out to have a far more complex relationship with colour. His early reading of Locke had made him regard hue as accidental; he felt that tonal values in colour, which defined form and spatial relationships, were the primary concern of the artist, including even Turner, whose works he had come to know chiefly through black-and-white engravings. Ruskin's growing devotion to Early Italian art in the late 1840s brought about a rapid revision of this position: with the example of Fra Angelico before him he came to believe that 'the purest and most thoughtful minds are those which love colour the most'; and he had fewer inhibitions than Berenson about positing a continuum between art and nature.[3] But even in the 1850s, after a close engagement with ancient and modern Pre-Raphaelites, Ruskin continued to adjudicate in favour of the primacy of form, and he annoyed his co-teacher at the Working Men's College, Dante Gabriel Rossetti, by insisting that a study of colour must come only after a thorough grounding in chiaroscuro. His great practical handbook of 1857 was entitled *The Elements of Drawing*.[4] At the time I did not fully understand the importance of giving as much attention to value (light and dark content) as to hue (spectral location), but I have come to see it more and more, and now agree with Ruskin's assessment of its central interest to Turner.

Berenson and Ruskin set me thinking about hierarchies in colour, but chance encounters in my college library with two other books made me realize that there was far more to colour than meets the eye. One was Paget Toynbee's *Dante Studies* (1902), which included an essay on the obsolete medieval colour-term *perse* whose meaning it seemed almost impossible to reconstruct on the basis of written evidence alone. The other was R. D. Gray's *Goethe the Alchemist* (1952), which persuaded me that colour-theory was not simply a few rules of thumb but a rich amalgam of physical and metaphysical ideas. When at the Council of Europe 'Romantic Movement' exhibition of 1959 I was able to examine Turner's two late paintings *Shade and Darkness – the Evening of the Deluge* and *Light and Colour (Goethe's Theory) – the Morning after the Deluge – Moses writing the Book of Genesis*, I knew that I had found a great painter who thought so too.

Neither Berenson nor Ruskin were historians, although they both knew a good deal of history and both, especially Berenson, devoted more attention to the art of the past than to that of their contemporaries. But they attended to this historical art primarily as critics. My spell as an undergraduate showed me that I was neither a good artist nor a good historian yet that history was to be my absorbing interest: I wanted to identify, isolate and understand sets of circumstances which are inseparable from the past, not to take the critical position of making of the past a sort of honorary present. Yet how art, which is so vividly present to us, can be set in its own (past) 'present' is an issue of the greatest difficulty, one which the most recent approaches to art-historical writing have only been able to accommodate by ignoring. Colour compounds the problem, for in what sense is

the colour which I perceive in an artefact not 'present'? I may recognize from the style of the work that it belongs to a particular time which is not ours but how can I say the same for its colours? Is not red the same whenever and wherever it is seen? To find the historical dimension of colour I had to look at artefacts and at the colour-language of the periods in question; as Paget Toynbee had warned me, this was an exceedingly problematic issue. The study of colour-vocabularies has been one of the most expansive areas of research since the 1960s: we know a good deal about the structure of colour-thinking, as expressed in language, in many hundreds of cultures and yet we know very little about how these structures came to be formed, how they relate to experience. Wittgenstein, for example, assumed that six colour-terms were adequate for most purposes, a figure almost certainly reached because he was thinking of the colour-circle of three 'primaries' and three 'secondaries', as published for instance by Goethe – a recent and rather specialized way of arranging colour-space.[5] Those who cook on gas know that it is the high-energy (short-wave) blue flames which do most of the heating and even those who do not are likely to be aware that it is the even shorter, higher-energy waves, the ultra-violet, which burn our skin. Yet in common usage it is the long-wave red end of the spectrum which is felt as warm and the blue as cool. We may think of a 'universal' experience of hot red (?) sun and cool blue (?) sea but in the written record this folklore seems to go back no further than the eighteenth century; the first colour-system to incorporate co-ordinates of cold and hot was probably the one published by George Field as late as 1835. So what is our 'experience' of colour in this case? Why are our linguistic habits so at odds with our knowledge?[6]

I said earlier that colour is within the experience of almost everyone and that the colours of nature are continuous with the colours of art. But, of course, artists have a special way of seeing colour and a special way of presenting what they see in the form of artefacts. As a schoolboy I went on a summer sketching holiday to Oxfordshire; one dull afternoon at Dorchester I encountered an extraordinary colour-composition of an old red telephone-box isolated on the edge of a wood in which the normally strident contrast of red paint against green foliage was softened and mediated by the 'warm' depths of the dark, tree-filled space behind the box itself. It was a stunning image of unity in contrast and I risked the traffic to make a hasty and unsatisfactory painting of it from the best viewpoint in the middle of the road. Some years later I read Adrian Stokes's *Colour and Form* and was surprised to see a vivid recollection of just such an experience, this time with a red post-box on a telegraph pole. Stokes concluded his long account of it in these terms:

> My experience was unique at that time. How long I had waited to see our glaring pillar boxes given by the light and season a structural relationship in the English countryside! For years they had stood out in my eyes, glaring irrelevantly. On this overcast May day, however, the young leaf-greens of intense luminosity and of the right area and disposition, had come to the rescue, had entered into companionship with the red, and *with each other*, like soldiers who make a solid pile of their (red) hats to prove their amity, the

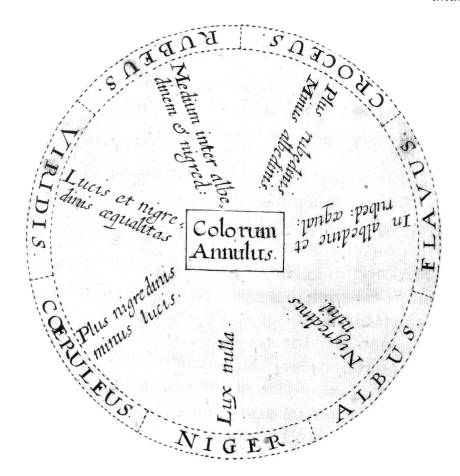

One of the most radical early attempts to reduce colour perceptions to a simple diagram was the physician Robert Fludd's colour circle, published in 1626 (see p. 171). Fludd arranges seven colours in a tonal sequence between white and black, but it will be seen he describes both red (*rubeus*) and green (*viridis*) as the median colour, with equal proportions of light and dark, white and black. (1)

distinctiveness of each as brother. And in my opinion every picture that really 'works', possesses in infinite reduplication this kind of relationship, this kind of *movement*.[7]

This experience of colour was available to many, it was perhaps even commonplace, but it was an aesthetic intent which gave it value. It is in pictures, or when we see in terms of pictures, that these colour-relationships take on a coherence. Hence the central importance of art for the study of colour in the larger social context.

As a student I had the good fortune to spend long periods in Florence and came to love those large painted embellishments to Italian fourteenth- and fifteenth-century choir-books, displayed so spaciously and luminously in the Convent of S. Marco and other Florentine libraries and sacristies. I was astonished that such beautiful objects had been so little regarded in the histories of Italian painting. I imagined that because of their perfect state of preservation they could show us what the pristine colouring of the much damaged and repainted altarpieces and frescoes of the period might have been. As it happened, I never did have the opportunity of pursuing my interest in Renaissance manuscript illumination very far; paradoxically, my only discussions here are of two miniaturists mentioned by Dante (none of whose works are known; *see* Chapter 4) and the disparaging remarks of sixteenth-century critics about this branch of painting (*see* Chapter 7). I was, in any case, quite mistaken about the import of the colour of these works, since the materials and technical conventions of manuscript paintings were quite different from those in work on panel or wall, which also differ markedly from each other. Berenson's belief that materials have almost no role to play in style should hardly have survived his first visit to S. Croce in Florence, where many chapels still furnished with stained glass, wall-painting and altarpieces from the Trecento show quite clearly that the colour-ranges in each of these media have very little in common. Perhaps, after all, his eye was too conditioned by his use of black-and-white photographs. The study of materials (developed for the most part out of the exigences of conservation) has brought a new concreteness to the historical understanding of art. It is important for us to know how an object was made and what it was made of because of the hierachy of values inherent in materials and techniques themselves, even now when synthetic pigments and media have taken over. A precious ultramarine in the fourteenth century had no more of an aesthetic value for its user than a synthetic or industrial paint for an American Colour-Field painter of the 1960s. This sort of analysis seems to be even more important for the historian than for the activity of conservation which provoked it, since the rhetoric of conservation-theory often seems to confuse conservation (preventing further preventable deterioration to the work) with restoration (bringing it back to a notional pristine condition). Only very limited sorts of small portable objects – enamels, illuminated manuscripts, cabinet pictures – are ever likely to be seen in their original condition and in something like their original circumstances, which brings us back to the earlier question of how much of the past can ever be seen at all.

A book which has been more than thirty years in the making can hardly expect to engage closely with the most recent phase in a rapidly evolving subject such as the history of art and I have to admit that some recent developments are hostile to the sort of project I have undertaken here. When I began looking at the history of art, its most controversial branch was iconography, as associated especially with the Warburg Institute in London. This seemed to reduce the 'subject' of painting essentially to written texts. I was fortunate to be taught by Edgar Wind who, although he had been a pupil of Warburg's, continued to approach the question from a far broader base than I had come to expect from that school and who believed that subject must also imply style.

Since that time the influence of E. H. Gombrich and especially Michael Baxandall at the Warburg has brought the formal characteristics of artefacts back into the centre of the discussion of their meaning; it is to their work that I owe much of my own approach. Iconography in its less expansive sense has been revived by the most vital of the newer tendencies in art-historical writing, which has given it a political edge. The New Art History has done a great service in bringing a new seriousness to a subject which might have lost itself in the routine pursuit of influential postures in the figure. However, because it has adopted theoretical tools from writers with no important visual interests, and because the ambiguity of visual images has made them seem poorly adapted to re-cycling as propaganda, there has been a turning away from the visual characteristics of artefacts towards a concern with the sort of representation which may readily be conveyed in verbal terms. It is another version of 'find the text' but this time the text is less likely to be found in historical literature than in social theory or psychoanalysis. But if the visibility of the visual arts is not seen as the proper concern of historians of these arts, the task of treating it will be left in the equally reductive hands of the commodity-fetishists of the media and the market.

Although I have had to deal with a number of controversial points, I do not intend this to be a polemical study, for there is no active debate about colour in Western culture to which my arguments might be usefully related. The neo-formalist German school of 'colouring-history' (*Koloritgeschichte*) is too non-contextual in its emphasis and too exclusively concerned with painting to bear more than tangentially on my own subject.[8] I

want simply to demonstrate that there is a set of issues which needs to be grasped. My list of references, though long, is very lean and intended simply to send the reader to my sources. I do not think a large-scale bibliography of colour is practicable at the moment but I have given an outline of what I would expect it to look like in a bibliographical article.[9]

So this book cannot be an historical survey of colour even from A to A. Such a history does not seem to be possible, although a number of bolder historians have attempted it since the 1960s.[10] What we still need is an overview of the chief landmarks in changing attitudes to colour and we do not yet know even which historical texts bear on the question, since the several useful historical studies of theories of colour, for example, have been concerned rather with the development of new knowledge than with its diffusion and acceptance by the community at large.[11] What I have tried to do is to find surviving types of monument which were the subject of contemporary commentary; for the earlier periods especially, these are very few and far between. I have tried to isolate techniques, such as mosaic and stained glass, drawing or oil-painting, which were clearly responses to particular aesthetic needs and to discuss their transformation as these needs themselves changed. Some chapters focus on these techniques; others look at more theoretical questions, such as the continual re-interpretation of an ancient text on four-colour painting, or the problem of how to see the rainbow, or the function of the palette, or the paradigm of music, all of which recur in many historical periods. Several themes return repeatedly, such as the feeling that verbal language is incapable of defining the experience of colour, or the notion from Antiquity to Matisse of an 'Orient' which was an exciting and dangerous repository of coloured materials and attitudes. These two themes were constantly interrelated in the belief that the rational traditions of Western culture were under threat from insidious non-Western sensuality. Thus as late as the 1940s Berenson was characterizing his experience of medieval stained glass outside its architectural framework as 'not so different from the Rajah's gloating over handfuls of emeralds, rubies and other precious stones'.[12] How artists and thinkers in the West negotiated these dangers is a theme of great interest and one which I hope will make my readers look at the traditions of Western art and psychology in a rather different way.

1 · The Classical Inheritance

Archaeology and philology · Greek theories of colour · Splendour and motion

TOWARDS THE END of the 1860s the Anglo-Dutch painter Lawrence Alma-Tadema exhibited a small picture, *Pheidias and the Frieze of the Parthenon. Athens*, in which the artist is shown, not as the greatest sculptor of Antiquity, but as a painter, putting the finishing touches to the rich polychromy of the relief, the fiery flesh-tones of the horsemen set off against a background of the deepest blue.[1] Alma-Tadema became famous for his careful reconstructions of the Classical past; this early intrusion of a strident colouring precisely where the dazzling purity of white marble had been thought, at least since the Renaissance, to be one of the noblest characteristics of ancient art was not an arbitrary one.[2] For during the first half of the nineteenth century archaeologists throughout Europe and Scandinavia had come to realize more and more that Greek architecture and sculpture had indeed been painted and in the most vigorous way. As early as 1817 the English scholar Sir William Gell had been able to assert of the Greeks that 'no nation ever exhibited a greater passion for gaudy colours'.[3] Even though the discussion of the colouring of the Parthenon Frieze itself had arrived at no very firm conclusions,[4] Alma-Tadema may well have been impressed by the 1862 report of the excavations of the Mausoleum at Halicarnassus in Asia Minor, where the sculpted frieze, attributed to Scopas (fourth century BC), was shown to have been brightly painted just as in his picture, the background ultramarine and the flesh 'dun red'.[5] To demonstrate the practice of colouring sculpture in the greatest period of Greek Classical art was a bold stroke, which would have been unthinkable in the period of high Neo-Classicism fifty years earlier.

Alma-Tadema was perhaps the most daring but he was not the first painter to exploit the archaeological discovery of Greek polychromy. Ingres's 1840 version of *Antiochus and Stratonice* introduced an interior of extraordinary richness, far beyond anything in his original conception of the subject in 1807. It is very likely that he drew on the impressive researches of J. I. Hittorff, whose magnificent study, *De l'Architecture polychrome chez les grecs*, had first appeared in 1830.[6] Many Neo-Classical architects were themselves turning to polychromy in these years; Karl Friedrich Schinkel's design for a new Royal Palace on the Acropolis at Athens, its interiors laden with inlaid and painted decoration, dates from the same year (1834) as Gottfried Semper's proposals for the use of polychromy in modern classical buildings.[7] By the 1840s the last of the English Neo-Classicists, John Gibson, perhaps following Hittorff's suggestions, made a timid attempt to re-introduce polychromy into sculpture itself, first with his portrait of Queen Victoria in 1846 and then, most importantly, with his *Tinted Venus* of 1851–6, shown in London at the 'International Exhibition' of 1862 in a

brightly coloured niche devised by the designer Owen Jones. It bore the inscription *Formas Rerum Obscuras Illustrat Confusus Distinguit Omnes Ornat Colorum Diversitas Sauvis* and *Nec Vita nec Sanitas Nec Pulchritudo Nec Sine Colore Iuventus* ('The gentle variety of colours clarifies the doubtful form of things, distinguishes the confused and decorates everything' and 'Without colour there is neither life nor health, neither beauty nor youth').[8] Nothing could demonstrate more decisively the death of the Renaissance and Neo-Classical aesthetic. The discovery of the pre-Classical remains of Mycenae and Knossos in the latter half of the nineteenth century reinforced the view that the Greek world had always been a highly coloured one.

Yet it is an irony of scholarship that in these very years the Classical philologists who approached the Greek experience of colour from the direction of language were reaching entirely opposite conclusions about its nature. The British statesman W. E. Gladstone, in his essay 'Homer's perceptions and use of colour', concluded that the poet's colour-system was 'founded upon light and upon darkness', that the organ of colour 'was but partially developed among the Greeks of his age' and that it had not developed much further by the time of Aristotle.[9] More detailed research into Greek colour-terminology tended to confirm Gladstone's views; the then only recently investigated phenomenon of colour-blindness was invoked to explain why the Greeks seemed to be so insensitive to the difference between blue and yellow.[10] But blue and yellow were precisely among those colours most frequently used in early Greek painting, and Gladstone's conclusions were soon contested by at least one scholar who had taken the trouble to compare language and artefacts.[11] We know now that language cannot be interpreted as a direct index of perception and that the phenomenon of colour is multivalent: besides the characteristics of hue and saturation, which modern spectators tend to regard as most important, is the characteristic of value, the degree of lightness in a given hue. It was this last characteristic which was of special interest to the ancient Greeks, an interest rooted in the Greek theory of colour.[12]

Greek theories of colour

As we should expect, the earliest written Greek records of colour, in the poetry of Alcmaeon of Croton (early fifth century BC), dwell on the antithesis between black and white, or darkness and light.[13] In the fifth century this antithesis provided the armature of the more developed theories of Empedocles and Democritus. Empedocles used the analogy of the painter's mixing colours (*harmonin mixante*) to illustrate the harmony of

Neo-Classical sculptors were reluctant to follow the discoveries of archaeologists very far. Although it was shown at the London International Exhibition of 1862 under a canopy which stressed the importance of colour (pl. 9), John Gibson's *Tinted Venus* (1851/6) had the colour restricted to hair, lips, eyes and gold ornaments, with only the palest tingeing of the flesh. (2)

the four elements, earth, air, fire and water, among themselves;[14] in an early formulation of the notion that 'like perceives like', he stated that the fiery element in the eye is what perceives white and the watery, black.[15] The late antique commentators on Empedocles, Aëtius and Stobaeus, had it that he followed a Pythagorean scheme of 'primary' colours, adding to black and white red and *ōchron*, a vague term which has been thought to designate a whole range of hues from red through yellow to green and must probably be understood to imply a faded quality in any of them.[16] Stobaeus noted that Empedocles linked his four colours with the four elements, although he did not specify which elements were appropriate to red and *ōchron*.

Democritus also spoke of four 'simple' (*hapla*) colours: white which was a function of smoothness, black which was a function of roughness, red which related to heat and *chlōron* which 'is composed of both the solid and the void'. 'The other colours are derived from these by mixture.'[17] When Democritus came to describe the nature of these mixtures, his formulations are difficult to follow. Gold and copper were mixed from white and red (of some interest when we come to consider the affinities of red and gold); purple (*porphuron*) was mixed from white, black and red – its large proportion of white made it pleasant to look at and could be deduced precisely from its brilliance (*lampron*). But indigo (*isatin*), according to Democritus, was mixed from deep black and a little *chlōron* (pale green); leek-green (*prasinon*) from crimson and indigo, or pale green and a purplish pigment. He added that sulphur is a more brilliant variety of this mixed *prasinon*, which refers aptly to the greenish cast of sulphur-yellow.[18] This must be the earliest recorded proposal that yellow and green are two species of the same genus of hue. Clearly we are dealing with a writer who either had little experience of practical colour-mixing or, as is more likely, used his terms to designate a far wider range of hues than we are accustomed to grouping together. Democritus also stated that *chlōron* might be produced from a mixture of red and white, which has led one commentator to suppose that he was thinking of the complementary after-image of a red patch on a white ground.[19] What is more important is the observation of Aristotle's follower Theophrastus (to whom we owe this account of Democritus's theory), that he need not have expanded his 'simple' colours beyond black and white, and that red and green are not true antitheses, since they do not have opposite 'shapes'[20] (colour being related to different geometric arrangements of atoms).

These theories of Empedocles and Democritus were taken up and developed by Plato and Aristotle in the fourth century and, through them, became the starting-point of all subsequent colour-systems until Newton. Plato's most extensive account occurs in his poem on the creation, in *Timaeus* 67d–68d, where he offered what he called 'a rational theory of colours'. White, said Plato, is the effect of the dilation of the ray which the eye sends out in the process of vision and black the effect of its contraction. A more violent 'fire' and dilation of the ray produces what we call 'dazzle' and an intermediate fire, blood-red. But Plato and his contemporaries had no means of assessing the quantities of light reflected from any coloured surface, nor was any means devised until the nineteenth century, and he concluded this passage with a cry of despair: 'The law of proportion ... according to which the several colours are formed, even if a man knew he would be foolish in telling, for he could not give any necessary reason, nor indeed any tolerable or probable explanation of them.' He none the less listed a number of mixtures, including an *ōchron* composed of white and flame-yellow (*xanthon*), itself a mixture of red, white and *lampron*. Plato's leek-green was a mixture of flame-colour (*purron*) and a darkener (*melan*).[21] He concluded:

> There will be no difficulty in seeing how and by what mixtures the colours derived from these are made according to the rules of probability. He, however, who should attempt to verify all this by experiment would forget the difference of the human and divine nature. For God only has the knowledge and also the power which are able to combine many things into one, and again to resolve the one into many. But no man either is or ever will be able to accomplish either the one or the other operation. [trans. Jowett]

Plato thus passed on the most meagre of colour-systems. Aristotle, with his more developed interest in experiment, produced a far more extensive and ramified body of doctrine, all of it, however, scattered among writings on many other subjects. It was his school of philosophy which left the only comprehensive treatment of colour to have come down to us from Antiquity.

In his treatise *On Sense and Sensible Objects* (442a), Aristotle stated that 'the intermediate colours arise from the mixture of light and dark.'[22] He also identified five unmixed intermediate colours: crimson, violet, leek-green, deep blue and either grey (which he conjectured might be a variety of black) or yellow (which might be classed with white, 'as rich with sweet').

Aristotle seems to be inclined towards a seven-colour scale from black to white here because of its closeness to the musical octave, which had just provided him (439b–440a) with an analogy for the method of generating intermediate colours by numerical ratios. In his account of the rainbow, however (*Meteorology* 372a), he seemed to regard red, green and purple as the only *unmixed* intermediate colours. Green appears elsewhere to be the central intermediate colour between (black) earth and (white) water (*On Plants* 827b; compare *Problems* XXXI, 959a). Red was closest to light and violet to dark (*Metereology* 374b–375a).

The Peripatetic *On Colours* presents few variations on the same theme, although the 'primary' colours here seem to be white (the colour of air, water and earth) and golden (the colour of fire), black becoming simply the colour of the elements in transformation (791a). Here too, in effect, the modification of light by darkness was the cause of the intermediate colours: red was the primary product of such a modification (791b). In

general the picture of the nature of the colours beyond light and dark was as uncertain as Plato's:

> We do not see any of the colours pure as they really are, but all are mixed with others; or if not mixed with any other colour they are mixed with rays of light or with shadows, and so they appear different and not as they are. Consequently things appear different according to whether they are seen in shadow or in sunlight, in a hard or soft light, and according to the angle at which they are seen and in accordance with other differences as well. Those which are seen in the light of the fire or the moon, and by the rays of the lamp differ by reason of the light in each case; and also by the mixture of the colours with each other; for in passing through each other they are coloured; for when light falls on another colour, being again mixed by it, it takes on still another mixture of colour. [793b, trans. Hett]

The admission that these problems in identifying colours was

J.A.D. Ingres, *Antiochus and Stratonice*, a sculptural and monochromic pencil and brown wash study of 1807. (3)

further evidence of the eye's incapacity to judge the true nature of things became enshrined in a tradition of sceptical thought from about the first century AD, when Philo of Alexandria cited an example which was to have a particular resonance in the Middle Ages: 'Have you ever seen a dove's neck changing in the rays of the sun into a thousand different shades of colour? Is it not magenta and deep blue, then fiery and glowing like embers, and again yellow and reddish, and all other kinds of colours, whose very names it is not easy to keep in mind?'[23]

Of course, what to one observer was a subject for despair to another was a cause of great sensual delight. In a brilliant set-piece description of a magnificent hall, the second-century Greek writer Lucian paused to consider the plumage of the peacock, which was also to be much in the mind of medieval commentators:

> Now and again he is a sight still more wonderful, when his colours change under the light, altering a little and turning to a different kind of loveliness. This happens to him chiefly in the circles that he has at the tips of his feathers, each of which is ringed with a rainbow. What was previously bronze has the look of gold when he shifts a little, and what was bright blue [kuanauges] in the sun is bright green [chlōrauges] in shadow, so much does the beauty of the plumage alter with the light. [The Hall 11, trans. Harmon]

The Peripatetic On Colours had insisted that the study of colour should be investigated 'not by blending pigments as painters do' but rather by 'comparing the rays reflected from . . . known colours' (792b). In discussing the rainbow Aristotle had stressed that the basic unmixed colours there were those 'which painters cannot manufacture' (Meteorology 372a). Yet from Empedocles onwards theorists of colour repeatedly drew on the experience of handling colour in art. Democritus is reported to have left treatises both on colour and on painting, neither of which have survived,[24] and Plato, who made frequent references to painting methods, especially in theatrical scene-painting, was thought in Antiquity to have been a painter in his youth.[25] An anonymous, probably Alexandrian Platonist of the sixth-century AD even claimed that the notions of colour-mixing expressed in the Timaeus arose from discussions in Plato's studio.[26] One of the most vivid of Aristotle's accounts of colour-contrast derives from his observation of textile-manufacture; it posed a question which was not addressed systematically until Chevreul took it up in the nineteenth century:

> Bright dyes too show the effect of contrast. In woven and embroidered stuffs the appearance of colours is profoundly affected by their juxtaposition with one another (purple, for instance, appears different on white and on black wool), and also by differences of illumination. Thus embroiderers say they often make mistakes in their colours when they work by lamplight, and use the wrong ones. [Meteorology 375a, trans. Webster]

This is a remarkably clear formulation of the problem now known as metamerism, by which colours that appear to match under one sort of light, seem different under another.

Records of a number of technical treatises by Classical artists have also come down to us but nothing of their contents.[27] The most intriguing are perhaps On Symmetry and On Colours (volumina . . . de symmetria et coloribus) attributed by the Elder Pliny to the mid-fourth-century BC painter and sculptor Euphranor (Natural History XXXV, xl, 128). Pliny's reference to volumes in the plural suggests that they were distinct treatises, but he may well have been dividing what had been a single concept in the earlier Greek discussion of colour. In the Meno (76d) Plato had defined colour itself, in terms which he had borrowed from Empedocles, as effluences from the surfaces of objects 'fitted' into the channels of sight in the eye by the process of perception: colour was itself a form of 'measuring together' (summetros) or symmetry.[28] Pliny may have been inclined to separate these concepts because, as a sculptor, Euphranor had a high reputation for his expertise in symmetry (usurpasse symmetriam). It was as a sculptural concept, the canon of proportions in the human figure, that the term came to have most resonance in the later Classical period. By Pliny's own day the Stoics had treated symmetry and colour as the two essential, but quite distinct, ingredients of beauty. This formulation, transmitted especially by Cicero, had the greatest impact on medieval aesthetics.[29]

Symmetry was a concept based on number: proportion could only function as a numerical relationship between a number of parts. With the exception of Aristotle's rather vague and random attempt to relate colours to the musical octave, there was in Antiquity no attempt to interpret colours in terms of number. Plotinus, a Greek philosopher living in Rome in the third century AD, excluded colour from the category of Beauty precisely on these grounds: 'All the loveliness of colour, and even the light of the sun, being devoid of parts and so not beautiful by symmetry, must be ruled out of the realm of beauty. And how comes gold to be a beautiful thing? And lightning by night, and the stars, why are these so fair?'[30] He was echoing the attitudes of his master, Plato, and, I suggest, of Euphranor. No painting attributable to Euphranor has survived but a Roman reference of the first century AD to his Poseidon at Athens talks of its 'most extraordinary splendour'.[31] It was this splendour, or brilliance in colour, understood as the effect of reflected light, which constituted its chief charm for the ancient observer.

Other Classical writers refer to the beauty of colour: Democritus talks rather obscurely of a 'most beautiful colour' (kalliston chrōma) composed of green, white and red, 'but the green component must be small, for any admixture would not comport with the union of white with red'.[32] In a well-known passage of the Philebus (53b) Plato referred to the intrinsic beauty of simple colours on the analogy of simple geometrical shapes; but he did not say which he understood these simple colours to be. Elsewhere, for example in the Republic (421c-d), he supported the conventional Classical preference for purple as the most beautiful colour, also endorsed by Aristotle in his discussion of colours and music.

The relationship of these theoretical ideas to the practice of Classical painters is very difficult to assess since almost no specimens of painting of the Classical period, with the exception of vase-painting, have come down to us. There are, however, some indications that the techniques of monumental painters were well understood by the theorists. One of Aristotle's hypotheses about the origin of the intermediate colours was that:

> the black and white appear the one through the medium of the other, giving an effect like that sometimes produced by painters overlaying a less vivid upon a more vivid colour, as when they desire to represent an object appearing under water or enveloped in a haze, and like that produced by the sun, which in itself appears white, but takes a crimson hue when seen through a fog or a cloud of smoke [*On Sense and Sensible Objects* 440a, trans. Beare]

The use of a semi-transparent white scumble in mural painting is known at least as early as 1400 BC at Knossos and a black under-layer has been noticed in the fifth-century BC Etruscan wall-paintings at Tarquinia, which may be by a Greek artist.[33] Much later, at Pompeii, the use of a black, pink, brown or grey underpainting for red had become standard in the most important schemes. Pliny, who died at Pompeii in the volcanic eruption of AD 79, described a number of red and blue undercoats used to achieve the most brilliant effects with the cheapest purple pigment (*Natural History* XXXV, xxvi. 45).[34] He also left the most important record of what may be a reflection of theory in painterly practice: the four-colour palette confined to black, white, red and yellow, which was attributed to the fifth-century painter Apelles and his contemporaries (*see* Chapter 2). Pliny's account, which was essentially a complaint about the florid painting of his own day, falls into a familiar Roman rhetorical pattern: painting is now thought worthless, he says, if it is not executed in a multitude of costly and exotic pigments. In another passage (*Natural History* XXXV, xil, 30), he indicated that these *floridi* colours were supplied by the patron and not by the artist, which suggests not simply their cost but also that they represented the taste of the consumer rather than that of the producer. The Roman architect Vitruvius also remarked on this practice in the late first-century BC (*Ten Books on Architecture* VII, 7–8). The theme of the decadence of modern extravagance was a common one in these years: Seneca, for example, contrasted the simplicity of the baths at Scipio's villa with the modern taste:

> But who in these days could bear to bathe in such a fashion? We think ourselves poor and mean if our walls are not resplendent with large and costly mirrors, if our marbles from Alexandria are not set off by mosaics of Numidian stone [*Crustis Numidicis*], if their borders are not faced over on all sides with complicated patterns, arranged in many colours like paintings, if our vaulted ceilings are not buried in glass [mosaic] [*nisi vitro absconditur camera*] [*Epistles* LXXXVI, 6f, trans. Gummere]

The reference to Egypt and Numidia is a crucial one, as is the reference to Indian colours in Pliny's complaint (*see* p. 39), for it was essential that the decadence should have an exotic, an oriental origin. Pliny's contemporary the Latin poet Petronius was already stigmatizing China and Arabia as the source of that luxury which was undermining Roman taste (*Satyricon* II, 88 and 119). It was an extension into art of the old controversy between the Attic and the Asian in rhetoric, where Attic stood for simplicity and directness and Asian for a soft and over-ornamented style.[35] In rhetoric itself the term *colores* came as early as Seneca in the first century to mean the embellishment

and amplification of the essential structure or material of an argument.[36] In the history of visual colour it is important that the materials which provided the basis of sensual delight should have been seen to come into Europe from the East, for this is a *topos* which recurs throughout this book.

For critics throughout Antiquity colour in painting had a profoundly ambiguous status: on the one hand it stood for the adventitious, the merely decorative, the false,[37] but on the other it was what gave painting life and truth. The antithesis was already clear in Aristotle who wrote in the *Poetics* (1450a–b) that 'the chalk outline of a portrait will give more pleasure than the most beautiful colours laid on confusedly'. Plato, on the other hand, spoke of 'a portrait which is as yet an outline sketch and does not represent the original clearly because it has still to be painted in colours properly balanced with one another' (*Statesman* 277b–c). For both philosophers the aim of art was the imitation of nature; colour might either further or hinder this aim. Even Philostratus, the novelist of the second to third century AD, who moved beyond imitation to a notion of the intuitive imagination in art,[38] contrasted the colours of cosmetics with the colours of painting, whose function was to imitate: 'if that was not its business, it would not be considered absurd, a pointless mixing of colours'. But, he continued, colours were not even essential to imitation, since verisimilitude could be achieved in monochrome if the drawing was good: 'If we draw one of these Indians even with a white chalk, he will obviously seem black; the snub nose, fuzzy hair, large jaws and (so to speak) bulging eyes have a black effect on the thing seen.'[39] Plutarch, in the first century AD, summed up the Classical attitude in a brilliant paradox:

> Just as in pictures, colour is more stimulating than line-drawing, because it is life-like, and creates an illusion, so in poetry falsehood combined with plausibility is more striking, and gives more satisfaction, than the work which is elaborate in metre and diction, but devoid of myth and fiction . [*Moralia* 16c, trans. Babitt]

The emphasis on the imitative function, which at the same time confers a decorative attractiveness, can be seen at work in late Hellenistic polychromy, such as a painted sarcophagus from Sidon, which has both naturalistic colouring and a decorative use of gilding.[40]

For the ancient critics colour, if not positively damaging, was at least not essential to representational painting: it has been argued that the ethos of Hellenistic art was seen to reside less in the use of colour than in a command of line.[41] In a period when execution was already considered to be inferior to conception, it was even suggested that 'a precise mixture of colours and appropriateness in the application of them' were matters best left by the master to his apprentices.[42] Such a view will not have been welcomed in the workshop itself but we are still very ill-informed about the details of ancient practice. One of the rare representations of an ancient painter at work, on a painted sarcophagus of the first century AD from Kertsch in South Russia, shows a paintbox with sixteen divisions. Even the painters of the small funeral-stelai at Volos are known to have used a palette of thirteen pigments, including two whites and three blacks as well as blue and green.[43] At Pompeii some twenty-nine different pigments have been identified, including ten reds, although the contemporary Roman murals from nearby Boscotrecase used a very limited palette of five pigments (including an earth green), whose range was somewhat increased by mixing.[44] An account of painting procedures given in the second century AD by Julius Pollux lists twelve colours, including flesh-tints (*andreikelon*) in an arrangement which seems quite arbitrary(*Onomasticon* VII, 129). As he was writing essentially for connoisseurs of rhetoric, we can learn rather little about practical attitudes to colour from this sort of lexical compilation.

Splendour and motion

For all their conventionality, the complaints of Pliny and Vitruvius about the extravagant polychromy of later Roman painting do reflect a development in taste which is attested by both monuments and Roman literature at large. We have seen that polychromy was by no means foreign to Classical Greece: one of the rare surviving documents of the economics of Greek taste concerns the interior decoration of the Asclepeion at Epidauros (4th century BC), where the expenditure for labour on wood inlay and the gilded ivory statue of the god was – excluding the precious materials themselves – two and a half times that on the colonnade of the temple and more than ten times the annual salary of the architect.[45] The fashion for encrusting walls with thin panels of coloured marble can certainly be traced to sixth-century Greece – the earliest example may be the Siphnian Treasury at Delphi, where now all traces of the marble itself have vanished – but it was used more widely in Rome after the first century BC.[46] Clearly, the Romans made far more use of the coloured marbles of Greece than the Greeks themselves had ever done.[47] A development of this sort may be seen most readily perhaps in the sequence of Roman mosaic pavements, from the simpler four-colour mosaics made from black, white, red and yellow pebbles or stone from the third century BC (Morgantina, Serra Orlando in Sicily), through the gradual introduction of coloured glasses – especially for bright reds, blues and greens in the second century BC (Pergamon) – to the chromatic splendour of the glass mosaics at Pompeii and Herculaneum or the first-century AD mosaic now in the museum at Corinth, where the most vivid blues, greens, yellows and red are woven into the geometric border.[48] In the Latin language, too, a decisive expansion of colour-terminology has been noted in the late first century AD, when the meagre list of five words for hues in Homer's poems had now expanded to over seventy terms, including some sixteen terms for reds, eight for blues and ten for greens.[49] Artistic practice and public perceptions of colour may indeed have gone hand in hand.

Yet we should not leap to the conclusion that a tonal outlook had been replaced by a chromatic one. If we look at Roman descriptions of their sumptuous buildings, we find that they are still seen primarily in terms of light, of brilliance, of splendour. The Roman poet Lucretius, for example, writing in the first century BC, praised the simple life: 'But what matter if there are no golden images of youths about the house, holding flaming torches in their right hands to illumine banquets prolonged into the night? What matter if the hall does not

sparkle with silver and gleam with gold, and no carved and gilded rafters ring to the music of the lute?' [*On the Nature of the Universe* II, 59–63, trans. Latham], He may have been drawing his images from that *locus classicus* of architectural description, Homer's account of the Palace of Alcinous (*Odyssey* VI, 82–130), but he was using it in a didactic poem and in a section where, following Democritus and Epicurus, he was anxious to demonstrate the physical unreality of colour.[50]

If we look at the techniques of painting and mosaic developed by the Romans, the emphasis can be seen to have been no less on lustre than these descriptions suggest. The painted walls of Pompeii and Boscotrecase were burnished until they shone like mirrors;[51] the pavements of Pergamon and Morgantina were ground smooth, waxed and polished not only to bring out the colour (as is now done by dousing them with water) but also to produce a highly reflective surface.[52] The effect to be achieved was surely akin to that which Pliny attributed to the thin coat of dark varnish used by Apelles to finish his paintings that 'caused a radiance in the brightness [*repercussum claritatis*] of all the colours and protected the painting from dust and dirt', and, 'by using a calculated system of lighting', acted so that 'the brightness of the colours would not be offensive to those who looked on them (it would be as if they were looking through transparent mica) and this same device, from a distance, might give an austere quality to colours which were too bright'.[53] An effect of at once enhancing and subduing the colours on a surface according to the changing angle of vision of a moving spectator is exactly what polishing will achieve. Apelles was indeed accustomed to working in the context of architecture: his celebrated paintings of the Venus Anadyomene were originally destined for the sumptuously polychromed temple at Kos.[54]

As Pliny's account of Apelles suggests, the Romans were highly sensitive to the effects of lighting on pictures: Vitruvius, for example, prescribed a north light for museums so that the lighting should be more constant.[55] A concern for sheen or lustre in coloured objects and in painting was also exemplified in late-antique colour-preferences, at least in those preferences which can be attributed with some confidence to that period.[56] The most obviously prized hue was purple, the most valuable dystuff in Antiquity. Purple dye made from a number of species of shellfish had been developed among the civilizations of Asia Minor and in Mycenaean Greece since the fifteenth century BC; already in the seventh century it was noticed by the lyric poet Alcman as being especially admired.[57]

That Greek sculpture was coloured came as a shock to the early Victorians, but by the 1860s the archaeological evidence was too strong to be resisted. Alma-Tadema, in a painting showing the fifth-century Athenians viewing the Parthenon frieze before the scaffolding was taken down, imagined the reliefs painted in strong, schematic colours that would make the bodies stand out in the distance.

4 SIR LAWRENCE ALMA-TADEMA, *Pheidias and the Frieze of the Parthenon, Athens*, 1868/9 (detail)

5

6

Mixing and matching

The range of colours used by Greek and Roman artists was certainly not limited to four (white, black, red and yellow), as was once believed. A panel from Saqqâra (**7**) is virtually the only known painting from the classical period which is so restricted. Works from all centuries, early (**5**) and late (**6**), show many colours, including bright blue. On a papyrus fragment from Antinoë, however (**6**), the blue-grey of the central charioteers may have been made from black. Pigments were rarely mixed on the palette, but where necessary the same effect was achieved by hatching (**8**).

5 Tomb of the Diver, Paestum, fifth century BC (detail)
6 Six charioteers, papyrus fragment from Antinoë, *c.* AD 500
7 Fragment of painted panel from Saqqâra, fourth century BC
8 Mummy-portrait from el-Fayum, Egypt, fourth century AD

7

8

Greek colouring restored

FORMAS RERVM OBSCVRAS ILLVSTRAT CONFVSAS DISTINGVIT OMNES ORNAT COLORVM DIVRSITAS SVAVIS

NEC VITA NEC SANITAS NEC PVLCHRITVDO NEC SINE COLORE IVVENTVS

9

Early in the nineteenth century the idea that Greek architecture and sculpture was pure white had to be given up. Ingres, greatest of French Neo-Classical painters, represented Greek interiors as vividly polychromed (**10**). His friend the French archaeologist and architect Hittorff published coloured reconstructions of Greek buildings (**11**) and imitated them in his own. Owen Jones in 1862 designed a temple (**9**) to house Gibson's famous *Tinted Venus* (pl. 2) carrying a series of inscriptions proclaiming the importance of colour for life and health, beauty and youth.

9 OWEN JONES, *Design for a temple to house Gibson's 'Tinted Venus'*, 1862
10 JEAN AUGUSTE DOMINIQUE INGRES, *Antiochus and Stratonice*, 1834/40
11 JAKOB IGNAZ HITTORFF, The Temple of Empedocles at Selinunte, from *Restitution du Temple d'Empèdocle à Selinunte, ou Architecture polychrome chez les Grecs*, 1851

The legendary Apelles

Apelles was the most famous painter in
Antiquity. None of his works survived, but it
became popular to paint reconstructions of
them based on written descriptions. Titian's
Venus Anadyomene (**13**) recreates one of his
paintings that was damaged at the bottom.
Tiepolo (**12**) shows a scene from his life, when
he was commissioned to paint Alexander the
Great's mistress Campaspe and fell in love
with her himself, upon which Alexander
generously surrendered her to him. The report
that Apelles used a four-colour palette seems
not to have interested either artist, for Titian's
sea is blue-green, and Tiepolo, naturally,
shows Apelles painting from a well-stocked
eighteenth-century palette such as he used
himself.

12 GIOVANNI BATTISTA TIEPOLO, *Alexander and
Campaspe in the Studio of Apelles, c.* 1736/7
13 TITIAN, *Venus Anadyomene (The Bridgewater
Venus), c.* 1520/5

Although the finds in the Royal Tomb of Philip II at Vergina (Thessaly, fourth century BC) include remnants of purple cloth spangled with gold-star medallions, purple was not apparently a royal prerogative until Roman times, when it came to be the object of a special cult. Pliny wrote of

> that precious colour which gleams [*sublucens*] with the hue of a dark rose . . . This is the purple for which the Roman *fasces* and axes clear a way. It is the badge of noble youth; it distinguishes the senator from the knight; it is called in to appease the gods. It brightens [*illuminat*] every garment, and shares with gold the glory of the triumph. For these reasons we must pardon the mad desire for purple, but why the high prices for the conchylian colour, a dye with an offensive smell and a hue which is dull and greenish, like an angry sea [*color austerus in glauco et irascenti similis mari*]? [*Natural History* IX, xxxvi, 126, Bailey]

As Pliny suggests, purple was a colour reserved for the highest officers in the state: in the form of a purple and gold robe, it could only be worn by a general in his triumph. Senators might wear broad stripes of purple round the openings of their tunics, and knights and other high-ranking officials narrower stripes. Cicero and other first-century writers had spoken of 'royal purple'[58] and by the time of Diocletian (early fourth century AD) it had come to be associated exclusively with the emperor. For anyone else to wear purple was tantamount to their plotting against the state. The ownership of any purple-dyed cloak or any cloth dyed with the finest purple or even an imitation of it incurred severe penalties, although by the fifth century there was widespread evasion and a lively black-market in purple cloth.[59]

The reasons for this cult of purple are very difficult to define. According to Theophrastus, Democritus had referred to a purple (*porphurios*) which was a mixture of white, black and red: red in the largest proportion, black in the smallest and white as intermediate between the two. 'That black and red are present is clear to the eye; its clarity [*phaneron*] and lustre [*lampron*] testify to the presence of white, for white produces such effects.'[60] The very names for purple in the earliest Mycenean and Homeric Greek texts seem to have had the secondary connotation of movement and change, which may perhaps be accounted for by the many colour-changes in the dyeing process but which is also of course the condition required for the perception of lustre itself.[61] The fourth-century BC poet Menander described a textile made of interwoven purple and white threads, which shimmered according to the fall of light, an effect akin perhaps to that of the shot stuffs of late Antiquity (*see* Chapter 3).[62] Two and a half centuries after Menander Lucretius wrote of 'the

---

Red, as the colour of light, was an important element of the interiors of Roman religious buildings. This wall at Pompeii would certainly have been polished, as well as painted, to enhance its brilliance. Coloured illustrations of these magnificent interiors became available to the public in the early 1830s, almost a century after the excavations.

14 CHARLES FRANÇOIS MAZOIS, Reconstruction of a wall, 'Edifice' of Eumachia, Pompeii, from *Les Ruines de Pompei*, 1829

bright sheen of purple robes' (*On the Nature of the Universe* II, 58). The beauty of purple was also attributed to its surface lustre by Pliny and Philostratus, who in his *Pictures* (I, 28) noted, 'though it seems to be dark, it gains a peculiar beauty from the sun, and is infused with the brilliancy of the sun's warmth'. Pliny's characterization of the many nuances of purple in his *Natural History* is, as usual, the fullest. Of the Tyrian purple made from *murex* he wrote, as we saw, that 'it brightens every garment' and although he claimed that a frankly red [*rubeus*] colour was inferior to one tinged with black (XI, xxxviii, 134), he went on to describe precisely how this blackness was achieved. Distinguishing between two types of shellfish yielding dyestuff, the small *buccinum* (? *purpura haemastroma*) and the *purpura* (*murex brandaris*), he explained (IX, xxviii, 134–5):

> The buccine dye is considered unsuitable for use by itself, for it does not give a fast colour, but it is perfectly fixed by the pelagian [*purpura*], and it lends to the black hue of the latter that severity [*austeritatem*] and crimson-like sheen which is in fashion [*nitoremque qui quaeritur cocci*]. The Tyrian colour is obtained by first steeping the wool in a raw and unheated vat of pelagian extract and then transferring it to one of buccine. It is most appreciated when it is the colour of clotted blood, dark by reflected and brilliant by transmitted light [*colore sanguinis concreti, nigricans adspectu, idemque suspectu refulgens*]. [trans. Bailey]

In a later chapter (IX, xxxix, 138), he noted that a paler shade of purple was fashionable in his own time.

Certainly true double-dyed Tyrian purple, like gold, had great rarity value for it was very uneconomical to produce, and the Phoenicians kept the secret of its manufacture for many centuries.[63] It was also a particularly durable colour: when Alexander the Great brought back his booty from the Persian campaign he found that a large quantity of Greek purple cloth had kept its sheen and freshness for nearly two centuries.[64] This durability made emperors like Diocletian and Constantine use it for burial shrouds.[65] In the process of dyeing with *murex*, several colours were produced at various stages, including yellow, blue and red, as well as the blue-green which is presumably the colour Pliny viewed with such distaste; we might have expected that these hues would have been equally prized.[66] 'Green purple' was indeed used in Byzantium to distinguish the curators of the Imperial court.[67] That these colours were far less important than purple must surely be attributed to the symbolic value of purple as a heavenly colour, a value which has been traced at least as far back as the early fifth century BC in a ceiling at Chiusi.[68] It was heavenly precisely because it was a bearer of light.

The most valued purple cloth was probably the deepest double-dyed variety, such as in Theodora's imperial robe at Ravenna,[69] yet we have seen from Pliny and many. other writers that it was the brilliance and lustre of the colour that was most noticed; it may well have been that, like Apelles's dark varnish, it was the miracle of purple to incorporate within itself darkness and light and hence the whole world of colour. Pliny's rather rudimentary test for the best purple must have been much in demand in late Antiquity and in Byzantium, for the identification of true purple (used exclusively by the Imperial family) in the face of the many imitations necessarily had the

34

force of law, whose breach might incur the penalty of death. The many edicts of the Emperors Gratian, Valentinian, Theodosius and Justinian suggest that this was a persistant problem. Their wording, which referred to the dyestuff (*sacri murici*, sacred whelks, or *triti conchylii*, crushed shellfish) rather than the hue, which is called *purpura* throughout, is an early instance of the recourse to clearly identifiable materials rather than uncertain appearances, as a criterion for judgment.[70] The legal codex of Ulpian (third century) went so far as to define *purpura* as all red materials except those which contained the other red animal dyestuff *coccum*, made from the insect *coccus illicus*.[71]

34
14
31–2

But if 'purple' could include so many colours, how could it bear the important meanings which it undoubtedly attracted in late Antiquity? It could do so first of all because it was a colour generally classed with red,[72] the chromatic representative of fire and of light. Red had, since the earliest times and in many cultures, heralded the divine.[73] It was used in Ancient Greece as a colour to sanctify weddings and funerals and as a military colour in both Greece and Rome to strike awe into the enemy. Before the fifth century, Greek funerary stelai had red-painted grounds (see the purplish-red grounds of some Hellenistic stelai at Volos), although these grounds later became blue. The interiors of some temples were painted red, such as the Temple of Aphaia on Aegina. Philostratus in his *Life of Apollonius of Tyana* reported a shrine of the sun at Taxila in India where, 'The walls of the shrine were of a red stone that had a golden sheen, giving off a light like the sun's rays' (II, 24). The Temple of Isis at Pompeii had red walls, and the background of the initiation scenes in the Villa of the Mysteries in the same town was probably red for the same sacred reason. Some red-painted statues of Roman gods are also known. Red was widely regarded as the colour of the sun; some Greek rites used red and white interchangeably in a solar context: a late third-century AD mosaic of Helios in the museum at Sparta shows the god with a reddish nimbus emitting reddish-yellow, red and white rays.[74]

Thus red also had a particular affinity with gold, that other supremely imperial 'colour' in Antiquity and early medieval times.[75] It was an affinity that affected the methods of both mosaic and panel-painting (*see* Chapter 3). Aristotle placed red next to light in his colour-scale, which must be emphasized here precisely because it returns us, through purple, to our primary concern with light.

For if the nature and identity of particular hues was a matter of uncertainty in the Greaco-Roman world, there was no doubt about the place of light. Light and life were cognate concepts;[76] to be alive was to see the light of the sun.[77] A touching epitaph on a late fifth-century BC tombstone in the Kerameikos in Athens, which shows a woman with her grandchild, reads: 'I am holding here the child of my daughter, the beloved, whom I held in my lap when, alive, we beheld the light of the sun, and now I am holding it dead, as I am myself dead.' Zeus, the chief of the gods, was the personification of the sky, as the source of brightness and of day. From Mycenaean times light was a sign of the epiphany of the god; even statues of gods, like the Palladium, could blind mortals. Hence perhaps the frequency of the subject of the rape of the Palladium on Antique gems, since gems themselves were repositories of light.[78] Dio Chrysostom

(*Orations* XII, 25.52) described Pheidias's gold and ivory statue of Zeus at Olympia as emanating light and grace: it was a radiant omen (*phasma lamprou*). The nimbus or halo of light became an attribute of divinity and appears on many statues from the time of Alexander the Great.[79]

Yet it was not until late Antiquity that light began to take on a transcendental colouring in the West. Greece was exceptional among ancient cultures in having no developed cult of sun and moon gods, nor a prominent place for sun and moon legends in its mythology: such cults, notably those of ancient Egypt, were regarded by the Greeks as barbaric. Then, in the second century AD, two Hellenized orientals, Julian the Chaldaean and his son Julian the Theurgist, published a number of oracles which brought light to the centre of late antique religion. In these oracles the sun was the hub of the cosmos and the element in which the supreme God revealed himself. The sun had purificatory and cathartic powers and its rays descended to earth to lift the soul of the initiate towards itself.[80] The magic practices of Theurgy which derived from these Chaldaean Oracles were in vogue until the fifth century. Among them was the conjuring of the God by a spirit-medium; this manifestation was, too, frequently accompanied by a shaped or more often a formless luminosity.[81]

The most distinguished contemporary discussion of these ideas occurs in the *Enneads* of Plotinus. His connection with the Theurgists has been hotly disputed but he certainly shared many concepts and images with them.[82] Plotinus is of particular interest because he was the most important thinker about light and colour in late Antiquity and, like his masters Plato and Aristotle, he showed a lively interest in the theory if not the practice of the arts. He was a religious philosopher chiefly concerned to explore the nature of the soul and the modes of its unification with the Supreme One. The One he repeatedly described as light and specifically as the sun (V, 3.12, 17) precisely because for Plotinus light in itself was a perfect image of oneness, of wholeness. He used this image in a beautiful passage describing the union of the soul with the One:

> Here, we put aside all the learning; disciplined to this pitch, established in beauty, the quester holds knowledge still of the ground he rests on, but, suddenly, swept beyond it all by the very crest of the wave of Intellect surging beneath, he is lifted and sees, never knowing how; the vision floods the eyes with light, but it is not a light showing some other object, the light is itself the vision. No longer is there thing seen and light to show it, no longer Intellect and object of Intellection; this is the very radiance that brought both Intellect and Intellectual object into being for the latter use, and allowed them to occupy the quester's mind. With this he himself becomes identical, with that radiance whose Act is to engender Intellectual-Principle . . . [VI, 7.36, trans. MacKenna]

Beauty, too, is identified by Plotinus with the One and with Light; for a moment, as we saw, he seems to accept the beautiful 'simple' colours of Plato's *Philebus*, 'devoid of parts' (although all Plotinus's examples are lights rather than colours: gold, lightning, fire, the stars) (I, 6.3): 'The beauty of colour is also the outcome of a Unification: it derives from shape, from the conquest of the darkness inherent in matter by the pouring-in of light, the unembodied, which is a Rational-Principle and an

Ideal-Form'. More often Plotinus regarded colours as modes of light alone (II, 4.5), engendered by the reflection of light (IV, 4.29) or the effect of light acting on matter (IV, 5.7). In talking of painting, he allowed that colour must be apportioned according to the function of each of the various parts (II, 2.11): 'people . . . ignorant of painting . . . complain that the colours are not beautiful everywhere in the picture: but the Artist has laid on the appropriate tint to every spot.'

Plotinus was especially sensitive to the subjective manifestations of colour (V, 5.7):

> The eye is not wholly dependent upon an outside and alien light; there is an earlier light within itself, a more brilliant, which it sees sometimes in a momentary flash. At night in the darkness a gleam leaps from within the eye: or again we make no effort to see anything; the eyelids close; yet a light flashes before us; or we rub the eye and it sees the light it contains. This is sight without the act, but it is the truest seeing, for it sees light whereas its other objects were the lit, not the light . . .

He had perhaps been impressed by Aristotle's observation that after gazing at the sun colours are produced in the eye even after it is closed, the sequence beginning with white and ending with black (*On Dreams* 459b). These subjective phenomena of colour were of special interest from the second century onwards and they prepare us for the more extreme subjectivity of art and theory in the early Middle Ages.[83] Plotinus's aesthetic thought was transmitted to the Middle Ages in the *Hexaemaron* of St Basil the Great (II, vii, 9f) but whether it had much effect on medieval aesthetics may be doubted.[84] Certainly his close identification of colour with light met with little favour in later centuries, which found the Peripatetic concern to distinguish them (*On Colours* 793b) more sympathetic.

Yet the ancient tradition of interpreting the values of colours according as they more or less embodied light was a very persistent one. Pliny's characterization of Tyrian purple was well known to the Middle Ages. Descriptions of the amethyst by Isidore of Seville, Bede and Marbode of Rennes related this stone, whose colour Pliny had compared to the finest purple stuffs (*Natural History* IX, xxviii, 135), to the hue of a dark rose,

as he had done (*nigrantis rosae colore sublucens*, IX, xxxvi, 126). This comparison may itself derive from a Greek source, since a version of it appears in Greek in some eighth- or ninth-century treatises, the Lucca MS and the *Mappae Clavicula*.[85] The stress on lustre which is such a feature of the Roman accounts of purple also emerges from some late Antique Greek technical literature, as well as from that of the medieval West. The Stockholm Papyrus of the late third or early fourth century AD includes three recipes for dying purple with substitute dyestuffs, which refer to lustre; one of them is prefaced by an admonition to 'keep this a secret matter because the purple has an extremely beautiful lustre'.[86] In the eleventh century the craftsman known as the Anonymous Bernensis claimed in a discussion of egg-tempera that his preparation would give a shine to red that was 'almost the effect of the most prized purple'. Isidore of Seville's derivation of the word *purpura* from *puritate lucis*, 'purity of light', had a long life in Western thought until the Renaissance.[87]

No less than the Ancients, medieval spectators found it difficult to isolate purple among a whole range of reds; they, too, sought to anchor their perceptions in materials rather than hues. Like the late-medieval terms 'scarlet' and 'perse' (*see* Chapter 5), 'purple' in the early medieval West came to designate not a hue but a thick quality of probably silk cloth, which might be of almost any colour, including white and green.[88] This confusion is rather engagingly exemplified in one of the mosaics in the fourteenth-century Church of Christ in Chora (now the Karije Djami) in Istanbul: in the scene of Mary's choice of coloured threads to weave into the curtain of the Temple (*see* Chapter 7), the skein of purple, clearly labelled *porphurion*, is rendered by the mosaicist in a bright vermilion red.[89]

Thus Greek and Roman Antiquity passed down to its posterity a set of assumptions about colour which were modified only slowly and which gave far more prominence to the value of light and shade than they gave to hue. Yet modified they were, and we can trace the nature of this modification if we focus on the posthumous fortune of the most famous of ancient artists, the painter Apelles.

35

Mosaic pavement border, Corinth, first century AD. This pavement was probably the earliest to be made entirely of glass cubes – a great luxury, but more significantly, inaugurating a much wider range of bright colours than had been available in stone. (15)

2 · The Fortunes of Apelles

The four-colour theory · The problem of mixture · Apelles in the Renaissance
Dürer and Titian · The idea of the primaries · Apelles in the studio

IN CONTRAST to the generally ambiguous notions about hues handed down to posterity by the ancient world is the story, formulated most clearly in Pliny's *Natural History*, that some of the best painters of Classical times had made use of a very deliberately limited palette:

> Four colours only – white from Milos, Attic yellow, red from Sinope on the Black Sea, and the black called *atramentum*– were used by Apelles, Aëtion, Melanthius and Nikomachus in their immortal works; illustrious artists, a single one of whose pictures the wealth of a city would hardly suffice to buy, while now that even purple clothes our walls, and India contributes the ooze of her rivers and the blood of dragons and of elephants, no famous picture is painted. We must believe that when the painters' equipment was less complete, the results were in every respect better, for . . . we are alive only to the worth of the materials and not to the genius of the artist.[1]

Pliny's account not only records the precise nature of the four colours but also attributes their use to four named painters, first of all to Apelles, who was born *c.* 370 BC and flourished in the 320s. He was the most famous of all ancient artists, in spite of the fact that none of his works had survived even until Pliny's day.[2] Nevertheless, Pliny and the other ancient writers on art were able to pass on anecdotes about Apelles's extraordinarily successful career and – most unusually – about his style. We have already encountered the story of his remarkable dark varnish, also called *atramentum*, like the black of the four-colour palette; another told of his virtuoso performance as a draughtsman, when he was able to outshine Protogenes with his supremely fine line.[3] Apelles was clearly one of those rare Greek artists whose works could be vividly imagined.

All subsequent discussions of the four-colour palette stem from Pliny or Cicero (*Brutus* 50) and perhaps the most recent is in V. J. Bruno's *Form and Colour in Greek Painting* (1977), where the palette is exemplified in painted tombs at Lefkadia in Greece and Kazanlak in Bulgaria, which date from the late fourth or early third centuries BC, thus slightly later than Apelles. Bruno has sought to establish the plausibility of Pliny's story by relating it to the pre-Socratic ideas of the four 'basic' colours of the four elements and by explaining the rather surprising absence of blue in the four-colour palette on the grounds that black pigments may be made to appear blue and that there was,

indeed, an overlap in the Greek terms for black and blue.[4] Whether or not Pliny in the first century was aware of the philosophical arguments relating colours to elements, and chose his four pigments according to those arguments, there is little reason to think that they were ever in the minds of the fourth-century BC painters. Empedocles, the earliest philosopher to whom a four-colour theory of the elements was attributed, makes no reference to it in the surviving fragments of his writings; his use of the term 'polychrome' (*polychroa* [*sic*]) to refer to the painter's palette in Fragment 23 suggests that he was not aware of any restriction of colours in workshop practice.[5] Neither Aëtius nor Stobaeus give details of the four colours they attribute to Empedocles's theory of the elements.[6] The earliest text to name four colours as basic was, as we have seen, the *On Sense* of Theophrastus, who was, as it happens, a near-contemporary of the painters named by Pliny: he reported that Democritus in the late fifth century had argued that these 'simple' colours were white, black, red and green.[7] Theophrastus did not suggest that Democritus had related these colours to the elements; in the *On Colours* (which may also be his work[8]) earth, air and water were all, as we saw, related to white and yellow to fire. It was not until the first or second centuries AD, in Aëtius (*Epitome of Physical Opinions* I, 15.8), in Galen (*On the Elements from the Hippocratic Opinions* I, 2) and in the pseudo-Aristotelian *On the World* (396b), that there seems to have been any agreement that there were four basic colours related to the four elements, and that these were black, white, red and yellow.

Perhaps the most promising rationale for the four-colour theory of Pliny is offered by the Hippocratic doctrine of the four humours, which were thought to express themselves in the colours of the human complexion. For Apelles had a high reputation as a painter of flesh (Plutarch, *Alexander* 4 and Lucian, *Pictures* 7) and he had inherited an older Greek tradition in painting which had represented differences in gender by lighter or darker skin.[9] A gifted portraitist such as Apelles might well have been expected to amplify this repertory. Some later commentators on the four-colour palette did relate it specifically to the painting of skin.

The medical school of Hippocrates, who was a slightly older contemporary of Apelles, had argued that man is made up of four 'humours': blood (red), phlegm (white) and yellow and black bile, which in a perfectly balanced mixture (*krēsios*) made up a perfectly balanced organism.[10] Yet in the corpus of Hippocratic writings we do not find this doctrine applied to the colour of flesh. It was certainly applied to the four diagnostic colours of the tongue (*Epidemics* VI, 5.8) but it was not until Galen in the second century AD that it was extended to the complexion and hence became available to painters of the

Nicoletto Rosex, *Apelles*, *c.* 1507/15. The most famous painter of ancient Greece contemplates a board bearing four geometrical shapes, perhaps the graphic equivalents of the four elements, the four seasons, and the four colours of his palette. (16)

figure.[11] Nor do the ancient writers on physiognomics take up this doctrine, although they were much concerned with the colour of the complexion as an index of personality.[12] More important, there is very little indication of the use of such colouring in the most impressive body of ancient portrait-painting, the tempera or encaustic mummy-effigies of Roman Egypt, which employ a similarly restricted palette for flesh.[13] Most of them were painted about the time that Galen's interpretations of Hippocratic doctrine were spreading throughout the Roman world.

8

In other examples of Greek painting the absence of blue in the palette attributed to the four-colour artists continues to be a serious problem. The argument, revived by Bruno, that *atramentum* may have been a blue-black pigment which, mixed with white or used as a semi-transparent glaze, can be made to appear blue, is convincing in itself but it hardly applies to the history of the Greek palette as we know it. As we saw in Chapter 1, there were many blue pigments in use from Mycenaean to Hellenistic times; they were not blue-black but bright, saturated blues made for the most part from the Egyptian blue frit called *kuanos* in Greek and *caeruleum* in Latin.[14] It is blues of this sort that we see in the Bronze Age wall-paintings of Thera and Knossos, at Mycenae and Vergina as well as in the sixth-century tombs at Kizilbel in Lycia, the fifth-century Tomb of the Diver near Paestum and in the fourth-to-third-century paintings of Lefkadia and Kazanlak.[15] This is also the type of blue used in the fourth-century Kertsch-style ceramics which have been associated with the style of Apelles himself.[16] Hellenistic works which have been regarded as copies of paintings by Apelles or other four-colour painters, such as the *Alexander Keraunophon* and the 'Alexander mosaic' from Pompeii, also make use of a range of blues and greens.[17] A fragment of panel-painting from Saqqâra in Egypt appears to use a four-colour palette; it is particularly interesting in relation to Apelles since Pliny stated that he painted almost exclusively on panel. This fragment, from a portable shrine, is painted in white, black, red and yellow ochre and their mixtures grey and pink. There is no blue.[18] It is certainly not impossible that this small provincial work might reflect the most advanced aesthetic of its period, but it hardly seems to be enough to outweigh the improbable notion that a group of artists (and their patrons) should have abandoned the use of a beautiful and familiar pigment on purely aesthetic grounds, and that this voluntary restraint should have found no echo in the practice of their followers in late Antiquity.

5

7

The key both to Pliny's account of the four-colour painters and to the later interpretations of Apelles's practice is surely aesthetic choice: as suggested in Chapter 1, Pliny was above all concerned to show that the simplicity of the Ancients was preferable to the modern proliferation of gaudy and expensive materials. Like Cicero, he was giving an historical justification to a familiar Roman critical theme, the complaint against modern, exotic taste also voiced by Vitruvius, Seneca, Varro and Petronius.[19] So anxious was Pliny to establish the virtuous sobriety of his Classical artists that he fell into a serious inconsistency in his various accounts of Apelles's practice. The four colours he listed so precisely are all in the category of *colores austeri*, as opposed to the *colores floridi* he attacked (*Natural History* XXXV, xii, 30). In a passage on early monochrome painting (XXXIII, xxix, 117), Pliny also accounted for the abandonment of the florid colours cinnabar and minium in favour of the austere ochres *rubrica* and *sinopis*, on the grounds that the former were considered by later artists to be too vivid. But in his account of Apelles's dark varnish (*see* p. 16), he claimed that one effect of this substance was to tone down florid colours (*nimis floridis coloribus austeritatem occulte daret*): just that class of pigments which he had earlier suggested Apelles had been careful to avoid.[20] It may well be that Pliny's Greek sources distinguished various phases in this painter's career, in which he first used florid colours under a dark toning varnish and later a restricted palette of austere colours – the sort of development which we know in the careers of Dürer or Titian or Rembrandt. However this may have been, it seems clear that Pliny was prepared to sacrifice historical consistency in order to promote a Roman ideal of *austeritas*. He may have been thinking, for example, of the four-colour palette used by the white-ground Greek *lekuthoi* painters of the fifth century BC; but his theory seems to owe more to the general notion of the irreducible number of 'simple' colours current in his own time.

The problem of mixture

One of the most persistent arguments for the authenticity of the four-colour theory is that the small number of basic pigment-colours could have been substantially expanded by intermixture: one eighteenth-century scholar calculated that these four colours alone could yield 819 variations.[21] It is an argument which would have much to recommend it if it could be shown that mixing was a usual procedure among Classical painters and if it were not for a body of ancient opinion which condemned it. In Fragment 23, Empedocles compared the mixture of the elements in the material world with the painter's blending (*mixante*) of pigments in their preparation of temple-offerings;[22] in a discussion of the mixing-bowl mentioned by Herodotus (*History* 1.25), Plutarch spoke of 'pigments ground together, losing their own colour in the process', mentioning especially mixtures of red and yellow ochre and of black and white (*Moralia* 436bc). But elsewhere Plutarch voiced the painter's strongest objection to mixtures: 'Mixing produces conflict, conflict produces change, and putrefaction is a kind of change. This is why painters call a blending of colours a deflowering [*phthora*: Aristotle's term for a 'passing away'] and Homer [*Iliad* IV, 141] calls dyeing "tainting"; and common usage regards "the unmixed and pure as virgin and undefiled".'[23]

Portraiture is perhaps the context in which we should expect to find mixtures for the painting of flesh, for here the problems of matching tints in nature with colouring materials must soon have been apparent. Plato refers the mixture of several colours specifically to flesh-painting (*Cratylus* 424e).[24] Both here and in the encyclopaedia of Julius Pollux a flesh-tint is given a special term: *andreikelon* (*Onomasticon* VII, 129). Yet there is some reason to think that even flesh-tints were sought in an unmixed state: in his discussion of red-ochre (*miltos*), Theophrastus stated that it was found naturally in many different nuances, 'hence painters use it for flesh tints'.[25]

As Plutarch's remark suggests, there was a lively discussion about the nature of mixture in Antiquity: was it, as the

Platonists and Peripatetics held, that only the qualities of substances were truly mixed, while the substances themselves remained in some looser form of association; or was it, as the Stoics maintained, that the substances were themselves fused together and hence destroyed? The crucial question was whether the process was reversible, whether the compound could be reduced again to its elements. Composition by juxtaposition (*sunthesis, parathesis* or *mixis*) was reversible; fusion (*sunchusis*) was not, for it led to the destruction (*phthora*) of the elements.[26] Aristotle (*On Generation and Corruption* 328a) distinguished two types of mixture as homogeneous physical mixture and purely perceptual 'optical' mixture. The latter notion was attributed to Democritus the atomist by Aristotle's commentator Alexander of Aphrodisias in the third century AD.[27] Plutarch's record of studio-language suggests that painters deplored fusion and the less drastic optical method was indeed a part of ancient technique: the building-up of tones by superimposed hatchings, rather than by tones established and mixed beforehand, can be seen both in the wall-paintings of Pompeii and in the rarer examples of tempera-painting on panel, such as a mummy-portrait dating from the fourth century AD.[28] Another form of 'optical' mixture practised in Egypt and Classical Greece was the glazing of a transparent colour over an opaque one, a method noticed by both Aristotle (*On Sense* 440a) and Pliny (*Natural History* XXXV, xxvi, 45).[29] Here, too, the mixture was easily resolvable into its component parts, as we can see from the frequent flaking of the upper layers.

Apelles was known in Antiquity as a painter in wax encaustic (Statius, *Silvae* I. 1, 100; Lucian, *Pictures* 23), which was the ancient method that approximates most closely to modern painterly techniques of mixing, especially in the painting of flesh. In the mummy-portraits of Hawara and el-Fayum and in the Early Christian encaustic icons of Sinai, we often have a sense of a more spontaneous blending and working-together of tones on the panel itself, which reminds us of the oil-painters of sixteenth-century Venice and sometimes even of Rembrandt.[30] Pollux's account of painting methods, although it lists thirteen colours, places particular emphasis on mixing and seems to refer chiefly to encaustic: the term *mixai* is applied to wax and four terms are listed in connection with the mixture of colours: *kerasai, mixai, symmixai* and *syncheai*.[31] Yet even the most painterly of the mummy-portraits, such as a second-century *Priest of the Sun* from Hawara, show an extensive use of hatchings to model the flesh.[32] Also, the palette of the encaustic painter as given by Pliny and Pollux was far from restricted, suggesting that in any case mixtures were not much in demand.[33] Encaustic was one of the few ancient techniques to have survived unmodified into the Middle Ages: it is documented in the ninth century in Byzantium and the group of sixth- and seventh-century encaustic icons in the monastery of St Catherine on Mount Sinai is among the most impressive monuments of Early Christian painting.[34] Yet in the fourth century, Gregory of Nyssa, one of the most widely read Greek Fathers, who must have been especially familiar with this technique, compared the soul to the painter precisely because both could separate the already mixed into its constituent parts; his analogy referred to the 'elemental' colours of the four-colour painters – black, white, red and yellow.[35]

Perhaps the most telling indication that mixtures were not common in ancient times is the absence of a tool for making them, namely the palette.[36] Another is the extraordinary ignorance of the principles and effects of mixtures which seems to have prevailed among the educated. It has been well argued by Bruno that the difficult passage on mixture in Plato's *Timaeus* (*see* p. 12) can be made to yield a perfectly cogent meaning if the colour-terms are correctly understood but Plato deliberately discouraged investigation.[37] None of the mixtures he listed was, strictly, inter-chromatic: all were made with 'lighteners' or 'darkeners', elements with which Greek scientists felt themselves to be rather more at home. In the second century AD Aulus Gellius reported an interesting discussion between the philosopher Favorinus and the ex-consul Fronto on the subject of Greek and Latin colour-terms, which reveals the prevailing uncertainties about basic colours and mixtures. Following Democritus, the simple colours were taken to be red (*rufus*) and green. *Fulvus* (classified as a type of red) was a mixture of red and green and *flavus* (also taken by Fronto to be a red), of red, green and white.[38] Both *fulvus* and *flavus* seem to us to be varieties of yellow, only to be mixed from red and green by an additive, optical process such as was hinted at by Aristotle in his account of the rainbow (*Meteorology* 347a, 7–8).[39] Gellius has no reference at all to blue and the discussion does not suggest that a knowledge derived from the practical experience of colour-mixing was current in his day. A century later, an account of the rainbow by Alexander of Aphrodisias also suggests that mixture was not the usual procedure among painters. Aristotle had claimed that it was impossible for painters to represent the phenomenon since, although they did some mixing, no mixtures could produce the rainbow-colours red, green or violet. In his commentary on this passage Alexander considerably extended the argument:

> That the ... colours of the rainbow can neither be procured nor imitated by painters, and that red [*phoinikoun, puniceus*] is closer to white than green [*prasinon, prasinus*] and violet [*halourgon, halurgus*] is clear from the following. The natural red pigments are cinnabar [*kinnabari*] and dragon's blood [*drakontion*] which are made from the blood of animals;[40] red is also made from a mixture [*mixis*] of talc [*koupholithos*] and purple [*porphuron, purpureum*], but this is much inferior to the natural colours. Natural green [*prasinon*] and violet are *chrysocolla* and *ostrum*, the one made from blood and the other sea-purple.[41] But the artificial colours cannot match them: green is indeed made from blue [*kuanon*] and yellow [*ōchron*], but violet from blue and red, for the contrasting energies of blue and yellow make green, but those of blue and red, violet. And in these cases the artificial colours are far inferior to the natural ... That red is closer to white than green and violet is evident from their origin. For red is made from talc, which is white, but green from ochre, which is a weaker white, for a [gradually] darkened light appears first to be changed into this colour, thus red is closer than green to white ... But again [it is clear] that green is closer than violet to white, since the former is made from yellow, but violet from red ... and yellow is closer than red to white ...[42]

From this account, which seems to be the earliest attempt to establish a value-scale between white and black, it appears that although painters sometimes mixed cheaper substitutes for natural pigments, they did not, so far as Alexander knew, attempt to match the colours of nature with mixtures on the palette.

The *Attic Nights* of Gellius and Alexander's commentary on Aristotle's *Meteorology* were both familiar texts in the Middle Ages and the Renaissance, when they were often reprinted. Their rather loose classification of hues and their uncertainty about mixtures may well have contributed to the delay in the development of notions of primary colours until well into the sixteenth century.

Apelles in the Renaissance

The reputation of Apelles was kept alive during the Middle Ages in biographies of artists and popular stories, but it was not until the fifteenth century that the nature of his art became a widespread topic of discussion. The competition with Protogenes to draw the finest line attracted the attention of the artists and theorists Alberti and Ghiberti in Florence; Apelles's painting *Calumny*, the subject of a famous description by Lucian, became a favourite topic both in literature and in art.[43] The first portrait of him in his professional role seems to be a print by the north Italian engraver Nicoletto Rosex, produced in the early sixteenth century.[44] Rosex presented the artist in a romantic landscape setting as a silent poet, alluding to the celebrated dictum attributed to Simonides that painting is silent poetry. Apelles contemplates a board bearing geometrical figures, which is resting against the base of twin broken columns, the emblem of strength, and perhaps an allusion to Apelles's famous power over princes.[45]

Perhaps the most surprising feature of this portrait is the object of Apelles's meditation. It recalls that remarkable joint 'picture' by Apelles and Protogenes, the three lines, which Pliny recorded as having survived at Rome until the time of the Caesars: 'and among the numerous works by excellent painters it was like a blank [*inani similem*], and it was precisely this that lent it surpassing attraction and renown' (*Natural History* XXXV, xxxvi, 83). The architect's square resting at the foot of the panel and the callipers depicted on the base of the ruined monument suggest that the artist is primarily a geometer, as he had been presented in Ghiberti's first *Commentary* where the competition with Protogenes had been interpreted as a competition in perspective.[46] But if Apelles was simply a geometer, the inclusion on his panel of the lowest of the four figures, the octagon, is puzzling, for the three 'primary' figures of the circle, the triangle and the square were usually considered in the Renaissance to be a sufficient symbol of the whole of plane geometry.[47] On the other hand, if we regard the figures of Apelles's diagram to be symbolic of solids – the sphere, the pyramid, the cube and the octahedron – we fall into another numerical difficulty, for the doctrine of the primary bodies attributed in late Antiquity of Pythagoras and much discussed in north Italy around 1500 involved a series of five regular solids: the pyramid, the cube, the octahedron, the icosahedron and the dodecahedron.[48] The absence of the sphere is especially striking but Aëtius had characterized the dodecahedron as 'the sphere of all', an idea repeated by Luca Pacioli in his *De Divina Proportione* (*On Divine Proportion*) published in Venice in 1509.[49]

A different series, of *four* geometrical solids, had been established by Plato in his discussion of the structure of the elements (*Timaeus* 52d ff) and elaborated by Theon of Smyrna early in the second century AD.[50] According to this view, all the elements were based on a combination of triangles, descending in complexity from the most rarified, fire (pyramid), through air (octahedron) and water (icosahedron) to the densest, earth, a cube composed of forty-eight triangles surrounded by six equilateral pentagons. If Rosex intended to refer to this scheme of solids and elements, why, by including a circle, did he allude to the sphere, which had no direct part in it? According to the Platonic doctrine, the circle in Apelles's diagram should correspond to the icosahedron, for the pyramid, the cube and the octahedron are clearly symbolized in his other plane figures. The icosahedron, constructed from twenty equilateral triangles, is not a solid that can be reduced to an easily legible plane figure. Pacioli treated it as the most comprehensive solid, with the exception of the dodecahedron (*De Divina Proportione* XLVI), and showed that it could circumscribe even the dodecahedron itself (XXXIX). He amplified Plato's discussion of water in the *Timaeus* by suggesting that the very large number of surfaces in this figure had led the philosopher to think 'that it suited the sphere more readily because of its downward rather than upward motion when scattered', i.e. that this figure was indeed closely related to the sphere.[50] If Rosex was following the Platonic schema, and if he expected his public to identify the circle with the icosahedron and with water and the other three figures with the other elements, it seems entirely likely that he felt this to be appropriate to the subject of his print precisely because of Apelles's reputation as a four-colour painter, and because of the association between the four colours and the four elements that had been such a commonplace since late Antiquity.

Rosex's engraving is not coloured, however, and the reading of his four shapes as colours is not as straightforward as it might first seem. None of the ancient commentators related specific colours to specific elements, except for the author of *On Colours*, who named only two colours, yellow and white. On the other hand, the Democritan view that the elements were not themselves coloured – that colour was only a secondary quality of matter – persisted well into the Middle Ages.[52] The earliest writer to allocate different colours to the elements seems to have been the second-century AD Athenian astrologer Antiochos who, like Theon of Smyrna, drew up an elaborate table of correspondences in which black was the colour of earth, red of air, white of water and yellow of fire.[53] There is no reason to think that this four-colour scheme (the same as that of the four-colour painters) was known in the fifteenth century. When Alberti came to relate colours to the elements in his treatise on painting, his correspondences were quite different because he did not regard black and white as basic colours at all. For him, red corresponded to fire, blue to air, green to water and ash-colour (*cinereum*) to earth.[54] Rosex's contemporary Leonardo da Vinci rehabilitated black and white as 'simple' colours, 'for painters cannot do without them', but he identified the elements with four colours between them: his equivalents were Alberti's, except that where Alberti had excluded yellow and introduced green, Leonardo allocated yellow to earth.[55]

Thus, seen in the light of contemporary north Italian theory, the diagram in Rosex's engraving would read, from the top:

Circle–icosahedron–water–green
Triangle–pyramid–fire–red
Square–cube–earth–yellow
Octagon–octahedron–air–blue

But this would be to assume the universal acceptance of the Platonic equivalents, which was clearly not the case. Leonardo, for example, disputed the identification of the cube with earth; for him the pyramid was the more stable body, for it had fewer surfaces than the cube and was thus a more appropriate symbol of earthly stability.[56]

6   The question is further complicated by the survival into the Renaissance of another four-colour scheme, derived from the late-antique symbolism of the imperial horse-races. Here the association was chiefly with the four seasons, which Alberti introduced into his treatise on architecture as green for spring, red for summer, white for autumn and dark (*fuscus*) for winter.[57] The late-antique and Byzantine authors who had dicussed the question in relation to the Imperial Circus, notably Tertullian, Cassiodorus and Corippus, had not followed this scheme. They all agreed with Alberti about spring and summer but Tertullian and Corippus assigned blue to autumn and white to winter, and Cassiodorus the reverse.[58] Theon of Smyrna had proposed:

Spring–pyramid [i.e. fire–red]
Summer-octahedron [i.e. air–blue]
Autumn–icosahedron [i.e. water–green]
Winter–cube [i.e. earth–yellow]

and Antiochus of Athens:

Spring–red
Summer–yellow
Autumn–black
Winter–white

Thus around 1500 we are presented with a number of arbitrary and conflicting options for linking 'basic' colours to 'basic' forms. No clear reasons for preferring one colour to another had yet emerged, probably because there was still remarkably little interest in that aspect of colour now regarded as the most important one, namely hue.[59] It seems clear that, if Rosex's
16   portrait of Apelles was understood to refer to the four-colour palette, his public would have been hard put to it to identify which shapes these colours were, even with the help of Pliny's story.

Dürer and Titian

Apelles's fame made his the most appropriate name to invoke in a learned compliment to a modern artist and it was frequently used in the Middle Ages, sometimes in the most unlikely places.[60] (Pacioli's references to Leonardo's art as surpassing those of Apelles and the sculptors Myron and Polyclitus fall into this purely adulatory category.[61]) The growing interest in the imagined formal qualities and subject-matter of Apelles's work during the fifteenth century may lead us to expect more critical

and more concrete allusions to him in the High Renaissance, especially in contexts where painters and scholars were becoming more interdependent in their treatment of the Classical past. Two painters of the sixteenth century closely associated with humanist scholarship were Dürer, whose Classical interests were for a time remarkably close to those of Erasmus, and Titian, whose circle in the middle years of the century included a number of scholars and polymaths working for the Venetian publishing houses of Giolito and Marcolini. Both artists were compared to Apelles more persistently than any before them, and in both cases it was their mastery of colour which seems chiefly to have invited the comparison.

Dürer and Erasmus at first cultivated their interest in Apelles independently of each other. The painter had been described as *altero Apelle* by the humanist Conrad Celtis as early as 1500.[62] A few years later Dürer was using the loss of all the ancient writings on art, including those of Apelles (Pliny, *Natural History* XXXV, xxxvi, 79) as a stimulus to compiling his own treatise on painting, most of which was itself never to be published.[63] Thus it was Apelles the theorist who seems chiefly to have concerned the painter; for the humanist Erasmus, on the other hand, it was Apelles the satirist: in 1506 he had edited Lucian's *Slander*, the only early source of information about the *Calumny* of Apelles, and in response to the bitter attacks on his first edition of the New Testament ten years later, he employed Ambrosius Holbein to cut a version of this subject for the title-page of the second edition.[64] Erasmus and Dürer met in The Netherlands in 1520, when the painter took the scholar's likeness twice. For Erasmus he soon became *nostrum Apellem*.[65] But it was at the end of the painter's life that Erasmus made his most telling comparison between Dürer and Apelles: he introduced into his *Dialogue on the Proper Pronunciation of Latin and Greek* (1528) a passage on Dürer's prints in which he claimed that the painter was able to achieve with a single colour what Apelles had only been able to achieve with several, 'albeit few'.[66] It was astonishing that, whereas the Greek painter had been supreme through his use of these few colours, the German was supreme in his day without the benefit of any save black. Erasmus could here have been reflecting his friend's view of the virtues of a restricted palette: Philipp Melancthon recalled how the painter had told him he had abandoned in old age the complexity and vivid colouring of his early work (*floridas et maxime varias picturas*) in favour of greater simplicity; Dürer's only surviving discussion of colour, a note on drapery-painting of about 1512/3, presumably part of his projected treatise on painting, already emphasized the chromatic simplicity of relief as opposed to the complexities demanded by the rendering of shot materials.[67] But that Erasmus did not think of the colours in this sense, and that he did not refer to them either in his notes to Pliny's *Natural History* (which he published in 1516) or in the introduction to the new edition of 1525, where he re-told the story of Apelles's damaged *Venus*,[68] suggests that the four-colour palette was of no interest to him and that it had no special significance for Dürer either.

Could Pliny's story have been of any direct concern to painters when the significance and even the identity of the four colours remained so obscure? Certainly in the seventeenth century it was suggested that the story found a sympathetic echo among earlier painters in Venice, especially with Titian. In his life of Giorgione the seventeenth-century writer Carlo Ridolfi was anxious to show that this painter was the first to employ an extensive range of mixtures for the more perfect imitation of nature, particularly for flesh,

> which was imitated by Giorgio with a few colours [*tinte*] adequate to the subject he undertook to express, which procedure was also followed (if we are to believe their writers) among the ancients, by the illustrious painters Apelles, Aëtion, Melanthius and Nikomachos, who used no more than four colours [*colori*] to constitute flesh tints.[69]

Modern analysis of Giorgione's flesh-painting has certainly shown an avoidance of 'florid' pigments and it is particularly interesting that Ridolfi confined the restricted palette to this area.[70] It was as a flesh-painter, too, that he regarded Titian as the closest follower of Giorgione, although he was equally certain of Titian's special interest in blue, which in combination with red in drapery 'never interferes with the figures'.[71] Another seventeenth-century Venetian commentator, Marco Boschini, cited Titian's preference for a palette limited to black, white and red in underpainting, which may also refer to the preparation of flesh areas.[72] Titian's personal interest in Apelles can hardly be doubted: his three-quarter-length *Bridgewater Venus* was clearly inspired by the story of Appelles's *Venus Anadyomene*, whose lower portion was damaged (Pliny XXXV, xxxvi, 91),[73] but even in this picture Titian did not avoid the use of blue outside the areas of flesh.

13

It became a commonplace to link the names of Titian and Apelles in that large body of Venetian art-criticism which grew up about the middle of the sixteenth century in the writings of Pietro Aretino, Anton Francesco Doni and Lodovico Dolce. All were in direct contact with the painter and all show a knowledge of the life of Apelles as told by Pliny.[74] In several letters between 1540 and 1548, including one to Titian himself, Aretino compared the painter to Apelles but, although it was Titian's colour which chiefly aroused his admiration, he nowhere mentioned the four-colour story as an example of his mastery.[75] Doni, in his dialogue on painting of 1549, made a comparison between Apelles and Titian as physiognomists and, although he showed a particular interest in pigments (especially their capacity to render flesh), he, too, made no reference to Pliny's story.[76] Perhaps the most striking evidence of the lack of interest in the four-colour story in Titian's *ambiente* is offered by Dolce, who was one of the most prolific *poligrafi* working for Giolito and one of the most vigorous supporters of Titian, whose work he praised particularly in the dialogue *L'Aretino*, published by Giolito in 1557. Here Dolce professed a special liking for the brownish softness in flesh-tints he attributed to Apelles who, he said, had particularly cultivated brown; surprisingly, he did not go on to associate this sombre tonality with a restricted palette.[77] Dolce was familiar with Pliny's story in its most modern form: in 1565 he published *Dialogo . . . nel quale si ragiona della qualità, diversità e proprietà de i colori*, much of which is taken direct from Pliny but also from the *Libellus de Coloribus* of Anthonius Thylesius, first published in Venice in 1528. Thylesius had linked Pliny's account of the 'florid' and 'austere' colours to the four-colour palette, a passage Dolce

reproduced in his own version.[78] He amplified Thylesius's protest that he wrote as a philologist, not as a philosopher or a painter, by claiming that the painter's view belonged to the 'divine Titian',[79] but again he made no attempt to suggest that Titian was working according to four-colour principles. If the four-colour theory had enjoyed any currency at all among Venetian painters from the 1540s to the 1560s, we may be sure that scholar-journalists such as Aretino, Doni and Dolce, avid for copy, would have made the most of it.[80]

Even in the latter half of the sixteenth century, when Pliny's story had come to be examined more closely in the light of painterly practice, its significance for the interpretation of Titian's methods did not seem to be very great. The volume on painting in a remarkable illustrated catalogue (*On the Pictures placed in Andrea Vendramin's Museum*) compiled for the Venetian collector Andrea Vendramin in the 1620s, which includes reproductions of many works attributed to Giorgione and Titian, has a Latin preface extracted from the *Gallus Romae Hospes* (1585, 1609) of Louis de Montjosieu (Demontiosius). Montjosieu's work, reprinted several times in the seventeenth century under the title *Commentarius de Pictura*, includes one of the most important early discussions of the four-colour palette (*see* p.35); here I want to notice that although the surrounding matter on the history of ancient painting is reproduced by Vendramin's cataloguer the analysis of the four-colour theory is not.[81] Clearly it was of no interest to him and it is very likely that as late as the 1620s it had not been associated with Venetian technique. Ridolfi's linking of the limited palette to Giorgione in 1648 was, like Pliny's own account, part of a polemic against the garishness of modern painting, particularly against the flesh-tints of 'grey, orange and blue' which he had noticed among 'some moderns', by whom he probably intended Federico Barocci and Rubens.[82] There is little reason to suppose that the sombre palette was ever an issue with the earlier Venetian painters themselves, who would have found the exclusion of blue difficult to accept. It is an irony of history that, through the work of philologists such as Montjosieu in the late sixteenth century, blue had become firmly established as a component of the four-colour palette and that this palette could be at the centre of the development of the modern system of 'primary' colours.

The idea of the primaries

Closely related to the question of colour mixture is that of the irreducible number of colours needed to re-constitute the whole range of visible hues, a question we generally take for granted but which even nineteenth-century colour theory did not settle, proposing as it did different numbers and sets of primary colours according to whether colour was seen from the point of view of the physicist, the psychologist or the painter.[82] The early history of the idea of the primaries is complex: it seems clear that the very late development of the modern subtractive triad of red, yellow and blue, in the context of painting, was itself witness to the reluctance to experiment with mixtures which we have seen. A further obstacle was the linguistic problem of classifying colours in a range of specific substances. Pliny, in his account of the four-colour painters, was able to distinguish between pigments and abstract colour terms: the white of Milos was 'ex albis', the red of Sinope 'ex rubris', *atramentum* was 'ex nigris'; but here two of the terms were simply the names of the places of origin of the materials. Pliny's fourth colour – also identified by its place of origin – *sil* from Attica, was such a doubtful term that it became the subject of an important controversy in the sixteenth century. Favorinus, according to Aulus Gellius, recognized the poverty of Greek and Latin colour-terms, as compared with the capacity of the eye to discriminate between nuances of colour, and he made his abstract colour-categories far more wide-ranging than we would do. His *rubor* included purple (*ostrum*) on the one hand and yellow (*crocum*) on the other.[84] The technical literature of the Middle Ages for the most part avoided an engagement with abstract colour-terms and simply listed specific colorants.[85] A number of late medieval texts do show an awareness of the problems of abstract colour classes but they too pass quickly to the discussion of pigments. The fourteenth-century Neapolitan *De Arte Illuminandi* (*On the Art of Illumination*), for example, attributed to Pliny the view that there are three 'principal' colours, black white and red, and that all the others are 'intermediate'. The author then proceeded to show that the illuminator required eight *naturales colores* and listed the classes *niger, albus, rubeus, glaucus, azurinus, violaceus, rosaceus* and *viridis*; but finally he classified the pigments yielding these hues according to whether they were natural or artifical and arrived at a figure of some twenty colouring agents.[86] Similarly the late fourteenth-century Tuscan writer and painter Cennino Cennini began the chapter on colours in his *Libro dell' arte* (*Book of Art*) by stating that there are seven 'natural' colours, then opted for four 'mineral' colours – black, red, yellow and green – the last three of which are 'natural', but needed to be helped artificially by white, ultramarine or azurite and *giallorino*.[87] Clearly Cennini was concerned neither with the status of 'natural' colours nor with the precise distinction between these and the 'artificial' ones; he had little interest in theory but felt, significantly, that he must make some gesture towards it at the start of his account.

Several early sixteenth-century Venetian writers deplored the prevailing confusion about the nature and number of basic colours;[88] indeed, with the increasing use of mixtures brought about by the development of the oil technique, we might well expect that some more empirical approach to the problem would emerge in the course of the century from a painterly milieu. It has rightly been suggested that the most important feature of the first modern colour-systems, which make their appearance about 1600, is the new prominence given to blue.[89] Although blue had been an important colour throughout the Middle Ages, it does not seem to have formed part of a set of 'basic' colours: we have seen that green was far more usual in such sets. In the sixteenth century, when Titian showed a particular liking for blue, the view that it was essential to the basic set began to gain ground and, by a curious linguistic error, to be incorporated into the context of Pliny's four-colour system. The problem was the precise identification of Attic *sil*. In the *Natural History* (XXXIII, lvi, 158) Pliny had stated that both *sil* (yellow ochre) and *caeruleum* (probably azurite) occur in gold and silver mines: this may have led to a confusion of the two pigments, a confusion all the easier in the later Middle Ages

when a term for yellow, *cerulus* (perhaps from *cera*, wax), was in use.[90] A late fifteenth-century Venetian commenator on Pliny, Ermolao Barbaro, was possibly the first to make the confusion,[91] soon followed by a number of other writers. Cesare Cesariano, in his commentary to the magnificent 1521 Como edition of Vitruvius, stated categorically that *sil* was ultramarine (although he here confused lapis lazuli and azurite); Thylesius in 1528 accepted that *silaceus* was 'among the blues'.[92] Only in the middle of the century did the topic become important in the context of painterly mixture. In a treatise on monetary values, written probably after 1563 when he became deputy director (*luogotenente*) of the Florentine Accademia del Disegno, Vasari's friend Vincenzo Borghini adduced Pliny's attack on the abuse of expensive pigments, citing the four-colour story; but he was unable to provide a colour-equivalent for *attico*, as he had done for all the other terms, as if he was uncertain whether the Greek painters could ever have managed without blue.[93] A decade later a French encyclopedia of the arts, Pierre Grégoire's *Syntaxeon Artis Mirabilis*, proposed, following an earlier French commentator on Vitruvius, Georges Philander, that *sil* was *ianthinus*, a shade of violet, but he also added the important suggestion that from the four colours all others could be mixed.[94] The most substantial discussion of the whole question was made in 1585 in the *Commentarius de Pictura* (*Commentary on Painting*) by the French mathematician, philosopher and bear-leader Louis de Montjosieu, who had arrived in Rome two years earlier. He was one of the first scholars to test the descriptions of ancient styles by reference to contemporary practice, rejecting the view that the competition between Apelles and Protogenes had been a demonstration of drawing supremely thin lines, since he had not found such an emphasis in the work of modern draughtsmen such as Raphael, Michelangelo, Salviati, Polidoro da Caravaggio, Correggio or Titian.[95] When he came to Pliny's account of the four colours he found Philander's alternative of purple or yellow for *sil* confusing: he stated clearly (61) that one of the four colours must have been blue: 'For it is certain that these four colours, white, black, red and blue, are the fewest that are needed in painting, and from a mixture of which all the others are composed.' However, Montjosieu went on to list a number of mixtures which may cast doubt on his practical experience: we may accept his grey (*cineraceus*) composed of black and white and his brown (*fulvus*) made from red and black; but his green was a mixture of red and blue and his yellow (*luteus*) a mixture of green and red, which suggests that he was still thinking very much in Classical terms, for there is no indication that he was concerned with the optical mixture which might give this result.[96] What is important is that Montjosieu stressed the dependence of all colours upon these basic four, that Attic *sil* (as opposed to other types of *sil*, which might be violet or yellow) was always blue, and that his views were several times republished and widely read during the sixteenth and seventeenth centuries.

The several accounts of the primary colours which appeared about 1600, which established the modern subtractive triad of red, yellow and blue, appealed to the experience of mixing in painting although, for the most part, they were written by physicians.[97] The Irish chemist Robert Boyle, writing in mid-century, summed up the way in which painters had guaranteed for natural philosophers the identity of the newly discovered primary set, in *Experiments & Considerations Touching Colours* (1664) 219–21:

> There are but few Simple and Primary Colours (if I may so call them) from whose various compositions all the rest do as it were Result. For though Painters can imitate the Hues (though not always the Splendor) of those almost Numberless differing colours that are to be met with in the Works of Nature, and of Art, I have not yet found, that to exhibit this strange Variety they need imploy any more than *White* and *Black*, and *Red*, and *Blew*, and *Yellow*; these *five*, variously *Compounded*, and (if I may so speak) *Decompounded*, being sufficient to exhibit a Variety and Number of Colours, such, as those that are altogether Strangers to the Painters' Pallets, can hardly imagine.

The growing conviction that the primary colours were three, and that black and white stood in some sense outside this triad, even if they could still be regarded as colours, threw the interpretation of Pliny's account still further into confusion. The archaeologist J. C. Boulenger hedged his bets in the 1620s by claiming that modern painters mixed their hues from *either* three *or* four colours, without naming them.[98] The three (or five) colour scheme, which Boyle clearly presented as a novelty, cannot be seen to have been generally accepted until the end of the century. Furthermore, if Attic *sil* was now identified as blue it could not also be a yellow, so Apelles's four colours were no closer to being assimilated to the new triad of primaries.[99] The French mathematician Marin Cureau de la Chambre, in a treatise on the rainbow of 1650, was still worrying over the discrepancies of Pliny's story. Apelles was known to have been a wonderful painter of lightning but if *sil* were blue, his four-colour palette could not include yellow 'which is proper for the representation of brightness'. The ancient authors must have been referring not to classes of abstract colours but to pigments, and it was well known, said Cureau, that *sils* were both yellow and blue; so he could conclude that yellow, like blue and red, 'is a simple and primary colour'.[100] The German painter Joachim von Sandrart, too, found it hard to reconcile Pliny's account – which he attributed to the painter Euphranor (*see* Chapter 1) – with the modern doctrine of the primary colours: he proposed that black and white be removed from the series, which must surely have been 'the four bright [*bunte*] colours red, yellow, blue and green, necessary to paint the whole creation'.[101]

Apelles in the studio

Thus the problem of the number and identity of these basic colours continued to be a perplexing one: Roger de Piles, writing at the end of the seventeenth century in the context of the French Academy of Painting, called the four colours of the ancients 'capitales' but did not specify them, although in his adaptation of Ridolfi's account of Venetian flesh-painting he excluded black and white from their number.[102] Similarly, the anonymous French translation of Pliny's Book XXXV, which appeared in London in 1725, glossed the four colours as 'Simples & primitives', without further comment.[103] But during the eighteenth and nineteenth centuries, as the red–yellow–blue reading of the primaries became the orthodoxy among theor-

ists of art, so Pliny's story came to be interpreted entirely in its terms. The second (1762) edition of A. J. Dézallier d'Argenville's *Abrégé de la vie des plus fameux peintres* noted that a system of five primaries – Boyle's – had been 'à peu près' that of the four-colour painters of Antiquity, a verdict quoted with approval by the critic C. L. von Hagedorn in Germany.[104] Hagedorn observed that Pliny had been concerned to recall painters to a primitive simplicity of colouring, an endeavour he thoroughly supported, and this was again to be the nub of the story during the Neo-Classical period. He also claimed that painters rarely noticed that they had more than four colours on their palettes, forgetting the black and the white, and he concluded, somewhat opaquely: 'And if they make a mystery of this, that does not disprove my thesis; for often the artist, palette in hand, paints with such impetuousity that he would be hard put to it to give a detailed account of his mixtures'.[105] Yet Hagedorn was writing at a time when the setting of the palette (*see* Chapter 10) was still a thoroughly organized affair, and its range of pigments was far from restricted to four. How did the artist of the eighteenth century imagine that Apelles had set his? The Renaissance interpreters of the theme of the *Calumny* had given no sign that they were anxious to follow Apelles in respect of colour; they made, for example, an abundant use of blue.[106] Several artists of the eighteenth century who showed Apelles at work were also happy to represent him as one of themselves. In an *Allegory of Painting* Sebastiano Conca (1680–1764) showed Apelles painting Campaspe, the mistress of Alexander the Great, as Venus: his palette seems to be set for flesh with only reds, yellow and white but there is blue in the picture on the canvas, as well as in other parts of Conca's scene.[107] A similar subject by Francesco Trevisani (1656–1746) also presents Apelles with a far from restricted palette, including vermilion, as does Tiepolo in two versions of *Alexander and Campaspe in the Studio of Apelles*. Apelles's palette in the later version (*c.* 1735/40) is set in the standard eighteenth-century sequence from white, near the thumbhole, through yellows and reds to black, a total of six colours.[108] *12*

Possibly the first visual indication of the effect of both the excavations at Herculaneum, where a number of representations of artists at work had been uncovered, and the philological study of the four-colour story, is presented by the otherwise thoroughly Tiepolesque frontispiece by Friedrich Oeser to Winckelmann's *Gedanken* of 1756, which shows the painter Timanthes – described by Cicero (*Brutus*, 70) as a four-colour artist – at work on his most famous subject, *The Sacrifice of Iphigenia*.[109] Timanthes does not use a palette but seems about to take his colours from four pots at his feet; a closer examination reveals a shadowy fifth put behind the others and it is likely that Oeser, like Dézallier d'Argenville, intended to allude to the story of the limited palette only in the most general way. Later painters were more precise: David, in an unfinished picture, showed Apelles painting Campaspe from only four saucers of paint and without a palette.[110] In 1819 J. M. Langlois won the larger Gold Medal at the Paris Salon with a *Generosity of Alexander* that also shows the painter using only three pots of colour (although he does have another in front of him and uses a palette).[111] Another late French Classicist, Antoine Ansiaux, also presented Apelles in his *Alexander offering Campaspe to* *17* *18*

Apelles with a conventional modern palette bearing only the three primaries, red, yellow and blue, in tonal order from light to dark.[112] A French theorist of the 1820s, David's pupil J. N. Paillot de Montabert, insisted that the three colours of the primary triad, plus black *or* white, were just the four the ancients had used, a view re-stated by Ingres's pupil J. C. Ziegler in the 1850s.[113] Ziegler was familiar with the *De la loi du contraste simultané des couleurs* (1839; *Principles of Harmony and Contrast of Colours*) of the chemist and colour-theorist M. E. Chevreul, which had claimed summarily that the ancients had used a palette of five primaries, including the red–yellow–blue triad, and that mixtures may have been produced 'spontaneously' (i.e. optically) by the effects of the simultaneous contrasts Chevreul had expounded.[114] By the time of Chevreul, the understanding of the four colours in terms of some 'primary' combination had become quite uncontroversial and it does not seem to have been of much concern to later students of Greek art until Gladstone, as we saw, raised the question of the Greeks' colour vision.

Painters in the Romantic period were conscious that Pliny's account of the four colours could still be understood as practical advice. There were, indeed, painters who found the effort to reconcile the conflicting evidence hardly worth the trouble. The Norwich portrait-painter Thomas Bardwell, who was also the author of a widely read and much reprinted *Practice of Painting* (1756), had been inclined to be sceptical of the supposedly practical details handed down by Pliny (1f):

> For my part, I cannot believe, that the four capital colours of the Ancients would mix to that surprising perfection we see in the works of *Titian* and *Rubens*. And if we have no certain knowledge of *their* methods of Colouring who lived in the last Century, how should we understand theirs who lived Two Thousand years ago?

Sir Joshua Reynolds was far more typical in seeking to accommodate Pliny's account to contemporary practice: he disputed a view, still current in the eighteenth century, that Apelles had laboured under a disadvantage in restricting his palette. He interpreted the story of the dark varnish as a mistake of Pliny's in interpreting the sobriety of Apelles's paintings, which was due, according to Reynolds, not to an overall toning-down but to 'his judicious breaking of those [four] colours to the standard of nature'.[115] Later, in his notes to Du Fresnoy's *De Arte Graphica*, Reynolds came to interpret the account of the varnish as a description of glazing and scumbling but he continued to commend the restricted palette: 'I am convinced the fewer the colours, the cleaner will be the effect of those colours, and that four are sufficient to make every combination required. Two colours mixed together will not preserve the brightness of either of them single, nor will three be as bright as two ...'[116] Too many mixtures would be an infringement of the simplicity implicit in Apelles's practice. Towards the end of his life Reynolds based his own pictures on simple underpaintings of white, black, indian red and raw umber, 'representatives', as a commentator put it, '(however negative) of the three primary colours'.[117] In Reynolds, too, there is a hint of the lingering ancient prejudice against mixture in a more comprehensive sense. In a note to Du Fresnoy he referred to 'that harmony which is produced by what the ancients called the *corruption* [*corruptio*, i.e. *phthora*] of the

Friedrich Oeser, *Timanthes painting 'The Sacrifice of Iphigenia'*, frontispiece to J.J. Winckelmann's *Gedanken*, 1756. Oeser's Timanthes paints from four or possibly five pots, arrayed on the ground. (17)

J.M. Langlois, *The Generosity of Alexander*, 1819. The late Neo-Classical version of Apelles's studio shows a limited number of pots but also a nineteenth-century palette. (18)

colours, by the mixing and breaking them till there is a general union of the whole, without any thing that shall bring to your remembrance the painter's palette, or the original colours', which he found characteristic of the Bolognese and Dutch schools.[118] This method of achieving harmony he found inferior to the Venetian practice, best exemplified in Rubens, where 'the brightest possible colours are admitted, with the two extremes of warm and cold, and those reconciled by being dispersed over the picture, till the whole appears like a bunch of flowers'.[119]

It is especially ironic that Reynolds should have thus asserted the essentially Antique virtues of the limited palette, for this must also have been the emphasis of his enemy William Blake, who attacked him precisely because he felt he was guilty of Rembrandtesque mixing and who condemned the works of Titian and Rubens as 'sickly daubs'.[120] But about 1800 Blake himself looked at Rembrandt and the Venetians with great interest.[121]. It was probably during his two subsequent years of colour-study, described in a letter of November 1802, that he began to cast about more widely for appropriate models and came across the story of Apelles. Writing shortly after Blake's death, J. T. Smith, who had known the visionary well for many years, recorded:

> As to Blake's system of colouring . . . it was in many instances most beautifully prismatic. In this branch of the art he often acknowledged Apelles to have been his tutor, who was, he said, so much pleased with his style, that once when he appeared before him, among many of his observations he delivered the following: 'You certainly possess my system of colouring; and I now wish you to draw my person, which has hitherto been untruly delineated'.[122]

Blake's portrait of Apelles may be identifiable with the well-known drawing *The Man who taught Blake Painting in his Dreams*. This portrait dates from about 1819 but it is not easy to place the artist's encounter with his ancient teacher. He alluded to the competition with Protogenes in the *Descriptive Catalogue* of 1809, and also in his *Notebook*, which was in use for many periods from the 1780s.[123] But the 'prismatic' palette, recognized by Apelles during this encounter, was certainly developed in the watercolours prepared for his patron Thomas Butts in 1803. In his letter to Butts of the previous November, Blake showed that he had made an extensive study of Reynolds's writings, where he will have found the discussion of the palette of the ancients quoted above. The lesson which he claimed to draw from Reynolds's (which he reinforced in his later marginalia to Reynolds's *Literary Works*) was that the 'broken' hence 'corrupt' colour of the Venetians was injurious to grandeur, which could only be the product of simplicity.[124] It is not at all clear how far Blake took Apelles's message to be a serious recommendation of the restricted palette: the florid tonality of many of the later illuminations with their frequent use of gold suggests that austerity was never a constant aesthetic with him. The technique of even the simplest of the late watercolours, the *Dante* series, makes a good deal of play with mixed and 'broken' tints. Blake's early biographer, Alexander Gilchrist, described his pigments as 'few and simple' but went on to list five, including cobalt blue, one of the newest synthetic pigments, which the painter would supplement occasionally with ultramarine, gamboge and vermilion. The palette of *Painting* in the *Enoch* lithograph of 1821 shows a range of six colours.[125] It must remain debatable how far Blake's reading of Apelles's colour practice was, like that of his French contemporary François Gérard, a reductive one.[126]

Thus from Antiquity until the nineteenth century Apelles stood, as a colourist, for an ideal aesthetic simplicity, understood by each period which looked to him in terms of the prevailing notion of basic or primary colours. His story gives us the clearest indication of how theory often provided an uncomfortable fit with practice and how each generation could only look at the colour of the past with the colour in its own eyes.

William Blake, *The Man who taught Blake Painting in his Dreams, c. 1819.* (19)

3 · Light from the East

Monumental mosaics · Meaning in mosaic · Light and liturgy · Realism and movement · The colours of Divine Light · The colours of Islam

WRITING IN GAZA in the first half of the sixth century AD the orator Chorikos concluded his account of the Church of St Stephen there with a rather surprising picture of a group of Early Christian connoisseurs:

> Let us invite men who have examined the shrines of many cities, each one an expert in a different kind of work, and in the presence of such judges let our church be tried as in a court against the famous temples of the world. Let one, for instance, be a connoisseur of painting, not only the kind that uses pigments, but also of mosaic, which imitates it; let another be a judge of marbles, be they named after the place where they are quarried or after their colour; another an expert on capitals; let another clearly evaluate the amount of gold, in case there is a deficiency or an excess – both errors of taste. Let someone else carefully observe the roof (unless he declines to do so because of its height), for here there are costly timbers, covered with coffering for the sake of both strength and beauty. When all the judges have come together, and each one allotted the aspect he happens to know better than the others, then our church will unanimously be declared the victor.[1]

This is an attitude towards Christian art which is thoroughly secular: a church interior is to be admired for the beauty of its proportions, its precious materials and its craftsmanship; there is no suggestion that any of these serve a religious or even a generally expressive function.[2] The only hint that there is something about this building beyond the immediate aesthetic impression is in the reference to the types of marble in columns and revetments, since Chorikos had written earlier that they offered a double benefit:

> [they provide] the church [with material] for decorous workmanship and are a source of honour to the cities that sent them, since a man who has seen them and admired them at once praises the donor. Among the columns, the most remarkable are the four, dyed by nature with the colour of imperial raiment, which define the area forbidden to those who are not members of the holy ministry ... The Lower part [of the apse] gleams with different kinds of marble. In the centre is a window, wide and tall in proportion, entirely encompassed by a single kind of stone, though diversified by art, which completes the revetment along both edges of the window and adorns the walls on either side. It does not cease here, but mounts up on both sides and reaches the band, itself of the same [kind of] stone, that lies above the window. In this way, bands of well-fitting marble cover the wall. They are so joined together as to appear to be a work of nature, and so variegated with their natural colours as to resemble altogether a hand-painted picture. Indeed, painters whose business it is to select and copy the most beautiful objects there are, should they need to represent columns or gorgeous plaques – and I have seen that sort of thing in paintings – will find plenty of excellent models here.[3]

Chorikos's appreciation of the origin and colour of the marbles at St Stephen's was echoed even more vividly by his contemporary Paul the Silentiary, in his description of Sta Sophia in Constantinople:

> Upon the carved stone wall curious designs glitter everywhere. These have been produced by the quarries of sea-girt Proconnesus. The joining of the cut marbles resembles the art of painting, for you may see the veins of the square and octagonal stones meeting so as to form devices: connected in this way, the stones imitate the glories of painting ... Yet who, even in the thundering strains of Homer, shall sing the marble meadows gathered upon the mighty walls and spreading pavement of the lofty church? Mining [tools of] toothed steel have cut these from the green flanks of Carystus and have cleft the speckled Phrygian stone, sometimes rosy mixed with white, sometimes gleaming with purple and silver flowers. There is a wealth of porphyry stone, too, besprinkled with little bright stars that had laden the river-boat on the broad Nile. You may see the bright green stone of Laconia and the glittering marble with wavy veins found in the deep gullies of the Iasian peaks, exhibiting slanting streaks of blood-red and livid white; the pale yellow with swirling red from the Lydian headland; the glittering crocus-like golden stone which the Libyan sun, warming it with its golden light, has produced on the steep flanks of the Moorish hills; that of glittering black upon which the Celtic crags, deep in ice, have poured here and there an abundance of milk; the pale onyx with glint of precious metal; and that which the land of Atrax [Thessaly] yields, not from some upland glen, but from the level plain: in parts vivid green not unlike emerald, in others of a darker green, almost blue. It has spots resembling snow next to flashes of black so that in one stone various beauties mingle.[4]

The appreciation of marbles for their provenance and their coloured veining goes back to the Roman poet Statius in the first century AD.[5] It is not surprising that Chorikos and Paul drew on this tradition for they were writing within the literary convention of *ekphrasis* – the description of works of art – which at Gaza was practised especially by Procopius and John of Gaza.[6] Their accounts should not be dismissed as mere literary exercises, for the architectural features to which they drew attention were precisely those on which Early Christian and Byzantine patrons and craftsworkers lavished the greatest expense and skill. Columns of green-veined cipolin marble from Carystus in Euboeia were indeed sent to the Christians in Gaza.[7] The finely drilled and carved capitals are perhaps the most distinguished form of Byzantine sculpture on a monumental scale. Although very few roofs of this period have survived (see the reconstructed fifth-century roof of Sta Sabina in Rome or the twelfth-century roof of the Palatine Chapel in

39

21 Palermo), there is good evidence that they were particularly sumptuous. The mosaic of the Nile, with its meadows and birds, as Chorikos described it on the aisle walls at St Stephen's, is known at least in the form of mosaic pavements from late

20 Antiquity – at Palestrina, and Piazza Armerina in Sicily – to the Christian churches of Aquilea in north Italy of the late fifth century and, not far from Gaza, the church of St John the Baptist at Gerasa.[8] The imagery of these Nile landscapes, soon assimilated to that of the four rivers of Paradise in Early Christian apses (for example, in SS Cosmas and Damian in Rome), has not so far been found on walls, but there is no reason to doubt the substantial accuracy of Chorikos's account.[9]

The orator had stated that the first and greatest merit of the church was its proportions and the second its marble cladding; he concluded, 'Gold and other colours give brilliance to the whole work'. Symmetry and colour were still the primary categories of beauty, as they had been in Classical times. For the Byzantine spectator, as for the Classical, the foremost aspect of colour to be appreciated was its value as light. The most characteristic items of Early Christian liturgical equipment, the sheen of silk vestments and hangings, the gold and silver of lamps and vessels, the jewels and enamels of processional icons, reliquaries and books – all were developed in the early Christian

Palestrina, Temple of Fortune, Nile scene, first to third century AD. Images of the Nile were frequent subjects in Roman mosaic pavements such as this, leading on to the Early Christian theme of the four rivers of Paradise, and to the Byzantine notion of the mosaic itself as 'flowing', like a river. (20)

centuries primarily as receptacles and images of light. Yet it was their background of silver and gold mosaic 'as it were, gushing from an abundant golden fountain', as Chorikos put it in his *ekphrasis* of the Church of St Sergius at Gaza,[10] which shows most clearly how a specialized technique was put to the service of an aesthetic ideal.

Monumental mosaics

The monumental mosaic is perhaps the most original medium of Early Christian art, and in its transference from pavement to wall and vault, the technique itself was modified with the specific object of exploiting the effects of light. At first, wall and pavement mosaics ran parallel in their style and imagery. The pebbles of the early Greek mosaics gave way to regularly cut tesserae (cubes) about the third century BC,[11] and soon the naturally coloured stone tesserae were supplemented by a sprinkling of artificially coloured terracotta or glass, which brought a vast increase in chromatic range. The earliest surviving pavement entirely of glass is at Corinth, which   15 matches in richness the wall and niche mosaics of contemporary Pompeii and Herculaneum. Its borders include naturalistic vegetation which breaks with the geometric patterns of earlier Roman mosaics. This tendency increased in some of the highly polychromatic pavements of the fifth century AD at Argos and the late fifth-century pavement excavated in an Early Christian basilica at Heraclea Lyncestis (Bitola) in Macedonia: its florid rendering of the Garden of Eden relates directly to the imagery of several Early Christian apses in Rome and Ravenna (SS Cosmas and Damian, Arian Baptistry).[12]

Conversely, the earliest intact vault-mosaics which survive – the *criptoporticus* of Hadrian's Villa at Tivoli (early second century AD), the ambulatory of Sta Costanza in Rome and the   26 vaults of the Rotunda of St George in Thessaloniki (late fourth and late fifth centuries respectively) – echo the geometrical designs of earlier pavements.[13] The Tivoli vault, although it is in an exceptionally dark passage and can only be seen by artificial light, makes only a little use of glass (for blues) but the rough pebble-like tesserae are loosely set to catch the light at several angles.[14] All the early literary references to vault mosaics in the first century AD allude to glass; indeed, until the word *musivum* (the origin of our 'mosaic') gained currency in the second to fourth centuries, *vitris* (glass) seems to have been the only term for wall and vault mosaics.[15] The decisive break with the methods of pavement mosaics probably came with the introduction of metallic tesserae – first gold, then silver – which   27–30 can be traced fairly certainly to the early third century, specifically to the gold halo of the risen Christ in the vault mosaic of the Mausoleum of the Julii under St Peter's in Rome.[16] The place and date are interesting in that they coincide with the appearance of a related specialized technique, that of gilded glass vessels, large quantities of which have been found in the Catacombs of Rome: in them, as in the gold tesserae, a layer of gold foil is sandwiched between two layers of glass.[17]

This, then only sparing, use of metallic tesserae is the first clear indication that the Early Christian mosaic was to be primarily a vehicle of light. In the Mausoleum of the Julii, the analogy gold–light is overt, since Christ here appears as the nimbed *sol invictus*. In the second prominent monument to use gold cubes, Sta Costanza, they are both more decorative and more subtle. The mosaics with subjects from the Old Testament, which also had decorative surrounds including gold mosaic, have now vanished[18] but the ambulatory mosaics which survive have gold only at the liturgical focus of the design, in the two vaults flanking the high altar, which is lit by windows in a turret above. We may assume that the lost mosaic of Christ and the Apostles in this turret also incorporated gold: it was compared in the sixteenth century to Sta Pudenziana (*c.* 401/7) in Rome, where there is also a notable use of highlighting in gold on the robe and halo of Christ.[19] From these modest beginnings, gold mosaic spread over the whole background in the Rotunda of St George at Thessaloniki, where there is also perhaps the earliest use of silver cubes.[20] It spread also to the scarcely modulated cladding of dome or apse in S. Vittore *in caelo aureo* in the Ambrosian Basilica of Milan (?late fifth century) and to Sta Eirene in Istanbul, with its iconoclastic decoration of the eighth century.[21] From the precious focus of the most heaven-like precinct of the temple, it became in later centuries, notably in the twelfth-century Royal Chapel at Palermo and in the Cathedral at Monreale where gold is lavished over the surfaces like a bath of *Ambre Solaire*, simply another field for conspicuous display.[22]

With the introduction of metallic cubes went the development of techniques of setting that also took the practice of wall mosaics further and further away from the practice of the pavement. At Pompeii and Herculaneum the flush setting of glass tesserae in and around the niches of fountains seems to have aimed for the same sort of polished surfaces as the floors.[23] As the technique for walls and vaults developed, a deliberately irregular surface was created, giving especially in the case of gold a soft, fluid effect which is particularly striking in the dome of the chapel of S. Vittore in Milan and in the 'Mausoleum' of Galla Placida at Ravenna.[24] A more controlled irregularity was created by raking some metallic cubes downward at an angle of up to 30°, so as to reflect light down to the spectator below – a technique used especially for haloes and mandorlas as in the monastery of St Catherine on Sinai of the mid-sixth century, in the fifth- and seventh-century mosaics of S. Demetrios in Thessaloniki, and in the ninth-century panel over the Imperial door in Sta Sophia at Constantinople;[25] and for inscriptions, as at Poreč in Croatia and again at Sta Eirene and S. Demetrios.[26] These irregularities of surface seem more characteristic of Early Christian than of later medieval mosaics: in Sta Sophia they seem to have been abandoned in most work of the ninth and tenth centuries.[27] There are no examples in the Nea Moni on Chios of the late eleventh century and by the close of the Middle Ages, when the first substantial technical literature on methods of setting made its appearance in Venice, the Classical ideal of a smooth surface, with no visible gap between the cubes, had reasserted itself, as can be seen in the early fifteenth-century work in the Mascoli Chapel in S. Marco.[28]

The technique of Early Christian mosaic may be divided broadly into two types. One was the more peculiarly Greek method using smaller stone cubes for modelling flesh and a more linear method of setting; this was found widely in Constantinople. The other was the use of larger glass tesserae

Flickering light from stalactite patterns of carving bring the ceiling of the Palatine Chapel at Palermo close to the Byzantine aesthetic of colour in motion. (21)

throughout and a more random 'impressionistic' setting; this is the style of the early mosaics of Rome. I shall look more closely at the 'Greek' style in a discussion of naturalism but I want to emphasize here that the two styles, however distinct in their effects, were able to co-exist from Antiquity onwards. The well-known mosaic pavement of Dionysus on a panther in the House of the Masks at Delos is in the minutest of techniques but is framed by panels of centaurs in a loose impressionistic style, which is also that of a contemporary group of musicians in a neighbouring room.[29] And at S. Lorenzo fuori le Mura in Rome (sixth century), the head of St Lawrence is in the same style and entirely in glass, while the head of the contemporary St Paul uses smaller stone tesserae for the flesh, in a linear setting.[30] It may be that the early 'Greek' technique related more closely to those Hellenistic subjects like the Battle of Alexander or the two small theatrical scenes in Naples which were clearly reproductions of paintings. To conclude that the 'Roman' style is more specifically appropriate to the medium and thus more autonomous[31] seems hasty, for mosaic has shown precisely that it is infinitely adaptable. If the 'Roman' technique exhibits a more completely homogeneous surface, and is thus freer from illusionism (the adaptation of the material and style to the characteristics of the subject), it shares this homogeneity with, for example, late antique wool-tapestry, where the demands of the medium itself – the regular repetition of the same units of

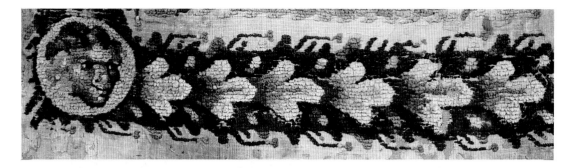

Tapestry and mosaic commonly work with equal-sized, regularly spaced units of colour, to create a homogeneous visual effect, although mosaic has far greater flexibility (see pls. 27–30). Both the loop-tapestry fragment from Akhmin (fourth century AD) and the mosaic pavement made in Antioch use optical mixing techniques. The circular pattern at the left of the mosaic recalls the bands of colour spun on a potter's wheel in an experiment with mixtures described by Ptolemy. (22,23)

(Opposite) A mosaic panel from Hadrian's Villa, a copy of a painting, uses exceptionally fine tesserae to render the sheen of doves' feathers and lustre of the drinking vessel by means of hatching. (24)

colour – impose a uniform texture, with an effect very close to this type of mosaic.

Any understanding of illusionism must surely depend on the context of the work under discussion; this is conspicuously so with one aspect of mosaic technique that can be closely related to the contemporary theory of colour, namely 'optical mixture'. The local setting of tesserae not in regular lines but in a 'staggered' or checkerboard arrangement has been noticed in all periods of medieval mosaic and it is particularly striking in the 'Greek' style, where it contrasts with the more usual linear setting. It seems in general to have been used for flesh, where a softness of modelling was appropriate (the general use of smaller tesserae for the modulation of flesh itself shows a nice understanding of the principles of optical mixture), or for lustrous surfaces like fish skins or animal coats or more positively luminous ones like haloes or the rainbow or water.[32]

These patterns are so striking that they must have been the result of a thoroughly self-conscious method. The theoretical basis for optical mixture had been laid down clearly in the second century AD by Ptolemy, who had identified two causes of optical fusion in colours: the first, by distance, meant that the angle of vision formed by rays of light from very small patches of colour was too small for them to be identified separately by the eye, hence many points of different colours seemed, together, to be the same colour. The second cause was persistence of vision, whereby if a coloured object was moving, an after-image would be superimposed on the successive image and a mixture of the two would result. Ptolemy illustrated this second phenomenon by the spinning of a parti-coloured wheel, such as a potter's wheel – precisely the tool for optical mixtures used by many colour-theorists in the nineteenth century, including several, such as Clerk Maxwell and Ogden Rood,

who were cited by the Neo-Impressionists.[33] The disc with a radial pattern of black, white, yellow, red and green squares in a staggered pattern, on a fragment of third- or fourth-century mosaic from near Antioch may reflect the sort of disc for mixing that Ptolemy had in mind.

Yet we should not conclude from this that these early mosaicists were Neo-Impressionists *avant la lettre*;[34] if they were, the looser and more homogeneous 'Roman' style would be far closer to the aims of pointillism than the more local 'Greek' use of 'staggered' textures. But when we look at the crucial question of viewing-distance the range is very great. The small panels from Hadrian's Villa were originally set in pavements and were thus to be seen from a distance of from three to a little over five feet (a metre to a metre and a half): their technique is very fine. That of the pavement at Heraclea Lyncestis is far coarser, although the viewing distance is the same. The dome mosaics of the Rotunda of St George are some sixty feet (eighteen metres) above ground level, yet the detail of the heads is in a fine linear style; it has been suggested that they were set on the ground, in the Classical manner, and transferred wholesale to the walls.[35] On the other hand, the mosaics on the vault of the small Chapel of S. Zeno in S. Prassede in Rome are about fifteen feet (four-and-a-half metres) above the spectator, yet they are set in the coarsest style and in electric light or in photographs the contrasts of colour are very strident. Only in a subdued light do the colours begin to fuse, although the texture of the surface is still very clear. Similarly, the chequerboard pattern of cubes on the neck of the Virgin is clear to the spectator in the large *Deesis* mosaic in the Church of Christ in Chora in Istanbul: here it is impossible to go far enough away to make the colours fuse. The typical movement of the spectator under the mosaic decoration of vaults and the upper areas of walls – where

they are so often sited – is opposite to that of the spectator of easel-paintings: they must be parallel and not perpendicular to the surface, which makes it very difficult to adjust the viewing distance and achieve optical fusion. What we miss in these antique and medieval examples is not so much the understanding of a theory, as that relentless empiricism which was to characterize Seurat's career.

Ptolemy also analysed other instances of optical mixture, already the subject of scattered observations by Aristotle and his commentators: the heightening of contiguous colours by contrast or the softening of their edges by colour-spread.[36] It is the understanding of this latter phenomenon which surely accounts for those touches of brilliant vermilion that were so often used in and around areas of flesh in the early mosaics of the 'Roman' type.[37] They are not highlights or any part of a system of tonal modelling but simply colouristic touches to give warmth to the skin. A quite opposite intention seems to lie behind the use of a range of greens, sometimes very bright greens, in the modelling of flesh, which is particularly noticeable in some late medieval examples in Greece.[38] It may be that this pronounced green is taken over from the green underpainting for flesh, which sometimes appears through transparent shadows and was used as early as the frescoes of Pompeii although it was not standardized perhaps until Middle Byzantine painting.[39] In mosaic it has the purely surface effect of cooling down the whole complexion.

As the use of gold ground spread, mosaic artists found means to modulate the excessive uniformity of vast areas of gold, at first by reversing some cubes to show the colour of their glass body (as at Sta Maria Maggiore in Rome, S. Appolinare Nuovo in Ravenna and at St Catherine's on Sinai) and later by scattering a few silver cubes (Sta Eirene) or sometimes both, as

in the ninth-century apse mosaic in Sta Sophia.[40] Here, too, we are dealing with a purely colouristic device based on the phenomenon of colour-spread. That the gold cubes in Italy should sometimes have had a basis of red glass is interesting: in the often loose setting of such gold grounds the cubes project up to a quarter of their thickness from the plaster bed, allowing the colour of the glass body to be diffused over the gold by reflection and giving it that reddish cast which was so prized in Antiquity. The setting-bed itself was often coloured red, so that the plaster between the cubes would add to their rosy flush.[41] A beautiful instance of the affinity the Byzantines felt between gold and red is in a mosaic votive panel of the seventh century in S. Demetrios in Thessaloniki, which shows the saint and a donor in a blue *tablion* with an identical pattern to that on the white *himation* under it. The golden triangles on the white become a brilliant red on the blue: as in Aristotle's scale of colours (*On Sense* 442a), red is, as it were, only the shadow side of light.

The outlines of haloes against gold in Middle Byzantine mosaics are usually red, which may have to do with their symbolic function as light but may also reflect the old aesthetic preference for these two colours in conjunction. Gregory of Nyssa wrote of a river 'which glows like a river of gold drawn through the deep purple of its banks and reddening its current with the soil he washes.'[42] He was talking of an experience of pure colour which was especially grateful to the Byzantine eye.

It may be felt that these rather slight and scattered instances of the application of a theory of colour in mosaic painting do not reflect any notable curiosity or scientific culture on the part of Early Christian or Byzantine artists, who were, it might be thought, simply carrying out the wishes of their patrons and working according to barely conscious rules of thumb. For the moment it would be rash to suggest that these craft workers did

28

more than share some low-level (and ancient) assumptions about light and colour with the intellectuals of their day. Yet there is some reason to think that the educated spectator of the time was capable of bringing a general knowledge of science to bear on the experience of art. Some striking instances of this are in the *Homilies* of Photius, Patriarch of Constantinople in the ninth century. In these sermons given to Imperial gatherings in the capital, Photius alluded repeatedly to optical theory: in March 863 he spoke of

> this holy and august temple [Sta Sophia] which one might well call ... the eye of the universe, and especially so today when, mixing the white and the black [an allusion to the dress of the congregation], out of which colours the natural constitution of the eye is wrought, you have filled with your bodies the voids of this wondrous place, forms, as it were, the socket of the eye ...[43]

The image may be thought overwrought until we remember that the sermon was delivered in a space whose gilded dome was not at all unlike the socket of a vast eyeball, the sun-like organ of vision according to Platonic theory, and that the reference to the black and white, as well as evoking the dark eyes of his audience, alluded to the Empedoclean view of the function of black and white in perception.[44] A few years later in the same place Photius justified a defence of images (he was celebrating the victory of the Iconodules over the Iconoclasts) by an appeal to the ancient Greek doctrine of sight as the superior sense: 'For surely, having somehow through outpourings and effluence of the optical rays touched and encompassed the object, it too [like hearing] sends the essence of the thing seen to the mind, letting it be conveyed from there to the memory for the concentration of unfailing knowledge.' Here, too, Photius adopted one of the several contending theories of vision current in his day, that of the Pythagoreans and Hipparchus of Alexandra, who argued that the eye sends out rays which seek and grasp the objects of sight and return them to the mind.[45] In a sermon at the inauguration of the Palatine Chapel Photius even made a passing reference to the mosaic pavement: 'Democritus would have said, I think, on seeing the minute work of the pavement and taking it as a piece of evidence, that his atoms were close to being discovered here actually impinging on the sight'.[46] These apparently far-fetched allusions are in no way surprising, for Photius was a formidable scholar – he compiled a lengthy list and abstracts of the books he had read, the *Myriobiblion*, which includes many titles no longer available to us. In particular, his manuscript of Johannes Stobaeus's *Eclogues*, which summarized in its first book Classical ideas on physics including those of Empedocles and Democritus on vision and colour, was more complete than any now extant.[47]

Speaking of the decoration of the mosaic-filled interior of the Palace Chapel (the church of the Virgin of Pharos), Photius declared: 'It was as if one had entered heaven itself with no one barring the way from any side, and was illuminated by the beauty in all forms shining all around like so many stars, so is one utterly amazed.'[48] The luminosity of the ecclesiastical interior was an image of the heavenly light: it was not simply for aesthetic enjoyment or conspicuous display that mosaic was developed as the supremely luminous form of painting, but as the vehicle of a Christian iconography of light.

The *Chi-Rho* symbol of Christ is set in the centre of a starry vault – an emanation of light that grows weaker as it gets further from its source. Compare the 'Divine Darkness' (pl. 33) of the *Transfiguration* mosaic at Sinai. (25)

Meaning in mosaic

Mural mosaic was a luxury medium; the examples which we now know were for the most part the result of imperial or royal or papal patronage; the precious materials were, like others, subject to both plunder and legitimate re-use. As funds dwindled programmes of decoration begun in mosaic had sometimes to be finished in painting; in the less visible areas, the application of a scattering of tesserae sometimes did duty for a large mosaic surface, the rest being filled with fresco. Within the mosaic materials themselves there was a hierarchy of values from marble to glass and finally to stone or terracotta cubes: when the more valuable ran out, mosaicists sometimes had to make do with the cheaper.[49] Thus, at least in its early phases, we should expect to find the medium used only in the most significant areas of ecclesiastical buildings. (There are many documents of the use of mural mosaic in secular buildings in Byzantium but the Stanza del Re Ruggero at Palermo seems to be the only surviving example.) If we look at the iconographic programmes of these areas, we become aware of the intimate connection between the subject-matter and the means of its expression.

Both the literary and the archaeological evidence for the Classical use of glass mosaic in walls and vaults refer predominantly to fountains and baths.[50] Even the etymology of the term mosaic (*opus musivum*) reflects the belief that it was especially appropriate to the haunts of the Muses, or nymphs, namely watery grottoes.[51] Thus the use of mosaic decoration in some of the earliest Christian baptistries (Naples, *c.* 400; Albenga and Ravenna, late fifth century) was in a continuing tradition. But the imagery of the decoration of these early baptistries was also especially appropriate to the medium, for the rite of baptism was, as its original Greek name *photisma* (illumination) implies, a conferring of light. A Neo-Platonic text of the late third century, the *Symposium* of Methodius of Olympus, comments on the presence of the moon under the feet of the woman clothed with the sun (*Revelations* 12: 1) and links it to baptism:

> for moonlight seems to bathe us like lukewarm water, and all humidity derives from the moon. The Church must preside over the baptised as a mother: it is thus that her function is called moon [*selene*], since those who are renewed shine with a new glow [*selas*], that is, with a new brightness, which is why they are also called 'newly illuminated': the Church shines in their eyes, through the phases of the Passion, the full moon of the Spirit . . . until the radiant and perfect light of the full Day.[52]

Hence baptism was often celebrated at night and, especially at the time of the Easter vigil which stressed the theme of the Resurrection, baptistries were lit by lamps; the mosaics, which as at Naples and Albenga on the Italian Riviera sometimes have representations of starry skies in their vaults, became especially significant.[53] The orientation of the baptistry, like that of the church, was often towards the east;[54] according to a fourth-century instruction to the candidate, he or she was to turn first to face the west, 'the realm of the visible darkness', and to 'deny the dark and shady ruler' (Satan):

> when you have denied Satan and all association with him, and completely loosed the ancient bond with Hell, God's Paradise will be opened to you, which he planted towards the rising sun, from which our ancestor Adam was driven for transgressing the Commandment. To show this symbolically you must turn from the setting to the rising sun, towards the realm of light. Then you will be told to say, 'I believe in the Father, and in the Son, and in the Holy Ghost, and in the Baptism of Penitence'.[57]

25   At Albenga, the mosaic vault with the monogram of Christ in a starry firmament is in the eastern apse of the building, opposite the entrance; in Naples the phoenix, emblem of Resurrection, is also to the east of the vault, to figure the dawning light of illumination.[56] This imagery of Paradise, set 'eastward in Eden', and of Christ as the rising sun was also common in that other major area of the earliest mosaic decoration, the apse. Very little is known of possible mosaic wall or vault decoration in pre-Christian temples,[57] but if an early seventeenth-century Roman drawing of a now vanished Lupercal Chapel to Romulus and Remus is to be credited, by the third century AD mosaic was used for apse-decoration in a pagan context.[58] Certainly in the majority of Roman churches mosaic was at first confined to apses,[59] many of them (SS Cosmas and

32 Damian in Rome and S. Vitale in Ravenna are the best-known examples) showing images of the future Epiphany of Christ that was, according to Early Christian traditions, to take place in the east.[60] That these are scenes of dawning light is often made clear by the clusters of rosy clouds above and around the figures. So crucial did this visible indication of the time of day appear that

in the twelfth-century apses of S. Clemente and Sta Francesca Romana in Rome, whose crowded compositions did not allow them to be deployed in the main picture-space, these clouds are packed into small compartments on either side of the hand of God, at the top of the design.[61]

A later image of Christ, common both in Western apse mosaics and in the central dome of Byzantine churches, is the figure of the *Pantokrator* or Ruler of the World. This image, too, is a manifestation of light, for Christ often carries a scroll or book bearing the text from St John's Gospel, 'I am the Light of the World'. Even where, as at Daphni, Hosios Loukas or Arta in western Greece, and in the Pammacaristos (Fethiye Djami) in Istanbul, the book is closed, its glittering bejewelled cover is a surrogate for this legend.[62] The ninth-century Anglo-Saxon poet Aethelwulf seems to have been thinking in terms of this Pantokrator figure when he spoke of 'Books which present the exalted utterances of God the Thunderer' and refers specifically to their conspicuous gold covers.[63] Gospel book-covers in the early Middle Ages were indeed essentially items of display, for use on the altar or in processions,[64] and were thus precious liturgical objects in their own right, could be stored separately from books and transferred from manuscript to manuscript.[65] Inscriptions like that on the Lindisfarne Gospels might mention not only the scribes and authors but also the goldsmith who made the cover 'with gold and with gems and also with gilded silver – pure metal', as well as the maker of the leather-covered boards.[66] The cover by Billfrith for this manuscript is lost but many others survive, their extravagant encrustation with gems, their lavish use of gold and ivory and enamel making it clear that they could be seen very readily as an embodiment of Divine Light.

36–7

The figure of the Virgin, who also appears frequently in early apse mosaics, can equally be understood as entering this realm of light. The eighth-century theologian John of Damascus in a *Homily* on the Birth of the Virgin, invoked her in these terms: 'Hail thou gate, looking towards the East, from which there appeared the Rising of Life, diminishing for men the setting of death', and in a tenth-century epigram on an icon of the Virgin, Constantine of Rhodes wrote: 'If one would paint thee, O Virgin, stars rather than colours would be needed, that Thou, the Gate of Light, should be depicted in luminosities . . .'[67] In the twelfth-century apse at Torcello, the *titulus* beneath the Virgin refers to her as 'Star of the Sea' and as 'the Gate of Salvation', since she as the second Eve has now replaced the first. In this role she stands near the gate of Paradise at the bottom of the vast mosaic of the Last Judgment on the west wall.[68] Here and in Sta Sophia, Hosios Loukas and Kiev, Mary bears a star on her forehead, but a particularly moving example of her luminous role is in the sixth-century apse mosaics in the cathedral at Poreč on the Istrian coast of Croatia. The Virgin (with a star on her forehead) and Child are seated beneath the figure of Christ Pantokrator on the triumphal arch and crowned with blue and pinkish clouds. At the sides of the apse are two scenes from her life, the Annunciation and the Visitation. Both scenes, which presented the promise of Christ's coming, take place on the edge of the sea from which rise, in rosy striations, the first indications of the dawning day.[69] The development of a simple gold ground, at Sta Sophia in Thessaloniki in the seventh century, for example, sometimes gave added intensity to this image of the Virgin: all figurative imagery has gone; there is neither sunlit cloud nor the mandorla of light which from this date was to serve so often as the most characteristic hieroglyph of super-human majesty; she became simply the luminous focus of a bowl of light.[70]

That the donors and craftworkers of these mosaic pro-grammes were well aware of their function is clear from the many inscriptions which they appended to them in the West, for these inscriptions often refer to the light-creating qualities of the cubes. A typical formulation runs round the base of the apse-conch in SS Cosmas and Damian in Rome: 'This hall of God shines with its adornment of mosaics,[71] a hall where the precious light of faith gleams even more brightly.'[72] Some-times, as in the now ruined church of the late fifth-century monastery of St Andrew the Apostle at Ravenna, the *titulus*, which refers chiefly to the marble revetment, is long enough and literary enough to constitute an *ekphrasis* of the decoration itself. It begins:

> Either light is born here, or, confined here, rules freely. Perhaps it is the earlier light, whence comes now the beauty of the sky. Perhaps the modest walls generate the splendour of daylight, now that external rays are excluded. See the marble blossom, a quiet glow, and the reflections from every compartment [*percusa*] of the purple vault. The gifts of Peter dazzle because of the mastery of the workman [*auctoris precio*] . . .[73]

The conceit that the church interior rivalled the light of day was one which became a commonplace in early medieval aesthetics, dependant on the dominant role of artificial lighting. Before we can understand the leading themes of Early Christian and Byzantine colour-aesthetics, we must look more closely at the physical conditions in which this decoration was seen.

Light and liturgy

It has been shown that in the early Byzantine church, for example in the 'Mausoleum' of Galla Placida at Ravenna, the windows themselves and the controlled light which entered through them were part of a complex iconography of light. As a Syrian hymn put it: 'There shines in the sanctuary a single light, entering through three windows in the wall: another eloquent symbol of the Trinity of Father, Son and Holy Spirit.'[74]

One of the greatest obstacles to the modern appreciation of medieval buildings is the fact that for the most part the lighting conditions for which they were created no longer apply. If the present-day visitor to the dingy interior of Sta Sophia in Istanbul is surprised at the dazzling evocations of Procopius or Paul the Silentiary, this is not simply due to the grimy condition of the marble revetment and the sadly unlucid vaulting, which give it rather the appearance of a run-down Victorian railway station (not, indeed, unlike the present condition of the Pera Palace Hotel on the other side of the Golden Horn). It is also due to the reduction in the number of windows in the course of many restorations since the sixth century to about half the original figure. Before the collapse of the dome in 558, each of the half-domes had windows around its base; those around the eastern half-dome were reduced from fifteen to five in order to

strengthen the structure and in the interests of symmetry similar reductions were made on the west. The semi-circular tympana to north and south originally had far larger semi-circular windows than at present.[75] Similar modifications were made at S. Marco in Venice, where the extension of the mosaic programme paradoxically meant the blocking-up of many windows, although here the darkening led to the construction of two large rose-windows in the south wall and the large lunette on the north in the late fifteenth century and the enlarging of many windows in the seventeenth.[76] Although the disposition of the light is now very different from that in the original twelfth- and thirteenth-century church, S. Marco still offers perhaps the most authentic experience of a Byzantine church interior available to us.

At Monreale in Sicily some thirty-four windows were made or enlarged during the restorations of 1816, so that there is much more light in the nave now than in the twelfth century.[77] Here, too, the lightening effect is increased by the seventeenth-century substitution of panes of clear glass for the original pierced lead *transennae*, or window-screens, which has also been the case with many Early Christian monuments. At S. Apollinaire in Classe, outside Ravenna, the present *transennae* have been shown to be far less substantial than the original ones, and the excavation of coloured glass fragments both at S. Vitale in Ravenna and in Istanbul suggests that, at least from the twelfth century, such glass was used in conjunction with fresco and mosaic in the interior: here, too, the result must have been considerably less light.[78]

Whatever the effect of a modification of light from outside, through the use of small openings or coloured glass, it seems clear that the Early Christian or Byzantine church was to be experienced as not so much a receptacle as a generator of light. As the early eulogist of Sta Sophia, Procopius, put it: 'You might say that the interior space is not illuminated by the sun from the outside, but that the radiance is generated within, so great an abundance of light bathes this shrine all round.'[79] Interior space was above all to be seen by artificial light. It is clear to the modern observer that, for example, the ninth-century apse-mosaic of the Virgin and Child, which was inserted rather awkwardly into the eastern half-dome of Sta Sophia over existing windows, was never intended to be seen by daylight, for against the light from these windows it is almost invisible from the body of the church. The spectator has the same difficulties at Torcello and, in a reverse sense, in Sta Sophia with the tenth-century Alexander mosaic in the North Gallery, which is placed high under a vault that receives no direct light from the windows. Only if we could see them at night by artificial light would they be properly visible.

This is precisely the way in which Byzantine mosaics were usually seen, for much of the ritual of the Eastern Church was nocturnal. Any visitor to Greek or Russian Orthodox services even today will notice the vast role played in them by the many candles and lamps. From the end of the second century the Eucharist in the Eastern Church was celebrated just before dawn: St Jerome, who visited Constantinople from the West in the fourth century, noted: 'in all the Churches of the East, when the Gospel is going to be read, candles are lighted, even though the sun may already be up – not to dispel the darkness, but demonstrating a sign of joy.'[80] Vespers, too, was held in the evening twilight and lamps and candles were lit during the first half of the service (called *luchnikon* because of this): at Easter, according to the Exultet hymn for the Easter Vigil, they were to last until the morning star – Christ – had risen. From the second century the vespertine service also included a hymn to 'joyful light' (*phōs ilaron*), anticipating the dawn.[81] The Spanish nun Egeria, visiting the Church of the Resurrection in Jerusalem at the end of the fourth century, described the evening service thus:

> Every weekday at the tenth hour [4 p.m.], called *licinicon* – we call it *lucernare* – the people gather in the Anastasis [Resurrection]. All the lamps and candles are lit, and an infinite light is created. The light is not brought in from outside but from within the grotto, where a lamp burns night and day, that is from the room behind the grille. The psalms of light are also sung ... great glass lanterns are burning everywhere, and there are many candles in front of the Anastasis, and also before and behind the Cross. By the end of all this it is dusk ...[82]

Many monastic services were vigils and it is recorded that after the completion of the Church of Christ in Chora in Constantinople, its founder, Theodore Metochites, attended the nocturnal services with the monks to observe the effect of the interior decoration of mosaic and marble.[83]

Hence the emphasis on lamps and candles, which also played such an important role in the ceremonial of the Byzantine court.[84] The rhapsody on Sta Sophia by Paul the Silentiary closes with a long and astonishing account of the lighting arrangements in the church: 'But no words are sufficient to describe the illumination in the evening: you might say that some nocturnal sun fills the majestic temple with light.' He went on to describe the great double ring of lamps with silver reflectors under the dome, the rows of lamps down the aisles, around the edges of the galleries and the base of the dome, along the chancel screen and even on the floor, concluding;

> Countless other lights, hanging on twisted chains, does the church of ever-changing aspect contain within itself; some illumine the aisles, others the centre or the east and west, others shed their bright flame at the summit. Thus the bright night smiles like the day and appears herself to be rosy-ankled ...[85]

In 1200 Archbishop Anthony of Novgorod saw eighty silver candlesticks in the dome and others throughout the church, and another visitor from Novgorod in the fourteenth century noticed the

> enormous and innumerable quantity of lamps ... some in the chapels and the rooms, others on walls and between the walls, in the aisles of the church where the great icons are, and where there also burn lamps of olive oil, and we sinners went joyfully, with tears in our eyes, offering candles according to our means, just as before holy relics ...

Even in the far smaller church of S. Demetrios in Thessaloniki a late fifteenth-century traveller counted some six hundred lamps burning on the name-day of the saint.[86]

The effect of this lighting on mosaics is difficult for us to sense, accustomed as we are to daylight or (as usually in Italian churches) the even glare of electric floodlights. Paul the Silentiary was surely right when he suggested that it was an effect of continual movement, for the breeze and the air distributed by the processions must often have caught the flames. The flickering light played over the soft and irregular surface of the vault mosaics, making them even less substantial than they seem to us and certainly more porous, more gentle and more alive. At the same time, it is very unlikely that they gave an impression of more vivid local colour.

Realism and movement

Although Byzantine aesthetics has been given a good deal of attention in recent years, there is still very little agreement about what its leading characteristics were. Two main schools of thought have developed: one, that Byzantine attitudes to the arts were governed by essentially Hellenistic ideas of truth and verisimilitude,[87] and the other, that they aimed to create a hieratic distance and an essentially unreal spiritual effect.[88] The casual spectator might find the latter the more compelling but an examination of the documents and of the methods of image-making gives far stronger support for the former. Quite apart from the many *ekphraseis*, which understandably reflect more or less the attitudes of their Hellenistic literary models, the extensive literature arising from opposition – triumphant opposition – to the iconoclastic movements of the eighth and ninth centuries is, of its very nature, strongly in favour of a close resemblance between image and prototype.

Writing in the early eighth century, before his conversion to Iconoclasm, the Emperor Leo III told the Caliph Omar II 'we have always felt a desire to conserve [the images of Christ and his Disciples] which have come down to us from their times as their living representations ...'. Earlier still the Council *In Trullo* of 691 had repudiated the Hellenistic type of Christ, insisting that he be shown in his historically accurate, bearded (i.e. Syrian) appearance.[89] Even the Iconoclasts, at the Ecumenical Council of Hiereia in 754, characterized the art of painting images as 'deceptive.'[90] Many popular stories of miraculous icons depend upon the fact of their complete verisimilitude; that this was the expectation of the Byzantine artist himself is attested by an engaging anecdote told to Anthony of Novgorod on his visit to Sta Sophia:

> There was also a great mosaic of the Saviour, which lacked a finger of the right hand, and as the artist completed it, he said, looking at it 'Lord, I have made you just as you were when alive.' A voice came out of the picture and said, 'And when did you see me?' And the artist was silent and died, and the finger remained unfinished. Then it was made out of gilded silver.[91]

Artists had both written and graphic models available to them to learn the exact appearance of their subjects. The list of the features of a vast range of religious personalities, familiar in the eighteenth-century compilation of Dionysius of Fourna, go back to the physiognomics of the type of Ulpian the Roman, of the ninth or tenth century.[92] Anthony of Novgorod also pointed to the thoroughly Classical procedure of using a 'master' model – in this case two icons in Sta Sophia – for the likenesses of saints.[93] The urgent need for an exact likeness in icon-making was also understood in secular portraiture, as we read from a ninth-century Islamic account which praised Byzantine artists for their unusual gifts:

> If one of their painters paints a portrait without omitting anything, he is still not satisfied, and is willing to present him as a young man, a mature man, or an old man, as required. Even that does not satisfy him, and he paints him weeping or laughing. That also is not enough for him, and he represents him as handsome, charming and distinguished-looking. However, he is still discontented, and distinguishes in his painting between a quiet and an embarrassed laugh, between a smile and a laugh strong enough to make tears flow from one's eyes, between joyous laughter and mocking or threatening laughter.[94]

These signs of mobility in facial features, even allowing for their literary origins in physiognomics, were far more appreciable to contemporaries than they are to us, as we may see if we try to interpret the expression on the face of the Pantokrator.

The role of colour in the establishment of this realism also followed the traditional Hellenistic pattern. The Greek Fathers of the fourth century, in their occasional and well-informed remarks on the nature of painting, were content to observe that colour was used to give greater truth to the first sketch. Even Gregory of Nyssa, for all his delight in pure colour-sensations, restated Aristotle's severe judgment when he wrote, 'anyone who looks at the picture that has been completed through the skilful use of colour does not stop with the mere contemplation of the colours that have been painted on the panel; rather he looks at the form which the artist has created in colour.'[95] For Gregory, as perhaps for most of us, these ways of looking were entirely distinct. The emphasis was repeated by the Council of 754, Photius and John of Damascus in the ninth century, and in the twelfth by Constantine Manasses who, in an *ekphrasis* of a mosaic in the Great Palace at Constantinople, preferred painting to sculpture precisely because it was able to use chiaroscuro to portray 'the roughness of skin and every kind of complexion, a blush, blond hair, a face that is dark, faint, and gloomy, and again one that is sweet, comely and radiant with beauty.' The attitude is one that comes directly from one of the Elder Philostratus's *Pictures* (I, 2).[96]

Against this emphasis on verisimilitude must be set the frequent inability of artists to discriminate between individuals and a reliance on verbal inscriptions, which had a strong theological justification throughout the Byzantine world. As John of Damascus wrote in the eighth century, 'Divine grace is given to the materials by the naming of the person represented in the picture'.[97] But among the writers who discuss the realism of painting we find hardly any support for the aesthetic value of colour in itself.[98] In the fourth century St Gregory Nazianzus confessed that he had a weakness for deep, florid colours, but these, he said, confuse the imagery; the simple palette of Zeuxis, Polyclitus and Euphranor – whose works he can hardly have known – were much to be preferred. It is a fitting irony that his own works should have received some of the most florid and sumptuous illumination of the Middle Ages.[99] And we saw with what pleasure Paul the Silentiary compared the polychrome marbles of Sta Sophia to painting: for him, the glories of painting must surely have been the glories of colour.

This concern for realism shown by commentators on Byzantine art was reflected in its methods. Although there are some striking examples of artists ignoring the needs of the spectator for visibility and intelligibility (for example the small narrative panels in Sta Maria Maggiore in Rome and S. Apollinare Nuovo in Ravenna and the frescoes in the side-chapels in Staro Nagoričane in Macedonia), Byzantine artists showed considerable interest in illusionism. Optical corrections to allow for the viewing position of the spectator were widely practised: they have been noticed in Sta Eirene in Constantinople, in Sta Sophia in Thessaloniki, at Ravenna and in Sta Sophia in Kiev.[100] In mosaics at Rome (Chapel of John VII) and at Ravenna (S. Vitale) there was also an attempt to render jewelry 'illusionistically' by the use of single large tesserae or shaped mother-of-pearl, although the more usual practice was to shape jewels from several tesserae in a 'representational' way. The handling of flesh and drapery in mosaic also indicates a striving for realism. The standard Byzantine practice of using far smaller tesserae for flesh was clearly to produce subtler modelling than in the more broadly handled draperies and backgrounds. In the draperies themselves, a painterly discrimination between opaque highlights, using marble or matt glass, and transparent glass shadows has been noticed both in Rome (Sta Maria Maggiore) and in Ravenna (Basilica Ursiana fragments).[101] In the Church of Christ in Chora at Istanbul (presumably in the panel of the Virgin in the nave and the *Deesis* in the narthex) it has been noticed that the reverse is true and that the highlights on the drapery are glass, whose glossy surface suggests light itself, and the reduced intensity of hue which that brilliance produces.[102]

All these examples refer to the realistic treatment of the figure; in none of them is there a hint of a spirituality beyond appearances, still less that the artist might convey such a spirituality through expressive deformations. The one suggestion of such an attitude that I have encountered is in a ninth-century sermon by Leo VI, in which he referred to a Pantokrator figure in a dome as truncated in order 'to offer a mystical suggestion of the eternal greatness inherent in the One represented, that is, that His incarnation on earth did not detract from His sublimity …'[103] Yet there is a whole class of Byzantine and Early Christian literature on art that does not deal with the figure but is concerned with sublimity and the means of achieving it in art: this is the description of the interiors of buildings, of which we have seen several examples. They are the most original and the most important evidence of a specifically early medieval aesthetic.

Gold highlights could be used in ceiling mosaics in a way that was not possible in the level medium of pavements. In a bay of the ambulatory of Sta Constanza in Rome (built as a mausoleum for the daughter of Constantine) they pick out the bowl with drinking doves, and indicate proximity to the focus of the building, at first a tomb but now the high altar.

26 Rome, Sta Costanza, vault mosaic in a bay of the ambulatory, fourth century AD

27

27 Istanbul, Christ in Chora (Karije Djami), *Deesis*, *c.* 1320
28 Rome, S. Prassede, Chapel of S. Zeno, vault mosaic detail, ninth century
29 Istanbul, Sta Sophia, panel of *Leo VI kneeling before Christ*, ninth century
30 Ravenna, 'Mausoleum' of Galla Placida, *The Good Shepherd*, fifth century

28

29

Luminous colour

It was through mosaic that the artists of the Early Christian and Byzantine churches were able to convey their message of salvation. They achieved an astonishing degree of expressiveness in this difficult medium, in which bright colours, including gold, were fused into little glass cubes, the tesserae (**30**), giving an enhanced brilliance, and by varying the angles of their surfaces, creating sparkle and shimmer as the spectator moved. Tesserae might be set at an angle at strategic places, such as haloes (**29**), to reflect light downward, or optical techniques could be used to create a variety of effects. Flesh (**28**) was warmed by a random scattering of red tesserae, for example, or a chequerboard type of shading gave an optical shimmer to soft or lustrous subjects (**27**). The examples range from the fifth to the fourteenth century.

The colour of Divine Light

Throughout the Middle Ages the Classical tradition that red was
the colour of light continued to find expression in art. In one of the
mosaics of St Mark's in Venice (**31**), the light of Creation itself is red
as it is separated from darkness (blue). In many Early Christian apse
mosaics, the theophany of Christ takes place among the rosy clouds
of dawn (**32**).

31 Venice, S. Marco, atrium mosaic, *The separation of light from darkness*,
thirteenth century
32 Rome, SS. Cosmas and Damian, apse mosaic, sixth century

32

The colour of Divine Darkness

33 Sinai, Monastery of St Catherine, apse mosaic, *The Transfiguration of Christ*, sixth century

In the Transfiguration the 'light' emanating from Christ's mandorla becomes whiter as it recedes from its source, and here at Sinai it even turns the Apostles' garments blue. This unusual characteristic (for the normal behaviour of light, see pl. 25) may be a reflection of the view propagated by the sixth-century theologian the Pseudo-Dionysus, that at this moment in Christ's life, 'a cloud and darkness were about him' (Psalm 96/7, 2).

34

The colour purple

Redness and lustre seem to have been the two most prized qualities of ancient and medieval purple. In the Empress Theodora's robe at Ravenna it was probably the shine, not the hue, which proclaimed it the true Imperial purple; and in the scene of Mary receiving the skein of wool (**35**), although an inscription calls it 'porphurion' it is clearly a vermilion red.

34 Ravenna, S. Vitale, *The Empress Theodora and her ladies*, c. 540
35 Istanbul, Christ in Chora (Karije Djami), *The Virgin receiving the skein of wool*, c. 1320 (detail)

35

33

The illuminating book

37

The Gospel itself was a vehicle of light. In a
copy of Beatus's Commentary on the
Apocalypse (**36**), Christ, in a cloud supported
by seraphim, holds the Book with a jewelled
cover. Another such Gospel-book appears on
the altar in the Uta Codex (**37**).

36 *Christ appearing in the Clouds*, from a
Commentary on the Apocalypse by Beatus of Liebana,
c. 1109
37 *St Erhard Offering Mass*, from the Uta Codex,
eleventh century (detail)

36

The ultimate model of these *ekphraseis* was Homer's description of the Palace of Alcinous, which Odysseus approached with some misgivings (*Odyssey* VII, 82–130):

> For a kind of radiance, like that of the sun or moon, lit up the high roofed halls of the great king. Walls of bronze, topped with blue enamel tiles, ran round to left and right from the threshold to the back of the court. The interior of the well-built mansion was guarded by golden doors hung on posts of silver which sprang from the bronze threshold. The lintel they supported was of silver too, and the door handle of gold . . . [trans. Rieu]

Here Homer first sets the tone of the description, then takes the eye briskly round the interior space. He hints at the splendour of the ceiling but not at the character of the pavement, although an early commentary on this passage had it that it was of gold.[104] Later Homer's brief account was elaborated into a type of set-piece description by Lucian in the second century AD and by Nonnos in the fifth. Lucian in *The Hall* dwelt at length on he gilded ceiling, like a starry sky at night, mentioning too the painted walls with their suggestion of spring flowers. Nonnos (*Dionysiaca* XVII, 67–90), on the other hand, turned the whole building into a lavish display of precious stones and metals and drew attention to the intricate patterns in the mosaic pavement; he concluded that his visitor 'turned his wandering gaze to each thing in order'. The early medieval *ekphrasis* developed these models by amplifying all their characteristics and by giving particularly extended attention to ceiling and floor. Thus, already in the early fourth century the author of a life of Constantine the Great described the ceiling of the Church of the Holy Sepulchre in Jerusalem as composed of carved coffering 'which, like a great sea, extended over the entire basilica in a continuous intertwining, and, being entirely overlaid with radiant gold, made the whole church gleam with flashes of light.'[105] It was an image which fascinated the early Middle Ages in the West: Paulinus in the fifth century used it of his new ceiling in the basilica at Nola in South Italy, with its 'shimmering' coffers; in the seventh century Venantius Fortunatus introduced it into his account of the church of Bishop Felix at Ravenna and in the ninth Giselmanus into his of the Church of St Vincent in Paris.[106] This vivid image of the coffered ceiling as a shimmering sea stands out from the more obvious metaphor of a sunny or starry heaven.[107]

The pavement, in mosaic or the marble slabs whose striations recalled the striations of salt-foam on the breaker or the ship's wake, was also frequently compared to the sea or rivers in these descriptions: the use of green Thessalian marble lent itself especially to such an analogy. In his account of the mosaics of the Great Palace in Constantinople, from the period of Andronikos Paleologus the elder (1282–1328), Nicephorus Xanthopoulos extended this image to the whole room: 'What is spread on the floor, and what clothes the whole space like a dress worked in colours might at first sight be called a sea, which, moving on all sides in the gentlest waves, is suddenly petrified.'[108] The analogy is second only to the image of the pavement (and sometimes the whole church interior) as a flowery meadow, another with a good Classical pedigree.[109] Sometimes the idea of the sea and the meadow co-existed, for all this cosmic imagery was part of the early medieval attempt to see the church as expressive of the whole universe.[110] The relationship of pavement to sea was sometimes a response to the imagery of the pavement itself, as in the vast late fifth-century fishing pavement of the Cathedral at Aquilea (whose motifs go back to the Temple of Fortune at Palestrina and whose style reflects secular pavements at Piazza Armerina in Sicily) and a group of pavements in churches around the Adriatic – notably Sta Eufemia at Grado – and in north Italy, from the sixth to the twelfth centuries, which include a particular wave-like pattern.[111] We are reminded, too, that the great rivers and the ocean had been singled out by Longinus in the first century AD as among the sublimest images of nature (*On the Sublime* 35).

The most important feature of the sea-imagery for both ceilings and pavements is that they conveyed a vivid sense of the gentle but ceaseless movement of natural things; the interpretation of the Byzantine and Early Christian interior as movement was perhaps the most original characteristic of post-Classical *ekphrasis*. The twelfth-century description of the pavement in Sta Sophia in Constantinople, by Michael of Thessaloniki, stated categorically: 'The floor is like the sea, both in its width and in its form; for certain blue waves are raised up against the stone, just as though you had cast a pebble into the water, and had disturbed its calm . . .'.[112] It extended to every feature of the interior space: Chorikos's hint that the gilded vault mosaics were flowing fountains, echoed by Michael Psellus in the eleventh century,[113] was expanded in the twelfth by Michael of Thessaloniki into an image of liquid movement that brought tears to the eyes of the spectator and involved church and observer in a single action: 'The brightness of the gold almost makes the gold appear to drip down; for by its refulgence making waves to arise, as it were, in eyes that are moist, it causes their moisture to appear in the gold which is seen, and it seems to be flowing in a molten stream.'[114] This intense subjective involvement in the experience of the church interior had already been expressed by Procopius in his sixth-century account of Sta Sophia:

> All [the] elements, marvellously fitted together in mid-air, suspended from one another and reposing only on the parts adjacent to them, produce a unified and most remarkable harmony in the work, and yet do not allow the spectators to rest their gaze upon any one of them for a length of time, but each detail readily draws and attracts the eye to itself. Thus the vision constantly shifts around, and the beholders are quite unable to select any particular element which they might admire more than all the others . . .[115]

In his account of the new church of St George of Mangana, Psellus went out of his way to stress that it was the size and grandeur of the building which impressed and, above all, its manifold detail:

> It was not merely the exceptional beauty of the whole, composed as it was of most beautiful parts, but just as much the individual details that attracted the spectator's attention, and although he could enjoy to his heart's content all its charms, it was impossible to find one that palled. Every part of it took the eye, and what is more wonderful, even when you gazed on the loveliest part of all, the small detail would delight you as a fresh discovery . . .[116]

This sense of ecstatic bewilderment was induced partly by the

20

38

intricate planning, both horizontal and vertical, of the Byzantine church, so unlike the simple sweep of the Western basilica towards the apse, and by the often confusing lay-out of the many narrative paintings or mosaics, at its most extreme in the Macedonian painted churches of the fourteenth century, such as Staro Nagoričane. This meant that the narrative sequence had to be sought with some difficulty in order to be understood.[117] It was an attitude towards viewing a church which also had important consequences for style – not least, for example, in delaying the exploitation of the late-Classical single-point perspective system in monumental painting – and for the handling of colour, for it is only to the moving eye that the metallic elements in mosaic and fresco are fully visible. But when the gold and silver surfaces are at their most reflective, the adjacent coloured areas are least chromatic: light destroys colour and the spectator must move on to enjoy the coloured images again.[118] This functional separation between light and colour in Byzantine mosaics, which reflects the Aristotelian distinction between them that dominated the early Middle Ages and was still strongly present in the Arab theorists of the tenth and eleventh centuries,[119] could only be reconciled in an aesthetics of movement; it was this aspect of Byzantine aesthetics which was perhaps most important. The early Renaissance polemic against the use of real gold in painting and the great reduction of its use in mosaic, for example in the Mascoli Chapel in Venice,[120] was closely associated with the re-assertion of a single-point perspective system and hence the reduction of lateral movement in the spectator.

Mosaic pavement of Sta Eufemia, Grado, sixth century. The wave-like pattern embodies the poetic notion of the mosaic pavement as a shining sea. (38)

The colours of Divine Light

If light and colour were distinct, albeit related phenomena, what was the colour of light, and more specifically of Divine Light? Some years ago Patrik Reuterswärd addressed this question in a playful essay and concluded that it was either red or blue.[121] But if we look at a related group of Byzantine churches whose similar iconographic programmes gave many opportunities for the deployment of Divine Light – Hosios Loukas (c. 1020), Nea Moni on Chios (mid-eleventh century) and Daphni (before 1080) – we find a situation which is rather more complicated than that. Hosios Loukas, which has the most complete cycle of mosaics, includes a scene of Pentecost in the dome where the red flames of the Holy Spirit are enclosed in white rays with a dark bluish-grey edge; this pattern is also seen in the heavenly rays descending on Christ at the Baptism. The same formula is used in these scenes at Nea Moni but at Daphni, where the use of silver cubes is generally very marked, the rays in the Baptism include silver too. In the Nativity at Hosios Loukas the rays descending on the infant Christ are gold, where silver is again used at Daphni; in the scene of the Transfiguration in Nea Moni, Christ's dazzling effulgence is gold, while in the painted rendering in the crypt at Hosios Loukas and in the mosaic at Daphni it is blue, white and silver, where the mosaic artist has made the rays flashing from Christ's body gold and grey within the area of his mandorla, to contrast with the blue-silver of the mandorla itself, and silver and grey outside it, to contrast with the gold background of the whole picture. At Daphni too is one of the most eloquent evocations of the Divine Light: in the astonishing space between Gabriel and Mary in the scene of the Annunciation light is caught and held in the cupped surface, whose bareness of imagery is especially striking by comparison with the crowded figures of the other three pendentifs of the dome. There the light catches the figures of Christ or the Holy Spirit (as a dove); here their presence must surely be implicit in the reflected light itself. For it occupies just that place in the composition reserved for the Christ-child or the dove of the Holy Spirit in some Annunciations in the Mani (southern Peloponnese) and in a well-known icon at Sinai.[122] Here Divine Light is indubitably a beautiful pale gold.

Perhaps the question 'what colour is Divine Light?' is badly framed, for we have seen that it was not hue but luminosity with which the early medieval artist was chiefly occupied. Certainly it could be red, especially in the later Middle Ages.[123] It is notable that the miraculous light which appeared in the Holy Sepulchre in Jerusalem at Vespers on Good Friday was described in the twelfth century as 'not like an ordinary flame, but [it] burns in a marvellous fashion, and with an indescribable brilliance, red like cinnabar'.[124] Yet the red was surely important not for its hue but because it stood for the finest sort of light.

Divine Light may also be blue: blue grounds seem to have preceded gold grounds in the earliest wall mosaics[125] and blue was the dominant colour in many of the mandorlas which surround Christ in representations of the Transfiguration and the *Anastasis* from the sixth century onwards, as it is of the emanation from God's hand in the Byzantine churches just discussed. There is something very curious about the form of

39

Daphni, *The Annunciation, c.* 1080. The emanation of the Holy Spirit is conveyed by no more than the reflection of light on gold mosaic. (39)

these mandorlas and these emanations: for the most part they reverse the sequence of brightness-zones that we should expect from a light-giving body (described clearly by Plotinus in his discussion of divine emanation in *Enneads* IV, 3.17); they proceed from dark at the centre, round the body of Christ or the hand of God, to light at their furthest extremity. There are exceptions to this scheme – Christ's mandorla in the Last Judgment at Torcello, in the central dome of S. Marco in Venice and in the fresco Transfiguration at Nea Moni, for example – but in general this 'normal' sequence is reversed.[126] Nicholas Mesaretes in the twelfth century put his finger on the reason for

this curious inversion when he described the scene of the Transfiguration in the (now destroyed) Church of the Holy Apostles in Constantinople, which must have conformed to the usual type:

> The space in the air supports a cloud of light and in the midst of this bears Jesus, made more brilliant than the sun, as though generated like another light from His Father's light, which as though with a cloud is joined to the nature of man. For a cloud, it is written, and darkness were about Him, and the light produces this [cloud] through the transformation of the higher nature to the lower, because of this union which surpasses all understanding, and is of an unspeakable nature . . .[127]

Thus the darkness arose when the Divine Light took on flesh; but there was another dimension to Mesaretes's commentary, for he was able to appeal to a Biblical tradition of Divine darkness, a tradition which had been given particular prominence by one early Byzantine theologian.

The ancient Jewish notion that God dwelt in ineffable darkness[128] became firmly Christianized in the sixth century in the writings, probably by a Syrian monk, attributed to Dionysius the Areopagite, the pagan philosopher converted by St Paul at Athens (Acts 17: 34) and who, according to a legend often represented in Byzantine art, had attended the Virgin at her death. Pseudo-Dionysius was one of the most frequently cited theologians of the early Middle Ages,[129] according to whom, 'we posit intangible and invisible darkness of that Light which is unapproachable because it so far exceeds the visible light' (*On the Divine Names* VII, 2), and in a letter, 'The divine darkness is that "unapproachable light" where God is said to live'.[130] That Christ is emanating darkness in the Transfiguration is suggested by the darkened bodies of the three Disciples on the sides towards him, especially clear in the earliest known monumental rendering of the subject, in the apse in St Catherine's on Sinai, where the tunics of SS Peter and James (respectively, a light brown and a light purple) turn deep blue where Christ's rays strike them.[131] The Divine effulgence seems to have similarly surprising effects in the Church of Christ in Chora mosaic of the Dormition of the Virgin where Christ's mandorla (grey and blue) turns the golden seraphim grey-blue where it overlaps them; in the Nativity the grey-white light from heaven does the same for the oxen. Conformably to the sense of bafflement which is conveyed in the Gospel accounts of the Transfiguration, blue is the colour of the Divine Darkness which transcends light. The mosaic at Sinai seems to be the earliest representation of this type and it was especially appropriate to the Dionysian interpretation of God's nature there since Sinai was the site where Moses 'went into that darkness where God was' (Exodus 20: 21), the episode shown in another mosaic at St Catherine's and an example of the 'truly mystical darkness of unknowing' to which Pseudo-Dionysius drew attention in his *Mystical Theology*.[132]

At the Transfiguration, too, however, Christ's garment became a dazzling white: in his commentary on the story, the second-century Greek writer Origen amplified the idea that 'since there are even degrees among white things, his garments became as white as the brightest and purest of all white things, that is light.'[133] The Greek and his early Latin translators did indeed have several terms for white at their disposal: Origen used *lampron* as well as *leukon* and his translator *candidus*.[134] He might still have been able to use *phaion*, now translated as 'grey' but originally meaning 'shining' as well.[135] *Lampron* (bright) was such a fundamental concept in Greek thought about colour that it appeared together with *phaion* as one of the 'twelve' colours (actually ten) capable of being distinguished by the eye in a fragment of Ptolemy's *Optics* (probably from the lost first book) widely known in Byzantium.[136] The list also includes three terms for dark colours and it is not surprising that Greek and Latin also had several ways of characterizing 'black': it is the other side of the coin of what has seemed to philologists to be a simplification of colour groupings into 'light' and 'dark'.[137]

Red and blue were not simply Divine but also the colours of mundane light and darkness, as they appear in the thirteenth-

century mosaics of the Creation in the atrium of S. Marco in Venice; in the eleventh-century colour-scale devised by the Byzantine lexicographer Suda, red also appears next to white and blue to black.[138] If early medieval painters grouped the colours according to those which had an affinity with light and those which were close to darkness, they hardly had the means to develop a very complex language of colour symbolism.[139] In liturgical vestments, where we might have expected to find such a language developing, there was no general agreement about the significance of colours: here, too, red was usually assimilated to white for joyous feasts and violet and indigo to black for feasts of penance and mourning. For Pope Innocent III, who attempted to codify liturgical colours for the Western Church at the end of the twelfth century, green, following Aristotle, was the median colour, 'intermediate between white, black and red', and could thus be used for less clearly characterized feasts. The Eastern Church had no colour-canon but showed a preference for bright colours and white, even for funereal occasions. White and black remained for both Eastern and Western churches the most important points of the colour-scale.[140]

Modern studies have tended to narrow the gap between designers and executant craftworkers in medieval mosaic production, to stress the freedom of action of the setters, especially in the matter of colour choice.[141] Certainly the transmission of ideas through model-books concentrated on forms, so far as we know, and in the few known examples of the use of manuscript illuminations by mosaicists – the most familiar example is that of the Cotton Genesis in the British Library and the atrium mosaics of S. Marco – the influence does not extend to the colour.[142] Dionysius of Fourna, following the Gospels of Mark and Luke, prescribed white for the garments of the transfigured Christ, and so they were usually rendered; but at Nea Moni Christ is in gold, at Daphni he wears a pale green cloak over a pink tunic, and at Nerezi in Macedonia in the twelfth century and on an iconostasis beam at Sinai in the thirteenth he is in red over green. Yet if we look at the clothing of some familiar Biblical figures such as St Peter, we find that from Venice to Sinai and over a period of eight or nine centuries he wears the same class of colours, if not precisely the same hues: a yellow or brownish cloak over a bluish or greenish tunic. The medieval spectator would not have been able to recognize Peter by his colours alone: in the scene of Christ washing the Disciples' feet at Nea Moni, three other Apostles wear exactly the same combination of colours as he does; and yet his garments invariably belong to the family of the blues and browns. The medieval painter was concerned less with precise individual hues than with a general class.[143]

Given the concentration on effects of light manifested in the development of early medieval mosaic, it is perhaps surprising that mosaicists made little use of a formal device which became very common in the drapery painting of the later Middle Ages: colour-change, by which draperies could be modelled not with a darker value of their own hue but with another hue which might be of the same value and thus maintain an overall high tonality. A model of colour-change effects had perhaps been available to artists since late Antiquity in the form of 'peacock stuffs', or shot materials. These have been identified in a first-century AD mosaic with a scene from a comedy in Naples (blue-green) and were described in the third century by Alexander of Aphrodisias, although no early examples of the fabrics themselves have survived.[144] The history of these textiles remains confused because we must rely for the most part on ambiguous verbal descriptions. It is not clear, for example, whether the silk dyed with orseille (*sericum auricellatum*), dipped in indigo and then showing shimmering colours similar to those of the peacock (described by the south Italian doctor Urso of Salerno at the end of the twelfth century), was a shot material (in which the woof is of one colour and the weft of another) or simply had a sheen.[145] Certainly by the eleventh century Tinnīs, near Alexandria, was famous for a cloth called būkalamūn, 'the colour of which changes according to the different hours of the day', one type of which was red and green, and was compared to jasper and peacock's feathers.[146] In the early fourteenth century, discussions of colour-illusions began to add silk stuffs to the more traditional examples of the dove's neck and the rainbow. Peter Aureol, for example, about 1316, related these 'silk cloths which in different positions show different colours' to the dove's neck, but went on to say that they were indeed illusions, which suggests very strongly that if they were shot materials, he had not examined them very closely.[147] At about the same time *cangiacolore* (colour-change) stuffs begin to be mentioned in Italian inventories, notably at Assisi.[148]

In handbooks of painting, however, there is little hint of these 'shot' effects: Theophilus in his twelfth-century treatise makes no reference to any other than tonal shading, nor does Dionysius of Fourna, some of whose material goes back to the eighth or ninth century; the first hints that colour-changes might be used does not appear until the late additions in 'Heraclius' in the late thirteenth century. Most of these examples could also be regarded as 'tonal'.[149] Yellow-green colour-changes are common enough from the fourth to the twelfth centuries, but we have seen the status of yellow as a type of green in Antiquity (p. 12) and they continued to be regarded as members of the same genus of hue as late as the fifteenth century.[150] I have noticed red-green colour-change in the mosaics of Nea Moni and in the wall-paintings of Moni Mavriotissa at Kastoria in northern Greece. From the twelfth century a very wide range of combinations – blue or green on purple, yellow on blue or red, red on white are some of the more striking – may be seen in monuments all over the Byzantine world.[151] The device is perhaps more common in painting than in mosaic and may be a function of the method, known from the eleventh century onwards, of working on a blue or black ground, from dark to light (whereas the mosaic setters worked from light to dark), and needing to create the light entirely out of colour.[152]

Do these developments (which accompanied the decline of mosaic as an important medium of expression) testify to a new sensitivity to hue during the course of the Middle Ages? There are certainly some reasons for thinking that they might. Knowledge of the subjective effects of colours grew and spread during the period. Galen wrote of the miniature painters who 'especially when they are working on white parchment' and their eyes tire easily, 'place nearby grey or dark-coloured objects, to which they keep looking away, thus resting their eyes'.[153] This clearly reflects the Greek idea that vision is essentially dependent on light and dark. But two centuries later Basil of Caesarea referred to blue and green as the colours which were specifically restful and it was for this reason that the poet Baudri of Bourgueil in the eleventh century preferred to write on green rather than black wax tablets.[154] Aristotle had seen green as the happy medium between light and dark; in Antiquity it had also been associated with the magical virtues of the emerald and other green stones, which were powdered and used as an eye-salve, but now the idea was given a more subjective, a more psychological inflection.[155]

The colours of Islam

If we examine the colour of a wide range of Byzantine artefacts in every medium, it becomes clear that a good deal of the vivid local colour, which has given them their reputation for a peculiarly highly developed colour-sense, derives from the ornament, much of which was developed from late-antique motifs, from the landscape and architectural backgrounds, which have a similar origin, above all from the costumes of the figures, who stand or kneel, stiffened by the weight of the jewelled and embroidered stuffs they are so avid to display. These costumes are the least Hellenic ingredient in Byzantine art and in many cases they are specifically oriental. In S. Apollinare Nuovo in Ravenna it is the brightly clothed Persian Magi who present the Holy Virgins to Mary – the Virgins who are themselves dressed in richly flowered dalmatics, with Asian belts and the oriental *loros* underneath them, whereas the white-robed martyrs opposite are led by St Martin in a plain purple tunic. These same Magi are figured on the hem of the Empress Theodora's cloak in the mosaic at S. Vitale, their presence underlining the pervasive influence of oriental fashion from the sixth to the ninth centuries and also that it was fashionable women who were its most important transmitters to the West.[156] Charlemagne indulged his wife and her entourage, as well as the many churches he endowed, with the rich imported stuffs and gold brocade that he denied himself and discouraged in the male members of his court.[157] At Palermo on Christmas Day 1185 the Arab traveller Ibn Jobaïr noted that the Christian women wore silk stuffs and gold brooches, variegated veils and gold-embroidered shoes, perfume and paint, 'like musulman women'.[158]

This was not a taste for women only: a love of luxurious jewels and stuffs, especially oriental stuffs, had come to Byzantium with the Roman army of the Emperor Constantine, the first Roman emperor 'to wear a diadem decorated with pearls and precious stones', according to an early chronicler.[159] Constantine's biographer described his entrance to the Council of Nicea (325) 'like some heavenly messenger of God, clothed in raiment which glittered as it were with rays of light, reflecting the purple radiance of a glowing robe, and adorned with the brilliant splendour of gold and precious stones ...'. The same writer described, somewhat disapprovingly, how the barbarians would attend the Emperor at his palace in Constantinople: 'like some painted pageant, [presenting] to the Emperor those gifts which their own nation valued, some offering crowns of gold, others diadems set with precious stones, some bringing

40

34

The Persian costumes of the Three Magi at Ravenna (sixth century) caught the attention of western artists and were widely imitated. It may be an indication of the fluidity of colour-description at the period that the ninth-century restorer of these mosaics listed the cloaks as blue (signifying matrimony) for the purple, yellow (*flavo*, signifying virginity) for the white, and variegated (signifying penitence) where we find green. (40)

fair-haired boys, others barbaric vestments embroidered with gold and flowers.'[164] The bright tunics and trousers which now became a feature of Roman army uniform reflect Hunnish influence, and further Hunnish and Persian garments were introduced by Justinian in the sixth century.[161] The costumes represented in the mosaics of Piazza Armerina (probably early fourth century) show those *segmenta* – inlaid decorative panels of woven design of animals, birds, human figures – which were so much in demand in North Africa from the first century AD and had spread throughout the Roman Empire by the end of the third.[162] A taste for Persian fabrics became so strong that in the seventh century the Emperor Heraclius brought Iranian weavers to Constantinople, and oriental stuffs were widely imitated within the Empire.[163]

The fashion for rich stuffs was not confined to costume. Those swags of seemingly pointless materials which drape so many buildings in early medieval pictures are symbols of the innumerable hangings with which churches in Byzantium and the West were decorated on feast-days – hangings which included the most precious oriental textiles. The Spanish nun Egeria was greatly impressed by the church interiors at Jerusalem and Bethlehem late in the fourth century:

> The decorations really are too marvellous for words: All you can see is gold, and jewels and silk; the hangings are entirely silk with gold stripes, the curtains the same, and everything they use for

services at the festival (Epiphany) is made of gold and jewels. You simply cannot imagine the number, and the sheer weight of the candles and tapers and lamps and everything else they use for the services.[164]

Although textiles with Christian subject-matter had been produced at least since the late fourth century, many of these church hangings and even vestments used the traditional pagan designs of flowers, animals, hunting scenes and, after the rise of Islam in the eighth century, Kufic inscriptions in praise of Allah, which were later imitated on stuffs produced in the West. Thus in the late eighth century Pope Leo III presented St Peter's with a hanging for the ciborium of the high altar bearing tigers embroidered in gold, and ten years later Pope Gregory IV gave a curtain from Alexandria for the main door, with 'men and horses', probably a hunting silk.[165]

This presentation of entirely secular and often pagan imagery in a Christian setting might have been expected to stimulate the kind of allegorical interpretations which had arisen when the hunting and fishing pavements of late Antiquity had been taken into churches. Yet this does not seem to have happened: an early ninth-century text, the *Antirrheticus* of the Patriarch of Constantinople, Nicephorus Gregoras, provides a remarkably early discussion of the distinction between subject-content and decorative content which has had a good deal of resonance in modern aesthetics. Arguing against the Iconoclasts, Nicephorus stated that what was venerated by the Iconodules was the sacred objects themselves, not the decorations on them, not even the image of Christ. The many living things – he listed wild animals, horses and birds – represented in the sanctuary were there not to be honoured and venerated 'but because of the decorativeness of the stuffs into which they are woven'. Holy icons were not like this, since they were holy in their own right and designed to recall the Archetypes.[166] That the concept of pure decoration should have been associated with textiles is interesting, for it was in the enjoyment of textiles that medieval spectators expressed the purest interest in colour for its own sake. Gregory of Nyssa in his *Life of Moses* retold the story of the vestments made for the officiants at the Tabernacle (Exodus 39: 1–3): 'blue is interwoven with violet, and scarlet mingled with white, and among them are woven threads of gold; the variety of colours shine with remarkable beauty'.[167] Gregory's version is striking not only because he emphasizes the whiteness of the linen far more than his model, but also because, like other Byzantine writers, he is concerned with the visual effect – the beauty – of the result, where the Hebrew writer simply admires the clever workmanship, and the Graeco-Jewish commentators Josephus and Philo of Alexandria stress the elemental symbolism of the colours.[168] One of the most vivid and precise descriptions of a work of art in the Middle Ages is Reginald of Durham's account of the textiles shrouding the remains of St Cuthbert in Durham Cathedral, which were exposed and examined in August 1104:

> He was clad in tunic and dalmatic, in the manner of Christian bishops. The style of both of these, with their precious purple colour and varied weave, is most beautiful and admirable. The dalmatic which, as the outer robe[,] is the more visible, offers a reddish purple tone, quite unknown in our time, even to connoisseurs. It still retains the bloom of its original freshness and beauty, and when handled it makes a kind of crackling sound because of the solidity and compactness of the fine, skilful weaving. The most subtle figures of flowers and little beasts, very minute in both workmanship and design, are interwoven in this fabric. And for more grace and beauty its appearance was frequently changed and variegated by strands of another colour mingled with it ... a yellow colour seems to have been laid down drop by drop; by virtue of this yellow the reddish tonality in the purple is made to shine with more vigour and brilliance ...[169]

As Aristotle had hinted, and as his late-antique commentators had emphasized,[170] it was the workers with textiles who had developed the most intimate knowledge of the harmony and contrast of colours.

Since the cause of this appreciation of pure hue was probably oriental in origin and since with the rise of Islam in the seventh century a culture was to develop in Asia and the Arab world which was as self-conscious and articulate as any in the West and was, in particular, to make the most important advances in medieval optics, it might well be expected that the art and ideas of the Middle East would offer a quite distinct aesthetic or, at least, a distinctly different emphasis from those developing in Europe. Certainly the most original and uncompromising of all medieval colour-styles is found in manuscript-painting in northern Spain, on the borders of the Arab world, in the highly schematized illustrations of the tenth to twelfth centuries to Beatus's *Commentary on the Apocalypse*, which were so exciting to colourists like Picasso and Léger when they were brought to light again in the 1920s. Modern critics have emphasized the autonomy of colour in this remarkable group of some twenty surviving manuscripts and have underlined the lucid, almost diagrammatic quality of the colour-areas of high saturation – what one of them described as 'the brilliant, unearthly zones of an abstract cosmos'.[171] It is still not clear what precisely the relations between this style and Mozarabic art really were but certainly its visual origins were very various.[172] The diagrammatic quality of these illuminations is in the spirit of the manuscript tradition of Isidore of Seville's *On the Nature of Things*, with its early development of a range of scientific schemata, especially those based on the circle.[173] Although the Beatus manuscripts differ considerably among themselves in their choice and handling of colour, all deploy an unusually wide range of hues to articulate sets of clearly demarcated colour contrasts.[174] What is perhaps most striking about these large and sumptuous books is their complete lack of metallic colours: where Baudri of Bourgueil specifically mentioned the Arab origin of the gold which embellished the manuscript of his poems,[175] in the Beatus series we find an unusually widespread use of yellow paint, unparalleled perhaps until El Greco at the close of the sixteenth century. These Beatus yellows have not, so far as I know, been analysed but some of them look like saffron, a vegetable dyestuff grown in the Middle East which the Crusades had introduced very widely into Europe by the twelfth century.[176] Yellow has had a bad press in modern times and is now thought to be the least popular colour;[177] but there were good reasons for regarding it as an especially harmonious hue in the later Middle Ages. The yellow angels who are so conspicuous in the *Silos Apocalypse* may be understood in terms of a gloss by Bernardino de Busti in the fifteenth century, where the colour (*flavus*) expressed the balance between the red of justice and the white of compassion.[178]

Visually this yellow seems to bear little relationship to gold and unlike the early medieval Irish manuscripts whose repertory of interlace seems to derive largely from metalwork,[179] the Spanish organization and handling of colour reflects a highly developed taste in textiles. Of the subtle modulation of the coloured areas by repeated lines and dots, characterized by the tiny horseshoe pattern in the *Silos Apocalypse*, Meyer Schapiro has written: 'It is a method of dosage of color that suggests an Impressionist flecking and breaking, but is related also to the play of colored points and threads in a woven fabric.'[180] It is perhaps more than a coincidence that one of the most extended and original metaphors in Beatus's *Commentary on the Apocalypse* should be drawn precisely from textiles and their dyes. The mystery of the Trinity, wrote Beatus, could be understood in terms of the way pure undyed woollen cloth was made up of three elements: the warp, the thrum and the woof. But this pure white cloth was often darkened (*fuscantur*) by a range of coloured dyes. Some cloths smile (*subrideant*) with vermilion, some with green, some with yellow, some with scarlet, others with different red or black colours – the range indeed which we see in the illuminated manuscripts of his work (but all of them postdating the eighth-century text). Yet for

Beatus these colours were the manifold heresies which defiled the purity of the Godhead, heresies which his own career as a theologian was dedicated to uprooting and which in fact were the pretext for his vast commentary on the *Apocalypse of John*.[181] We are reminded of the apocryphal *Gospel of Philip*, where God himself was described as a dyer, capable of conferring through baptism a permanent dye on all his creatures but with only a single colour, white; in particular of the episode where Jesus, on a visit to a dyeworks, throws seventy-two colours into the vat and brings them all out white.[182]

Beatus's reservations about polychromy were thus firmly in line with the late-antique aesthetic of light outlined here. The Islamic attitudes to which his illustrators were more or less close were no less Hellenic in character. The magnificent mosaic decorations of the Dome of the Rock in Jerusalem (691) and in the Great Mosque at Damascus (*c.* 715) do not differ in style or colour from their Western counterparts; indeed, they often employed Byzantine craftworkers.[183] Nor were Islamic attitudes to such work very different from those in the West: a ninth-century text attributed to Hunain Ibn Ishāq suggests that Greeks, Jews and Christians decorated their temples with the common aim of the 'refreshing of souls and the engagement of hearts' and a little later the philisopher al-Razi wrote that the therapeutic effect of pictures derived, apart from the subject, from 'beautiful, pleasant colours – yellow, red, green and white – and the forms are reproduced in exactly the right proportions' – an entirely Hellenic formulation.[184] Islamic descriptions of buildings emphasized their light-giving materials and their capacity to stun the spectator in ways which are close to Western examples.[185] The role of light in Islamic mysticism was analagous to that in early Christianity and it was probably derived from a theory of perception which included the ideas of Plato and Plotinus.[186] The theory of colours in the ninth-century Syrian Job of Edessa's *Book of Treasures* was largely Greek: black and white were the primary colours, from which the intermediate red, saffron-yellow, green and golden-yellow derived. The colours were linked to the elements, white to dryness and black to humidity; the eye itself contained black and white, and hence all the colours, within it.[187] Avicenna (980–1037) was particularly preoccupied by the question of the relationship of values to hues, which he was able to describe only as a series of discrete scales between white and black for each hue, and for grey.[188] As we shall see (Ch. 9), it took many centuries for colour-theorists to see that a co-ordinated colour space must be three-dimensional. Avicenna's concern with value was even greater than that of his Greek forbears.

Even Alhazen, who wrote the most comprehensive treatise on optics in the Middle Ages and specifically developed the study of subjective colour-phenomena, did not reject the tonal emphases of Aristotle or Ptolemy, who provided him with his starting-point. He experimented with colour mixtures on a spinning disc, noticing that the 'stronger' colour tends to overcome the 'weaker' (*Optics* I, 31; II, 19f), but strength and weakness seem to have been understood entirely in terms of value, the lighter colours being the stronger. In a section on the effects of colour-contrast (I, 32), such contrasts were explored only in a tonal context: red spots on a white ground seemed black, but on a black one white; the ground should be grey to show their true colour; green on a yellow ground seemed simply darker (not greener or yellower) than on a darker ground. A discussion of beauty (II, 59) was similarly unspecific about light and colours: the moon and the stars, flowers and coloured cloth were all described simply as beautiful; there was beauty in both similarity and contrast, and harmony and proportion were primary sources of it. But Alhazen (who died *c.* 1038) brought no developments in understanding the interaction of hues.[189]

The structure of colour-terminology in Arabic was very similar to that in the European languages of the Middle Ages, with an emphasis on light and dark and a relative imprecision in the discrimination of hues.[190] It is very striking that perhaps the two most distinct contributions of early Islamic craft-skill to the arts – the lustre-ware ceramics produced in Egypt from about the seventh century, in imitation of metalwork, and the monochrome silks manufactured in Persia in the ninth century and at Antioch or Damascus in the eleventh – should have depended for their effect entirely on creating sensations of light.[191]

To find light used in the service of colour, rather than colour in the service of light, we must turn to the stained glass which became the most important new medium of European monumental painting from the middle of the twelfth century.

The immaterial glow of stained glass gave colour a new mystical dimension in the Early Middle Ages. Among the most densely symbolic of such windows are those made for Abbot Suger of St-Denis in the mid-twelfth century. The top roundel, a modern reconstruction, is based on Revelations V, 1–6, and shows the Lion and the Lamb unsealing the Book. Below, the Ark of the Covenant with a crucifix surmounts the *Quadriga of Aminadab*, and is flanked by the symbols of the four Evangelists, who proclaim that the new life of the New Testament creates a new Covenant with God. Suger, following the Pseudo-Dionysus, argued that sensory impressions derived from bright colours drew the onlooker 'from the material to the immaterial', bringing the divine into human life. Glass becomes a medium for mysteries.

41 St-Denis, Chapel of St Peregrinus, 'Anagogical' window, *c.* 1140 (detail)

QVI·EVS·ES·MAGNUS

LIB VVS·LEO·SO   VIG·E·AGNVS

AGNVS·SIVE

LEO·FIT·CARO

IVNCTA·DEO

FFDERIS·PV ARCA·C·SVCE   FEDERE·MAIORI·VVLTIBI·VITA

SISIS · · IVNCIV   MORE·ITE·

MV A·DRIGE·II

ARCA·MINA·PAB·

42

Transparency and gems

43

In the twentieth century the preciousness of gems relates to their transparency, but in the Early Middle Ages all matter was thought to incorporate light, so that the 'sapphire', the 'gem of gems', could be shown as the opaque *lapis lazuli* (**43**) in an inventory of the jewels of St Albans compiled in the thirteenth century (note the gem at the foot of the page). With the spread of stained glass transparency became more and more prized; even a silver chalice (**44**) might incorporate the quality with a decoration of windows. Precious gems also had healing and magical qualities by virtue of their divine associations. The walls of the Heavenly Jerusalem (**42**) were traditionally built of sapphires (oval), emeralds (rectangular) and pearls, and the same combination appears in the Shrine of Charlemagne (**45**), formerly in the treasury of St-Denis but destroyed in the Revolution.

44

42 Rome, Sta Maria Maggiore, detail of mosaics of the Triumphal Arch, *The Heavenly Jerusalem*, fifth century

43 MATTHEW PARIS, *The Jewels of St Albans*, MS inventory, 1257

44 The Mérode Cup, French or Burgundian, early fifteenth century

45 The *Escrin de Charlemagne*, ninth century (now lost). Watercolour by E. Labarre, 1794

45

4 · A Dionysian Aesthetic

The new light · Suger's aesthetics · The blues of St-Denis
From glass-staining to glass-painting · Workmanship versus materials
The secularization of light · Dante on the psychology of light

IN HIS ACCOUNT of the rebuilding of the Carolingian Abbey Church of St-Denis, on the northern outskirts of Paris. Abbot Suger remarked in the 1140s that he had ordered a mosaic to be inserted over the door in the new north portal, even though this was 'contrary to modern use'.[1] Wall mosaics had indeed gone out of fashion in northern Europe by the twelfth century; Suger's use of a modest one here was probably a self-conscious tribute to an older Christian tradition, which he would have encountered at Rome and perhaps also at Nola near Naples, where seven hundred years earlier Bishop Paulinus had clad his basilica of St Felix in extensive mosaic decorations. Paulinus had supplied these with just the sort of *tituli* that Suger was to display so conspicuously at St-Denis.[2] In order to gain space and light for his much visited shrine of St Felix, Paulinus had removed the wall separating two earlier churches and had put up *versiculi* (a term also used by Suger) proclaiming how these twin halls had given access to a new light (*nova lux*).[3] Suger's enlargement of his upper choir was the occasion of a very similar inscription:

> Once the new rear part is joined to the part in front,
> The church shines with its middle part brightened,
> For bright is that which is brightly coupled with the bright,
> And bright is the noble edifice which is pervaded by the new light
> [*lux nova*]...[4]

Whereas the Early Christian tradition had developed the glass mosaic to embody these notions of luminosity, the incipient Gothic of St-Denis developed the stained-glass window; Suger made it very clear that he regarded this as one of his own special achievements. In a probably slightly earlier account of the consecration of St-Denis in 1144 Suger wrote of the glazing of the chapels around his new Upper Choir, 'by virtue of which the whole [church] would shine with the wonderful and uninterrupted light of most luminous windows, pervading the interior beauty'.[5]

Yet if to the medieval spectator light could be manifested as well in mosaic as in glass windows, to the modern observer these windows seem to have very different characters. Between the mid-twelfth-century glass of, say, Chartres's west façade and the thirteenth-century glass of, say, the Chapter House at York Minster there seems to be little enough in common. The richness and low tonality of the first – which was to be accentuated in the thirteenth century – confers on the interior an almost tangible gloom[6] but the predominance of white or grisaille glass at York allows that space to be bathed in light.

This manifest change in the aesthetics of stained glass, which took place during the course of the thirteenth century,[7] is reflected in a number of texts of the later Middle Ages and the Renaissance. In the Temple of the Supreme God of the early fourteenth-century French *Roman de Perceforest*, 'there were no windows, except such as were necessary to give a modicum of light, to be able to see the way round the Temple, and to see and recognize the image of God; for the wise men said that a place of worship should have neither brightness nor painted decoration to which the people could direct their imaginations.' The anonymous author went on to say that the new, open fashion in the design of temples 'hinders worship and simplicity ... evil vanity [has] made glass and windows to give ample light, so that worship and repentance, which formerly inhabited these temples, have become suspicious, and are fled because of the great brightness.'[8]

This theme became a commonplace in the Renaissance. The churches in Thomas More's *Utopia* (1516), for example, were 'al sumwhat darke': 'Howbeit that was not donne through ignoraunce in buildinge, but as they say, by the counsel of the priestes. Bicause they thought that over much light doth disperse mens cogitations, whereas in dimme and doubtful lighte they be gathered together, and more earnestly fixed upon religion and devotion.'[9] Later in the same century a German commentater joked that in former times hearts were lighter and churches darker, by virtue of the many-coloured glass windows.[10] These developments towards the lightening of stained glass were not, as has sometimes been claimed, a question of economy but one very largely of aesthetic choice. The earliest surviving specialized treatise on glass-painting, compiled by Antonio da Pisa about 1400, stressed that coloured windows should include at least a third of white (colourless) glass, which will make the work more joyous (*allegro*) and also more easily read (*comparascente*). At Siena in the 1440s work on a coloured oculus by Guasparre di Giovanni da Volterra was suspended because some citizens felt that it would darken the cathedral, making it less *bello*.[11]

For most modern spectators light has seemed to be the key to the understanding of stained glass throughout the whole span of the Gothic centuries, and some have characterized the idea of

---

In many medieval churches no surface was left uncoloured. Painted ornament, narrative scenes in fresco, imitation mosaic and even *trompe l'œil* cloth-of-gold hangings all contributed to the sumptuous effect. At Assisi the generally lighter colours of the glass allowed the fresco cycles to be clearly seen.

46 Assisi, S. Francesco, Upper Church, North wall of the Isaac bay, *c.* 1300

'gothic gloom' as a figment of the Enlightenment or of the Romantic imagination.[12] Others have relied on largely thirteenth-century texts to reconstruct a 'metaphysic of light' in relation to stained glass, a 'metaphysic' in which light is seen as the primary creative force and an analogue of the Divine. The analogy is attractive but it can hardly be understood without some consideration of the various degrees within the concept of light, current in the early Middle Ages and codified in the optical writings of the thirteenth century. In the literature on the six days of Creation, which goes back to St Basil the Great, the primary light (*lux*) was distinguished from the light of the heavenly bodies (*luminaria*) created later as derivations from *lux*. Isidore of Seville wrote that '*Lux* is substance itself, and *Lumen* what flows from *Lux*, that is the whiteness of *Lux*, but writers confuse these two' (*Etymologies* XIII, x, 12ff). Indeed they do; the terms seem to have been used more or less indiscriminately until the thirteenth century when it was generally accepted, by scientific writers at least, that *lux* referred to light-sources and *lumen* to light seen, as it were, from the terrestrial, receiving end.[13] But some writers, and most importantly here Johannes Scotus Eriugena in the ninth century, seriously attempted to discriminate between these terms. Eriugena asked in his commentary on the Pseudo-Dionysion *Celestial Hierarchy* 'whether the Father of lights [*luminum*] is in himself light (*lux*)'.[14] In some conventional formulae, like the *Lux nova*, the light of the Christian dispensation, used by Paulinus and by Suger, or the text *Ego sum Lux mundi* held by the Pantokrator, the identification of *lux* with the Divinity is clear. It was a term used on candlesticks, these light-spreading analogues of the Divine presence, such as the Gloucester Candlestick of the early twelfth century.[15]

The relationship of light to colour was a matter of some debate in these centuries but there was general agreement that colour was at best a secondary attribute of light, its most material aspect, accident rather that substance. Colour was related to *lumen* rather than to *lux* and was thus at two removes from the highest form of light. The late-antique Roman philosopher Boethius was emphatic that colour was an accident; of the later Arab writers most concerned to figure out the relationship of light and colour, and most influential in the West, Avicenna, Alhazen and Averroes – although Alhazen was able to distinguish light from colour and allow colour some independent power – all made light a far more important structural concept.[16] We have already seen how early attempts to construct colour-scales put blue next to black or darkness and blue is the colour most characteristic of twelfth-century French glass.[17] That this reflected not simply a specialized academic doctrine but a general response to colour values is suggested by the use of blue glass in the Cruxifixion Window at Poitiers (*c.* 1180) as a surrogate for the black of Christ's hair and beard.[18]

It may appear paradoxical to suggest that the type of stained glass which is the glory of the Romanesque and early Gothic periods in France should have represented light at its least divine, but the paradox remains only if we regard luminosity as the central preoccupation of the early glass-designers. I want to show here that this was hardly the case; to do so I must start by examining the texts by Suger which more than any others have allowed modern commentators to project back into the twelfth century the attitudes of the thirteenth – the texts which the leading modern expert on Suger has, in an unguarded moment, called 'an orgy of neo-Platonic light metaphysics'.[19]

Suger's aesthetics

Suger's accounts of his re-modelling of St-Denis must be the central documents for the study of the aesthetics of early medieval glass because of their detail and length and because they describe the most influential cycle of early windows. In his *On Administration* Suger recounted how he 'caused to be painted, by the exquisite hands of many masters from different regions a splendid variety of new windows, both below and above; from that first one which begins [the series] with the *Tree of Jesse* in the chevet of the church, to that which is installed above the principal door in the church's entrance.'[20] He gave the subjects of a few of his favourite windows in the chevet but not the total number of windows glazed, nor the subject-matter of more than these few. According to which modern reconstruction of the church we accept,[21] we must assume that there were between fifty-eight and sixty-eight window-openings, 'above and below' (i.e. four registers, including the crypt, which also appears to have been glazed with painted glass); a further eleven have been estimated for the narthex, none of which have survived.[22] If we take Suger at his word and include the windows of the Carolingian nave,[23] something like ninety to a hundred windows must have been glazed by him. The figure of seven hundred *livres*, plus the gift of all the blue glass – the most expensive item – which Suger mentioned with satisfaction, would probably have been ample to glaze all these openings in the style of the surviving windows, which would certainly have made the building as dark as Chartres.[24]

So it is rather surprising that in the *On Consecration* Suger should characterize the effect of his circuit of ambulatory chapels, whose rich and florid style of glazing we know so well, as essentially one of light. Some of these chapel windows were almost certainly filled with grisaille glass, but Suger's grisaille, some of which survives at St-Denis, was itself densely patterned with lozenges of griffins in complex red and green borders, and its capacity to transmit light is very much less than that of the contemporary grisaille developed by the Cistercians.[25] The prestige of white colourless glass, which was the most difficult to manufacture and which Isidore (*Etymologies* XVI, XVi, 4) had described as the noblest, had survived into Suger's day. In eastern France and Germany there was a tradition of white grounds for figures: the 'backgrounds of the clearest white' mentioned by the German Theophilus in his treatise *Of Divers Arts* of the 1120s and exemplified by the earliest extant windows, the prophets at Augsburg which date from perhaps a decade or so later.[26] It is particularly surprising that Suger should have ignored this tradition in favour of blue grounds since his glassworkers, 'from different regions', must surely have made him aware of it, even if he had not seen glass of this type on his travels. It is possible that he was given the lavish supply of blue glass in the period between the *On Consecration*, which speaks of the beautiful and 'wonderful' light from the windows, and the *On Administration*, which makes no reference to it. But since at this time white glass would have been almost as

41

expensive as blue, and hence unlikely to be removed, this scarcely seems plausible.

Suger's two accounts thus present us with a number of difficulties in interpretation. How seriously are they to be taken? Do these texts represent accurate as well as vivid descriptions of what the Abbot achieved, or were they largely propaganda designed to impress the Abbey Chapter and to justify the enormous expense? Suger borrowed his account of the Carolingian church almost *verbatim* from an earlier chronicle; we have seen that the language of the verses he displayed on various parts of his building was sometimes very close, in its stress on light, to the Early Christian *tituli*. They thus laid emphasis on just those aspects of the traditional cult of luminosity which his modern style of glazing might have been expected to make obsolete.

If Suger's fascination with light was rather a conventional, even old-fashioned, attitude, can his creation of a mysterious gloom at St-Denis be attributed to anything more serious than a liking for lavish display? I believe it can, for the thought behind some of the verses and behind the account (*see below*) of how the splendour of the decorations led his spirit 'in an anagogical manner' to the 'purity of Heaven' have suggested that he was familiar with the theological writings of Pseudo-Dionysius, whose identity had in the ninth century been assimilated to that of St Denis, the Apostle of France and the patron of Suger's Abbey. St Paul had rallied Dionysius and the Athenians for setting up an altar to 'The Unknown God'; mystical ignorance was a keystone of the Dionysian doctrine, which presented a two-fold, positive and negative, experience of the Divine. Although some modern commentators have chosen to ignore it, there can be no doubt that for Pseudo-Dionysius the negative was the superior way and that Suger shared a concern for it with a number of associates and contemporaries such as Hugh of St Victor and St Bernard's friend William of St Thierry.[27] One indication that Suger was indeed involved in the negative aspect of the Dionysian theology is the elaborate and detailed programme he devised for the 'anagogical windows' in the chapels of his Abbey, of which, from his account of it in the *On Administration*, we may infer that he was inordinately proud. It was an appropriately Pauline scheme, seeking to expound the Christian traditions of esoteric and exoteric religion. In the Old Testament the truth is shrouded in the Law, but in the New it is revealed by the Gospel.[28] This conception of hiding and revealing is articulated in the windows through a series of symbolic roundels of extraordinary abstruseness; in particular,

41 the panel of the *Quadriga of Aminadab* in the 'Anagogical' window, which has been aptly characterized as 'a sort of sacred hieroglyph', seems to correspond very closely to a passage in the Dionysian *Celestial Hierarchy* which embodies that theologian's view of the nature and function of religious symbolism itself. Divine matters, said Dionysius, may best be conveyed by incongruous images (*dissimilia signa*): God may be presented as having many faces or feet, like a great bull or a ferocious lion; he may be said to have an eagle's feet or a bird's plumage; we may see in the heavens fiery wheels or material thrones, many-coloured horses and great captains bearing arms, and other expressive symbols from the Scriptures. These images have been provided to raise the spirit towards the Divine: they are *anagogicas sanctas scripturas*. Dionysius continued:

That metaphors without resemblance [*dissimiles similitudines*] are more apt to elevate our souls, I think no man of sense would question; for it is likely that sacred figures of a more precious nature would probably induce men to err, since they would be induced to believe that there are in the heavens brilliant essences like gold, or men fashioned of light, brilliant and beautifully dressed, emitting rays of harmless fire; in short, that we find there all those sorts of celestial forms of which we read in the Scriptures.[29]

The three animal symbols of the Evangelists and the wheels of the Quadriga were brought together in Suger's window with the figures of the crucified Christ and his awesome Father looming over the whole in proportionate disproportion, to create just that sort of paradoxical enigma recommended by Pseudo-Dionysius to puzzle the minds of simple men.

Suger's chief access to the theology of Pseudo-Dionysius was through the translations and commentaries of Eriugena, who is especially interesting to us because, unlike Pseudo-Dionysius, he was concerned to relate his mystical experience to the phenomena of the physical world.[30] In his treatise *Periphyseon: On the Division of Nature*, from which Suger seems to have borrowed a number of ideas used in his *On Consecration*, Eriugena took up and reinforced the Dionysian concept of negative symbolism outlined above, suggesting that metaphors like frenzy, intoxication, forgetfullness, anger, hatred or concupiscence are, for the simple-minded, more appropriate to God than life, virtue, breath, cloud, brightness, sunrise, thunder, dew, shower, water, river, earth or even the remoter images suggested by Pseudo-Dionysius such as lion, ox, eagle or worm.[31] In a discussion of the operations of the light of the sun later in the same book, Eriugena made the surprising claim that it becomes brighter not as it is closer to its source but the nearer it approaches earth, for it is only by mixing with the substantial vapours of the material world that it can be apprehended at all by the material senses.[32] Thus on a purely physical level the light of the distant heavens was also darkness, that 'incomprehensible and inaccessible light', in the Dionysian formulation, of the dwelling-place of God; the luminous darkness of Suger's windows at St-Denis was a perfect analogue of the Divine presence in his church. Was it not in the very nature of glass, according to Isidore of Seville (*Etymologies* XVI, xvi, 1) that it at the same time shut out and made manifest, thus providing Suger with the appropriate medium for his iconographical programme?

The blues of St-Denis

Perhaps we have been misreading the glass at St-Denis by suggesting that it was anything more than an expensive vehicle for an ambitious decorative scheme. Stained glass was, after all, no novelty in the 1140s; it has only seemed so because of the almost complete lack of extant examples from the previous four centuries. Whatever the origins of figurative stained-glass decoration in the West – the earliest documents suggest that it was first introduced into apse-decoration in Rome as a development from the mosaic schemes in use there and took over their function as a luminous manifestation of the Theophany[33] – by 32 the twelfth century it had come to be used in France on a very substantial scale.[34] Suger's exclusive concentration on the subject-matter of the east windows at St-Denis suggests that for him they were, too, appropriate to the most sacred part of the building. His boast about the extraordinary extent of the glazing, and the devotion of some windows (not mentioned by Suger and possibly later[35]) to the lives of saints and the exploits of Charlemagne foreshadow those vast glazing schemes of the late twelfth century and the High Gothic period when the medium became, like the mosaics of Norman Sicily, just another vehicle for painted decoration, another opportunity for *varietas* and a further pretext for conspicuous display.

The emphasis on material values which emerges again and again from Suger's account of his church was shared by many commentators in his time. His biographer, William of St Denis, writing in the 1150s just after Suger's death, dwelt on the preciousness of the materials, the onyx and sardonyx, the prase and other precious stones, the silks and purple and gold cloths used in the Abbot's decorations, but he did not give the stained glass more than an afterthought.[36] This emphasis was that of the Abbot himself: Suger devoted far more space to enumerating the abundant gemstones than to describing the glass, which was itself always identified as *saphirorum materia*. This was perhaps no more than the common generic term for stained glass in the period;[37] Theophilus noted (II, 12) that it was indeed the French who were especially adept at making 'precious sheets of sapphire, very useful in windows'. But the indication of preciousness here is important for it was also a major feature of Suger's account of his windows. In the mid-twelfth-century dispute between the Cistercians and the Cluniacs about legitimate decoration, *vitreae saphiratae* were to be considered almost as synonymous with 'beautiful and precious windows'.[38] In the later Middle Ages blue glass was by far the most expensive variety but it is not easy to see why this should have been so in Suger's time, for the most costly ingredient of Gothic blue glass, cobalt, which would have been imported from Saxony or Bohemia or from as far afield as Persia, was only one of the possible colouring-agents for this glass: it could have been produced with the far more commonplace ingredients of manganese and copper. These have, indeed, been found to be in the commonest use in French window-glass before the thirteenth century.[39] Perhaps the most important clue to the prestige of this glass was not its chemistry at all but Theophilus's observation that the French were skilled at making panes of blue window-glass from ancient vessels, probably a reference to the Roman scent-bottles of opaque blue glass that were common in the Rhineland between the second and fourth centuries AD but which had probably become very scarce by the twelfth.[40] Another source of blue glass for re-use was Byzantium (Theophilus also mentions the re-cycling of ancient mosaic cubes), where it was possibly employed in windows as early as the beginning of the twelfth century; this glass would also have been an expensive imported material.[40]

It has been noticed that the stylistic affinities of some of the motifs in the glass at St-Denis are with metalwork and jewellery.[42] It seems, indeed, to belong to that phase in the development of French stained-glass design where the practice of all these arts was closely related, a relationship reflected in the prominence given jointly to glass-painting and metalwork in Theophilus's treatise and in the arrangement of the workshops

at the Abbey of Cluny in the first half of the eleventh century, where goldsmiths, enamellers and 'glass masters' shared the same cell.[43] This is not at all surprising, when glass as a substance was seen to belong to the family of stones and metals and when an important branch of the glassmakers' art had for long been the manufacture of artificial gems.[44] Theophilus gives a method for applying such gems to stained glass itself, a practice which so far has only been identified in some glass from thirteenth-century Germany.[45]

The chief reason, however, for Suger's pride at the display of 'sapphire material' at St-Denis surely lies in the significance of the sapphire itself. In *On Administration* he spoke of the satisfaction, even excitement, with which he contemplated the *Cross of St Eloy* (the goldsmith-saint) and the 'crista', the so-called *Escrin de Charlemagne*, on the high altar of his church, displaying as they did all the nine stones of Paradise enumerated in Ezekiel 28: 13:

> To those who know the properties of precious stones, it becomes evident, to their utter astonishment, that none is absent from the number of these (with the only exception of the carbuncle), but that they abound most copiously. Thus when – out of my delight in the beauty of the house of God – the loveliness of the many-coloured gems has called me away from external cares, and worthy meditation has induced me to reflect, transferring that which is material to that which is immaterial, on the diversity of the sacred virtues: then it seems to me that I see myself dwelling, as it were, in some strange region of the universe which neither exists entirely in the slime of earth nor entirely in the purity of Heaven; and that, by the grace of God, I can be transported from this inferior to that higher world in an anagogical manner.[45]

A knowledge of the 'properties' and of 'the diversity of the sacred virtues' seems crucial to Suger's conception of the anagogical process'; his engagingly frank admission that neither cross nor shrine included a carbuncle must depend on his knowledge that the true carbuncle shone brightly in the dark and on his inability to guarantee that the red stones of the *Escrin*, the sards listed by him or the *rubis* noted in the late twelfth- or early thirteenth-century chronicle,[47] possessed this rare and fascinating characteristic. Although some ancient and Islamic lapidaries had referred to the magic properties of some gemstones, the systematic interpretation of the nature of stones in magic and moral terms was a very recent development, due chiefly to the popular verse and prose lapidaries written by Marbode of Rennes about 1090. An older Western tradition of interpreting stones, for example in Bede's commentary on the Apocalypse,[48] had been based on the twelve stones which made up the fabric of the Heavenly Jerusalem (Revelation 21: 18–21; Suger, *On Consecration* IV); this allegorization of the twelve stones was particularly cultivated in Suger's day. The elaborate cast censer in the form of the Heavenly Jerusalem described by Theophilus included 'representations of the twelve stones', each of which was assigned to one of the Apostles, 'according to the significance of his name'. Although the idea that the twelve stones might be related to the twelve Apostles was an old one, it does not seem to have been detailed until the beginning of the twelfth century in the *Sermones* of the German poet Sextus Amarcus whose attribution to each depended upon the 'virtues'

45

inherent in the stones themselves.[49] The special status of these twelve stones was reflected in the design of many precious objects, such as the *Escrin de Charlemagne* itself. Along the top of the reliquary casket in this shrine was a sequence of large blue and green stones, separated by round pearls. According to the detailed inventory of the treasure of St-Denis, drawn up in 1634, the oval blue stones were 'saphirs' and the oblong green stones 'grosses presines d'esmeraudles'.[50] This trio of oval blue *cabochons*, square-cut green stones and pearls is one which we also encounter in the representations of the Heavenly Jerusalem in the mosaics of the Triumphal Arch in S. Maria Maggiore in Rome and at S. Vitale in Ravenna, and it was common in the mosaic border-decorations of many Early Christian churches.[51] The combination epitomized the twelve stones of the walls and the pearls of the gates of the Heavenly Jerusalem. In Revelation 21 the first stone is given as *jaspis*, a green stone often confused with *smaragdus* (the fourth of the series), and here given the characteristic oblong shape which depended on the crystalline structure of the emerald. The second, and in the present context, more important stone, was the *saphirus*.[52]

Suger's appeal to the 'sacred virtues' of his gemstones suggests very strongly his familiarity with the verse lapidary of Marbode of Rennes, where all stones were seen to be impregnated with virtues by Divine power (*On Stones* 34). Marbode gave pride of place to *saphirus* for its manifold capacities to protect its bearers from harm, release them from prison or other shackles, reconcile them with God and dispose them to prayer, to cure disease of the body by cooling the inner organs, prevent excess of perspiration, cure sores when powdered and mixed to a paste with milk, to clear eyes and cure headaches and ailments of the tongue. It was, in short, a sacred stone, the 'gem of gems' (41–3). In Marbode's primary source, the possibly late-antique Greek writer 'Damigeron', a Latin version of whose lapidary is known in a number of twelfth-century French manuscripts, the role of *saphirus* was stated even more uncompromisingly. He who possessed this stone 'is armed against all deceit and all ill-doing, and against the strategems of all other stones. This natural power is said to be divine: the stone is vigorously honoured by God' (96).[53] It is thus no surprise that Suger was so proud to have whole registers of windows fashioned from this material.

Yet it is perhaps surprising that his immediate analogy for the blue glass of St Denis should have been not with a transparent, light blue stone but with a dark and mottled opaque one; for the *saphirus* of the ancients and of the early Middle Ages was not our sapphire (blue corundum) but *lapis lazuli*, which continued to be one interpretation of the word until well into the middle of the thirteenth century.[54] In its adjectival form *saphirinus*, the blue stone, seems to have embodied no connotations of clarity: it could be used of the distinctly opaque textiles, Frisian felts, which were presumably dyed with a dark indigo.[55] Bede, in his commentary on the Apocalypse, had indeed made a comparison between the colour of the stone and the clear blue of the sky (*quasi coelum cum serenus est*) and, by a beautiful inversion, Hugh of St Victor in Suger's day transferred the luminous attribute of the stone back again into the transparency and clarity of the sky.[56] That he was inclined to do so suggests that the connotations of *saphirus* had now changed, that *lapis lazuli* had been succeeded by the transparent blue stone *iacinthos* which,

although it was numbered among the twelve stones, had enjoyed no particular reputation during the early Middle Ages. *Iacinthos* was thought to be found in three colours, red, yellow and blue, of which the most valuable was red, for this was not simply resistant to but also enhanced by fire.[57] The chief visible characteristic of the blue variety was its watery transparency. Theophilus's account of the manufacture of blue window-glass makes it clear that it was opaque blue glass from ancient mosaic cubes or *vascula* which was turned into semi-transparent material by the addition of clear colourless (*clari et albi*) glass, in order to make the 'precious panes of sapphire'.[58] In the discussion of the embellishment of windows with artificial gems, the *iacinthos* – to be placed in the by now traditional arrangement between the emeralds (*smaragdos*) – were to be made from *particulis saphiri clari*, fragments of clear sapphire glass.[59] In this treatise of the 1120s, as in the contemporary writings of Hugh of St Victor, we are witnessing a shift in the understanding of the characteristics of blue stones: the physical attributes of *iacinthos* are now seen to belong to *saphiri* and conversely the moral connotations of *saphiri* are transferred to *iacinthos*. It is not at all surprising that the blue stones of the *Escrin de Charlemagne*, including those beautiful watery sapphires which decorate the only surviving fragment, the crest, should in the earliest (ninth-century) acount of the shrine be referred to as iacinths, whereas in 1634 they were described as sapphires.[60] It is tempting to suggest that this transference in the designation of 'sapphire' from an opaque to a transparent stone was accelerated, if not positively stimulated, by the outstanding beauty of blue stained glass.

From glass-staining to glass-painting

The remarkable stylistic change from the type of glass seen at Chartres and St-Denis to that characterized by the Chapter House windows at York has been interpreted largely as a function of the growing control of the medieval architect over every aspect of construction and decoration, and of his wish to allow his own notable achievements to be properly seen.[61] This view is supported by the increasingly architectural patterns of the glass-designers themselves in the late thirteenth and especially the fourteenth centuries,[62] and by the shift in the training and attitudes of glass-painters from the earlier affinities with crafts like jewelling and metalwork to closer association with painting. In the fifteenth century, too, we witness a separation of the functions of the glass-designer (now usually a painter) and those of the executant painter.[63] The growing luminosity of late medieval glass was aided by advances in glass-technology (particularly in that most difficult of glasses to manufacture, clear white glass) and by the discovery of new materials, such as silver-stain, developed about 1300, which enabled many elements such as hair and draperies to be painted freely in the pale yellow which is so characteristic of fourteenth-century glass.[64] But institutional and technical developments should not obscure the essentially aesthetic and conceptual character of this change, whose background in the thirteenth century was the revaluation of the role of light itself.

That the Pseudo-Dionysian fascination with luminous obscurity was no longer of any general interest by the mid-thirteenth century is suggested by an anonymous description of the two rose windows in Lincoln Cathedral, written probably around 1230. The poetic account begins in a rather conventional way by invoking the power of the luminous nave and choir windows to overcome the 'Stygian tyrant', continuing: 'And two are greater, like two lights, their circular blaze, looking upon the directions of north and south, surpass through their double light all the other windows. The others can be compared to the common stars, but these two are one like the sun, the other like the moon.' Then the author turns to the more immediate and exciting image of the rainbow: 'In this manner these two candles lighten the head of the church, and they imitate the rainbow with vivid and various colours; not indeed imitate, but excel, for the sun makes a rainbow when it is reflected in the clouds: these two sparkle without sun, glitter without cloud.'[65] The image is particularly interesting in the context of Lincoln since the poem was written while Robert Grosseteste was Bishop there, who in the 1230s was much occupied with the rainbow, concluding in a short treatise on it that it was not, as earlier theorists had supposed (and as the poet implied), the product of light reflected from a dark cloud but of a much more complex set of six modifications of light – including darkening, but also refraction – which produced the six rainbow colours.[66] Thus, according to the poet at least, the artists of the rose windows were close to a new understanding of the rainbow as the product of light alone. .

The Dionysian teaching was, as we have seen, a two-fold one: it is the positive, exoteric aspect of this doctrine which we find uppermost in the several thirteenth-century discussions of the nature of the beautiful. A more expansive interest in this topic was itself an important feature of Scholastic philosophy. Pseudo-Dionysius had raised the question in his treatise *On the Divine Names* (IV, 5). The chapter was the subject of extensive commentaries in the thirteenth century by Thomas Gallo and Albertus Magnus and his pupil Aquinas, as well as forming the basis of a short treatise by another pupil, Ulrich Engelberti of Strasbourg.[67] The tendency of all these writings was to tip the balance of the traditional, Ciceronian and Augustinian definition of the beautiful as proportion united with softness (*suavitas*) of colour in favour of light (*lumen* or *claritas*) as its single efficient cause. Colours, for example, were seen to be the more beautiful the more light they incorporated. Albertus Magnus is particularly interesting on the way in which forms in the crafts (*forma artis*) are less luminous (*clara*) in baser materials and more luminous in nobler,[68] for this reflects a widespread thirteenth-century re-assessment of precious stones and other materials as above all the vehicles of light. Pseudo-Dionysius had referred to only four types of gemstones, classed according to their colours, all of which were at the light end of the scale. The white (*leukas*) symbolized light, the red (*eruthras*) fire, the yellow (*xanthas*) gold; a fourth colour, the troublesome *chlōras*, which Eriugena and the mid-twelfth-century translator of the Dionysian corpus Jean Sarrazin interpreted as 'pale' (*pallidas*), stood for youth and the flowering of the soul.[69] Many late twelfth- and thirteenth-century writers on gemstones traced their origin to light itself; Herrad of Landsberg in her encyclopaedic *Garden of Delights* (*c*. 1176/96) characterized the twelve stones on Aaron's breastplate (Ezekiel 28:13) as the

vestments of the first angels, which she saw moving like a glittering army.[70] Hildegard of Bingen wrote in the lapidary included in her *Physics* (*c*. 1151/8) that every sort of stone was compounded of fire and water and that precious stones and gems were generated in the rivers of the eastern world, where the sun is hottest. The sapphire, for example, was created at noon and thus incorporated more fire than air or water.[71] This view was expanded by Vincent of Beauvais in his widely read encyclopaedia, the *The Great Mirror* of the 1260s, where he recorded that the most valuable stones and glasses were those created closest to the sun which thus had the virtue of being most resistant to fire.[72] Thomas of Cantimpré, in another influential encyclopaedia written in the first quarter of the thirteenth century, also maintained that precious stones were those washed out of the east by the rivers of Paradise and that the most valuable were precisely those most replete with light. The darkest were those composed of the most earthy 'vapours', the lightest of the most watery, the blue of the most airy and the red the most fiery. But Thomas made it clear that the carbuncle was by far the most important stone because it could transform night into day. Even the most inferior quality of carbuncle, the *balaustus* (balas ruby), he regarded as nobler than the sapphire and the jasper.[73]

Albertus Magnus in his alphabetical lapidary, the *Book of Minerals* (*c*. 1250), gave the fullest account of the background to this change from the primacy of the sapphire to the primacy of the carbuncle: he cited an unspecified body of Hermetic writings which

> say that this is the reason why precious stones, more than anything else, have wonderful powers – because, that is, they are in substance more like things above in their brightness and transparency. On this account some of them say that precious stones are stars composed of elements.
>
> For in the upper [spheres], they say, there are, as it were four colours, which are also the colours found most frequently in precious stones. One of these is the colour of the starless sphere, which is called sapphire by everyone; and this colour is pre-eminently that of the *saphirus* from which it is named... The second colour is that of most stars, which is called bright, shining white; and this is the colour of *adamas* [diamond], beryl, and many other stones. The third is called fiery and flashing; this is the sun and Mars and certain other [stars]; and this is pre-eminently [the colour of] the carbuncle ... And therefore they say that the carbuncle is the noblest, having the powers of all other stones; because it receives a power similar to that of the sun, which is nobler than all other heavenly powers.

In his account of the carbuncle here, Albertus stated that it was to the other stones as gold to the other metals: 'When it is really good it shines in the dark like a live coal, and I myself have seen such a one.'[74]

His account of the colours of stones also stressed their transparency, and in his earliest discussion of their nature in the *Book of Minerals* he related this transparency to that of glass.[75] In the Aristotelian tradition, transparency was a central issue with writers on optics because it was seen both as the condition of the propagation of light and images and as essential for the production of colours; in many contexts in these writings we encounter the example of a ray of light passing unmodified through glass. This was an image already used by St Bernard as a metaphor for the Immaculate Conception, but there the implication was that the glass, which remained intact although penetrated by the sun's rays – a miraculous instance of the co-extension of two material bodies – was colourless.[76] Now, however, the glass was usually coloured, to illustrate some aspect of the proposition that light and colour are distinct but that light, the vehicle (*hypostasis*) of colour, has the capacity to activate it.[77] In several instances the glass was descibed as a window, and although we may be dealing with mental experiments rather than actual experiences, the frequency of the allusion and the rather different forms in which it was presented suggest that during the thirteenth century stained glass was usually expected to transmit light, rather than to retain it in the manner of gemstones and some twelfth-century windows.[78] It is striking that an early thirteenth-century and an early fourteenth-century text both specified red glass to illustrate this point, for unless it is 'flashed' onto a clear glass base or is lightened by some complicated interfusion with colourless glass, ruby glass appears almost black and has very little power to transmit light at all.[79] As in Antiquity, redness was given almost supernatural powers.

This intense interest in the characteristics of transparency affected the presentation of gemstones themselves. Jewellers had always made use of, for example, the natural crystalline structures of the emerald and rock crystal; quite elaborate cutting and facetting had been practised on stones such as the garnet, the beryl, the amethyst and the cornelian since Roman times.[80] But the exploitation of the refractive properties of colourless or highly transparent stones like the diamond seems to begin in earnest only in the thirteenth century; it depended on an increasingly precise knowledge of the phenomenon of the refraction of light through transparent media of varying densities, which only the optical researches of that century could supply.[81] We are moving towards the Renaissance, when the diamond with its elaborate facetting became what it has usually remained, the most precious of stones.[82]

The passion for clarity and translucency which permeates the language and the imagery of Gothic poetry[83] is also reflected in developments in metalwork, especially in the new translucent enamels introduced in the late thirteenth century, at their most magnificent in the Royal Gold Cup (British Museum) or the Mérode Cup (Victoria and Albert Museum), which includes, indeed, the motif of stained-glass windows in the technique known as *plique à jour*.[84] Some of these techniques used colourless enamels over a coloured ground or foil, in a manner similar to the contemporary setting of coloured gemstones. It is, too, in the manuscript illumination and mural painting of the later Middle Ages that we encounter an increased use of glazes over a light or coloured ground and the finishing with varnish, which was to be exploited fully with the refinement of oil painting in the fifteenth century.[85]

Workmanship versus materials

This chapter has attempted to show that the medieval values of art depended on the physical as well as the metaphysical

Bishop Henry of Blois (before 1171) presenting a gift of a 'brass' shrine in which – according to the inscription and contrary to the medieval love of rich materials – 'art is above gold and gems'. The reliquary appears to be decorated with three roundels. (47)

characteristics of raw materials. Medieval people were no strangers to the glamour of expense and, as Suger's writings suggest, self-advertisement could be effective precisely in terms of cash-values.[86] Many precious objects from the early Middle Ages seem to us to be little more than agglomerations of precious stuff. The notable preference for polishing rather than cutting gemstones in this period, which often produces bizarre contrasts with the refined Classical intaglios with which they were so often set, may well have been due not only to a shortage of skills but also to a reluctance to waste any of the valuable material. The high social status of goldsmiths in the period (we recall that Suger claimed to own a wonderful cross by the canonized goldsmith St Eloy) was also, it would seem, chiefly a function of their elevating contact with noble materials.[87]

Nevertheless, it would be hasty to assume that the monetary evaluation of the raw materials and their symbolic functions exhaust the range of categories in the medieval appreciation of art. Suger supplied his readers with what was perhaps the most frequently cited aesthetic tag from Classical poetry, Ovid's climax to his account of Mulciber's silver doors for the Palace of the Sun: *Materiam superabat opus*, 'the workmanship surpassed the material'.[88] The force of the idea is of course lost unless the material itself is precious and all the early uses of the tag are in the context of metalwork or jewellery. But throughout the Gothic period, when there was, in general terms, a revaluation of the role of the artisan and an increasing respect for some categories of manual skill,[89] the phrase and the concept seem to have been applied more and more to ordinary materials of little intrinsic worth, with a shift in favour of a more exclusive delight in sheer craftsmanship.[90] Perhaps the most graphic indication on this changing attitude is the inscription on a mid-twelfth-century enamel plaque, possibly from a cross made at Winchester, which shows Bishop Henry of Blois holding the shrine of St Swithun. The difficult inscription has been translated as follows: 'Art is above gold and gems: the Creator is above all things. Henry while living gives gifts of brass to God; whom, equal to the Muses in intellect and superior to Marcus in oratory, his renown makes acceptable to man, his morals to God above.'[91] What is striking here is the opening phrase, *Ars Auro Gemmisque Prior*, and the explicit reference to the base metal copper or brass (*aes*). The plaque is made of an opaque *champlevé* enamel on copper, the implication being that these ordinary materials are, because of their fine workmanship, superior to mere gold and gems.[92] At exactly this time the philosopher John of Salisbury developed a radical notion that art is a transformer of nature, improving on nature's own methods by her *methodon*, or purposeful plan, 'which avoids nature's wastefulness and straightens out her circuitous wanderings'.[93]

Such a recognition of the craftworker's transformation of base materials into a valuable object also perhaps accounts for the increasing number of allusions to artificial (glass) gems in late medieval inventories. Although they were often drawn up as a guide to valuing the gems as pledges – the compilers sometimes pointed out that the artificial stones had no value[94] – there was now at least a frank admission that what in earlier periods had seemed to be genuine natural stones were in fact the product of human skill.[95] The use of glass to counterfeit stones had been practised since Antiquity and there were simple tests to detect it; but the admission that many stones on important liturgical objects were in fact cheap substitutes does not seem to have been a feature of the earlier descriptions. During the thirteenth century, just as light began to lose its transcendental status and to be studied simply as a manifestation of the terrestrial laws of optics,[96] so gems began to be accepted not for their magical properties but simply as elements in a design and as evidence of technical skills.

The secularization of light

Even in fourteenth-century Byzantium and fifteenth-century Russia a revived interest in Pseudo-Dionysius served to reinforce the modern view that light was essentially an earthly, physical phenomenon which only symbolism could really associate with the Divine. It has been suggested that the Calabrian monk Barlaam, who went to Constantinople in the early fourteenth century in search of pagan philosophy and stayed to combat the movement of mystical spirituality called Hesychasm, was influenced by Western Scholasticism. However this was, Barlaam found himself using Dionysius's concept of the unapproachable God to underline the separation of the realms of the earthly and the Divine. He cited the example of the Transfiguration, arguing that the light which overwhelmed the Apostles on Mount Tabor was a purely earthly light, apprehended by their senses alone; it could only be a symbol of the Divine, not divine in itself.[97] Paradoxically, Barlaam's opponents, who eventually won the day and who argued for a continuum between God and man through the incarnation of Christ, also stimulated a demand for a more naturalistic rendering of light and the modelling of the human figure, most vividly in the Russian painter Andrei Rublev (1370?–*c.* 1430), whose interest in the observation of nature has been emphasized by both contemporaries and modern critics.[98]

Perhaps the clearest indication that by the fourteenth century the Neo-Platonic and early medieval understanding of light as an intrinsic property of matter and a direct emanation of the Divine had given way to an almost exclusive interest in its function as revealing the optical properties of surfaces, is in the remarkable display of painted decoration in the Upper Church of S. Francesco at Assisi, which was undertaken in the years around 1300. Its extent and variety seems to be unprecedented: the lowest register of the nave and transepts has a band of fictive hangings with geometrical designs, which are close to several of those represented in the Old Testament and St Francis cycles above, and to the designs of the Spanish 'Alhambra' silks of the late thirteenth century.[99] Above this sumptuous base is a painted cornice supporting the lowest register of frescoed scenes, and above them another cornice, partly carved and coloured, supporting two registers of scenes and the stained-glass windows that are perhaps the most unexpected feature of the decoration. The rich, jewel-like windows of the choir give way in the transepts to far lighter panels and in the nave to an array of pale colours and white.[100] Yet the design of even the latest windows is old-fashioned by northern standards and still reflects the traditional links with metalwork rather than with architecture or painting. The borders of the St Francis window share some of the decorative motifs of the most impressive example of early Italian translucent enamel, the Guccio di Mannaia cup, made for Pope Nicholas IV and given by him to the church about 1290.[101] The link is also reflected in the palettes of both the glass-painters and the enameller,[102] suggesting that the lightening in tone of the glass was less an echo of northern fashion than a response to the need to combine stained glass and fresco in the same scheme, a combination which was to be characteristic of central Italian monumental decoration until the High Renaissance.[103]

The vaulting-ribs in each bay are decorated with a repertory of geometrical patterns adapted chiefly from Cosmatesque mosaic, which is also represented prominently in the narrative scenes and the fictive architecture of the Upper Church.[104] It was a type of painted decoration that followed Giottesque painting wherever it was practised throughout the fourteenth century.

All these decorative ideas have strong papal associations, since they had been more or less the prerogative of papal patronage and they fit well with the Roman and papal emphases of the narrative cycle.[105] In the nave they are also characterized by an extraordinay subtlety and restraint. Although the Spanish silk and gold cloth which was a model for the textile-painting would have given an excellent pretext for the application of real gold, it was hardly introduced at all; the same is true of the Cosmatesque ornament, although there was much gold and glass in the abundant Cosmati mosaic in the earlier Lower Church. The choir and transept vaults of the Upper Church were partly gilded and there are still traces of what might have been intended as the beginning of gold mosaic work on the vault of the crossing.[106]

In a document of 1311 the basilica of S. Francesco was described as 'lumen et status salutifer … totius civitatis et districtus Asisij' (the light and health-giving condition... of the whole city and district of Assisi).[107] The use of the term *lumen* may be a casual one but it corresponds closely to the character of the decoration, which replaces reflective, apparently light-generating surfaces or dense, light-holding glass with the soft textures of cloth – whose beauty depends on the fall of light on its folds – light-transmitting pale glass and the matt surfaces of fresco, which allows far greater play than mosaic to the representation of light-effects like shadow in the figurative scenes.[108]

For the aesthetic context of the novel decoration of S. Francesco we might well turn to St Bonaventure, Minister General of the Franciscans, under whose direction the first statutes of the order to embody clear aesthetic recommendations, the Statutes of Narbonne (1260), were framed. These Statutes are remarkable in that they refer specifically to stained-glass windows; they permit far more of them than did the twelfth-century Statutes of the Cistercians, whose fear of *curiositas* affected all subsequent monastic attitudes towards art, including those represented by the Franciscans at Narbonne. This Council sanctioned coloured figurative windows behind the high altar, listing the Cruxifixion, the Virgin, St John, St Francis and St Anthony as admissable subjects, which suggests that the framer of this Statute (III, 18) may have had in mind the already existing windows at Assisi, the order's mother-church, that show the life of Christ and its Old Testament types.[109] Bonaventure had a liking for glass: he used the example of the making of glass from ashes as a striking instance of the presence of light in even the most despised of substances.[110] Nor can he be regarded as an ascetic, since he presented a precious silver ciborium to S. Francesco.[111] In the exceptionally sensitive account of artistic production which he gave in his *On the Subordination of the Arts to Theology*, Bonaventure laid great emphasis on knowledge, pleasure and the desire for praise, motivations which can be seen in the extravagant inscriptions displayed by the Cosmati on many of their works.[112] He was not always careful to distinguish among *lux*, *lumen* and *splendor* (reflected light), categories of light which taxed the ingenuity of so many of his contemporaries,[113] but it now seems clear that he was chiefly concerned to explore the nature of *lumen*, a type of light which did not lend itself to metaphysical speculation.[114] In his aesthetics, the emphasis on harmony and proportion and the characterization of colour as mixture were in tune with the rejection of absolutes implicit in the decoration of the Upper Church.[115]

Dante on the psychology of light

Bonaventure may help us to understand the aesthetic tone of this decoration but he cannot tell us much about the assumptions of a wider and essentially secular public. We have a guide to these assumptions in the vernacular encyclopedia appended to a group of Dante's love poems and composed in the first decade of the fourteenth century. The casual references to vision, light and colour in the third part of the *Feast*, together with many passages in the *Divine Comedy*, especially the *Paradise*, give us some sense of an unspecialized level of knowledge about these topics in the period. Dante showed himself to be particularly fascinated by the passage of rays of light through transparent substances, such as glass,[116] but also by their reflection from polished surfaces. The phenomenon of dazzle, which in a Bonaventuran vein he characterized as destroying the harmony of the eye, was one to which he returned again and again in the *Comedy* and not simply in the

Paradise, that blinding zone of light.[117] This is a significant emphasis, for dazzle is a subjective, psychological phenomenon and we see in Dante, as in S. Francesco, an interpretation of the role of light and colour in essentially human terms.

Dante's sympathy with this shift in the aesthetics of light may best be seen in a well-known passage in Canto XI of the *Purgatory*, where the poet recognizes in the ranks of the Proud a miniature painter he may perhaps have encountered in the flesh in Bologna in the 1280s:

> 'Oh,' diss' io lui, 'non se' tu Oderisi,
> l'onor d' Agobbio e l'onor di quell'arte
> che "alluminar" chiamata è in Parisi?'
> 'Frate,' diss'egli, 'più ridon le carte
> che pennelleggia Franco Bolognese:
> l'onor è tutto or suo, e mio in parte . . .' [79–84]

('Oh,' I said to him, 'are you not Oderisi, the honour of Gubbio, and the honour of the art that is called "illumination" in Paris?' 'Brother,' he said, 'the pages Franco of Bologna paints smile more: the honour is now his – and mine in part . . .') Art-historical commentators on this passage have usually wanted to match surviving manuscripts with the hands of Oderisi da Gubbio, who is recorded at Bologna between 1268 and 1271, and of Franco Bolognese, who is entirely undocumented.[118] Yet what strikes the casual reader most about this passage is Dante's self-conscious choice of a French term, *alluminar* (his version of *enluminer*), rather than the standard Italian word *miniare* (from *minio*, red oxide of lead). Did he simply need a rhyme for 'Oderisi'? I think not, for the French term gave him, as the Italian did not, the crucial implication of light.

The earliest texts to apply the Latin word for 'lamp-lighter', *illuminator*, to painters in miniature date from the first half of the twelfth century, precisely the time when Theophilus uses the tem *illuminare* to refer to high-lighting in painting.[119] An early usage by William of Malmsbury links illumination specifically with gilding. This seems to have been a common association in Italy in Dante's time, where the northern term had been introduced at least in papal circles, perhaps as a result of the removal of the popes to Avignon.[120] But whatever the origins of the usage, there can be little doubt that Dante intended an allusion to light, for the point of the contrast he drew was that Oderisi was an honour to the art of illumination but Franco was even more so: Franco's pages smiled more than his.

The notion of 'smiling' colour in painting Dante may have found in Alain of Lille or more probably in Baudri of Bourgeuil, who used the same image to evoke a manuscript of his poems decorated with gold and vermilion or green by Gerard of Tours, so that the letters 'smiled',[121] But Dante had a profounder interest in the coupling of smiling and light. St Bernard had already in his sermons on the Song of Songs described the motions of the mind as lights shining from the body – but had been rather surprised that laughter should be among them.[122] For Dante the link was inevitable: he used *ridere* in the sense of 'light up' elsewhere in the *Purgatory* (I, 19) but he also gave the idea a psychological twist in *Paradise* (XIV, 76–88); in the *Feast* (II, viii, 11) he asked: 'What is a smile if not a flashing-out [*corruscazione*] of the soul's delight, that is a light [*lume*] manifesting what is within?' That a smile lights up the

77

The Jaulnes Virgin, Sens, 1334, one of many smiling images of Mary. (48)

The Great Angel of the Apocalypse, *Douce Apocalypse*, 1270. (49)

face, and especially the eyes, was a commonplace of descriptions of women in the French and Italian romances of the period; in French usage *riant* ('laughing', 'smiling') became almost a synonym for *cler*.[123]

Such a visually and psychologically compelling notion could not but find an expression in art. Around 1270 broadly smiling angels make their appearance in the sculpture of Rheims; in the almost contemporary *Douce Apocalypse* the association of smiling and light is quite explicit in the Great Angel of Chapter X, 1–7, whose *facies . . . erat sol*.[124] The artists of this sombre and painterly manuscript supplemented the traditional symbolism of precious materials with a new complexity of psychological expression, which became increasingly subtle in the long series of French sculptures of the Virgin and Child of the early

fourteenth century. In the Jaulnes Virgin at Sens the regal splendour of the crowned and enthroned Mother is perfectly counterpointed by her warm and engaging smile.[125]

By the fifteenth century, in the writing of the Florentine Neo-Platonist and Dante scholar Marsilio Ficino, the experience of the light of Heaven itself had become an experience of laughter. 'What is light in the heavens?' he asked in a little treatise *On Light*: 'Abundance of life from the angels, unfolding of power from the heaven, and laughter of the sky.'[126] By the Renaissance, light had become not only an essentially optical property, it was a psychological one as well. Symbols were giving way to experience but, as I hope to show in the next chapter, experience had long been enrolled in the shaping of these symbols themselves.

5 · Colour-Language, Colour-Symbols

Basic colour terms · The colours of heraldry · Secular and sacred in colour-meaning
Post-medieval perceptions of heraldic blazon

And indeed the pure colours do not even have special commonly used names, that's how unimportant they are to us. [Ludwig Wittgenstein, *Remarks on Colour* II, 67]

I SHOWED in Chapter 1 how in the nineteenth century the scholarly understanding of early colour-terminology hardly kept pace with the archaeological investigation of ancient polychromy and it must be admitted that in our own times the gap has widened even further, because the remarkable development of studies in colour-languages over the past twenty years has not been matched by a comparable development in the study of colour in the visible world, particularly in the world of art. For the student of languages the chief problem has been to account for the fact that although the human eye is capable of discriminating some millions of colour-nuances, most colour-languages, in all cultures and throughout recorded history, include a vocabulary of from eight to eleven 'basic' terms.[1] The notion of 'basic' terms is a relatively recent one which has been brought very much into the foreground by a seminal study, *Basic Color Terms*, published by Brent Berlin and Paul Kay in 1969 – it has generated most of the important discussion ever since.[2] From a survey of ninety-eight spoken languages or dialects, Berlin and Kay proposed a model for the universal development of colour-vocabularies, which showed a seven-stage evolution. At Stage I a language would have terms for black and white; at Stage II, red would be added; at Stage III green or yellow; at Stage IV yellow or green; at Stage V blue; at Stage VI brown; at Stage VII purple or pink or orange or grey, or several of these, until the series of eleven 'basic' terms was completed. The detailed criticism of Berlin and Kay's work, chiefly by linguists and ethnographers, has generally concerned levels above Stage II, although it has been pointed out that Stage I languages rarely distinguish 'black' and 'white' but rather 'dark' and 'light' or 'cool' and 'warm' or 'moist' and 'dry' colours. From the point of view of the historian of culture, what is most unsatisfying about Berlin and Kay's approach to colour-language is the assumption that subjects tested will respond in a 'natural' way to the presentation of small chips of coloured plastic from the Munsell System used by the researchers, a system which itself grew out of nineteenth-century assumptions about 'primary' colours.[3]

Colour-salience as revealed by language must be related to the wider experience of colour in a given culture, this experience differing among the different groups within this culture to whom colour is of some concern.[4] Children may be one such sub-group, in whom the development of a colour-vocabulary may be close to the Berlin and Kay scheme,[5] but women, as a group, are not and they have long been recognized as being particularly precise and discriminating in their handling of colour.[6] Other distinctions may be drawn between groups who have a more of less professional interest in colour,[7] one of the most interesting of which for the historian is the group of horse-breeders and traders, who have played an important role in European cultures since Antiquity and beyond. Late-antique writers like Palladius in the fifth century and Isidore of Seville in the seventh listed thirteen horse-colours in Latin, some of which are rare and highly specialized terms.[8] Byzantine Greek offers a shorter list of some eleven terms but some of these are also extremely obscure.[9] An Arab–Latin glossary of around 1000 lists eight colours and a Spanish thirteenth-century treatise on horses fourteen.[10] In the horse-breeding countries of Eastern Europe and Central Asia in more recent times the number of terms for horse-colours has been appreciably larger, from some thirty among the Kirghiz of the Steppes to nearly twice that number in western Russia.[11] Clearly when the need arose, colour-discrimination expanded to meet it and precise terms were devised to communicate these nuances to other people.

And yet, of course, colour-space has never been more than partially and crudely mapped by colour-language. There has been a far more remarkable tendency towards the 'basic' than towards the development of more and more subtle discriminations. Most of the ethnographic material gathered for the study of colour-vocabularies has come from non-European cultures, but exactly the same story could be read from the examination of European texts and artefacts. Already in late Antiquity the Roman philosopher Boethius pointed to the fact that 'black' was used to describe rational man, irrational crow and inanimate ebony, and 'white' equally to refer to swans and marble, men and horses, stars and lightning – which meant that colour was a mere accident, quite incapable of informing us about the true nature of things.[12] Berlin and Kay's first three terms, black, white and red, have shown themselves to form the most fundamental colour triad in Africa and Asia and also throughout Europe; in a study of the most salient terms in modern fiction, these three have been found to be used far more than any others.[13] Even though many people are capable of discriminating a very wide range of nuances, and of communicating many of these discriminations, it remains that for most purposes a highly reduced and abstract colour-vocabulary is all that seems to be required. It is also clear that for many people, unless they are professionally engaged in colour-technology, this reduced colour-vocabulary has a powerful effect on perception itself. So colour-perception and colour-language turn out to be closely bound up with each other; since symbolizing is essentially a linguistic function, the available colour-vocabulary must have a decisive role in the creation of any language of colour-symbols.[14] As colour-terminology is so vague, this presents real problems for the modern reader of historical texts, no less than for contemporary speakers of different languages.

The problem was already a familiar one in Antiquity. We saw in Chapter 2 how in the second century AD Aulus Gellius introduced the question of colour-vocabularies into his *Attic Nights* (II, xxvi), where Favorinus pointed out that the eye sees far more *facies* (nuances) of colour than language can distinguish and that Greek was rather more discriminating in this respect than Latin. The Latin *rufus*, he said, comprehended many colours, from purple to gold, where Greek had four terms – *xanthos eruthros*, *purros* and *kirros* – to cover the same area as *rufus*. Favorinus's companion Fronto retorted by listing seven Latin terms for red: *fulvus, flavus, rubidus, poeniceus, rutilus, luteus* and *spadix*. The precise identification of two of Fronto's terms, *flavus* and *rubidus*, might well have been rather crucial in ancient medicine, for two late-antique north Italian Latin translations of the very popular Greek medical writer Oribasius – in the course of a discussion of the colour of urine as symptom – used either *flavus* or *rubeus* as a translation of Oribasius's *xanthos*, a term which, in Classical Greek, could refer to fair hair, or honey or wine or the whitish-yellow of parched grass.[15] Clearly there was no consensus about the appropriate term for a given and important phenomenon, even within the same language in the same geographical area.

We have also seen how in the case of purple late-antique lawyers sought to stabilize the concept by referring not to a chromatic term but to a method of manufacture; medieval users of colour attempted to do the same with their textiles by isolating not the hue but the quality of cloth that the most precious dyestuff were used to colour. This has, of course, created some puzzles for the post-medieval interpreter of medieval texts. In Spain *purpura* was, as early as the tenth century, the name of a silk fabric, not a colour. It continued to be so in Europe at large until the Renaissance, so that we find many 'purples', from white and yellow to blue and black, as well as red and green.[16] That purple had come to mean essentially a hue by at least the middle of the seventeenth century is suggested by the heraldic controversy mentioned below (p. 82). The history of the much more recent colour-term 'scarlet' suggests a similar progression from material to abstraction. The two colours had a close relationship as dyestuffs in Jewish culture; but the term 'scarlet' itself appeared in the German-speaking world in the eleventh century to signify a fine shorn woollen cloth of great value. 'Scarlets' of many colours from black and blue to white (undyed) and green are documented in the early literature but since the complement to the most valuable woollen textile of the period was, understandably, the most valuable dye (which in the Middle Ages was the bright red *kermes* or *coccus*), it seems that by the thirteenth century the most usual 'scarlet' was that dyed with this colour. Hence came the confusion of the colour with the cloth. The thirteenth-century French prose romance *Merlin* was already able to use the term *escrelate* as the paradigm of all bright reds and by the following century it could refer simply to the red dye itself.[17]

Very much the same pattern of development may lie behind the more mysterious medieval term *perse*, which has remained problematic because it fell out of use in the sixteenth century. The origin and nature of *perse* have resisted analysis for many years: linguists have similarly found the word to apply to many hues from light blue to dark red. When it first appears at Reichenau in the eighth century it is used as a synonym for the purplish-blue *hyacinthinus*; one of its last recorded appearances, in Dolce's *Dialogue on Colours* in the middle of the sixteenth century, is as the colour of rust (*ferrugineo*).[18] Nor is there any agreement among modern scholars on the origin of the word: some have derived it from late Latin *pressus*, one of Palladius's horse-colours.[19] Others have related it, through *pressus*, to a group of Spanish and Portuguese words meaning 'black'.[20] Others again have traced the term to the blossom of the peach (*persica*), which is usually a bluish-pink, or to the similarly coloured Persian lilac or to the blue-violet cornflower (*persele*).[21] Certainly in northern Europe in the later Middle Ages the word, when applied to cloth, seems to have meant the darkest and most expensive shade of blue (called *satblaeu* in Flemish), although a fifteenth-century heraldic writer stated that while bluish, *pers* was not as dark as blue.[22] One of the most circumstantial texts, in a late fourteenth-century French handbook of household management, underlines the problem of interpreting *perse*. In a chapter on the cleaning of garments the anonymous author stated that stains on a *robe de pers* could be removed with a detergent, 'And if any other colours of cloth whatever are stained . . .', as if *pers* was a colour; but at the end of this passage she or he wrote 'To take spots out of a silk, satin, camelot, damask or other dress (*robe*) . . .', as if *pers* was one of a number of cloths rather than a colour.[23] The notion that *perse* may be related to 'Persian' has found little favour with recent scholars,[24] but that one of the earliest, eleventh-century texts speaks of 'a tunic of gold *perse* cloth' (*tunicam de panno perso inaurato*) might well suggest a Persian origin.[25] Perhaps, like 'purple' and 'scarlet', *perse* was a term primarily used of cloth, in this case a silk originally from the Orient (although it was later imitated in the West), which was usually dark but could be supplied in a range of hues. If so, it was another example of the way in which medieval users of colour were able to stabilize their fluid perceptions of hue by focusing on the material substance.

The colours of heraldry

Perhaps the most striking instance of this sort of stabilizing strategy is in the late-medieval artificial colour-language of heraldic blazon. It is astonishing that the records of an obsession with kinship and power, which are perhaps the most visible and most attractive survivals of the medieval in the modern world, have never been investigated thoroughly by anthropologists. A characteristic document of the power of armorial devices in maintaining status is the contract of 1541 between a Spanish grandee and the Dominican monks of S. Telmo in northern Spain, for whom he was having a new church and convent constructed. The contract stipulated that the arms of the patron and his wife were to be displayed in perpetuity, in stone and in painting, on columns, pillars, walls, vaults, arches, doors and other parts throughout the main chapel, church and convent, 'and that no other arms whatsoever of any other person of any rank whatsoever should be erected or permitted to be erected for ever and ever'.[26] We are reminded of the proliferation of the

Knights jousting, from a fifteenth-century English Military Roll. The knights are named, but when helmetted in the field they could only be identified by their coats of arms, devised by the heralds in accordance with the rules of blazon. The colours and tinctures of blazon at the period included *or* (gold), *argent* (silver), *azure* (blue), *gules* (red), *vert* (green) and *sable* (black, after the precious black fur) – an evolving vocabulary of value. (50)

heraldic logo of that great commercial sponsor Henry VIII in King's College Chapel, Cambridge, only a few years earlier, although these arms never seem to have been coloured. Conversely, reformers like St Antoninus, Archbishop of Florence in the fifteenth century, specifically included coats of arms among the superfluous vanities which should be kept away from churches.[27]

Heraldry has for the most part remained in the hands of the genealogists. Only in the past twenty years or so have historians of ideas begun to look into the structure of these visible tokens of kinship, by focusing not so much on historical coats of arms as on those of fictional characters such as the Knights of the Round Table.[28] Of most concern here is the development of a language of blazon, which has its beginnings in the twelfth century and had become standard throughout Europe by the sixteenth; in several respects it ran counter to the ordinary colour-vocabularies of the European languages. The history of blazon as a language has never been traced, but what is clear is that it took several centuries to reach its final form and that it was essentially the creation of an increasingly professional body of heralds – guardians of the right of families and later institutions to bear arms, and controllers of the forms these arms could take.

Hereditary devices or badges were not unknown to the ancient Athenians[29] but it was not until about the eleventh century in northern France that the armorial shield seems to have been conceived of as a precise means of recognition in battle.[30] The enamelled effigy of Geoffrey Plantaganet of Anjou at Le Mans, of about 1151, may include one of the first authentic representations of a coat of arms, since the device of golden lions on blue had been noticed at his investiture as a knight in 1123 or 1127 and it re-appeared as the arms of his grandson at the end of the century.[31] The spread of the practice of jousting from

France to the rest of Europe during the early twelfth century made signs of identification more and more essential;[32] with this increase in numbers went the need for regulation and the development of the office of herald. But it took many decades for a specialized language of blazon to evolve. The earliest descriptions of shields are in French romances, which use the same colour-language of *vermeil* or *rouge, blanc, or* and *azur* that had been used by the author of the *Chanson de Roland* in the late eleventh century.[33] *Or* and *azur* later became technical terms of blazon, because they were the most precious metal and the most precious and exotic blue pigment,[34] but at this early stage other words for yellow and blue might serve just as well. Benoit de Sainte-Maure's *Roman de Troie* (c. 1155) also describes shields of *argent, vert, porpre* or *porprin*, these last terms causing great confusion in the later vocabulary of heraldry. In the following decade Chrétien de Troyes's *Érec et Enide* introduced a tournament near Edinburgh (Tenebroc) in which banners and shields were described with several terms for blue and gold, as well as another troublesome term, *sinople*. At this time it probably meant 'red' – it was regularly paired with *azur* (ll. 2097–119) – but it later came to mean green. The poems of Chrétien de Troyes witness the emergence of professional heralds, although he seems to have had little sympathy with them: in *Lancelot: le Chevalier de la Charette* (1180s) he introduces a tournament at which the Queen is instructed about the identity of certain knights from their coats of arms, not by a herald, but by other noble spectators (ll. 5773–99); when a herald is introduced into the poem (ll. 5563ff) he makes a mistake about the crucial arms of Lancelot.

It was not until the mid-thirteenth century that collections of coats of arms known as armorial rolls testify to the much greater importance of the heralds and to a greater standardization of

50

53

terms. The exactly contemporary French Bigot Roll and the English Glover's Roll use a vocabulary of eight terms – six tinctures (hues) and two furs. The tinctures are now *or, argent* (in both rolls still also called *blanc*), *azur, gules, vert* and *sable* (called *noir* in the Bigot Roll and sometimes in Glover's Roll), and the furs *ermine* and *vair*.[35] The new term for red is *gules*, deriving from the Latin *gula* (throat) and used of the fox-fur collars, including the head with its open mouth, that were fashionable in the twelfth century.[36] *Gules* also came to heraldry from poetry, where it had been in use at least since the 1230s, in a poem, *The Tournament of Antichrist*, which had seen it as the attribute of lechery and gluttony (*gula*).[37] The other new term was *sable*, also deriving from the fashion in furs but whose black colour came from dyeing rather than from the natural appearance of the skin. By the fifteenth century, sable was the most expensive fur of all, known as 'black gold'.[38] The two other terms were derived directly from furs, the ermine, a semiprecious fur – which was, however, regarded as the finest in the Arab world of the later Middle Ages,[39] and *vair* (the squirrel, *sciurus varius*), whose characteristically stylized wave-patterns can already be seen in the lining of Geoffrey of Plantaganet's cloak. *Vair* was generally regarded in the later Middle Ages as the most valuable fur of all and it gave its name to the craft of furrier in German (*Buntwerker*) and in the dialects of Venice, Florence and Flanders.[40]

53

Thus the vocabulary of blazon was essentially a vocabulary of value: the two most precious metals, the most precious pigment (*lapis lazuli* or ultramarine) and the four most precious furs. The looser heraldic language of the poets had been streamlined according to a very precise understanding of aristocratic taste.[41] The only surprises in this arcane language are the presence of a rather ordinary green, *vert*, and the absence of purple. The importance of green as a colour in the Middle Ages can scarcely be overestimated. We have seen how it was regarded in Antiquity as the especially pleasing median colour and how Innocent III sanctioned it in the thirteenth century as a liturgical colour for the same reason. He was joined in this by the Scholastic writer William of Auvergne, who thought green even more beautiful than red because, he said (echoing the Peripatetics), it 'lies between the white which dilates the eye and the black which contracts it.'[42] But the problem in heraldry was the humdrum French word *vert*, which although long used in blazon was now confusing since it was a homophone with *vair*.[43] In practice the problem was generally alleviated by using the adjectival form *vairé*,[44] but in spoken Norman-French this must still have presented difficulties; the solution was eventually to substitute the term *sinople*, a poetic word echoing *sinopis* which, as in Antiquity, was generally used to denote red but which had, paradoxically, come to stand for green by the early thirteenth century.[45] (*Sinople*, however, continued to mean red in poetic usage for another two centuries.) In the most comprehensive of early heraldic treatises, Jehan Courtois, as Sicily Herald, had to explain in the 1430s to Alfonso the Magnanimous, King of Aragon and Sicily, that it meant green in this context, and not the rather trivial green of dyes and paints but the beautiful refreshing green of nature.[46] It was, none the less, an excellent addition to this specialized vocabulary for it was ancient and exotic and had a meaning only the initiated

could understand. Although never a very widespread heraldic tincture, it was firmly accepted into the canon by the early fifteenth century.[47]

Purple also presented problems to the heralds and, unlike *sinople*, it was never generally accepted. About 1250 the historian and painter Matthew Paris included it as one of his reds, together with *rubeus* and *gules*, in his rather precise descriptions of a series of emblazoned shields.[48] But, predictably, this was exactly the problem: as William Caxton put it in his late fifteenth-century translation of Christine de Pisan's *Book of Fayttes of Armes and of Chivalrye* (1408/9), 'the second coloure is purpre that we call red'.[49] The earliest surviving treatise on heraldry (*c.* 1280/1300) had already pointed out that very few people thought of purple as a heraldic colour,[50] and almost the only early blazon to include it as a distinct tincture was the arms of the King of Spain, whose lions were *purpure* in two copies of Glover's Roll (*c.* 1235), although *azure* in another; the same is true of the rather later Walford's Roll (*c.* 1275), which has *azure* in one sixteenth-century copy.[51] Seventeenth-century Spanish heraldic writers compounded the confusion by using *purpura* for the red of the field but usually the term for the lions was a more straightforward red: *rojo*.[52] It is no surprise that in one of the last classic treatises of heraldry, C. F. Menestrier's *L'Art du blason justifié* of 1661, the author sought to ban purple, citing the vexing case of the Spanish King's arms and arguing that it was impossible for heraldic artists to decide how to render this tincture: 'Painters and illuminators do not know what colour to use for the so-called purple: some make it out of mauve, others wine-colour, some the colour of mulberries [*meures*], which is a dark violet, others a colour like that of the husk of mulberries [*sac des meures*], which is lighter.'[53] It was in heraldry indeed that the demise of the concept of royal purple came about. An anonymous, early fifteenth-century French heraldic treatise stated that purple was not simple but a mixture of all the other tinctures, and a little later Sicily Herald explained that since this made it the humblest (*la plus basse*) of colours, some authorities excluded it altogether from the canon. He himself, however, took the more traditional view that purple was the proper attribute of kings and emperors – he clearly did not foresee the fate of the Spanish arms, now blazoned in *gules*.[54]

Secular and sacred in colour-meaning

The slow assimilation of *sinople* as green and the virtual exclusion of *purpure* from the language of blazon suggests that the requirements of that highly artificial vocabulary were abstraction, in that it should be removed from everyday language, and at the same time the concreteness of association with objects of great material worth. Even the four furs were included because of their monetary value not because the animals from which they came (the fox, the sable, the ermine and the squirrel) had any special place in the medieval bestiary, which fulfilled an essentially moral function. But if these terms were so abstract, and if symbolism depends upon words, how could they fulfil those symbolic tasks which, especially in the later phases of heraldry in the fourteenth and fifteenth centuries, were increasingly thrust upon them by heraldic writers and the wider public? They did so by using the standard strategies of medieval symbolizing, by the free use of the imagination and by a refusal to think in terms of the universal.

Romanticism and the Jungian psychology of archetypes have led us to expect that a symbol should have some universal validity, should respond in some way to a deeply felt human need. But this was not the way symbolism was understood in the Middle Ages. Then symbols were fluid; inventions of the imagination, whether or not they were subsequently endorsed by repetition in some institution such as the Church. They were functions of the 'colours' of rhetoric, those ancient techniques of amplification and embellishment that enjoyed such a vivid life in medieval theories of poetry.[55] Thus in an early Byzantine hymn the Virgin might be compared to a score of objects from nature and art, and a late fourteenth-century English preachers' manual could give sixteen meanings to the peacock.[56] The theorists of symbolism from Augustine to Dante emphasized this ambiguity: in the twelfth century, for example, the exceptionally full discussion of symbols by Peter of Poitiers included the argument that the same object might have opposite connotations – the lion, because of its ferocity was sometimes compared to the devil but since it was fearless it could also be compared to Christ.[57] So it is not at all surprising that modern students of medieval colour-symbolism have been hard put to it to reach any general conclusions about the meanings of individual colours, even when they have been able to identify them. The regal purple of Christ's robe may be the same as the scarlet of sin.[58] In the essentially secular context of heraldry the urge to symbolize was accommodated on the one hand by an eclectic borrowing from religious ideas, a solution which proved in the long run to be very popular, and on the other by a more scholarly attempt to extract colour-meanings from the material characteristics of the colours themselves.

Early signs of a wish to attribute meaning to heraldic colours appear in the writings of Matthew Paris. The division of the shield of Prince Henry (who had died very young in 1183) into fields of red and black gave Matthew the occasion to think of red as a colour of life and black of death.[59] He was also attracted to the idea of the knight as bearer of the 'Shield of Faith' (*Scutum Fidei*, from St Paul's metaphor in Ephesians 6:16), a theological diagram, which had probably originated with Robert Grosseteste, presenting the relationship of Father, Son and Holy Ghost in the form of a coloured triangle. The field was green, a colour sometimes associated with faith, although not it seems in later heraldic contexts.[60] The roundels bearing the names of the Persons of the Trinity are in red and blue.[61] This combination of red, blue, and green was also deployed in the rather earlier diagrams of the Trinity by the Italian theologian Joachim of Flora, where in one instance the Father was beige, the Son red and the Holy Spirit blue, and green was used, as here, to express the unity of the Godhead. But neither in Joachim nor in the artists of the *Scutum Fidei* was there any standard distribution of colours.[62] This impressive image is interesting chiefly as an indication that by the middle of the thirteenth century it was possible for a medieval spectator to interpret a coat of arms in metaphysical or moral terms.

A far more comprehensive indication that arms might be read in this way is offered by a stirring account of some dozen shields and their bearers in the thirteenth-century Icelandic

Didrecks Saga, in which the guests at the banquet of King Theodoric (Didreck) of Bern were all knights with expressive armorial bearings. Theodoric himself bore a red shield, as did another knight, Hildebrand, to show that he was Theodoric's man. That the author of the saga was familiar with some of the functions of heraldry is shown by his attribution of the same coats of arms to members of the same family. Most of his moral interpretations of the shields depended upon the animal devices on them but there was also some interpretation of colour. Heine the proud, for example, carried a blue shield which signified his cold breast and his grim heart; Fasold and his brother Ecke bore shields with a red lion, whose colour expressed their love of fighting.[63] In the *Didrecks Saga* one knight, Hornbogi of Wendland, and his son Amelung bore brown shields, signifying worth and courtesy. This underlines the Germanic culture within which this poem was composed, for brown was a tincture of blazon common in Germany from the early thirteenth century but which did not find a place (as *tanné* or *tawny*) in French or English heraldry until more than a century later.[64] Another symbolizing development in late heraldic usage was the association of the tinctures with precious stones, whose tradition of moral interpretation was well established. The late fourteenth-century German herald Peter Suchenwirt introduced pearls, rubies, diamonds, emeralds, mother-of-pearl and 'brown sapphire' into his blazon, in a number of heraldic poems.[65] By about 1400 the idea had been taken up in France and England, where it was immediately expanded into a comprehensive system of correspondences.[66] The anonymous French treatise in the Bibliothèque Mazarine in Paris provides each tincture not only with its appropriate gems and moral qualities but also with its metal, its humour, its element, its planet and signs of the zodiac and its day of the week. Thus *azur* connoted the sapphire, praise, beauty, *hauteur*, the sanguine temperament, the planet Venus, Gemini, Libra and Aquarius, air, fine silver (because this was used in the manufacture of a number of fine blue pigments) and Friday.[67] When Sicily Herald came to propose a similar scheme in the mid-fifteenth century his correspondences were by no means the same: he agreed about sapphire air and the sanguine temperament but his moral associations for *azur* were with loyalty, 'science' and justice; he introduced childhood but also autumn; his blue planet was Jupiter and his blue day Tuesday.[68] These correspondences had a particular vogue in English heraldic writing in the fifteenth century, where there were further local variations: we seem to be dealing with the free associations of rhetoric rather than with any practical concerns. Yet we learn that at the end of the century professional heralds making a visitation – an inspection of family records to maintain the proper heraldic procedures – of the north of England were using the vocabulary of precious stones.[69] Small wonder that the instructions to heralds drawn up by Thomas Duke of Clarence about 1420 included the study of books on the properties of colours, plants and stones, 'so that by this [reading] they may more properly and conveniently assign arms to each person'.[70]

The association of the colours of blazon with astrology and with the calendar brought them into the realm of costume, and we know that in fifteenth-century Italy, where Sicily Herald was employed by Alfonso at Naples, this was an aspect of the interpretation of colour which had some resonance at the courts. Alfonso's son-in-law Leonello d'Este, Duke of Ferrara, was known to choose the colour of his clothing according to the position of the planets and the days of the week;[71] Alfonso himself was always a careful dresser, preferring black, which, as Sicily Herald explained, signified melancholy and prudence; it was the colour most in demand for clothing in his day, 'pour la semplicité qui est en elle'. Black was the equivalent of the diamond and some of the best black cloths were as expensive as scarlet.[72]

Certainly we might expect the moral values of heraldry to be expressed first of all in clothing: a popular mid-thirteenth-century French poem, the *Ordene de Chevalerie*, described how at his investiture a knight would first be dressed in a white robe to show his cleanliness of body, then in a scarlet cloak to remind him of his duty to shed blood in the defence of the Church. He would then put on brown stockings to remind him of the earth in which he must finally lie and at the end of the ceremony he would tie on a white girdle to signify his chastity.[73] Dress had always been regarded as expressive. One of the earliest medieval debates about colour was the long discussion (*c.* 1127–49) between St Bernard of Clairvaux and Peter the Venerable on the subject of whether monks should wear white like the Cistercians or black like the longer established Benedictines at Cluny. St Benedict himself, the founder of Western monasticism, had left the matter open, recommending the cheapest cloth or leather available, but Peter the Venerable now insisted that only black could express the appropriate humility, penitence and abjectness of the monks in this vale of tears. White was expressive of joy and even glory, as in the Transfiguration of Christ, and was thus quite unsuitable for this purpose. Peter brought anthropological as well as theological and historical arguments to bear on the question: black, he said, was a funeral colour in Spain, for example. The debate is an indication of a remarkably sophisticated level of interpretation in questions of colour-meaning.[74] We are reminded of the dismay aroused in Pope Alexander VI's Master of Ceremonies in 1495, when the Pope wanted to dress in white a procession praying for the abatement of a great storm which had flooded the Tiber and left many casualties: white, explained the official, expressed 'happiness and rejoicing' and he was able to persuade Alexander to substitute the more appropriate violet.[75]

As these examples suggest, it was within the Christian Church that the expressive value of colour in vestments had been most commonly recognized. Yet the history of the liturgical colours shows that there was similarly little agreement about their precise connotations. Black and white presented few problems. Pope Innocent III, the promoter of one of the earliest canons of liturgical colour about 1200, proposed that red should be used for the feasts of the Apostles and martyrs because of its association with blood and the Pentecostal fire; but his contemporary Siccardus of Cremona argued that red vestments and hangings signified charity.[76] It may well be that the growing thirteenth-century interest of the heralds in the meaning of the tinctures was stimulated by the concern of the Church to establish a more standard canon, reflected in the popular and bulky *Rationale Divinorum Officiorum* of Guillaume Durand, Bishop of Mende. Certainly Sicily Herald referred to the liturgical use of red for the feasts of martyrs and his black Friday was discussed by Durand as appropriate to the Friday penitential feasts.[77] From the point of view of the liturgy, yellow had the same function as green, which must have depended upon their traditional confusion, and violet the same function as black. But in both the secular and the religious spheres painters were becoming more precise in their use of allegorical colour. Ambrogio Lorenzetti, for example, in his *Good Government* fresco (1338–9) in the Palazzo Pubblico in Siena, coded his figures of Temperance, Justice, Fortitude and Prudence with a scheme of colours – blue, green, diamond and carbuncle – derived from a recent exposition of the meaning of gemstones; in his *Maestà* at Massa Marittima he even labelled the three theological Virtues Faith, Hope and Charity by words as well as colours.[78] There can be little doubt that colour and its meaning was becoming a more central concern in the lay consciousness of medieval Europe. Secular love-poems such as Hadamar von der Laber's *Die Jagd der Minne* (*c.* 1335/40) included lengthy sections on the amorous connotations of colours, in this case six: green, white, red, blue, yellow and black; in fifteenth-century Germany there was a popular poem devoted to the six or seven colours and their interpretation in a multi-coloured dress, which later became a rhyming game.[79]

Another way in which heraldic blazon came to bear meaning was far more specialized and more scholarly. From the

56

The arming of a knight, in a late fourteenth-century illumination of Benoit de Sainte-Maure, *Roman de Troie*. (51)

Heraldic blazon

52

The enamel funerary plaque of Geoffrey Plantagenet (**53**) shows the earliest known truly heraldic device, of rampant lions on shield and bonnet. He is also wearing a cloak lined with squirrel-fur (*vair*), whose formalized design became the heraldic version of this blazon. Geoffrey's device of lions may well symbolize what the inscription proclaims, that he was a courageous defender of the Church, but it was perhaps not for a century that the colours of blazon were read symbolically. The virtuous knight from Peraldus (**52**) carries the green Faith on his shield, but true to the improvisatory character of medieval symbolism, this was only one of the colours attributed to that Theological Virtue.

52 Knight bearing a 'Shield of Faith', from Peraldus, *Summa de Vitiis, c.* 1240/55
53 Funeral effigy of Geoffrey Plantagenet, 1151/60

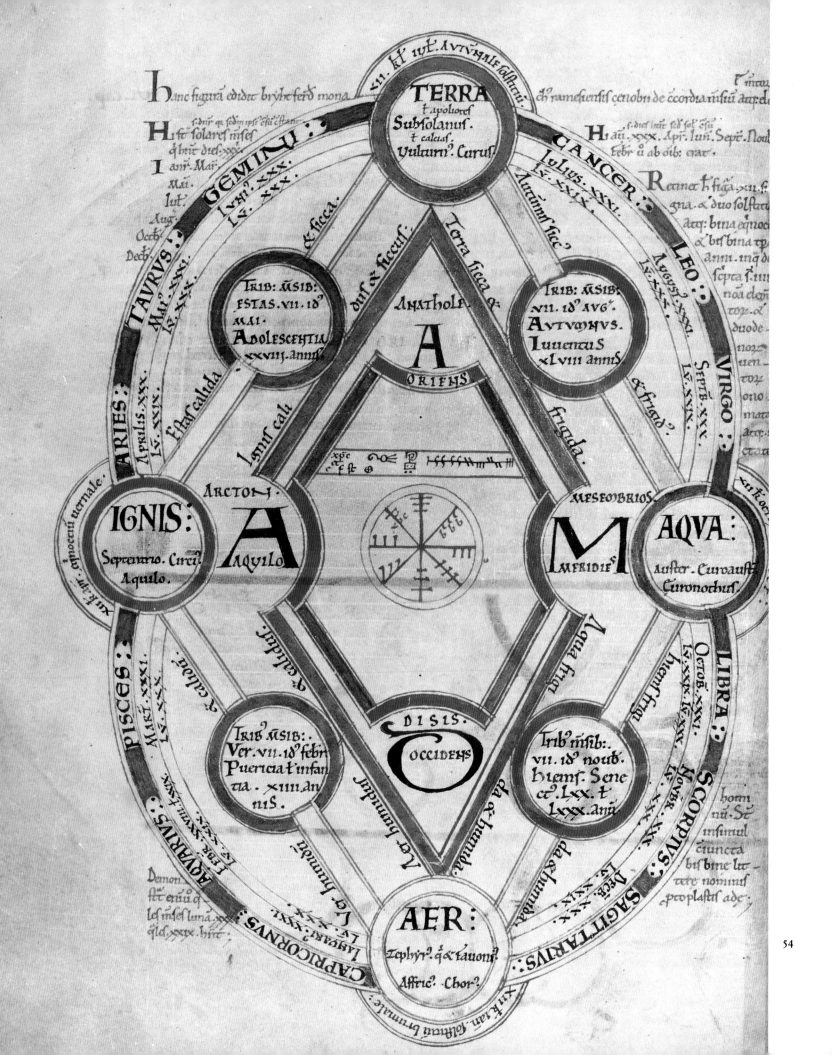

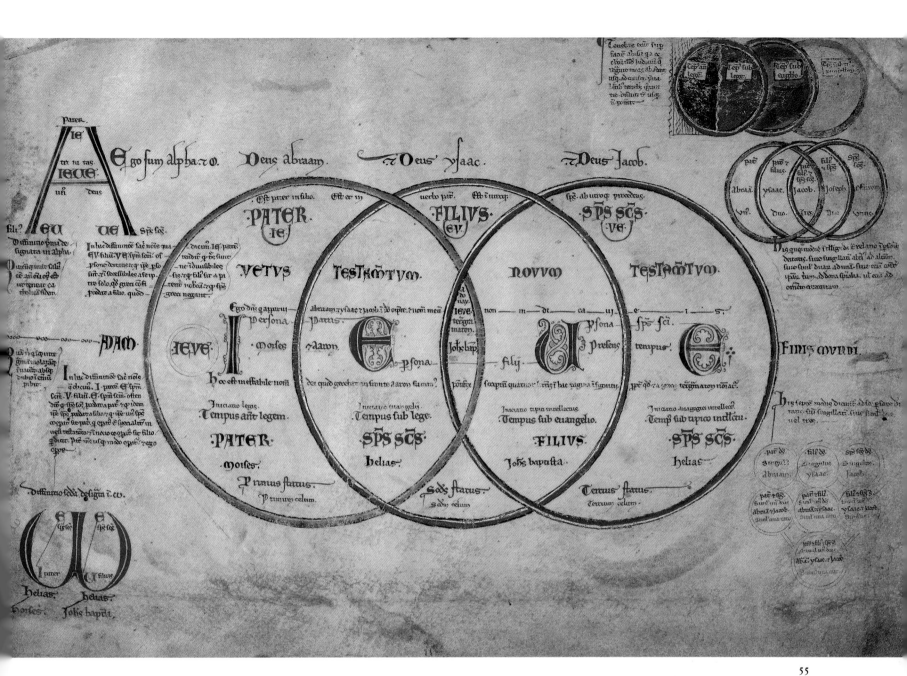

Diagrams of colour

The medieval love of systems which gave us these magnificent diagrams should not lead us to suppose that colours were symbolic in any standard way. Byrtferth's correlation of the four humours, the four seasons, the four points of the compass, and so on (**54**), was only one of many similar schemes which provided an abundance of colours for each of the four elements. A single manuscript of Joachim of Flora (**55**) has different colour-equivalents for the Son and the Holy Spirit on different pages. Colour provided imaginative embellishment, rather than expressing any notion of objective truth.

54 Attributed to Byrtferth of Ramsey, *The four-fold system of Macrocosm and Microcosm*, from a collection of scientific texts, *c.* 1080/90

55 *The Holy Trinity*, from Joachim of Flora, *Liber Figurarum*, twelfth century

fourteenth century the right to display particular armorial shields had to be defensible at law;[80] an Italian jurist, Bartolo of Sassoferrato, seems to have been the first to draw up criteria for the attribution of blazon in arms. For Bartolo there were five tinctures; he argued on scientific grounds that gold was the noblest colour since it represented light; the next was red (*purpureus sive rubeus*), since it represented fire, which was the noblest of the elements. Thus only princes might bear gold and red in their arms. The third tincture was blue, the representative of air, 'which is a diaphanous and transparent body, and particularly receptive to light'. Of the remaining two colours, black and white, said Bartolo, citing Aristotle, white was noble because of its lightness and black the least noble, since it was opposite to white. This hierarchy of colours, besides relating to the social hierarchy, could also, according to Bartolo, affect the arrangement of blazon on shields or banners, with the nobler colours uppermost and the others downwards in succession.[81]

These highly constricting recommendations do not seem to have been acted upon even in Italy, and towards the end of the century an obscure English heraldic writer, Johannes de Bado Aureo ('John of the Golden Bucket', or 'Measure'), launched a critique of Bartolo's ideas, with a much greater battery of scientific writing behind him. Johannes drew on the opinions of his master, one Francis, of whom nothing is known. Master Francis had divided the colours into three groups: the primary, white and black; the secondary (*medius*), blue, yellow and red; and the tertiary (*submedius*). Black could not be the least noble colour, although it was inferior to white, because it belonged to the primary set. Of the secondary set, blue was the first, because it represented the 'noble air' and was composed equally of light and dark. The next was yellow (*aureus*), which was not as noble as white since it was not as close to light. Red was, confusingly, also equidistant between white and black and the reason why it was more appropriate to princes than any other colour was because it signified ferocity and fortitude. Green, on the other hand, as a tertiary colour mixed from the two secondaries blue and yellow, was not properly admissible in arms at all and indeed it had not been used by the 'ancients'.[82] Unlike the other heraldic writers, who associated the diamond (*adamas*) with black, Master Francis gave it to blue, and one of the reasons why blue was nobler than yellow was because this colour was sent by an angel from God to form the basis of the Emperor Charlemagne's arms, which were three gold flowers on an azure field.[83] Yellow, continued Master Francis, was inferior because, according to Avicenna, it needed the admixture of red, white and black and it could also be produced from 'the vilest colour in the world', that is the tertiary green. Red was inferior to blue because in its noblest form, fire, it required the presence of blue air to give it light.[84]

This juggling with the constituents of colour in order to construct a hierarchy of tinctures more 'scientific' than Bartolo's

is typical of the late Scholastic splitting of hairs. But when in the 1430s Bartolo's scheme came under attack from the Italian humanist Lorenzo Valla, it was on the grounds not of his physical descriptions of the tinctures but largely on the basis of everyday experience embodied in ordinary language. We can see, said Valla, that the sun is not golden, a colour which we would call *fulvus, rutilus* or *croceus*, but rather silvery (*argenteus*) or white (*candidus*). But why should white be considered superior to all other colours, as Bartolo had it inconsistently later in his treatise? Do we prefer pearls and crystal to carbuncles, emeralds, sapphires or topazes; or white linen to red or purple silk? And as for black, both the raven and the swan are sacred to Apollo, and the eye, which is the sole judge of colour, has been made black in the centre: it can hardly be the most despised of colours. And what of the order of precious stones prescribed by God for the decoration of Aaron's breastplate or for the walls of the Heavenly Jerusalem? Enough said, concluded Valla; it is stupid to want to lay down the law about the dignity of colours.[85] Note that Valla did not ridicule the principle of attributing values to colours as such but Bartolo's reductive and illogical system. After he was expelled by the law-students of Pavia for his attack on the jurist, Valla moved in 1437 to Naples, to the court of Alfonso I, whose Sicily Herald, as we have seen, had incorporated a very wide network of colour-associations into his *Blason des Couleurs*.[86]

Just as the legal-scientific system of late heraldic blazon came under attack from an Italian humanist, so the more popular and unsystematic correspondences of Sicily Herald were held up to ridicule by the greatest French Renaissance writer, François Rabelais. Rabelais's monstrous comic creation Gargantua, true to the current fashions, had to be furnished with a family device, which was blazoned argent (*blanc*) and azure (*bleu*): white because it meant 'joy, pleasure, delights and rejoicing', to Gargantua's father, and blue because of its reference to celestial things. But, said Rabelais, readers might object that white signifies faith (as in Lorenzetti's *Maestà*) and blue constancy. Who says so? Some ridiculous little book call *Le Blason des Couleurs*, so disreputable that it has prudently no name attached to it and which is hawked around by cheapjacks. It is nothing short of tyranny to want to impose these regulations on the making of badges 'without any other demonstration or valid arguments'.[87] Rabelais went on to say that he himself hoped some day to write a book proving 'as much by philosophical reasoning as by ancient authority' what colours there are in nature and what is signified by each of them (as far as we know, he never did so). Later in *Gargantua* he turned to the Aristotelian arguments for the opposition of white and black, used by common consent for rejoicing and for mourning. He cited Valla against Bartolo and a whole range of ancient authors to show that just as white expands the eye, so it expands the heart, and concluded that in Gargantua's blazon 'blue certainly means the sky and celestial things by the same symbolism by which white signifies joy and pleasure'.[88]

In spite of such weighty criticisms, the explication of the meanings of heraldic blazon became very much a part of courtly entertainment in Italy during the Renaissance. Early in the sixteenth century Lodovico Gonzaga composed a treatise on the subject (now lost) and it was originally considered as one of the

56

Faith. Hope and Charity form the steps up to the Virgin's throne, and each is given its appropriate colour – white, green and red.

56 Ambrogio Lorenzetti, *Maestà*, c. 1335 (detail)

possible topics of conversation in that most influential of Italian treatises of courtesy, Baldassare Castiglione's *Book of the Courtier* (1528).[89] F. P. Morato's *On the Meaning of Colours*, which owes a good deal to Sicily Herald, ran into a dozen editions in the sixteenth century alone and an Italian version of Sicily Herald's own *Blason*, which had been published in French in 1495 and again in 1528, was reprinted twice in Venice towards the end of the century. A rival Italian publication, Luca Contile's *Discourse of Devices* (Pavia, 1574), followed the same pattern but chose a rather different set of correspondences between the tinctures and the days of the week (blue Thursday, black Friday *and* Saturday). None of the Italian publications used the standard French vocabulary of blazon, which was never adopted in Italy.[90]

Post-medieval perceptions of heraldic blazon

The idea that heraldic blazon embodied an authentic language of colours was reinforced in the many seventeenth-century treatises on heraldry in which the art coagulated into its present form, and it re-appeared most influentially in Baron Portal's great Romantic synthesis of colour-meanings early in the nineteenth century.[91] Portal revived the medieval notion of the ambivalence of colour-symbols in his 'Rule of Opposition', by which red, for example, might equally signify love and hate.[92] But, even if he was aware of it, Portal was not able to accommodate the antithetical *perceptions* of a common term such as *sinople*, whose red/green connotations exemplified the nineteenth century's principle of complementarity.[93] Complementarity depended chiefly on the physiological pheno-menon of coloured after-images: one colour-sensation 'deman-ded' another. For the Middle Ages the relationship of red and green was probably closest because they were both seen as the median term on the colour-scale,[94] and beauty and harmony were understood to consist in the mean between extremes.[95] In costume the combination of red and green was one of the most popular in the later Middle Ages, especially in northern Europe (the Church Synods at Cologne and Liège decreed in 1281 and 1287 that priests were not to wear these colours without special reason).[96] Whether this pairing is to be accounted for primarily on aesthetic or on economic grounds is a nice question: we know that in Tuscany at least in the late fourteenth century these were by far the most expensive colours of cloth, more than a third more costly than blue.[97] Nor was the confusion between red and green unique in medieval colour perception. It is perhaps even more surprising to us that three words in Latin and French much used in the later Middle Ages, *glaucus, ceruleus* and *bloi*, could be used to signify either blue or yellow, another pair which came to be known as complementary in the later nineteenth century.[98] There may be a technological back-ground to both these anomalies, for just as medieval glassmakers used the same copper oxide to manufacture red and green glass, simply varying the time of heating,[99] so a comparable chemical colour-change, from yellow to blue, must have been noticed during the manufacture of the blue vegetable dyestuff woad, whose leaves, shielded from light, were an intense yellow and only turned blue on exposure to it. Both colour-phases were described as *isatis* (woad).[100] Since we are dealing with large

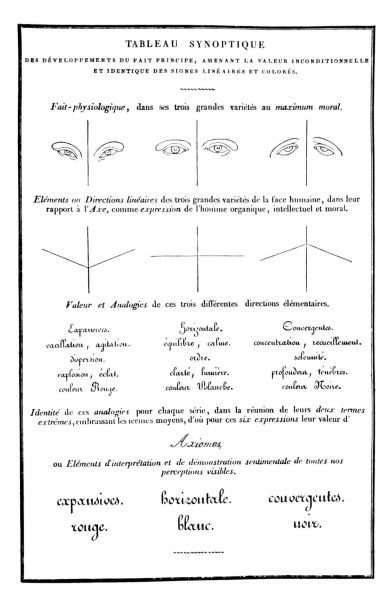

A more psychological way of interpreting colour symbolism developed during the nineteenth century, and began to affect the interpretation of blazon. D.P.G. Humbert de Superville's 'Synoptic Table' of 1827 characterizes red as 'violent' and 'expansive'; blazon identified the colour with vertical lines, in accordance with its dynamic power. (57)

speech-communities, however, technology seems perhaps too specialized an occupation to have affected perception in such a widespread way. Other commentators have referred to the facts of colour-vision, which may manifest deficiencies precisely in the perception of the red/green and yellow/blue pairs. However we account for these anomalies – and there have been few extended discussions of the problem – these extreme examples of the fluidity of colour terms in the medieval period make it very clear that we must be wary of translating colour symbolism into modern psychological language, as was done so frequently in the later nineteenth century.

It may indeed be doubted whether the colours of heraldic blazon were ever as important as the forms they embellished.

Although plain coloured shields were very common in the romances, they hardly figure at all in historic coats of arms, where meaning has always tended to reside in the heraldic devices. Many of the earliest arms were on monochromatic seals or tiles[101] and when, from the fifteenth century, engraving was applied to the reproduction of armorial bearings, there was no attempt for more than a century to devise a graphic system for suggesting the different tinctures, and no widely accepted system of this sort for a century after that.[102] A Flemish system of 1623, using diagonal hatchings for gold and dots for blue, never became general.[103] The first widely adopted system, using dots for gold, vertical hatching for gules, horizontal for azure and so on, was published by P. Silvestre de Petra-Sancta in *De Symbolis Heroicis* (1634) and *Tesserae Gentilitae* (1638); it was spread very widely by the theoretical treatise on heraldry by Marc de Vulson de la Colombière in 1639.[104] The system was still current in the nineteenth century and even became part of the general vocabulary of colour, being used outside the heraldic context, for example by Moses Harris in the plates for his *Natural System of Colours*, originally about 1776. It is something of a paradox that this graphic scheme, devised as a matter of pure convenience in the seventeenth century, many decades after the code of colour-meanings in blazon had reached a more or less general acceptance throughout Europe, should in the intensely psychologizing atmosphere of *fin-de siècle* Paris have been seen to embody some profound psychological truths. Already in the Romantic period the Dutch mythographer D. P. G. Humbert de Superville had published an outline of the

relationship between the direction of lines and the impact of colours, but this had rested on a very far-fetched notion of cosmic correspondences.[105] The relationship was given an empirical, psychological and mathematical twist by Seurat's friend Charles Henry in his *Protracteur Chromatique* of 1888; in an article a few years later in the *Revue de Paris* the aesthetician Paul Souriau brought the whole question into the context of the hatchings of traditional blazon:

> At first sight it is not easy to imagine how we can establish any sort of analogy between parallel lines drawn in such and such a direction, and green or orange. Nevertheless, the horizontal strokes, which agree with the habitual movements of the eyes better than the others, have a sort of sweetness which makes them appropriate for expressing nature's neutral tints, the tone of distant objects, the softly gradated nuances of sea or sky. On the other hand the vertical strokes, since they present the opposite to our eye, something abnormal and misleading, will rather express sharp and lively colours. Why in the engraving of blazon is red symbolized precisely by the vertical lines and blue by the horizontal? . . . Instinct leads [the engraver] to express differences of colour by differences of direction.[106]

Souriau was writing at a time when experimental psychology, especially in France and Germany, had made it seem possible to see choices and combinations of colours in artefacts as the expression of psychological states; but we shall see that this was scarcely more certain a procedure than it had been for the symbolizers of the later Middle Ages.

The coat of arms of George Field (1777–1854) illustrates the persistence of graphic conventions for armorial colours into the modern period. Gold is symbolized by dots, blue by horizontal lines. (58)

The story of Noah, from Aelfric's *Paraphrase of the Pentateuch and Joshua*, eleventh century. The medieval illuminator has tried to convey with many bands the 'thousand colours' of Virgil's account of the rainbow. (59)

6 · Unweaving the Rainbow

From Titian to Testa · The Romantics · Prismatics and harmony
Twentieth-century epilogue

... Do not all charms fly
At the mere touch of cold philosophy?
There was an awful rainbow once in heaven:
We know her woof, her texture; she is given
In the dull catalogue of common things.
Philosophy will clip an Angel's wings,
Conquer all mysteries by rule and line,
Empty the haunted air, and gnomed mine –
Unweave a rainbow.
(John Keats, *Lamia*, 1819)

IN ONE of the earliest histories of optics the eighteenth-century English chemist Joseph Priestley remarked that 'of all the optical appearances in nature, the *rainbow* is perhaps the most striking. Accordingly, we have found that it has always engaged the attention of philosophers.'[1] So indeed it had and has continued to do so ever since.[2] Another contention of Priestley's, that in the bow 'the *regular order of the colours* was a . . . circumstance that could not have escaped the notice of any person',[3] raises many problems, for his own abundant evidence suggests that the number and even the order of the colours has been far from clear to all observers, and in both the literary and the visual record we have a very large number of differing analyses. This will hardly come as a surprise if we recall that the identification of the colours in the far more easily standardized spectrum of white light has presented difficulties to spectators in laboratory experiments even in recent times.[4] A young late nineteenth-century observer could see only four colours in a well-defined bow, which should help us to understand the very common four-colour bows of the Middle Ages; the almost equally familiar two-colour bow of medieval art may be partly explained by the greater salience of the red and the green still often observed in the spectrum.[5] What is clear is that the very delicacy of the transitions in the bow, which was to commend it to some theorists as a model of colour-harmony, makes it extremely hard to number and name the colours. This has made the phenomenon especially apt for interpretation according to any of a number of prevailing schemata.

Like all the phenomena of the heavens the rainbow and the related manifestations of prismatic colour, such as haloes and parhelia, have been the subjects of intense scrutiny by astronomers in many cultures and all periods.[6] In Jewish myth the bow could be a hopeful portent, as in the story of God's convenant with Noah, and in the Judaeo-Christian tradition it could be the symbol of Divine power at the Last Judgment, recorded in Ezekiel (1:28) and the Revelation of St John (4:3). In a secular context the bow could usefully indicate both good and bad fortune: as late as 1806, when Napoleon conferred a crown on the Kürfurst Friedrich August of Saxony, the rainbow which appeared in the neighbourhood was read as a good omen, but in the event it proved to be an augury of further war and the eventual partition of the new kingdom.[7]

In spite of its enormous religious and political significance, the problem of analysing and representing the rainbow remained intractable. Ancient writers from Homer to Isidore of Seville had handed down notions of the bow varying from one to six chromatic divisions; Ovid and Virgil had indicated the impossibility of counting by proposing a thousand.[8] Nor had the order remained stable: Aristotle's well observed sequence of red (*phoinicoun*), green (*prasinon*) and purple (*halourgon*) had in late Antiquity become yellow, red, purple, orange, blue and green in the Stoic philosopher Aëtius and the Roman historian Ammianus Marcellinus.[9] The few surviving visual records give rather more evidence of a considered study of the phenomenon itself among the Greeks and Romans. If the probably sixth-century illustrator of the *Vergilius Romanus* (a manuscript whose prototype was perhaps of the fourth) condensed the author's thousand colours into three – red, white and green[10] – mosaicists made the most of their opportunities for conveying the shimmering, luminous qualities of the phenomenon. The remarkable rainbow mosaic from Pergamon of the second century BC introduced ten colours in thirty rows of tesserae, blending at the edges and with yellow at the centre. The far more modest fragment of pavement from a third-century AD Roman bath at Thessaloniki has a sequence of five colours – red, pink, white, yellow and green with, like the shawl of Iris in the *Vergilius Romanus*, white as its luminous centre.[11]

What is striking in a number of medieval renderings of the bow is their closeness to some contemporary conception of the number and disposition of the colours in observable rainbows, where the colouring of other objects in the image is fanciful or conventional. In the sixth-century *Vienna Genesis*, for example, the rainbow marking God's Covenant with Noah is shown in the two colours of blue-green (water) and red (fire), as set out in the almost contemporary eighth homily on Ezekiel by St Gregory the Great and quoted, despite the growing number of rival versions, until well into the Renaissance.[12] Other artists preferred the Aristotelian three-colour bow, which did not fail to be glossed as late as the seventeenth century as a symbol of the Trinity;[13] Aelfric's Anglo-Saxon *Paraphrase of the Pentateuch and Joshua* illustrated the story of Noah with a rainbow divided into six bands of colour but with each band divided into a number of smaller units. These suggested again the vagueness of Virgil's 'thousand colours', which had passed into medieval Old Testament literature through St Jerome's commentary on Ezekiel.[14]

64–5

64

59

Allegory of Judgment, Cesare Ripa, *Iconologia*, 1611. (60)

Rainbow in the story of Noah, from the *Weltchronick* (*Nuremberg Chronicle*) by Hartmann Schedel, 1493. Four bands are in line with the fourteenth-century theory of Theodoric of Freiberg, but elsewhere the *Chronicle* lays down that there are two bands (red and green) in accordance with St Gregory. (61)

There are even examples of medieval rainbows which approach the Newtonian seven-colour formula: one is in a magnificent Norman Book of Hours executed in the second quarter of the fifteenth century, when the study of refraction in northern and central Europe was already well developed. It reminds us that Dante had revived a seven-colour theory in the *Divine Comedy* and had even conceived of the secondary bow as a reflection and hence an inversion of the first.[15]

The illuminator of the Aelfric manuscript also made a distinction between the quasi-historical bow of the Noah story and those other Biblical bows of the *Maiestas Domini* (Christ in Glory) whose mandorlas were described in Ezekiel and Revelation simply by analogy with the rainbow.[16] It is as if in showing such a singular and significant event as the Covenant, the illuminator was anxious to get as close as possible to its literal truth. A similar attempt in the sixteenth century is implicit in the contrast between what must be one of the earliest, as it is certainly one of the most beautifully observed, rainbows in a landscape, Grünewald's *Stuppach Madonna*, and the wholly transcendental glory of the Isenheim *Resurrection*.[17] Grünewald's bow was not his own invention; it depended, like the rest of the rich symbolism in his picture, on the *Revelations* of St Bridget of Sweden, where the Virgin described herself as a rainbow, mediating between earth and heaven against the dark clouds of sin and worldliness.[18] Yet the painter did not follow his source slavishly: the dark clouds are not behind the arc,[19] both ends of the bow are not firmly planted on the earth and, possibly through the effect of the Madonna's own nimbus, the sky inside the arc gives a convincing effect of heightened luminosity. In his sensitivity and close observation, this Lutheran painter contrasted strikingly with Luther himself, who opposed Aristotle's

rainbow theory on the grounds that it clashed with his own observations (he seems to have noticed a solar halo), but admitted bafflement and, with the excuse that reason is more reliable than the eye, retreated to the traditional, two-colour version of St Gregory.[20]

We saw that the second important Christian symbolic use of the rainbow was apocalyptic, and the ambivalence of the image continued to be felt until the Romantic period. Before the ninth century the rainbow glory had transferred its properties to Christ's throne – which for St Jerome had been of sapphire[21] – and it was this type of *Maiestas Domini*, sometimes with a second bow as a footstool, which was developed for the specific representation of Christ in Judgment right up to the work of the Rococo decorators.[22] It was also this type that was adopted by the iconographer Cesare Ripa as the emblem of Judgment (*Giuditio*) itself, in his early Baroque dictionary of allegories.[23] Given a Newtonian interpretation, Ripa's image might bring us close to Blake's *Ancient of Days*,[24] but he used his rainbow, like his contemporary Tommaso Campanella, not as representing a reduction to rigid simplicity but as the aggregation of strands of experience into a psychological complex: 'To explain the rainbow, we shall say that everyone who rises to public notice in any way must learn judgment from a multitude of experiences, just as the rainbow results from the appearance of many colours brought together by the sun's rays.'[25]

From Titian to Testa

The emblem of Judgment is not the only rainbow in Ripa's *Iconologia*, for in his commentary on the personification of the Italian province Umbria, he made an exceptionally long excursus on the bow spanning the falls of Piediluce on Lake Velino. This, he was careful to explain, is not a rainbow but rather 'special, and only formed on days when the sky is very clear'.[26] The same bow had been celebrated by Pliny in his *Natural History* (II, lxii, 153) and it became in the later eighteenth century an important staging-post on the Grand Tour. But the element of surprise and wonder in Ripa's account may help us to understand why the phenomenon was so rarely introduced into earlier attempts at a more independent sort of landscape. It we look at a picture-book of the Renaissance, Hartmann Schedel's *Weltchronik* (1493), which has been noticed for its wilful duplication of images, we find among a dozen comets and incidences of fire from heaven a record of only two rainbows, which are represented as quite distinct. The story of Noah has a bow with four bands, although the text (xi) asserts the truth of St Gregory's symbolic two-colour bow against the theorists of five and six colours, but the great rainbow seen to the accompaniment of fire from heaven in the reign of Pope John IV has three colours and, said the text (cli), it did not fail to suggest in the minds of many the coming of the end of the world.

Despite the indications in Ripa's *Umbria* and somewhat earlier in Leonardo[27] of an interest in the rainbow for its own sake among an unspecialized public, it can scarcely be found in the newly emerging genre of landscape in the sixteenth century. Pinturicchio's *Departure of Aeneas Sylvius for Basle* hardly qualifies as pure landscape but the rainbow and its attendant clouds were not in the preparatory drawings. Although they might be interpreted as foreshadowing the stormy journey or, conversely, the Pope's extraordinary success on his political mission,[28] it is very likely that they represent that loosening of landscape imagery which has been noticed in the period and may, in other examples too, account for the appearance of the rainbow where it is hardly demanded by the story.[29] Yet, in spite of a developing interest in sensational effects of weather – in Giorgione's *Tempesta* or Dosso Dossi's *Adoration* or Altdorfer's *Battle of Alexander* – the landscape theorists of the period did not use the rainbow as an example of the reach of colour, even though in the Italian comparison of the arts, the *paragone*, from Castiglione at the beginning of the century to Cristoforo Sorte at the end, it was the versatility of colour in the portrayal of storms and night-scenes, of dawn light and conflagrations, which was seen as the particular glory of landscape art.[30]

One of the few sixteenth-century Italian painters to make much use of the motif of the rainbow was Titian, who introduced bows of great complexity, sometimes with upwards of six colours, into his compositions *Venus and Adonis* and *Diana and Callisto*.[31] Titian's predominantly warm rainbows beginning and ending their sequence with warm pinks and purples – may partly be due to the poor or dirty condition of some of the paintings but they are also very much in tune with the account of the bow in an encyclopaedia by Giorgio Valla, published in Venice in 1501. Valla listed five colours, three of which, *puniceum, ostrinum* and *purpureum*, were reds.[32] It may be more than a coincidence that the Florentine philosopher Antonio Brucioli chose Titian – whom, he said, surpassed nature in the proportions and colours of his figures – as the interlocutor with the architect Serlio in a discussion of the nature of the rainbow in one of his dialogues. Brucioli set the conversation in Titian's house and started it with a reference to a bow in one of his paintings. Titian asks about the rainbow of the Covenant and is assured that it had the two colours of water and fire which, in balance, assured mankind that no further flood would occur in foreseeable time. Yet the scientific explanation of the bow is entirely Aristotelian, introducing the three colours purple (*pagonazzo*), green and red.[33] If Titian read this dialogue, it can hardly have meant very much to him.

For most of the nineteenth century Grünewald's *Stuppach Madonna* was regarded as the work of Rubens.[34] For Constable, as for Reynolds, Rubens's landscapes meant 'rainbows upon a stormy sky – bursts of sunshine, – moonlight, – meteors . . .'. He numbered the rainbow landscape which is now in the Wallace Collection, London, among the painter's finest works.[35] That this was a Romantic and even a specifically English conception is suggested by the fact that Rubens's most liberal early biographer, Roger de Piles, never devoted any specific attention to the motif.[36] (He had introduced the idea of those 'accidents of light' – of which the rainbow was certainly one of the most striking and which became a commonplace of nineteenth-century landscape criticism[37] – and he had discussed two rainbow landscapes by Rubens in the collection of the Duc de Richelieu.) Moreover, versions of at least five of the seven rainbow landscapes known at present were in English collections early in the nineteenth century.[38] Clearly the taste had something to do with the English love of weather.

Rubens, who used the rainbow equally to accompany disaster – as in the *Shipwreck of St Paul* (Adler 36) – and the summery hopefulness of the harvest, may have developed an interest in its pictorial qualities in the Elsheimer circle in Rome, for there is a small panel by Elsheimer's imitator Johann König, where the bow is introduced rather freely into *The Road to Emmaeus*.[39] De Piles described the *Shipwreck* as having been painted in Italy and the Louvre *Rainbow* has also been assigned to the painter's Italian period (the Hermitage version is thought to be rather later).[40] But Rubens's rising interest in the phenomenon soon became far more diverse: he began to introduce it into figure subjects, of which the first was perhaps *Juno and Argus* (*c.* 1610). Here Iris and her emblem were brought into the Ovidian story of many-eyed Argus. The picture, which was painted at the time of Rubens's involvement in the illustrations for François d'Aguilon's treatise on optics, has been interpreted as an allegory of optics and especially colour.[41] It may well have been the starting-point for an even greater interest in the rainbow, for the painter introduced it no less than three times into his great cycle of the life of Marie de' Médicis, and we know from a letter that he discussed at least one with his adviser Peiresc.[42] The presence of the bows may not be due solely to the rather exaggerated good fortune of the Queen, for the badge of her predecessor Catherine de' Médici had been a rainbow with the motto *Luce apporto, e bonaccia* (I bring light and stability).[43] This may well have been Rubens's intention even if, as in other instances in the cycle, it was not a case of mistaken identity.[44]

The symbolic rainbows of Rubens were composed of red, yellow and blue or green, but in his landscapes they were much more complex and bear witness to a degree of observation which, although erratic, has deserved better of the critics. It was not long after the completion of the Medici Cycle in 1625 that Descartes worked out his fundamental theory of the rainbow both mathematically and with newly developed principles of observation and experiment.[45] But Rubens, like Goethe, who excused his illogical lighting for the higher imperatives of good picture-making,[46] was only a (proto) Romantic because he was everything; to the painters and critics of the Romantic period to whom observation was as important as imagination, it was this high-handedness in the face of the data of the out-of-doors which helped to make him in their eyes no more than a model of technique. Ruskin noted of the Wallace Collection painting, which may well have been a good deal darker than it is now, that the bow was 'a dull blue, *darker* than the sky, in a scene lighted from the side of the rainbow. Rubens is not to be blamed for ignorance of optics, but for never having so much as looked at a rainbow carefully.'[47] Turner, who saw the Louvre landscape in 1802, had been equally damning:

> The Rainbow appears to me the most considered as a picture. Not but this as well as the rest of his landscapes is defective as light and the propriety of nature. The woman in blue strikes the eye and prevents it straying to the confused and ill-judged lines, but as to the figures in the Middle which is lit from the opposite side, a proof that he wanted light on that side and rather chose to commit an error than continue the light by means of the ground to where the sky is placed. Then it is led by the yellow within the trees to the sky and

Pietro Testa's *Triumph of Painting on Parnassus* (detail), a witness to the painter's (ultimately fatal) obsession with the rainbow. Goethe owned an impression of this engraving. (62)

thence to the Bow, which is hard and horny by the use of the vivid Blue in the distance, which is another instance of his distorting what he was ignorant of – natural effect.[48]

It is certainly in the seventeenth century that we must look for a proto-Romantic attitude to the rainbow but it is to be found less in Rubens than in Jacob Ruisdael and Pietro Testa.

As Rembrandt was for Goethe the thinker among seventeenth-century painters, so Ruisdael was the poet. It was for his poetry and economy of means, so different from the exuberance of Rubens, that he was admired by Romantic painters as diverse as Delacroix and Samuel Palmer, Constable and Caspar David Friedrich. The Romantic understanding of Ruisdael focused on a symbolic interpretation of his imagery, nowhere more so than in that sudden burst of colour in two versions of *The Jewish Cemetery* at Dresden and Detroit. Of the Detroit version J. Smith wrote in 1835:

> The grandeur and solemnity of the scene is strikingly enhanced by the rolling stormy clouds, in which may be perceived the evanescent colours of a rainbow. In this excellent picture the artist has evidently intended to convey a moral lesson of human life, and in addition to this there is a sublimity of sentiment and effect reigning throughout the composition which renders it worthy of the powers of Nicolo Poussin.[49]

Smith's interpretation was essentially the same as Goethe's

commentary on the Dresden version.[50] But neither critic seems to have known that the cemetery was Jewish and had been studied by Ruisdael in some unusually detailed drawings.[51] Nothing is known of the circumstances of the commission but whether the painter had introduced the rainbow as the Christian symbol of judgment or the Jewish symbol of reconciliation, it is clear that the pictures were for Ruisdael, as they became for the Romantics, far more than picturesque topography.

The case of the Lucchese painter Pietro Testa is very different because although we know a good deal about the man very few of his works have survived. Goethe owned a number of his prints, including two with the rainbow,[52] but in general Testa seems to have been virtually unknown in the Romantic period when his psychology and his obsession with observation, stimulated very much by Leonardo da Vinci, would have made him a congenial figure. His seventeenth-century biographer Baldinucci wrote:

> His temperament was somewhat melancholy and as a result he always had a peculiar bent for very old things, and for depicting night scenes and changes in the atmosphere and in the sky. His works prove how much he had to study from the life, until one day a doleful accident befel him. He was standing on the bank of the Tiber, drawing and observing some reflections of the rainbow in the water, when, whether because he was jostled, or because of the softness of the slippery bank, or for whatever other reason I know not, he tumbled into the river . . .[53]

Testa drowned in 1650 and, although this is not the only account of his death in Baldinucci,[54] it is possible that in the broader sense at least we have in Testa the first martyr to optics, since some of the precepts he left in his notes on painting point to the laborious and 'scientific' preparation of his pictures and help to explain why so few were made:

> The practice of painting is a continual observation of the beautiful, and an absorbtion of it, so to speak, through the eyes, and with the hands to put it well into practice through lines and colours and chiaroscuro, always copying [*imitando*], and at the same time endeavouring to find out why the object seen is and seems to be what it is . . . From imitation we move to observation and from thence to mathematical certainty as by stages . . . When a good technique has been acquired we move on to the understanding of causes [*al'intendere per le sue chause*]. When these are understood, since we are now well-informed and eager, we start work on the picture . . .[55]

Testa introduced the rainbow into a painting and an engraving of *The Triumph of Painting*. The painting cannot now be traced but to judge from a poor photograph of it[56] he seems to have understood the contrast of light and dark inside and outside the bow (Alexander's dark band) and to have counted six bands of colour; this might well support Baldinucci's account of his interests. The rainbow as a symbol of chromatics became commonplace on the title-pages of optical treatises and painters' handbooks, but as an idea it had a particular attraction for the Romantics for it suggested an area where art and nature might meet on an equal footing: Testa's brief career and the intensity of his optical interests look forward to the work of the German painter-theorist Philipp Otto Runge.

TAB. LXVI.

Rainbows and what caused them had been subjects for investigation and speculation since Antiquity. Until the close of the Middle Ages the rainbow was thought to be a sort of reflection of the sun on a dark cloud, rather than the result of the variable refraction of light through drops of water, represented here by circles in an elegant eighteenth-century diagram by J.J. Scheuchzer. Scheuchzer shows the workings of single refraction in the lower, primary, bow, and of double refraction (with an inversion of the order of the colours) in the upper, secondary bow, while the circular bow is demonstrated in the spray of a waterfall. Although this account is based directly on the work of Sir Isaac Newton (*Opticks*, 1730), at the same time it fulfils the far more traditional function of explaining the bow marking the Old Testament Covenant between God and man in the Book of Genesis.

63 The formation of the rainbow, J.J. Scheuchzer, *Physica Sacra*, 1731

GENESIS Cap. IX. v. 12.17.
Iridis demonstratio.

I. Buch Mosis Cap. IX. v. 12.17.
Untersuchung des Regenbogen.

Fig. I.

64 God's Covenant with Noah, the *Vienna Genesis*, sixth century
65 Noah's Ark, from a Book of Hours, Normandy, *c.* 1430/40
66 MATTHIAS GRÜNEWALD, *Stuppach Madonna*, 1517/19

64

The bright bow of promise

Christian imagery teems with representations of rainbows, but they are rarely shown in the same way. For the scene of God's Covenant, the Early Christian artist of the *Vienna Genesis* (**64**) used a two-colour scheme: the green of water signified the Deluge and the red band below the fire of Judgment Day. The Norman illuminator (**65**) may have been aware of fourteenth-century research which suggested that the colours were formed in prismatic order by the refraction of light, for he paints a bow with the colours of the spectrum; in the Renaissance Grünewald (**66**) illustrated the analogy between the Virgin Mary and the rainbow which he had found in the *Revelations* of St Bridget of Sweden, while perhaps drawing partly on an earlier metaphor of Mary as a rainbow in St Bonaventure (*Laus Virginus*, 6), which dwelt on the blue as an image of virginity and the red as an image of charity, two colours prominent in Grünewald's bow.

65

66

The natural phenomenon

68

The mysterious beauty of the rainbow has often been observed and painted, but it was chiefly the Dutch and Flemish masters of the seventeenth century who introduced it into the repertory of landscape. Ruisdael (**68**) still had symbolic concerns, using the bow together with ruins, flowing water and tombstones as an image of transience and mortality, but Rubens (**67**) seems to have been interested largely in its brilliant effect. His treatment of the bow, predominantly in pink, blue and yellow, is often barely credible from the point of view of lighting, but his rainbows look more like delicate atmospheric phenomena than any before the nineteenth century.

67 PETER PAUL RUBENS, *Rainbow Landscape*, 1636/8
68 JACOB VAN RUISDAEL, *The Jewish Cemetery*, 1670s (detail)

67

69

The uses of the rainbow

Since it included all the colours of light in a fixed order, the rainbow offered painters a 'natural' key to the harmony of colours. Both Angelika Kauffmann (**69**) and her friend Goethe (**70**) were interested in the idea – although the anti-Newtonian Goethe has arranged his colours in an 'Aristotelian' sequence (engendered at the junction of light and dark seen through a prism), with blue at the top. In the Romantic period, rendering the fleeting appearance of the bow also became a sought-after test of the painter's sharpness of observation and dexterity of hand. According to his own inscription, Glover's watercolour recorded the bow 'while the effect lasted' (**71**), and Turner swiftly brushed the changing effects of light into a tiny sketchbook (**73–4**). Constable's growing interest in unusual phenomena in the 1830s led him to document this extraordinary double bow near his home in Hampstead (**72**).

70

69 ANGELIKA KAUFFMANN, *Self-portrait as 'Painting'*, *c.* 1779
70 After JOHANN WOLFGANG VON GOETHE, *Mountain Landscape with Rainbow*, 1826
71 JOHN GLOVER (1767–1849), *A Rainbow*
72 JOHN CONSTABLE, *London from Hampstead, with a double rainbow*, inscribed 'between 6 & 7 o'clock Evening June 1831'
73–4 J.M.W. TURNER, *Durham Cathedral with a Rainbow*, 1801

71

72

73

74

The purest form of rainbow art – a series of *Rainbow Splashes* made and photographed in remote English beauty-spots by the artist Andy Goldsworthy in 1980. They are in direct succession to the bows admired by tourists such as Scheuchzer's (pl. 63), visiting the waterfalls of Italy and Switzerland since Classical times.

75 ANDY GOLDSWORTHY, *Rainbow Splash, River Wharf, Yorkshire, October 1980*

The Romantics

If Romantic artists interested in the problems of chromatics and weather looked back to the example of their sixteenth- and seventeenth-century predecessors, this was because the eighteenth-century tradition of landscape had comparatively little to offer. It followed, broadly speaking, the styles of Claude, Salvator Rosa and Nicholas or Gaspard Poussin, who had hardly used the more extravagant effects of light; where in Watteau or Gainsborough the Rubensian landscape provided a model, it was shorn of Rubens's less conventional observations. Nor was the most important and most international of the eighteenth-century approaches to landscape, the Picturesque movement, favourable to chromatics, for it too proposed a set of norms which were themselves based on the experience of Salvator, the Poussins and Claude. Characteristically enough, Salvator himself, who seems to have been the first painter to use the word 'pittoresco' of landscape, in a letter to G. B. Ricciardi of May 1662 in which he enthused over the mountain scenery between Loreto and Rome, went on to describe the falls of Terni on Lake Velino – those falls which in the Romantic period were to be a constant source of rainbow studies – only in terms of the 'orrida Bellezza' of their half-mile of crashing water and flying spray.[57] Salvator of course may simply have run into dull weather and not seen a bow. His eighteenth-century English follower William Gilpin – who toured the British Isles for many years preparing a dozen guides to the Picturesque appreciation of scenery, which to judge from many translations and several satires were widely read throughout Europe – never reported having seen a rainbow on his travels. Gilpin's rather timid recommendations about colouring make it unlikely that he would have wanted it to be introduced into the painted landscape even if he had. Only after his death were some of his designs embellished with colours and rainbows in John Heaviside Clark's *Practical Illustrations of Gilpin's Day* (1811).[58] Not that Gilpin was uninterested in the weather: he had studied it for many years and had prepared a book on weather-forecasting.[59] It was perhaps this very searching for regularities, for the norm, which made him advise landscape artists 'to avoid every uncommon appearance in nature'.[60] But for the following generation it was the uncommon in every sphere which was so attractive and which, through the habit of observation, itself became normal.

The permanent rainbows over the waterfalls at Tivoli had become an important tourist-attraction early in the nineteenth century.[61] An English traveller wrote of them in 1830:

At the different points of view are little cabins (which would be very picturesque if they were less rudely constructed) for the accommodation of artists and other travellers ... The rainbows are very various, seen from different points: from the middle, where the river rushes from the vortex of the great fall to plunge into another, the stream appears to be painted with a broad layer of divers colours, never broken or mixed till they are tossed up in a cloud of spray, and mingled with it in a thousand variegated sparkles. Above, an iris bestrides the moist green hill which rises by the side of the fall; and, as the spray is whirled up in greater or lesser abundance, it perpetually and rapidly changes its colours, now

disappearing altogether and now beaming with the utmost vividness. The man told me that at night the moon forms a white rainbow on the hill ...[62]

By the classic falls of Terni Pope Pius VI had constructed a summer-house, and other shelters were put up for tourists at other vantage-points there to give a perfect view of the bows.[63] Even in Switzerland, where so many rival sublimities were apt to distract the traveller, the rainbows at the falls of Schaffhausen became a standard sight and Swiss view-painters such as Caspar Wolf began in the 1770s to introduce bows into their work.[64] In 1816 Byron was fascinated by a bow at the Jungfrau Falls, 'principally purple and gold; the bow moving as you move; I never saw anything like this ...'[65] But the excitement of discovery may best be illustrated by the accounts of three nineteenth-century painters.

In 1823 the landscape-painter Carl Rottman wrote to his fiancée from Murnau, a village in the mountains to the south of Munich (later to be made famous by Kandinsky and Münter):

I am thinking of an indescribable storm effect which I must show you some day, for I have partly sketched it and partly noted it down in words – since as usual the whole thing was over in a few minutes. The atmosphere was a fiery grey, like the dark waters of the Wallersee, and the mountains at the other side of the lake. On the right was a chapel of the monastery in the pine-woods lit up on a green hill; and a rainbow arched down into the water on the left, and in the middle of it a stream of red rain coming down through the lightning. I should have been pretty well carried away with astonishment and the thrill of it, if it had gone on any longer, but the impression that this sort of thing leaves with me is quite remarkable ... a strange mixed feeling ... of unknown life, of the world of spirits.[66]

A decade later the young French painter Paul Huet visited the Vallon d'Enfer in the Auvergne and recorded a comparable experience in a letter to his sister: 'I had never seen anything quite so extraordinary, twenty or thirty miles of horizon around me and at my feet the wildest of precipices; below me, in the direction we had come from, dense clouds with rainbows springing from them; above my head a clear sky ...'[67] In 1850 the American genre-painter and biographer of Constable, C. R. Leslie, noted in his diary his first sight of that rarest and most Romantic of natural phenomena, the lunar bow:

I remarked, as we often see it in the solar bow, that the mist on which it appeared was of a uniformly darker shade outside the arch. The prismatic colours were not perceptible to my eye, but it appeared of a soft pale light nearly white. It seemed the ghost of the magnificent double bow which I had seen in the morning not very far from the same place in the heavens.[68]

Constable himself in a remarkable watercolour recorded an unusual rainbow effect over Hampstead Heath and a sepia drawing by John Sell Cotman fixed the 'curious and beautiful' phenomenon of the parhelion, which he observed in 1815.[69] In his youthful sketchbook of 1824 Samuel Palmer projected a painting of 'A Twilight in Saturn with the ring diverse color'd and ... all manner of colours ... Or ... Like an immense rainbow'.[70] But these more abstruse phenomena rarely occur in

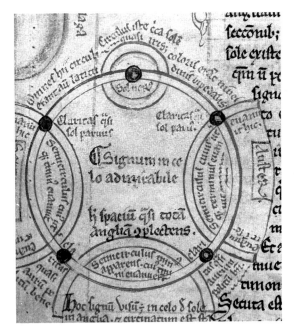

The rare and curious parhelion, a bow formed in ice crystals around the sun, as recorded by two distinguished painters. Matthew Paris represented the 'wonder in the sky' that he saw in 1233; John Sell Cotman fixed the 'curious and beautiful' phenomenon in a drawing of 1815. (76,77)

anything more ambitious than memoranda. Rottman introduced only a number of common bows into the Greek landscapes he prepared for King Ludwig I of Bavaria;[71] Constable's rainbows in his large landscapes are similarly rather standard; I have discovered only one large lunar bow, in a wonderful and eccentric painting by Caspar David Friedrich.[72] Although in England as early as 1808 an anonymous critic, after recording several appearances of the lunar halo, asked 'why should it not attract attention as well in Art as in Nature?',[73] the only example of such a rarely experienced phenomenon I know is the solar halo of Turner's *Staffa: Fingal's Cave* (1832).[74] That the experience lying behind this picture affected the artist deeply is suggested by the way it provoked one of the very rare letters relating directly to his art.[75]

The problems of the exceptional effects of weather were for landscape-painters not only problems of observation but also, as we have seen, problems of pictorial tradition. Sir Joshua Reynolds, in a rather confused passage in his fourth *Discourse* (1771), did not endorse the use of 'accidents of light' in landscape painting, and his successor as President of the Royal Academy, Benjamin West, noted on Bromley Hill, south of London in 1813 'the freshness of the fields and the general appearance of the landscape, but observed that however agreeable in nature, such scenes and colours wd not do in landscape painting'.[76] Nevertheless, towards the end of the eighteenth century, perhaps stimulated by some hints in Roger de Piles, the view that the landscape could be animated by changes in the sky and the weather was gaining ground; it was here that the northern countries had the advantage over the south. A precocious English essay on landscape of 1783 argued: 'We have . . . a great advantage over Italy itself, in the greater variety and beauty of our Northern skies, the forms of which are often so lovely and magnificent, where so much action is seen in the rolling of the clouds; all this is nearly unknown to the placid southern hemisphere [*sic*].'[77] In a letter of 1838 Paul Huet complained that it was his northern background which made the clear skies of the Midi so difficult to manage.[78] Even Blake, whose contempt for the 'vegetative eye' (that is, the observation of nature) is hardly in question, showed in his watercolour of Felpham and in a passage of his *Public Address* of 1809 that he was on the side of 'accidents of light'.[79] The tension between the rival schools of thought was perhaps acutest in the work of Pierre Henri de Valenciennes who as a pupil of Vernet inherited the Franco-Roman tradition of sketching from nature in oil and produced, perhaps as early as the 1780s, many free and subtle studies, including a number of rainbows.[80] But it is clear from his sketchbooks that Valenciennes saw landscape composition very much in terms of Gaspard Poussin; his larger paintings do little more than gather his observations of light and shadow into an essentially seventeenth-century format.

Not that a belief in that format was invariably hostile to the most refined atmospheric effects, for the rainbow was introduced into the mainstream of nineteenth-century German landscape by the Austrian Josef Anton Koch, whose compositions were usually well-swept versions of the Poussinesque type. Koch had been much affected by his experience of the rainbows spanning the Rhine falls at Schaffhausen in 1791[81] but in his first important oil, of 1805, the motif was introduced as an

Caspar David Friedrich, *Landscape with Lunar Rainbow*, 1808. Friedrich, like Turner (pl. 85), interested himself in the rainbow in many moods. His apparently moonlit mountainscape provides the weary traveller with a rare and oddly tapering moonbow. (78)

attribute of the Sacrifice of Noah.[82] Koch was also an admirer of Rubens and it was probably his example which led him to bring the bow into heroic landscapes where it had no obvious place, such as the large canvases in Munich and Karlsruhe and the *Rider Returning in a Thunderstorm* (c. 1830).[83] He became the acknowledged master of the southern school of German landscape. His most important followers – Rottman, the Scot G. A. Wallis and the Nazarene landscape-painter Ferdinand Olivier – all showed an interest from time to time in the rainbow as a motif, although it was usually in ways which must be read as symbolic.[84] This was a double concern: the marriage of sharpened and extended observations with a symbolic or even metaphysical purpose, which constituted the originality of Romantic landscape. In both these aspects the great barrier which separated the Romantics from their seventeenth-century forbears was not eighteenth-century landscape or even the cult of the Picturesque, but Sir Isaac Newton, for whom poetry had been 'a kind of ingenious nonsense'.[85]

Prismatics and harmony

Perhaps the most agreeable episode in Romantic anti-Newtonianism was the 'immortal dinner' with Wordsworth, Keats and Charles Lamb given by the heroic painter B. R. Haydon on the evening of 28 December 1817. He recalled:

> Lamb got exceedingly merry and exquisitely witty . . . he then in a strain of humour beyond description, abused me for putting Newton's head into my picture [*Christ's Entry into Jerusalem*] – 'a fellow' said he, 'who believed nothing unless it was as clear as three sides of a triangle'. And then he and Keats agreed that he had destroyed all the poetry of the rainbow, by reducing it to the prismatic colours. It was impossible to resist him, and we all drank 'Newton's health and confusion to mathematics'.[86]

Critics have enjoyed this passage, but their attention has usually focused on Keats, who crystallized his objection to Newton in *Lamia* a few years later, or on Wordsworth, who was far from being an anti-Newtonian but had a personal and poetical interest in the integrity of the rainbow and, after some hesitation, also joined in the toast.[87] Haydon himself, whose diaries demonstrate a profound interest in problems of colour and technique and who had a deeply religious apprehension of nature,[88] was among Newton's warm admirers. For the problems presented to the painter by Newtonian optics were very different from those Newton offered the poet. The poetic prejudice against unweaving the bow was certainly persistent: Ruskin – who at the age of seven had been a child of the Enlightenment and who had a written a didactic poem on the rainbow whose tone was still that of a Thomson or an Akenside[89] – by the time he came to write the third volume of *Modern Painters* in the late 1840s was pronouncing: 'I much question whether any one who knows optics, however religious he may be, can feel in equal degree the pleasure of reverence which an unlettered peasant may feel at the sight of the rainbow.'[90] Here Ruskin was wholly the poet; but if we look at the circles of painters, we are more likely to find anti-Newtonianism among those with an eighteenth-century background, such as Louis-Bertrand Castel or Goethe, James Barry or William Blake, than in the Romantic period itself, when Newton was admired by Haydon and Runge, Palmer and Olivier, the Nazarene Friedrich Overbeck and Turner.[91] Even Dante Gabriel Rossetti, who had a foot in both painterly and poetic camps and was an admirer of both Blake and Keats (whose response at the 'immortal dinner' he later thought 'splendid' and 'magnificent'[92]) found a place for Newton, together with Columbus, Cromwell, Haydon, Isaiah, Joan of Arc and many others among the lower ranks of the immortals.[93]

Poets like Keats and Thomas Campbell seem to have taken the early eighteenth-century interpretation of Newton's rainbow at face-value: science had indeed unwoven the bow and all the Romantics did was to reverse the moral. I shall keep for Chapter 9 a discussion of the nature of Newton's theory and of its following in the eighteenth and nineteenth centuries. Here I only note that the ancient debate about the number of colours in the rainbow was now transformed into a debate about the number of colours which could be called 'primary': how many strands of colour, in short, went into its weaving? Newton had seemed to propose three, although his rainbow spectrum was divided into seven hues;[94] other theorists proposed as few as one.[95] That this debate was a source of perplexity to painters was to be expected. The Irish historical painter James Barry was Newtonian enough to include him among 'those great and good men of all ages and nations, who were cultivators and benefactors of mankind' in his *Elysium* (1783–1801) decorating the Society of Arts in London,[96] but in his Royal Academy lecture on colour in the early 1790s he summarized the painter's difficulties in accepting Newtonian optics:

> For my own part, I feel but little conviction or satisfaction in the splendid theories deduced from prismatic experiment, which have been handed down for some time past with so much confidence; where it is pretended to be demonstrated by this three-sided wedge of glass, that the solar light is not homogeneal . . . but is combined of seven differently coloured pencils or rays of different refrangibility . . . such experiments appear to be, if not foreign to the real object of enquiry, yet at least very vague and inconclusive, and have been made by men little practised in the progressional affinities or differences of colour. To offer one instance of this, our philosophers have pretended to discover in the rainbow just seven primitive colours in that phenomenon. But if they mean by primitive colours, colours simple and uncompounded of any others, why seven, when there are but three? If they mean only to enumerate the differences, without regarding the actual fact of the procreation of the compounds from the primitives, why more than six?, or, why not double that number, or even more, if all the intermediaries are attended to? . . . we may quote the testimony of Aristotle, who has, with his usual accuracy, fallen upon the tripartite division.[97]

It was Barry's younger friend William Blake who developed the most bitter opposition to Newton in England. Yet, in contrast with the earlier poet Christopher Smart or with Blake's German contemporary Novalis who scathingly derived the term 'Enlightenment' from a toying with the more trivial aspects of light,[98] *Newton's* optics was barely mentioned in Blake's polemic; in the frequent rainbows and rainbow glories that appear throughout his work, the number and sequence of colours is always essentially Newtonian.[99]

Blake divided his light in a Newtonian way because he needed an image in colour of the divided state of the material world; to his admirers this colour was simply 'beautifully prismatic'.[100] To the more facetious critics of Turner or John Martin 'prismatic' meant diseased: they both seemed to have prisms for eyes.[101] In no aspect of Romantic painting more than colour was the feverish casting about for formulae and recipes the subject of speculation and attack. In the rainbow and the prism artists found, so they thought, a scheme of colour-harmony sanctioned by masters such as Leonardo, Raphael and Rubens and recommended by nature herself. 'If you wou'd have

the neighbourhood of one Colour, give a Grace to another' said an eighteenth-century English version of Leonardo's *Trattato*, 'imitate Nature, and do that with your Pencil, which the Rays of the Sun do upon a cloud, in forming a Rainbow, where the colours fall sweetly into one another, without any stiffness appearing in their extremes.'[102] Leonardo's recommendation embodied something of a paradox, for Aristotle and his followers had laid great emphasis on the impossibility of painting the rainbow, whose light-bearing colours could not be matched by anything available in the way of pigments.[103] Chapter 2 showed how Aristotle's commentator Alexander of Aphrodisias (who first recorded the dark band which bears his name) had looked in some detail at the reasons why the immaterial, unmixed colours of the bow could not be rendered by material mixtures. I shall show in Chapter 9 how this separation of immaterial from material colours was not resolved until the seventeenth century. This Peripatetic problem had not, of course, deterred even medieval artists from attempting to record these remarkable phenomena in colour. Matthew Paris, in some brilliantly observed studies, painted the parhelia which were seen near Worcester and Hereford in 1233. He wrote that some of more than a thousand spectators 'in commemoration of this extraordinary phenomenon, painted suns and rings of various colours on parchment, so that such an unusual pheno-menon might not escape the memory of man.'[104] Yet the notion that the rainbow was unpaintable persisted well into the nineteenth century, when a German commentator noted that even the most brilliant efforts of Rubens, Poussin and Koch had not disproved it.[105]

Leonardo's advice owed nothing to optics or even to the theory of painting, for it was a paraphrase of a passage in a late Antique treatise on music by Boethius who in his turn was elaborating on an earlier discussion of musical harmony by Ptolemy. In *On Music* (V, v) Boethius had written:

> Just as when a rainbow is observed, the colours are so close to one another than no definite line separates one colour from the other – rather it changes from red to yellow, for example, in such a way that continuous mutation into the following colour occurs with no clearly defined median falling between them – so also this may often occur in pitches.[106]

What was surely the most exciting possibility for Leonardo was that a link between the chromatic *sfumato* of the rainbow and musical pitch might also be a link with the principles of colour-harmony. Boethius was not forgotten in this context in the seventeenth century, when the Dutch scholar Franciscus Junius discussed the Greek concept of *harmogen* – harmony, reported by Pliny (XXXV, xi, 29) as a transition from one colour to another. It was, said Junius:

> an unperceivable way of art, by which an artificer stealingly passeth over from one colour into another, with an insensible distinction . . . when we behold how the sea and sky do meet in one thinne and misty Horizontal Stroke, both are most strangely soft and confounded in our eyes, neither are wee able to discerne where the one or other doth begin or end: water and aire, severall and sundry coloured elements, seeme to be all one at their meeting . . . Yet doth the Rain-bow minister to us a clearer proof of this same *Harmoge*,

76

The President of the Royal Academy, Benjamin West, lecturing on the prismatic principles of colour harmony in painting in 1817 (portrait by Thomas Lawrence). West's diagram of a sphere graded with a sequence of prismatic colours is displayed on the wall behind the easel. (79)

when she beguileth our sight into the scarce distinguished shadowes of melting, languishing & leisurely vanishing colours. *For although there doe shine a thousand severall colours in the Rain-bow, sayth Ovid . . . their transition for all that deceiveth the eyes of the spectators; seeing her colors are all one where they touch, though farther off they are much different.*[107]

The example of the bow thus suggested to painters how they might manage subtle transitions from one colour to the next, a skill very much deployed in the shot draperies of Mannerism and recommended, perhaps independently of Leonardo, by Veronese's patron Daniele Barbaro.[108] It was not the only way, though, in which the bow might be seen as a model for chromatic harmony. Another seventeenth-century Dutch theorist, Karel van Mander, who gave rather detailed instructions about how the six rainbow colours might be matched by pigments, also argued that the bow demonstrated an intrinsically harmonious juxtaposition of these colours: blue looked especially well next to purple, purple to red, red with orange-yellow and so on.[109] In Romantic England such notions received the stamp of Academic authority: when in 1804 the Royal Academy Council was debating the removal of Sir James Thornhill's copies of the Raphael Cartoons, the President, West, stressed the advantages of studying these copies, rather than

prints, 'as *the arrangement of the colours* could be known by them . . . and that arrangement was as masterly as the Composition was superior.'[110] Again, in 1817, West

spoke nearly half an hour and *Extempore*, and with great self-possession, also with a readiness of delivery beyond what had been before heard from him . . . to prove that the *order of Colours in a Rainbow* is the true arrangement of colours in an Historical picture – viz: exhibiting the warm and brilliant colours in a picture where the principal light falls & the *cool colours* in the shade; also that as an accompanying reflection, a weaker rainbow often accompanies the more powerful rainbow, so it may be advisable to repeat the same colours in another part of the picture . . . He remarked that in the picture in the *Vatican* at *Rome* [i.e. the *Stanza of Heliodorus*] *Raphael* had not attended to this principle, but that He felt and arranged his colours agreeably to it in the *Cartoons* . . . was manifest.[111]

It was at this impromptu lecture that West showed a painting of two spheres or globes, one colourless and the other tinted with prismatic colours, the latter of which was to 'show how the colours of the rainbow expressed the different degrees of light, half-light and reflection, and shewed how perfectly well the arrangement of these colours was adapted to the purposes of painting'.[112] This was the apparatus shown next to a small copy of the Raphael cartoon *The Death of Ananias* in the formal portrait of West painted by Lawrence in 1818.[113] The pictures of globes were described in great detail by a member of West's audience on that occasion, the landscape-painter A. W. Callcott, who said that the first, more purely tonal one on the left at the lecture was larger than the second, prismatic one on the right. The first was a dark brown with a slight variation on the light side, beginning with a reddish tone, then a yellowish, then blue and 'wholly neutral'. The second was composed

of the most positive colors commencing with red this changing into orange from this to yellow, from yellow to green, from green to blue & from this to darkness. Then on the reflected side the same order of colors was repeated . . . The arrangement on this ball was the only unerring principle on which colors of light and dark could be arranged in a picture.[114]

Callcott noted that West applied his theory to several of Raphael's Cartoons, including the *Ananias*,[115] but that he did not mention the *Gate of the Temple* (*The Healing of the Lame Man*) whose colour-organization was in direct contradiction to it. Only in the course of the lecture did Callcott remember that the order of colours in the secondary rainbow was reversed, although West had not allowed for it.

This exposition of West's rainbow theory was by no means the first, for he had been toying with it long before he attained high academic office. In a memorandum compiled for a German pupil in the late 1780s, West had used Rubens as an exemplar of the arrangement which he later saw supremely in Raphael; but at this stage he was thinking more in terms of the balance of warm and cool colours according to the rainbow order, any infringement of which would 'bring on such distraction and discord to the Eye that it turns away disgusted as the Ear [to] a discordant sound'.[116] In an Academy lecture of 1797 he had argued that blue, grey or purple were the best grounds for showing up the prismatic colours, 'for those colours partake of the complexion of the watery sky in which the rainbow appears'.[117] The practical conclusions he drew from this do not seem to be either very original or very consistent. What was new was the projection of these precepts derived from a study of nature on to the interpretation of the Old Masters. Here, as he later confessed, 'he could only trace the observance of this rule, as a principle, in the later works of Raffaelle ... He admitted that in Titian's "Peter Martyr" the arrangement of colour is on a plan exactly contrary.'[118] And yet, however improbably in practice, the assumptions that lie behind this theory – that nature has revealed the secret of colour harmony in the structure of the prismatic spectrum – were far from peculiar to West and continued to occupy the attention of painters from the Romantics to Cézanne.[119]

We saw how West had first articulated his notions of the rainbow as a guide to colouring in the context of Rubens, and it was Rubens, whose idiosyncratic analysis of the colours of flesh had long been recognized as 'prismatic' or 'primary',[120] who first suggested a version of the rainbow theory among the French Romantics. Delacroix's pupil Andrieu recalled how as a young man his master had found new principles of colouring in the rainbow, condensed as it were into a drop of water, and introduced the idea into his first major painting, the *Barque of Dante* (1822).[121] Andrieu may have had the story from Delacroix himself, although the water-drops on the torso of a tormented soul are now far brighter than any of the other colours in the painting and could well belong to a re-working of the picture in the late 1840s. But they are a thoroughly Rubensian motif and may have been adapted from some drops in the Medici Cycle, then in the Luxembourg Palace, from which Delacroix made a number of painted studies in the early 1820s. In a later conversation with George Sand, Delacroix, like some of his English contemporaries, spoke of a Rubens nude child in terms of 'the rainbow melted into the flesh'.[122] Unlike West or Turner, however, Delacroix was little inclined to pursue colour-theory very far or for very long – although he turned to it again towards the end of his life (*see* Chapter 9). Painters, he suggested in a draft entry for his uncompleted *Dictionary of Fine Arts*, should avoid illusions of universality and stick to their lasts.[123]

Far more theoretically engaged was the German Romantic painter Philipp Otto Runge, who was convinced that the developments of chromatics since Newton must form the basis of the new landscape painting, which would eventually absorb all the other genres.[124] Unlike West, he felt that the rainbow-spectrum presented too monotonous a series to form the basis of colour-composition and to represent the infinite variety and texture of natural things.[125] *The Times of Day*, of which only *Morning* came to be painted, were to be, as Runge stated clearly in a letter, a practical manifestation of 'the astounding difference between invisible and visible, transparent and opaque colours'.[126] He drew a Newtonian rainbow in the decorative and symbolic border of *Day*, to represent the visible colours of nature which 'fade into white [*geht in Ermattung des Weissen über*]', instead of rising to the perfection of [transparent] light, as they did in *Morning*.[127] Clearly, like Blake, he thought the formation of material colours was a tragic degradation of light; commentators who have interpreted the rainbow here as a

symbol of the heavenly pact are surely wide of the mark.[128] It has been suggested that Runge introduced the Mosaic snake among the passion flowers of the border in reference to St John's Gospel (3:14), where it symbolized the striving of the earthly man for God; the idea is even clearer in an earlier version of the design, where the Mosaic Tables of the Law were introduced in place of the flowers.[129] But just as Turner's *Light and Colour (Goethe's Theory)*, which also introduced the snake for a similar purpose, cancelled the optimism of its imagery in the bitter pessimism of its caption,[130] so Runge in *Day* presented the rainbow as a materialization of light, final reconciliation with God coming only at the end of the series, which he designed but did not live to paint.

Runge's interest in the rainbow-spectrum was, his many experiments show, as much technical as philosophical: he willingly divided light into the Newtonian seven parts or into the three primary colours; to do so was essential to his symbolic system. Like many other painters of his day, he was being less than Romantic. But the scientific analysis of the rainbow did not stop with Newton, whose scheme begged many questions which were to tease artists and scientists alike. Henry Howard told his Royal Academy students in the 1840s:

> The simplest mode of harmony is where one of the primary colours is pure, and the other two are combined ... The fullest and richest harmony is where the seven prismatic hues are all displayed together. In either of these cases there is a just proportion of cold colour necessary to counter balance the warm. It would seem to follow, that, to produce an agreeable effect of light in painting, the same proportion of warm and cold colour should be adopted as we perceive in a dissected solar ray; but ... these proportions do not appear to have been accurately ascertained.[131]

Despite the attempts of Samuel Galton and Matthew Young to establish the proportions of the prismatic colours in white light at the beginning of the century,[132] Howard was right; the question was hardly illuminated by the observation of the rainbow in natural conditions.

Joseph Priestley's history of optics devoted a chapter to eighteenth-century observations of the rainbow and related phenomena, which showed many deviations in colour, width and number of arcs from the Newtonian norm.[133] As early as 1722 the Rector of Petworth in Sussex had observed and recorded four completely distinct bows, from which he concluded 'that the rainbow seldom appears very lively without something of this Nature; and that the supposed exact Agreement between the Colours of the Rainbow and those of the Prism, is the reason that it has been so little observed'.[134] He also noted the difficulty of recording the fleeting appearance of the bow, precisely what was to fascinate many observers in the Romantic period. As Wordsworth wrote in his *Ode on Intimations of Immortality* (II), 'The Rainbow comes and goes

---

Philipp Otto Runge, *Day*, 1803. At the top of his allegorical drawing Runge introduces a seven-banded rainbow, over-arching the triangular symbol of the Holy Trinity, which he interpreted in terms of the three primary colours: blue (the Father), red (the Son) and yellow (the Holy Ghost). (80)

…'. In Act I of the Second Part of *Faust*, Goethe drew the moral:

> Der Wassersturz, das Felsenriff durchbrausend,
> Ihn schau ich an mit wachsendem Entzücken.
> Von Sturz zu Stürzen wälzt er jetzt in tausend,
> Dann abertausend Strömen sich ergiessend,
> Hoch in die Lüfte Schaum an Schäume sausend.
> Allein wie herrlich, diesem Sturm erspriessend,
> Wölbt sich des bunten Bogens wechseldauer,
> Bald rein gezeichnet, bald in Luft zerfliessend,
> Umher verbreitend duftig-kühle Schauer!
> Der spiegelt ab das menschliche Bestreben.
> Ihm sinne nach, und du begreifst genauer:
> Am farbigen Abglanz haben wir das Leben.

'I watch the water-fall, with heart elate,/The cataract pouring, crashing from the boulders,/Split and rejoined a thousand times in spate;/The thundrous water seethes in fleecy spume,/Lifted on high in many a flying plume,/Above the spray-drenched air. And then how splendid/To see the rainbow rising from this rage,/Now clear, now dimmed, in cool sweet vapour blended./So strive the figures on our mortal stage./This ponder well, the mystery closer seeing;/In mirrored hues we have our life and being.'[135] Despite his passionate plea for the study of colour in nature, the basis of Goethe's exposition of a theory of colour depended on experiments with the prism, for he was anxious to refute Newton on his own ground. Only one, unimpressive, rainbow drawing has been associated with his illustrations to the *Theory of Colours*[136] and the promised supplementary section on the phenomenon never appeared during the poet's lifetime.[137] In an undated fragment he did, however, treat the bow, which he claimed had led students of chromatics into an

David Lucas, mezzotint after John Constable, *Salisbury Cathedral from the Meadows: The Rainbow*, c. 1835. Constable was probably prompted to study the rainbow as a geometrical problem by Lucas's large print after his landscape of 1831 (National Gallery, London). In the print the atmospheric conditions necessary for the appearance of the bow are more correctly observed than in Constable's original painting, where it functioned largely as a symbol of hope. Constable's diagrams of c. 1833 record the formation of colours in drops of water. (82,83)

obsession with refraction. Although he observed Alexander's dark band between the arcs of the double bow, he does not seem to have realized that the differences of luminosity outside and inside the arc would support his own theory of the generation of colours through the interaction of light and dark.[138]

The evanescent phenomenon had fascinated Goethe all his life. About 1770 his urge to write poetry had been renewed by the sight of a double bow in Alsace, 'more marvellous, more colourful, more pronounced, but also more fleeting than I had ever seen';[139] in the late 1820s, when the passage quoted from *Faust* was written, he was still planning his supplement to the *Theory* on that difficult topic.[140] Only a month before his death in 1832 he was still returning to the subject in correspondence with the antiquarian and collector Sulpice Boisserée, whom he warned never to feel that he had reduced it to manageable terms.[141] It was surely to this life-long preoccupation that the scientist and painter Carl Gustav Carus referred in his *Allegory on the Death of Goethe* where a rainbow arches behind the poet's lyre. Carus had been a friend and correspondent of Goethe for many years up to 1831 and in the early 1820s he had discussed several colour-problems with the poet.[142]

In landscape-painting perhaps the most subtle expressions of the physiognomy of this fleeting phenomenon were in the work of two English artists, Constable and Turner. One of Constable's biographers has used the rainbow to characterize his subject[143] and it did indeed become one of his preferred motifs. When, in his lectures on landscape in the 1830s, Constable came

70

81

Carl Gustav Carus, *Allegory of the Death of Goethe*, 1832. Carus includes a rainbow in his memorial, as the phenomenon which had engaged Goethe's curiosity for most of his life. (81)

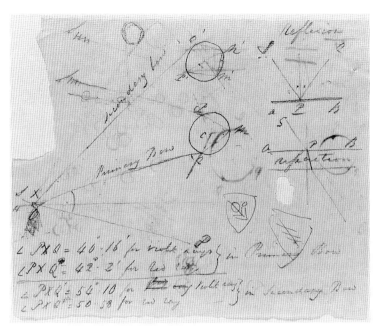

between *Salisbury Cathedral from the Meadows* with the superficially similar *Medieval Town by a River* by the German architect and painter Karl Friedrich Schinkel. Both were to a degree symbolic pictures: Constable described the sentiment of his as 'solemnity, not gaiety';[147] his wife had died while he was planning the design and he was also shaken by the Catholic Emancipation Act of 1829, which seemed to cut the Anglican Church at the root. It has been suggested that the bow offered Constable a symbol of reconciliation with life and that its ending on the house of his friend Archdeacon Fisher suggested too that there was hope for the Church.[148] The subject may stand on its own, too, as representing the weather effect of the title he gave it in 1836: *Summer Afternoon: a retiring Tempest.*

82

84

Schinkel, on the other hand, designed his picture as a pendant to his *Greek Landscape*,[149] to exemplify a contrast between the earth-bound Greek and the heavenward-striving Gothic architecture. The rainbow, which Schinkel had picked up from Koch in Rome,[150] was simply a symbolic attribute, reinforcing the notion that the Gothic 'expresses and manifests the Ideal, so that Idea and Reality are completely fused, so that in the outward appearance of the building we see what connects us directly with the supernatural, with God, whereas before only the earthly, with all its limitations, was the subject of works of art'.[151] He introduced none of the necessary weather-conditions and, like Koch, who made drawings for his rainbow compositions without including the bow,[152] he probably painted it directly on to the canvas. As it happens, this was probably Constable's procedure in the *Salisbury*, too: none of the surviving sketches, including the full-size one,[153] show the bow (there are a number of earlier, unrelated rainbow studies[154]). It reminds us that Constable's process of picture-making was essentially traditional, for no thoroughgoing outdoor painter would have imagined that such a complex atmospheric phenomenon could be understood outside the

to deal with the art of Paolo Uccello, it was the *Sacrifice of Noah*, for the Chiostro Verde in Sta Maria Novella in Florence, 'the whole arched by the rainbow', that he chose for illustration.[144] Constable's own rainbows have aroused the admiration of a meteorologist[145] but the idea that he was 'never guilty of giving the wrong sequence of colours in either primary or secondary bow' is surely exaggerated, for in the first recorded rainbow study, a small oil dated 1812, he failed to reverse the secondary colours.[146] At least before the 1830s Constable's interest in rainbows was no more purely scientific than his interest in clouds, and he did from time to time represent impossible situations of weather. But how unusually convincing his treatment of the rainbow is may be seen in a comparison

In the *Medieval Town on a River* (1815) Karl Friedrich Schinkel uses the rainbow much as it had been used in the Middle Ages, as a symbol – here, of the aspiration of the soul towards God. His bow is too implausibly narrow and the sky too uniformly dark to suggest the true atmospheric conditions in which a rainbow might be observed. (84)

J. M. W. Turner, *Buttermere Lake, with part of Cromackwater, Cumberland, a shower*, 1798. Thompsons' poem *The Seasons* spoke of 'every hue' in the 'grand ethereal bow', but Turner's painting is truer to the phenomenon he had observed. It shows the rare fog bow, in which the drops of water are very small, and the bow is almost white. (85)

context of a total landscape effect. Turner, for example, does not seem to have made rainbow studies as such but sometimes made written notes of its colours on a complete landscape sketch[155] and in two small early watercolours of Durham Cathedral he showed his recognition that it was the fleeting consequence of a changing effect of weather and lighting.

73–4

The study involved in introducing the bow into the *Salisbury*, his most important late picture, had a notable effect on Constable's conception of landscape in the 1830s. The composition was reproduced in mezzotint by David Lucas and Constable took endless pains to ensure the accuracy of the print which is, as has been pointed out, truer to the necessary weather-conditions than the painting.[156] Constable changed the title to *The Rainbow*, which, he later said, 'forms the subject of the picture'.[157] 'If it is not exquisitely done,' he wrote to Lucas in 1835, 'if it is not tender – and elegant – evernescent [*sic*] and lovely – in the highest degree – we are both ruined. I am led to this having been very busy with rainbows – and very happy in doing them – by the above rules.'[158] What these 'rules' were is not clear but it is possible that the painter consulted his friend the colour-theorist and technologist George Field, who had been adapting his ingenious circular prism, the Chromascope, for the projection of a semi-circular spectrum. This, he claimed, 'affords a method by which a rainbow, of any arc or diameter, may be superinduced upon a picture, into which the artist may design to introduce the phenomenon, so as to try its effect, and the best way of producing it'.[159] During the production of Lucas's plate the width of the bow decreased from $1\frac{1}{2}$ inches to $\frac{7}{8}$

82

173

inch (3.8 to 2.2 centimetres), which may reflect the use of some proportioning device such as Field's.[160]

Rainbows became more numerous in Constable's work of the last years and he began to produce coloured preparatory sketches, such as the two for the large watercolour of *Stonehenge*, one of which is perfectly plausible in the disposition of the sky.[161] This is the period when we find Constable interesting himself in scientific meteorology and copying diagrams to illustrate the formation of colours by refraction through a drop of water.[162] A measure of his achievement as a painter of the rainbow may be had by comparing the sensitivity of his late double bows with those of Koch, who seems never to have noticed the inversion of the colours, or with the work of English landscapists like John Glover, who missed the effect even in front of the motif, or, even more astonishingly, a Pre-Raphaelite such as Millais, whose second bow in the *Blind Girl* was only corrected (for a supplementary fee) when this inversion was pointed out to him.[163]

83

71

When Constable's *Salisbury* was exhibited in 1831, the critic of *The Morning Chronicle* called it 'Mr Constable's coarse, vulgar imitation of Mr Turner's freaks and follies',[164] and if any painter has the right to the title of 'Rainbow-master' in the Romantic period, it is surely Turner. His first exhibited rainbow, in *Buttermere Lake*, already announces an unusual sensibility, for in tune with the sombre landscape it is almost white; the painter had to edit severely a passage on the rainbow from Thomson's *Seasons* in order to provide a suitable caption for his own representation.[165] Thomson had written:

85

Meantime, refracted from yon eastern cloud,
Bestriding earth, the grand ethereal bow
Shoots up immense; and every hue unfolds,
In fair proportion running from the red
To where the violet fades into the sky.
Here, awful Newton, the dissolving clouds
Form, fronting on the sun, thy showery prism;
And to the sage-instructed eye unfold
The various twine of light, by thee disclosed
From the white mingling blaze. (*Spring* 11.203–12)

Turner's version of 1798 ran:

Till in the western sky the downward sun
Looks out effulgent – the rapid radiance instantaneous strikes
Th'illumin'd mountains – in a yellow mist
Bestriding earth – the grand ethereal bow
Shoot up immense, and every hue unfolds.

A watercolour sketch of 1797 with a number of revisions in the bow suggests that Turner was not quite sure how to handle this evanescent effect; yet the painting has all the elements of Turner's later interest in landscape colour: the diaphanous bow atmospherically extended into a reflection in the water. It was the starting-point of a long series of rainbow studies and pictures in sketches and watercolours, oils and engravings throughout a long career. The delicacy of observation in these works is unprecedented: in a written note of 1818 Turner recorded the variations in the width of the bow, according to the conditions of the background, sky.[166] He was also very conscious of the limitations of medium: I know of no rainbow oil after *Buttermere* until the early 1830s, by which time Turner had brought the technique of oil painting to a pitch of refinement comparable to his watercolours. The 1840s were Turner's greatest rainbow period, for it was then that he used the image as a vehicle of expression, of the gathering pessimism of his last years. In 1847, when his failing health allowed him to offer only a rather clumsily reworked canvas for hanging at the Royal Academy Exhibition, he made a last, faint gesture of Varnishing-Day magic by painting the rainbow into Daniel Maclise's *Sacrifice of Noah*.[167] Two years later, when he next exhibited, only one of his paintings was new, an early marine which he had taken six days to transform, again with a rainbow, into the fragile brilliance of *The Wreck Buoy*.[168] Turner's captions of this time make it perfectly clear that the rainbow was no symbol of hope or reconciliation. In 1837 he prepared a vignette of a rainbow-landscape to illustrate Thomas Campbell's poem *The Pleasures of Hope*, whose well-known opening scene invoked the enchantments of aerial perspective which might stand as a commentary on Turner's own work. But Campbell, whose poem included a eulogy of Newton, based his optimism on domestic happiness and the salvation of the soul, both ideas being closed to Turner as an unbelieving and unmarried father who lived in squalor. Apart from the rainbow, the artist chose to illustrate only those episodes in Campbell's *Poems* which could be interpreted as disasters: the foundering ship, the fall of Warsaw to Napoleon, the awful origin of the Mosaic Law. In a later poem devoted to the rainbow in Campbell's collection, which Turner must have read although he did not illustrate it, the poet doubted the adequacy of science to interpret the meaning of the bow:

When Science from Creation's face
Enchantment's veil withdraws,
What lovely visions yield their place
To cold material laws![169]

When Turner's own portmanteau-poem, *The Fallacies of Hope*, re-appeared after a long absence in the Royal Academy Exhibition catalogue of 1839, it was to amplify an allegory of great abstruseness called *The Fountain of Fallacy*, the dispenser of 'rainbow-dew'.[170] The prismatic bubbles in *Light and Colour (Goethe's Theory)* were, according to this poem, 'Hope's harbinger', but they were also 'ephemeral as the summer fly, which rises, flits, expands and dies'.[171] In the last group of paintings Turner exhibited, the year before his death, it was *Aeneas relating his Story to Dido* which included the last rainbow – in this case a moonbow – a picture whose caption might well have given the title to that same lugubrious poem:

Fallacious Hope beneath the moon's pale crescent shone
Dido listened to Troy being lost and won.[172]

Twentieth-century epilogue

Fascination with the rainbow as a pictorial motif has continued into our own century, particularly with the Neo-Romantics of South Germany before the First World War. Wassily Kandinsky had already introduced a quite orthodox, seven-coloured bow into his gouache *Tunisian Sheep Festival* in 1905 and, like his friend Franz Marc, was also interested in the phenomenon about the time of the formation of the Blaue Reiter (Blue Rider) group a few years later.[173] Much later, it has re-appeared in the purest form of all in the ecological performance art of Richard Long and Andy Goldsworthy. But we may agree with Paul Klee, who told his students at the Bauhaus as early as the 1920s that it had ceased to have any compelling symbolic or theoretical power.[174]

Franz Marc, *Blue Horses with Rainbow*, 1913. (86)

7 · *Disegno* versus *Colore*

Alberti and Grey · Ghiberti and perception · Colour-symbolism in the Quattrocento
The importance of materials · Leonardo da Vinci
Venetian colour in the sixteenth century

THE ANCIENT NOTION that an adequate representation might be made with line alone, colouring being an inessential adjunct to form, received a new impetus in the developing art practice and criticism of the Italian Renaissance. A key text, Philostratus's *Life of Apollonius of Tyana* (*see* Chapter 1), was translated into Latin by the Florentine Alemanno Rinuccini by the end of the Quattrocento and into Italian by the Venetian journalist Dolce in 1549. The ancient model of the historical progress of art in Pliny (XXXV, v, 15–16), in the first-century AD rhetorician Dionysius of Halicarnassus (*Isaeus* 4) and in Isidore of Seville (*Etymologies* XX, 19.16) presented a development from line in the earliest period to chiaroscuro and finally to colours. That this process could be seen as the making of a single work, even by late medieval lay people, is suggested by an ingenious spiritual exercise proposed in the early fourteenth century by the Franciscan mystic Ugo Panziera. According to Panziera the first act in making Christ vividly present to the mind is to imagine his name; the second to imagine him drawn (*disegnato*), the third with his outline shaded (*ombrato*), the fourth embodied (*incarnato*), which includes a notion of colouring, and finally turned from a flat image into three dimensions (*rilevato*).[1] But neither here nor in the ancient histories was there any sense that the earlier stages were more important than the last. It was not until the Romans attacked bright pigments – because of their association with luxury – that colour was seen to be inferior to design. These were attitudes which re-emerged among the Italian humanists of the fourteenth century. Giovanni Conversino of Ravenna, for example, wrote that a painting was admired not so much for 'the purity and exquisite quality of the colours (*colorum puritatem ac eleganciam*), as for 'the arrangement and proportion of its parts': only the ignorant were attracted simply by the colour. None the less, the beauty of the pigments (*pigmentorum pulchritudo*) could add to the beauty of proportion.[2] Certainly in the iconoclastic movements of the Middle Ages and in Lenten observance towards their close there was occasionally an appeal for monochromatic images. In the late fourteenth-century grisaille painting on silk, the *Parament of Narbonne*, and in related liturgical vestments made for Lenten use, we have perhaps the first great post-antique works of specifically monochrome drawing.[3]

A belief in the sufficiency of drawing has much to be said for it on psycho-physiological grounds. Infants tend to focus on contour in their process of discovering their environment; colour-blindness often goes undetected for many years because hue-perception is functionally less important than the perception of light and dark values. Late twentieth-century work on the mechanisms of colour-vision suggest that the eye has two independent systems of polychromatic and monochromatic receptors. It has also been well known since the early nineteenth century that sensations of colour – yellow, green and light blue – may be stimulated by the rapid alternation of light and dark, an effect not uncommon when watching black-and-white television.[4] We are all used to experiencing the world as black and white images in photography and film: these images are the successors of the monochrome engravings first produced in the fifteenth century that until the nineteenth were usually regarded as adequate even for the reproduction of paintings – and by painters themselves. In sixteenth-century Venice, where the polemic of the colourists against the 'designers' developed for the first time, it was still not unusual for painters to present their ideas to patrons in the form of a grisaille.[5] Here I want to look especially at the development of monochromatic art and trace the polemic of *disegno* (drawing, design) against *colore*.

Alberti and Grey

There can be little doubt that in Italy by the end of the fourteenth century there was widely developed sense of the distinction between design and colour as aesthetic values. In a letter of 1395 two Tuscan patrons spoke of a Crucifixion which was 'drawn [*disegnato*] so well that it could not be improved, even if Giotto had drawn it'.[6] Then, as now, Giotto was seen to be supreme as a designer and draughtsman.[7] About the same time the earliest theorist of Italian art, Cennino Cennini, who having been taught by Agnolo Gaddi, the son of Giotto's pupil Taddeo Gaddi, was proud to be seen as Giotto's great-grandson, yet recognized that Agnolo's colour was more 'beautiful and fresh' (*vago e fresco*) than that of his more Giottesque father.[8] True to his Tuscan tradition, Cennini also gave a good deal of attention to several techniques of drawing, including the elaborate preparation of softly modelled brush drawings on tinted paper, of which one example by Taddeo Gaddi has survived.[9] Nevertheless there is in Cennini no sense of any antithesis between drawing and colour: both were seen as fundamental to painting (iv) and chiaroscuro drawing on tinted paper was seen to be a stage on the way to colouring (xxxii).

Cennini compiled his book of recipes in the 1390s, addressing himself essentially to professional artists. When forty years later two other Tuscans, the architect and humanist Leon Battista Alberti and the sculptor Lorenzo Ghiberti, turned to the theory

Fra Bartolomeo, *Pala della Signoria*, *c.* 1512. Though little more than a vast monochrome drawing in oils, this fine example of Florentine *disegno* was thought worthy to serve as an altarpiece in the church of S. Lorenzo from the sixteenth to the eighteenth century. (87)

96

of art, they had very different audiences in mind: it mattered to them very much to distinguish between the various facets of the visual process.

Alberti was an amateur painter and claimed in his treatise *On Painting* to be writing as a painter; yet his shorter Italian version, probably of 1435, was dedicated to the architect Brunelleschi and the fuller Latin version (*De Pictura*) to the Prince of Mantua: it was far from being a practical text-book.[10] But particularly in its Latin version the treatise includes a discussion of colour which throws important light on the understanding of chiaroscuro in the early Quattrocento. Alberti divided painting into three parts: circumscription, or drawing the outline, composition and 'reception of lights' (*receptio luminum*), which included colour (II, 30). That colour was thus for Alberti a function of light was important for his lengthy and repetitive treatment of black and white (II, 46–7):

> while the kinds [*genera*] of colours remain the same, they become lighter or darker according to the incidence of lights and shades ... white and black are the colours with which we express lights and shades in painting; and ... all the other colours are, as it were, matter to which variations of light and shade can be applied. Therefore, leaving other considerations aside, we must explain how the painter should use white and black ... all his skill and care should be used in correctly placing these two ... You can very well learn from Nature and from objects themselves. When you have thoroughly understood them, you may change the colour with a little white applied as sparingly as possible in the appropriate place within the outlines of the surface, and likewise add some black in the place opposite to it. With such balancing, as one might say, of black and white a surface rising in relief becomes still more evident. Go on making similar sparing additions until you feel you have arrived at what is required ... if ... the painter has drawn the outlines of the surfaces correctly, and clearly sketched the border-line between lighter and darker, the method of colouring [*ratio colorandi*] will be easy. He will first begin to modify the colour of the surface with white or black, as necessary, applying it like a gentle dew up to the borderline. Then he will go on adding another sprinkling, as it were, on this side of the line, and after that another on that side of it, and then another on this side of this one, so that not only is the part receiving more light tinged with a clearer [*apertior*] colour, but the colour also dissolves progressively like smoke into the areas next to each other. But you have to remember that no surface should be made so white that you cannot make it a great deal whiter still. Even in representing snow-white clothing you should stop well on this side of the brightest white. For the painter has no other means than white to express the brightest gleams of the most polished surfaces, and only black to represent the deepest shadows of the night. And so in painting white clothes we must take one of the four kinds of colours [*quattuor generibus colorum*] which is clear and bright [*apertum et clarum*]; and likewise, in painting, for instance, a black cloak, we must take the other extreme which is not far from the deepest shadow, such as the colour of the deep and darkening sea. This composition of white and black has such power that, when carried out skilfully, it can express in painting surfaces of gold and silver and glass. Consequently those painters who use white immoderately and black carelessly should be strongly condemned. I should like white

to be purchased more dearly among painters than precious stones. It would be a good thing if white and black were made from those pearls Cleopatra dissolved in vinegar, so that painters would become as mean as possible with them, for then their works would be more agreeable and nearer the truth. It is not easy to express how sparing and careful one should be in distributing white in a painting ... If some indulgence must be given to error, then those who use black extravagantly are less to be blamed than those who employ white somewhat intemperately; for by nature, with experience of painting, we learn as time goes by to hate work that is dark and horrid [*atrum et horrendum*], and the more we learn, the more we attune our hand to grace and beauty. We all by nature love things which are clear and bright [*aperta et clara*]. So we must the more firmly block the way in which it is the easier to go wrong.[11]

I have given this passage *in extenso* because it seems to me to be one of the most important statements in the history of colour and as fruitful for the development of Renaissance attitudes towards painting as Alberti's far better-known discussion of the single-point perspective system. The account of *sfumato* modelling is not of itself very original: Cennini had used the same term (*a modo d'un fummo bene sfumate*) in his chapter on chiaroscuro drawing (xxxi). Unlike Cennini, however, Alberti was concerned to provide a rationale for his modelling procedure; his use of the term *apertus* ('open') for light colours shows that he had in mind the Classical theory of the functioning of light and darkness in the eye (*see* p. 16). For all his disclaimer that he was not writing for philosophers (I, 9), his instructions were backed by what appears to be the first coherent account of the values (light/dark content) of hues, towards which medieval writers such as Avicenna at the end of the tenth century and Theodoric of Freiberg in the fourteenth had been groping in vain.[12]

In a more theoretical discussion of light and colour earlier in his book (I, 9–10), Alberti had argued, against the ancient and medieval tradition, that 'the admixture of white ... does not alter the basic kind [*genus*] of colours, but creates *species*. Black has a similar power, for many species of colours arise from the addition of black.' For the painter, he continued:

> white and black are not true colours, but, one might say, moderators of colours [*colorum alteratores*], for the painter will find nothing but white to represent the brightest glow of light, and only black for the darkest shadows. Furthermore, you will not find any white or black that does not belong to one or other of the kinds of colours.

This last, crucial, observation explains what Alberti meant in Book II when he said that white and black objects should be painted not with the extremes of white and black pigments, but with values of the four genera of hues, slightly darker than absolute white and lighter than absolute black. It also helps us to interpret what has seemed to be a puzzling feature in Alberti's account of the four colours. He associated the four *vera genera* of colours with the four elements (*see* Chapter 2), identifying red with fire, blue (*celestis seu caesius* in Latin, *celestrino* alone in Italian) with air, green with water and ash-colour (*cinereum* in Latin, *bigia e cenericcia* in Italian) with earth. Starting from modern preconceptions about the 'primary' colours, some recent commentators have sought to introduce yellow into this set, by arguing that *bigia* and *cenericcia* could have been understood as 'dark yellow'.¹³ Quite apart from the extreme fluidity of the colour-terms used in the supporting texts (only one of which, Cennini, pre-dates Alberti), the *De Pictura* states quite clearly (I, 9) that the colour of the earth is a mixture of black and white (*Terrae quoque color pro albi et nigri admixtione suas species habet*). Two of the sixteenth-century manuscripts of the Italian version are helpful here because they gloss the identification of the earth with *bigia* and *cenericcia* with the note: 'and because the earth is the detritus [*feccia*] of all the elements, perhaps we are not wrong to say that *all* the colours are called grey [*bixi*] like the detritus of the earth'.¹⁴ All colours were thus seen to partake of grey: grey was the key to the tonal coherence of the pictorial composition, as Alberti's perspectival system was the key to the coherence of its linear space.

We saw that since Antiquity yellow had been repeatedly interpreted not as an independent hue but as a light species of green, and this continued to be so in Alberti's Italy.¹⁵ What he needed was not a fourth 'primary' but a colour which would express the mean between black and white seen as absolutes, just as saturated red and green were both means between the extremes of their genera, and his sky-blue (emphasized in Latin by the use of two terms, since blue was usually considered to be a dark colour) the mean in the scale of blue. It was essential to his understanding of the art of the colourist that Alberti should give equal status to grey and the other three 'true' colours, from which many mixtures (*species*) could be produced.¹⁶

In his account of the management of 'black' and 'white' Alberti stated that they could represent shining objects, even – and somewhat paradoxically until we remember that they are coloured – gold. His repeatedly expressed wish that gold and gems should be rendered in paint (e.g. II, 25) has often been seen as a new Renaissance attitude towards materials, in marked contrast to the medieval reverence for precious metals and colours, as represented by Cennini's Chapter xcvi. But when Alberti reviewed the question at some length in his second book (49), mentioning the gold ornaments on the costume of Queen Dido, he made it quite clear that from the single viewpoint required by his system of perspective (52), the use of real gold would make an ambiguous impression, since from some angles the gold would appear light and from others dark, which would destroy the carefully arranged tonal unity of his picture. Alberti had no objection to the use of precious materials as such, for he went on to say that the architectural elements in painting (perhaps he was referring to frames) might well be of such materials, since 'a perfect and finished painting is worthy to be ornamented even with precious stones.' Quite apart from the well-known taste among humanist collectors for International Gothic art which made much use of such materials, we shall see later in this chapter that all kinds of patron stipulated in contracts that precious metals and pigments were to be used in the execution of religious art. What is perhaps most striking about Alberti's book is that it made no reference to any but secular painting: although he was a notable designer of churches, he was here thinking exclusively of the decoration of palaces, where the light-levels were higher and more even than those creating the environment of religious painting and sculpture. In his rather later treatise on architecture Alberti emphasized light-reflecting surfaces in secular buildings, ad-

vocating the use of waxed and polished plaster on the ancient model, as well as what he called the 'newly discovered' technique of painting with linseed oil, both of which were very durable and gave the effect of jewels or 'flowing glass'.¹⁷ Both these techniques were primarily for decorative use but, more surprisingly, Alberti also recommended mosaic in imitation of painting, because of the sparkle of its highly reflective cubes (an argument which was appealed to a century later, in the context of the debate between drawing and colour, by a Florentine critic, Anton Francesco Doni, in his polemic against the perishable oil-painting of the new Venetian masters).¹⁸ So Alberti was thinking of the demands of painting as being quite different in different architectural contexts; the secular subjects he described in *De Pictura* were clearly to be executed on a portable scale.

For all the great and novel emphasis on black, white and grey in Alberti's book, it was in no sense an argument for *disegno* against *colore*. If a painting should be well drawn (*bene conscriptam*), it should also be excellently (*optime*) coloured (II, 46). In contrast to the ancient painters who were thought to have restricted their palettes, Alberti argued that 'all the kinds and species of colours' should appear in a painting, *cum gratia et amenitate* (II, 48). He proceeded to describe a file of nymphs in the train of Diana, one dressed in green, the next in white (*candidus*), the next red (*purpureus*), another yellow and so on, 'in such a way that light colours are always next to dark ones of a different genus'. This famous passage may be applied very effectively to the group of muses deployed across Mantegna's *Parnassus* painted much later for Isabella d'Este, where they appear in 'azure to royal blue [...] gold to orange, now green, now rose, now gleaming white'.¹⁹ Perhaps, too, Mantegna had felt the force of Alberti's remark that there is a kind of sympathy (*coniugatio* in Latin, *amicitia* in the Italian) between certain colours, for in individual figures he used the contrasts of red and green and red and blue which Alberti had specified: 'If red [*rubeus*] stands between blue [*coelestis*] and green [the Italian has the looser formulation 'near', *presso*] it somehow enhances their beauty as well as its own [here the Italian is far more specific, stating that they confer on each other honour and visible respect, *vista*]. White [*niveus* in Latin, *bianco* in Italian] lends gaiety [*hilaritas, letitia*], not only when placed between grey (*cinereus*) and yellow, but almost to any colour'. Here, although there are clearly medieval precedents for the notion of the harmony of, for example, red and green, and the whole conception of fulness and variety has a very medieval flavour,²⁰ Alberti was probably echoing contemporary workshop principles. His contrasting and complementary pairs of red and blue, particularly his view that a large proportion (one third) of white will always render the whole work 'joyful' and highly visible (*comparascente*), appears slightly earlier in a treatise on glass-painting by Antonio da Pisa, who was working in Florence about 1400.²¹ Alberti's love of light, gay colours also emerges from his treatment of clothes in another book, on the family, where one of the interlocutors recommended above all those which are 'joyful' (*lieti*) and clear (*aperti*), both terms encountered in the *De Pictura*.²² Thus Alberti brought an unusually wide range of experience to bear on what was effectively the first sustained theoretical discussion of visual art.

92

Ghiberti and perception

Alberti's understanding of the 'reception of light' on surfaces was, as he said, the result of 'experiment' (I, 8) and he was generally diffident about invoking the authority of the 'philosophers'. But his contemporary Lorenzo Ghiberti had no such qualms: in the longest section of a very substantial treatise on art, the *Commentaries* (late 1440s), the sculptor plunged into the centre of the most abstruse branch of medieval optics, to discover the behaviour of light in the most complicated circumstances and, more particularly, the interrelation of eye and brain in perception. Ghiberti's text is long and unwieldy, incorporating a more than respectable proportion of direct quotations from ancient and medieval sources; this has led most commentators to bypass its problems and to treat it as irrelevant to his highly original art.[23] But in the present context the *Third Commentary* offers a number of important insights into the development of an attitude towards light and shade that emerged half a century later as the debate between the claims of *disegno* and those of *colore*. Ghiberti opened his discussion with the bald assertion, 'O most learned [reader], nothing can be seen without light',[24] which alerts us at once to his double preoccupation with light and with seeing: that is, with the subjective effects of light or its absence. His experience as a designer of stained glass at a time when there was frequent opposition to the darkening effects of this glass in church interiors (*see* Chapter 4), will have made him sensitive to the relationship of colours to levels of illumination, a topic which he often broached in his book.[25] He was even more concerned with the lighting of sculpture and since contemporary sculpture was sometimes coloured, he was able to bring colour into this argument too. A common topic of discussion among the thirteenth-century perspectivists so often quoted by Ghiberti had been the effect of strong or weak lights on the appearance of hues,[26] a topic also implicit in Alberti's definitions. This was of the first interest to Ghiberti; in a discussion of fine sculptural detail, invisible in a weak light, he turned his attention to colour:

> Again we find how solid bodies [*corpi densi*] coloured with sparkling colours such as blues and sky-blues [*azzurini e celesti*] in dark places and in a weak light will appear as murky [*torbidi*][27] colours, and when they are in a luminous and light place, they will appear sparkling and light, and the more so the more the light on them increases. When the light is small that body will appear dark, and vision will not be able to distinguish its colour and it will seem almost black . . .[28]

Unlike the rather generalizing perspectivists, Ghiberti, as we might expect from an artist designing glass, was careful to refer to specific colours, which suggests that he had tried the experiments himself.[29] But it was a specificity also characteristic of the professional perspectivists of his day, such as the Pole Sandivogius of Czechel (*c.* 1410–76) who, while working very much along the lines proposed by Alhazen and Witelo, brought greater refinement and concreteness to their ideas.[30] As objects of perception, light and colour now seemed less separable than in earlier centuries, an interrelationship that was particularly clear in the growing number of depictions of night scenes in the fourteenth and early fifteenth centuries, both in Italy and in northern Europe. Taddeo Gaddi's several representations of night in the cycle of the Life of the Virgin in the Baroncelli Chapel at Sta Croce in Florence (1332–8) already show a severe reduction of local colour but not its total elimination, as there is in scotopic vision, using the photoreceptors on the retina called rods.[31] Among Ghiberti's younger contemporaries we might well have expected to find examples of night scenes without colour in a scientifically oriented writer such as Piero della Francesca. Indeed we do in his *Stigmatization of St Francis* in the predella of the Perugia altarpiece but not in the slightly earlier *Dream of Constantine* in S. Francesco at Arezzo.[32] One of the most striking instances of the new perception is in a close associate of Ghiberti himself, Fra Angelico, who in his *Annunciation* at Cortona shows a fully lit foreground in rich colour set against a distant night-scene with the Expulsion in a colourless grisaille.[33] Monochrome images were thus not simply a matter of taste or technique: in the Quattrocento they could be seen to reflect the processes of vision itself. *88*

Colour-symbolism in the Quattrocento

The development in the fifteenth century of a sense that *colore* and *disegno* were antithetical was hindered by this growing recognition that colour was a perceptual function of light and that it incorporated tonal values willy-nilly, and also by the heavy investment of the early Quattrocento in symbolic attitudes surviving from the Middle Ages. We saw in Chapter 5 how both the Este and the Medici families took up in their liveries the colours associated with the Theological Virtues. But I have also shown the contingency and local character of systems of medieval colour-symbolism, features long familiar in Renaissance symbolism, where several different and conflicting 'systems' were in place at the same time.[34] Lorenzo Valla's attack on the heraldic scheme of Bartolo of Sassoferrato and Rabelais's on that of Sicily Herald are signs that even contemporaries were finding such symbolizing tedious. Several writers in sixteenth-century Venice began to compare the various opinions and to find that they had very little in common. In a series of dialogues on love, where, of course, the expressive force of colours was seen to play a vital role, Mario Equicola in 1525 admitted the dangers of talking of colours at all, because of the differences in ancient and modern terms and because different authorities gave different equivalents for the colours of the elements or the planets; worse, 'the meanings of colours are somewhat different among the Italians, the Spanish and the French'.[35] Equicola sought to resolve the problem by proposing that 'variety' should govern colour-juxtaposition, variety conceived in terms of chemistry: those colours whose chemical constituents were the same should not be put side by side. Another Venetian writer of this period, Fulvio Pellegrini Morato, suggested more significantly in a book on colour-symbolism that the eye should be the only judge of colour-assortments, irrespective of meaning. He proposed grey (*berettino*) with tawny (*leonato*), yellow-green with red or flesh-pink, blue (*turchino*) with orange, maroon with dark green, black with white and white with flesh-pink, which combinations should, above all, please the eye. An assortment of colours according to their meaning, said Morato, might even have a very disagreeable aesthetic effect.

The tapestry-like meadow and the deployment of rich stuffs and precious ornament in Fra Angelico's *Annunciation* suggest an attitude to colour more medieval than Renaissance. Yet the monochrome treatment of the distant scene of the *Expulsion*, which is shown at night, indicates that the painter was aware of the more scientific approach to colour-vision which his collaborator Lorenzo Ghiberti was beginning to introduce into the discussion of art.

88 Fra Angelico *The Annunciation, c.* 1434

89

The value of dyes

89 Attributed to BENEDETTO DI BINDO, *Madonna of Humility* and *St Jerome translating the Gospel of John*, Siena, *c.* 1400
90 SASSETTA, *St Francis renouncing his heritage*, 1437/44
91 JAN VAN EYCK, *The Virgin with Chancellor Rolin*, *c.* 1437 (detail)

Since the brightest dyestuffs of the later Middle Ages were also the most expensive, sometimes they had spiritual connotations. In the left panel of the diptych (**89**) the Virgin Mary has been spinning brightly coloured threads to be woven into the curtain of the Temple. All the colours of the threads were used at some time or another to represent her costume. In the traditional Italian fashion she is dressed in a purplish-blue mantle, probably painted in the most expensive pigment blue, ultramarine. In many of van Eyck's paintings such as this scene (**91**), where she is shown as Queen of Heaven, and described on the border of her mantle as 'like a garden of roses', the Virgin is in red. Red was the most precious cloth in the late Middle Ages, suitable to be worn by Fathers of the Church such as Jerome (**89**). When St Francis renounces all his possessions for a life of poverty, they are represented by a red robe (**90**).

90

The joy of variety

In a canvas painted for Isabella d'Este,
Mantegna has followed Leon Battista Alberti's
advice that friezes of figures should be dressed
in contrasting colours to give the greatest
variety, including a good deal of white to
make the other colours more 'joyful'.
(*Overleaf*)

92 ANDREA MANTEGNA, *Apollo and the Nine Muses*,
detail of *Parnassus*, *c.* 1497

91

93 Leonardo da Vinci,
Ginevra de'Benci, c. 1474
94 Michelangelo, lunette with *Eleazar*,
Sistine Chapel, Rome, *c.* 1510

The colour of drawing

It has been usual to contrast Florentine *disegno* (drawing) and
Venetian *colore* (colour). Yet two of the greatest Florentine
draughtsmen, Leonardo and Michelangelo, were also supreme, and
supremely diverse, colourists. Leonardo gave a tonal coherence to
foreground and landscape background in his portrait of *Ginevra
de'Benci* (**93**) which surpassed his Netherlandish models (pl. 92), and
which depended on the same mastery of chiaroscuro that he showed

in his drawings (pl. 98). Michelangelo, who despised oil painting,
introduced an unprecedented range of colours into his frescoes in the
Sistine Chapel (**94**) and, as the recent cleaning has revealed, he
adopted at the same time a very bright palette which looks backward
to the Quattrocento, and an astonishing use of shot effects which
looks forward to Mannerism.

94

The use of small colour-studies in the very thorough preparation of altarpieces such as Barocci's, as well as the adoption of the soft, 'painterly' medium of pastel in drawings (see pl. 100), suggests that by the second half of the sixteenth century, at least in central Italy, the traditional opposition of *disegno* and *colore* had lost its force. It was, however, revived on a more theoretical level by the French Academy of the later seventeenth century and again in France in the 1820s.

95 FEDERICO BAROCCI, *Il Perdono di Assisi*, 1574/6

It is notable that Morato's views were copied in the 1560s by Lodovico Dolce, who was close to Titian.[36]

In the early Quattrocento the symbolism of colour, even in a religious context, had begun to take on a very materialist inflection. One panel in Sassetta's series *The Life of St Francis*, in which the young saint is seen giving his cloak to a poor knight, has allowed a modern commentator to propose that the ultramarine of the garment would have given it special symbolic resonance to contemporary observers.[37] These observers might well have been interested in the cloak of mid-blue, with its deep purple shadows, which might (or might not) have been read as shot silk; but they would surely have been more impressed by the rich wine-red gown that the saint did not give away but kept to discard when on the eve of his religious career he renounced his earthly father. The investigation of damage to these red areas in both the panels has revealed that Sassetta sought to enhance the brilliance of the fabric by grounding it with a layer of silver leaf under the transparent crimson glaze.[38] The pious spectators might even have recalled that at an earlier stage in his life Francis, fearing death, had thought it prudent to dispose of some supremely luxurious *pannis scarlaticis* at Foligno and, although they would probably not have been aware of this, the painter himself might have thought that the pigment he used for Francis's dress, the insect dye *kermes*, was appropriate precisely because it was the primary dye of scarlet cloth.[39] For scarlet was still by far the most expensive cloth in fifteenth-century Tuscany: in a Florentine dyers' manual crimson (*chermisi*) was characterized as 'the first and the highest and the most important colour that we have', so that it was specifically cited in the Florentine sumptuary regulations of 1464.[40] Writing to her son in Naples not long after the painting of Sassetta's altarpiece, Alessandra Macinghi Strozzi, of the Florentine patrician family, was delighted that her daughter had been given for an engagement present a waistcoat of crimson velvet, which, she said, was 'the most beautiful cloth in Florence'.[41] On the other hand, in Tuscany blue cloths were of very minor importance, hardly worth mentioning, said the Florentine manual, and could be dyed at nearly half the cost of crimson.[42] Similarly, the ultramarine which is lavished over the building in Sassetta's picture would surely have been read as an architectural wash rather than as a precious pigment in the painting itself: we have accounts of the wholesale painting of plastered walls and vaults in the secular architecture of early Quattrocento Tuscany, even in blue and gold; in a Bolognese text of the period there are two recipes for cheap blues for walls.[43] Although many among Sassetta's public will have themselves been patrons or donors and known the cost of paintings and their materials, it is surely more plausible to imagine that even they looked rather at the subject of the picture than at its precious techniques.

In this sense the use of evidence from contracts is rather misleading. Renaissance contracts were specialised legal documents which, as they referred to materials and workmanship, represented the interests of the commissioning patron in the face of the professional artist, whose own interests were represented, and whose production was regulated, by the guild.[44] Not that these interests were necessarily at odds: in fact the references to materials in contracts echo the requirements of the guilds that cheaper colours and so on were not to be substituted for the most valuable ones: the fourteenth-century regulations of Florence, Siena and Perugia, for example, forbade substitutions of silver for gold, tin for silver, azurite for ultramarine blue, indigo or other vegetable blues for azurite, minium for vermilion: just the precious pigments which we find stipulated in Italian contracts well into the sixteenth century.[45] That precious pigments such as gold, ultramarine and vermilion were sometimes provided by the patron is suggested by a number of recorded cases not referred to in contracts themselves. A document of 1459 suggests that while Sano di Pietro was working on a fresco of the Madonna begun by Sassetta in a gateway at Siena the town authorities had charge of the gold and ultramarine; twenty years later Ghirlandaio's patron for the *Last Supper* at Passignano noted in his account book that the colours had been provided by himself.[46] A particularly intriguing case is that of Francesco Gonzaga, Marquis of Mantua in 1493, one of whose agents in Venice sent a batch of colours for Mantegna by a 'Master [*maestro*] who makes ultramarine blue, and other perfect colours: who comes to live and die in the service of your Lordship'. Nothing more is known of the colour-maker but it would surely have been quite extraordinary to have one specifically attached to a court, even one so active in artistic patronage as that of Mantua.[47] The control of expensive pigments by patrons may be interpreted as a bid for durability but it also recalls the criticisms of Vitruvius and Pliny in Antiquity (*see* p. 15) and may be read as an indication of a patron-led taste at odds with that of the artists themselves.

Patrons and contracts might prescribe which materials were to be used but they could not dictate how exactly they were to be employed. A memorandum on Fra Angelico's *Linaiuoli Tabernacle* in Florence stipulated 'colours gold and blue and silver of the best that can be found' (and suggested that the painter's conscience might allow him to reduce the fee); but the central figure of the Madonna in the main panel is in a very pale, desaturated and now slightly greenish blue (?azurite), whereas her smaller self in the *Adoration of the Magi* below is in a saturated and immediately recognizable ultramarine.[48] Piero della Francesca's contract for the the S. Agostino altarpiece in Sansepolcro in 1454 made the usual stipulations about 'good and fine colours', gold and silver, but in one of the figures, the St Michael – where we might well have expected a deployment of gold and silver similar to that in Filippo Lippi's slightly later *St Michael* – the golden armour has been painted in an Albertian vein and gold is reserved exclusively for the saint's halo.[49] An early fifteenth-century Sicilian contract suggests that a patron might even seek to control this manner of handling the precious materials, so that they would be apparent to all spectators and seen to be well up to the expected level of display. In 1417 Corardus de Choffu was to paint for two patrons an altarpiece of the Virgin, which was to be executed

> as well as he knows how to and is able to do it, with fine colours and especially fine gold, fine ultramarine blue and fine lake, ... with used. Which colours, gold, blue and lake are to be used in a similar way to those which are on a certain image [*ycona*] in the chief church at Palermo, on the altar formerly constructed there by one Master Florem de Cisario ...[50]

Thus in the references to materials in contracts we are dealing essentially with legal conventions; they were often regarded as inessential, just as references to standards of workmanship were not invariably included in guild regulations. They can hardly be used as indications of aesthetic or symbolic attitudes without further qualification; the suggestion that they became less prominent in the later Renaissance is not borne out by the documents. Andrea del Sarto's 1515 contract for the *Madonna of the Harpies* required that the robe of the Virgin be painted with ultramarine blue of at least five broad florins the ounce, just as two hundred years earlier Pietro Lorenzetti's gold used in the altarpiece in the Pieve at Arezzo had to be 'at one hundred leaves to the florin'; and the stipulation of 1320 that here the Virgin and Child and four of the other figures should employ 'select ultramarine blue' was already interpreted by the painter in the most liberal fashion, for the Virgin is not dressed in blue at all, but in gold brocade.[51]

Nothing suggests more that the religious colour-symbolism of the Renaissance must be subsumed under a more secular semiology of material value than this question of the colour of the Virgin's robe, so often mentioned in Italian contracts in terms of the most expensive grade of ultramarine. The heavenly blue of the Virgin's mantle has indeed seemed axiomatic to some twentieth-century commentators, just as it was to some writers of the later Middle Ages, for the access to an understanding of her nature offered by colour. For the Catholic phenomenologist Hedwig Conrad-Martius in the 1920s, Goethe's assertion that blue was a 'negation' showed why the colour was especially emblematic of Mary's humility; while for a more recent cultural historian the traditionally male connotation of the colour gives an insight into her 'fields of operation which are above gender' (*übergeschlechtlicher Gewaltenbereiche*).[52] When modern historians of art have encountered Mary in other than this supposedly canonical colour, they have tried to argue it away on technical or liturgical or expressive grounds.[53] Yet it was shown long ago that blue was far from common for the mantle in northern Europe before 1400,[54] and it was certainly not invariable after that date. Perhaps the strongest tradition of late medieval and Renaissance colour-usage is encapsulated in a *89* small diptych attributed to the Sienese painter Benedetto di Bindo, dating from about 1400. The Virgin has interrupted her work to feed the Christ Child and has left on the table the bobbins of coloured thread with which she has been occupied: white, vermilion and two nuances of blue. The darker blue is that of her own mantle. The allusion is to that episode in her life recorded in the *Protoevangelium of James* which we encountered in fourteenth-century Byzantium (*see* Chapter 1). Mary was *35* among the group of virgins chosen to weave the curtain of the Temple from gold, cotton or linen, hyacinth-blue, scarlet and purple. They drew lots for who was to spin which colour and the young Mary drew first the scarlet and then the purple; while she was spinning at her house, the angel Gabriel visited her and foretold the birth of her Son.[55] As Benedetto di Bindo's image indicates, there was a direct link between the colours of the Temple Curtain and those of the Virgin's robes, for both Jewish and Christian traditions attached great symbolic importance to the colours of that sacred drapery.[56] For the first-century AD Jewish writer Flavius Josephus (*Jewish Wars* V, v, 4) the curtain was emblematic of the universe, with the colours symbolizing the four elements: scarlet fire, white linen earth (because it was a vegetable fibre), blue air and purple water (because it was derived from a shellfish).

These equivalents were taken up by many other writers in Byzantium and the West, who brought further attributes to bear on this most resonant set of four colours. Isidore of Seville (*Etymologies* XIX, xxi, 1–8) added a widely influential mystical interpretation: the blue signified heaven, the purple martyrdom, the scarlet charity and the white linen chastity and purity. In the twelfth century Hugh of St Victor related this double exegesis to the material constituents of man in the four elements and his spiritual side through the four cardinal virtues, wisdom, justice, temperance and fortitude.[57] Hugh also argued that Mary's role as Queen of Heaven made purple a particularly appropriate colour for her and in the Byzantine tradition she had often been robed in purple: when in the seventh century her mantle was transferred for safe-keeping from the church at Blachernae to Hagia Sophia, it was found to be of a miraculously imperishable purple wool.[58] It was a Byzantine icon of the Virgin and Child, dressed in a pale red robe and a blue overmantle, which is said to have been the prototype for this combination of colours, so common in Western Europe from the fourteenth century.[59] In ultramarine, with its purplish cast – *si bello violante*, as Cennino Cennini calls it (Lxii) – and very high price, Western painters found the perfect pigment equivalent of Imperial purple, hence its use to serve this noble function in so many versions of the image of the Madonna. Her second chosen colour for the weaving of the Temple Curtain was scarlet, which was very frequently used in combination with the blue in her dress. In The Netherlands in the fifteenth century, where scarlet was by far the most valuable dyestuff for textiles, the Virgin was often clothed predominantly in this colour, which *91* because of the loose connotations of the Latin *purpureus* (*see* Chapter 1) could itself be read as purple without difficulty.[60]

The Virgin's companion in the Benedetto di Bindo diptych is *89* St Jerome, occupied with his translation of St John's Gospel into Latin. The saint is dressed as a cardinal and is thus depicted in two very expensive varieties of red, vermilion for his hat and crimson for his robe. Were Alberti to have described this image to his literary friends in Latin he might well have picked up the distinction; among his own family he would probably have been content with a single vernacular term for both.[61] On the other hand, according to the tightly regulated dress codes of official Venice in the High Renaissance – where, we are surprised to learn, both scarlet and deep purplish *pavonazzo* could be colours of mourning, black having been pre-empted for other social functions – a nice perception of the difference between a yellowish or a bluish red was essential to reading the political signs. The guardian of official orthodoxy, the diarist Marin Sanudo, was careful to note the colour of the Doge's costume and that of his Council: during the war crisis in 1509, he saw on the important feast of Corpus Christi that Doge Loredan, during a campaign of austerity, continued to wear his usual crimson velvet, while some of the senators wore scarlet and others black or *pavonazzo*, according to the degree of sorrow they wished to express.[62] Like the theorist of colour Morato, political commentators were having increasingly to use their eyes.

In the history of the official dress of the Roman Church, the distinctions in St Jerome's costume were also far from trivial. Pope Innocent IV had decreed in the thirteenth century that his cardinals should wear the red hat, the emblem of martyrdom for their faith, but their traditional purple robe was retained until 1464, when Paul I allowed them to dress in scarlet. This was a direct consequence of the closure of the Byzantine purple trade after the Turkish conquest of 1453 and the discovery of a rich supply of alum, an essential ingredient in *kermes* dyeing and formerly imported from Turkey, in the Papal territories in 1462.[63] Why then do so many painters of cardinals before 1464 give the robe the same colour as the hat or, as in our Sienese example, a red which is only faintly purplish?[64] As we have seen so often, the answer must be that our modern discrimination of purple and red was still quite foreign to the early Renaissance and that, as in the case of the Virgin's robe, scarlet, purple and the painter's vermilion, crimson lake, and ultramarine were cognate colours, united in symbolic value by their beauty, rarity and extraordinary cost.

The importance of materials

It is no surprise that the *maestro* of pigments who was bringing a batch to Mantegna in 1493 came from Venice, for Venice in the Renaissance was the great emporium of artists' colours, not least the ultramarine blue which came from Budakshan (in what is now Afghanistan) and hence from 'beyond the sea', as opposed to azurite or 'German blue', which was imported from northern or central Europe.[65] Patrons knew that if they wanted the best materials they might have to bear the extra cost of fetching them from Venice, and contracts sometimes allowed for this cost. Thus Filippino Lippi's contract for frescoing the Strozzi Chapel at Sta Maria Novella in Florence (1487) included a provision that some of the fee should be kept in hand for when 'he wants to go to Venice'; Pinturicchio's contract for the extensive series of frescoes in the Piccolomini Library at Siena (1502), which were to be painted 'with gold, ultramarine azure, green glazes and other colours as are in accordance with the fee', also allowed for 200 gold ducats to be paid at the outset 'in Venice to buy gold and necessary colours'.[66]

Venice, besides selling the raw materials, was also a manufacturer of the processed pigments ready for use.[67] But here it had a rival in Florence, where the lay confraternity of the Gesuati in the Convent of S. Giusto alle Mura made a particular speciality of the highest quality lapis lazuli and azurite blues.[68] It would be hard to overestimate the importance of this increasing specialization in the manufacture and sale of artists' materials, for it went hand in hand with the growing independence of artists as a class and the shift in emphasis from workshop and guild to academy for their training during the course of the sixteenth century. Even Cennini had avoided detailing the various and complicated recipes for artificial vermilion made from mercury and sulphur, saying that if he wanted them, the painter could make friends with *frati* (xl), by whom he may well have meant the Florentine Gesuati.[69] Leonardo da Vinci, whose notebooks give ample evidence of an active interest in the chemistry of painting materials, was also a patron of the confraternity: his contract for the unfinished *Adoration of the Magi* includes the unusual condition that he should get his colours from them.[70] By the middle of the sixteenth century the processing of raw pigments into paints must have become very rare in the painters' studios, even in Venice: a painter from the Veneto, Paolo Pino, in his *Dialogue on Painting* (1548) wrote contemptuously that he would not go into the nature of the various colours which, he said, everyone knew, and even those who sold them knew how to use them in pictures. Beauty, said Pino, did not mean ultramarine at sixty *scudi* the ounce, nor a beautiful lake, colours which are just as beautiful in the box as in the painting.[71]

Specialization was partly a function of the increasingly sophisticated technology of paint-manufacture, most noticeable in the development of oil painting in the fifteenth century, for which the purification of oils and the distillation of spirits for thinners required skills and apparatus not usually found in the artists' workshops. Here again the Gesuati showed that they were able to supply the needs of a developing fashion.[72] The vast contribution of conservationists to the study of historical techniques in the 1970s and 80s has at last laid to rest the pleasant, surprisingly universal, story of the 'discovery' of oil painting by Jan van Eyck. Oils had been used in the making of paintings for some centuries: Urso of Salerno, a doctor, gave towards the close of the twelfth century what may be the first account of the distinct techniques of oil and egg-tempera, mixed with the juice of fig-shoots.[73] What seems to have happened in the fourteenth and fifteenth centuries is that these two methods became more and more mixed, so that well into the sixteenth century in Italy it has sometimes proved very difficult to identify precisely the medium of a given work.[74] What Van Eyck brought to the technique was essentially a complicated method of glazing transparent colours over a light ground and about the precise origins of this refinement there is still little agreement. It has been pointed out that Van Eyck had associations with painting on glass,[75] and it is also clear that several of his contemporaries also painted sculpture, where a traditional technique of glazing such transparent colours as red and green over gold or silver leaf was also well developed.[76] Another technique related to the new oil methods is painting on a fine canvas (*Tüchlein*) with thin paints bound in glue and water, which was much used in The Netherlands in the early fifteenth century. We may well imagine that the painters, including Van Eyck, who used this method might have wished to transfer the very thin layers and continuous modelling, which depended on a fluid medium, to the more durable and more expressive context of panel painting.[77] That they were able to do this depended on their development of distilled thinners (which are, however, documented in The Netherlands from the early fourteenth century).[78] Whatever the origins of the new Netherlandish method, its consequences were vast. The smooth, jewel-like surfaces of Van Eyck and his supremely refined detail could easily be transformed – by thickening the oil, by adding resins and by making the complicated palette-mixtures that were now permissible because each particle of pigment was locked into an envelope of oil which protected it from the chemical action of its neighbours – into the combination of broad impasto and subtle glazing which first developed in Venice in the sixteenth century. Most importantly, in the new capacity for the illusionistic treatment of detail, as well as the durability of the medium as opposed to

91, 105

13

Workshop of Taddeo Gaddi, *Presentation of the Virgin*, after 1330. The use of a toned ground (as here) was already traditional in Tuscan drawing before the fifteenth century, and the sense of cohesion it could provide was soon to be exploited in oil painting. (96)

Then on top of this put as it were with a white shadow [*una ombra di bianco*], whatever you want to do, that is, give form to figures or buildings or animals or trees, or something [else] that you have to do, with this white [*biacca*], which should be finely ground. And so should all the other colours be finely ground, and each time you should let them dry well, so that they combine [*s'incorpori*] well with each other.

Forms should be made with white and shadows with any colour, 'and then with a light touch give them a thin coat with the colour you have to cover them.'[81]

The reference to the thin layers of finely ground pigments suggests that Filarete had been well informed about Netherlandish procedures but what is most striking about this account is its prescribing white drawing on coloured grounds, for this does not correspond to northern practice but was used, for example, by Uccello in oil painting in these years.[82] The recommendations remind us of central Italian techniques of drawing as they had developed since the fourteenth century. Drawing, often in silverpoint, with a good deal of white heightening on a toned paper, was a method which became one of the best-known graphic techniques in the Italian Renaissance and was practised by Uccello himself.[83] The importance of the tinted ground is that it established the tonal unity of the image from the start; when Vasari came to discuss the various methods of drawing a century later he wrote:

> Other drawings in light and shade are executed on tinted paper which gives a middle shade; the pen marks the outlines, that is the contour or profile, and afterwards half-tone or shade is given with ink mixed with a little water which produces a delicate tint: further, with a fine brush dipped in white lead mixed with gum, the high lights are added. This method is very pictorial and best shows the scheme of coloring [*e questo modo è molto alla pittoresca e mostra più l'ordine del colorito*].[84]

Uccello's sense of colour was no less conceptual than his sense of linear space; he liked sharp contours and bright contrasts which work against the sense of an overall tonal unity; but when married to a feeling for perceptual coherence and to a method of working from nature this technical device of the mid-toned ground was able to work a revolution in the understanding of tonal relationships within the picture. The technique of drawing on toned paper was, in fact, especially developed among Florentine painters such as Filippino Lippi and Ghirlandaio, for whom the close study of nature was a primary concern. This concern was not confined to Italy. Dürer was no stranger to the blandishments of 'the most beautiful colours', when it came to persuading a patron to increase his fee.[85] As an outdoor sketcher he saw at the same time that the function of colour was to match the tones of nature; in the only fragment of his treatise on painting to have survived (*see* Chapter 2) – the passage on drapery painting – he argued for a tonal unity which avoided both the extremes of light and dark and the extremes of colour-contrast in shot materials: the sort of broad and unified effects we see in the *Apostles* (1526).[86] Dürer's great German contemporary, the sculptor Tilman Riemenschneider, was also introducing a conception of overall tonal unity into wood sculpture in these years, by abandoning the traditional polychromy and

the colours, oil technique slowly led to that devaluation of pigments as indicators of worth in painting, reflected in the scathing remarks of Pino and Dolce. Yet although this was originally a Netherlandish development, it was in Italy that it first made its aesthetic mark.

The new Flemish methods first came into Italy in the 1430s and 40s in the work of Filippo Lippi in Florence and Antonello da Messina in Naples.[79] That it had already become quite a widespread but also very expensive practice by the 1450s is suggested by a document referring to the painting of the refectory at S. Miniato al Monte outside Florence by Andrea del Castagno and Paolo Uccello. In February 1454 they were paid an extra ten florins for their work, done, in the event, in oil 'which they were not obliged to do'.[80] Not long after this in Milan, the architect Antonio Averlino (Filarete) gave the first substantial account of oil painting in any language, citing Van Eyck and Van der Weyden, from whose Milanese pupil Zanetto Bugatti he may have learned the details. The technique, said Filarete, could be used on panel or on wall and the ground might be of any colour, including white (*biacca*):

'colouring' particular areas of his relief-altarpieces with a repertory of graphic marks loosely related to the new tonal conventions of engraving that were developing in Germany at this time, notably in the hands of Dürer. The now fragmented and dispersed Münnerstadt Altar of the early 1490s, Riemenschneider's first large-scale work and the earliest monochromatic altar in Germany, caused such a scandal that in response to parish pressure it was painted by another sculptor, Veit Stoss, early in the sixteenth century.[87]

So monochrome, and the related downgrading of the inherent values of unmodulated colours, had become a central part of the visual experience of Western Europe by 1500. The theorist of this development, as well as its most distinguished exponent in painting was Leonardo da Vinci.

Leonardo da Vinci

In Leonardo the prejudices of Vitruvius and Pliny against extravagant colouring and the developing practices of the Quattrocento towards a more coherent and lower-toned harmony of the picture-surface came together in the most commanding and influential of painterly styles. The study of a wide range of medieval writers on optics had brought him into touch with many ideas about the supremacy of light; it is by no means clear why he turned so decisively against them – perhaps out of a well attested spirit of rivalry and a belief in the importance of novelty[88] – but turn against them he did. He translated the preface to Pecham's *Perspectiva Communis* (1269/79) where, 'Among all the studies of natural causes and reasons, light most delights the contemplators'; but when in the opening passage of his book Pecham wrote that 'when the eye sees bright lights, it suffers greatly and endures pain' (I, 1.1), Leonardo softened this to 'the sight when seeing light suffers somewhat'.[89] Light as a subjective effect was already losing its power. Leonardo's reading in his medieval sources, particularly Alhazen, Bacon, Witelo and Pecham, brought him into touch with a range of problems in physiological optics and much of his work may be seen, like Ghiberti's, as an attempt to test, refine and extend these issues by reference to his own experience of nature, which was vast.

His approach is well illustrated by his treatment of the blue colour of the sky. Medieval scholars had argued that it was due to the mixture of white air with the darkness of space. The thirteenth-century Tuscan encyclopaedist Ristoro d'Arezzo, for example, had drawn his explanation from an experience of art: 'Although according to the learned the sky ought not to have any colour, let us see the reason why it seems a blue colour. Learned painters who use colours, when they want to simulate [*contrafare*] blue colour, put two opposite colours together, the light and the dark, and from this mixture results blue colour.' The same was true of deep water and of the different blues of the sky by day and by night: 'And because it is the nature of the dark and the light, when they mix together, to produce blue colour, accordingly learned painters who use the mixture of colours, . . . when they want to simulate a light blue put in more of the light, and when they want to simulate a dark blue they put in more of the dark.' The sky cannot be blue because of blue vapours, said Ristoro, because then the stars would seem blue, 'And the proof

[*segno*] of this is that if you put a transparent blue glass, or green, or red, or another colour [between you and the object] you would see them of that colour, and especially if you see on the other side [of the glass] things with a light colour.' The blue sky with white stars, Ristoro concluded, 'seems more noble and delightful to the eye than any other colours'.[90] Leonardo's account incorporated several of these ideas but his approach to the problem was quite different. In the *Codex Hammer* (1506/9) he wrote:

I say that the blueness we see in the atmosphere is not intrinsic colour, but is caused by warm vapour evaporated in minute and insensible atoms on which the solar rays fall, rendering them luminous against the infinite darkness of the fiery sphere which lies beyond and includes it. And this may be seen, as I saw it, by any one going up Monboso, a peak of the Alps which divide France from Italy . . . There I saw above me the dark sky, and the sun as it fell on the mountain was far brighter here than in the plains below, because a smaller extent of atmosphere lay between the summit of the mountain and the sun. Again as an illustration of the colour of the atmosphere I will mention the smoke of old and dry wood, which as it comes out of a chimney, appears to turn very blue, when seen between the eye and the dark distance. But as it rises, and comes between the eye and the bright atmosphere, it at once shows an ashy colour [*cenerognolo*]; and this happens because it no longer has darkness beyond it, but this bright and luminous space. If the smoke is from young, green wood, it will not appear blue, because not being transparent and being full of superabundant moisture, it has the effect of condensed clouds which take distinct lights and shadows like a solid body. The same occurs with the atmosphere, which when overcharged with moisture appears white, and the small amount of heated moisture makes it dark, of a dark blue colour; and this will suffice us so far as concerns the colour of the atmosphere; though it might be added that, if this transparent blue were the natural colour of the atmosphere, it would follow that wherever a larger mass of air intervened between the eye and the element of fire, the azure colour would be more intense; as we see in blue glass and in sapphires, which are darker in proportion as they are larger. But the atmosphere in such circumstances behaves in an opposite manner, inasmuch as where a greater quantity of it lies between the eye and the sphere of fire, it appears much whiter. This occurs towards the horizon. And the less the extent of atmosphere between the eye and the sphere of fire, the deeper is the blue colour, as may be seen even on low plains. Hence it follows, as I say, that the atmosphere assumes this azure hue by reason of the particles of moisture which catch the rays of the sun. Again, we may note the difference in particles of dust, or particles of smoke, in the sunbeams admitted through holes into a dark chamber, when the former will look ashy [*cenereo*] and the thin smoke will appear of a most beautiful blue; and it may be seen again in the dark shadows of distant mountains when the air between the eye and those shadows will look very blue, while the brightest parts of those mountains will not differ much from their true colour. But if any one wishes for a final proof let him paint a board with various colours, among them an intense black; and over all let him lay a very thin and transparent white. He will then see that this transparent white will nowhere show a more beautiful blue than over the black – but it must be very thin and finely ground.[91]

The unfinished oil painting of 1481 (*Adoration of the Magi*) and pen and wash sketch of *c.* 1478 (*The Madonna and Child with cat*) show how remarkably similar Leonardo's drawing and early painting procedures could be in the use of broad tonal areas of light and dark. (97,98)

This wide-ranging discussion introduces a number of recurrent themes in Leonardo's investigation of nature: the importance of mountains for the study of aerial perspective; the fascination with smoke, that traditional pre-occupation of the Quattrocento artist concerned with tonal modelling, but here brought into the realm of colour;[92] and the wish to test ideas about the natural world by experiments in painting. Where Ristoro put painting before the study of nature at large – and was content with one or two experiments – Leonardo only arrived at it after a long series of examples and then in a way which suggests that he had not really attempted the experiment. The creation of a beautiful blue-grey by overlaying a white ground with transparent black had long been known in the studio – it was to be used by Titian, for example in the sash of Tarquin in the late *Tarquin and Lucretia* in Cambridge[93] – but the reverse procedure, white over black, was far more problematic, not least because of the difficulty of finding a near-transparent white. The white-lead (*biacca*) specified by Leonardo is a particularly dense and covering white; and one modern scholar who has repeated the painter's 'experiment' has found it to result only in 'unpleasant greys with a greenish cast'.[94]

Leonardo's handling of the problem of the blue colour of the sky is characteristic of the obstacles presented to the student anxious to understand Leonardo's attitudes to colour: an abundance of graphic but disparate examples strung together without pause and without a clearly articulated theme. It seems to be empiricism run mad. Leonardo's notes, although they were clearly intended to form the raw material of one or more publications, are repetitive and sometimes contradictory, and this is not the place to enter into the many intractable problems of dating and interpretation which they present.[95] Here I can only indicate some of the main issues in the painter's approach to colour and attempt to relate his theory to his extraordinary practice.

Perhaps the most immediately impressive feature of Leonardo's view of colour in both theory and practice is his revaluation of darkness. I showed in the context of mosaic and again of stained glass how darkness came to have a positive, mystical value in the earlier Middle Ages and that this was largely the result of a particular reading of Pseudo-Dionysius. The revival of interest in the Dionysian corpus in the Italian Renaissance, with new translations by Ambrogio Traversari (a scholar in touch with Ghiberti) in the 1430s and by Marsilio Ficino in 1490, might simply have reinforced the exoteric links between this theology and the metaphysics of light. Yet there is some reason to suppose that in painterly circles at least, after 1500, the negative and mystical elements of his doctrine re-asserted themselves. Fra Bartolommeo's 1515 *Madonna della Misericordia* places a dark cloud immediately below the figure of Christ in a way which is both Dionysian and in the spirit of the painter's mentor, Savonarola;[96] Fra Bartolommeo was also one of the first to adopt Leonardo's new principles of structural chiaroscuro. Leonardo may not have been aware of, or interested in, the Dionysian mystical theology but there is no doubt that he conceived of darkness in a far from passive way: 'Shadow is of greater power than light [*lume*]', he wrote about 1492, 'in that it can impede and entirely deprive bodies of light and the light can never chase away all the shadows of bodies.'[97] He planned to write seven books on the taxonomy of shadow, notes for several of which have survived. What was perhaps of the greatest practical importance for painting was his distinction between shadow (*ombra*) and darkness (*tenebre*), for he argued that shadow stood between light and darkness and it could either be infinitely dark or have an infinite degree of absence of darkness.[98] Where the medieval metaphysics of light required a plurality of types of light and was amplified by the Neo-Platonist Ficino, who held colour to be 'opaque light' and in his twelve-tone scale of colour from light to dark included four tones at the light end,[99] Leonardo posited an infinite scale of shades. In a note of about 1508 he berated contemporary painters who 'give to all shaded [*infuscate*] objects – trees, fields, hair, beards and furs – four degrees of darkness in each colour they use: that is to say first a dark foundation, secondly a spot of colour somewhat resembling the form of the details, thirdly a somewhat brighter and more defined portion, fourthly the lights which are more conspicuous than the other parts of the figures; still to me it appears that these gradations are infinite upon a continuous surface which is in itself infinitely divisible.'

And he went on to give a mathematical proof of this proposition.[100] This concept of the infinity of shadows forms the philosophical underpinning of Leonardo's *sfumato*, that method of infinitely subtle gradation of tone for which he developed a number of new graphic media and techniques. The late sixteenth-century report of Lomazzo attributed to him a new type of soft pastel, which he used to study the heads of Christ and the Apostles in the *Last Supper* in drawings, none of which have survived although others in soft red chalk have.[101] A very large-scale drawing such as the cartoon of the *Madonna and Child with St Anne* uses charcoal and probably chalk, as white chalk heightening, and there seems to be a good deal of smudging with the fingers in the heads.[102] Conservation has revealed fingerwork in a number of Leonardo's paintings, too, from the early *Annunciation* and *Ginevra de' Benci*, to the late, London, version of the *Madonna of the Rocks*: the fine texture of

the fingertips provided the subtlest means of making the nuances that Leonardo required in modelling and, by a sort of sympathetic magic in the handling, transmitted some of its own softness to the painted flesh.[103]

True to the Florentine traditions of the Quattrocento, Leonardo made use both of tinted paper for his drawings, even on the scale of the London cartoon, and also the all-over or partial underpainting of both wall and panels in one or more darkish tones.[104] As he wrote of drawing in his *Treatise on Painting*, 'To draw objects in relief, painters should stain the surface of the paper with a tint that is medium dark, and then put on the darkest shades, and finally the principal lights in little spots, which are those first lost to the eye at a short distance.'[105] Nothing demonstrates more clearly the overriding role of shade in Leonardo's conception of the making of an image; even when he began with a light ground, as in many drawings, or in the oil-paintings which he had barely begun, such as the *Adoration* or the *St Jerome*, he seems to squeeze his limited lights slowly out of a matrix of darkness.

Leonardo has been regarded as the father of chiaroscuro but this technical concept does not appear as such in his written works, except in the *Treatise*, where it is described as a science of great importance (*di gran discorso*). It may well be that the idea, which became current in Italy only in the 1520s, was interpolated into his notes by the editors of the *Treatise* in the following decades.[106] If so, his failure to think in terms of a specific concept which might be set beside *disegno* and *colore* could well be due to a continuing ambiguity in his attitude towards colour, which is exemplified in his use of the term *bello*, or 'beautiful'.

It has long been recognized that in some contexts Leonardo's *bello* simply had the connotation of 'light' or 'bright'.[107] Green might thus be made more *bello* by adding yellow; the light sky near the horizon is more *bella* than at the zenith; if colours are set in a luminous space they will have the more *bellezza* the more the light has *splendore*.[108] This may be no more than the survival of the exoteric Dionysian aesthetic but, as another section of the *Treatise* demonstrates, it had important consequences for the handling of colour:

> *Which nuance [parte] of one and the same hue shows itself as more beautiful in painting*
> Here we must note that the degree of the same colour that looks more beautiful in nature is either that which has the lustre, or that which has the highlight, or that which has the mid-tone, or that which has the true transparent shadows [*scure vero in trarasparentia (sic)*]. Here we must understand which colour we need, since different colours have their beauties in different values of themselves; and this shows us that black has its beauty in the shadows and white in the light and blue and green and tawny in the mid-tones, and yellow and red in the lights and gold in reflections and lake in the mid-tones.[109]

Here Leonardo was setting up a model of beauty in colouring which depended on a tonal or value scale – in which red was close to light – and which it would have been especially difficult to translate into painting while giving due attention to relief. In an early note (1492), subsequently incorporated into the *Treatise*, Leonardo had argued that 'You should invest your figures with the brightest colours you can, since if you make

Mariotto Albertinelli, *The Annunciation*, 1506–10. Striving to enhance the chiaroscuro in his altarpiece, Albertinelli developed a new and forceful white, although he ruined the painterly qualities of the work with constant revision. (99)

them of a dark colour they will be of little relief and little in evidence from afar . . . if you make a vestment dark there will be little difference between light and shadow, but in the bright colours there is great variety.'[110] And in some disparaging remarks about paints, which look forward to the Venetian attitudes of the sixteenth century, he asked:

> Which is of greater importance: that the form should abound in beautiful colours, or display high relief? Only painting presents a marvel to those who contemplate it, because it makes that which is not seem to be in relief and to project from the walls; but colours honour only those who manufacture them, for in them there is no cause for wonder except their beauty, and their beauty is not to the credit of the painter, but of him who has made them. A subject can be dressed in ugly colours and still astound those who contemplate it, because of the illusion of relief.[111]

I have quoted enough to suggest that Leonardo found himself facing a dilemma in respect of beauty, which he came to feel must be sacrificed in the interest of relief. Yet it seems that he saw this sacrifice chiefly in terms of dress, where he was also able to deploy, at least in a minor way, those harmonious contrasts which he identified in colour-pairs, such as the yellow and blue of the Virgin's robe and its lining in the early *Madonna of the Pink* or the London *Madonna of the Rocks*. These swags of sculpturesque and rather random drapery, although they clearly originated in Netherlandish art, were used for purely abstract effect and it is not surprising that from the 1470s onwards several workshops in Florence, notably Verrocchio's, where Leonardo trained, made a particular study of elaborate draperies as an exercise in the handling of light and shade.[112] Leonardo's dangerously experimental techniques of painting have deprived us of any certainty that we see his works as he saw them: The 'rosy and pearly tints' which Vasari's informant described in the *Mona Lisa* have long since fled, although the overall tonality of this picture may perhaps be guessed from the recently cleaned workshop version of *St John the Baptist* in Milan.[113]

Leonardo's belief in illusion, in the capacity of painting to render precisely the effects of nature, has a degree of fanaticism without precedent. In the *Treatise* he argued that, when working outdoors, the painter should compare his colours directly with those of his subject, 'so that the colour you make may coincide with the natural colour', by holding samples painted on paper against the real scene.[114] His brilliant observations of the effects of colour in shadow and in reflection and the powerful impressions of colour-contrast have led some commentators to think forward to Impressionism:

> If you see a woman dressed in white in the midst of a landscape, that side which is towards the sun is bright in colour, so much so that in some portions it will dazzle the eyes like the sun itself; and the side which is towards the atmosphere, – luminous through being interwoven with the sun's rays and penetrated by them – since the atmosphere itself is blue, that side of the woman's figure will appear steeped in blue. If the surface of the ground about her be meadows and if she be standing between a field lighted up by the sun and the sun itself, you will see every portion of those folds which are towards the meadow tinged by the reflected rays with the colour of that meadow . . .[115]

We seem to be looking at a Renoir of the 1870s. But Leonardo introduced such examples only to discount them; what concerned him was what he called the 'true' colour of objects, unmodified by environmental reflections, whose effect, he said, might be 'very ugly'.[116] Similarly, strong contrasts of tone, which made things 'ambiguous or confused' to the painter, were to be avoided.[117] Just as Alberti had advised against the use of tonal extremes, so Leonardo now recommended an even, subdued lighting for the painter, especially for portraits. He should paint the walls of a courtyard black and cover it with a lined awning to diffuse the light, 'Or when you want to take a portrait do it in dull weather, or as evening falls, making the sitter stand with his back to one of the walls of the courtyard. Note in the streets, as evening falls, the faces of the men and women, and when the weather is dull, what softness and delicacy you may perceive in them.'[118]

In order to be able to match his perceptions Leonardo experimented with complicated pigment mixtures and with new sorts of oil and turpentine media, with the disastrous consequences so evident in the *Last Supper*.[119] But he had already programmed himself for disaster by an attitude which sought to reconcile the irreconcilable demands of hue and of tone. We do not know why the *Adoration* and *St Jerome* were abandoned at such an early stage; Leonardo was already buying some expensive pigments for the former in 1481 but he does not seem to have used them and seems rather to have been attempting to create colour through overlaid glazes.[120] We may imagine that Leonardo struggled with this painting rather as, thirty years later, Fra Bartlommeo's assistant Mariotto Albertinelli struggled with his *Annunciation* which, though signed and delivered, is now an over-worked ruin, both in the lights and in the darks. Vasari reported how the painter tried to reconcile softness (*dolcezza*) and force:

> This work was undone and re-done by Mariotto several times before he could bring it to completion, switching the colour from light to dark, now more lively and fiery, now less, but he could get no satisfaction from it; and because his hand did not seem to have carried out the idea in his mind, he wanted to find a white more powerful [*fiero*] than lead-white, so he set himself to purify it so as to be able to carry the light even beyond [the value of] the main lights in his own way. Nevertheless, since he was not able to execute what his genius envisaged, he rested content with what he had done . . .

Albertinelli's patrons, the Compagnia di S. Zenobi, were not happy with the result but they were overruled by a committee of assessors made up of painters.[121]

Juggling with tonalities was perhaps the logical consequence of an emphasis on matching the precise tones of nature in the painting, an emphasis so marked that what is apparently only a large drawing in oils, Fra Bartolommeo's *Pala della Signoria*, could be accepted for display on an altar.[122] This was the apotheosis of *disegno* but, as I have tried to show, it was *disegno* with a colouristic background and colouristic force.

Venetian colour in the sixteenth century

When in the sixteenth century the criticism of Titian's style polarized the debate of *disegno* versus *colore*, the Florentine master of drawing was seen to be not Leonardo but Michelangelo. The cleaning of the frescoes of the Sistine Ceiling and the less controversial cleaning of the *Doni Tondo* in Florence have revealed Michelangelo to be a colourist of unsuspected originality and power, fully in command of a highly saturated palette in some respects close to that of the mid-Quattrocento. We can no longer be surprised that one of his first acts on receiving the commission to decorate the Sistine Chapel in 1508 was to send for some 'beautiful blues' to the Gesuati in Florence.[123] It is a palette and a manner of painting, too, that makes Michelangelo far more the forerunner of the sharp Mannerist colourists, Andrea del Sarto, Pontormo, Bronzino and even Rosso Fiorentino in the 1510s and 1520s,[124] than he seemed before the cleaning. This is the sort of colourism to which Titian's supporter Lodovico Dolce might have been alluding when in a letter of about 1550 he contrasted a *Sta Caterina* of the Venetian master with

> that diversity of colours which most painters nowadays affect in their works, which, quite apart from our knowing that they are used to give relief to the figures and please the eyes of the ignorant, are also outside the bound of probability. For it is not often – perhaps never – that you see men of so many liveries [*divise*] together, so that some are clothed in red, others in yellow, others in purple [*pavonazzo*], others in blue and still others in green.[125]

In the dialogue on painting which Dolce published at this time, he looked at drapery painting in more detail, echoing Leonardo and Paolo Pino:

> Let no one think that the power of colour consists in the choice of beautiful colours, like beautiful lakes, beautiful blues, beautiful greens and so on, since these colours are just as beautiful without being set to work, but rather it consists in knowing how to handle them appropriately. [Some painters] don't know how to imitate the different nuances of cloth, but put the colours on fully saturated as they stand, so that in their works there is nothing to praise but the colours.[126]

Another critic in Dolce's circle, Pietro Aretino, had already compared such crude palettes to those of the miniaturists who could paint nothing but strawberries and snails, or imitate velvet and belt-buckles, using the pretty colours of stained glass.[127] It is something of an irony that Titian himself asked Aretino in 1548 to procure him half a pound of lake 'so fiery and splendid in its madder colour that by the side of it the crimson of velvet and silk become less beautiful'.[128]

The requirement of Venetian *colore* was thus colour not in the sense of bright hues and sharp contrasts but rather a particularly rich and resonant handling of the brush. Pino argued that the skilful painter should be able to substitute one colour for another and still achieve the required effect.[129] But this was also a matching function to be achieved by mixture,[130] and the mixtures of the Venetian oil-painters of the sixteenth century – Titian chief among them – were unprecedentedly complex.[131] The soft shadowing of Leonardo, especially on the face, was introduced into Venice around 1505 by Giovanni Bellini in his altarpiece in Sta Zaccaria and by Giorgione in his great altarpiece at Castelfranco. All this helped to lower the overall key and chromaticity of the picture, a tendency increased by the use of tinted grounds of the sort we have seen in Florence, both in drawing and in oil painting.[132] The palette of the sixteenth-century Venetian painters was scarcely distinguishable from that used in the fifteenth century but the thickening of the medium, the development of impasto and the acceptance of mixtures were signs that the painter's handling was now the chief object of admiration to the connoisseur. This notion of conspicuous handling had also developed from the practice and appreciation of drawing.

During the course of the sixteenth century the dispute between *disegno* and *colore* took on the character of an intellectual exercise in the growing number of more or less official art academies, the first of which, the Florentine Accademia di Disegno, was founded in 1563 and attracted the interest even of the leading Venetian artists, who were anxious to join. The ambiguities in the notion of *disegno* between a repertory of graphic techniques, a capacity to render a three-dimensional volume on a two-dimensional surface by means of these techniques and the ability to visualize and execute an idea in graphic form became inextricably interwoven, providing food for discussion in and among these academies for several centuries. The rather less crucial ambiguities between *colore* as the chromatic embellishment of the picture and the tonal arrangement of a composition were less fully explored, since *colore* was regarded, for reasons which we have seen developed essentially in the fifteenth and sixteenth centuries, as at best a secondary consideration.

95

100

The later sixteenth century refinement of these ideas may be illuminated best by the work of a painter who brought drawing and painting together more closely than any other, a painter neither from Florence nor Venice, but from the Marches, Federico Barocci. Barocci's exceptionally careful method is attested both by his early biographer Bellori and by many surviving sequences of work. After Barocci had settled on a subject he made life-studies in charcoal, chalk and frequently pastel, a medium he had made particularly his own, although Bellori claimed that he had been stimulated by the pastels of Correggio, none of which are now known. Then Barocci made models of the individual figures in clay or wax, draped according to their role in the composition, followed by a chiaroscuro study of the whole arrangement in oil or gouache, from which a full-size cartoon was made in charcoal and powdered gesso or pastels. This cartoon was transferred to the primed canvas. Then the painter made a small coloured 'cartoon' in oil, in order to work out the colour-relationships, 'so that all the colours should be concordant and unified among themselves without hurting each other, and he said that just as the melody of voices delights the hearing, so the sight is entertained by the consonance of colours joined to the harmony of the linear composition. And so he called painting music.'[133] Finally Barocci painted the large canvas on which he blocked out the general colour-areas using a soft pastel-like palette and a melting *sfumato* very close to the first pastel and oil studies from the life.[134] His was perhaps the first working procedure in painting to emphasize equally drawing and colour,[135] although it is notable that even he made his 'inventions', the chiaroscuro compositional sketches, before the colour 'cartoons'. Nevertheless we are not far from the seventeenth century and from El Greco, whose colour has a great deal in common with Barocci's and who confessed in an interview a few years before his death in 1614 that colouring was far more difficult than drawing, and that Michelangelo 'was a fine chap but did not know how to paint'.[136] El Greco had of course been active in Venice and was here echoing Venetian opinion. Among painters in that city in the late sixteenth century the practice of 'drawing' sketches in oils became a very standard one. The Venetian Marcantonio Bassetti, working in Rome in the early years of the seventeenth century, described how his 'academy' there, which used brush and 'colori' to make studies from the life, was seen by his Roman friends to be very much 'alla veneziana', but they agreed with him that 'inasmuch as you draw, you also paint'.[137]

Federigo Barocci, pastel study for the head of St Francis in the *Perdono di Assisi*. (pl. 96). (100)

8 · The Peacock's Tail

*Colour indicators · Leonardo on alchemy · Alchemical gendering in Jan van Eyck
Alchemy in the Sistine Chapel · Spiritual metaphors in metallurgy*

Pale, and Black, wyth falce Citrine, unparfyt Whyte & Red,
Pekocks fethers in color gay, the Raynbow whych shall overgoe
The spottyd Panther wyth the Lyon greene, the Crowys byll bloe as lede;
These shall appere before the parfyt Whyte, & many other moe
Colors, and after the parfyt Whyt, Grey, and falce Citrine also:
And after all thys shall appere the blod Red invaryable,
Then hast thou a Medcyn of the thyrd order of hys owne kynde Multyplycable.[1]

THIS BUNDLE of colour-images from a fifteenth-century poem by Sir George Ripley indicates one area of experience where a precise identification of colours was always indispensable: in the practice of alchemy, for from the earliest times in Hellenistic Egypt, it was closely intertwined with colour-technology. Alchemy began, it seems, with the many changes in the superficial appearance of metals and dyes in their working, that is, with technology – although modern studies of the earliest literature of this technology (the collections of recipes in papyri at Stockholm and Leyden) have suggested that even at this stage much of it was ideal desk-exercise rather than practical laboratory experiment.[2] The notion of alchemy as charlatanry has persisted, even among those historians of science who have seen in it the prelude to modern chemistry; one of the more entertaining attacks on alchemy by such a historian is an essay by George Sarton, 'Ancient Alchemy and Abstract Art', in which both are seen as 'a treasure of nonsense available to every irrational endeavour'.[3] Nowadays we might be inclined to substitute economists for abstract artists and invoke the occult power of the market.

When in the twelfth century Hellenistic alchemy reached the Latin West, largely through translations of Arabic versions,[4] it was not at first looked upon with any suspicion; indeed many of its concepts, based as they were on Aristotelian categories such as the four elements, were in no way unorthodox. As early as the tenth century the bishop-artist Saint Bernward of Hildesheim, who had some reputation as an alchemist, had made a pair of large candlesticks that an inscription describes as made without gold or silver, although modern analysis has shown them to be largely silver-gilt.[5] But the technological hubris of the early experimenters is well exemplified in the thirteenth century by Roger Bacon's *Opus Tertium*, where he stated categorically that 'Alchemy is operative and practical; it teaches how to make noble metals and colours and many other things better and more abundantly by artifice than they are made by nature.'[6] It was this sort of attitude which brought upon Bacon the censure of the Church. The reference to colours is crucial, since one of the most ancient examples of the manufactured pigment was artificial vermilion made from sulphur (fire) and mercury (water), two substances considered to be the basic components of all metals.[7] The making of vermilion may help us to understand why gold was equated with red in the alchemical process.[8]

The arrogance of the alchemists in the face of nature, coupled with their usually self-serving concentration on the most precious metals and dyes, led them increasingly, during the course of the thirteenth century, to be outlawed by the Church. In response they developed a far more hermetic approach to their art: they plundered both the metaphorical language of Christianity and the specialized terminology of heraldry in order to shroud their operations in mystery; they fell into the secretive habit of foisting their literature onto respected religious and scientific authorities such as St Thomas Aquinas and Albertus Magnus.[9] This spiritualization of alchemy in the later Middle Ages has made the practice of great interest to modern psychologists in search of archetypal imagery, notably the school of Jung, several of whose publications still provide the fullest overview of the later alchemical tradition.[10] It also offers an insight into the attraction of alchemy to many artists, from Bernward of Hildesheim in the tenth century to Marcel Duchamp, Marc Chagall and Max Beckmann in the twentieth.[11]

In our context, the great fascination in alchemy, however, was that its adepts daily held in their hands the materials for making the colour-changes which were essential to completing the alchemical Great Work, the Philosophers' Stone which could transmute base metals into gold. As early as the thirteenth century it was recognized that workers with the materials of nature could be divided into those who, like painters and sculptors, generated extrinsic forms because they dealt with secondary qualities such as colour, and those like physicians and agriculturalists, who generated the forms of nature from the inside by acting on the four primary qualities, hot, cold, wet and dry.[12] But the process of transformation could still be monitored only by observing changes in surface appearance, which were largely changes in colour. I have already shown how in the manufacture of stained glass and the dyeing of cloth, colour-changes in the course of the same lengthy process could be exploited for the production of different coloured materials; conversely, in the seventeenth century the chemist Robert Boyle's development of standard colour-indicators for acids and alkalis (for example, our litmus paper) was able to draw on the experience of colour-technologists in the arts.[13]

From the earliest times a colour-sequence was seen to be essential to understanding transmutation but, as we should by now expect, the establishing of such a sequence was not a straightforward matter. The oldest version, in writings attributed to the Gnostic Zosimus, of the third or fourth century AD, started with black and proceeded through white to yellow and violet, stages which were given the names *melanosis* (blackening), *leukosis* (whitening), *xanthosis* (yellowing) and *iosis* (transforming to violet).[14] In the Latin alchemical tradition yellow was dropped and the final stage was changed from violet (originally representing purple?) to red. The sequence also became far more complicated and by the fourteenth century had embraced further hues and more indeterminate terms such as grey and the 'rainbow' or 'peacock's tail', which was applied to the shimmering irridescent surface of the heating metal. Thus a fourteenth-century treatise by Simeon of Cologne reported black as the putrefaction of the base metal; followed by red, but not the 'true red' because it turns yellow; then green 'which is its soul' (*anima*); then peacock-colour ('know that almost all colours, which today prevail in the world and which may be devised, appear before the white'); then 'true white' in which red is hidden, but between true white and true red is a certain ash-grey colour, which is not to be despised; and finally the 'crowned king, red' (*rex diademate rubeo*).[15] The validity of these observations and categories is not in question here, although they survived in the same form until the development of modern chemistry in the eighteenth century.[16] What is more interesting in the colours of transmutation is their falling into a dynamic series which might give insights into colour-relationships and that, in a particularly vivid way, they represented colours inherent in black or white. As Simeon of Cologne put it: 'know that white is hidden in blackness'.

The dynamic of colour-change could issue in a picture of colour as in a natural sequence, like that of the rainbow-spectrum: already in the thirteenth century it was suggested that this sequence might be visualized as a circle. Albertus Magnus wrote of the metals that, since they are similar in essence and differ only in their form, 'one may pass easily from one to another, following a circle'.[17] In the sixteenth century a follower of Paracelsus, the most important alchemical writer of the Renaissance, devised what is perhaps the first colour-diagram based on a segmented circle: Hieronymus Reusner's image of the White (silver) Queen as an 'imperfect thing' serves as a prelude to the perfection of the Red (gold) King:

105

> What made me white, that makes me red. The white and the red come out of the same root. This thing transforms [*verkehrt*] a thousand parts of quicksilver into the purest, clearest silver ... Now, my dearest, you have learned how to make the white, and it is time to talk of the red. But if you do not make the white first you cannot make the true red happen or become, since none can go from the first to the third without its happening through the other, and you cannot go from the black to the yellow except through the white alone because the yellow is made up of much white and a proportion of the purest black; thus whiten or make white the black and make the white red, and you have mastery.[18]

Implicit in this movement is the notion that the 'root' of all the colours is the same; here the most potent metaphor was the peacock's tail which, like the rainbow, represented the totality of colours. We saw how the early 'shot' fabrics of Hellenistic Egypt were described in terms of the peacock and in the early

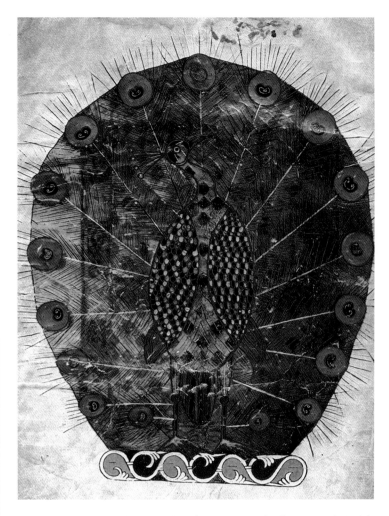

The Peacock, symbol of immortality, from Gregory the Great, *Moralia in Job*, written and illuminated by the Spanish monk Florentius in 945. (101)

Christian church the bird was frequently depicted on textiles as well as in sculpture and mosaic because it was a symbol of incorruptibility and immortality, shedding and renewing its magnificent tail-feathers every year. A seventh-century Byzantine writer underlined the physical beauty of the bird's varied colouring:

> How could anyone who see the peacock not be amazed at the gold interwoven with sapphire, at the purple and emerald-green feathers, at the composition of the colors of many patterns, all mingled together but not confused with one another? ... Once again, whence comes the beautiful peacock? The bird is refulgent and star-like in aspect, clad in purple plumage, because of which, boastful and arrogant in its appearance, it streams alone through all of the other birds. This purple has twined patterns on the bird without its tail, and has mixed a plentiful stream of many colors.[19]

One of the fullest accounts of the 'peacock's tail' stage of the alchemical process is in an alchemical notebook of Newton, in which he described how he mixed a 'star regulus' of antimony, prepared with iron, silver, common mercury and a little gold; this, by a lengthy and complicated process, would produce a mercury capable of dissolving all metals, especially gold.

I know whereof I write, for I have in the fire manifold glasses with gold and this mercury. For they grow in these glasses in the form of a tree, and by a continued circulation [analogous to the peacock's semi-circular tail] the trees are dissolved again with the work into new mercury. I have such a vessel in the fire with gold thus dissolved, where the gold was visibly not dissolved through a corrosive of atoms, but extrinsically and intrinsically into a mercury as living and mobile as any mercury found in the world. For it makes gold begin to swell, to be swollen, and to putrefy, and also to spring forth into sprouts and branches, changing colours daily, the appearances of which fascinate me every day.[20]

Among the Gnostics of the second century AD, so much of whose thought fed into the theory of alchemy, the idea of such an array of peacock colours emerging from a single white egg was the supreme mystery, analogous to God's bringing out the many from the one.[21] We may recall that in a contemporary Coptic Gospel, his son achieved the reverse miracle, by extracting one colour from the many (*see* p. 64). The presence of all colours *in potentia* in white was expressed perhaps most clearly in one of the many treatises attributed to Albertus Magnus and published in an extensive seventeenth-century anthology of alchemical texts:

> All colours that can be conceived by men in the world appear there [in white] and then they will be fixed and complete the Work in a single colour, that is the white, and in that all colours come together. The whitening is namely the beginning and the strength and will not be changed further into various colours, except the red, in which the final goal lies. The becoming grey however appears in the blue- and red-making and is not called a colour.[22]

Since Newton acquired this text in 1669, during the early stages of his work on the nature of colours, it may not be too fanciful to suggest that his crucial and revolutionary concept of the presence of all colours in white light, independently of the modification of this light by darkness (as earlier theories had required), owed something to his wide experience of the theory and practice of alchemy.[23]

Leonardo on alchemy

In one of the earliest novels about the life of an artist, the German Romantic writer Ludwig Tieck sent his hero, Franz Sternbald, to Florence where he met the sculptor friend of Leonardo da Vinci, Giovan Francesco Rustici. Rustici was also an alchemist and in conversation with him the young Sternbald mused that everything must needs be transformed into gold in the hands of the artist, so why not metals?[24] We should not project Tieck's high Romantic view of the artist's calling back into the period he was describing, although indeed it had some of its origins there; we should also remember that Leonardo was one of the most outspoken critics of alchemy in the Renaissance. Leonardo's attack depended on a fervent belief in the supremacy of nature which,

> is concerned with the production of elementary things. But man from these elementary things produces an infinite number of compounds; although he is unable to create any element except another life like himself – that is, in his children.

Old alchemists will be my witnesses, who have never either by chance or by experiment succeeded in creating the smallest element which can be created by nature; however the creators of compounds deserve unmeasured praise for the usefulness of the things invented for the use of men, and would deserve it even more if they had not been the inventors of noxious things like poisons and other similar things which destroy life or mind ... Moreover, by much study and experiment they are seeking to create not the meanest of Nature's products, but the most excellent, namely gold, true son of the sun, inasmuch as of all created things it has most resemblance to the sun ... And if gross avarice must drive you into such error, why do you not go to the mines where Nature produces such gold, and there become her disciple? She will in faith cure you of your folly, showing you that nothing which you use in your furnace will be among any of the things which she uses in order to produce this gold. Here there is no quicksilver, no sulphur of any kind, no fire or other heat than that of Nature giving life to our world; and she will show you the veins of the gold spreading through the lapis or ultramarine blue, whose colour is unaffected by the power of the fire.

> And examine well this ramification of the gold and you will see that the extremities are continuously expanding in slow movement, transmuting into gold whatever they touch; and note that therein is a living organism which it is not in your power to produce.[25]

It was of little importance to Leonardo in this fanciful account that he had never seen a vein of lapis lazuli and that the 'gold' he described here was the particles of iron pyrites which are usually found mingled with the stone.

Leonardo's polemic has been dated to about 1508 so it is perhaps no accident that during a period spent in Florence at this time he was lodging with Rustici, who was soon to devote a good deal of time, as Vasari put it, 'trying to congeal mercury', that is, practising alchemy.[26] Among Leonardo's notes on metallurgy are a recipe for a 'varnish' (?patina) and an account of a mould expressed in alchemical language which may well relate to his friendship with the sculptor. One of them reads:

> The mould [*sagoma*] may be of Venus (copper), or of Jupiter (tin) and Saturn (lead), and frequently thrown back into its mother's lap. And it should be worked with fine [ ] and what is moulded should be of Venus and Jupiter impasted over Venus. But first you should try Venus and Mercury mixed with Jupiter and make sure the Mercury disperses. Then fold them well in together so that Venus and Jupiter shall be allied as thinly as possible.[27]

Although in these recipes Leonardo's use of a specialist language and a hermetic style shows that he had access to alchemical sources, it would be unrealistic to assume that alchemical ideas were the preserve of specialists at this time. Vasari records, for example, how the painter went to Rome in 1513 to see the new Medici Pope, Leo X, who was a devotee of alchemy and other occult sciences, and for whom he made some amusing toys.[28] The Medici had a long record of sharing these interests, going back at least to Cosimo il Vecchio, for whom Marsilio Ficino made a translation of a work attributed to the ancient Magus Hermes Trismegistus and who was himself the author of an alchemical treatise.[29] Martin Schaffner's homely

104 vision of the Heavenly Universe is a cheerful reminder that the alchemical notion of occult correspondences among planets, elements, humours, seasons, colours and so on[30] was a commonplace of aristocratic and even bourgeois Europe by the early sixteenth century. For the remainder of this chapter I shall look at a number of ways in which it was manifested in a quite unspecialized form in the work of some artists whose connections with alchemy are well documented. The link is essentially between a concern for technical experiment and an understanding of the symbolic content of alchemical ideas.

Alchemical gendering in Jan van Eyck

The earliest written account of the art of Jan van Eyck to have come down to us is that of 1456 by the Italian humanist Bartolomeo Fazio, historian and secretary to Alfonso V of Naples. In praising 'the leading painter of our time', Fazio emphasized, predictably perhaps for a scholar, that he was not unlettered since Eyck was familiar with geometry and 'is thought to have discovered many things about the properties of colours recorded by the ancients, and learned by him from reading Pliny and other authors'.[31] The notion of an artist learned in the theory of his craft seems convincing, although we know little or nothing of the 'authors' who might have come his way. But the collection of technical manuscripts gathered together by the French scholar Jehan le Begue in 1431 may give us some idea of what was known in Van Eyck's time in the north. Some of the recipes in Le Begue's collection, in a manuscript dated 1409, used the names of planets to refer to metals, as we have seen in Leonardo, and the compiler provided a key, lest they should not be understood by the layman.[32]

Whatever the technical literature (apart from Pliny) that Van Eyck consulted, the clearest evidence of his familiarity with the metaphysics of the alchemists is in his portrait *Giovanni Arnolfini and Giovanna Cenami*. To a painting that has been the subject of numerous iconographical analyses I hesitate to add yet another reading.[33] But it seems to me that any understanding of its symbolism must depend upon its visual coherence, which is based on its stability of format, solemnity of mood and symmetry of composition. The two protagonists stand on either side of a central axis, established at the top of the picture by the round mirror and at the bottom by the little dog (?Fido); their respective attributes are also carefully arranged on either side. Giovanni Arnolfini (if it be he) has the outdoor light through the window on his side, the light from the Paradise-garden 'eastward in Eden', since we can see the orange-trees beyond and their fruit on ledge and chest.[34] On her side Giovanna Cenami (if it be she) has domesticity: the bedroom and the brush with which it is swept and dusted hanging from the carved figure of a female saint overcoming a dragon on the chair.[35] Both husband and wife – for this is a marriage-portrait – have jewelry. Giovanni has a string of amber beads hanging by the mirror,[36] Giovanna a double necklace of pearls. This jewelry is perhaps the best introduction to the nature of a third level of interpretation in Van Eyck's painting, besides its status as a realistic picture of the betrothed in their home and its role as representing a sacrament, by the inclusion of the Passion of Christ in the scenes around the central mirror.[37] The third,

perhaps most fundamental, level concerns the gendering of the elements and the presentation of the mysterious union of fire and water.

In a very lengthy account of amber in the *Natural History* (XXXVII, xi, 36–51), to which Fazio referred, Pliny reported that the Greeks called it *electron*, from their term for the sun, *Elector*, 'the shining one'; he went on to cite the opinion of a Greek writer, Nicias, that it was produced by moisture from the sun's rays in the evening and washed westwards by the ocean to the shores of Germany. Pliny would have none of this, arguing rightly that amber was a hardened pine-resin, but he did agree about the association with fire, since rubbing brought out its 'hot spirit' (*caloris anima*), which had the power to attract, and it was very easy for it to catch fire. He also reported the opinions of one Callistratus that when taken powdered as a medicine or carried as an amulet amber served to remedy attacks of madness (*lymphationes*, from *lympha*, 'water') and problems with the urine – probably by sympathy with the clear and the yellow. One variety, *chryselectrum* or 'gold-amber', said Callistratus, was highly inflammable but could cure fevers when worn as an amulet or necklace, and if powdered and mixed with other substances, including honey, and a resin familiar to painters, mastic, could cure affections of the stomach and ears and weak sight. The best amber, Pliny held, was the dull yellow (*fulvus*) variety, transparent but not too fiery: 'not a fiery glow, but a mere suggestion of it, is what we admire in amber'. Best of all was that sort which looked most like white Falernian wine, quite transparent and glowing gently. This seems to correspond very well with what we see in Van Eyck's picture, where the transparent beads pick up and concentrate the light from the window; it establishes their identity as emblematic of heat and light.

Pliny was far less circumstantial about pearls (IX, liv, 107–9), although he retold a number of anecdotes about their prodigious value in the Roman world. He accepted the view that pearls are produced in oysters filled with a 'dewy pregnancy' and that their colour depends upon the complexion of the sky. Since sunlight is apt to give them an unpleasant reddish tan, deep-sea pearls are the most brilliant because they are out of reach of the sun's rays.[38] Thus the pearl is emblematic of water.

The idea of the marriage of man and wife as a marriage of fire and water takes us to what may have been the most important key to the elemental reading of the Arnolfini marriage-portrait: its painted frame of matt gilt with marbled shutters, which seems to have been destroyed by fire in the eighteenth century. This frame was decorated not only with the arms of an early owner, Don Diego de Guevara, but also, according to an inventory of 1700, with a verse of Ovid which stated how the man and the woman in the painting 'were linked to each other'.[39] The frequent use of often long and complicated inscriptions on Van Eyck's surviving frames makes it more than probable that this one was original and that it was essential to the understanding of the scene. A vague reference to Ovid may be a rather slender peg on which to hang an interpretation, but there are in Ovid at least two accounts of 'marriage' which would fit the theme rather well. The first is in that most popular of his poems in the later Middle Ages, the *Metamorphoses* (I, 430–3):

Quippe ubi temperiem sumpsere umorque calorque,
Concipiunt, et ab his oriuntur cuncta duobus,
Cumque sit ignis aquae pugnax, vapor umidus omnes
Res creat, et discors concordia fetibus apta est.

('For when moisture and heat unite, life is conceived, and from these two sources all living things spring. And, though fire and water are naturally at enmity, still heat and moisture produce all things, and this inharmonious harmony is fitted to the growth of life.' [trans. Miller]). In his verse treatise on Roman religious festivals, the *Fasti* (*Festival Calendar* IV, 785–90), Ovid applied this scientific view of the creation to the ritual of Roman marriage, in which the couple touched fire and water on the threshold of their new home:

An, quia cunctarum contraria semina rerum
Sunt duo discordes, ignis et unda, dei,
Iunxerunt elementa patres aptumque putarunt
Ignibus et sparsa tangere corpus aquae?
An, quod in his vitae causa est, haec perdidit exul,
His nova fit coniunx, haec duo magna putant?

('Are we to suppose that, because all things are composed of opposite principles, fire and water, – those two discordant deities – therefore our fathers did conjoin these elements and thought meet to touch the body with fire and sprinkled water? Or did they deem these two important because they contain the source of life, the exile loses the use of them, and by them the bride is made a wife?' [trans Frazer])[40] Either or both these quotations, extracted or combined, could have provided an appropriate epigraph for Van Eyck's picture.

As it happens, Ovid's *Metamorphoses* was cited as an important repository of alchemical lore in one of the several fourteenth-century attempts to rationalize and spiritualize alchemy, the *Pretiosa Margarita Novella* of Petrus Bonus of Ferrara, written about 1330.[41] A chapter of this treatise is devoted to the alchemical notion of male and female and to the generative powers of cold and wet in conjunction with hot and dry.[42] Besides Ovid and Virgil, Moses, David and Solomon were cited as alchemical authorities, as was St John the Evangelist who, according to Bonus, completed the unfinished alchemical writings of Plato, for alchemy was 'above nature, and is divine'. Bonus's book was, in effect, a sustained attempt to reconcile alchemy with Christianity, since God is the prime alchemist and his son the Philosophers' Stone itself: Bonus cited the Persian writer al-Razi (Rhazes) that heat and dryness destroy cold and wetness 'by divine reason'.[43] The identification of Christ as the Stone and of the cycle of his Passion as the process of the Great Work gives a new force to the ten scenes around the mirror in Van Eyck's picture, from his night in the Garden of Gethsemane at the bottom to his Crucifixion at the top and down again to the Resurrection. The mirror, like the Great Work, is a *speculum humanae salvationis*.[44]

It is important to emphasize that the imagery of alchemy in the Arnolfini portrait was in no way unorthodox or esoteric: it was in tune with that late medieval tendency in alchemy to legitimize the art by assimilating it to the prevailing scientific and religious systems. Van Eyck would have been especially implicated because of his search for new painterly materials;

what is most immediately striking about its effect in his picture is not the detailed use of imagery but the effect on his colour.

Giovanni Arnolfini, as befits a merchant of Lucca, is wearing a black beaver hat and a black dress, stockings and shoes: the sign, according to Courtois (Sicily Herald), of dignity and loyalty in merchants.[45] Over this sombre dress he wears a fur-trimmed deep-purple surcoat, which seems, even in its present rather degraded state, to glow with some inner fire. This has been identified with the Italian *chlamys* (purple cloak) and *crosina* (fur cloak) prescribed for marriage ceremonies.[46] But purple, of course, had its own significance: Courtois referred it to 'abundance of goods', citing Christ's purple robe preserved at Argenteuil, which grew as he did. Following Isidore of Seville, Courtois also characterized purple as 'purity and light', 'for it grows naturally in those countries of the world which the sun illuminates most'. The noblest scarlet is dyed purple and violet as well as red, he said; and it may well be that it is fine scarlet of Ghent that Arnolfini is wearing in his house in neighbouring Bruges. It was a colour between red and black but closer to red; it was thus, like amber, a sign of light and heat.

Giovanna Cenami wears a blue dress covered with a green cloak lined with white fur. Blue, according to Courtois, stood for loyalty, friendship, nourishment and childhood, as well as for a sanguine temperament; it is a colour between water and air but closer to air than to water. As is appropriate to Van Eyck's purpose, green shows the youthful beauties of spring in nature; it was also, says Courtois, created by heat in matter half-way between moist and dry but closer to moist. Among the Seven Sacraments, he added, it represented the Sacrament of Marriage.[48] Thus Van Eyck, the Arnolfinis and any well-informed fifteenth-century spectator will have been able to extract some very rich resonances even from the paired colours of the costumes in this painting. The overall impression must have been that a bourgeois marriage was also, on an elemental level, a coming-together of water and fire.[49] The painter and his subjects must have been disappointed that such an over-determined union was not, in the event, to be productive of children;[50] but the merchant Arnolfini (for whom, incidentally, alchemy was prohibited[51]) had ways at least of multiplying gold.

Alchemy in the Sistine Chapel

Van Eyck's adoption of alchemical notions in the Arnolfini portrait was, insofar as such a comprehensive philosophy could be casual, distinctly understated. In Italy during the Renaissance, on the other hand, there were artists who made no secret of their aspiration towards the most material rewards of the alchemical quest. One such was the Florentine Cosimo Rosselli, a painter of mediocre talents called to high things. In his essentially hostile biography Vasari mentioned that Rosselli spent his all in pursuit of alchemy, with the usual lack of success,[52] but another story, which became one of the most famous in the whole of art-historical writing in Italy, suggests that some aspects of Rosselli's alchemical outlook did indeed survive to make him a kind of dubious fortune.

Vasari described how the painter and his assistants Piero di Cosimo, Ghirlandaio, Botticelli and Perugino were commis-

Cosimo Rosselli was derided for lavishing precious pigments and even gold on the frescoes commissioned for the Sistine Chapel (*c.* 1481). That he did so may reflect his interest in alchemy, for Moses (seen here condemning the merely material gold of the Golden Calf) was widely regarded during the Middle Ages and the Renaissance as a great alchemist. (102)

102

sioned in 1481 by Pope Sixtus IV to decorate the walls of his new chapel in the Vatican with ten scenes from the Life of Moses and the Life of Christ. Rosselli was given three scenes but because of Ghirlandaio's absence in Florence during 1482 he took on a fourth, making him the most employed artist of the group. The surviving contract for this work is unusual in that it stipulates only that the murals should be painted 'very diligently and truly and as well as they and any of their assistants can do it and as it was begun'.[53] There was no reference to materials, but Vasari wrote that the Pope was said to have proposed a prize for what he judged to be the best work, and

> Cosimo, feeling himself to be weak in invention and drawing, tried to hide his defect by covering the work with the finest ultramarine blues and other bright colours, and by highlighting his subject with much gold, so that there was neither tree nor grass, nor drapery nor cloud that was not highlighted, believing that the Pope, who understood little of this art, would thus award him the prize . . .

When the work was unveiled, the others laughed at it, but the joke was finally on them,

> because those colours, as Cosimo had imagined, immediately so dazzled the eyes of the Pope, who did not understand much about such things, although he delighted greatly in them, that he thought Cosimo had done much better than all the others. And so, when he had awarded the prize to him, he ordered the others to cover their pictures with the best blues that they could find, and to touch them up with gold, so that they should be similar to Cosimo's both in colouring and in richness.[54]

There are some difficulties about accepting this scathing anecdote at face-value, since it is clear that the other painters did not ruin their scenes with overpainting as Vasari claimed. Ghirlandaio's *Calling of Peter and Andrew*, for example, exhibits very little gold at all, although it might have been that he did not come back from Florence to finish it. Expensive gilded

decorations were, in any case, a sort of Vatican convention: they were used by Fra Angelico for his frescoes in the Chapel of Nicholas V in the 1440s, and in the 1490s they were even more conspicuous in the gilt relief of Pinturicchio's decorations for the Borgia apartments, designed to appeal, as Vasari again complained, to people who understood little of that art.[55] Rosselli had already used a good deal of bright colour and gold in his two or three figures of the Popes between the windows of the Sistine Chapel and it has been proposed that Sixtus was so pleased with these that he took Cosimo away from that task and gave him the lion's share of the major new series underneath.[56]

What seems clear is that the two Rosselli subjects in which an unusual pairing of subjects suggests the direct intervention of Sixtus in the programme, the *Moses Giving the Law* and the *Sermon on the Mount*, are those which are most smothered with the painter's most extravagant colours.[57] This is particularly so in the Moses who, unusually, turns his back on the worship of the Golden Calf. We have already encountered Moses the alchemist and a few years before this commission Marsilio Ficino had restated this view in his *De Christiana Religione* (1474), arguing that he was to be identified with Hermes Trismegistus.[58] Rosselli was thus exemplifying the late medieval aspiration to Christianize the Great Work by showing how Moses rejected the vulgar worship of material gold and turned towards the spiritual gold of revelation. This argument was reinforced by Cosimo's equally unusual treatment of the *Last Supper* (or *The Institution of the Eucharist*), where the table is laden not with food but with a single golden chalice. Behind Christ are represented the scenes of his Passion. It was a message which Rosselli thought – mistakenly as it turned out – to underline by the prolific use of the most valuable pigments.

The earliest account of the new paintings in the Sistine Chapel – a conventional eulogy by a humanist – spoke simply of the 'pleasant and appropriate' colours (*colores . . . suaves et appositi*) but it may have been written before Rosselli's most extravagant scene of the *Golden Calf* had been completed.[59] When Michelangelo came to re-paint the ceiling of the chapel from 1508 to 1512, taking his cue for the tonality of his own work from the fifteenth-century frescoes underneath, he was clearly expected by Pope Julius II to complete his work with gold and ultramarine (applied on top of the fresco in *secco*) in the canonical papal way. Michelangelo's follower and biographer, Condivi, who also tells us that the master ground his own colours for the work, recorded a typical conversation between the artist and the patron:

The incandescent vision of Christ as embodied light may well depend on observations made by Grünewald during the processing of metals, for he was probably engaged in the manufacture of colours. The blue-green fringe of the fiery nimbus is perhaps the earliest representation of a negative after-image. The robe of vermilion, the manufactured red whose components of mercury and sulphur were thought to constitute all metals, may identify Christ alchemically as the 'Red King', the Philosophers' Stone.

103 MATTHIAS GRÜNEWALD, *The Resurrection*, Isenheim Altar, *c.* 1515 (detail)

104

104 MARTIN SCHAFFNER, *The Heavenly Universe*, wooden table-top, 1533
105 *The White Rose*, from H. REUSNER, (ed.) *Pandora: Das ist die edelst Gab Gottes*, c. 1550
106 JAN VAN EYCK, *Giovanni Arnolfini and Giovanna Cenami (The Arnolfini Marriage)*, 1434

Colour and power

The hidden structures which the
Renaissance philosophers detected in the
world included assumptions about colour.
Schaffner (**104**) makes this clear in his poems
on the correspondences of the 'sevens': planets,
liberal arts, metals, virtues and days of the
week, on this table-top made for a Strasbourg
goldsmith. Thus Venus corresponds with
green, music, copper, Friday and obedience.
Van Eyck (**106**) shows in the colours worn by
his couple at their betrothal, deep purple and
green, as well as by their jewels, that they
partake of the elemental union of fire and
water. The power of Alchemy was especially
manifested by colour: Reusner's diagram of
the penultimate phase of the Great Work of
transmuting base metals into gold (**105**) shows
the White Queen, prelude to the arrival of the
Red King, and includes a segmented half-
circle, signalling the alchemical progression
from black to red through white.

105

106

It [the ceiling] still lacked the final touches of ultramarine *a secco*, and the gold in some places, so that it should seem richer. Julius . . . wanted Michelangelo to put them in, but he, considering the trouble he would have had setting up the scaffolding, replied that what was missing was not important. 'You still need to re-touch with gold', retorted the Pope, to which Michelangelo responded as familiarly as he was used to with his Holiness: 'I don't see that men wore gold [then]'. And the Pope: 'It will be mean [*povera*]'. 'Those that are painted here', he replied, 'were also poor.' And they joked together, and so it remained as it was.

Condivi added that Michelangelo had 3,000 ducats for the work, of which he spent only 20 to 25 on colours.[60]

Vasari re-told this story in the second version of his *Life of Michelangelo* (1568) but added a reminiscence of the affair of Sixtus IV and Rosselli, specifying that it was certain backgrounds (*campi*), draperies and skies (*arie*) which were to be retouched with blue and gold.[61] I showed in the last chapter how careful Michelangelo was to get the best blues at the beginning of the work, and the recent cleaning has shown his use of gold in the fictive bronze medallions and other parts of the lunettes,[62] so that his reputation as a despiser of such display must be seriously qualified.

Whatever the rationale of Rosselli's handling of colour in the Sistine Chapel, Vasari's attack on it meant that it was handed down as a prime example of the ignorance of patrons. In Venice Lodovico Dolce used the story to put down those who thought they were praising Titian by saying that he 'coloured well' (*tinge bene*): were that the case, many women would be his equals; the greatest merit of painting was in the disposition of forms and the imitation of nature, in which, said Dolce, Titian excelled.[63] In the Baroque period, too, Vasari's story was introduced by the painter Pietro da Cortona into a discussion of delight to show that the sensual pleasure of the eye can dazzle the light of reason; later on, in the eighteenth century, when facility of handling had again become a requirement in Italy, Rosselli's absurdities were used to point the moral that over-working a painting would ruin it.[64] But nowhere was there any sense that subject-matter and style of colouring might be one.

Spiritual metaphors in metallurgy

Unlike Van Eyck, Rosselli was no technical innovator but access to alchemical attitudes and imagery through technical experimentation was not an uncommon experience among Renaissance artists. Besides oil painting, which can no longer be regarded as a peculiarly Renaissance development, the most important innovations in visual expression were in printmaking, especially etching, which developed in Germany and Italy in the early years of the sixteenth century. The artist who most of all brought a free style of etching into the repertory of

Italian art was Parmigianino, of whom Vasari reported that towards the end of his life,

> having begun to study alchemical matters, he abandoned pictorial matters entirely, thinking to make a quick fortune by congealing mercury . . . he wasted the whole day in moving bits of coal, logs and glass retorts about, and other such games . . . and thus, little by little he burned himself out with his stoves . . . and from being refined and gentle he became, with his unkempt beard and long hair, almost a wild man and unlike what he had been . . . melancholy and strange.[65]

It is perhaps no accident that one of Parmigianino's etchings, the *Woman Seated on the Ground*, is a figure of Melancholy based *109* ultimately on Dürer's great engraving of 1514, whose complex *110* imagery is almost an anthology of alchemical ideas about the structure of matter and the role of time.[66] Black melancholy was the lot of the alchemist at the beginning of his quest, as illumination was its final goal.

The heating crucible to the left of Dürer's image is the clearest sign of its alchemical context, just as in a drawing by the northern Italian artist Giulio Campagnola the urn accompany- *108* ing the two philosophers suggests the same complex of ideas.[67] Dürer and Campagnola were among the first printmakers to etch plates with acids;[68] Campagnola was a learned artist[69] in the circle of the poet Giovanni Aurelio Augurelli, whose alchemical poem, *Chrysopoeia* of 1515, dedicated to Pope Leo X, was one of the more popular productions of its type in the sixteenth century. What is remarkable about Augurelli's approach to alchemy is that, in the tradition of pastoral poetry in northern Italy, he linked the search for the Philosophers' Stone with the landscape that provided its raw materials. In Book III of his poem, for example, he recommended that fireproof crucibles should be made from the white clay of the Euganean Hills. He also spoke of the landscape-painting that could be produced with the colours the landscape provided, which brought him directly into relation with the practice of Campagnola and Giorgione.[71] Augurelli brought a quite new emphasis to alchemical writing, in particular the belief that the natural world and the seasons were the framework of the alchemist's enterprise: spring was the season when the laboratory should be equipped to commence the Great Work.

It was this emphasis on the cosmic significance of alchemy, as harnessing all the forces of nature, that also informed Parmigianino's use of alchemical imagery. *The Madonna of the Rose* offers at first sight a picture of such remarkable sensuality *107* that in the eighteenth century it was thought to have begun as a *Venus and Cupid*.[72] It was originally painted for the journalist Pietro Aretino, and it is in his popular devotional writings that we find the conceptions of Christ and his Mother which link this picture to the newer interpretations of the Great Work.[73] In the present context it is important that at every turn in the life of Christ, Aretino pointed to the cosmic implications of Christian events. After the Annunciation Mary was filled with the light of the high sun, glowing with it like a lamp in an alabaster vase; Joseph proclaimed the coming of 'the precious stone, foreseen by the Patriarchs', on which was engraved without art the image of a King; at Christ's birth the ice melted and the desert places of the world were covered with spring green, and when

---

Is there alchemical imagery too in Parmigianino's *Madonna*? The infant Christ holds the red rose in his role as the Red King.

107 PARMIGIANINO, *The Madonna of the Rose*, 1528/30

Giulio Campagnola's mysterious landscape drawing of *c.* 1510 may be hinting (with the crucible-like urn) that the materials of alchemical transformation were available in the countryside of the Veneto. (108)

he returned after seven years in Egypt the green also vanished, 'for the parting of Christ turned it to autumn'. In short, 'when Christ was being born, living, dying and being resurrected, the heavens, the earth and the abyss all felt it'.[74] Thus the globe on which Christ rests in Parmigianino's picture is directly express-ive of his cosmic role, and the red rose, too, plays a part in this imagery: at Gethsemane that part of the sky to which Christ's prayer rose became so serene that 'it was revealed like red roses in a glass vase'; at the Ascension dawn let fall 'the most beautiful, the sweetest and the most coloured roses she had ever gathered from her sacred places'.[75] When Christ died on the cross,

> behold how the earth trembled and behold how the rocks were split asunder, behold how the winds moaned, behold the veil of the Temple rent, the mountains clashing together, the sun obscured, the air sullied. The seas roll back, the rivers stop in their course, the lakes overflow, the shores rage with storms. The leaves turn yellow, birds no longer fly, fish swim nor game run; the herds lose their pasture and the flocks their watering; the elements were confounded together and seemed to want to return to their primal state . . .

Similarly, when Christ appeared again to the Apostles, he was 'the dawn of the dawn, the day of the days and the sun of the sun'.[76]

None of these images was entirely new – the rose held by Christ in Parmigianino's painting, for example, had had a long history in Christian iconography, as symbolizing his Passion – but their emphasis in Aretino's popular book suggests how much a wide public in northern Italy was prepared to read the Christian story in terms of the movement of the natural world, that is, in terms coloured by alchemical ideas. In the sixteenth century even the medieval romance the *Roman de la Rose* was being given a specifically alchemical gloss.[77] The brilliant blood-red coral bracelet around Christ's wrist also had a long history in ancient and medieval thought as an amulet warding off all manner of diseases (coral can be seen worn round the neck

of the Christ-child in many fifteenth-century pictures, as a sign of the staunching of blood) but here its proximity to the globe suggests its more universal power to control the tempest.[78]

The Mannerism of Parmigianino and Aretino was simply a reworking of very traditional ideas, presenting them in an elegant and fashionable form. Other artists were able to penetrate more deeply into the experience of alchemy and to bring its processes into the visualization of spiritual experience in a new way. We seem to see this in Grünewald's astonishing vision of the resurrected Christ in the Isenheim Altar where, perhaps for the first time in painting, a human figure is presented as created out of light. The movement of light and heat had, of course, been recognized in the Middle Ages and had formed part of the visionary vocabulary of St Hildegard of Bingen in the twelfth century. In one of the visions recalled in her treatise *Scivias*, for example, she described

> the most serene light (*lux*), and in that light the sapphire-coloured image of a man, who was burning with the gentlest red-glinting fire. And that serene light infused the whole of that reddish fire, and that reddish fire the whole of that serene light, and that serene light and that red-glinting fire the whole image of this man – thus one light in one power . . .

This was a manifestation of the mysterious co-existence and co-extension of the Father (serene light), the Son (sapphire image) and Holy Spirit (red-glinting fire); but with the painterly techniques and visualization at her disposal, Hildegard was able to present these ideas visually only in the form of diagrams.[79]

Grünewald was more fortunate, for not only had he to a high degree the developed representational skills of a Renaissance painter but it now seems clear that he had a considerable experience of metallurgy and chemistry, as a manufacturer of colours. At his death he left a large quantity of pigments, notably artificial colours, which suggests that he was engaged in their manufacture. Among them was the vermilion which appears so dazzlingly in Christ's robe and which was, because of its constituents mercury and sulphur, the golden-red crown of

103

The Blake text image (id 1):

A Memorable Fancy

I was in a Printing house in Hell & saw the method in which knowledge is transmitted from generation to generation.

In the first chamber was a Dragon-Man, clearing away the rubbish from a caves mouth; within, a number of Dragons were hollowing the cave.

In the second chamber was a Viper folding round the rock & the cave, and others adorning it with gold silver and precious stones.

In the third chamber was an Eagle with wings and feathers of air, he caused the inside of the cave to be infinite, around were numbers of Eagle like men, who built palaces in the immense cliffs.

In the fourth chamber were Lions of flaming fire raging around & melting the metals into living fluids.

In the fifth chamber were Unnam'd forms, which cast the metals into the expanse.

There they were reciev'd by Men who occupied the sixth chamber, and took the forms of books & were arranged in libraries.

Alchemy was a natural interest for printmakers working with metals and acids. Parmigianino's etching of a woman seated on the ground echoes the imagery of Albrecht Dürer's complex engraving *Melencholia* (1514), where the heating crucible and rainbow offer the clear suggestion that the travails of alchemy were among its subjects. William Blake's *A Memorable Fancy* (1793) uses the traditional symbolism of alchemy to describe the effects of etching in his 'Printing house in Hell', and equates the chemical action of acids with spiritual cleansing. (109,110,111) the alchemical quest.[80] Grünewald's religious sympathies may well have allowed him to agree with Luther that

> The art of alchemy is really the philosophy of the ancients, which appeals to me very much ... on account of its allegories and secret meanings, which are quite beautiful, such as the resurrection of the dead on the last day. For just as fire in a furnace draws out and separates the best in matter, and releases spirit, life, juice and power into the heavens ... so God will do the same through the Last Judgment: he will sift out, divide and separate the justified from the godless, as if in a fire.[81]

In all the visionary elements in this altarpiece, Grünewald has represented the effects of incandescence: in the nimbus around the risen Christ he has made his red light so intense that it has induced an after-image of blue-green. This is the sort of observation which could only have been made by the painter in a metal-worker's furnace: the unearthly light is in fact earthly but far beyond the experience of most of Grünewald's public.[82]

Grünewald's spiritualization of metallurgy was the highest point in the visual history of alchemy, although there were many finely illustrated alchemical texts in the sixteenth and seventeenth centuries.[83] But in the Romantic period another great artist and visionary re-introduced the dual notion of alchemy as a chemical process and a spiritual quest into the arena of visual art – William Blake. Blake it was who kept an *110* impression of Dürer's *Melencholia* beside his engraving table[84] and there can be no doubt that in the search for a technique in which to print and publish his illuminated books of poems, he looked deeply into the literature of alchemy which, by his time, was very extensive.[85] In one of the earliest of his books, *The Marriage of Heaven and Hell* (1793), Blake related his original method of printing specifically to the search for spiritual purification, in doing so drawing on the terminology of traditional alchemy: 'But first the notion that man has a body distinct from his soul is to be expunged; this I shall do by painting in the infernal method, by corrosives, which in Hell are salutary and medicinal, melting apparent surfaces away, and displaying the infinite which was hid'.[86] How this was to be *111* done Blake showed a little later in his 'Memorable Fancy' of a printing-house in Hell, where in the first chamber a Dragon-Man was clearing away rubbish from the mouth of the cave which houses the press; in the second a viper was adorning the cave with gold, silver and precious stones; in the third an Eagle, with plumage of air 'caused the inside of the cave to be infinite';

in the fourth were 'lions of flaming fire, raging around & melting the metals into living fluids'; in the fifth were unnamed forms casting the metals into the expanse; and finally in the sixth chamber men arranged these metals as books into libraries. Blake's chief source for this imagery seems to have been the seventeenth-century German experimental alchemist Johannes Glauber, whose collected works had been published in English in 1689. For Glauber the Dragon symbolized the corrosives salt and nitre, as well as sulphur, and the eagle and the lion were also acids and fixed salts: 'Whatsoever the acid spirit thereof [*sal ammoniac*], or the Eagle with its sharp claws cannot effect, its fixed salt, or the fiery Lion, will accomplish'.[87] The gold and bejewelled serpent also appears in Blake's *Milton* as the creature of 'dark fires' and may represent the 'rainbow' or 'peacock's tail' phase of the Great Work, although in seventeenth-century sources it could also stand for mercury of arsenic.[88] Blake was describing the progressively refined corrosion of his metal plates in terms of a traditional chemical allegory.

In another 'Memorable Fancy' at the end of the book, Blake presented an angel in conversation with a devil, whose definition of God at first angered the angel but then convinced him, so that he too was transformed into a devil (no bad thing in Blake's view of the relationship between Heaven and Hell). Blake showed the angel receiving the devil's words very much in the same fluid state that Grünewald had given to the angels in his Isenheim Altar: 'The Angel hearing this became almost blue; but mastering himself he grew yellow, & at last white, pink and smiling.' At the end of the Fancy the angel 'stretched out his arms, embracing the flame of fire [i.e. the devil] & he was consumed and arose as Elijah'.[89]

In this chapter I have tried to show that alchemy in the Western world was far from being a purely esoteric subject; that it drew many of its notions and much of its language from the prevailing conception of the structure and value of matter; that it took on a spiritual colouring at the end of the Middle Ages; and that its two strands, the technological and the spiritual, remained intertwined at many levels until the Romantic period, when only the spiritual content of the art could survive under the assault of modern chemical doctrines and was eventually rescued by twentieth-century psychology. The perception of colour played a central role in the presentation of alchemical ideas, which in turn made colour a language of movement. It was finally to emerge as the colour-music of the twentieth century.

9 · Colour under Control: The Reign of Newton

The colours of light · Darkness visible · The problem of colour scales · Newton's Opticks *and the uses of classification · Colour-space from Newton to Seurat*

That God is Colouring Newton does shew;
And that the devil is a Black outline, all of us know.
(William Blake, *To Venetian Artists*)

THE SEVENTEENTH CENTURY saw the most thoroughgoing and far-reaching changes in the European understanding of colour as a physical phenomenon. Early in the century a German scientific encyclopaedia was still describing colour in an essentially Aristotelian and medieval way: the 'noblest' colours were white, yellow, red, purple, green, blue and black, and the 'simple' ones black and white alone. There were two sorts of colours: the 'true' colours of substances and the 'apparent' colours of the rainbow and other accidents of lighting. There were still two types of light, the medieval *lux* and *lumen*.[1] A century later the picture was transformed: The Danish physician C. T. Bartholin wrote in his textbook, *Specimen Philosophiae Naturalis* (1703), that all colours were equally real, that black and white were not colours since they did not arise from the refraction of light, which is the cause of colours, and the 'primary' colours were red, yellow and blue. On the other hand, all colours were equally unreal, since they had no existence outside the eye.[2] Bartholin's testimony is particularly interesting because he does not seem to have been aware of Newton's work which, until the publication of *Opticks* the year after Bartholin's book, had been available only in Cambridge lectures and in a number of papers in the *Philosophical Transactions* of the Royal Society a quarter of a century earlier.

The development of a unified theory of light and colour had been proceeding very fast since the beginning of the seventeenth century. The mathematician and astronomer Johannes Kepler had already argued in Prague in 1604 that the distinction between 'apparent' and 'true' colours was unfounded and that all colours, except black and white, were transparent.[3] The ancient distinction between apparent and real colours and between *lux* and *lumen* were rejected by Descartes in his *Dioptrique* of 1637, although they continued to be respected by other writers until the middle of the century.[4] The notion that the colours were dependent not on the interaction of black and white but on the various degrees of refraction of light and that they were, indeed, inherent in light, had been advanced and to some extent demonstrated by Mersenne in 1634, by Marci in 1648 and by Grimaldi in 1665.[5] Yet Newton's predecessor as Lucasian Professor of Mathematics at Cambridge, Isaac Barrow, was still arguing in the late 1660s, albeit somewhat diffidently, that white and black were the origin of all colours.[6] Newton himself in the same decade felt bound in his early experiments at Cambridge to test this traditional view by examining black and white prints or monochrome drawings; he found that

No colour will arise out of yᵉ mixtures of pure black & white for yᵉ pictures drawne wᵗʰ inke would be coloured or printed would seem coloured at a distance & yᵉ verges of shadows would be coloured & Lamb black & Spanish whiteing would produce colours whence they cannot arise from more or lesse reflection or shadows mixed wᵗʰ light.[7]

Not long after this a Dutch pupil of Rembrandt, Samuel van Hoogstraten, ridiculed the theory of an English amateur, Sir Kenelm Digby, whose Aristotelian notion of the origin of colours was reinforced by seeing a series of experiments at the English Jesuit College at Liège in which black and white surfaces were viewed through a prism and the tonal junctions were seen to have coloured fringes. Digby, a friend and patron of Van Dyck, had been rash enough to assert that the nature of the 'middling colours' was clear from the way painters mixed their colours on the palette: if white prevailed strongly over a dark colour, red and yellow resulted; if the reverse, the product was blues, violets and sea-greens. Hoogstraten found this quite impossible to accept, pointing out that the only binary mixed colours produced on the palette were green from yellow and blue and purple from red and blue, 'as in the rainbow'.[8] Digby had conceivably been thinking of the glazing methods much used by Van Dyck, by which (as we saw in Chapter 2) a blue might be made by glazing black over white; but Hoogstraten was alluding to one of the most important seventeenth-century colour doctrines to have been suggested by the experience of artists: that all hues could be reduced to three 'primaries'. I showed in Chapter 2 how the theory of the primaries impinged upon the older four-colour theory attributed to the Greeks; here I want to emphasize that in the first half of the seventeenth century the triad of red, yellow and blue, which was certainly not new,[9] became a central principle of colour-organization among painters in many parts of Europe. Poussin's *Holy Family on the Steps* is as much an exposition of the notion of the three primaries and the three secondaries, laid out across the foreground of the painting, as it is a demonstration of perspectival construction.[10] It might well be that Poussin made the extraordinary range of subtle greys in the clouds and architecture of the background from these same three base colours.

Interest in the idea of primary colours first emerged in the literature of science: perhaps the first writer to outline it in its modern form was V. A. Scarmilionius, Professor of Theoretical Medicine in Vienna and a physician to the Emperor Rudolph II, to whom his *De Coloribus* (1601) was dedicated. Scarmilionius proposed a sequence of five 'simple' colours: white, yellow, blue (*hyacinthinus*), red and black, in this unusual order. He gave only two mixed colours (although red, yellow and blue were effectively 'mixtures' of black and white), *puniceus* (?orange) and green. He was concerned that there should be five basic colours only because, as I shall show in Chapter 13, he wanted to elaborate a musical theory of colour-harmony and needed the colours to relate to musical fifths.[11] Robert Boyle, whose debt to painters in the formulation of a three-colour theory was noticed (*see* p. 35–6), pointed out that with the three primaries and black and white, 'the skilfull Painter can produce what kind of Colour he pleases, and a great many more than we have yet Names for.' But Boyle went on to argue that this knowledge was particularly useful to the natural philosopher:

> much of the Mechanical use of Colours among Painters and Dyers doth depend upon the knowledge of what Colours may be produc'd by the Mixtures of Pigments so and so Colour'd. And ... 'tis of advantage to the contemplative Naturalist, to know how many and which Colours are Primitive (if I may so call them) and Simple, because it both eases his Labour by confining his most solicitous Enquiry to a small number of Colours upon which the rest depend, and assists him to judge of the nature of particular compounded colours, by shewing him from the Mixture of what more Simple ones, & of what Proportions of them to one another, the particular Colour to be consider'd does result ...[12]

In England the technological and commercial advantages of such a reduction of colours were repeatedly emphasized: Sir William Petty's account of dyeing, published by the Royal Society in the 1660s, grouped all the several dyestuffs under the three headings of red, yellow and blue, which, with the addition of white, were responsible for 'all that great variety which we see in Dyed Stuffs'.[13] When, early in the eighteenth century, the first experiments in full-colour printing were made in England 124–7 by the German painter J. C. Le Blon, he made great play with the reduction to three 'primitive' colours, which was the economic basis of his method; he even had sets of colour-separations pulled to instruct the 'curious'.[14] Indeed some of the newly developing science museums, to whom Le Blon was clearly appealing, might now have a section on painting and dyeing materials, arranged under these primary categories.[15]

Of course, the problem of the primaries was very far from being solved in the seventeenth century, nor was it until the middle of the nineteenth when James Clerk Maxwell did so simply by ruling it out of court. Newton in his early lectures had made the by now standard reference to painters, who were able to make all colours from red, yellow and blue; but the thrust of his optical work was to show that *all* rays in the spectrum – including green, orange and violet – were independently colour-bearing and could not be seen as mixed from any other colours; hence the number of 'simple' or 'primitive' colours is infinite.[16] As we shall see, this was quite incomprehensible to many eighteenth-century Newtonians. Newton's most important rival, the pioneer of the microscope, Robert Hooke, had proposed in the 1660s an equally problematic conception of the primaries in scarlet and blue, the former being sometimes 'diluted' to yellow. He found that by using hollow prisms filled with blue and yellow-red liquids,

> all the varieties of colours imaginable are produc'd from several degrees of these two colours, namely Yellow and Blue, or the mixtures of them with light and darkness, that is, white and black.

And all those most infinite varieties which Limners [i.e. miniature painters] and Painters are able to make by compounding those several colours they lay on their Shels or *Palads*, are nothing ellse, but some *compositum*, made up of some one or more, or all of these four.[17]

Hooke's work stimulated the Dutch scientist Christiaan Huyghens to maintain that only yellow and blue were required to constitute white light.[18] It is perhaps no more than a remarkable coincidence that in these same years the greatest Dutch connoisseur of the visual attributes of light, Vermeer, should in 117 so many of his pictures have made yellow and blue the dominant colours on his supremely luminous palette.[19]

But, as Scarmilionius and Hooke already admitted, the radically reduced palette of 'primaries' was of little practical use to painters, since the physical characteristics of pigments, particularly their greater or lesser opacity, could not match the ideal colours of the spectrum.[20] This was an extension of the problem articulated by Aristotle in relation to the colours of the rainbow, which in the nineteenth century was to issue in the distinction between the 'subtractive' primaries of pigments and the 'additive' primaries of light. What is surprising in the seventeenth-century debate about 'primaries' is that until Van Hoogstraeten made a passing reference to it in the 1670s, and despite the scientific appeal to painterly usage, the notion of 'primary' does not seem to have played a part in the painterly discussion of colour. That early visual anthology of colour ideas, Rubens's *Juno and Argus*, which has rightly been related to the 114 comprehensive treatment of colour in François d'Aguilon's *Optics* of 1613 – for which Rubens provided the illustrations and 183 which offered one of the first clear expositions of the new scheme of primaries and secondaries – was painted with a far from limited palette; nor did the painter, it seems, ever limit himself in any way. Even the unusually restricted palette of the London *Samson and Delilah*, dating from precisely the period of his collaboration with d'Aguilon, made use of a number of reds and yellow and, in the almost complete absence of blue, the bright purples and greens of the draperies were mixed with black.[21] Although d'Aguilon classified three types of mixture in painting – on the palette, using glazes, and optical mixtures using juxtaposed dots of pure colour – he did not refer to a fourth method, widely used by Rubens and his school, of the semi-transparent medium. This, according to the principles of Rayleigh's law of the scattering of reflections from small particles, and in the painterly technique of scumbling, could produce new nuances of great subtlety over a dark or light ground. Well might d'Aguilon protest that the complexities of painterly mixture were beyond the scope of his treatise and leave their investigation to artists themselves.[22]

Similarly Poussin, whose attitude to colour seems on the face of it to be so much more schematic than Rubens's and whose painterly methods, making a very limited use of glazes, were certainly more straightforward than his, used a palette of a dozen or so pigments.[23] Rubens certainly and Poussin possibly wrote on light and colour but these works were never published – perhaps an indication of their quality, since the authors' fame as artists would surely have guaranteed them a market as writers – and they are now lost. It is likely that their treatments were

The great illusionist ceilings of the Roman Baroque depended critically on the discrimination of many tones of light and shade. Giovanni Lanfranco's dome of the *Assumption* (1621/5, S. Andrea della Valle) was perhaps the earliest to convey vast and continuous space through tone; Baciccio's Gesù ceiling is one of the most breathtakingly expansive (see also pl. 121). The imaginary 'section' through the Gesù nave shows what the spectator on the ground *seems* to be seeing. (112,113)

little more than the collections of notes such as we have seen in Ghiberti or Leonardo or Pietro Testa. Leonardo's unsystematic *Treatise*, edited in the sixteenth century by Francesco Melzi, was eventually published in France with illustrations by Poussin in 1651.[24] But whatever Rubens and Poussin discussed, it is unlikely that the newly fashionable topic of the primaries was on their agenda. The more scientific spirit of the age certainly made itself felt in several of the seventeenth-century discussions of *disegno* and *colore*, from the amateur Girolamo Mancini at the beginning of the century to the painter Carlo Maratta at the end, in both of whom the superiority of drawing to colour was related to their relative capacities to convey the being, or essence, of a figure. We are already close to John Locke's discrimination of primary attributes of matter such as figures and secondary such as colour, published at the end of the century.[25] But even in the extensive studies of colour which were promoted during the second half of the century by the French Academy, the nature and status of colour was rarely in question. In 1672 the painter Blanchard was asked to lecture on 'the disposition of colours and their properties' but it is not clear whether this was to be about pigments and their use in pictures or about the nature of colour itself.[26] Even Roger de Piles, and the other supporters of Rubens and the 'colourist' party in France, argued that very few 'rules' of colouring could be

devised, which put the subject beyond the reach of rational enquiry.[27] André Félibien, the chief spokesman of the *Poussiniste* faction, put the scientific investigation of colours beyond the scope of the painter, who was, he said, interested only in their 'effects'.[28] We already sense the arrival of the modern period, when the increasing specialization and professionalization of the arts as well as the sciences have meant that the study of colour is fragmented and has proceeded along a number of distinct and unrelated lines.

Darkness visible

If the seventeenth century was, for students of optics, the century of light *par excellence*, when colour had finally been relegated to a derivative, subordinate position, it was also, for painters, supremely the century of darkness. The Italian utopian writer Tommaso Campanella wrote at the beginning of the century that the decadent, even hellish customs of that age of materialism were expressed in the universal love of black in dress.[29] But we know that black had been among the highest fashion colours for the European aristocracy for the previous two hundred years and that for almost as long it had been spreading downwards to the bourgeoisie.[30] So general was the taste for black clothes among all the wealthy classes in the

118

seventeenth century that a portrait-painter such as Frans Hals in Holland or Nicholas de Largillière in France was obliged to develop a subtle eye and a refined technique for rendering what van Gogh noticed in Hals as 'no less than twenty-seven blacks'.[31] Largillière's procedure for painting black silk, satin and velvet was of such a carefully structured complexity that he called it 'la couleur géometrale'.[32]

Campanella's negative assessment of black in a moral and religious sense was by no means the norm. Sir Thomas Browne, in Neo-Dionysian vein, wrote ecstatically in the 1650s:

> Light that makes things seen, makes some things invisible; were it not for darkness & the shadow of the earth, the noblest part of the Creation had remained unseen, & the Stars in the heaven as invisible as on the fourth day, when they were created above the Horizon, with the Sun, or there was not an eye to behold them. The greatest mystery of Religion is expressed by adumbration, & in the noblest part of Jewish types, we finde the Cherubims shadowing the Mercy-seat: Life itself is but the shadow of death, and souls departed but the shadows of the living: All things fall under this name. The Sunne it self is but the dark *simulacrum*, & light but the shadow of God . . .[33]

What for Browne was productive of beauty and meaning in the heavenly bodies had been for the astronomer Kepler the very condition of their being known and understood, hence his praise for the shadows of eclipses and of night.[34] In the course of the century darkness was allowed to be more positive than even Leonardo had felt possible: the Jesuit Athanasius Kircher argued that it could not be mere privation of light, since it had the power to induce blindness; in a long analysis of the problem he concluded: 'Thus darkness, shadow and obscurity [*obscuritas, umbra umbratioque*] are not ordinary states of privation of *lux* or *lumen*, but are real entities which are called positive.'[35]

120 The most visible manifestation of this new assessment of darkness was a remarkable style of painting which spread from Rome to the rest of Italy and from Italy throughout Europe: tenebrism, whose creator was Caravaggio. Where the spiritual writers had sought, like the painters of the High Renaissance, to find a balance between light and darkness, darkness now took over most of the picture: Reynolds, who was used to studying the Old Masters by making thumbnail diagrams of their distribution of light, reckoned that Rembrandt introduced only an eighth proportion of it into his compositions.[36] Where earlier painters such as Tintoretto had made much use of night and artificial light effects, the tenebrists used these effects in daylight without any pretext except the closeness of the room and the smallness of the windows.

The style of Caravaggio and his 'school' was well characterized by one of its earliest critics, Girolamo Mancini:

> This school has the peculiarity of lighting [the picture] with a unified light that comes from above without reflections, as it were from a single window in a room with the walls painted black, so that with the lights and shadows very light and very dark, they give relief to the picture, but in a way that is not natural, and unthought of in earlier centuries or by older painters such as Raphael, Titian, Correggio and others.[37]

It is curious that Mancini found this lighting unnatural, for most of Caravaggio's early critics – perhaps dazzled more by his subject-matter – described his colour as far too natural.[38] Caravaggio's stylistic origins were with the highly wrought realism and dramatic lighting of the sixteenth-century Brescian school of Savoldo and Moretto. This training may have been given a tenebrist reinforcement by the positive attitude to shadow in the circle of his early Roman patron, Cardinal Francesco Maria del Monte, whose brother published a book on perspective in 1600 which emphasized that drawing and shadow were the fundamentals of painting.[39] But this breadth of shadow had the effect of neutralizing the local colours to an unprecedented degree; Caravaggio's early biographer G. P. Bellori noted that the painter showed no interest in beautiful individual colours such as vermilion and bright blues, which he always subdued, 'saying that they were the poison of tones [*tinte*]'.[40]

Caravaggio was certainly asked to use such bright colours by his Roman patrons: the contracts of 1597 and 1599 for the Contarelli Chapel in S. Luigi dei Francesi, of which *120* scheme *The Calling of St Matthew* is a part, made the usual Renaissance stipulations about ultramarines and other blues but, as seems not unusual in Rome at this time, they were to be provided by the patron, not the painter.[41] Perhaps painters by this date were only too pleased to be spared the cost. In the Contarelli Chapel Caravaggio does seem to have taken some pains to pick up in his *St Matthew* altarpiece the golds and reds of the earlier frescoes of the Cavaliere d'Arpino. The shocking contrast between his approach to colour and that of a more classicizing artist can be seen in the smaller and slightly later Cerasi Chapel in Sta Maria del Popolo, where Annibale Carracci's *Assumption of the Virgin* (1600/01), probably already in place when Caravaggio started his own work, seems to belong to a totally different world from Caravaggio's *Crucifixion of St Peter* and *Conversion of St Paul* (1601). We are reminded of the heterogeneous colour-schemes of the Trecento, such as those in Sta Croce in Florence, where there was no common colouristic ground between stained glass, fresco and gilded altarpieces.[42]

The Caravaggesque approach to shadow, although less controversial than his vulgar treatment of religious subjects, continued to vex artists in other parts of Italy. In 1625 the Florentine perspectivist Pietro Accolti warned students at the Academy not to lose the 'abundance and variety of colours' in great highlights and deep shadows, as so many artists now did, and he appealed for a rather Albertian use of contrasting hues to give relief.[43] When tenebrism spread to distant Spain, where expensive pigments were far less easily come by than they were in Italy, painters like Velazquez, Ribera and Zurbarán were able to achieve much more homogeneous colour compositions, in which the abrupt transition from brightly coloured lights to murky neutral shadows is far less marked than in Caravaggio himself. A more limited palette, a simpler technique and a greater reliance on palette mixtures make this Spanish Caravaggism the most important watershed between an attitude to colour that put great emphasis on the raw materials and one wholly concerned with design and handling: what Annibale Carracci laughingly characterized as 'good drawing and colouring with mud'.[44]

Colour itself is the subject of Rubens's painting, an allegory of vision. Juno with her peacock and Iris with her rainbow examine the many eyes of the decapitated Argus, some of which they have already inserted into the peacock's tail. While he was working on this picture Rubens was perhaps already making illustrations for François d'Aguilon's treatise on optics, which appeared in 1613 (pl. 183), and he himself was the author of a (now lost) treatise on light and colour.

114 PETER PAUL RUBENS, *Juno and Argus*, 1611

115

116

117

The idea of the primaries

The colour triad red, yellow and blue had been used in the Middle Ages (**115**) because it could be represented in the three most precious pigments, vermilion, gold and ultramarine. In the seventeenth century (**116**, **117**) it received a renewed impetus because, with white and black, it was seen as in some sense 'primary'. Vermeer's approach (**117**) perhaps relates to a later-seventeenth-century view that blue and yellow were the basic colours of light; but he also had a medieval attitude to materials, and used the most expensive ones.

115 MASTER OF S. FRANCESCO, *Cruxifixion*, Umbria, thirteenth century
116 NICHOLAS POUSSIN, *The Holy Family on the Steps*, 1648
117 JOHANNES VERMEER, *The Artist in his Studio* (detail), *c.* 1666–7

The limited palette

The Dutch tenebrists (painters of shadows) reduced their palettes virtually to monochrome. Hals's and Rembrandt's paintings were probably portraits, but even the demands of matching flesh-tones have not led to the use of a very wide range of hues. Hals (**118**) is most concerned with nuances of black and white (van Gogh said he created twenty-seven blacks), and Rembrandt (**119**) in this late work was manipulating his limited palette by glazing and scumbling (essentially of black, white, yellow and red) into a brilliant, rich harmony.

118 FRANS HALS, *Standing Man*, 1639–40
119 REMBRANDT VAN RIJN, *The Jewish Bride*, probably 1666

118

119

From darkness to light

Caravaggio (120) was one of the first painters to restrict his light-source – here a high window – in daylight scenes, thus throwing most of his subject into shadow and creating a sense of high drama. In the much larger ceiling composition (**121**), carefully graded tonal recession from the damned souls cast into outer darkness at the bottom to the glowing letters of the monogram of Christ in the centre, produces an effect of extraordinary spaciousness (see also the imaginary projection of Baciccio's ceiling, pl. 113).

120 CARAVAGGIO, *The Calling of St Matthew*, 1599/1600
121 BACICCIO, *The Adoration of the Name of Jesus*, 1668/82, ceiling of the Gesù, Rome

120

121

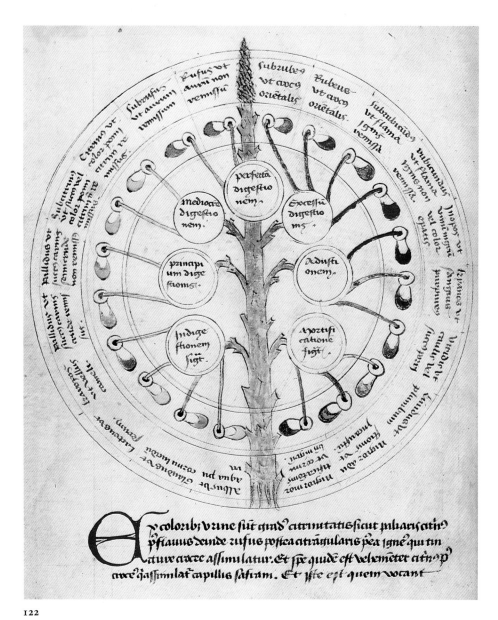

122

Making colour prints

From three colours all the rest can be produced – this is the idea basic to colour-printmaking, which depends on an economy of plates and processes. Le Blon's colour mezzotints (**124–7**) were probably the first to apply this notion, and he issued sets of separations to illustrate the novel principle. Most of the information is carried by the blue plate (**124**) which was printed first, and in this case the sequence was completed with red (**126**). Plate 127 shows a proof in two colours. But Le Blon's materials were far from perfect, and his enterprise failed because of the need for extensive hand-finishing.

124–7 JACOB CHRISTOPH LE BLON after F.H. Rigaud, *Portrait of Cardinal de Fleury*, colour separations, before 1738

Establishing colour circles

The circular arrangement of colours used by most artists seems to originate in a medieval scale devised for physicians diagnosing disease by uroscopy. In a fifteenth-century scale (**122**) the colours run from white to black through a series of yellows and reds. Newton's circular version of his prismatic scale (pl. 134) offered greater coherence by showing the relationships of neighbouring hues, and was quickly taken up by painters. The eighteenth-century colour circle of Claude Boutet (**123**) replaces Newton's two blues, indigo and blue, with two reds, fire-red and crimson. Other circles reduced Newton's seven colours to six: three 'primaries' and three 'secondaries'.

122 The colours of urine, from JOHN OF CUBA, *Hortus Sanitatis*, fifteenth century
123 Colour circle, from CLAUDE BOUTET, *Traité de la peinture en mignature*, 1708 edn

123

124

125

126

127

The problem of colour-scales

One of the most striking novelties in the artistic culture of Baroque Italy was a general interest in identifying styles of art. The drawing of Michelangelo and the colouring of Titian had been clichés of sixteenth-century criticism but now Mancini sought to distinguish, perhaps for the first time, at least four 'schools' of Italian painting and a number of individual styles as well. In the middle of the century the Roman painter Pietro da Cortona used the Contarelli Chapel as a lesson in contrasting the 'natural' idiom of the Caravaggio oils and the 'mannered and graceful', 'beautiful and genteel' frescoes of the Cavaliere d'Arpino in the vault above.[45] This chapel was only one of several examples where the sharp juxtaposition of light, frescoed vaults and dark canvases on the walls demonstrated the vast range of tonality now available to the modern painter. Another striking instance involves a single artist, Giovanni Lanfranco, in the Chapel of SS Agostino and Guglielmo (c. 1616) in the Roman church of S. Agostino, where even Bellori commented on the darkness of the oils.[46] But it was in the great illusionistic ceilings of the Roman Baroque – where space was opened up from near ground-level to the seemingly infinite distance of the highest heavens, beginning more or less with Lanfranco's dome of S. Andrea della Valle (1621–5) and developing through Pietro da Cortona's Barberini ceiling (1633–9) to Baciccio's Gesù in the 1670s and Andrea Pozzo's S. Ignazio twenty years later – where the capacity to convey the extremes of light and dark in painting was stretched to its farthest limit.[47] The task that faced the illusionistic ceiling-painter was considerable: preparatory oil studies by Baciccio for the Gesù show a far more colouristic handling of the space than in the final ceiling fresco, where the more monochromatic angels merge into the atmosphere itself.[48] The painter had to sacrifice chromatic richness and variety to a more precisely graded tonal scale, running from the dark clouds and draperies below the gilded frame up to the glowing letters of the Name of Jesus. What the Baroque decorator introduced to the art of painting was not simply extremes of darkness and light but a carefully graded scale linking them together: as Molière said of Pierre Mignard's slightly earlier cupola of the Val-de-Grace in Paris,

> Les distributions, & de l'ombre, & de lumière,
> Sur chacun des objets, & sur la masse entière;
> Leur degradation dans l'espace de l'air,
> Par differens de l'obscur & du clair . . .[49]

To depict the triumph of Light over Darkness, Delacroix had to use very bright and sharply contrasted colours, red against green and yellow against violet. The format of his ceiling in the Salle d'Apollon of the Louvre was dictated by the seventeenth-century architectural setting, which was (and is) rather poorly lit from one side. It was perhaps with this problem in mind that he proposed to consult the French expert on colour-contrast, M.E. Chevreul, in 1850.

128 EUGÈNE DELACROIX, *The Triumph of Apollo*, 1850/1

('The distribution of shade and light over each object, and over the whole composition; their gradation in aerial perspective by distinctions of dark and light . . . ') But how could these tonal scales be constructed? The Aristotelian theory of colour had supposed that hue was itself a function of the mixture of light and dark, so the idea that each hue, or genus, of colour could be arranged in a series of lighter or darker species presented extraordinary difficulties of organization and was, for the most part, left out of consideration. It was particularly difficult to understand before the development of any adequate techniques of recording and calibrating the degree of reflection of light from a surface. Aristotle's colour-system had been a linear scale, which seemed at one moment to have a median of red and at another, green; a further complication was the instability of Greek colour-terms. An attempt by Hipparchus (second century BC) to identify six degrees of luminosity in stars is recorded by Ptolemy (*Almagest* VII, i) but he gave no details. We have no further evidence of visual scales until in the fourth or fifth century Chalcidius introduced a simple tonal scale of five terms – white, yellow (*pallidum*), red, blue and black – into his commentary on Plato's *Timaeus*.[50] In the twelfth century, Urso of Salerno in a discussion of the colours arising from mixtures of the elements – blue air, black earth, red fire and white water – argued that there were too many intermediate tones to list and anyway he did not know their names. 'However, a good painter could really, by making them, demonstrate rather than name the many median colours mixed from the colours of the elements.'[51] If Urso had been able to persuade a painter to carry out this interesting task, we might well have had a scale of some complexity but nothing like it has yet come to light. In what is by far the most detailed and circumstantial medieval discussion of a colour-scale, in the *Liber de Sensu et Sensato* attributed to Roger Bacon, a scale (*gradus*) of twenty or twenty-one colours was proposed but the only way of arranging them was by their composition, according to the various authorities Bacon had consulted. In Latin the scale ran: '*flavus* or *lividus, albus, candidus, glaucus, ceruleus, pallidus, citrinus, puniceus, rufus, croceus, rubeus, rubicundus, purpureus, viridis, venetius, lividus* [!]*, lazulus, fuscus, niger*'. From the lengthy discussion which preceded this scale, the various terms may be identified as follows:

1. —*flavus* = golden-yellow, related to white
2. —*lividus*: Aristotle has this as equal to *flavus*, and a white, but it is also the colour of lead (which produced white lead), so it might be a dark grey as in 17 below.
3. —*albus* = white
4. —*candidus* = shining white
5. —*glaucus* (*karopos* in Greek) = a yellow with more white than yellow and red in it; the colour of camel-hair
6. —*ceruleus* = wax-yellow
7. —*pallidus* = pale yellow, according to Avicenna
8. —*citrinus*: = doctors say that this yellow is reddish in urine. Avicenna says that it includes *igneus* (fire-colour) and *croceus* (11)
9. —*puniceus* = ?orange; [in *Opus Maius* VI, xii Bacon says that this is one of the grades of *glaucus* (5) of which the other is *caeruleum* (6)]
10. —*rufus* = red-gold (? as in red-lead)

11.—*croceus*: as in oriental crocus and blood

12.—*rubeus* (*alburgon* in Greek) = the median colour between white and black: moderate heat and cold in medium matter

13.—*rubicundus* = darker red

14.—*purpureus* (*kianos* in Greek) = purple

15.—*viridis* = green

16.—*venetius*: Averroes says that this is an ebony colour between blue (*azurum*) and black, but Isidore says that it is *ceruleo* (6), so there may be two colours of this name

17.—*lividus* = lead-grey

18.—*lazulus* (lapis lazuli) = a blue-black, but with a beautiful shine, which suggests that it has some white in it. Some say it is a medium blue; if so, it should be between *viridis* and *venetius*

19.—*fuscus* = dark (not qualified)

20.—*niger* = black

This list suggests that despite all his efforts Bacon had the greatest difficulty setting out a coherent scale and that, quite apart from the ambiguities in *glaucus* and *ceruleus*, he was particularly uncertain about the values of the yellows and the blues. Nevertheless he made a remarkably effective attempt at a scale running from shining white (although elsewhere in this discussion Bacon has the order *candor, albus, flavus* at this point), through yellow and orange, red and purple, green and blue, to black.[52]

Since Bacon, in his discussion of the relationship of light to colour, drew frequently from the *On the Soul* of Avicenna, it is surprising that he did not discuss Avicenna's important attempt to overcome the problems inherent in the arrangement of a tonal scale without any means of testing the quantity of reflected light from a given hue. Avicenna had recognized before Alberti that within each hue there were species of colour differing in their lightness and darkness and that there was even a 'pure' (i.e. achromatic) sequence from white to black through grey. The twelfth-century Latin translation of Avicenna isolated three such sequences: the first 'pure' way, through *subpallidum* and *pallidum*, the second through pale red (*subrubeus*) and red and the third through green and indigo.[53] In the thirteenth century, when Vincent of Beauvais included these scales in his encyclopaedia *The Great Mirror*,[54] Albertus Magnus amplified them a little by adding *fuscus* to the achromatic scale, *croceum*, *purpureum* and *indicum* to the red scale and *viride clarum* and *intensa viriditas* to the green scale. The contemporary Persian commentator al Tûsî saw that all the hues had their proper species of light and dark and proposed a scale for yellow through orange, for red through purple and violet, and for green and blue, as well as grey.[55] Al Tûsî's work seems to have been known to Theodoric of Freiberg, who introduced this scheme into his *On Colours* (*c.* 1310) but did not develop it.[56]

The linear scales of the Renaissance introduced a greater refinement in the arrangement of values. Ficino in the late fifteenth century, for example, included a dark red (*rubeus plenior*) and a light red (*rubeus clarior*) in his series and Cardano a century later proposed a precisely calibrated scale of values between black (1) and white (100), in which *fuscus* stood at 20, blue at 25, green at 62 and yellow at 65–78.[57] Such scales

Scala Rubedinis.

Gradus ejus.	Grana ceruſſæ.	Grana Cinna- baris.	Utriuſque proportio minima.
11ᵘˢ.	Satura Rubedo.		
10ᵘˢ.	gr. 40.	gr. X	C. 4. Ci. gr. I.
9ᵘˢ.	gr. 60.	gr. IX.	C. 6 ⅔ Ci. gr. I.
8ᵘˢ.	gr. 80.	gr. VIII.	C. 10. Ci. gr. I.
7ᵘˢ.	gr. 100.	gr. VII.	C. 14⁴⁄₇ Ci. gr. I.
6ᵘˢ.	gr. 120.	gr. VI.	C. 20. Ci. gr. I.
5ᵘˢ.	gr. 140.	gr. V.	C. 28. Ci. gr. I.
4ᵘˢ.	gr. 160.	gr. IV.	C. 4. Ci. gr. ¹⁄₁₀ gr.
3ᵘˢ.	gr. 180.	gr. III.	C. 6. Ci. ¹⁄₁₀ gr.
2ᵘˢ.	gr. 200.	gr. II.	C. 10. Ci. ¹⁄₁₀ gr.
1ᵘˢ.	gr. 220.	gr. I.	C. 22. Ci. ¹⁄₁₀ gr.
Simplex albedo, baſis ſcalæ.			

Francis Glisson, a physician concerned with the colours of hair, devised perhaps the first system to coordinate hues and values in a coherent way. His tables (1677) give the precise proportions of each pigment to be used in every mixture. The 'scale of redness' lists mixtures of vermilion with lead-white, from pure white to saturated red at step eleven. The 'scale of blackness' (below) distinguishes twenty-three steps between white and black. (129,130)

Scala Nigredinis.

Gradus ejus.	Grana ceruſſæ.	Grana a- tramenti fuliginei.	Utriuſque proportio minima.
23ᵘˢ.	Simplex Nigredo.		
22ᵘˢ.	100.	gr. XXII.	C. 4 ⁴⁄₁₁ F. I.
21ᵘˢ.	150.	gr. XXI.	C. 7 ⅓ F. I.
20ᵘˢ.	200.	gr. XX.	C. 10. F. I.
19ᵘˢ.	250.	gr. XIX.	C. 13 ⅓ F. I.
18ᵘˢ.	300.	gr. XVIII.	C. 16 ¹³⁄₁₉ F. I.
17ᵘˢ.	350.	gr. XVII.	C. 20 ¹⁶⁄₁₉ F. I.
16ᵘˢ.	400.	gr. XVI.	C. 25. F. I.
15ᵘˢ.	450.	gr. XV.	C. 30. F. I.
14ᵘˢ.	500.	gr. XIV.	C. 35 ⁵⁄₇ F. I.
13ᵘˢ.	550.	g. XIII.	C. 42 ⁴⁄₁₁ F. I.
12ᵘˢ.	600.	gr. XII.	C. 5. F. ¹⁄₁₀
11ᵘˢ.	650.	gr. XI.	C. 5 ¹⁰⁄₁₁ F. ¹⁄₁₀
10ᵘˢ.	700.	gr. X	C. 7. F. ¹⁄₁₀
9ᵘˢ.	750.	gr. IX.	C. 8 ⅓ F. ¹⁄₁₀
8ᵘˢ.	800.	gr. VIII.	C. 10. F. ¹⁄₁₀
7ᵘˢ.	850.	gr. VII.	C. 12 ¹⁄₁₀ F. ¹⁄₁₀
6ᵘˢ.	900.	gr. VI.	C. 15. F. ¹⁄₁₀
5ᵘˢ.	950.	gr. V.	C. 19. F. ¹⁄₁₀
4ᵘˢ.	1000.	gr. IV.	C. 25. F. ¹⁄₁₀
3ᵘˢ.	1050.	gr. III.	C. 35. F. ¹⁄₁₀
2ᵘˢ.	1100.	gr. II.	C. 55. F. ¹⁄₁₀
1ᵘˢ.	1150.	gr. I.	C. 115. F. ¹⁄₁₀
Simplex Albedo, baſis ſcalæ.			

continued to be devised in the seventeenth century,[58] but it was also at this time that the first serious attempts to integrate the dimensions of hue and value into a single colour-system appeared. The earliest such system seems to have been the colour-sphere of the Swedish mathematician Sigfrid Forsius, which was devised about 1611. Forsius proposed a four-colour circle of red, yellow, green and blue, plus grey, forming the central axis of his solid. However, he had clearly not attempted to construct it or to co-ordinate his two dimensions of hue and value in a coherent way: orange, for example, should have appeared between red and yellow at the equator, as it did in Forsius's two-dimensional colour-circle, but in the diagram of the sphere it appeared as the first stage between yellow and black.[59] This problem of co-ordination does not appear to have been solved until the second half of the century when an English doctor, Francis Glisson, devised what seems to be the first coherent three-dimensional colour-solid, the ancestor of all the modern systems, which he suggested (although we have no record of his success) could be constructed with named pigments. Glisson accepted the primaries of red, yellow and blue; his grey-scale had twenty-three steps between black and white and was to be constructed using lead-white and black ink (*atramentum*) or ivory-black; his yellow scale used orpiment, his red scale vermilion and his blue scale azurite (*bice*), since ultramarine was too light and indigo too purplish in hue.[60] Modern estimates of the perceptible steps on the grey-scale propose around two hundred, and modern colour-systems work with from ten to twenty.[61]

These efforts to articulate a coherent colour system, particularly a tonal scale, came together in Baroque Rome in the circle of painters and literati around the patron Cassiano dal Pozzo, who shared with them an interest in the writings of Leonardo da Vinci. The most important painter of the group was Poussin but its chief theorist was a lesser artist, Matteo Zaccolini, who around 1620 had written, but did not publish, what promises to be the most important, as it is certainly the most compendious, seventeenth-century treatise on optics for artists.[62] Zaccolini devoted a great deal of thought and experiment to establishing scales in aerial perspective, both the linear scale of colours as they were transformed into the blue of the atmosphere at various distances – in the order black, green, 'pale' (yellow-green), purple (*pavonazzo*), tan, red, yellow, white – and the progression of each hue – green, purple, red, blonde (*biondo*), yellow and blue, as well as grey – in a tonal sequence of eight steps.[63] Zaccolini's treatment was concerned to relate the abstract ordering of tones to specific pigments used by painters, giving details about how to make mixtures: tan (*tané*), for example, was made from red and black and was similar to a type of *pavonazzo* that 'the Roman painters call *pavonazzo di sale*', which had a lot of dark red but was mixed without a trace of blue (*turchino*); the most beautiful green was to be mixed with light blue (*biadetto*) and Naples yellow (*giallorino*), with ultramarine and *giallo santo*, not with ochre and smalt or 'ordinary blue' because they destroy each other.[64] Perhaps the most important feature of Zaccolini's treatise for us is its Leonardesque interest in the colours of the natural world and how these might be interpreted in terms of the painter's scales. Red mixed with the grey called *berettino* or *ceneritio*, mixed from white and black, makes the sort of violet seen in the clouds at sunrise or sunset. When red in the sky turns to blue, at one point a mixed colour is produced, like dried roses, or *pavonazzo*, and clouds may change suddenly from one colour to another.[65] The scientific painter (*il scientifico Pittore*) will know how to exploit such phenomena, he says, so it is perhaps not surprising that the most concrete results of Zaccolini's approach were shown in landscape painting. The emphasis on the clear discrimination of planes by colour reminds us of Poussin's lucid landscape spaces and Poussin is known to have made many notes from Zaccolini. The most striking parallel, however, is in a working procedure developed in Rome by another French painter, Claude Lorrain. According to his early painting-companion Joachim von Sandrart, Claude

lay in the field before day-break and into the night, so that he could learn to represent the reddening dawn, the sun's rising and setting, as well as the evening hours really naturally, and when he had closely observed the one or the other, he quickly mixed [*temprirte*] his colours accordingly, ran back home with them, and applied them in the work he was engaged in with much greater naturalness than any one before him.

Sandrart also stressed that Claude knew how to modulate the 'hardness' of colours by mixing them so that they no longer looked like themselves but rather like those 'which he needed to represent [*entbilden*]'; he did so as 'a master of perspective'. In a later passage Sandrart remarked that Claude only painted 'the view from the middle to the farthest distance, fading away towards the horizon and the sky', for which, of course, he needed precisely the perspectival knowledge codified by Zaccolini.[66] What precisely were Claude's methods? Did he set his palette in the field with a series of graded tones? Or did he simply arrange these tones on board or paper? We know that his most devoted eighteenth-century follower, Claude-Joseph Vernet, used a book of home-made colour-samples to speed his work as an outdoor sketcher, simply referring to them by number.[67] In either case, Claude's samples must have been set out as a scale. Some light may be thrown on this practice by a note among the manuscripts of the Flemish doctor at the Court of Charles I, Theodore Turquet de Mayerne. De Mayerne recorded a recipe, unfortunately unattributed, for the painting of a landscape (*La terre ou pais*), working from the far distance, which should be done in 'the most beautiful ashes [? of ultramarine] and white, with a touch of lake'; the next plane was to be painted with ashes, blue and lake, with a little massicot [bright yellow], the next with ashes, yellow ochre and a little *Schitgeel*; finally the foreground with ashes, *Schitgeel* and a little lake.[68] This was evidently a conceptual formula quite unlike Claude's observation but it shows how artists of the period were used to thinking of landscape space in terms of carefully gradated colour.

A similar procedure to Claude's was also recommended by another acquaintance of his, the history and landscape painter J.H. Bourdon, in a lecture to the French Academy in 1669. In the course of a discussion of the best times of day for the landscape artist, which like Claude he held to be morning and evening, Bourdon spoke of a particularly vivid sunset in which 'the more bizarre the accidents [of light], the more it is necessary to make notes of them, and as they are of very short duration one must be quick to copy them as they are.' He then rather weakened the force of his argument by advising that these extreme effects were nature's vices and should not be used in painting without modification. Bourdon went on to give an account of the colour structure of such natural effects: before dawn the sky should have few clouds:

if there are any, they should be luminous only at their edges. The base or blue of the sky should also tend towards darkness; and observe that in the parts closest to the horizon the blue should be of a lighter tone, both so that the sky can better form a vault, and because it is in this place that the light grows ... the sky should be coloured with a vermilion flush [*incarnat*] which, spreading out parallel to the horizon, will form, up to a certain height, alternately gilded and silvered bands, which will get less brilliant the farther they are away from the origin of the light.

Again, Bourdon spoils the effect of this highly specific observation by concluding that he was simply describing a painting by one of the Bassanos.[69]

Zaccolini's scales could only have been applied in a milieu which believed in the precise analysis of landscape out of doors and there is now more and more evidence that landscape was treated in this way in the seventeenth century. Outdoor oil-sketches and drawings from a Roman ambiance, or accounts of the apparatus used to make them, are emerging in increasing numbers; from northern Europe there is even a little support for the view that full-scale landscape pictures might be painted in front of the motif.[70] Such a method relies, of course, as Sandrart said of Claude, on the capacity to match perceptions with mixtures of paints; such mixing became the norm in seventeenth-century painting practice.

The treatment of colour in the early seventeenth-century German encyclopaedia quoted at the beginning of this chapter was already unusual for its rather detailed – and thoroughly eccentric – account of the *nobiliores colores* as mixed: for example, the blues were composed of much green and a little black, and green itself from a mixture of black with less red.[71] So, too, a number of technical treatises for artists, such as the anonymous *Paduan Manuscript* of the mid-century, gave a good deal of space to mixtures, sometimes of up to five colours.[72] At the same time it became a common practice for painters to ground their canvases with a mid-tone mixed from all the waste colours scraped from their palettes.[73] Caravaggio and Rubens were painters much given to palette-mixtures early in the century, when the ancient distrust of 'corrupting' colours (*see* Chapter 2) which had been reinforced by the use of intrinsically valuable pigments in the Middle Ages and the Renaissance, was now no longer a serious issue.[74] The most learned of the Baroque historians of ancient art, the Earl of Arundel's Dutch librarian Franciscus Junius – whose book, *The Painting of the Ancients* (for all its indigestible density), was consulted by many artists including Rubens and Poussin – cited the classical term *corruptio* without any sense of disparagement: in seventeenth-century usage it had become a quite neutral technical term.[75]

The painter most prized in this period for his capacity to 'break' colours in complicated mixtures was Rembrandt, whose follower Sandrart was even more enthusiastic about this capacity in him than in Claude:

> It must be to his great credit that he knew how to break colours away from their own character in the most rational and artful way, and to use them harmoniously to depict nature's true and vivid life; and in doing so he opened the eyes of those who in the common way are rather dyers than painters, in that they set the hard, raw colours quite bold and hard next to each other, so that they have no relationship with nature, but only with the colours in colour-boxes at the dealer's, or the stuffs straight from the dye-works ...[76]

The transition in Rembrandt's practice from the use of a wide palette of ten to a dozen pigments in the 1620s and early 1630s, including the very expensive azurite, vermilion and malachite green, to the use from about 1650 of roughly half this number of

largely earth pigments, is well established; it is equally clear that a late palette such as that for *The Jewish Bride* was not lacking in brilliance.[77] In his early years Rembrandt was even prepared to paint on gilded copper, a technique he shared with Vermeer, whose old-fashioned attitude to precious materials I have already hinted at.[78] But it is perhaps indicative of Rembrandt's thoroughly modern attitude to colour that in the 1630s a so-far unique instance of his use of ultramarine, in *Self Portrait with Saskia*, should be in a complex mixed brown and was probably an accidental transference from a dirty brush.[79] Rembrandt's late style did not depend entirely upon palette mixtures – a painting such as *The Jewish Bride* makes use of the whole technical range of thick impasto, transparent glazes and semi-opaque scumbling – but there can be little doubt that Sandrart was substantially right. Even as early as the *Night Watch* (1642) the painter used palette mixtures of up to eight pigments in the same layer, nearly all the colours used in the painting as a whole.[80]

This new attitude to mixing necessarily had an important aesthetic dimension. Although the medieval notion of the harmony of juxtaposed colours, as articulated by Alberti, was still current in Europe, a newer notion of the creation of harmony through the mixture of all the tones in a painting from the same ingredients began to spread. It had been adumbrated in Leonardo's chiaroscuro but its real origin was in the doctrine of primary colours. The French painter J.-B. Jouvenet (1644–1717) was praised precisely for his capacity to harmonize his colours in this way so that, it was said, 'they seemed to have been produced by a single palette'.[81] I hope to show in Chapter 10 the extraordinary implications of this view.

Newton's Opticks *and the uses of classification*

This painterly concern with mixtures, with shadow and with the colour-scale from white to black ran counter to the most important seventeenth-century research into light and colour, crowned in 1704 by the *Opticks* of Sir Isaac Newton. The only scale in Newton is the prismatic one which, in his Cambridge lectures of 1669/70, he characterized rather exotically in its principal (*insigniores*) steps as 'scarlet, or purple [*purpureus*], red-lead, lemon yellow, golden-yellow or sun-golden [*Heliocryseus*], dark yellow, green, grass-green, sea-green, blue, indigo and violet': eleven steps which he was late to reduce, significantly, to seven.[82] Newton's theory – which denied that there was any specifically 'primary' set of hues, by arguing that all the rays of refracted light were 'primary', 'homogeneal' or 'simple' and that some, such as green, violet and even yellow, could be manifested in either a simple or a compound form – might have seemed to fly in the face of any technological experience; yet for many years, and in every European country, the *Opticks* or popular versions of it became part of the standard equipment of the painter.

One of the earliest technical encyclopaedias, published soon after the appearance of the *Opticks*, Harris's *Lexicon Technicum*, carried an account of colour which was essentially Newtonian but also a list of twenty-one 'simple' pigments grouped in a random order between white and black.[83] This ambiguity in the notion of 'simple' as it referred to the colours of light and the colours of matter – or rather of two sorts of colours of matter, for Newton regarded light as material – is felt in perhaps the earliest attempt to rationalize colour-mixing along Newtonian lines, by Newton's Cambridge collaborator, the mathematician Brook Taylor. In an appendix to a new edition of his treatise on linear perspective, Taylor tried to apply Newton's mixing diagram and in doing so discovered not only that light colours overcome dark but also that the products of pigment mixture were quite unpredictable:

> If the nature of the material Colours, which are used in Painting, was so perfectly known, as that one could tell exactly what Species of Colour, how perfect, and what degrees of light and shade each Material has with respect to its Quantity, by these Rules one might exactly produce any Colour proposed, by mixing the several Materials in their just proportions. But ... these Particulars cannot be known to sufficient exactness for this purpose, besides the Tediousness that would be in Practice ... If the Colours were as dry powders, which have no effect upon one another, when mix'd, these observations would exactly take place in the mixing of them. But some colours are not of such a Nature, that they produce a very different effect upon their Mixture, to what one would expect from these principles. So that it is possible there may be some dark materials, which when diluted with white, may produce cleaner, and less compounded Colours than they gave when single; as some Colours do very well to glaze with, which don't look well laid on in a Body. But these Properties of particular Materials I leave to be consider'd by the Practitioners in this Art.[84]

The gap between the scientists and the artists was widening and the first enterprise that sought to exploit the growing prestige of Newton's name as a theorist of colour, J. C. Le Blon's Picture Office for the manufacture of coloured reproductions of paintings, which was set up in England about 1717, was soon to experience this gap. In a treatise on harmony, published in English and French in 1725, Le Blon wrote:

> Painting can represent all *visible* Objects with three Colours, *Yellow, Red,* and *Blue*; for all other Colours can be compos'd of these *Three*, which I call *Primitive* ... And a *Mixture* of those *Three* Original Colours makes a *Black*, and all *other* colours whatsoever; as I have demonstrated by my Invention of *Printing* pictures *and* Figures with their natural *Colours*.
>
> I am only speaking of *Material* colours, or those used by *Painters*; for a *Mixture* of *all* the primitive *impalpable* Colours, that cannot be felt, will not produce *Black*, but the very contrary *White*; as the great Sir ISAAC NEWTON has demonstrated in his Opticks.[85]

The chequered career of Le Blon and his manufactory, and the eventual abandonment of this approach to colour-printing by his successors in France, is evidence enough that full-colour printing with three plates was quite impracticable while pigments or inks approximating to the 'primary' red, yellow and blue were not available. We know that in France later on in his career Le Blon used Prussian blue and a dark yellow lake but that for a red he had to develop a complicated mixture of madder-lake, carmine and a little natural cinnabar (vermilion). He was also obliged to use a fourth, black, plate and to make extensive recourse to hand-finishing the other colours, which subverted the economics of the whole project.[86] Among all

these confusions of theory it was perhaps no accident that one of the first proposals to teach colour at a European academy of art, that for the new Royal Academy in Vienna in 1772, should have included the principles of colour-mixing as well as the more traditional copying of paintings.[87]

Yet in the first half of the eighteenth century very few appeared to notice the problematic nature of Newton's colour ideas. The *Opticks* seemed to lend itself very directly to the imagination; Blake's sardonic verses at the head of this chapter were backed by a century of poetic eulogy. We saw in Chapter 6 how James Thomson attributed to Newton rather than to God the unravelling of the mystery of the rainbow; now even a devotional writer such as J. J. Scheuchzer was anxious to show that the 'subtilissimus & accuratissimus' Newton had finally revealed its secret, so that where the medieval interpreters of the colours had referred to the Covenant or the Trinity, the torturing of white light into colours by refraction was now seen to be emblematic of Christ's Passion.[88] A precocious English plea that landscape painting should demonstrate the functioning of nature used as its paradigm the Newtonian laws of light and colour:

> The Laws of Light and Colours, which, properly speaking, produce all the various Phaenomena of the visible World, would afford ... an inexhaustible fund of the most agreeable entertainment ... In short, Pictures which represent visible Beauties, or the Effects of Nature in the visible world, by the different modifications of Light and Colours, in consequence of the Laws which relate to Light, are samples of what these Laws do or may produce.[89]

It was clearly for natural scientists rather than for artists or poets that the clarification of the nature and order of colours brought about by Newton had been a most urgent requirement. As Richard Waller, a Fellow of the Royal Society, complained in 1686, no standard of colour had yet been established for philosophers.[90] Where in earlier scientific usage colour had been more or less confined to the diagnostic technique of medicine, the scientific community now needed it for the task of cataloguing the whole of creation. Waller had provided a visual standard of painted samples but earlier naturalists had to rely on the uncertain language of colour-terms or, in the case of the magnificent *Hortus Floridus* of the Dutch artist Crispyn van de Passe, on almost equally uncertain instructions for painting each copy. This multi-lingual anthology of garden-flowers presented its own problems because of the vagueness of technical terms in the various languages; Van de Passe's English translator excused himself in an end-note,

> the names of the colours so much differinge from the original language, that neither by search of bookes, nor conference with painters, nor marchants beyond the seas, could sufficientlie expresse the same to an Englishman's understandinge. Yet by some that made profession of that arte, being persuaded that they had all one generall name; whereof I myself knew better, have done them all, or the most part of them, to be understoode of any Englishman, onely in one coloure which the dutchemen call schÿt-geel, which translated signifyeth a shitten yellow. I have in place thereof

(because of not offending modest eares) called it throughout the whole book a sad yellow. It is that which the Lattines, french and spanish, call Buxus, that is box coloure, which is a sad or deadlyke yellow.[91]

Although there was a moment in the late seventeenth century when it seemed that colour might itself provide an insight into the principles of vegetable classification,[92] this conjecture was soon overtaken by the sexual system of Linnaeus (Karl von Linné). It was the cataloguing activities of Linnaeus and his followers that provided the greatest stimulus to the development of the colour-systems of the eighteenth and nineteenth centuries. Sometimes these systems were evolved by naturalists themselves and the most ambitious early attempt to establish a comprehensive set of colour standards addressed itself to naturalists, painters, manufacturers, artists and artisans, in that order, and was, indeed, attacked by artists for its exclusive concentration on the 4,800 local colours which were of use in a scientific context.[93] One of the most intelligent of the new colour-theorists, the Viennese entomologist Ignaz Schiffermüller, even suggested in 1771 that since animals, plants and minerals now had their fully articulated systems, it was time that colour was treated as a 'natural' system in the same way.[94]

Such a system was essential to the descriptive vocabulary of the naturalists, as it has seemed to be for some historians of art in our own time.[95] The painter William Williams told a touching story of an old entomological illustrator who,

> living in a remote country, unacquainted with artists, or any rational system of colours, with a patience that would have surmounted any difficulties, had collected a multiplicity of shells of colour, of every various tint that could be discerned in the wing of that beautiful insect [the butterfly]; for he had no idea that out of two he could make a third, by this method he had accumulated two large hampers full of shells, which he placed on each side of him, and sometimes the individual tint he wanted, was half a day's labour to find out. What excellence must he have arrived at, had he known how to have mixt his tints.[96]

Here coloured shells performed a systematic function but in the eighteenth century they also had aesthetic importance. If Rembrandt's wonderful etching of a *Conus marmoreus* L. might well have fitted the setting of the Baroque *Wunderkammer*, Boucher's equally wonderful design of shells fits no less clearly into the aesthetic context of the Rococo. Basing themselves on the objects listed in Boucher's posthumous sale of 1771, his biographers the brothers Goncourt evoked the sensuous pleasures of such a collection: *132*

131

> As he grew older, he collected about him precious stones, whose bewitching rays warmed his vision, his talent, into life; he encumbered his studio with their rocky brilliance, with quartz, rock crystal, Thuringian amethyst; tin, lead and iron crystals; pyrites and marcasite. Native gold, clusters of unwrought silver like vegetation, copper iridescent like the feathers of doves and peacocks, fragments of lapis, Siberian malachite, jasper, flint, agate, sardonyx, coral, the contents of Nature's jewel-box seemed to have been poured out onto his shelves and tables. And to this wonderful museum of celestial colours garnered from the earth was added a

Shells require a system of colour standards for classification but can offer permanent colour standards themselves. Both Rembrandt and Boucher formed collections. François Boucher's frontispiece to *Conchyliologie* (1780) is a fanciful arrangement which juxtaposes exotic shells and pearly flesh. Rembrandt's etching of 1650 presents his shell for inspection like a rare specimen in a *Wunderkammer*. (131,132)

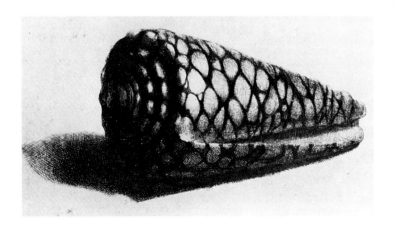

collection of shells, with their thousand delicate shades of colour, their prismatic sheen, their changing reflections, their rainbow glisten, their pale, tender pinks like a drenched rose, their greens as soft as the shadow of a wave, their moonlit whites; there were conchs, purpurae, oysters, scallops, mussels, flor of pearl, mother of pearl and enamel, arranged like sets of gems in Boule showcases, in cabinets of amaranth wood, or spread out on tables of Oriental alabaster beneath carved wood candelabra.[97]

One Austrian entomologist, G. A. Scopoli, devised a colour-mixing system with spinning discs of the sort which, so far as I know, had not been used since the Middle Ages but was to be developed very extensively in the nineteenth century. Scopoli was unable to mix the hues of high saturation needed to match the brilliant colours of his insects; nor, of course, was he able to record his disc-mixtures in a more permanent, stable form[98] His work is one of the many indications that the characteristically empirical approach to colour systems in the eighteenth century was unable to take the problem very far.

Colour-space from Newton to Seurat

Although Newton's *Opticks* should properly have removed colour from a central place in the study of light,[99] it did no such thing; what Newton bequeathed to posterity, almost by accident, was two ideas of compelling power. The first was that colour-relationships could best be visualized in a circular arrangement, and the second, closely related to this, was the idea
54 of complementarity. We saw in a table of elements how readily the medieval mind gave itself to expressing complicated ideas in simple diagrams and, in the tradition of Isidore of Seville, some of these diagrams were circular.[100] Yet it is a further indication of the difficulty philosophers experienced in reaching a clear idea of colour-relationships that no colour-diagram appears to have been devised before the fifteenth century, when a circle of twenty hues was published in an anonymous *Treatise on Urine*.
122 Colour was of course an essential diagnostic in urology and this circle, which runs from white to black, includes only those colours which are relevant to this diagnosis; but it was the ancestor of a more abstract circle published by the magus
1 Robert Fludd in the 1620s.[101] In this seven-part circle black and white are adjacent, green is the median colour and is next to red, which is also described as embodying equal parts of white and black. The choice of a circular arrangement seems to be quite arbitrary in both these cases.
134 Newton's colour-mixing diagram, on the other hand, although it is clearly based on Descartes's arrangement of
185 musical intervals, has a clear inner coherence because it was simply an attempt to roll up the prismatic spectrum. It runs from red to violet in an unbroken sequence of hues whose place depends upon their intimate relationship to those on either side of them. With some modification of the number and area of the component hues, this circular arrangement has remained standard in painterly colour-theory until the present day. The first sign that this might be so was in the coloured circle published in an anonymous supplement on pastel in the 1708
123 Hague edition of the *Traité de la peinture en mignature* attributed to Claude Boutet, a work first published in 1673, which ran into

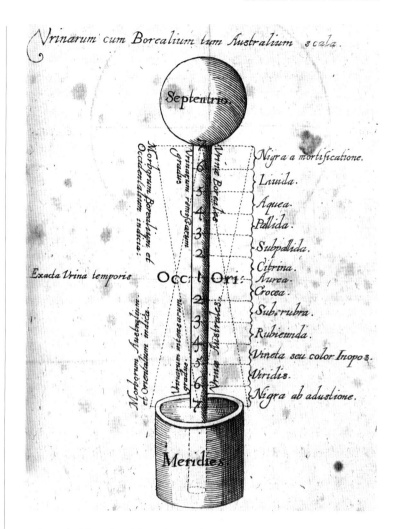

Robert Fludd's scale of the colours of urine, from *Medicina Catholica*, 1629. The colours are graded between north and south, both black through excess, with orange (*aurea*, golden) in the centre. As well as devising his own scale, Fludd re-published the medieval twenty-colour urine circle (pl. 122) in the same book. (133)

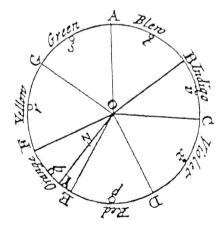

Sir Isaac Newton, colour wheel (*Opticks*, 1702). Newton sets out the colours of the spectrum in their order and proportion, locating the components of mixtures geometrically, and enabling mixtures of prismatic colours to be predicted. (134)

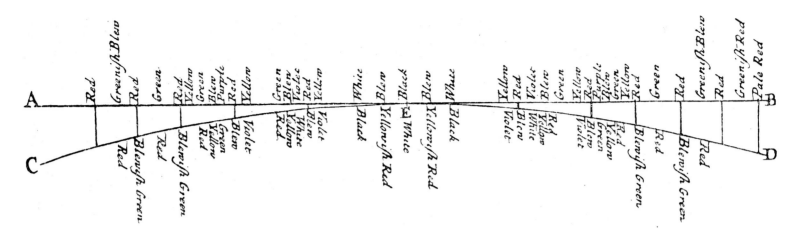

Isaac Newton's 'colours of thin plates' (*Opticks*, 1704), also known as 'Newton's rings', record the colours that appear on either side of two transparent plates when they are pressed together and illuminated by reflected and transmitted light. The pairs (listed in the diagram) gave rise to the notion of complementary colours, from black and white at the centre of pressure to bluish-green and red at the extremities. (135)

more than thirty editions by the end of the eighteenth century.[102] Newton, for reasons which I shall discuss in Chapter 13, had divided his blue into two but 'Boutet', more concerned with the practice of painting, made his division in the red section, knowing, like Le Blon after him, that a 'pure' red could only be a mixture of the yellowish *rouge de feu* and the blueish crimson. A more significant asymmetry was introduced into the circle in the 1780s by the Berlin painter Johann Christoph Frisch, who proposed an eight-part circle since, he argued, the eye recognizes a greater distance between blue and red and blue and yellow than between yellow and red. He proposed two steps, violet and purple, between blue and red, and two, sea-green and leaf-green, between blue and yellow. This was probably the first attempt to ground a colour-system on perception and it had little echo until the work of Wilhelm von Bezold in the 1870s and, particularly, Wilhelm Ostwald's twenty-four part colour-circle at the beginning of the twentieth century.[103]

On the contrary, the symmetrical circle of three 'primaries' and three 'secondaries' became deeply rooted in the understanding of all concerned with the fine and the decorative arts. This was because it seemed not only to embody the six key colours but also to express their complementary relationship: red was opposite green, which was the product of the other two primaries, yellow and blue, and so on. The importance of polar opposites was deeply rooted in Western thought: we saw in Chapter 1 how Theophrastus could not accept the Democritan theory because he could not see among the colours any contraries but black and white. Leonardo had described the most beautiful colour-contrast as the direct opposite (*retto contrario*); but he had no single view of what these opposites were – sometimes blue was contrasted with green and white, green with dark violet or blue, white with blue or black – which suggests that he had never laid colours out in the form of a

diagram.[104] Newton's view of opposite colours was of a quite different order: in a paper of 1672 he had already regarded red and blue, yellow and violet, and green and 'a purple close to scarlet' as opposite.[105] His work on the concentric rings of colours generated when two plates of thin glass are pressed together showed him that by reflected and transmitted light the same circles were variously white and black, red and blue, yellow and violet, and green and 'a compound of red and violet'.[106] Although it is not a completely symmetrical circle, Newton's mixing diagram, which first appeared in the *Opticks* of 1704, has these opposites very nearly in place. Newton showed himself to be unhappy with the idea of a mixture of white with as few as three colours but claimed that he had been able to mix his 'mouse-colour' (the grey that he regarded as 'white' in pigment mixtures) with only two: one part red-lead to five of copper-green.[107] So the 'opposites' were those pairs which mixed to white.

The first use of the term 'complementary' seems to be in a paper of 1794 by the American scientist Benjamin Thompson, Count Rumford, in the context of the colours of shadows (complementary to the colour of the light which causes them) and of colour-harmony: two colours are harmonious when one of them is balanced by the product of the two remaining primaries.[108] Rumford had been stimulated by the work of Robert Waring Darwin on 'ocular spectra', that is the coloured after-images perceived when a patch of a particular colour is looked at closely for a considerable time. The after-image of a patch seemed to be its complement, which gave many writers on harmony, notably Goethe, an added confirmation that the eye 'demanded' certain pairings.[109] It is notable that although all these early observations of after-images pointed out quite correctly that the complement of red, for example, is not green but blue-green, the by now canonical circular arrangement and the doctrine of secondary mixtures made green the almost universally accepted 'complementary' of red.

In due course these ideas filtered into the literature of art. One of the most coherent of the early circular systems, the entomologist Moses Harris's *Natural System of Colours* of the early 1770s, had been dedicated with his approval to Reynolds; its second edition of 1811 was dedicated to his successor as President of the Royal Academy, West.[110] In 1803 the scientist Isaac Milner was invited by the landscape-gardener Humphrey Repton to contribute an essay, 'Theory of Colours and

135

134

153

Shadows', to a book on gardening, in which Milner said that Repton ('the gentleman who consulted me on this subject of shadows') was in the habit of using a little diagram of the colour relationships to assist him while painting.[111] Such diagrams became part of the standard equipment of painters in England and France by the 1820s, and by the middle of the century a French chemist was asserting confidently:

> The colour circle [spectre circulaire] of six colours was known to Titian, Giorgione, Murillo and Rubens, since all the complementary effects and all the harmonies which can be obtained by the colour-circle can be found eminently in their works, and harmony can only be known by those who know antagonism.[112]

Colour harmony had come to mean particular sets of contrasts, a view given the greatest authority by the exhaustive experiments of another French chemist, Michel Eugène Chevreul. Called in the 1820s to improve the brightness of the dyes used in the Gobelins manufactory, Chevreul discovered that their apparent dullness was due not to the quality of the dyestuffs but to the subjective effect of optical mixture: adjacent threads of complementary or near-complementary hues were mixing in the eye to a neutral grey. After extensive experimentation Chevreul, at the suggestion of the physicist Ampère, presented his discoveries in the form of laws: 'In the case where the eye sees at the same time two contiguous colours, they will appear as dissimilar as possible, both in their optical composition and in the height of their tone'; and 'In the Harmony of Contrast the complementary assortment is superior to every other'.[113] The transforming effects of colour contrast had, of course, been familiar since Aristotle and had reached quite a sophisticated level of analysis among his commentators in the Middle Ages, such as St Thomas Aquinas, who noticed that purple looks different on white and on black, and gold better on blue than on white: this was familiar enough to painters and dyers.[114] As we have seen, Leonardo was also concerned about the changes in appearance wrought on colours by contrast and was as anxious as Chevreul to remove these contrasts to reveal the true nature of his subject. As Chevreul put it, 'to imitate the model faithfully, we must copy it differently from what we see it (§333)'. His findings, first published in 1828 and soon incorporated into public lectures at the Gobelins and elsewhere, were widely reported in the art press from the mid-1830s;[115] in 1839 Chevreul expanded them into a large illustrated book in which they were applied to a vast range of topics, from painting to the decorative arts, gardening and dress. *The Law of Harmonious Colouring* was translated into German and English and became perhaps the most widely used colour-manual of the nineteenth century.

Chevreul's taste in painting was conventional: he referred only to the sixteenth- and seventeenth-century masters Titian, Albano and Rubens in his book (§322); among contemporaries his closest associations were with painters who stood somewhere between the contending factions of Classicism and Romanticism in his day.[116] One important friend was Horace Vernet, one-time Director of the French Academy in Rome, whose speciality was battle-painting. He may have been attracted to the scientist by his belief that military uniforms should be in the most highly-contrasted colours, which would

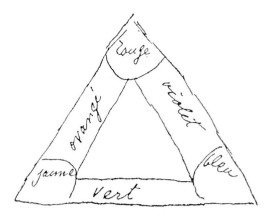

Delacroix adapted his colour triangle of *c.* 1830 from Mérimée's colour scale (pl. 176) to show the three 'primaries' (red, blue and yellow) in the corners, and their 'secondary' mixtures (violet, green and orange) between. Delacroix added a note (also based on Mérimée) that a mixture of a primary and a secondary colour (such as yellow-violet) gave a better grey than black and white. (136)

allow them to be used longer since the subjective effect of simultaneous contrast would compensate for the fading dyestuffs (§§658ff).[117]

One painter whose relationship to Chevreul remains problematic is Delacroix, who had shown some interest in colour theory from an early age but whose distaste for the positivism of the period cannot have endeared him to an outstandingly dogmatic scientist such as Chevreul.

In 1852 Delacroix wrote:

> I have a horror of the common run of scientists . . . they elbow one another in the antechamber of the sanctuary where nature hides her secrets, and are always waiting for someone more able than themselves to open the door a finger's breadth for them . . . Scientists ought to live in the country, close to nature; they prefer to chat around the green tables of the academies and the Institut about the things that everyone knows as well as they do; in the forest, on the mountains you observe natural laws, you do not make a step without finding a subject for admiration.[118]

A triangular colour-diagram in a Delacroix notebook of around 1830 comes not, as has sometimes been supposed, from Chevreul, but from a handbook on oil painting by the painter J. F. L. Mérimée, with whom Delacroix was closely associated in 1831.[119] Delacroix was perfectly familiar with the complementary circle: he sketched one in a notebook about 1839 and towards the end of his life seems to have kept a painted version in his studio.[120] This was the period when he was most anxious to inform himself about the principles of contrast, when he acquired a set of notes taken in 1848 at lectures by Chevreul and when, about 1850, he proposed to visit the chemist himself but was prevented by illness.[121] Chevreul's view that the high contrast of 'flat painting' should be adopted by artists working on large-scale mural and ceiling decoration was particularly important to Delacroix, who in the 1840s had been executing such schemes for the libraries of the Chamber of Deputies and

136

176

	Violet.	Bleu indigo.	Bleu cyanique.	Vert bleu.	Vert.	Jaune vert.	Jaune.
Rouge.	Pourpre.	Rose foncé.	Rose blanchâtre.	Blanc.	Jaune blanchâtre.	Jaune d'or.	Orangé.
Orangé.	Rose foncé.	Rose blanchâtre.	Blanc.	Jaune blanchâtre.	Jaune.	Jaune.	
Jaune.	Rose blanchâtre.	Blanc.	Vert blanchâtre.	Vert blanchâtre.	Jaune vert.		
Jaune vert.	Blanc.	Vert blanchâtre.	Vert blanchâtre.	Vert.			
Vert.	Bleu blanchâtre.	Bleu d'eau.	Vert bleu.				
Vert bleu.	Bleu d'eau.	Bleu d'eau.					
Bleu cyanique.	Bleu indigo.						

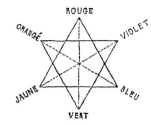

Auguste Laugel's table of colour mixtures (*L'Optique et les arts*, 1869) shows the component colours red, blue, yellow, etc., at the left and top, and their products, such as white, at the intersections. The scheme had been devised by Helmholtz, who formulated it using additive disc-mixtures. Laugel's colour-star was based on a diagram he had found in one of Delacroix's notebooks, and he claimed that though it was crude (it shows the subtractive primaries and complementaries of Chevreul), it was more practical for painters than Helmholtz's scheme. (137,138)

the Senate and also in the Paris church of St Denis du Saint-Sacrément.[122] In these works Delacroix developed a style of modelling in forceful hatchings of brilliant reds and greens in the flesh. Renoir, who was a close student of Delacroix's technique, argued that this was the only context in which he would have needed a knowledge of complementarity.[123] In 1850 Delacroix was embarking on a new monumental task, the ceiling of the Salle d'Apollon in the Louvre, which may have been his most immediate reason for wanting to talk to Chevreul. In 1851 an English critic spoke of this ceiling as showing how France 'is largely imbued with the ideas of modern science' and mentioned the problem of painting so high above the spectator. Certainly the colours, which outraged another critic in 1853, were originally brighter than they have become, so that van Gogh recalled the ceiling in the 1880s as simply a simultaneous contrast of yellow and violet.[124] It was about the time of the *Apollo*, too, that the writer Maxime du Camp witnessed Delacroix making complicated mixtures by overlaying threads of coloured wools and arguing that the best pictures he had seen were certain Persian carpets; he was also becoming more aware of the phenomenology of sunlight on surfaces out of doors.[125]

Of enormous consequence for Delacroix's great reputation as a colourist was his encounter at this time with the critic Charles Blanc, Director of the Arts under the brief Socialist government of 1848–50 and writer of one of the most important textbooks for artists in the second half of the century.[126] Blanc's *Grammaire des arts du dessin* of 1867, whose title was itself indicative of the new positivism, argued that the traditional view that colour, unlike drawing, could not be taught was quite mistaken and that it was Delacroix, 'one of the greatest colourists of modern times', who demonstrated most clearly the falsity of this position. Delacroix understood the laws, even the 'mathematical rules' of colour, and these laws and rules were essentially those enunciated by Chevreul.[127] Blanc was not, however, a great admirer of colour *per se*: he regarded it as the

'feminine' part of art, which must take second place to the 'masculine' drawing, and he felt that Delacroix's sacrifices to colour had sometimes been too great.[128] For Blanc, the great masters of colour were the Orientals but their superiority was shown in the less important branch of the decorative arts. The hatchings of red and green which Blanc saw in Delacroix's central dome in the library of the Luxembourg Palace seemed to him to function like the colour-mixtures in a cashmere shawl.[129] Thus he found Chevreul's principles exemplified most extensively in the painter's oriental subjects, such as the *Women of Algiers* (1834) to which he devoted a lengthy analysis but, as Lee Johnson has shown, edited the optical data in the interests of Chevreulian system, and focused on just those colourful decorative accessories which he felt were essentially demeaning to high art.[130] It is true that Delacroix was fascinated by oriental textiles and artefacts – many ceramics are still preserved in his studio at place Furstenberg in Paris – but we also know from a comparison between preparatory studies and final paintings that he was prepared to make many colour-changes as the work proceeded – and not usually in the direction of Chevreulian principles.[131]

Chevreul's career was a very long one, in the course of which his views on colour scarcely changed. His ideas were re-published in different forms but they were not revised and treatises based on his principles of the 1820s continued to be published in France at least until 1890.[132] Yet the study of colour had undergone great changes in mid-century because of the more precise analysis of the processes of vision, which cast doubt on the whole notion of primary colours and on the colour-circle based on them. There was a revival of interest in the early nineteenth-century work of Thomas Young, who had argued that the colour-receptors in the eye are sensitive to red, blue and green light; both Hermann von Helmholtz in Germany and James Clerk Maxwell in England showed that white light could be re-constituted from a mixture of only yellow and blue. Newton's coherent system was now re-complicated by the formal distinction to be made between additive and subtractive mixtures.[133] Chevreul appealed to the experience of painters and other artists against what he took to be the totally erroneous doctrines of Helmholtz and his followers in France;[134] but the publication of a translation of Helmholtz's great *Handbook of Physiological Optics* in 1867 had been succeeded by a spate of popular manuals designed to bring these doctrines within the scope of practising artists, the first of which, Auguste Laugel's *L'Optique et les arts*, appeared only two years later.[135] As recently as 1857 a physicist and amateur critic, Jules Jamin, had argued along seventeenth-century lines that since the painter, unlike the scientist, was exclusively concerned with effects, and since the powers of nature were beyond the powers of art, the 'realism' vaunted by the current school of French landscape painting was utopian to a degree.[136] But now, with the rise of Impressionism, a whole series of artists' handbooks, drawing on Helmholtz, proclaimed that the newly-discovered truths of optics were indeed being exemplified in painting. Thus Edmond Duranty, a critic who had read Armand Guillemin's Helmholtzian *La Lumière* of 1874, felt that 'for the first time painters have understood and reproduced, or tried to reproduce, these phenomena'.[137] A somewhat later text used by the writer J. K. Huysmans in his interpretation of Impressionism, Eugène Véron's *L'Esthétique* of 1878, presented Helmholtz's findings about mixture in the form of a table; but he made it clear that the only way in which this could be used was in the context of optical contrast:

> But these theories are of little use to painters as aids in the preparation of tints, because the coloured powders which they employ are unfitted for their application. They are, however, a great help to the comprehension of the effects resulting from the juxtaposition of different colours. Whenever complementary colours are placed side by side, they enhance each other's brilliancy . . .[138]

The proper exploitation of these discoveries would need a wholly new technique; in his characterization of the Impressionists Véron laid emphasis on their 'direct observation and unflinching sincerity' rather than on theoretical analysis, for their 'principle of the discolouration of tints when in full sunshine'.[139]

Thus, when the self-styled *impressionniste-luministe* Georges Seurat exhibited the first example of what he called *chromo-luminarisme* or *peinture optique*,[140] *Sunday Afternoon on the Island of La Grande Jatte*, at the final Impressionist exhibition in 1886, the theoretical ground was well prepared. This large picture had been in existence for two years but during the winter of 1885–6 Seurat re-worked much of its surface with a texture of more or less uniform dots and strokes, which made it, in Meyer Schapiro's words, the first self-consciously 'homogeneous' painting, as it is also the first that makes an optical theory the justification for a technique.[141] Perhaps the most substantial change in the colour-organization of the whole canvas was the shift from a more conventional Chevreulian notion of contrasts to a more subtle Helmholtzian one. The 1884 sketch for the couple in the right foreground of the picture sets up a series of complementary contrasts in which the red skirt of the woman is set against the green grass.[142] At some stage, probably in 1885,

Seurat decided to change this skirt to a purplish blue, as he did in a small oil sketch;[143] for, according to the Helmholtzian scheme, of which Seurat might have learned from Ogden Rood's *Modern Chromatics* (1879) or, more importantly, from conversations with the scientist Charles Henry (whom he met in October 1885), deep blue-purple and dark green were complementary.[144] Another, more significant, addition to the *Grande Jatte* was its painted border, which changes hue according to the hue of the area of painting against which it is set.[145] This thoroughly abstract device is a good index of Seurat's current beliefs about colour-contrast: it is clear that he sometimes felt, as in the right-hand edge of the painting and in the bottom centre, that blue was the appropriate contrast to orange (a Chevreulian pair) and sometimes that a bright purplish red was the complement of dark green, as Helmholtz and Rood had sought to demonstrate. These contrasting views of contrast are also evident in the smaller landscape, *The Bec du Hoc*, begun in Normandy in 1885, when the more expressive brushstroke was still very much apparent, but provided with some uniformly dotted revisions and a coloured border probably during 1886. Here the blue-red of the border is set against the blue-green of the sea and the blue-orange against the very pale whitish blue of the sky, but the contrast to the pale green grass is largely red.[146]

So Seurat's attitude to theory was eclectic, not to say *ad hoc*, and this eclecticism is reflected in the substantial list of his early reading which he sent to the critic Felix Fénéon in 1890.[147] The list included Rood's up-to-date textbook in the French version of 1881 – although Seurat did not say that he had read it, only that it had been brought to his notice – and Charles Blanc's *Grammaire*, which may indeed have been the immediate source for Seurat's extensive note on value-contrast from Chevreul (which he entitled *Refléxions sur la peinture*) and also for the quite un-Rood-like notion that sunlight is orange.[148] But above all Blanc, as we saw, had presented Delacroix as the scientific colourist *par excellence*; when Seurat made notes of the colour of some Delacroix oriental sketches in 1881, he concluded that they showed 'the strictest application of scientific principles seen through a personality'.[149] It was perhaps at this time too that Seurat took notes from some passages in Delacroix's *Journal* recording colour contrasts in nature:

> From my window I see the shadow of people walking in the sun on the sand [which is] violet itself, but gilded by the sun; the shadow of these people is so violet that the ground becomes yellow.
>
> Is it too daring to say that in the open air, and above all in the effect which is before my eyes, the reflection must be produced by the ground which is gilded being lit by the sun, that is to say yellow, and by the sky which is blue, and that these two induced [*produis*] tones would necessarily have a green tone? . . . all my life I have painted white drapery truly enough in colour [*ton*].
>
> So here are the testimonials of which a scholar might be proud; I am even more so at having painted well-coloured pictures before being aware of these laws . . .[150]

Seurat's early training and tastes were well calculated to inspire him with scientific ambitions. A series of articles on vision published in 1880 by the painter and aesthetician David Sutter included the following instruction, against which Seurat placed his cross. 'We must find a clear and precise formula for the rules of harmony of lines, of light and of colours, and give the scientific basis [*raison*] for these rules ... In the arts, everything must be willed.'[151] This is in essence the aesthetic credo which Seurat passed on to a friend at the end of his life; but being a scientific painter, in particular a scientific colourist, was no simple matter and throughout his short career he continued to use the superannuated but more easily remembered Chevreulian scheme of contrasts: red against green, blue against orange, yellow against violet, which Sutter published here, although on the basis not of Chevreul but of Goethe.[152] Seurat was very reluctant to expand on his principles, leaving that to his friend Fénéon, whose Roodian account of the *Grande Jatte* has shaped all subsequent interpretations of the technique of Neo-Impressionism, but who as early as 1888 was remarkably diffident about the scientific input into the method.[153] There is some reason for thinking that the ex-Impressionist Camille Pissarro, who in a letter to the dealer Paul Durand-Ruel of November 1886 generously pointed to Seurat as the first painter 'who had the idea of studying profoundly and applying the scientific theory', was himself rather more familiar with the scientific literature than his mentor. It is not always remembered that in his outline of the history of his own work Seurat drew attention to a (now unidentified) painting by Pissarro, shown at a private gallery early in 1886, which was 'divided and pure', that is, had, so Seurat thought, the essential characteristics of the Neo-Impressionist division of light into its coloured constituents.[154] In the letter to Durand-Ruel Pissarro referred quite correctly to the crucial roles of Maxwell and Rood in measuring the precise constituents of the complementaries; about the same time he was in touch with another painter, Louis Hayet, who was experimenting with the construction of colour-circles of from 40 to 120 divisions. Hayet presented Pissarro with five circles, only one of which, the simplest, forty-hue version, appears to have survived.[155] It represents an attempt to fill a Chevreulian, forty-part format with the information derived from Rood's far more complex colour-space, and may be compared with the way in which Seurat, when he drew a little diagram of the colour circle in 1887, tried in vain to fit the six-part Chevreulian scheme of complementaries into the eight-part circle of Charles Henry, based on Helmholtz's complementary contrasts. Seurat probably shared the opinion of Laugel that although the Helmholtzian scheme represented the truth about the colours of lights, in practice the crude (*grossier*) diagram of Delacroix, based on his note of about 1839, was far more useful.[156] Even Pissarro continued to put Chevreul at the head of those scientists who had made it possible for painters to feel confident about their understanding of light.[157]

Recent studies of Seurat's technique have tended to erode the traditional view that he was an essentially scientific artist.[158] What they have not done is to show that his new methods produced an optical context of such complexity that no painter could be expected to have dealt with its problems and retain freedom as an artist: this was one of the reasons why Pissarro soon turned his back on the Neo-Impressionist technique.[159] Seurat wanted to create high contrasts in large areas of tone but he also wanted to increase luminosity by the use of optical mixtures and these are incompatible with high contrast, which depends on sharp contours. We can see in the *Grande Jatte* how he tried to firm up his contours by making his dots smaller towards the edges of forms, hence more easily fusible at a constant viewing distance. This optical fusion was itself problematic, since different hues fuse at different distances.[160] Unlike Pissarro, who was most concerned with optical mixture, Seurat seems to have shown little interest in the question: he painted his large picture in a very confined space, in which empirical judgments of this sort would have been quite impossible.[161]

Newton had apparently brought order into the chaos of colour and had thus made it for painters as communicable a subject as drawing. Yet, as the Viennese physiologist Ernst Brücke stated quite categorically in a handbook for artists which had some influence in France, the enormous developments in the science of optics in the nineteenth century made it out of the question for the painter to be up-to-date in the manner of a Leonardo da Vinci.[162] So far from marking the beginnings of a scientific aesthetic, the optical concerns of the Neo-Impressionists signalled its demise, and helped to usher in that disdain for the methods and discoveries of the natural sciences which has had important consequences for the painterly study of colour in the twentieth century.

138

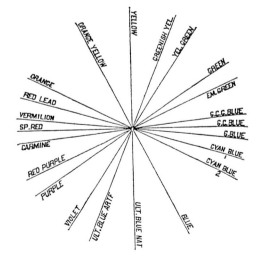

Ogden Rood's contrast diagram (*Modern Chromatics*, 1879) shows only those complementary contrasts established by disc-mixing techniques with specific pigments – hence both its asymmetrical appearance and its usefulness to painters. Seurat is known to have owned a copy of the French version of 1881. (139)

10 · The Palette: 'Mother of All Colours'

The palette as system · The well-tempered palette · Delacroix's palettes
The palette as painting

Praise be to the palette for the delights it offers . . . it is itself a 'work', more beautiful, indeed, than many a work. (Wassily Kandinsky, 1913)[1]

ONE OF THE least studied aspects of the history of art is art's tools. Historians of science are beginning to see what a fundamental effect the design and limitations of the available technology have had on the development of scientific concepts[2] but there is little sign yet that the same is being done for the technology of art. Here, with few exceptions, the study of equipment has so far been largely in the hands of those who feel that good craftsmanship has been lost and ought to be recovered.[3] The palette is one of the more important tools in the history of painterly ideas, since its development is relatively easy to trace in pictures of artists at work.[4] The method of its setting-out also has an important history, which takes us from the tool itself to the notion of 'palette' as the overall tonality of a picture. It is this history which I want to outline here.

The use of the palette as a small portable surface on which colours could be held and mixed is not clearly attested in Antiquity or the Middle Ages, for reasons which seem closely related to the early dislike of mixing as such (*see* Chapter 2).[5] Most depictions of medieval painters at work show the pigments in shallow containers such as shells or saucers, often with a wide range of colours, as in the five or six shown in an English fourteenth-century encyclopaedia, or the ten or eleven in the late fifteenth-century Flemish representation of an episode in the life of the ancient Greek painter Zeuxis.[6] The earliest representations of palettes in Europe, all in the hands of the women painters included in Boccaccio's *Livre des Femmes Nobles et Renommées* (*De Claris Mulieribus*) in two fifteenth-century Burgundian manuscripts now in Paris, show smallish bat-like palettes with a handful of colours placed in the centre, so that it is still unlikely that much mixing was done.[7] It is, of course, impossible to judge what medium the women were using in these fanciful illustrations of around 1400 but it could well have been oil; it was surely the binding power of oil, with its capacity to make a stiff and lastingly flexible paste, which made oil-colours possible to hold easily on the palette. Certainly what seems to be the earliest known description of palettes, in the accounts of the Dukes of Burgundy in the late 1460s, states clearly that they were for oil-colours: *trenchers of wood for them* [painters] *to put oil colours on and to hold them in the hand.*[8] There was still no reference to mixing and the early representations of palettes after the Burgundian ladies, all of which occur in northern painting *c.* 1500, show small surfaces holding the few pigments used to paint each section of the picture separately, with no sign of blending between each little pile of paint.[9]

One of the most interesting of these early representations of the artist at work is the panel of *St Luke painting the Virgin* by the Swiss painter Niklaus Manuel Deutsch, from a now fragmented altar. The Virgin is represented in the standard way, with a smallish, blue cloak, palette of white, several blues and a red-brown, which cover a good part of the surface; but in the background his assistant is preparing a far more extensive palette, set with a large number of pigments along the edge and presumably intended for making a quite different painting. The setting of a palette with many colours at the edge and a large bare area in the centre is a sign of extensive mixture: technical analysis of Niklaus Manuel's picture has shown that he did indeed use many mixtures in a complicated medium of oil and probably emulsion. He also used a range of more than twenty pigments, which might well fit the palette in the background.[10] This arrangement is similar to that in a Flemish painting of St Luke (*c.* 1520) where the saint's own palette is set in two lines totalling eight colours parallel to the edge, with the lightest (white) close to the thumb-hole and the darkest (blue) at the farthest end.[11] What these images suggest is that mixing practices were developing very rapidly in oil painting in the early sixteenth century, which was making it important to organize the palette in a quite new and regular way.[12]

Most of our examples of early palettes are from northern Europe but Vasari gives us a memorable picture of the Florentine painter Lorenzo di Credi, the fellow-pupil with Leonardo in the studio of Verrocchio and a close imitator of Leonardo's early style. His chief claim to our interest is his extraordinarily meticulous and solid technique. Vasari described how Lorenzo would prepare his very finely ground colours and distilled oils, and how 'he made on his palettes a great number of colour mixtures, so that they went gradually from the lightest tint to the darkest, with exaggerated and truly excessive regularity [*con troppo e veramente soverchio ordine*], so that sometimes he had twenty-five or thirty on his palette, and for each of them he kept a separate brush'.[13] We should very much like to know what this *ordine* was and how Lorenzo arrived at it; what seems clear is that his was the ancestor of those obsessively nuanced tonal palettes of pre-mixed colours which we find so often in the eighteenth and nineteenth centuries. Vasari disapproved of this degree of attention to the arrangement of the colours and there is nothing so regular among the surviving representations of palettes in the sixteenth century, either in Italy or the north. The only common principle seems to be that the black and the white shall be kept as widely separated as possible.[14] As late as the 1580s a north Italian technical handbook could remark that the palette was essentially a surface on which to dilute the colours with oil and that the mixtures of colours 'are made little by little as one works, since this time one veils, rather than covers, those details of painting which have already been well executed'.[15] Here the author, G. B. Armenini, is clearly assuming that mixtures are made by glazing on the painting and not beforehand on the palette.

We saw in earlier chapters how around 1600 a new interest in colour-systems based upon a notion of primaries and their mixtures began to affect artists; in due course this interest brought about a completely new attitude to the role of the palette. Technical practices are notoriously conservative and there is, so far as I know, little evidence of new arrangements until the 1620s. One of the first evidences of change is in the palette held for St Luke in Domenichino's pendentives for the dome of S. Andrea della Valle in Rome, which shows a line of colours along the edge from white near the thumb, through a bright red and a bright yellow to the darks, including yellow-brown and brown. We shall see in Chapter 13 on music and colour how sensitive Domenichino was to precise tonal scales; we know from the English traveller Richard Symonds how Domenichino's pupil Giovanni Angelo Canini would set his palette about 1650 in two rows, one of unmixed pigments from white, yellow-ochre, vermilion and so on to charcoal black, but without blue, and the second row of mixtures of up to three of these pigments. Canini spoke, significantly, of 'putting his palette in order'; he made what was for his day a remarkable use of mixtures, and Symonds described how in *Anthony and Cleopatra* he painted a river-bank, 'wch was colourd a sad greene, he tooke a masse of Terra Verde & mixt it dipping his pencill into all the scuri [dark colours] as Terra Rossa, Lacca, Terra d'ombra, Black a little, yet a sad greene prvayld in the colouring above all'. When Symonds looked closely at the clouds in another painting by Canini, mixed out of six pigments, he found that it was 'sch a pleasant mistigaglia'.[16]

Rubens made more use of the juxtaposed touches of pure pigments, and of glazes; although the future Queen of France was instructed in painting, the palette Rubens gave to her in the 1620s in his *Education of Marie de Médicis* is still small, with a large dose of white in the centre.[17] Rembrandt in this decade may also have used distinct palettes for each part of the painting: *The Artist in his Studio* at Boston, probably a self-portrait of about 1629, shows the traditional small palette, as well as a much larger one hanging on the wall.[18] But the portrait by Gerrit Dou of about the same date shows him working with a larger oval palette, on which the colours are set in a tonal order round the edge.[19] This order Rembrandt maintained throughout his life: it is hinted at in his moving self-portrait of 1660 in the Louvre and was adopted by pupils such as Aert de Gelder, in his revealing self-portrait painting an old woman. One of the problems revealed by these palettes is an uncertainty about the position of bright red in the tonal scale. Rembrandt, for example, felt that it was brighter than yellow-ochre, placing it next to white; de Gelder placed it beyond yellow and many other artists put it with other bright – and precious – pigments, such as ultramarine, apart from the main series and usually in much smaller quantities.[20]

Around 1630 the arrangement and use of the palette became as never before a subject for discussion in painterly circles. Turquet de Mayerne recorded at least two palettes, both

145

unattributed, one which runs through nine pigments from white to ivory- and lamp-black, with vermilion next to white, and the other of twelve colours in the same sequence, with an extra brown, and (?ultramarine) ashes and the lead-based yellow massicot at the end, out of sequence beyond black. Mayerne observed that 'the first function of the palette is to arrange the colours, the second to temper them with oil, and the third *alliance et meslange*' – the most comprehensive definition we have encountered so far; he also had a clear idea that arrangement was a principle, since in a later note on a palette set for portrait painting, he remarked that it was essential to put the light colours at the top (i.e. near the the thumb-hole) and the dark at the bottom.[21] It was increasingly assumed that the palette should be laid out as a general one for the whole of the picture: an English handbook of the early 1630s stated that it should include 'a small quantitie of every such colour you are to use', going on to list at least fourteen.[22] It was also clear that it should now be a tool for mixing. Pierre Le Brun, writing in Paris in 1635, characterized it as 'the mother of all colours, for from the mixture of three of four principal colours [the painter's] brush will create and, as it were, cause to bloom all kinds of colours'; he went on to describe a palette for flesh-painting which included ten pigments, blues and greens among them, and was to be set for the painter by his 'garçon'.[23] The common practice, going back to the Renaissance, of leaving an assistant to set the palette, must also have increased the need to make a regular and repeated order of colours which could become a habit. Le Brun also stated that the white must be placed in the centre of the palette, an arrangement we saw in Rubens and which was not uncommon in the first half of the seventeenth century: a good example is the otherwise very unusual palette of Judith Leyster, in her self-portrait of *c.* 1635.[24]

What is most striking about the new rational and tonal organization of the palette is that variations were as much local as personal. Velazquez, for example, painting himself into *Las Meniñas* (1656), used a tonal palette of ten colours, with vermilion before the white and a wider range than usual of browns and blacks, just as we should expect of him, but also essentially the range and the arrangement prescribed in a contemporary Spanish manual.[25]

Probably the first treatise to give a good deal of attention to the palette as such was Roger de Piles's *Les Premiers Élémens de la Peinture Pratique*, written in collaboration with and illustrated by the painter J.-B. Corneille and published in 1684 under his name. The *Élémens*, as its title suggests, was directed at beginners but it included very detailed instructions for painting in oil and in fresco and for making miniatures. De Piles argued that there were eight 'capital' colours, from which all others could be made by mixture, and his diagram of the order in which they were 'almost always' placed showed the by now conventional sequence, with yellow-ochre next to white. The only curiosity seems to be the placing of yellow lake (*stil de grain*) as the median colour, between lake and *terre verte*.[26] Another diagram showed a palette set for painting flesh, with vermilion placed as in the Spanish examples before the white, adding Naples yellow, carmine and ultramarine in a separate series. Half-tints for a head, said De Piles, were made with three values of a greenish

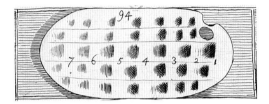

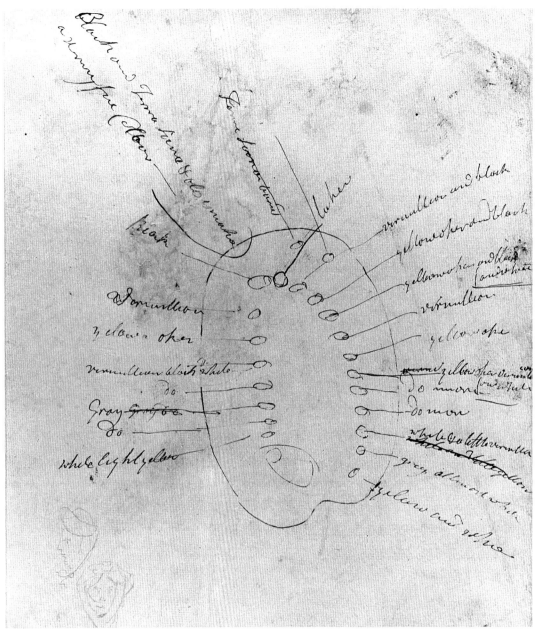

Palettes can tell us much about painters' attitudes to colour. Two English palettes of the eighteenth century show contrasting approaches to setting. Hogarth's palette (*The Analysis of Beauty*, 1753) has no room for mixing. Black, white, and five 'bloom tints' (red, yellow, blue, green and purple) are placed in spectral sequence from the top at No. 4, each hue graded in seven values, from dark to light (see also pls. 143–4). George Romney's drawing of his palette shows a tonal arrangement of twenty-two colours, many of them pre-mixed. The artist painted chiefly portraits, and his palette probably reflects the need to match flesh-tones. (140,141)

mix, each with a little less white, and shadow tones in two values, only the darkest with black. These tones were not mixed in the process of painting but pre-mixed and set out over the whole palette in two tonal series amounting to ten tones, getting progressively darker away from the thumb-hole. They might however be modified by further mixing, according to the needs of the developing painting, but this should be kept to a minimum and the models to follow for the handling of 'virgin tints' were Veronese and Rubens.[27]

A slightly later French manual by the amateur Bernard du Puy de Grez also laid great emphasis on mixture, citing a painter friend who first prepared tints with his palette-knife on the palette, then further blended them with his brush in the act of painting. This is an early reference to the knife that was so much used by Rembrandt as a tool for painting itself and which can be seen in use in a portrait of the marine painter Willem van de Velde the elder by Michel van Musscher of about 1665/7.[28] Elaborate pre-mixed palettes began to be very common in the

last quarter of the seventeenth century, a tendency which was to continue for two hundred years. In the 1670s, for example, Sir Peter Lely would arrange up to forty mixed tints on his palette for portraits and his rival in England Gerard Soest used three or four tones of each of his own major colours.[29] This proliferation both of 'primary' pigments and of mixed tones increased throughout the eighteenth century. In a lecture to the French Academy in 1752 the *animalier* J.-B. Oudry suggested that all available colours should be used and that each of them should have five or six pre-mixed light tones and as many mid-tones as the painter could manage, to avoid 'tiring' them by mixing with the brush. The pre-mixed tones should be arranged in tonal sequence 'in order better to evaluate the tone of each of them and compare it with the others'.[30] We are close to the large palettes of two ranges of pre-mixed tones used by Jacques-Louis David in his teaching[31] but, as we shall see, even these were simple compared with the highly orchestrated arrangements of Delacroix in the Romantic period.

158

The well-tempered palette

In a late seventeenth-century treatise on watercolour-painting the French artist Hubert Gautier expressed puzzlement at the way oil-painters often seemed to make a secret of the arrangement of their palettes. His surprise at the rather standard tonal settings which now prevailed may seem less unusual if we consider his own bizarre chemical theory of colours, which made black, white, violet and yellow the primaries, and blue and green derivatives, so that, for example, the alkaline violet would be turned red by mixture with an acid.[32] But the growing individualism of eighteenth-century art brought a range of unorthodox palette arrangements, from those of unschooled artists such as the barely teenaged Gainsborough in a recently discovered self-portrait,[33] to the elderly Welsh landscape-painter Richard Wilson, who moved from a rather straightforward setting of some nine pigments and mixtures in the 1750s to a far more eccentric range of eight or nine pigments and a dozen pre-mixed tints twenty years later.[34] The commercial value of some personal style of laying out the palette was quickly appreciated by writers of handbooks, such as J. C. Le Blon, who published some outstandingly complicated hand-coloured illustrations of portrait palettes in his *Coloritto* of 1725, and Thomas Bardwell, a painter and author of one of the most popular treatises of the period, whose palettes prescribed for portraits, with more than twenty pigments and tones, seem to have been far more complex than those he used in his own practice.[35] This individualism is also reflected in a new curiosity about the palettes of well-known painters, evident in Paul Sandby's sketch of Wilson's, or the portrait-painter George Romney's own remarkable diagram, showing an unusual *141* arrangement with all the mixtures round the edge.[36] This curiosity was to last well into the twentieth century; Sandby's was the ancestor of those anthologies of palettes which began to appear in technical handbooks in the nineteenth century and have been even more cultivated in the next.[37]

Perhaps the most idiosyncratic of all eighteenth-century palettes was that of William Hogarth. In an early self-portrait Hogarth represented a palette for flesh-painting made up of white and vermilion and their mixed tones.[38] But in the course of preparing his treatise *The Analysis of Beauty* in the 1750s, he devised a far more ambitious scheme, based on the analysis of colour-relationships. Starting from Leonardo's account of the rainbow (*see* p. 108), Hogarth proposed that the vigour of the primary tints could be maintained by observing the way in which, in the bow, the adjacent colours were mingled without losing their identity. The painter, said Hogarth, 'by means of a certain order in the arrangement of the colours upon his palette, readily mixes up what kind of tint he pleases.'[39] What this order should be he expounded in the commentary to Plate II of his *140* book, where the ideal palette is at the centre of the upper frame. The five 'original' colours of painting are, besides white and black, red, yellow, blue, green and purple, which Hogarth placed in a vertical scale, as 'bloom tints' or what painters called 'virgin tints', at No. 4 in his diagram, as the median and most brilliant class of colours, in spectral order from the top. To the left each of these hues moves into white, at 7, 6 and 5; to the right, 1, 2 and 3 'would sink into black, either by twilight, or at a

moderate distance from the eye'. Nos 5, 6 and 7 are almost as beautiful as class 4, since they gain in light, whereas it is the opposite with black. Hogarth went on to show how all the colours on this palette might be used, at row 7, to make a painting of the marble bust, No. 96 on his plate, in the right-hand margin, with a 'very fair transparent and pearl-like complexion'.[40] His chief concern was to keep his tints clear and distinct, as he admired them in Rubens, and he left no space in his arrangement for palette-mixing, or for black and white as such. It was a palette which must have been virtually impossible to use: although he kept the spectral arrangement on the palette shown in his self-portrait of a few years later, Hogarth there *143* started the sequence with white, added an extra red (?crimson) and left a good deal of space for making tints in the process of painting.

I know of only one painter hardy enough to take Hogarth's advice literally, the American historical artist John Trumbull, who showed himself at the age of twenty-one with a copy of *144* Hogarth's *Analysis* and a palette derived from the argument resting on it. But even Trumbull simplified Hogarth considerably and since the English artist was so disparaging about the dark end of the scale, the American started with the fully saturated hues and graded them in a series of six values towards white.[41] In the event, Trumbull's self-portrait seems to have been no more than a youthful demonstration-piece; later in his career he showed himself holding palettes with much more conventional tonal settings.[42]

The growing practice of laying out a series of pre-mixed tints, and of limiting the possibilities of mixture in the process of painting, was, in effect, to impose a more or less nuanced grid onto the perceptions of the motif. Where Claude had mixed his tones out of doors and taken them back to his studio to make a painting, an eighteenth-century painter, even the unconventional J.-B. Desportes, who was responsible for some of the freshest outdoor oil sketches of the period, would take a 'loaded palette' on his expeditions into the country – and 'loading' meant loading in every sense.[43] It had long been felt that the colouring of a painting might reflect rather the character of the painter's taste than the character of his subject.[44] Oudry in his 1752 lecture recalled how his master Nicholas de Largillière loved to watch Flemish painters at work because he could see how the relationship of tints on the palette affected the same relationship in the subject they were painting: 'what he had no less admired was that beautiful harmony which he always saw throughout the gradations of these tints, and which seemed to respond in advance to what he would find in the picture'.[45]

Painters in their studios began to be represented from the late Middle Ages onwards. In the sixteenth century, St Luke the artist uses a small and limited palette for painting the blue cloak of the Virgin, and does not appear to be mixing his colours very much. But in the background an assistant prepares a far more extensive palette, running from white to black, perhaps the palette used by Niklaus Manuel for painting this very picture, in which a wide range of mixed pigments has been identified.

142 NIKLAUS MANUEL DEUTSCH, *St Luke painting the Virgin*, 1515

The personal palette

143

144

143 William Hogarth, *Self-portrait painting the Comic Muse, c.* 1758 (detail)
144 John Trumbull, palette set according to Hogarth's precepts, detail of *Self-portrait*, 1777

During the eighteenth century the invention of palette arrangements began to be almost as personal as style. In his book the *Analysis of Beauty* (1753), Hogarth proposed an elaborate, essentially spectral palette (pl. 140), but he does not seem to have used more than a very simplified version of it himself (**143**). Possibly the only painter to take it seriously was the young American John Trumbull (**144**), who in an early self-portrait showed a similarly reduced adaptation of it resting on his copy of 'Hogarth'.

145 Aert de Gelder, *Self-portrait as Zeuxis* 1685 (detail)

Rembrandt's pupil de Gelder presents himself as the ancient Greek painter Zeuxis, who was said to have died laughing at his portrait of an old woman, here represented incongruously as Venus. Yet his palette is of a classic late seventeenth-century type, arranged in tonal sequence from white at the thumbhole, through yellow, red and brown to black. There is plenty of room for mixing.

145

Of the Impressionsists, the artist most concerned with colour theory was probably Pissarro, who later joined Seurat's group of Neo-Impressionists. In a witty demonstration-piece he shows how a far from schematic landscape painting was created out of a palette of six brilliant colours: white, yellow, red, purple, blue and green. Like Seurat's (pl. 148), this was an 'outdoor' palette and could be fitted neatly into a portable paintbox.

146 CAMILLE PISSARRO, *Palette with a landscape, c. 1878*

Where in the late seventeenth century the phrase 'made with the same palette' had characterized a painting whose overall union of tones had brought the whole into a pleasing harmony,[46] now in the eighteenth it became a term of abuse for a work which too obviously reflected the arrangement of the raw materials. We saw in the last chapter how the German critic Hagedorn argued that it was the task of mixture to destroy the evidence of palette-arrangements – the work should no longer 'smell of the palette' – and the English portrait-painter John Hoppner sneered at his rival Romney, whose palette as revealed in his paintings might 'readily be traced back to the colour-shop'.[47] It was a new twist to the Renaissance debate about truth to nature or truth to materials; what is certain is that by about 1750 the notion of the palette as simply another tool had given way to the notion of a particular range of colours characterizing a painting, or even a particular painter's work as a whole. By the end of the century a number of English landscape artists felt that the character of the picture was directly dependent on the setting of the palette.[48] In the Romantic period a group of artists, meeting at the house of the critic William Hazlitt, probably about 1815, debated his question,

> Whether a particular set of colours arranged on a painter's palette did not influence his style of art? – so much so indeed, as to be a question whether any artist would not have painted in the same style, scale of colour, and peculiarities, with any given palette, – say, for instance, of Titian, Rubens, or Rembrandt, – and that a painter, with the palette so set of any one of these three, would have painted in the precise style of Titian, Rubens, or Rembrandt?

The Scottish genre-painter David Wilkie thought that he would, assuming that Titian's palette had been set 'with the *peculiar* and *particular* primitive colours, so arranged with gradations of tints and variations'. Hazlitt and Haydon dissented, as did the teller of the story, the now forgotten historical artist William Bewick, who pointed to an anecdote about Van Dyck on a visit to Frans Hals, taking Hals's palette to paint a portrait – but very much in his own style.[49] Wilkie, of course, who had made his reputation with modern versions of Teniers, was soon to become a not insensitive interpreter of Titian, Rubens and Murillo. Another English critic of this period, the associationist Richard Payne Knight, supported the idea that colour was not a determinant of style, or the chief carrier of meaning, by observing that 'no person ... ever found pleasure in hearing verse recited in a language which he did not understand, or in contemplating the materials of the picture spread out on the palette'.[50] The later development of Romantic and Symbolist aesthetics was to show how very far this was from being the case.

A new dimension in the understanding of the palette as a formative influence on the making of paintings may be seen in the parallel increasingly drawn between its function and that of a musical instrument. Already in the 1820s a Swiss painter's manual had presented its gradations of colour as analogous to the notes on a piano keyboard; certainly the range of thirty-six mixtures from nine basic hues proposed in this book reminds us of the developing resources of the piano technology in the Romantic period, not to mention the new orchestration of a Berlioz or a Wagner. 'Tuning' the palette was seen to resemble tuning an instrument: 'To tune a colour-tone, and to bring it into harmony with another, which is there for comparison, is just as swiftly to be achieved by the painter, as by the musician who tunes his instrument by comparison with another, and even swifter, if he is practised at it.'[51] But as the nineteenth century advanced, it was the lush sonorities of complex and subtly nuanced mixtures which came to determine the instrumental role of the palette. It was the age of Wagner-worship, in which the art of one of Wagner's greatest French idolators, Henri Fantin-Latour seemed to expose hitherto unknown possibilities of tonal refinement. That Symbolist lover of black, Odilon Redon, wrote of Fantin in 1882 that even his handling of tone was not without its shortcomings: 'His palette, which is the true, the only palette, is a perfect piano which gives all the degrees of colours taken to itself, admirable for painting the brilliance of flowers, dazzling stuffs, but doubtless incomplete when he asks of it that fundamental *grey* which distinguishes the masters, expresses them and is the soul of all colour.'[53] We remember that it was another Wagnerite, Vincent van Gogh, who discovered twenty-seven blacks in Frans Hals.[53] Fantin's friend Whistler went some way towards answering Redon's objection and he, too, was impressed by the analogy with music. Not surprisingly in the painter of *Arrangement in Black: Portrait of Señor Pablo de Sarasate* (1884), Whistler was conscious of the palette's relationship less to the piano than to the violin: he told a pupil in the late 1890s that, 'being the instrument on which the painter plays his harmony, it must be beautiful always, as the tenderly cared-for violin of the great musician is kept in condition worthy of his music.' Whistler would spend up to an hour preparing his mixtures, which he laid out on his palette in two scales: from red to black and from yellow to blue.[54] An English contemporary of Whistler's, however, G. A. Storey, gave the most circumstantial account of the uses of the well-tempered palette: Storey arranged his nineteen colours

> like the keys of a piano, or at least affording the possibility of obtaining perfect chromatic scales by mixture ... When the colours are arranged in a settled and rational order ... they are found the more readily; and after some practice the artist comes to be able to play upon them as a musician plays upon his instrument, well knowing how and where to find the elements of his combinations.

A painter of genre, he expanded on his theme:

> I play upon it in this way, – If I want blue, for instance, I take, say Antwerp blue and white: it is too crude. I take some black: it is not purple enough. I take some lake etc. So one colour counteracts another, or modifies it; and although the number of different tints or shades of colour is infinite, this method of producing them is the simplest thing in the world. We only require to know our colours on the keyboard well – to know exactly what they can do – and then making a tint becomes very like striking a chord in music.[55]

Delacroix's palettes

Undoubtedly the great virtuoso of the palette in the nineteenth century was Delacroix, to whom both Fantin and Whistler paid homage in Fantin's group portrait of 1864. Fantin, indeed, was sometimes said to have adopted Delacroix's palette himself; it,

View of Delacroix's studio in 1853, with some of the complicated palette arrangements that he put on display among his paintings. (147)

or rather they – for there were many Delacroix palettes – were probably the best-known in the whole period. Paradoxically in an artist to whom the musicality of painting was one of its most important attributes, Delacroix compared his palette not to an instrument but to the arms of the warrior, 'the sight of which gives him confidence and boldness'.[56] Confidence was certainly something which he might expect to gain from his own palettes, for he considerably extended the old practice of changing their arrangement according to the character of the subject. From at least the early 1840s each Delacroix painting had its own 'palette', which he had pondered at great length and which made the execution of the work itself relatively swift and straightforward. This was an approach to colour-organization particularly associated with the great decorative schemes where the workshop assistant who executed the work needed to be given detailed instructions for the colour compositions.[57] A Delacroix pencil-note of 1844, relating to the decoration of the Library of the Palais Bourbon, suggests how these palettes were to be set and recorded: tones contrasting and even complementary to each other were to be laid out side-by-side on the palette at the same level of value and they were to be grouped together numerically with all those of a similar value.[58] This sort of complex tonal arrangement can still be seen in the loaded palettes preserved at Delacroix's studio in Paris, although the deterioration of the pigments makes it difficult for the unaided eye to work out the rationale of each grouping now. One of his assistants, Andrieu, gave further details of how they were set up:

> Delacroix before starting on his large decorative pictures spent whole weeks combining on his palette the tonal relationships,

which he transferred to bits of canvas pinned to the wall of his studio. On each of these tones he carefully noted the composition and the destination (reflection, shadow, half-tone and light, name of the figure, the feeling to be expressed, impasto or glaze, etc.).[59]

These collections of numbered painted strips soon got into circulation. Those for the *Justice of Trajan* (1840) and *Christ in the Garden of Olives* (presumably the painting of 1827, a sign that Delacroix worked in this way from a remarkably early date), for example, were known in the 1850s among quite a wide circle of artists;[60] many were kept after Delacroix's death by Andrieu and were acquired at his sale by Degas, who, apparently, could use only the simplest of them, since sometimes they numbered more than fifty tones.[61]

These numbered series of tones for each of the large compositions formed a remarkable reference library for Delacroix himself and they are a telling indication of his essentially conceptual approach to the tasks of the colourist. Another indication is the practice recorded by Charles Blanc of using samples from his huge collection of sealing-wafers for letters, which, like the shells collected by the English entomologist quoted in Chapter 9, he had collected in all hues and all values of each hue. These Delacroix would apply to his canvas in a sequence of tones in order to judge the effect at a distance. Nothing suggests more strongly than these 'palettes' and this collection of wafers the justice of Blanc's remark that Delacroix possessed 'the mathematical rules of colour'; but they were rules which the painter constructed very much for his own purposes and using his own eye.[62]

147

The palette as painting

Delacroix, like Whistler, loved his palettes: Andrieu reports that during his master's terminal illness he sent for one on which to work out some mixtures and the pupil knew that he was dead, he said, only when he found the colours dry.[63] But their extraordinarily complicated arrangement shows that the tool had become an even more personal thing than it had been in the eighteenth century. The 1860s seem, like the 1620s, to be a watershed, when the tonal setting going back some 250 years – my choice of exceptional examples to discuss should not dispel the impression of overwhelming standardization that emerges from an examination of self-portraits – ceased to be regarded as a norm. It is not easy to trace the breakdown of this norm, although the handbook of Thénot in 1847 already regarded it as far from binding.[64] One of its clearest symptoms is a homage to Chardin by Philippe Rousseau, *Chardin et ses modèles* (1867), where the palette which is included runs from red near the thumb-hole through blue to white, yellow and browns: quite unlike the very orthodox tonal palette which we know Chardin himself was used to, from its frequent appearance in his still-lives, the *Attributes of the Arts*.[65]

For whatever reason, from the 1850s in France and elsewhere the notion that the palette should be organized along tonal lines lost its attraction. Painters as different as Gustave Courbet in France and the more academic Alfred Stevens in Belgium presented themselves to the public in a sort of painterly *déshabille*, with palettes arranged according to no recognizable principle.[66] The same goes for Gustave Moreau (significantly the master of Matisse), James Ensor, Sir Edward Burne-Jones, John Singer Sargent and Lovis Corinth, to mention only painters trained in the third quarter of the nineteenth century.[67] Even a French handbook of the 1870s, although it was committed to 'valeurs', the French version of tonal painting, and opposed to Impressionism, proposed a colour-sequence on the palette running from madder lake to ivory black, with yellows in the middle, which seems to us to be quite unreasoned.[68] Sargent and Corinth were both much affected by Impressionism and it was among the Impressionists that, not surprisingly, the idea of a tonally based order was first widely disputed. Sargent's portrait of Monet at work in the 1880s shows a palette in a fine state of confusion; but as early as the 1860s Monet's arrangement had been far from traditional, as can be seen in his *Studio Corner* (1861).[69] Other associates of the Impressionists, such as Bazille and Guillaumin, also used idiosyncratic arrangements in these years.[70] A decade later the more scientifically oriented Camille Pissarro gave an amusing demonstration of the generative powers of what he called the 'six rainbow colours', by making them form a landscape on his
146 palette itself.[71] Here indeed was the palette as 'mother of all colours'!

Pissarro's arrangement without black was a sort of compromise between the tonal scale and the spectrum, and we saw earlier how Hogarth had tried to offer a rational alternative to the tonal palette by invoking the rainbow. The 'primary' or 'spectral' palette was one of the most common variations on the traditional tonal form throughout the nineteenth century. The German Nazarene painter Wilhelm von Schadow showed

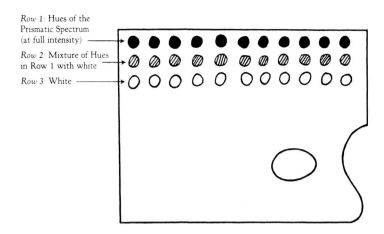

Row 1: Hues of the Prismatic Spectrum (at full intensity)

Row 2: Mixture of Hues in Row 1 with white

Row 3: White

The palette (*c.* 1891) used by Seurat at the time of his death is set with a row of 11 pure hues, running in spectral sequence from yellow to green; a row of these hues mixed with white; and a row of pure whites, for use in further mixtures. (148)

himself with a 'primary' palette of red, yellow and blue, in descending order of luminosity, to black, in a self-portrait of about 1815 in Berlin;[72] the American artist Charles Willson Peale, perhaps taking his cue from Trumbull, was using a similarly restricted range in a quasi-spectral order in the 1820s.[73] David's pupil Paillot de Montabert, in his compendious handbook of 1829, argued that the three 'generating' colours were, theoretically, sufficient and that it was only the unscrupulous colour-manufacturers who foisted unnecessary pigments on the ignorant artist. Since it was not yet possible to find categorically 'pure' primaries, each of the three should be bought or mixed in four values.[74] A German painter and theorist of the late 1840s proposed an extraordinarily extended 'prismatic' palette, divided into 'warm' and 'cool' sequences and still running from white to black in twenty-three stages.[75] Even the most famous of the 'spectral' palettes, those of Signac and Seurat in the 1880s, made a compromise between the idea of a   148
spectral sequence and a tonal one, using eleven pigments from yellow near the thumb-hole to green at the far end, and with separate whites for mixing next to each of these hues.[76] There are a number of anomalies about this palette: Fénéon described its arrangement as 'l'ordre du prisme', which it clearly is not, and Signac, who claimed to have introduced Seurat to it in 1884, recalled in old age that his own sequence at this time ran 'from yellow to yellow . . . in order or gradation of the prism'.[77] What is certain is that this was not the only spectral palette available at the time; it is something of an irony that the simplest was published in 1891 by an arch-opponent of Impressionism and of scientific theory, J.-G. Vibert, the painter of cardinals at   149
play and teacher of the most traditional techniques at the École   179
des Beaux-Arts.[78] Vibert's spectral palette used thirteen hues to match the spectrum as closely as possible, just as Signac and Seurat used eleven or twelve: we are not dealing with the sort of restricted palette characteristic of the Impressionists until the end of their lives.[79]

The spectral palette was not the only more or less organized arrangement of the modern period. The German theorist

Hundertpfund's attempt to arrange sequences of warm and cool was the ancestor of a scheme by the Nabi painter Paul Sérusier who, believing in the incompatibility of warm and cool in the same composition, devised separate palettes for each tonality. And not only for painting: the dealer Ambroise Vollard recalled an encounter with the painter in a Paris street when Sérusier told him, 'You see that woman in a violet coat in front of us? When I saw you beside her in your brick-coloured overcoat, you have no idea how much those two colours screamed at being juxtaposed. It really made me ill.'[80] From about 1908 Sérusier proposed that painters should use two separate palettes, but some years later he tried to combine the arrangement on a single surface, with the warm colours, topped by yellow, set apart from the cold, of which white, almost a light blue, was the highest value. He made something of a fetish of these distinctions: he had, for example, given up using Naples yellow because he thought that some manufacturers made it up from yellow ochre plus white – which could only belong to the cold scale.[81]

Sérusier's intense involvement with systems was not matched by his capacities as a practical colourist; but the most considerable colourist of our century, Henri Matisse, also had a highly developed sense of order. 'To put order into colour-relationships is to put order into your ideas', he told an interviewer in 1925.[82] For Matisse order could only be established on the canvas in the course of painting; the many loaded palettes which he left around him, and his several representations of them in paintings and drawings, not to

150

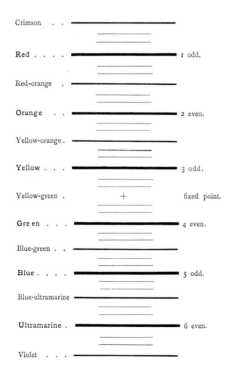

J.-G. Vibert's diagram of a spectral palette (*The Science of Painting* 1890/92) divides it into 37 degrees, represented by the lines, with the centre marked by a cross. Complementaries are represented by an odd and an even number, and found by adding or subtracting 3. Hence the complementary of yellow, at 3, is ultramarine, at 6. (149)

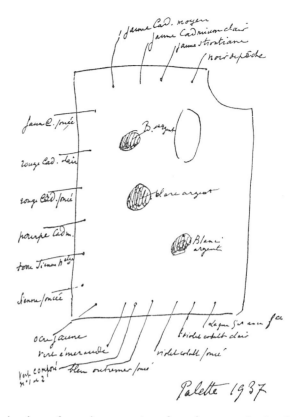

Palette 1937

Matisse's palette of 1937 shows a setting of 17 colours, running in what seems like an arbitrary sequence from peach-black at the thumb-hole to madder lake, with several cadmium yellows and reds, cadmium purple and lemon-yellow, yellow and brown ochres, two cobalt-violets, dark ultramarine, viridian and two mixed greens. In the centre are placed large mounds of white. (150)

mention the accounts he gave to the press, defy analysis, for they differ markedly among themselves and seem to have no common principles of organization.[83] Some of the surviving palettes are very lightly touched with colour and may well have been, like his paintings, improvised as Matisse's work progressed.

The setting of the palette was clearly aspiring to the condition of painting. Matisse's contemporaries Paul Klee and Wassily Kandinsky had already seen that what happened in the paintbox or on the palette was more crucial to the making of art than what happened in nature, in the ostensible subject. In a diary note of 1910 Klee described as a 'revolutionary discovery' the recognition of his relationship to his box of colours: 'I must one day be able to fantasize on the colour-piano of neighbouring watercolour pans.'[84] And in the first important manifesto of non-representational art, Kandinsky wrote about 1912:

Letting one's eyes wander over a palette laid out with colours has two main results:
(1) There occurs a purely physical effect, i.e. the eye itself is charmed by the beauty and other qualities of the colour. The spectator experiences a feeling of satisfaction, of pleasure, like a gourmet who has a tasty morsel in his mouth. Or the eye is titillated, as is one's palate by a highly spiced dish. It can also be calmed or cooled again, as one's finger can when it touches ice. These are all physical

sensations, and as such can only be of short duration. They are also superficial, leaving behind no lasting impression if the soul remains closed . . .

(2) The second main consequence of the contemplation of colour, i.e. the psychological effect of colour. The psychological power of colour becomes apparent, calling forth a vibration from the soul. Its primary, elementary physical power becomes simply the path by which colour reaches the soul . . .[85]

With such powerful effects from the palette alone, we might well wonder what role in the articulation of colour was left to painting itself.

One of the chief stimuli to this new, expressionist understanding of colour had been the art and writing of van Gogh, whose letters to his brother Theo were not fully published in German until 1914 but had been included in anthologies much earlier. In his long process of self-education, van Gogh had soon come up against the problem of matching his perceptions – the colours of his subjects – with the pigments available to him, and he had asked, 'Mightn't I presume . . . that a painter had better start from the colours on his palette than from the colours in nature?' (Letter 429). He had begun with the by then quite academic tonal arrangement of the eighteenth century; but his encounter with Impressionism in Paris in 1886 had thrown this order into confusion, just as it caused him to re-organize his colour-compositions on a hue-based, essentially complementary structure which we shall look at more closely in Chapter 11.[86] Paris also introduced Vincent to the idea of the importance of the palette for the understanding of the painter's personality. The collecting of palettes – usually unloaded – by admired masters had certainly begun in England in the 1820s but Delacroix was probably the first to use an Old Master's palette for the purposes of study. He had been given a loaded palette ostensibly of Van Dyck's and used its constituents, including 'Vandyke brown', in planning his own mural schemes of the 1840s.[87] Delacroix's personal palette-arrangements, displayed so prominently among the paintings in his studio, seem to have started a fashion for showing these tools in public exhibitions. One appeared at a dealer's exhibition in 1885 and in a mixed show, including a handful of other modern artists' palettes, in Paris in 1887. When, in the following year, the Louvre opened a new room of modern French art, these palettes were again on show and attracted the notice of the press, since 'on each of them we recognize the painter's manner of painting'.[88] Vibert in the 1890s mentioned a private collection of artists' palettes, which 'still showed all the tones improvised in the act of painting, and on many of them the artists had painted a little, according to his own method' – a collection which Vibert said was destined for the Louvre and would be a great lesson for future generations.[89] It is not clear what became of this collection but after the turn of the century Paris saw a number of exhibitions entirely of palettes: one of a hundred at Bernheim Jeune in 1908 and in 1911 a sale of 123 at the Georges Petit gallery, which might conceivably have been the collection mentioned by Vibert. We are used nowadays to seeing palettes as a feature of both temporary exhibitions and permanent displays of painting but I imagine that very few modern spectators look upon them as anything more than just another tool.

152

151

147

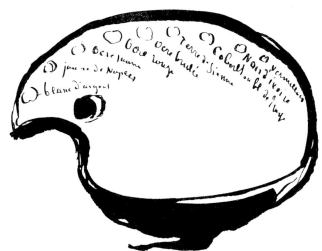

Van Gogh's drawing of his palette in 1882 shows 9 colours, running tonally and quite conventionally from white at the thumb-hole to vermilion, placed unusually beyond black. Vincent described it as, 'a practical palette with healthy colours. Ultramarine, carmine, and the like are added when strictly necessary.' The *Self-portrait* of 1888 illustrates a palette with an arbitrary non-linear arrangement, largely of orange, red, blue and green, suggesting the disintegrating influence of Impressionism. (151,152)

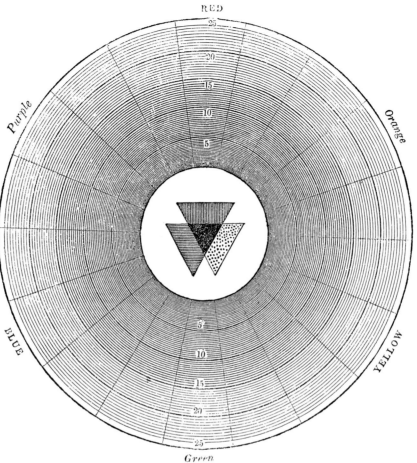

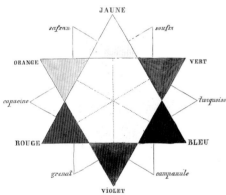

Eighteenth- and nineteenth-century colour-theorists were attracted to shapes such as circles and stars which emphasized the polar opposites. Moses Harris's colour circle (*Prismatic Colours, c.* 1776, above) was one of the earliest entirely symmetrical arrangements, and also suggested a solid by the darkening of the hues towards the centre. The stars (left and right) of Charles Blanc (1867) and Jules-Claude Ziegler (1850) are especially interesting for their exotic terms for tertiary colours, based on flowers and vegetable colorants. (153–5)

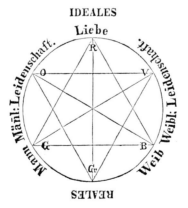

Philipp Otto Runge (1809) used the star in a more mystical vein (above) to suggest the contrast between the ideal world of love, red, and the real world of green. The masculine passions are represented by the warm side of the circle (yellow and orange) and the feminine by the cool (blue and violet). (156)

11 · Colours of the Mind: Goethe's Legacy

Colour as perception · The impact of Goethe · The morality of colour · 'Painting is recording coloured sensations' · From Matisse to abstraction

NEWTON's *Opticks* had sought to put the study of light and colour on an objective, quantitative, basis. In his experiment to determine the chromatic constituents of the spectrum he had enrolled the services of 'an Assistant, whose Eyes for distinguishing Colours were more critical than mine'.[1] Whether or not this 'assistant' was a rhetorical fiction, his role was to confirm that the analysis of the spectrum was in some sense independent of the observer, Newton. Newton deliberately avoided engagement with the colour-observations which could not be subsumed under the quantitative law: 'as when by the power of Phantasy we see Colours in a Dream, or a Mad-man sees things before him which are not there; or when we see Fire by striking the Eye, or see Colours like the Eye of a Peacock's Feather, by pressing our Eyes in either corner whilst we look the other way.'[2]

We saw in Chapter 9 how powerfully Newton's belief in a quantifiable colour-order affected the study of colour in art until the nineteenth century; we shall see in the last chapter how it recurred rather more fitfully among the Constructivist artists of the twentieth century. But after Newton it was increasingly the subjective colour-phenomena which he had left out of consideration that occupied the attention of scientists who developed the modern study of colour vision. In the seventeenth and eighteenth centuries, as in Classical Antiquity, scientists recognized that these phenomena had been identified and investigated first of all by painters and dyers.[3]

Writing in 1815 on 'accidental' colours (i.e. the subjective colours produced by psychological processes less extreme than those mentioned by Newton), the Italian mathematician Pietro Petrini argued that it was Leonardo da Vinci who had first noticed the blue 'complementary' shadows at sunrise and sunset.[4] He went on to describe in some detail the effect of colour juxtapositions:

> The mutual reaction of colours placed close to each other, so that their appearance changes more or less noticeably, has long been known to painters and has been named *contrast* by them. They noticed, for example that a very slightly bluish [*turchineggiante*] patch changes to a delicate blue [*azzurro*] if it is surrounded by a very light edge of red-violet. And there is no nuance which cannot be changed into a very delicate, but also lively tint of the same hue by being placed on a ground of its complementary. You may also effect a change of tone in a given colour equally successfully by means of the neighbouring colour of the ground, or by a border which serves as a ground. An orange card on a red ground will seem almost yellow; on a yellow ground it will seem almost red. If it is placed on a green ground, it will seem to be an even darker red, and on a violet ground it will take on a lemon-yellow or sulphur

colour. But on an indigo or purple ground, it will take on its own proper hue, that is, the hue it has when on a white ground, but certainly more intense than in this latter case.[5]

These observations were to be amplified and codified in the 1820s into a 'law of simultaneous contrast' by Chevreul, but Petrini was quite right to suggest that they had long been current in the studios of painters. They formed part of that empirical approach to colour which gathered momentum in late seventeenth-century Holland and was particularly cultivated in France. One of the first painters to advocate a purely perceptual procedure in colour-composition was the Dutch classicizing artist Gerard de Lairesse, whose *Het Groot Schilderboek* (*Art of Painting*, 1707) was one of the most widely translated and studied treatises of the eighteenth century. Lairesse held the harmonizing of colours in painting, as opposed to proportion, or even aerial perspective, to be 'mere chance'; he described the use of chance in some notes on dividing the picture into three coloured masses, light, half-tint and shade, which he laid out on his palette:

> then I took cards, and severally painted them with one of the aforesaid tempered colours; when they were dry, I placed and replaced and shifted them so long till I had satisfied my judgement: sometimes, when this would not answer my purpose, I shuffled them; and then took a parcel of them at random, which, if they happened to please, were my directors.[6]

This was an even more radically abstract process than Delacroix's judging the effects of his coloured wafers.

In a no less popular handbook Roger de Piles argued that two factors determined colour in painting: the accuracy of perceiving tones and the skill to give them their due weight. The first was achieved by constant comparison between the colours of the motif and the colours on the palette; the second by a study of the effects of colours in juxtaposition and in space, where aerial perspective came into play.[7] This method of constant comparison on the palette and in nature at large was advocated by the French portrait-painter Largillière, whose pupil Oudry recorded how he was instructed to paint a group of white flowers by surrounding it with several other white objects for comparison. Oudry himself, in a lecture of 1749 to the French Academy, described a still-life of a silver vase which looks forward to his beautiful *White Duck* of 1753. The vase was to be surrounded with linen, paper, satin or porcelain so that 'the different whites will make you assess the precise tone of white that you need to render your silver vase, since you will know by the comparison that the colours of one of these white objects will never be those of the others.'[8]

158

The discrimination of nuances which had made Boethius despair of the objectivity of colour was now to be eagerly embraced. This exacting study of colour-scales and relationships was most readily available in the context of still-life, always the most abstract of painterly genres and one in which Oudry's younger contemporary Chardin especially shone because, it was said, he kept his subjects at such a distance that he was no longer troubled by details and could concentrate on shape and colour alone.[9] Such focusing on the tones of contingent areas also affected French landscape, for the leading eighteenth-century French specialist in this genre, Claude-Joseph Vernet, one of the earliest advocates of outdoor sketching in oil, argued in a short essay of the 1760s or 70s that 'if you really want to see the colour of things, you must always make comparisons between them', citing the innumerable greens of foliage or meadow.[10]

This close painterly attention to the nuances and changes of colour-effects in nature and art led, not surprisingly, to discoveries which were only later recognized and codified by optical science. One of the most striking was the Purkinje shift, by which at twilight the switch from rod (scotopic) to cone (photopic) vision produces a change in the perceived intensity of the blue and red areas of the spectrum. The phenomenon has been named after the Bohemian physiologist J. E. Purkinje, who described it precisely in 1825,[11] but it had already been noticed in a studio context in 1685 by Philippe de la Hire, the mathematician who was trained as a painter in the tradition of his father:

> The light which illuminates hues changes them considerably; blue appears green by candlelight and yellow appears white; blue appears white by weak daylight, as at the beginning of night. Painters know hues whose brilliance is much greater by candlelight than by daylight: there is also a number of hues which are very bright by daylight but lose their beauty entirely by candlelight. For example, verdigris appears a very fine colour by candlelight; and when it is weak, that is to say, when it is mixed with a large quantity of white, it appears as a very beautiful blue. Those ash pigments [cendres] one describes as either green or blue appear by candlelight to be an extremely beautiful blue. The reds which contain lake appear by candlelight as very bright, and others like carmine and vermilion seem dull.[12]

By the beginning of the nineteenth century twilight had come to be regarded in England as 'the painter's hour', since it facilitated the study of the massing of light and dark without the distractions of colour. Yet many artists recognized that it had the disadvantage of distorting the relationship of the warm and cool colours. Reynolds's pupil James Northcote observed that 'the reds look darker than by day, indeed almost black, and the light blues turn white, or nearly so'; in a lecture of 1818 Turner seems to have alluded to the same effect when he described red as 'the first ray of light and the first which acknowledges the diminishing of light'.[13] It was, ironically, the decline of tonal painting in the nineteenth century which led to the obsolescence of the 'painter's hour' so that the American colour-theorist Ogden Rood, himself an amateur painter, could attribute the first discovery of this phenomenon to Purkinje, rather than to the traditional experience of artists. When he was painting *The*

Dance about 1910, Matisse was startled to see its powerful reds and blues vibrating in twilight, for this was a threshold phenomenon he clearly did not recognize for what it was.[14]

Colour-contrasts and the Purkinje shift were striking evidences of the instability of colour perceptions. Towards the end of the eighteenth century another and very different phenomenon in the psychology of colour came to be investigated by scientists, namely colour-constancy: the stabilizing control by which the brain maintains a constant perception of colour under varying conditions of lighting. The classic analysis was in a paper of 1789 by the French mathematician Gaspard Monge but he had already recognized it some time earlier, while teaching at the royal École de Génie.[15] At exactly the same time the Venetian architect and theorist Francesco Milizia described the effect in the context of painting, referring to the colour scarlet seen under direct sun, under the light of the sky, by artificial lights or through a more or less dense and extended medium, which none the less still appeared to be scarlet. Unlike Monge, who argued for constancy as a function of our perception of surface, Milizia interpreted this not as the result of psychological adjustment but as reflecting the incapacity of language to describe all the nuances of colour as perceived.[16] Monge had long interested himself in painterly problems (for example aerial perspective, in which he acknowledged Leonardo to be the supreme master[17]) and in later editions of his *Géométrie descriptive* he discussed aspects of coloured shadows and colour contrast as they affected painting, as well as repeating his earlier discoveries on constancy.[18] His ideas on this phenomenon were brought into the context of art chiefly by his pupil L. L. Vallée in *Traité de la science du dessin* (1821), which included a very up-to-date account of contrast and complementarity, as well as instructions about how to deal with the inadequacy of paints to convey the more extreme lighting effects of nature.[19] Colour-constancy emphasized local colour – the colour of an isolated surface illuminated by white light (a notion increasingly contested during the nineteenth century by painters such as Delacroix, who drew attention to the transforming effects of context and lighting[20]). The primacy of local colour was maintained in early nineteenth-century France by Delacroix's rival Ingres, who argued that the ancients had rightly kept their figures distinct and that this could be aided by heightening the contrast of colours:

> The essential qualities of colour are not to be found in the *ensemble* of masses of lights or darks in the picture; they are rather in the brightness and individuality of the colours of objects. For example, put a beautiful and brilliant white drapery against an olive-dark body, and above all distinguish a blonde colour from a cold colour, and a fleeting colour from that of coloured figures in their local tints...[21]

A belief in local colour is a belief in colour as substance: in *Antiochus and Stratonice* Ingres drew on the new understanding of Greek polychromy developed by his friend the architect Hittorff (*see* Chapter 1).[22] But it was precisely this emphasis on the materiality of colour which attracted the bitter criticism of Delacroix, in conversation with the novelist George Sand. Ingres, he said, confused colouring with colour:

10

The imperatives of observation

The discipline of still-life offered especially rich opportunities for the manipulation of colour. It became an essential feature of the French eighteenth-century emphasis on observation, and was also a means for 'editing' what was observed. Chardin depicted his subjects from a distance (**157**) in order to lose detail and thus reveal their 'essential' character of form and colour, rendering them in broad painterly style. Oudry's vision was more sharply focussed, and he developed a precise technique of visual comparison which, notably in this wonderful arrangement of whites (**158**), was to turn this genre of painting into pure demonstrations of the powers of perception.

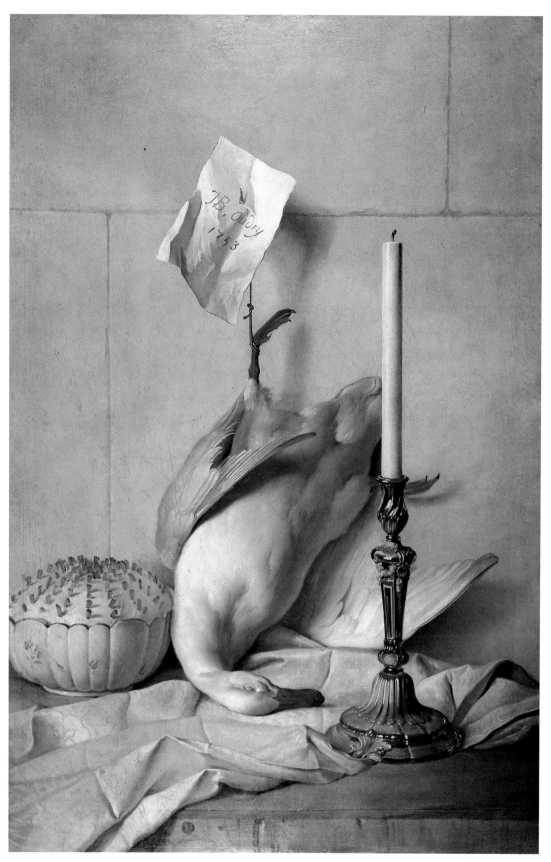

158

157 JEAN SIMEON CHARDIN, *A Vase of Flowers*, c. 1760/3
158 JEAN-BAPTISTE OUDRY, *The White Duck*, 1753

157

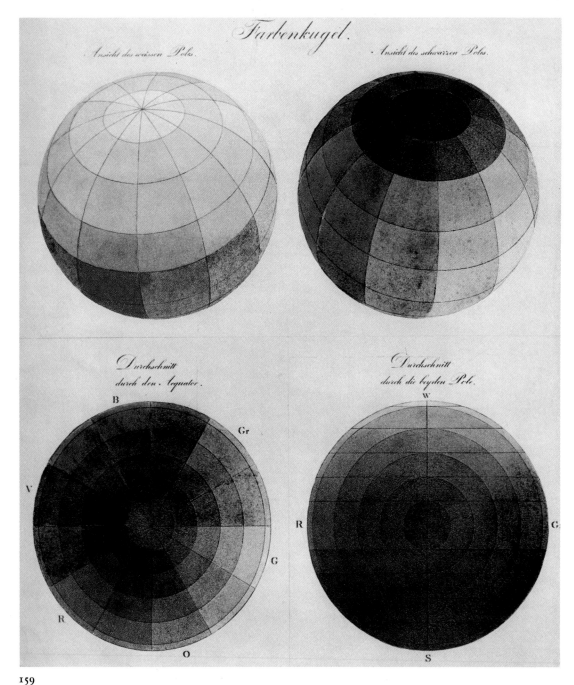

159

159 PHILIPP OTTO RUNGE, *Colour Sphere*, 1810
160 FRIEDRICH SCHILLER and JOHANN WOLFGANG
VON GOETHE, *The Temperament-vane
(Temperamentrose)*, 1799
161 J. M. W. TURNER, *Colour-Circle No. 2, c.* 1825
162 PHILIPP OTTO RUNGE, *The small 'Morning',*
1808

160

161

Romantic artists sought to extract new meanings for colours from their positions in space. Runge's sphere (**159**) was one of the earliest attempts by a painter to co-ordinate hues and values (light-dark content) into a coherent whole. He used a set of three primaries – red, yellow and blue – arranged in a complementary scheme around the equator. In the book that accompanied this diagram Runge scarcely ventured beyond the visible data, but in fact he shared a belief in the moral connotations of colour with his contemporaries, the poets Schiller and Goethe (**160**) who related the polarities of colour to the traditional four temperaments – optimistic, melancholic, phlegmatic and

choleric. Such theoretical concerns find an outlet in the series called 'Times of Day' – Morning – Noon – Evening – Night – in which colour could be used schematically. In Runge's *Morning* (**162**) red is the dominant colour for the dawn of life, with its Christ-like baby and Venus rising from the sea, and the red lily (*amaryllis formosissima*), rising in the border. Turner too (**161**) saw a universal significance in the three primaries. He started from the complementary diagram of Moses Harris (pl. 153), but subordinated the primaries in his own diagram to light – the yellow which he later made the keynote of his allegory of the creation of light out of darkness (pl. 169).

194

The colours of passion

163

His vision of the café at Arles was Van Gogh's most ambitious attempt to convey an emotional situation through colour. 'I have tried to express the terrible passions of humanity by means of red and green', he wrote to Theo. 'The room is blood red and dark yellow with a green billiard table in the middle; there are four citron-yellow lamps with a glow of orange and green. Everywhere there is a clash and contrast of the most disparate reds and greens . . .'

163 VINCENT VAN GOGH, *The Night Café*, 1888

164

166

165

Gauguin's quarrel with Van Gogh sprang partly from his distaste for the polar contrasts favoured by his friend: he himself came more and more to work with 'mysterious' close-tones and subtle resonances, bluish-greens, purplish-reds and orange-yellows (**164**). The same rejection of sharp chromatic contrasts characterizes the late paintings of the two most perceptually aware artists of the nineteenth century, Monet and Cézanne (**165**, **166**), who used the bright palette of Impressionism, but tended to unify their compositions by focussing each one on a single segment of the colour-circle, and working in a nuanced range of warm or cool tones.

164 PAUL GAUGUIN, *The Loss of Virginity*, 1890/1
165 PAUL CÉZANNE, *The Winding Road*, c. 1902–6
166 CLAUDE MONET, *Poplars (Banks of the Epte)*, 1891

The responsive eye

167 HENRI MATISSE, *The Red Studio*, 1911
168 HENRI MATISSE, Chapel of the Rosary of the Dominicans, Vence, 1948/51

The unprecedentedly powerful all-over colour in Matisse's *Red Studio* (**167**) may have been the result of the intense green of the painter's sunlit garden, which stimulated him to 'see' his grey studio walls as red. Much later, at Vence (**168**), he experienced the red after-image as an effect of light pouring in through the blue and green design of his stained-glass windows. In each work, Matisse's colour is wonderfully harmonious, for the eye, as Goethe had observed, compensates for a strong stimulus of one colour by creating the complementary colour as an after-image – making the circle whole.

He has studied with great delicacy the effects of light on marbles, gilding and fabrics, but he has forgotten one thing: reflections … He has not the slightest inkling that everything in nature is reflection and that colour is essentially an interplay of reflections. He has scattered little bits of sunlight over all the objects placed in front of him as if they had been recorded in a daguerrotype; there is no sun, no light, no air in any of that … He puts a bit of red on a cloak, some lilac on a cushion, some green here, some blue there, a vivid red, a spring green, a sky-blue. He has a taste for dress and a knowledge of costume. He has interspersed in his coiffures, in his fabrics, in his fillets, a lilac of exquisite freshness, coloured borders and the attraction of a thousand pretty ornaments, but they do nothing at all to create colour. The livid and leaden tones of an old wall by Rembrandt are far richer than this abundance of clashing tones applied to objects which he will never get to relate to one another by reflections, and which remain crude, isolated, cold and gaudy.[23]

This is an exact analysis but it rests on a very partial interpretation of 'colour'. Ingres and Delacroix came to represent the opposing poles of the nineteenth-century version of the debate of drawing *versus* colour but both were supreme colourists: if in them two antithetical principles of colour were at work, there can be no doubt that they were both principles and that each of them had the sanction of an experience of colour valid well beyond the bounds of art.

A more familiar instance of the prevailing empiricism of colour-practice in the nineteenth century is the notion of optical mixture. This, as we saw, had been understood since Antiquity but was given the cachet of a 'scientific' method only by Neo-Impressionism. Broken tones of contrasting dotted or hatched colours had long been used in several contexts to ensure greater visibility at a distance, in large decorative schemes executed in fresco, or the distemper-painting of theatrical scenery, as well as, paradoxically, in the smallest of miniature paintings.[24] It was the traditions of fresco which kept the idea of optical mixture most alive in the nineteenth century, when Ingres's pupil Victor Mottez, for example, discussed it in his 1858 edition of Cennini, arguing that the brilliance and softness of Pinturicchio's frescoes

An allegory of light, Turner's painting of the scene on the morning after the Deluge was exhibited with the caption:

> The ark stood firm on Ararat; th'returning sun
> Exhaled earth's humid bubbles, and emulous of light,
> Reflected her lost forms, each in prismatic guise
> Hope's harbinger, ephemeral as the summer fly
> Which rises, flits, expands, and dies.

Turner's eccentric treatment of the Noah story, perhaps influenced by Baroque ceiling painting (see pl. 121), replaced the rainbow of the Covenant with an irridescent bubble which (as his caption says) was even more ephemeral. Indeed, the overall theme of this luminous painting is one of pessimism.

169 J.M.W. TURNER, *Light and Colour (Goethe's Theory) – the Morning after the Deluge – Moses writing the Book of Genesis*, 1843

in the Piccolomini Library in Siena was due to his use of hatching and 'pointillism'.[25] But these usages, besides being purely empirical, were also very local. What the Neo-Impressionists did to this tradition, by basing themselves on a scientific concept of mixing lights rather than pigments, was to construct the whole surface of their paintings (which were to be seen close to as well as at a distance) from a more or less homogeneous structure of coloured dots or patches, which drew attention to their function by being so unusual and so very easy to see.

The impact of Goethe

Purkinje's studies of the subjective effects of vision had been stimulated during his medical training by a reading of Goethe's substantial three-part study of 1810, *Farbenlehre* (*Theory of Colours*)[26] which more than any other publication directed the attention of scientists as well as the wider public to a range of physical and psychological colour-phenomena throughout the nineteenth and early twentieth centuries. This was partly due to Goethe's international reputation as a poet and thinker and partly to his strident polemic against Newton, to the unpicking of whose *Opticks* he devoted the whole of his second part, but most of all perhaps to his reliance on the eye as a sufficient tool for the study of colour and his directing his readers to many examples of colour-phenomena in the world around them, which they could experience for themselves. Unlike Newton, who had retreated to his dark chamber at Trinity College, Cambridge, where the sunlight was permitted to enter only through the smallest of apertures to form a spectrum on a screen which only his 'assistant' could divide, Goethe based his inferences on experiments in which he inspected the junctions of light and dark areas through a prism and observed the coloured fringes which appeared where the image of the edges was displaced. Goethe's 'screen' was his own retina. He concluded that light was homogeneous, that it created colour only when disturbed by darkness and that the two extreme tonal hues of yellow and blue interacted by a mysterious process he called 'augmentation' (*Steigerung*), to form the third principal colour, red, which, since it was the most noble, he named *Purpur*.

Goethe's experimental methods were, of course, quite traditional. The prism experiments had been worked out by Thomas Harriott by 1590, published in the mid-seventeenth century by Sir Kenelm Digby in Paris and G. B. Hodierna in Sicily,[27] and were familiar to Newton in the 1660s. Characteristically, Goethe also used a homely and unspecialized experience to exemplify coloured fringes:

> If, when the sky is grey, we approach a window, so that the dark cross of the window-bars be relieved on the sky; if after fixing the eyes on the horizontal bar we bend the head a little forward; on half closing the eyes as we look up, we shall presently perceive a bright, yellow-red border under the bar, and a bright light-blue one above it. The duller and more monotonous the grey of the sky, the more dusky the room, and, consequently, the more previously unexcited the eye, the livelier the appearance will be; but it may be seen by an attentive observer even in bright daylight.[28]

Similarly, the striking effects of complementary after-images were illustrated by Goethe in his report of a very concrete experience:

> I had entered an inn towards evening, and, as a well-favoured girl with a brilliantly fair complexion, black hair, and a scarlet bodice, came into the room, I looked attentively at her as she stood before me at some distance in half shadow. As she presently afterwards turned away, I saw on the white wall, which was now before me, a black face surrounded with a bright light, while the dress of the perfectly distinct figure appeared of a beautiful sea-green.

Here the secret was, of course, the prolonged scrutiny which the poet gave to the figure of a pretty girl.[29]

This is not the place to examine the differences between the Newtonian and the Goethean accounts of colour in any detail;[30] suffice it that at the end of his life Goethe came to regret his intemperate polemic against the English scientist and, although he continued to regard his work on colour as his most important achievement, he was prepared to leave the second part out of any new edition of the *Theory*.[31] Nevertheless, he added very little in principle to his colour work after 1800 and showed a surprising indifference to the more recent developments of chromatics even where, as with Thomas Young's work on colour-vision and the wave theory of light, they might have helped him consolidate his anti-Newtonian position.[32] Physicists found little to stimulate them in Goethe's theory, since they argued correctly that his account of the production of colours could be explained along Newtonian lines; but it did focus on a number of physical phenomena which were to be more thoroughly investigated later in the century, one of which was the role of the turbid medium in the scattering of light. Goethe, as usual, illustrated what he called this 'basic phenomenon' (*Urphänomen*) of the production of colours by the modification of light with a number of homely instances, including one of the simplest, smoke, 'which appears to us as yellow or reddish before a light ground, but blue before a dark one.' But he nowhere discussed the crucial question of the size of particles in the medium which, again, had been considered by Young.[33]

It is more understandable that the *Theory of Colour* should have made an important contribution to the developing science of the physiology of perception, from Purkinje and Helmholtz's teacher Johannes Müller in the 1820s to Ewald Hering in the 1870s: certainly Purkinje and Müller were unstinting in their acknowledgment of the poet.[34] Goethe's emphasis on the polar structure of both the formation of colours from light and dark and their reception by the eye made his system the ancestor of Hering's opponent-colour theory. It was this, too, which made his scheme, rather than Newton's, so attractive to Romantic philosophers such as Schelling, Schopenhauer and Hegel. Schelling had been in touch with Goethe even before the publication of the full version of the *Theory* and he adopted many of the poet's ideas, notably that of polarity, in his *Philosophie der Kunst* (1802/3).[35] Schopenhauer's treatise *Über das Sehn und die Farben* (*On Vision and Colours*, 1816) sought to turn Goethe's theory into a much more rigorously subjective system by arguing, in a way which was ultimately fruitful for Hering, that the retina itself was stimulated by the complementary poles of red and green, orange and blue and yellow and violet.[36] Hegel in his turn supported Goethe's views against

Newton in his *Enzyklopädie* (1817) and later lectures; his pupil L. D. von Henning gave what were probably the first academic lectures on Goethe's book in Berlin in 1822, with apparatus lent by the poet himself.[37] All these thinkers, however, were attracted primarily to the logical structure of Goethe's ideas and were hardly concerned with experiment or even experience, for which they depended on the example of painters.

Even Goethe's scientific opponents sometimes argued that, however unlikely his theory might be in the context of physical optics, it was of great use to painters – another early indication of the growing division between colour-theory for artists and colour-theory for the world at large. It is true that Goethe's early interest in colour seems to have been stimulated by his experiences of art on his Grand Tour in the 1780s and that conversations with painters on that trip provided him with much material for the *Theory*. In 'Confessions of the Author', for example, which the poet appended to the final, historical part of his book, he described how he asked the Swiss painter Angelika Kauffmann to paint a picture 'in the old Florentine way', by beginning with a grisaille underpainting which she then glazed in colours. It was an experiment which lay behind the traditional view expressed in the *Theory* that 'The separation of light and dark from all appearance of colour is possible and necessary. The artist will solve the mystery of imitation sooner by first considering light and dark independently of colour, and making himself acquainted with it in its whole extent.'[38] Kauffmann may also have helped Goethe to formulate some of his more novel and fundamental attitudes towards colour, such as the primacy of the tonal opposites yellow and blue, for this had been an idea published by an earlier admirer of hers, the anti-Newtonian journalist and later revolutionary, Jean-Paul Marat, to whom she had been close in England in the 1760s.[39] Another Swiss artist, Heinrich Meyer, became Goethe's advisor on artistic matters over many years and was also set to testing colour ideas by him from the earliest period of his researches.[40] Meyer provided Goethe with a channel for studying colour in landscape, an important support for his principles in the *Theory*; for although the poet was an enthusiastic amateur artist, he was always plagued by technical difficulties, never developing a technique adequate to the representation of the effects he was most anxious to study.[41] In an unpublished essay on the eye Goethe made painting the arbiter of truth itself: 'Painting is truer for the eye than reality itself. It presents what man would like to see and should see, not what he habitually sees.'[42]

There are many questions surrounding the role of painting in Goethe's conception of colour. He seems, for one thing, to have been surprisingly reluctant to introduce the theory of colour into the several programmes for training artists with which he became involved. In his periodical *Propyläen*, of the late 1790s, he appears to have proposed a discussion of how painters might be instructed in these matters but nothing was ever published, except some hints on warm and cool colours in the account of a French system of drawing.[43] In an article on art-training by Meyer, revised by Goethe, nothing more theoretical was proposed than the making of coloured rather than simply drawn academy studies from the life; at the Weimar Drawing School in Goethe's day only a 'simple method of colouring' was taught.[44] When the Weimar Prize Competitions for painting and drawing, sponsored by Goethe in the hope of raising the standard of German art, were finally abandoned in 1806, he thought that he might introduce colour into some future series, but nothing ever came of the scheme.[45]

Nor did artists at first show much interest in Goethe's colour ideas. The *Theory* was much in demand in Rome in 1811 when a new generation of German artists, the Nazarenes, deeply interested in colour-symbolism, was establishing itself there; but only one late associate of the group, J. D. Passavant, better known as an art historian, seems to have studied it and we know nothing of whether he put it to use in his work.[46] One of the first German artists to publish his own theory of colours after the appearance of Goethe's book, the Munich painter Matthias Klotz, showed himself anxious to be distanced from the poet's ideas, some of which he claimed had been borrowed unacknowledged from himself.[47] Not until after Goethe's death do we encounter a colour theory for artists based substantially on the *Theory*, in a work by the Weimar theatre-artist Friedrich Beuther, and even here Goethe was barely mentioned.[48] In Germany in the 1840s Goethe's book had a low reputation among artists, and although by the middle of the century this had ceased to be so, it still seems to have been neglected in painterly handbooks until long after then.[49]

Only two artists in the early nineteenth century engaged with Goethe's theory in any thoroughgoing way. One was Turner (*see below*) and the other Runge, who had known of the poet's ideas on colour from around 1800, when he took part in the Weimar Prize Competition. In 1803 he met Goethe and from that date until his early death in 1810 they were in more or less continuous communication. Like Goethe, Runge hoped to see the functions of colour exemplified in painting: his most important project, uncompleted at his death, was a series of four Times of Day, which would articulate the universe of colour in

162 a set of allegorical compositions. Only the first two, *Morning* and *Day*, were even begun in colour, and since their imagery was subject to continual revisions their detailed meaning is still far from clear. In tandem with these allegories was Runge's book,

158 *Farben-Kugel* (*The Colour Sphere*), begun around 1807 and finally published in 1810. The paintings and the book show the opposite extremes of Runge's engagement with colour: on the one hand the quasi-mystical sense of colour as a power in nature, manifesting Divine truths by its division into the basic blue (the Father), red (the Son) and yellow (the Holy Ghost);[50] on the other a dry and summary 'mathematical figure', as Runge called it, designed to show the relationship of colours to each other and to aid the understanding of colour harmony.[51] The reference to mathematics at once distances Runge's approach from Goethe's; although the poet published an extract from an early draft of Runge's work in his *Theory*, with a note that they were essentially in agreement, this was only because Runge had touched none of the most contentious aspects of his ideas.[52] Nor did he do so in his *Kugel* of 1810 and he continued to keep a certain distance from Goethe's concepts, claiming that they could be of little use to him.[53]

Runge was an energetic experimenter; he made many disc-mixtures in which he found that palette and disc produced quite different results, and that the closest analogy to disc-mixing in painting was through the use of semi-transparent glazes.[54] His

most original contribution to the theory of colour was indeed in the matter of transparency: it figured largely in the letter published by Goethe and it became crucial to Runge's practice. He explained to a friend that the latest, large version of the *Morning* was to be painted – like Kauffmann's study for Goethe – in grisaille and then glazed in colours.[55] This friend, the Austrian painter F. A. von Klinkowström, had made a copy of Correggio's *Nativity* (*The Night*) as a demonstration of how the Old Masters used glazing to achieve the finest colour harmony. It became one of Runge's most treasured possessions: he had it brightly lit and set by his bedside to contemplate in his dying hours.[56] Runge also experimented in the *Times of Day* with a technique of glazing transparent colours over a gold ground, which at this time was thought to be a method characteristic of Correggio.[57] Yet, although he was able to make a blue by scumbling white over black, he did not use this interest in transparency to explore the turbid medium so dear to Goethe. It was precisely because it was uncontroversial that his sphere, the first colour-solid to co-ordinate the complementary circle with the poles of light and dark, became so influential in the development of colour-order systems later in the century.[58] Runge's brief career is another instance of the division between scientific aspirations and artistic expression that gathered momentum during the Romantic period, despite the efforts of Romantic scientists such as Henrich Steffens, who contributed an essay, 'The Meaning of Colours in Nature' to Runge's *Farben-Kugel*, to bring the two together. Runge was perfectly aware of this division: he wrote to his brother Gustav that he had to forget the 'mathematical figure' of his treatise when he was painting, 'since those are two different worlds which intersect in me'.[59]

Turner, for his part, had always been concerned with the interrelation of light and colour and around 1820 had been, like Runge, attempting to fit the scheme of three primary colours, red, yellow and blue, into the times of day, although he found, as had Runge, that it was necessary to play with a number of alternative solutions, one of which was the red of dawn and sunset, and the 'yellow morning'.[60] Aristotelian and anti-Newtonian attitudes towards colour were as common in England at this time as they were in Germany or France: Turner's instincts were, no less than Runge's or Goethe's, to emphasize the polarities of light and dark and to arrange the scale of colours in a tonal order. His treatment of Moses Harris's complementary circle in the lecture diagrams he prepared to 153 show at the Academy in the 1820s shows a perverse insistence that light and dark were the primary poles of colour experience: 'Sink the yellow until it light into the red and blue, and hence two only: light and shadow, day and night, or gradation light and dark.'[61] So when Turner came in the early 1840s to read Eastlake's translation of Goethe's *Theory*, he gave it some attention. One passage that struck him was the table of polarities in which the poet had sought to show how colour, unlike light, was 'at all times specific, characteristic, significant':

Plus	*Minus*
Yellow	Blue
Action	Negation
Light	Shadow

Brightness	Darkness
Force	Weakness
Warmth	Coldness
Proximity	Distance
Repulsion	Attraction
Affinity with Acids	Affinity with Alkalis

Against this table Turner noted in his copy, 'Light and Shade'.[62]

Turner had been exhibiting pairs of paintings with an essentially warm–cool or light–dark contrast since the mid-1830s; now in 1843 he used Goethe's scheme predictably in two episodes from the story of Noah's Flood, the first of which, *Shade and Darkness – the Evening of the Deluge* showed the last disobedient families, tarnished by 'negation' and 'weakness', who were about to be swept away by the Flood, in a landscape which was brooding, dark and blue. Its companion, *Light and* 169 *Colour (Goethe's Theory) – the Morning after the Deluge – Moses writing the Book of Genesis*, provided the plus side of the polarity: its dominant yellow space is full of action, brightness and force in the vortex of figures whirling around Moses, suspended like one of the angels adoring the Name of Jesus in Baciccio's *Gesù*, which Turner may well have studied on one of his visits to Rome. And the title of this painting drew the spectator's attention specifically to Goethe's book.

As so often in Turner, the relationship of the painting to Goethe's ideas is far from being straightforward; certainly Turner did not endorse them as a whole. The use of his name only in relation to the second painting may be taken to suggest Turner's view that Goethe had not given enough attention to shade: against a passage of the *Theory* (§744), where the poet had defined darkness in the traditional way simply as an absence of light, he noted 'nothing about Shadow or Shade as Shade and shadow Pictorially or optically'. He also found Goethe's account of the production of red through the 'augmentation' of yellow and blue 'absurd', so that no more than Runge was he a follower of the poet.[63] What Turner's use of Goethe's polarities does suggest is that he had a sense of the moral force of colour, an aspect to which Goethe devoted a substantial section at the end of his book, and which was to prove perhaps the most durable of his approaches.

The morality of colour

There can be little doubt that Romanticism gave colour-symbolism a new life. I showed in Chapter 5 how the late-medieval scheme of colours for the days of the week was echoed in the 1820s by the German touring and gardening prince Hermann Pückler-Muskau.[64] The equally arbitrary set of colours representing moral values, published by Lairesse at the end of the Baroque period – yellow for glory, red for power and love, blue for divinity, purple for authority, violet for humility and green for servitude – were re-introduced into Romantic England by Lairesse's last editor.[65] Yet there was a new and more psychological inflection to the search for a morality of colour among painters. The young Nazarenes Franz Pforr and Friedrich Overbeck described how in Vienna shortly before their move to Rome in 1810 they discovered that they could use in their work the observation that people naturally chose the colours of their dress according to their characters;[66] Turner, whom we have already seen looking for the 'natural' sequence of primary colours in the times of day, dismissed Lairesse's equivalents on the grounds that 'They must be left with those who framed them as emblematical conceits and typical allusions'.[67] An associate of Turner's, the landscape painter Augustus Wall Callcott, was even more emphatic in his rejection of conventional symbols. In an unpublished essay on colour he wrote:

> A kind of association was formerly made between colours and Expression and particular colours were made use of as [*illegible word*] of the passions and feelings. This is now done away with as trifling and absurd, things which have no real connection and which cannot assist the suppositions of the imagination, by their own natural relation cannot long meet with estimation unless their origin is connection with some classical Event or favourite circumstance. The powers of colours upon the feelings are very feeble and it is only in association with peculiar circumstances of the countenance [?] and particular effects of nature that I at present feel they have any influence whatever.[68]

Even Humbert de Superville, searching for a 'natural' system of colours among ancient religions, and attributing the late medieval heraldic scheme of the colours of the planets to Aristotle, argued in the 1820s that the meaning of colours was by universal consent and that women were particularly able to respond to their moral connotations.[69] Humbert was familiar with Goethe's *Theory of Colours*, where in the concluding section of the 'Didactic Part' the moral theory of colours received its most influential formulation.[70]

Already in the late 1790s Goethe had been devising with his friend the poet and dramatist Friedrich Schiller – another member of the Weimar Friends of Art – a scheme of correspondences based partly on the ancient and medieval quadripartite system of the four elements, the four humours, the four points of the compass, the four seasons, the four times of day, the four ages of man, the four phases of the moon and so on. In this elaborate parlour-game, which issued in the *Temperament-* 160 *rose*, red came surprisingly to stand for air, midnight, north, winter and old age, as well as for melancholy, reason, humour and judgment, the ideal and unity.[71] Goethe emphasized that Schiller was here the organizing genius – perhaps he was one of the 'pedants' who shared *Purpur* with rulers and tyrants and were melancholics by temperament – and this rather ossified approach to colour values may be in line with Schiller's conventional and now Neo-Classical view of the superiority of line to colour as a conveyer of 'truth'.[72] But it is clear that to the traditional polarities had been added the newly discovered complementarity: green, the opposite of *Purpur*, now stood for the sanguine temperament, for example, and for sensuality and memory. In the *Theory* Goethe was able to draw a distinction between 'symbolic' colour, 'Coinciding entirely with nature', and 'allegorical colour', where, 'the meaning of the sign must be first communicated to us before we know what it is to signify' (§§916–7) – a distinction which rested on the belief that colours had a direct, not simply a mediated, effect on the mind and feelings.[73] It was a powerful idea which was to be crucial in the early development of German abstraction but in the nineteenth century it seems to have found a more receptive audience in France.

Goethe's theory had little support in France in the early years; but both anti-Newtonianism and a belief in the affective power of colour had been very much alive there during the Enlightenment period and they continued into Romanticism.[74] By the middle of the nineteenth century Goethe's colour-ideas had become absorbed into the French literature of art; in Blanc's *Grammaire des arts du dessin* the poet's name was linked with Delacroix because of their common interest in complementary after-images.[75] Blanc also sought in another book to show that Delacroix had been very much concerned with colour's '*harmonies morales*'.[76]

Blanc's books were perhaps the most fertile texts on colour in France during the second half of the nineteenth century, for they were read with attention by a younger generation of artists whose approach to these 'moral harmonies' of colour was central to their work. Two of them were Vincent van Gogh and Paul Gauguin, whose stormy friendship in 1887 and 1888 produced not only an important debate on the nature of colour-relationships but also an impressive body of paintings which bear directly on this debate. Van Gogh like Runge was a largely self-taught artist with an insatiable curiosity about the procedures of painting and an acute feeling of unease about the existing practices. Just as Runge had been gripped by Forestier's article on new methods of art-teaching in Paris, published in Goethe's *Propyläen* in 1800,[77] so van Gogh was much impressed in 1884 by his reading of Blanc's account of Delacroix in *Les Artistes de mon temps*, lent to him by his painter friend Anton van Rappard. As he wrote to his brother Theo shortly afterwards, his experience of colour, again like Runge's, was interwoven with his experience of the world at large:

The *laws* of the colours are unutterably beautiful, just because they are *not accidental*. In the same way that people nowadays no longer believe in fantastic *miracles*, no longer believe in a God who capriciously and despotically flies from one thing to another, but begin to feel more respect and admiration for, and faith in nature – in the same way, and for the same reasons, I think that in art, the old fashioned idea of innate genius, inspiration etc., I do not say must be put aside, but thoroughly reconsidered, verified – and greatly modified.[78]

Van Rappard was essential to van Gogh's programme for teaching himself through reading as well as through looking. It was probably he who as early as 1881 had introduced van Gogh to a handbook which was to affect his understanding of colour throughout his brief career as a painter. A.-T. Cassagne's *Traité d'aquarelle* of 1875 was far from being a simple technical manual: it introduced a wide range of theoretical issues in painting and a number of extended quotations from earlier nineteenth-century artists, which were clearly very impressive to the beginner. Black, said Cassagne, was the most fundamental colour in nature, entering into all three primaries to form an infinite variety of greys, those greys which were an important feature of van Gogh's palette in Holland and with which he was still seeking to come to terms in Arles.[79] It may well have been a hint by Cassagne which set him thinking in 1884 about how to paint a series of the four seasons in terms of contrasted complemen-

tary pairs: spring as green and pink, autumn as yellow and violet, winter as black and white and summer as blue and orange.[80]

Complementarity was perhaps the colour-principle closest to van Gogh throughout his career, reinforced by his reading of Blanc's *Grammaire*, which be bought after having enjoyed *Les Artistes*. Blanc had visualized the complementary colours as victorious allies when juxtaposed in a pure state but as deadly enemies when mixed; it was this dynamic of the colour-pairs which especially intrigued van Gogh.[81] At Arles in 1888 he introduced it into his *Night Café*, of which he wrote to Theo in September (CL 533):

I have tried to express the terrible passions of humanity by means of red and green. The room is blood red and dark yellow with a green billiard table in the middle; there are four citron-yellow lamps with a glow of orange and green. Everywhere there is a clash and contrast of the most disparate reds and greens in the figures of the sleeping hooligans, in the empty, dreary room, in violet and blue. The blood-red and yellow-green of the billiard table, for instance, contrast with the soft tender Louise [*sic*] XV green of the counter, on which there is a pink nosegay. The white coat of the landlord, awake in a corner of that furnace, turns citron-yellow, or pale luminous green . . .

But in another letter (CL 534) he laid more emphasis on the clashes of the various greens and sulpher-yellow in the picture; with him it was always a vexed question what precisely it was that made colour expressive. This was an uncertainty made more acute by his close association with Gauguin towards the end of his visit to Paris in 1886–7.

Gauguin was also a self-taught painter and like van Gogh and Seurat he read Blanc's *Grammaire* some time early in the 1880s.[82] Like van Gogh too, he had experimented with Seurat's dotted technique in Paris in 1886[83] so he was already something of a connoisseur of the most advanced attitudes towards colour. His *Still-Life with a Horse's Head*, which includes a Japanese doll and fans, shows that he was also an admirer of the Japanese artefacts – much lauded by Blanc – which were to engage so much of van Gogh's attention during his Paris period. They certainly became close friends during the visit,[84] and one common concern which is likely to have been eagerly discussed between them was the oriental principles of colour harmony. During the winter of 1885–6 Gauguin had circulated a translation of a fragment of what he claimed was an eighteenth-century Turkish treatise, which included a number of precepts about colour:

Who tells you that you ought to seek contrast in colours?
What is sweeter in an artist than to make perceptible in a bunch of roses the tint of each one?
Although two flowers resemble each other, can they ever be petal by petal the same?
Seek for harmony and not contrast, for what accords, not what clashes. It is the eye of ignorance that assigns a fixed and unchangeable colour to every object; as I have said to you, beware of this stumbling-block.[85]

Van Gogh in 1886 was working on a long series of flower compositions, including roses, which were intended precisely to reveal 'oppositions of blue with orange, red and green, yellow and violet, seeking *les tons rompus et neutres* to harmonize brutal extremes. Trying to render intense colour and not a grey harmony' (CL 459a). It was this insistence on complementaries, even while attempting to modify them, that Gauguin was later to criticize most bitterly in his work.[86] He probably witnessed in Paris one of the most startling examples of its operation in the version which van Gogh made of Hiroshige's colour-print, *Plumtree Teahouse at Kaneido (Plum Trees in Flower)*, where the soft greens and salmon-pinks were heightened into bright complementary greens and reds, the whites turned to yellows and the few blues extended and set off by a wholly invented bright orange frame.[87] That this was an especially impressive transformation to Gauguin is suggested by his use of the design a year later in his *Vision after the Sermon (Jacob Wrestling with the Angel)*, whose highly contrasting palette he described in a letter to van Gogh.[88] For a moment, and for an unusually dramatic subject, Gauguin adopted the more strident tonalities he had described, like Blanc, in military terms in his *Notes synthétiques* about 1884.[89]

Vincent for his part was well able to learn from Gauguin's subtler tonalities, which he used in the several 'greys' of the self-portrait presented to his friend in September 1888,[90] as well as in his 'portrait' of Gauguin's chair, in contrast to the painting of his own more robust yellow chair in its red and blue room. In a number of paintings done at Arles, notably *Les Alyscamps*, he adopted a resonant but muted palette and the strongly marked outlines which were being developed by Gauguin and his circle at Pont Aven.[91] He had long been aware of the range of options open to a painter anxious to work according to the 'laws' of colour. In one of his many didactic letters to Theo in 1885 (CL 428) he had listed contrasts of complementary hues, contrasts of kindred hues and contrasts of values, rather as Adolf Hoelzel and Johannes Itten were to do forty years later; but he came down in favour of the primacy of complementaries. Yet only a few days later he was arguing, '*Much, everything*, depends on my perception of the infinite variety of tones of one *same family*' (CL 429). All these principles of colour organization had been explored in his painting since the Dutch years; what Gauguin did was to open his eyes to new colours and new combinations.

One passage from his reading about Delacroix's methods which stayed in van Gogh's mind referred to 'an unnameable nuance of violet' on that master's palette. The etcher Félix Bracquemond, his source in this instance,[92] was particularly worried by colour-names which, with the development of synthetic dyestuffs and pigments and the growth of commerical fashion, seemed to be running out of control. Some of these new names, such as Magenta, the aniline crimson named after a French battle of 1859, are still with us; but two mentioned as ephemeral by Bracquemond, *cuisse de nymphe émue* ('thigh of an excited nymph'), which might be anything from pink to lilac or even yellow, and *Bismark*, a leather-brown, have left no trace.[93] If, as Bracquemond hoped, colour and values were to become a language with its own grammar,[94] how could it do without names? It was precisely the gap between perception and language which intrigued van Gogh and was to become an important aspect of Gauguin's Symbolist aesthetic of colour – a gap which gave the edge to painters over the Symbolist poets.[95]

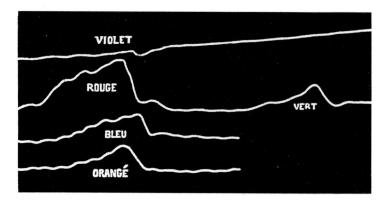

The lines of the graph plot the contraction of the muscles of the hand and forearm under the influence of various coloured lights, which (according to Charles Féré, *Sensation et Movement*, 1887) could be felt even with the eyes closed. Violet has the least effect, red the most. (170)

In the early 1880s Gauguin had used a very commonplace and limited vocabulary of colour terms – red, yellow, blue, green – when, for example, he annotated his sketches.[96] In his correspondence with van Gogh in 1888 he had used studio language: *vermillion, vert eméraude, ocre, ultramarine, chrome 2* and so on. Van Gogh used a mixture of more general words and technical terms, the first more commonly when writing to Theo and the latter when talking to other artists or to himself on drawings.[97] One of the colour diagrams which had attracted Gauguin in his studies was the colour-star adapted by Blanc from the version in *Études céramiques* by Ingres's pupil J.-C. Ziegler. In this star the primary and secondary colours were given their usual names, but the tertiaries had been much less susceptible to standardization, so that Ziegler had devised for them the quite personal terms of 'sulphur', 'turquoise', 'garnet' and 'nasturtium', as well as the technical terms indigo and cadmium (yellow-orange), which Blanc changed to 'bell-flower' and saffron.[98] This instability in the names of tertiaries, not to mention those of their 'unnameable' derivatives, must have appealed especially to Gauguin, for he used these nuances extensively in his paintings of the 1890s, such as *The Loss of Virginity* and *Manao Tupapau* (1892), where colour became the chief vehicle of mystery:

154–5

164

> Since colour is in itself enigmatic in the sensations which it gives us (*note*: medical experiments made to cure madness by means of colours) we cannot logically employ it except enigmatically, every time we use it not to define form [*dessiner*], but to give musical sensations which spring from it, from its peculiar nature, from its inner power, its mystery, its enigma . . .[99]

The nameless colours were not only mysterious but could speak directly, without associations, to the feelings. In these remarks Gauguin seems to be referring to the work of the French physiologist Charles Féré, who in the 1880s was testing and treating hysterics under various sorts of coloured light in a programme of what came to be called Chromotherapy, which gathered momentum during the 1890s, especially in Germany.[100] It was generally discovered that red light had a somewhat exciting and blue light a somewhat calming effect,

170

conclusions not unfamiliar to readers of Goethe's *Theory*, which was frequently invoked in the German literature of this branch of healing.[101]

The revival of interest in Romanticism, together with this new concern with the immediate psychological effects of colours, brought Goethe's *Theory* into prominence again around the time of the First World War, chiefly on account of its psycho-physiological ideas. It was now the turn of artists to claim Goethe for themselves; one critic in the 1890s had already argued that 'Naturalism, Pleinairism, Symbolism; Impressionists, Pointillists, and whatever these isms and ists may be called, can all appeal to Goethe'.[102] The most far-reaching revival of interest in Goethe's principles appeared after 1900, in the circles of German artists who came to be known as Expressionists. One of the first, the Dresden painter Ernst Ludwig Kirchner, a founder of the Brücke (Bridge) group, had tried to work in a Neo-Impressionist style around 1906, had studied Helmholtz, Rood and, surprisingly perhaps, Newton, but had finally discovered Goethe's *Theory* and thought it the most appropriate to his interests. Goethe's after-image effects showed that only strongly coloured stimuli needed to be painted into the picture, not the results of these stimuli in the nineteenth-century representational manner.[103] German Expressionist painting, like German Expressionist poetry, released colour from its traditional role of identifying objects; in this sense it was informed by the same concerns as experimental psychology, which sought, with some difficulty, to isolate the effects of colours entirely from associations.[104] It is something of an irony that one of the few scientists to support the physical aspects of Goethe's *Theory* in these years, Arnold Brass, should have attacked the 'green skies' and 'violet meadows' or 'yellow streams' of this type of modern art.[105] Brass in Munich may have been thinking of the Munich-based painter Wassily Kandinsky who came, it seems, to Goethe's *Theory* rather late, after he had published the first edition of his manifesto *On the Spiritual in Art* (1912), in which the most thoroughgoing Expressionist theory of colour was given a classic formulation. Kandinsky's access to Goethe at this date was chiefly through the Theosophist Rudolph Steiner[106] and it has been the occult and spiritualist elements in Kandinsky's theory, mediated largely by Steiner, which have been emphasized in recent studies. His aims were certainly spiritual but the taxonomy of this spirituality in its visible manifestations owed a great deal to the contemporary psychological debate.

In his book Kandinsky introduced precisely the topic of the non-associative psychological effects of colours which was occupying psychologists: after an account of the various types of synaesthesia (the simultaneous triggering of several senses by the same stimulus), Kandinsky continued:

> This explanation [in terms of association] is, however, insufficient in many instances that are for us of particular importance. Anyone who has heard of colour therapy knows that coloured light can have a particular effect upon the entire body. Various attempts to exploit this power of colour and apply it to different nervous disorders have again noted that red light has an enlivening and stimulating effect upon the heart, while blue, on the other hand, can lead to temporary paralysis. If this sort of effect can also be observed

in the case of animals, and even plants, then any explanation in terms of association completely falls down. These facts in any case prove that colour contains within itself a little studied but enormous power, which can influence the entire human body as a physical organism.[107]

The reference to red and blue depends upon a book on colour-therapy by Arthur Osborne Eaves, *Die Kräfte der Farben* (1906), in his copy of which Kandinsky noted the contrasting effects of blue and red with the symbols for centripetal and centrifugal forces later used in Table I of *On the Spiritual in Art* to characterize blue and yellow.[108] But he had become familiar with some of the research of colour-therapists in a number of German and French publications as early as 1901.[109] His own colour-system, with its polar arrangement of black and white, blue and yellow, red and green and orange and violet, although it did not depend on any earlier system, relates to the circular 'opponent-colour' scheme proposed by the Viennese physiologist Ewald Hering[110] and the polar progression from yellow to blue, the 'primary' contrast, to the work of the psychologist Wilhelm Wundt. Wundt described how the psychological transition from yellow to blue, or from liveliness to rest, could be by one of two routes: a stable route through green and a highly unstable one through red, purple and violet.[111] This was a way of thinking about the dynamics of colour close to Kandinsky: it may have been because he was well aware of this tradition in German experimental psychology that he included a note to the effect that his conclusions depended upon 'empirical-spiritual experience', and not on any 'positive science'.[112]

The conception of colour as a labile polar phenomenon was not confined to Kandinsky in the circle of the Blaue Reiter (Blue Rider) of which he was a co-founder in 1911. Already some years earlier Franz Marc, the painter of animals and co-editor with Kandinsky of *Der Blaue Reiter* almanac, had been discussing the subject of the colour circle with a third artist who joined the group, August Macke; Marc wrote:

> *Blue* is the *male* principle, sharp and spiritual, *yellow* the *female* principle, soft, cheerful and sensual, *red* the *material*, brutal and heavy and ever the colour which must be resisted and overcome by the other two. If, for example, you mix the serious, spiritual blue with red, then you augment the blue to an unbearable mourning, and the reconciling yellow, the complementary colour to violet, will be indispensable (the woman as consoler, not as lover!). If you mix red and yellow, you give the passive and female yellow a Megaera-like, sensual power, for which the cool, spiritual blue – the man – will again be indispensable, and certainly blue sets itself immediately and automatically next to orange; the colours love each other. Blue and orange, a thoroughly festive chords [*Klang*]. But if you now mix blue and yellow to green, you bring red, the material, the 'earth' to life, but here I, as a painter, always feel a difference: with green you never put the eternally material, brutal red to rest, as you do with the other colour-chord (just imagine objects decorated in green and red!). Blue (the heaven) and yellow (the sun) must always come to the aid of green again, to *subdue the material*. And then, another thing … blue and yellow are not equidistant from red. In spite of all spectral analysis I can't get over my painter's belief that yellow (the woman) is closer to the earthly red than blue, the male principle … [113]

171
172

TABLE I.

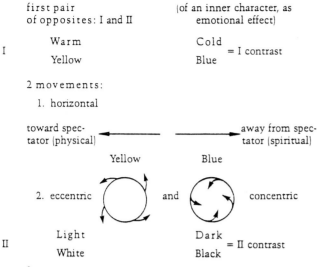

We can easily imagine how Marc came to conceive the idea of the Blue Rider, the spiritual controller of one of his red or yellow horses.[114]

This gendering of colour had had its parallel in an essay by Runge, although Marc's interpretation of the colours was almost the opposite of his, which saw the cool colours of the circle related to the feminine and the warm to the masculine 'passions' and red to love.[115] It is possible that Marc was directly affected by Runge's scheme, since the Romantic artist had risen to prominence in Wilhelmine Germany because of the 'Jahr-hundertsausstellung' (Centenary Exhibition) of German art from 1775 to 1875, held in Berlin in 1906. This great exhibition had been arranged by Hugo von Tschudi who, because of his positive attitude to modern, particularly French, movements, was soon after dismissed from the Berlin Museum and moved to Munich, where be became close to the circle of Marc and Kandinsky (who dedicated the *Almanac* to his memory). In the catalogue to the 'Jahrhundertsausstellung' Tschudi had written of Runge in terms very likely to commend him to his new friends: 'He is a mystic, and writes a scientific theory of colour; every flower, every colour has a symbolic meaning for him and he sees the task of painting in the representation of air and light and the movement of life; he speaks of the new art, and [yet] paints with the means and the attitudes of the Old Masters.'[116] But whatever the source of Marc's idea, it was one which was entirely up-to-date and had also been recorded in the literature of experimental psychology.[117]

Few, if any, of the many approaches to colour among members of the Blaue Reiter cannot be paralleled in the technical publications of experimental psychology in this period; many were presented in a single series of interviews, chiefly with professional people, including some art-historians and painters, conducted by G. J. von Allesch before the First World War but not published until 1925.[118] Allesch's object was to identify patterns of colour-preference, which he was conspicuously unable to do; but in the process he assembled some of the most detailed accounts of spiritual and sensual responses to colour in subjects from a wide range of ages, nationalities and professions: they should give pause to those modern commentators who consider the views of the Blaue Reiter to be eccentric or entirely personal.[119] One of the assumptions developed within this school of psychology was precisely that at the level of sensual apprehension, pleasure in bright, saturated colour was common to all periods and peoples and that only the higher levels of aesthetic appreciation were the result of acculturation: this was very much how form was promoted by the large collection of artefacts gathered from many civilizations, presented in the illustrations to the *Blaue Reiter* almanac.[120] Had cheap colour-reproduction been available in 1912, the editors might well have offered similar observations for colour; as it was, they included only some of their own coloured woodcuts in the *de luxe* edition.

To judge from his short autobiogaphical essay *Reminiscences* (1914), Kandinsky was a natural synaesthete: speaking of the first paintbox of his adolescence, he wote, 'It sometimes seemed to me as if the brush, as it tore pieces with inexorable will from this living being that is colour, conjured up in the process a musical sound. Sometimes I could hear the hiss of the colours as

156

Wassily Kandinsky, first and third colour diagrams from *On the Spiritual in Art*, 1912. Kandinsky's conception of colour was essentially dynamic, and in the third diagram he sought a polar arrangement of black versus white, green versus red, orange versus violet, each arising 'from a modification of red by yellow or blue', and so on. (171,172)

Table III

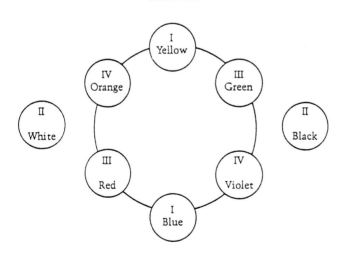

The pairs of opposites represented as a ring between two poles = the life of the simple colors between birth and death.

(The Roman numerals indicate the pairs of opposites.)

they mingled.'[121] Synaesthesia was also one of the most active areas of experimental psychology in these years and one in which the 'empirical-spiritual' was especially hard to disentangle from 'positive science'. When we look at colour and music (Chapter 13) we shall see that in the linkage of colours with musical sounds, Kandinsky's responses were very much in line with a long tradition now being renewed in a systematic way. It was this commonest variety of synaesthesia, called *audition colorée* ('colour-hearing'), that particularly interested the psychologists and in 1890 the Congrès Internationale de la Psychologie Physiologique set up a committee to investigate it: some five hundred cases were reported by 1892.[122] Kandinsky will have read of the phenomenon in articles by Scheffler and Gérome-Maësse and he made notes on an inconclusive essay by Freudenberg on its most widespread manifestation, the identification of colours and vowel-sounds. This had been proposed as early as A. W. Schlegel in the Romantic period but it had been given a new stimulus in the 1870s by Rimbaud's poem 'Voyelles', which begins 'A noir, E blanc, I rouge, U vert, O bleu: voyelles'.[123] Even though it was thought by some that Russian – Kandinsky's native tongue – was particularly rich in synaesthetic sounds[124] and although *audition colorée* had a particularly vigorous life in Russian art and literature,[125] Kandinsky seems to have kept this aspect of the phenomenon at a distance until his period as a teacher at the Bauhaus in the 1920s.[126] But once again he was caught up in the mainstream of experimental colour-psychology.

'Painting is recording coloured sensations'

Goethe's engagement with the problems of the psychology of perception involved a number of levels, including the fundamental question for the painter of what it is precisely that we see. In a remarkable passage of the introduction to the *Theory of Colours* he expressed this problem in a way which was to resonate as long as representation was a central preoccupation of painting:

> We now assert, extraordinary as it may in some degree appear, that the eye sees no form, inasmuch as light, shade and colour together constitute that which to our vision distinguishes object from object, and the parts of an object from one another. From these three, light, shade and colour, we construct the visible world, and thus, at the same time, make painting possible, an art which has the power of producing on a flat surface a much more perfect visible world than the actual one can be.[127]

In some ways this was simply a return to the neo-medieval idealism of a Bishop Berkeley in the early eighteenth century[128] but the application specifically to painting was new. Goethe was not a painter: his extensive visual oeuvre is confined almost entirely to wash drawings and he never addressed the problems of painting from nature; but as nineteenth-century painting, especially in France, took a more empirical and positivist turn in the 1860s and 70s, Goethe's idea became an urgent issue. It was of course the Impressionists who first seemed to paint simply what they saw and appeared to see only what Goethe had suggested. But what exactly did he suggest? Monet, the most radical Impressionist, even towards the end of his career took a

surprisingly simple view of the visual experience of the painter:

> 'When you go out to paint, try to forget what objects you have before you, a tree, a house, a field, or whatever. Merely think, here is a little square of blue, here an oblong of pink, here a streak of yellow, and paint it just as it looks to you, the exact colour and shape, until it gives your own naive impression of the scene before you.'
>
> He said he wished he had been born blind and then had suddenly gained his sight so that he could have begun to paint in this way without knowing what the objects were that he saw before him.[129]

This belief in the virtues of naivety was a return to Ruskin's teaching of the 1850s, specifically to the *Elements of Drawing*, which enjoyed a high reputation in France at the end of the century.[130] In a remarkable passage of his slightly earlier essay *Pre-Raphaelitism*, Ruskin had contrasted the antithetical approaches to landscape of John Everett Millais and Turner, the former keen-sighted and concerned to record every detail of what he saw while he saw it and hence occupied with the most permanent features of the scene; the latter long-sighted and anxious to render the most fleeting effects of light and weather and hence dependent very much on his memory and invention.[131] But Impressionist landscape was both concerned with transient effects of light like Turner's and was to be executed in front of the motif like Millais's; its extraordinarily novel qualities of brushwork and colour can be attributed for the most part to these two barely reconcilable demands. We learn from his extensive correspondence that Monet was remarkably unreflective about these problems: for him landscape painting was largely a matter of overcoming the relative feebleness of his painting materials and the vagaries of the weather. Around 1890 he developed a method of working on a series of canvases in succession, for as few as seven minutes each in the case of the *Poplars* and on as many as fourteen at a session in the case of *Rouen Cathedral*.[132] There is no reason to think that he did not believe in the rhetoric of 'naturalness' and 'objectivity' with which these works were launched, even when they came to be recognized as too decorative to be 'natural', and when he completed them more and more in the studio.[133] Monet was entirely unconcerned about the problematic nature of his own subjectivity, the effect of prolonged scrutiny of the motif on his eyes and his perceptions. This was very much the concern of contemporary physiological psychology in the tradition of Helmholtz, no stranger to Goethe's science and whose ideas were dominant in the French positivist aesthetics of the 1870s and 80s (*see* Chapter 9).

Not so Cézanne and it is to Cézanne that we must look for the supreme and surprisingly complete exemplification in painting of the attitudes towards colour and perception current in contemporary French physiology and philosophy. In a lecture in 1855 Helmholtz had stated, 'we never perceive the objects of the external world directly. On the contrary, we only perceive the effects of these objects on our own nervous apparatuses, and it has always been like that from the first moment of our life.'[134] In the 1860s he developed what he called the Empirical Theory of Vision, by which he meant that visual perception was not the result of immediate apprehension based on intuition or innate capacities, but rather of a process of learning through expe-

166

rience.[135] This was surely the debate which lay behind a casual remark of Cézanne's in a letter of 1905 to Émile Bernard: 'Optics, which are developed in us by study, teach us to see.'[136] Cézanne was not, it seems, a great reader of theory, although the idea of theory became more and more attractive to him towards the end of his life.[137] If we can credit the recollections of his friend Joachim Gasquet that they once discussed Kant on subjectivity, it may be that this related to Helmholtz's debate with the Kantians about the nature of perception and the organization of the mind.[138].

The most popular exponent of Helmholtzian physiology in France was undoubtedly the polymath Hippolyte Taine, whose survey of modern theories of the mind, *De l'Intelligence* (1870), ran into a dozen editions during Cézanne's lifetime. The painter is at least likely to have heard of Taine's ideas, since his close friend the novelist Émile Zola claimed to have read him as early as the 1860s and to have adopted his positivist attitude towards the world.[139] Taine, like Helmholtz, drew widely on his experience of painting, especially in his discussion of the role of memory, where he cited the well-known school of memory-training run by Henri Lecoq de Boisbaudran – frequented by Fantin-Latour – where the perception of colour was developed by means of progressively more complex charts of coloured nuances.[140] Taine took a rather more radical view than Helmholtz of the role of the mind in shaping the objective array of colours: 'All our sensations of colour are . . . projected out of our body, and clothe more or less distant objects, furniture, walls, houses, trees, the sky and the rest. This is why, when we reflect on them afterwards, we cease to attribute them to ourselves; they are alienated and detached from us, so far as to appear different from us'.[141] He later cited an instance well-known to us by now from Ruskin and Monet, the case of a woman whose sight had been restored and had at first seen only 'patches' (*taches*):

> Colourist painters know this state well, . . . their gift consists in seeing their model as if it were a *tache* of which the only element is colour more or less diversified, toned down, enlivened and mixed. So far no idea of distance and the position of objects [in space] except when an inference [*induction*] derived from touch sites them all opposite the eye . . .[142]

From the 1880s onwards Cézanne developed a painterly vocabulary of mostly regular *taches*, with which he more or less covered his canvas. As he told Bernard: 'To read nature is to see her, underneath the veil of interpretation, as coloured *taches* following one another according to a law of harmony. These large coloured areas [*teintes*] can thus be analysed into modulations. Painting is recording coloured sensations.'[143] If we examine a spacious and luminous late landscape such as *Winding Road* (*c.* 1900), we shall surely find it difficult to identify the function of these subtly modulated *taches* 'following each other according to a law of harmony', which, with the exception of a few gables, roofs and tree-trunks, do not reveal themselves in any obvious way. In particular, they seem to offer no points of focus in the way in which we might expect them to constitute a scene around a number of salient points. And yet they convey a marked sense of depth. In a letter to Bernard about the time of this painting, Cézanne associated reds and yellows with light

and blues with air, but here they all seem to function more as local colours.[144] We have the assurance of a number of painters and critics that it is possible, with patience and persistence, to replicate a Cézanne-like way of looking at the world, although those painter-critics such as Roger Fry, Ernst Strauss or Lawrence Gowing who have interpreted his work both verbally and visually stopped short of attempting the sort of modulation by colour which gave many of his late paintings such luminosity.[145] What this highly specialized manner of looking seems to have involved was the fixation on a small area of the scene – what Cézanne called the 'culminating point' – in order to identify its tone and colour characteristics in isolation from its context. After recording its precise quality the painter would move to another point, which might be at a considerable distance from the first, so that in time his canvas or paper might show a number of discrete areas of working; the progress of the painting would depend upon his capacity to knit these areas together into a coherent whole.[146] This was the antithesis of the common Impressionist procedure of covering as much of the surface as possible from the first.[147]

We know from many barely started canvases or watercolour sheets and from the account by Bernard of Cézanne at work on a watercolour in 1904[148] how a subject might begin with the darkest points or junctions of surfaces; we know far less about how it was brought to a conclusion. Indeed the whole notion of finish, as his critics soon recognized, became irrelevant to Cézanne's method.[149] He was, after all, a man of independent means and little concerned until the last years with the sale of his work. The pictures came increasingly to represent less a statement about a motif – although his imperious attitude to the motif is clear from the way he organized it even before he started painting[150] – than notes of his reactions to it over a period of time. His dealer Ambroise Vollard, who claimed to having submitted to 115 sittings for his portrait, clearly had every occasion to observe Cézanne's meticulous working procedures, his many soft brushes, each carefully cleaned after each stroke, laid on in very liquid glazes like watercolour, layer after layer. In this instance the painter left two or three small patches of bare canvas on the hands, hoping at some time to identify the precise tone which would be necessary to complete them: if he were to finish the painting casually with any ill-considered nuance, he would have had to repaint the whole thing 'starting from that place'.[151]

If Cézanne began by establishing his darks and working up the scale, he must soon have run into that familiar obstacle to representational painting, the inadequacy of the scale of light in the picture to match the scale of nature, an inadequacy which had even been quantified by Helmholtz.[152] Cézanne's determination to render values by colours – to 'modulate' rather than to model – must have complicated his task even further. Like Whistler and the painters of the École des Beaux Arts, he set out his scale of mixtures on the palette before he started working and did not mix as he went along; this must of itself have imposed some conceptual coherence on his rendering of his perceptions from the outset.[153] But Bernard, who recorded most of these details, did not say precisely what Cézanne's scale was – how much he used mixed colours at all, for example – and it is only from other parts of his memoirs that we learn how

165

Cézanne resisted the suggestions of an Impressionist such as Pissarro, or a Symbolist like himself, to restrict the palette. In 1904, according to Bernard, Cézanne was using nineteen pigments arranged in a strictly tonal sequence.[154] The paintings themselves suggest that now, in contrast to the 1870s, mixture was something which he tried to avoid, so it is not surprising that, even with white and five yellows, Cézanne found no possibilities left to him at the top of the scale and had to leave his canvas or paper blank. That it was the lightest lights which were thus left unpainted has made it possible for us to read many of these late images as whole.

What is clear is that this need to abandon paintings at various stages of their making became a source of great anxiety to Cézanne. In a letter to Bernard of October 1905 he wrote: 'Now, being old, nearly 70 years, the sensations of colour, which give the light, are for me the reason for the abstractions which do not allow me to cover my canvas entirely nor to pursue the delimitation of the objects where their points of contact are fine and delicate; from which it results that my image or picture is incomplete.' A year later to his own son: 'I must tell you that as a painter I am becoming more clear-sighted before nature, but that with me the realization of my sensations is always painful. I cannot attain the intensity that is unfolded before my senses. I have not the magnificent richness of colouring that animates nature.'[155] The frustrations coming from a lifetime of testing the psycho-physiological question, 'what do our perceptions look like?' produced not only anxiety but also the visual tensions which give such vitality to Cézanne's last works.

From Matisse to abstraction

Cézanne came to be the single most important presence in French painting before the First World War. Of his younger admirers Henri Matisse was perhaps the most able to explore the implications of his late style and to account for that exploration in an articulate verbal commentary. Matisse had studied with the Symbolist Gustave Moreau who, although a professor at the École, took an imaginative view of colour which was closer to van Gogh and Gauguin than to the French academic tradition.[156] But as he admitted himself, Matisse was 'a good half a scientist' and we remember that even in later life he took to working in a white coat.[157] He read Signac's *D'Eugène Delacroix au néo-impressionnisme* as soon as it came out in 1898 or 1899 but at that time he used the dotted technique so vaguely as to suggest the experiment was based entirely on reading and that he had not yet examined any works by the Neo-Impressionists themselves.[158] Five years later Matisse was in direct contact with Signac and another exponent of the method, H.-E. Cross, in the south of France. Although he later played down his interest in the 'scientific' colour of this group, arguing against the constraints inherent in Signac's preoccupation with complementaries and that the only way to establish them was to study the paintings of the great colourists,[159] there are signs that Matisse himself was now inclined to be doctrinaire. His most important Neo-Impressionist work, *Luxe, calme et volupté* (1904–5) incorporates a set of complementary contrasts, vermilion and green, yellow and violet, which are far harsher than those in the contemporary work of Cross and Signac, who was more inclined to juxtapose related tones which would fuse to an optical shimmer. Maurice Denis called Matisse's picture 'the diagram of a theory'; Matisse himself admitted that he felt he had to heighten the contrasts more than Cross had recommended – he certainly had a reputation among the other Fauve painters in 1905 for a more rigid observance of theory than they.[160] When he opened his private art-school in Paris in 1908, the theories of Chevreul, Helmholtz and Rood were, according to one of his pupils, among the subjects discussed. Matisse's belief that red, green and blue sufficed 'to create the equivalent of the spectrum' suggests an unusually careful reading of Rood's *Modern Chromatics*, but not thorough enough for him to have been aware of the Purkinje Shift.[161] But this year also marked a change in direction from a more or less conceptual to an entirely perceptual theory of colour and, as a consequence, towards painting in flatter and flatter tones.

Matisse's *Notes d'un peintre* (1908) includes perhaps the most sophisticated theory of colour to have been written by an artist in this century:

> I study my method very closely: if I put a black dot on a sheet of white paper, the dot will be visible no matter how far away I hold it: it is a clear notation. But beside this dot I will place another one, and then a third, and already there is confusion. In order for the first dot to maintain its value I must enlarge it as I put other marks on the paper.
>
> If upon a white canvas I set down the sensations of blue, of green, of red, each new stroke diminishes the importance of the preceding ones. Suppose I have to paint an interior: I have before me a cupboard; it gives me a sensation of vivid red and I put down a red which satisfies me. A relation is established between this red and the white of the canvas – Let me put a green near the red and make the floor yellow; and again there will be relationships between the green or yellow and the white of the canvas which will satisfy me. But these different tones mutually weaken one another. It is necessary that the various marks I use be balanced so that they do not destroy each other. To do this I must organize my ideas; the relationship between the tones must be such that it will sustain and not destroy them. A new combination of colours will succeed the first and render the totality of my representation. I am obliged to transpose (*obligé de transposer*), until finally my picture may seem completely changed when, after successive modifications, the red has succeeded the green as the dominant colour. I cannot copy nature in a servile way; I am forced (*forcé*) to interpret nature and submit it to the spirit of the picture . . .[162]

For Cézanne's despairing bondage to colour in nature Matisse was substituting the bondage to colour in the picture. In this he was following the imperatives of van Gogh in 1888 who although he had thought of his colours as 'arbitrary' also felt that they 'follow of their own accord'.[163] Matisse's formulation of a similar idea in an essay on colour towards the end of his life reinforced his own feeling that he was not in control: 'I use the simplest colours, I don't transform them myself, it is the relationships which take charge of them (*qui s'en chargent*).'[164]

Matisse's newly formulated attitude to colour in 1908 was not an entirely coherent one: just after the passage quoted above he stated that he must have 'a clear vision of the whole from the beginning' and a little later that the chief function of colour was to serve expression. But it seems clear from the course of his major works up to the War that his radically perceptualist, empiricist approach was the dominant one. Many paintings, notably *Still Life in Venetian Red* (1908), *At the Painter's Studio* (?1909–10) and *Zorah on the Terrace* (1912), show signs of the most extensive repainting; perhaps the most startling early instance of this is *Harmony in Red* which, as we now know from an early colour-photograph, began life as a *Harmony in Green*.[165] Of the great pair of canvases *Dance* and *Music* of 1910, the first was the climax of a number of versions and was painted with assurance and directness but the second bears the marks of substantial changes of mind. Matisse began at precisely this time to keep photographic records of the metamorphoses of his works.[166] From 1911 a thinner, watercolour-like treatment, with no opportunities for *pentimenti*, became more and more evident and shows how much more developed Matisse's capacity to visualize had become; but even now, and indeed until the end of his life when the use of paper cut-out 'jigsaws' made commitment to a first idea irrelevant, the evidences of radical changes in composition and colour were a recurrent feature of his work. So important were these changes to his method that by the mid-1910s he had developed a special scraper to remove the earlier paint, in order to work faster and avoid overloading the surface with tired impasto.[167]

One of the most compelling results of this radical perceptualism and the transformations it induced was the *Red Studio* (1911). This painting still has an exceptionally luminous, fresh surface and yet it, too, was originally a blue-grey interior, corresponding more closely to the white of Matisse's studio as it actually was. This quite powerful blue-grey can still be seen even with the naked eye around the top of the clock and under the thinner paint on the left-hand side. What forced Matisse to transform his studio with this dazzling red has been debated: it has even been suggested that it was stimulated in the most perceptual of ways by the after-image of the greens from the garden on a hot day.[168] Certainly he suggested to a questioning visitor in 1912 they they should go for a walk in his garden.[169] Matisse's extraordinary sensitivity to this type of psychological effect is again suggested by a story he related about an experience in the chapel he decorated with drawings and stained-glass at Vence in the years around 1950. Recalling the sun filtering through the design of leafage in the windows, Matisse told an interviewer:

> That effect of colour has real power … So much power that, in certain lights, it seems to become a substance. Once when I found myself in the chapel, I saw on the ground a red of such materiality that I had the feeling that the colour was not the effect of light falling through the window, but that it belonged to some substance. This impression was reinforced by a particular circumstance: on the floor in front of me there was some sand in a little pile that the red colour was resting on. That gave the effect of a red powder so magnificent that I have never seen the like in my life. I bent down, put my hand in the sand and picked up a good fistful, raised it to my eyes and let it trickle through my fingers: a grey substance. But I haven't forgotten that red and one day I should like to be able to put it on canvas …[170]

What is most astonishing about this story is that the windows at Vence are glazed entirely with yellow, green and blue; there is no red, so Matisse's experience must have been of a negative after-image.

Matisse was used to taking the starting-point for paintings from the flowers in his garden and at Issy-les-Moulineaux, where his studio was in 1911, there were many reds among these flowers.[171] He told the Italian Futurist painter Gino Severini how the intense experience of, say, a single blue patch, might take over the whole of a picture, which may well be what happened here in the *Red Studio*, the most brilliant fruit of Matisse's perceptual stance.[172]

In his *Notes* Matisse had argued that 'an artist must recognize, when he is reasoning, that his picture is an artifice; but when he is painting, he should feel that he has copied nature'.[173] He always required the stimulus of a living presence, whether human, animal or vegetable, but his approach to painting nevertheless came as an inspiration to the non-representational painters who around 1910 were casting about for a *modus operandi* and a rationale. Kandinsky may have been in touch with Matisse in Paris; certainly he read the *Notes* when they appeared in German in 1909[174] and they may be felt in one of the very few places where he wrote not in general terms about art and life but of his own work. In an account of the large and turbulent *Composition VI*, based on an idea of the Deluge, the painter told how it reached its final form, after the main design had been laid in:

> Then came the subtle, enjoyable and yet exhausting task of balancing the individual elements one against the other. How I used to torture myself previously when some detail seemed to be wrong and I tried to improve it! Years of experience now taught me that the mistake is rarely to be found where one looks for it. It is often the case that to improve the bottom-left-hand corner, one needs to change something in the upper right. If the left-hand scale goes down too far, then you have to put a heavier weight on the right – and the left will come up of its own accord. The exhausting search for the right scale, for the exact missing weight, the way in which the left scale trembles at the merest touch on the right, the tiniest alterations of drawing and colour in such a place that the whole picture is made to vibrate – this permanently living, immeasurably sensitive quality of a successful picture – this is the third, beautiful and tormenting moment in painting …[175]

Kandinsky was describing a psychological drama acted out on his canvas, one still full of the residual symbols of his early phase of abstraction; but his means for conveying this drama were far from pre-ordained. He had begun with a large number of drawn and painted sketches, as befitted a subject of such narrative complexity, but even when he had finally fixed on a design, the act of painting moved through a series of psychological adjustments which characterized the new art of process. We shall see in the final chapter how many abstract painters in our century have developed this sense of process; it has been perhaps the most lasting contribution of the psychological theory of colour to the practice of art.

12 · The Substance of Colour

Venetian secrets · Technology and ideology · The impact of synthetic colours · Time the painter
Colour as constructive material

Beyond the conditioning which he receives from the world around him and the place in which he finds himself, the artist must yield, up to a certain point, to the possibilities and limitations of the medium he uses. Pencil, charcoal, pastel, oil paint, the blacks of the print, marble, bronze, clay or wood: these are all his companions and collaborators, and they too have something to say in the fiction he is about to produce. Materials have secrets to reveal; they have their own genius; it is through them that the oracle speaks ... (Odilon Redon, 1913)[1]

TOWARDS the end of the 1790s the Royal Academy in London was shaken by a scandal which reflected very seriously on the technical knowledge and competence of its leading members. A young woman, Ann Jemima Provis, claimed to have discovered an old manuscript recording the exact methods of the sixteenth-century Venetian painters, among the papers of an ancestor of hers who had travelled in Italy. Provis had exhibited miniatures at the Academy in the 1780s and it was on the recommendation of a miniaturist among the academicians, Richard Cosway, that she was introduced to the President, Benjamin West, who was induced to try out what came to be known as the 'process' or the 'Venetian Secret'. The process had three salient features, the first of which was a highly absorbent ground that took most of the oil from the colours and was usually dark, sometimes, as James Gillray showed in his brilliant satire on the 'Secret', even black. The second feature was the use of pure linseed oil, so highly refined as to have the consistency of water; and the third was the use of the so-called 'Titian Shade', a mixture of crimson lake, indigo or Hungarian (Prussian) blue or Antwerp blue, with ivory black: a mixture used to lay out the composition in chiaroscuro – the procedure seen to be characteristic of Titian in France – and over which the brightest colours were to be glazed. Then the painting was to be allowed to dry completely and finally varnished.[2] This 'Secret' which Provis's father once thought might be worth one thousand pounds was sold to various academicians for ten guineas each and much of it was communicated by demonstrations and supplementary information over a period of months: the whole enterprise has a very *ad hoc* feel about it. Its products, notably paintings by West, were shown at the Royal Academy exhibition in 1797, to general disappointment.[3] Edmond Malone, who in the first edition of Reynolds's *Works* (1797) had welcomed the 'Secret' as something the first President should have lived to use, dismissed it as useless in the second edition (1798).[4] Gillray immortalized the whole sorry affair in his print, where Reynolds, with ear-trumpet and spectacles, is seen rising from the grave: it had been his attempts to fathom the Venetian technique, and the decay of his works partly as a result of these reckless experiments, that

had fuelled the wish of the academicians to discover the Venetian secret; but it turned out that the Provis 'Process' was equally unstable.[5]

This did not prevent the continued search for Venetian secrets in England. Since the dark absorbent ground was a major feature of the process, two other experimenters, Timothy Sheldrake and Sebastian Grandi, drew attention to their work on this aspect of the method, with the significant difference that they chose the more public forum of the Society of Arts, which had been testing artists' materials for several decades.[6] Another aspect of the secret was the medium used by the Venetian masters, which the Irish painter Solomon Williams claimed to have discovered: it too a brief vogue among academicians, notably Farington, until its limitations were revealed.[7] As late as 1815 another young woman, a Miss Cleaver, arrived on the scene with a new 'Venetian Process', this time using wax crayons. Richard Westall, who had been one of the Provis supporters, now tried the new recipe and exhibited a *Cupid and Psyche* painted according to its principles at the Royal Academy in 1822; the patron and amateur Sir George Beaumont, who had actually been a pupil of Provis, asked his friend Constable to test it. Constable did not like it, and Cleaver and her 'secret' quickly sank from view.[8]

In the course of the 1797 affair the landscape-painter Paul Sandby, one of Provis's leading critics, recalled that Cosway had found an Italian book 'published at Venice in Titian's time', where 'the whole process is fully displayed'.[9] This book was probably one of the very few technical treatises of the sixteenth century, G. B. Armenini's *De' Veri Precetti della Pittura*, first published at Ravenna in 1587 but whose second edition of 1678 had indeed appeared in Venice. Armenini's book was an example of the sort of early treatise increasingly attracting attention among artists in the Romantic period: when it was printed for a third time in 1820, its editor, Stefano Ticozzi, did not fail to note that in an age obsessed by the idea of *disegno* (he was talking of course of Neo-Classical Italy) the precepts and methods of colouring described by these Old Masters – the 'secrets' which Armenini had brought out into the light – were especially important.[10] The first half of the nineteenth century was remarkable for the attempt to provide authentic texts describing Old Master techniques, even pre-Renaissance masters whose work was only just beginning to be taken seriously. The *Of Divers Arts* of Theophilus had already been published simultaneously in Germany and England in 1781 but rather as a literary curiosity than as a practical handbook; yet Cennini's *Book of Art*, first published in Italy in 1821, was soon studied by Blake and Haydon in England and in due course by Ingres in France.[11] It heralded a spate of early technical texts, a spate

George Field in his laboratory, around 1843. The 'Metrochrome' (shown to his right, on the table) contains glass wedges filled with red, yellow and blue liquids, designed to measure the strength of colours. (173)

which gathered momentum in England in the 1840s, where the controversies over the medium to be used for decorating the new Houses of Parliament stimulated two of the most important studies to publish or be based on original sources, Charles Eastlake's *Materials for a History of Oil Painting* (1847–69) and the *Original Treatises on the Arts of Painting* (1849), gathered and translated by Mary Merrifield, who had already translated Cennini into English in 1844. The techniques of the sometimes distant past were to be studied now on the basis of authentic documents but the problem exposed by the vogue for spurious 'secrets' remained: how could modern artists procure the materials which had seemed to guarantee the lasting reputation of the Old Masters?

The profession of colour-manufacturer and dealer had been gaining ground in the sixteenth century; in seventeenth-century Holland we find the first records of shops selling raw and prepared pigments together with other painters' apparatus and, in some cases, pictures themselves.[12] These dealers grew in numbers and importance all over Europe during the eighteenth century and until surprisingly late some painters themselves prepared the raw pigments for use: Bouvier's handbook of the 1820s assumed that its readers (?in Switzerland) would be grinding their own colours and a stray remark by van Gogh in a letter of 1885 shows that even he was still buying raw pigments and having them ground at Neunen or grinding them himself.[13] But these were exceptional circumstances, outside the major art centres. For most artists during the nineteenth

century, materials were to be bought ready-prepared, although they might well be prepared especially to order, as they were for example by Mme Haro for Delacroix, who liked his colours more liquid than most.[14] With the developing mass-production of paints in the course of the century, a painter such as van Gogh was obliged to shop around in Paris to get the quality he wanted at the price his brother could afford: the colourman Julien (Père) Tanguy, whom he immortalized in a number of portraits, was not in fact his favourite supplier and he was increasingly inclined to buy from Tanguy's rival, Tasset and L'Hôte.[15] It would be a delicious irony if the portraits were painted with Tasset's colours but it is not clear when van Gogh started dealing with the cheaper colourman, who is first mentioned in letters from Arles, after he had left Paris. In any case he was using both suppliers' colours until the end of his life.

Technical handbooks devoted more and more space to assessing the merits and defects of pigments, since it was considered unlikely that artists themselves would be able to test their materials.[16] In London, a Professor of Chemistry was appointed at the Royal Academy in 1871, and in Paris, where the great chemist Louis Pasteur had occasionally lectured at the École in the 1860s, a colourman was regularly in attendance in the 1880s and 1890s, but it was not until early in the 1900s that a laboratory was set up to test commercial colours at the school.[17] With the mass-production of colours went the development of synthetic pigments, which of course involved the directed research and development programmes which could only grow out of the mass demand created by the professional and amateur art-boom of the nineteenth century. How this expansion first came about is well illustrated by the careers of two prominent theorists and colour-manufacturers, J.-F.-L. Mérimée in France and George Field in England.

Technology and ideology

Mérimée, born in 1757, had trained as a painter, first with the late-Baroque Doyen and then with the precocious Neo-Classicist Vincent. In the 1790s he had made a sufficient impression to be installed with a scholarship among the privileged students at the Louvre but as a result of his marriage in 1802 he was obliged to take to teaching and he abandoned painting completely after 1815.[18] Like Reynolds and the supporters of the Venetian Secret, Mérimée felt that the decadence of modern technique could be remedied by a study of the methods of the Old Masters; but unlike them he saw salvation not so much in the Venetian painting of the sixteenth century as in Early Netherlandish art. As he wrote at the beginning of his most important publication, *De la Peinture à l'huile* (1830):

> The paintings of *Hubert* and *Jan Van Eyck*, and those of several painters of the same period, are far better preserved than most paintings of the last century. The methods by which they were executed, passed down entirely by tradition, have not reached us in their original form, and we may be allowed to believe that these paintings, whose colours, after three centuries, amaze us by their brilliance, were not painted in the same way as those which we see perceptibly altered after only a few years.[19]

During the 1790s, first privately and then at the École Polytechnique, Mérimée set out to discover by experiment the medium used by the Early Netherlandish masters – this even before a taste for their art had been more generally rekindled by the arrival of their works in the booty which Napoleon's Netherlands campaigns had brought to the Louvre. He concluded that their secret had been the mixture of varnish – a dissolved resin – with the oil medium.[20] What was most unusual about Mérimée's handbook of 1830 was the introduction, side-by-side, of personal experiments, the recipes attributed to Old Master (now going back to Theophilus in the Middle Ages), the testimony of contemporary painters such as the Correggesque Pierre-Paul Prud'hon, who was said to have used the copal varnish of Theophilus at the end of his life (doubtless on the advice of Mérimée)[21] and, most important of all, the contributions of research chemists who in Napoleonic France had been directed specifically to meet the needs of painters. Mérimée recorded how the chemist Louis-Jacques Thénard was set by the Minister of the Interior, Count Chaptal (himself a chemist), to discover a substitute for the costly ultramarine and did so by synthesizing cobalt blue in 1802.[22] Mérimée was also commissioned by Chaptal to make experiments with colours at this time, which suggests that his capacities as a chemist were already recognized; but the only colour for which he gained a reputation was a brilliant madder-lake, known as *carmin de garance*, well known in France in the 1820s.[23]

Another original characteristic of Mérimée's handbook was its introduction of a theory of harmony based on complementarity and using a colour-circle of six hues that, he said, should be copied and used by every student of art. His ideas were less radical than Chevreul's: he resisted the notion that the complementaries could be used harmoniously in full saturation and argued that it was chiaroscuro which should regulate the contrast of hues.[24] Yet Mérimée's reputation as a theorist must have been as great as his reputation as a chemist, since about 1812 he collaborated with the textile technologist Gaspard Grégoire on the commentary to a colour-chart of 1351 painted samples, for which he provided Grégoire with a diagram of complementaries essentially the same as his own circle of 1830.[25] For his primary red Grégoire chose a carmine which he described as the most beautiful colour since it was the median between yellow and blue; this may well have been the madder carmine developed by Mérimée.[26] A few years later Mérimée was also called upon to supply the colour-scale for a botanical work by C. F. Brisseau de Mirbel, which he did with a circle of twelve divisions that, he said, had been devised with the help of Grégoire's tables.[27] The close collaboration between artists, technologists and natural scientists could hardly be better demonstrated than in Mérimée's career.

Yet the handbook on oil painting does not seem to have been particularly well received by painters. Mérimée's friend the Neo-Classicist François-Xavier Fabre said that it might be useful to beginners but would have no effect on his own practice.[28] I have found it cited only by Delacroix (see p. 173), a painter whose work in the 1820s Mérimée seems to have thought would 'direct our school towards colouring' but whose poor drawing made him a dangerous model.[29] The book was

translated into English in 1839 but it seems to have been almost entirely forgotten in France after Mérimée's death in 1836.

After the defeat of Napoleon, Mérimée had been sent to London to study the English colour-industry, which may account for the many English examples in his book. One of the friends he made was Reynolds's pupil and biographer James Northcote. Reynolds appears, perhaps rather surprisingly, in *De la Peinture à l'huile* as 'the greatest colourist of his time', who had discovered the methods of Titian, Rubens and Rembrandt. Yet Mérimée did not approve of the *Anglomanie* in French art of the 1820s, in particular the effect of Constable on French Romanticism.[30] Since he is known to have had a special interest in English landscape painting and seems to have known of Constable's work as early as 1817 when he arrived in London, it would be pleasant to find that he was the French *paysagiste* who called on Constable some time in the 1820s to learn his method of painting. Another visitor on that occasion was George Field (born in 1777), a colour-maker who in many ways shared Mérimée's interests and who became a particular friend to Constable.[31]

The voluminous publications by Field dealt with many subjects besides colour, and his much prized pigments, as well as his close contacts with a wide range of English artists in the early years of the century, make him perhaps the ideal English counterpart to Mérimée – with these important distinctions, that his work was carried out without the benefit of state support and that although he claimed to have studied with the chemists Sir Humphrey Davy and Michael Faraday, his contact with the leading scientists of the period seems to have been very slight.[32]

Field had not been trained in art, although he became an amateur painter and picture-restorer. He had intended from the start to become a technologist and he began in the 1790s with what was then a very traditional English project, the attempt to grow and process the madder plant to manufacture the red dyestuff which was the most permanent version of that colour then known for cloth. By about 1800, however, Field had shifted his attention to the question of painters' materials and was producing madder as a lake pigment in London. His understanding of the needs of artists was certainly heightened by his close involvement in an exhibiting society, The British School, which ran from 1802 to 1804 and showed at least one of Solomon Williams's paintings using the 'Venetian process', as well as works by many artists who were worried by the weaknesses in English technique. Pigment-technology took Field to colour-theory and theory back to technology, since he was anxious to develop precisely those pigments which exemplified the harmony he saw operating in nature. Like many colour-technologists in his day, Field was an anti-Newtonian, believing that colours had their origin in black and white:

> If the authority of Newton herein is wanting, we have Nature and Reason in its favor, and these are the authority of God. For if Colours were really analyzable from light or white, then by a synthesis of Inherent or Transient Colours White or Light might be recomposed: but tho' Black may be composed of a due admixture of pure, deep, primitive colours ... it is not possible to compose white by any mixture of colours whatever ...[33]

The reference to God is crucial because, like Runge, Field was at work on a universal theory of triads in nature, of which the Holy Trinity was the supreme exemplar and the triad of primary colours the most visible of earthly manifestations. He had opened a colour-factory near Bristol in 1808 and had met the founder of the Bath Harmonic Society, Dr Henry Harington, who had just published a remarkable pamphlet, *SYMBOLON TRISAGION, or the Geometrical analogy of the Catholic doctrine of triunity, consonant to human reason and comprehension; typically demonstrated and exemplified by the natural and invisible triunity of certain simultaneous sounds* (1806). The publication included a contribution from the Rev. William Jones, who had asked Harington in a letter:

> Is it the effect of chance, can we think, that there is the like wonderful Trinitarian coincidence in optics, as in sounds, and if possible more adequate? When we refract the pure light by a prism, it is manifested to the eye under the three primary simple colours of red, yellow and blue; each of them so distinct, that we can lay our finger on them separately, and say, this is not that, and that is not the third; yet we say truly of each by itself, that is *light*: but when they are joined, the same that were three are now one without distinction, the glory equal, the majesty co-eternal.[34]

This belief informed the whole of Field's career as an experimenter; in a much later note to his 1808 *Chromatics* he was able to persuade himself that the primary colours were related closely to the principal minerals, or earths: 'Thus *Alumine* appears to be the natural basis of *Reds*, Silex of *Blues* and *Lime* of *Yellows*'.[35] Such linkage of specific colours to specific minerals was not Field's invention: it had appeared at the end of the eighteenth century in a far more humdrum painters' handbook by Constant de Massoul; but there the minerals iron, copper, gold and so on were shown to be capable each of producing a range of hues and there was no sense of system, least of all the tight triadic scheme to which Field devoted his career as a thinker.[36] Although he was able to develop a wide range of pigments, including the tertiaries citrine, russet and olive, so that all the colours in his *Definitive Scale* had been developed and manufactured by himself; although he sometimes made specific pigments for particular customers, such as the Extract of Vermilion specially developed for Sir Thomas Lawrence,[37] Field gave particular attention to his three primary hues, his madders, his lemon yellow and his ultramarine (which he persisted in refining from lapis lazuli in the face of competition from the new French synthetic product of the 1820s). But this concentration was for ideological not commercial reasons.

The problem of the primaries in the nineteenth century had many dimensions. If a system of harmony was to be based on the relationship of primary colours to their complementaries, it was important to know which were the 'primary' pigments and to be able to manufacture them for the use of artists. The first attempt to base a theory of harmony on the primary colours had probably been that of Louis-Bertrand Castel in the 1720s: he had chosen the recently developed synthetic Prussian blue *or* indigo, a good but unspecified red lake and for yellow the earth colour umber (*terre d'ombre*) which is usually rather brown.[38] It was a far from straightforward question and Field was heir to a number of other solutions, none of them satisfactory. The

economics of early colour-printing had also required the purest primaries to mix a full range of colours from only three plates. The pioneer colour-printer Le Blon had used Prussian blue, the darkest of the yellow lakes and a mixture of lake, carmine and vermilion to approximate the red of the spectrum (*see* p. 169).[39] The technologist Robert Dossie, describing Le Blon's methods in the middle of the eighteenth century, pointed to the continuing inadequacy of the available inks, which needed to be pure, bright and transparent, arguing that the best blue might be Prussian blue but that the best lakes, even if they could be procured, did not match it in purity and the only acceptable yellow was the vegetable colour Brown Pink, which was neither sufficiently bright nor sufficiently powerful to balance the others.[40] Towards the end of the eighteenth century this practical problem was addressed by a German technologist, A. L. Pfannenschmidt, who produced not only a handbook on the mixture of the three primary colours but also a set of pigments which was based on long experiment to establish standard hues; for he argued, even the same manufacturer might market different nuances under the same name at different times, citing vermilion, which often veered markedly towards yellow.[41] His standard red seems to have been a carmine, 'the most beautiful red colour', his yellow gamboge and his blue natural ultramarine.[42]

Pfannenschmidt had at first attempted to produce sets of hues in light and dark values but he had soon abandoned this ambition and in 1792 was supplying sets of twelve standard colours: blue, yellow, red, green, fire-colour (?orange), violet, mixed black, yellow-brown, yellow-red, brown, unmixed black and white; all were keyed to a triangular diagram, which included their intermixtures, to a total of sixty-four nuances. He also supplied a set of ten watercolour pigments which had been developed to give each of them equal power.[43] In the tradition of eighteenth-century empiricism, Pfannenschmidt's technique of assessment was entirely visual: the purity of the primaries was to be judged by binary mixtures which should show no trace of brown or black and the proportion of the ingredients in these mixtures was established when they showed no preponderance of either component. The results of these optical judgments led to the weighing of the components and these weights gave Pfannenschmidt the numerical values recorded in his triangle.[44]

The whole mystique of 'Old Master' colouring was exposed to ridicule when a young miniature-painter called Ann Jemima Provis claimed to have discovered a manuscript 'going back to Titian', revealing the secrets of his art. She is shown putting them into practice in the upper part of this satirical print by Gillray. She sold the 'Venetian Secret' to the President of the Royal Academy, West – seen slinking off to the right – and to many other distinguished academicians, some of them depicted here. But it was soon exposed as a hoax. An earlier 'expert' on Venetian technique, Sir Joshua Reynolds, is shown with his ear-trumpet, rising from the grave.

174 JAMES GILLRAY, *Titianus Redivivus*, 1797

175

Pigments and theory

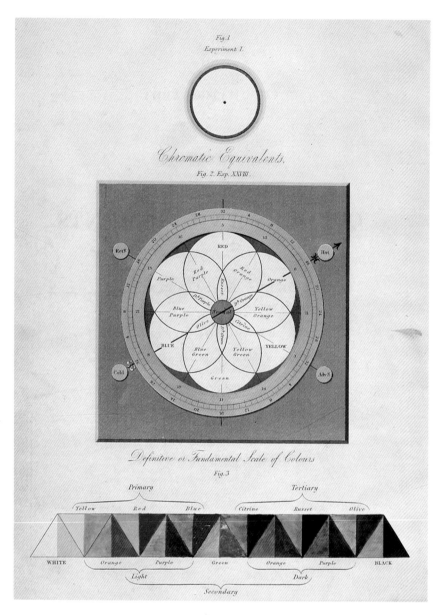

175 George Field, Frontispiece to *Chromatography; or a Treatise on Colours and Pigments, and of their Powers in Painting*, 1835
176 J.F.L. Mérimée, Chromatic scale, from *De la Peinture à l'huile*, 1830
177 William Holman Hunt, *Valentine rescuing Sylvia from Proteus*, 1850/1

175

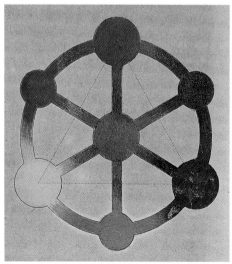

Colour theory proliferated in the nineteenth century. Mérimée (**176**) showed with his circle that complementary colours mix to harmonious greys, an idea that attracted the interest of Delacroix. Field's diagram (**175**) illustrated the harmonic proportions of colours in light, as well as the dynamics of warm and cool, although his linear scale shows that he also had a traditional notion of the values between black and white. Field developed a set of 'pure' primaries to give practical expression to his ideas. It was the brilliant and stable properties of his pigments, rather than the theories, that appealed to painters such as Holman Hunt (**177**), and contributed to the astonishingly bright colours of the Pre-Raphaelites.

176

177

Seurat was the first painter to invoke optical principles in support
of his technique, and indeed, to evolve a technique based on his
theory. The dotted brushwork creates a visual shimmer through
partial optical mixture, and the border of this large canvas provides
carefully calculated 'complementary' contrasts to the scene. Seurat
tried to keep his colours pure and little-mixed, but, like Holman
Hunt (pl. 177), he sometimes used pigments that faded or darkened,
and, unlike Hunt, he took no technical steps to ensure that they
remained stable. The peppering of brownish spots on the light grass
was not intended by the artist, but is due to the irreversible darkening
of the then recently introduced synthetic pigment, zinc yellow.

178 GEORGES SEURAT, *Sunday Afternoon on the Island of La Grand Jatte*, 1884/6
(detail)

His cumbersome system and his colours seem to have made little impact on thinking about colours in the nineteenth century: I have found little reference to them in the later literature, except by the French taxonomist J.-B. Lamarck, who in the 1790s sought to accompany his eccentric ideas about the formation of colours by the action of the 'fixed fire' within all matter, with a numerical scale of colours and their mixtures. Like Pfannenschmidt, Lamarck based his mixtures on weight but their working out led him into many practical difficulties, which he was not inclined to address: he confessed that he did not have the practical skills necessary to make the experiments but 'any artist who is prepared to take the trouble would easily be able to bring them to a successful conclusion'. For primaries he suggested ultramarine (although its cost might make Prussian blue a better proposition), carmine, which was closest to 'natural' red, and gamboge, which, although not as close to spectral yellow as orpiment, could at least be mixed with lead white with impunity.[45] The problem of standardization which Pfannenschmidt had attempted to solve frustrated the efforts of many technologists until Wilhelm Ostwald in the 1920s collaborated with the German paint-industry to produce sets of carefully calibrated hues and their nuances which, it was asserted, could be used to establish a rational system of harmony on a mathematical basis.

153 Many colour-theorists specified their primaries rather precisely. Where the entomologist Moses Harris had used vermilion, King's yellow (artificial orpiment) and ultramarine, the painter and conchologist James Sowerby proposed gamboge, carmine and Prussian blue and Field himself used ultramarine, madder and the vegetable colour Indian yellow in his earliest diagrams.[46] In France, Grégoire's tables of 1812 used gamboge, carmine and indigo, but still in the late 1820s Paillot de Montabert was arguing that colourmen, who were ignorant of the principle of the three primaries, were flooding the market with many superfluous pigments, while chemists had not yet developed the pure standard hues. Indigo, said Paillot, was the only 'primary' which was so far capable of remaining pure in its lightest and darkest values, for the available yellows and reds were unable to render good darks. If no single primary could fulfil its function along the whole scale of values, then each hue should be manufactured in four grades with different ingredients.[47] By the 1850s Clerk Maxwell's work on the nature of the colours of light had made the notion of a specific set of 'primaries' irrelevant, since all that was needed to reconstitute white light was three co-ordinates sufficiently widely spaced along the spectrum. Nevertheless, during the first half of the century a good deal of thought and much experiment had gone into the attempt to match spectrally pure primaries with commercially available colours.

Field's efforts bore only limited fruit. In order to establish his primaries and their harmonic relationship he had had to devise an instrument for colour-measurement, the Chromometer 173 (later Metrochrome), based on the principle of the absorption of light through coloured filters. This instrument allowed Field to establish what he called Chromatic Equivalents: the proportions of each primary needed to constitute a harmonious balance of the three in white light, as set out in the colour-circle for 175 *Chromatography* in 1835. The ratio of three for yellow to five for

red to eight for blue was not reached without considerable experiment; the primary tinctures used in the liquid-filled filters of the last version of the Metrochrome were copper sulphate, liquid madder and saffron or turmeric. Field's Chromatic Equivalents aroused some interest among interior decorators in the 1840s and 50s, notably Owen Jones, who used them in his experimental painting of part of the interior of the Crystal Palace for the Great Exhibition of 1851 and again in his sumptuous pattern-book *The Grammar of Ornament* a few years later. But the work of Maxwell and Helmholtz, and developments in colour-measurement on the basis of precise spectral analysis, showed that Field's ratios were quite arbitrary, and they were hardly quoted again after this time.[48]

It is something of an irony that the bright primary hues manufactured by Field for largely theoretical reasons were not those he himself preferred. His taste had been formed around the turn of the century on the rather mellow tones of early English Romantic landscape-artists, particularly Richard Wilson, whose works formed the nucleus of his own collection of art. Field had developed a set of unmixed tertiary hues because these were for him in some ways the most important colours. 'The chaste eye', he had written in his first publication on colour-theory, 'receives greater satisfaction from the harmony of the tertiaries in which the three primitives are more intimately combined, and for the same reason the correct eye demands a concurrence of the three primitives in every harmony'. Yet he had stated in an earlier unpublished note that 'it is ... a rule, in which Chemistry and Chromatics equally coincide, that the *Artist should use his colours as pure and unmixt as possible*'; so that it was essential to offer unmixed pigments all the way round the colour-circle of twelve hues.[49]

Field's pure hues were much in demand and they receive the sanction of Merrifield when she argued in the notes to her 1844 version of Cennini that the technologist's experiments had, for the most part, substantiated Cennini's view of the twelve 'best' pigments from the point of view of permanence, and directed her readers to the study of *Chromatography*.[50] It was these unusually pure and transparent colours which around 1850 allowed the Pre-Raphaelites to cover their white-lead grounds 177 with the thinnest of glazes and achieve an unprecedented brilliance of hue.[51]

The impact of synthetic colours

Mérimée and Field gave a guarded welcome to the several new synthetic pigments – notably yellows, blues and greens – developed in the early years of the nineteenth century but neither of them lived to see the revolution in synthetic dyestuffs of the 1850s and 60s. The synthesis of the coal-tar colour mauve by Sir William Perkin in 1856 and of artificial alizarin red by Graebe and Lieberman in 1868 were just two of the chemical discoveries which resulted in the release of a host of new dyestuffs and pigments on to the market in the third quarter of the century. Artists' manuals now devoted more and more attention to the stability of these new substances. Around 1890 the École des Beaux-Arts in Paris employed the genre painter J.-G. Vibert to give a course of instruction in technique, which, in its published form at least, was much concerned with problems of permanence. For Vibert the invention of synthetic aniline was a catastrophe for painting: he proposed that a commission on quality-control should be set up by the Société des Artistes Français and a laboratory at the École itself.[52] A contemporary French theoretical writer, Adrien Recouvreur, also regarded the situation as critical: 'Colours have never altered so much as they do today. Drawing is more and more the probity of art [a quotation from Ingres] since if we do not react against the current free-wheeling attitude, it will be art's only lasting characteristic.'[53] Recouvreur argued that one of the few remedies for the instability of modern colours was to buffer pigments against each other and against the atmosphere by locking them in a good varnish. Indeed Vibert did develop a range of fine, fast-drying and transparent varnishes which were manufactured and marketed by Lefranc and Co.[54] Instability was the other side of the coin of the new freedom offered by a range of brilliant pigments representing areas of the spectrum such as yellow, green and violet, which had been poorly served by more traditional materials. It might even be imagined that these new colours were the condition of the more or less universally admitted aspiration of the Impressionists to paint light itself.

For between the Middle Ages and the late nineteenth century it had been widely felt that art was hopelessly handicapped by the limitations of its materials in the face of nature. The twelfth-century Spanish-Arab philosopher Averroes had argued that since the colours of art (*colores et tincture . . . ratio extrinseca*) are finite and the colours of nature (*in ratione intrinseca*) infinite, there were many colours which art (in this case notably dyeing) could not make: he was arguing against the very possibility of the imitation of nature which so animated the researches of Leonardo da Vinci, Runge and Monet.[55] But with the rise in the seventeenth century of the idea of matching appearances on the canvas, it became clearer and clearer where the limitations of pigments lay. In his lecture to the French Academy in 1669, J. H. Bourdon argued that the painter should never attempt to paint a landscape under the midday sun, since pigments are quite incapable of doing justice to this effect of light and the sun itself should always be hidden.[56] A similar admonition was also heard in the Academy among the supporters of both Poussin and Rubens in the following decade.[57] The expansion of painterly tasks in the eighteenth century and the increasing use of optical devices such as the camera obscura, by means of which more precise comparisons between the real and the painted image could be made, together with the more sophisticated psychology of perception gaining ground among artists, led some to argue that, as in the musical scale, it was not absolute values but proportional relationships which counted in painting and that the deficiencies of materials could be counteracted by 'skill and management'.[58] This attitude began to prevail in the nineteenth century, especially in France before the advent of Impressionism.

In his *Géometrie descriptive* (cited by Charles Blanc in the 1860s, *see* Chapter 11) Gaspard Monge had argued that only an exaggeration of luminous effects in painting could compensate for the feebleness of the artists' means and give the truth of subjective impressions rather than the objective conditions of light.[59] Jules Jamin's 1857 article on optics and painting

expanded on the need of painters to make many compromises, both because of the limits of their perception of precise difference and, again, because of the weakness of their materials. Jamin had been busy with his photometer which, like the camera obscura of the eighteenth century, offered painters an 'objective' reading of a scene, against which to measure their own rendering; the results of his experiments had shown that it was essential for the artist to paint down from the tone of nature, 'and to weaken proportionally all nature's brightness'.[60] Although he admired the fidelity to the motif of modern artists such as Descamps, Jamin argued that 'realist' painters should stop attempting to reproduce nature and concern themselves with more spiritual things.[61] Undoubtedly the most influential formulation of this problem was in Helmholtz's contemporary lecture, 'On the relation of optics to painting', in which he discussed at some length the discrepancy between the light of nature and the light of art, concluding:

> The representation which the painter has to give of the lights and colours of his object I have described as a translation, and I have urged that, as a general rule, it cannot give a copy true in all its details. The altered scale of brightness which the artists must apply in many cases is opposed to this. It is not the colours of the objects, but the impression which they have given, or would give, which is to be imitated, so as to produce as distinct and vivid a conception as possible of those objects.[62]

As the discussion of Cézanne suggested, painting the impression of objects was every bit as problematic as painting 'objects' themselves; but it might well have been thought that the heightened contrasts of painting which these writers, and many others in the period, expected of painters might now be achieved very effectively with the help of the new intense colours on their palettes. One critic of the 1880s asserted that that was precisely what they were doing and he did not like what he saw:

> The artist will give objects not the colours which they reflect in reality, but those which they would have for a dazzled eye. He must heighten the reds, yellows and greens, and tone down the blues and the violets . . . These considerations are perhaps of some interest from the point of view of the new school of *plein air*. Its promoters do not seem to have taken enough account of the fact that as the intensity of light increases all pure colours approximate to white or whitish yellow. They think they can enrich the range of their hues [*teintes*] with new tones; daylight and especially full sunlight does nothing but impoverish them. The true colourists have proceeded in quite a different way; it is on the contrary in chiaroscuro that the Titians and the Rembrandts sought and found their most beautiful effects.[63]

It was at the top end of the scale that the open-air painters were encountering the greatest difficulties, as Cézanne had discovered. Already in the 1840s Field had pointed to the revolutionary effects of the brighter pigments even he was producing: the inferior materials of the Old Masters, he said, had meant that 'their key of colouring was necessarily lower, and compelled them to harmonize much below nature'.[64] How did the Impressionists and the Post-Impressionists use their new media to respond to the challenge?

Advances in conservation technology have made it possible to be more or less certain of the composition of many nineteenth-century paintings.[65] We now know that the Impressionists were particularly concerned about the permanence of their pigments: Monet stated at the end of his life that he had abandoned the use of the rather unstable chrome yellows in favour of the newer cadmiums, which do indeed appear more and more in his work after the 1870s.[66] The cadmiums had been developed in the 1840s and the only more recent pigments on Monet's palette were cobalt violet and viridian (*vert eméraude*), which had first been marketed a decade later; he continued to use mixed violets for many years to come. Renoir was perhaps the greatest traditionalist among the Impressionists and one of the few to use the ancient – and slow – technique of glazing. Yet he used chrome yellow and viridian in the 1870s and one of the reds in *Boating on the Seine* (*c.* 1879) probably includes a synthetic dyestuff.[67] In the 1890s Renoir's palette included more and more earth colours, traditional lakes and particularly the lead-antimony yellow called Naples yellow, one of the oldest known synthetic pigments then undergoing a revival in the improved version manufactured by Lefranc. It could well have commended itself to Renoir because it had been identified with the manufactured yellow described by Cennini as *giallorino*.[68] Renoir may have discovered Cennini in 1884 while working on a technical handbook of his own, the *Abrégé de la grammaire des arts*, a book which has not survived although something of its tone may be guessed from the letter to Henri Mottez published in the 1911 reprint of his father's French version of Cennini. While he recognized that circumstances had changed for the artists of the nineteenth century, Renoir believed that the true methods of the Ancients lived on: 'If the Greeks had left a treatise on painting, you may well believe that it would be identical to Cennini's. All painting, from that of Pompeii, done by Greeks, to that of Corot, passing through Poussin, seems to have come from the same palette.'[69] The increasing classicism of Renoir's style is well known and at the end of his life he ventured to experiment, rather unsuccessfully, with fresco.[70] When about 1904 Matisse tried to persuade him to exchange his very traditional vermilion for a cadmium red, which would have been more permanent in the spirit medium Renoir was using, he refused to try even the sample of cadmium Matisse gave him, saying that he did not want to change his ways.[71]

All the new pigments used by the Impressionists have been identified in some paintings belonging to one of the largest collections of nineteenth-century German art, the Schack-Galerie in Munich, but no artist represented there had any interest in Impressionist *plein-air* methods so there is no intrinsic link between these materials and a particular style of painting.[72] What can be seen is that the Impressionists made conspicuous use of the bright yellows, greens and violets to match their sensations in the open air. On the other hand, the painters and theorists in France who were most cautious about the new materials were themselves no strangers to the strong effects of outdoor colour. Georges Meusnier ('Karl Robert') explained to his readers:

A white wall in full sunlight is never white: it is pinkish white, yellowish white, greenish white, according to the reflections which

J.-G. Vibert's illustration for his satirical short story 'The Delights of Art' (*The Century Magazine*, 1896), in which a sunbeam discusses with the curtain the merits of the cardinal's *éclatiste* painting. (179)

it receives. It is the same for all the colours [*tons*], to such an extent that in the studies of some masters you will see the well-lit greens of the foreground rendered in pure blues or tender pinks made of white and cobalt or white and lake.[73]

Similarly Vibert attacked the Impressionists – the *éclatistes* ('dazzlers') – for painting 'only with intense colours and without shading any of the tones'.[74] Yet in his *Science de la peinture* he presented a vivid picture of one of his cardinals moving through his garden:

Let us follow a cardinal, dressed in red, whilst he walks in his gardens. At every instant the colour seems different, according to whether he receives the blinding rays of the sun, or the white reflections from a cloud, or shelters under the verdant shade of a leafy grove. Whether we see him on the intense green of the sunny lawns, under the dark green of the cypress, on the silvery surface of a lake, or under the azure of the sky, he still changes. He changes always, becoming pale before a bank of geraniums, and red before the marble of the statues; he gets dark in proportion as the daylight fades, until he becomes a dark purple, and is dressed in black like a simple priest, as he returns to his palace by the dusky shades of twilight.[75]

It was less their vision itself than their highly individual interpretation of that vision which set the Impressionists apart from many painters of the Establishment.

Time the painter

Among the later French outdoor painters it was probably Cézanne who remained truest to the Impressionist caution about materials – he had, of course, been a close associate of Pissarro in the 1870s. At no point in his career does Cézanne seem to have used any of the new synthetic pigments except viridian.[76] When he saw Bernard's limited palette in 1904 he was astonished: 'You paint with just these? Where is your Naples yellow? Where is your peach-black, where is your siena earth, your cobalt blue, your burnt lake? . . . It is impossible to paint without these colours.'[77] Like Renoir, Cézanne's use of transparent glazes – his technical traditionalism – his many earth colours, did not simply arise from a wish to render the brilliant yet earthy landscape of Provence but also, again like Renoir, from an urge to keep in touch with the art of the museums.

The contrast with van Gogh's attitude to his materials could hardly be more marked. Half Cézanne's pigments were well known for their stability; of the other half, only the chrome yellow had a poor reputation for it at the end of the nineteenth century and had often been replaced by cadmiums. But a large order for new paints which van Gogh sent his brother Theo from Arles in 1888 listed a dozen of the brightest available pigments, four of them – malachite green (probably copper aceto-arsenate), cinnabar green (a mixture of chrome yellow and Prussian blue), geranium lake (an aniline colour) and orange lead (?chrome orange) – among the most fugitive then on the market.[78] He was well aware of the dangers of these materials; in his next letter to Theo he admitted: 'All the colours that the Impressionists have brought into fashion are unstable, so there is all the more reason not to be afraid to lay them on too crudely – time will tone them down only too much.' And time has indeed been at work on some of his later paintings, although not perhaps in quite the way he anticipated.[79]

By 'Impressionists', van Gogh may have understood the Neo-Impressionists (with whom he had been in close contact in Paris in 1886–8), for Seurat had used some unstable pigments in paintings such as the large *Grande Jatte* and had noticed some deterioration in them as early as 1887.[80] In the case of this painting the main culprit seems to have been zinc yellow (zinc chromate), which has darkened both on its own and in several mixtures with blue and orange. This pigment is rarely mentioned in the contemporary literature and had perhaps been very little used in France since its introduction about 1847.[81] Seurat's choice of it may have been an early stage in his search for a good mixing yellow, a search implied in a remark by Camille Pissarro to his son in 1887 that Seurat and Signac should know about the (quite unsatisfactory) results of mixtures of cadmium yellow with emerald green, 'even blacker than the chrome yellow mixture'.[82] Clearly the Neo-Impressionists were concerned to match the spectral colours with the brightest pigments available and were finding this difficult to achieve. The 'spectral' palette which Signac claimed to have adopted in the early 1880s (*see* p. 187) included the stable cadmium yellows but also viridian and a cerulean blue, a new variety of cobalt stannate produced after 1860, which is now regarded as a stable pigment but which in late nineteenth-century France, where it was marketed as *bleu céleste*, had the reputation of tending to fade.[83] The greying effect produced by the Neo-Impressionist dotted technique had been noticed by critics as early as 1886, but it came to be even more significant after 1900 in a climate of increasing dissatisfaction with Seurat's original version of the style and the use of much larger coloured units. This was partly a function of an imperfectly digested theory, which overlooked the mixture of complementaries to an optical grey;[84] but it may also have been a result of these experiments with pigments whose properties were little known and whose lasting qualities had simply not been tested.

Van Gogh's perplexing belief that time would inevitably mellow his pictures took up a very old notion in the history of art but gave it a quite contemporary twist. The degree to which some artists had been ready to collaborate with time is one of the most vexed questions in modern picture-conservation; for restorers' estimates of it will inevitably determine how far they wish to bring the work in question back to its 'original' condition. In the early nineteenth century some painters pre-empted the action of time by toning their pictures themselves, but the evidence for this practice in earlier periods is extremely inconclusive.[85] What seems clear is that a century or so after the development of oil-painting in Italy the yellowing and darkening of pictures, which was largely a function of their having been varnished, was beginning to be prized as part of their aesthetic effect. Van Dyck, for example, was thought to have tried with his paints to imitate the yellowed flesh in Titian's mellowed paintings.[86] Collectors expected Old Master paintings to be mellowed: in 1657 a Veronese was returned to a dealer by Leopoldo de' Medici because of its 'troppa freschezza'.[87] On the other hand it became the task of the painter to anticipate and compensate for the effects of ageing. Some seventeenth-century painters deliberately painted lighter than they intended because of their perception of the effects of time; this became something of a critical commonplace in the more perceptually oriented climate of the eighteenth century.[88] But it was by no means a universal aspiration: a wish to make old pictures look like new must have been felt as early as the Romantic period, when it was rebutted in Dresden by the painter Ferdinand Hartmann, supported by Goethe and his advisor Heinrich Meyer.[89] There was inevitably a confused diversity of opinions but it was at least clear that the great weakness of time as a painter was its lack of discrimination: painters had known for many centuries that pigments do not age uniformly – as Hogarth put it in the *Analysis of Beauty*, 'much time disunites, untunes, blackens, and by degrees destroys even the best preserved pictures'.[90] The deterioration in van Gogh's paintings, as in Seurat's, has been quite local and it is almost impossible for us now to reconstruct the balance of some of their colour-compositions. Nevertheless, as in the case of Cézanne's 'unfinished' canvases, several generations of the public have learned to see them 'whole'.

Colour as constructive material

Hue and value are of course not the only properties of the painter's pigments; Impressionism, as well as the painterly movements which preceded and followed it have made us sensitive to the qualities of surface texture, in which rough canvas, stiff paints and vigorous brushwork all play their part. Texture, which may include matt or glossy variations, is almost as susceptible to ageing as hue: re-lining the canvas or even prolonged hanging can smooth heavy impasto in the most disturbing way and such smoothing can remove the evidence of the artist's intense involvement with material. Although, as we saw, Delacroix as a young painter liked his colours unusually liquid, he grew to enjoy the pleasure of managing a stiff paste and felt towards the end of his life that the physical manipulation of pigment was not unlike the sculptor's handling of clay.[91] Delacroix's physical attitude towards his materials was passed on to Impressionism, which added a belief in the relief-like character of the perceived subject, most palpably felt perhaps in Cézanne's paintings of the 1870s but characterized most sharply by Alfred Sisley, who kept alive the immediacy of early Impressionism until the end of his life. Sisley wrote that he favoured a great variation of surface in the same picture, 'Because when the sun lets certain parts of the landscape appear soft, it lifts others into sharp relief. These effects of light, which have an almost material expression in nature, must be rendered in material fashion on the canvas.'[92]

It was above all in Russia early in this century that texture (*faktura*), depending on the medium and its handling, acquired the status of an independent aesthetic category. In an essay, 'Towards a Theory of Painting', written just after the First World War, the art critic Nikolai Tarabukin argued: '[Material] colours themselves have an autonomous aesthetic value which is not exhausted by hue. They have a specific aesthetic potential which is an element in the sum of colouring . . . it is clear that the same art-object affects us differently according to whether it is painted in oil, watercolour or distemper.' Tarabukin compared the medium to the timbre of a musical instrument, which is determined by the material from which it is made. Modern artists, he said – he must have meant the Impressionists and Post-Impressionists, as well as Russian painters such as Mikhail Larionov whose handling of paint owed so much to them – draw attention to the substances of their paintings, 'which are no longer the inferior element that they were for the masters of the past'.[93] In the modern movements related to Constructivism colour came to be regarded as a 'material' on the same constructive level as any other.[94] Chapter 14 will show how this attitude helped to fill the vacuum left by the demise of colour-theory in painting after the Second World War. For the moment I want to investigate Tarabukin's interesting comparison of the effects of colour to those of musical timbre, which will take us into perhaps the most abstract area of the relationship between our conception of colour and our experience of the visual world.

180

146, 166

The 'white on white' paintings of Kasimir Malevich (1917/18) explored both the capacity of white to convey infinity, and *factura* (texture), a prominent concern of Russian painters at the time. (180)

Paolo Veronese, *The Marriage Feast at Cana* (detail), 1563. In Venice, the home of *colore*, the virtuoso performances of painters were often compared to the skills of performing musicians. Veronese's musicians are his painter-friends Titian on the viola de gamba, Tintoretto and Veronese himself on the violas, Veronese's brother on the *lira da braccio*, and perhaps Jacopo Bassano on the flute. (181)

13 · The Sound of Colour

The Greek chromatic scale · Medieval and Renaissance colour harmonies · Arcimboldo's colour-music
Music and colour in the seventeenth century · Castel's ocular harpsichord · The Romantics
Sonority and rhythm · Moving colour

THE EXPERIENCE of colour in the West has always been closely interwoven with the experience of music. In ancient Greece, one kind of musical scale (*genos*), introduced by Plato's friend Archytas of Tarentum in the fourth century BC, was named 'chromatic'. It was divided into semi-tones and was regarded as simply 'colouring' its two neighbouring scales, the diatonic (divided into full tones) and the enharmonic (divided into quarter-tones).[1] Some Greek theorists considered 'colour' (*chroïa*) to be a quality of sound itself, together with pitch and duration; it may have been thought akin to what we now describe as timbre.[2] What most impressed the Greeks, it seems, was the capacity of colour, like sound, to be articulated in a series of regularly changing stages whose differences were perceptible in an equally regular way – for Aristotle and his school light and dark appear to have been cognate with clear and muffled sound or even high and low pitch.[3] As early as Plato's time the description of melody as 'coloured' had become part of a professional jargon of which he did not approve. Conversely, the musical terms 'tone' and 'harmony' soon became integrated into the critical vocabulary of colour in visual art.[4]

In a society in which music was widely regarded as having a powerful moral effect, the chromatic scale was credited with a distinct character quite different from those of the diatonic and the enharmonic: its closer tones (not, of course, as close as in the enharmonic scale) seemed to give it a particular quality of movement, of changeability, which was set against the firmer and more decisive diatonic; it carried the moral connotations of sweetness and mournfulness; it was, according to Ptolemy, more 'mathematical' and more 'domestic' than the 'theological' or 'political' diatonic; it could even turn men into cowards.[5] In the Christian Middle Ages one of the three types of the Greek chromatic scale was held to be soft and licentious so that, according to the Early Christian writer Clement of Alexandria, writing in the late second century,

> temperate scales are to be admitted, but the pliant scales are to be driven as far as possible from our robust minds. These through their sinuous strains instruct one in weakness and lead to ribaldry, but the grave and temperate melodies bid farewell to the arrogance of drunkenness. Chromatic scales, then, are to be left to 'colourless' carousals and to the florid and meretricious music.[6]

Thus in its earliest associations with music, just as in its scientific connotations, colour seems to have shown its capacity for manifesting the changing and unstable world of the everyday.

According to most accounts, the chromatic scale was developed rather later than the diatonic and perhaps even than the enharmonic; certainly the more nuanced character of its tuning appears to have made it far more difficult to play. In the history of Greek string-playing the late sixth-century BC kitharist Lysander of Sicyon was said to have introduced a more colourful (*chrōmata enchroa*) style even before the development of the scale itself by Archytas of Tarentum. In the most comprehensive of all the ancient treatises on music, Aristides Quintilianus, writing probably in the second or third century AD, argued that the technical sophistication of the chromatic scale made it accessible only to well-trained musicians.[7] We have a situation in which a more archaic, direct, 'masculine' style is amplified by a newer, more complicated and softer one: a sequence parallel to the development of the figurative arts from the Archaic to the Hellenistic, except that in music these styles co-existed and seem to have had a functional rather than a purely chronological significance.

For some of the Peripatetics, colour was to be distinguished from music, even purely instrumental music, in that it had no moral power (Aristotle *Problems* XIX, 27, 29). The affective power of music depended on its status as action and its importance in that it provided the most comprehensive imitation of action in human affairs. In a passage which indicates that there was already a lively debate on the status of the various arts in late Antiquity, Aristides argued that painting and the other visual arts, working through signs alone, could convey only a 'tiny fragment' of life as a whole, whereas music had a direct effect on both the body and the soul, through the rhythms which imitated bodily rhythms, through the accompaniment to poetry which imitated human thought and action, and through dance, which gave this action visual form.[8] Most important of all, the numerical intervals and ratios of music could indicate the structure of the soul and even of the universe at large; here Aristides was generous to the painter, whom he saw equally as working through proportional systems:

> If we consider painting ... we shall find that it does nothing without the help of numbers and proportions: it is through numbers that is hunts for the proportionate measures [*summetriai*] of bodies and mixtures of colours [*chrōmatōn kraseis*], and from these it gives the pictures their beauty. We may also observe that this same art uses numbers to imitate a thing's fundamental nature: for it is the kind of proportion which brings beauty to natural bodies that painters are pursuing in the dimensions [*metra*, measures] of their shapes and the mixtures of their colours [*chrōiōn sunkrasesi*] ...[9]

The analogy between musical sound and colour seems to have been most compelling to the Greeks because both could be organized in more or less regularly stepped scales: even the technical terms *tonos* and *harmogē* reported by Pliny (XXXV, xi, 29) probably referred to different types of scalar arrangement.[10]

But the striking asymmetry between the potential of sound for mathematical treatment and that potential in colour is well illustrated by the fact that there are more than a dozen Greek musical treatises still extant (although only a handful of short compositions with which to compare them) but only one on colour, the Peripatetic *On Colours*, which includes no account of the 'proportions' of colours among themselves. Plato had derided any attempt to discover the proportions of colours in mixtures (*see* Chapter 1), a question only God could fathom (*Timaeus* 67d–68d). Aristotle, who did entertain the possibility that colours might be quantified, was not able to take his suppositions very far: in his discussion of the production of colours by the mingling of particles of white and black (*On Sense and Sensible Objects* 439b) he had argued:

> It is thus possible to believe that there are more colours than just white and black, and that their number is due to the proportion of their components; for these may be grouped in the ratio of three to two, or three to four, or in other musical ratios (or they may be in no expressible ratio, but in an incommensurable relation of excess or defect) so that these colours are determined like musical intervals. For in this view the colours that depend on simple ratios, like the concords in music, are regarded as the most attractive, for example purple [*halourgon*] and red [*phoinikoun*], and a few others like them – few for the same reason that the concords are few –, while the other colours are those which have no numerical ratios; or it may be that all are expressible in numbers, but while some are regular in ratio, others are not; and the latter, when they are not pure, have this character because they are not in a pure numerical ratio [trans. Hett].

Aristotle's hesitation is clear and even if we identify his purple with the consonance of the fifth and his red with the fourth, so that white forms the octave – the three main consonances recognized by the early Greek theorists[11] – we do not know the order of the colours he placed in between.

In what must be one of the earliest accounts of a synaesthetic colour-musical experience – Plato's myth of Er in Book X of the *Republic* – the moving image of the solar system, in which each of the eight circling orbits was coloured and accompanied by the eight pitches (*tonoi*) sung together by sirens to produce a single *harmonia*, none of the colours mentioned was pure.[12] Constructing visual consonances was a good deal harder than establishing aural ones: perhaps the only other Greek attempt to describe such a synaesthetic experience in detail, Plutarch's vision of Timarchus in *Moralia* (590a), avoided direct comparisons altogether. It became the task of succeeding centuries to find a way of exemplifying a relationship that ancient theory had proposed but ancient practice had been unable to make concrete: it may fairly be said that the task has never been brought to a satisfactory conclusion.

Medieval and Renaissance colour harmonies

The double disability of 'colour' in music – that it produced a sound which was morally enervating and that its capacity for proportionality was not clearly understood – was handed down to the Middle Ages and the Renaissance and indeed to all periods in which the music of the ancients, however obscure, was still a living ideal. One theorist of the late eleventh century, Rudolph of St Trond, sought to introduce a notational system which represented the modes (*tropoi*) of plainsong – which he mistakenly identified with the ancient Greek modes – by colours: thus the Dorian was to be written in red, the Phrygian in green, the Lydian in yellow and the Mixolydian in purple.[13] This system, which was designed simply for clarity, found little echo even in the manuscripts of Rudolph's own work. When in the late fifteenth century the Milanese theorist Franchino Gaffurio re-introduced the idea of the colours of the Greek modes, he associated them with the temperaments or humours attributed to each of those modes since ancient times. The Dorian, he argued, was a phlegmatic mode, which painters would represent with a 'crystalline' colour, the Phrygian a bilious mode, represented by orange (*igneo colore*), the Lydian a joyful mode rendered in sanguine red and the Mixolydian conveyed by painters in an undefined mixed colour.[14] Although Gaffurio was close to painters, including Leonardo da Vinci, and although his ideas were felt in sixteenth-century Italian musical theory, these moral colour-correspondences were his own and appear to have had no effect on later thought or practice.

Far more promising was the Aristotelian notion of the proportionality of colours in a scale between black and white, which was repeated throughout the Middle Ages and well into the Renaissance – although the identification of the two 'harmonic' colours could not remain the same, since the most precious red of Antiquity, Aristotle's purple, had now given way to the most precious modern red, scarlet (*coccineus*).[15] One of the few medieval attempts to develop Aristotle's thought was in the *Great Mirror* of Vincent of Beauvais, where it was argued that although there were numerous colours only seven of them could embody proportions and thus appear pleasant. He did not name these seven but mentioned that a pink mixed from a good deal of white and a little red and a green modified with a little yellow pleased the eye just as a musical fifth or fourth pleased the ear. Thus pink formed a consonance of a fifth to the octave of white and light green a fourth.[16] This sort of exploration of harmonic colour-scales implied the more complex construction of those scales characteristic of the thirteenth century (*see* pp. 165–6) but the manifest confusion about the order of the colours made it virtually impossible to translate them precisely into musical terms.

The prestige of musical theory was assured during the Middle Ages by its inclusion in the Quadrivium of the mathematical arts taught in the universities.[17] Colour had no such advantage, since it did not form a distinct branch even of mathematical optics and we have seen how it continued to resist quantification down to the time of Newton. Around 1300, the Byzantine musical theorist Manuel Bryennius had claimed that only hearing, of all the senses, was able to quantify its sensations.[18] When, during the Renaissance, the debate among the rival arts for the distinction of being recognized as liberal was revived, painters could find little support in the colouristic element of their practice and appealed for the most part to the newly developed systems of linear perspective. This is the more surprising in that the *paragone* developed first of all in Milan in the circle of Leonardo and Gaffurio, had almost certainly originated from the revived interest in the *On Music* of Aristides which, as we saw, had pointed to proportionality in the painter's mixing of colours as well as in the drawing of the figure.[19] We might well have expected Leonardo to draw on this argument in his defence of painting against the claims of music and poetry but, like his friend the mathematician Luca Pacioli, he relied entirely on the geometrical arguments associated with anatomy and perspective.[20] Leonardo's reading of Boethius will also have reminded him that it was not enough either for the musician to create consonances or for the colourist to have a merely intuitive understanding of colour and form: they must also, said that philosopher, be able to give a rational account of these phenomena.[21] In the case of the colouristic painter, this was far easier said than done.

Perhaps the chief obstacle to Leonardo's own treatment of colour-harmony in an Aristotelian way was this very devotion to the idea of the geometric basis of painting. Following Aristotle's definition in *Categories* (VI, 4b–5a), or perhaps the version which Boethius (*On Music* II, iii) attributed to Pythagoras, Leonardo understood geometry as the science of continuous quantity, which was where painting began: the point becomes the line, which becomes the plane, which in turn becomes the three-dimensional solid.[22] But as Ptolemy had argued in the passage on the rainbow in his *Harmonics*, which had come via Boethius to Leonardo (*see* p. 108), musical harmony depended on ratios, that is, on discontinuous, arithmetical quantity. Thus the continuous transitions of the colours in the rainbow could be no model for it. If Leonardo was able to think of colour-harmony at all, it could only be in the ancient Greek sense of a 'fitting-together', rather than in the more modern one of a pleasing concord of 'sounds'.[23] Discrete objects might be set proportionately, hence harmoniously, in continuous space.[24] In the case of colour only Leonardo's gradations of *sfumato* modelling could express the continuous quantities of geometry and this could hardly be brought to bear on the harmonious assortment of colours as understood in Quattrocento Italy. It is perhaps no surprise that Leonardo's virtuosity as a practising musician was chiefly exercised on the *lira da braccio*, a bowed string instrument with two continuously sounding open (drone) strings, or that his contribution to the repertory of wind playing was a precocious *glissando* flute, whose sound he compared to the continuous modulation of the human voice. There was, for Leonardo, a *sfumato* of aural pitch as well as of visual tone.[25] His dilemma was a further indication of the confusion which persisted until the scale of hues and the scale of values could be co-ordinated into a three-dimensional colour-space.

Renaissance developments in the theory of musical harmony brought it closer to the realm of colour-mixing, as a function of the expansion of oil-painting in the sixteenth century. The late-medieval elision of 'consonance' and 'harmony', expressed by Gaffurio in the frontispiece to his *De Harmonia* as 'Harmonia est discordia concors', developed around 1500 into a concentration on the three-note chord, Boethius's harmonic mean, 3:4:6, in which the ratio of the three parts to each other was equal to the ratio of the extremes. In the third quarter of the sixteenth century the Venetian theorist Gioseffo Zarlino argued that it was a triumph of modern counterpoint to have amplified the

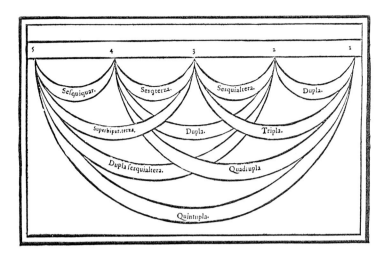

Gioseffo Zarlino, table of harmonic proportions (*Istitutioni Harmoniche*, 1573). (182)

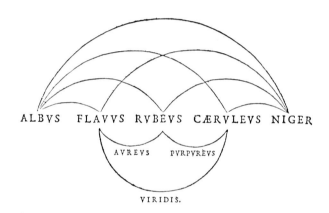

François d'Aguilon, colour scale (*Opticorum Libri Sex*, 1613). D'Aguilon introduces into the realm of colour the diagram of Pythagorean musical consonances as it had been shown in theoretical texts ever since Antiquity. His intention here was to show the relationships between colours, rather than suggest harmonies. (183)

ancient tetrachord of four tones ($1 + 2 + 3 + 4 = 10$) – whose ratios gave the octave, the fourth and the fifth – with concords deriving from the first six numbers, which added the major and minor thirds (5:4, 6:5) and the major sixth (5:3).[26] This at once brought musical consonance into a potential relationship with the new scale of primary and secondary colours. It is surely no coincidence that the first modern colour-diagram, showing the relationship of the three primaries and the three secondaries and their derivations from black and white, should have been based on the sort of (admittedly very ancient) diagram of musical consonances published in Zarlino's *Istitutioni Harmoniche*. Similarly, at the close of the sixteenth century it seemed to be possible for the first time to demonstrate the visual concord of colours on a musical instrument – the first experiment in colour-music as a form of synaesthetic art which was to tax the ingenuity of many technologists, and the patience of their audiences, well into the twentieth century.

183

182

Arcimboldo's colour-music

The growing empiricism in sixteenth-century Italian musical theory, especially marked in the greater attention to problems of tuning, was matched by a shift in the perceived relationship of music to painting, where colour was associated more and more with the quality of sound and painters compared to musicians in their capacity as performers to create this quality. In his *Dialogo di Pittura* of 1548 Paolo Pino based his claim that painting was a liberal art on its links with the Quadrivium but went on to argue that invention (*disegno*) was its chief claim to liberality, and that this invention, like musical composition, must be manifested in performance: 'Notwithstanding that some say making [*operar*] is a mechanical act because of the diversity of colours and the outlines [drawn by] the brush, just as the musician raises his voice and deploys his hands with various instruments, nonetheless we are all liberal because of the same perfection [of performance].'[27]

Federico Barocci at the end of the century felt that in working out the colour-compositions of his paintings in small sketches he was searching for a *concordia ed unione* of colour, united to a harmony of shape, the whole analogous to that by which singers delighted the ear. He told his patron, Duke Guidobaldo di Montefeltro, who encountered him in the act of painting, that he was 'harmonizing this music'.[28] These attitudes had been very much part of the Venetian *ambiente*; Veronese had pointed to them when he included portraits of some of his painter-friends as performing musicians in the vast *Marriage Feast at Cana*, where Titian, otherwise known as something of a keyboard player, was given the *viol da gamba*; Tintoretto, who made his own instruments, and Veronese himself, violas; and Veronese's brother Benedetto Caliari a small *lira da braccio*. The flautist seems to be Jacopo Bassano.[29]

Performance and the pre-occupation with scales came together, perhaps for the first time, in the experiments of the Milanese painter Giuseppe Arcimboldo, working at the court of the Emperor Rudolph II in Prague towards the end of the sixteenth century. According to the writer Gregorio Comanini, who was apparently active in Milanese musical life when Arcimboldo returned there in the late 1580s,[30] he had developed at Prague a scale of values between white and black stepped according to the double octave of musical tones in the Pythagorean system. He had also extended his investigations to the scale of hues and persuaded a musician at Rudolph's court, Mauro Cremonese dalla Viuola, to locate on his *gravicembalo* (a keyboard instrument used for accompaniment) the consonances established by the painter 'with colours on a sheet of paper'.[31] That Arcimboldo should have started with a grey-scale of fifteen values reminds us that he was brought up in Milan not long after the death of Leonardo (his father, also a painter, had been a friend of Leonardo's follower Luini)[32] and where, later in the century, Girolamo Cardano had published his series of colour-scales, including the quantified scale of brightness (*see* Chapter 9).[33] Like Zarlino, and unlike some of the ancient theorists, Arcimboldo equated darkness with high pitch and he probably constructed his scale from white to black by mixing weighed quantities of black with white paint according to the ratios 4:3 for the fourth, 3:2 for the fifth, 2:1 for the octave, 9:8

for the whole tone, 3:1 for the twelfth and 4:1 for the double octave. Comanini argued that the painter was even able to surpass Pythagoras in his ability to divide the whole tone into two nearly equal semi-tones.[34] But when we move from the value scale to the hue scales, Comanini's account becomes exceptionally difficult to interpret, for he says that the gradual darkening of the white in the grey scale 'reducing it to sharpness' (*riducendolo ad acutezza*) was also followed in the other colours:

> using white for the lowest part which is found in the cantus firmus [*canto*], and green and blue for the higher parts, since of these colours the one follows and darkens the other, for white is darkened by yellow, and yellow by green, and green by blue, and blue by *morello*, and *morello* by *tané*; just as the bass is followed by the tenor and the tenor by the alto, and the alto by the superius [*canto*].

He seems to be envisaging a motet for five male voices in which each vocal line is characterized by a hue, starting with white for the basso profondo, or cantus firmus, and ending with a dark brown (*tané*), for the falsetto superius, each of which voices is capable of spanning a double octave as in the Pythagorean grey-scale. Arcimboldo was apparently groping towards a three-dimensional conception of colour-space but either he or his commentator Comanini had little idea of its implications. What is most surprising is the absence of red in this scheme, since, as we saw, red had been a very important point on the Aristotelian colour-scale which lies behind Arcimboldo's work.[35]

Mauro Cremonese was apparently seeking to exemplify the harmonic order of the scale on his *gravicembalo*; this has led at least one modern commentator to suggest that Arcimboldo was supplying a sort of colour-coded notation in the tradition of Rudolph of St Trond.[36] Others have seen in these experiments the seeds of the synaesthetic experience of the 'colour-piano', although there is nothing in Comanini's account to suggest that Arcimboldo wrote any 'compositions', or that the plotting of his colour-consonances on the keyboard gave any pleasure to the eye. It is clear that the painter at this time had no means of gauging the proportions of black and white in the intermediate hues and that his Aristotelianism was still an obstacle to linking the notion of musical consonances practically to the idea of colour-harmonies.

It is perhaps more fruitful to think of Arcimboldo's work as part of that dominant strand in the intellectual life of Rudolph's court which sought to trace and articulate the correspondences of universal harmony. His best-known paintings presented analogies between the human temperaments and the elements, or seasons, in bizarre heads constructed from the visual manifestations of fire or water, spring flowers and so on.[37] Several other members of this court showed an interest in musical colour-scales after Arcimboldo left in 1587: the Italian Professor of Medicine at Vienna, V. A. Scarmilionius of Foligno, argued on the analogy of the five simple consonances of early Pythagorean theory (octave, twelfth, double octave, fifth, fourth) that the simple colours must also be five: black, white, yellow (*flavus*), blue (*hyacinthinus*) and red. Rudolph's court-physician, the alchemist and gemmologist Anselm de Boodt, also assumed this five-step scale of principal colours.[38] Just before he joined the Imperial court in Prague in 1600, the

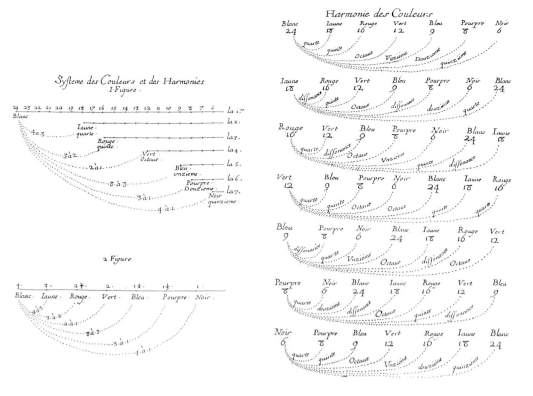

Marin Cureau de la Chambre, table of musical harmony of colours (*Nouvelles Observations et Conjectures sur l'Iris*, 1650). Cureau shows an Aristotelian scale of five hues between black and white, with each colour numbered so that harmonic proportions could be established along musical lines. Thus white was given the value 24 and black 6; yellow at 18 formed an interval of a fourth with white, red at 16 a fifth, green at 12 an octave, and so on. Black at 6 forms a fifteenth, or double octave. (184)

mathematician Johannes Kepler, working at another Hapsburg court in Graz, conceived of a tonal scale of hues between light and dark. It could be observed in the sequence of colours in the sky at dawn and dusk and in the rainbow, and might be calibrated just as musical notes were identified by their geometrical proportions from among the infinite 'voices' in the continuum of sound. Kepler even argued, anticipating Newton, that the colours of the rainbow might depend upon their angles of refraction and might thus be quantified in a musical way.[39] But he was no more able than his predecessors to shake off the Aristotelian view that the hues lay on a linear scale between light and dark, so he could not integrate the idea of the spectrum into a sequence of values.

Arcimboldo's bold attempt to exemplify his colour-music analogy by having it 'played' on a keyboard was very much in line with the efforts of musicians in his day to devise instruments which would play ever more subtly differentiated scales. Among these musicians were painters such as Domenichino, who is known to have made keyboard instruments capable of playing enharmonic quarter-tones.[40] Characteristically, he claimed that these experiments were part of his revival of ancient music and his wish to combine the Dorian, Lydian and Phrygian modes in a single scale.[41] But if the flesh-palette of two rows of fifteen nuances between white and black used by his pupil Canini depended upon his own practice, it seems more than likely that a preoccupation with musical and colour-scales went hand in hand. Certainly as an associate of Matteo Zaccolini, Domenichino might have been expected to ponder these connections, for Zaccolini numbered the colours on his nine-hue scale according to their spatial effect and compared the

power of white and yellow to that of the most forceful musical chords.[42] Among Domenichino's teachers, Agostino Carracci had been particularly devoted to string-playing: it would be pleasant to imagine that the lute-playing landscapist with his elaborately set palette in a painting attributed to Paul Bril is demonstrating an attitude to the association of musical and colour-scales with which Domenichino must have been brought up.[43] The painterly search for ever more nuanced tonal scales in the early seventeenth century (discussed in Chapter 9) thus had a significant musical dimension.

188

Music and colour in the seventeenth century

Although it was based on an ancient diagram of consonances in the musical scale, François d'Aguilon's scheme of simple and mixed colours did not of itself indicate any harmonious relationships between hues. The Aristotelian harmonic system could not, in any case, be illustrated in this way, since it referred not to the assortment of colours but to the intrinsic pleasingness of individual hues, deriving from the proportionate mixtures of black and white from which they were constituted. Developments in seventeenth-century optics, which suggested that light was a movement of particles of matter and colours a function of the various speeds of that movement, just as musical pitches were a function of various degrees of vibration, seemed to change and strengthen the basis of the colour-music analogy; but the lingering Aristotelian scale still made it difficult to separate the notion of mixtures of light and dark from the mixtures of hues among themselves. In d'Aguilon's scale purple, for example, as a mixture of red and blue, came before blue in

183

231

184 the progression from light to dark; but in other scales of the period, notably that of Marin Cureau de la Chambre, purple was considered to be a darker tone than blue and was placed next to black.[44] The French mathematician Marin Mersenne made one of the most elaborate attempts to relate musical consonances to colours by identifying the 'simple' colours (*nuances*) with the Greek musical scales: green with the diatonic, yellow with the chromatic and red with the enharmonic. Within each of these scales or *nuances*, the scale of tones or semi-tones corresponded to the scale of *couleurs*, or values, of these simple colours. But Mersenne also regarded the mixture of colours across these various *nuances* as productive of harmony, so that, for example, the mixture of blue and yellow, 'the painter's two primary colours', produced green, the most agreeable middle tone, the Greek *mese*.[45] Aristotle's perfectly consonant reds had now been joined by that favourite colour of the later Middle Ages, green, whose especially harmonic relationship with red was soon to be interpreted in terms of complementary contrast.

The extended and more coherent colour-scales of the Baroque made it possible to devise more complete correspondences with musical scales: Cureau de la Chambre in 1650 was *184* able not only to plot the consonances in a double octave from white to black but also to number the hues along this scale, so that combinations of colours were seen to have harmonic relationships with each other. Thus red at 16 was dissonant with blue at 9 and yellow at 18 but formed an octave with purple at 8 and a fourth with green at 12. It was Cureau's example that was invoked in the lectures on painting at the French Academy given be Félibien in the 1680s;[46] even earlier than this, in the *De Arte Graphica* (1667) of Du Fresnoy, chromatics was at last returned from musical discourse to the context of colour in art.[47]

It was left to Newton at the end of the century to free the colour-scale from the Aristotelian tonal scheme and to develop Kepler's and Descartes's quantification of colours in the spectral sequence, so that this sequence could be related more plausibly to the quantified musical scale. Newton had been much concerned with musical theory since the 1660s. (Around 1700 he collaborated with Brook Taylor and the composer J. C. Pepusch on a treatise on the subject which is still unpublished.[48]) Already in his Cambridge lectures of 1669 Newton had argued for a 'musical' division of the spectrum of white light,

> not only because it agrees with the phenomena very well, but also perhaps because it involves something about the harmonies of colours (such as painters are not altogether unacquainted with, but which I myself have not yet sufficiently studied) perhaps analogous to the concordances of sounds. It will even appear more probable by noting the affinity existing between the outermost purple and red, the extremities of the colours, such as is found between the ends of the octave (which can in a way be considered as unisons).[49]

Yet, as we saw in Chapter 6 the division of the spectrum into discrete areas presented Newton with as many problems as the articulation of the Aristotelian scale: his first, eleven-fold division (*see* p. 168), was soon reduced to five 'more prominent' colours, which was then amplified in 1672 with orange (*citrius*) and indigo – to make the parts 'more elegantly proportioned to

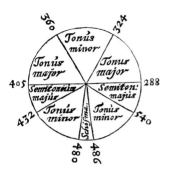

René Descartes, circle of major and minor tones (*Compendium Musicae*, 1650). This musical diagram suggested the form of Newton's colour wheel (see pl. 134). (185)

one another' – and the blue extremity changed from 'purple' to 'violet'.[50] The introduction of indigo, a species of blue, was especially problematic and can only have been justified by the need to make up the seven tones in the musical octave, although Newton was anxious to claim that his 'friend', who marked the divisions for him, had not been privy to his ideas before he did so.[51] Just as he appealed to a 'friend' to perform this function, so in thinking about the details of colour-harmony, Newton appealed to the authority of painters. In a draft for an unpublished section of *Opticks*, written probably in the 1690s, he stated:

> green agrees with neither blew nor yellow for it is distant from them but a note or tone above & below. Nor doth orange for the same reason agree with yellow or red: but orange agrees better wth an Indigo blew than wth any other colour for they are fifts. And therefore painters to set off Gold do use to lay it upon such a blew. So Red agrees well wth a sky coloured blew for they are fifts & yellow wth Violet for they are also fifts. But this harmony and discord of colours is not so notable as that of sounds because in two concord sounds there is no mixture of discord ones, in two concord colours there is a great mixture, each colour being composed of many others.[52]

Newton had, however, taken some time to formulate these detailed examples of colour harmony: in his letter to the Royal Society of 1675 he had proposed that 'golden' (i.e. orange, the Latin *aureus*) was concordant with blue, rather than the 'indigo blew' of this later draft, or the 'Indigo' of the published version of *Opticks* in 1704 (Bk III, Pt I, Qu. 14). Nor was his conception of the musical scale constant: in the 1669 lectures he used a Dorian scale of five tones and two semi-tones from G to G and in the *Opticks* a scale from D to D, both of them based on the medieval system of modes unaffected by modern developments.[53] Newton's influential colour-circle in *Opticks* was *134* adapted, indeed, from the diagram of the tempered diatonic octave published by Descartes in his *Compendium Musicae*, *185* written in 1618 and old-fashioned even then.[54] But in spite of these weaknesses, Newton's proposals gave a more comprehensive and a more detailed account of the analogy between aural and visual sensations. The great authority of the *Opticks* has made this appear to be a legitimate and potentially fruitful area of inquiry until our own day.[55]

Castel's ocular harpsichord

Newton had stated quite clearly his belief in the analogy between the diatonic scale and the spectrum but it was only in the more speculative 'Queries' in Book III of *Opticks* that he ventured to suggest that the perceived harmonies of sound and colour might be related to their both being vibratory phenomena.[56] Yet this gave a new lease of life to the ancient belief in universal harmony,[57] and it was not long before eighteenth-century empiricists tried to exemplify the idea in the practical form adumbrated by Arcimboldo and Mauro Cremonese. The first and most famous of these was the French Jesuit Louis-Bertrand Castel, who in the 1720s began work on the construction of an 'ocular harpsichord', which would play colour-sequences in the manner of a traditional keyboard. Castel had reviewed Coste's translation of Newton's *Opticks* somewhat coolly in 1723 and although he claimed that Newton had personally helped him in the late 1720s, it is clear that whatever stimulus *Opticks* may have given to his researches, his earliest debt was to his fellow-Jesuit Kircher's *Musurgia Universalis* (1650).[58] The problem was, of course, that Kircher's thirteen-part scale of two octaves running from white to black was scarcely compatible with Newton's seven-tone spectral scheme. A further complication was added by Castel's friendship with the composer and theorist Jean-Philippe Rameau. Rameau, in his *Traité de l'harmonie réduite à ses principes naturels* (1722) also reviewed by Castel, amplified the sexpartite theory of Zarlino by reference to the overtones recently investigated by the pioneer of acoustics, Joseph Sauveur: each pitch embodied three 'natural' tones fundamental to harmony – the fifth and the major and minor thirds. These three consonances were primary and gave rise to three 'secondary' consonances, the fourth and the major and minor sixths.[59]

It was Rameau who had encouraged Castel to embark on his experiments with the ocular harpsichord. When the instrument reached something like a developed form in the 1730s, Castel was using a scale of thirteen notes running from C (blue) to B (violet), which was closely related to Rameau's six primary and secondary consonances.[60] In the 1720s Castel had argued in a Newtonian fashion that just as white contains all colours, so a sound (*le son*) embraces all sounds; but now he held that black, or the closely related blue, was the 'fundamental' of all colours, as for Rameau the bass was the fundamental of all pitched sounds. He reinforced this view by pointing out that dyers used blue woad as the basis for their blacks and that the colour-printer Le Blon began his three-colour process by printing the blue plate.[61] Castel's 12 hues were each capable of modification by light or dark in 12 steps, giving 144 nuances, which he compared to an organ spanning 12 octaves in the chromatic scale.[62] If his contemporary Rameau provided the basis of his notions of musical harmony, Castel derived his ideas of colour-harmony and discord from the late seventeenth-century French writers Félibien and especially de Piles, whose feeling for the dissonance of ultramarine blue with vermilion, exemplified in paintings by Titian and Veronese, he found particularly compelling.[63]

All this remained very much at the level of theory. In the 1720s Castel had enlisted the help of an instrument builder,

124–7

Design for 'Musique Oculaire', 1769. G.G. Guyot's simple table-top apparatus rotated a drum carrying transparent coloured paper inside a lantern. Apertures allowed the illuminated slips to be seen on a scale equivalent to a musical octave. If it was ever built, the device represented the only practical eighteenth-century equivalent of Castel's abortive 'ocular harpsichord'. (186)

Rondet; their prototype, using coloured slips of paper which rose above the cover of the harpsichord, seems to have been in use by 1730. In the following decade a carpenter and joiner, Touronde, was also employed to help, but the account given by a friend of the German composer G. P. Telemann (published by Telemann in 1739) is so vague as to suggest that nothing had yet been performed. Telemann's informant said that strings, wires or wooden keys were used to expose a colour box, or compartment, or picture, or a brightly painted lantern, and that the instrument was only 'nearly' finished.[64] A model using a hundred candles, reported as having been exhibited in 1754 and 1755, was also apparently far from perfect. The performance with a much larger instrument using some 500 lamps behind 60

Η ΜΟΥΣΙΚΗ ΜΗΔΕΝ ΕΣΤΙΝ ΕΤΕΡΟΝ Η ΠΑΝΤΩΝ ΤΑΞΙΝ ΕΙΔΕΝΑΙ.

PANHARMONICON

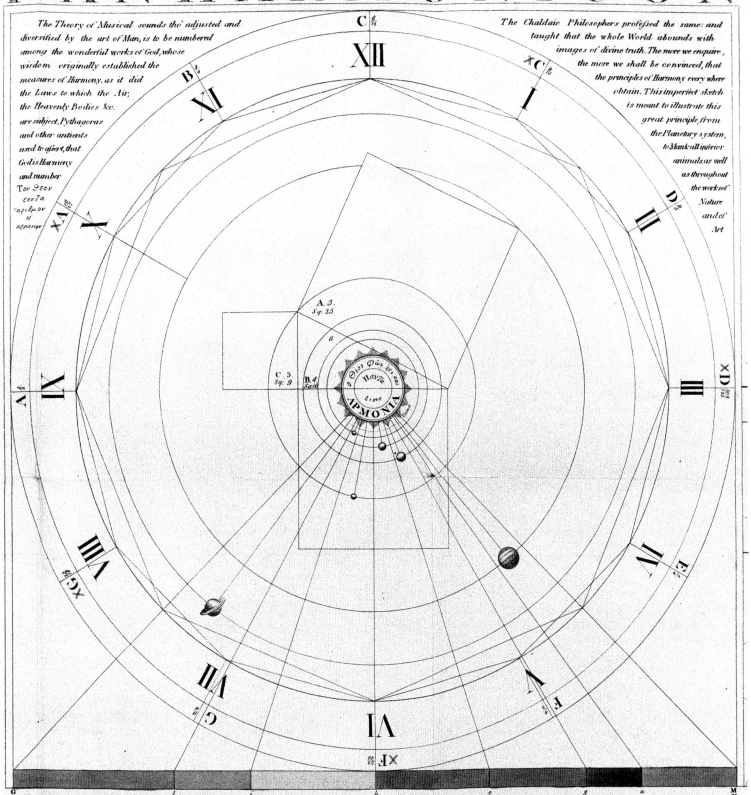

The Theory of Musical sounds tho' adjusted and diversified by the art of Man, is to be numbered among the wonderful works of God, whose wisdom originally established the measures of Harmony, as it did the Laws to which the Air; the Heavenly Bodies &c. are subject, Pythagoras and other antients used to assert, that God is Harmony and number. Τον Θεον εοντα ϰαριθμον ϗ αρμονιαν.

The Chaldaic Philosophers professed the same: and taught that the whole World abounds with images of divine truth. The more we enquire, the more we shall be convinced, that the principles of Harmony every where obtain. This imperfect sketch is meant to illustrate this great principle, from the Planetary system, to Mank all inferior animals, as well as throughout the works of Nature and of Art

According to Sir Isaac Newton's wonderful discovery, a ray of light passing through a prism (suppose from M to G) the line M G will be divided in the same proportions as a musical Chord by the spaces M a, a g, g e, e k, h i, i l, and l G, the respective colours of the ray. If G M be supposed continued as a direct line, and extended to X, & i X be equal to G M and the whole line considered as a musical Chord, G M will be minor Octave to the fundamental G X. Then G X (considered as a continued line) l X, i X, k X, e X, g X, a X, will be in proportion to one another as, 1, ⅞, ⅚, ¾, ⅔, ⅗, ½ and so represent the Chords of the Key & a tone, a 3rd minor a 4th a 5th a 6th major, a 7th & an 8th in that Key: & the intervals M a, a g, g e, e k, k i, i l, l G are the spaces which the respective colours occupy; viz. Violet, Indigo, Blue, Green, Yellow, Orange, Red.

Sir Isaac Newton also, by the same profound sagacity, discovered another truth equally wonderful and curious with the former; which is, that if we suppose musical Chords extended from the Sun to each Planet, in order that these Chords might become unison, it will be requisite to increase, or to diminish their tension in the same proportion as would be necessary to render the gravity of the Planets equal. So that, thus far at least, the celebrated harmony of the Spheres is proved and established, by philosophical principles, and absolute demonstration.

This great and exalted genius also demonstrated what the celebrated Kepler discovered, that the squares of the periodic Times, and the cubes of the mean distances of the Planets, are to each other in a ratio compounded of the direct ratio of their quantity of matter, and the inverse ratio of their magnitudes.

coloured glass filters, each $2\frac{1}{2}$ inches (6.4 cm) in diameter, advertised for 1757 (the year of Castel's death) at the Great Concert Room in Soho Square in London did not, it seems, take place.[65] The technical hitches which dogged Castel's colour-harpsichord over a period of nearly twenty-five years were very much the shape of things to come. Although it was widely discussed – and as widely rejected – in eighteenth-century philosophical literature throughout Europe, on a practical level Castel's experiments issued only in an engaging toy for demonstrating 'Musique oculaire', published by G. G. Guyot in 1769. Guyot started from Castel's book *L'Optique des couleurs* but he rejected its scale of analogies and did not risk prescribing his own scale to fill the five spaces for colours which were to be exposed and illuminated in the lantern-like table-top instrument.[66] When Castel's idea was invoked again in the nineteenth century by the Belgian physiologist J. A. F. Plateau, it was to signal an instrument for the display of moving colours based not on the principle of musical correspondence but on the psychological facts of the persistence of vision.[67]

The Romantics

The search for universal principles of harmony gathered momentum in the Romantic period but as the options in the study of both colour and musical theory increased, it became less and less likely that any consensus would be reached on the basis of a close analogy between musical and colour scales. One of the more comprehensive systems was evolved in the late eighteenth century by the little-known English historical painter Giles Hussey. He moved from a perception of the geometry of the human figure to a Newtonian scale of colour-music correspondences in three octaves, running from A (red) to A♭ (violet), a system which formed the basis of the great diagram of universal harmony, the *Panharmonicon*, of his biographer Francis Webb.[68] Hussey's view of the privileged status of music compared to painting, even at this late date, is suggested by his design of *Prosperity of Music with the Dejection of Painting*, recorded in 1773 in the collection of his most important patron, Matthew Duane.[69] A rather later system, based on the triad red (E), yellow (C) and blue (G), was elaborated by Field and first published in 1820 – but, as usual with Field, amplified and reworked in numerous later publications.[70] Field was much affected by the Romantic attempts to detach music from imitation and to relate it directly to feeling. He argued: 'it is evident colors have a science as distinct from any association with figure or forms . . . as that of musical sounds is from the figurative language of poetry.'[71] But when in a later book Field sought to link the expressive power of musical form to the various types of colour scale, he could do so only by referring to the Greek tradition of the chromatic and enharmonic scales.[72]

Hussey and Field were still looking for objective criteria in their comparison of colours to sounds but what chiefly distinguished the colour–music analogy in the Romantic period was not only its greater subjectivity but also the appreciation that styles of handling colour in painting could be paralleled by styles of musical performance. The subjectivity of harmonic colour-groupings now had an objective status: the investigation of 'accidental' colours in the second half of the eighteenth century meant that there was now some optical equivalent to Rameau's overtones, or Giuseppe Tartini's 'resultant tones' (a third, lower, tone heard involuntarily when two tones are sounded loudly), which might offer a physiological basis for harmonic juxtapositions of colours.[73] The development of these 'accidental' sequences gave a new impetus to the idea that colour, like music, could embody movement.[74] One of the most engaging visual evocations of this colour-movement was in a pamphlet of 1844 by the otherwise unknown D. D. Jameson. There the elegant woodcut designs reproduced compositions of coloured paper which were to serve as a sort of notation for the popular tunes that formed the repertory of Jameson's 'colour-music', to be performed by a coloured piano-keyboard which activated shutters in front of a dozen flasks of coloured liquids arranged in prismatic order. Lamps were to shine through the bottles into a darkened, tin-lined room: 'With each note, a strong colour is evolved in the dark room and reflected by its sides; and the duration and extension of this colour are greater or less according to the tune and position of the note which it represents and accompanies.'[75] Jameson's far from transparent theory drew freely on several sources: he combined Goethe's table of plus and minus colours (*see* pp. 203–4), which he related to mood, for example, with Field's Chromatic Equivalents of Red 5, Yellow 3 and Blue 8, which represented the proportions of these colours in white light and also the three major consonances in the musical octave. He argued that recent research had shown silence to be the product of the simultaneous sounding of the 'three primary notes', as 'darkness is eliminated by the interference of undulations of light'.[76] It is very unlikely that Jameson's instrument was ever built but he argued that the 'ocularised tune' of the pasted paper arrangements and hence of his woodcut reproductions might, if only 'in a very low degree', 'unless indeed to a perfect eye', produce the same sensations as those attending the performance of colour-music. We may imagine them on a larger scale having something of the presence of a late painting by Nicholas de Stael.

The notion of the painter's palette as a keyboard became a commonplace in the nineteenth century (*see* Chapter 10):[77] Delacroix had as a young man copied the very group of painter-musicians in Veronese's *Marriage Feast at Cana*.[78] It was perhaps in his theory of art that the modern concept of the painter as performer received its earliest formulation. Echoing the eighteenth-century German painter A. R. Mengs, who went about his last painting, *The Annunciation*, whistling a sonata of Corelli so that it might be in that composer's style, Delacroix, according to a friend, was always whistling or singing a favourite aria of Rossini's while at the easel.[79] He regarded the daily scale-practice he attributed (implausibly) to the virtuoso violinist Paganini – the subject of an animated portrait – as especially incumbent upon painters.[80] In conversation with

Francis Webb's *Panharmonicon* (1814) includes Newton's spectrum beneath the harmonic circle as the key to harmonic proportions, visual and aural, throughout the universe. (187)

another virtuoso performer, Chopin, he elaborated his idea that the liaison between musical notes, 'the logic of their succession', and what he called their 'aural reflection' was a precise parallel to the reflections of colours in nature and in painting. This aural liaison was, of course, very much a function of a string or keyboard style.[81] We are entering a period when painters were not only the friends of composers and performers but might, like Ingres or Matisse or Klee, use their own very ample experience as performers to illuminate their practice as visual artists.

It was Delacroix's most devoted follower, Vincent van Gogh, who brought this practical obsession with the sonority of colour most vividly into the era of Symbolism. In Holland in 1885 he took piano lessons in order to learn about the nuances of colour-tones. But his elderly teacher soon dismissed him, 'for seeing that during the lessons Van Gogh was continually comparing the notes of the piano with Prussian blue and dark green, and dark ochre, and so on, all the way to bright cadmium yellow, the good man thought that he had to do with a madman'.[82] The deep frustration of both teacher and pupil may be better appreciated if we remember that van Gogh's chief musical inspiration was Wagner.[83] Although his obsession with nature made him reluctant to be thought of as 'a musician in colours', his active conception of his role as a painter touched the idea of musical performance at several points. He wrote to his sister in 1888 that he wanted painting to be witnessed by an audience like a violin or piano concert and the following year he argued to Theo that his coloured versions of the designs of Millet and Delacroix, worked from monochrome reproductions in the asylum at St Rémy, were to be understood as interpretations: 'I improvise colour on it ... and then my brush goes between my fingers as a bow would on a violin, and absolutely for my own pleasure' (CL w. 4, 607).

Sonority and rhythm

Ever since Castel's experiments in the eighteenth century, critics had argued that the attempt to create colour-music rested on a false analogy. In that period the most vocal and influential had been Jean-Jacques Rousseau who in the *Essay on the Origin of Languages* (1764) had pointed out that sounds could not be identified individually, as colours could.[84] With the increasingly precise measurement of the various forms of electromagnetic radiation during the nineteenth century, it became clear that the characteristics of visible and audible vibrations were quite distinct; in particular the band of the visible spectrum was much narrower than that of the frequencies of audible sound. One of the first aesthetic texts to make these distinctions clear, G. T. Fechner's *Vorschule der Aesthetik* (1876), also introduced the discussion of a type of psychological association between colour and sound which was to become a central issue among colour-musicians by the end of the century: the synaesthetic phenomenon of colour-hearing.[85] *Audition colorée* was usually experienced in speech (*see* Chapter 11) but from the earliest times it had also been felt by synaesthetes as a function of music, and musical examples were often discussed in the growing literature on the subject around 1900. In the *Theory of Colours* Goethe had drawn attention to a pamphlet on colour-harmony

by J. L. Hoffmann, in which setting the palette had been compared to tuning the instruments of the orchestra and these instruments to the individual colours. Thus yellow suggested the clarinets, bright red the trumpets, crimson the flutes, ultramarine the violas and violins and so on.[86] Hoffmann was familiar to students of *audition colorée*[87] although the spate of new research did not always support his scheme of equivalents. The association which did prove remarkably durable was the scarlet of the trumpet, which had been brought into the literature of psychology much earlier by Locke's example of a blind man who was driven to use this analogy. It recurred regularly, at least until Schoenberg alluded to it in the brass section of his total art-work *Die Glückliche Hand* (1910–13), where the red lighting during fanfares of brass changes to yellow with the rising notes of the trumpet.[88] Similarly the evocation of blue by the sound of the flute (not Hoffmann's equivalent) began to be noticed in the Romantic period and gathered momentum from the 1870s, when it acquired some experimental support.[89] Thus Kandinsky was drawing on a sizable body of received opinion when he claimed in 1912: 'Represented in musical terms, light blue resembles the flute, dark blue the 'cello, darker still the wonderful sounds of the double bass; while in a deep, solemn form the sound of blue can be compared to that of the deep notes of the organ.'[90]

Under the influence of late-nineteenth-century psychology the analogy between colour and musical sound had ceased to be based on quantifiable pitch and had shifted to the more mysterious qualities of instrumental timbre, a shift made easier in the German-speaking countries where the term for timbre is precisely 'sound-colour' (*Klang-farbe*).[91] It may be paralleled by the emphasis on rich orchestral 'colour' which had been growing since Berlioz and Wagner and may be seen neatly encapsulated in the *Klangfarbenmelodie* of Schoenberg's pupil Webern – a contributor to the *Blaue Reiter* almanac – among his *Six Pieces for Orchestra* (1909). The association might well come most readily to performing musicians, so it is perhaps no accident that Kandinsky was a cellist and that for him the dark blue of the cello was the most inward and spiritual of colours.[92] The violinist Matisse similarly objected to Neo-Impressionism not only because of its mechanical character but also because of its 'jumpy' surface, 'only a tactile vitality comparable to the "vibrato" of the violin or voice'.[93] String-players were especially conscious that the tactility of colour could be matched by a tactility of sound.

Developments in orchestration went hand in hand with new attitudes towards musical harmony, which were chiefly focused on what came to be known as the 'emancipation of dissonance' and eventually atonality. In the Munich circle of the Blaue Reiter the notion of dissonance in Schoenberg was much discussed in relation to colour in painting. Franz Marc, co-editor of the almanac to which Schoenberg also contributed, argued that the composer's atonality could be related to Kandinsky's, in that the independence of each note was like the discrete patches of Kandinsky's paint surrounded by white canvas. Schoenberg's refusal to recognize the categories of consonance and dissonance also occupied Marc incessantly in his painting, allowing him to overcome the prismatic order of the complementary colours and to set complementaries at any distance from each other.[94]

The linked themes of colour, music and landscape are compellingly evoked in this portrait, which may be of Bril himself. Around 1600 the idea that scales of colour, represented by the freshly-set palette, and scales of sound shared some affinity became commonplace (see pl. 181). The vigorously brushed landscape on the easel suggests a similar order of virtuoso fingering to that of the lutenist.

188 Attributed to PAUL BRIL (1554–1626), *Artist playing a lute*

237

189

In the twentieth century the musical affinities of colour have been felt by artists in widely differing ways. Around 1913 Kandinsky (**192**) painted a number of complex canvases of almost symphonic proportions, in which, he felt, shapes and colours evoked vibrations in the spectator akin to the various timbres of instruments in the orchestra – his own instrument was the 'cello, which he 'saw' as dark blue. Klee, on the other hand, paid homage in this large and stately composition (**189**) to the structural principles of Baroque counterpoint, which he also explored as a teacher at the Bauhaus (**190**). Mondrian, in his last major work, left unfinished in New York (**191**), was stimulated to a new vitality by the staccato piano style of the latest phase of American jazz.

Structure and resonance

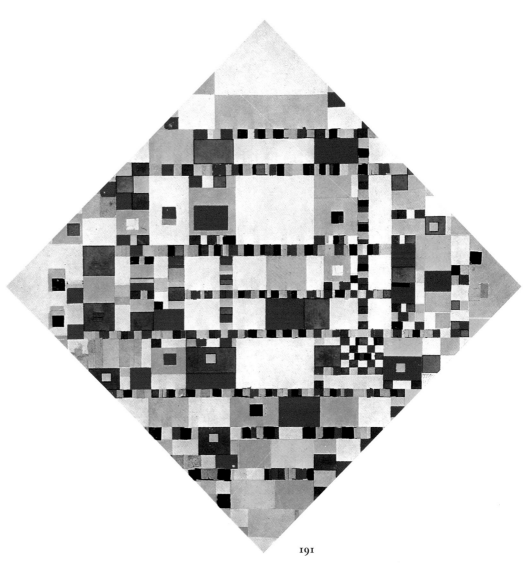

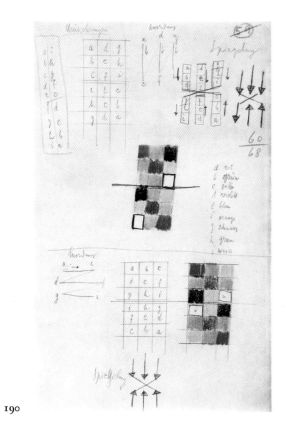

189 PAUL KLEE, *Ad Parnassum*, 1932
190 PAUL KLEE, Exercises in mirror-reversal in
coloured grids, probably *c.* 1922
191 PIET MONDRIAN, *Victory Boogie-Woogie*, 1943/4
192 WASSILY KANDINSKY, *Composition VI*, 1913

Marc reported that Kandinsky was more cautious but hoped to be able to supplement the old-fashioned harmonies of pure colours with 'dirty' dissonances like Schoenberg's.[95] Already in the first letter to Schoenberg in January 1911 Kandinsky had argued that today's dissonances would be tomorrow's consonances. In *On the Spiritual in Art*, published at the end of the year, he came down firmly on the side of a non-hierarchical view of musical or colour-tones:

> From the fact that we live in a time full of questions and premonitions and omens – hence full of contradictions . . . – we can easily conclude that harmonization on the basis of simple colours is precisely the least suitable for our own time. It is perhaps with envy, or with a sad feeling of sympathy, that we listen to the works of Mozart. They create a welcome pause amidst the storms of our inner life, a vision of consolation and hope, but we hear them like the sounds of another, vanished, and essentially unfamiliar age. Clashing discords, loss of equilibrium, 'principles' overthrown, unexpected drumbeats, great questionings, apparently purposeless strivings, stress and longing (apparently torn apart), chains and fetters broken (which had united many), opposites and contradictions – this is our harmony.[96]

It was from about this time that the idea of 'laws' of colour-harmony like the imperatives of musical consonance, although they continued to be promoted by the devisers of colour-order systems such as the German chemist Wilhelm Ostwald or the American painter Albert H. Munsell, ceased to be of much vital aesthetic interest.[97]

Kandinsky's judgment of Mozart in 1911 makes it at first sight rather surprising that he should use an eighteenth-century analogy when discussing the need of the modern colourist for some sort of grammar. He repeated throughout the publications of the Blaue Reiter period a remark of Goethe's that a 'well-established and approved theory', like the thorough-bass (*Generalbass*) in music, was also required in painting and this became an aesthetic slogan of the group.[98] Kandinsky's emphasis is the more curious that Schoenberg had argued in his *Harmonielehre* of 1911, a text very familiar to him, that the thorough-bass was now entirely outmoded.[99] It does, however, point to a very general admiration for eighteenth-century principles among early twentieth-century artists searching for a basis in painterly structure and also to the failure of visual artists to understand the character of the latest developments in other arts. From Kandinsky the idea of the importance of a *Generalbass* spread to other avant-garde artists anxious for new structures. The Swedish pioneer of abstract film, Viking Eggeling, in 1918 designed *Material for a Thorough-Bass of Painting*, and the Dutch leader of De Stijl, Theo van Doesburg, in 1923 also described his elementary rectangular forms as a *Thorough-Bass of Painting* – again rather surprisingly since in the accompanying text he expressed his hostility to the Baroque.[100] Perhaps the most striking indication of the uncertainties that the newest musical aesthetic presented to visual artists was the almost universal respect of the avant-garde for Johann Sebastian Bach.

Bach's high reputation was not quite the invention of the late nineteenth century, since Mendelssohn had performed his *St Matthew Passion* in 1829 and the Leipzig Bach Society, responsible for the publication of the complete works, had been founded in 1850. But there can be little doubt that interest in Bach increased enormously among composers and critics towards the end of the century. Of the early twentieth-century composers who claimed a special affinity with him, Schoenberg and Busoni were particularly close to the most innovative painters.[101] What fascinated composers and painters alike was the tight yet flexible structure of the Bach fugue; comparison with the fugue became a fashionable way of characterizing painting with little ostensible subject-matter but a marked preoccupation with structure. Robert Delaunay's work (*see* Chapter 14) was described in these terms by both Marc ('pure sounding fugues') and Klee, who noted in a review of 1912 that one of his window-paintings was 'as far away from a carpet as a Bach fugue'.[102] Delaunay's American followers in Paris, the Synchromists, underlined the musicality of some of their compositions and one of them, Morgan Russell, an amateur composer, sometimes worked with a Beethoven score in front of him.[103] Russell's formal interests derived chiefly from a study of Michelangelo's sculpture but he and his friend Stanton Macdonald-Wright approached colour with a similar high-mindedness, and argued in 1913:

> Mankind has until now always tried to satisfy its need for the highest spiritual exaltation only in music. Only tones have been able to grip us and transport us to the highest realms. Whenever man had a desire for heavenly intoxication he turned to music. Yet color is just as capable as music of providing us with the highest ecstasies and delights.[104]

Russell used the terminology of tonic, dominant and counterpoint to describe his principles of colour-construction. His *Four-Part Synchromy No. 7* clearly reflects a fugal form and *Creavit Deus Hominem* – a thoroughly Bach-like title – also proclaims its contrapuntal structure.[105]

Russell and Macdonald-Wright had been taught in Paris by a Canadian artist, Percyval Tudor-Hart, who had developed a psychological colour-theory of some complexity. He claimed that pitch was equivalent to luminosity and timbre or 'tone' to hue but at the same time that the twelve notes of the chromatic scale were equivalent to these 'chromatic colours', in which C represented red and A blue-violet.[106] The confusion which must have arisen from such incompatible ideas may lie behind Russell's later rejection of 'all [Tudor-Hart's] complicated systems and academic humbug'.[107] But the attempt to marry the traditional interpretation of the colour-music analogy as based upon mathematical principles with the newer psychological emphasis on the quality of sound also affected the far more considerable theory and practice of Paul Klee.

Klee was a gifted violinist with an interest in music which helped to shape both his painting and his teaching. He was not in

193 in right margin

Baroque principles of musical structure lie beneath Morgan Russell's colour composition, and Michelangesque sculpture beneath its form.

193 MORGAN RUSSELL, *Creavit Deus Hominen (Synchromy No. 3: Color Counterpoint)*, 1914

Theo van Doesburg, *Ragtime (Composition in Greys)*, 1918. (194)

the Bauhaus with Lyonel Feininger (who was composing thoroughly eighteenth-century fugues on his harmonium at this time), are generally confined to sequences of a single hue. In his Bauhaus lectures he devoted far more time to the quantifiable element of value than to hue.[109] Yet Klee did attempt to analyse hue in terms of 'weight', giving greater psychological prominence to the primaries red, yellow and blue than to the secondaries and tertiaries, and to the complementaries among contrasts. He applied fugal reversal and reflection to hues as well *190* as to tones in his 'magic-square' compositions. Colour was less susceptible than line and tonal gradation to the quasi-diagrammatic treatment of so much of Klee's earlier work: it was only when he came to work on a large scale in the 1930s, with paintings such as *Ad Parnassum* (based on an idea of the *189* treatise on counterpoint *Gradus ad Parnassum* of 1725 by J. J. Fux) or the twelve-tone *New Harmony* that colour-sonorities could be felt as a dominant principle of pictorial organization as well as a creator of mood.[110]

Among the admirers of Bach in these years perhaps only the Swiss artist Johannes Itten was able to use his musical experience in the construction of a coherent theory of colour: this became possible because of a fortunate meeting in 1919 with the twelve-tone composer Josef Matthias Hauer in Vienna. Itten had already been contrasting what he saw as the linear melodic structure of Bach and the late Gothic painter Meister Francke, with the harmonic content of Schoenberg and van Gogh: 'In the linear the temporal movement of breathing-rhythms can be clearly represented as a horizontal order. With the coloured or harmonic (musical) the order of breathing-rhythms is represented as simultaneous or vertical (music) . . . A linear [order] can be determined far more precisely than a coloured, even in music.'[111] The meeting with Hauer, who had just published his *Über die Klangfarbe* (*On Timbre*, 1918), gave Itten the opportunity of pursuing these studies with far greater precision and they entered into an intensive exchange of ideas over a number of years. Hauer gave the painter a sound-colour circle of twelve equally spaced notes, divided into warm colours for the fifths and cool for the fourths.[112] The colour-system which Itten published in 1921 was also a twelve-tone one, but it was arranged in spectral order and also sought to co-ordinate twelve equally spaced hues with a value scale of seven steps, which (like Klee, who was now his colleague at the Bauhaus) he related to the intellectual, whereas the 'sound-colour' expressed the emotions.[113] Also like Klee, Itten developed the coloured grid as a flexible format for establishing colour harmonies which, as he told his students from the 1920s onwards, must reflect the personality types of those who composed them.[114]

One of the styles of modern music which had a more than usual resonance for the colour-style of some avant-garde painters was jazz, which arrived in Europe from America about the time of the First World War. It was quickly taken up by the De Stijl group, particularly Mondrian who published an important essay, 'Jazz and Neo-Plastic' in 1927. Mondrian's Theosophical background and his continuing spiritual cravings did not allow him to see modern jazz as more than a rather superficial and transitional stage on the way towards the new society but he none the less felt that 'the passage from art to life is seen most clearly in jazz and in Neo-Plasticism'[115] and he had

principle hostile to modern music but he felt that if painting were to catch up with contemporary developments in musical theory it must start with the Baroque, since 'Music already saw and solved the question of abstraction in the eighteenth century, but this was muddled again by the programme-music of the nineteenth. Painting is only now taking it on board.'[108] But Klee had a thoroughly modern sense of colour as quality which, unlike line and chiaroscuro, could not be quantified. In an early attempt to construct a value-scale of hues, he noticed that the value structure (*Schattenbild*) was rational and the colour structure irrational, so that they could only be reconciled with difficulty (*Diary*, 1910, no. 879). Thus the group of paintings of *221* stepped tonal sequences executed in 1921, including *Hanging Fruit* and *Fugue in Red*, which may have arisen from contact at long been an enthusiastic modern dancer. As early as 1915 in Holland he had been observed 'ramrod straight, his head tilted upwards, making "stylized" steps' and we might imagine that he was the model for van Doesburg's syncopated grid-like 194 *Ragtime (Composition in Grey)* of a few years later.[116] In the 1920s Mondrian painted a number of *Fox-Trot* compositions and developed the view that rhythm was the unifying feature of life and art, whether visual or musical, and its most characteristic manifestation the jazz-bar, where the repetitive rhythms of the machine or of nature were modified according to a more human need.[117] The Fox-Trot was of course based on a square formation and its solo-instruments were the saxophone and the trumpet, which helped to give it an essentially linear character. When Mondrian moved to New York in 1940 the prevailing version of jazz was Boogie-Woogie, a piano-based style often using two instruments, whose staccato 'riffs' and runs up and down the keyboard gave it a sparkling and fragmented character which Mondrian, abandoning his black lines, picked 191 up in the colouristic grid of his last paintings. Here again, a musically inspired style of painting was developed not on the basis of a system but in response to an aural experience.

Moving colour

Mondrian's preoccupation with rhythm was timely for it was among his contemporaries that Castel's aspiration for moving, rhythmic colour formations seemed within sight. This was very largely a question of technology and, not surprisingly, it began with theatrical lighting. As early as the 1780s the improved oil-lamp of Argand made it possible for scenic artists such as P. J. de Loutherbourg in London to control the level of stage-lighting to an unprecedented degree and to introduce subtle effects of movement.[118] The development of gas lighting and its derivative the lime-light about 1820 put even more power at the designer's disposal. In the 1840s the English scientist Charles Babbage devised a ballet including a largely abstract scene in which four coloured lime-lights would project a red, yellow, blue and purple light which would move and overlap to produce a rainbow effect playing over the white-clad dancers.[119] The risk of fire prevented its production but this was a risk which became markedly less with the development of electric lighting in the 1870s, which also gave the promise of compositions on a far larger scale than ever before. An early colour-organist, the American painter Bainbridge Bishop, wrote in 1893:

> The invention of the electric light renders it possible to use colour-harmony as an accompaniment to a church organ and sacred music. This can be done on a grand scale. The whole end of a cathedral, behind and over its organ, could be arranged as a tablet or ground on which to display the colour-harmonies. Beautiful effects could be produced by a combination of statuary and gauze curtains, which, as the music pealed forth, would flash and fade with the softly melting hues of coloured lights with the chant of adoration ...[120]

By the turn of the century the technical capacities of electrical stage-lighting had made it possible to write moving colours into the plot, as Kandinsky did with his three stage pieces of 1909,

The Yellow Sound, The Green Sound and *Black and White*, and as the Swiss designer Adolph Appia projected for a production of Wagner's *Parsifal* three years later.[121] None of these projects was realized but in New York in 1915 there was a performance in music and colour which was to take on something of the allure of Castel's ocular harpsichord a century and a half earlier – Alexander Scriabin's *Prometheus: a Poem of Fire*.

Scriabin's *Opus 60* (1910/11) was his first and last attempt to 195 introduce a colour accompaniment to his music, although at the time of his death in 1915 he was planning an even larger work, *Mysterium*, which would include odours as well as coloured lights. He had been in touch with the Theosophical movement in Brussels in 1906, particularly with the Symbolist painter Jean Delville, but the moral and spiritual connotations he gave to his colour-scale of twelve tones had little in common with that published by the international Theosophical Society in Besant and Leadbeater's *Thought Forms* (1901). Scriabin's blues, for example – E, C♭ and G♭ – which connoted dreams, contemplation and creativity, are not far from the Theosophists' 'devotion to a noble ideal' or 'pure religious feeling'; but his joyous yellow (D) cannot easily be compared with their 'highest intellect', nor can his violet or purple (D♭), 'will of creative form', be seen as very close to their 'love for humanity'.[122] But at the end of their book Besant and Leadbeater introduced three examples of musical thought-forms, perceived by a clairvoyant at recitals on a church organ of Mendelssohn's *Songs without Words No. 9*, the soldiers' chorus from Gounod's *Faust* and the overture to Wagner's *Meistersingers*. The Mendelssohn produced a very linear composition in the three primary colours, the Gounod a much larger and more complex formation with a whole spectrum radiating outwards in a sort of expanding globe, but the Wagner was perceived as 'a vast bell-shaped erection, fully nine-hundred feet in height':

> The resemblance to the successively retreating ramparts of a mountain is almost perfect, and it is heightened by the billowy masses of cloud which roll between the crags and give the effect of perspective ... the broad result is that each mountain-peak has its own brilliant hue – a splendid splash of vivid colour, glowing with the glory of its own living light, spreading its resplendent radiance over all the country round. Yet in each of these masses of colour other colours are constantly flickering, as they do over the surface of molten metal, so that the coruscations and scintillations of these wondrous astral edifices are far beyond the power of any physical words to describe.[123]

This florid description might well have been an important stimulus to Scriabin, whose E♭ (humanity) and B♭ (lust or passion) included a 'glint of steel' on their flesh-pinks.[124]

Scriabin was something of a synaesthete and had discovered this gift at a concert in the company of Rimsky-Korsakov, when they had agreed that a piece in D major appeared yellow.[125] His early conception of the colour accompaniment to the *Prometheus Symphony* had been extremely ambitious: he had wished to flood the whole auditorium with coloured lights and at one stage he anticipated Kandinsky in proposing that a dancer should mimic the light-changes with appropriate gestures.[126] But when the *Symphony* came to be performed, the colour element was far more modest. The colour-keyboard

Colour organ (*luce*) appears at the top of Scriabin's score for the *Prometheus Symphony*. The organ's colours were projected on to a multi-layered screen above the orchestra, seen in this impression of the opening performance in New York in 1915. (195,196)

used in the first Moscow performance of 1911 failed to function and we know nothing of it. Subsequent concerts in Russia, Germany and England did not include a colour instrument, although Henry Wood in London had hoped that this part would be arranged by the leading English colour-organist, A. W. Rimington.[127] So the first complete performance was at the Carnegie Hall in New York in 1915, where the colour-keyboard was provided by an unknown designer working for the Electrical Testing Laboratories of New York, using vacuum or gas-filled tungsten lamps made especially by the General Electric Company. The lights were projected on to a series of meshes or gauzes of varying translucency in an eight by ten-foot (two and a half by three metre) box-like structure above the orchestra. Scriabin's score demanded two simultaneous light-projections, one to follow the orchestra tone by tone and the other to underline the general tonality of the parts of the symphony. They might last for many bars, so that the many-layered screen was required, where, as a critic reported,

> The effect ... was that the observer saw the light of one hue displayed upon the rear gauzes, and the light of a different hue displayed upon the front gauzes, the one being visible through the other. The final result of this was a beautiful combination of hues not precisely identical in any two portions of the screen, and varying in appearance as does changeable silk in dress materials when shown under strong light.[128]

Another New York critic found it difficult to relate the shape of the colour-score to that of the music: 'In the midst of what seemed to be one phase the lights would change half a dozen times. There was no variation in intensity as the music grew more emphatic; at the height of its proclamation there was the same pleasing variety of yellows, oranges, violets, purples and emeralds as there was at the beginning.'[129]

Scriabin's conception, if not its execution, found an echo in Kandinsky's published stage-piece *The Yellow Sound*, which like *Prometheus* began and ended with blue.[130] This piece was not performed until the 1960s but already before its publication in *Der Blaue Reiter* it was influential on the staging of Scene III of Schoenberg's *Die Glückliche Hand*, which includes a crescendo of lights changing from a dull red to yellow, through dirty-green, violet, blue-grey and blood red.[131] Schoenberg's piece also had to wait some years for a production: one of the earliest was at the Kroll Opera in Berlin, with sets by Oskar Schlemmer, who had long been working on ballets with elaborate light-scores under the influence of Scriabin and of Kandinsky's scenario for *The Yellow Sound*.[132] Kandinsky himself was finally able to see one of his abstract stage-compositions, to a version of Mussorgsky's *Pictures at an Exhibition*, performed at Dessau in 1928.[133] Technology, in this case high-wattage filament lamps, was at last catching up with aesthetics.

Schoenberg, indeed, had hoped as early as about 1913 that his drama might be presented in the newest art medium of all, the motion picture, and that Kandinsky might be one of the painters invited to design the sets and hand-colour the film stock under Schoenberg's direction. But he also felt that the relative weakness of this colouring might need the support of supplementary lights flooding the auditorium.[134] Abstract film was

196

very much in its infancy in these years but, like the colour-score of Scriabin, it too developed in the shadow of Theosophy and of Wagner. The Italian brothers Arnaldo Ginna and Bruno Corra, whose experiments with hand-painted abstract film go back to 1911 or 1912, had attended Theosophical lectures in Bologna and Florence and read widely in the literature, including Rudolph Steiner, Besant, Leadbeater and Edouard Schuré, who had described Wagner as the last of his 'Great Initiates'.[135] Like Scriabin and Schoenberg, Ginna and Corra imagined flooding their audiences with lights during their wordless 'chromatic dramas', but after disappointing experiments with a colour-keyboard of twenty-eight keys they turned to film.[136] One of Corra's early pieces was a colour version of Mendelssohn's *Spring Song*, and others were intended to be accompanied by extracts from Chopin, although Corra also composed some scores of his own. The brothers saw that film would allow them to use far stronger lighting than hitherto and also to mix colours optically through the effect of the persistence of vision. It is not clear which, if any, of their films were shown in public, but one of their short demonstration pieces suggests a style close to the film-maker Oskar Fischinger's work in the 1930s:

> [it was] composed of seven colours, the seven colours of the solar spectrum in the form of small cubes arranged initially on a horizontal line at the bottom of the screen against a black background. These move in small jerks, grouping together, crashing against each other, shattering and re-forming, diminishing and enlarging, forming columns and lines, interpenetrating, deforming etc.[137]

Technical difficulties hampered the work of the early film-makers no less than of the stage-designers and colour-organists. Hand-painted film stock was exceptionally unstable: Fischinger had to work in black and white during the 1920s until a reliable colour-film, Gasparcolor, was developed early in the following decade, when he also had the possibilities of a co-ordinated sound-track. For his early colour work he could only collaborate with the Hungarian colour-keyboard performer Alexander László, who was perhaps the best-known artist in this medium throughout the 1920s.[138] László came to colour-music from the musical end, using the services of visual artists such as Fischinger or the painter Matthias Holl to design his compositions. He adopted the recently published colour-theory of Ostwald and seems to have known of the work of Feininger and Klee: like them, he had no fixed idea of the relationship of specific sounds to specific colours, regarding it rather as a question of feeling.[139] Typically for the period, his work aroused a good deal of interest among experimental psychologists investigating synaesthesia but its life in the concert repertory was very short.[140] As in the case of Ginna and Corra and Fischinger (another admirer of Bach), there was something of a disjunction between the modern repertory of László's visual forms and the Baroque or Romantic style of the music, which made it at best a rather hybrid medium of entertainment.[141]

The 1920s and 30s were the high period of colour-music, which appeared in a bewildering variety of forms, most of which have now disappeared without trace.[142] In the majority the analogy between the physical characteristics of light and sound had ceased to play any shaping role.[143] In some

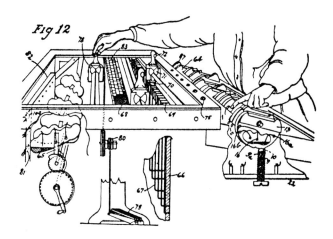

Mary Hallock Greenewalt's design for 'A Light-Color Play Console', 1927, with keys to supply 'starlight' and 'moonlight'. (197)

manifestations, such as the *Colour-Light Plays* developed by Ludwig Hirschfeld-Mack and Kurt Schwertfeger at the Bauhaus in 1922, the stimulus seems to have been purely formal.[144] However, in most cases the enormous technical and financial problems and the equally vast public indifference to this form of art meant that it could only be sustained by the strong spiritual conviction that it gave in some sense a privileged access to the divine.[145]

Two of the most spiritual but also the most successful exponents of the medium worked in the United States. Mary Hallock Greenewalt began as a concert pianist but, stimulated by theatrical lighting, she became interested in colour-music about 1906 and gave her first concert, in Philadelphia, in 1911. She toured extensively the following year and seems to have performed regularly until the late 1930s on a series of increasingly sophisticated instruments, one of which was awarded a gold medal at the Philadelphia Exhibition of 1926. Sometimes she played in chapels: as she told a convention of the Illuminating Engineers' Society in 1918, colour-music was 'an art that can play at will on the spinal marrow of the human being, remind him of the Holy Ghost and the utter sheerness of beauty'.[146] Greenewalt did not believe in a close analogy between colour and music but like Bainbridge Bishop and Rimington she was much stimulated by her experience of nature. She often composed colour-accompaniments to pieces with strong programmatic associations, such as the first movement of Beethoven's 'Moonlight' Sonata or Debussy's 'And the moon descends on the Temple which was' (from the second series of *Images*, 1907). The console which she patented in 1927 included a 'moonlight' key among several pre-established varieties of natural light.[147]

Thomas Wilfred, a Danish-American folk-singer, had begun to experiment with light and colour as a teenager in Copenhagen but it was not until his arrival in New York in the 1910s that he came to work seriously on a large-scale instrument. This was under the influence of the visionary architect and theorist of the fourth dimension, Claude Bragdon, who designed Wilfred's first studio on Long Island and with whom he formed a society, The Prometheans, to develop the new art.[148] Bragdon had

197

already built his own colour-organ and had given concerts in 1915 and 1916, but Wilfred developed his 'Clavilux' on a different principle, and had the first model ready by 1921.[149] Bragdon was probably the intellectual force behind Wilfred's practice: he dismissed the physical analogy between light and sound, emphasizing the imaginative autonomy of the medium, and he directed attention to the representation of four-dimensional space:

> Colour without form is a soul without a body; yet the body of light must be without any thought of materiality. Four dimensional forms are as immaterial as anything that could be imagined and they could be made to serve the useful purpose of separating colours one from another, as lead lines do in old cathedral windows, than which nothing more beautiful has ever been devised.[150]

When, about 1930, Wilfred designed his Art Institute of Light, it naturally took the form of a church, and he wrote in an essay of 1947 that his screen was like 'a large window opening on infinity, and the spectator imagines he is witnessing a radiant drama in deep space'.[151]

Wilfred's first 'Clavilux' did not apparently give an impression of deep space but rather a two-dimensional surface;[152] but the rapid development of new models in the early 1920s meant that by the time his work was shown at the Paris 'Exposition des Arts Decoratifs' and in London in 1925 his style could convey the fourth dimension of space–time that Bragdon had so eagerly sought. His London concerts in May of that year included the very Bragdonian contrast of two compositions, *The Factory* and *The Ocean*, 'four-dimensional stage settings for a fantastic play'. Some of his work on this occasion reminded one spectator of late Turner, 'by some magic caused to fade and glow, to recede and to advance'.[153] One of Wilfred's most appreciative critics, Sheldon Cheney, said of a performance on a model-C 'Clavilux' in the Long Island Studio, 'One had that feeling of detachment, of extasy, which is a response only to the most solemn religious or aesthetic experience', and he suggested

that 'perhaps ... this is the beginning of the greatest, the most spiritual and radiant art of all'.[154]

The element of ritual attending this remote, silent display – for Wilfred used no musical accompaniment – must have been paramount, but towards the end of his life Wilfred admitted rather petulantly that to the majority of 'worldly' people, his work would appear 'monotonous and uninteresting'.[155] Those who have sat through what he regarded as his masterpiece, *Lumia Suite, Op. 158* (1963–4), playing to an all-but empty basement in the Museum of Modern Art in New York, will hardly disagree; but they will also perhaps feel that Wilfred was tempting fortune with his massive works of the 1940s and 50s, the *Vertical Sequence No. II* of 1941, which ran for 2 days, 12 hours and 59 minutes, or the oddly titled *Nocturne (Op. 148)* of 1958, which filled 5 years, 359 days, 19 hours, 20 minutes and 48 seconds. This was surely hubris rather than spirituality.

Colour-music was an art form which was always about to be the most important twentieth-century art but never quite became it. It was, wrote Willard Huntington Wright (brother of Macdonald-Wright) in 1923, 'the logical development of all the modern researches in the art of colour'.[156] Yet it was not until the late 1920s that much attention was given to the crucial question of how a spectator might perceive, and respond to, rhythmically moving abstract forms.[157] If the physics of sound is not precisely similar to the physics of light, their respective psychological effects have perhaps even less in common. Experiments in colour-music on all levels, from disco-light-shows to therapeutic abstract film, have of course continued into our own times[158] but after nearly a century of development, it is sobering to hear a prophecy of as late as 1958:

> the time will come when ... in an atmosphere of semi-darkness, colours of every variety will be projected on to a screen, expressive of and corresponding to the content of the music. Thus will that dream of Scriabin's be realized, the unity of colour and sound; and through its realization the audiences of the future will experience the healing and stimulating effects of that very potent conjunction.[159]

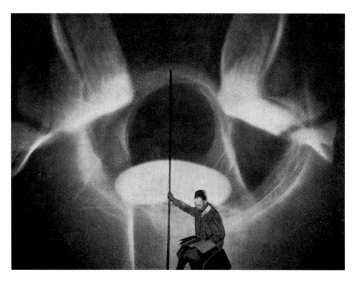

Thomas Wilfred rehearsing a composition. (198)

14 · Colour without Theory: The Role of Abstraction

The grammar of colour · De Stijl · Colour at the Bauhaus · Empiricism in Italy and France
Empiricism as theory · The materials of abstraction

By THE late nineteenth century colour had become a central, and in some places *the* central preoccupation of European painters and their public. The outdoor painting of the Impressionists as well as the indoor painting of Symbolists such as the Swiss artist Arnold Böcklin seemed to guarantee that modern art would be characterized by an urge towards more and more powerful colouristic effects. 'Whichever endeavour we look at,' wrote the critic Waldemar von Seidlitz in 1900, 'a decisive striving for colouristic fulness is emerging everywhere at the end of the nineteenth century.'[1] In an article on the psychology of colour which attracted the notice of Kandinsky, another German critic, Karl Scheffler, saw as early as 1901 that: 'Our time, which, more than any other, depends on the past for its forms, has produced a kind of painting in which colour is independent.'[2] Thus it was colour that was to supply the spearhead of non-representational art; it seemed to open up a new era of unprecedented visual freedom, and although we have seen in the work of Matisse that this freedom was rather submission to another sort of creative bondage, a belief in the autonomy of colour animated artists and designers in many areas of visual art. How did this belief come to be so widely shared?

Seurat had already announced that the traditionally conceived relationship of drawing to colour could no longer be sustained: 'If, scientifically, with the experience of art, I have been able to find the laws of pictorial colour, can I not discover a system, equally logical, scientific and pictorial, that will permit me to harmonize the lines of my painting as well as the colours?'[3] Seurat was clearly under the influence of Blanc, whose *Grammaire* had argued that the 'fixed laws' of colour could be taught like music and whose 'grammar' of drawing already co-existed with a 'grammar' of colour, a more and more popular notion as the nineteenth century ended.[4] So colour became the paradigm of visual law, and could also be seen as a language with its own grammatical structures: Chevreul had provided one of the earliest formulations of the idea of colour as a universal language;[5] by the time of the First World War, it had become something of a commonplace, to be set unproblematically beside form in Kandinsky's *On the Spiritual in Art*.[6] To the rather rudimentary colour-systems of the nineteenth century were now added the more nuanced and extensive schemes of Ostwald in Germany and Munsell in the United States, both based on the new techniques of psychological testing for colour-discrimination and thus having some claim to represent 'universal' colour-relationships. Yet the very complexity of these colour-order systems put them beyond the reach of most artists in the early twentieth century and helped in the end to take them away from theory at all.

Ostwald came to colour late in life, at the end of a distinguished career as a physical chemist (having won the Nobel Prize in 1909). He was also an enthusiastic amateur artist who around 1900 became involved with a group of Munich painters, including the society-portraitist Franz von Lenbach, who were anxious about the instability of artists' pigments and might well have welcomed a chemist who had long made his own painting materials into their circle.[7] Ostwald's experience resulted in a small handbook, the *Malerbriefe* (*Letters to a Painter*) of 1904, which advocated an experimental approach to the technique of painting. It seems to have been received rather coolly by artists, apart from the young Klee, who reported to his future wife that it was 'an excellent scientific handling of all technical matters'.[8] (Yet Klee became one of Ostwald's bitterest opponents in later years.) It was an encounter at Harvard in 1905 with Albert Munsell, who had begun his career as a painter in Paris, that turned Ostwald decisively in the direction of the theory of colour, the work which he was to claim, like Goethe, as the highest achievement of his life.[9]

Munsell had recently published his first handbook, *A Colour Notation* (1905), based on a circle of ten colours and a spherical arrangement borrowed from Runge; but, according to Ostwald, he was unable to give an adequate scientific account of its principles, falling back on the notion of 'artistic feeling'. Ostwald spent the next decades attempting to remedy these defects in the essentially empirical earlier systems by applying new techniques of colour-measurement and a mathematical approach to colour-psychology. In 1912 he joined the colour-committee of the Deutsche Werkbund, the architecture and design association which was seeking to introduce a measure of standardization into German industrial design. From this period date his concentration on colour-problems and the spate of publications which was soon to dominate the literature of colour throughout Europe. At the Cologne 'Werkbund' exhibition of 1914 Ostwald arranged a *Farbschau* ('colour-show') of industrial paints and dyes, which he hoped would demonstrate the need for a fundamental, systematic, study of colour principles; from his first handbook, *Die Farbenfibel* (*The Color Primer*, 1916), this is what he set out to do.[10] As well as being a patriot who at the height of the Great War substituted the German botanical terms *kress* and *veil* for the French loan-words *orange* and *violet*, Ostwald was an outspoken Socialist who believed that art was essentially a social product and that the age of individualism must now give way to the age of organization.[11] When works of art seemed to him to offend against the 'laws' of colour harmony he had uncovered, he had no hesitation in 'correcting' them. Although he believed that the Japanese had long had an instinctive sense of 'aesthetic norms', which they applied in architecture and furnishing, he found that certain of their colour prints, based only on empirical studies, did not match his standards of harmonious colouring. He prepared improved versions of them which, he assured his readers, were recognized by connoisseurs to be 'more Japanese' than the originals.[12] This high-handed treatment of much-admired artefacts in the name of science gave Ostwald a certain notoriety in the art world of his day, particularly in the confused aesthetic atmosphere of the Bauhaus in the 1920s. As it happens, his first important effect was felt not in Germany but in Holland, where his ideas were taken up almost immediately by the De Stijl group and where they had a particular impact on one of the first non-representational painters of that movement, Piet Mondrian.

De Stijl

By 1917, when the De Stijl magazine started publication, Mondrian had already proved himself to be a painter of great strength and versatility, having moved over the previous twenty years from tonal landscape painting in the tradition of the Hague School, through Impressionism, Fauvism and a late version of Divisionism to Cubism, always showing a feeling for great simplicity of colour and construction and a preference for symmetrical compositions. Along the way he had encountered a number of theories of colour. His version of Pointillism had little to do with Seurat, since the dune landscapes of 1909 which were its chief vehicle used very large and separated units in a decorative way, with no attempt at optical fusion or the reconstitution of light through contrast. They are like enlarged details of the beach scenes of the Symbolist Jan Toorop, with whom Mondrian was in close touch at this time. As he wrote to a critic, 'I believe it definitely necessary in our period that paint be applied as far as possible in pure colours set next to each other in a pointillist or diffuse manner'.[13] In a speech opening the first exhibition of the Moderne Kunstkring in Amsterdam in 1911 (a modernist art society of which Mondrian was an officer), Toorop called for a spiritually pure style using straight or 'quietly undulating' vertical and horizontal lines, together with 'contrasting complementary colours'.[14] Mondrian's notion of complementarity was a very fluid one: in a sketchbook of about 1914 he mentioned the opposites red (external) and green (internal) in the context of thoughts on the antagonism between the material female and the spiritual male[15] but later he saw yellow and blue as equally opposed to red, as 'inward' to 'outward'[16] and later still he seems to have regarded blue as the most fundamental opposition to red, an opposition already felt in his early *Red Cloud, Red Tree* and *Red Mill* (1907–11).[17]

More important were Toorop's interest in Theosophy and Mondrian's joining of the Dutch Theosophical Society in 1909. The idea of the spiritual content of colours had its origins in Theosophy, for example in the colour charts of Besant and Leadbeater's *Thought Forms* (1901) and *Man Visible and Invisible* (1902), which were translated into Dutch in 1905 and 1903, respectively. Here red was presented as pride, avarice, anger or sensuality, according to its degree of purity; blue as high spirituality, devotion to a noble ideal, or pure religious feeling; yellow as highest intellect and green as sympathy, adaptability or, in its muddiest manifestation, selfishness. These values were represented most directly by Mondrian in *Evolution* (1910–11), a triptych showing the awakening of a woman to spiritual enlightenment in three stages. On the left the woman, whose abundant hair suggests that she is still close to nature, is painted in a bluish green which according to the Theosophical chart signifies 'religious feeling tinged with fear'. The flowers which flank her head are the turbid ochery red of anger or sensuality and their centres the black of malice. In the second stage, on the far right, her body has become a bluish violet, perhaps the purple of 'devotion mixed with affection'; her hair is more restrained and the flowers have become six-point stars, white in their triangular centres, then pale yellow, then darker yellow ('strong intellect'), then a palish blue-green. The yellow stars are evidence of 'an attempt to attain an intellectual conception of cosmic order'.[18] In the final stage, the elevated centrepiece of the triptych, the initiate has opened her eyes which, like her body, are a bright blue; her hair is a set of luminous triangles and the flowers are now white triangles on white circles against a bright yellow ground: she is like Theoclea, priestess of Delphi in one of Mondrian's favourite Theosophical texts, Edouard Schuré's *Les Grands Initiés* (*The Great Initiates*, 1889), who, in the presence of Pythagoras, was

> visibly becoming transformed beneath the thought and will of the master as by a slow incantation. Standing in the midst of the astonished elders, she untied her raven-black locks and thrust them back from her head as though she felt flames of fire playing in and about them. Her eyes, transfigured and wide open, seemed to behold the solar and planetary gods in their radiant glowing orbs.[19]

This was Mondrian's most explicitly theosophical painting. It was also the last occasion when he seems to have believed that women were capable of spirituality: in his later thought – probably under the influence of Italian Futurism – the female was essentially the tragic, sensual, natural element in the world order which must be brought into balance by the intellectual and spiritual activity of the male. Nevertheless, her characteristic red played a major role in a group of his paintings around 1921 and again around 1930.

Mondrian soon became disenchanted with the 'astral colours' of Theosophy because they were not 'real'[20] but Schuré had offered him a far more manageable set than Besant and Leadbeater. Just as the alchemists of the later Middle Ages had drawn on the Christian myths to lend plausibility to their ideas, so the Theosophists of the nineteenth century looked to the natural sciences for confirmation of their own conceptions of matter and often found just what they were seeking. The early nineteenth-century industrial chemist K. L. Reichenbach, for example, had conducted experiments with sensitive subjects – mainly women – which showed him that they were able to see magnetic forces in perfect darkness and that these forces were manifested as red, yellow and blue lights, sometimes undulating with a vibratory movement.[21] Red, yellow and blue were, of course, still the most widely accepted set of primary colours; Mondrian made them, in a very desaturated form, the basis of a number of his Cubist compositions of 1914, planned and sometimes executed in Paris, notably *Oval Composition*.

Primary colour

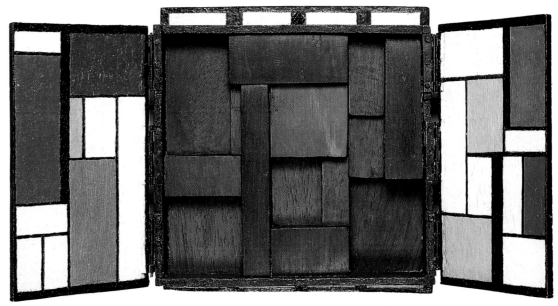

200

199

Colour theory began to assume the imperative tone of an ideology among some early modernists. Yet even within the Dutch De Stijl group, whose members were especially concerned with 'primary' colour around 1920, there was no firm consensus on what it might be. Rietveld (**199**) opted for red, yellow, blue, thinking that this triad was the basis of colour-vision; Mondrian (**201**), under the influence of Ostwald (pl. 205), felt the need for green, which he sometimes elided with yellow, while Vantongerloo in this triptych (**200**) chose to use a quasi-Newtonian spectral series.

199 GERRIT RIETVELD, *Red-Blue Chair*, *c*. 1923 (painted version)
200 GEORGES VANTONGERLOO, *Triptiech (Triptych)*, 1921
201 PIET MONDRIAN, *Composition C*, 1920

201

202

Colour as system

202 Illustration of 'film color', from Josef Albers, *Interaction of Color*, 1963 (XVII–1)
203 *Advancing and Retiring Colors*, from Emily C. Noyes Vanderpoel, *Color Problems. A Practical Manual . . .* , 1902
204 Goethe-triangle, Barry Schactman and Rackstraw Downes after Carry van Biema, from Josef Albers, *Interaction of Color*, 1963 (XXIV–1)
205 WILHELM OSTWALD, *Section through the colour-solid*, from Josef Albers, *Interaction of Color*, German ed. 1973 (XXIV–2)
206 JOSEF ALBERS, *Homage to the Square*, 1950

203

Ostwald's colour-solid (**205**) was one of the first diagrams to emphasize the material, repeatable quality of the coloured units, thereby suggesting they might be copied and used directly by painters and designers. He cut out the units from coloured paper, a method of colour-experimentation taken up by Josef Albers, who published silkscreen reproductions of cut-paper arrangements made mainly by his students.

204

One of these (**202**) deals with 'film-color' (a term for transparency adopted by D. Katz in *The World of Colour*, 1930) while the other (**204**), a triangle, embodies the expressive colour chords which Albers attributed to Goethe. Albers's long series of paintings *Homage to the Square* (**206**) was based on these school-exercises, but goes far beyond mere textbook illustration (**203**) in creating colour dynamics through spatial articulation.

Farbton 1

Farbton 13

205

206

Decoration and expression

Early abstract painters were particularly concerned to increase the expressive, as against the merely decorative qualities of colour. Balla's experiments with the dynamics of colour contrast were, however, themselves conducted in the context of a commission for interior decoration (**207**). Sonia Delaunay's applied arts, such as this bedspread for her son (**209**), had a decisive impact on her own painting as well as that of her husband Robert Delaunay – characterized as *Simultané* because of the central importance of simultaneous contrasts of colour. Robert Delaunay's *Disc* series of 1913, however (**208**), uses descriptive forms for sun and moon, showing that at this stage he was still interested in the expressive power of the subject, rather than depending solely on colour.

207 Giacomo Balla, *Iridescent Interpenetrations No. 13*, 1912
208 Robert Delaunay, *Sun, Moon, Simultané I*, 1913
209 Sonia Delaunay, *Patchwork coverlet*, 1911

209

The materiality of colour

210 Helen Frankenthaler,
Mountains and Sea, 1952
211 Morris Louis, *Golden Age*, 1959
212 Mark Rothko, *Orange Yellow
Orange*, 1969

210

American painters in the 1950s were particularly anxious to explore new technical possibilities. Helen Frankenthaler used thin oil paints on unprimed duck (**210**), and stimulated Morris Louis (**211**) and Kenneth Noland (**213**) to find synthetic (acrylic) staining colours which would work better with this transparent technique on a large scale. Rothko (**212**) also experimented with degrees of transparency, using unpredictable mixtures of oil, thinners and egg tempera, which have sometimes led to a rapid deterioration in his paintings.

254

211

The shape of colour

Noland and Davis both followed Albers (pl. 206) in searching for a 'neutral' form which would allow their colour free rein. They felt they had found it in stripe painting, a type of abstraction widely practised in the 1960s. Yet the regular repeats and hard edges of this motif inevitably affect our perception of the colours by simultaneous and successive contrast; and this ultimate colouristic style of painting shows us that, as in the past, colour and form are inseparable.

213

213 KENNETH NOLAND, *2-1964*
214 GENE DAVIS, *Limelight/Sounds of Grass*, 1960

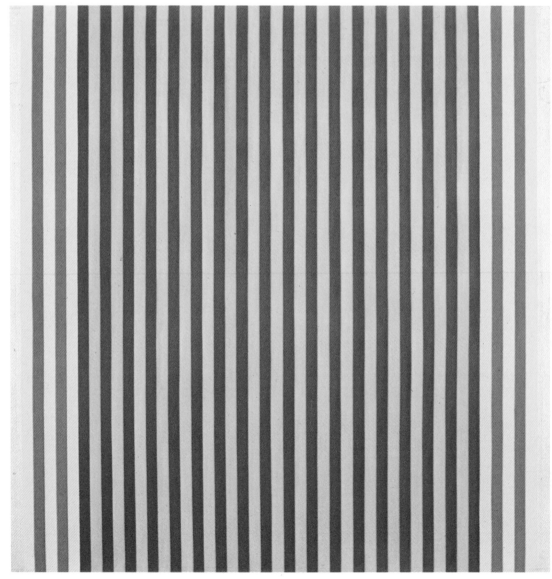

214

His interest in this set was strengthened when, having returned to Holland during the Great War, he worked at the village of Laren near Amsterdam and met a former Theosophist, M. H. J. Schoemmackers, and the painter Bart van der Leck. Schoenmaekers, an ex-priest, was promoting a movement he called Christosophie; he had already published *Mensch en Natuur: een mystische Levensbeschouwing* (*Man and Nature: a Mystical Contemplation*, 1913), which included a table of cosmic movements presenting man as the vertical and architectural and woman as the horizontal and musical.[22] He was now engaged on a book, *Het Nieuwe Wereldbeeld* (*The New World Image*, 1915), which sought to reconcile positivism and mysticism in a way particularly congenial to Mondrian. In it he argued that red, yellow and blue were the only colours, since all the others derived from them. Yellow was the vertical movement of the light-ray itself: it was expansive and moved towards the spectator, aspiring to be the middle point of spatial movement. Blue was the opposite colour to yellow, soft, supple and retiring, horizontal like the firmament. Red was the uniting of yellow and blue in an 'inner' way, unlike their common mixture, which produced green. Pure red had the radial movement of life, visual art and volume: it did not jump forward but hovered – like Mondrian's 1907 *Red Cloud* – before the horizontal blue expanse. The joy of colour was the joy of mankind striving towards higher things, the light in which all colour is contained.[23] Although Schoenmaekers mentioned that he found Goethe's ideas 'rather vague', his debt to them is clear. Mondrian, who quoted Schoenmaekers's *New World Image* in his own pamphlet of 1920, 'Die Nieuwe Beelding in de Schilderkunst' (Neo-Plasticism in Painting), also noted Goethe's view that 'colour is troubled light'.[24]

He wrote:

> Reduction to primary colour leads to the visual internalization of the material, to a purer manifestation of light. *The material, the corporeal* (through its *surfaces*) causes us to see colourless sunlight as natural colour. Colour then arises from *light* as well as from the *surface*, the *material*. Thus natural colour is *inwardness* (light) in its most outward manifestation. Reducing natural colour to primary colour changes the most outward manifestation of colour back to the most inward. If, of the three primary colours, yellow and blue are the most inward, if red (the union of blue and yellow – see Dr H. [*sic*] Schoenmaekers, *The New World Image*) is more outward, then a painting in yellow and blue alone would be more inward than a composition in the three primary colours.

He was here modifying Schoenmaekers's Goethean view of red as the supreme colour in the light of his earlier Theosophical experience; in due course they fell out and he was soon to claim that the Dutch Christosophist was far less important to him than the founder of the Theosophical Society, Madame Blavatsky.[25]

In 1916 Mondrian's belief in the primacy of red, yellow and blue was strengthened by his meeting with Bart van der Leck, who had a background in the applied arts and also believed that these were the colours expressive of light.[26] Early that year van der Leck had begun to reduce his palette to the three saturated primaries plus black and white; under the influence of Mondrian's 'plus and minus' paintings of 1915, he decomposed his flat figures into groups of coloured lines, calling them simply 'compositions'.[27] Mondrian and van der Leck were very close at this time but that the older painter did not at once adopt the younger's 'pure' primaries was almost certainly due to the arrival in Holland, and in this circle, of another impressive approach to the question of primary colour, that of Ostwald.

The *Farbenfibel* of Ostwald seems to have been introduced to the De Stijl circle by the Hungarian painter and designer Vilmos Huszár. He gave it an appreciative review in the journal *De Stijl* in August 1918, arguing that at last an objective way of checking subjective colour-impressions had been found and that the geometry of formal design could now be matched by a geometry of colour.[28] In his article Huszár published a Dutch version of Ostwald's colour circle of a hundred hues but it is not clear whether this came from a Dutch edition: his own copy was the second German edition of 1917. It is unlikely that Huszár had encountered Ostwald's work before the end of that year: a letter of September outlining a simple theory of three primaries and three secondaries, plus black and white, shows no sign of its impact.[29] But a number of works of 1918, now known only in photographs, suggest that the painter had by then discovered the German theorist and was anxious to put his ideas into practice. Two compositions with colour-planes, *3 Klank+ = 3K met Zwart* (*Colour-chord with 3 Tones+ = 3 Tones with Black*) and *4 Klank* (*Colour-chord with 4 Tones*), have titles including terms derived from Ostwald, and the colour-circle in Huszár's copy of *Die Farbenfibel* has a moveable equilateral triangle improvised by him which allowed him to plot the triads of 'harmonious' hues.[30] The *Colour-chord with 4 Tones* would presumably have given him the opportunity to include four primaries, for Ostwald was a follower of Hering and gave an unusually large place to green in his system, although this was hardly appreciable in his very simplified circle of 1916.[31] More significant was Huszár's experimentation with grey, since Ostwald's single most important contribution to the theory of colour was his notion of grey as a colour and of the grey content of all colours, which guaranteed their harmonious juxtaposition. In 1918 Huszár painted a composition entirely in grey planes.[32] To judge from the photograph, one of the lost paintings of 1918 seems to be made up of more than a hundred small rectangles of colour applied to the picture-surface rather as Ostwald applied rectangles of tinted paper to his diagrams.[33] Even if it was not made in this way, it seems to give clear evidence that a new, systematic type of colour-plane painting was being made possible by the publication of a colour-theory for artists of a wholly new order of subtlety.

Ostwald became something of a cult-figure in De Stijl: the journal announced his new publications and promised (but failed) to review them,[34] although in 1920 it did reprint an article on colour-harmony in which he announced that he had constructed a colour-organ.[35] But what effect did his ideas have on the most considerable of the De Stijl painters, Piet Mondrian? As usual, it is not easy to say.

On the face of it, Mondrian's handling of colour in 1917 and 1918 shows some striking parallels with Ostwald's doctrines. He was mixing a good deal of white with his three 'primary' colours in the earliest of his colour-plane paintings, in order to unite them tonally and, it seems, to keep them as closely tied as possible to the plane of the picture. These paintings were

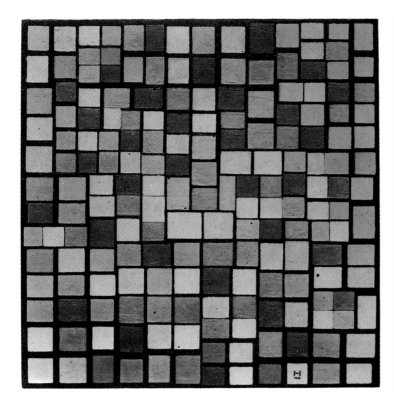

The grid (borrowed from experimental psychology) became widely interesting to non-representational artists around 1920, and Vilmos Huszár's *Composition*, 1918, is one of the earliest to be based on it. The painting is known only from this black and white photograph, but it appears to be made of cut-out rectangles glued to a backing, the same technique Ostwald used to prepare his colour scales (see pl. 205). (215)

themselves, in their use of large rectangles and, most important, in their, for Mondrian, quite novel asymmetry, very close to Huszár's experiments in these years.[36] Yet the two artists do not seem to have had any direct contact until June 1918, when Huszár visited Mondrian, who was surprised to find how close their approaches were.[37] In 1918 Mondrian had also begun a series of grey paintings, notably *Lozenge with Grey Lines*, and he continued to use grey as a prominent 'colour' until the mid-1920s, including many different values of it in his early Neo-Plastic compositions. In his discussion of colour in *De Stijl* in 1918, he somewhat eccentrically regarded grey as part of his basic set of six colours since, 'just as yellow, blue and red can be mixed with white and remain *basic colour*, so can black' – a view which simply revived but did not solve the ancient problem of what to do with the non-chromatic colours.[38] His argument in favour of very desaturated primaries owed nothing to Ostwald: defending these pale colours against van Doesburg's criticisms early in 1919, Mondrian argued that they were close to nature because the time was not yet ripe for full primary statements: 'I use those mute colours *for the time being*, adjusting to present-day surroundings and the world; this does not mean that I would not prefer a pure colour.'[39]

Mondrian's detailed knowledge of Ostwald must remain doubtful; he had not read Huszár's review by September 1918, although the Hungarian had assured him that his (Mondrian's)

painting accorded with Ostwald's principles. Mondrian told van Doesburg that 'one day' he would read it but, although we know he discussed Ostwald's ideas of harmony with the sculptor-painter Georges Vantongerloo in Paris in 1920, it is by no means certain how much he really knew.[40] Two paintings of 1919, *Composition: Chequerboard, Light Colours* and *Composition: Chequerboard, Dark Colours*, do however suggest a strong influence from the colour theorist. Each painting has a rectangular grid of 256 squares filled with an irregular arrangement of colours: in the first, pale primaries plus several greys and in the second blue, a rather bluish red and a hot orange which Mondrian described in the 1920s as 'old gold'.[41] The regular grid was a figure which had been introduced into the repertory of 'Gestalt' studies in 1900 by the Berlin psychologist F. Schumann;[42] it betrays a clear interest in system and we might almost imagine that Mondrian chose his values in these cases from the upper and lower cones of Ostwald's colour-solid.

205

Perhaps the best evidence that Mondrian felt obliged to come to terms with the Ostwaldian ideas circulating among the members of De Stijl around 1920 was his attitude to green. Green, with its indissoluble association with nature, came to be anathema to him, as it was already to Kandinsky; there are many anecdotes of the Dutch painter's manoeuverings to avoid having to look out of the window at fields or trees.[43] Yet in a number of paintings of this date he used a distinctly greenish yellow or even an apple-green as his third primary, as if he wanted somehow to accommodate Ostwald's primary yellow *and* green. We have seen that since Antiquity yellow and green had rarely been clearly distinguished; the psychological techniques of Mondrian's own day had also uncovered marked confusions of interpretation in this area of the spectrum.[44] Mondrian's notion of primariness was as fluid as his notion of opposites: as late as 1919 he was still able to describe a lozenge painting (now lost) as 'ochre and grey'.[45] Not until the 1920s did he seek a categorically 'pure' red, and found, as had so many painters before him, that he could only achieve his aim by glazing a bluish transparent pigment such as crimson over an opaque orange-red, such as vermilion.[46]

201

Although the idea of the primaries was so prominent in De Stijl, in this as in so much else there was little agreement among the individuals as to the meaning of the term. We have seen that both Mondrian and van der Leck thought of the primaries as three and that they were, in some sense, the constituents of light; we have also seen that Huszár moved, after reading Ostwald, from a three-colour to an infinite number theory. When van Doesburg read his copy of the *Farbenfibel* he noted in the margin that Ostwald's four colours were 'Rubbish', since in fact there were only three primary, three secondary and three non-colours. In spite of the more economical scheme, without secondaries, which he presented in his Bauhaus Book, *Grundbegriffe der neuen gestaltenden Kunst* (*Principles of Neo-Plastic Art*, 1925), he continued to use all nine, both in his painting and decorative work, until his death in 1931.[47] The member of the group who perhaps more than any other defined its ethos was the furniture-designer and architect Gerrit Rietveld, who provided its icon, the Red-Blue Chair. Coming as he did from a craft tradition of furniture making, he was equally undoctrinaire about colour. His painted furniture started with nursery

199

pieces and the primary-coloured version of his chair (still sometimes attributed to the early years of De Stijl) does not seem to have been conceived until the time he was working on the Schröder House at Utrecht in 1923 or 1924.[48] More importantly perhaps, Rietveld's developing view of the fundamental character of the three primaries red, yellow and blue, was based on the quite mistaken idea that three receptors in the retina are severally sensitive to each of these colours.[49] They thus represented for him the structure of colour-vision.

The most extravagant of all the De Stijl theories of colour was that promoted by the Belgian Vantongerloo, about whom Mondrian wrote to van Doesburg from Paris in September 1920:

> he has invented an entire system based on the eternity, or rather the unity of the seven colours and the seven tones! ! ! As you know, he uses all seven of them, for goodness sake, just like the rainbow. With his Belgian intellect he has created an operative system which, as I see it, is based on nature. He hasn't the faintest idea of the difference between the *manner of nature* and the *manner of art* . . .[50]

During the period of his early contact with De Stijl, about 1918, Vantongerloo had adopted the canonical three-colour primary palette[51] but during 1920 he had developed a neo-Newtonian theory of harmony (of which a symptom is the description of the purple in *Triptiek* as 'indigo-violet'), which demanded the full gamut of prismatic hues. He seems to have believed that harmony could be achieved by mixing the precise tones and proportions of the prismatic colours to a neutral grey on a spinning disc; it was this which led him to reject Ostwald's non-empirical system of establishing the grey content of his hues.[52] In an article of 1920 Vantongerloo set out his theory of the 'absolute spectrum' (*le spectre de l'absolu*) of light as one stage in the unified spectrum of vibratory phenomena, through sound, heat, light and 'chemical rays'. Red was the first stage of the spectrum of colour, coming immediately after heat, whose vibrations were of a lower frequency; then came blue, then yellow, then indigo-violet, orange, green-blue, blue-indigo, violet, green and indigo, 'the seven [*sic*] colours of the rainbow'. 'The scientific knowledge of colour', said Vantongerloo, 'allows the artist to manifest the ideas of art by means of a pure plasticism quite different from the preceding plasticism' and it allowed him to remain within the domain of colour without introducing anything of 'nature'.[53] Vantongerloo certainly had a non-Newtonian conception of three-dimensional colour-space, for he argued that the artist could work with the scale of a single colour, such as that from red to violet,[54] and in a later essay he gave an account of his painting *Composition in Indigo-Violet* (1921) in which the coloured planes were balanced mathematically to form a unity.[55] In concluding his manifesto of 1920, he admitted disarmingly, 'I know no philosophy and am totally ignorant of science but I do know that art is a product of two processes, of which the one is philosophical: speculation, and the other scientific: empiricism.'[56] Yet he was mathematical enough to supply seven pages of equations sufficiently abstruse, I suspect, to have exhausted the capacities of most of his painter-readers.[57] They remind us that at exactly the same time the very numerate lectures on light and colour by Seurat's former friend Charles Henry, now Director of the Laboratory of the Physiology of Sensations at the Sorbonne, were being presented to a painterly and architectural readership by Le Corbusier's group, L'Esprit Nouveau.[58] Clearly artists in the new age of technology were expected to absorb and use an unprecedentedly large body of colour-information in mathematical terms, and very few were able to do so.

Mondrian, in his utopian way, when he first encountered Vantongerloo's ideas early in 1920 was less perturbed than, as we have seen, he subsequently became. As he wrote to van Doesburg: 'I find his use of purple and the 7 colours a bit premature: perhaps later that can be done. In theory, it can be defended, it even seems to be better.'[59] But he was puzzled by the inconsistencies in Vantongerloo's attitude: if harmony depended upon a balance of *all* the seven spectral colours, how could Vantongerloo refrain from using *all* of them in *all* his paintings, for example in *Triptiek*, where according to an annotated drawing the now yellowish colour was originally 'orange'.[60] In the circle of these early constructivists, as among the members of the Blaue Reiter, we are made acutely aware that a belief in universality based upon standardization and its technology was still no more than an aspiration. As Huszár had written in his article on Ostwald, 'Nothing is more subjective than the reaction to colour, which depends on the nature of the individual.'[61]

200

Colour at the Bauhaus

As we might have expected, Ostwald's work played an even more central role in the colour-culture of modernist Germany. His key position in the Werkbund and his several wartime publications gave him a high public profile; he organized the first of the still-running German Day-Conferences on Colour within the framework of the Werkbund conference at Stuttgart in September 1919. The occasion was remarkable for the bitter debate which developed between Ostwald and his supporters and a group of artists led by the Stuttgart painter and teacher Adolf Hoelzel, who had been one of the earliest non-representational painters in Germany. In a lecture to this conference, Hoelzel stated that he used some fifteen theories of colour in his teaching, including those of Chevreul, Helmholtz, von Bezold, Rood, Brücke and Ostwald himself, all of them reworked theoretically and practically for the benefit of artists. Ostwald's recommendation that hues should be tempered with white, for example, might well suit gouache and pastel but could hardly be used, as Rubens had shown, in oil or tempera. Goethe, said Hoelzel, was the most comprehensive guide, since his system was based on polarity, as was Hoelzel's own, which posited seven types of contrast, of which complementarity was the most important for establishing harmony. Although his scheme of complementaries drew on both von Bezold and Ostwald, Hoelzel argued that the eye must be final arbiter and art and science could never be equal partners in the study of colour. Even Ostwald's own lecture at the conference had shown, he said, that context and lighting played a decisive role which his system did not take into account.[62] Further, in an essay reviewing the controversy Hoelzel argued that the instability of colour-values in various concrete situations, modified by the activity of the eye, was one reason why the art of children and primitive peoples often seemed so much more original and harmonious than the calculated harmonies of the scientists.[63] A group of artists and art-historians around Hoelzel on this occasion petitioned all the German ministries of education to prohibit the use of Ostwald's system and it was indeed banned in Prussia.[64]

Hoelzel's subjectivist views might well have had little influence on the larger course of colour-study outside his immediate circle had not a number of his pupils become students and teachers at the new German institute for the teaching of architecture and design, the Bauhaus, which had been set up in Weimar in spring 1919. The Bauhaus was formed by amalgamating the Weimar Hochschule für bildende Kunst (Academy of Art) and the Kunstgewerbeschule (School of Applied Arts), the latter of which had long been directed by the distinguished Belgian painter and designer Henry van de Velde. Van de Velde, who in the 1880s and 90s had been a Neo-Impressionist painter of some note, had developed at Weimar what he called 'the iron discipline of rational design', arising from 'artistic laws' including those of colour as expounded by Chevreul, Rood, Maxwell and Charles Henry.[65] He organized the programme of the Kunsgewerbeschule in 'workshops and laboratories', entrusting the teaching of colour-theory and ornament, characteristically, to a female assistant. We do not know whether any colour-theory was taught at the Weimar Academy under the painter Fritz Mackesen but Hoelzel at least, in the tradition of Blanc, made no distinction between the theory as applied to the fine and the decorative arts.[66] His pupil Itten carried this attitude into the Bauhaus, where he became one of the first appointees in the summer of 1919.

The founding-director of the Bauhaus, the architect Walter Gropius, had met Itten in Vienna, where after leaving the Hoelzel school in Stuttgart he had opened his own school during the war. Itten now has the reputation of being a mystic – as indeed he seems to have been – and the chief representative of that 'Expressionist' phase of the early Bauhaus which gave way to a more 'Constructivist' orientation after his departure in 1923. But this is to underestimate his efforts to discover – in the wake of Hoelzel – the basic formal vocabulary of art, parti-cularly the grammar of colour, which must have suggested to Gropius that he was just the sort of 'radical artist' he needed for his new institution.[67] Itten's fundamental belief in the harmony of contrasts derived directly from the seven-fold contrasts of Hoelzel's theory, but he added to it an interest in the colour-sphere of Runge, whose scheme was the basis of his own twelve-point colour-star.[68] Runge was also revived at the Bauhaus by another teacher who had been a pupil of Hoelzel, the painter, sculptor and theatre-designer Oskar Schlemmer, and by Klee, both of whom joined the staff in 1920.[69] Both Itten and Klee were hostile to the new colour-system of Ostwald.[70]

As well as trying to attract strong artistic personalities of the avant-garde, Gropius was clearly concerned to find artists who had already shown their capacities as teachers: in addition to Itten, two of his early appointees, the painter Georg Muche and Klee himself, had worked briefly during the War at the Berlin school run by Herwarth Walden, the proprietor of the Sturm gallery and its journal, at this time the chief platform for German Expressionism.[71] But in spite of, perhaps because of,

the importance of the individual Bauhaus artists, it remains very difficult to discover what precisely was taught at the new institution and to whom. It seems that Itten's chief function was to devise and teach the Preliminary Course (*Vorlehre*), the most original and most influential of the Bauhaus's innovations, which was to become obligatory for all students, no matter what their workshop specialization came to be. Although it bore the stamp of Itten's course at Vienna and, of course, of Hoelzel's teaching, the *Vorlehre* seems to have been evolved during 1920: it was first mentioned at a meeting of masters and students in October that year[72] and it first appeared as obligatory in the Prospectus of January 1921. Here, however, it was described as a course in form and materials only; the physical and chemical theory of colour, 'in connection with rationalized methods of painting', was mentioned only under 'supplementary subjects of instruction'.[73] Itten appears to have occupied himself mainly with the study of materials and with drawing, while colour was handled by his assistant Hirschfeld-Mack, the first graduate of the Bauhaus, who had also been a Hoelzel pupil (*see* Chapter 13). Hirschfeld-Mack was chiefly concerned with colour-scales and contrast, using among other things the exercises with cut paper which were to have such an important effect on the teaching methods of Josef Albers.[74] But it is very difficult to distinguish material from the *Vorlehre* from later work: one of Mack's collage demonstrations of colour-form co-ordinates, dated 1922, for example, was apparently made in Kandinsky's *Farbseminar* for more advanced students.[75] Having completed the *Vorlehre*, Bauhaus students proceeded to the various workshops, where Itten, for example, was 'form-master' for sculpture, metal, wall-painting, joinery, glass and weaving (but it is still uncertain precisely what sort of theoretical teaching he undertook in these contexts).[76]

A similar uncertainty surrounds Klee's teaching on colour. His first lecture-series, 'Beiträge zur bildnerische Formlehre' (Contributions to the Theory of Plastic Form), was given in the winter of 1921/2 and did not include any discussion of colour. An expanded series in 1922/3 included two lectures dealing chiefly with colour-dynamics, briefly mentioning the theories of Goethe, Runge, Delacroix and Kandinsky. Klee was at this time form-master in the glass workshop (perhaps occasionally in the book-bindery as well) but the only reference in these lectures to the main work of the Bauhaus is to interior decoration. Here he argued for rooms painted successively in various tones of the complementary pairs, in order to achieve a 'totality' throughout the whole suite – an idea remarkably close to Goethe's decoration of his house at Weimar with a series of successively coloured interiors arranged according to comple-mentary contrast.[77] At Dessau, where the Bauhaus moved in 1925, Klee taught these colour topics as part of a Basic Course (*Grundlehre*) which seems to have been distinct from the *Vorlehre* and which by 1928 at least was being given in the weaving-workshop where Klee was form-master.[78] Klee and Kandinsky were at last able to introduce a programme of imaginative painting classes at Dessau, a move very much against the grain of the original Bauhaus idea; it may well have been in the context of these classes that their ideas about colour were given their fullest rein.

Kandinsky was probably the Bauhaus master most consist-

159

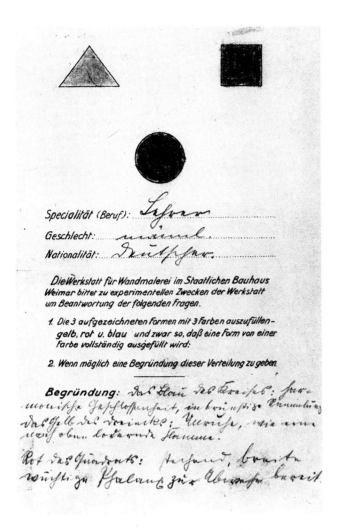

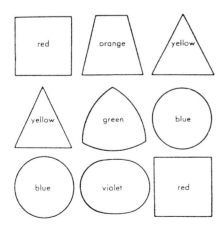

Completed questionnaire for the wall-painting workshop at the Bauhaus, 1923. Alfred Arndt, a student, explains that he has chosen a yellow triangle for its flame-like nature, a red square for its solid yet attacking defensiveness, and a blue circle for its intensely closed, inward-looking quality. (216)

Johannes Itten, a former Bauhaus teacher, correlates the primaries as, the square, red, matter; the triangle, yellow, thought; the circle, transparent blue, spirit in eternal motion. The secondaries are shown as, the trapezoid, orange; the spherical triangle, green; the ellipse, violet. Itten's secondary forms seem as eccentric as those of most theorists. (217)

ently involved in the teaching of colour. He came to the school in 1922, having already elaborated a detailed programme of instruction for the reformed Moscow Institute of Artistic Culture (Inkhuk) after the Revolution of 1917. This programme gave a very prominent place to colour which, according to Kandinsky, must be investigated in the context of physics, physiology, medicine (ophthalmology, chromotherapy, psychiatry), as well as 'the sciences of the occult, where we can find many valuable guidelines in the context of supersensory experiences'.[79] The reference to the occult was dropped at the Bauhaus and Kandinsky's rather shaky grasp of the physics of colour – suggested by his confusion of additive and subtractive mixture in the Moscow programme – was much improved. He developed his Bauhaus 'Colour-Course and Seminar' in the context of the wall-painting workshop, which he took over from Schlemmer on his arrival in 1922. Here, as he put it in a protocol of 1924, colour, as physical and chemical substance and as psychological effect, was the sole 'material' of practice.[80] In an essay for the catalogue of the Bauhaus Exhibition of 1923 Kandinsky stressed again that colour must be examined from the points of view of physics, chemistry, physiology and psychology;[81] it was the last of these aspects, which, as we saw, had informed Kandinsky's study of colour from his Munich years before the War, that provided his most original contribution to the subject at the Bauhaus.

Already in Moscow Kandinsky had taken over the idea of the questionnaire from the experimental psychologists: he had issued for Inkhuk in 1920 a lengthy list of twenty-eight questions aiming to discover 'the root of a general law', which included much on responses to colour: 'which colour is most similar to the singing of a canary, the mooing of a cow, the whistle of the wind, a whip, a man, talent; to a storm, to repulsion, etc.? Can you express through colour your feelings about science and of life etc.?'[82] The list also included a question about 'basic' colours and 'basic' shapes, which is what survived in the far shorter but more widely distributed questionnaire for the wall-painting workshop at the Bauhaus in 1923. Kandinsky had sensed in Munich that yellow was an acute, angular figure, that blue was deep and centripetal and that red, which could be either warm or cool, lay somewhere in between.[83] These hints were codified in an illustration to the Russian version of *On the Spiritual in Art* (1914), into an equation between red and the square, blue as the circle and yellow as the triangle, which had a profound effect on the Russian investigation of colour-form coordinates after the Revolution.[84] But it was also influential in Germany and it may well have been from his reading of Kandinsky's book in 1914 that Itten developed his own set of equivalents.[85] This clearly became part of his Bauhaus teaching: in 1922 one of his pupils, Peter Keler, made a painted cradle for Itten's son using these correspondences. Given that Itten left under a cloud, as a dangerously irrational personality in the institution, it is not surprising that Kandinsky should have attempted to re-establish his scheme on the basis of a scientific experiment. Hirschfeld-Mack recalled that an enormous sample of one thousand cards was sent out 'to a cross section of the community' and that 'an overwhelming majority' opted for the by now standard equivalents.[86] Carelessly, the results were never published, and just as in Moscow the painter Liubov

216

217

Popova had allocated red to her circle and blue to her square,[87] so within the Bauhaus there were several divergences of view. At a discussion between masters and students Klee remarked mischievously that at least the yellow egg-yolk was circular.[88] Schlemmer (who, curiously, had not been sent a questionnaire) also voiced his dissent to a friend and former Hoelzel-pupil Otto Mayer-Amden:

> The consensus, by I do not know how many votes, was: the circle blue, the square red, the triangle yellow. All the experts agree on the yellow triangle, but not on the others. Instinctively I always make the circle red and the square blue. I am not quite sure of Kandinsky's explanation, but it goes something like this: the circle is cosmic, absorbent, feminine, soft; the square is active, masculine. My contrary contention: a red circular surface (a ball) occurs in a positive sense (actively) in nature: the red sun, the red apple (orange), the surface of red wine in a glass. The square does not occur in nature; it is abstract . . . or metaphysical, for which blue is the proper colour . . . And when 'neutrals' free of preconceptions also decide that red = circle and blue = square, I can only ask: why do I paint my circles red? Should I sacrifice my instinct to a rational explanation?[89]

But Kandinsky's scheme was incorporated not only into the decoration and catalogue of the Bauhaus Exhibition of 1923 but also into his Bauhaus Book *Punkt und Linie zu Fläche* (*Point and Line to Plane*, 1926),[90] so that it was a particularly impudent gesture of Schlemmer's to include in his going-away present to Gropius in 1928, a collage entitled *Punkt-linie-fläche (Kandinsky)*, the caption 'the circle is eternally red'.[91] When the Swiss Marxist architect Hannes Meyer came to take over the directorship of the Bauhaus from Gropius, he singled out these ideas about colour and form as symptomatic of the unseriousness of even the Dessau period: for Meyer they were no more than a game, another example of art stifling life.[92]

We cannot be sure which Bauhaus students received the benefit of Kandinsky's views on colour. After Itten's departure he seems to have taken over the colour element of the *Vorlehre*: a timetable of 1923 or 1924 shows that he taught it for only one hour a week, in a class open to all students, including those already in the workshops.[93] At Dessau, under the direction of Moholy-Nagy and Albers, colour is said to have disappeared from the *Vorlehre* altogether[94] but Kandinsky certainly taught a very extended compulsory course, including colour-theory and colour-form-theory to students in their first semester there.[95] And it was at Dessau that he began to introduce the serious discussion of Ostwald.

At Weimar, although Gropius – a leading figure in the Werkbund since before the War – made a brief reference to Ostwald's (and Runge's) colour-order system in the catalogue of the 1923 Exhibition (which apparently showed them side-by-side in the Bauhaus foyer),[96] his work had hardly been taken on board. Kandinsky, for example, still used the six-colour complementary circle favoured by most of his colleagues.[97] However, at Dessau Ostwald's presence came to be increasingly felt, he was invited to lecture in 1927 and his lectures provided a framework for not uncritical discussion in Kandinsky's colour-course.[98] Ostwald's system was advertised in 1928 as forming the basis of colour-teaching in the course on lettering run by Joost Schmidt; a version of his twenty-four-part circle hung in the wall-painting workshop when it was directed by Hinnerk Scheper.[99] Even Klee was investigating the Ostwaldian arrangement around 1930[100] and in 1931 the chemist became one of the directors of the Circle of Friends of the Bauhaus.[101] After the closure of the Dessau Bauhaus in 1932, its successor, which opened briefly in Berlin under Mies van der Rohe, also gave a good deal of attention to colour, including its chemistry and psychology and even perhaps its 'psycho-technology', since Kandinsky was still professor for 'artistic design' as well as 'free painting'. But we know nothing of the details.[102]

This outline of the colour-interests in the Bauhaus is far from comprehensive. In particular I have omitted some of the more marginal manifestations of Bauhaus colour-ideas, such as the several theatrical events mounted by Schlemmer, Kurt Schmidt, Moholy-Nagy and Kandinsky, and the activities at Weimar of Gertrud Grunow, who arrived in 1921 at the behest of Itten to teach a type of eurhythmics which depended on the unified laws of colour and sound. One of her pupils recalled:

> The student had to stand with outstretched arms, close his eyes, and concentrate on a colour of the spectrum 'Don't think about it, feel it, be permeated by it, eradicate everything else. When you have it, then go on to the next colour.' Miss Grunow claimed to know intuitively whether or not the student had really experienced the colour. 'That's not it', she would cry, 'do it over again.' There were actually some who believed her, just as she probably believed in herself, but most of us were sceptical.[103]

I have tried to show that scepticism was not confined to these more eccentric activities but affected the central teachings of the institution as well.

At no time, therefore, during the short but tortuous history of the Bauhaus, except perhaps at its close, was there a coherent view of the nature and functioning of colour among its teachers and most students must have come away with a very confused idea of its significance. Only Kandinsky seems to have been prepared to take on board the most recent developments of colour-order systems in his research into the psychology of perception, and even he remained thoroughly eclectic in his sources. For his colleagues the systematic study of colour seemed to have stopped essentially in the mid-nineteenth century, before the complications introduced by Helmholtzian and Maxwellian science. This lack of coherence and eclecticism was to have a profound effect after the Bauhaus. In the United States, it affected the resistance to theory as manifested in the work of Josef Albers, who had been one of the longest surviving students and teachers at the Bauhaus and who now sought to replace theory with a thoroughgoing empiricism.

Empiricism in Italy and France

In his autobiography, Ostwald described how his understanding of the harmony of colours had come to him while he was preparing the plates for the *Farbenatlas* (*Colour Atlas*) of 1918: the complementary colours of equal value he now found beautiful in themselves, although until that moment he had considered harmony to reside in the balance of tonal values alone.[106] Thus even the mathematician showed himself to be an empiricist and indeed, ever since Chevreul's 'méthode *a posteriori*', empiricism had been a prominent component of scientific colour-theory throughout Europe. It was to become even more prominent among artists in the twentieth century, as the scientific approach to colour, with its increasing emphasis on standardization and quantification, became less and less attractive to them. One of the most comprehensive of the early twentieth-century handbooks for artists was Gaetano Previati's *Principi scientifici del divisionismo* (*Scientific Principles of Divisionism*, 1906), which, despite its title, was the attempt of a painter to win back the initiative from the natural scientists.[105] In his theory of 'Divisionism', the Italian version of French Neo-Impressionism, Previati none the less drew heavily on Rood and Brücke, who were, indeed, practically the most recent authorities cited by him, more than thirty years after they had first been published. The painter felt, predictably, that the scientists had given far too little emphasis to shadow as a positive element in painting. He also made an interesting distinction between the effects of *successive* contrast, created by the eye's restless scanning of a scene, which because of the relative feebleness of means the artist must paint into the picture, and the effects of *simultaneous* contrast, which are equally powerful in nature and in art.[106]

This second conclusion was a radical advance on nineteenth-century attitudes; perhaps the first artist to take it seriously was the Italian Futurist Giacomo Balla, who had been involved with Divisionism about 1910–12 and whose *Street Lamp*, which may be as late as 1912, was the starting point for a series of colour-studies for a scheme of decoration painted in Düsseldorf between 1912 and 1914.[107] Some thirty studies of these 'Iridescent Interpenetrations' in watercolour and in oil have survived. They show, as Balla himself wrote to his family from Germany, the results of 'an infinity of tests and re-tests': an empirical method which produced an astonishing series of hard-

207

edged geometric designs of an unprecedented optical activity.[108] But although some of them were painted in oil on canvas and exhibited in 1913, Balla does not seem to have conceived of them as independent pictures; they had very little effect on his later style as an easel painter or even on his designs for Diaghilev's abstract accompaniment to Stravinsky's *Fireworks*, staged in Rome in 1917. Their optical force, due to the juxtaposition of repeated hard-edged forms in contrasting hues, notably the 'modern' complementaries blue and yellow,[109] was to be developed only by the Op artists of the 1960s.

Previati's *Principi* was published in French in 1910[110] and was probably noticed soon after this by Robert Delaunay, who in an essay on light two years later used the Italian term 'divisionniste' rather than the more usual French 'Néo-Impressionniste', or 'pointilliste'.[111] Like Balla, Delaunay may have derived his interest in using the motif of the window as a vehicle for exploring the effects of light and transparency from Previati. In a series of some twenty-two *Windows* painted between 1911 and 1913, he moved from a style using a mosaic of brightly coloured touches in a tidied-up Divisionist manner (*Window on the Town No. 3*) to the more broadly modulated, Cubist-like colour planes, sometimes with sharply juxtaposed edges and much play with semi-transparent scumbles over a light ground or over other colours.[112] The dominant colouration of this series is in contrasts of orange-yellow, purple and blue-green, unusual combinations which suggest a knowledge of Rood's circle.[113] But as late as the end of 1912 or early 1913 Delaunay was disinclined to accept the suggestion of Franz Marc that he worked in a scientific manner:

> I am mad about the forms of colours but I do not look for a scholastic explanation of them . . . None of the finite sciences have anything to do with my technique [*métier*] of moving towards light. My only science is choosing among the impressions which light in the universe offers to my craftsmanly awareness [*conscience*], and which I try to group together by giving them an order, and an adequate life in representation . . .[114]

Delaunay's flattening of the coloured patches in these paintings, and their heightened contrasts, may well have been stimulated by the work of his Russian wife, Sonia Delaunay-Terk, whose painterly origins in Fauvism had given her a vivid sense of the behaviour of bright colours even more extensive than his, schooled as it was in the later traditions of Neo-Impressionism.[115] In 1911 Sonia Delaunay had made a collage-like patchwork coverlet for their baby, the first of a series of works in paper collage and other media using sharp juxtapositions of flat areas of colour. The violets, yellows and dull greens of this textile may be related to the palette of Robert's later *Windows* but its most important feature is its patchwork of forms, which recurs in the later collages of 1912 and 1913.[116] Sonia claimed that this coverlet was the start of a series of experiments with a 'cubist conception' in other objects of applied art and in paintings;[117] but she always maintained that she worked intuitively, and that it was her husband who was the 'scientist': 'My life was more physical', she recalled in 1978, 'he would think a lot, while I would always be painting. We agreed in many ways, but there was a fundamental difference. His attitude was more scientific than mine when it came to pure

139

209

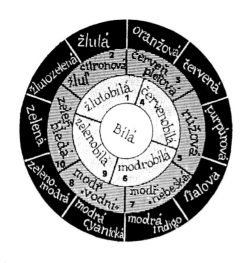

KEY
1 warm white
2 lemon-yellow
3 flesh pink
4 light pink
5 pink
6 cool white
7 light blue
8 sea-blue
9 green-white
10 light green

The Czech painter Frantisek Kupka made this version of Newton's colour wheel about 1910. He arranges orange, red, purple, violet, indigo, blue, green-blue, green, yellow-green and yellow, clockwise from the top around the perimeter, and their modifications circling white at the centre. It was an interest in colour-theory which led him to pioneer the emancipation of colour from any descriptive role, possibly inspiring the similar develoment in the work of Robert Delaunay (pl. 208). Kupka went on to paint a series of canvases with the title 'Discs of Newton' (now in Paris and Philadelphia). (219)

painting, because he would search for justification of theories.'[118] But it was clearly only a difference of degree and the concept of simultaneity (*simultané*) which both Robert and Sonia used to characterize their style of 1912–13 – a concept of going back, of course, to the 'simultaneous contrast' of Chevreul but now given a more practical inflection in the context of easel-painting by Previati – was based essentially on experimentation. In Robert's work the most conspicuous example of this is clearly *Disc*, a painting traditionally given to 1912 and set at the beginning of the series *Circular Forms*, but almost certainly to be placed at the end of this series, late in 1913.[119] *Disc* is, in fact, the most radical embodiment of a conception of colour-movement that Robert was developing in the summer of 1913: he argued at the time that complementary contrasts produced slow movements and 'dissonances' (colours close to each other on the diagrammatic circle) fast ones.[120] We might then imagine that in *Disc* the radial movement outwards from the red-blue centre is slow towards the top right, for example, and faster towards the top left, and that the concentric movements are also sometimes slow (blue-orange) and some-times fast (blue-green). But in the fullest account of this work, written more than twenty years later, Delaunay described red and blue together as 'extra-rapid', so that it is not at all certain what scheme of complementarity he had in mind: neither Chevreul's nor Rood's can be in question. Indeed, as the repeated changes in parts of the canvas show, *Disc* was far from being a systematic, *a priori* conception.[121]

Although its radical abstraction has made *Disc* the most important ancestor of 'optical' painting, it does not seem to have been thought of as an autonomous work of art until Robert Delaunay exhibited it in 1922. A version was shown at the Berlin 'Herbstsalon' in the autumn of 1913, as a backdrop to a

piece of painted sculpture, now destroyed; a very similar composition was placed among the discs in a large painting, *Homage to Blériot*, exhibited the following year.[122] In 1912 and 1913 Delaunay was resisting the interpretation of his paintings as abstractions by German artists such as Klee: he saw his work grounded in nature, which is clearly manifested in the 'representational' distinctions made between sun and moon in the *Disc* series of 1913.[123] The evocation of the intense energy of the sun by jagged and fragmented shapes and the introduction of the dynamic helical form, which was to be developed by Delaunay in the more truly non-representational works of the 1920s, suggest that he had not yet been able to represent, or even conceive of, movement in terms of 'pure' colour. That he had indeed done so was a myth which, impelled by his own later commentaries, has continued to shape the understanding of non-representational colouristic painting until our own times.

Empiricism as theory

The empirical attitudes and the vagueness or confusion of theory in Balla and Delaunay was developed in the most far-reaching way by Josef Albers, in whose hands empiricism became itself a theory. Albers had joined the Bauhaus as a student in 1920; by 1922 he was working as a journeyman in the new glass-painting workshop, with Klee as form-master; soon afterwards he began to teach the practical study of materials on the *Vorlehre*, which, as Professor, he co-directed with Moholy-Nagy on the move to Dessau in 1925. He stayed at the Bauhaus until it was finally closed in 1933. We saw that colour played very little part in Albers's Bauhaus teaching, although he made a liberal use of it in his glass assemblages at Weimar and at Dessau in his flashed and sand-blasted glass panels.[124] It was not, it seems, until he emigrated to the United States in 1933, to teach at Black Mountain College in North Carolina, that Albers began to investigate the properties of colour in any systematic way. His work at Black Mountain was the background to the longest series of colour-experiments, *Homage to the Square*, which began in 1950, the year Albers transferred to Yale University, and continued until his death in 1976. This series, in its turn, was to stimulate and shape the most important of his publications and the most influential as well as the most beautiful of modern books on colour, *Interaction of Color* (published in 1963 and in a short paperback version in 1971).

Albers's approach to colour drew on ideas which had been presented to him over many years. His preference for working with cut paper, which 'being a homogeneous material, permits us to return to precisely the same tint or shade again and again', recalls the collage exercises practised at his earliest art-school in Bottrup in Germany before the First World War, as well as Hirschfeld-Mack's methods at the Bauhaus.[125] The notion of expressive colour-chords – based on the various groupings of hues in a nine-part colour-triangle, the first of his systems and theories, which Albers called the 'Goethe-Triangle' – derives through Hirschfeld-Mack from the teaching of Hoelzel.[126] Most important of all, the sort of psychological texts introduced by Kandinsky into his courses at the Dessau Bauhaus included, for example, the problem of the extreme relativity of colour sensations and the failure of the mind to make correct

208

206

202 204

204 207

judgments about colour, as well as the phenomenology of transparency, which increasingly informed Albers's colour-work in the 1930s and came to play a large part in his book.[127]

Yet, although Albers claimed that it was his feeling that Ostwald's theory was inadequate for the artist which led him to an intensive engagement with colour at Black Mountain College, so that we might expect that he was determined to replace it,[128] in the event he kept theory very much at a distance, writing at the beginning of *Interaction*, 'This book . . . does not follow an academic conception of "theory and practice". It reverses this order and places practice before theory, which, after all, is the conclusion of practice.'[129] This conception was very congenial to a tradition of 'learning by doing' deeply rooted in American educational theory since the work of Liberty Tadd around 1900.[130] But the anti-theoretical stance had also been naturalized in the context of the American avant-garde by Alfred Stieglitz, who had launched his New York gallery An American Place in 1929 with something like an anti-manifesto:

> *No* formal press views
> *No* cocktail parties
> *No* special invitations
> *No* advertising
> *No* institution
> *No* isms
> *No* theories
> *No* games being played
> *Nothing* asked of anyone who comes
> *No anything* on the walls except what *you see there* . . .[131]

Such a way of negation became something of a litany for American modernists after the Second World War and Albers was prominent among them. In an interview about his *Homage to the Square* in 1950 he protested that he used 'No smock, no skylight, no studio, no palette, no easel, no brushes, no medium, no canvas, no variation in texture or *matière*, no personal handwriting, no stylization, no tricks, no twinkling of the eyes. I want to make my work as neutral as possible.'[132] In this yearning for neutrality, influential as it became, Albers showed most clearly how inadequate his conceptual framework was to account for the power of his paintings.

It was not simply that his account of Goethe's theory, or of the Weber-Fechner law – that an arithmetical progression in perceptions requires a geometrical progression in the stimuli – which he illustrated with one of Klee's most brilliant water-colours of 1921, betrayed a rather slight acquaintance with the literature.[133] After all, he told an interviewer, 'I don't care to be scientific, and explore all the possibilities'.[134] More important than this, Albers seems to have believed that the demonstrations of colour dynamics, both in his paintings and in *Interaction of Color*, functioned independently of form. This is the more surprising in that his own painting of the 1930s and 40s frequently used soft contours, quite unlike the hard edges of his later work, and he must have been aware of the powerful colouristic effects in the large-scale and soft-edged paintings of Mark Rothko and Morris Louis, for example, in the 1950s and early 1960s.

By around 1950 colour had become for Albers what he called 'autonomic';[135] he articulated this idea especially in the context

Albers reproduced Paul Klee's watercolour *Hanging Fruit* of 1921 in *Interaction of Color* (1963) to illustrate the Weber-Fechner law that equal perceptual steps must be the result of a geometrical progression (1,2,4,8...), rather than an arithmetical progression (1,2,3,4...). (220)

of *Homage to the Square*: 'For me, color is the means of my idiom. It's automatic. I'm not paying "homage to a square". It's only the dish I serve my craziness about color in.'[136] The square was neutral and in particular static: it had no movement of its own until it was brought to life by colour.[137] But if we compare Albers's *Homage* format of nesting squares with a square diagram of 'Advancing and Retiring Colours', we can see that the painter has already set up a very pronounced asymmetrical movement by setting the squares close to each other at the bottom of his frame; in some cases he even created a much more traditional sense of perspectival recession by 'mitering' the corners.[138] The architect Buckminster Fuller watched Albers's class at Black Mountain making exercises with 'squares within squares' in 1948 and recognized that 'the varying band widths were proportional to the magnitude of any one given color's

265

juxtapositional properties, as those brought out certain scientifically predictable and intuitively sensed harmonious effects.' But Albers seems to have wanted to exclude any sense of predictability, of hypothesis, from his account of the functioning of this powerful *Gestalt*.[139] Everything was left to empirical test.

In this he was followed by one of his most successful pupils at Black Mountain, Kenneth Noland, who came in the 1960s to be an early member of the group loosely known as the Washington

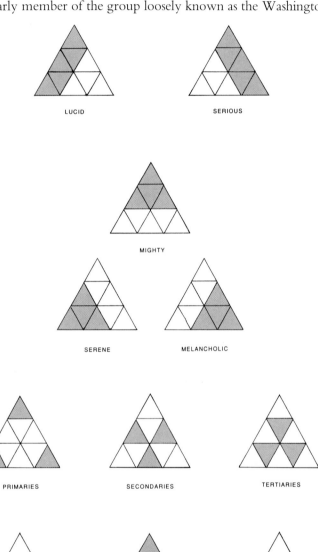

LUCID　　　　　　　SERIOUS

MIGHTY

SERENE　　　　　　MELANCHOLIC

PRIMARIES　　　SECONDARIES　　　TERTIARIES

COMPLEMENTARIES WITH THEIR MIXTURES WHICH ARE DOMINATED BY THEIR PRIMARIES

Josef Albers's 'expressive colour combinations' (*Interaction of Color*, 1963) divided the 'Goethe Triangle' (pl. 207) into eight smaller triangles which could be grouped in various regular ways to demonstrate 'expressive' colour chords. (221)

Color-Field Painters. Noland sought to distance himself from Albers, whom he characterized as 'too much a scientist',[140] but he was nevertheless profoundly affected by the German master's colour ideas. Like Albers, who as early as 1940 had claimed that the content of art was 'the performance – how it is done', Noland laid his emphasis on process: he and his friend Morris Louis in the early 1950s 'wanted the appearance to be the result of the process of making it'.[141] He also hoped to drain his canvases of anything but colour: 'No graphs, no systems, no modules', he asserted in 1968, when the Neo-Constructivist 'systems' painting and Minimalism were in the ascendant, 'No shaped canvases. Above all, no *thingness*, no *objectiveness*. The thing is to get that color down on the thinnest conceivable surface, a surface sliced into the air as if by a razor. It's all color and surface. That's all.'[142] Like Albers too, Noland believed that colour could be released from shape. In 1966 he explained, 'With structural considerations eliminated I could concentrate on color. I wanted the freedom to exercise the arbitrariness of color' and, a little later, 'Structure is an element profoundly to be respected, but, too, an engagement with it leaves one in the backwaters of what are basically cubist concerns. In the best color painting, structure is nowhere evident, or nowhere self-declaring.'[143] But Noland's highly determined lozenges, chevrons and, most of all, stripes, of the 1950s and 60s give the lie to this astonishing version of Albersian renunciation. Stripes, which in the 1960s played a similar role to the chequerboard among abstract painters around 1920, were used in a score of different ways by Op artists and Color-Field painters but none of them can have been unaware of the profound optical effects to be derived from the bunching of these coloured strips. Albers, after all, had demonstrated it in a number of exercises in *Interaction of Color*, although he argued for the 'shapelessness' of the motif and Noland made the same point when explaining why he preferred a horizontal format to the vertical of Louis and others.[144]

Another Washington painter, Gene Davis, who made stripes his own in the late 50s and 60s, felt that they provided 'a simple matrix to hold the color and do not distract the eye too much with formal adventures'.[145] Like Noland he distrusted what he saw as Albers's system-building, arguing that the painting must grow empirically under the painter's eye and hand:

> I seldom think about color. You might say I take it for granted. Color theories are boring to me, I'm afraid. In fact, sometimes I simply use the color I have the most of and then trust to my instincts to get out of trouble. I never plan my color more than five stripes ahead and often I change my mind before I reach the third stripe. I like to think that I am somewhat like a jazz musician who does not read music and plays by ear. I paint by eye . . .[146]

We have leapfrogged over the *Gestalt* investigations into form and colour in the 1910s and 20s and are back with Matisse in 1908.

The materials of abstraction

Empiricism was not the only device which the colour-painters of the mid-century sought to outflank the complexities and contradictions of modern theories of colour. One of the hallmarks of Albers's art was its meticulous attention to technique: towards the end of the 1940s in the *Variant* series, and in *Homage to the Square* in the following decades, he made a practice of recording the precise identity of the pigments employed, as well as the principles of formal construction, on the back of each support.[147] He came to regard any mixtures as destructive of colour and light, using pigments direct from the tube, and sometimes, as in his last *Homage* of 1976, waiting until he could find the right colour not just from the same manufacturer but even from the same batch of paint.[148]

180   We saw in Chapter 12 that it was chiefly in Russia just after the First World War that surface texture (*faktura*) was understood to be a primary aesthetic element in painting.[149] *Faktura* was seen to be the result of a distinctly modern approach; as Tarabukin wrote in his treatise of 1916–23: 'We have seen in respect of colour that the modern painter is distinguished by the very special reverence he has for his materials, to the point that even when he is working with colours he gives through them the feeling of material as such, parallel to the effect produced by coloured sensations.'[150] The reform of the Moscow art-institutions in 1918 included a plan to establish not only an experimental colour-workshop but also an associated factory for manufacturing paints.[151] This attention to painterly materials was also very much alive at the Bauhaus, which taught the chemistry as well as the physics and physiology of colour, and Bauhaus artists, notably Klee, made an imaginative use of many types of coloured pigment in their paintings. After the closure of the school, during the Nazi period, when he was forbidden to exhibit and sell his work, Schlemmer could make a living only by testing materials for a paint manufacturer.[152]

    In the United States during and after the Second World War, the vast scale and dense working of Abstract Expressionist canvases stimulated experimentation with cheaper industrial materials; here too the use of such materials came to take on a positive aesthetic value.[153] Mark Rothko had once worked as a
212 theatrical scene-painter and it may well have been that experience which fostered his taste for the brilliant but highly fugitive pigments which have proved disastrous in large canvases such as the series painted for Harvard University in 1961.[154] But it was the staining plastic and acrylic paints used by a group of Washington painters in the 1950s which helped to give materials as such a crucial place in the understanding of
210 painting itself. Helen Frankenthaler was perhaps the first to use raw unprimed duck as a support for very diluted students' oil-colours or commercial enamels applied as a stain, and it was from their contact with her that Noland and Louis adopted and expanded the technique from the early 1950s.[155] During that decade Louis met the New York paint manufacturer Leonard Bocour, who had been developing cheaper, mass-produced paints for artists in response to the new demands for quantity. Bocour had marketed an acrylic polymer emulsion since 1956 which was quickly taken up by the Washington painters; it is
211 tempting to believe that Louis's use of the thinnest veils of dilute

Frank Stella at work. The use of house-painting materials and methods emphasizes the impersonal, industrial nature of Stella's approach. (222)

colour owed something to his making the most of the free 'end of batch' portions with which the manufacturer supplied him. Certainly he told Bocour that 'part of my thesis is that materials influence form'.[156] Eventually Bocour, who was proud of having introduced 'big tubes for big paintings' in the 1940s, was producing acrylics for Louis and Noland in gallon cans.[157]

    During the post-war period in Europe too the virtues of paint as such were being revalued even more radically in the work of the French painter and performance artist Yves Klein, who had a synthetic blue developed especially for himself under the name IKB (International Klein Blue), which he used as a dry powder with a special resin medium or binder, Rhodopas M 60 A, to 'protect each grain of pigment from any alteration'. The extraordinarily yielding and caressing velvety surfaces of Klein's blue monochromes, very small and icon-like by American standards, give us a sense of the 'spiritual absolute' to which he was aspiring;[158] it is clear that his emphasis on materials was not related to any belief in their absolute autonomy. His friend, Arman (Armand Fernandez) went further in the direction of pure materialism, in 1965 producing a work with squirting paint-tubes sandwiched between plexiglass sheets, entitled *Life in the Town for the Eye*.[159]

    In the Minimalist context of New York in the 1960s it was Frank Stella who more than anyone set the materials of painting 222 on an aesthetic pedestal. During his student years Stella had

267

worked as a house-painter; he was urged not simply to use industrial colours, as the Abstract Expressionists had done, but to use them in an industrial way. In several series of canvases in this decade Stella made a virtue of the even application of commercial paint, and in some he used aluminium and other metallic enamels. As he said in a radio interview in 1964:

> The artist's tools or the traditional artist's brush and maybe even oil paint are all disappearing very quickly. We use mostly commercial paint, and we generally tend toward larger brushes. In a way, Abstract Expressionism started all this ... I didn't want to make variations; I didn't want to record a path. I wanted to get the paint out of the can and on to the canvas. I knew a wise guy who used to make fun of my painting, but he didn't like the Abstract Expressionists either. He said they would be good painters if they could only keep the paint as good as it is in the can. And that's what I tried to do. I tried to keep the paint as good as it was in the can.[160]

Stella had studied both painting and the history of art at Princeton University, where his courses included something on colour-systems,[161] yet he remained very much within the American empiricist tradition, one little troubled by discursive thought. 'Thinking about colour abstractly', Stella remarked, 'hasn't done me any real good'.[162] In a series of lectures given at Harvard University in 1983, however, he rejected his earlier emphasis on 'materiality' (which he identified appropriately enough with the legacy of Kandinsky) in favour of the more spatially sophisticated 'Baroque' legacy of Picasso, which was more in tune with Stella's flamboyant three-dimensional painted constructions of these years:

> Picasso saw the danger ... of materiality – the danger that the new, open, atmospheric space of abstraction would be clogged up and weighed down by the mass of its only real ingredient: pigment.

Picasso's concern articulated the fear that abstraction, instead of giving us pure painting, would merely give us pure paint – something we could find on store shelves as well as on museum walls.[163]

Yet it is not difficult to see how Minimalist art, with its abolition of hierarchy and compositional relationships in general, could have little use for modern colour systems, which have been intrinsically concerned with relationships. It is less easy to understand how even the more technologically and experimentally oriented branches of modern colour-painting should have been so little interested in recent colour research, or should so readily have adopted the half-truths of nineteenth-century and modern popular science.[164] Even one of the more abundantly colouristic artists of the systems movement in the 1960s, the Swiss painter Richard Paul Lohse, showed no particular interest in exploring the dimensions of colour in anything but a mathematical, topographical sense. Like other Minimalists, and in the tradition of Russian Constructivism, Lohse sought a place for art in utopian social engineering; unlike the Constructivists, he derived his aesthetic concepts exclusively from his reading of the history of modernist art. Colour and form were perceived as even more autonomous than they had been in the inter-war years.[165] Yet this is perhaps no more than we should expect from the fragmentation of late twentieth-century academic and cultural practices. It is no more surprising that a distinguished colour scientist, W. D. Wright, after a long career investigating colour-discrimination and measurement, should recognize only towards the end of it that black has a positive psychological value and is not perceived simply as an absence of light.[166] The struggle to understand the nature of colour, whether physical or psychological, and to use that understanding in the shaping of our coloured environment has been the central subject of this book; it is a struggle that is still going on.

ACKNOWLEDGMENTS

A CATALOGUE OF INDEBTEDNESS is always difficult to write, doubly so when, as here, the theme has occupied me for most of my working life. Very few friends and acquaintances have not been sounded for their opinions or advice on the question of colour and although I have disregarded much of it, much more has worked itself, yeast-like, into the texture of my argument, so that I am really at a loss to identify the origin of many ideas. These are thus acknowledgments of a sort of collective responsibility and I am very happy that they should be so. The early stages of this work in London were speeded by exchanges with Bob Ratcliff and Stephen Rees-Jones at the Courtauld Institute and particularly with Anne Rees-Mogg at the Chelsea School of Art. Paolo Vivante first directed me to the philological dimension of colour and Robin Cormack has sent me further along that road. J. B. Trapp, Richard Gordon, David Cast, John Onians and Jean-Michel Massing have helped me considerably with the Classical sources; Nigel Morgan, Sandy Heslop, Michael Camille and John Mitchell with the medieval. David Chadd has, almost inadvertently, given my musical discussion in Chapter 13 whatever plausibility it may have; Alex Potts has, as usual, encouraged me to think of more interesting questions. John Mollon and Philippe Lanthony have put me in touch with the literature of physiology and Ann Massing with several key technical sources. I have been given generous access to important manuscript material by Jon Whiteley, Ian McClure and Peter Staples and received many important publications from Maria Rzepińska, Thomas Lersch, Lorenz Dittmann, Heinz Matile, Alan Lee, Georges Roque and Janis Bell. Crucial hints have been dropped from time to time by Bob Herbert, Robin Middleton, Stefan and Anna Muthesius, Paul Hills, Tim Hunter, Philip Conisbee, David Charlton, Charlotte Klonk, Oliver Logan, Anna Rowland and Carol McKay. Douglas Druick gave much assistance with material on Seurat's *Grande Jatte*. Paul Joannides has satisfied many bookish queries.

But if my debt to these many personal contacts is great, it is even greater to the several institutional libraries which have maintained their services to scholarship against all the odds. It might have gone without saying that this book would never have been possible without access not simply to specialist collections such as the Faber Birren collection at Yale, the Colour Reference Library at the Royal College of Art in London, the Wellcome Medical Library and the library of the Hamilton Kerr Institute but also, and especially, to the great general libraries such as the British Library and the Library of Congress, the Cambridge University Library and the library of the Warburg Institute, as well as smaller ones such as that at the University of East Anglia, the National Gallery library in Washington, and the library of my own Faculty of Architecture and History of Art at Cambridge. This should have gone without saying but nowadays it must be said.

Chapter 2 originally appeared in a slightly different version in *The Journal of the Warburg and Courtauld Institutes*, vol. 44, 1981; most of Chapter 4 in *Art History*, vol. 5, 1982, and *Akten des XXV Internationalen Kongresses für Kunstgeschichte*, vol. 6, 6, 1986. They are here reprinted with the permission of the respective editors. Chapter 12 was partly prepared while I was a Visiting Fellow at the Yale Center for British Art; Chapter 14 could not have been completed without a brief spell as Paul Mellon Senior Visiting Fellow at the Center for Advanced Study in the Visual Arts in Washington, where I had the good fortune to secure the help of Milton Brown. I am grateful for the generosity of both these institutions.

As always, my family has shown great patience in supporting and nourishing my obsessions.

J.G.

NOTES TO THE TEXT

Numbers in square brackets after the author and date are cross-references to the Bibliography

Introduction

1 Berenson 1949 [**1**], 127f. For his most sustained attack on colour as a value in art, Berenson 1950 [**2**], 74–9. He was nevertheless one of the earliest art-historians to approve of the use of coloured reproductions, *c.* 1920: see Berenson 1965 [**3**], 90.
2 See espec. Berenson's preface to Thompson 1936 [**24**], and Berenson 1950 [**2**], 49–58. For a critique of this position, Camesasca 1966 [**7**], 389ff, and ch. 12 below.
3 For Ruskin's early preference for value (chiaroscuro) rather than hue, Ruskin 1843 [**18**], Pt II, sect. i, ch. v; sect. ii, ch. ii, §20. For his opening to the spiritual value of colour, Ruskin 1853 [**19**], ch. v, §30–6. The development has been discussed by Hewison 1976 [**12**], 197ff, who has pointed to the early influence of Locke.
4 For Ruskin on the ultimate primacy of form, Ruskin 1856 [**20**], Pt IV, ch. iii, §24. For the Working Men's College, Burne-Jones 1912 [**6**], 191–2.
5 Wittgenstein 1977 [**26**], III, 52. Wittgenstein mentions a colour circle in II, 80 and often alludes to Goethe. Even an exceptionally well-read Wittgensteinian such as Jonathan Westphal (1991 [**25**]) makes several dubious inferences about the 'facts' of colour because of his philosophical preoccupation with the present.
6 See espec. Reynolds 1852 [**17**], II, 335. A psychological testing of 25 American undergraduates in 1926 seemed to show that green and blue were perceived as far 'warmer' than red or purple (Morgensen and English 1926 [**15**], 427–8). A more recent study has also argued that the association of colours with temperature is a question of acculturation (Marks 1978 [**14**], 218ff).
7 Stokes 1937 [**23**], 149.
8 For a brief characterization of this school, Gage 1990 [**9**], 520–3.
9 Ibid 518–41.
10 Birren 1965 [**4**]; Brusatin 1983 [**5**]; Dittmann 1987 [**8**]; Rzepińska 1989 [**22**].
11 Halbertsma 1949 [**11**]; Pastore 1971 [**16**]; Lindberg 1976 [**13**].
12 Berenson 1950 [**2**], 75.

1 The Classical Inheritance

1 For the problems of interpreting the polychromy of the Parthenon frieze, Jenkins and Middleton 1988 [**95**], espec. 204f. Also Richter 1944 [**128**], Suppl. 321–3.
2 For the Italian Renaissance belief in the essential whiteness of Classical architecture and sculpture, Cagiano di Azevedo 1954 [**54**], espec. 153ff. The most important development came, however, in the 18th century with Winckelmann (1882 [**148**], xxvii). For the continued resistance to the idea of polychrome sculpture in the Romantic period, Flaxman 1838 [**70**],

185–9; David d'Angers 1958 [**61**], I, 182–3, 347; II, 32; Ruskin, II, 1846 [**132**], Pt III, sect. II, ch. iv, §9.
3 Gell 1817–19 [**78**], 160. The polychromy on the Ionic Temple of Ilissus at Athens had been noted as early as the middle of the 18th century by Stuart and Revett, I, 1762 [**142**], 10 and pl. VIII, fig. 3. Also Barry 1809 [**34**], 537–8. The development of this discovery of Greek polychromy, especially after Winckelmann, has been studied by Reuterswärd 1960 [**127**], ch. 1 and espec. van Zanten 1976 [**152**].
4 See espec. Eastlake 1848 [**67**], 63–4, 79–80, 114.
5 Newton 1862 [**111**], II, i, 185, 238. He found the sculpture here less 'ethical' than that of Pheidias (237).
6 *Ingres* 1967–8 [**94**], no. 25. For Hittorff, van Zanten 1976 [**152**], 29ff; Billot 1982 [**41**]; Middleton 1976 [**108**], 55ff.
7 Semper 1834 [**138**] and van Zanten 1976 [**152**], 52ff, 162ff; Grisebach 1924 [**85**], 164 and fig. 98. For a reconstruction of the Parthenon in full polychromy, see Leo von Klenze's painting *The Acropolis with the Preaching of St Paul* (1846), Hederer 1964 [**89**], 175 and van Zanten, ibid., 170ff.
8 The *Venus* with its canopy *in situ* are reproduced in Matthews 1911 [**106**], facing 230. For Gibson and Hittorff, Cooper 1971 [**57**], 91, nn. 14, 17; Darby 1981 [**60**], 37–53.
9 Gladstone 1858 [**81**], III, 488 (expanded in Gladstone 1877 [**82**], 366ff). He did admit (495) that the surviving samples of ancient pigments told a different story: 'The explanation, I suppose, is, that those, who had to make practical use of colour, did not wait for the construction of a philosophy, but added to their apparatus from time to time all substances which, having come within their knowledge, were found to produce results satisfactory and improving to the eye.'
10 See espec. Schultz 1904 [**136**], 187–8. For a modern survey of the question Grossman 1988 [**86**].
11 Hochegger 1884 [**91**], espec. 38ff. His interdisciplinary approach has remained the exception in this branch of colour-study; for a recent application of it to ancient Egyptian art, Baines 1985 [**32**], 282–97. See also Schultz 1904 [**136**], 80f, 108; Platnauer 1921 [**120**], 155ff, 162; André 1949 [**27**], 12; Osborne 1968 [**114**], 274.
12 Kranz 1912 [**99**], 126.
13 Freeman 1966 [**71**], frs 22–3; Beare 1906 [**35**], 14ff.
14 Empedocles's most recent editor has argued that the philosopher's idea of mixture here means the setting of colours side by side (M. R. Wright 1981 [**150**], 180). See also p. 30 above.
15 Freeman 1966 [**71**], frs 22–3.
16 Aëtius *Placita* I, 15. 3 (1st or 2nd

century AD) in Diels 1879 [**63**], 313; Stobaeus (5th century AD) 1792 [**140**], 362ff. On *ōchron*, Schultz 1904 [**136**], 73.
17 Stratton 1917 [**141**], 132ff (includes the whole text of Theophrastus *On Sense*).
18 Ibid., n. 183 supposes a lacuna in the MS at this point and suggests that the reference to sulphur comes from another recipe. Siegel 1959 [**139**], 153, however, had no difficulty in testing Democritus's mixtures and found them to be quite possible. Also van Hoorn 1972 [**92**], 55 and n. 41.
19 Stratton 1917 [**141**], n. 187. This seems unlikely, since even Aristotle's 4th-century account of after-images does not identify their colours correctly (*On Dreams* 459b).
20 Stratton 1917 [**141**], 82. Aristotle (*Categories* VIII, 10b) had argued that, unlike black and white, red (*purron*) and yellow (*ōchron*) have no contraries.
21 I have followed Bruno 1977 [**50**], 89ff in the interpretation of this difficult passage.
22 See Charlton 1970 [**55**], 45 on Aristotle's indefinite use of the terms *leukos* and *melas*; also Platnauer 1921 [**120**], 153f; Bruno 1977 [**50**], 91f.
23 Philo 173 in Annas and Barnes 1985 [**28**], 38f; also 31f and 42. Diogenes Laertius (*Lives of the Philosophers* VII, 52) reported that the Stoics believed that only white and black could be the proper objects of perception.
24 Freeman 1966 [**71**], 92–8.
25 The evidence is assembled by Schuhl 1952 [**135**]. Keuls 1978 [**97**], 69 argues for the improbability of this tradition. Aristotle's familiarity with painters has been emphasized by Bertrand 1893 [**38**], 145ff.
26 See *Anonymous* 1962 [**29**], XIII, 13–15, pp. 6–7.
27 The Byzantine Suda lexicon attributes a book on *graphikes* and *skematon* to the late 4th-century painter Protogenes; Reinach's supposition (1985 [**125**], no. 497) that *skematon* refers to colour seems improbable, although the use of *skematon*, 'figure of the dance', in Plato's definition of colour (*chroa*) in *Meno* 76d suggests that the two terms were linked (cf. F. A. Wright 1919 [**149**], 31). Also Gaiser 1965 [**75**], 180f. For *skema*, Pollitt 1974 [**122**], 64.
28 For the more formal connotation of 'symmetry', Pollitt 1974 [**122**], 14ff.
29 Cicero *Tusculan Disputations* IV, 31–2 (*cum coloris quadam suavitate*); also Plotinus, n. 30 below.
30 Plotinus *Enneads* I, 6.1, trans. MacKenna; also V, 8.4 and VI, 7.33 on 'Intellectual Beauty'.
31 Valerius Maximus in Pollitt 1965 [**121**], 173; the Latin is in Reinach 1985 [**125**], no. 355. On *splendor*, Pollitt 1974 [**122**], 227ff. The other literary references to Euphranor have been collected by

Reinach 1985 [**125**], nos 351–7.
32 Stratton 1917 [**141**], 132ff.
33 Heaton 1910 [**88**], 209; Duell and Gettens 1940 [**66**], 94. In general see Borelli 1950 [**45**], 55ff.
34 Swindler 1929 [**144**], 420ff; Augusti 1967 [**30**], 36f. On green underpainting for flesh at Pompeii, Seibt 1885 [**137**], 16.
35 The classic study is Willamowitz-Möllendorf 1900 [**147**], 1–52.
36 Seneca *Controversies* IV, iii.3, cit. Baldwin 1924 [**33**], 98ff.
37 For the 'colours' of rhetoric and falsehood, Trimpi 1973 [**145**], 25ff.
38 Pollitt 1974 [**122**], 52ff.
39 Philostratus *Life of Apollonius of Tyana*, trans. Jones, 1970, 59–60. Philostratus's view has been traced to Aristotle by Bermelin 1933 [**37**], espec. 160ff, 179. For the taste for monochromes in Hellenistic painting, Bruno 1985 [**51**], 42ff. For other late antique discussions of colour as aiding imitation, Lucian *Pictures* 7 (Reinach 1985 [**125**], no. 54), Dio Chrysostom *Discourse* 12 (trans. Cahoon, 1939, II, 60–85).
40 Reuterswärd 1960 [**127**], 60ff.
41 Kuels 1978 [**97**], 102ff.
42 Pollitt 1974 (full edn) [**122**], 151ff, citing Lucian *Zeuxis* 5.
43 Preusser, von Graeve and Wolters 1981 [**123**], 23ff.
44 Augusti 1967 [**30**], 123ff; von Blanckenhagen and Alexander 1962 [**42**], 63. The mixtures are a blue-grey from terre verte, lime white and black, and a brown from iron oxide, lime white and black, both ready-mixed before application. For the problems of mixture, pp. 30–2 above.
45 Burford 1972 [**53**], 136–7. See also Pausanius's account of the interior of the Temple of Zeus at Olympia (V, xi, 1–10).
46 Swift 1951 [**143**], 127–8 and review by K. Lehmann, *Art Bulletin*, XXXVI, 1954, 71.
47 Swift 1951 [**143**], 72–4; Friedländer 1964 [**72**], 330–9; Gnoli 1971 [**83**], 5ff. Gnoli gives many beautiful plates of the coloured marbles used in Antiquity.
48 L'Orange and Nordhagen 1965 [**113**], 35; Phillips 1960 [**119**], 244; Salzmann 1982 [**133**], 43.
49 André 1949 [**27**], 12, 25ff, 399. There is no direct correlation between the varieties of colour terms and the varieties of pigments (see Augusti 1967 [**30**], 123ff), although the proportions are roughly the same. Reds form by far the largest group in both words and pigments; it is notable that Homer's short list includes two reds, *eruthros* and *phoinikous* (purple-red).
50 Rist 1972 [**129**], 63; Hahm 1978 [**87**], 75ff.
51 W. Klinkert, 'Bemerkungen zur Technik der Pompejanischen Wand-Dekorationen' (1957) in Curtius 1960 [**59**], 439ff; von Blanckenhagen and Alexander 1962 [**42**], 63.
52 Fuhrmann 1931 [**73**], 110.

53 *Natural History* XXXV, xxxvi 97. See Pollitt 1974 **[122]**, 245–6 for the text of this difficult passage. For the content, p. 30 above.
54 For Apelles as exclusively a panel-painter and for the painting of many Greek murals on panel, Robertson 1975 **[130]**, I, 244, 494 and II, 659, n. 152.
55 *Ten Books on Architecture* VI, 7. For other references, Beccatti 1951 **[36]**, 29.
56 Alexander of Aphrodisias, writing in the 3rd century AD, calls white 'the colour, par excellence, and the finest of colours' (Gätje 1967 **[77]**, 371–3) but I have found no other support for this view.
57 Alcman, *Maiden Song* (fr. 1D, 64f), trans. Bowra 1961 **[46]**, 44f. For Mycenaean Greek, Gallavotti 1957 **[76]**, 12f and in general Reinhold 1970 **[126]**, 9f.
58 Reinhold ibid., 8.
59 Avery 1940 **[31]**, espec. 76ff; Lopez 1945 **[104]**, 10; Reinhold ibid., 63.
60 Stratton 1917 **[141]**, 136–7.
61 See 'Colore' in *Enciclopedia dell'arte ... orientale* 1959 **[69]**, 770f; König 1927 **[98]**, 141.
62 Menander, fr. 667 K^2, cit. Collard 1970 **[56]**, 34. On the history of 'shot' materials, pp. 60–1 above.
63 Jensen 1963 **[96]**, 109 estimates that 12,000 animals produced only 1.5 g of dye.
64 Reinhold 1970 **[126]**, 30 from Plutarch *Alexander* 36 and Diodorus Siculus, 17, 70.
65 Avery 1940 **[31]**, 79.
66 Blümner 1912 **[43]**, I, 242; Jensen 1963 **[96]**, 110f; Roosen-Runge 1967 **[131]**, II, 25ff; espec. 'Färbung' in Pauly-Wissowa 1894–1978 **[117]**, suppl. III, 1918, cols 465–6. The preparation of indigo from woad was scarcely less unpleasant and was devastating to the medieval economy, yet it never acquired the status of purple (Thompson 1936 **[24]**, 136ff). For colour-changes in indigo dyeing, Leggett 1944 **[101]**, 19f.
67 *Book of the Eparch* 1970 **[44]**, 245.
68 Lehmann 1945 **[102]**, 11.
69 Neuburger 1969 **[110]**, 186ff.
70 For the edicts, Reinhold 1970 **[126]**, 63 and espec. Hunger 1965 **[93]**, 84–5. The late 9th-century *Book of the Eparch* **[44]**, 245 prohibited silk dyers from manufacturing purple dyes referred to simply as *vlattia* (dyes) and by the names of garments, i.e. *scaramaggia* (tunics).
71 Schmidt 1842 **[134]**, 102; 106f also gives the fullest list of the bewildering variety of ancient purple stuffs. Obermiller 1931 **[112]**, 422 has suggested that price would have been the only guide because of the multitude of beautiful imitations.
72 See espec. André 1949 **[27]**, 88–104; Quintilian *Institutes of the Orator* XI, 1.31. Many modern observers still class purple as a red: see König 1927 **[98]**, 126; Gipper 1964 **[80]**, 63.
73 Wunderlich 1925 **[151]** and review by S. Eitrem, *Gnomon*, II, 1926, 95–102; Cumont 1949 **[58]**, 33–45; Delcourt 1965 **[62]**, 13–30; Gerschel 1966 **[79]**, 608–10, 624ff.
74 Reuterswärd 1960 **[127]**, 56ff, 198ff, Pausanius **[118]**, II, 2.5 (with Levi's note, I, 136), VII, 26.4, VIII, 39.6 all refer to statues of Dionysius and may, of course, allude to wine.
75 Tertullian *On Idolatry* XVIII referred to the high reputation of gold and purple among the Egyptians and Babylonians. See Wunderlich 1925 **[151]**, 41 on the interchangeability of red and gold and André 1949 **[27]**, 138 on the Roman preference for a reddish cast in yellow.
76 Bultmann 1948 **[52]**, 4. See also Bremer 1973 **[47]**, 1974.
77 Bierwaltes 1957 **[39]**, 13.
78 Ibid., 14–19. For Classical and Renaissance gems, Kris 1929 **[100]**, I, 20f. On light concentrated in stones, Pliny XXXVII, xi, 37.
79 Brendel 1944 **[49]**, espec. 18f.
80 Lewy 1956 **[103]**, espec. 192f, 399ff.
81 Dodds 1971 **[64]**, 298f.
82 Bierwaltes 1961 **[40]**, 334–62; Dodds ibid., 285ff.
83 Ptolemy *Optics* II, 107; Galen *On the Usefulness of the Parts of the Human Body* X, 3; Kleomedes in Schultz 1904 **[136]**, 117. See also Proclus in the 5th century: 'We must not look for the good in the manner of knowledge ... but by abandoning ourselves to the divine light and by closing our eyes' *Platonic Theology* I, 5).
84 Mathew 1963 **[105]**, 20 has denied that Plotinus was well known in the Middle Ages. Proclus has sometimes been regarded as his transmitter, but no earlier than the 11th century (Proclus *Elements of Theology*, ed. E. R. Dodds, 2nd edn 1963, xxx). An extreme case for Plotinus's influence is in Grabar 1946 **[84]**, 15ff. See also Pollitt 1974 **[122]**, 57f. On the key Byzantine concept of the relation of the image to its archetype Plotinus offers conflicting views (IV, 3.11; VI, 4.10) and he perhaps thought the status of art more elevated (V, 8.1) than would have been acceptable later. Nor do we find his preference for images rather than propositions (V, 8.5) much followed in medieval practice, which is characterized in all periods, but espec. the earliest, by a marked use of the written word together with the image. See ch. 3 below.
85 Gage 1978 **[74]**, n. 28.
86 Ibid., n. 29.
87 Ibid., n. 30. The attempt by Edgeworth 1979 **[68]**, 281–91 to detach purple from connotations of brightness seems to rest on too narrow a selection of source-materials, although he is right to suggest that a red would fit his contexts perfectly well. Isidore *Etymologies* XVIII, xix; Rabanus Maurus *De Universo* XXI, xxi in *Patrologia Latina* **[116]**, CXI, col. 579); for later examples, Meier 1977 **[107]**, 201.
88 Gage 1978 **[74]**, n. 31; Dodwell 1982 **[65]**, 145–9. Dodwell's identification of *purpura* with shot-silk taffeta, endorsed by Owen-Crocker 1986 **[115]**, 135, is fraught with difficulties (see pp. 60–1 above). Owen-Crocker shows that the Anglo-Saxon translation of *purpura* was *godweb* (good or godly cloth). For red, grey (*subnigra*) and white *purpura* in 13th-century Hildesheim, *Mittelalterliche Schatzverzeichnisse* 1967 **[109]**, 40–1.
89 According to the *Protoevangelium of James*, Mary received both a purple and a scarlet skein to spin for the temple veil (10. 1–2): J. Lafontaine-Dosogne, 'Iconography of the cycle of the Life of the Virgin' in Underwood 1967–75 **[146]**, IV, 183–4. For a contemporary confusion between a purple (*ozus*) and scarlet (*coccinus*) in a more official context, Pseudo-Kodinus 1966 **[124]**, 146.

2 The Fortunes of Apelles

1 Jex-Blake and Sellers 1968 **[248]**, 97. The most informative commentary is now in Pliny 1978 **[296]**, which includes important material from other ancient writers.
2 For the literary sources, Reinach 1985 **[125]**, nos 400–86. The fullest discussion of Apelles's career is Lepik-Kopaczyńska 1963 **[257]**.
3 For the various later interpretations of these 2 stories, Gombrich 1962 **[226]**, 51–55; Mahon 1962 **[263]**, 463f; Plesters 1962 **[294]**, 453ff; Gombrich 1963 **[227]**, 90ff; Kurz 1963 **[253]**, espec. 94; van der Waal 1967 **[345]**; Gombrich 1976 **[228]**, espec. 15–16.
4 Both these solutions had been suggested by earlier scholars: for the relation of the 4 colours to the elements, Seibt 1885 **[137]**, 31; Berger 1975 **[167]**, 54. The function of black as a blue had been noticed in the 17th century by Félibien (1981 **[209]**, 14) and in the 18th by Lambert 1772 **[255]**, 16; Requeno 1787 **[303]**, I, 25; H. Meyer, 'Hypothetische Geschichte des Kolorits' in Goethe 1957 **[225]**, 59; also Berger loc. cit. For the equivalence of black and blue in Greek, Schultz 1904 **[136]**, 36; Schefold 1963 **[320]**, 5.
5 Pointed out by Keuls 1975 **[252]**, 15.
6 The evidence is reviewed by Bruno 1977 **[50]**, 57.
7 Stratton 1917 **[141]**, 132ff. Chlōron is the crucial term in this context: the earliest usages do not seem to have given it a specifically chromatic content but rather the connotations of 'pale', 'bright', 'fresh', 'moist' (Handschur 1970 **[237]**, 150ff; Irwin 1974 **[247]**, 31f). Dürbeck has translated it in this passage as 'yellow', although the terms for yellow attributed to Empedocles by ancient authors were *ōchron* (Aëtius) and *pyrrochrous* (Galen). The first unambiguous use of *chlōron* to connote 'yellow' is in Apelles's older contemporary, the medical writer Hippocrates (Dürbeck 1977 **[200]**, 37, 50ff, 108ff, 113).
8 Gottschalk 1964 **[229]**, 85.
9 The fullest discussion is in Lepik-Kopaczyńska 1963 **[257]**, 36ff. The distinction of skin colour is especially striking in the Herculaneum *Theseus Victorious*, discussed as a close copy of a 4th-century Greek original by Scheibler 1978 **[323]**, 299ff. The convention survived at least as late as early Cézanne: see his *The Rape* (*c.* 1867) in the Keynes Collection.
10 Hippocrates *The Nature of Man* ivff; for the whiteness of phlegm, vii. For a general account of the humours in Antiquity, Evans 1969 **[208]**, 17ff.
11 Galen 1562 **[218]**, 8ff.
12 Foerster 1893 **[212]**, I, 74–5. A 14th-century Fr. physiognomical MS (Jordan 1911 **[249]**, 685), which adopts the Hippocratic scheme of the 4 humours and 4 colours, equates melancholy not with black but with yellow (*luteus*). The 9th-century Galenic *Isagoge* of Hunain Ibn Ishāq lists 4 colours of hair and 5 of unhealthy skin, including a grey (*glaucus*) deriving from melancholy (Grant 1974 **[231]**, 707).
13 Stout 1932 **[332]**, 86 (4 pigments); Ramer 1979 **[302]**, 5 (6 pigments); Hart 1980 **[238]**, 22 (5 pigments).
14 For the history of this pigment, Forbes 1964–72 **[213]**, III, 224ff; Filippakis, Perdikatsis and Paradellis 1976 **[211]**, 143ff; Profi, Weier and Filippakis 1976 **[301]**, 34ff; Cameron, Jones and Philippakis 1977 **[182]**, 157–60; Profi, Perdikatsis and Filippakis 1977 **[299]**, 107ff; Fuchs 1982 **[216]**, 196ff.
15 Profi, Weier and Filippakis 1974 **[300]**, 105–12; Filippakis, Perdikatsis and Assimenos 1979 **[210]**, 54ff. For Kizilbel and Karaburun, Mellink 1971 **[270]**, 247–8; for *Tomb of the Diver*, Napoli 1970 **[278]**, 103ff and espec. pls 3, 30, 37; for Lefkadia and Kazanlak, Bruno 1977 **[50]**, ch. 9 and pls 5b, 6, 10, 11, 13a.
16 E.g. the pelike of *c.* 330 BC (National Museum, Athens, no. 1718), which has a palette of red, black white, blue and gold leaf. For the link with Apelles, Pollitt 1972 **[298]**, 159.
17 Mingazzini 1961 **[272]**, espec. 15. For the Alexander mosaic, which has been regarded as reflecting the 4-colour palette and the style of Apelles since its discovery in 1832, Fuhrmann 1931 **[73]**, 203ff; Rumpf 1962 **[311]**, 240f. Fuhrmann noted a green stone in Alexander's costume and there are many others in the plant and rocks and in the draperies to the bottom left. Bruno (1977 **[50]**, 75) denied the presence of green but the dispute may be no more than semantic, since he allows (76–7) that the painted original must have used mixtures including blue.
18 Cook 1977 **[186]**, 197–8. Here Cook briefly refers to the Chiton as 'pale blue' but in his fuller report (of which he kindly allowed me to see a typescript) he modified this to 'bluish-grey', which indeed it appears to be.
19 Cicero *Brutus* 70; Vitruvius *Ten Books on Architecture* VII, v, 7–8; Seneca *Epistles* LXXXVI, 6f; CXIV, 9; CXV, 9; Varro *On Country Matters* III, 2:3f; Petronius *Satyricon* II, 88, 119. The fullest discussion is in Jücker 1950 **[250]**, 143, 155ff; also Bruno 1977 **[50]**, 68ff.
20 For the fullest discussion of *colores floridi et austeri*, Pollitt 1974 **[122]**, s.v. *austerus*. Although he discusses the 4-colour theory in this context, Pollitt does not seem to see the inconsistency.
21 Tobias Mayer, cit. by Bertand 1893 **[38]**, 139. For an extended discussion of the 4-colour theory in the light of the account of the primaries discussed by Rood 1879 **[306]**, Veckenstedt 1888 **[342]**, 29ff. The possibility of substantial mixing is also implicit in the theses of Lepik-Kopaczyńska 1963 **[257]** and Bruno 1977 **[50]**.
22 M. R. Wright 1981 **[150]**, 179ff argued that 'mixing' here means setting colours side by side. Bollack 1969 **[173]**, II, i, 122ff points out that the context of this passage shows that mixture is prior to the act of painting and that the phrase '*harmonēi meixante*' simply has the connotation of 'mixed closely together'. For the lack of mixtures in archaic painting, Walter-Karydi 1986 **[346]**, 26ff.
23 Plutarch *Quaestiones Conviviales*, 725c; cf. also *From E to Delphos*, 393c and Plato *Philebus* 51–3. The notion of mixing as death or passing away goes back at least to Empedocles and Anaxagoras (Solmsen 1960 **[329]**, 372).
24 Here, too (see n. 22 above), the analogy is with letters side-by-side in a word, so that the idea of a more intimate blending may not have been in Plato's mind. Forbes 1964–72 **[213]**, III, 222 notes some pinks made from red and white. For the term for flesh-painting, Keuls 1978 **[97]**, 68.
25 Theophrastus *De Lapidibus* 51; see also Pliny *Natural History* XXXV, xiii, 31.
26 Wolfson 1970 **[352]**, I, 374ff; Todd 1976 **[338]**, espec. 59ff. For the late

medieval discussion in the West, Maier 1952 [**264**], 4ff.
27 *On Mixture* 214 in Todd 1976 [**338**], 110–11. The term for 'mixture' here is *krasis*. Todd (184) argues that the attribution of the idea to Democritus is Alexander's own invention.
28 Hatchings in the shadows at Herculaneum were already noticed by Cochin and Bellicard in their *Observations sur les antiquités de la ville de Herculaneum* (1754) and at Pompeii by the Nazarene painter Peter von Cornelius, who described them as like 'worn carpets' (Berger 1975 [**167**], 69). The literary evidence for 'optical mixture' has been discussed by Keuls 1975 [**252**], 10ff and 1978 [**97**], 70ff, 78f.
29 For glazing in Egypt, Forbes 1964–72 [**213**], III, 229, 247 and in Greek encaustic, Schmid 1926 [**325**], 86f. For the literary references, Borelli 1950 [**45**], 55ff.
30 See espec. the late 1st-century AD portrait of a youth from Hawara (Sainsbury Collection, University of East Anglia, no. 326) and one in the British Museum, NG1265 (Shore 1972 [**327**], pl. 5).
31 *Onomasticon* VII, 128–9. For a German translation, Berger 1917 [**166**], 182ff. Berger stresses (195–6) that Pollux's very incomplete account is not that of a professional.
32 Shore 1972 [**327**], pl. 8 (NG2912); cf. also pl. 16 (NG3139).
33 *Natural History* XXI, xlix, 85; XXXV, xxxi, 49. Scheibler 1974 [**322**], 92ff also suggests that the encaustic painters' palette was far brighter than that of the 4-colour painters. For the use of glazes in encaustic, Berger 1975 [**167**], 206ff; Schmid 1926 [**325**], 86f.
34 Loumyer 1914 [**259**], 147ff; Weitzmann 1976 [**348**], nos B1, B2, B3, B5, B9, B10, B16, B17.
35 *On the Soul and Resurrection, Patrologia Graeca* 857–66 [**116**], XLVI, 73b ff.
36 The evidence for the use of the palette in ancient painting was assembled by Bümner 1912 [**43**], IV, 1879, 459ff and contested by Berger 1975 [**167**], 173ff, who showed convincingly that there was no substantial reason to assume such use. Keuls 1978 [**97**], 61, n.10 points to the lack of word for palette in either Greek or Latin. For the paintboxes of the Egyptians, where colours were ready-mixed before use, with separate brushes for each colour, Forbes 1964–72 [**213**], III, 244f.
37 Bruno 1977 [**50**], 89ff. The first Latin translation of this ch. of the *Timaeus*, by Marsilio Ficino, interpreted the terms in a similar way, distinguishing *niger* from *nigredo* and characterizing *xanthon* as yellow (*flavus*): Plato *Opera Omnia*, Venice, 1581, 415).
38 Aulus Gellius *Attic Nights* II, xxvi. Dürbeck 1977 [**200**], 38ff is the only modern discussion of this passage and has translated *viridis* as 'yellow' to accommodate the sense.
39 For *flavus* as *xanthos* and *fulvus* as *pyrros*, Ficino's translation of Plato (see n. 37 above); Keuls 1975 [**252**], 15. Aristotle, however, refers to the product of red and green as white.
40 Cinnabar is the usual term for red sulphate of mercury (HgS) but Alexander is probably thinking of *vermiculum* or *kermes* made from the dried insect *coccus illicis* (cf. Pliny XXXIII, iii, 7; XXXV, xxxii, 50). Dragon's blood is a reddish resin produced by a variety of palm, in Antiquity regarded as the product of a duel between an elephant and a dragon (Pliny XXXIII, iii, 7). On these pigments, *De Arte Illuminandi* 1975 [**193**], s.v. *Sanguis draconis*.
41 *Chrysocolla* was in fact a basic carbonate of copper ($CuCO_3$).
42 For the Greek text, Hayduck 1899 [**240**], 161; for William of Moerbeke's Latin translation (1260), Smet 1968 [**328**], 252–4. Heinrich Bate of Mecheln, who extracted this version of Alexander's commentary in his early 14th-century encyclopaedia (1960 [**162**], 126–7, 129f), added the important qualification that *halurgus* is 'violaceus', that *cyanus* is 'fuscus' (dark) and that ochre is 'vitellinus' (the colour of egg-yolk).
43 The fullest discussions are Cast 1981 [**183**] and Massing 1990 [**269**].
44 Hind 1938–49 [**242**], V, no. 29. Hind (107ff) gives the fullest account of the mysterious Rosex (de Rubeis, Rosa). The figure of Apelles seems to depend on that of the philosopher in Filippino Lippi's *Triumph of St Thomas Aquinas* in Sta Maria sopra Minerva, Rome (Scharf 1950 [**318**], fig. 76), which may allow us to date the print between 1507, when Rosex is documented in the city, and 1515, when records of him cease.
45 For the broken column representing *fortezza* in the Mantegnesque repertory, from which Rosex drew so many graphic ideas, Wind 1969 [**351**], 2, 18–19. See also Fabio Segni's phrase in his early 16th-century epigram on Botticelli's *Calumny*: 'Terrarum reges parva tabula monet' (Vasari 1962–6 [**341**], I (1962), 204).
46 Ghiberti 1947 [**220**], 24.
47 See *Geometria* in the *Tarocchi* series (Hind 1938–49 [**242**], pl. 343) and the tablet at the foot of the astrologer in Cecco d'Ascoli, *Acerba*, Venice, 1524 (*Gazette des Beaux-Arts*, VIe sér., XXVII, 1945, 209).
48 Nahm 1964 [**277**], 59.
49 Pacioli 1889 [**280**], 84–5. Pacioli attributed the notion to Plato, basing himself on *Timaeus* 55c.
50 Cornford 1937 [**188**], 51, 70.
51 Pacioli 1889 [**280**], 96f, Cf. *Timaeus* 49c, where water is shown to perform a complete upward and downward cycle. Plato's contemporary Timaeus of Locris (Fr. 101c) had a scheme of four basic colours, black, white, red (*phoinikoun*) and bright (*lampron*) but he did not relate them to the elements.
52 The influential 10th-century Arab writer Alfarabi also sustained the view that the elements were themselves uncoloured but manifested colour when mixed (Dieterici 1892 [**195**], 139). See also the extended discussion by the 12th-century south Italian writer Marius, 1976 [**268**], 58ff, espec. 63: the ancients 'never made any reference to colour' when they discussed the elements. This view was restated *c.* 1200 by Daniel of Morley (1917 [**191**], 11f).
53 Seznec 1953 [**326**], 47. Marius 1976 [**268**], 63 cites a contemporary view that earth is black, water white, air yellow and fire red; a 15th-century French *Lumen Luminum de Coloribus* proposes the same 4 colours as 'principales' but without reference to the elements (cit. Thompson 1934/5 [**336**], 468). Writing *c.* the 1220s, Wiliam of Auvergne gave the equivalents air–blue, fire–red, water–purple (since purple derives from a sea-creature) and earth–grey (*bissus*): 1674 [**350**], I, 32); in the most sustained medieval account of the relationship of colours to elements, Theodoric of Freiberg (1304/10) has fire–red, air–yellow, water–green and earth–blue (1914 [**334**], 82–3).
54 Alberti 1972 [**153**], 46. Although he refers elsewhere to the 4-colour painters (86) he does not relate their colours to the elements. In his own Italian version, Alberti stresses that ash-colour is a form of grey (*bigio*); the attempt of Gavel 1979 [**219**], 49–51 to interpret this as a yellow is not convincing: he had a good earthy yellow available to him in *ochria* (see Cennini 1971 [**184**], xlv). But see Marius 1976 [**268**], 58 for earth as black, white, red or yellow. S. Y. Edgerton 1969 [**204**], 123ff glosses over some important differences between the views of the Ancients and of Alberti. See p. 119 above.
55 Pedretti 1965 [**289**], 56. Green and yellow had often been confused since Antiquity.
56 Uccelli 1940 [**339**], 1.
57 Alberti 1966, [**153**], 741.
58 For a useful tabulation of these equivalents, Tertullian 1961 [**333**], lxxxiv f and for Corippus, the substantial discussion by A. Cameron in Corippus 1976 [**187**], 144–6.
59 See Gage 1978 [**74**], 105ff.
60 A 10th-century Byzantine example is discussed by Mango 1963 [**268**], 65–6; a German example of *c.* 1500 in Huth 1967 [**245**], 69; several other medieval and Renaissance instances in Panofsky 1969 [**283**], 223.
61 Pacioli 1889 [**280**], 33; Speziali 1953 [**331**], 302f.
62 Wuttke 1967 [**353**], 322; also Dürer 1956–69 [**201**], I (1956), 255, 290.
63 Dürer ibid., II (1966), 99f; also 109, 113 (1512), 135 (1523); III (1969), 438 (1527/8).
64 Förster 1887 [**214**], 93f. *Erasmi Epistolae* 1906–58 [**206**], III (1913), no. 809; also his Apologia for the 1518/19 edn, 82. For Dürer's own *Calumny*, Massing 1990 [**269**].
65 *Erasmi Epistolae* 1906–58 [**206**], nos 1398 (1523), 1536, 1558 (1525).
66 Dürer 1956–69 [**201**], I (1956), 297. The fullest commentary on this text is Panofsky 1951 [**282**].
67 Dürer 1956–69 [**201**], I (1956), 289; II (1966) 393f (cf. 94ff). Dürer's note is hardly the chapter on colour itself, as claimed by Hofmann 1971 [**243**], 17. Kuspit 1973 [**254**], 188f shows that this and related remarks reported by Melancthon are part of the humanist's argument for the simple style in language. See Dittmann 1987 [**196**], 119 for Dürer's neglect of his own principles in practice.
68 *Erasmus Epistolae* 1906–58 [**206**], III (1913), 503f; VI (1926), 16f and letter 1544.
69 Ridolfi 1914 [**305**], I, 107.
70 See H. Ruhemann's technical analysis of the Berlin *Portrait of a Youth* in Richter 1937 [**304**], 126, which identifies only black, white, red and brown. In the early Pala di Castelfranco, Giorgione used 4 reds, 3 yellows, ultramarine, 3 greens and black and white but no samples were taken from the flesh areas (Lazzarini et al., 1978 [**256**], 46–7). Gioseffi (1979 [**222**], 95) has made a rather surprising comparison between Giorgione's '4-colour' palette and the 4-colour problem in mathematics.
71 Ridolfi 1914 [**305**], I, 154, 209. A 19th-century restorer, Palmaroli, thought that Titian used ultramarine as an underpainting for flesh (Kurz 1963 [**253**], 94) and it has been identified in the shadows of Ariadne's flesh in *Bacchus and Ariadne* (Lucas and Plesters 1978 [**260**], 40). The most attentive early modern analyst of Venetian flesh-painting found no blue in Titian's usage (Grunewald 1912 [**235**], 133ff). Grunewald stressed Titian's liking for yellow in flesh and there are several yellows on the back of the man offering tribute in the London *Tribute Money*, and on the wrist of Diana in the London *Death of Actaeon* is a bright yellow which seems the same as that in the foliage of the nearby trees.
72 Boschini 1674 [**177**], 27. Crowe and Cavalcaselle (1881 [**189**], II, 125) converted this story to a dictum 'according to a tradition still preserved'. Boschini based his account on the information of Titian's pupil Palma Giovane, whose testimony has been accepted by most modern scholars (Kennedy 1964 [**251**], 167f; Panofsky 1969 [**283**], 16–18). Grunewald 1912 [**235**], 202 links the story to the late painting of flesh but both the works cit. in n. 71 above are late and yellow was not in Titian's alleged triad.
73 Kennedy 1964 [**251**], 162; Wethey 1969–75 [**349**], III, no. 39. Cf. the patent of knighthood granted to Titian by Charles V in 1533 (Wethey ibid., II (1971), 7) and the letter of 27 September 1559 from Titian to Philip II (Tietze-Conrat 1944 [**337**], 120).
74 For Titian's membership of the Accademia Pellegrina, which included Doni and Dolce, by 1552, Grendler 1969 [**233**], 58.
75 Aretino 1957–60 [**155**], I, 156, 242f; II, 192, 198, 200, 221. For Aretino's borrowings from Pliny, Beccatti 1946 [**163**], 1–7; for his aid to Titian as a letter-writer, Ridolfi 1914 [**305**], 208.
76 On colours, Doni 1549 [**198**], 7r; on flesh-painting, 9v, 14v; on Apelles (and Titian), 37v ff.
77 Roskill 1968 [**308**], 152–3. Roskill (299) links this with Apelles's dark varnish, which is also referred to as *bruno* in a letter of G. B. Adriani to Vasari in 1568. For Apelles, Roskill 104–7, 138–9, 148–9, 150–1, 156–7, 174–5.
78 Thylesius *Libellus de Coloribus* (1528) in Goethe 1957 [**225**], 118. Dolce 1565 [**197**], 17r where he insisted, astonishingly, that painters still used only the white of Milo. He referred to Thylesius's book on 6v.
79 Thylesius in Goethe 1957 [**225**], 111; Dolce 1565 [**197**], 7r. Dolce also referred to Titian on 51v and 64r.
80 There is no mention of the 4-colour theory in Pino (1548), although Pino, a painter, was interested in technique, admired Titian and told several stories about Apelles. Nor was it especially noticed by Lodovico Domenichi in the commentary to his translation of Pliny (Venice, 1561), although he made several references to contemporary artists, including Titian (2nd edn 1573, 1087, 1110). For Domenichi, who had been close to Doni in the 1540s, Grendler 1969 [**233**], 52ff, 66ff.
81 Borenius 1923 [**175**], 12ff; Montjosieu 1649 [**274**], Pt III, 59ff.
82 Ridolfi 1914 [**305**], 107. For the later interpretation of Rubens's flesh-painting in terms of a few simple, bright and optically mixed colours, Gage 1969 [**217**], 62f; Sonnenburg and Preusser 1979 [**330**], III, n.p.

83 For modern views of the arbitrariness of the 'primary' set, Gloye 1957/8 [**224**], 128ff; Frodl-Kraft 1977/8 [**215**], 102ff.
84 But see p. 26 above for purple as red and for the antique taste for reddish gold. The 5th-century BC writer Ion of Chios also tells a story about 'purple' which suggests that the Greeks were perfectly aware of the discrepancy between colour-perception and colour-terminology (Russell and Winterbottom 1972 [**312**], 4–5).
85 See the list of 13 colours in a 12th-century MS of the *Mappae Clavicula* (Roosen-Runge 1967 [**131**], I, 185ff). A slightly amplified version with 15 colours is in the 14th-century Fr. (?) *Liber de Coloribus* (Thompson 1926 [**335**], 288). The 15th-century Portuguese *Livro de como se fazan as Côres* lists 10 principal colours, most of them names of pigments (1928–9 and 1930 [**258**], 130 and 80 respectively). M. F. Edgerton 1963 [**203**], 194 points out that the word *color* in a 15th-century Ger. *Tractatus de Coloribus* usually refers to a colouring-agent rather than a concept. An exception to this general rule is in the 13th-century additions to *Eraclius*, which list black and white in several varieties and then the intermediates *rubeus, viridis, croceus, purpureus, prasinus, azur* and *indicus*, only the last of which is clearly a pigment, although the list includes 2 blues and 2 greens (Merrifield 1849 [**271**], I, 244–5).
86 *De Arte Illuminandi* 1975 [**193**], 36ff. Since the attribution of a 3-colour theory to Pliny is clearly an error, some earlier editors amended the reading *Pliniam* to *physicam*.
87 Cennini 1971 [**184**], xxxvi, 35. These pigments have been analysed in detail by Bensi 1978/9 [**164**], 37–85. The division into 'natural' and 'artificial' is an ancient one; for Vitruvius (VII, vii) the 'natural' colours were yellow-ochre (*sil*), red-ochre, minium, white, green and yellow (orpiment). His epitomizer Faventinus (*c.* AD 300) omitted *sil* but added the blues *chrysocolla, armenium* and *indicum* (Plommer 1973 [**297**], 74ff). For the medieval interest in Faventinus, in the context of pigments, Gransden 1957 [**230**], 370. For Michelangelo Biondo the 'natural' colours were blue, red, yellow and green, plus black and white (1549 [**170**], 21r).
88 E.g. Mario Equicola, *Libro di natura d'amore* (1525) in Barocchi 1971–7 [**161**], II (1973), 2153; F. P. Morato *Del significato dei colori* (1535) in ibid. 2176; also Borghini 1584 [**176**], 230.
89 Parkhurst 1973 [**287**], espec. 425.
90 The earliest unambiguous use of *ceruleus* or *caeruleus* as a yellow I have noticed is in Matthew Paris's illustrated inventory *The Jewels of St Albans* (1257, British Libary, Cotton Nero DI, f.146): 'gemmam oblongam coloris cerulei, videlicet topazium' refers to a stone painted yellow. Luard's edn (Paris VI, 1882 [**285**], 383) reads 'caerulei'. The *Summa Philosophiae* (1265/75) attributed to Robert Kilwardby refers to 'color caeruleus et maxime scintillans, qualis est topasius Chrysopassus itemque Chrysolitus' (i.e. yellow stones; McKeon 1948 [**262**], 10ff; text in Grosseteste 1912 [**234**], 631). For the topaz as a yellow stone, Marbode of Rennes 1977 [**267**], 50f. Pliny (XXXV, xxii, 39) and Isidore of Seville (XVI, ix, 10) had referred to the island of Topazios as a source for ochre, which may be the origin of the idea. Young (1964 [**354**], 43) notes that Virgil calls the usually yellow Tiber *caeruleus*. Theodoric of Freiberg (1914 [**334**], 60) has 'caeruleus seu citrinus, quem Xancton vocant' from the Greek *xanthos*. The 8th-century *Glossaria Abstrusa* and *Abolita* give *caeruleus* and *ciruleus* as *viridis, glaucus vel niger* (*Glossaria Latina* 1926–31 [**223**], III (1926), 20, 110–11; *Mittellateinisches Wörterbuch*, s.v. *caeruleus*). *Glaucus*, usually translated as 'grey', could also mean yellow (see Bacon 1897–1900 [**156**], II, 197; 1937 [157], 70ff;' MacLean 1966 [**261**], 40). Theodoric of Freiberg (44) has 'citrinus sive glaucus' as does the 15th century collection of lapidaries at Prague (Rose 1875 [307], 345).
91 E. Barbaro 1534 [**159**], 378. In Pt II (465), where he discussed the 4-colour painters, Barbaro was less certain that *sil* could be a blue, as well as yellow ochre. For his otherwise empirical approach to editing Pliny, Branco 1963 [**180**], 193ff.
92 Vitruvius 1521 [**343**], cxxv, with reference to VI, xiv, where imitation *Attic sil* was described as an infusion of violets, although the resulting colour, called *sillacetus* in the later Middle Ages, was a yellow (Merrifield 1849 [**271**], I, 36, 251). Thylesius in Goethe 1957 [**225**], 118. Philander 1544 [**290**], 232 noted Barbaro's view but preferred to regard *sil* as 'coloris purpurei violacei (qui et ianthinus dicitur)'. Veronese's patron Daniele Barbaro took the more comprehensive view that *sil* was a variety of ochre, 'ma di colore alquanto diverso, o che pendesse all'azzurro, o al purpureo, & violino' (D. Barbaro 1629 [**158**], 323).
93 Barocchi 1971–7 [**161**], I, 632–3. It was partly at Borghini's request that G. B. Adriani supplied the resumé of the history of Greek painting to Vasari for the 2nd edn of the *Vite* in which the competition with Protogenes and the dark (*bruno*) varnish were mentioned but not the 4 colours (Vasari 1878–85 [**340**], I (1878), 15ff).
94 Grégoire 1576 [**232**], 563ff; see the index: 'Coloribus quattuor omnes alios misceri'. Elsewhere (242) Grégoire described black and white as the chief colours and proposed a scale with 5 intermediates: *albus, glaucus, puniceus, ruber, purpureus, viridis, niger*. Scaliger 1601 [**316**], 1047 included *sil* among the blues.
95 Montjosieu 1649 [**274**], 59–60. He proposed instead that the 'lines' were the 3 tonal areas corresponding to highlight, mid-tone (*splendor*), in which the hue was clearest, and shadow. This solution is close to Gombrich 1976 [**228**], who has solved the problem of the 4th colour rather neatly by proposing a blue ground for the panel. It was probably Montjosieu's example that led Carlo Dati (who cites him in 1667 [**192**], 169) to consult Ciro Ferri on the nature of Apelles' line but Ferri was inclined to the 'outline' theory (Minto 1953 [**273**], 116).
96 These mixtures were followed by Vossius 1650 [**344**], 74f but were attacked by Schefferus 1669 [**319**], 161f (see Ellenius 1960 [**205**], 181ff). Schiffermüller 1772 [**324**], 38f cited them as an instance of how even learned men could err if they neither experimented themselves nor consulted artists who did.
97 Scarmilionius 1601 [**317**], 122, where, however, it is argued that certain colours cannot be mixed from these primaries. Boodt 1609 [**174**], I, viii, 8 (see Parkhurst 1971 [**286**], 3f). Scarmilionius, who was professor of theoretical medicine at Vienna, dedicated his treatise to Rudolph II, one of whose physicians was de Boodt, whose view of the primaries may depend on his. Another theorist discussed by Parkhurst (1973 [**287**], 242ff) was Louis Savot but I have been unable to trace a 3-colour theory in Savot 1609 [**315**]. Savot does offer a 4-colour theory based on Pliny (Index, 6r ff; cf. 13v, 17v ff) which interprets *sil* as *bleu* and appeals to the 'daily experience' of craftworkers, including painters. All these authors were students of medicine; colour was particularly important to physicians, for the study of urine, as a diagnostic tool. The Peripatetic *On Colours* as well as Thylesius were often printed as appendices to J. Actuarius *De Urinis* (e.g. Paris 1548, 259).
98 Boulenger 1627 [**178**], 106; cf. 10, 14 on Pliny's 4-colour story, reproduced without comment. For a comparable vagueness, Pierre le Brun *Recueil des essais des merveilles de la peinture* (1635) in Merrifield 1849 [**271**], II, 771–3.
99 Van Mander (1916 [**265**], 302ff) clearly regarded Attic *sil* as yellow, for he congratulated the moderns on having 4 yellows where the ancients had but 1. See also Schiffermüller 1772 [**324**], 36, 38.
100 Cureau de la Chambre 1650 [**190**], 159f. The reference to lightning is to Apelles's painting of Alexander the Great holding a bolt of lightning, and presumably the painting of lightning itself, both recorded by Pliny (XXXV, xxxvi, 92, 96).
101 Sandrart 1675 [**313**], 86. The Latin version (1683 [**314**], 69) had an additional section on Classical painting, including a reference to Apelles's 4 colours, but without comment.
102 De Piles 1699 [**292**], 131, 257–8. He later (1708 [**293**], 352) argued that the 4 colours could only be an underpainting, which would be finished in lighter 'aerial' tones.
103 Pliny 1725 [**295**], 44.
104 Hagedorn 1775 [**236**], II, 201 (original Ger. edn 1762).
105 Ibid., 202f. Anxious to save Pliny's story, he also stressed that it could only apply to flesh-painting, since there was clear evidence in Pliny (XXXIII, iv, 11) and at Herculaneum that blue was used by the ancients (201, 204).
106 Förster 1887 [**214**], 35ff, 45–6, 48–9.
107 Col. pl. *Apollo*, LXXVI, 1962, 397.
108 Trevisani in col.: *Connoisseur*, CXCIII, 1976, 209; Montreal version of Tiepolo in Morassi 1955 [**275**], pl. II. The absence of blue was a standard feature of 18th-century palettes for flesh, yet Webb 1760 [**347**], 80n. cast doubt on the authenticity of Pliny's story because the 4 colours cited were incapable of forming 'a perfect carnation'.
109 See Pliny XXXV, xxxvi, 73. For Oeser's Tiepolesque prototype, see Morassi 1962 [276], 13, 42, and fig. 233.
110 See *De David à Delacroix* 1974/5 [**194**], no. 37, pl. 147, dated *c.* 1814.
111 This may be the *Alexandre cédant Campaspe* (Salon 1817) pl. 18.
112 The painting was with Wildenstein, London, in 1981.
113 Paillot de Montabert 1829 [**281**], II, 245–6 and VII, 367–8; Ziegler 1852 [**355**], 15. It is not clear whether Ingres was as interested in Apelles's colour as he was in his line (*Ingres* 1947 [**246**], I, 57): in the *Apotheosis of Homer* (1827, Louvre) Apelles, wearing his standard blue cloak, holds a palette seen from the back; in the watercolour at Lille, his cloak is pink and his palette faces the spectator but bears no colours. In the 1820s the English theorist Charles Hayter (1826 [**241**], 14–15) proposed that the ancients had used the 3 primaries plus black.
114 Chevreul 1854 [**185**], §342. In the 1820s B. R. Haydon was showing Thomas Phillips that the range of the 4-colour palette could be extended by contrasts, including the 'management' of black to look blue (Haydon 1926 [**239**], I, 395). Phillips remained doubtful that the whole range of colour could be represented with the 4 colours, rather than the modern primaries (Phillips 1833, [**291**], 352–3).
115 Northcote 1818 [**279**], I, 40.
116 Reynolds 1852 [**17**], II, 328f.
117 Eastlake 1847–69 [**202**], II, 255ff.
118 Reynolds 1852 [**17**], II, 337; cf. 328.
119 Ibid., 337, and 339 on the pre-eminence of this system. Du Fresnoy (1667 [**199**], ll. 339–40) had characterized the *corruptio colorum* as specifically Venetian. For Reynolds as a glazer, H. Buttery in Hudson 1958 [**244**], 248ff.
120 Blake 1956 [**171**], 612 (*Descriptive Catalogue*).
121 Bindman 1977 [**168**], 125ff.
122 Bentley 1969 [**165**], 468; for the drawing, Butlin 1981 [**181**], no. 753.
123 Blake 1956 [**171**], 617 and 590. where Apelles and Protogenes are called 'fresco' painters. Blake 1973 [**172**], 32: 'Ghiottos circle or Apelles line were not the work of Sketchers drunk with wine'.
124 Bindman 1977 [**168**], 136ff. For the marginalia, Blake 1956 [**171**], 791ff.
125 Gilchrist 1942 [**221**], 60. For *Enoch*, Bindman 1978 [**169**], no. 413 and for technique and dating, Essick 1980 [**207**], 161–3. Blake's own palette (Victoria and Albert Museum, London) is too badly preserved to reveal much about the order of colours to optical inspection.
126 C. Lénormant, *Gérard, peintre d'histoire*, 2nd edn 1847, 55, cit. Rubin 1975 [**309**], 787–9.

3 Light from the East

1 Mango 1972 [**501**], 72.
2 The non-religious character of much Byzantine *ekphrasis* has been emphasized by Macrides and Magdalino 1988 [**494**], 51. Chorikos does refer to the iconography of the symbolic scenes in other parts of his account.
3 Mango 1972 [**501**], 69–70.
4 Ibid., 85–6.
5 Gnoli 1971 [**83**], 25ff. A renewed interest in the collection of examples of these marbles is an aspect of that 19th-century revival of polychromy described in ch. 1 above (see Mielsch 1985 [**521**], 9–11).
6 Abel 1931 [**357**], espec. 6, 8ff; Downey 1959 [**420**], cols 938ff.
7 Abel 1931 [**357**], 12f.
8 Ibid., 26, n. 1.
9 For this type of imagery, Maguire 1987 [**496**].
10 Mango 1972 [**501**], 63.
11 Salzmann 1982 [**133**], espec. 59ff.
12 On this pavement, Tomašević 1973 [**586**], 37ff and for the subject-matter, Maguire 1987 [**496**], 36ff.
13 On Tivoli, Lugli 1928 [**490**], 168ff; on Sta Costanza, Stern 1958 [**577**], 59ff.
14 Lugli 1928 [**490**], 172 and fig. 14.
15 For *vitris*, Pliny [**296**], XXXVI, lxiv, 189; Statius, *Silvae*, I, 5, 42–3; Seneca,

Epistolae, LXXXVI, 6f. For *musivum*, Svennung 1941 [579], 175ff; Calabi-Limentani 1958 [396], 14; A. Walde, *Lateinisches Etymologisches Wörterbuch*, II, 1954, s.v. *museum*. The Greek usage derives from the Latin and is no earlier than the 6th century AD (P. Chantraine, *Dictionnaire etymologique de la langue grècque*, III, 1974, s.v. *moũsa*). Lavagne (1983 [482], 262ff) has stressed the link between the oriental taste for gemstones and the taste for glass in Marcus Aemilius Scaurus, to whom the new fashion was attributed.

16 Perler 1953 [539]; L'Orange and Nordhagen 1965 [113], 74 (pl. 39). For gold mosaic in a pavement at Antioch, Levi 1947 [487], I, 630ff; Dyggve 1962 [421], 220; in an Early Christian oratory on the Via Augusta at Aquileia, Fiorentini Roncuzzi I, 1971 [430], 54. A 9th-century *ekphrasis* of a church in Constantinople condemns the use of gold in pavements as 'excessive luxury' but without citing any e.gs after Homer (Frolow 1945 [434], 46). See also Brenk 1971 [389], 18–25.

17 Vopel 1899 [594], 3, 18f.

18 Stern 1958 [577], 188.

19 Cf. ibid., 163 that the turret seems to have been an afterthought. See also ibid., 206ff. For the gold highlights in Sta Pudenziana, Kitzinger 1963 [471], 108f. Oakeshott 1967 [532], 64 suggests that the metallic tessserae in Sta Costanza may have been added during the extensive 1836–43 restorations but Stern (1958 [577], 193f) shows on the basis of a 16th-century drawing that at least one of these vaults must have been restored substantially as it was.

20 Torp 1963 [588] (good col. pls), espec. 46ff; Pelakanidis 1963 [538], 34–6. For the dating, Kleinbauer 1972 [474], 27 and Speiser 1984 [574], 130f.

21 For S. Vittore, Bovini 1970 [386], 146ff; for Sta Eirene, George 1912 [438].

22 Demus 1949 [409], for a survey of these mosaics.

23 Joly 1965 [461], 51–73. But a small fountain-niche from Baia (? 2nd century AD; Fitzwilliam Museum, Cambridge) shows a far looser setting and more irregular tesserae.

24 First half of 5th century. For good col. pls, Zovatto 1968 [611]. For the technique, Deichmann II, 1974 [406], 70. His observations of the size of the tesserae in the lunettes of the Good Shepherd and St Lawrence are not convincing; nor are Nordhagen's on the flatness of Italian as opposed to Byzantine setting (1983 [531], 83, n. 32).

25 Forsyth and Weitzmann 1965 [433], pls CXXIV-CXXVIII; Cormack 1969 [402], 30; Hawkins 1968 [451], 155 and fig. 11.

26 George 1912 [438], 51ff. Other e.gs of raking adduced in the literature, e.g. in the halo of the symbol of St Luke in S. Apollinare in Classe, Ravenna (Bovini 1954 [381], 10; L'Orange and Nordhagen 1965 [113], 62) and the small cross on the triumphal arch at Hosios David in Thessaloniki (Frolow 1951 [435], 205), do not seem to have the effect of accenting the fall of light but this may simply be the result of too even modern lighting.

27 Underwood and Hawkins 1961 [591], 194. It seems to me that the settings of Hosios Loukas and Daphni in Greece are also flush. For the mosaics of the Nea Moni, Mouriki 1985 [522], expec. 98.

28 Reali 1858 [548], 12ff; Muraro 1961 [527].

29 Bruneau 1972 [390], 245.

30 Oakeshott 1967 [532], 57, captions to pls 17, 18.

31 As in Fiorentini Roncuzzi 1971 [430], 13. For the *Battle of Alexander*, Fuhrmann 1931 [73]; for the small panels in Naples, Bieber and Rodenwaldt 1911 [379], espec. 17f. For an opposite view, that the 'Roman' technique is a 'stale continuation of the illusionistic ancient mosaic art', Nordhagen 1965 [530], 165–6. It is arguable that the 'Roman' technique relates just as closely to the 'impressionistic' mural paintings of the catacombs.

32 See the e.gs cit. Gage 1978 [74], 114–15.

33 Ptolemy 1956 [546], (II, 95–6) 59–61: 'Now we see . . . how, because of distance or the speed of movement, the sight in each of these [cases] is not strong enough to perceive and interpret the parts individually'. Alexander of Aphrodisias (3rd century) discussed the case of optical mixture at a distance in his commentary on Aristotle's *On Sense* 440a, 16–30 (Alexander of Aphrodisias 1901 [361], 53–7).

34 Demus wrote (1949 [409], 383ff) that the technique of using several smaller tesserae for each detail from the late 5th century (e.g. at S. Vitale in Ravenna) 'was very much in the way of nineteenth-century pointillism. Like illusionistic painting in general, this technique of mosaic was meant for the distant view. Looked at from a distance the colour-dots appear as modelled forms . . . The evolution from the fourth to the eighth century may be likened to the stylistic developments of modern French painting from Monet to Seurat.' For a discussion of this passage, Gage 1978 [74], 112ff.

35 L'Orange and Nordhagen 1965 [113], 57.

36 Ptolemy 1956 [546] (II, 10ff) 15–17. Schultz 1904 [136], 103.

37 They are espec. prominent in the nave mosaics of Sta Maria Maggiore, in the Chapel of S. Zeno in S. Prassede, Rome, and in the Chapel of S. Aquilino in S. Lorenzo, Milan, as well as in the narrative cycle in S. Apollinare Nuovo, Ravenna. For an example in an earlier pavement, see the heads of Dionysus and a maenad from Utica (*c.* 400 AD) in the British Museum (54g, k). The tesserae at the Rotunda of St George have an average of 005cm^2 and those at S. Prassede about 0.67cm^2 (*Dictionnaire d'archéologie chrétienne et liturgie* 1935 [412], col. 70).

38 See espec. the 13th-century mosaics of the Parigoritissa at Arta (good col. pls in Orlandos 1963 [534]); Underwood 1967–75 [146], II, pls 33, 34, 45, 69, 70.

39 Winfield 1968 [606], 128; J. Plesters in Talbot-Rice 1968 [582], 229.

40 Bovini 1954 [381], 7; Forsyth and Weitzmann 1965 [433], 16; George 1912 [438], 47; Mango and Hawkins 1965 [502], 125.

41 The 12th-century treatise of Theophilus specifies white glass as a basis for gold mosaic (1961, 46). At Sta Maria Maggiore the gold tesserae are on a base of several colours: greenish, brown, yellowish, pink as well as colourless (Astorri 1934 [368], 56). Mr E. Hawkins has kindly informed me that he has found no examples of gold on a red glass base outside Italy. Some gold cubes in the museum at Pula in Istria (Croatia) have a green glass body, as do some at Ravenna, Aachen and Germigny-des-Près (from mosaics in Ravenna): del Medico 1943 [508], 98–9. Red setting-beds have been found, e.g., in a 9th-century mosaic in Cyprus (Megaw and Hawkins 1977 [510], 132ff) and in Sta Sophia, Istanbul, from the 9th century, although earlier and later examples there are set in yellow. This difference may be attributable to the different functions of the underpainting: the red was to affect the final appearance of the mosaics, the yellow simply to give the painter an overall guide to the colour-composition. For the related use of a red ground for gold leaf in MS illumination from *c.* the 8th century, S. M. Alexander 1964 [363], 42ff. A red silk core was used for some medieval gold thread (G. M. Crowfoot in Battiscome 1956 [373], 433), although yellow core was also widespread (Falke 1921 [429], 26).

42 Letter 20, trans. Mathew 1975 [505], 218–19.

43 Photius 1958 [540], 140.

44 Stratton 1917 [141], 71f. 'The passages [of the eye] are arranged alternately of fire and water: by the passages of fire we perceive white objects; by those of water, things black; for in each of these cases [the objects] fit into the given [passages].' For Empedocles and Plato *Timaeus* 67c f, Kranz 1912 [99], 126.

45 Photius 1958 [540], 294. Haas 1907 [449], 354–62 gives a good summary of these theories, including the eclectic Early Christian opinions. Paul the Silentiary had held the opposite view to Photius, namely that vision was a function of rays emanating from the objects seen (Mango 1972 [501], 86, 87).

46 Photius 1958 [540], 187. Mango refers this passage puzzlingly to Aristotle *Metaphysics* 985b; Photius's source is surely Alexander of Aphrodisias *On Mixture*, 214 in Todd 1976 [338], 110–11.

47 See Pauly-Wissowa 1894–1978 [117], IX, cols 2549ff; for *Myriobiblion*, Photius 1959–77 [541], II, 1960, 149–59.

48 Photius 1958 [540], 185.

49 On the re-use of materials, del Medico 1943 [508], 85; Mango 1972 [501], 132; Frolow 1951 [435], 202; Mouriki 1985 [522], 103. On changes in medium, Frolow 1951 [435], 184. On hierarchy of materials, Underwood 1967–75 [146], I, 179f. On substitution of materials, Bovini 1954 [381], 105, 1957 [382], 24; Cormack 1969 [402], 40; Cormack and Hawkins 1977 [403], 218; Mouriki op. cit., 101, 102; Belting, Mango and Mouriki 1978 [378], 89; Megaw and Hawkins 1977 [510], 132ff.

50 Statius and Seneca, see n. 15 above; Koldewey 1884 [476], 39f; Karageorghis 1969 [464], pls 175–6; Bovini 1954 [381], 16.

51 See refs in n. 15 above.

52 Methodius 1958 [515], 222.

53 De Bruyne 1957 [392], 356, 360; Maier 1964 [497], 11.

54 Khatchatrian 1962 [467].

55 Cyril of Jerusalem, cit. Dölger 1918 [417], 3–4.

56 Sciaretta 1966 [567], 29f (although Khatchatrian 1962 [467], 63 had suggested that there were originally 2 entrances at Albenga, on the E. side of the building, flanking the apse with the mosaics). De Bruyne 1957 [392], 360 also points out that the monogram in the vault must be read looking W.

57 Bovini 1954 [381], 17f notes a cupola mosaic in the Temple of Diana, Baia, and in other pagan temples.

58 L'Orange and Nordhagen 1965 [113], 45 and pl. VII.

59 The most useful catalogue of these decorations is Waetzoldt 1964 [597].

60 See espec. Dölger 1925 [418], 198ff.

61 In this sense, Kitzinger's characterization of the 'magnificent evening sky' in S. Pancrazio seems implausible (1977 [472], 42). The example at Poreč includes perhaps the most spectacular of these dawn skies but it may be the result of a late 19th-century restoration (Conti 1988 [401], 302–3).

62 Capizzi 1964 [397], 191ff, 128ff (for Byzantine hymns referring to the *Pantokrator* in terms of light).

63 Aethelwulf 1967 [359], 51, l. 639.

64 For display on the altar, Sauer 1924 [560], 177f; Henderson 1987 [453], 126. For processions, Tschan II, 1951 [589], 76; Steenbock 1965 [575], 52ff.

65 The Bamberg inventory of 1127 lists 'sex tabulos ad imponendos libros auro et gemmis ornati' (*Mittelalterliche Schatzverzeichnisse* I, 1967 [109], 17).

66 Kendrick et al. 1960 [466], II, 10. Also Eddius 1927 [423], 37; Symeonis Monachus, 1882–5 [580], I, 67–8.

67 John of Damascus, cit. Kantorowicz 1963 [463], 141ff; Constantine of Rhodes, cit, Runciman 1975 [555], 87. This understanding of the Virgin as unlocking Paradise was, by the 10th century, embodied in Byzantine court ceremonial. In the Christmas Day court liturgy, chanters in the Imperial progress, by the clock of Sta Sophia, repeated the verse 'The Virgin, at Bethlehem, has re-opened Paradise, which was in Eden' (Constantine VII 1935–40 [400], I, 31).

68 Andreescu 1976 [367], 258ff has dated the apse mosaic to the late 12th century, about a century after the mosaics on the W. wall; but she postulates an earlier fresco in the apse which may have included the same iconography.

69 For the remarkable iconography of this programme, Maksimovic 1964 [499], 247ff; but see also n. 61 above.

70 Grabar 1955 [442], 305ff; Sacopoulo 1975 [558].

71 *Metallis*, often translated as 'enamels', referring to glass mosaic; but Goldschmidt 1940 [439], 137 points out that *metallum* derives from the Greek *metallon*, a (marble-)quarry. A reference to *vitrei metalli* in the 6th-century poem of Corippus (I, 99) may be read in this sense rather than as the 'glassy metal' proposed by his recent translator (Corippus 1976 [187], 89 and 133n.). Since there is frequently a mixture of marble and glass even in Roman mosaics, it seems better to translate *metallis* with the less specific 'mosaics'. In SS Cosmas and Damian there is very little gold.

72 Oakeshott 1967 [532], 94. The Roman *tituli* have been collected by E. Diehl 1963 [414]. For the 6th-century *tituli* at Poreč, Maksimovic 1964 [499], 247–8; for the similar 13th-century inscription on the ciborium mosaics there, Demus 1945 [408], 238ff. Some Byzantine e.gs are in the *Greek Anthology* 1969 [447], I, 1–18.

73 Bovini 1964 or [383], 180f. The inscription is now largely effaced but survives in a 15th-century copy of the 9th-century *Liber Pontificalis Ecclesiae Ravennatis*.

74 Mango 1972 [501], 59; Palmer 1988 [535], 132. Also L'Orange 1974/5 [533], 191–202.

75 Michelis 1963 [519], 221ff; Kähler 1967 [462], 30ff; Mainstone 1988 [498], 124–6.

76 Demus 1960 [**410**], 87n., 207. For a similar blocking-up of windows in Sta Maria Maggiore, Rome, Karpp 1966 [**465**], 10; for the Palatine Chapel, Palermo, Beck 1970 [**377**], 151.
77 Demus 1949 [**409**], 110.
78 For *transennae*, Schöne 1979 [**566**], 46ff. A catalogue of surviving e.gs in Günter 1968 [**448**], 80ff. For glass, Schöne, ibid. 53f; Günter, ibid. 83; Megaw 1963 [**509**], 349–67; Mango 1962 [**500**], 43.
79 Mango 1972 [**501**], 74. This reflects the Kontakion for the 2nd inauguration of Sta Sophia at Christmas 562 (Palmer 1988 [**535**], 141).
80 *Contra Vigilantium*, cit. Mathews 1971 [**506**], 149; Dölger 1925 [**418**], 107ff.
81 Dölger 1936 [**419**], 10ff.
82 Egeria 1960 [**424**], 31ff; 1971 [**425**], 123f.
83 Underwood 1967–75 [**146**], I, 15; see also Metochites's own account in I. Ševčenko, 'Theodore Metochites, the Chora and the intellectual trends of his times' in Underwood, IV, 66–7, which emphasizes simply the sense of community.
84 Cf. Constantine VII, 1935–40 [**400**], I, 5, 12.
85 Mango 1972 [**501**], 89–91.
86 Khitrowo 1889 [**468**], 91f, 118, 264. For the 180 lamps, chandeliers and candelabra presented by Constantine to the Lateran Basilica in Rome, the *Liber Pontificalis* in Davis-Weyer 1971 [**405**], 12. For the 27 lights used in even a small domestic chapel in north Africa in the 2nd century, Dix 1945 [**416**], 24–5. In the museum at Sfax, Tunisia, is a 6th-century mosaic panel from the Baptistry at La Skhirra, depicting 4 gemmed crosses, each hung with 2 lamps. Some of the few surviving glass lamps from the Byzantine period have been studied by A. Grabar 1971 [**444**], 107ff.
87 For this view, see espec. Mango 1972 [**501**], xiv–v; Mango 1963 [**266**], espec. 64ff; Maguire 1974 [**495**], espec. 128ff. For the earlier period Wallace-Hadrill 1968 [**598**], 97f.
88 Michelis 1952 [**517**], espec. 39ff; ibid., 1955 [**518**]; Mathew 1963 [**105**], espec. chs 1, 3; Lazarev 1967 [**484**], espec. 24f; Rüth 1977 [**556**], 757, which extends a symbolic reading of late Byzantine art back into its earlier history. James and Webb (1991 [**459**], 1–17) have sought to reconcile these two traditions by an appeal to the rhetorical context of ekphrasis.
89 Meyendorff 1964 [**516**], 127; C. Diehl 1910 [**413**], 305.
90 Anastos 1955 [**365**], 179. For the 'realistic' basis of icons, see also P. J. Alexander 1958 [**362**], espec. 199.
91 Khitrowo 1889 [**468**], 95.
92 Dionysius of Fourna 1974 [**415**]; for Ulpian, Mango 1972 [**501**], 214–15.
93 Mango 1972 [**501**], 237; also a 14th-century example on 249; Pausanius 1971 [**118**], II, 477, where Onatas, son of Mikon, when asked by the Phigalians for a statue of Demeter, found a copy or a painting of the ancient wooden idol, and found out most . . . by a vision of it in his sleep, and made the Phigalians a statue in bronze'. For the Christian adoption of pagan attitudes to idols, P. J. Alexander 1958 [**362**], ch. II.
94 Rosenthal 1975 [**554**], 44. On the whole question of the portrait, Spatharakis 1976 [**572**]. A 4th-century text of Athanasius of Alexandria, emphasizing the importance of a recognizable likeness of the Emperor, has been repr. by Bryer and Herrin 1977 [**393**], 181, no. 10. See also the decree of the Seventh Ecumenical Council, cited by Sahas 1986 [**559**], 101.
95 Gregory of Nyssa *Commentary on the Song of Songs* I, i in Mathew 1975 [**505**], 220; see also St John Chrysostom in Mango 1972 [**501**], 47–8.
96 For the Council of 754, Anastos 1955 [**365**], 179; Photius 1958 [**540**], 290; for John of Damascus, *Patrologia Graeca* [**116**], XCIV, col. 1361D and Mathew 1963 [**105**], 118; Manasses, cit. Maguire 1974 [**495**], 127–8. The closest prototype for this view seems to be Plato *Statesman* 277b-c.
97 Lange 1969 [**480**], 235.
98 The decorative (i.e. unrealistic) use of colour in animals in the Byzantine 'inhabited scroll' mosaic pavements has been noted by Dauphin 1978 [**404**], espec. 404ff.
99 *Carmen de se ipso et de Episcopis* in *Patrologia Graeca* [**116**], XXXVIII, col. 1220); Galavaris 1969 [**436**].
100 Underwood 1959 [**590**], 239; Kostof 1965 [**478**], 102f; Lazarev 1966 [**483**], 69.
101 For Sta Maria Maggiore, Astorri 1934 [**368**], 59.
102 Frolow 1951 [**435**], 303.
103 Mango 1972 [**501**], 203; see also Mesaretes in ibid., 232. Later admirers of the Pantokrator figure simply marvelled at the discrepancy between its real and its apparent size: Nicephorus Gregoras in ibid., 249; Clavijo 1928 [**399**], 74.
104 Bultmann 1821 [**394**], 251. See also the 9th-century sermon of Leo VI (Mango 1972 [**501**], 203, 205, and espec. Frolow 1945 [**434**], 46).
105 Mango 1972 [**501**], 13.
106 Paulinus *Carmen* XXVII, 387–8 (Goldschmidt 1940 [**439**], 52ff, 96, 136); Venantius Fortunatus *Opera Poetica* III, vii, in *Monumenta Germania Historica* IV, i, 1881, 57; Giselmanus *Vita Droctovei* in *MGH Scriptores Rerum Merovingiarum* III, ed. Krusch, 1896, 541. See also Sidonius Apollinaris, on a church at Lyon dedicated 469 or 470, *Letter* II, 10 in Davis-Weyer 1971 [**405**], 55: 'Within is shining light, and the gilding of the coffered, ceiling allures the sunbeams golden as itself. The whole basilica is bright with diverse marbles, floor, vaulting and windows all adorned with figures of most various colour, and mosaic green as a blooming mead shows its design of sapphire cubes winding through the ground of verdant glass.'
107 For the heaven image, Mango 1972 [**501**], 26, 58, 63, 83, 86, 197–8, 219, 229. See also the mid-7th-century *titulus* in S. Stefano Rotondo, Rome (cit. Bovini 1964b [**384**], 105–6); Nicephorus Kallisti Xanthopoulos (14th century) *Church History* in Richter 1897 [**551**], 368, no. 980; Beck 1970 [**377**], 122, and for the ceiling of the Palatine Chapel in general, Ettinghausen 1962 [**426**], 44ff.
108 Richter 1897 [**551**], 368, no. 980; other examples in Mango 1972 [**501**], 101, 102, 197, 205; Mango and Parker 1960 [**503**], 239–40, 243. For the traditional description of the 12 slabs of green Proconessian marble in front of the sanctuary of S. Marco, Venice, Günter 1968 [**448**], 38. The petrification of the sea, an idea which may derive from Statius IV, ii, is analogous to the idea of ice in the 11th-century Romance *Digines Akrites* (Mango 1972 [**501**], 216) and to the vitrified sea in Alfano da Salerno's contemporary poem on Monte Cassino (Acocella 1963 [**358**], v. 150). A late Western example is in Baudri of Bourgueil's *Carmen* 134 (once 196), on the quarters of the Countess Adèle, whose mosaic pavement was described as a 'glass sea' (*vitreum Mare*) and was perceived to be in movement like the sea (Baudri of Bourgueil 1979 [**374**], 168, ll. 728ff). For links with Mosaics representing the ocean, Barral y Altet 1987 [**372**], 41–54. The analogy with textiles was not uncommon: see Mango 1972 [**501**], 104, 194, 216; Mesarites 1957 [**514**], 890. For the textile origins of the vault-pattern in the Mausoleum of Galla Placida, Kitzinger 1977 [**472**], 54.
109 Athenaeus XII, 542D, cit. Robertson 1965 [**552**], 84f; Horace *Epistles* I, 10, 19ff; Statius II, ii; *Greek Anthology* 1969 [**447**], I, 10, 60–2 (of walls); Prudentius *Crowns of Martyrdom* in Davis-Weyer 1971 [**405**], 14 (mosaics under arches). For the Byzantine period, Mango 1972 [**501**], 37, 76, 164, 209; Runciman 1975 [**555**], 96; Frolow 1945 [**434**], 54; Zovatto 1963 [**610**], 47; Davis-Weyer 1971 [**405**], 138.
110 E.g. Mango 1972 [**501**], 205; John the Geometer (10th century) *Carmen* 96 in *Patrologia Graeca* [**116**], CVI, col. 943ff; Maguire 1987 [**496**], espec. 37 for a 6th-century *ekphrasis* by Avitus.
111 On the Aquilean Mosaic, Zovatto 1963 [**610**], 63ff; for the wave-pattern, ibid., 141, 161ff; Stern 1957 [**576**], 387, fig. 4 (Salona); Barral y Altet 1985 [**370**], 24ff, 45ff, 79ff.
112 Mango and Parker 1960 [**503**], 239ff.
113 Mango 1972 [**501**], 219.
114 Mango and Parker 1960 [**503**], 237.
115 Mango 1972 [**501**], 75; also Photius on the Church of the Virgin of the Pharos: 'it seems that everything is in ecstatic motion, and the church itself is circling round. For the spectator, through his whirling about in all directions and being constantly astir, which he is forced to experience by the variegated spectacle on all sides, imagines that his personal condition is transferred to the object' (ibid., 185). Both these passages were studied by Wulff 1929/30 [**608**], 536–9. See also Frolow 1951 [**435**], 206 and Michelis 1964 [**520**], 259. The idea was taken up in the West by Theophilus 1961 [**583**], 61–3.
116 Psellus 1953 [**543**], 188–90.
117 For the iconographic programmes from the 11th to the 13th centuries, Lafontaine-Dosogne 1979 [**479**], I, 287–329. Lazarev (1966 [**483**], 32) has estimated that at Sta Sophia in Kiev the spectator must move from W. to E. and circulate 3 times clockwise under the dome in order to read the frescoes in sequence.
118 One of the few art-historians to have appreciated this is Prandi 1952 [**542**], 291f.
119 See the discussion in Smith 1983 [**570**], 154ff.
120 Alberti 1972 [**154**], 92–3 on opposition to gold in painting. Elsewhere he recognized that the effect of mosaic came from irregular reflections from its surface (1966 [**153**], VI, x, 509).
121 P. Reutersward, 'What color is Divine Light?' in Hess and Ashbery 1969 [**454**], 109ff.
122 On the Annunciation including the Christ Child, I. Rogan in an unpublished paper given at the Fifteenth International Byzantine Congress, Athens, 1976; on the Sinai icon with the dove, Weitzmann 1971 [**599**], 169–70.
123 See, e.g., Christ's halo in the crypt paintings at Prousa, Greece (10th or 11th century); in the *Anastasis* in the Church of Sta Barbara at Soganli, Cappadocia (early 11th century); a 12th- or 13th-century Transfiguration mosaic (Louvre, Paris) and this scene in the 14th-century wall-paintings in the Church of the Hodegetria, Mistra; Cavallini's scene of the Dormition in his mosaics at Sta Maria in Trastevere (1291). See also pp. 74–5 above for stained glass.
124 Khitrowo [**468**], 1889, 75f. The appearance of this light was still a feature of the Good Friday Vespers about 1400 (ibid., 174) and it has been noted as recently as the second World War (S. Runciman *A Traveller's Alphabet*, 1991, 206), when it formed part of the celebrations of the morning of Holy Saturday.
125 Brehier 1945 [**388**], 19–28.
126 For examples, Gage 1978 [**74**], 125, n. 40.
127 Mesarites 1957 [**514**], 872. The references are to Psalm 97, 2; Mark 9:7 and Luke 9:34.
128 Aalen 1951 [**356**], espec. 81, 319; Hempel 1960 [**452**], 355–8, 367f; Scholem 1974 [**565**], espec. 5, 23f.
129 Koch 1956/7 [**475**].
130 Pseudo-Dionysius 1987 [**545**], 107, 265; cf. Puech 1938 [**547**]; Ivanka 1959 [**458**], cols 350–8.
131 See also the 14th-century MS in Paris reproduced by Reutersward in Hess and Ashbery 1969 [**454**], 114.
132 Pseudo-Dionysius 1987 [**545**], 137. For other links between him and Sinai, Gage 1978 [**74**], 111.
133 McGuckin 1986 [**491**], 157–8,
134 The texts are in *Patrologia Graeca* [**116**], XII, col. 1070.
135 Reiter 1962 [**550**], 77ff.
136 The list is recorded in a *Life of Ptolemy* in the library of Photius (1959–77 [**541**], VII, 1974, 128f) and copied in the Suda *Lexikon* (1935 [**578**], III, s.v. *opsis*, 602) but without the attribution to Ptolemy. The colours may correspond to those 'quidem splendidos' mentioned by Ptolemy (1956 [**546**], IX, 4) as seen 'simpliciter'. They are black, white, orange (*xanthos*), *phaion*, yellow (*ōchron*), red (*eruthros*), blue (kuanos), purple (*halurgos*), *lampron* and dark brown (*orphninon*). The most useful discussion of these terms is Mugler 1964 [**523**]. The lost first book of Ptolemy's *Optics* has been discussed by Lejeune 1948 [**485**], 19–20. See also Smith 1988 [**571**], 189ff.
137 For *kuaneos*, *porphurios* and *oinoros* (wine-colour) as related to black, Blümner 1891 [**380**], 188. Blümner also cites Servius on Virgil's *Georgics* III on the distinction between *candidus* and *albus*.
138 Suda 1935 [**578**], IV, s.v. *phaion*, 709–10.
139 One modern attempt to identify such a symbolism is Haeberlein 1939 [**450**], 78ff. The ancient link between colours and elements persisted: see Kirschbaum 1940 [**469**], 209–48. One of the rare contemporary descriptions of colour symbols, in the 9th-century account of the mosaics in S. Apollinare Nuovo, Ravenna, does not describe the colours as they now are, although this section (the Magi) was inserted at the instigation of the writer, Bishop Agnello (Mango 1972 [**501**], 108). The changes may be due to restorations, although this has not been noted in a discussion of Agnello's additions (Bovini 1966 [**385**], 65ff). For the colours of the Magi, McNally 1970 [**493**], 667–87.

140 Braun 1907 [**387**], 729ff. Lubeck 1912 [**489**], 802f argues for some constancy in the use of black, white and red in the Eastern Church but also mentions that red was used as a mourning colour. For a well documented and extensive listing of liturgical usage, see 'Farbe (Liturgisch)' in *Reallexikon zur deutschen Kunst-Geschichte*, VII, 1981 [**549**], cols 54–139.
141 Demus 1949 [**409**], 140, 145; Forlati 1949 [**432**], 86; Frolow 1951 [**435**], 204; Kitzinger1960 [**470**], 130, n. 106; Mango and Hawkins 1965 [**502**], 117; Young 1976 [**609**], 269–78; Kitzinger 1977 [**572**], 71–2; Lavagne 1977/8 [**481**], 431–44; C. Balnelle and J.-P. Darmon, 'L'Artisan-mosaïste dans l'Antiquité tardive: refléxions à partir des signatures' in Barral y Altet 1986 [**371**], 235–45; X. Barral y Altet, 'Commanditaires mosaïtes et execution specialisée de la mosaïque de pavement au Moyen Âge', ibid., 255–62.
142 Scheller 1963 [**564**]. Only Scheller's 4, 6, and 20 give indications of colour; Dionysius of Fourna (1974 [**415**], 38, 39, 40) also gives very few. The written instructions to painters in the 4th-century MS the Quedlinburg Itala Fragments do not mention colour (Davis-Weyer 1971 [**405**], 24–5). For some medieval MSS which do have indications of colours to be applied, sometimes in terms of pigments and sometimes of abstract classes, Gousset and Stirnemann 1990 [**441**], 189–98; Speciale 1990 [**573**], 339–50. On MSS as models, E. Kitzinger, 'The role of miniature painting in mural decoration' in Weitzmann et al. 1975 [**600**], espec. 109 on the Cotton Genesis, whose colour has recently been recontructed in Wenzel 1987 [**601**], 79–100. For mosaics see also Bruneau 1984 [**391**].
143 For further details of Peter's colours, Gage 1978 [**74**], 108. Rüth 1977 [**556**], 798 sees Peter as one of the few figures with a more or less fixed colour iconography but he also points out that Joseph sometimes wears the same combination and has the same physiognomy. Certainly physiognomy was always more important than colour for recognizing the Apostles: Mango 1972 [**501**], 42 and Davis-Weyer 1971 [**405**], 78–9.
144 Schultz 1904 [**136**], 103; Bieber and Rodenwaldt 1911 [**379**], 2.
145 Urso von Salerno 1976 [**592**], 110.
146 Serjeant 1972 [**568**], 142–3.
147 Tachau 1988 [**581**], 96, n. 34 (cf. 327, n. 36, 329, n. 43).
148 E.g. 1338 Inventory, nos 207, 208, 227, 239, using the terms *qui colorem mutat* and *cagnacolore* (Alessandri and Penacchi 1914 [**360**], 86–7). Mr Donald King has kindly informed me that a Pisan brokerage list of 1323 mentions *tartarini dicti cangia colore*, which both points to a central Asian origin and suggests that the term was a novel one.
149 Theophilus 1961 [**583**], 5f, 14f. It is conceivable that Theophilus was thinking of tonal rows modelling forms in mosaic, but in what is perhaps the most complicated 13th-century modelling, the columns in the scene of prayers for the recovery of the body of St Mark in S. Marco, Venice, no more than four steps can be identified (Demus 1984 [**411**], figs. 9, 10). The limit so far discovered is five (Winfield 1968 [**606**], 136ff. See also Dionysius of Fourna 1974 [**415**], 8); 'Heraclius' in Merrifield 1849 [**271**], I, ch. LVI, 250–7 has combinations of white, red and blue; brown-black and blue-green (*vergaut*); ch. LVIII has a red-green combination but otherwise the triads can be seen as the same genus of colour.
150 For mosaics, Logvin 1971 [**488**], pl. 58; for enamels, Gauthier 1972 [**437**], nos 45/6, 48, 88, 90. For an example as late as 1436, Müntz and Frothingham 1883 [**526**], 65.
151 D. Winfield in Talbot-Rice 1968 [**582**], 196–7 notes this in an Apostle in the scene of Doubting Thomas at Trebizond but the only Apostle in these colours is shaded tonally; he probably means the figure in the short green tunic, modulated with red, in the Miraculous Draught scene immediately below.
152 On the *proplasmus* or black ground, Underwood 1967–75 [**146**], I, 304ff; Winfield 1968 [**606**], 100ff.
153 Galen *On the Usefulness of the Parts of the Body* X, 3.
154 Basil in Wallace-Hadrill 1968 [**598**], 50; Baudri 1979 [**374**], no. 196.
155 For the green stones, Theophrastus 1965 [**584**], 65; Pliny [**296**], XXXVII, xvi, 62–3; Pseudo-Aristotle 1912 [**544**], 134, 151.
156 Martinelli 1969 [**504**], 51ff. Von Falke (1921 [**429**], 9), however, has linked the *segmenta* in the Theodora panel with 5th-century Greek stuffs rather than with Persia. See also the *tzitzakion*, the Imperial overgarment imported to Byzantium in the 8th century by the daughter of the Khan of Khazares, who married Constantine V. Its name probably derives from the Turkish *tschitschek*, 'flower' (Ebersolt 1923 [**422**], 52). Also Kondakoff 1924 [**477**], 7–49. The 14th-century official *Book of Offices* variously noted that particular costumes were of Persian or Assyrian origin (Pseudo-Kodinus 1966 [**124**], 181–2, 218–19).
157 Sabbe 1935 [**557**], 760–1, 813ff, 820ff, 1283.
158 Ibn Jobaïr 1949–65 [**455**], III (1953), 391.
159 Mango 1972 [**501**], 10.
160 Eusebius, cit. MacMullen 1964 [**492**], 438ff, where the whole question of the barbaric tastes of the army is discussed.
161 Ebersolt 1923 [**422**], 38f, 125, 143.
162 Carandini 1961/2 [**398**], 9ff. For a col. pl. of a *segmentum*, Lemberg and Schmedding 1973 [**486**], pl. I, and pl. II for a late 4th-century Egyptian wall-hanging showing figures with such panels on their tunics. The most recent study of the mosaics of Piazza Armerina has argued for their N. African workmanship (Wilson 1983 [**605**], 44).
163 Delvoye 1969 [**407**], 126–7.
164 Egeria 1960 [**424**], 35; 1971 [**425**], 127.
165 De Waal 1888 [**595**], 315, 318.
166 Nicephorus Gregoras *Antirrheticus* in A. Grabar 1957 [**443**], 177–9.
167 Mathew 1975 [**505**], 219.
168 Flavius Josephus *Antiquitates Judeorum* III, 183; Philo of Alexandria *Vita Mosis* II, 88. Another Byzantine writer, Cosmas Indicopleustes (*Topographie chrétienne*, II, 1970 [**587**], V, 35, 62–3), also refers in general to the symbolic link with the elements but adds that the colours were quite beautiful.
169 Schapiro 1977 [**562**], 12; Battiscombe 1956 [**373**], 107ff. The immediacy of the account is the more remarkable that Reginald was not an eye-witness and was writing 70 years after the event. There is nothing similar in the earlier anonymous account of the opening of the tomb, written after 1122 (Battiscombe ibid., 99–107). The vestments do not survive since they were removed and used in the Cathedral, where Reginald may, of course, have seen them (ibid., 111).
170 See espec. the 6th-century commentary on Aristotle's *Meteorology* quoted and trans. by Schultz 1904 [**136**], 103.
171 Schapiro 1977 [**562**], 35. See also Mentré 1983 [**512**], n.p. Picasso's debt to this Spanish style is clear both in the colour and the forms of his 1930 *Crucifixion*. Léger's interest in the early 1940s was suggested by Schapiro 1979 [**563**], 326. Itten used 2 pages from the Paris *Apocalypse of St Sever*, from this group, to illustrate his *Art of Color*, 1961 [**457**].
172 See espec. Werckmeister 1965 [**602**], 933–67 and A. Grabar in discussion (ibid., 977ff). At least one MS has marginal annotations in Arabic (Madrid, Archivos Historicos Nacionales 1097B; see Mundo and Sanchez Mariana 1976 [**525**], no. 11). The question has been reviewed in Klein 1976 [**473**], 287ff.
173 Isidore 1960 [**456**], 15–17; Evans 1980 [**427**], espec. 42ff. Mentré (1984 [**513**], 192) has linked the anti-naturalistic quality of the Beatus illustrations to Isidore's idea of painting as fiction (*fictura*: *Etym* XIX, xvi).
174 Klein 1976 [**473**], 238ff has identified some dozen 'primary colours' (*Hauptfarben*) and 6 'basic' colours: white, yellow, sepia, minium, blue, green. For col. illustrations from a handful of MSS, Mundó and Sanchez Mariana 1976 [**525**]; Williams 1977 [**604**], .
175 Baudri 1979 [**374**], 9 (*Carmen* I, ll. 95ff).
176 Wackernagel 1872 [**596**], I, 188f.
177 Pastoureau 1983 [**536**], [1989] [**537**]. For a more cautious assessment of the early documentation, Volbehr 1906 [**593**], 355–65.
178 Mariale (1502), cit. Meier 1977 [**107**], 195f.
179 Henderson 1987 [**453**], 19ff (espec. on the orpiment of the *Book of Durrow*), 106ff.
180 Schapiro 1979 [**563**], 323.
181 For Beatus's career, Williams 1977 [**604**], 27; Beatus 1930 [**376**], 377. A 12th-century Parisian writer, Andrew of St Victor, in a commentary on Isaiah 16–18, also detailed the significance of the idea of scarlet sins and pure wool in terms of pigments and dyes, by pointing out that wool and other soft threads were dyed with *coccinus*, while paper and other hard substances were coloured with *vermiculum* (cit. Smalley 1952 [**569**], 389–90). There seems to be some confusion of terms here since *coccus* and *vermiculum* were usually identical.
182 *Gospel of Philip* 1963 [**440**], III, 24/30, 28f. Till regards the text as a 4th-century translation from the Greek. The number 72 is intriguing, since Coptic colour-terms were generally as limited as in other ancient languages. (Till 1959 [**585**], 331–42).
183 O. Grabar 1964 [**445**], 70, 82–8. For col. pls, Ettinghausen 1962 [**426**], 18–27.
184 Rosenthal 1975 [**554**], 73, 265–6.
185 Cf. the 10th-century decription of the Palace of Ghumdan in Yemen in O. Grabar 1973 [**446**], 79 and Ibn Jobaïr's account of the Martorana in Palermo, where the 'sparkling fires' of the gilded glass windows 'ravish the sight and will be capable of throwing the souls into a disquiet which we pray God to guarantee' (1949–65 [**455**], III (1953), 390–1).
186 Nicholson 1914 [**528**], 50ff; Menendez y Pelayo 1910 [**511**], 83–90. On the tradition of Plotinus, Fakhry 1970 [**428**], 33–9.
187 Job of Edessa 1935 [**460**], 130ff.
188 Avicenna 1956 [**369**], II, 78. Avicenna's 13th-century Persian commentator, Nasîr al Dîn al Tusî, increased the number of hues to include yellow and blue but retained the tonal progression in each (Wiedemann 1908 [**603**], 88f.
189 See espec. Bauer 1911 [**375**]. There is still no modern edn of Alhazen's *Optics* but an excellent Eng. trans., 1989 [**364**]. One 13th-century commentator, Kamāl al Dīn al-Farāsī, did turn his attention to the various saturation of different colours, asking, e.g., why pure blue and purple-red seemed the strongest colours in the rainbow (Winter 1954 [**607**], 207–8).
190 Fischer 1965 [**431**], espec. 233ff.
191 For lustre-ware, Scanlon 1968 [**561**], 188–95; Caiger-Smith 1985 [**395**], espec. 24, 59; for monochrome silks, Müller-Christensen 1960 [**524**], 37ff.

4 A Dionysian Aesthetic

1 Panofsky 1979 [**783**], 46–7. The mosaic was removed in 1771. Verdier [*c.* 1974] [**820**], 708, n. 39 suggested that it may have been a mosaic-encrusted stucco relief of a Carolingian type.
2 For Suger's visit to Italy, as far S. as Bitonto, S. McK. Crosby, 'Abbot Suger's program for his new Abbey Church' in Verdon and Front (eds) 1984 [**821**], 193f.
3 Goldschmidt 1940 [**439**], 44.
4 Panofsky 1979 [**783**], 50–1. A 9th- or 10th-centry MS of Paulinus's *Epistles*, which detailed his building campaigns, was in the library of the Abbey of Cluny in Suger's day (Delisle 1884 [**667**], 345) and is now BN nouv. acquis. MS Lat 1443. For Suger's friendship with the Abbot of Cluny, Peter the Venerable 1967 [**786**], I, 272–3 (who knew his Paulinus: ibid., 288f) and Oursel 1958/9 [**780**], 54–5. Among several parallels of language and thought in Paulinus and Suger is their liking for symbols of the Trinity in the arrangement of doors and in ceremonial (Goldschmidt 1940 [**439**], 44; Panofsky 1979 [**783**], 44–6, 154–5).
5 Panofsky 1979 [**783**], 101.
6 The figure of 1–5 foot-candles inside the cathedral, as opposed to 8000–9000 outside, given by Johnson 1964 [**736**], 10, contested by Sowers 1966 [**809**], 220 who found in a September–October period that the outside reading could be 200–800 foot-candles and the interior reading for the W. windows 3 foot-candles for a sky reading of 200 foot-candles.
7 Lillich 1970 [**748**], 26ff.
8 *Roman de Perceforest* 1951 [**791**], II, 316f, 256–7. The sense of darkening in the later 12th century is implicit in the widespread enlarging of windows to take the darker glass but retain the older light-levels (Grodecki 1949 [**709**], 9, 10, n. 20).
9 More 1551 [**770**], II, ix.
10 Johann Matthesius *Sarepta oder Bergpostill* (1562) in Oidtmann 1929 [**776**], 467. See also Vasari I, 1962 [**341**], 152f.
11 Antonio da Pisa 1976 [**620**], 25. For Siena, Milanesi 1854–6 [**766**], II, 197–8.
12 E.g., Grodecki 1977 [**717**], 12ff; ibid., 1986 [**718**], 343, 353. For the Fr. development of the notion of the 'darkness' of the Middle Ages, Voss 1972 [**825**], 28–33.

Grodecki's interpretation has a polemical edge for he was concerned to rebut the outcry among many Fr. artists and the general public that the restoration of the glass of Chartres West had left the windows far too bright and had in particular dampened the effect of the blues (see *Revue de l'art*, 1976, XXXI, 6ff). See also Grinnell 1946 [**708**], 182ff; Schöne 1979 [**566**], 38ff; von Simson 1988 [**805**], ch. 2; F. Deuchler, 'Gothic Glass' in Hess and Ashbery 1969 [**454**], 34ff; for a wide-ranging general survey, Nieto Alcaide 1978 [**773**].

13 For a summary of the hexaemeral tradition, G. F. Vescovini *Studi su la prospettiva medievale*, 1965, 16f; for the 13th-century discrimination of *lux* and *lumen*, Schmid 1975 [**799**], 9ff. That even a scientist like Bacon in the 13th century did not feel obliged to use the terms consistently, Lindberg 1983 [**750**], 356–67.

14 *Patrologia Latina* [**116**], CXXII, col. 128.

15 See the inscription on the grease-pan: LUCIS ON' VIRTUTIS OPUS DOCTRINA REFULGENS (Oman 1958 [**777**], 1). It has been translated 'This flood of light, this work of virtue, bright with holy doctrine instructs us so that Man shall not be benighted in vice' (N. Stratford in *English Romanesque Art, 1066–1200* 1984 [**678**], no. 247) and 'Carrying the candle is the task of righteousness. In light is the Church's teaching, whose message redeems man from the darkness of vice' (C. Sydenham, *Burlington Magazine*, CXXVI, 1984, 504).

16 Boethius 1906 [**636**], 313, 346–7; A. Smith 1983 [**570**], 154ff (Avicenna and Alhazen); Gätje 1967 [**697**], 294–5 (Averroes).

17 For early scales see pp. 165–6 above. See also Avicenna 1956 [**369**], III, 1–4; Grosseteste *De Iride* in Grosseteste 1912 [**234**], 77; Bacon 1897–1900 [**156**], II, 19; Albertus Magnus *De Sensu* II, ii in Hudeczek 1944 [**732**], 130.

18 For col. pl., Grodecki 1977 [**717**], 73, fig. 58.

19 Panofsky 1979 [**783**], 21.

20 Ibid., 72–5.

21 S. McK. Crosby in ibid., 239; Conant 1975 [**658**], 727ff, figs 4, 6.

22 Grodecki 1976 [**716**], 25–8. Grodecki estimated a total of some 52 or 54 windows glazed. On 27 he suggests that some surviving fragments of border (cf. 130–1) may be from the W. windows.

23 Grodecki 1976 [**716**], 27 argued that Suger's statement can hardly have included the transept (which was only beginning to be built when *On Admin.* was written) or the nave, which was about to be demolished. The plan in Formigé 1960 [**689**], 66–7, fig. 49 shows 20 windows in the nave. The precise fenestration of the Carolingian church is unknown but a description of 799 gives a figure of 101 windows, very close to Suger's church (Bischoff 1984 [**635**], 215f). Brown and Cothren 1986 [**648**], 36, n. 150 suggest that Suger did not claim literally to have glazed the whole church and could, practically, only have glazed a much smaller number of windows; but Kidson 1987 [**737**], 10 notes that he glazed at least 30 in the choir.

24 For Suger on the cost, Panofsky 1979 [**783**], 52–3. In mid-14th-century London blue glass cost from 4 to 6 times as much as white and about a 3rd more than red (Brayley and Britton 1836 [**643**], 176–80; Salzman 1926/7 [**796**]). The only early window price I know is that for the major window at Soissons, which cost 30 Paris *livres* in *c.* 1220 (Grodecki 1953 [**711**], 175). If this was the Jesse Window (fragments formerly in Berlin), it was probably about twice the size of the Jesse window at St-Denis; if we take account of price-inflation in France during the 12th century (Duby 1971 [**670**], 363 gives a rate of 10–20 times for agricultural produce between the first Crusade and the mid-13th century) we reach an astonishingly low figure of some 2 Paris *livres* for each of the main windows at St-Denis.

25 For the St-Denis grisaille, Grodecki 1976 [**716**], 122ff; for Cistercian grisaille, Zakin 1974 [**838**], 17ff; M. Lillich, 'Monastic stained glass: patronage and style' in Verdon and Front 1984 [**821**], 218.

26 Theophilus 1961 [**583**], II, xxi. For col. pl., Grodecki 1977 [**717**], 51 and for the tradition of white grounds in eastern France, Grodecki 1949 [**709**], 12.

27 Panofsky 1979 [**783**], 19. Lillich in Verdon and Front 1984 [**821**], 222ff has contested this judgment most vigorously. Suger's interest in Dionysian theology has been doubted by Grodecki 1986 [**718**], 221 and more stridently by Kidson 1987 [**737**], 5ff. But his close dependence on the Dionysian language of Hugh of St Victor and Richard of St Victor has been established by G. A. Zinn, 'Suger, Theology and the Pseudo-Dionysian tradition' in Gerson 1986 [**700**], 36. See Hugh's *Expositio in Hierarchiam Caelestem* II in *Patrologia Latina* [**116**], CLXXV cols 967, 977, de Bruyne 1946 [**650**], II, 215f and Weisweiler 1952 [**830**]. I have been unable to document von Simson's claim that Hugh was a friend of Suger's (1988 [**805**], 120) but their affinities of thought have been studied by Rudolph 1990 [**794**], which is, however, also critical of a Dionysian emphasis in the interpretation of Suger's thought. For William of St Thierry *Aenigma Fidei*, *Patrologica Latina* [**116**], CLXXX, cols 422f and *Dictionnaire de spiritualité*, 1953–, [**668**], s.v. 'Denys l'Areopagite', cols 335ff.

28 For this programme, von Simson 1988 [**805**], 120–2; espec. Grodecki 1961a [**712**], 19ff; Hofmann 1968 [**729**], 63; Esmeijer 1978 [**680**], 14–15.

29 *Celestial Hierarchy* II. I have used Eriugena's version in the synoptic collection of all Pseudo-Dionysius's Latin texts, 1950 [**789**], II, cols 742ff.

30 See espec. Panofsky 1944 [**782**], 95ff.

31 Eriugena 1968–81 [**679**], I (1968), 194f, and in general, Bierwaltes 1977 [**632**], 127ff. Suger's borrowings were noted by von Simson 1988 [**805**], 125n.

32 Eriugena 1968–81 [**679**], II (1972), 186ff.

33 The *Liber Pontificalis* 1886–1957 [**745**], refers (ch. 98) to Leo II's work in St John Lateran *c.* 800: 'simul et fenestras de absida ex vitro diversis coloribus conclusit atque decoravit' (at the same time he also enclosed and decorated the windows of the apse with variously coloured glass). The note adds that the other windows in the basilica were repaired not with glass but with translucent marble (*ex metallo cyprino*). The same source (106) records work by Benedict III half a century later in the apse of Sta Maria in Trastevere: 'Fenestras vero vitreis coloribus ornavit et pictura musivi decoravit' (He ornamented [it] with colour-glazed windows and embellished it with mosiac pictures). The earliest known use of this method was in Syria in the mid-8th century (Frodl-Kraft 1970 [**692**], 20). The Eng. coloured window-glass excavated at Monkwearmouth and Jarrow was sometimes painted to simulate striated translucent marble (Cramp 1968 [**662**], 16; 1970 [**663**], 327ff). The earliest surviving Fr. glazed apse is that of St Nicholas at Caen (Héliot 1968 [**724**], 89ff) of 1083/93 but a nearly contemporary record has Bishop Hoel of Le Mans also decorating his chancel with glass (Grodecki 1961b [**713**], 60). The glazing of Poitiers also began from the E. end in the 12th centry (Grodecki 1951 [**710**], 138). For the spiritual meaning of Early Christian apse windows, P. Reuterswärd, 'Windows of Divine Light' in Rosand 1984, [**792**], 77–84; for the programme of apse-mosaics and paintings, Ihm 1960 [**734**]. In the Carolingian period Rabanus Maurus attempted to derive the word 'apse' from light itself: 'Absida graeco sermone latine interpretatur lucida; eo quod lumine accepto per arcum resplendeat' ('Apse' in Greek means 'lucid' in Latin: that which shines in a bow of received light) (*De Universo* XIV, xxiii in *Patrologia Latina* [**116**], CIX col. 403); the derivation is from *apsis* = rainbow (Aristotle *Meteorology*, II, 2.3).

34 See espec. Mortet 1911 [**772**], 85, 94.

35 Brown and Cothren 1986 [**648**], 3.

36 William of St Denis *Vita Sugerii* II in Lecoy de la Marche 1867 [**742**], 391f. For the context, Glaser 1965 [**703**], 268. A later 12th century panegyric by Radulphus Phisicus dwells on the gemstones but makes no reference to the glass at all (1962 [**790**], 763ff).

37 See Oidtmann 1929 [**776**], 47; Lehmann–Brockhaus 1955–60 [**744**], II, no. 4616.

38 Martène and Durand 1717 [**759**], col. 1584.

39 Bettembourg 1977 [**629**], 8–9; Bouchon et al. 1979 [**641**], 19. For traces of cobalt in glass from St-Denis, Crosby et al. 1981 [**665**], 81. For the sources of cobalt in the Middle Ages, Rumpf 1961 [**795**], 17ff; Bezborodov 1975 [**630**], 64f.

40 Theophilus 1961 [**583**], bk II, xii. For Roman glass coloured with cobalt, Geilmann 1962 [**699**], 186f, who also mentions cobalt in mosaic glass from Ravenna, the source of spoils in northern Europe of the type also mentioned here by Theophilus (cf. del Medico 1943 [**508**], 85, 97).

41 For blue glass excavated in Constantinople, Megaw 1963 [**509**], 362, who relates it to the *saphiri graeci* mentioned by Theophilus (II, xix). For a later date and a possible Western origin, Lafond 1968 [**740**], 234ff. D. B. Harden 1969 [**723**], 98 and Frodl-Kraft 1970 [**692**], 14–16 have suggested a Byzantine origin for Western glass-technology. The windows of King Hugon of Constantinople's palace in the Old Fr. epic *Pèlerinage de Charlemagne* were of *brasme ultramarin*, which might mean a blue stone or glass; but this poem may be as late as the late 13th century (Faviti 1965 [**688**], 124).

42 Grodecki 1961c [**714**], 184; 1986 [**718**], 255f; Crosby 1966 [**664**], 28; Crosby et al. 1981 [**665**], 67, 84, 86 and nos 15, 16; Stratford 1984 [**811**], 215.

43 Mortet 1911 [**772**], 139.

44 The idea that glass is a stone or a metal goes back to ancient Egypt (Trowbridge 1928 [**819**], 19ff; Ganzenmüller 1956 [**694**], 131) and was transmitted to the West by Isidore of Seville (*Etym* XVI, xvi) and by the *Secreta Secretorum* of the late 9th-century writer Al-Razi (Rhazes), who valued it as highly as real gemstones (1912 [**619**], 87). That glass was a stone was assumed by technical writers such as the 9th-century author of the *Mappae Clavicula* (1974 [**757**], 116). See the formal comparisons in Engels 1937 [**676**], 57 and Johnson 1964 [**736**], 57ff; also the fragment from St Pierre de Chartres illustrated in *Franse Kerkramen* 1973/4 [**690**], no. 4.

45 Theophilus 1961 [**583**], II, xxviii; Oidtmann 1929 [**776**], 36; Grodecki 1977 [**717**], 35, 350.

46 Panofsky 1979 [**783**], 65. Verdier [*c.* 1974 [**820**], 701 has linked this passage appropriately with Pseudo-Dionysius 1950 [**789**], *Celestial Hierarchy* XV, vii, 336c.

47 Viard 1927 [**822**], 257. One of the more extravagant accounts of the carbuncle is in the *Pèlerinage de Charlemagne* (ll. 441f) ; for its Byzantine background, Schlauch 1932 [**797**], 500ff.

48 Bede *Explanatio Apocalypsis* II, 21 in *Patrologia Latina* [**116**], XCIII, cols 97–8. Bonner 1968 [**638**], 10 has been able to find no earlier source for Bede's lapidary here.

49 Theophilus 1961 [**583**], III, lxi. Sextus Amarcus 1969 [**802**], 183ff; also ibid., 29 on this tradition of exegesis. Manitius dates these poems to *c.* 1100–1120 and points out (33) that the passage on stones was copied in the 13th century. If Sextus was Theophilus's source it helps to confirm the now generally accepted date for *Of Divers Arts* (Hanke 1962 [**721**], 71ff; L. White 1964 [**835**], 227ff; van Engen 1980 [**677**], 161).

50 Montesquiou-Fezensac 1973 [**768**], 108.

51 The earliest example seems to be in Sta Maria Maggiore (Brenk 1975 [**644**]; see also Matthiae 1967 [**762**], figs 89, 101–2, 136, 145, 177, 196, 228, 229, 338–9. For S. Vitale, C.-O. Nordström 1953 [**774**], 23–5; K. R. Brown 1979 [**649**], 57. For S. Apollinare in Classe, Deichmann 1958 [**666**], pls XII–XIV. For the same arrangement in Byzantine metalwork, Hahnloser 1965–71 [**719**], tav. I, II, and II, no. 72 and tav. LX). Theophilus (1961 [**583**], II, xxviii) reports the continuing popularity of the combination in the West; for western MSS, Grabar and Nordenfalk 1957 [**707**], 155; de Hamel 1986 [**720**], pl. 36.

52 In what seems to be the only precise account of the distribution of these stones, a 12th-century German poem on the Heavenly Jerusalem (in Schroeder 1972 [**801**], I, 96–111), *jaspis* is given to the foundations and *saphirus*, *smaragdus*, *calcedonius* and *sardonix* to the walls (see Lichtenberg 1931 [**746**], 14ff).

53 Evans 1922 [**682**], 212–13. 'Damigeron' has been thought by some commentators to be as late as the 6th century AD.

54 Isidore of Seville (*Etym* XVI, ix), following Pliny ([**296**], XXXIII, xxi 68) stated that *saphirus* was never transparent and he referred to its purple cast, as did the early Christian lapidary of Epiphanius (in *Patrologia Graeca* [**116**], XLIII, col. 297).

55 See the felts sent by Charlemagne to Haroun al-Raschid (*Monumenta Germaniae Historica Scriptores Rerum Germanicarum* 1960 [**769**], 63).

56 Bede in *Patrologia Latina* [**116**], n.47; Hugh of St Victor, ibid., CLXXVI cols 820f.

57 The earliest, 5th-century AD account of this stone (Solinus 1958 [**808**], 135f) was confined to the blue variety but a late 9th-century text by Costa Ben Luca described the three types and his version passed on to Marbode (1977 [**267**], 17f). Herrad of Landsberg however, described *iacinthos* simply as blue (Lipinsky 1962 [**752**], 146; Lipinsky also has important material from 15th-century lapidaries).

58 Theophilus 1961 [**583**], II, xii. Dodwell's trans. is 'white' but *album* should read 'colourless' here as in II, vi, xv, xvii. The use of *saphirus* in the context of mosaic cubes is found as early as the 9th century in a description by Sedulius of Liège (Traube III, 1896 [**817**], 198).

59 Theophilus 1961 [**583**], II, xxviii; also *Mappae Clavicula* 1974 [**757**], 67, 88.

60 For the earlier account, Hubert 1949 [**731**], 72–3. The early 13th-century account already refers to 'saphirs' (Viard 1927 [**822**], 257); Montesquiou-Fezensac 1973 [**768**], 90ff, 285ff. See also Albertus Magnus 1967 [**614**], 41, 97f, 115f.

61 Martindale 1972 [**760**], ch. IV espec. 80–1.

62 Becksmann 1967 [**627**], 14ff, 42.

63 Wenzel 1949 [**832**], 54f. For the late medieval association of painters and glaziers in the same guilds, Cahn 1979 [**651**], 11. An early 14th-century Eng. treatise, *Ad faciendum emallum*, suggests that jewellers were no longer familiar with the recipes of glass-painters (1846 [**612**], 172).

64 M. P. Lillich, 'European Stained Glass around 1300: the introduction of silver stain' in Liskar 1986 [**753**], 45–60.

65 Morgan 1983 [**771**], 35f. The most accessible Latin text is in Lehmann-Brockhaus 1955–60 [**744**], I (1955), no. 2372.

66 The link with Grosseteste was suggested by F. Nordström 1955 [**775**], espec. 258 but has found little echo. Grosseteste's rainbow theory has been studied by Eastwood 1966 [**671**], 313ff. The Last Judgment in the North Rose, *c*. 1200/35, includes a 'Christ as Judge' seated on a yellow and purple bow (Morgan 1983 [**771**], H.I.).

67 For Gallo, de Bruyne 1946 [**650**], III, 58ff; Pseudo-Dionysius 1950 [**789**], I, 673ff and espec. 683; Albertus Magnus 1972 [**616**]; Aquinas 1950 [**621**], trans. Coomaraswamy 1938 [**661**], 66ff; Engelberti 1925 [**675**], trans. Coomaraswamy 1935 [**660**], 35ff. Lillich in Verdon and Front 1984 [**821**], 225f has suggested the discrediting of Eriugena as a suspected heretic in the 13th century as one reason why the Dionysian negative theology sank into oblivion until the Renaissance but her argument is weakened by a reference (250, n. 84) to a mid-13th-century MS from St-Denis (London, Lambeth Palace 382) which includes the parallel versions of Eriugena, Sarrazin and Gallo.

68 Albertus Magnus 1972 [**616**], 189.

69 Pseudo-Dionysius 1950 [**789**], *Celestial Hierarchy* XV, vii. For *chloron*, see ch. 2, n. 7 above.

70 Herrad of (Landsberg) Hohenbourg, 1979 [**725**], I, 89.

71 Hildegard of Bingen *Physics* IV, *Patrologia Latina* [**116**], CXCVII, cols 1247ff.

72 Vincent of Beauvais 1624 [**823**], XI, ch. cvi. He specifically mentions the sapphire.

73 Thomas of Cantimpré 1973 [**814**], 355, 359; also Arnoldus Saxo 1905 [**622**], 70.

74 Albertus Magnus 1967 [**614**], 61 and 77. For the association of the carbuncle with gold in alchemy, Ganzenmüller 1956 [**694**], 85ff and for its reputation in medieval literature, Ziolkowski 1961 [**839**], 313ff; A. R. Harden 1960 [**722**], 59ff. On the identification of the garnet with the carbuncle in the early Middle Ages and their high value, Arrhenius 1985 [**623**], 23ff. Bartholomeus Anglicus's widely used *De Proprietatibus Rerum* (*c*. 1230) [**625**], suggested that the sapphire was the mother of the carbuncle (XVI, ch. 86). Both these stones were called 'la gemme des gemmes' in the late 13th century: Studer and Evans 1924 [**812**], 120, 126.

75 Albertus Magnus 1967 [**614**], 14ff.

76 See M. Meiss in Gilbert 1970 [**701**], 49ff. For Bacon's discussion of transparency (*Opus Maius* Pt IV, dist. iv, ch. i), Hills 1987 [**727**], 66.

77 Grosseteste 1912 [**234**], 202; Albertus Magnus 1968 [**615**], 108, 123; Bacon 1897–1900 [**156**], II, 409, 412, 456, 510, 519; Pecham 1970 [**785**], 89, 159; Bartholomeus of Bologna 1932 [**626**], 373f.

78 On the importance of transparency in stained glass, Schöne 1979 [**566**], 39n.

79 William of Auvergne 1674 [**350**], Supplementum 207; Theodoric of Freiberg in Wallace 1959 [**826**], 370f. For ruby glass, Johnson 1964 [**736**], 53–7. Gauthier 1981 [**698**], 35, 38 notes the special status of *rouge claire* enamel at this time.

80 For cutting Indian beryl, Pliny XXXVII, xx, 76–7, followed by Isidore *Etym* XVI, vi. For cutting other stones with saws, Theophilus 1961 [**583**], II, xcv. A Roman necklace with facetted amethysts is in the Victoria and Albert Museum, London (1852–1863) and 9th- and 10-century Viking necklaces with finely facetted cornelians are in the National Museums of Antiquites at Helsinki and Stockholm and the Oslo University Museum of National Antiquities.

81 In the mid-13th century Bacon had noted that diamonds were not cut in the manner described by Pliny (XXXVII, xv, 55–61), by softening with goats' blood, but with fragments of the same stone (Pt VI, i, II, 1897 168; III, 1900, 180). A French inventory of 1322 refers to an emerald 'taillé à manière de dyament' (Falk 1975 [**683**], 12), which suggests that diamond-facetting was commonplace by this time. For the study of refraction in the later Middle Ages, Grant 1974 [**231**], 420ff; Eastwood 1967 [**672**], 406ff; Lindberg 1968/9 [**749**], 24ff.

82 The diamond was already regarded as the most important of stones in the 11th-century Byzantine lapidary of Psellus (1980 [**788**], 77) but as late as the beginning of the 15th century in Venice rubies were commanding prices twice as much as even facetted diamonds and continued to be more expensive than diamonds for some centuries (Sirat 1968 [**806**], 1075–6). But see also Heyd 1936 [**726**], 655f for higher values of diamonds in the early 16th century. For the problem of identifying the diamond in the early gem literature, Barb 1969 [**624**], 66–82.

83 For German and French literature, Weise 1939 [**829**], 477ff; Lydgate 1891 [**754**], ll. 46ff.

84 Lightbown 1978 [**747**], 64, 78ff; Gauthier 1981 [**698**].

85 Thompson 1936 [**24**], 144f and espec. *De Arte Illuminandi* 1975 [**193**], 193. For

fresco, Tintori and Meiss 1962 [**815**], 90, 133. For the language of glazing, Ploss 1960 [**787**], 73, n. 14, 321, n. 57.

86 At a popular level this curiosity about price can be seen in a romance such as Chrétien de Troyes's *Erec et Enide*, ll. 1578ff, where a dress of *vert porpre* is said to have been trimmed with more than 200 marks of beaten gold; but, as Chrétien's recent editor shows, the figure varies from MS to MS and in one is as low as ½ mark (1987 [**652**], 314)! Suger did not go so far as to put a price-tag on his objects but this was not uncommon (Schlosser 1896 [**798**], 297 ; Krempel 1971 [**739**], 24; Gowen 1976 [**706**], 168).

87 For the social role of the medieval goldsmith, Claussen 1978 [**656**], 47ff.

88 *On Administration* XXXIII; Ovid *Metamorphoses* II, 5. For Suger's frequent use of the tag, Panofsky 1979 [**783**], 164. For other early examples, Schlauch 1932 [**797**], 513; Söhring 1900 [**807**], 502; Frisch 1971 [**691**], 39.

89 Alessio 1965 [**618**], 83, 156ff; Sternagel 1966 [**810**], 121; Ovitt 1983 [**781**], 89–105; for an extensive survey, Whitney 1990 [**836**], .

90 Two architectural examples, relating to design rather than materials, are in Mortet 1911 [**772**], 166ff and von Simpson 1982 [**804**], 597–613.

91 Colish 1968 [**657**], 36ff; for a different trans. Gauthier 1972 [**437**], 361, no. 112. The context of the idea has been sketched by Bialostocki 1967 [**631**], 56ff.

92 For earlier precedents for this emphasis, Tatarkiewicz 1970–74 [**813**], II, 25–6. The incription on a pair of candlesticks at Hildesheim (11th century) states that they are not made of gold or silver (Tschan II, 1951 [**589**], 129). For Alexander of Hales (13th century) on art transforming nature by putting noble forms into base material or vice versa, de Bruyne 1946 [**650**], III, 115.

93 *Metalogicon*, cit. Eco 1988 [**673**], 94 but see also 95–6 for Scholastic views on the limitaton of art. The popularity in the 13th and 14th centuries of some preaching manuals called *Lumen Animae*, which cite recipes attributed to Theophilus (though not found in his book), are a further indication of a concern for technology at this time (Rouse 1971 [**793**], 5–113).

94 E.g. Hoberg 1944 [**728**], 168.

95 Ibid., 17, 25, 184, 253, 255–6; Braun 1907 [**387**], 322–3. The earliest reference to glass gems I have found is in early 9th-century Germany (*Mittelalterliche Schatzverzeichnisse* I, 1967 [**109**], 90); see also Gallo 1967 [**693**], 279, 283 and for the general picture, Holmes 1934 [**730**], 195–6, 199.

96 Vescovini *Studi su la prospettiva medievale*, 1965, 174ff.

97 Meyendorff, 'Spiritual trends in Byzantium in the late 13th and early 14th centuries' in Underwood 1967–75 [**146**], IV, 101–6.

98 Onasch 1962 [**778**], espec. 15, 19; also 11–12 on Barlaam and 25ff on the controversy in Russia.

99 The only writer to give much attention to the decoration is Schöne 1957 [**800**], 50–116; 1979 [**566**], 32–6, 237f. Belting 1977 [**628**], 214ff is chiefly confined to the Roman and antique elements in the vaults and fictive architecture. For the textile designs, Klesse 1967 [**738**], 25, 34ff, 49, 56, nos. 1, 6, 7, 16, 17, 22, 29, 30–3, 50. For col. reproductions of similar designs, May 1957 [**763**], frontispiece and

fig. 63. None of the textiles described in the early inventories of S. Francesco is called Spanish but many in the Papal inventories were (Molinier 1885, 28f and 1886 [**767**], 647ff).

100 Marchini 1973 [**758**], 19ff.

101 Gauthier 1972 [**437**], 205ff, 387ff, no. 166; Bemporad in Middeldorf 1980 [**765**], 123ff, no. 49.

102 Gauthier 1972 [**437**], 215.

103 For earlier examples of this combination, Grodecki 1975 [**715**], 45–6 and for an excellent discussion of the relationship between glass and fresco in Gaddi's Baroncelli Chapel in Sta Croce in Florence, Hills 1987 [**727**], 75–81. For some of the difficulties faced by modern spectators in relating glass to painting at Assisi, Martindale 1988 [**761**], 179f; Borsook 1980 [**639**], 23–7.

104 Euler 1967 [**681**], 78f, 85ff; Belting 1977 [**628**], 217; Toulmin 1971 [**816**], 180.

105 Espec. Belting 1977 [**628**], ch. II and 38ff.

106 Tintori and Meiss noticed gold in the hangings of only one scene (1967 [**815**], 148); see also J. Gardner, review of Belting 1977 [**628**], in *Kunstchronik* XXXII, 1979, 65; White 1981 [**834**], 371. Professor White has kindly confirmed my observation that real gold was used in the vault decoration at the E. end. For inscriptions referring to gold and glass in Cosmati work, Giovannoni 1908 [**702**], 280; Hutton 1950 [**733**], 35. Since the Cosmatesque altar in the Upper Church has been entirely restored, the relation between it and painted Cosmatesque decoration is best studied in the Lower Church. Gardner 1973 [**695**], 40f has pointed to the mosaic origins of even the narrative style of the St Francis cycle.

107 Zaccaria 1963 [**837**], doc. 147.

108 For cast shadows in these scenes, Tintori and Meiss 1967 [**815**], 139f and for elsewhere in the Lower Church, McGinnis 1971 [**755**], 63–4.

109 Bihl 1941 [**634**], 51f. Brooke dates Statute III, 18 to *c*. 1247–57 but there is nothing so specific in the Dominican Constitutions of 1228 and 1241 to which she compares it (1959 [**647**], 259) and it may well be later. For the Cistercian Statutes of 1134, de Bruyne 1946 [**650**], II, 133, also on *curiositas* 134f. For the iconography of the choir windows, Marchini 1973 [**758**], 25ff. The earliest known Franciscan glass, the three E. windows of the Barfüsser Kirche at Erfurt (1230–5), related to Assisi by Wenzel 1952 [**833**], 69f, also has a Life of Christ and a Jesse, together with a Life of St Francis (Drachenberg et al. 1976 [**669**], 11ff).

110 Bonaventure 1882–1902 [**637**], II (1885), 321 and IV (1889), 1025. For an assessment of the central role of light in Bonaventure's thought, Lindberg 1986 [**751**], 17ff.

111 Alessandri and Penacchi 1914 [**360**], 1338 Inventory no. 32. In 1253 Innocent IV had granted the friars the right to own and use precious objects and vestments (Zaccaria 1963 [**837**], docs 35–6).

112 Bonaventure 1882–1902 [**637**], V (1891), 322f. For the Cosmati, Glass 1980 [**704**].

113 Trevisano 1961 [**818**], 183ff.

114 Bigi 1961 [**633**], 396, 419.

115 For 'harmony', Bonaventure 1882–1902 [**637**], V (1891), 300f, in which colour is preferred as a mean between extremes. Bonaventure does not adopt Aquinas's modification of Cicero's *suavi-*

tas to *claritas* (de Bruyne 1946 [**650**], III, 298ff). On colour as a mixture of the elements, Bonaventure 1882–1902 [**637**], IV (1889), 1025; for Scholastic interest in mixture around 1300, Maier 1952 [**264**], 19ff. Even Duccio made use of many mixtures in the *Maestà*, starting from a limited palette of 7 pigments (Brandi 1959 [**642**], 197ff).

116 Dante *Feast* III, vii, 4. He cites Albertus Magnus *De Intellectu et Intelligibili* I, iii, 2 but he must also have been impressed by the long discussion in Bartholomeus of Bologna 1932 [**626**], 233, 237f on light passing through stained-glass windows. For his knowledge of Bartholomeus, Simonelli 1967 [**803**], 208f.

117 Passera 1921 [**784**], 13f.

118 Bottari 1967 [**640**], 53–9; Fallani 1971a [**684**], 135ff; ibid., 1971b [**685**], 137ff; ibid., 1973 [**686**], 103ff; Conti 1981 [**659**], 7, 39; R. Gibbs, *Burlington Magazine*, CXXVI, 1984, 639.

119 For France, Orderic Vitalis II, 1969 [**779**], 86; for Germany, Lehmann-Brockhaus 1938 [**743**], no. 3007; for England, Lehmann-Brockhaus 1955–60 [**744**], I no. 1859. Theophilus 1961 [**583**], 6–10. Brunello has noticed the word in an 8th-century MS (*De Arte Illuminandi* 1975 [**193**], 3). The best survey of the question is Wattenbach 1896 [**828**], 347, also 256, 363ff. Wattenbach cites the 13th-century Chronicle of Salimbene to show that the term was still something of a novelty in that period, although it had been known in Italy since the 12th century.

120 For William of Malmsbury, Lehmann-Brockhaus 1955–60 [**744**], I, no. 1859; cf. also Walsingham I, 1867 [**827**], 94 (before 1259). For references in inventories, Ehrle 1885 [**674**], 43, 346, 347; Wenk 1885 [**831**], 278ff, 284; Alessandri and Penacchi 1914 [**360**], nos 300, 308. Bolognese usages of *illuminator* in Brieger et al. 1969 [**646**], 37; Malaguzzi Valeri 1896 [**756**], 267.

121 Alain de Lille 1955 [**613**], 57, 94: see Ciotti 1960 [**655**], 257–67; Baudri of Bourgueil 1979 [**374**], no. I, p. 9.

122 Eco 1988 [**673**], 10.

123 Weise 1939 [**829**], 88, 112f, 265, 447ff.

124 Christe and James 1981 [**654**], facsimile 32, cf. 21ff, 66, 72f, 77, 93. An iconographic link with Rheims has been made by P. Kurmann, 'Le portail apocalyptique de la cathédrale de Reims' in Christe 1979 [**653**]. The Great Angel in the slightly earlier *Trinity Apocalypse* is not smiling (Brieger 1967 [**645**], facsimile folio 10v).

125 For the De Jaulnes Virgin, *Les Fastes du Gothique* 1981/2 [**687**], no. 25. For illustrations of the type, Vloberg 1936 [**824**], 69–93. For the literature of smiling, Ménard 1969 [**764**]. Weise 1939 [**829**] gives many Fr. and Ger. lilterary examples of the Virgin as a source of light (112ff, 214, 455).

126 Ficino *De Lumine* V, 16, cit. Lindberg 1986 [**751**], 23. See also *Epistolae*, Venice 1495, folio lxx^v and the comment by John Colet in Jayne 1963 [**735**], 114. Lavin 1981 [**741**], 193ff does not notice this expansion of the idea of light and smiling in Ficino but (203) relates Leonardo da Vinci's smiling *John the Baptist* (Paris, Louvre) to the identification of St John's feast (6 January) with the Feast of the Holy Lights. For Leonardo's reading of Ficino, Garin 1965 [**696**], 69–70.

5 Colour-Language, Colour-Symbols

1 There seems to be no general agreement among psychologists about the number of discriminable colour-sensations: H. Terstieg, 'The CIE colour-coding system' in Mollon and Sharpe 1983 [**931**], 563, proposes 1 million and only 8 commonly recognized names; U. Eco, 'How culture conditions the colors we see' in Blonsky 1985 [**853**], 167, cites the Optical Society of America's estimate of from 7.5 to 10 million sensations. This seems to be a desk-exercise.

2 For a discussion of Berlin and Kay's effect on language studies, Grossman 1988 [**86**], 16f.

3 For a critique of these methods, Kuschel and Monberg 1974 [**916**], 213ff; Sahlins 1976 [**949**], 12; Grossmann 1988 [**86**], 21.

4 Bolton 1978 [**854**], 306, 310.

5 Merrin et al. 1975 [**930**], 54–60; Bornstein 1975 [**856**], 401–19.

6 Chapanis 1965 [**867**], 338; Grossmann 1988 [**86**], 6. It is well known that women are far less prone than men to visual colour-deficiencies: Barlow and Mollon 1982 [**847**], 197; for a dissenting voice, Wasserman 1978 [**975**], 69ff.

7 Wattenwyl and Zollinger 1981 [**976**], 303–15. The tests described in this study showed that art students in Switzerland and Israel had more difficulty than science students in naming colours quickly because they were more concerned with individual nuances.

8 Isidore *Etymologies* XII, i, 48; Palladius *Opus agriculturae* IV, 13, cit. M. L. Wagner [**974**], 1916/17, 234. Some of these terms were not what we term 'colours' but refer to markings on the coat.

9 Schwyzer 1929 [**951**], 93–100.

10 Steiger 1958 [**961**], 768, 778. Old High German terms have been estimated to be 11 ('Farbe' in *Handwörterbuch des deutschen Aberglaubens*, II, 1929/30, col. 1190).

11 Radloff 1871 [**946**], 302f: Köhalmi 1966 [**913**], 46 (about 40 terms); Sundberg 1985 [**963**], espec. 156f (58 terms, 16 of them 'basic'); Hill 1972 [**904**], 120f has found 20 terms in modern Slavic usage, some of them quite unknown to lay people.

12 Boethius 1906 [**636**], V, 10, 24, 313, 346f.

13 The fundamental study is de Vries 1965 [**970**], 351ff. For the study of colour terms in 17 contemporary novels, which found white used 957 times, black 694 and red and blue almost equal at 477 and 482 respectively, with the next most used colour, grey, far behind at 400, R. M. Evans 1948 [**884**], 230–1.

14 On this relationship, Lucy and Schweder 1979 [**922**], 599f. Also Kouwer 1949 [**914**], 9f.

15 Oribasius I, 1940 [**934**], 125, 127: for the Greek, Oribasius 1851–76 [**933**], V, 76 Bk II, §44: V, 78, Bk II, §55 and Mugler 1964 [**523**], s.v. *xanthos*. For the colours of wine, Fitton Brown 1962 [**888**], 192–5.

16 May 1957 [**763**], 62f. For variously coloured 'purples' in French romances, Goddard 1927 [**894**]; for the same in the Vatican in 1436, Müntz and Frothingham 1883 [**526**], 60ff. For various *purpura* in MS illumination, Silvestre 1954 [**956**], 138–9. See also p. 27 above.

17 Weckerlin 1905 [**977**], 85; J. H. Munro, 'The mediaeval scarlet and the economics of sartorial splendour' in Harte and Ponting 1983 [**899**], 59. As late as the early 14th century documents still refer to 'scarlets' of several colours (Weckerlin, ibid., 12; R. van Uytven, 'Cloth in mediaeval literature of western Europe' in Harte and Ponting, ibid., 158). For references to *kermes* as *escarlate*, Poerck 1951 [**941**], **213ff.**

18 Dolce 1565 [**197**], 13v. For the definition in the Reichenau Glossary, H. Meier 1963 [**927**], 106. The fullest studies are Toynbee 1902 [**965**], 307–14; Mann 1923 [**924**], 186–96; Hoepffner 1923 [**905**], 592–7.

19 M. L. Wagner 1916/17 [**974**], 234; H. Meier 1963 [**927**], 106f.

20 H. Meier 1963 [**927**], 106f.

21 For peach-blossom, Du Cange in Toynbee 1902 [**965**], 307–14; for Persian lilac, Mann 1923 [**924**], 189; for *persele*, Brereton and Ferrier 1981 [**862**], 271 and 329n. The interpretation of this passage from a late 14-century text is complicated by the author's inclination to see the flowers of the cornflower (*perseau*), purple corn-cockle (*neelle*) and pink rose-mallow (*passe-rose*) as of all the same colour and all red (*vermeille*).

22 Poerck 1951 [**941**], 167; Sicily Herald 1860 [**954**], 88. For the cost of English *pers* in the late 13th-century as second only to scarlet, whereas light blues were much cheaper, Carus-Wilson 1953 [**866**], 90.

23 Brereton and Ferrier 1981 [**862**], 133.

24 H. Meier 1963 [**927**], 106.

25 Robert Guiscard's gift to Monte Cassino, *c.* 1085, in Lehmann-Brockhaus 1938 [**743**], no. 2844. For Persia as the chief intermediary in the silk trade between China and the West, Falke 1921 [**429**], 2f.

26 Fernandez Arenas 1982 [**887**], 95. For the building as it survives, Azcona 1972 [**843**].

27 *De Ornatu Ecclesiae* in *Summa Major*, (Antoninus 1959 [**841**]) Pars III, tit. xii, cap. x, §ii, col. 546f. For Antoninus as an opponent of art, Gilbert 1959 [**893**], 76.

28 Brault 1972 [**860**]; Pastoureau 1982 [**935**]; ibid. 1983 [**936**]; ibid. 1986 [**937**]; ibid. 1989a [**938**].

29 Seltman 1924 [**952**], espec. 24.

30 Bouly de Lesdain 1897 [**858**], 69–79; Gras 1951 [**895**], 198–208.

31 Bouly de Lesdain 1897 [**858**], 71; Dennys 1975 [**876**], 29f argues that this shield is only proto-heraldic since we do not know whether it was used by Geoffrey's son, Henry II Plantaganet, King of England.

32 Barker 1986 [**846**], 4–6, 176–83.

33 For *Chanson de Roland*, Bouly de Lesdain 1897 [**858**], 70; for mid-12th century *Roman de Thèbes*, A. Wagner 1956 [**973**], 12f.

34 See German text of *c.* 1156 in which 'Greek' *lazur* was described as *optimus color* (Schlosser 1896 [**798**], 234) and a Florentine 13th-century treatise in which *azura* is 'nobilior ceteris coloribus' (Thorndyke 1960 [**964**], 58). See also Kurella and Strauss 1983 [**915**], 34ff.

35 Glover's Roll (*c.* 1235), ed. in London 1967 [**921**], 89ff and in Brault 1973 [**861**], 31–7. Bigot Roll in Brault ibid., 16–28.

36 Goddard 1927 [**894**], 131–3. For the derivation, Tobler-Lommatsch *Altfranzösisches Wörterbuch*, 1925–, s.v. *gole*.

37 Huon de Meri 1976 [**910**], 75, 84; Prinet 1922 [**943**], 43ff.

38 Delort 1978 [**875**], 1228, 1270ff.

39 Serjeant 1972 [**568**], 210; Delort 1978 [**875**], 29ff, 1261.

40 Delort 1978 [**875**], 42ff, 531ff (hierarchy of furs in the 14th century), 1245ff (prices).

41 A Latin armorial text written in Switzerland in the 1240s, Konrad von Mure's *Clipearius Teutonicorum*, still used a very loose vocabulary of black, 3 yellows (*croceo, auro, gilvo*) 3 blues (*lasurio, blaveus, glaucus*), 3 whites (*niveo, albus, candore nitentem*), 3 reds (*rubeo, rubro, rufus*) and green: Ganz 1899 [**891**], 172–85,

42 Gage 1978 [**74**], 108.

43 Cf. M. Plouzeau, 'Vert Haeume: approaches d'un syntagme' in CUERMA 1988 [**873**], 598ff. Plouzeau denies the problem.

44 See e.g., in the Chifflet-Prinet Roll (1297, Brault 1973 [**861**], no. 80) the arms of Gobiert de Montsablon, 'a trois pens vairés d'argent et de vert au chief d'or'. In Glover's Roll the spelling is very various: verre, verré, verrée, vaireè, vierre, varrieè, varreè.

45 Pastoureau 1986 [**937**], 25 trace the use of *sinople* as green in a heraldic context to the anonymous romance *Durmart le Galois*, written in Picardy in the late 1210s. The use of the term in French to denote red also seems to have a heraldic origin: in the *Liber de Coloribus Faciendis* of Peter of St. Audemar the use of the term *sinopis* to describe a particularly beautiful vermilion is attributed to shield-makers, *scutarii* (Merrifield 1849 [**271**], I, 143). For the date and authorship L. van Acker (ed.), *Petri pictoris carmina nec non Petri de sancto audemaro librum de coloribus faciendis* (Corpus Christianoum continuatio mediaevalis XXV), 1972, 163–6.

46 Sicily Herald 1860 [**954**], 46f. As late as the mid-16th century the Imperial Hungarian Herald Johann von Francolin felt bound to explain that the *sinope, sinoble, sinople* used by heralds was 'auf die recht Frantzösisch sprach', *verdt* (Berchem et al. 1939 [**851**], 154f).

47 Nicholas Upton also wrote that he had when young written in disparagement of green but now wished to retract this (1654 [**967**], 123).

48 Tremlett 1967 [**966**], 7, 36–57.

49 Christine de Pisan 1937 [**868**], 290; see also Haye 1901 [**901**], 283 (1456). Both depend on Bonet 1949 [**855**], 206 (1387).

50 Dean 1967 [**874**], 25. For the date, Dennys 1975 [**876**], 60f. Humphrey Smith 1956 [**908**], 19f. notes only 3 English examples using purple *c.* 1300.

51 For Glover's Roll, London 1967 [**921**], 106; for Walford's, Brault 1973 [**861**], 38, 46, 57.

52 Argote de Molina 1957 [**842**], 86 (*rojo*); Salazar de Mendoza 1618 [**950**], 37: *campo de goles o purpura ... leon rampante bermejo*. See also Bouton III, 1884, [**859**], 185f.

53 Menestrier 1661 [**929**], 54; cf. 55 and 67 on the arms of Spain.

54 Douet d'Arcq 1858 [**879**], 322; Sicily Herald 1860 [**954**], 47ff.

55 See espec. Brunetto Latini IV, 1883 [**918**], Pt III, ch. xiv, 53ff on comparison as the most 'beautiful' of the 8 colours of rhetoric. On the tradition in general, Faral 1924 [**886**], 49f and for the medieval opposition, 92–3.

56 Maguire 1987 [**496**], 8ff; Coulton 1953 [**872**], 554.

57 Peter of Poitiers 1938 [**940**], 4. For a survey of medieval ideas about symbols, Chydenius 1960 [**869**].

58 Haupt 1941 [**900**], 84–6. Lists of antithetical meanings were already drawn up by Wackernagel 1872 [**972**], 234–40. The dictionary of medieval colour-symbolism Christel Meier has been compiling will take account of these ambiguities: see C. Meier 1974 [**926**], espec. 387–95; 1977 [**107**], espec. 147ff; also Brückner 1982, [**863**], 24–5.
59 Tremlett 1967 [**966**], 59 and no. 13.
60 The earliest literary example of green as faith I have noticed is in the Latin song of *c.* 1000, *Civis celestis patrie*, where green *jaspis* and the emerald are its bearers (Dronke 1972 [**880**], 77). See also Gervais du Bus 1914/19 [**892**], 200f (1310/14): *de foi loyale et d'esperance*.
61 For the history of the *Scutum Fidei*, M. Evans 1982 [**883**], 22ff; Lewis 1987 [**920**], 195ff.
62 Reeves and Hirsch-Reich 1972 [**947**], 194.
63 Didreck 1924 [**877**], chs 172–86, 224ff; Didreck 1951 [**878**] is the original Icelandic.
64 Seyler 1889 [**953**], 125 cites several examples from early 13th-century romances. The earliest use of *tawny* I have found is in the English mid-15th century 'Ashmolean Tract', ed. Humphrey 1960 [**907**], 165f. The author implies that it is used only in the Empire and in France.
65 Suchenwirt 1827 [**962**], 3ff.
66 The earliest instance I have found is in *Mowbray's French Treatise* in the College of Arms, London, which probably dates from the end of the 14th century (Campbell and Steer I, 1988 [**865**], 63, no. L.12c, folios 32–35v).
67 Douet d'Arcq 1858 [**879**], 324.
68 Sicily Herald 1860 [**954**], 38ff, 56ff.
69 Hunter Blair 1930 [**909**]. The stones are mixed with more traditional tinctures (e.g. 96, 118).
70 A. Wagner 1956 [**973**], 138.
71 A. C. Decembrio *De Politia Literaria* (*c.* 1462), cit. Gundersheimer 1973 [**897**], 106f.
72 Sicily Herald 1860 [**954**], 43ff, 86f. For Alfonso's taste for black, Vespasiano da Bisticci 1963 [**969**], 73. In 1376 Charles V of France had bought a quantity of brown (*tanné*) cloth for 'Friday robes' (*pour robes des vendredis*): J. Evans 1952 [**882**], 27. For the Romantic revival of the idea, Pückler-Muskau 1831–6 [**944**], IV, 289 (black Friday).
73 Keen 1984 [**912**], 7; the story is repeated in one of the MSS of Sicily Herald (1867 [**955**], 75f).
74 Peter the Venerable 1967 [**786**], I. Letters 28, 111, 150 (Bernard's letters are missing). For the earlier history of monastic dress, Oppenheim 1931 [**9**], espec. 79f. See also Pastoureau 1989b [**939**], 222–4 on the variable interpretation of 'black' in the Benedictine robes of the 13th century. Black was, of course, a very expensive colour (see below).
75 Burchard 1884 [**864**], II, 252f. Violet was the liturgical requivalent of black.
76 For Innocent III's *De Sacro Altaris*, Braun 1907 [**387**], 749ff; for Siccardus *Mitrale*, Wickham Legg 1882 [**979**], 99. Both these ideas were introduced by Durandus of Mende (Guillaume Durand) 1859 [**881**], 30, 130). The only recent discussion of the question overlooks these disagreements (Pastoureau 1989a [**938**], 217ff). An exhaustive history and survey of liturgical colours in both the Roman Catholic and Protestant churches is provided by the *Reallexikon zur deutschen Kunstgeschichte*, VII, 1981, s.v. 'Farbe (Liturgisch)'.
77 For red, Sicily Herald 1860 [**954**], 35f; Durandus 1859 [**881**], 130; for black, Sicily Herald ibid., 56f; Durandus ibid., 131. The link between armorial and liturgical colour-developments was suggested by Pastoureau 1989b [**939**], 221f but in the context of his implausible idea that they were both abstract systems.
78 Skinner 1986 [**957**], 52 has traced the scheme of the Siena frescoes to Brunetto Latini's encyclopaedia of the 1260s, *Li Livres dou Tresor*; but an Italian writer closer in time to Lorenzetti, Francesco da Barberino (1264–1348), has a scheme of the same Virtues which gives green to Prudence, white to Justice and red to Fortitude (1875 [**890**], 423ff). For the *Maestà*, Borsook 1966 [**857**], 32–3. It has been pointed out that the colours of the Theological Virtues, red, white and green, correspond to the livery-colours of the Medici in Florence (Ames-Lewis 1979 [**840**], 129, 137, 143) and that they borrowed them from the Gonzaga at Mantua; but they were also the colours of the Este at Ferrara and were glossed in the same way (Gundersheimer 1972 [**896**], 51, 86, 109). Mantegna made prominent use of the red, white and blue of the Gonzaga and Este arms, which were also the colours of the planets Mars, Venus and Mercury, in his paintings for these patrons (Lehmann 1973 [**919**], 165f, 172).
79 Hadamer von de Laber 1850 [**898**], 243–50; *Von den Farben* in Lassberg 1820/5 [**917**], I, 153–8, on which see Bartsch 1863 [**848**], 38ff.
80 See espec. Squibb 1959 [**959**], 14–16.
81 Bartolo *De Insigniis et Armis* (1358), chs 23–27 in Jones 1943 [**911**], 244–7.
82 Johannes de Bado Aureo *Tractatus de Armis* (?c. 1394) in Jones ibid., 96–9. Nothing is known of Johannes, who has even been identified with the early 15th-century heraldic writer Nicholas Upton, apparently the only writer to cite the *Tractatus*, which was first published with Upton's own *De Studio Militari* in 1654 (cf. n. 47 above for Upton on green).
83 Jones ibid., 103.
84 Ibid., 109.
85 L. Valla *Epistola ad Candidum Decembrium* in Baxandall 1986 [**849**], 168–71.
86 For Valla in Naples, Bentley 1988 [**850**], 108–22.
87 Rabelais 1966 [**945**], 35f. Rabelais has, of course, misread his *Blason*.
88 Ibid., 38–41.
89 Cian 1951 [**871**], 167. One of Gonzaga's tasks was to have been to explain the *reasons* for the meanings attributed to colours, which makes the loss of his book particularly regrettable.
90 For a survey of these and other publications on colour-symbolism, Cian 1894 [**870**], 314–29.
91 Portal 1979 [**942**], 21n.
92 Ibid., 32f.
93 This was pointed out by Vallier 1979 [**968**], 12f. For German poetic comparisons of red and purple being as green as, or greener than, grass, Zingerle 1864 [**980**], 391ff.
94 Gage 1978 [**74**], 108.
95 Thus in the 13th century Witelo mentioned *roseus* and *viridis* as the most beautiful colours (Baeumker 1908 [**845**], 172 and on the beauty of green in nature, 173).
96 G. Taubert, 'Erwähnung von Textilien in Mittelhochdeutschen Epen' in Flury-Lemberg and Stolleis 1981 [**889**], 17. For this combination in late Gothic panel painting and stained glass, Frodl-Kraft 1977/8 [**215**], espec. 114; E. Frodl-Kraft, 'Farbendualitäten, Gegenfarben, Grundfarben in der gotischen Malerei' in Hering-Mitgau et al. 1980 [**902**], espec. 294.
97 Melis I, 1962 [**928**], 570.
98 For *glaucus* and *ceruleus*, see p. 35, n. 90 above. For *bloi*, Weise 1878 [**978**], 288. The dual colour of the topaz made it possible to give it a 2-fold interpretation: blue for heaven and gold for the Godhead (Bach 1934 [**844**], vv.4389ff). Although the tradition of Isidore had mentioned 2 colours in the topaz, only 1, *golden*, was named (Marbode 1977 [**267**], 50f). Sextus Amarcus, 12th century, claimed that the topaz was white, red and green and thus symbolized the unity of the Theological Virtues in St Paul (1969 [**802**], 183ff). For the Old High German *blao*, König 1927 [**98**], 150. For the Slav languages, Herne 1954 [**903**], 71; McNeill 1972 [**923**], 21. A late medieval French MS on physiognomy seems to use the term *bloi* in both senses, yellow for the skin and blue for the eyes: both signify courage (Jordan 1911 [**249**], 702f). A student of Greek colour-terms has found evidence that *karopos* may have meant both amber and light blue but rejects this as incredible (Maxwell-Stuart 1981 [**925**], 21f). Frodl-Kraft 1977/8 [**215**], 99 has pointed to the stained glass of the Sainte-Chapelle, Paris (completed 1248), as an example of blue–yellow tonality; here a good deal of its force is due to the ubiquitous blue–gold of the French royal arms, gold lilies on a blue field.
99 Gage 1978 [**74**], 107.
100 Forbes 1964–72 [**213**], IV (1964), 110.
101 Pastoureau 1986 [**937**], 90f.
102 Pastoureau 1982 [**935**], 133 has discounted the earlier idea that seal-engravers sought to indicate colours by hatchings. Different capital letters were occasionally used in the 16th century to indicate colours (Seyler 1889 [**953**], 591ff).
103 *Pompa funebris optimi potenties principis Alberti Pii archiducis &c. veris imaginibus expressa a Jac. Francquart*, Brussels, 1623, pls XXIX–L.
104 Vulson de la Colombière 1639 [**971**]. The system was first used in Germany in 1643 (Seyler 1889 [**953**], 591) and was canonized in Siebmacher's *Wappenbuch* (1655). For England, Evelyn 1906 [**885**], 127.
105 Humbert de Superville 1827 [**906**], 8–22. For the context, Stafford 1972 [**960**], 311–35.
106 Souriau 1895 [**958**], 859. Souriau's aesthetics of dynamism has been discussed by Roque 1990 [**948**], 15–18.

6 Unweaving the Rainbow

1 Priestley 1772 [**1110**], II, 588.
2 Boyer 1959 [**1009**]; Nussenzveig 1977 [**1097**], 116–27; *Regenbögen* 1977 [**1114**], 175–252.
3 Priestley 1772 [**1110**], I, 50.
4 Raehlmann 1902 [**1112**], 11ff; Westphal 1910 [**1155**], 182–206; Boigey 1923 [**1002**], 18–19; Dimmick and Hubbard 1939 [**1028**], 242–54; Beare 1963 [**995**], 248–56.
5 W. Preyer *Die Seele des Kindes*, 2nd edn, 1884, 16 in Waetzoldt 1909 [**1153**], 355. The colours were red, yellow, green and blue, the same set as that proposed in the 14th century by Theodoric of Freiberg (Boyer 1959 [**1009**], 113), except that Theodoric has purple rather than blue. For 2-colour salience, Beare 1963 [**995**], 250, fig. 1 and the Norse *Stjórn*: 'Though the rainbow seems to have six colours in it, it has two [red and dark green] that are predominant' (cit. Dronke 1972 [**880**], 71). See also the n. in a coloured copy of Rolewinck's *Fasciculus Temporum* (Strasbourg, 1493) that the bow has 2 main colours, although some say 4 or 6 (cit. Rösch 1960 [**1122**], 422f).
6 For Buddhism in Afghanistan, B. Rowland, Jr, 'Studies in the Buddhist art of Bāmiyān: the Bodhisattva of Group E' in Baratha Iyer 1947 [**986**], 46ff. For South American Indian cultures, Levi-Strauss 1970 [**1079**], 246ff; the Art Gallery in Perth, W. Australia, has a collection of Aboriginal bark paintings illustrating the N. Arnhemland myth of the Wannelak sisters and the rainbow snake. For the modern history of parhelia and glories, Greenler 1980 [**1056**]. The history of the related confusions of the colours of stars studied by Boll 1918 [**1003**] and Malin and Murdin 1984 [**1082**], 1–24, 88–90.
7 Menzel 1842 [**1087**], 259.
8 Dürbeck 1977 [**200**], 42ff; Isidore of Seville 1960 [**456**], 284f; Ovid *Metamorphoses* VI, 65–7, cit. Seneca *Quaestiones Naturales* I, 3.4; Virgil *Aeneid* IV, 700 and V, 88.
9 For Aëtius, O. Gilbert 1907 [**1050**], 609f; Ammianus Marcellinus *History* XX, ll.27 (trans. J. C. Rolfe, II, 1940). Ammianus gives a surprisingly reasoned account of his bizarre series.
10 Rosenthal 1972 [**1124**], 45; col. pl. in Eggenberger 1973 [**1030**], 34.
11 For the Pergamon mosaic, Merkev 1967 [**1088**], 81–2; for a col. reconstruction, Kawerau and Wiegand 1930 [**1072**], pl. VIII.
12 For St Gregory, *Patrologia Latina* 1844–55 [**116**], LXXVI (1854), cols 67–8; Hugh of St Victor, in the 4th book of his encyclopaedia *De Bestiis et aliis Rebus*, has the same colours but reverses the order, which had not been specified by Gregory (ibid., CLXXVII, col. 149). For the Renaissance see below.
13 Boyer 1959 [**1009**], 48–9; Stornajolo 1908 [**1142**], 41 pl. 39; Cornelius a Lapide 1865 [**1019**], I, 134; Picinello 1697 [**1105**], 96.
14 British Library Cotton Claudius B.IV, folio 16v in Henderson 1962 [**1063**], 189, fig. 35b; St Jerome in *Patrologia Latina* 1844–55 [**116**], XXV (1845), col. 31. The idea was repeated in the 16th century by Dolce 1565 [**197**], folio 6v. One colour-formula which seems to be very rare in represented bows is the 4-colour bow related frequently in the literature to the 4 elements, humours and seasons (several e.gs in Wackernagel 1872 [**972**], I, 146f; Hellmann 1904 [**1062**], 39f, 87; Maclean 1965 [**1081**], 144–5, 213ff; M.-T. Vorcin, 'L'arc-en-ciel au XIIIe siècle' in CUERMA 1988 [**873**], 231–4). As seen in ch. 2 above, there was very little agreement in the Middle Ages about the identity of these elemental colours.
15 Dante *Purgatorio* XXIX, 76–8; *Paradiso* XII, 10–12; Austin 1929 [**984**], 316–17, which quotes Landino's 15th-century commentary that Dante really intended 4 colours, red, sanguine, green and white; Boyer 1959 [**1009**], 108–9, and 62 for a Greek 7-colour theory attributed to Ptolemy.
16 British Library Cotton Claudius B.IV, ff. 2, 4v. Also Meyer 1961 [**1089**], 83.

17 Weixlgärtner 1962 [**1154**], 95–6; Behling 1968 [**997**], 11–20. For a possibly more earthly prototype for the Isenheim glory, see p. 152 above.
18 Weixlgärtner 1962 [**1154**], 95–7.
19 Weixlgärtner attributes this to possible damage through repeated cleaning and restoration.
20 Weixlgärtner ibid., 20; Thiel 1933 [**1147**], 168–9.
21 *Patrologia Latina* 1844–55 [**116**], XXV (1845), col. 31. See also a 12th-century Limoges enamel, Cluny Museum, Paris, where the rainbow-throne is in 2 values of blue, although other colours are used elsewhere in the design.
22 See e.g., Rogier van der Weyden *Last Judgment*, Beaune; Stefan Lochner *Last Judgment*, Cologne, Wallraf-Richartz Museum; Jerome Bosch *Paradise, Hell and Last Judgment*, Vienna, Akademie; J. B. Zimmermann *Christ in Judgment*, ceiling fresco Wieskirche, Bavaria. Also Cornelius a Lapide 1865 [**1019**], I, 134.
23 Ripa 1611 [**1119**], 198–9. The origin of the emblem has not been traced by Mandowsky 1939 [**1084**], and may be Ripa's own invention, although an Elizabethan jewel is said to have shown a figure of VIRTUTE (or VIRGO) holding compasses and standing on a rainbow (Graziani 1972 [**1054**], 251, n. 9).
24 Butlin 1981 [**181**], nos. 268–71. Ripa's emblem is mentioned by Blunt [**1938**], 53ff in connection with this design but that Blake knew Ripa has been denied by Navnavutty 1952 [**1094**], 261. The link between Blake's *Newton* and Ripa's *Judgment* is one of idea, not design.
25 Ripa 1611, [**1119**], 198–9. For Campanella, Garin 1950 [**1048**], 275.
26 Ripa 1611 [**1119**], 275–7.
27 Richter 1970 [**1118**], I, 229–30, 300.
28 Carli 1960 [**1013**], col. pl. 126; drawing (Florence, Uffizi) in van Marle 1923–38 [**1086**], XIV (1933), 269, fig. 176. Carli 1974 [**1014**], 12 argues that Pinturicchio's bow derives from a fresco by Sodoma. See also Piccolomini 1960 [**1104**], 30, 36.
29 C. Gilbert 1952 [**1049**], 202–16; Gombrich 1966 [**1053**], 107–21. There is, e.g., a rainbow in the *Beheading of John the Baptist* by Niklaus Manuel Deutsch I, Basle, Kunstmuseum.
30 Castiglione 1946 [**1017**], 127; Sorte in Barocchi 1960–62 [**992**], I, 275. Most of the 16th-century accounts seem to derive from Castiglione.
31 Wethey 1969–75 [**349**], III (1975), nos 11 (*c.* 1566), 43, 44 (*c.* 1560–5).
32 Valla 1501 [**1152**], XXI, xxxvii; XXII, xxiii.
33 Brucioli 1537–8 [**1010**], II, xix, 32v–35v. Brucioli was an important translator of Aristotle into Italian. His *Dialoghi* was briefly noticed by C. Dionisotti, 'Tiziano e la letteratura' in Pallucchini 1978 [**1099**], 268–9.
34 Weixlgärtner 1962 [**1154**], 93.
35 Reynolds *Discourse* IV, 1771; Leslie 1951 [**1078**], 299.
36 De Piles 1743 [**1106**], 127–8.
37 Teyssèdre 1963 [**1146**], 266–7. De Piles did refer to the bow to distinguish it from the colouring of clouds (1743 [**1106**], 129). Deperthes (1822, [**1027**], 4–5) referred to Rubens as a master of the accidents of light but without mentioning the rainbow.
38 Adler 1982 [**982**], no 29, 36, 39, 40, 47, 54, 55.
39 Cologne, Wallraf-Richartz Museum. König's *Noah's Sacrifice* (Berlin, Staatliche Museen, Dahlem, 1843) has a double bow (no inversion) with a similar triad of white, yellow and blue-grey, as does a gouache of the subject (Hazlitt, Gooden and Fox, *European Drawings: Recent Acquisitions*, London, 1988, no. 48 in col.).
40 Teyssèdre 1963 [**1146**], 267; Glück 1945 [**1051**], no. 15. The Hermitage version of *Pastoral Landscape with a Rainbow* seems to be an early example of the correct observation of darker sky outside the bow.
41 Parkhurst 1961 [**1102**], 34–50.
42 Peiresc to Rubens, 27 October 1622 in Rubens 1887–1909 [**1126**], II, 57. The substance of the conversation has not survived but it may have referred to the *Marriage of Marie de Médici and Henri IV at Lyon* since Peiresc's immediately following remark about a 'victoria romana in habito di Minerva' tallies with the figure in the chariot in that picture.
43 Paradin 1557 [**1101**], 64; Picinello 1687 [**1105**], ch. XVIII, §255. Needless to say, it was hardly an appropriate sign for the queen who presided over the St Bartholomew's Day massacre in 1572.
44 For Rubens's confusion of the royal birth-signs, 1887–1909 [**1126**], III, 10–11.
45 For Descartes, Boyer 1959, [**1009**], ch. 8.
46 Goethe to Eckermann, 18 April 1827, in Gage 1980b [**1043**], 205–6.
47 Ruskin 1900–12 [**1129**], XXII, 212n. The painting is Adler 1982 [**982**], no. 55.
48 Finberg 1909 [**1036**], I, 192. The painting is Adler ibid., no. 40.
49 J. Smith 1829–42 [**1137**], VI (1835), 25–6.
50 J. W. von Goethe *Ruysdael as a Poet* in Gage 1980b [**1043**], 213–15. Goethe did not mention the rainbow, which was not reproduced in the sepia copy by C. Lieber in Goethe's collection. It may not have been visible in the picture, which Smith described as very dark at this time. For an earlier interpretation on similar lines, C. F. von Ramdohr in Friedrich 1968 [**1039**], 153; for Constable's moralizing reading of other Ruisdaels, Leslie 1951 [**1078**], 319.
51 Rosenberg 1928 [**1123**], 31–2 and figs 59–60. Both drawings were engraved in 1670. A recent discussion of the context of the pictures is in Sutton 1987 [**1144**], 100.
52 For *The Triumph of Painting* and *Summer*, from the *Four Seasons* (Cropper 1984 [**1022**], fig. 56), in Goethe's collection, Schuchardt 1848–9 [**1132**], I, 87, nos. 833–4.
53 Baldinucci V, 1728 [**985**], 479–80.
54 For a discussion of the various interpretations of Testa's death, Sutherland-Harris 1967 [**1143**], 35–69.
55 Cropper 1984 [**1022**], 236, cf. 218, 240, 244.
56 Lopresti 1921 [**1080**], 75, fig. 10.
57 Bottari I, 1822 [**1007**], 450–1.
58 For Gilpin's tours, Barbier 1963 [**990**]; for his influence, Hussey 1927 [**1067**], Manwaring 1925 [**1085**]. For his colour, Barbier 1959a [**988**], nos 71, 81; for Clark's treatment of *Gilpin's Day*, ibid. 1963 [**990**], 85.
59 Barbier 1959b [**989**], 25–6.
60 Hussey 1927 [**1067**], 124. Another leader of the Picturesque movement, Uvedale Price, did refer to Rubens's weather effects, as 'sublime and picturesque' (Price 1810 [**1109**], I, 130–1).
61 Valenciennes 1800 [**1150**], 217; Rehfues 1804–10 [**1115**], IV, 150–1; Rogers 1956 [**1121**], 275.
62 Wilson 1927 [**1156**], I, 253.
63 Carus 1835 [**1015**], II, 64–5: Rogers 1956 [**1121**], 205–6.
64 See his study for *Obere Staubbachfall im Lauterbrunnental* (Aarau, Kantonale Kunstsammlung, Raeber 1979 [**1111**], no. 181), *Das Wehr bei Mühletal östlich Innerkirchen* (1776, Zürich, Landesmuseum, ibid., 252) and the 2 versions of *Schneebrücke und Regenbogen in Gadmental* 1778 (Basle, Kunstmuseum, and Bern, Kunstmuseum, ibid., 381, 382).
65 Byron, *Journal*, 23 September 1816. He also increased the reputation of the Terni rainbow by including it in *Childe Harold's Pilgrimage* IV, 69–72 and note.
66 Decker 1957 [**1025**], 132. The sketch no. 174, fig. 325 corresponds closely to this account.
67 Miquel 1962 [**1091**], 87.
68 Leslie 1860 [**1077**], I, 193–4; see also Valenciennes 1800 [**1150**], 217.
69 Kitson 1937 [**1073**], 166. Cotman's early patron Sir Henry Englefield had described his experience of this phenomenon in 1802 and may have communicated his interest to the painter (Englefield 1802 [**1031**], 1–4, illustration p. 3). It is possible that Cotman's monochrome drawing, which exists in 2 versions, was for a similar scientific illustration.
70 Grigson 1960 [**1057**], 15. A few pages later Palmer made a trial rainbow spectrum (Butlin 1962 [**1011**], 163) but no compositions of the subject are known.
71 Bierhaus-Rödiger 1978 [**999**], nos 251, 467, 615, 626.
72 Friedrich's strong sense of the bow's religious significance is clear from his use of it behind the Crucifix in a lost drawing (Börsch-Supan and Jähnig 1973 [**1006**], 229) and from some remarks *c.* 1830 in Friedrich 1968 [**1039**], 112. A MS illumination attributed to Pinturicchio in the Vatican (Vat. Barb. Lat. 614, folio 219v) also has a 3-colour rainbow immediately behind the Cross. For the identification of Friedrich's as a lunar bow, *Caspar David Friedrich* 1974 [**1040**], no. 80. For discussions of the lunar rainbow in Germany in the period, *Gilberts Annalen der Physik* XI, 480; *Schweiggers Journal* LIII, 1828, 126, cit. Menzel 1842 [**1087**], 274.
73 *Artists' Repository*, III, 1808, 93.
74 Butlin and Joll 1984 [**1012**], no. 347. The halo was first identified by Bell 1901 [**998**], no. 182.
75 Gage 1980a [**1042**], no. 288. Turner did not mention the halo.
76 Farington 1978–84 [**1033**], 13 July 1813. It was West who probably told Constable that his skies should be 'a white sheet thrown behind the objects': Leslie 1951 [**1078**], 85, cf. 14.
77 [Pott] 1782, [**1107**], 52–3. See also Turner on the advantages of the British weather in an Academy lecture *c.* 1810 (Gage 1969 [**217**], 213–14).
78 Miquel 1962 [**1091**], 112–13.
79 Butlin 1981 [**181**], no. 368; Blake 1956 [**171**], 633.
80 Valenciennes 1956/7 [**1151**], nos 3, 4 are on the backs of calendars for 1785 and 1786; nos 17 and 86 are dated 1817; nos 72 and 100 include rainbows. See also Valenciennes 1800 [**1150**], 219–20, 227, 260.
81 Musper 1935 [**1093**], 182–5. Koch reported that the falls were said to surpass Terni but his sketch shows no bow (183)
82 Frankfurt, Städel Institute; version of 1814/15 in Berlin, Schloss Charlottenburg (Jaffé 1905, [**1068**], 37).
83 For Koch and Rubens, Jaffé ibid., 321. The Karlsruhe version is possibly from 1805 (ibid., 42–3) and the Munich picture 1815; for the Stuttgart *Rider*, Council of Europe 1959 [**1020**], no. 235.
84 Rottmann copied Koch's Munich landscape as a young man (Decker 1957 [**1025**], no. 14). Wallis's *Heidelberger Schloss*, including a rainbow, is in the Frankfurt Goethe-Haus; for a linked drawing, Baudissen 1924 [**994**], 38, fig. 7. Other landscapes with rainbows are nos 12, 20. For Wallis's relationship to Koch, ibid., 17. Olivier was in the Koch circle in Vienna *c.* 1816 (Grote 1938 [**1058**], 122, 156–7) when he used the bow in his *Hubertuslegende* (ibid., 127–30, fig. 67) and later in the *Babylonian Captivity* (1825/30, ibid., 335–6, fig. 213).
85 Abrams 1958 [**981**], 300.
86 Haydon 1926 [**239**], I, 269; more drily in Haydon 1960–63 [**1060**], II, 173.
87 Haydon 1876 [**1059**], II, 54–5, Abrams (1958 [**981**], 306) forgets that he did drink in the end.
88 See his enjoyment of a Devon sunrise recorded by Redding 1858 [**1113**], I, 123.
89 Ruskin *Praeterita* I, iii, §63.
90 Ruskin *Modern Painters* III, 1856, Pt IV, ch. xvii, §42.
91 For Goethe, Barry, Runge and Turner, see pp. 108, 110, 112, 114–15. For Palmer, Palmer 1892 [**1100**], 314, 319, 328; for Olivier, his poem *Schönheit* in Grote 1938 [**1058**], 4; for Overbeck, Overbeck 1843 [**1098**], 10, where Raphael is dressed in white 'as symbolical of the universality of his genius, uniting all the qualities which we gaze on with wonder in their separate states, in others, as the beams of light include the seven prismatic colours'.
92 Rossetti 1895 [**1125**], II, 328, 19 January 1876.
93 Hunt 1905 [**1066**], I, 159–60.
94 Newton 1730 [**1095**], I, ii, prop. V, theor. iv, Experiment 15. In Experiment 9 at least 5 primaries are implied.
95 Field 1845 [**1035**], 182–5.
96 Barry 1783 [**993**], 116, 120–1; for a discussion of the painting, Pressly 1981 [**1108**], 113–22, 294–8.
97 Barry 1809 [**34**], I, 524–6 (?1793). See also Dayes 1805 [**1024**], 299.
98 Novalis 1956 [**1096**], 100. For Smart, Greene 1953 [**1055**], 327–52.
99 I have discussed this in some detail: Gage 1971 [**1041**], 375–6.
100 J. T. Smith 1920 [**1138**], II, 384; see also Samuel Palmer in Palmer 1892 [**1100**], 243.
101 Field 1845 [**1035**], 69, 116–18; for the identification with Turner, see Field's index. For Martin, *Somerset House Gazette*, 15 May 1824, 81.
102 Leonardo 1721 [**1075**], 72 (1956 §185).
103 For the 'nobler' colours of the bow as opposed to pigments, Pecham 1970 [**785**], 236 from Aristotle *Meteorology* 372a; also Grosseteste 1912 [**234**], *De Iride*, 77. See also Pecham ibid., 234 for these nobler colours as 'light-bearing'. At one moment, Leonardo seems to have adopted a specifically anti-Aristotelian stance in relation to painting the rainbow, since he argues that the principle of the mixture of the painter's colours might itself help to explain the phenomenon (Richter 1970 [**1118**], I, 229, §287). He also noticed the mingling of colours in the centre of the bow (MS E, cover, verso, cit. Duhem 1906–13 [**1029**], I, 173f where Leonardo's

approach is seen to be close to that of the 14th-century Timon the Jew, on whom see Crombie 1961 [**1021**], 261ff).
104 Lewis 1987 [**920**], 71ff.
105 Menzel 1842 [**1087**], 265.
106 Boethius 1989 [**1001**] 167. His source is Ptolemy *Harmonics* in Barker II, 1989, [**991**], 283, which does not, however, detail the colours. For Leonardo's knowledge of Boethius's *On Music*, Solmi 1976 [**1140**], 104.
107 Junius 1638 [**1071**], 280 (with a reference to Boethius V, 4). See also 258 that the term *harmoge* was borrowed from music. Another discussion of this term proposes implausibly that it means optical fusion (Keuls 1978 [**97**], 77f). See also p. 108 above.
108 Barbaro 1568 [**987**], 176.
109 Van Mander 1973 [**1083**], 188–91 (VII, 22–2).
110 Farington 1978–84 [**1033**], 24 March 1804.
111 Ibid., 4 December 1817. From the notes taken by Callcott at this lecture we know that apart from the students and himself, Henry Howard, Fuseli, Turner, William Owen, Thomas Phillips, Henry Thomson, Chalon, Mulready and Prince Hoare attended (Oxford, Ashmolean Museum MS AWC 1h folios 1701, 204ff) and we may assume that C. R. Leslie was also present since it was he who reported to Farington.
112 *Annals of the Fine Arts*, II, 1818, 537f.
113 On the portrait, Schweizer 1982 [**1133**], 437.
114 Callcott, see n. 111 above, 205v–207v.
115 'In the course of the observations on the Annanias [*sic*] Mr West pointed out in his management of the blue color between the Red and yellow of the leading apostles the feeling Raphael had for making beautiful shapes in colors remarking that in order to avoid making two spots of the Blue on the breast and under the yellow tunic of St Peter he had not only extended it to the disciple immediately [ ] but the one also by his side' (folio 207v). After the lecture Howard asked West which was the highest red in the *Ananias*, to which West replied that of the right, at which Howard objected that it was not the red in the picture nearest the source of light, as his theory demanded. West countered this and a similar objection that the brightest yellow was on St Peter by claiming that Raphael wished to direct the spectator's attention to these 2 figures (folio 205v).
116 Forster-Hahn 1967 [**1037**], 381–2. A hint of a theory of warm and cool arrangement based on the rainbow was already suggested by West's American associate Copley as early as 1774 (1914 [**1018**], 240). In the late 1770s students at the Royal Academy were being taught (by an unnamed tutor who may have been West) that fruits like peaches and pears also displayed a prismatic sequence in their modelling (Sowerby 1809 [**1141**], 3–4). See also the recipe for painting sunsets in Hayter 1815 [**1061**], 168.
117 Galt 1820 [**1046**], II, 115; Farington 1978–84 [**1033**], 11 December 1797.
118 Leslie 1860 [**1077**], I, 57–8. For a rainbow landscape by West, von Erffa and Staley 1986 [**1032**], no. 478.
119 See the version in the treatise of the Norwich watercolourist John Thirtle (1777–1839) in Allthorpe-Guyton 1977 [**983**], 31 and no. 20 for a watercolour of a 6-coloured bow. Thirtle seems to depend chiefly on Leonardo and van Mander. For Cézanne, see p. 210 above.
120 J. B. Descamps *Les Vies des peintres flamands* 1753, I, 310, in Eastlake 1847–69 [**202**], I, 492–3; Hogarth 1955 [**1064**], 133; Reynolds *Discourse* VI, 1774.
121 *Musée de Montpellier* 1876 [**1092**], 361–3. For a col. detail, Johnson 1963 [**1069**], pl. 5. For the painting (now in the Louvre), Johnson 1981–9 [**1070**], no. 100 and pl. II.
122 Sand 1896 [**1130**], 84–5.
123 Delacroix 1980 [**1026**], 13 January 1857.
124 Runge 1959 [**1128**], 62, 111; also 16 January 1803 letter in Runge 1840/1 [**1127**], II, 195.
125 Runge 1959 [**1128**], 20–1, 24, 49, 92; cf. Howard 1848 [**1065**], 155.
126 Runge 1840/1 [**1127**], I, 60–1; See also to Steffens, March 1809, 151.
127 Ibid., 61.
128 D. Runge in Runge ibid., 228: Milarch (1821) in ibid., II, 533.
129 Traeger 1975 [**1149**], nos 272, 282a-b.
130 Gage 1969 [**217**], 186–7.
131 Howard 1848 [**1065**], 154–5.
132 Galton 1799 [**1047**], 509–13. He assumed that the proportions he discovered could be the basis of harmonious interior decoration and dress; his ideas were spread by the poet Erasmus Darwin (1806 [**1023**], I, 257–60). Young 1800 [**1157**], 393 noted, like Galton, that in disc-mixing Newton's proportions were unreliable, since they depended on the horizontal spectrum.
133 Priestley 1772 [**1110**], II, 588–630; cf. Boyer 1959 [**1009**], 276–8.
134 Priestley ibid., 590–1; Boyer ibid, 278.
135 *Faust* II, 'Anmutige Gegend', trans. P. Wayne.
136 Femmel 1958–73 [**1034**], Va (1963), 7 and no. 352.
137 *Farbenlehre, Polemischer Teil* (1810) §609.
138 Goethe 1953 [**1052**], 661–5; see also his *Tagebuch*, 19 August 1797, (Weimar edn III Abt., vol. 2. 1888, 83) and a letter from Dornburg to his son, 14 July 1828, on the importance of Alexander's dark band (Weimar edn IV Abt., vol. 44, 1909, 191).
139 Goethe *Dichtung und Wahrheit* II, ch. xi.
140 Goethe *Gespräche mit Eckermann*, 1 February 1827.
141 Goethe to Boisserée, 25 February 1832 (Weimar edn IV Abt., vol. 49, 1909, 250)
142 Carus 1948 [**1016**], 18–19, 27–8, 38–9.
143 Shirley 1949 [**1136**], espec. 87, 171–2.
144 Reynolds 1984 [**1117**], no. 36.14; cf. Leslie 1951 [**1078**], 304. Constable's drawing, which was taken from an uncoloured engraving, and is generally in sepia, gives the bow in pink, yellow and grey-blue from the top.
145 Bonacina 1937 [**1004**], 485–7.
146 Reynolds 1961 [**1116**], no. 117.
147 Beckett IV, 1966 [**996**], 427.
148 Shirley 1949 [**1136**], 171–2; Boulton 1984 [**1008**], 29–44. For a summary, Parris and Fleming-Williams 1991 [**1103**], no. 210.
149 Syndow 1921 [**1145**], 247.
150 Schinkel to Grass, 1804, in Baudissen 1924 [**994**], 17.
151 Schinkel III, 1863 [**1131**], 158.
152 Council of Europe 1959 [**1020**], n. to no. 235.
153 Reynolds 1984 [**1117**], 29.13 29.42, 29.43, 31.2–5.
154 E.g. Reynolds 1961 [**1116**], no. 183a; 1984 [**1117**], 27.11; Parris and Fleming-Willliams 1991 [**1103**], nos 206–9,
155 E.g. London, Clore Gallery for the Turner Bequest, TB, CI, 40; CXLI, 17a–18; CLX, 73a–74.
156 Bonacina 1937 [**1004**], the impossibility of some of Constable's rainbow effects has been pointed out by Schweizer 1982 [**1133**], 427.
157 Constable to Lucas, 19 January 1837, Beckett IV, 1966 [**996**], 433.
158 Constable to Lucas, 6 September 1835, ibid., 421.
159 Field 1845 [**1035**], 198. He had been using the Chromascope since at least 1819. For his relationship with Constable, Gage 1989 [**1045**], 48–52.
160 Shirley 1930 [**1135**], no. 39, 202.
161 Reynolds 1984 [**1117**], 36.3, 36.4, 36.6. The topography is based on a pencil sketch of 1820 which has no bow (20.17).
162 Ibid., 33.49–52. For Constable's interest in scientific meteorology, Thornes 1979 [**1148**], 697–704.
163 Millais 1899 [**1090**], I, 240. Glover's watercolour is inscribed 'painted from nature while the effect lasted'.
164 Shirley 1949 [**1136**], 192.
165 The bow has been studied from a meteorological point of view by Bonacina 1938 [**1005**], who points out the incorrectness of the lighting outside and inside the arcs (605), and by Seibold 1990 [**1134**], 80–1, who is more sympathetic. Turner's watercolour sketch (London, Clore Gallery, TB, XXV, 84) has been studied by Ziff 1982 [**1158**], 2–4 in the context of Turner's caption.
166 London, Clore Gallery, TB, CLXVI, 52a.
167 George Jones in Gage 1980a [**1042**], 8. For the painting, *Daniel Maclise*, 1972, London, Arts Council, exh. cat., no. 98.
168 Butlin and Joll 1984 [**1012**], no. 428. The picture was still bright enough in 1898 for the inaccuracy of the colour-sequence in the secondary arc to be noticed.
169 Thomas Campbell, 'To the Rainbow' (1st version 1819) in *Poetical Works* 1837, 102–3. Turner's watercolours for this book are now in Edinburgh, National Gallery of Scotland.
170 For the painting, Butlin and Joll 1984 [**1012**], no. 376; for the subject, Gage 1987 [**1044**], 224–5.
171 For the subject, Gage 1969 [**217**], 186–7.
172 Butlin and Joll 1984 [**1012**], no. 430. The painting was destroyed earlier this century and is known only in a very poor black-and-white photograph. The rainbow (not mentioned by Butlin and Joll) was noticed by Bell 1901 [**998**], no. 266.
173 See Kandinsky's *Murnau with Rainbow* (1909) in Munich (Roethel and Benjamin 1982 [**1120**], no. 310) and *Section of Composition IV* (1910/11) in London (ibid., no. 367). Marc's drawing *Landscape with Animals and Rainbow* in Vienna was used for a painting behind glass of 1911, where, however, the colours are arranged differently (L.-G. Buchheim *Der Blaue Reiter*, 1959, 53, 143). See also Marc's drawing *Blue Horses with Rainbow*, pl. 86. Robert Delaunay, who was closely associated with the Blaue Reiter, painted a number of subjects with rainbows before the First World War (*La Flèche de Nôtre Dame* 1909/14, col. pl. in Francastel 1957 [**1038**], 145; see also nos 126, 127, 147) and a bizarre 11-colour bow in 1925 (ibid., 752, col. pl. in *Robert et Sonia Delaunay*, 1985, Paris, Musée de l'Art Moderne de la Ville de Paris, exh. cat., 98). The rarity of the rainbow in the work of the Impressionists and Post-Impressionists is striking. I have found it only in an early Monet, *Jetty at Le Havre* (1868, in J. Rewald *The History of Impressionism*, 4th edn, 1973, 155) and in Camille Pissarro's *The Plain of Epluches (Rainbow)* (1877, in C. S. Moffett *The New Painting: Impressionism 1874–1886*, 1986, 232). Among Post-Impressionists I have found it only in a Seurat study for *Baignade* (1884, Berggruen Bequest to National Gallery, London; see P. Smith 1990 [**1139**], 384 on its idealism) and in Signac's *Entrance to the Port of Honfleur* (1899, Indianapolis Museum of Art). Perhaps the problem was that the bow was still being used symbolically in late 19th-century French painting, e.g. in J.-F. Millet's *Spring* (1873, Paris, Louvre).
174 Klee made much of the bow as a 'linear representation of colours' (Klee 1964 [**1074**], 467–9).

7 *Disegno* versus *Colore*

1 Ugo Panziera *Della mentale azione*, cit. Assunto 1961 [**1165**], 223. See also Abelard 1927 [**1159**], 316–17; Vincent of Beauvais 1624 [**823**], XI, ch. xix.
2 Baxandall 1986 [**849**], 62. A later humanist, Antonio de Ferrariis, associated what he considered to be an irrelevant taste for decorated books with an equally irrelevant florid style of writing (*Il Galateo*, *c.* 1500, in Garin 1982 [**1224**], 110f).
3 For St Donatus of Besançon's rejection of colour in images, Assunto 1963 [**1166**], 74. For grisaille in Lent, Smith 1957/9 [**1303**], 43–54; Philippot 1966 [**1279**], 225–42. For the *Parament de Narbonne*, *Fastes* 1981/2 [**687**], no. 324; see also the mitre no. 324 bis. The somewhat earlier grisaille illuminations to the *Hours of Jeanne d'Evreux* (ibid., no. 239) have coloured grounds and are more closely related to enamelled silver than to drawing. Giotto's even earlier grisaille frescoes in the Scrovegni Chapel, Padua, imitate monochrome sculpture.
4 Cohen and Gordon 1949 [**1205**], 99ff; Bornstein 1975 [**1184**], 416; Ratlif 1976 [**1286**], 321; Mollon 1989 [**1271**], 31–2.
5 See, e.g., Andrea Vicentino's *modello* for the painting in the Sala del Maggior Consiglio, Doge's Palace (*c.* 1577), now in Minneapolis Institute of Arts, *Gray is the Color* 1973/4 [**1233**], no. 19. The important 16th-century taste for monochrome oil sketches, espec. in Venice, has been studied by Bauer 1978 [**1171**], 45–59.
6 Mazzei 1880 [**1265**], II, 404.
7 See the brilliant characterization of the colour of the Scrovegni Chapel as subordinate to design in Hills 1987 [**727**], 52–4. Technical examination has shown that they are based on a chiaroscuro underpainting in black or brown (L. Tintori, 'Tempera colors in mural painting of the Italian Renaissance' in Hall 1987 [**1237**], 69).
8 Cennini 1933 [**1201**], 46; 1971 [**184**], lxvii, 78. There are no certain attributions to Cennini as a painter (Boscovits 1973 [**1187**], 201–22). Vasari described Taddeo Gaddi's murals in the Baroncelli Chapel as particularly 'fresh' (Ladis 1982 [**1250**], 33).

For the colour of Cennini's master, Cole 1977, [**1206**], 41.
9 Cennini 1971 [**184**], xxvii–xxxiv, espec. xxxi. Gaddi's *Presentation in the Temple* (pl. 96) is discussed by Ames-Lewis 1981 [**1164**].
10 Both versions are now available together in Alberti 1960–73 [**1161**], III (1973). For their relationship, Simonelli 1972 [**1301**], 75–102, whose argument that the Italian precedes the Latin has not been accepted by Grayson (Alberti ibid., 305, n. 2) or by C. Parkhurst, 'Leon Battista Alberti's place in the history of colour theories' in Hall 1987 [**1237**], 185, n. 1. My quotations are lightly emended from Alberti 1972 [**154**].
11 Alberti ibid., 88–91.
12 See Ch. 9 below.
13 Gavel 1979 [**219**], 49–51. His argument has been much extended to *cenericcio* by Parkhurst in Hall 1987 [**1237**], 187–8, n. 8.
14 Alberti 1960–73 [**1161**], III (1973), 311 (my emphasis). The notion of earth as the *fex elementorum*, the dregs of all the other elements, had been discussed by Bacon in his *Liber de Sensu et Sensato* (1937 [**157**], 30).
15 Müntz and Frothingham 1883 [**526**], 65.
16 Maltese 1976 [**1254**], 245 is thus close to the truth when he interprets *cenericcio* as 'grey-content', although he is using the 20th-century Ostwaldian concept, which does not quite express Alberti's meaning.
17 Alberti 1966 [**153**], 503–5.
18 Ibid., 509. Alberti's patron Giovanni Ruccellai, whose Florentine palace he designed, also showed a notable taste for ancient mosaics, although he is not known to have patronized the medium himself. On his view of the mosaics at Sta Costanza, Rome, Ruccellai 1960 [**1293**], 74. For Doni, Barocchi 1971–7 [**161**], I (1973), 587–9.
19 P. W. Lehmann, 'The sources and meaning of Mantegna's *Parnassus*' in Lehmann 1973 [**919**], 90. Some personal contacts between Alberti and Mantegna have been proposed by Srutkova-Odell 1978 [**1305**], 101ff, who applies this account of draperies to the London *Agony in the Garden*.
20 On variety, Zubov 1958 [**1329**], 260ff. D. Summers, 'The stylistics of color' in Hall 1987 [**1237**], 207 has adduced Alhazen I, 3, 120 and Witelo 1572 [**1323**], IV, 48 as pointing to the pairing of pink and green in medieval theories of beauty, although neither text speaks of juxtaposition. The modern scholar who has argued most strongly for Alberti's medieval attitude to colour, S. Y. Edgerton, referred this pairing to the draperies of Christ in the Brancacci Chapel murals by Masaccio, the only painter to be referred to in the *Della Pittura* (Italian version only): S. Y. Edgerton 1969 [**204**], 110, n. 1; but cleaning has revealed this pair to be pink and blue (Berti and Foggi 1989 [**1178**], 98–9). Sicily Herald, who has a ch. on the beauty of colours in juxtaposition, disliked red and green together, although he said they often appeared in liveries; but he found various combinations with white 'very beautiful' and thought that in painting green 'resjouyst' the other colours (Sicily Herald 1860 [**954**], 113f, 116). For e.gs from Romances, Michel 1852–4 [**1268**], I, 190ff.
21 Antonio da Pisa 1976 [**620**], Antonio also used Alberti's term 'onore' to refer to the effect of green.
22 Alberti 1960–73 [**1161**], I, 202.
23 The best edn is now Bergdolt 1988 [**1177**], which traces the use of earlier sources in great detail.
24 Ibid., 4, derived from Witelo 1572 [**1323**], II, definition I, 61.
25 I have given e.gs in Gage 1972 [**1222**], 364–5; see also Hapsburg 1965 [**1238**].
26 Hills 1987 [**727**], 67.
27 This is the term used in one of Ghiberti's most frequently cited sources, John Pecham (1970 [**785**], 86).
28 Bergdolt 1988 [**1177**], 20 The immediate source is Alhazen I, 4, 20 (1989 [**364**], 54), who gives the colours red, lapis lazuli, wine-coloured, purple. Ghiberti's blue nuances seem to come from dyeing (Rebora 1970 [**1287**], 8). For a similar observation of the change of colour in darkness by a Venetian comtemporary of Ghiberti's, Giovanni da Fontana (*c.* 1395–1455), Canova 1972 [**1199**], 23.
29 Gage 1972 [**1222**], 364–5.
30 Rosińska 1986 [**1291**], 127, n. 40. Sandivogius argued that vision cannot tell us what a colour is, only 'discussion and science' can do that; he gave the example of seeing colours in a dark place, where they seem black, not the green or red they really are. For the crucial importance of Ghiberti's chief source, Alhazen, for 14th-century optical developments in Italy, Vescovini 1965 [**1319**], espec. 18. On 33f Vescovini shows how Ghiberti expanded the concrete references to colour in his version of a passage from Alhazen. See also Vescovini 1980 [**1320**], 370, 373.
31 See the discussion in Hills 1987 [**727**], 81–3 and col. pls XIII and XV. For scotopic and photopic (cone) vision, Barlow and Mollon 1982 [**1169**], 103–4. This feature of the mechanism of vision was not identified until the 19th century.
32 The development was noticed by Weale 1974 [**1321**], 27.
33 For Ghiberti and Angelico's collaboration on the *Linaiuoli Tabernacle* (1433), Middeldorf 1955 [**1269**], 179–94.
34 Baxandall 1988 [**1173**], 81.
35 Equicola 1525 [**1213**], 183.
36 F. P. Morato *Del Significato de Colori*, Venice, 1535, in Barocchi 1971–7 [**161**], II (1973), 2177; Dolce 1565 [**197**], 36r.
37 Baxandall 1988 [**1173**], 11. See the col. pls in Wyld and Plesters 1977 [**1327**], 16. In his 1st edn (1972, 10–11) Baxandall mistakenly used the panel reproduced here.
38 Wyld and Plesters ibid., 11.
39 Thomas of Celano 1904 [**1309**], 12; Wyld and Plesters ibid., 11 for *kermes*.
40 Gargiolli 1868 [**1223**], 30; Herald 1981 [**1242**], 151.
41 Guasti 1877 [**1235**], 5f.
42 Gargiolli 1868 [**1223**], 53f, 78f.
43 Mazzei 1880 [**1265**], II, 385f, 412f; Merrifield 1849 [**271**], II, 400 (§§56–7).
44 For the role of the guilds in contracts, Glasser 1977 [**1228**], 29.
45 For Florence (1316), Fiorilli 1920 [**1218**], 48; for Siena (1356) and Perugia (1366), Manzoni 1904 [**1259**], 32f, 87f. The Siena regulations were renewed in 1405.
46 Pope-Hennessy 1939 [**1285**], 156; Neri di Bicci 1956 [**1272**], 225 (1464); Rosenauer 1965 [**1290**], 85.
47 Kristeller 1901 [**1249**], 487, document 53. An ambiguity in the language makes it unclear whether the pigments mentioned (not listed in the surviving version) were ordered for or by Mantegna. For an analysis of the materials used by Mantegna and other artists in Isabella d'Este's Studiolo at Mantua, Delbourgo et al. 1975 [**1211**], 21–8.
48 Langton Douglas 1902 [**1251**], 163, document II. The *Tabernacle* is illustrated in Baxandall 1988 [**1173**], 9.
49 For the S. Agostino contract, with full Eng. trans., Meiss 1941 [**1267**], 67–8. For Lippi's letter about his altarpiece, including St Michael, Baxandall ibid., 3–4.
50 Bresc-Bautier 1979 [**1192**], 216.
51 Shearman 1965 [**1299**], II, 391, document 30; White 1979 [**1322**], 35. For the Lorenzetti Madonna in colour, Hills 1987 [**727**], pl. XXII.
52 Conrad-Martius 1929 [**1207**], 362; the reference is to Goethe 1957 [**225**], §779; Brückner 1982 [**863**], 23.
53 E.g. D. Dini and G. Bonsanti, 'Fra Angelico e gli Affreschi del Convento di San Marco (*c.* 1441–50)' in Borsook and Superbi Gioffredi 1986 [**1186**], 17 (Virgin in light red); J. Ruda, 'Color and representation of space in paintings by Fra Filippo Lippi' in Hall 1987 [**1237**], 42 (Virgin in lavender or green); M. Barasch, 'Renaissance color conventions: liturgy, humanism, workshops' in Hall ibid, 141 (El Greco's *Espolio* at Toledo, Virgin in dark violet).
54 Coulton 1953 [**872**], 264, 550ff (mostly Fr. e.gs).
55 Hennecke and Schneemelcher 1959–64 [**1241**], I, (1959), 284f.
56 For the early Jewish tradition, Scholem 1974 [**565**], 10f.
57 Hugh of St. Victor *Sermon* 46 in *Patrologia Latina* 1844–55 [**116**], CLXXVII, col. 1025.
58 Cameron 1981 [**1198**], 51–3. Purple-clad Virgins in the Western tradition include a crucifix of 1257 by Simone and Machilone of Spoleto (Rome, Museo Nazionale di Palazzo Barberini) and another attributed to the Master of the Bigallo (same collection); and Fra Angelico's fresco from Fiesole (Paris, Louvre no. 1294). These types of mourning Virgin can be expected to be in violet but there is also a *Madonna and Child* by Gentile da Fabriano (Washington, National Gallery) where the Madonna is in purple and the Child in blue. For the imperial connotations of the purple-clad Virgin in the 6th and 7th centuries, Nilgen 1981 [**1274**], espec. 20.
59 Nixdorff and Müller 1983 [**1275**], 129.
60 An early modern student of Van Eyck's *Lucca Madonna* noticed the many reds, including a deep purple, which go to make up its extraordinary richness (von Bodenhausen 1905 [**1180**], 63).
61 In *De Pictura* II, 48 Alberti uses the Latin terms *purpureus* and *rubeus* to describe the dress of the nymphs but in the Italian version both terms are rendered by *rosato* (Alberti 1960–73 [**1161**], III (1973), 86).
62 Newton 1988 [**1273**], 84; also 18, 26 for the reds of mourning. But even Sanudo might on occasion confuse *cremesino* with *scarlatto* (86).
63 R. Sachtleben, 'Mit den Farbstoffen durch die Jahrhunderte' in Kramer and Matschoss 1963 [**1248**], 254.
64 Some e.gs of the uniform treatment of hat and robe in vermilion are in the frescoes by Ugolino in Orvieto Cathedral, an illustration of the *Concistoro Papale* in Vatican MS Vat. Lat. 1389 3v (Conti 1981 [**659**], col. pl. xxviii); St Jerome in Gentile da Fabriano's *Valle Romita Altarpiece* (*c.* 1410/12, Christiansen 1982 [**1204**], col. pl. A); Antonio da Fabriano *St Jerome* (1451, Baltimore, Walters Art Gallery). For discrimination, see the *Annunciation and Saints* (*c.* 1360) attributed to Barna of Siena in Berlin (Dahlem); the miniature by Lorenzo da Voltolina of the teaching of Henricus de Allemania (*c.* 1380, same collection). Bartolommeo di Tommaso's *Funeral and Canonization of St Francis* (Baltimore, Walters Art Gallery) and Sassetta's *Recognition of the Fransiscan Order* (London, National Gallery) use both conventions in the interests, apparently, of spatial articulation; the miniature of the Papal Consistory by the 'Maestro di 1328' (New York, Pierpont Morgan Library) includes cardinals robed in grey, pale blue and pale pink, but all hatted in vermilion.
65 For Venice as a centre of the pigment trade, L. Lazzarini, 'The use of colour by Venetian painters, 1480–1580' in Hall 1987 [**1237**], 117–19.
66 Borsook 1971 [**1185**], 803; Chambers 1970 [**1202**], 26–7. For Gentile da Fabriano's purchases of colours from an apothecary (*spezier*), Armanino da Nola in Venice, while he was working in Brescia in 1414, Christiansen 1982 [**1204**], 150ff. For Domenico Veneziano's sending from Florence to Venice for blue (from a branch of the Medici Bank) in 1439, Wohl 1980 [**1324**], 341; for Raphael's sending to Venice for pigments in 1518, Golzio 1971 [**1230**], 75f; for the Dossi brothers sending from Ferrara, Gibbons 1968 [**1227**], documents 9, 29, 176. For Parmigianino visiting Venice to buy pigments in 1530, A. E. Popham, *Burlington Magazine*, XCI, 1949, 176. For Lotto's dealings with a Flemish colour-dealer in Venice, Lotto 1969 [**1253**], 170–1, 211–12, 221, 316. When Michael Coxie in the Netherlands wanted 'azure' for his copy of Van Eyck's *Ghent Altarpiece*, he could get it only in Venice (van Mander 1916 [**265**], 200v), perhaps from Lotto's supplier.
67 Guareschi 1907 [**1234**], 343ff.
68 Uccelli 1865 [**1313**], and espec. Bensi 1980 [**1176**], 33–47. After the destruction of the convent in the 1529 seige of Florence, their recipes came into the public arena in Alessio Piemontese 1975 and 1977 [**1162**], folio 84v ff and espec. folio 55v ff respectively.
69 For vermilion, Thompson 1933 [**1310**], 62ff; Gettens et al. 1972 [**1226**], 45ff.
70 Milanesi 1872 [**1270**]. Another document of July 1481 mentions that Leonardo bought an ounce of blue and an ounce of yellow (*giallolino*) from them.
71 Pino 1954 [**12821**], 47–8.
72 Eastlake 1847–69 [**202**], I, 9–10, 327–8.
73 Urso von Salerno 1976 [**592**], 115f; *Sic et pictores colores suos cum oleo et clara ovi et lacte ficus conficiunt, ut accidentali viscositate parietibus vel lignis inseparabiliter hereant illiniti* ('Thus painters make up their colours with oil and egg-white and fig-milk, so that the qualities of the paint-strokes will, by means of this stickiness, adhere inseparably to the walls or the wood panels'). The technique of mixing egg with the juice of fig-shoots was still used for wall-painting in Cennini's time (1933 [**1201**], lxxii, xc) and, as Eastlake pointed out, the mixture of egg-yolk and fig-juice is already mentioned by Pliny in the context of medicine (XXIII, lxiii, 119). Since Urso was a doctor, it is tempting to imagine that he or one of his

colleagues introduced the idea to painters. No Salernitan panel paintings earlier than the 2nd half of the 13th century appear to have survived (Garrison 1949 **[1225]**, 229, 489A; Bologna 1955 **[1181]**, 3, 4) and their technique has not been analysed. The earliest known oil-paintings on panel, from late 13th-century Scandinavia, have been studied by L. E. and U. Plahter, 'The technique of a group of Norwegian Gothic oil paintings' in Bromelle and Smith 1976 **[1194]**, 36–42.

74 Johnson and Packard 1971 **[1246]**, 145ff; Bowron 1974 **[1188]**, 380ff. For a sensitive discussion of mixed media from the 14th to the 16th centuries, del Serra 1985 **[1297]**, 4–16.

75 J. A. van de Graaf, 'Development of oil paint and the use of metal plates as a support' in Bromelle and Smith 1976 **[1194]**, 45–8.

76 Taubert 1978 **[1308]**, 19 mentions the standard reference to drying oils in medieval recipes for painting statues. For glazes over silver in the Herlin Altar (1466), Bachmann et al. 1970 **[1167]**, 381ff. For the painting of statues by Robert Campin and Rogier van der Weyden, Rolland 1932 **[1289]**, 335–45. An unusually detailed contract of 1516 for a sculpted retable at Tournai mentions that in the *Crucifixion* and the *Christ bearing the Cross* the ground should be of fine matt gold 'et le reste glacié à olle' (de la Grange and Cloquet 1888 **[1232]**, 233–5). Sassetta's glazing over silver in the St Francis altar (see p. 129 above) used an egg-tempera, not an oil medium.

77 Wolfthal 1989 **[1325]**, espec. 27, 32 for technique. Bouts's *Entombment* in this technique has been contrasted with his oil *Virgin and Child* (both London, National Gallery) by Bomford et al. 1986 **[1182]**, 39–57.

78 Coremans 1950 **[1209]**, 114, n. 3. Vasari's story that Van Eyck's paintings could be smelled has suggested his use of volatile thinners to Ziloty 1947 **[1328]**, 142. For a survey of more recent work on Netherlandish oil technique, Périer-d'Ieteren 1985 **[1278]**, 15ff. The importance of the many lost Netherlandish mural paintings of the late 14th and early 15th centuries, as well as the link with painted statuary, has been stressed by Hagopian van Buren 1986 **[1236]**, 101–3, 112.

79 Ames-Lewis 1979 **[1163]**, 255–73; Wright 1980 **[1326]**, espec. 42–6; Ruda 1984 **[1294]**, 210–36 takes a far more cautious view of the Italian debt to northern Europe but deals with iconography rather than technique.

80 Fortuna 1957 **[1221]**, 43.

81 Filarete 1972 **[1216]**, II, 667f. Bugatti was in Brussels with his master 1460–3 and Filarete is thought to have completed his treatise in 1464.

82 Bromelle 1959/60 **[1193]**, 94 (orange-red priming); Massing and Christie 1988 **[1262]**, 35–6. Sjöblom 1928 **[1302]**, 47f and 84ff cites Filarete's account and argues that Van Eyck and other Netherlandish masters also used dark grounds but this cannot now be sustained.

83 Degenhart and Schmitt IV, 1968 **[1210]**, no. 302 and pl. 278.

84 Vasari 1960 **[1316]**, 213.

85 Dürer to Jacob Heller, 1508/9 in Uhde-Bernays 1960 **[1314]**, 9–11.

86 See the ch. headings on colour for his projected treatise (*c.* 1508) in Dürer 1956–69 **[201]**, II, 94f; for the section on drapery, see ch. 2, n. 66 above.

87 Baxandall 1980 **[1172]**, 42–8.

88 See the rueful passage (*Cod. Atlant.* 119v) in which Leonardo decribed himself as the late-comer at the fair, picking up only those goods which have been rejected by others before him (cit. Garin 1965 **[696]**, 58).

89 *Cod. Atlant.* 207va, trans, Kemp 1981 **[1247]**, 129. For Pecham's original and Leonardo's translation, Solmi 1976 **[1140]**, 226–7.

90 Ristoro d'Arezzo (1282), II, 8, 16, 1976 **[1288]** 220ff.

91 Richter 1970 **[1118]**, I, 237–8, §300. Ristoro was summarizing the view of the Arab writer Al-Kindi, where Leonardo started from the far more sophisticated analysis of Alhazen (Spies 1937 **[1304]**, 17–19).

92 Both themes have been examined in some detail by Veltman 1986 **[1317]**; for mountains, 278ff; for smoke, 317.

93 Jaffé and Groen 1987 **[1245]**, 168f.

94 Maltese 1983 **[1256]**, 218.

95 Veltman 1986 **[1317]**, and Farago 1991 **[1215]**, have made valiant attempts to bring order to the notes on several aspects of aerial perspective and chiaroscuro.

96 Steinberg 1977 **[1306]**, 85, where there is also a discussion of the quotation from the *De Divinis Nominibus* on a 1509 painting by Fra Bartolommeo. See also *Firenze e La Toscana* ... 1980 **[1219]**, nos 79 (in col.), 84 (*Madonna della Misericordia*). It is possible that the astonishing dark God the Father of Titian's *Assumption* (1516/18) has a Dionysian significance, although Goffin 1986 **[1229]**, 96f thinks he is the source of light in the painting. Elsewhere (94, 103) she notes appropriately that he is in a cloud, as in Exodus 16:10. At the end of the century Annibale Carracci in Venice complained that the dazzling light from the 2 large choir windows made the painting exceptionally hard to see (Fanti 1979 **[1214]**, 160). For a substantial discussion of the theological connotations of cloud painting in the High Renaissance, Shearman 1987 **[1300]**, I, 657–68. Shearman **[661]** cites Gregory the Great's commentary on Ezechiel, where clouds with the brilliance of electrum – an alloy of gold and silver – are characterized: a passage in which Gregory paraphrases Pseudo-Dionysius (*Celestial Hierarchy* 336 A–C; 1987 **[545]**, 188).

97 Kemp 1981 **[1247]**, 97; Richter 1970 **[1118]**, I, §119. See also the discussion by Barasch 1978 **[1168]**, 53–4.

98 Richter ibid., §121. For Leonardo's categories of shadow, Barasch ibid., 53 and n. 38.

99 Ibid., 177f.

100 Richter ibid., I, §548. For another discussion of Leonardo's Aristotelian concept of infinity in connection with *sfumato*, Zubov 1968 **[1331]**, 67.

101 Meder 1923 **[1266]**, 116, 122ff, 136. For a red chalk drawing on red-toned paper for *Judas* in col., Ames-Lewis 1981 **[1164]**, 49, pl. VII.

102 For the materials, Harding et al. 1989 **[1239]**, 22–4.

103 Brachert 1970 **[1189]**, 84ff ; 1974 **[1190]**, 177ff; 1977 **[1191]**, 9ff.

104 For drawings Meder 1923 **[1266]**, 92; for paintings Brachert 1977 **[1191]**, 12; Hours 1954 **[1243]**, 17–18; 1962 **[1266]**, 124ff. For the unusual black underpainting of Christ's red sleeve in the *Last Supper*, Matteini and Moles 1979 **[1263]**, 130ff.

105 *Treatise* §144: Leonardo 1956 **[1076]**, 73. For grounding in green, Richter 1970 **[1118]**, I, §628.

106 Verbraeken 1979 **[1318]**, 91ff. *Treatise* §§6, 43 (*questo è il chiaroscuro, che i pittori dimandono lume et ombra*). For the suggestion that these passages are due to the editors, Folena 1951 **[1220]**, 61.

107 Shearman 1962 **[1298]**, 30, 44, n. 44.

108 Leonardo 1956 **[1076]**, §§196, 215, 226, 241.

109 Ibid., §190. However, in §§187 and 188 Leonardo had said that *all* colours look best in their illuminated parts.

110 Veltman 1986 **[1317]**, 329f.

111 Leonardo 1956 **[1076]**, §108; cf. §§110, 434.

112 For yellow and blue as harmonious, ibid., §182. For the drapery studies, Cadogan 1983 **[1197]**, 27–62.

113 Vasari 1903 **[1315]**, 34–5. Vasari had not seen the picture himself: Pedretti 1957 **[1276]**, 133. For the lighting Filipczak 1977 **[1217]**, 518ff. The Ambrosiana *St John* has been published by Bora 1987 **[1183]**, col. fig. 13.

114 Leonardo 1956 **[1076]**, §872; cf. §§192 and 765 on lighting the painted landscape in the same way as the natural landscape. Examples of this working from nature are the annotated drawings of mountains at Windsor (nos 12.412 and 414), on which see Gould 1947 **[1231]**, 239ff. These are, however, in red chalk on toned paper, heightened with white.

115 Richter 1970 **[1118]**, I, §566. Leonardo is elaborating on an idea of Alhazen's (I, 3, 116: 1989 **[364]**, 44).

116 Pedretti 1968 **[1277]**, 28, 50. For a general discussion with further references, Zubov 1968 **[1331]**, 141.

117 Agostini 1954 **[1160]**, 20.

118 Richter 1970 **[1118]**, I, §520. for Leonardo's knowledge of Alberti's writings, Zubov 1960 **[1330]**, 1–14.

119 For mixtures see espec. Richter ibid., §619. For oils, Marazza 1954 **[1260]**, 53. For the technique of the oil murals, Travers Newton 1983 **[1312]**, 71–88.

120 Milanesi 1872 **[1270]**, 229. The only technical analysis so far available is Sanpaolesi 1954 **[1296]**, 40ff. For the glazes, Maltese 1982 **[1255]**, 172f.

121 Vasari 1962–6 **[341]**, III, (1963), 505f.

122 Vasari 1878–85 **[340]**, VI, 203 speaks of such works 'solamente disegnata ed aombrata con l'acquarello in su gesso' which Fra Bartolommeo left to be finished by Bugiardini. For the altarpiece, *Firenze e La Toscana* ... 1980 **[1219]**, no. 80. Shearman 1965 **[1299]**, I, 136 considers the notion of broken colours to have been transmitted to Andrea del Sarto from Venice via Fra Bartolommeo, who was there in 1509.

123 Poggi et al. I, 1965 **[1284]**, 66–7. For the Sistine ceiling Mancinelli 1983 **[1257]**, 362–7; Chastel et al. 1986 **[1203]**, espec. 223 on the palette and 244 on technique. For the Quattrocento tonality, G. Colalucci, 'Le lunette di Michelangelo nella Capella Sistina (1508–12)' in Borsook and Superbi Gioffredi 1986 **[1186]**, 78; Mancinelli 1988 **[1258]**, 12. For dissenting voices, Conti 1986 **[1208]**; Beck 1988 **[1174]**, 502–3 . For the *Doni Tondo*, *Il Tondo Doni* ... 1985 **[1311]**; Buzzegoli 1987 **[1196]**, 405–8.

124 For Sarto, Shearman 1965 **[1299]**, ch. VIII: 'Colour'; for Pontormo and Rosso, Maurer 1982 **[1264]**, 109ff; Caron 1988 **[1200]**, 355–78; Rubin 1991 **[1292]**, 175–91. For Bronzino, see espec. his sharply coloured *Holy Family* (*c.* 1525, Washington, National Gallery) with Mary in red, green and dark blue and Joseph in orange and violet.

125 Roskill 1968 **[308]**, 208.

126 Ibid., 154–5; see also Pino 1954 **[1282]**, 62.

127 Aretino 1957–60 **[155]**, I, 45f, 57. By strawberries and snails Aretino meant the borders of Fr. and Flemish Books of Hours of the late 15th century, e.g. Harthan 1977 **[1240]**, 118–19, 123.

128 Aretino ibid., II, 235.

129 Pino 1954 **[1282]**, 69.

130 Ibid., 46–7. See also the account of painting a fire (a task Pino regarded as particularly difficult) by the late 16th-century Veronese artist Cristofero Sorte, who gave the precise mixtures he used for various parts of the subject (Barocchi 1960–62 **[1170]**, I, 291–2).

131 L. Lazzarini, 'The use of color by Venetian painters, 1480–1580: materials and technique' in Hall 1987 **[1237]**, espec. 120ff. See also the remarks on spontaneous mixing in Piccolpasso 1934 **[1280]**, 63–4.

132 For the Venetian invention of papers coloured in the pulp, Meder 1923 **[1266]**, 112–13, and Pino 1954 **[1282]**, 43 on the uses of these *carte tinte* for achieving unity. For 'Giorgione', Ruhemann 1955 **[1295]**, 281; for Sebastiano del Piombo in fresco, Tantillo 1972 **[1307]**, 33–43; for Tintoretto, Plesters 1980 **[1283]**, 36, 39, 41.

133 Bellori 1976 **[1175]**, 206. Barocci's procedure is summarized by Emiliani 1975 **[1212]**, liv-v. The chiaroscuro study for the *Absolution of St Francis* is in St Petersburg, Hermitage, and the colour 'cartoon' in Urbino, Galleria Nazionale delle Marche (Emiliani ibid., no. 74). For the importance of the oil studies from nature, Pillsbury 1978 **[1281]**, 170–3. M. A. Lavin (*Art Bulletin*, XLVI, 1964, 252–3) has drawn attention to the systematic element in Barocci's handling of colour and suggested that he may have had access to the sections on light and shadow in the earliest MS of Leonardo's *Treatise*, in the Ducal Library at Urbino until 1626.

134 Barocci's methodical laying-out of his canvas is seen in the late unfinished *Lamentation* (Emiliani 1975 **[1212]**, no. 280). For the pastel-like painting technique, Lavin 1956 **[1252]**, 435–9; C. Dempsey, 'Federico Barocci and the discovery of pastel' in Hall 1987 **[1237]**, 62–4.

135 The sculptor Baccio Bandinelli, a pupil of Albertinelli, seems to have thought that Andrea del Sarto had a very particular 'modo di colorire' and tried in vain to learn the secret of it; he was not successful and we know nothing of it (Vasari 1962–6 **[341]**, IV (1963), 302.

136 F. Pacheco 1649 in Fernandez Avenas 1982 **[887]**, 166. See also El Greco's notes on the difficulties of colour in his copy of the Barbaro edition of Vitruvius (Marìas and Bustamente 1981 **[1261]**, 78ff).

137 Bauer 1978 **[1171]**, 52. There are many Bassetti monochrome sketches in the English Royal Collection (Blunt and Croft-Murray 1957 **[1179]**, nos 1–24; see also Brugnoli 1974 **[1195]**, 311ff).

8 The Peacock's Tail

1 George Ripley *Twelve Gates* in E. Ashmole (ed.), *Theatrum Chemicum Britannicum*, 1652, I, i, 188, cit. Read 1939 **[1390]**, 147. On Ripley, Holmyard 1957 **[1360]**, 182–5.

2 The best edn of the Stockholm and Leyden Papyri, now dated early 4th century, is Halleux I, 1981 [**1357**]. Halleux is less categorical about the function of the texts than Pfister 1935 [**1385**], 7–53, who argued that they were never practical. A far tighter fit between early medieval technology and alchemy has been proposed by A. Wallert, 'Alchemy and medieval art technology' in Martels 1990 [**1373**], 154–61. Wallert is particularly illuminating about a curious recipe for 'Spanish gold' in Theophilus III, xlviii (1961 [**583**], 96–8) which he interprets as based on an alchemical version of the sulphur-mercury theory of metals, and about a recipe for 'artificial azure' in the 15th-century Bolognese manuscript (Merrifield 1849 [**271**], II, 387), whose product must be vermilion, not blue, and is also an alchemical type of sulphur–mercury compound.
3 Sarton 1954 [**1398**], 170ff.
4 Wallert in Martels 1990 [**1373**], 155–6 argues convincingly that even before the transmission of Arabic alchemy to the West, many of its concepts were preserved in texts such as the 8th-century *Compositiones Lucenses* and *Mappae Clavicula*. He cites the recipes for making vermilion from sulphur and mercury, for which see below.
5 Now in St Margaret, Hildesheim; Tschan II, 1951 [**589**], 129–40. I have been unable to trace the *Secretum Secretorum quod sub poena aeternae damnationis relinquo meis successoribus*, cit. J. M. Kratz *Der Dom zu Hildesheim*, 1840, III, 11 and n. 1.
6 Bacon 1859 [**1334**], 39ff. See also his fuller account, *De Expositione Enigmatum Alkimie*, in ibid 1912 [**1335**], 85f, on the application of the doctrine of the elements and humours, and 84, where 'reddening' is decribed as making gold and 'whitening' silver. For an earlier phase in the revaluation of art, see pp. 75–6 above.
7 Thompson 1933 [**1310**], 62–9. The manufacture of vermilion is discussed in the 14th-century *Liber Claritatis Totius Alkimicae Artis*, 1925/7 [**1371**], VII (1926), 265, where artificial vermilion is described as *lapide quem occultaverunt philosophi*. The treatise is attributed to the ? 9th-century Arab writer Jābir ibn Hayyān (Geber), the chief proponent of the sulphur–mercury theory (Read 1939 [**1390**], 17–18).
8 Hopkins 1938 [**1362**], 343.
9 For religious imagery, see below; for heraldry, Obrist 1983 [**1379**], 170ff; for pseudonymity, Pseudo-Aquinas 1977 [**1388**], 22–114; Kibre 1942 [**1368**], 502–5.
10 The chief studies are still Jung 1953 [**1366**], and espec. 1963 [**1367**]. For an overview, Luther 1973 [**1372**], 10–20.
11 For Duchamp, Golding 1973 [**1356**], 85–93; J. H. Moffitt, 'Marcel Duchamp: Alchemist of the Avant-Garde' in Tuchman 1986 [**1407**], 257–71. For Chagall, Compton 1985 [**1344**], no. 22: *Homage to Appollinaire* 1911/12. For Beckmann, G. Schiff, 'Max Beckmann: die Ikonographie der Triptychen' in Buddensieg and Winner 1968 [**1340**], 276.
12 Paul of Taranto *Theorica et Practica*, cit. Newman 1989 [**1377**], 434, 442–4.
13 Eamon 1980 [**1351**], 204–9.
14 Hopkins 1938 [**1362**]; ibid., 1927 [**1361**], 10–14. Since the term for the alchemical still, *kerotakis*, is the same as for the palette in wax painting, Hopkins suggests (11–12) a link with the 4-colour palette attributed to the Greek painters (ch. 2 above).
15 Simeon of Cologne 1918 [**1401**], 65. A 15th-century writer described a sequence after 170 days' cooking of black, red, yellow, green 'peacock-colour', before the final 'water of gold': Forbes 1961 [**1354**], 17–20. For the later use of the colour-sequence, Read 1939 [**1390**], 145–8. One late text even has blue as the final stage of the process: *Tractatus Aureus Hermetis*, cit. Jung 1963 [**1367**], 14. In illuminated MSS blue was often the colour of silver (Obrist 1983 [**1379**], 210f).
16 Crosland 1962 [**1348**], 30–2, 66–73.
17 Cit. Read 1939 [**1390**], 26.
18 Reusner 1588 [**1393**], 48–50.
19 Cit. Maguire 1987 [**496**], 30.
20 Dobbs 1975 [**1350**], 178; for the Latin text with alchemical symbols, ibid. 251. For the image of the tree in traditional alchemy, Szulakowska 1986 [**1404**], 53–77.
21 *Reallexikon zur deutschen Kunstgeschichte*, IV, col. 743f, s.v. 'Ei'.
22 *De Lapide Philosophorum* in Zetzner 1659 [**1410**], IV, 858. For Newton's purchase of this 6-volume compilation, Dobbs 1975 [**1350**], 131ff.
23 For Newton's theory and its immediate antecedents, Sabra 1967 [**1396**], espec. 67, 242. Dobbs (ibid., 224f, 231) has traced Newton's notion that the smallest particles of metal were black (Newton 1730 [**1095**], 259–60)and his belief in the transmutation of light into matter and back (374) to his experience as an alchemist.
24 Tieck 1798 [**1405**], IV, ch. iv.
25 Lightly emended from I. A. Richter 1952 [**1395**], 10–11. The Italian text is in Reti 1952 [**1392**], 722. C. Vasoli, 'Note su Leonardo e l'alchimia' in *Leonardo e l'età della ragione: Atti del Convegno, Milan* 1982 [**1255**], 69–77 suggests that Leonardo's scepticism was shared by some alchemical writers themselves, such as Petrus Bonus of Ferrara (see p. 143 above). The mixture of gold with the blue stone was mentioned by Bartholomeus Anglicus, *De Proprietatibus Rerum*, XIX, viii.
26 Vasari 1878–85 [**340**], VI (1881), 606–9. Vasari tells us that while he was working on his bronze group of *St John between the Levite and the Pharisee* (1509, Florence, Orsanmichele) Rustici could tolerate no company but Leonardo's, who also helped him (604).
27 J. P. Richter 1970 [**1118**], I, 641. The other passage on 'varnish' is §637. Richter's trans. mixes some of the metaphors and gives 'iron' for 'Jupiter'. These terms also occur in a painterly context in the 13th-century Portuguese treatise *Livro de como se fazan as Côres*, I, 1930 [**258**], 71–83; 1928–9, 97–135, which also discusses the terms on 119ff. Pedretti 1977 [**1384**], II, 18–19 dates Leonardo's notes to *c.* 1515 and relates them to his work on mirrors. Boni 1954 [**1337**], 405 suggests that they are concerned with a patina for bronze. It is possible that the note, not in Leonardo's hand, in *Codice Atlantico* 244vb which includes the alchemical term for gold (*sole*) was supplied by a friend such as Rustici (Reti 1952 [**1392**], 664).
28 Vasari 1903 [**1315**], 41.
29 Carbonelli 1925 [**1343**], ix–xi. For Leonardo's knowledge of Hermes Trismegistus, Solmi 1976 [**1140**], 142f.
30 For a detailed description of the tabletop and its scheme of correspondences, Scheckenburger-Broschek 1982[**1400**], 52.
31 Baxandall 1986 [**849**], 106 and for the Latin, 165.
32 *Experimenta de Coloribus* in Merrifield 1849 [**271**], I, 66–9. The large collection of the Le Begue MSS is ibid., 16–321.
33 The classic analysis of Panofsky (1934) in Gilbert 1970 [**701**], 1–20 has now been superseded by Bedaux 1986 [**1336**], 5–28. For excellent fig. details of the painting, Dahnens 1980 [**1349**].
34 For the fruit, Purtle 1982 [**1389**], 125.
35 Bedaux 1986 [**1336**], 19–21 has suggested that this saint, traditionally identified as St Margaret, patroness of childbirth, may be St Martha, patroness of housewives. The suggestion is strengthened by reference to the tradition that St Martha subdued *her* dragon (represented in the carving) with just such a brush, the *aspergillum*, used to sprinkle holy water.
36 Panofsky 1966 [**1382**], I, 203 argued that the beads were crystal and referred to the purity of the wife but they are clearly yellow and were identified as amber by Eastlake 1847–69 [**202**], I, 289f. He mentioned them in connection with the early development of amber varnish. See also Schabaker 1972 [**1399**], 396, n. 54, who points to Bruges as a centre for the manufacture of amber paternosters.
37 Bedaux 1986 [**1336**], 15f gives the greatest attention to the sacramental status of the painting.
38 An early Christian tradition in the Greek world that the pearl was the product of lightning striking into the sea and reaching the oyster, thus creating a union of fire and water, does not seem to have been current in the West until after Van Eyck's time (Ohly 1977 [**1380**], 297ff). Ohly (307) cites a poem by Venantius Fortunatus in which Mary is referred to as crystal, amber (*electrum*), gold, purple (*ostrum*), pearl (*concha alba*) and emerald.
39 *Los versos declaran cómo se engañan* [sic] *el uno al otro* (Allende-Salazar 1925 [**1332**], 191, n. 6). Allende-Salazar's transcription gives the nonsensical *engañan* = deceive, which must be *enganchan* = link (cf. Eng. 'engage'). Dahnens 1980 [**1349**], 197 trans. 'plight their troth'. It is not inconceivable that Arnolfini's shifty look and the tradition of Dutch brothel-scenes in the 17th century led the compiler of the inventory to detect some deceit, just as he read the single burning candle (the token of a legal contract) as indicating a night scene.
40 For the large number of medieval MSS of the *Fasti*, Reynolds 1983 [**1394**], 266ff. Bedaux 1986 [**1336**], 14, without referring to Ovid, suggests that the verses may have referred to the *consensus* of the couple, which Aquinas considered to be the *causa efficiens* of marriage.
41 Petrus Bonus *Pretiosa Margarita Novella*, Ch. IX, cit. Zetzner 1622 [**1410**], 661. There is a new Italian edn by Crisciani 1976, who has published an introduction to Bonus in English (1973) [**1347**], 165–81). See also Holmyard 1957 [**1360**], 138–45.
42 Bonus cit. Zetzner 1622 [**1410**], 709. Another, late 14th-century alchemical text, the *Liber Phoenicis* (1399), attributed to Solomon the notion that the Philosophers' Stone was 'husband and wife' and cited 'Aristotle' on the conjunction of wet and dry, cold and hot, and one 'Mircherio' (?Mercury) on that of fire and water (Carbonelli 1925 [**1343**], 9, 59).
43 Bonus cit. Zetzner ibid., 648–50, 661 and 648.
44 See the fine detail in Dahnens 1980 [**1349**], 200, also 203. Christ's Passion as an analogy of the Great Work was also discussed in an early 15th-century *Buch der Heiligen Dreifaltigkeit*, which adds a number of unorthodox scenes to the standard cycle (Ganzenmüller 1956 [**694**], 244–6).
45 Sicily Herald 1860 [**954**], 43f, 86f.
46 Bedaux 1986 [**1336**], 13.
47 Sicily Herald 1860 [**954**], 47f, 85f. Sicily, who was a Netherlander from Hainault, copied Isidore's definition of purple as light from Jean Corbichon's 1372 Fr. trans. of Bartholomeus Anglicus (M. Salvat, 'Le Traité des couleurs de Barthelemi l'Anglais' in CUERMA 1988, [**873**], 384). For scarlet of Ghent, R. van Uytven, 'Cloth in mediaeval literature of western Europe' in Harte and Ponting 1983 [**899**], 158–9.
48 Sicily Herald 1860 [**954**], 38f, 46f, 56ff, 83f, 87ff.
49 The *Buch der Heiligen Dreifaltigkeit* proposed equating red with fire and green with water (Ganzenmüller 1956 [**694**], 245). For other equivalents, see pp. 32–3 above.
50 Dahnens 1980 [**1349**], 199.
51 See the prohibition of the practice of alchemy for the merchant, who was concerned only with *cose stabili*, in Cotrugli 1602 [**1346**], 83.
52 Vasari 1878 [**340**], III, 190.
53 For the commission, Ettlinger 1965 [**1352**], 25–8. The contract is reprinted on 120–1.
54 Vasari 1878–85 [**340**], III, 187–9.
55 Vasari *Vita di Bernardino Pintoricchio* in Vasari III, 1971 [**1408**], Testo 574f (1550).
56 Steinmann 1901–05 [**1402**], I, 201, 222. The leadership of the group has been debated. Vasari stated that Botticelli was leader but Ettlinger (1965 [**1352**], 30–1) has argued convincingly that Perugino had this role. Mesnil 1938 [**1375**], 79, argued that the unity of style in the series derived from Ghirlandaio. But it remains that Rosselli executed 1 more scene than any of them. Horne 1908 [**1363**], 103 pointed out the use of bright colours and gold by members of the team before the Sistine commission.
57 Ettlinger ibid., 89–90.
58 Ficino *Della Religione cristiana, prima versione in lingua toscana dello stesso Ficino*, Florence 1568, 112, cit. Calvesi 1962 [**1341**], 236–7.
59 Monfasani 1983 [**1376**], 11. The account, by Andreas Trapezuntius, is dated April/May 1482. For the sequence of work, Ettlinger 1965 [**1352**], 27–8.
60 Condivi 1964 [**1345**], 52. In fact Michelangelo was paid double this sum for the work and the figure for expenditure on colours seems very modest.
61 Vasari VII, 1965 [**1408**], 139–41. The term *campi* had been interpreted as 'strokes of paint' by Stumpel 1988 [**1403**], 228 but I do not find his arguments convincing.
62 Conti 1986 [**1208**], 42–5. But cf. Mancinelli 1988 [**1258**], 15 that the medallions were heavily restored in the 18th century. Condivi (1964 [**1345**], 50) is surprisingly ambiguous about the use of gold in these medallions: he says '*si son detti* finti di metalli' (my emphasis). For Michelangelo's use of gold in the *Doni Tondo*, Buzzegoli 1987 [**1196**], 405–8.
63 Roskill 1968 [**308**], 207–9: undated letter from Dolce to Gaspare Ballini.
64 Ottonelli and Berrettini 1973 [**1381**], 58f, [Bottari] 1772 [**1339**], 234ff. The story is put into the mouth of the late Baroque painter Carlo Maratta.
65 Vasari IV, 1976 [**1408**], Testo 543–5.

The story is given more fully in Vasari's 2nd edn and the evidence for and against it is weighed by Freedberg 1950 [**1355**], 143, who inclined to discount it, and by Fagiolo dell'Arco 1970 [**1353**], who makes it the basis of a wide-ranging alchemical interpretation of Parmigianino's imagery.

66 The most thoroughgoing interpretation of Dürer's *Melancholia* as an alchemical allegory is Calvesi 1969 [**1342**], 37–96, which suffers somewhat from the documentary overkill. The identification of the distant bow with the rainbow has been challenged by Horst 1953 [**1364**], 426, 431, n. 9, who argued that it is a precisely observed ring of Saturn. See also Ploss et al. 1970 [**1387**], 24–6 on Dürer and alchemy, perhaps the best modern survey of alchemy from all points of view.

67 This was pointed out by Hartlaub 1953 [**1358**], 65. The drawing is discussed in Tietze and Tietze-Conrat 1970 [**1406**], no. 579.

68 Hind 1910, [**1359**], 492.

69 Kristeller 1907 [**1370**], 3.

70 *Ioannis Aurelii Augurelli P. Ariminensis Chrysopoeia Libri III*, 1515. There is a Fr. trans. of 1550. Augurelli cites Campagnola as a painter of landscape in Bk III. For the connection, Pavanello 1905 [**1383**], 96–7.

71 For the green, yellow and red pigments mined in the Veneto, Lazzarini in Hall 1987 [**1237**], 118. See also the reference by Augurelli to the 'pigmentum aureum' (i.e. orpiment) of the painters at the end of Bk I.

72 Freedberg 1950 [**1355**], 80, 141.

73 For a general study, Weise 1957 [**1409**], 170ff.

74 Aretino 1539 [**3133**], 9v, 16, 17v, 29f. The book was reprinted as late as 1945.

75 Ibid., 69v–70, 80, 117v.

76 Ibid., 100v, 118.

77 Joret 1892 [**1365**], 242, 246, 255. For the *Roman de la Rose*, Kirsop 1961 [**1369**], 146.

78 Evans 1922 [**682**], 22, 24, 36, 185.

79 Dronke 1972 [**880**], 98. For the diagrams, Meier 1972 [**1374**], 245–355.

80 Saran 1972 [**1397**], 228ff. See particularly 231f for cinnabar, citing a late 15-century recipe-book produced by Dominican nuns in Nuremberg, which used alchemical terminology in the recipe for vermilion (Ploss 1962 [**1386**], 121–2). Grünwald's inventory of 1528 was first printed by Zülch 1938 [**1411**], 373–5. His effects also included a quantity of '*alchemy grün*', i.e. manufactured green.

81 Luther *Sämmtliche Werke*, LXII, Pt IV, vol. X, 1854, 27f, cit. H. C. von Tavel, 'Nigredo-Albedo-Rubedo: ein Beitrag zur Farbsymbolik der Dürerzeit' in Hering-Mitgau et al. 1980 [**902**], 310. This important study treats the alchemical iconography of a panel in Niklaus Manuel's *St Eligius Altar*, exactly contemporary with Grünewald's Isenheim altar.

82 The only parallel I have found is in the sky of Konrad Faber von Kreutznach's portrait of Justinian and Anna von Holzhausen (Frankfurt, Städel Institute, no. 1729).

83 For a survey, Read 1952 [**1391**], 286–92.

84 Gilchrist 1942 [**221**], 303.

85 For the technique, Essick 1980 [**207**], ch. 9.

86 Blake 1956 [**171**], 187.

87 J. Glauber *The Prosperity of Germany*, cit. Crosland 1962 [**1348**], 9, 16.

88 Blake 1956 [**171**], 388. See Nurmi 1957 [**1378**], 206–7 for an identification with the rainbow. For the serpent in chemistry, J. J. Becher *Oedipus Chemicum*, 1669, cit. Crosland 1962 [**1348**], 17. The very varied colouring of the several copies of Blake's books makes interpretation of the colour impossible but suggests his fluid interpretation of symbolism as such.

89 Blake 1956 [**171**], 191.

9 Colour under Control

1 Goclenius 1613 [**1494**], 393ff.

2 C. T. Bartholin *Specimen Philosophiae Naturalis*, Oxford 1703, ch. VII (trans. Kuehni 1981 [**1533**], 230ff).

3 Kepler 1980 [**1530**], 114f. The background to Kepler's theory has been sketched by Lindberg 1986 [**751**], 29–36. An interesting medieval survival in Kepler's view is his uncertainty whether the carbuncle has its own light (ibid., 134).

4 Prins 1987 [**1578**], 293–4.

5 M. Mersenne, *Questions théologiques, physiques, morales et mathématiques*, Paris 1634, 105 cit. Darmon 1985 [**1468**], 89f; Marcus Marci, *Thaumantias*, Prague, 1648, 98 and F. M. Grimaldi *Physico-Mathesis de Lumine, Coloribus et Iride*, Bologna, 1665, 399 cit. Marek 1969 [**1555**], 393–406.

6 Barrow 1860 [**1425**], 107–8. Newton prepared Barrow's lectures for publication.

7 Shapiro I, 1984 [**1603**], 83, n. 10.

8 [Digby] 1658 [**1473**], 321; Hoogstraten 1678 [**1518**], 224. Digby was shown these experiments by Francis Hall (alias Line) *c.* 1640. Similar experiments had been conducted in the late 16th century by Thomas Harriot; they were repeated by Newton and formed the basis of Goethe's anti-Newtonianism. For Hoogstraten's use of mixed greens, Plesters 1987 [**1574**], 82 and for his use of glazes, 83. His omission of orange from binary mixtures may be due to his belief that it was a red.

9 Another striking example of the red–blue–yellow palette in the Middle Ages is one of the last products of Giotto's workshop, the *Polyptych* of *c.* 1333/4 (Bologna, Pinacoteca).

10 For the perspective, Kemp 1990 [**1529**], 126–7. A programmatic use of primary and secondary colours in Poussin's *Healing of the Blind* (1650, Paris, Louvre) has been argued by O. Bätschmann, 'Farbgenese und Primärfarbentrias in Nicholas Poussins "Die Heilung der Blinden"', in Hering-Mitgau 1980 [**902**], 329–36; trans. in Bätschmann 1990 [**1426**].

11 Scarmilionius 1601 [**317**], 111–12. He places his *puniceus* between *flavus* and *viridis* in his scale (117), which also has a *purpureus* but no *ruber* in this form, so I interpret *puniceus* as 'orange'.

12 Boyle 1664 [**179**], 219–21, 232.

13 Sir William Petty, 'An Apparatus to the History of & common Practices of Dying' in Sprat 1959 [**1616**], 295–302.

14 For Le Blon, Lilien 1985 [**1546**]; Gage 1986 [**1490**], 65–7. For colour-prints in general, Friedman 1978 [**1485**]; S. Lambert 1987 [**1541**], 87–106.

15 See, e.g., the Tradescant Museum (1656) in Allan 1964 [**1415**], 263: blacks, yellows, reds, blues, whites as used by dyers and painters.

16 Shapiro I, 1984 [**1603**], 436f, 460f, 506f; also Westfall 1962 [**1638**], 357.

17 Hooke 1961 [**1519**], 74f.

18 Huyghens in *Philosophical Transactions* XLVI, 1673, reprinted in Cohen 1958 [**1460**], 136.

19 Kühn 1968 [**1534**], 155–202, espec. 168 on Vermeer's unusual use of ultramarine; Sonnenburg 1973 [**1610**], after 11. Vermeer's fascination with light has always been noticed, but see espec. Seymour 1964 [**1601**], 323–31. For Charles le Brun's view that yellow and blue are the colours of air and light, see Félibien cit. Badt 1969 [**1423**], 339.

20 For Hooke's quite substantial discussion of this question, Hooke 1961 [**1519**], 76–8.

21 Plesters 1983 [**1573**], 38–46. Kemp 1990 [**1529**], 104 has argued that the painting exemplifies particularly closely several of d'Aguilon's ideas of light. The palette of 10 pigments, including 4 blues, and the complexity of palette-mixtures in the Antwerp *Descent from the Cross* (1610) have been studied by Coremans and Thissen 1962 [**1464**], 121ff, 126. The later portrait *The Gerbier Family* used some 20 pigments, as well as complex mixtures (Feller 1973 [**1479**], 59–64). A group of paintings of all periods in Munich has yielded some 15 pigments (Sonnenburg and Preusser 1979 [**330**], n.p.). The collection of Rubens's materials preserved at Antwerp includes 14 pigments (Hiler 1969 [**1516**], 137).

22 Aguilonius 1613 [**1413**], 41. For scrumbled mixtures 'Optische Farbwirkungen' in Sonnenburg and Preusser 1979 [**330**], n.p. Rubens's collaboration has been discussed by Jaeger 1976 [**1522**]; Judson and van de Velde 1978 [**1527**], 101–15. The link with *Juno and Argus* was made by Parkhurst 1961 [**1102**], 37–48 and another with the Vienna *Annunciation* (1609/10) by Jaffé 1971 [**1523**], 365–6. See also Held 1979 [**1509**], 257–64 and for a general account of d'Aguilon in Eng., Ziggelaar 1983 [**1644**].

23 Delbourgo and Petit 1960 [**1472**], espec. 52–4; Rees-Jones 1960 [**1579**], 307; Plesters and Mahon 1965 [**1575**], 203.

24 For the records of Rubens's *De Lumine et Colore*, which survived in MS until the 18th century, Gage 1969 [**217**], 222, n. 10. Poussin's 1649 self-portrait (Berlin) shows him holding a book inscribed *De Lumine et Colore* but it is not known whether this was his own work or the lengthy extracts from Zaccolini he is known to have made. His biographer Félibien denied that he had written anything of his own (Pace 1981 [**1565**], 16). See also Cropper 1980 [**1465**], 570–83.

25 Mancini 1956 [**1553**], I, 162 (*disegno as essere individuale*); Bellori 1976 [**1430**], 632 (*disegno as principio formale*). Maratta's didactic print of *c.* 1680 sums up his argument: students busy themselves with drawing, perspective, anatomy and the study of the Antique, while a palette and brushes stand idle (Kutschera-Woborsky 1919 [**1537**], 9–28). See also Domenichino to Angeloni *c.* 1632 in Mahon 1947 [**1551**], 120. In all cases these remarks arise from the Milanese theorist G. P. Lomazzo's proposal (*Trattato dell' Arte della Pittura*, Milan, 1584, 24) that drawing is the *materia* and colour the *forma* of painting. See also Le Brun in 1672 that *dessin* imitated *les choses réelles* and colour only *accidentels* (Imdahl 1987 [**1521**], 36). For Locke, 1975 [**1548**], 295, 300–301. This was only a refinment of the ancient discussion of the colours of the elements

(see ch. 2, 32–3).

26 Teyssèdre 1965 [**1620**], 206–7.

27 Le Blond de la Tour (1669) cit. Teyssèdre ibid., 71; de Piles (1672) in ibid., 194, n. 3 and 491, n. 2.

28 Pace 1981 [**1565**], 25. This attitude may have influenced Félibien's reluctance to believe that Poussin had written on the subject. He none the less agreed with the scientists that the primary colours were red, yellow and blue (Teyssèdre ibid., 308).

29 *Sopra i colori delle veste*, Campanella 1956 [**1452**], 852.

30 Piponnier 1970 [**1568**], espec. 189, 264; Scott 1981 [**1598**], 171ff. For 16th-century Italy, Newton 1988 [**1273**], 9, 72; Bombe 1928 [**1439**], 53 (Florence in 1534). Most of the recipes in the mid-16th-century Venetian dyers' manual *Plictho* were for black or red (Rosetti 1969 [**1589**], xvi). In 1530 Pietro Aretino wrote thanking the Duke of Mantua for a black and gold outfit he called 'gli abiti de i principi' (M. Gregori, 'Tiziano e l'Aretino' in Pallucchini 1978 [**1099**], 282). But by the end of the 17th century in Venice black was being prescribed for all men and women by the sumptuary laws (Bistort 1912 [**1435**], 150ff.)

31 Van Gogh 1958 [**1626**], no. 428 (1886), cit. F. S. Jowell, 'The rediscovery of Frans Hals' in *Frans Hals* 1989 [**1503**], 77. Hals's town, Haarlem, was particularly noted for its manufacture of black cloth (B. M. Dumortier, 'Costume in Frans Hals' in ibid., 58, n. 36).

32 J. B. Oudry (Largillière's pupil) in Rosenfeld 1981 [**1586**], 320.

33 Brown 1658 [**1445**], ch. III. Rzepińska 1986 [**1594**], 107 cites an alchemical treatise by Blaise Viguère, *Traité de feu et de sel*, Paris, 1618, which articulated ideas of darkness very close to Browne's.

34 Kepler 1980 [**1530**], cit. Rzepińska ibid., 102. The astronomical significance of shadows had stimulated the study of their projection in Antiquity and the Middle Ages (Kaufmann 1975 [**1528**], 262–7).

35 Kircher 1646 [**1531**], bk II, pt ii, 54, cit. Rzepińska ibid., 111.

36 Reynolds 1852 [**17**], II, 332–3. According to him, even Rubens introduced light into only a little more than a quarter of his picture. Some examples of this method of study are in Reynolds's sketchbook, Sir John Soane's Museum, London, folios 155, 159, 162, 177–8.

37 Mancini 1956 [**1553**], I, 108.

38 Mahon 1947 [**1551**], 37, n. 39, 65, 95.

39 Guidobaldo del Monte *Perspectivae Libri Sex*, Pisa, 1600, I, 2, cit. Spezzaferro 1971 [**1614**], 83, 89f. For Caravaggio's training, Baumgart 1955 [**1427**], 63.

40 Bellori 1976 [**1430**], 229.

41 Röttgen 1965 [**1591**], 48, 49f. See also the 1602 contract (54). For a similar stipulation in the Cavaliere d'Arpino's 1591 contract for the frescoes in the same chapel, Röttgen 1964 [**1590**], 205. A particularly interesting instance of this practice is in the 1612 contract for Domenichino's frescoes of the life of St. Cecilia, Polet Chapel, same church, where the patron agreed to provide ultramarine according to the painter's own taste (*sia tenuto darlo lui* [Domenichino] *a suo gusto, tanto della quantita, quanto della qualita come a lui* [Domenichino] *meglio parera*: Spear 1982 [**1612**], 328). In the early 1620s Guercino appealed to Pope Gregory XV for payment for his huge altarpiece *Sta Petronilla*

(now Rome, Capitoline Museum), including a special fee for the large quantity of ultramarine lavished over several figures, 'it being usual that painters never put this down to their own cost' (Pollack II, 1931, [**1577**], 564). For a very late example of this, see the frescoes of the Casa Bartholdy in Rome (now Berlin, Nationalgalerie), painted by a group of Nazarenes in 1816–17, for which the patron Niebuhr supplied the ultramarine (Seidler 1875 [**1599**], 304).
42 For the Cerasi Chapel, Hibbard 1983 [**1515**], 118ff.
43 P. Accolti *Lo Inganno degli Occhi*, Florence, 1625, 150, cit. Cropper 1980 [**1465**], 577f.
44 Malvasia 1841 [**1552**], I, 2. See also the remark by the Spanish theorist Palomino (1715/24) that to achieve the right effects even the dust of the street might be used (Veliz 1986 [**1628**], 164). Palomino (154) also noted with disapproval that the patron still often supplied the most expensive colours. It may be significant that no Spanish contracts stipulating the use of specific colours have yet come to light (McKim Smith et al. 1988 [**1550**], 97), although a Madrid example of 1654 specified 'fine and bright colours' (59); at this time ultramarine might have been used for the mantle of the Virgin (Veliz ibid., 118). For Spanish colour-principles, Soehner 1955 [**1609**], espec. 12f; Spinner 1971 [**1615**], 173. For the palettes of Velasquez and Zurbarán, Sonnenburg 1970 [**1610**], n.p.; Veliz 1981 [**1627**], 278–83.
45 Mancini 1956 [**1553**], I, 108–11; Ottonelli and Berrettini 1973 [**1381**], 25f. Cortona's colouristic interests have been emphasized by Poirier 1979 [**1576**], 23–30. For the Cavalier d'Arpino's work in the Contarelli Chapel, cleaned in 1966, *Il Cavaliere d'Arpino* 1973 [**1453**], 177. The juxtaposition of frescoes by Raphael and Sebastiano del Piombo in the Farnesina, Rome, must have been just as shocking and stimulating to spectators in the High Renaissance but does not seem to have generated the same comparisons.
46 Bernini 1982 [**1432**], 44f and figs 33–41. The vault frescoes were cleaned in 1959.
47 For an early description of Lanfranco's cupola, which stresses his range of tones from light to dark, Turner 1971 [**1625**], espec. 323. For Baciccio, Engass 1964 [**1477**], 31–43.
48 Baciccio may have taken his cue for this yellow–brown–white tonality from Federico Zuccari's cupola fresco of the Virgin adoring the Holy Trinity in a neighbouring chapel, dating from the end of the 16th century.
49 Molière X, 1949 [**1562**], 209, ll. 153–6.
50 For Hipparchus, Padgham and Saunders 1975 [**1566**], 57. Chalcidius 1963 [**1454**], 375f. Alexander of Aphrodisias's account of the rainbow (*see* p. 31 above) although it implies some scalar thinking, was not yet a coherent scale.
51 Urso von Salerno 1976 [**592**], 185.
52 Bacon 1937 [**157**], 70–77.
53 *Avicenna* 1972 [**1421**], 205f. Bacon's identification of *pallidus* with yellow has no basis in Avicenna's text and it was generally regarded as achromatic (see p. 74 above). It seems possible that the scheme of 12 steps, each in red and green, discussed in the early 12th century by Theophilus (I, 16) for painting the rainbow, was influenced by Avicenna, although the translation seems to be rather later than his book. He was, of course, describing the standard red-green bow of the early Middle Ages. For a detailed working-out of this scheme, see Theophilus 1963 [**1621**], 23–5.
54 Vincent of Beauvais 1624 [**823**], *Speculum Naturae* II, ch. lxviii.
55 For Albertus Magnus, *De Sensu*, II, 2, cit. Hudeczek 1944 [**732**], 130; for al Tûsî, Wiedemann 1908 [**603**], 88f.
56 Theodoric's account in *On colours* VI, however, does not include the notion of a grey-scale, as Parkhurst (Hall 1987 [**1237**], 174–6) suggests, since it is concerned with the black and white content of hues as hues. I have left out of consideration the theory of Robert Grosseteste, which Parkhurst has attempted to reconstruct as a three-dimensional solid (ibid., 168–72). Grosseteste proposed a list of 7 unnamed hues which could be arranged in a sequence from white to black and *another* unnamed 7 from black to white again (Parkhurst claims that there was only one set of 7). But as Parkhurst himself recognizes, this scheme was fraught with practical difficulties and was attacked by Bacon (1937 [**157**], 74–5) on these grounds. See espec. Parkhurst ibid., n. 18.
57 Barasch 1978 [**1168**], 178–80. For Renaissance scales see also Gavel 1979 [**219**], 45–6.
58 See, e.g., the carefully argued scale from white, pale green, yellow, red, purple and blue to black in Vossius 1662 [**1632**], 61ff.
59 Forsius 1952 [**1483**], 316ff. An Eng. trans. in Feller and Stenius 1970 [**1480**], 48–51 includes some rather misleading drawings after Forsius's diagrams, reprinted by Parkhurst in Hall 1987 [**1237**], 183.
60 Glisson 1677 [**1493**], ch. IX: 'De coloribus pilorum', 54–61. On blue *bice*, Harley 1982 [**1504**], 48–9. Glisson's approach may have been stimulated by the tables in Zahn 1658 [**1643**], fund. I, synt. 2, ch. IX, which show the progression of hues from black to white: green, e.g., has white, pale-yellow, yellow, green, blue, blue-black, black.
61 Chandler 1934 [**1455**], 69; Gage 1984 [**1489**], 256.
62 For Zaccolini, Bell 1985 [**1429**], 227–58. My account is based on Bell 1983 [**1428**], the Italian text of Zaccolini's treatise, which will soon be published in translation.
63 Bell 1983 ibid., 295, 356–64.
64 Ibid., 307, 335, 340–1.
65 Ibid., 295, 311, 326.
66 Sandrart 1925 [**1595**], 209f. The passage has been examined in some detail by Gowing 1974 [**1497**], 90–6 and Conisbee 1979 [**1462**], 415–19.
67 Conisbee ibid., 424.
68 Berger IV, 1901 [**1431**], 122–4. For *schitgeel*, n. 91 below.
69 J. H. Bourdon *Conference sur la lumière* (1669) in Watelet and Levesque I, 1792 [**1636**], 405–6, 413. Bourdon mentioned a meeting with Claude, whose sunrises he espec. admired (406).
70 Sutton 1987 [**1144**], 10–11 and 430 on Rembrandt's *Ice Scene near Farm Cottages*.
71 Goclenius 1613 [**1494**], 393f. It is remarkable that he grouped *glaucus, coesius, lividus, cinericius* and *pallidus* under *caeruleus*.
72 Merrifield 1849 [**271**], II, 650–7.
73 This practice has been identified as early as Tintoretto (Plesters 1980, [**1572**], 36, 39); for its use by the young Rembrandt, van de Wetering 1977 [**1640**], 63; for Jan Steen *c.* 1660, Butler 1982/3 [**1449**], 46.
74 For Caravaggio, Greaves and Johnson 1974 [**1498**], 20; for Rubens, Coremans and Thissen 1962 [**1464**], 126.
75 Junius 1638 [**1071**], 272. The book appeared in Latin, Eng. and Dutch. For Rembrandt's possible knowledge of it in the late 1630s, Gage 1969 [**1487**], 381. See also Félibien on 'couleurs rompuës' in 1676 (Pace 1981 [**1565**], 167, n. 115.1).
76 Sandrart 1925 [**1595**], 203. This is my free trans. from a difficult passage. Sandrart's thought is close to 16th-century Venetian attitudes (p. 137 above). His sympathy for Rembrandt's style and technique is clear in his *Good Samaritan* (Milan, Brera). See also the emphasis on harmony through mixture in Rembrandt's pupil Hoogstraten 1678 [**1518**], 223, and 291 for Rembrandt's technique.
77 Groen 1977 [**1499**], 74; Coremans 1965 [**1463**], 183f; Kühn 1976 [**1535**], 27f. Catalogues of substantial collections of Rembrandts which include technical analyses are de Vries et al. 1978 [**1633**], and Bomford et al. 1988 [**1440**].
78 See n. 19 above and Froentjes 1969 [**1486**], 233–7; Sonnenburg 1976 [**1611**], 11. The technique was noted in the work of Holbein (silver leaf) in the 17th century (Mayerne n.d. [**1559**], 110) and was used locally in the 15th (p. 129 above).
79 Kühn 1977 [**1536**], 226.
80 Van de Wetering et al. 1976 [**1641**], 95f.
81 Restout 1863 [**1583**]. A rather different interpretation of the palette's affecting style was suggested by Hagedorn 1775 [**236**], II, 170, who said that 'feeling the palette' in a painting was to feel the falseness and exaggeration of the local colours, which must be modified by mixing.
82 Shapiro I, 1984 [**1603**], 460f, who conjectures plausibly that Newton intended to write *puniceus* for *purpureus*.
83 Harris 1708–10 [**1505**], I, s.v. 'Colour'. In II an article on 'Colour' is also derived from *Opticks*.
84 Taylor 1719 [**1619**], 67–70. For his paintings and collaboration with Newton on the theory of music, see P. S. Jones in *Dictionary of Scientific Biography*, XIII, 1976, 265–8.
85 Le Blon [1725] [**1543**], 6. The date was established by Lilien 1985 [**1546**], 140–1, who also published a facsimile of this 1st edn.
86 Gage 1983 [**1488**], 19–20 and 1986 [**1490**], 67. One of the first popularizers of Newton's *Opticks*, Francesco Algarotti, already in 1737 showed that Le Blon left his paper white since he could not constitute it from his primary colours (Algarotti 1969 [**1414**], II, 150). See also Cominale 1754 [**1461**], 133.
87 Wagner 1967 [**1634**], 42.
88 Scheuchzer I, 1731 [**1596**], 61. The poetic tradition of the *Opticks* has been explored by Nicolson 1946 [**1564**]; Greene 1953 [**1055**], 327–52; Murdoch 1958 [**1563**], 324–33; Guerlac 1971 [**1500**]. The visual tradition of eulogy of Newton has been less studied but see Haskell 1967 [**1506**], 218–31 and *The European Face of Isaac Newton* 1973/4 [**1478**].
89 Turnbull 1740 [**1624**], 145–6. The link with the *Opticks* had been made on 133–4.
90 Waller 1686 [**1635**], 25. See also Harley 1982 [**1504**], 36. The only precedent for Waller's colour-atlas seems to have been Elias Brenner 1680 [**1441**] but, as Waller pointed out, this atlas, which provided 31 colour-samples grouped under white, yellow, red, green, blue and black and was directed primarily at miniaturists, dealt only with 'simple' colours. Waller included about 120 samples.
91 'E. W.' in *A Garden of Flowers; Wherein Very Lively is Contained a True and Perfect Discription of al the Floures Containd in these Foure Followinge Bookes, as also the Perfect True Manner of Colouring the same, with their Naturall Coloures . . .*, Utrecht, 1615, end of bk IV. *Schijt-geel* is recommended as a good glazing colour by C. P. Biens (1639), cit. de Klerk 1982 [**1532**], 55–6 (Eng. summary 57ff). The difficulty of interpreting the colours in 16th-century herbals has been discussed by Arber 1940 [**1418**], 803. For some early attempts to catalogue animals using colour-names in a more or less systematic way, Charleton 1677 [**1456**], 61–71, which refers to Glisson's system (see p. 167 above); Buonanni 1681 [**1448**], 87–96, which refers back to Savot 1609 [**315**]. It is notable that Buonanni, whose work was based on the collection of shells left by Athanasius Kircher to the Jesuit College at Rome, did not extract a three-colour theory from Savot's book (see p. 274, n. 97 above) but listed as his primaries white, black, yellow, red, purple, green and blue (*turchino*).
92 J. Pitton de Tournefort (1694), cit. Dagognet 1970 [**1466**], 31f. For the view that colour was of no taxonomic significance, Linnaeus 1938 [**1547**], 138–42.
93 C. F. Prange *Farbenlexicon*, Halle, 1782 and review in Meusel's *Miscellaneen artistischen Inhalts*, IX, 1781, cit. Rehfus-Dechêne 1982 [**1581**], 15f. Another set of standards directed primarily at naturalists was J. C. Schäffer *Entwurf einer allgemeinen Farbenverein*, Regensburg, 1769.
94 Schiffermüller, 1776 [**324**], 6–7. For the date and context, Lersch 1984 [**1545**], 301–16. Schiffermüller was co-author with M. Denis of *Systematisches Verzeichniss der Schmetterlinge der Wiener Gegend*, Vienna, 1776, where, in spite of the usual references to problems of terminology (38–9), there appears to be no reference to his system.
95 Gage 1990 [**9**], 538.
96 Williams 1787 [**1642**], 39f. It is a symptom of the still disorganized character of Eng. science that as late as 1823, after the publication of Symes 1821 [**1618**], a meteorologist could still look forward to 'a systematic arrangement of colours . . . by reference to flowers and other standard substances. It would be well if we had a nomenclature for colours which expressed them by reference to the proportion of the primitive tints of which they may be compounds' (Forster 1823 [**1484**], 85n).
97 Goncourt 1948 [**1496**], 89. For the vogue for shell-collecting in Boucher's circle, Dance 1966 [**1467**], 61.
98 Scopoli 1763 [**1597**], n.p. Scopoli used a disc divided into 8 equal segments; his 'primaries' were vermilion, gamboge, Prussian blue, black (*atramentum indicum*) and white lead, with a mixed green. Some of his mixtures are surprising, including a *corallinus* from 6 parts of red and 4 of green. The *Insecta Musei Graecensis* of the Jesuit N. Poda (1761) does not use a colour-notation, although Scopoli is

mentioned in it as a friend, so the technique may have been devised in the early 1760s. Schiffermüller 1776 [**324**], 2n. was very critical of these experiments. Those by Peter Shaw in the 1730s seem to have been concerned only with testing Newton's theory of the heterogeneous character of white light (Shaw 1755 [**1604**], 304).

99 Thus colour plays no part in G. Cantor's study *Optics after Newton: Theories of Light in Britain and Ireland, 1704–1840*, 1983.

100 Isidore 1960 [**456**], 15–17, 202bis, 212bis, 216bis, 296bis. For diagrams in Cassiodorus and Joachim of Flora, Esmeijer 1978 [**680**], 38, 125f. See also Evans 1980 [**427**], 32–5.

101 See D. Huë, 'Du crocus au jus de Poireau: remarques sur la perception des couleurs au Moyen-Âge' in CUERMA 1988 [**873**], 165ff. For Fludd, Godwin 1979 [**1495**], 65, who notes a 15th-century version in Oxford, Bodleian Library, MS Savile 39, folio 7v.

102 For the complicated bibliography of 'Boutet', Parkhurst and Feller 1982 [**1567**], 229, n. 14. A 2nd wheel in the treatise increased the number of mixed tones to 8.

103 Frisch (1788), cit. Lersch 1984 [**1545**], 314; Bezold 1876 [**1434**], 114; for Ostwald p. 247 above.

104 Gavel 1979 [**219**], 95. This was true of many later proposals: R. Agricola in a discussion of *Difference* listed blue and yellow as *contrarii* and indigo, red and green as widely separated (Agricola 1967 [**1412**], I, xxvii, 161). Zahn 1658 [**1643**], fund. I, synt. 2, ch. IX argued that the most opposite colours were the liveliest in juxtaposition but did not specify them. H. Testelin *Tableau sur la couleur* (1696) gave red and green, yellow and blue as particularly helpful for enhancing each other's brilliance (cit. Teyssèdre 1965 [**1620**], 298). Lairesse 1778 [**1539**], 120–1 gave a long list of harmonious pairs but like Leonardo's they were very fluid: light yellow, e.g., suited violet but also purple and green, and pale red suited green and blue.

105 Cohen 1958 [**1460**], 85.

106 Ibid., 206 (1675).

107 Newton 1730 [**1095**], I, ii, prop. V., theor. iv, experiment 15. See Shapiro 1980 [**1602**], 234; H. G. Grassmann (1853) in MacAdam 1970 [**1549**], 57ff. On the history of Newton's work on the colours of thin plates, Westfall 1962/5 [**1639**], 181–96; Sabra 1967 [**1396**], ch. 13.

108 Rumford 1802 [**1592**], I, 319–40. Matthaei 1962 [**1557**], 72–4 traces the term to the Fr. scientist J. H. Hassenfratz in 1801.

109 R. W. Darwin 1785 [**1470**], reprinted in E. Darwin 1796 [**1469**], I, 568. R. W. Darwin pointed out that his work started with an analysis of Newton's colour-wheel. Rumford had made similar experiments in 1793 (Rumford ibid., 336–7) and they were also made the basis of a theory of harmony by Venturi 1801 [**1629**], 113ff. For Goethe, see ch. 11 below.

110 I date Harris's book to the early 1770s because it is dedicated to Sir Joshua Reynolds, who was knighted in 1769 but does not mention Harris's *Exposition of English Insects* of 1776, in a long title which refers to other of Harris's publications. The *Exposition* used a modified version of the *Natural System*, which is known in a copy at Yale and another in Munich, Bayerische Staatsbibliothek, neither of which has the last plate with samples of colour-mixtures. The Yale copy was published in facsimile by F. Birren in 1963 but with re-worked col. pls which are quite misleading; the pls of the Munich copy are reproduced in Lersch 1984 [**1545**], pls 3a, b.

111 Repton 1803 [**1582**], 218.

112 Regnier 1865 [**1580**], 13–15. This view had already been offered more cautiously by Rumford (1802 [**1592**], I, 336); in 1792 a young Eng. painter, Henry Howard, had noticed the 'oppositions' of e.g. crimson and brownish green in a Titian in Venice (Howard 1848 [**1065**], liii).

113 Chevreul 1854 [**185**], §§16, 237. For the influence of Ampère, Chevreul 1969 [**1459**], iv.

114 Aquinas 1952 [**1417**], 630, §289. See also Alhazen 1989 [**364**], I, 99; II, 58.

115 See *Le Magasin Pittoresque*, II, 1834, 63, 90–1; 'Dr E. V.', 'Cours sur le contraste des couleurs par M. Chevreul', *L'Artiste*, 3rd series, I, 1842, 148–50, 162–5; C. E. Clerget, 'Lettres sur la théorie des couleurs', *Bulletin de l'Ami des Arts*, II, 1844, 29–36, 54–62, 81–91, 113–21, 175–85, 393–404. In 1842 Chevreul's lectures were advertised at the Paris Salon (Herbert 1962 [**1512**], 77).

116 I have discussed these associations in a forthcoming paper, 'Chevreul entre Classicisme et Romantisme'.

117 For Vernet, see the well illustrated cat. *Horace Vernet*, 1980, Académie de France à Rome.

118 Delacroix 1980 [**1026**], 6 May 1852; cf. 2 September 1854.

119 For Delacroix's note, Dittmann 1987 [**1474**], 284, and in trans., with the triangle, by Kemp 1990 [**1529**], 308. He and Mérimée served on a government committee in 1831 (L. Rosenthal 1914 [**1588**], 5) and he owned a Mérimée watercolour of horses (Bessis 1971 [**1433**], 213, no. 123).

120 For the 1839 circle, Johnson 1963 [**1069**], 56, pl. 34. This is still the best study of Delacroix's colour but see also Badt 1965 [**1422**], 46–74; Howel 1982 [**1520**], 37–43.

121 The lecture notes, in an exercise book, are now in the Cabinet de Dessins at the Louvre (MSS Anonymes I d.80). They are not in Delacroix's hand but include a number of corrections which may be by him. The 24-colour circle in them may be related to Delacroix's late *cadran* described by Silvestre 1926 [**1608**], I, 48. For the painter's proposed visit to Chevreul, Signac 1964 [**1607**], 76; since Delacroix, who lived until 1863, does not seem to have attempted a 2nd visit it is possible that it was intended to be more social than educational: at the time Delacroix was suing for membership of the Institut, of which Chevreul was President.

122 Lecture-Notes, 13 January 1848, n.p. Cf. the memoirs of Delacroix's assistant on some of these schemes, Planet 1928 [**1571**], 399, 435f.

123 Vollard 1938 [**1631**], 215.

124 Van Gogh 1958 [**1626**], Letter 503. For the ceiling, Johnson 1981–9 [**1070**], V, 115–31; Matsche 1984 [**1556**], espec. 478–82. For other col. details, Sérullaz 1963 [**1600**], pls 105, 108.

125 Du Camp 1962 [**1451**], 270; Delacroix 1980 [**1026**], espec. 7 September 1856.

126 For Blanc and Delacroix, Matsche 1984 [**1556**], 470; Delacroix 1935–8 [**1471**], II, 374f, 391; IV, 526. See also Spector 1967 [**1613**], 95, 163, n. 7.

127 Blanc 1867 [**1436**], 24, 595–8, 600–4; 1876 [**1437**], 62–4.

128 Blanc 1867 [**1436**], 22, 24, 608ff.

129 Blanc ibid., 604ff. For orientalism, ibid., 595, 606f; 1876 [**1437**], 72–4; 1882 [**1438**], 222, 390, 404f, 473ff.

130 For the *Women of Algiers*, Blanc 1876 [**1437**], 68ff; Johnson 1963 [**1069**], 69; for accessories, Blanc 1867 [**1436**], 609f.

131 For the *Women of Algiers*, Johnson 1963 [**1069**], 42–3, pls 23–4; ibid., 1981–9 [**1070**], III, no. 356. For Delacroix copies from authentic oriental sources, Johnson 1965 [**1525**], 163f; 1978 [**1526**], 144ff; D. A. Rosenthal 1977 [**1587**], 505–6.

132 See espec. Chevreul's remarks about the Eng. trans. of his work in the early 1850s (1879 [**1458**], 2^{e}séc., LXI, 241f). For new versions, see espec. the most magnificent of them, 1864 [**1457**], and the 1889 edn of *De la Loi du contraste simultané*, reprinted 1969 [**1459**]. One of the last colour-handbooks on Chevreulian lines seems to be Lacouture 1890 [**1538**], dedicated to his memory.

133 See espec. Maxwell (1856) in Maxwell I, 1990 [**1558**], 412–13. The distinction between additive and subtractive mixing had been described clearly by Forbes 1849 [**1482**], 165 and hinted at by Hayter 1826 [**1508**], 6. The 'paradox' of the mixture of blue and yellow lights to white had also been reported much earlier by the German mathematician J. H. Lambert (1760 [**1540**], 528). Forbes knew Lambert's other major publication, the *Farbenpyramide* of 1772 (Forbes ibid., 161f).

134 Chevreul 1879 [**1458**], 14, 55, 178ff, 248ff, appealing to the experience of painters to expose them. The development has been discussed by Sherman 1981 [**1606**].

135 Laugel 1869 [**1542**], which recommended (7, n. 1) Helmholtz's *Handbook of Physiological Optics* (1867) as the best guide.

136 Jamin 1857 [**1524**], 624–42. Cf. Sheon 1971 [**1605**], 434–55. This view was not so far from Helmholtz's as expressed in the 1850s in the 'On the relation of optics to painting' in Helmoltz 1900 [**1511**], II, 73–138.

137 E. Duranty *La Nouvelle Peinture*, 1876, in Geffroy 1922 [**1492**], 88–90. For Duranty and Guillemin, Marcussen 1979 [**1554**], 29. Duranty also owned another book which took a Helmholtzian line on primaries and secondaries and reprinted his essay on painting: Brücke 1878 [**1447**].

138 Véron 1879 [**1630**], 220. For Véron and Huysmans, Reutersvärd 1950 [**1584**], 108–9. Another Fr. account of Helmholtzian complementaries in these years was Guéroult 1882 [**1501**], 174. For the same texts read at this time by outdoor painters in Italy, Broude 1970 [**1442**], 406–12.

139 Véron 1879 [**1630**], 243.

140 For *impressioniste-luministe*, Seurat to Signac 1887 in Dorra and Rewald 1959 [**1475**], lx; for *chromo-luminarisme*, 'chère à Seurat', Signac 1964 [**1607**], 151; for *peinture optique*, Seurat to Fénéon, 1889, in de Hauke and Brame 1961 [**1507**], I, xx.

141 M. Schapiro in Meyerson 1957 [**1560**], 251. Camille Pissarro recognized the importance of this new, impersonal, quasi-mechanical touch but found in the long run that the sacrifice was too great (Anquetin 1970 [**1416**], 430). The fullest account of the genesis of the *Grande Jatte* is now Thompson 1985 [**1622**], 97f.

142 Thompson ibid., col. pl. 114.

143 Minervino 1972 [**1561**], col. pl. xvii.

144 Rood's colour circle, of which Seurat owned a tracing, is reproduced with a copy in Homer 1970 [**1517**], 41 (captions reversed). For Seurat's reading of Rood, Gage 1987 [**1491**], 449. In that article (451, n. 24) I discounted the influence of Rood on the *Grande Jatte* but I was thinking then of the small-scale deployment of contrasted dots, rather than of the large colour areas discussed here. For Seurat's meeting with Henry, Fénéon 1970 [**1481**], I, xv; for Henry's interest in Helmholtz and his attack on Chevreul's circle in 1885, Argüelles 1972 [**1419**], 94f.

145 The best available colour-reproductions of the picture with its border, taken after cleaning, are in Art Institute of Chicago, *Museum Studies*, XIV, 1989, pls 2, 6, 8, 12.

146 Minervino 1972 [**1561**], col. pl. xxviii. The present dotted frame is not Seurat's, which was white (R. Alley, *Catalogue of the Tate Gallery's Collection of Modern Art*, 1981, 682f, no. 6067). Prof. R. L. Herbert first pointed out to me the mixture of Chevreulian and Helmholtzian complementaries in the small *Poseuses* (P. Smith 1990 [**1139**], 383, col. pl. II).

147 The letter is translated in Broude 1978 [**1443**], 16. The fullest discussion of the painter's reading is Herbert et al. 1991 [**1514**], 384–93.

148 For Seurat's note, de Hauke and Brame 1961 [**1507**], I, xxiv and Blanc 1867 [**1436**], 599f. For orange sunlight, Gage 1987 [**1491**], 449–50; Blanc ibid., 608. A sustained attack on the 'scientific' notion of white sunlight had already been launched by Regnier, who argued that it was a 'light, slightly orange yellow' (1865, [**1580**], 2–3).

149 Herbert et al. 1991 [**1514**], 394–6. For one of Seurat's annotated sketches, Russell 1965 [**1593**], fig. 69.

150 Piron 1865 [**1569**], 416ff. For Seurat's copy in the Signac archive, Herbert ibid., 23.

151 Sutter 1880 [**1617**]. For Seurat's cross, Rey 1931 [**1585**], 128.

152 Sutter ibid., 218–19. For Seurat's colour-circle, Gage 1987 [**1491**], 450–1.

153 Fénéon 1970 [**1481**], I, 117 cit. Halperin 1988 [**1502**], 101.

154 Halperin ibid., 139.

155 For the letter to Durand-Ruel, Bailly-Herzberg 1980– [**1424**], II, (1986), 75. The Hayet circle was no. 28 in *Artists, Writers, Politics* ... 1980 [**1420**]; for Hayet's despairing letter about it, Dulon and Duvivier 1991 [**1476**], 60. Both are now in Oxford, Ashmolean Museum and the circle was reproduced in col. by Dulon and Duvivier ibid, 169. Pissarro's preference for the optical mixture of tones close to each other on the circle has sometimes been related to his earlier practice as an Impressionist (Herbert 1970 [**1513**], 29; cf. Brown 1950 [**1444**], 15) but Rood had also recommended the harmonies of the 'small interval' (Gage 1987 [**1491**], 453).

156 Laugel 1869 [**1542**], 151–2.

157 See espec. his letter to Lucien 23 February 1887 (Bailly-Herzberg 1980– [**1424**], II (1986), 131).

158 M. Schapiro in Meyerson 1957 [**1560**], 248; Weale 1972 [**1637**], 16ff; Lee 1987 [**1544**], 203–26; see also the responses by D. A. Freeman and myself, *Art History*, XI, 1988, 150–5, 597.

159 Pissarro to van de Velde (1896) in *Pissarro* 1981 [**1570**], 124.
160 As pointed out by Brücke 1866 [**1446**], 282ff.
161 Gage 1987 [**1491**], 452.
162 Brücke 1878 [**1447**], 7.

10 The Palette

1 Kandinsky 1982 [**1686**], I, 372.
2 See, e.g., 'Intruments in Experiment' in Gooding, Pinch and Schaffer 1989 [**1674**], 31–114.
3 One of the best and most useful examples of this sort of literature is Ayres 1985 [**1646**]. Two important items of painterly equipment, paint-containers and brushes, have been investigated by Harley 1971 [**1677**], 1–12; and 'Artists' brushes – historical evidence from the sixteenth to the nineteenth century' in Bromelle and Smith 1976 [**1194**], 61–6.
4 See espec. the collection of nearly 300 photographs gathered by Faber Birren and now at Yale. Kaufmann 1974 [**1687**], 51–72 has postage-stamp size illustrations of the whole collection.
5 The 'palette' of 6 colours described by Bazin et al. 1958 [**1649**], 3–22 is simply an area of the panel used for testing pigments, all of which are unmixed.
6 Jacobus *Omne Bonum*, British Library MS Roy 6EVI, folio 329r, where the 9 saucers hold 5 or 6 tints (pl. in Martindale 1972 [**760**], 20); Cicero: *Rhetoric*, Ghent University Library MS 10, folio 16v (col. pl. in Bellony-Rewald and Peppiatt 1983 [**1652**], 25).
7 Baticle et al. 1976 [**1648**], 9–10. *Marcia*, from BN MS Fr 12420, folio 101v was reproduced in col. in Behrends and Kober 1973 [**1651**], 12.
8 *De trençoirs en bois pour iceulx mettre couleurs à olle et pour les tenir à la main.* Laborde 1851 [**1693**], II, 354, no. 4669.
9 See, e.g., the blue drapery palette of *St Luke painting the Virgin* (1487), col. pl. in Kaufmann 1974 [**1687**], 53; Derick Baegert's red-drapery palette (?) of 9 colours in *St Luke painting the Virgin* (*c.* 1485–90), col. pl. in *Herbst des Mittelalters* 1970 [**1679**], pl. VI and no. 39; follower of Quentin Massys *St Luke painting the Virgin* (*c.* 1500), London, National Gallery (no. 3902), which has a flesh palette of some 6 colours, including a blue-green (see Stout 1933 [**1730**], 191); Colÿn de Coter *St Luke* (before 1493), also with a blue robe palette, col. pl. in Perier d'Ieteren 1985 [**1711**], fig. 27, also 55ff.
10 Kühn 1977 [**1692**], 160–7.
11 Stout 1933 [**1730**], 186–90. Stout suggests that this is a fanciful arrangement, since there are too few colours for the painting in hand, and in particular no reds, but this would not be a problem if the palette were a 'local' one.
12 One symptom of these new methods was the attempt in 1546 by the Guild of St Luke at 's-Hertogenbosch in Holland to preserve the traditional Netherlandish method of oil painting with superimposed glazing, by banning the newer use of a single layer of mixed pigments, a quicker, cheaper and less durable procedure, See Miedema 1987 [**1704**], 141–7 (with English summary).
13 Vasari IV, 1976 [**1408**], 303.
14 Some examples I have noticed are – for Italy – Dosso Dossi *Jupiter and Mercury* (*c.* 1530), Vienna, Kunsthistorisches Museum; the self-portraits by Alessandro Allori (1535–1607) and Gregorio Pagani (1558–1605), Florence, Uffizi; Palma Giovane's self-portrait, Milan, Brera (*The Genius of Venice* 1983/4 [**1671**], no. 69); Annibale Carracci's *Self-Portrait with other Figures* (*c.* 1585), Brera (Posner 1971 [**1715**], no. 25); *Self-Portrait with an Easel* (*c.* 1604), St Petersburg, Hermitage, (Posner no. 143), replica in Uffizi repr. in col. by Bonafoux 1985 [**1654**], 83; *Apparition of the Virgin to SS. Luke and Catherine* (1592), Paris, Louvre. For the north, Marten van Heemskerk *St Luke painting the Virgin* (*c.* 1530/50), Rennes (col. pl. in Bellony-Rewald and Peppiatt 1983 [**1652**], 26; also *Le Dossier d'un tableau* 1974 [**1665**], Havel 1979 [**1678**], pl. IV and 45); Katharina van Hemessen *Self-Portrait at the Easel* (1548), Basle, Kunstmuseum (col. pl. in Bonafoux 1985 [**1654**], 102); Joseph Heintz Snr. *Self-Portrait with his Siblings Muriel and Salome* (1596), Berne, Kunstmuseum (col. pl. in *Prag um 1600* 1988 [**1716**], no. 128, pl. 31). These examples have been discussed by Schmid 1948 [**1724**], 73–5, but his technical information is out of date and he confuses a 'restricted' with a 'local' palette. Antonis Mor (1517–76) Uffizi (Kaufmann 1974 [**1687**], no. 7); Joachim Wtewael *Self-Portrait* (1601), (col. pl. in Lowenthal 1986 [**1698**], frontispiece); Jorge Manuel Theotocopuli's palette in El Greco's portrait of him at Seville (*c.* 1600/5) has the same small number of pigments as the El Greco palette reconstructed in Lane and Steinitz 1942 [**1695**], 23, but their arrangement of it seems to be an ideal construct.
15 G. B. Armenini 1988 [**1645**], 144 (1977, 193).
16 Beal 1984 [**1650**], 244; for the other references, 140ff, 225, 247.
17 For a colour reproduction, von Simson 1968 [**1727**], 19.
18 See espec. van de Wetering 1977 [**1640**], 65, and idem. 'Painting materials and working methods' in de Bruyn et al. 1982 [**1657**], 24.
19 The identification of the figure as Rembrandt has been disputed by W. Sumowski (*Gemälde der Rembrandt-Schüler*, I, 1983 [**1731**], no. 262), but the picture on the easel is clearly in his early style. Dou's own self-portraits (New York Metropolitan Museum, and a Private Collection) follow this scheme (Kaufmann 1974 [**1687**], no. 39; col. pl. in Ayres 1985 [**1646**], 53).
20 A fine example of this is B. van de Helst's portrait of Paul Potter (*c.* 1654) where the bright colours are placed in the middle of what is still a surprisingly small palette for this date (Kaufmann 1974 [**1687**], no. 38). An interesting variant in the order of the light colours is in the work of Frans Francken II, who liked to place pale yellow *before* white, then vermilion and darker yellows (see his *Christian Allegory*, Budapest Museum of Fine Arts, and his *Interior of a Gallery*, Berlin-Dahlem, Gemäldegalerie).
21 Mayerne n.d. [**1559**], 108–9, 130.
22 Bate 1977 [**1647**], 132.
23 Merrifield 1849 [**271**], II, 770–3.
24 Slive 1970–74 [**1728**], III, no. D69. The palette of another major woman-painter of this period, Artemesia Gentileschi, shown in her self-portrait, Rome, Galleria Nazionale del Palazzo Barberini, is a straightforwardly tonal one. Another flesh-palette with white in the centre is that of the Spanish artist Esteban March in the Prado self-portrait (Kaufmann 1974 [**1687**], no. 26).
25 For the treatise, Veliz 1986 [**1628**], 110, 113, and fig. 28. The palette also keeps vermilion and carmine in a separate sequence, as does Murillo's palette in his self-portrait, London, National Gallery, (no. 6153 and Kaufmann 1974 [**1687**], 43).
26 [De Piles] 1684 [**1713**], 40–41. For the collaboration with Corneille, Picart 1987 [**1712**], 30, 147. Schmid 1948 [**1724**], 47–51 gives a summary of the main points of the treatise, which he still attributes to Corneille.
27 [De Piles] 1684 [**1713**], 46–9, 70.
28 Du Puy de Grez 1700 [**1717**], 245f. Although he reports this as the practice of a friend, it may be a reminiscence of Félibien 1725 [**1669**], V (1679), 16, where mixing with the knife on the palette and with the brush on palette and canvas is mentioned. The Musscher portrait is reproduced in colour in Jackson-Stops 1985 [**1684**], no. 305. Du Puy de Grez was still arguing that white should be placed in the middle as well as in the sequence at the edge (256–7, 269).
29 Kirby Talley 1981 [**1688**], 333, 342. For France see, e.g., Martin Lambert *Portrait of H. and C. Beaubrun* (1675), col. pl. in Ayres 1985 [**1646**], 118, and Jean-Charles Nocret (1647–1719) *Portrait of the two Nocret* in Havel 1979 [**1678**], pl. XVII.
30 Oudry 1861 [**1709**], 109. See his palette in the *Allegorie des Arts* of 1713 at Schwerin, repr. in col. in Venzmer 1967 [**1733**], pl. I.
31 See the palettes in M. Cochereau's view of David's studio, Paris, Louvre, and those in a drawing of *c.* 1800 by J.-H. Cless, Musée Carnavalet (repr. in Levitine 1978 [**1697**], fig. 17). The David palette given by Lane and Steinitz 1942 [**1695**] has 17 pigments but no mixtures.
32 Gautier 1708 [**1670**], 5, 26. For 17th-century work on colour-indicators, Eamon 1980 [**1351**].
33 Corri 1983 [**1662**], 210ff, with col. repr. facing p. 195. The attribution to Gainsborough has not been universally accepted.
34 For the early palette see the portrait of Wilson by A. R. Mengs (1752), Cardiff, National Museum of Wales (Constable 1954)[**1660**], frontispiece); for the later arrangement, sketch by Paul Sandby, reconstructed in Whitley 1968 [**1739**], I, 384.
35 For Le Blon, Lilien 1985 [**1546**], col. pl. 47 and pp. 202, 221, 225. For Bardwell, Kirby Talley and Groen, 1975 [**1689**], 65ff, 101.
36 Williams 1937 [**1740**], 19ff.
37 Thénot 1847 [**1732**], 2ff (palettes of David, Gros, Ingres, Watelet, Lapito, Thénot, Bouton, Renoux, Dauzats, Gudin, Bracarsat, Werboekhoven); Moreau-Vauthier 1923 [**1706**], 23–24 (palettes of Dagnan, David, Delacroix, Derain, Aman-Jean, André, Bail, Bonnat, Bougereau, Carolus-Duran, Chabas, Collin, Cormon, Cottet, Desvallières, d'Espagnet, Doigneau, Dupré, Denis, Domergue, Gaudura, Girardot, Gérome, Harpignies, Ingres (not the same as in Thénot's list), Levy Dhurmer, Maillart, Matisse, Maufra, Ménard, Millet, Morot, Picard, Pissarro, Point, Ricard, Renoir, Rixens, Roll, T. Rousseau, Saint-Gernier, Simon, Ulmarin, Valloton, Whistler, Zuluoga); A. Ozenfant, in *Encyclopédie Française* 1935 [**1666**], XVI, 30–5–6 (palettes of Signac, Renoir, Bonnard, Matisse, Utrillo, Dufy, Derain (not the same as Moreau-Vauthier's), Braque, Lhote, Léger, de Chirico).
38 Col. pl. in *Manners and Morals* 1987 [**1701**], no. 73.
39 Hogarth 1955 [**1064**], 98.
40 Ibid., 127–30. The palette of Hogarth's early associate Joseph Highmore, in a self-portrait of *c.* 1725–35 at Melbourne, is set only with white, red, blue and yellow.
41 For the portrait, Cooper 1982 [**1661**], no. 33. A detail of the palette is on p. 93.
42 Cooper 1982 [**1661**], no. 114 (*c.* 1802 repr. in colour on cover); no. 114, *c.* 1821 (both Yale University Art Gallery).
43 Conisbee 1979 [**1462**], 421. I have been unable to find an illustration of Desportes's palette setting.
44 See, e.g., A. Mascardi's *Dell'Arte Historica*, Rome 1636, 403, where the habit of identifying artists on the basis of their colour is dismissed as merely sensual (cit. Cropper 1984 [**1022**], 143).
45 Oudry 1861 [**1709**], 111. Among the 'Flemings' were probably Gerard Edelink, whose portrait Largillière painted about 1690 (Norfolk, Virginia, Chrysler Museum), and which shows a palette with an unusually wide range of 10 pigments being much blended on the palette (col. pl. Rosenfeld 1981 [**1586**], cover).
46 Thus du Puy de Grez 1700 [**1717**]; Restout 1863 [**1583**]. A self-portrait of Jean Jouvenet, to whom Restout here refers, and showing a standard tonal palette, is in the museum at Rouen.
47 Hagedorn 1775 [**236**], II, 170; also Laugier 1972 [**1696**], 152; Hoppner 1908 [**1680**], 102. For later expressions of the same idea, Bon 1826 [**1653**], s.v. 'Palette'; Sutter 1880 [**1617**], xcv and xcvii, where he claimed that colour-relationships were very hard to judge on the palette.
48 Joseph Wright of Derby in Carey 1809 [**1658**], 20; Farington 1978 [**1033**], 16 June 1798.
49 Landseer 1978 [**1694**], I, 123–7.
50 R. P. Knight, *Edinburgh Review*, XXIII, 1814, 292.
51 Bouvier 1828 [**1655**], 165–7, 249; see also Paillot de Montabert 1829 [**281**], VII, 390.
52 Redon 1979 [**1718**], 156. For Fantin's palette, *Fantin-Latour*, 1982 [**1668**], 56. For a 'Wagnerian' dimension to Seurat's divisionism, Smith 1991 [**1729**], 26–8.
53 See p. 156 and Van Gogh 1958 [**1626**], Letter 507, which shows that Vincent felt Wagner's problem was the subdivision of tones.
54 Pennell 1908 [**1710**], II, 25, 231, 274f. The reconstruction by Lane and Steinitz 1942 [**1695**], 25 is not reliable.
55 'Technical Notes', *The Portfolio*, VI, 1875, 111. See also Morley Fletcher 1936 [**1707**], 37.
56 Delacroix 1923 [**1663**], 75; see also *Journal*, 21 August 1850: 'My freshly arranged palette, brilliant with the contrast of colours, is enough to kindle my enthusiasm' (ed. Joubin 1950 [**1664**], I, 392, not in 1980 edn).
57 One of the first records of a palette set for a specific painting is that for Louis de Planet's copy of Delacroix's *Jewish Wedding at Algiers* (1841). Planet stressed that Delacroix did not want his colours and pre-mixed tones to be blended much on the palette (Planet 1928 [**1571**], 388f). Planet also gave a precise account of the 11 mixtures Delacroix made up for some work in the Library of the Palais Bourbon in 1843 (435f).

58 Louvre, Cabinet de Dessins, *Autographes de Delacroix* (C. D. A. Boite 4).
59 Piot 1931 [**1714**], 2. One of the most detailed reconstructions of a Delacroix palette is in Lane and Steinitz 1942 [**1695**], 23.
60 Huet 1911 [**1682**], 229.
61 Piot 1931 [**1714**]; Rouart 1945 [**1723**], 46 says that Degas's enthusiasm had been aroused by hearing the many descriptions of palettes in Delacroix's *Journal*, which was read to him by his maid. Gigoux 1885 [**1672**], 80 mentions photographs of these 'dessins de la palette', which were able to pick up the 'colorations', underlining their tonal character.
62 Blanc 1876 [**1437**], 66f.
63 Piot 1931 [**1714**], 67–8.
64 Thénot 1847 [**1732**], 54–8.
65 See the paintings in *Chardin* 1979, [**1659**], nos 30, 123, 125 and in the Hammer collection. The revival of interest in Chardin in 19th-century French still-life painting has been analysed by McCoubrey 1964 [**1700**], 39–53.
66 G. Courbet *L'Atelier du Peintre* (1855, Paris, Musée d'Orsay); A. Stevens *The Painter and his Model* (1855, Baltimore, Walters Art Gallery).
67 For Moreau, see the loaded palette preserved in his museum in Paris (Mathieu 1977 [**1703**], 223); for Ensor, Haeserts 1957 [**1676**], 22, 98, 141, 166; for Burne-Jones, see his portrait of 1898 by P. Burne-Jones, London, National Portrait Gallery; for Sargent *An Artist in his Studio* (1904), Boston (Bellony-Rewald and Peppiatt 1983 [**1652**], 32); for Corinth *Self-Portrait with White Smock* (1918), Cologne, Wallraf-Richartz Museum; *Self-Portrait at the Easel* (1919), Berlin, National Galerie; *Self-Portrait with Palette* (1923), Stuttgart, Staatsgalerie; the palettes in each have a different arrangement. Corinth was the author of a handbook, *Das Erlernen der Malerei* (3rd edn 1920), which I have not seen.
68 Robert 1891 [**1722**], 84f.
69 For Sargent's portrait, House 1986 [**1681**], 140. See also Renoir's 1875 portrait of Monet, repr. in col. in Moffett 1986 [**1705**], 185.
70 For Renoir's *Bazille at his Easel* (1867) Callen 1982 [**1450**], 50–53; see also Bazille's self-portrait of 2 years earlier, Chicago Art Institute (Kaufmann 1974 [**1687**], no. 203); J.-B. Guillaumin *Self-Portrait* (1878), Amsterdam, Rijksmuseum Vincent van Gogh.
71 Shiff 1984 [**1726**], 206 gives this palette as (from the thumb-hole) lead white, chrome or zinc yellow, vermilion, alizarin crimson, ultramarine blue, emerald green. Pissarro's palette of the 1890s was essentially the same except that the alizarin was now madder, the ultramarine might be cobalt, and emerald was now Veronese green (Rewald 1973 [**1719**], 590).
72 W. von Schadow *Self-Portrait with his brother Rudolf and Thorwaldsen* (c. 1815/8, Berlin (East), National Galerie). I have not been able to see Schadow's article, 'Meine Gedanken über eine folgerichtige Ausbildung des Malers', *Berliner Kunstblatt*, September 1828, but from its title it sounds as though the palette arrangement may have some theoretical weight.
73 Richardson et al. 1982 [**1721**], 103.
74 Paillot de Montabert 1829 [**281**], IX, 184–8.
75 Libertat Hundertpfund (? a pseudonym), 1849 [**1683**], pl. 2 and p. 26.
76 W. I. Homer, 'Notes on Seurat's Palette' in Broude 1978 [**1443**], 117.
77 Signac (1935) in Homer 1970 [**1517**], 151. The palette held by Signac in a *c.* 1883 photograph seems to be tonal (*Gazette des Beaux-Arts* 6ᵉ pér. XXXVI, 1949, 98). An amusing pointillist palette with an apparently random arrangement is in Theo van Rysselberghe's *Portrait of Anna Boch* (*c.* 1889, Springfield, MA, Museum of Fine Arts).
78 Vibert argued that this palette, which was devised to make the location of complementary contrasts easier, would not serve all the time because of the impurities in pigments (Vibert 1892 [**1734**], 56). The first French edn of his work was published in 1891, but he seems to have been teaching at the École before that. Robert 1891 [**1722**], 77ff states that Vibert gave his course on technique 'cette année', but I have not been able to check the 1878 edition to see if he was already mentioned then. For Vibert's dislike of the Impressionists or 'éclatists', see his short story, *The Delights of Art*, *Century Magazine*, XXIX, 1895/6, 940–1.
79 For Monet's late palette of about 8 colours, including yellow-ochre and plus white, Gimpel 1927 [**1673**], 174. Renoir's late palette was similar: see the portrait of him by Albert André in the Art Institute of Chicago which shows a palette of 7 colours running from white to dark blue, and also including yellow-ochre (Kaufmann 1974 [**1687**], no. 249). In the most cogent attack on the spectral palette, the Scottish artist and curator D. S. McColl argued that the Impressionists had not restricted themselves to the 3 primaries, 'and if the number three is exceeded, there is no reason in theory for sticking at six rather than sixty or six hundred' ('*On the spectral palette and optical mixture*' in McColl 1902 [**1699**], 167).
80 Vollard 1959 [**1736**], 223.
81 Guichetau 1976 [**1675**], 116, n. 164. For the two palettes, (Sérusier 1950 [**1725**], 119–22, 169, and espec. Boyle-Turner 1983 [**1656**], 151–2.
82 Matisse 1972 [**1702**], 46, n. 9.
83 Two of the five or so Matisse palettes in the Musée Matisse, Nice, have been reproduced in col. in *Les Chefs d'Oeuvre du Musée Matisse et les Matisses de Matisse*, Tokyo, 1987/8 (catalogue by N. Watkins); another is in Moscow, Pushkin Museum. A self-portrait with palette (1918) is reproduced in col. in Watkins 1984 [**1737**], 148. Two descriptions of his palette were given by Matisse in 1923 (Moreau-Vauthier 1923, [**1706**], 30, repr. by Morse 1923 [**1708**], 26: 12 colours) and 1935 (*Encyclopédie Française* 1935 [**1666**], XVI: 17 colours).
84 P. Klee *Tagebuch* 1957 [**1691**], March 1910 §873.
85 Kandinsky 1982 [**1686**], I, 156–7. Already in the late 1890s, when they were both pupils of the Munich painter Franz Stück, Klee had noticed how closely Kandinsky examined his palette (F. Klee 1962 [**1690**], 5). A late Kandinsky palette has been reproduced in col. in Kandinsky I, 1980 [**1685**], pl. 28. Its arrangement is hard to recognize.
86 A loaded palette used by van Gogh at the end of his life at Auvers is now in the Louvre (Rewald 1978 [**1720**], 376). For reproductions of palettes in the self-portraits from 1885–89, Erpel 1964 [**1667**], 1, 31, 39, 40.
87 Piot 1931 [**1714**], 63, 82f. On Vandyke brown (Cassel Earth), whose name does not pre-date the 18th century, Harley 1982 [**1504**], 149f.
88 *Le Courier Francais*, 15 January 1888, cit. Welsh-Ovcharov 1976 [**1738**], 197; see also ibid., 220.
89 Vibert 1892 [**1734**], 63.

11 Colours of the Mind

1 Newton 1730 [**1095**], bk. I, pt. II, prop. III, prob. I. The 'assistant' first made his appearance as 'other judges' in Newton's Cambridge Lectures of 1669, and as a 'friend' in his letter to the Royal Society in 1675 (Shapiro I, 1984 [**1603**], 538f).
2 Newton 1730 [**1095**], bk. I, pt. II, prop. VII, theor. V.
3 The most vigorous early attack on Newton for ignoring the knowledge of colours so manifest in painters and dyers was by the French Jesuit inventor of the 'ocular harpsichord', Louis-Bertrand Castel (see Castel 1739 [**1783**], espec. 807; and for his instrument, Ch. 13). Probably the fullest account of the early work on subjective colours is Plateau 1878 [**1922**]. One important source not mentioned by Plateau is B. Castelli *Discorso sopra la vista* (1639): see Ariotti 1973 [**1746**], 4ff.
4 Petrini 1815 [**1917**], 1f. His reference is to the 1651 edition of Leonardo's *Trattato* §§328, 332. Petrini had already discussed coloured shadows in 1807 [**1916**], and he was something of an authority on ancient painting (see Petrini 1821–2 [**1918**]). The widespread 18th-century interest in 'accidental' colours is suggested by the long treatment of them in Diderot and d'Alembert's *Encyclopédie* [**1805**], Suppl. II, 1776, I, 636–41. For an early 19th-century instance of a painter, Caspar David Friedrich, demonstrating a contrast effect to a scientist, Carl Gustav Carus, Friedrich 1968 [**1039**], 203.
5 Petrini 1815 [**1917**], 51f.
6 Lairesse 1778 [**1539**], 118, 123. Lairesse also advised students to take detailed colour-notes of the juxtaposition of colours and tones, and their strengths, when studying the Old Masters (284–5). His book was published in five Dutch editions between 1707 and 1740, in French in 1787, in German in 1728 and 1784 and in English in 1738 and 1778, as well as in 19th-century editions in several languages. It has been discussed by Kaufmann III, 1955–7 [**1865**], 153–96. For Lairesse's own painting, D. P. Snoep, 'Classicism and history painting in the late seventeenth century' in Blankert el al. 1980 [**1764**], 237–45.
7 De Piles 1708 [**1921**], 271–2.
8 Oudry 1844 [**1908**], 39. For Largillière, ibid., 42f. It is tempting to think that the publication of this lecture in 1844 stimulated Courbet to paint a white vase on a white napkin, a task so difficult that it took 50 sessions (Courthion 1950[**1794**], II, 61). For the enthusiastic reception of Oudry's *Duck*, *J.-B. Oudry, 1686–1755*, Paris, Grand Palais, 1982/3, no. 152.
9 C. N. Cochin (1780), cit. Conisbee 1986 [**1790**], 59.
10 *Claude Joseph Vernet* ... 1976 [**1972**], Appendix. This 'letter' was first published in 1817, and reprinted in Cassagne 1886 [**1784**], 142 ff, used by Van Gogh. Delacroix (1980 [**1026**], 881), attributed this perception about greens to Constable.
11 Purkinje 1918 [**1924**], 118f.
12 P. de la Hire, *Dissertation sur les differens accidens de la Vuë*, I, v (1685), cit. Baxandall 1985 [**1755**], 90.
13 For Northcote, Fletcher 1901 [**1817**], 217–18; for Turner, Gage 1969 [**217**], 206. The engraver John Burnet complained that the engravers' habit of looking at pictures in twilight in order to 'detect' the light and shade for reproduction caused them to see red and blue in the wrong relationship (Burnet 1845 [**1780**], 23); see also Paillot de Montabert, 1829 [**281**], VII, 394f.
14 Rood 1879 [**306**], 189; see also Laugel 1869 [**1542**], 96; Forichon 1916 [**1818**], 137 (which depends heavily on Rood). For Matisse, Barr 1974 [**1752**], 136. This ignorance is perhaps surprising, since Matisse had been using Rood in his school in 1908 (Flam 1986 [**1816**], 223).
15 Monge 1789 [**1894**], espec. 133–47; for Monge's early work at the École de Génie in the 1770s, Vallée 1821 [**1969**], 349–50, 412f. For a modern account of colour-constancy, Beck 1972 [**1756**], ch. I.
16 Milizia 1781 [**1891**], 107–8. See also Brües 1961 [**1779**], 69–113.
17 Vallée 1821 [**1969**], 302ff.
18 Monge 1820 [**1895**], II, 130–6.
19 Vallée 1821 [**1969**], 304–5, 341, 349f, 374f. Milizia also pointed to the gap between the means of painting and of nature (Milizia 1781 [**1891**], 108).
20 See espec. the conversation 'Eugène Delacroix' recorded in Blanc 1867 [**1437**], 23f, a passage which espec. excited Van Gogh (see van Uitert 1966–7, [**1968**], 106ff). Blanc was also familiar with Monge's *Géométrie descriptive* (Blanc 1867 [**1937**], 600).
21 Delaborde 1984 [**1802**], 133. A slightly different version has been published by Boyer d'Agen 1909, [**1771**], 492; cf. also 487–8. Delaborde ibid., 137 and 152 seem to indicate changes of mind.
22 For their friendship, Naef 1964 [**1904**], 249–63. Ingres described Hittorff's work on polychromy as 'admirable' in a letter of 1851 (cit. Montauban 1980 [**1896**], 86).
23 Sand 1896 [**1130**], 77–9. It is notable that Delacroix thought of 'local' colour as appropriate to the underpainting (*ébauche*), which was transformed by 'accidental' colours in the final finishing (Delacroix 1980 [**1026**], 5 May 1852). Another coloured version of the *Antiochus and Stratonice*, on paper (1866), is at the Musée Fabre in Montpellier (London 1984 [**1877**], 60ff).
24 For the theatre, see espec. Baldassare Orsini, *Della Geometria e prospettiva prattica* (1771), cit. Mariani 1930 [**1885**], 80, who makes a link with 19th-century 'divisionism', although Orsini appealed only to 'buon gusto' and the gradations of nature. The 'pointillism' of the miniature painter was prescribed for flesh and draperies by Mlle Catherine Perrot, *Traité de la mignature* (1693), in Félibien 1725 [**1669**], lxxxv, but without any theoretical discussion: the method was required for using watercolour on an unabsorbent surface such as ivory. For a very clear account of the 'mosaic' of dots in Chardin's technique, Bachaumont 1750 in Ingrams 1970 [**1857**], 27.
25 Mottez 1911 [**1900**], 173. For 17th-century usages, Briganti et al. 1987 [**1775**], 237–8 (Annibale Carracci and Pietro da Cortona); Camesasca 1966 [**1782**], 271 (Domenichino and Baciccio); Rehfus-Dechêne 1982 [**1581**], 57, citing J. S. Halle *Werkstätte der heutigen Künste* ... Brandenburg/Leipzig, 1761, I, 313.

26 Purkinje to Goethe, 7 February 1823 in Kruta 1968 [**1869**], 39; dedication to *Beobachtungen und Versuche zur Physiologie der Sinne*, Purkinje 1918 [**1924**], §41.
27 For Harriott, J. A. Lohne in *Dictionary of Scientific Biography*, VI, 125: by measuring the widths of the fringes, Harriott was able to compute the refractive indices of green, orange and red rays. [Digby] 1658 [**1473**], 321, 329. For Hodierna, Serio et al. 1983 [**1953**], 67–8. Rainbow-coloured fringes around objects seen through a 'beryll' had already been noticed by Leonardo (Richter 1970 [**118**], I, §288).
28 Goethe 1840 [**1833**], 420. This trans. is reprinted at the end of the best-illustrated English version, ed. Matthaei (Goethe 1971 [**1836**]), although here the supplementary translations by Herb Aach are unreliable. Eastlake's trans. is hereafter referred to as TC.
29 TC [**1833**], §52. The somewhat *risqué* 'diagram' in watercolour reproduced in Goethe 1971 [**1836**], 84 may be based on this experience.
30 A number of substantial modern studies have appeared in English: Wells 1967–8 [**1974**], 69–113; Wells 1971 [**1975**], 617–26; Ribe 1985 [**1930**], 315–335; Burwick 1986 [**1781**]; G. Böhme, 'Is Goethe's theory of color science?' and D. C. Sepper, 'Goethe against Newton: towards saving the phenomenon' in Amrine et al. 1987 [**1742**], 147–73, 175–93; Sepper 1988 [**1952**]; Duck 1988 [**1807**], 507–19. For a brief survey of the later reception of the *Farbenlehre* from Helmholtz to Heisenberg, Gögelein 1972 [**1838**], 178–200, and Mandelkow 1980 [**1883**], 174–200.
31 Goethe, *Gespräche mit Eckermann*, 15 May 1831.
32 Young is a particularly interesting omission from Goethe's reading list, since the reviewer of the *Farbenlehre* in *Gilberts Annalen der Physik*, XXXIX, 1811 [**1829**], 220 had drawn attention to the link between Young's ideas in a paper of 1802, and Goethe's own. The poet's professional acquaintance, the opthalmologist Karl Himly, had been in touch with Young, and it was his copy of the 1802 paper that was passed on to Goethe (Ruppert 1958 [**1937**], no. 5295). The physicist Thomas Seebeck told Goethe of Young's work, but his professed lack of comprehension may have deterred Goethe from investigating further (Seebeck to Goethe, 25 April 1812 in Bratranek 1874 [**1774**], II, 318f). Young for his part attacked the *Farbenlehre* savagely and anonymously in the *Quarterly Review* (X, 1814, 427–8) concluding that it was 'a striking example of the perversion of the human faculties'. For Seebeck's mention of this review to Goethe in 1814, and the poet's neglect of it until more than a year later, Nielsen 1989 [**1905**], 163–4.
33 TC [**1833**], §160. For Young's work in 1801, Wells 1971 [**1975**], 618; but Ernst Brücke, investigating the phenomenon in the 1850s, attributed the renewed interest in it – although he noted that it had been discussed as far back as Aristotle – to Goethe (Brücke 1866 [**1446**], 94; and cf. id. 1852 [**1778**], 530–49).
34 See Müller 1826 [**1901**], ch. VII, and id. 1840 [**1902**], II, 292 (more critical of Goethe). Their personal relationship has been discussed by Scherer 1936 [**1944**]. For Goethe's relationship to Hering's and later researches on the perception of colour, Jablonski 1930 [**1858**], 75–81. Hering's view of the primary status of green had been anticipated in TC [**1833**] §802. Goethe's important part in the early study of colour-blindness has been discussed by Jaeger 1979 [**1859**], 27–38. For an American summary of his effect on the study of physiology, Boring 1942 [**1767**], 112–19.
35 Schelling III, 1959 [**1942**], 160–1. For his contact with Goethe between 1798 and 1804, Goethe (Leopoldina Ausgabe) 1957 [**225**], II, 3, 1961, xxxiv–xliii (hereafter LA).
36 Schopenhauer 1816 [**1948**]; also id. 1851 [**1949**], II, ch. VII, §103. The correspondence with Goethe between 1815 and 1818 has been gathered by Hübscher 1960 [**1856**], 30–55. See also Borsch 1941 [**1769**], 167–8.
37 Hegel VI, 1927 [**1845**], 175f; IX, 343. On Henning, R. Matthaei in Zastrau 1961 [**1979**], cols 2263–6; Hegel 1935–75 [**1846**], I (1970), 363–4. See also M. J. Petry, 'Hegels Verteidigung von Goethes Farbenlehre gegenüber Newton' in Petry 1987 [**1919**], II, 323–348.
38 TC [**1833**], §851; *Konfession des Verfassers*, in LA [**225**], I, 6, 1957, 416. Ingres was also impressed by this method of working, which he attributed to the Venetians (Boyer d'Agen 1909, [**1771**], 485, 492), and apparently to Raphael: see his *Raphael and the Fornarina* (1814) in the Fogg Museum and his grisaille version of the *Grand Odalisque* (1824/34) in the Metropolitan Museum, New York.
39 For Marat and Kauffmann, Farington 1978–84 [**1033**], 27 October 1793; Brissot 1877 [**1776**], 174; for Marat's view that yellow is the most 'deviable' ray of light and blue the least, see *Découvertes sur la lumière* (1780), cit. *The Monthly Review or Literary Journal*, LXVII, 1782, 294. Goethe's chapter on Marat in LA [**225**], I, 6, 1957, 394 drew attention to this idea.
40 Meyer's now lost painting *Castor and Pollux abducting the Daughters of Leucippus* (1791) was shown at Weimar in 1792 as painted 'according to the new prismatic experiments of Goethe' (LA [**225**], II, 3, 1961, 51). A number of other experimental drawings are mentioned in a Goethe letter of 1793 (ibid., 61). Meyer also interpreted the work of the Old Masters for Goethe: his discussion of the coloured stripes at the bottom of the Roman painting of a wedding (*The Aldobrandini Wedding*) in a letter of 1796, included the suggestion that it was a sort of 'key' to the harmony of the picture itself, and Goethe was particularly excited that the sequence was opposite to that in the rainbow: yellow and blue at the edges and *purpur* in the middle (ibid., 92–3); but this is not the sequence as it appears now (Maiuri 1953 [**1881**], 30).
41 See, e.g., Meyer's help with landscapes exemplifying various types of colour harmony in France in 1792 (LA [**225**], I, 3, 1951, 116–17). Goethe later employed another painter, C. K. Kaaz, to help him with colour techniques (Geller 1961 [**1827**], 17–25).
42 LA [**225**], I, 3, 1951, 437 (1805/6).
43 See *Goethes Werke* [**1835**], XIII, 1954, 157, 196. The article on Jean Baptiste Forestier's methods, 'Neue Art die Mahlerey zu lernen', was published in *Propyläen*, III, 1800 [**1832**], 110ff (repr. 1965, see espec. 824f., 827).
44 Meyer 1799 [**1891**], 156f (repr. 1965, 694f); for the Weimar school, Schenk zu Schweinsberg 1930 [**1943**], 22. See also the conventional programme of colour-study proposed by Goethe in 'Gutachten über die Ausbildung eines jungen Malers' (1798) in *Goethes Werke* [**1835**], XIII, 1954, 132.
45 Scheidig 1958 [**1941**], 491–2.
46 The demand for the *Theory* in Rome is described in a letter to Goethe by C. F. Schlosser, shortly after he mentions the arrival of the Nazarenes there (Schlosser to Goethe 2 September 1811, in Dammann 1930 [**1800**], 54f). Passavant's study of the book in Paris, just before leaving for Rome is mentioned in Cornhill, 1864 [**1793**], I, 56. One of Passavant's companions in Paris was the Berlin painter Wilhelm Wach, who in the 1820s was helping Purkinje to understand the neutralizing effects of complementaries (Purkinje to Goethe, 27 November 1825, in Bratranek 1874 [**1774**], II, 195f).
47 M. Klotz *Gründliche Farbenlehre*, Munich 1816, cit. Rehfus-Dechêne 1982 [**1581**], 88. Goethe had been indirectly in touch with Klotz since 1797 (LA [**225**], II, 6, 1959, 339–405).
48 Beuther 1833 [**1762**]; for Goethe, 8, 57.
49 For the 1840s, Hundertpfund 1849 [**1683**], 41–2; for the 1850s, Bähr 1860 [**1750**], espec. 6f.
50 Runge to his brother Daniel, 7 November 1802 in Runge 1840/1 [**1127**] (*Hinterlassene Schriften*), I, 17 (hereafter HS). These colours were linked to morning, noon, and night, but by January 1803 Runge had come to see red as morning (as in pl. 162) and evening, and blue as characteristic of day (ibid., 32). This Trinitarian interpretation of the primary colours is loosely related to one of Runge's chief spiritual sources, the 17th-century German mystic Jacob Boehme (see Steig 1902 [**1960**], 662 and Mösender 1981 [**1898**], 29f); but Matile (1979 [**1887**], 132) has pointed out that Boehme's 'primary' colours were not confined to three.
51 The fullest study of Runge's theory is now Matile 1979 [**1887**].
52 LA [**225**], I, 4, 1955, 257. See Gage 1979 [**1822**], 61–5. My interpretation differs somewhat from Matile's: see espec. his pp. 219–49.
53 See his draft of a letter to Schelling, 1 February 1810, HS [**1127**], I, 159–60.
54 See Runge to Goethe, 19 April 1808 in Runge 1940 [**1936**], 80–4. Runge had already been experimenting with discmixtures, which he described in a letter to Goethe of 21 November 1807 (ibid., 70–6), and Goethe wrote characteristically to Meyer on December 1 that this was under pressure from the 'Newtonians': 'I really can't explain myself either to him or to others' (Goethe 1919, [**1834**], 201–2).
55 Runge to Klinkowström, 24 February 1809 (HS [**1127**], I, 172). On the *Times of Day* as essentially an expression of the relationship of opacity and transparency, Runge to Ludwig Tieck, 29 March 1805 (ibid., 60–1). See also Rehfus-Dechêne 1982 [**1581**], 116ff.
56 F. von Klinkowström 1815 [**1867**], 195f. For Runge and his copy, A. von Klinkowström 1877 [**1866**], 200f; and for Klinkowström's rather modest assessment of it in 1807, see his letter to Runge in HS [**1127**], II, 344.
57 See Runge's painting of the central group of *Day* (1803, col. pl. in Traeger 1975 [**1149**], no. 285 and pl. 6). For Correggio's gold-ground, Fiorillo II, 1800 [**1815**], 284f, citing the opinion of Benedetto Luti (1666–1724).
58 The colour-circle of Moses Harris (above, p. 172) also represented a solid, running from saturated hues at the circumference to near-white at the centre, but its two-dimensional presentation seems to have prevented its being interpreted in this way. For the later history of the *Farben-Kugel*, Matile 1979 [**1887**], 360, n. 437.
59 Runge to G. Runge, 22 November 1808 (HS [**1127**], II, 372).
60 See Lecture V of 1818, in Gage 1969 [**217**], 206, also 210 (*c.* 1827). In his contribution to Runge's book (59), Steffens had also proposed a scheme of red morning, yellow midday and violet evening.
61 Gage 1969 [**217**], 210.
62 TC [**1833**], §696. Turner's notes have been printed in full in Gage 1984 [**1823**], 34–52. This edn also includes a brief account of Eng. anti-Newtonian thought in the early 19th century.
63 Gage 1984 [**1823**], 49 (TC [**1833**], §821); cf. also 47 (TC §744 and 745). It is notable that Turner's closest imitator, James Baker Pyne, at exactly the same time, and perhaps independently of a reading of Goethe, was publishing an anti-Newtonian account of the production of colours in nature by means of turbid media (Pyne 1846 [**1925**], 243–4, 277).
64 See p. 84 and n. 72.
65 Craig 1821 [**1797**], 173. Craig's edn of Lairesse dates from 1817.
66 Howitt 1886 [**1855**], I, 81. Pforr spoke of the innate character of each colour, and was careful to specify only those people who have a free choice in the way they dress. He applied his ideas in his 'friendship' painting, *Shulamith and Maria* (1809, Schweinfurt, Schäfer collection). An early attempt to base the moral meaning of colour on anthropological considerations is J. H. Bernardin de Saint-Pierre's 'Des Couleurs' in *Études de la Nature* (1784) in Bernardin de Saint-Pierre 1818 [**1760**], IV, 78–85, which reached the modern conclusion that black, white and red are the colours with the strongest cultural resonance.
67 Gage 1969 [**217**], 206 . Turner may be attacking Craig as well as Lairesse, since the watercolourist had been lecturing at the Royal Institution for many years, and his ideas were widely ridiculed at the Royal Academy (Farington 1978–84 [**1033**], 27 February, 14–15 March, 3 June 1806, 17 October 1811).
68 Oxford, Ashmolean Museum, MS AWC, I, d, folios 46r–47v.
69 Humbert de Superville 1827 [**906**], 9–10; Stafford 1979 [**1957**], 62, 77 n. 172, which cites an unpublished essay, *De la valeur morale des couleurs* (1828).
70 Stafford 1979 [**1957**], 74 n. 16.
71 *Vier Elemente*, in LA [**225**], I, 3, 1951, 507. For the *Temperamentrose*, 387–8.
72 Schiller to L. Tieck, in Landsberger 1931 [**1873**], 156–7.
73 See P. Schmidt 1965 [**1947**], 69–72.
74 Eighteenth-century French opponents of Newton's theory had included L.-B. Castel, J. Gautier d'Agoty and J.-P. Marat, all of whom were studied by Goethe. For the Romantic period, see, e.g., Déal 1827 [**1801**], which put a good deal of emphasis on the study of colour in landscape. For temperaments and colour in painting, Pernety 1757 [**1914**], 69, where melancholics were said to incline towards a yellow or greenish-grey tone,

phlegmatics towards a chalky one, and sanguine temperaments, not surprisingly, towards a liveliness in painting flesh.

75 The Swiss aesthetician David Sutter seems to have been the first in France to introduce Goethe's ideas into the discussion of colour for painters: see Sutter 1858 [**1964**], based on lectures at the École (262–3 for Goethe's complementary diagram, 271 for colours and moods). Sutter's equivalents in 1880 (cit. Homer 1970 [**1517**], 44), were not precisely the same as Goethe's. See also Faivre 1862 [**1810**], 49 on the rejection of Goethe's theory early in the century, and 166–233 for a summary of it. Faivre owed much to Eastlake's English translation of 1840, which, as he pointed out (344), had been directed at artists. For Blanc, 1867 [**1436**], 600, on complementary colours, citing Eckermann's *Gespräche*. An attempt to suggest the Delacroix knew Goethe's theory (Trapp 1971 [**1966**], 330–1) is unconvincing.

76 Blanc 1876 [**1437**], 62.

77 HS [**1127**], II, 44; for Forestier see n. 43.

78 Van Gogh 1958 [**1626**], no. 371 (hereafter CL). For the borrowing, CL R.48, for van Rappard, Brouwer et al. 1974 [**1777**]. Blanc had underlined Delacroix's instinctive command of the scientific laws of colour in 1876 [**1437**], 62–4, and another of Vincent's favourite books, Gigoux 1885 [**1672**], 184 had repeated this view. For his reading of Gigoux, CL [**1626**], 399, 401, 403, R.58.

79 Cassagne 1886 [**1784**], 22, 29; see CL [**1626**], 146 for Cassagne's book and van Rappard. Vincent summarized Cassagne on black and grey in a letter to Theo of 31 July 1882 (CL 221), and he returned to the question in 1885 (CL 371). See also CL B6 (June 1888) on black and white as complementaries. Another favourite book was Bracquemond 1885 [**1772**], a study by an etcher and ceramist close to the Impressionists but suspicious of their emphasis on colour. He rejected both Chevreul and Helmholtz as guides, and called upon scientists to establish an objective grey-scale (46–7, 244). Vincent read this book several times in 1885 and 1886 (CL 424, 456, R.58). For Bracquemond's views in general, Bouillon 1970 [**1770**], 161–77; Kane 1983 [**1864**], 118–21.

80 Cassagne 1886 [**1784**], 270–85. Only summer was not given a pair of colours, being regarded by Cassagne as rather the draughtsman's than the painter's season. See Van Gogh to Theo (?August) 1884 (CL [**1626**], 372).

81 He paraphrased Blanc 1867 [**1436**], 598 in CL [**1626**], 401 as 'the great principles which Delacroix believed in'.

82 Roskill 1970 [**1934**], 266–7.

83 *Post-Impressionism* ... 1979/80 [**1923**], no. 80.

84 There is some dispute about the date of their meeting: Rewald (1978 [**1927**], 502) proposed the autumn of 1886, but without documentation; Cooper (1983 [**1792**], 17) proposed a possible meeting through Bernard before April 1887, but the most generally accepted date is November 1887, after Gauguin's return from Martinique. What is clear is that they were closely associated by this time: Gauguin owned a number of Vincent's Paris paintings (Cooper ibid., 27–8).

85 Revised from Van Wyck Brooks's trans. in Nochlin 1966 [**1906**], 167. The status of the so-called 'papier de Gauguin' is still unclear: Fénéon in 1914 reported a general belief that it was by Gauguin himself, although he was undecided (Fénéon 1970 [**1481**], 282). The evidence has been reviewed most fully by Roskill 1970 [**1934**], 267–8 and by Herbert et al. 1991 [**1514**], 397–8. Some of the ideas in the *papier* are very close to Blanc's description of oriental practice in 1867 [**1436**], 606f.

86 See his note on Vincent of 1894 and a letter to Fontainas of September 1902 in Gauguin 1974 [**1824**], 294. See also the remarks to Daniel de Monfreid in Chassé 1969 [**1787**], 50.

87 Amsterdam, Rijksmuseum Vincent van Gogh (F.371). This process of heightening the contrasts has been discussed by Fred Orton in the most important study of Van Gogh and the Japanese print (Orton 1971 [**1907**], 10–11); for the cases of the other copies, *Van Gogh à Paris*, 1988 [**1971**], no. 62.

88 Gauguin to Van Gogh, 22 September 1988, in Gauguin I, 1984 [**1825**], 232. The blue/yellow of the angel is close to the costumes interpolated by Vincent into Hiroshige's design; (col. pl. and documentation in *Gauguin* 1989 [**1826**], no. 50).

89 Gauguin 1974 [**1824**], 24. See also his account to Van Gogh of the colour of another wrestling subject of 1888, *Boys Wrestling*, whose palette is none the less far more subdued (*Gauguin* 1989 [**1826**], no. 48; Gauguin I, 1984 [**1825**], 201).

90 F.476. For a col. pl. and a discussion of the results of the recent cleaning, Kōdera 1990 [**1868**], 56ff and pl. IV.

91 F.486. Even the rather dry technique on an absorbent ground is closely related to Gauguin (Laugui 1947 [**1875**], 37). Émile Bernard, Gauguin's companion at Pont Aven and one of the chief models for Vincent's 'cloisonnist' style, claimed much later that Vincent's interest in paintings with a single all-over colour tonality had been aroused by his (Bernard's) introducing him to the work of Louis Anquetin in Paris (Bernard 1934 [**1759**], 113–14; for Anquetin, *Van Gogh á Paris* 1988 [**1971**], nos 71–3).

92 Quoted in French (*nuance innommable violacée*) in CL [**1626**], 428; Van Gogh attributes this to Silvestre, but its source is Bracquemond 1885 [**1772**], 85f (*une teinte bistrée, violacée du nuance innommable*).

93 Bracquemond 1885 [**1772**], 55. See also Vibert 1902 [**1734**], 72. For the importance of naming to colour-memory, Bornstein 1976 [**1768**], 269–79.

94 Bracquemond 1885 [**1772**], 244.

95 F. Melzer rather misses the point of this dilemma when he speaks on the one hand of the neo-medieval 'strict codification' of colour in Symbolist verse, and on the other of a quasi-musical removal of a 'prescribed signifié' (Melzer 1978 [**1890**], 259).

96 See the drawing, *Un nuit à Vaugirard* (1881) in Gauguin I, 1984 [**1825**], pl. II.

97 The drawing for *Sailing Boats at Asnières* (1887, F.1409) is inscribed with a list of some 15 colours, only three of them the names of pigments. On the other hand, the *Still-Life with Coffee-Pot* (F.410) was described to Theo (CL [**1626**], 489) in ordinary terms of blue, orange, red and so on, but in a description to the painter Bernard (CL B.5) one of the blues became 'cobalt' and in the accompanying sketch there are 'chromes 1, 2 and 3', 'citron vert pale', 'bleu de roi', bleu myosotys' and 'mine orange'.

98 For Gauguin's copy, Roskill 1970 [**1934**], 267; Blanc 1867 [**1436**], facing 599, from Ziegler 1850 [**1980**], 199. The derivation is not acknowledged, but Blanc does cite Ziegler's book 603f (from Ziegler 1850 [**1980**], 230). Ziegler reprinted his star in 1852 [**355**], 16. His reference to cadmium yellow-orange must be one of the earliest to that pigment, which did not become generally available until the mid-1840s (Feller I, 1986 [**1811**], 67–8).

99 *Diverses choses* (1896/8) in Gauguin 1974 [**1824**], 179. The fullest treatment of Gauguin's colour is Hess 1981 [**1852**], 50–68. For *Manao Tupapau*, *Gauguin* 1989 [**1826**], no. 154.

100 Féré 1887 [**1812**], 43–6. He also refers to glazing maniacs' cells with blue or violet glass. The therapeutic effects of colour were alluded to in the Romantic period by Edward Dayes, a watercolour painter with an unbalanced personality, who committed suicide (Dayes 1805 [**1024**], 307–8n). For a brief history of Chromotherapy, Howat 1938 [**1854**], 1; and for two recent surveys of the subject, Anderson 1979 [**1743**]; Kaiser, 1984 [**1862**], 29–36 (highly critical).

101 e.g. Raehlmann 1902 [**1112**], 37; Goldstein 1942 [**1839**], 150; Heiss 1960 [**1848**], 381–2.

102 Malkowsky 1899 [**1882**], Beilage, 2. See also Berger 1911 [**1758**], 140; Friedländer 1916 [**1820**], 88; id. 1917–18 [**1821**], 141ff. Two artists who adopted Goethe's theory for a period were Arthur Segal (see his *Lichtprobleme der bildende Kunst* 1925 [**1951**] n.p.) and Auguste Herbin (see his *L'Art non-figuratif-non-objectif* 1949 [**1850**], espec. 23ff). For the importance of Goethe's physiological ideas, J. H. Schmidt 1932 [**1946**], 109–24.

103 Gordon 1968 [**1840**], 16. For Goethe's impact on Kirchner, *Goethe, Kirchner, Wiegers* ... 1985 [**1837**].

104 For poetry, Mantz 1957 [**1884**], 198–237, espec. 209; Motekat 1961 [**1899**], espec. 43–6. The freely-moving colours of Expressionist painting have been briefly characterized by L. Dittmann in *Künstler de Brücke* 1980 [**1870**], 45. For the debate on colour and association, Cohn 1894 [**1789**], 565f, Müller-Freienfels 1907 [**1903**], 241ff; Stefănescu-Goangă 1912 [**1959**], 284–335, espec. 332. All these studies refer to Goethe.

105 Brass 1906 [**1773**], 120. Brass stood in some ill-defined relationship to a group of Munich decorative painters (see his obituary by A. Piening in *Technische Mitteilungen für Malerei*, XXXII, 1915/16, 157–9; see also Richter 1938 [**1931**], 7–10).

106 According to an associate of Kandinsky's in these years, he did not engage in detail with Goethe's *Theory* until 1912, and then in the hope of substantiating Steiner's interpretation of it (Harms 1963 [**1844**], 36, 41, 90). Steiner's contact with Kandinsky has been discussed by Ringbom 1970 [**1932**], 79, 81–2, and the notes from Steiner's *Lucifer-Gnosis* published by Ringbom in Zweite 1982 [**1981**], 102–5, and 89, fig. 1. Steiner had edited the volume of Goethe's *Farbenlehre* for Kürschner's *Deutsche National-Literatur* (*Goethes Werke* XXV: *Naturwissenschaftliche Schriften*, III, 1891), with a polemical introduction and notes which stress that it had found 'general recognition' among artists (317, §900n).

107 Kandinsky 1982 [**1686**], I, 159.

108 Ringbom 1970 [**1932**], 86 and pl. 23; Kandinsky 1982 [**1686**], I, 178. The change of red to yellow was probably affected by Steiner's transmission of Goethe's fundamental 'primary' pair.

109 For example Scheffler 1901 [**1940**], 187; cit. Kandinsky 1982 [**1686**], I, 161n; Gérome-Maësse (Alexis Mérodack-Jeanneau) 1907 [**1828**], 657, cit. Kandinsky ibid., I, 196n. See Fineberg 1979 [**1813**], 221–46 for Kandinsky's links with Gérome-Maësse.

110 Hering 1878 [**1851**], 110: 'Every simple colour has a simple colour, every mixed colour a mixed colour as its opposite'. Cf. Kandinsky 1982 [**1686**], I, 189. For Hering, however, green was a simple, not a mixed colour.

111 Wundt 1902–3 [**1977**], II, 329; cf. Kandinsky 1982 [**1686**], I, 174–89.

112 Kandinsky 1982 [**1686**], I, 179n.

113 Marc to Macke, 12 December 1910, in Macke 1964 [**1879**], 28–30. It is not clear what Marc meant by 'spectral analysis' in this case. In the 1920s Kandinsky considered yellow to be masculine and blue femine (Kandinsky 1984 [**1863**], 52–3).

114 Although the spiritual value of blue and the brutality of red were a commonplace of Theosophical writing, the attempt by Moffitt 1985 [**1893**], 107ff to trace Marc's views to this source seems over-strained.

115 HS [**1127**], I, 164.

116 *Ausstellung* 1906 [**1747**], I, xix.

117 Stefănescu-Goangă 1912 [**1959**], 320. Here several subjects found yellow to be gentle and feminine, while red was serious and masculine.

118 Allesch 1925 [**1741**], 1–91, 215–81.

119 It should be emphasized that the question of colour-preference among Europeans is still a vexed one, although many writers seem to think it is settled. The standard order of preference for single colours: blue, red, green, violet, orange, yellow, has been proposed by the largest-scale study to date, Eysenck 1941 [**1809**], 385–94, based on 21,060 cases, but very few of them tested by Eysenck himself. For colour-pairs, Granger 1952 [**1841**], 778–80. For a recent study of single colours which places blue and yellow at top and bottom but re-arranges the intermediate hues, McManus et al. 1981 [**1878**], 651–6; and for a survey of the literature, Ball 1965 [**1751**], 441ff. The most recent and widespread system of psychological testing with colour, the Lüscher Test, also uses notions of preference (see the Eng. pocket version, Scott 1971 [**1950**]): it has been criticized as too abstract: see Heimendahl 1961 [**1847**], 185–9; Pickford 1971 [**1920**], 151–4; Lakowski and Melhuish 1973 [**1872**], 486–9. Nevertheless the Swiss Neo-Constructivist Karl Gerstner has included the Test among the several useful systems available to artists, and Lüscher has admired his work (Stierlin 1981 [**1961**], 10, 164ff).

120 Cohn 1894 [**1789**], 601. For the *Almanac*, Lankheit 1974 [**1874**].

121 Kandinsky 1982 [**1686**], I, 372.

122 The best historical study is still Mahling 1926 [**1880**], 165–257, with an extensive bibliography. Interestingly, Mahling criticized Kandinsky for taking too much on trust (256–7). See also the popular account by Binet 1892 [**1763**], 586ff. The topic seems to have gone out of fashion among psychologists in the 1940s, perhaps because of the inconclusive results (Barron-Cohen et al. 1987 [**1754**], 761);

but it is discussed in some detail by Marks 1978 [**1886**], 83–90.
123 Scheffler 1901 [**1940**], 187; Gérome-Maësse 1907 [**1828**], which drew largely on the most extensive early collection of cases, Suarez de Mendoza 1890 [**1963**]. For Kandinsky's notes from a synaesthetic study by F. Freudenberg, Ringbom in Zweite 1982 [**1981**], 93, fig. 7; cf. Kandinsky 1982 [**1686**], I, 158n. For Schlegel, 'Betrachtungen über Metrik' in Schlegel I, 1962 [**1945**], 199–200: his analogies are rather symbolic than synaesthetic, as is the interpretation of Rimbaud's 'Voyelles' by Starkie 1961 [**1958**], 163ff.
124 Gérome-Maësse 1907 [**1828**], 656, (Basque was another fruitful language mentioned here).
125 The radically reductive linguistics of Velimir Khlebnikov and its relationship to the radical abstraction of Malevich has been studied by Crone 1978 [**1798**], espec. 147ff. For an English account of Khlebnikov's version of *audition colorée*, Cooke 1987 [**1791**], 84–5. Malevich was also a friend of the phoneticist Roman Jakobson (Barron and Tuchman 1980 [**1753**], 18; Padrta 1979 [**1909**], 40–1); and Jakobson continued to be interested in *audition colorée* in the context of phonetics (Jakobson 1968 [**1860**], 82–4; Jakobson and Halle 1975 [**1861**], 45n). See also Vallier 1975 [**1970**], 284ff. In the 1920s it was the Russian art-workshops which modelled themselves most closely on laboratories of experimental psychology and gave special attention, for example, to relationships between colour and form (Lodder 1983 [**1876**], 125ff; see also Belaiew-Exemplarsky, of the Moscow Psychological Institute, 1925 [**1757**], espec. 425).
126 Kandinsky 1984 [**1863**], 230 (1928).
127 TC xxxvii–xxxix (Goethe 1971 [**1836**], 213–14). See also p. 202 above. The poet Jules Laforgue used similar terms in his account of Impressionism in 1883: 'The Impressionist sees and renders nature as it is – that is wholly in the vibration of colour. No drawing, light, modelling, perspective, or chiaroscuro ...' (cit. Bomford et al. 1990 [**1766**], 84).
128 See *An Essay towards a New Theory of Vision*, 1709, §CLVIII. The 18th-century debate on the role of mind in shaping the visible world has been discussed in detail by Morgan 1977 [**1897**], espec. 70ff. on Condillac.
129 Perry 1927 [**1915**], 120.
130 Ruskin 1857 [**1938**], I, §5n: 'The whole technical power of painting depends on our recovery of what may be called the *innocence of the eye*; that is to say, of a sort of childish perception of these flat stains of colour, merely as such, without consciousness of what they signify, – as a blind man would see them if suddenly gifted with sight'. For the *Elements* in France, Signac 1964 [**1607**], 117. Monet is reported as saying in 1900 that 'ninety-per-cent of the theory of Impessionism is ... in "Elements of Drawing"'. (Dewhurst 1911 [**1804**], 296). See in general Autret 1965 [**1748**], 77ff.
131 Ruskin 1906 [**1939**], 21–2. Ruskin's view of Turner's eagle-eye has been confirmed by an analysis of his spectacles, preserved by Ruskin, and now in the Ashmolean Museum in Oxford (Trevor-Roper 1988 [**1967**], 92).
132 For the *Poplars*, Perry 1927 [**1915**], 121; for *Rouen Cathedral*, Monet to Alice Hoschedé, 29 March 1893, in Wildenstein 1979 [**1976**], 273.
133 Signac noted in 1894 'no, M. Monet, you are not a naturalist ... Bastien-Lepage [an essentially tonal painter] is much closer to nature than you! Trees in nature are not blue, people are not voilet ...' (cit. House 1986 [**1853**], 133). Only a decade earlier critics of the Impressionists had been prepared to claim that their superabundance of violet was perfectly natural: see the texts assembled by Reutersvärd 1950 [**1584**], 106–10. House 1986 has by far the fullest discussion of these technical questions, and on 110 he underlines the painter's reputation for being unconcerned about theory; see also Bernard 1934 [**1759**], 111–12. Monet's knowlege of complementary contrast is shown by an interview of 1888 (cit. Bomford et al. 1990 [**1766**], 88).
134 'Human Vision', 1855, cit. Pastore 1978 [**1913**], 357.
135 Helmholtz 1901 [**1849**], espec. 242, 263–4. These lectures were translated into French in 1869. See also Pastore 1973 [**1911**], 194–6.
136 Cézanne to Bernard, 23 October 1906 (Cézanne 1976 [**1786**], 317). See also the remarks recorded by Bernard: 'in painting there are two things, the eye and the brain; each must help the other: we must work towards their mutual development, at the eye by its vision of nature and the brain by the logic of organized sensations which give the means of expression' (cit. Doran 1978 [**1806**], 36).
137 The only scientific book recorded among is effects was an 18th-century textbook, although he may have known Regnier 1865 [**1580**], and books on anatomy and on perspective (Reff 1960 [**1926**], 303–9; de Beucken 1955 [**1761**], 304). For theory, Cézanne to Émile Solari, 2 September 1897 and to the painter Charles Camoin 22 February 1903 (Cézanne 1976 [**1786**], 260, 294) and Camoin to Matisse 2 December 1905 (Giraudy 1971 [**1831**], 9–10).
138 Gasquet 1921 in Doran 1978 [**1806**], 110. Doran is rightly cautious about the authenticity of this conversation, as recorded by the wordy Gasquet. For Helmholtz and Kant, Pastore 1974 [**1912**], espec. 376–86.
139 Giraud 1902 [**1830**], 188. Taine has been cited in the context of Cézanne by Shiff 1978 [**1955**], espec. 339, but without exploring his implications for Cézanne's style.
140 Taine 1870 [**1965**], I, 76–85. For Lecoq, Chu 1982 [**1788**], 278–80.
141 Taine 1870 [**1965**], II, 86ff. For Taine and Helmholtz, Pastore, 1971 [**1910**], 179–82.
142 Taine 1870 [**1965**], II, 122. For the use of *tache* in French art-criticism from the 1860s to the 1880s, Bomford et al. 1990 [**1766**], 92–3.
143 Doran 1978 [**1806**], 36.
144 Cézanne to Bernard, 11 April 1904 (Cézanne 1976 [**1786**], 301).
145 For seeing like Cézanne, Frankl; 1975 [**1819**], 125–30; Damisch 1982 [**1799**], 42.
146 A good example of this sort of beginning is the *Mont Sainte-Victoire* seen from Les Lauves, 1904/6 in Rubin 1977 [**1935**], no. 63; and for watercolour, *Mont Sainte-Victorie seen from the north of Aix*, ibid., 130.
147 Bomford et al. 1990 [**1766**], 97.
148 Doran 1978 [**1806**], 59. See also Cézanne's instructions to Bernard (ibid., 73) on painting a still-life, starting 'with the almost neutral tones' and then 'going up the scale to include more and more of the colours' (*aller en montant toujours la gamme et en serrant davantage les chromatismes*). This procedure has been discussed very sensitively by Badt 1943 [**1749**], 247.
149 See especially G. Geffroy in 1901, cit. Shiff 1978b [**1956**], 79. Geffroy seems to have taken a hint from Monet's letter to him in 1893, where the painter argued that the *Rouen* canvases were abandoned only when he felt tired of them (Wildenstein 1979 [**1976**], III, 272). For the modern debate about 'finish' in late Cézanne, Reff in Rubin 1977 [**1935**], 36–7. Ernst Strauss has re-stated the modernist view that many of these late canvasses with substantial areas of bare canvas can be regarded as complete (Strauss 1983 [**1962**], 182).
150 Cézanne's 'editing' of the motif can be readily seen in the landscapes he did side-by-side with Armand Guillaumin (see Rewald 1985 [**1928**], 110–11, 114–15: 1986 [**1929**], 132–3); and his elaborate arrangement of still-life in the late 1890s was recorded by Louis le Bail (Rewald 1986 [**1929**], 228).
151 Doran 1978 [**1806**], 8. Col. pl. in Rubin 1977 [**1935**], no. 4; for the brushes and method, Vollard 1938 [**1631**], 60.
152 Helmholtz reckoned that white in a picture indoors, for example, would have from 1/20 to 1/40 of the reflectivity power of the same white in sunlight (Helmholtz 1901 [**1849**], II, 97–8). See also, among many observations, Jamin 1857 [**1524**], espec. 632ff, 641–2; Laugel 1869 [**1542**], 89–100; Brücke 1878 [**1447**], 105; Guéroult 1882 [**1501**], 176; Vibert 1902 [**1734**], 68–9.
153 Bernard in Doran 1978 [**1806**], 61. For Whistler, see p. 185 above.
154 Doran 1978 [**1806**], 72–3, Pissarro's advice in the 1870s to restrict himself to three primaries and their derivatives, as reported by J. Gasquet, *Paul Cézanne*, 1926, 148f, does not seem to have been taken (see Shiff 1984 [**1726**], 206, 299f, n. 23; Bomford et al. 1990 [**1766**], 200). For Bernard's palette, limited to as few as two colours, Bernard to Ciolkowski (1908) in Chassé 1969 [**1787**], 80; Doran 1978 [**1806**], 61.
155 Cézanne 1976 [**1786**], 316–17, 327. In a letter of August 1906 Cézanne had told his son that he regretted his advanced age 'because of my colour sensations' (320), which may refer either to a feeling of incapacity to see, or to render what was seen. I have not been able to investigate the rather inconclusive suggestions of Hamilton 1984 [**1842**], 230ff that Cézanne's diabetes in old age (see Doran 1978 [**1806**], 24) affected his painting.
156 Cartier 1963 [**1783**], 351.
157 Matisse to Camoin 1914, cit. Matisse 1972 [**1702**], 94. Matisse added that this side of him conflicted with his romanticism, and left him exhausted.
158 See *Sideboard and Table* (1899) in Watkins 1984 [**1973**], 36–8.
159 Matisse 1972 [**1702**], 49; see also the interview with R. W. Howe, in Matisse 1978 [**1889**], 123.
160 For Denis, Flam 1986 [**1816**], 121; for Cross, Matisse to Tériade, 1929/30 in Matisse 1978 [**1889**], 58; see also ibid., 132; Derain to Vlaminck 28 July 1905 in Derain 1955 [**1803**], 154f, 161. Matisse's attitude to the Neo-Impressionists has been studied in detail by Bock 1981 [**1765**].
161 For Chevreul etc. Flam 1986 [**1816**], 223; for the spectrum, Duthuit cit. Watkins 1984 [**1973**], 63, who suggests that the red–green–blue palette of *Dance* (1910) depended on this knowledge (94) and that the greys in the *Piano Lesson* (1916) may have been chosen because of the discmixing of the complementaries in the painting – red–green, orange–blue – to grey (138). Rood's chapter on the Young–Helmholtz theory of vision had generally opted for Young's red–green–violet primaries of light (see e.g., Rood 1879 [**306**], 113ff), but he also reported the red–green–blue theory of Maxwell (121). Matisse's particular love of the light-creating triad red–green–blue has also been noticed in his late cut-paper compositions by J. H. Neff in Cowart et al. 1977 [**1795**], 33. See also Flam 1986 [**1816**], 283.
162 Matisse 1972 [**1702**], 46, and for the English, Matisse 1978 [**1889**], 37.
163 CL [**1626**], 429: 'It is true, I still often blunder when I undertake a thing, but the colours follow of their own accord, and taking one colour as a starting-point, I have clearly in mind what must follow and how to get life into it'.
164 *Le Chemin de la couleur* (1947) in Matisse 1972 [**1702**], 204; English in Matisse 1978 [**1889**], 116. Elsewhere, of course, e.g. Matisse 1978 [**1889**], 100 (1945), he spoke of colour as a means of liberation.
165 For the earlier state, Flam 1986 [**1816**], fig. 229 and p. 230.
166 For *Music*, Flam 1986 [**1816**], figs 288–9; for the 1930s, see the *Pink Nude* (1935) in Barr 1974 [**1752**], 472 (col. pl. in Watkins 1984 [**1973**], pl. 169), and *Music* (1939) in Watkins ibid., 187, 189.
167 Watkins (ibid., 138, 143) notes the use of this scraper in the *Piano Lesson* and *Bathers by a River* (both 1916).
168 Elderfield 1978 [**1808**], 86–8.
169 Matisse 1976 [**1888**], 92.
170 Ibid., 112 (1952).
171 Ibid., 94–5 (1919). A visitor in 1912 spoke of the 'flaming flowers' in June (Elderfield 1978 [**1808**], 86).
172 Severini 1917 in *Archivi del Futurismo* 1958 [**1744**], I, 214. The subject of the conversation was a Moroccan sketch 'from nature', possibly *Le Marabout* (1912/13), col. pl. in Cowart et al. 1990 [**1796**], no. 3.
173 Matisse 1972 [**1702**], 52.
174 For Kandinsky's probable contact with Matisse's patrons and associates in Paris, Fineberg 1984 [**1814**], 49f. He referred to the German version of the *Notes* in *On the Spiritual in Art* of 1912 (Kandinsky 1982 [**1686**], I, 151).
175 Kandinsky ibid., I, 386–7 (1913). For the painting and its sketches, Roethel and Benjamin, I, 1982 [**1933**], no. 464, and Hanfstaengl, 1974 [**1843**].

12 The Substance of Colour

1 Redon 1979 [**1718**], 128.
2 This account is based on three surviving versions of the 'process', which differ considerably in detail among themselves. The only published version is the paraphrase by Stephen Rigaud of the copy sold by Provis to his father, John Francis Rigaud (Rigaud 1984 [**2060**], 99–103). A MS copy sold to Joseph Farington, amplified by notes in his own hand, probably from conversations with Miss Provis, is in the library of the Royal Academy in London. Farington's *Diary* is our chief

source of knowledge for the progress of the affair, of which he gives an almost daily account between December 1796 and May 1797. A third version, possibly the earliest, is the MS *The Venetian manner of Painting particularly laid down, relating to the Practice, by A. J. P.*, in the collection of Dr Jon Whiteley, who kindly allowed me to study it. It does not mention the 'Titian shade', but gives 'a negative *Grey Tint* compounded of *Ivory Black, Indigo* and *Lake*'. The references to Hungarian or Prussian blue and Antwerp blue as key pigments in the two MSS suggest the rather recent origin of the 'Venetian Secret', since these were 18th-century pigments. For an account of the scandal, Gage 1964 [**2014**], 38–41.

3 West's 'process' paintings were *Cicero and the Magistrates discovering the Tomb of Archimedes* (von Erffa and Staley 1986 [**1032**], no. 22), sold Christie 22 November 1985 (69); *Cupid Stung by a Bee* (von Erffa and Staley, no. 133), *Portrait of Raphael and Benjamin West* (von Erffa and Staley, no. 543) and a lost *Crucifixion* (von Erffa and Staley no. 356).

4 Malone 1797 [**2039**], I, xxxii–xxxiiin.; 1798, I, lvi–lviii.

5 Farington 7 June 1797. For Reynolds's experiments, M. Kirby Talley, '"All good pictures crack": Sir Joshua Reynolds's practice and studio' in Penny 1986 [**2049**], 55–7, 62–7.

6 Sheldrake's *Dissertation of Painting in Oil*, 'in a manner similar to that practised in the ancient Venetian School', was submitted to the Society in the Spring of 1797, and won a Greater Silver Palette the following year (*Transactions of the Society of Arts*, XVI, 1798 [**2064**], 279–99). He thought his methods were close to Provis's (297) but this was disputed by one of his sponsors (Society of Arts, *Minutes of the Committee of Polite Arts*, 22 November 1797, 98). The *Dissertation* was reprinted in *The Artist's Assistant, or the School of Science*, 1801. Grandi, who had been trained by a Venetian master, also claimed that his coloured absorbent grounds were like Provis's (Farington 21 May 1797), and in 1806 won a Silver Medal from the Society for his method 'in the old Venetian stile', (*Transactions*, XXIV, 1806, 85; repr. in Fielding, *Painting in Oil*, 1839 [**2012**], 79–80).

7 See Farington 19 January, 26 February 1801; 10 July, 28 November, 6, 9 December 1802; 6 June, 25 July 1803. Farington's detailed account of the use of the 'vehicle" is in a notebook now in the Victoria and Albert Museum (P88–1921, folio 72v, dated 26 February 1801), but it does not give the ingredients. It was probably the 'true Venetian' medium discovered by John Singleton Copley, R.A. and reported by his son in August 1802 (Amory 1882 [**1983**], 230f).

8 Gage 1964 [**2014**], 40. For Westall, Wainewright 1880 [**2071**], 253–5; for Beaumont and Provis, Owen and Brown 1988 [**2046**], 94.

9 Sandby to Colonel Gravatt, October 1797 in Sandby 1892 [**2062**], 93.

10 Armenini 1820 [**1984**], xxxv; see also 108–9n.

11 For Blake, Gilchrist 1942 [**221**], 359f. John Linnell, who lent his copy to Blake about 1822, claimed that it was probably the first copy in England. It is possible that Blake or Linnell showed the book to Constable, who in an undated note copied out a passage (in translation) from ch. xxviii on nature as the perfect guide (Leslie 1951 [**1078**], 275). Haydon knew the *Book* by 1824 (*Diary*, ed. Pope II, 1960 [**1060**], 489) and was using its recipes by 1827 (ibid., III, 227, and cf. V, 84, 260 (1841, 1843)). For Ingres's purchase of the book in 1840, Ternois 1956 [**2067**], 173.

12 See the Leiden document of 1643 in Martin 1901 [**2040**], 86ff. Cornelis de Bie in 1661 assumed that a single colourmaker would supply a very large range of pigments (de Bie 1971 [**1991**], II, 208–11). For a London colour-shop in 1633, Bate 1977, [**1647**], 132.

13 Bouvier 1828 [**1655**], 9; Van Gogh CL [**1626**], no. 419a, to a colourman Furnée at The Hague (3 August 1885): 'I use only the colours I get brayed [i.e. ground] here'.

14 See Delacroix to Mme Haro, 29 October 1827, ordering 18 bladders of colours, all of them 'more liquid than the colours you prepare for everyone else' (Delacroix 1935–8 [**1471**], (1935), 200). See also Planet 1928 [**1571**], 47 for Delacroix's preference for liquid colours later in his career. His long relationship with the Haro family has been studied by Sauvaire 1978 [**2063**]. One colour which was usually made by the artist himself, a calcined Prussian blue called *Brun de Prusse*, was supplied to Delacroix by Haro (letter of 21 March 1846, in Delacroix 1935–8 [**1471**], II, (1936), 266): for the usual practice, Goupil 1858 [**2021**], 30.

15 See espec. CL [**1626**], 501, 503, 642, and 527, 532, 533, where van Gogh hopes Tasset will make experiments on the degree of grinding needed to bring out the best qualities in certain pigments. For Tanguy as colour-dealer, Bernard 1908 [**1989**], 600–14. The only study of large-scale pigment manufacture in the 19th century seems to be Kühn 1982 [**2033**], 35ff, but see also Bomford et al. 1990 [**1766**], 34–43, 50–72, and espec. the important review by Callen 1991 [**1999**], espec. 602–3.

16 A number of early proposals to teach chemistry to painters have been recorded in England: in 1770 the Incorporated Society of Artists employed a Dr Aussiter to lecture on the subject (Jones 1946–8 [**2030**], 23), and in 1807 a young Academy student, Andrew Robertson, was attending outside lectures on chemistry 'an art very necessary for a painter to know' (Robertson 1897 [**2061**], 150). In the 1840s the distinguished chemist Michael Faraday was assisting C. L. Eastlake in his researches into fresco painting (Faraday 1971 [**2006**], I, 423–5); Faraday also helped Turner with his pigments (Gage 1987 [**2016**], 225). In Rome in 1813 the Nazarenes were eager to read a new book on colours by a chemist, L. Marcucci and a restorer, P. Palmaroli, *Saggio analytico chimico sopra i colori minerali* (Howitt 1886 [**1855**], I, 316–17).

17 Lemaistre 1889 [**2037**], 43f; Prache 1966 [**2052**], 234; for the laboratory, Moreau-Vauthier 1923 [**1706**], 103. Notes on Pasteur's lesson of 10 April 1865, 'Obscurcissement de la peinture à l'huile', have been published in *Bulletin du laboratoire du Musée du Louvre*, (Suppl. to *Revue des Arts*, June 1956, 3–4).

18 For Mérimée's life, Pinet 1913 [**2051**].

19 Mérimée 1830 [**2042**], ix.

20 Ibid., 7–8; for the date of the researches, Pinet 1913 [**2051**], 72.

21 For Prud'hon and Theophilus, Mérimée 1830 [**2042**], 34, 71–5, 92.

22 Ibid., 168; Chaptal 1807 [**2000**], III, 373.

23 Berthollet 1824 [**1990**], II, 106–7; M. de L^{xxx}*c.* 1829 [**2034**], 83. Mérimée's discussion of madder forms one of the longest sections of his book (1830 [**2042**], 144–65).

24 Ibid., 293.

25 Grégoire *c.* 1812 [**2023**], 60f. For the date, Forichon 1916 [**1818**], 63. The views on complementarity in Grégoire (51–2) are essentially the same as those expressed in Mérimée's book.

26 Grégoire *c.* 1812 [**2023**], 6, 45. Mérimée's *carmin* in 1830, however, was a colour made not from madder but from *kermes* (124ff). He did not name the pigments he considered primary, although the slightly bluish red of his diagram could well be a carmine.

27 Mérimée, *Mémoire sur les lois générales de la coloration appliqués à la formation d'une échelle chromatique à l'usage des naturalistes* in Brisseau de Mirbel 1815 [**1994**], II, 909–24.

28 Pinet 1913 [**2051**], 81.

29 Ibid., 68. This seems to be a response to Delacroix's *Death of Sardanapalus* (1827). Mérimée seems to have had some direct contact with Delacroix in the 1820s, since his friend Rochard gave Delacroix a letter to take to him in 1825 (Ephrussi 1891 [**2005**], 461).

30 Mérimée 1830 [**2042**], 29–30. For his English experiences, Pinet 1913 [**2051**], 57–62. He translated Fuseli's Academy lectures, but none of his versions was published until after his death, when three appeared in *Les Beaux-Arts* in 1844. For Constable, Pinet 1913 [**2051**], 63.

31 Thornbury 1877 [**2068**], 262. For Mérimée and English landscape, Pinet 1913 [**2051**], 61, and for his reference to Constable in 1817, Ephrussi 1891 [**2005**], 462. There is a fleeting reference to Mérimée, based probably on the 1839 translation of his book, in Field's introduction to *Chromatics*, 1845 [**2010**], xn, but he does not seem to be mentioned in the large collection of Field's notebooks now with Messrs Winsor and Newton.

32 The following account of Field is based substantially on Gage 1989 [**2017**].

33 Field *Chromatics*, 1808, Winsor and Newton MS5 folio 540f. Field was still thinking in these terms as late as 1845 (Field 1845 [**2010**], 161). For another English anti-Newtonian technologist, Bancroft [**1986**], 1813.

34 Gage 1989 [**2017**], 30.

35 *Chromatics*, 1808, folio 522v. By the mid-1830s Field had developed an alkaline Lemon Yellow, and used a substratum of alumina for his madder lakes, hence the somewhat far-fetched linkage of this colour with alumina. He had also devoted much effort to the production of the highest quality natural ultramarine, a siliceous stone.

36 Massoul 1797 [**2041**], 123. See also 126ff for colours grouped under the categories of animal, vegetable and mineral. Massoul was also remarkable as a technologist for accepting the Newtonian account of colours (120ff), which he did not attempt to integrate into his discussion of pigments. Field's chief triadic text was Field 1816, much expanded in 1846 [**2011**]. This aspect of his thought has been discussed by Brett 1986 [**1993**], 336–50, although he seems to stretch the relationship with modernist theory too far.

37 Gage 1989 [**2017**], no. 52.

38 Castel 1739 [**2101**], 813.

39 Gage 1986 [**2015**], 67. Le Blon had eventually to add a fourth, black, plate, and to finish his prints with hand-colouring.

40 Dossie 1764 [**2003**], II, 182ff. Dossie stated that Le Blon sometimes had to use two printings to bring a colour up to strength. For Brown Pink, Harley 1982 [**1504**], 112–14.

41 Pfannenschmidt and Schulz 1792 [**2050**], 32. According to Michaud's *Biographie Universelle*, a first German edn of this work was publ. at Hanover in 1781, and a second in Leipzig in 1799. I have not found copies of this German version, and the French edn is also exceedingly rare. A copy of the first French edn, Lausanne 1788, is in the library of the National Gallery in Washington, and a copy of the second in the Bibliothèque Cantonal in Lausanne.

42 Pfannenschmidt and Schulz 1792 [**2050**], 34–5.

43 Ibid., 142–4.

44 Ibid., 37–40.

45 Lamarck 1797 [**2035**], 86. The reference to Pfannenschmidt is on p. 78, n. 5. Lamarck's system was reprinted almost verbatim in Latreille 1802 [**2036**], I, 349ff. Latreille hoped that the Musée d'Histoire Naturelle in Paris would engage famous painters to help in the execution of Lamarck's scale, which would further the essential work of the standardization of colours (350). He preferred a 10-part circle to the 12-part circle Lamarck had adapted from Pfannenschmidt.

46 Harris *c.* 1776 [**2026**], Sowerby 1809 [**1141**], 38–9; Field 1817 [**2010**], 56.

47 Grégoire, *c.* 1812 [**2023**], 45; Paillot de Montabert, 1829 [**281**], IX, 184–8. See also Hundertpfund 1849 [**1683**], 27–31, where of the basic colours chosen, only natural ultramarine was regarded as 'primary'. The others were Naples yellow and madder.

48 Gage 1989 [**2017**], 59–64. The early history of spectroscopy has been studied by Bennett 1984 [**1988**].

49 Gage 1989 [**2017**], 40.

50 Merrifield 1844 [**2043**], xi. Merrifield also cites Field's *Chromatography* on 117, 120, 123, 125, 138, 157. On 123, e.g., the madders developed by Field are cited as superior to Cennini's *lac lake*, which was badly affected by contact with lead. On 157 she cites Field on the use of stippled optical mixtures to achieve greater brilliance, probably a reference to Field 1841 [**2009**], 47.

51 For the Pre-Raphaelites and Field, Gage 1989 [**2017**], nos 21, 59–63. In a letter of 27 October 1879 (Oxford, Bodleian Library) Holman Hunt mentioned that he had read Merrifield's translation of Cennini as well as the 1841 edition of Field's *Chromatography*. Millais's reading of Field by 1847 is suggested by his palette shown in a self-portrait (Liverpool, Walker Art Gallery), which is set with a sequence of black and white and red, yellow and blue. Rossetti's interest in Field on the primaries is suggested not only by the palette of *Ecce Ancilla Domini* (1850, Tate Gallery), but also by a watercolour of 1853, *Dante drawing an Angel* (Oxford, Ashmolean Museum), which shows three pots of primary colours on the window-ledge.

52 Vibert 1902 [**1743**], 87, 103–7, 143. Vibert called his book , which went into eight printings in 1891 alone, 'the fruit of thirty years of study and experience'. For the laboratory at the École, n. 17 above.

53 Recouvreur 1890 [**2054**], 83. This book gave a good deal of space to the chemical constituents of colours and media, and argued (8) that the painter should take the trouble to learn about materials.

54 Recouvreur 1890 [**2054**], 105; Vibert 1902 [**1743**], 149–55. Matisse noted that he used Vibert's retouching varnish (Moreau-Vauthier 1923 [**1706**], 84).

55 Averroes 1949 [**1985**], 20f. For Leonardo 1956 [**1076**], I, 291; for Runge, HS [**1127**], I, 81, 180–1; for Monet see p. 209. Not that Monet was always content with his materials: in several letters of the 1880s he made the usual complaint about their inadequacy (Wildenstein 1979 [**1976**], II, Letters 394, 403, 460, 671), but he never seems to have reflected on how he might address these difficulties.

56 Bourdon in Watelet and Levesque I, 1792 [**1636**], 409–11.

57 Poussin's supporter Félibien argued that black and white were incapable of encompassing the extremes of luminosity and darkness in nature (*Entretiens* 1725 [**1669**], V (1979), 5); for de Piles (1677), Puttfarken 1985 [**2053**], 69. De Piles singled out brightness as inimitable. See also Hoogstraten 1678 [**1518**], 224.

58 The distinction between the camera obscura image and the painted picture was examined by Hamilton 1738 [**2025**], II, 384–5. For an extreme statement of the superiority of the camera to painting, Gautier d'Agoty 1753 [**2018**], 81–2. Another illustrator of natural history, Schiffermüller, argued for the superiority of nature to art in the matter of richness and brightness (1772 [**324**], 4ff n.). For the argument that art can overcome these deficiencies by manipulation, applied espec. to values of light and shade, Barry 1809 [**34**], I, 527–8.

59 Monge 1820 [**1895**], 130f. See also Vallée 1821 [**1969**], 374f on the freedom of the artist to manipulate his subject in order to compensate, a view which anticipates Cézanne's practice at the end of the century.

60 Jamin 1857 [**1524**], 632–8.

61 Ibid., 641–2.

62 Helmholtz 1901 [**1849**], II, 121–2. This opinion was quoted with approval by Brücke (1878 [**1447**], 105; cf. also 125), which also published a French version of Helmholtz's lecture. See also Brücke 1866 [**1446**], 153f.

63 Guéroult 1882 [**1501**], 176.

64 Field 1845 [**2010**], 119–20. Regnier 1865 [**1580**], iii, 115f also welcomed the new pigments, used with prudence, although he regarded the only 'pure' (i.e. primary) pigments as the traditional Naples yellow, madder and ultramarine (116).

65 The use of these new techniques is demonstrated by Bomford et al. 1990 [**1766**].

66 Trévise 1927 [**2069**], 49f. For chrome yellows replaced by cadmiums, Bomford et al. 1990 [**1766**], 63–4 and Jones 1977 [**2029**], 6. Pissarro was equally concerned about permanence (Fénéon 1970 [**1481**], I, 55–6), but continued to use chrome yellow until the end of his life (Rewald 1973 [**2059**], 590).

67 Bomford et al. 1990 [**1766**], 201 (no. 11).

68 Naples yellow appears in Renoir's work from the mid-1880s (Bomford et al. 1990 [**1766**], 201 (no. 14)); for the revival of the colour, ibid. 68–70. Renoir's heavy use of it in the '90s was recorded by Tabarant 1923 [**2066**], 289; see also Wainewright, Taylor and Harley 'Lead antimonate yellow' in Feller I, 1986 [**1811**], 219–26, 229–35. In Renoir 1962 [**2057**], 342 the painter noted that yellow ochre, Naples yellow and Siena earth were 'only intermediate tones' and could be replaced by mixtures of the brighter colours; see also M. H. Butler, 'Technical notes' in *Paintings by Renoir* 1973 [**2048**], 210. The identification of Cennini's *giallorino* with Naples yellow had been made in Mérimée 1830 [**2042**], 110–13 and espec. by Mottez (1858) 1911 [**2044**], 33n.

69 Mottez 1911 [**2044**], viii. For Renoir's book, Pissarro to Monet, 13 May 1884 (Bailly-Herzberg 1980 [**1424**], I, 299f). It has been associated with Renoir's proposal of 1884 to found a Société des Irregularistes to propagate an aesthetic or irregularity in all the arts, and to publish 'Une grammaire complet d'art' (Venturi 1939 [**2070**], I, 127–9). House 1985 [**2028**], 18, n. 33 has proposed that the discovery of Cennini dates from before 1881, when Renoir decided to go to Italy to study ancient and Renaissance techniques. It is notable that Degas, who also made use of Naples yellow in his pastels, was a reader of Cennini (Reff 1971 [**2055**], 162f and for the pastels, Maheux 1988 [**2038**], 87).

70 *Paintings by Renoir* 1973 [**2048**], no. 83.

71 Matisse 1976 [**1888**], 101.

72 Kühn 1969 [**2032**].

73 Robert 1891 [**1722**], 115.

74 Vibert 1895/6 [**1735**], 940–1.

75 Vibert 1902 [**1734**], 33. A cardinal subject set in a garden, *The Reprimand* (1874), is reproduced in Vibert 1895/6 [**1735**], 721; there seem to be very few of his works in public collections.

76 For the conservation evidence from paintings of the 1880s, Bomford et al. 1990 [**1766**], 201 (no. 15); Butler 1973 [**1996**], 77–85. For the lists of pigments in Cézanne's notebooks, Rewald 1951 [**2058**], 51; Gowing 1988 [**2022**], 91; Reff and Shoemaker 1989 [**2056**], 30, 133, 239.

77 Doran 1978 [**1806**], 61, 72–3.

78 CL [**1626**], 475. Vibert 1902 [**1734**], 284–91 usefully identifies the ingredients of these colours, often sold under confusing trade-names. Cézanne returned a cinnabar green to a colour-merchant in 1905 (Cézanne 1976 [**1786**], 314).

79 CL [**1626**], 476. In an earlier letter (474) he had remarked on the darkening of Théodore Rousseau's landscapes, so that 'his pictures are now unrecognizable'. See also CL 430 on the expense of permanent colours. The fading of his work has been studied by Cadorin et al. 1987 [**1998**], 267–73.

80 Signac to Lucien Pissarro, August 1887 in Dorra and Rewald 1959 [**1475**], LXI. For the *Grande Jatte*, Russell 1965 [**1593**], 229f; Fénéon 1970 [**1481**], I, 212. For its pigments, Fiedler 1984 [**2007**], 44–50, and 1989 [**2008**], 176–8.

81 For the history and characteristics of the pigment, Feller I, 1986 [**1811**], 201–2.

82 Camille to Lucien Pissarro, 31 May 1887, in Bailly-Herzberg II, 1986 [**1424**], 178.

83 For Signac's palette, Homer 1970 [**1517**], 151. For cerulean blue, Bomford et al. 1990 [**1766**], 56–7, and for the reputation of *bleu céleste*, Vibert 1902 [**1734**], 288, where it is grouped with, among others, Prussian blue as a ferric ferrocyanide, which indicates the difficulties Vibert (and historians) have in translating trade-terms into identifiable substances. My point is less that cerulean was an unreliable blue (its persistence on Signac's palette suggests that he was rather happy with it, and its manufacture may have improved with time) than that it was regarded as unreliable in the 1890s, and is thus an indication that painters like Signac were prepared to take risks in order to achieve brilliance. In 1891 Fénéon reported that, because of their permanence, Signac used the colours of the Belgian manufacturer Jacques Blockx, ground in an amber medium (Fénéon 1970 [**1481**], I, 197); and Signac was still specifying Blockx mixed greens in the 1930s (*Encyclopédie Française*, 1935 [**1666**], 16° 30–5–6). Blockx colours, espec. greens, were also much used by Matisse (Moreau-Vauthier 1923 [**1706**], 30; *Encyclopédie* 1935 loc. cit.), who had of course been close to Signac about 1904. Homer has identified one of the three reds on Seurat's surviving palette as alizarin crimson (Broude 1978 [**1443**], 117), a synthetic colour first developed in the 1860s, and quite stable. The pigments on this palette have, however, not so far been analyzed, and this remains a guess. It was not a question of using cheap materials: Seurat's supplier, Maison Édouard, where Tanguy had trained, was more expensive than Tasset and L'Hôte (for Seurat's patronage of Édouard, see the note on a drawing of 1885/6 in Herbert 1962 [**2027**], 188, no. 168 and Herbert et al. 1991 [**1514**], 179, n. 2; for the firm, Bomford et al. 190 [**1766**], 41f; and for prices, Van Gogh 1958 [**1626**], no. 507). Cézanne bought emerald green from Édouard (Reff and Shoemaker 1989 [**2056**], 133), although his major supplier seems to have been Gustave Sennelier (Daval 1985 [**2001**], 108f).

84 The lack of chromaticity in the *Grande Jatte* had been noticed in 1886 by Émile Hennequin (Broude 1978 [**1443**], 42), but he could not explain it. Signac, who was much troubled by it in 1892 (Cachin 1971 [**1997**], 71–2), had discovered the theoretical explanation by the end of the decade (Signac 1964 [**1607**], 42), and used it in his polemic in favour of 'divisionism'. In a letter of 1914, Severini used the same argument to contrast the greyed effect of French pointillism with the enhanced luminosity of analagous tones in Italian *Divisionismo* (*Archivi del Divisionismo* 1968 [**1745**], I, 312); but the Futurist Boccioni thought (1916) that even the Italians did not escape this greying (ibid., 58). A close reading of Blanc's *Grammaire* should have been enough to predict the greying effect of juxtaposed dots of complementary colours, since this is what his optical-mixing of stripes, stars and dots were intended to create (Blanc 1867 [**1436**], 604–6; cf. also Blanc 1882 [**1438**], 103–5). Amadée Ozenfant, who knew Seurat's work over many years, thought it was greying more and more (Ozenfant 1968 [**2047**], 50).

85 For Sir William Beechey's use of toning colours, Sully 1965 [**2065**], 36–7. The pre-17th-century evidence has been reviewed by Kockaert 1979 [**2031**], 69–72. For the 17th and 18th centuries, O. Kurz, 'Varnishes, tinted varnishes, and patina', *Burlington Magazine*, CIV 1962, 56–9; 1963 [**253**], 95.

86 Beal 1984 [**1987**], 143–4.

87 Conti 1988 [**401**], 96. Ironically, in the 18th century Veronese was singled out as a master who allowed time to harmonize his pictures (Algarotti 1764 [**1982**], 56–8). See also Fletcher 1979 [**2013**], 25–6 for a 17th-century 'smoked' Giorgione.

88 For anticipation, de Piles 1708 in Puttfarken 1985 [**2053**], 69; for A. Sacchi, Dowley 1965 [**2004**], 76f, n. 119; for F. Pacheco, McKim Smith et al. 1988 [**1550**], 110. For the 18th century Laugier (1771) 1972 [**1696**], 154–5.

89 Goethe 1871 [**2019**], 261.

90 Hogarth 1955 [**1064**], 130, n. 1. This was also noted by Mérimée 1830 [**2042**], 282. Mérimée felt that Rubens had intended time to turn his pictures into Titians (297); but Rubens has provided one of the most startling examples of the removal of a (19th-century) toned varnish. His *Gerbier Family* (Washington, National Gallery) lay under such a varnish until the 1970s and presented the critic Roger Fry with a lesson on 'a colour harmony built entirely and almost exclusively on coppery reds and reddish browns, and an almost neutral grey . . .'. The removal of this varnish has changed greys to blues and reds to greens (Buck 1973 [**1995**], 49–51).

91 Delacroix 1980 [**1026**], 23 February 1852.

92 Undated letter in Goldwater and Treves 1976 [**2020**], 309. The best discussion of Impressionist surfaces is Bomford et al. 1990 [**1766**], 93–8. For a more general treatment of texture Hackney 1990 [**2024**], 22–5.

93 Nakov and Pétris 1972 [**2045**], 111–12. See also 118–24, and espec. the remark that 'the modern painter is distinguished by the very special reverence he has for his materials'. See also A. Shevchenko in Bowlt 1976 [**1992**], 51–2, and espec. D. Burliuk, *Texture* (1912) in Barron and Tuchman 1980 [**1753**], 129f, for whom one of the most important examples was a Monet *Rouen Cathedral* in the Shchukin collection.

94 The circular diagram of Bauhaus courses devised for the 1923 exhibition (Wingler 1975 [**2072**], 52, fig. 17) included both colour-theory – in conjuction with space and composition – and 'colour' – with wood, metal etc. This scheme may have been devised by Klee, whose diagram of 1922 (Wingler 1975, fig. 1) is close to it; but it may also reflect the teaching of colour as material given in Weimar by Theo van Doesburg, and described in an article (1923 [**2002**], 12–13). He likened contrasts such as blue and yellow to the tensions between concrete and wood.

13 The Sound of Colour

1 For this characterization see the undated and anonymous treatise (Bellerman Anon. II, 26) in Najok 1972 [**2199**], 84–5.

2 Gaudentios *Introduction to Harmony* (3rd or 4th century AD) cit. Gavaert 1875 [**2133**], I, 85f. Gavaert interpreted *colour* as dynamic or harmonic function; but Palisca 1985 [**2204**], 129 calls it 'qualities that make sounds of the same pitch and duration differ'.

3 *Topics*, 106a, 9–32; 106b, 4–9; 107a, 11–17 in Barker, II, 1989 [**991**], 69–70; the Peripatetic *On audible things*, 801a–b (ibid. 101–3). Theophrastus's lost *On Music* seems to have equated lightness with a high pitch (ibid. 115).

4 Plato *Laws* 653c–660c in Barker I, 1984 [**2080**], 143 and n. 61, where this usage is interpreted as 'tone-colour' or nuances of tuning. For *tonos* and *harmogē*, Pliny XXXV, xi, 29.
5 For Ptolemy, *Harmonics*, III, vi in Barker II, 1989 [**991**], 378; see also Aristoxenus, *Elements of Harmony*, I, 23B (ibid. 141); Vitruvius 1521 V, [**343**], iv, 3; Najok 1972 [**2199**], 84–5; Adrastus of Aphrodisias in Barker ibid. 216; and for cowardice, the ?4th-century Hebih' Papyrus reporting and contesting a contemporary opinion (Barker I, 1984 [**2080**]2, 184). The *Musical Manual* of Nicomachus (?2nd century AD) argued that the chromatic scale was like changeable people who are said to have 'colour' (XII, 263 in Barker II, 1989 [**991**], 268).
6 Clement of Alexandria *Paedagogus*, II, iv, adapted from the translation in McKinnon 1987 [**2182**], 34. See also Remigius of Auxerre's 9th-century commentary on the *The Wedding of Philology and Mercury* of Martianus Capella, which in Bk IX transmitted a large body of Greek musical theory to the Latin West (Remigius 1965 [**2212**], II, 347). Macrobius's late 4th-century *Commentary on the Dream of Scipio*, much read in the Middle Ages and the Renaissance, also reported that the chromatic genus was frowned upon because it induced voluptuousness (II, iv, 13; 1952 [**2186**], 199). see also Boethius I 1989, [**1001**], xxi. The 14th-century Byzantine theorist Manuel Bryennius still regarded the chromatic *genos* as 'plaintive and pathetic' and 'downcast and unmanly' (1970 [**2091**], 114–15, 138–9).
7 Aristides Quintilianus *On Music*, I, ix in Barker II, 1989 [**991**], 418; Athenaeus *Deipnosophistae (The Banquet of the Philosophers)*, XIV, 638a in Barker 1984 [**2080**], 300. Lysander's style was said to resemble that of the wind instrument, the aulos, which had the almost exclusive capacity to play the even more nuanced enharmonic scale (Comotti 1989 [**2108**], 26f). Aristides claimed that the enharmonic scale could be played by only the most outstanding musicians.
8 *On Music*, I, i; II, iv in Barker II, 1989 [**991**], 400, 460–1.
9 *On Music*, III, viii in Barker ibid., 506.
10 Pollitt 1974 [**122**], 225 suggests that *tonos* may be compared to volume or pitch in music, but Pliny's characterization of it as existing between light and shade suggests another sort of scale, which was one of the several meanings of *tonos* in musical theory (Aristoxenus *Elements of Harmony*, II, 37 in Barker II, 1989 [**991**], 153–4, and espec. 17–27). *Harmogē* meant 'fitting-together', and in musical theory was also linked to the movement from one discrete note to another. Since the *harmonai* were related to musical modes, which were held to have a particular emotive effect, this idea may be related to the affective power of particular combinations of colours in compositions (cf. Barker I, 1984 [**2080**], 163–8).
11 See Gaiser 1965 [**75**], 212, n. 65 and 189ff. Sorabji 1972 [**2229**], 295–304 points out that in *Metaphysics* 1093a, 26 Aristotle recognized other consonances. See also Crocker 1963 [**2111**], 192
12 *Republic* 616b–617d in Barker II, 1989 [**991**], 57–8. The colours were 'whitish', 'reddish' and 'yellowish'. For analysis of this very difficult description, Lippman, 1963 [**2177**], 16f. Plato's myth was the subject of a multi-media entertainment designed by Bernardo Buontalenti for the wedding of the Grand Duke Ferdinand de' Medici in Florence in 1589 (Palisca 1985 [**2204**], 188–90).
13 Rudolf of St Trond 1911 [**2218**], 98. There seems to be nothing in the Western medieval tradition comparable to the 9th- and 10th-century Arab assimilation of colours to the four humours and four strings of the lute, for which see Farmer 1926 [**2124**], 18, 20.
14 Gaffurio 1518 [**2129**], bk IV, ch. IV, lxxxiv v; ch. V, lxxxv v, lxxxvi r. For Gaffurio's interpretation of the Greek modes in medieval terms, Palisca 1985 [**2204**], 11–12, 293–8; and on the *ethos* of the modes, 345.
15 E.g. Bate 1960 [**162**], 124–5 and Clichtove 1510 [**2106**], 218v, both of whom translated Aristotle's *halourgon* as *coccineus*. For Bate's skills as a practical and theoretical musician, Goldine 1964 [**2138**], 10–27.
16 Vincent of Beauvais 1624 [**823**], I, bk II, ch. lxvii. His musical theory, but not its colour, has been discussed by Göller 1959 [**2140**], 29–34.
17 Wagner 1983 [**2244**], espec. T. C. Karp, 'Music', 169–95; Whitney 1990 [**836**], 1–169.
18 Bryennius 1970 [**2091**], 174–9.
19 For Aristides' comparison of the arts, *On Music*, I, in Barker II 1989 [**991**], 400; *On Music*, II, iv, in ibid., 460. Aristides argued that music was superior as an art of *imitation*, and this continued to be the basis of the comparison in 16th-century Venice (Palisca 1985 [**2204**], 398–9). For Gaffurio's use of Aristides, ibid. 174ff, 204, 224f. See also his *On Harmony* lxxxvii r, on the need for harmony in music, painting, medicine and social relations. This paraphrases Aristides, who was also much used in the encyclopaedia of Giorgio Valla, who had taught at Milan when Leonardo was there in the early 1480s (Palisca ibid., 72ff; for Leonardo's use of Valla, Kemp 1981 [**1247**], 250–1).
20 Richter 1970 [**1118**], I, 76–81; Pacioli (1509) 1889 [**280**], I, 3 did, however, like Gaffurio, mention colour. Links between the careers and thought of Leonardo, Pacioli and Gaffurio have been explored by Onians 1984 [**2202**], 413–18, 421–3. For Leonardo and Gaffurio, see also Brachert 1971 [**2088**], 461–6.
21 Boethius, *On Music* I, i (Boethius 1989 [**1001**], 8). Boethius spoke of the 'learned' who perceive colour; the passage was repeated in the 16th century by Zarlino 1573, Proem, 2, but he regarded it simply as a pretext for treating theory and practice together. See also the classical revivalist Galilei 1602 [**2130**], 82–3, 86, who compared the simple rhythms which he favoured to drawing (*disegno*) and pitch to colour.
22 Richter 1970 [**1118**], I, 31–2 (§§1–2). For an excellent discussion of Leonardo's concern for continuity, Koenigsberger 1979 [**2170**], 68–75.
23 Leonardo, like Franciscus Junius in the 17th century may have had the *harmogē* recorded by Pliny in mind: his familiarity with Landino's translation of the *Natural History* has been demonstrated by Solmi 1976 [**1140**], 235–48. For the effect of polyphonic practice on a developing sense of harmony not as 'scale' but as a pleasing mixture of simultaneous sounds, Crocker 1962 [**2110**], espec. 4.
24 Richter 1970 [**1118**], I, 77–8 (§34).
25 For the *lira da braccio*, Winternitz 1982 [**2252**], 25–38, and for the flute, 192–3. Leonardo was also a fine singer.
26 Zarlino 1573 [**2256**], I, ch. xiiif. See Crocker 1962 [**2110**], 17–19. An anonymous English 15th-century treatise which sought to link musical notes with armorial blazon listed gold, silver, red, purple, green and black as the 'principal' musical colours, each of which had an 'equal proportion' from which all unequal proportions were derived, but this seems to have been an isolated sport (*Distinctio inter colores musicales et armorum Heroun* in Hawkins 1853 [**2150**], I, 247ff).
27 Pino 1954 [**1282**], 32–4. For musical empiricism, Lowinsky 1966 [**2179**], 136–41; Palisca 1985 [**2204**], 20f, 235ff; Koenigsberger 1979 [**2170**], 199f.
28 Bellori 1976 [**1430**], 206; see also the comparison between colour and singing in Armenini 1988 [**1645**], 126, which, as Gorreri notes, probably depends on Vasari 1878–85 [**340**] I (1878), 179–81.
29 For the identifications, Badt 1981 [**2078**], 155, 181, n. 1. For Titian, N. Pirotta, 'Musiche intorno a Tiziano' in *Tiziano* 1976 [**2234**], 29–34; M. Bonicatti, 'Tiziano e la cultura musicale del suo tempo' in ibid. 461–77. For Tintoretto, Weddingen 1984 [**2246**], 67–92. The musicality of Jacopo Bassano's handling of colour, 'like a well-tempered instrument touched by a masterly hand' was noted by Boschini, 1674 [**177**], Pref.
30 P. Preiss, 'Farbe und Klang in der Theorie und Praxis der Manierismus' in Pečman 1970 [**2205**], 167. Comanini's role as choirmaster of the Milanese Augustinians is not mentioned in M. Coccia's biography of him in *Dizionario Biografico degli Italiani*, but Coccia does list a publication, *Canzoniere spirituale, morale e d'onore*, Mantua, 1609.
31 G. Comanini *Il Figino, ovvero del fine della Pittura*, Mantua 1591, in Barocchi 1960–62 [**992**], III (1962), 368–70.
32 See the biography by E. Polovedo in *Dizionario Biografico degli Italiani*. Arcimboldo's grey-scale has been reconstructed by Caswell 1980 [**2103**], 157–8, who gives a full English translation of Comanini's text but unfortunately detaches the section on the hue-scale from its context (159).
33 Barasch 1978 [**1168**], 179–80. Cardano (1570 [**2093**], Prop. 168, 175) describes a system of value scaling closely related to Leonardo on aerial perspective.
34 Caswell 1980 [**2103**], 161, n. 19 points out that this inference rests on a misunderstanding of the Pythagorean system. Zarlino 1588 [**2257**], bk IV, ch. XVII, 174f. This discussion, published after Arcimboldo had returned to Milan, did not allow the possibility of dividing colour on a surface except by dividing the surface itself. For the more predictable equation of light with high pitch and shade with low, see Testa in Cropper 1984 [**1022**], 205, 223 and commentary 138ff; and Mersenne 1636/7 [**2193**], I, bk II, Prop. VI, 100ff.
35 Kemp 1990 [**1529**], 274 unaccountably translates *morello* (a dark, blackberry-like colour) as 'red'. Gavel 1979 [**219**], 93 and pl. III has attempted a coloured reconstruction of Arcimboldo's system, but ignores the evidence of the grey-scale entirely.
36 L. Levi, 'L'Arcimboldi musicista' in Geiger 1954 [**2132**]. 91–3. This interpretation has rightly been questioned by Preiss in Pečman 1970 [**2205**], 168.
37 See espec. Kaufmann 1989 [**2163**], and for the intellectual background, Evans 1973 [**2123**], espec. ch. VII.
38 Scarmilionius 1601 [**317**], 111–12. Elsewhere (117) Scarmilionius proposed a scale of *albus, flavus, puniceus, viridis, purpureus, caeruleus, niger*. He dedicated his book to the Emperor and mentioned (4) that he had visited Prague. For de Boodt, Parkhurst 1971 [**286**], 3ff; Evans 1973 [**2123**], 216f. The chief source on colour is de Boodt 1609 [**2085**], bk I, ch. 15.
39 Kepler to Mästlin 19/20 August 1599 in Kepler XIV, 1969 [**2165**], 50–51. These ideas about colour do not seem to have reappeared in Kepler's later work. See also Dickreiter 1973 [**2116**], 27–33.
40 Disertori 1978 [**2118**], 53–68; cf. also Spear 1982 [**1612**], 40ff.
41 Malvasia 1678 [**1552**], II, 339.
42 For Canini, Beal 1984 [**1650**], 140ff; for Zaccolini, Cropper 1984 [**1022**], 144. For the *archicembalo* of Nicola Vicentino, built by 1561 and capable of playing microtones on 132 keys, and with which Domenichino seems to have been familiar, Maniates 1979 [**2187**], 120, 141ff. Domenichino's work with keybooards is paralleled by another musician in his circle, G. B. Doni: see C. V. Palisca, 'G. B. Doni, musicological archivist and his "Lyra Barberina"' in Olleson 1980 [**2201**], 186–9.
43 For Carracci's skill on the lute and other string instruments, see his obituary in Malvasia 1678 [**1552**], I, 428, but his theoretical interest in music seems to have been strictly mathematical. Bril worked in Rome, but for other Dutch painter-musicians in the north, Raupp 1978 [**2211**], 106–29.
44 Cureau de la Chambre 1650 [**190**], 170ff.
45 Mersenne 1636/7 [**2193**], 100ff. Descartes also regarded green as the product of 'moderate action' and equivalent to the octave (Darmon 1985 [**1468**], 97), as did Athanasius Kircher in the complex system of correspondences he based on d'Aguilon's diagram (Kemp 1990 [**1529**], 280; cf. *Musurgia Universalis* 1650. bk IX, pt II, ch. V, Qu. 11; bk VII, ch I.). For an attempt to interpret Kircher's scale in modern terms, Wellek 1963 [**2248**], 168. For the musical activities of mathematicians at this time, Cohen 1984 [**2107**].
46 Cureau de la Chambre 1650 [**190**], 203ff. For his influence, Teyssèdre 1967 [**2233**], 208–10; Kemp 1990 [**1529**], 281
47 *Chromatices, tertia pars Picturae* in C. A. du Fresnoy *De Arte Graphica*, repr. in Sir Joshua Reynolds, *The Literary Works*, 1852, II, 273. Roger de Piles 1708 [**1921**], 163 already seems to have a vague idea of the painterly use of 'chromatique', and to equate it with discords, or with colouring in general.
48 For the early study of the Greek modes, Newton 1959 [**2199**], I, 388, n. 14, and for the collaboration with Taylor and Pepusch, P. S. Jones in *Dictionary of Scientific Biography*, XIII, s.v. 'Taylor'. The MS *On Musick* is among the Taylor papers at St John's College, Cambridge; it was known to D. Hartley (1749 [**2149**], I, 195), who noted that it was still primarily concerned with the Dorian scale of five tones and two semitones.
49 Shapiro 1984 [**1603**], I, 544ff.
50 Shapiro 1979/80 [**2227**], 109, n. 38; 1984 [**1603**], I, 542f.
51 For indigo, Biernson 1972 [**2082**],

526–30; McLaren 1985 [**2183**], 225–9. also letters from D. L. MacAdam and McLaren in ibid. XI 1986 [**2184**], 233–4. For the division of the spectrum, Newton 1959– [**2199**], I, 376–7: this letter to the Royal Society in December 1675 was first published in 1757.
52 Shapiro 1984 [**1603**], I, 546 n. 27. In another draft Newton noted 'The harmony & discord also wch the more skilfull Painters observe in colours' (n. 28).
53 Wellek 1963 [**2248**], 170. The Cambridge mathematician Robert Smith pointed out in 1749 that Newton's musical scale, while it agreed well enough with the prismatic colours, was 'not the properest for a system of concords', since it produced a major third, two minor thirds and two fifths, 'severally imperfect by a comma' (1749 [**2228**], 42–3, n. g).
54 Cohen 1984 [**2107**], 171. The link between the two circles was made by Sargant-Florence 1940 [**2220**], 103, 112, 172ff. Zarlino had used a series of circular diagrams to illustrate his six-part system of consonances as early as 1573 [**2256**] (31–2, 41, 43). Newton's first interest in the circular arrangement has been traced to a letter of 1694 (Newton 1959– [**2199**], III (1961), 345–6.
55 For Georges Vantongerloo *c.* 1920, *see* p. 259. Even more recently Carl Loef has argued for the adaptation of modern colour-systems which co-ordinate hue, saturation and value to the modern octave ('Die Bedeutung der Musik-Oktave im optisch-visuellen Bereich der Farbe' in Hering-Mitgau 1980 [**902**], 227–36).
56 Newton 1730 [**1095**], bk III, pt I, qu. 15.
57 See C. Avison *An Essay on Musical Expression* (1753), repr. in Le Huray and Day 1981 [**2154**], 61. As late as 1771 Benjamin Stillingfleet could be puzzled by the grounds for Newton's analogy, but still accept it, since 'it tends some way or other to the perfection of the universe' (1771 [**2232**], 146, §196).
58 For the review of Newton, Castel 1723 [**2095**], 1428–50, for Newton's supposed help, Castel October 1735, 2032f. There is no reference to Castel in the full account of the reception of Newton's *Opticks* in France from *c.* 1719, nor is there any extant correspondence with him (Newton, 1959– [**2199**], VII (1977), 116f). In his article announcing work on the harpsichord Castel mentioned Newton's important 'verification' of the link between colour and sound in his 'excellent' book, but also his own debt to Kircher (*Mercure de France*, November 1725, 2557, 2600f). The most important modern study of Castel remains Schier 1941 [**2221**], whose bibliography of Castel's writings is, however, unreliable.
59 Ferris 1959 [**2126**], espec. 234, 239. Castel's review of the *Traité* (*Journal de Trévoux*, October 1722 [**2094**]) has been reproduced in Rameau 1967–72 [**2210**], I, xxviiiff. Castel also reviewed Rameau's simplified *Nouveau Système de Musique Théorique* (1726) (Castel 1728 [**2098**], in Rameau ibid., II, xviiff).
60 For Rameau's encouragement, Castel August 1735 [**2099**], 1640 (in Rameau 1967–72 [**2210**], VI, 70ff). Castel's scale was presented most fully in Castel 1740 [**2102**], 221–4.
61 For the fundamental white, Castel 1726 [**2097**], 462f; for black as fundamental, Castel, 1735 [**2099**], 1630f, 1662, 2033–5; Castel 1740 [**2102**], 68, 73–7; for the practice of dyers and painters, ibid. 1661; for Le Blon, see Castel's review of *Coloritto* in Castel 1737 [**2100**], 1442f.
62 Castel 1740 [**2102**], 284–97.
63 For Félibien, Castel 1735 [**2099**], 1447, 1632; for the ideas of de Piles, who is not cited, ibid. 1453, from de Piles 1715 [**2206**], ch. XXI, 51f. Castel argued that vermilion fell between orange-red and fire-red at 7½ degrees of hue (*coloris*), and 8 or 9 degrees on the value scale (Castel 1739 [**2101**], 819). He often drew on de Piles without citing him: see his account of the relative neglect of colour-study in Castel 1740 [**2102**], 21–2, based on de Piles (1989 [**1921**], 166).
64 G. P. Telemann *Beschreibung der Augenorgel oder des Augenclavicimbals* (1739), repr. in Mizler 1743 [**2194**], II, 269–75. This was a translation from the French, but the French version in Castel 1740 [**2102**], 482–3 was itself a re-translation from Telemann's German.
65 See the anonymous *Explanation of the Ocular Harpsichord upon Shew to the Public* (1757) 1762, which Schier (1941 [**2221**], 183, n. 158) has attributed to Rondet. The history of Castel's instrument has been traced by von Erhardt-Siebold 1931–2 [**2121**], 353–7, and espec. Wellek 1935 [**2247**], 347–75 and 1963 [**2248**], 171–6, which cites an unpublished and undated MS of Castel's, *Journal des Travaux pour son clavecin oculaire* (Brussels, Royal Library). Mason's account, 1958/9 [**2189**], 103–16, derives entirely from Wellek.
66 Guyot 1769 [**2146**], 234–40. I owe my knowledge of this, and a photocopy, to the kindness of John Mollon.
67 Plateau 1849 [**2207**], 563–7. For an outline of Plateau's work on colour and movement, Roque 1990 [**948**], 19–23. His experiment seems to have stimulated the indefatigable Chevreul to make similar efforts with spinning discs, and, in consultation with a Paris organist, he rejected Castel's scale (Chevreul 1879 [**2105**], 183, 237ff).
68 F. Webb *Panharmonicon, designed as an illustration of an engraved plate in which is attempted to be proved, that the principles of harmony more or less prevail throughout the whole system of nature, but more especially in the Human Frame: and that where these principles can be applied to works of art, they excite the pleasing and satisfying ideas of proportion and beauty* [1814]. For the link with Hussey, 1–2, 10f. Hussey's chromatic system was published in Hussey 1756 [**2155**], 852. There has been no modern study of Hussey, but there are some interesting drawings by him in the British Museum, and a painting at Syon House, Middlesex. The most important sources for his ideas are G. Vertue *Notebook*, December 1745 (*Walpole Society*, XXII, 1933–4, 127–8); Maton 1797 [**2190**], I, 33–41; *Monthly Magazine*, October 1799, 725–6; Webb in Hutchins IV, 1815 [**2153**], 154–9.
69 Ozias Humphry *Pocket Book* I, British Library Add. MS 22949, folio 105v–106v. Some of Duane's Hussey drawings were acquired by West (Webb [1814], 10f; Hutchins IV, 1815 [**2153**], 159n).
70 Field 1820 [**2127**], 199, 202–3.
71 Ibid., 204. For his rejection of Castel's system, 226.
72 Field 1845 [**2010**], 56–60.
73 The painter Guiseppe Bossi invoked both Rameau and Tartini in one of the most systematic early studies of complementary contrast, Bossi 1821 [**2087**], 294–314.
74 The scientific poet Erasmus Darwin had already used the sequential nature of the after-images discussed by his son Robert Waring Darwin in 1786 as a sign of some necessary link with the sequence of musical sounds (*The Botanic Garden, II, The Loves of the Plants, 1789*, Interlude III, in Darwin 1806 [**1023**], II, 167–81). Count Rumford similarly felt that the palpably harmonic relationships of the complementaries would give a new impetus to 'instruments for producing that harmony for the entertainment of the eyes, in a manner similar to that in which the ears are entertained by musical sounds' (Rumford 1794 [**2219**], 107f); another scientist, Sir David Brewster, argued in 1819 that the kaleidoscope, presenting a succession of coloured shapes harmonized according to the principles of complementarity, 'realises in the fullest manner the formerly chimerical idea of an ocular harpsichord' (Brewster 1819 [**2090**], 68–9, 131–5). The kaleidoscope became something of a *topos* for the discussion of non-representational colour in the 19th century: the music critic Eduard Hanslick linked it with such 'trivial absurdities' as the colour-organ in 1854, and 20 years later the psychologist and aesthetician G. T. Fechner took up the idea more positively, adding his own experience of a disc-mixing apparatus such as Plateau's (both cit. Bujić 1988 [**2092**], 19–20, 287–9). The toy was still providing a model for non-representational moving colour for the early Italian theorists of abstract film, Arnaldo Ginna and Bruno Corra (*see* p. 245) *Arte dell'Avvenire*, 2nd edn, 1911 repr. in Verdone 1967 [**2242**], 185.
75 Jameson 1844 [**2159**], cit. Klein 1937 [**2169**], 188. Klein is the only modern writer to discuss Jameson's pamphlet, from which he quotes passages on 2–4, 80 and 188–9.
76 Jameson 1844 [**2159**], 20. For the borrowings from Goethe and Field, Klein 1937 [**2169**], 80. Field's equivalents had been published in Field 1835 (see Gage 1989 [**2017**], nos 45–6).
77 See espec. Bouvier 1828 [**1655**], 165f, 249 and Storey in *The Portfolio* VI, 1875, 111.
78 Johnson 1981–9 [**1070**], V (1989) no. 13A
79 Chenavard to Redon in Redon 1979 [**1718**], 63. For Mengs, Wittkower 1962 [**2253**], 149
80 Johnson 1981–9 [**1070**], I (1981), no. 93, and espec. Kemp 1970 [**2164**], 49ff. Reynolds had argued similarly that drawing demanded the same constant practice as a musical instrument (Reynolds 1975 [**2213**], 33).
81 Delacroix to Chopin, January 1841 in Sand 1896 [**1130**], 81ff. The idea is close to one of Hegel's in his lectures on aesthetics (Hegel XIV, 1927–8 [**1845**], 73–4). Some links between Delacroix and German Romantic musical thought have been proposed by Mras 1963 [**2197**], 270–1. See also the useful collection of the painter's remarks on music in Würtenberger 1979 [**2255**], 56–63.
82 A. Kerssemakers in Van Gogh 1958 [**1626**], II, 447.
83 Van Gogh ibid., no. 539 (?September 1888). See also p. Ch 10 p. 185, n. 53. For the cult of Wagner among Symbolist artists, Vaughan 1984 [**2241**], 38–48.
84 Le Huray and Day 1981 [**2154**], 100f. See also Herder *Kalligone* (1800) in ibid. 256.
85 For Fechner, Bujić 1988 [**2092**], 288–9; also Fechner II, 1898 [**2125**], 216. For a modern debate on the correlation between light and sound, Garner 1978 [**2131**], 225f; Davis 1979 [**2113**], 218f.
86 J. L. Hoffmann *Versuch einer Geschichte der malerischen Harmonie überhaupt und der Farbenharmonie insbesondere, mit Erläuterungen aus der Tonkunst, und vielen praktischen Anmerkungen*, Halle, 1786, in Goethe LA [**225**], I, 6, 1957, 395–9. Hoffmann also published a *Farbenkunde für Mahler und Leibhaber der Kunst*, Erlangen, 1798.
87 E.g. Suarez de Mendoza 1890 [**1963**], 16 (repeated by Gérome-Maësse 1907 [**1828**], 657).
88 Locke 1975 [**2178**], bk III, ch IV, sect. II. For the history of this example in England, Maclean 1936 [**2185**], 106ff; see also Fechner II, 1898 [**2125**], 216; Suarez de Mendoza 1890 [**1963**], 20 (repeated by Gérome-Maësse 1907 [**1828**], 658); Wundt 1902–3 [**1977**], II (1902), 351; Kandinsky 1982 [**1686**], I, 187; Dehnow 1919 [**2114**], 127. For Schoenberg, Crawford 1974 [**2109**], 588.
89 An instance in Ludwig Tieck has been noticed by Marks 1975 [**2188**]; Wundt 1902–3 [**1977**], II (1902), 352, n. 1 cites a reference in C. Herrmann, *Aesthetische Farbenlehre*, 1876, 45f; de Rochas 1885 [**2214**], 406f; Suarez de Mendoza 1890 [**1963**], 20; Souriau, 1895 [**958**], 860; Gérome-Maësse 1907 [**1828**], 658.
90 Kandinsky 1982 [**1686**], I, 182.
91 Both de Rochas 1885 [**2214**] and Wundt 1902–3 [**1977**], II (1902), 331 emphasized that timbre was the primary characteristic of music to be felt by synaesthetics. See also Fischer 1907 [**2128**], 525; Dehnow 1919 [**2114**], 127.
92 For a photograph of the young Kandinsky playing the cello, Roethel and Benjamin I, 1982 [**1933**], 32. For blue, Kandinsky 1982 [**1686**], I, 182.
93 Matisse to Tériade, 1929/30 in Matisse 1978 [**1889**], 58. As late as the 1950s Matisse conceived of his large-scale decorative works as the orchestral realization of the 'score' of the maquette, and did not want them to be seen together (Matisse to A. Barr (1954) in Cowart et al. 1977 [**1795**], 280f).
94 Marc to Macke, 14 January 1911 in Macke 1964 [**1879**], 40–1. See also his letter to Maria Marc, 5 February 1911 in Gollek 1980 [**2141**], 116. Paul Sérusier had already made dissonance a major element in his theory of colour in the 1890s: see his letter to Verkade of 1896 in Sérusier 1950 [**2226**], 72–5, also 20 November 1905 (119–22). Macke was studying Sérusier's theory in 1911 (Erdman-Macke 1962 [**2120**], 171 and cf. Vriesen 1957 [**2243**], 315 and no. 254).
95 Marc to Maria Marc, 10 February 1911 in Gollek 1980 [**2141**], 117.
96 Kandinsky 1982 [**1686**], I, 193. His letter to Schoenberg is translated in Hahl-Koch 1984 [**2147**], 21. See also P. Vergo in *Towards a New Art* 1980 [**2235**], 55–8.
97 See Arnheim 1974 [**2076**], 346–50; Whitfield and Slatter 1978 [**2249**], 199–206. For Ostwald's characterization of the palette based on his system as a 'colour-organ', Ostwald 1931–3 [**2203**], I, 166f, 173. The most extensive survey of theories of harmony in relation to colour-music is Klein 1937 [**2169**], 61–117.
98 Goethe had made the observation to Riemer in May 1807, and it had been reprinted in Goethe 1907 [**2136**], 94. See

also Goethe to Meyer, 30 June 1807, in Goethe 1919 [**1834**], 193. Kandinsky quoted the tag in *On the Spiritual in Art* (1982 [**1686**], I, 162, 176, 196), and in the *Blue Rider Almanac* (Lankheit 1974 [**2172**], 112, 170). Goethe had picked up the idea from his reading of Diderot, who had called the rainbow the *basse fondamentale* of painting (*Essai sur la peinture* (1766) in Diderot 1965 [**2117**], 678); but he misread his source so far as to imagine that Diderot had written of artists who arranged their palettes in the order of the spectrum, of which there is no suggestion in the French (Goethe 1962 [**2137**], I, 139–40). For his treatment of Diderot's essay in general. Rouge 1949 [**2217**], 227–36.

99 Schoenberg 1966 [**2225**], 8–9. In one of his references to the *Generalbass* in 1912 Kandinsky did admittedly show some scepticism about the possibility of such a fixed principle in the modern world (1982 [**1686**], I, 196).

100 Eggeling's *Material for a Thorough-Bass of Painting* was published in *Antologie Dada*, 15 May 1919: see O'Konor 1971 [**2200**], 201–4. Although he was familiar with Kandinsky's writing (ibid. 75f) his immediate stimulus was conversations with the composer Ferruccio Busoni, the second edn of whose *Entwurf einer neuen Aesthetik der Tonkunst* had been published in 1916 (see the extracts trans. in Bujić 1988 [**2092**], 388–94 and O'Konor 1971 [**2200**], 39, 101). Eggeling worked with light and was thus more interested in the additive than the subtractive primaries; but until his death in 1925 he worked almost exclusively in black and white (O'Konor ibid., 45, 56, 98). Van Doesburg's *Thorough-Bass of Painting* was illustrated in the journal *G: Zeitschrift für elementare Gestaltung*, 1923 (repr. in *Towards a New Art* 1980 [**2235**], 140). He was an admirer of Eggeling, discussing his work several times in *De Stijl* (IV, 5, 1921, 71–5; VI, 5, 1923, 58–62), as well as publishing an article by Hans Richter on him, which includes a definition of *Generalbass* as a language of form (*De Stijl*, IV, 7, 1921, 110). For van Doesburg's early interest in Kandinsky, Baljeu 1974 [**2079**], 16.

101 See Schmoll 1974 [**2224**], 325–43; Würtenberger 1979 [**2255**], 172–83, and espec. F. T. Bach, 'Johann Sebastian Bach in der klassischen Moderne' in von Maur 1985 [**2192**], 328–9.

102 Marc to Kandinsky, 5 October 1912, in Lankheit 1983 [**2173**], 193; Klee 1976 [**2167**], 108.

103 Levin 1978 [**2176**], 44.

104 Ibid., 129. For Russell's musical tastes, see also Levin in von Maur 1985 [**2192**], 370.

105 Levin 1978 [**2176**], 23. *Four-Part Synchromy*, not inappropriately for a fugal composition, is reproduced upside-down in von Maur 1985 [**2192**], 95. For a discussion of the arrangement of the panels, Agee 1965 [**2073**], 53.

106 Tudor Hart 1918 [**2239**, **2240**], 452–6, 480–6. In 1920 the *Cambridge Magazine* published a musical analysis of a still-life by Duncan Grant according to Tudor Hart's principles (X, 61 and fig. facing p. 1) and in 1921 Tudor Hart published a critique of Ostwald (ibid., 106–9). For a critique of his own theory, Klein 1937 [**2169**], 102–6. For col. reproductions of Tudor Hart's work, MacGregor 1961 [**2181**].

107 Levin 1978 [**2176**], 14.

108 Notes from a Klee lecture at Dessau, 1927/8 cit. Triska 1979 [**2236**], 78, n. 80. See also the conflicting recollections of the violinist Karl Grebe and Lyonel Feininger in Grote 1959 [**2144**], 63, 75; for Klee's dislike of jazz, ibid., 53, 70. See also the important discussion by C. Geelhaar in von Maur 1985 [**2192**], 423, 425. Grebe noticed the old-fashioned style of Klee's playing (see *Klee et la musique* 1985/6 [**2168**], 161).

109 For Feininger's 13 fugues, F. T. Bach in von Maur, 1985 [**2192**], 331–2, and H. H. Stuckenschmidt in ibid., 410, which also (35) reproduces Klee's *Fugue in Red* in colour. Feininger felt his love of Bach 'finds expression also in my paintings' (Hess 1961 [**2151**], 97f). For Klee's teaching of value-scales in 1924, Klee 1973 [**2166**], 335–407.

110 For a structural analysis of *New Harmony*, Kagan 1983 [**2161**], 76; and for *Ad Parnassum*, 85ff.

111 Diary, 3 November 1918 in Rotzler 1972 [**2216**], 61; P. Baumann, 'Das entscheidende Jahr' in *Johannes Itten* 1980 [**2158**], 31–4; for a structural analysis of Itten's 1916 painting *Der Bach-Sänger*, F. T. Bach in von Maur 1985 [**2192**], 331.

112 D. Bogner, 'Musik und bildende Kunst in Wien' in von Maur ibid., 350–2, and col. pl. p. 67.

113 Diary, July 1920 in Rotzler 1972 [**2216**], 72. For a reproduction of the colour-sphere, *Der Hang zum Gesamtkunstwerk 1983* [**2148**], 379. Itten seems to have devised his grey scale according to a geometrical progression (Diary, 5 July 1919 in Rotzler ibid., 65).

114 See Itten in *Johannes Itten* 1984 [**2157**], 176–7; and for a collection of these harmonies, Itten 1961 [**2156**].

115 Mondrian, 'Jazz and Neo-Plastic' in Holtzman and James 1987 [**2152**], 219.

116 Troy 1984 [**2238**], 645. For van Doesburg's painting of 1918/9, Blotkamp et al. 1986 [**2084**], 25–7. Mondrian's 'abstract' style of dancing in Paris was experienced by Nelly van Doesburg (1971 [**2119**], 180–1) and in New York by Max Ernst (1944 [**2122**], 25).

117 See Holtzman and James 1987 [**2152**], 222. For Mondrian's *Fox-Trot* painting (1920), Troy 1983 [**2237**], 93; for the others, K. von Maur, 'Mondrian und die Musik im "Stijl"' in von Maur 1985 [**2192**], 402.

118 Rosenfeld 1981 [**2215**], 62.

119 Guest 1948, [**2145**], 53–6.

120 Bishop 1893 [**2083**], 17. Bishop's attempts to develop his instrument, first demonstrated in New York in 1881, included the destruction of three versions by fire (12, 16).

121 S. Stein 1983 [**2231**], 61ff. For Appia, Bablet 1965 [**2077**], 263.

122 For Scriabin's scale, Motte-Haber 1990 [**2196**], 67. The Theosophical scale is in Besant and Leadbeater 1961 [**2081**], frontispiece. Scriabin's brother-in-law Boris de Schloezer attested to his knowledge of their writings (de Schloezer 1987 [**2223**], 66); for his general contact with Theosophy, H. Weber, 'Zur Geschichte der Synästhesie, oder, von der Schwierigkeiten, die luce-stimme in *Prometheus* zu interpretieren' in Kolleritsch 1980 [**2171**], 54–5. Kandinsky in 1912 described Scriabin's system as close to that of the Russian Theosophist A. Zakharin-Unkowsky, for whose relationship to Kandinsky see R. C. Washton-Long, 'Expressionism, Abstraction and the search for Utopia in Germany' in Tuchman 1986 [**1407**], 202. A comparative table of the colour-associations of Scriabin, Steiner, Kandinsky and Schoenberg has been compiled by D. Eberlein, 'Čiurlionis, Skrjabin und der osteuropäische Symbolismus' in von Maur 1985 [**2192**], 342.

123 Besant and Leadbeater 1961 [**2081**], 60–4.

124 See the discussion of Scriabin's annotated score (Bibliothèque Nationale, Paris) by J.-H. Lederer, 'Die Funktion der Luce-Stimme' in Kolleritsch 1980 [**2171**], 130f.

125 Myers 1915 [**2198**], 112. Scriabin disagreed with Rimsky about F♯, which he saw as violet, and Rimsky as green; the conductor of the first performance of the *Prometheus Symphony* in Moscow and St Petersburg, Koussevitsky, felt that it was strawberry-red (Klein 1937 [**2169**], 42).

126 De Schloezer 1987 [**2223**], 85; Eberlein in von Maur 1985 [**2192**], 342. For Kandinsky's experiments in revolutionary Russia with the dancer Alexander Sacharoff, who evolved dances translating the painter's watercolours into movement, J. Hahl-Koch in von Maur ibid., 355.

127 Klein 1937 [**2169**], 9. The outbreak of war prevented this concert's taking place. Rimington's own colour-correspondences were based on analogies between the musical scale and the spectrum, and were thus different from Scriabin's: his F♯ was green and his E yellow (A. W. Rimington. *Colour-Music. The Art of Mobile Colours*, 1911, 177).

128 Plummer 1915 [**2208**], 343, 350–1.

129 *New York Times*, 21 March, 1915, cit. Klein 1937 [**2169**], 248.

130 As was pointed out by Washton-Long 1980 [**2245**], 57ff. For Scriabin, Weber and Lederer, Kolleritsch 1980 [**2171**], 54, 134–6.

131 Hahl-Koch 1984 [**2147**], 96. For the link with Kandinsky, Crawford 1974 [**2109**], 587–94.

132 See Schlemmer's Diary, December 1912 in Schlemmer 1972 [**2222**], 7–8; for the 1912 correspondence with Schoenberg, von Maur 1979 [**2191**], I, 39. For Schlemmer's staging of *Die Glückliche Hand*, Curjel 1975 [**2112**], 378.

133 See his account in Kandinsky 1982 [**1686**], II, 750–1. The staging was by Paul Klee's son Felix: see his annotated score now in the Pompidou Centre, Paris (repr. in Derouet and Boissel 1985 [**2115**], 314); see also N. Kandinsky 1976 [**2162**], 153.

134 Hahl-Koch 1984 [**2147**], 101. Another painter suggested was Alfred Roller, whom Schoenberg knew for his innovative stage-lighting.

135 Ginna in Verdone 1967 [**2242**], 21. Ginna and Corra used the example of Wagner several times in their *Arte dell'Avvenire* (1910), 2nd edn 1911 repr. in ibid., 178, 183. Ginna cited Besant and Leadbeater's *Thought Forms* as similar in spirit to modern painting in *Pittura dell'Avvenire* (1915) (ibid., 208).

136 For chromatic dramas, Ginna and Corra (1910) in Verdone 1967 [**2242**], 185–7. They saw a precedent in the performances to light accompaniment of the American dancer Loïe Fuller, who described, in the tradition of Féré, how different lights obliged her to make different movements (L. Fuller *Quinze ans de ma vie* (1908), cit. Popper 1967 [**2208**], 28). For the colour-piano, Corra (1912) in Verdone ibid., 246.

137 Corra (1912) in Verdone 1967 [**2242**], 250; trans. from Apollonio 1973 [**2075**,] 69. See Fischinger's *Composition in Blue* (1935), some stills from which are repr. in W. Moritz, 'Abstract Film and Color Music' in Tuchman 1986 [**1407**], 296, 302.

138 Their collaboration is mentioned by S. Selwood, 'Farblichtmusik und abstrakter Film' in von Maur 1985 [**2192**], 420, n. 40. For Fischinger, see also Moritz in Tuchman 1986 [**1407**], 301–3, and Motte-Haber 1990 [**2196**], 212–13.

139 For Ostwald, László 1925a [**2174**], viii. László's grey-scale is repr. in von Maur 1985 [**2192**], no. 341b. He and Ostwald shared the same publisher, Unesma of Leipzig. Ostwald built his own colour–light–music apparatus in the late 1920s and offered it to Gropius at the Bauhaus. Ise Gropius noted that it was better than László's (Diary, 10 June 1927, kindly communicated by Dr Anna Rowland). László ibid., viii seems to confuse Klee's *Fugue in Red* with work by Feininger. For feeling, László 1925b [**2175**], II, 680–3.

140 See the bibliography in Mahling 1926 [**1880**], 170–1, and Anschütz 1926 [**2074**], 138; for a negative response by an experimental psychologist, Goldschmidt 1927/8 [**2139**], 8, 11, 31–2.

141 See von Maur 1985 [**2192**], 212; for Fischinger's Bach-inspired *Motion Painting No. 1* (1947), ibid., 226.

142 See the long and illuminating list of German patents for colour-music devices in Goldschmidt 1927/8 [**2139**], 71ff.

143 An exception was the colour-piano devised by a pupil of Itten's, which he described in a letter to Hauer of November 1919 (cit. Rotzler 1972 [**2216**], 67). It is just possible that this pupil was Ludwig Hirschfeld-Mack, who seems to have joined Itten's class at the Bauhaus in October.

144 See von Maur 1985 [**2192**], 216–17. The most circumstantial account of the origin of these compositions is in a letter from Hirschfeld-Mack to Standish Lawder in 1965, cit. Gilbert 1966 [**2134**], 13f. The forms are close to some of Klee's 1921 watercolours such as *Fugue in Red*. Reconstructions of several of Schwertfeger's compositions were filmed in 1967, and are available from various German Government Film Libraries. Hirschfeld-Mack's compositions were also interesting to psychologists, and perhaps his last performance was given at the invitation of Georg Anschütz at the Congress of Psychologists for Colour-Sound Synaesthesia, Hamburg 1930. See also Goldschmidt 1927/8 [**2139**], 8, 31.

145 This has been explored effectively by Moritz in Tuchman 1986 [**1407**], 297–311.

146 Greenewalt 1918 [**2142**], 2. For a chapel concert in 1939, Greenewalt 1946 [**2143**], 262.

147 The 1919 light-score for the Beethoven sonata, in red, green and purple, is repr. in Greenewalt 1946 [**2143**], 401; for Debussy, Greenewalt 1918 [**2142**], 15.

148 Zilczer 1987 [**2258**], 122.

149 For Bragdon's organ, which he soon abandoned, Cheney 1932 [**2104**], 187.

150 Bragdon 1918 [**2089**], 130; for autonomy, 139.

151 Wilfred 1947 [**2250**], 252. For the design, Stein 1971 [**2230**], 75; for the Institute, Bornstein 1975 [**2086**], 251.

152 Moholy-Nagy 1922 [**2195**], 100.

Some rather two-dimensional compositions by Wilfred, to which Moholy may be referring, were published in *Theatre Arts Magazine* in 1922, and are repr. by L. Henderson, 'Mysticism, Romanticism and the fourth dimension' in Tuchman 1986 [**1407**], 227.
153 Klein 1937 [**2169**], 18, 20. For Bragdon's dislike of industrial and his love of natural effects, Bragdon 1918 [**2089**], 127, 140. For the rapid succession of Wilfred's instruments, Stein 1971 [**2230**], 12–14, and for the performances by Wilfred's pupil, Fennimore Gerner, at the Paris Exposition des Arts Décoratifs, 1925, Moritz in Tuchman 1986 [**1407**], 229.
154 Cheney 1932 [**2104**], 180, 188.
155 Wilfred 1948 [**2251**], 90.
156 Wright 1923 [**2254**], 68.
157 Goldschmidt 1927/8 [**2139**], passim.
158 See the examples of both illustrated in Jones 1972 [**2160**], 24, 26, 28–30, 96.
159 C. Scott *Music, its Secret Influence throughout the Ages* (1958), cit. Godwin 1986 [**2135**], 286.

14 Colour without Theory

1 Von Seidlitz 1900 [**2384**], 52. This same tendency was recognized by an opponent of Impressionism, who linked the liking for colour with 'brute matter' (Caussy 1904 [**2280**], 639).
2 Scheffler 1901, [**2375**], 187. Kandinsky cited this article in 1912 (Kandinsky 1982 [**1686**], I, 161).
3 Cit. G. Kahn, 'Seurat' (1891) in Broude 1978 [**1443**], 22.
4 Blanc 1867 [**1436**], 595. The idea that colour, unlike drawing, is unteachable has a history going back at least as far as El Greco (*see* p. Ch. 7 p. 138 and Pacheco 1956 [**2360**], I, 440); Le Blond de la Tour and de Piles in Teyssèdre 1965 [**1620**], 69, n. 3, 194, n. 3; Lairesse 1738 [**1539**], 155; Castel 1740 [**2102**], 21–2; Valenciennes 1800 [**1150**], 402–3; for the 'grammar' of colour, Field 1850 [**2305**], Guichard 1882 [**2313**]. The Purists seem to have been the last theorists to sustain the old dichotomy of *disegno* and *colore* in favour of *disegno* (Ozenfant and Jeanneret 1918 [**2359**], 55).
5 See his assistant Arnaud on his 'langue universelle des couleurs' (1886) in Reynes 1981 [**2369**], 181.
6 Kandinsky 1982 [**1686**], I, 161. See also the Austrian poet Hugo von Hofmannsthal *Briefe des Zurückgekehrten* (1901) in Hofmannsthal 1951 [**2323**], 352.
7 Ostwald 1926–7 [**2358**], III, 355. There is a substantial entry on Ostwald in Supplement I to the *Dictionary of Scientific Biography (1978)*.
8 For the general reception of the book, Ostwald ibid., III, 356. It was translated into English as *Letters to a Painter on the Theory and Practice of Painting*, Boston, 1907. For Klee, Klee 1979b [**2334**], I, 430. Klee's diary entry for May/June 1904 (Klee 1957 [**1691**], no. 561) was far less positive.
9 Ostwald 1926–7 [**2358**], I, 30, and III, 358, 403; for the meeting with Munsell, III, 63f. See also Nickerson 1976 [**2351**], 70.
10 For the *Farbschau* in 1914, Ostwald 1917 [**2355**], 367. The *Farbenfibel* has been translated by F. Birren, based on a later edn, as Ostwald *The Color Primer* [**2357**].
11 Ostwald, 'Normen', *Jahrbuch des deutschen Werkbundes, 1914, 77, repr. in Junghanns 1982 [***2329**], 172.
12 For the 'norms' of Japanese design, Ostwald in Junghanns 1982 [**2329**], 172. For Ostwald's 'improvements', Ostwald 1922 [**2356**], 2–3. This book also included (111) an attack on Expressionism.
13 Holtzman and James 1987 [**2152**], 13. For the beach scenes of Mondrian and Toorop, Herbert 1968 [**2318**], nos 147, 174.
14 R. P. Welsh, 'Sacred geometry: French Symbolism and early Abstraction' in Tuchman 1986 [**1407**], 83.
15 Welsh and Joosten 1969 [**2402**],21.
16 'The New Plastic in Painting' (1918) in Holtzman and James 1987 [**2152**], 36. The book of which this article formed a part was largely written in 1914 and 1915 (ibid., 27). Mondrian was still arguing in these terms in the late 1920s: see E. Hoek, 'Piet Mondarian' in Blotkamp et al. 1986 [**2084**], 69.
17 'Natural reality and abstract reality' (1919/20) in Holtzman and James 1987 [**2152**], 86, 100.
18 Besant and Leadbeater 1961 [**2081**], 52, fig. 40: For a col. pl. of *Evolution*, C. Blotkamp, 'Annunciation of the new mysticism: Dutch Symbolism and early Abstraction' in Tuchman 1986 [**1407**], 101, fig. 17.
19 Schuré 1912 [**2383**], II, 61. The white light playing round Mondrian's central figure may be identified with the 'intelligible light' of the female, Mitra (ibid., 38–9).
20 Holtzman and James 1987 [**2152**], 36.
21 Schuré 1912 [**2383**], II, 40–2, quoting Reichenbach *Researches on Magnetism Electricity and Light*, 1850. For a brief account of Reichenbach, W. V. Farrar in the *Dictionary of Scientific Biography*.
22 Schoenmaekers 1913 [**2379**], 94; also 97 for the male as intellectual and the female as corporeal.
23 Schoenmaekers 1915 [**2380**], 223–7. For radial movement, Schoenmaekers 1913 [**2379**], 94.
24 Holtzman and James 1987 [**2152**], 36. Schoenmaekers had referred to Goethe's *Theory of Colours, Didactic Part* [**1833**], §§765, 780, 794, 802.
25. See his letter mentioning Blavatsky's *Secret Doctrine* to van Doesburg in 1918 (Blotkamp in Tuchman 1986 [**1407**], 103); also Hoek in Blotkamp et al. 1986 [**2084**], 49. But Blavatsky had no theory of colour, introducing a number of traditional three, four, five and seven-colour theories into her eclectic compilation, *The Secret Doctrine*, 1888 [**2271**], I, 125, 464, and II, 622, 628–9. The book had been translated into Dutch in 1908–9.
26 The best account of van der Leck in English is by C. Hilhorst in Blotkamp et al. 1986 [**2084**], 153–85. For his views on colour and light, see his essay,'De plaats van het moderne schilderen in de architectuur', *De Stijl*, I, i, 1917, which is available in a French trans. in *Bart van der Leck* 1980 [**2393**], 57–8.
27 See Hilhorst in Blotkamp et al. 1986 [**2084**], 163. For colour reproductions of van der Leck's work at this time, R. W. D. Oxenaar, 'Van der Leck and de Stijl, 1916–1920' in Friedman 1982 [**2306**], 68–79.
28 V. Huszár, 'Iets over die Farbenfibel van W. Ostwald', *De Stijl*, I, 10, 1918, 113–18.
29 Letter to C. Beekman, September 1917 in Ex and Hoek 1985 [**2301**], 196.
30 The circle is reproduced in col. in Ex and Hoek ibid., 168, fig. 67. The triangle is there set at 00 (yellow), 67 (blue) and 33 (crimson), as is the pencilled-in triangle on van Doesburg's copy, inscribed by him in 1918 (Doig 1986 [**2297**], 88, fig. 33). Huszár's paintings are reproduced in S. Ex, 'Vilmos Huszár' in Blotkamp et al. 1986 [**2084**], 98–101, which is the best account in English; but see also Bajkay 1984 [**2267**], 311–26, which has a rather imaginative account of Huszár's use of Ostwald.
31 See Ostwald 1931–3 [**2203**], I, 83 for the role of green. In a letter to Beekman of 4 March 1919 Huszár wrote that Ostwald had shown him that the primary colours were not three, but infinite (Ex and Hoek 1985 [**2301**], 203).
32 For grey, see Huszár's 1918 review (above, n. 28), 115. The best reproduction is in Ex and Hoek 1985 [**2301**], 48, fig. 72, and cf. 49–50 for a general discussion of it.
33 See the reproduction by Ex in Blotkamp et al. 1986 [**2084**], 98, fig. 85.
34 *De Stijl*, II, 12, 1919, 143.
35 'Die Harmonie der Farben', *De Stijl*, III, 7, 1920, 61. The article had originally appeared in *Innen-Dekoration* in 1919.
36 For Mondrian and symmetry, 'The New Plastic in Painting' (1917) in Holtzman and James 1987 [**2152**], 40. The statement was reprinted in *De Stijl*, V, 12, 1922, 183.
37 Ex in Blotkamp et al. 1986 [**2084**], 99.
38 Holtzman and James 1987 [**2152**], 36. Grey remained a difficult concept in De Stijl: van Doesburg regarded it as the non-chromatic equivalent to red, which would require a more Goethean conception of the relationship of blue to yellow than he seems to have supported (van Doesburg 1969 [**2296**], fig. I. and p. 15). This discussion of colour had not appeared in the first version of this work (1919), (1983, 22).
39 Mondrian to van Doesburg, 13 February 1919, cit. Hoek in Blotkamp et al. 1986 [**2084**], 54–5. Mondrian's ambivalence about the relationship of his work to 'nature' was very marked at this time (ibid., 50).
40 Mondrian to van Doesburg, 3 September 1918, cit. Ex in Blotkamp et al. 1982 [**2273**], 107. This passage is not included in the version of the letter trans. in Blotkamp et al. 1986 [**2084**], 103. For Vantongerloo, N. Gast in ibid., 249.
41 Blotkamp 1975–6 [**2272**], 103.
42 Schumann 1900 [**2382**], 11–12.
43. See, eg., the stories in Holtzman and James 1987 [**2152**], 7.
44 Westphal 1910 [**1155**], espec. 226–9. Westphal pointed to the painterly experience of at least one observer making these confusions. For other Mondrian paintings in public collections, using yellow-green and green at this date, *Composition with Red, Blue and Yellow-Green* (1920), Ludwigshafen, Wilhelm-Hack Museum (repr. in K. S. Champa, *Mondrian Studies*, 1985, 83 and pl. 14); *Composition XIII* (1920), Private collection, reprod. Cologne, Galerie Gmurzynska. *Mondrian und De Stijl*, 1979, 181.
45 Hoek in Blotkamp et al. 1986 [**2084**], 59.
46 Carmean 1979 [**2279**], 79, 83. This catalogue includes a technical examination of *Diamond Painting in Red, Yellow and Blue* (1921), which was repainted in 1922/4, 1925 and 1925/7.
47 Doig 1986 [**2297**], 90. See, e.g., *Composition in Discords* (1918) and the designs for the cinema and dance-hall at the Café Aubette in Strasbourg in 1927 (Baljeu 1974 [**2079**], 36, 172–3). In *De Stijl*, VII, 1926, 40f of van Doesburg showed that he was not averse, in theory as well as in practice, to using earth colours as 'variants'. In the late 1920s he was particularly concerned about the theory of colour, and hoped to bring out a second Bauhaus Book, a *Neue Gestaltungslehre* which would begin with a whole volume on colour (Doesburg to Moholy-Nagy, 16 August 1928 in van Doesburg 1983 [**2296**], 118f).
48 M. Küper, 'Gerrit Rietveld' in Blotkamp et al. 1986 [**2084**], 272–3.
49 Rietveld 'Insight' (1928) in Brown 1958 [**2275**], 160.
50 Mondrian to van Doesburg, 5 September 1920, in Holtzman and James 1987 [**2152**], 133.
51 *Composition*, reprod. in black and white by Gast in Blotkamp et al. 1986 [**2084**], 244, fig. 229, where it is dated 1918.
52 Ibid. 249.
53 'Unité' (1920) in Vantongerloo 1924 [**2394**], 26–9, 37. The fullest account of Vantongerloo's theory is Roque 1983 [**2370**], 105–28.
54 Vantongerloo 1924 [**2394**], 39.
55 'L'art ancien et l'art nouveau' (1921) in Vantongerloo 1924 [**2394**], 18–19. The painting is repr. by Gast in Blotkamp et al. 1986 [**2084**], 253, fig. 240 (black-and-white).
56 'Unité' in Vantongerloo 1924 [**2394**], 40. It may be significant that the only book on physics found in Vantongerloo's library was a French textbook published in the year of his birth, 1886 (Gast in Blotkamp et al. 1986 [**2084**], 257, n. 58).
57 'Unité' in Vantongerloo 1924 [**2394**], 29–36. His later and very precise structural use of algebra has been analysed by Couwenbergh and Dieu 1983 [**2286**], 86–104.
58 Henry, n.d. [**2317**], espec. VII, 728–36 on complementary colours.
59 Mondrian to van Doesburg, 19 April 1920, cit. Gast in Blotkamp et al. [**2084**] 1986, 248.
60 Mondrian to van Doesburg (1920) in ibid., 254.
61 Huszár 1918 (above, n. 28), 115. Vantongerloo in 1931 was anxious to detach himself from the ideas of other members of De Stijl, and to argue that they had had almost no contact with each other (letters to B. Oud in *Internationaal Centrum voor Structuuranalyse en Constructivisme, Cahier* I, 1983, espec. 132, 138, 149).
62 A. Hoelzel, 'Einziges über die Farbe in ihrer bildharmonischen Bedeutung und Auswertung' repr. in Venzmer 1982 [**2397**], 222, 223–5.
63 Hoelzel 1919 [**2322**], 580.
64 Ostwald 1926–7 [**2358**], III, 394, 437f. Hoelzel's version of the affair is in Hoelzel 1919 [**2322**], 577–80. One of the 'historians' was probably P. F. Schmidt, who had published a swingeing account of Ostwald's presentation (Schmidt 1919 [**2378**], 704ff). For the Werkbund context and the atmosphere at the Stuttgart conference, see also Campbell 1978 [**2278**], 138–9 and Parris 1979 [**2362**], 67–76.
65 Van de Velde 1962 [**2396**], 293–4; cf. also van de Velde 1902 [**2395**], 187f. For his painting, Herbert 1968 [**2318**], 187–90.
66 Hoelzel 1919, [**2322**], 577.
67 See Gropius to his mother *c.* April 1919 in Isaacs I, 1983 [**2325**], 212; also to Ernst Hardt, 14 April (ibid., 208). Bruno

Adler, the editor of Itten's first publication at Weimar, *Utopia: Dokumente der Wirklichkeit* [**2260**], which published Itten's colour-star, argued that his Hoelzelian concern for the 'grammar' of art distinguished him from the Expressionists (Adler in Baird 1969 [**2266**], 18f). See also Muche 1965, [**2348**], 166 on Itten's 'pedagogical chess-board motif', as the basis for his formal teaching at the Bauhaus.

68 For contrasts, Itten *Fragmentarisches* (1916) in Rotzeler 1972 [**2216**], 211; for Runge, *Adler* 1921 [**2260**], 79–81; for the colour-star, see n. 67.

69 For Schlemmer and Runge, O. Schlemmer 1927 [**2376**], I; see also T. Schlemmer 1972 [**2377**], 121. For Klee on Runge as the theorist most relevant to painters, Petitpierre 1957 [**2363**], 53. Cf. also Poling 1976 [**2365**], 18; Klee 1979a [**2333**]. transcript 81; Triska 1979 [**2236**], 59–60.

70 For Itten, see his letter of 1 July 1920 to another former member of the Hoelzel circle, Hans Hildebrandt, In Rotzeler 1972 [**2216**], 72. For Klee, Petitpierre 1957 [**2363**], 53; and letter to Hildebrandt in Klee 1961 [**1074**], 522. Klee's strictures on the notion of colour-laws and on the grey content of colours in the 1921/2 Bauhaus lectures were clearly aimed at Ostwald (Klee 1979a [**2333**], transcript 101–2).

71 For Muche at the Sturm school, Muche 1965 [**2348**], 163f, 229, and Jacoba van Heemskerk to H. Walden, 15 August 1917 in *Jacoba van Heemskerk* 1983/4 [**2316**], 108, no. 45. For Klee, van Heemskerk to Walden, 27 August 1916 in ibid., 102, no. 30. Muche's work could be very close to Klee's at the end of the War: see for example his *Dreiklang* (1919, Nationalgalerie, Berlin).

72 I owe this information to the kindness of Dr Anna Rowland. Cf. Also C. Wilk, 1981 [**2405**], 20, n. 12.

73 Wingler 1975 [**2072**], 44–5. This was essentially the context of colour-study outlined in the 1919 prospectus (ibid., 33).

74 See espec. the student exercises by Hirschfeld-Mack and Vincent Weber at the Bauhaus Archiv in Berlin (Berlin, *Bauhaus Archiv-Museum* 1981 [**2269**], nos 33–5, 38–40). Among the experimental rings of Mack's 'optischer Farbmischer', produced from *c.* 1923 in the joinery workshop at the Bauhaus, and now available in reproduction from the Bauhaus Archiv, are colour circles based on Goethe, Schopenhauer and von Bezold, as used by Hoelzel. Itten's much later recollection of colour exercises at the Bauhaus includes the use of checquerboards (from 1917) 'to free the study of colour-effects from associations of form', but none of them can now be identified (Itten 1964 [**2326**], 41). R. Wick, basing himself on the recollections of Muche, stated that Mack took over colourteaching in conjunction with Itten's *Vorkurs* from 1922–3, and that Itten himself had taught it earlier; but he has this course beginning in 1919 and cannot be relied on (Wick 1982 [**2404**], 99–100, 110, n. 90).

75 See Poling 1982 [**2366**], 72, and fig. 61.

76 R. Wick in *Johannes Itten* 1984 [**2157**], 120.

77 Klee 1979a [**2333**], transcript 93. For Goethe's scheme see the modern reconstruction in Goethe 1971 [**1836**], fig. 122.

78 Klee 1979b [**2334**], II, 1019, where he talks of the 'damned *Vorlehre*' (1926); for

the timetable of *Grundlehre* in 1925/6, including his 'elementare Gestaltung', ibid., 1035. Cf. also 1078 for *Vorkurs* in 1928. The *Grundlehre*, which included value-scales, primary colours, the coloursphere and peripheral colour-scale (1020), seems to have been taught specifically to weaving students (1077–9; cf. *Gunta Stölzl* 1987 [**2390**], 129); it was not mentioned among the compulsory basic design courses in a programme of that year (Wingler 1975 [**2072**], 144).

79 Kandinsky 1982 [**1686**], I, 460.

80 Wingler 1975 [**2072**], 80.

81 Kandinsky 1982 [**1686**], II, 501.

82 The questionnaire was first reproduced by Rudenstine 1981 [**2374**], 111, and discussed by C. V. Poling in *Kandinsky: Russian and Bauhaus Years* 1983 [**2330**], 27–8, and Lodder 1983 [**2342**], 80 and 280, n. 46. For a German trans. of the whole, *Wassily Kandinsky* 1989 [**2331**].

83 Kandinsky *On the Spiritual in Art* in 1982 [**1686**], I, 163, 180–9.

84 Bowlt 1973/4 [**2274**], 20–9.

85 Wick in *Johannes Itten* 1984 [**2157**], 116. Hoelzel had proposed a circular red and rectangular blue, as well as a triangular yellow (van Biema 1930 [**2270**], 186).

86 Hirschfeld-Mack 1963 [**2320**], 6. In an experiment conducted by the psychologist R. H. Goldschmidt, apparently during much of the 1920s, a single observer, tested at intervals of more than a year, associated yellow with the triangle (but on one occasion with the square), blue with the circle, and red with the square (except for a single occasion, when the association was with the triangle). Green was associated with the ellipse; the form-correlations with the secondary colours in this type of experiment in Germany and Russia were quite non-standard and often bizarre (see pl. 217). Goldschmidt unfortunately gives no details of his procedures (Goldschmidt 1927/8 [**2139**], 38).

87 Lodder 1983 [**2342**], 280, n. 46.

88 G. Pap in Neumann 1970 [**2350**], 79. In the end, however, Klee adopted Kandinsky's equivalents (Triska 1979 [**2236**], 77, n. 53).

89 T. Schlemmer 1972 [**2377**], 188. Schlemmer's 'instinct' was also that of his master, Hoelzel (*see* n. 85).

90 Kandinsky 1982 [**1686**], II, 591–2.

91 Von Maur 1979 [**2191**], II, no. A, 318a.

92 Wingler 1975 [**2072**], 164.

93 Whitford 1984 [**2403**], 102. The timetable shows that Klee taught form for 1 hour, Moholy-Nagy form-studies for 8 hours, Klee drawing and the life-class for 2 hours each, Kandinsky analytical drawing for 2 hours and Albers practical work for 10 hours: this puts the role of colour in the early Bauhaus into some sort of perspective.

94 T. Lux Feininger in Farmer and Weiss 1971 [**2303**], 47. There is no reference to colour in the fullest account of Albers's teaching on the Basic Course: Herzogenrath 1979/80 [**2319**], espec. 257–64.

95 Wingler 1975 [**2072**], 144.

96 Ibid., 64. Grohmann's statement that Ostwald lectured at the Bauhaus in both Weimar and Dessau (1958 [**2312**], 175, 201) has not been documented; and the bitterly anti-Ostwaldian views of two other Weimar masters, Schlemmer and Schreyer are well attested (von Maur 1979 [**2191**], II, 344; Schreyer 1929 [**2381**], 276).

97 Soupault 1963 [**2387**], 54.

98 For the lectures, Isaacs I, 1983 [**2325**], 415. This may have been at the invitation of the designer Herbert Bayer (Cohen 1984 [**2283**], 341). Kandinsky's Bauhaus lecture notes have been poorly edited and translated by P. Sers in his French edn of the painter's writings (*Écrits* III, 1975), and separately as a paperback: Kandinsky 1984 [**1863**]. The discussion of Ostwald's lecture is on 84 of this latter version, sandwiched between notes of 1929 and 1925, and there is another reference to the lecture in June 1927 on 221. For Kandinsky's use of Ostwald, Poling 1982 [**2366**], 60, 66–7. One of his chief sources in these years, Felix Krueger's journal *Neue Psychologische Studien*, was not uncritical of Ostwald (e.g. II, 1926, 9).

99 Wingler 1975 [**2072**], 145 and photographs, 466–7. See also Poling 1973 [**2364**], 33.

100 Klee 1979b [**2334**], II, 1151.

101 Poling 1973 [**2364**], 32.

102 Hahn 1985 [**2314**], 24–5, 63, 102.

103 Von Erffa 1943 [**2300**], 16–18. Grunow's contribution to the 1923 Exhibition catalogue, 'The creation of living form through colour, form and sound', has been trans. in Wingler 1975 [**2072**], 69–71.

104 Ostwald 1926–7 [**2358**], III, 409f.

105 The scientist in question was the opthalmologist L. Guaita, whose *La Scienza dei colori e la pittura* had been published in 1893: see *Archivi* 1968 [**1745**], I, 288f for Previati's letter to his brother of 24 January 1894. Guaita was none the less cited in Previati 1929 [**2368**], 60.

106 Previati 1929 [**2368**], 201f.

107 For the dating of *Street Lamp* (MOMA, New York), C. Green in *Abstraction: Towards a New Art* 1980 [**2259**], 102, who dates it 1912; Lista 1982 [**2341**], no. 208 dates it 1910/11 and suggests (no. 202) that a pencil study, also in New York, is formally related to the Düsseldorf decorations.

108 Lista 1982 [**2341**], nos 247–50, 256–81, 395. The letter (no. 248) is quoted on 505. There were a number of points of contact between Balla and Previati's ideas at this time. Balla's Divisionist *Window at Düsseldorf* (Lista no. 251) seems to have been stimulated by a passage on a luminous landscape seen through a window in Previati (1929 [**2368**], 154ff). His term for the Düsseldorf experiments, 'compenetrazioni', was frequently used by Previati (see Fagiolo dell'Arco 1970 [**2302**], 47, n. 12), and forms of iridescence were sometimes related to Previati's illustration of the colours of heated and chilled mica and glass plates (1929 [**2368**], 71–2; see also Martin 1968 [**2345**], 176 n. 1).

109 It is notable that another Italian Futurist, Gino Severini, also saw blue and yellow as complementary (Severini (1913) in Apollonio 1973 [**2075**], 124). Balla's own *Manifesto del Colore* (1918, Lista 1982 [**2341**], 473) confined itself to generalities. See also Severini's rather well-informed discussion of a colour-order system, citing Charles Henry's primary scheme, as well as those of Helmholtz and Maxwell (Severini 1921 [**2386**], 92–9). Blue and yellow were also regarded as complementary by the abstract film-maker Bruno Corra (see p. 245): see his essay 'Musica Cromatica' (1912) repr. in Verdone 1967 [**2242**], 248. It is striking that Corra's brother Ginna, when he showed two abstract canvases in Florence in 1912, had them catalogued as 'decor-

ations for a living-room', even though their titles, *Neurasthenia* (1908) and *Romantic Walk* (*Passeggiata Romantica*, 1909) were highly descriptive (ibid., 12).

110 Previati *Les Principes scientifiques du divisionnisme (les techniques de la peinture)*, Paris, 1910. See also the notice of the original Italian edn by Milesi in *Les Tendances nouvelles*, XXIX (1907) [**2346**], 537–9.

111 R. Delaunay, 'La Lumière' (1912) in R. Delaunay 1957 [**2291**], 147. For the general use of the term 'pointilliste' in France, Severini to G. Spovieri, 16 January 1914 in *Archivi* 1958 [**1744**], I, 312. Signac had been at pains to explain the difference between the 'divided' touch and the mere 'point', but he did not use the term 'divisionist' (Signac 1964 [**1607**], 103–12).

112 *Window No. 3* repr. in col. in *Guggenheim Museum* 1971, 92–3. One of the earliest and most representational of the series in the non-dotted style is repr. in col. in *Robert et Sonia Delaunay* 1985 [**2294**], 64, no. 29. This catalogue reproduces a number of the series, and there are other collections of col. reproductions in Vriesen and Imdahl 1967 [**2398**], figs 7–9 and *Robert Delaunay* 1976 [**2293**], 127–34. The fullest studies are by Spate 1979 [**2388**], 187–203, and for the dating 375–6; and Winter 1984 [**2407**], 34–42. For Previati's discussion of transparency and its techniques, 1929 [**2368**], 77, 142ff; cf. also A. Morbelli *La Via Crucis del Divisionismo* (1912/14) in *Archivi* 1968 [**1745**], I, 142–4, which cited the example of medieval stained glass, also of great interest to Delaunay (Buckberrough 1979 [**2276**], espec. 110).

113 These were the colours especially noticed in the *Window* paintings by August Macke in a letter of 1913 (Vriesen 1957 [**2243**], 116, n. 8). Delaunay mentioned Rood in reference to simultaneous contrast in 1912 (R. Delaunay 1957 [**2291**], 159); for his knowledge of this text, Buckberrough 1982 [**2277**], 125–31.

114 R. Delaunay 1957 [**2291**], 182–3, and for the date, Spate 1979 [**2388**], 355 n. 14. He was responding to an undated letter from Marc about his essay 'La Lumière', cit. Hess 1961 [**2151**], 91.

115 She claimed much later that she and Robert were simply 'continuing' Fauvism (Oppler 1976 [**2353**], 385).

116 The earliest of these seems to be the *Simultaneous Contrast* (?1913) in collage and gouache, repr. in col. in *Sonia Delaunay* 1980 [**2295**], 135, no. 47.

117 S. Delaunay 1956 [**2292**], 19. Buckberrough in *Sonia Delaunay* 1980 [**2295**], 113 n. 67 argues for this influence on Robert; see also Spate 1979 [**2388**], 201 and Cohen 1975 [**2282**], 61.

118 S. Delaunay (1978) in *Sonia Delaunay* 1980 [**2295**], 40; cf. also 82 for their discussions in the 1930s.

119 For the dating of *Disc* and the whole series Spate 1979 [**2388**], 376–7.

120 R. Delaunay 1957 [**2291**], 184 (1913); cf. also 60 (*c.* 1924). The most detailed formal analysis of *Disc* is in Albrecht 1974 [**2265**], 30–6.

121 R. Delaunay 1957 [**2291**], 217. For the revisions, Buckberrough 1982 [**2277**], 223–6.

122 Repr. in col. in Vriesen and Imdahl 1967 [**2398**], pl. 13. For the 1913 sculpture and its setting, Spate 1979 [**2388**], 223, fig. 169.

123 See espec. Delaunay to Macke, early

1913 in R. Delaunay 1957 [**2291**], 186; for the date, Vriesen 1957 [**2243**], 265. Delaunay's *Discs* contrast with the far more theoretically oriented *Discs of Newton* by Frantisek Kupka (1911–12; Paris, Musée Nationale d'Art Moderne and Philadelphia Museum of Art); see Rowell 1975 [**2372**], 67–76 and Kupka 1989 [**2338**], 156–7 for his idiosyncratic tenpart 'Discs of Newton' devised *c.* 1910. Kupka seems to have regarded these as spinning discs (ibid., 155).

124 The best survey of Albers's life and work is now *Josef Albers* 1988 [**2264**].

125 Albers 1967 [**2262**], 10. For the work at Bottrup in Westphalia, Weber 1984 [**2400**], 5. For the copying of paintings in cut paper, Albers 1963 [**2261**], Folders XIX, 1–3, 16–17 and commentary 38.

126 For the Goethe-Triangle, Albers 1963 [**2261**], Folder XXIV –1, commentary 45 and text 68. For Albers's closeness to Hirschfeld-Mack, see his letter to R. Arnheim, 14 March 1963, cit. *Leonardo*, XV, 1982, 174, and Torbruegge 1974 [**2391**], 198. Mack's version of the triangle is in the Bauhaus-Archiv in Berlin (no. 3818/12: see Poling 1982 [**2366**], 152, n. 84). Albers also told Arnheim that Mack showed him Carry van Biema's book on Hoelzel, which includes the fullest discussion of this 'Nine-part triangle' in the section 'Einige Hauptbegriffe aus Goethes Farbenlehre' (van Biema 1930 [**2270**], 107ff). Arnheim (*Leonardo*, XV, 1982, 175) argued that the diagram is 'more confusing than instructive', since it includes only three of the six possible tertiary colours and these are 'arbitrarily chosen'. In the revised paperback edition of Albers 1963 [**2261**] (1975, 66) Goethe's name has been replaced by 'equilateral'. A widespread Bauhaus concept that 'less is more', which was particularly crucial for Albers's approach, may also go back to Hoelzel's 'a few lines (*Striche*) may often be much more' (Hoelzel 1915, cit. Parris 1979 [**2362**], 266 and pl. 83).

127 For relativity, Fiedler 1926 [**2304**], espec. 390ff. For transparency, Fuchs 1923 [**2307**], 145–235 (trans. as 'On Transparency' in W. D. Ellis (ed.), *A Source-Book of Gestalt Psychology,* 1950). Fuchs's figures on 154 and 166 are close to some in Kandinsky's Bauhaus courses.

128 See the interview with D. Mahlow, 'Statt eines Vorworts' in the German paperback edn of *Interaction of Color*, Cologne, 1970, 8. Albers none the less felt that Ostwald provided 'a most comprehensive system of colour harmonies' (Albers 1963 [**2261**], commentary 47). In the late 1920s Malevich had also thought this about Ostwald, whose work was much used in Russia (Malévitch 1977 [**2344**], 116).

129 Albers 1963 [**2261**], text 10. The idea had already been articulated in an academic context by Reynolds and Turner (Gage 1969 [**217**], 53).

130 For Tadd's work, O. Stelzer, 'Erziehung durch manuelles Tun' in Wingler 1977 [**2406**], 51.

131 Lisle 1986 [**2340**], 233.

132 De Kooning 1950 [**2290**], 40.

133 For the Weber-Fechner law, Albers 1963 [**2261**], Folder XX, text 58–62, commentary 39–41. Albers's misunderstanding has been pointed out by Lee 1981 [**2339**], 102. This law may have been the subject of some demonstrations by H. Holl and F. Hausgirg at Black Mountain College, which caused Albers to leave the room, and some of his students to abandon his course (Harris 1987 [**2315**], 126, and cf. 20 (*c.* 1941). The Yale mathematician Charles E. Rickart also found it hard to interest the artist in his mathematical interpretation of his work ('A structural analysis of some of Albers's work' in *Joseph Albers* 1988 [**2264**], 58.). A modern analysis of some of the edge-phenomena exploited by Albers uses examples of work by his Yale pupil Richard Anuskiewicz (Jameson and Hurvich 1975 [**2327**], 125–31; and for Anuskiewicz's reminiscences of Albers's teaching, *Paintings by Josef Albers* 1978 [**2361**], 22–3).

134 Welliver 1966 [**2401**], 68.

135 See the 1952 statement repr. in *Josef Albers* 1988 [**2264**], 12, and the 1949 statement on the *Variant* series, cit. Gomringer 1968 [**2311**], 104f.

136 Welliver 1966 [**2401**], 68–9.

137 Holloway and Weil 1970 [**2324**], 463.

138 Examples of this 'mitering' are in *Homage to the Square: Insert*, 1959, National Museum of American Art, Washington D.C., and *Homage to the Square: Mitered*, 1962, Bottrup, Albers Museum (in *Josef Albers* 1988 [**2264**], no. 212). This is a type not considered in the taxonomy of the series given by Albrecht 1974 [**2265**], 70–96, although he does discuss the implied perspective of the others (78).

139 Fuller 1978 [**2308**], 311f. See also the photographs of Black Mountain classes in 1944 and 1948 (Harris 1987 [**2315**], 82; *Josef Albers* 1988 [**2264**], 290). For the empiricism implicit in changes made in the process of painting some of the *Homage* series, Weber in *Josef Albers* ibid., 40. The English stripe painter Patrick Heron was also more conscious of the function of shape and edge (Knight 1988 [**2337**], 34 (1969)).

140 Moffet 1977 [**2347**], 15.

141 Moffett ibid., 39. For Albers's 1940 lecture, Dubermann 1972 [**2298**], 60.

142 Noland in Johnson 1982 [**2328**], 50. The reference to shaped canvases is clearly

to Frank Stella's work of the mid-1960s; but Noland himself used this sculptural device a decade later.

143 Moffett 1977 [**2347**], 50.

144 Albers 1963 [**2261**], Folder XVIII, 7–10. The taxonomy of stripe paintings has been discussed by Kerber 1970 [**2332**], espec. 251, nn. 9, 10.

145 *Josef Albers* 1965/6 [**2263**], 9.

146 Tucker 1971 [**2392**], 16. cf. Noland, 'you can be fairly arbitrary about at what point you start ... I pick a color and go with it' (Moffett 1977 [**2347**], 45). For Davis on Albers's 'law of interaction of color', which he rejected, 'because that law emphasizes the intelligibility of the pictures before it emphasizes their stimulating – to the verge of chaotic excitement – character', Serwer 1987 [**2385**], 44.

147 See, e.g., *Josef Albers* 1965/6 [**2263**], 30; *Josef Albers* 1988 [**2264**], 37–8, 40.

148 *Josef Albers* 1988 [**2264**], 44 and no. 246; *Josef Albers* 1965/6 [**2263**], 29. Albers claimed that he had this instinct for materials and technique from his father, who had been an all-round craftsman *Josef Albers* 1988 [**2264**], 15).

149 Burliuk 1912 in Barron and Tuchman 1980 [**1753**], 129f; Shevchenko 1913 in Bowlt 1976 [**1992**], 51–2.

150 Tarabukin in Nakov and Pétris 1972 [**2045**], 124. See also A. Grishchenko's 'Colour dynamics and tectonic primitivism' group of 1918/19 in Bowlt 1976 [**1992**], 43, and Rodchenko's 1921 plan to put *faktura* into the programme of the State Art Workshops (Vkhutmas): Lodder 1983 [**2342**], 123–4.

151 See an article of 1919 repr. in Gassner and Gillen 1979 [**2309**], 44.

152 Von Maur 1979 [**2191**], I, 283–94, II, G. 605–57.

153 For the cheapness of materials, *Franz Kline* 1979 [**2336**], 12, 21, 24, n. 11. Kline recorded that when he was taken up by the fashionable dealer Sidney Janis in 1956, Janis asked him to switch to the more usual materials, and charge the gallery for them.

154 For Rothko's scene painting, Hobbs and Levin 1981 [**2321**], 116. The fugitive pigments used in this type of temporary painting were mentioned by Polunin 1927 [**2367**], 22n. For other examples of Rothko's experiments with glue, egg-tempera and modern synthetic paints, Clearwater 1984 [**2281**], 42; Cranmer 1987a [**2287**], 189–97; Cranmer 1987b [**2288**], 283–5; Cohn 1988 [**2284**], espec. 10, 17, 27; Barnes 1989 [**2268**], 39, 58–61; Mancusi-Ungaro 1990 [**2343**], 134–7.

155 Rose *c.* 1972 [**2371**], 54–5; Moffett 1977 [**2347**], 101f, n. 3. Noland also recognized the inspiration of Jackson Pollock's use of unconventional paints and methods, 'with the same kind of

intrinsic qualities that you could find out of the use of the materials' (Moffett ibid., 19). For Pollock, E. Frank, 'Notes on Technique' in O'Connor and Thaw 1978 [**2352**], IV, 264.

156 Interview with Paul Cummings, 8 June 1978: transcript in Archives of American Art, 35; and 39 for Louis as a 'steady customer' for the free 'ends of batch'.

157 Bocour loc. cit. 33, 50. See also Elderfield 1986 [**2299**], 34, 182f.

158 Klein in *Yves Klein* 1983 [**2335**], 194. IKB was developed by Édouard Adam, who could produce this synthetic ultra-marine more cheaply and in larger quantities than other suppliers. Klein procured a patent for his formula in 1960, although he described the mixture incorrectly in the specification (*Yves Klein* ibid., 247).

159 Paris, Galerie Beaubourg, col. repr. in *Colour Since Matisse* 1985 [**2285**], 46. See also Gerhard Richter *256 Farben*, 1974, housepaint on canvas, col. repr. in J. van der Marck, 'Inside Europe outside Europe', *Artforum*, XVI, 1977, 51.

160 Stella in Johnson 1982 [**2328**], 116.

161 Rubin 1970 [**2373**], 76; Stella 1986 [**2389**], 164.

162 Rubin ibid., 82.

163 Stella 1986 [**2389**], 71.

164 I am thinking particularly of the use of the Lüscher system by the Swiss Neo-Constructivist Karl Gerstner (Stierlin 1981 [**1961**], 164ff, 193). I haved not considered here the distaste for technology among some Abstract Expressionists, which has been studied by Craven 1990 [**2289**], 72–103, nor their dislike of verbal discourse, which has been discussed in Gibson 1990 [**2310**], 195–211. There were, of course, far more thoroughgoing programmes of colour-experimentation by some modern artists I have not mentioned, e.g. Louis Fernandez, whose *L'Apprentissage élémentaire de la peinture* (*c.* 1933) included a carefully worked out section on colour-measurement, extracted in *Abstraction-Création, Art non-Figuratif* II, 1933, 14f; but these investigations have never fed into the mainstream.

165 For an analysis of Lohse's approach to colour structures, Albrecht 1974 [**2265**], 114–55; see espec. 126 for Albrecht's very general sense that Lohse owed something to 'the colour theory and technology of his time'.

166 Wright 1981 [**2408**], 236–7. Some materials for the history of the reception and language of black in art have been gathered by Stephanie Terenzio in *Robert Motherwell and Black*, 1980; see also H. Weitemeier *Schwartz*, Düsseldorf, Kunsthalle, 1981.

BIBLIOGRAPHY

CONCORDANCE

Chief documents (or publications including chief documents) and primary sources for each period are indicated below by the reference number of their bibliography entries.

1 Antiquity

Nos. 28, 29, 55, 63, 71, 77, 118, 121, 122, 125, 140, 141, 150, 173, 212, 218, 240, 248, 277, 296, 297, 312, 333, 338, 343, 361, 394, 447, 544, 546, 636, 933, 934, 1001, 1357, 1454, 2080, 2186, 2199.

2 The Middle Ages

Nos. 44, 109, 124, 131, 156, 157, 162, 184, 187, 191, 193, 203, 231, 234, 249, 258, 267, 268, 271, 285, 328, 334, 335, 336, 350, 359, 360, 363, 364, 369, 374, 376, 399, 400, 414, 423, 424, 425, 439, 440, 455, 456, 460, 468, 491, 514, 515, 529, 540, 541, 543, 545, 551, 570, 578, 579, 580, 583, 587, 592, 595, 603, 612, 614, 615, 616, 619, 621, 622, 625, 626, 635, 637, 650, 652, 660, 661, 675, 679, 688, 691, 725, 742, 743, 744, 745, 754, 757, 759, 767, 769, 772, 779, 783, 785, 786, 788, 789, 790, 791, 798, 801, 802, 808, 812, 814, 817, 822, 823, 827, 831, 844, 848, 851, 855, 859, 861, 862, 868, 874, 878, 879, 881, 886, 890, 891, 892, 898, 910, 917, 918, 921, 940, 956, 962, 964, 1062, 1201, 1241, 1265, 1288, 1304, 1309, 1323, 1334, 1335, 1371, 1386, 1388, 1401, 1410, 1417, 1421, 1621, 1985, 2091, 2182, 2212, 2218.

3 The Renaissance

Nos. 153, 154, 155, 158, 159, 161, 170, 176, 197, 198, 201, 206, 220, 232, 274, 289, 290, 308, 339, 340, 341, 548, 620, 701, 766, 770, 841, 849, 864, 887, 901, 909, 945, 954, 955, 969, 987, 1010, 1017, 1076, 1118, 1152, 1161, 1162, 1170, 1177, 1185, 1192, 1202, 1213, 1216, 1224, 1228, 1230, 1231, 1232, 1235, 1253, 1259, 1267, 1270, 1272, 1277, 1280, 1282, 1284, 1287, 1291, 1293, 1315, 1316, 1343, 1345, 1346, 1376, 1393, 1395, 1408, 1411, 1412, 1439, 1589, 1645, 2093, 2106, 2129, 2256, 2257.

4 The seventeenth century

Nos. 174, 177, 178, 179, 190, 192, 199, 209, 265, 271, 305, 313, 314, 315, 316, 317, 319, 344, 950, 967, 969, 985, 1019, 1022, 1071, 1083, 1095, 1105, 1119, 1126, 1175, 1214, 1271, 1381, 1410, 1413, 1415, 1425, 1428, 1430, 1431, 1441, 1445, 1448, 1452, 1456, 1460, 1473, 1483, 1493, 1494, 1518, 1519, 1530, 1531, 1532, 1533, 1548, 1552, 1553, 1559, 1562, 1565, 1577, 1590, 1591, 1595, 1599, 1603, 1608, 1616, 1625, 1628, 1632, 1635, 1643, 1647, 1650, 1669, 1670, 1688, 1713, 1746, 1991, 2085, 2130, 2165, 2178, 2193, 2199a, 2360.

5 The eighteenth century

Nos. 17, 34, 148, 160, 236, 255, 303, 324, 347, 415, 1023, 1037, 1047, 1064, 1075, 1106, 1107, 1109, 1110, 1339, 1414, 1461, 1469, 1470, 1505, 1539, 1540, 1543, 1547, 1549, 1583, 1592, 1596, 1597, 1604, 1619, 1624, 1636, 1687, 1709, 1717, 1724, 1739, 1760, 1776, 1785, 1805, 1857, 1891, 1892, 1894, 1908, 1914, 1921, 1982, 2003, 2018, 2025, 2026, 2030, 2035, 2039, 2041, 2050, 2060, 2064, 2094, 2095, 2096, 2097, 2098, 2099, 2100, 2101, 2102, 2117, 2146, 2149, 2150, 2154, 2155, 2190, 2194, 2206, 2210, 2213, 2219, 2228, 2232.

6 The nineteenth century

Nos. 18, 19, 20, 21, 61, 70, 132, 165, 171, 172, 185, 225, 239, 241, 246, 281, 291, 306, 355, 906, 944, 958, 983, 989, 993, 996, 1011, 1015, 1018, 1024, 1026, 1027, 1031, 1033, 1035, 1039, 1046, 1052, 1057, 1059, 1060, 1061, 1065, 1066, 1077, 1078, 1090, 1096, 1098, 1100, 1115, 1121, 1127, 1128, 1129, 1130, 1131, 1138, 1141, 1150, 1156, 1157, 1416, 1420, 1434, 1436, 1437, 1438, 1443, 1446, 1447, 1451, 1457, 1458, 1459, 1471, 1481, 1482, 1484, 1496, 1501, 1507, 1508, 1510, 1511, 1514, 1524, 1538, 1542, 1558, 1569, 1571, 1580, 1582, 1585, 1607, 1617, 1618, 1626, 1629, 1630, 1631, 1653, 1655, 1656, 1658, 1663, 1664, 1672, 1680, 1683, 1694, 1710, 1714, 1718, 1722, 1725, 1732, 1734, 1735, 1750, 1759, 1762, 1763, 1769, 1770, 1771, 1772, 1774, 1778, 1780, 1784, 1786, 1789, 1793, 1794, 1797, 1801, 1802, 1806, 1810, 1812, 1815, 1817, 1823, 1824, 1825, 1829, 1832, 1833, 1834, 1835, 1836, 1845, 1846, 1849, 4851, 1852, 1855, 1866, 1867, 1869, 1871, 1882, 1895, 1900, 1906, 1915, 1916, 1917, 1918, 1922, 1924, 1925, 1931, 1936, 1938, 1939, 1942, 1944, 1945, 1948, 1949, 1963, 1964, 1965, 1969, 1977, 1978, 1980, 1984, 1986, 1990, 1994, 2000, 2006, 2009, 2010, 2011, 2012, 2019, 2020, 2021, 2023, 2034, 2036, 2037, 2042, 2043, 2044, 2054, 2061, 2065, 2068, 2070, 2071, 2083, 2087, 2090, 2092, 2105, 2125, 2127, 2136, 2137, 2153, 2154, 2159, 2207, 2214, 2305, 2313, 2396, 2383.

7 The twentieth century

Nos. 23, 26, 457, 852, 884, 914, 1056, 1074, 1082, 1112, 1155, 1184, 1205, 1207, 1271, 1286, 1366, 1368, 1631, 1666, 1673, 1686, 1690, 1691, 1699, 1702, 1706, 1707, 1725, 1736, 1741, 1744, 1747, 1753, 1754, 1757, 1768, 1773, 1786, 1791, 1792, 1803, 1804, 1806, 1809, 1818, 1828, 1831, 1839, 1841, 1844, 1850, 1852, 1854, 1860, 1861, 1863, 1874, 1879, 1880, 1888, 1889, 1903, 1931, 1940, 1950, 1951, 1954, 1959, 1989, 1992, 2001, 2002, 2045, 2047, 2066, 2069, 2072, 2074, 2075, 2079, 2081, 2089, 2104, 2113, 2114, 2119, 2120, 2122, 2135, 2139, 2142, 2143, 2144, 2147, 2152, 2156, 2160, 2162, 2166, 2167, 2169, 2172, 2173, 2174, 2175, 2195, 2198, 2203, 2208, 2216, 2222, 2225, 2226, 2239, 2240, 2242, 2249, 2250, 2251, 2254, 2260, 2261, 2262, 2266, 2270, 2275, 2280, 2290, 2291, 2293, 2296, 2300, 2304, 2307, 2309, 2316, 2317, 2333, 2334, 2337, 2338, 2334, 2346, 2348, 2349, 2350, 2352, 2354, 2355, 2356, 2357, 2358, 2359, 2363, 2367, 2368, 2374, 2375, 2376, 2377, 2379, 2380, 2381, 2384, 2386, 2387, 2389, 2393, 2394, 2395, 2396, 2397, 2401, 2402, 2403, 2404, 2406, 2408.

Introduction

1 BERENSON, B. 1949. *Sketch for a Self-Portrait.*
2 —. 1950. *Aesthetics and History.*
3 —. 1965. *The Selected Letters of Bernard Berenson*, ed. A. K. McComb.
4 BIRREN, F. 1965. *History of Color in Painting. With New Principles of Color Expression.*
5 BRUSATIN, M. 1983. *Storia dei colori*, 2nd edn (Fr. edn, *Histoire des couleurs*, 1986).
6 BURNE-JONES, G. 1912. *Memorials of Edward Burne-Jones*, 2 vols.
7 CAMESASCA, E. 1966. *Artisti in bottega.*
8 DITTMANN, L. 1987. *Farbgestaltung und Farbtheorie in der abendländischen Malerei.*
9 GAGE, J. 1990. 'Color in western art: an issue?', *Art Bulletin*, LXXII.
10 GRAY, R. D. 1952. *Goethe the Alchemist*
11 HALBERTSMA, K. T. A. 1949. *A History of the Theory of Colour.*
12 HEWISON, R. 1976. *John Ruskin: The Argument of the Eye.*
13 Lindberg, D. C. 1976. *Theories of Vision from Alkindi to Kepler.*
14 MARKS, L. 1978. *The Unity of the Senses.*
15 MORGENSEN, M. F. and ENGLISH, H. B. 1926. 'The apparent warmth of colors', *American Journal of Psychology*, XXXVII.
16 PASTORE, N. 1971. *Selective History of Theories of Visual Perception, 1650–1950.*
17 REYNOLDS, SIR J. 1852. *The Literary Works*, 2 vols, ed. H. Beechey.
18 RUSKIN, J. 1843. *Modern Painters*, I.
19 —. 1853. *The Stones of Venice*, II.
20 —. 1856. *Modern Painters*, IV.
21 —. 1857. *The Elements of Drawing.*
22 RZEPIŃSKA, M. 1989. *Historia Koloru w dziejach malarstwa europejskiego*, 2 vols, 3rd edn.
23 STOKES, A. 1937. *Colour and Form.*
24 THOMPSON, D. V. JR. 1936. *The Materials and Techniques of Medieval Painting.*
25 WESTPHAL, J. 1991. *Colour: A Philosophical Introduction*, 2nd edn.
26 WITTGENSTEIN, L. 1977. *Remarks on Colour* (1950), ed. A. Anscombe.

1 The Classical Inheritance

27 ANDRÉ, J. 1949. *Étude sur les termes de couleur dans la langue latin.*
28 ANNAS, J. and BARNES, J. 1985. *The Modes of Scepticism: Ancient Texts and Modern Interpretations.*
29 *Anonymous Prologomena to Platonic Philosophy.* 1962. Ed. L. G. Westerinck.
30 AUGUSTI, S. 1967. *I Colori pompeiani.*
31 AVERY, W. T. 1940. 'The Adoratio Purpurae and the importance of the Imperial Purple', *Memoirs of the American Academy in Rome*, XVII.
32 BAINES, J. 1985. 'Color terminology and color classification in ancient Egyptian color terminology and polychromy', *American Anthropologist*, LXXXVII.
33 BALDWIN, C. SEARS. 1924. *Ancient Rhetoric and Poetic.*
34 BARRY, J. 1809. *The Works*, 2 vols.
35 BEARE, J. I. 1906. *Greek Theories of Elementary Cognition from Alcmaeon to Aristotle.*
36 BECCATTI, G. 1951. *Arte e gusto negli scrittori latini.*
37 BERMELIN, E. 1933. 'Die kunsttheoretischen Gedanken in Philostrats Apollonius von Tyana', *Philologus*, LXXXVIII.
38 BERTRAND, E. 1893. *Études sur la peinture et la critique d'art dans l'antiquité.*
39 BIERWALTES, W. 1957. *Lux Intelligibilis. Untersuchungen zur Lichtmetaphysik der Griechen*, Ph.D. thesis, Munich University.
40 —. 1961. 'Die Metaphysik des Lichts in der Philosophie Plotins', *Zeitschrift für philosophische Forschung*, XV.
41 BILLOT, M. F. 1982. 'Recherches au XVIIIᵉ et XIXᵉ siècles sur la polychromie de l'architecture grècque' in *Paris, Rome Athènes: le voyage en Grèce des architectes français au XIXᵉ et XXᵉ siècles*, Paris, École des Beaux-Arts, exh. cat.
42 BLANCKENHAGEN, P. H. von and Alexander, C. 1962. 'The paintings from Boscotrecase, with an appendix on technique by G. Papadopulos', *Mitteilungen des deutschen Archäologischen Instituts* (Römische Abteilung), Ergänzungsheft, VI.
43 BLÜMNER, H. 1912. *Technologie und Terminologie der Gewerbe und Künste der Griechen und Römern*, 4 vols (only I published), 2nd edn.
44 *The Book of the Eparch.* 1970. Ed. I. Dujčev.
45 BORRELLI, L. 1950. 'Qualche scheda sulla tecnica della pittura greca', *Bolletino dell'Istituto Centrale del Restauro*, II.
46 Bowra, C. M. 1961. *Greek Lyric Poetry*, 2nd edn.
47 BREMER, D. 1973. 'Hinweise zum griechischen Ursprung und zur europäischen Geschichte der Lichtmetaphysik', *Archiv für Begriffsgeschichte* XVII.
48 —. 1974. 'Licht als universales Darstellungsmedium', idem., XVIII.
49 BRENDEL, O. 1944. 'Origin and Meaning of the Mandorla', *Gazette des Beaux-Arts*, XXV.
50 BRUNO, V. J. 1977. *Form and Colour in Greek Painting.*
51 —. 1985. *Hellenistic Painting Techniques: the Evidence of the Delos Fragments.*
52 BULTMANN, R. 1948. 'Zur Geschichte der Lichtsymbolik im Altertum', *Philologus*, XCVII.
53 BURFORD, A. 1972. *Craftsmen in Greek and Roman Society.*
54 CAGIANO DI AZEVEDO, M. 1954. 'Il colore nella antichità', *Aevum*, XXVIII.
55 CHARLTON, W. 1970. *Aristotle's Physics, Books I and II.*
56 COLLARD, G. 1970. 'On the tragedian Chaeremon', *Journal of Hellenic Studies*, XC.
57 COOPER, J. 1971. 'John Gibson and his Tinted Venus', *Connoisseur*, CLXXVIII.
58 CUMONT, F. 1949. *Lux Perpetua.*
59 CURTIUS, L. 1960. *Die Wandmalerei Pompeis*, 2nd edn.
60 DARBY, E. 1981. 'John Gibson, Queen Victoria, and the idea of sculptural polychromy', *Art History*, IV.
61 DAVID D'ANGERS, P. L. 1958. *Carnets*, 2 vols, ed. A. Bruel.
62 DELCOURT, M. 1965. *Pyrrhos et Pyrrha: Recherches sur les valeurs du feu dans les légendes helleniques.*
63 DIELS, H. 1879. *Doxographi Graeci.*
64 DODDS, E. R. 1971. *The Greeks and the Irrational*, 2nd edn.
65 DODWELL, C. R. 1982. *Anglo-Saxon Art – a New Perspective.*
66 DUELL, P. and GETTENS, R. J. 1940. 'A method of painting in Classical times', *Technical Studies in the Field of Fine Arts*, IX.
67 EASTLAKE, C. L. 1848. *Contributions to the Literature of the Fine Arts.*
68 EDGEWORTH, R. J. 1979. 'Does *purpureus* mean 'bright'?' *Glotta*, LVII.
69 *Enciclopedia dell'arte antica, classica e orientale*, II, 1959.
70 FLAXMAN, J. 1838. *Lectures on Sculpture*, 2nd edn.
71 FREEMAN, K. 1966. *Ancilla to the Pre-Socratic Philosophers.*
72 FRIEDLÄNDER, L. 1964. *Darstellungen aus der Sittengeschichte Roms* (1922).
73 FUHRMANN, H. 1931. *Philoxenos von Eretria.*
74 GAGE, J. 1978. 'Colour in history: relative and absolute', *Art History*, I.
75 GAISER, K. 1965. 'Platons Farbenlehre', *Synusia: Festgabe für Wolfgang Schadewalt.*
76 GALLAVOTTI, C. 1957. 'Nomi di colori in Miceneo', *La Parola del passato*, XII.
77 GÄTJE, H. (ed.). 1967. 'Die arabische Übersetzung der Schrift des Alexander von Aphrodisias über die Farbe', *Nachrichten der Akademie der Wissenschaften in Göttingen (Phil-Hist Klasse).*
78 Gell, Sir W. 1817–19. *Pompeiana. The Topography, Edifices and Ornaments of Pompeii.*
79 GERSCHEL, L. 1966. 'Couleur et teinture chez divers peuples indo-européens', *Annales economies, sociétés, civilisations*, XXI.
80 GIPPER, H. 1964. 'Purpur', *Glotta*, XLII.
81 GLADSTONE, W. E. 1858. *Studies on Homer and the Homeric Age*, 3 vols.
82 —. 1877. 'The Colour-sense', *The Nineteenth Century*, II.
83 GNOLI, D. 1971. *Marmora Romana.*
84 GRABAR, A. 1946. 'Plotin et les origines de l'esthétique médiévale', *Cahiers archéologiques*, I.
85 GRISEBACH, F. 1924. *C. F. Schinkel.*
86 GROSSMANN, M. 1988. *Colore e lessico.*
87 HAHM, D. E. 1978. 'Early Hellenistic theories of colour and the perception of colour' in P. Machamer and R. G. Turnbull (eds), *Perception: Interrelations in the History and Philosophy of Science.*
88 HEATON, N. 1910. 'The mural paintings of Knossos, an investigation into the methods of their production', *Journal of the Royal Society of Arts*, LVIII.
89 HEDERER, O. 1964. *Leo von Klenze.*
90 HITTORFF, J. I. 1830. *De l'Architecture polychrome chez les grecs.*
91 HOCHEGGER, R. 1884. *Die Geschichtliche Entwicklung des Farbensinnes.*
92 HOORN, W. van. 1972. *Ancient and Modern Theories of Visual Perception.*
93 HUNGER, H. 1965. *Reich der neuen Mitte: der christliche Geist der byzantinischen Kultur.*
94 Ingres. 1967–8. Paris, Petit Palais, exh. cat.
95 JENKINS, I. D. and MIDDLETON, A. P. 1988. 'Paint on the Parthenon sculptures', *Annual of the British School at Athens*, LXXXIII.
96 JENSEN, L. B. 1963. 'Royal Purple of Tyre', *Journal of Near Eastern Studies*, XXII.
97 KEULS, E. 1978. *Plato and Greek Painting.*
98 KÖNIG, J. 1927. 'Die Bezeichnung der Farben', *Archiv für die gesamte Psychologie*, LX.
99 KRANZ, W. 1912. 'Die ältesten Farbenlehren der Griechen', *Hermes*, XLVII.
100 KRIS, E. 1929. *Meister und Meisterwerke der Steinschneidekunst in der italienischen Renaissance.*
101 LEGGETT, W. F. 1944. *Ancient and Medieval Dyes.*
102 LEHMANN, K. 1945. 'The Dome of Heaven', *Art Bulletin*, XXVII.
103 LEWY, H. 1956. *Chaldean Oracles and Theurgy.*
104 LOPEZ, R. S. 1945. 'The silk industry in the Byzantine Empire', *Speculum*, XX.
105 MATHEW, G. 1963. *Byzantine Aesthetics.*
106 MATTHEWS, T. 1911. *John Gibson.*
107 MEIER, C. 1977. *Gemma Spiritualis: Methode und Gebrauch der Edelsteinallegorese von frühen Christentum bis ins 18 Jahrhundert*, I.
108 MIDDLETON, R. 1985. 'Perfection and colour: the polychromy of French architecture in the eighteenth and nineteenth centuries', *Rassegna* XXIII.
109 *Mittelalterliche Schatzverzeichnisse*, I, 1967. Zentralinstitut für Kunstgeschichte, Munich.
110 NEUBURGER, A. 1969. *The Technical Arts and Sciences of the Ancients.*
111 NEWTON, C. T. 1862. *A History of the Discoveries at Halicarnassus.*
112 OBERMILLER, J. 1931. 'Die Purpurfarbe im Sprachgebrauch', *Archiv für die Geschichte der Mathematik, der Naturwissenschaft und der Technik*, XIII.
113 ORANGE, H. P. L. and NORDHAGEN, P. J. 1965. *Mosaics.*
114 OSBORNE, H. 1968. 'Colour concepts of the ancient Greeks', *British Journal of Aesthetics*, VIII.
115 OWEN-CROCKER, G. 1986. *Dress in Anglo-Saxon England.*
116 *Patrologia Latina*. 1844–55; and *Patrologia Graeca*. 1857–66. Ed. J.-P. Migne.
117 PAULY-WISSOWA. 1894–1978. *Real-Encyclopaedie zur Altertumswissenschaft.*
118 PAUSANIUS. 1971. *Guide to Greece*, trans. P. Levi.
119 PHILLIPS, K. M. 1960. 'Subject and technique in Hellenistic-Roman mosaics: a Ganymede mosaic from Sicily', *Art Bulletin*, XLII.
120 PLATNAUER, M. 1921. 'Greek colour-perception', *Classical Quarterly*, XV.
121 POLLITT, J. J. 1965. *The Art of Greece 1400–31 B.C. (Sources and Documents in the History of Art).*
122 —. 1974. *The Ancient View of Greek Art: Criticism, History and Terminology*, Student Ed.
123 PREUSSER, F., GRAEVE, V. von and WOLTERS, C. 1981. 'Malerei auf griechischen Grabsteinen', *Maltechnik/Restauro*, LXXXVIII.
124 PSEUDO-KODINUS. 1966. *Traité des offices*, ed. J. V. Verpeaux.
125 REINACH, A.-J. 1985. *Textes grecs et latins relatifs à l'histoire de la peinture ancienne* (1921).
126 REINHOLD, M. 1970. *The History of Purple as a Status Symbol in Antiquity.*
127 REUTERSWÄRD, P. 1960. *Studien zur Polychromie*, II, *Griechenland und Rom.*
128 RICHTER, G. M. A. 1944. 'Polychromy in Greek Sculpture', *American Journal of Archaeology*, XLVIII, 4 (Suppl.).
129 RIST, J. M. 1972. *Epicurus: an Introduction.*
130 ROBERTSON, M. 1975. *A History of Greek Art*, 2 vols.
131 ROOSEN-RUNGE, H. 1967. *Farbgebung und Technik frühmittelalterlichen Buchmalerei*, 2 vols.

132 RUSKIN, J. II, 1846. *Modern Painters.*
133 SALZMANN, D. 1982. *Untersuchungen zu den Antiken Kieselmosaiken.*
134 SCHMIDT, W. A. 1842. 'Die Purpurfärberei und der Purpurhandel im Altertum' in *Die griechischen Papyrusurkunden der königlichen Bibliothek zu Berlin.*
135 SCHUHL, P. 1952. *Platon et l'art de son temps*, 2nd edn.
136 SCHULTZ, W. 1904. *Das Farbempfindungssystem der Hellenen.*
137 SEIBT, W. 1885. *Helldunkel I: von den Griechen bis Correggio.*
138 SEMPER, G. 1834. *Vorläufige Bemerkungen über bemalte Architektur und Plastik bei den Alten.*
139 SIEGEL, R. E. 1959. 'Theories of vision and color perception of Empedocles and Democritus: some similarities to the modern approach', *Bulletin of the History of Medicine*, XXXIII.
140 STOBAEUS, J. 1792. *Eclogarum Physicarum et Ethicarum Libri Duo* (with a Latin trans. by A. H. L. Heeren).
141 STRATTON, G. M. 1917. *Theophrastus and the Greek Physiological Psychology before Aristotle.*
142 STUART, J. and REVETT, J. 1762. *The Antiquities of Athens*, I.
143 SWIFT, E. H. 1951. *Roman Sources of Christian Art.*
144 SWINDLER, M. H. 1929. *Ancient Painting.*
145 TRIMPI. W. 1973. 'The meaning of Horace's *Ut Pictura Poesis*', *Journal of the Warburg and Courtauld Institutes*, XXXVI.
146 UNDERWOOD, P. A. (ed.). 1967–75. *The Karije Djami*, 4 vols.
147 WILLAMOWITZ-MÖLLENDORF, U. VON. 1900. 'Atticismus und Asianismus', *Hermes*, XXXV.
148 WINCKELMANN, J. J. 1882. *Geschichte der Kunst des Altertums*, ed. J. Lessing.
149 WRIGHT, F. A. 1919. 'A note on Plato's definition of colour', *Classical Review*, XXXIII–IV.
150 WRIGHT, M. R. 1981. *Empedocles: the Extant Fragments.*
151 WUNDERLICH, E. 1925. *Die Bedeutung der roten Farbe im Kultus der Griechen und Römer, erläutert mit Berücksichtigung entsprechende Bräuche bei anderen Völkern.* Religionsgeschichtliche Versuche und Vorarbeiten, XX, 1.
152 ZANTEN, D. VAN. 1976. *Architectural Polychromy of the 1830s.*

2 The Fortunes of Apelles

153 ALBERTI, L. B. 1966. *De Re Aedificatoria*, ed. G. Orlandi and P. Portoghesi.
154 —. 1972. *On Painting and On Sculpture*, ed. C. Grayson.
155 ARETINO P. 1957–60. *Lettere sull'arte*, 4 vols, ed. E. Camesasca.
156 BACON, R. 1897–1900. *Opus Majus*, 3 vols, ed. R. Bridges.
157 —. 1937. *Opera Hactenus Inedita*, ed. R. Steele.
158 BARBARO, D. 1629. *I dieci libri dell'architettura di M. Vitruvio* (1556/7), Venice.
159 BARBARO, E. 1534. *In Plinii Naturalis Historia Libros Castigationes* (1493), Basel.
160 BARDWELL, T. 1756. *The Practice of Painting.*
161 BAROCCHI, P. (ed.) 1971–7. *Scritti d'arte del cinquecento*, 3 vols.
162 BATE, Heinrich, of Mecheln. 1960.

Speculum Divinarum quorundam Naturalium, ed. E. van de Vyver.
163 BECCATTI, G. 1946. 'Plinio e l'Aretino', *Arti figurativi*, II.
164 BENSI, P. 1978/9. 'La tavolozza di Cennino Cennini', *Studi di storia dell'arte*, II.
165 BENTLEY, G. E., JR. 1969. *Blake Records.*
166 BERGER, E. 1917. *Die Wachsmalerei des Apelles und seiner Zeit.*
167 —. 1975. *Die Maltechnik des Altertums* (1904).
168 BINDMAN, D. 1977. *Blake as an Artist.*
169 —. 1978. *The Complete Graphic Works of William Blake.*
170 BIONDO, M. 1549. *Della Nobilissima Pittura*, Venice.
171 BLAKE, W. 1956. *Poetry and Prose*, ed. G. Keynes.
172 —. 1973. *Notebook*, ed. D. Erdman.
173 BOLLACK, J. 1965–9. *Empédocle*, 3 vols.
174 BOODT, A. DE. 1609. *Gemmarum et Lapidum Historia*, Hanau.
175 BORENIUS, T. 1923. *The Picture Gallery of Andrea Vendramin.*
176 BORGHINI, R. 1584. *Il Riposo*, Florence.
177 BOSCHINI, M. 1674. *Le Ricche Miniere della pittura veneziana*, Venice.
178 BOULENGER (BULENGERUS), J. C. 1627. *De Pictura, Plastica & Staturia*, Lyons.
179 BOYLE, R. 1664. *Experiments & Considerations Touching Colours*, London.
180 BRANCA, V. 1963. 'Ermolao Barbaro e l'Umanesimo Veneziano' in *Umanesimo Europeo e Umanesimo Veneziano.*
181 BUTLIN, M. 1981. *The Paintings and Drawings of William Blake.*
182 CAMERON, M. A. S., JONES, R. E. and PHILIPPAKIS, S. E. 1977. 'Analysis of Fresco samples from Knossos', *Annual of the British School at Athens*, LXXII.
183 CAST, D. 1981. *The Calumny of Apelles: a Study of the Humanist Tradition.*
184 CENNINI, C. 1971. *Il Libro dell'arte*, ed. F. Brunello.
185 CHEVREUL, M. E. 1854. *Principles of Harmony and Contrast of Colours*, trans. C. Martel.
186 COOK, B. 1977. 'Painted panel from Saqqâra', *British Museum Yearbook*, II.
187 CORIPPUS, Flavius Crescentius. 1976. *In Laudem Justini Augusti Minoris*, ed. and trans. A. Cameron.
188 CORNFORD, F. M. 1937. *Plato's Cosmology.*
189 CROWE, J. and CAVALCASELLE, G. 1881. *The Life and Times of Titian*, 2 vols, 2nd edn.
190 CUREAU DE LA CHAMBRE, M. 1650. *Nouvelles Observations et conjectures sur l'iris*, Paris.
191 DANIEL OF MORLEY. 1917. *Liber de Naturis Inferiorum et Superiorum*, ed. K. Sudhoff, in *Archiv für die Geschichte der Naturwissenschaften und der Technik*, VIII.
192 DATI, C. 1667. *Vite dei pittori antichi.*
193 *De Arte Illuminandi.* 1975. Ed. F. Brunello.
194 *De David à Delacroix.* 1974/5. Paris, Grand Palais, exh. cat.
195 DIETERICI, F. 1892. *Alfarabis philosophische Abhandlungen.*
196 DITTMANN, L. 1987. *Farbgebung und Farbtheorie in der abendländischen Malerei.*
197 DOLCE, L. 1565. *Dialogo nel quale si ragiona della qualità, diversità e proprietà de i colori*, Venice.
198 DONI, A. F. 1549. *Disegno*, Venice.

199 DU FRESNOY, C. A. 1667. *De Arte Graphica*, Paris.
200 DÜRBECK, H. 1977. *Zur Charakteristik der griechischen Farbenbezeichnungen.*
201 DÜRER, A. 1956–69. *Schriftlicher Nachlass*, 3 vols, ed. H. Rupprich.
202 EASTLAKE, C. L. 1847–69. *Materials for a History of Oil Painting*, 2 vols.
203 EDGERTON, M. F. 1963. 'Tractatus de Coloribus', *Mediaeval Studies*, XXV.
204 EDGERTON, S. Y. 1969. 'Alberti's Colour Theory: a Mediaeval Bottle without Renaissance Wine', *Journal of the Warburg and Courtauld Institutes*, XXXII.
205 ELLENIUS, A. 1960. *De Arte Pingendi: Latin Art Literature in Seventeenth-century Sweden and its International Background.*
206 *ERASMI EPISTOLAE.* 1906–58. 12 vols, ed. P. S. Allen.
207 ESSICK, R. N. 1980. *William Blake, Printmaker.*
208 EVANS, B. C. 1969. 'Physiognomics in the Ancient World', *Transactions of the American Philosophical Society*, N.S., LIX, pt 5.
209 FÉLIBIEN, A. 1981. *Life of Poussin*, ed. and trans. C. Pace.
210 FILIPPAKIS, S. E., PERDIKATSIS, B. and ASSIMENOS, K. 1979. 'X-Ray analysis of Pigments from Vergina, Greece (Second Tomb)', *Studies in Conservation*, XXIV.
211 —, — and PARADELLIS, T. 1976. 'An analysis of blue pigments from the Greek Bronze Age', *Studies in Conservation*, XXI.
212 FOERSTER, R. 1893. *Scriptores Physiognomici*, 2 vols.
213 FORBES, R. J. 1964–72. *Studies in Ancient Technology*, 9 vols, 2nd edn.
214 FÖRSTER, R. 1887. 'Die Verläumdung des Apelles in der Renaissance', *Jahrbuch der Preussischen Kunstsammlungen*, VIII.
215 FRODL-KRAFT, E. 1977/8. 'Die Farbsprache der gotischen Malerei', *Wiener Jahrbuch für Kunstgeschichte*, XXX/XXXI.
216 FUCHS, R. 1982. 'Gedanken zur Herstellung von Farben und der Überlieferung von Farbrezepten in der Antike, am Beispiel der in Ägypten verwendeten Blaupigmente', *Festschrift Roosen-Runge.*
217 GAGE, J. 1969. *Colour in Turner: Poetry and Truth.*
218 GALEN, 1562. *In Hippocrates Librum de Humoribus Commentarii*, Venice.
219 GAVEL, J. 1979. *Colour: A Study of its Position in the Art Theory of the Quattro- and Cinquecento.*
220 GHIBERTI, L. 1947. *I Commentari*, ed. O. Morisani.
221 GILCHRIST, A. 1942. *A Life of William Blake*, ed. R. Todd.
222 GIOSEFFI, D. 1979. 'Giorgione e la pittura tonale' in *Giorgione: Atti del Convegno Internazionale, Venice.*
223 *Glossaria Latina.* 1926–31. IUSSU Academiae Britannicae Edition, 5 vols, ed. H. J. Thomson and W. M. Lindsay.
224 GLOYE, E. E. 1957/8. 'Why are there primary colours?', *Journal of Aesthetics and Art Criticism*, XVI.
225 GOETHE, J. W. VON. 1957. *Zur Farbenlehre. Historischer Teil*, ed. D. Kuhn (Leopoldina Ausgabe der Schriften zur Naturwissenschaft).
226 GOMBRICH, E. H. 1962. 'Dark Varnishes: variations on a theme from Pliny', *Burlington Magazine*, CIV.
227 —. 1963. 'Controversial Methods and Methods of Controversy', *Burlington*

Magazine, CV.
228 —. 1976. *The Heritage of Apelles.*
229 GOTTSCHALK, H. B. 1964. 'The De Coloribus and its Author', *Hermes*, XCII.
230 GRANSDEN, K. W. 1957. 'The interpolated text of the Vitruvian Epitome', *Journal of the Warburg and Courtauld Institutes*, XX.
231 GRANT, E. 1974. *A Source Book in Medieval Science.*
232 GRÉGOIRE, P. 1576. *Syntaxeon Artis Mirabilis*, 2nd edn, Leiden.
233 GRENDLER, P. F. 1969. *Critics of the Italian World, 1530–1560.*
234 GROSSETESTE, R. 1912. *Die Philosophischen Werke*, ed. L. Bauer.
235 GRUNEWALD, M. 1912. *Das Kolorit in der venezianische Malerei*, I: *Die Karnation.*
236 HAGEDORN, C. L. VON. 1775. *Réflexions sur la peinture*, 2 vols.
237 HANDSCHUR, E. 1970. *Die Farb- und Glanzwörter bei Homer und Hesiod.*
238 HART, H. V. 1980. 'Chemical analysis of the Fayum portrait', *North Carolina Museum of Art Bulletin*, XIV.
239 HAYDON, B. R. 1926. *Autobiography and Memoirs*, 3 vols, ed. T. Taylor, 2nd edn.
240 HAYDUCK, M. (ed.). 1899. *Commentaria in Aristotelem Graeca*, II, ii.
241 HAYTER, C. 1826. *A New Practical Treatise on the Three Primary Colours.*
242 HIND, A. M. 1938–49. *Early Italian Engraving*, 7 vols.
243 HOFMANN, W. J. 1971. *Über Dürers Farbe.*
244 HUDSON, D. 1958. *Sir Joshua Reynolds.*
245 HUTH, H. 1967. *Künstler und Werkstatt der Spätgotik*, 2nd edn.
246 *Ingres raconté par lui-même et par ses amis.* 1947. 2 vols.
247 IRWIN, E. 1974. *Colour-Terms in Greek Poetry.*
248 JEX-BLAKE, K. and SELLERS, E. 1968. *The Elder Pliny's Chapters on the History of Art*, 2nd edn.
249 JORDAN, L. 1911. 'Physiognomische Abhandlugen: Die Theorie der Physiognomik im Mittelalter', *Romanische Forschungen*, XXIX.
250 JÜCKER, H. 1950. *Vom Verhältnis der Römer zur bildenden Kunst der Griechen.*
251 KENNEDY, R. W. 1964. 'Apelles Redivivus', *Essays in Memory of Karl Lehmann.*
252 KEULS, E. 1975. 'Skiagraphia once again', *American Journal of Archaeology*, LXXIX.
253 KURZ, O. 1963. 'Time the Painter', *Burlington Magazine*, CV.
254 KUSPIT, D. B. 1973. '"Melanchton and Dürer": the search for the simple style', *Journal of Medieval and Renaissance Studies*, III.
255 LAMBERT, J. H. 1772. *Beschreibung einer mit Calauschem Wachse ausgemalten Farben pyramide*, Augsburg.
256 LAZZARINI, L. et al. (eds). 1978. *Giorgione: La Pala di Castelfranco Veneto.*
257 LEPIK-KOPACZYŃSKA, W. 1963. *Apelles, der berühmteste Maler der Antike.*
258 *Livro de como se fazan as Côres*, Todd Memorial Volumes, I, 1930; trans. D. S. Blondheim, *Jewish Quarterly Review*, XIX, 1928–9.
259 LOUMYER, G. 1914. *Traditions, techniques de la peinture médiévale.*
260 LUCAS, A. and PLESTERS, J. 1978. 'Titian's "Bacchus and Ariadne"', *National Gallery Technical Bulletin*, II.
261 MACLEAN, J. 1966. 'De

Kleurentheorie in West-Europa (1200–1500)', *Scientiarum Historia*, VIII.

262 McKEON, C. K. 1948, *A Study of the Summa Philosophiae of the Pseudo-Grosseteste*.

263 MAHON, D. 1962. 'Miscellanea for the Cleaning Controversy', *Burlington Magazine*, CIV.

264 MAIER, A. 1952. *An der Grenze von Scholastik und Natur-Wissenschaft*, 2nd edn.

265 MANDER, K. VAN. 1916. *Het Schilderboeck* (1604), ed. R. Hoecker.

266 MANGO, C. 1963. 'Antique Statuary and the Byzantine Beholder', *Dumbarton Oaks Papers*, XVII.

267 MARBODE OF RENNES. 1977. *De Lapidibus*, ed. J. M. Riddle.

268 MARIUS. 1976. *On the Elements*, ed. R. C. Dales.

269 MASSING, J. M. 1990. *Du Texte à l'image. La calomnie d'Apelle et son iconographie*.

270 MELLINK, M. J. 1971. 'Excavations at Karatas-Samayuk and Elmah, Lycia, 1970', *American Journal of Archaeology*, LXXV.

271 MERRIFIELD, M. 1849. *Original Treatises on the Arts of Painting*, 2 vols.

272 MINGAZZINI, P. 1961. 'Una copia dell'Alexandros Keraunophonos di Apelle', *Jahrbuch der Berliner Museen*, III.

273 MINTO, A. 1953, *Le Vite dei pittori antichi di C. R. Dati e gli studi erudito-antiquari nel seicento*.

274 MONTJOSIEU, L. (Demontiosius). 1649. *Commentarius de Pictura (Gallus Romae Hospes*, 1585) in Vitruvius, *De Architectura*, ed. J. de Laet, Antwerp.

275 MORASSI, A. 1955. *G. B. Tiepolo*.

276 — . 1962. *G. B. Tiepolo: A Complete Catalogue of the Paintings*.

277 NAHM, M. C. 1964. *Selections from Early Greek Philosophy*, 4th edn.

278 NAPOLI, M. 1970. *La Tomba del Tuffatore*.

279 NORTHCOTE, J. 1818. *The Life of Sir Joshua Reynolds*, 2 vols, 2nd edn.

280 PACIOLI, L. 1889. *De Divina Proportione* (1509), ed. C. Winterberg.

281 PAILLOT DE MONTABERT, J. N. 1829. *Traité complet de la peinture*, 9 vols.

282 PANOFSKY, E. 1951. '"Nebulae in Pariete": Notes on Erasmus' eulogy of Dürer', *Journal of the Warburg and Courtauld Institutes*, XIV.

283 — . 1969. 'Erasmus and the Visual Arts', *Journal of the Warburg and Courtauld Institutes*, XXXII.

284 — . 1969. *Problems in Titian, mostly Iconographic*.

285 PARIS, M. VI, 1882. *Chronica Majora* (Rolls Series, ed. H. R. Luard).

286 PARKHURST, C. 1971. 'A color-theory from Prague: Anselm de Boodt, 1609', *Allen Memorial Art Museum Bulletin*, XXIX.

287 — . 1973. 'Louis Savot's nova-antiqua color theory, 1609', *Album Amicorum J. G. van Gelder*.

288 — . 1973. 'Camillo Leonardi and the Green-Blue Shift in sixteenth-century painting' in P. Bloch et al. (eds), *Intuition und Kunstwissenschaft. Festschrift für H. Swarzenski*.

289 PEDRETTI, C. 1965. *Leonardo da Vinci on Painting; a Lost Book*.

290 PHILANDER, G. 1544. *In Decem Libros M. Vitruvii Pollionis de Architectura Annotationes*, Rome.

291 PHILLIPS, T. 1833. *Lectures on the History and Principles of Painting*.

292 PILES, R. DE. 1699. *Abrégé de la vie des peintres*, Paris.

293 — . 1708. *Cours de peinture par principes*, Paris.

294 PLESTERS, J. 1962. 'Dark Varnishes – some further comments', *Burlington Magazine*, CIV.

295 PLINY THE ELDER. 1725. *Histoire de la peinture ancienne extraite de l'Histoire Naturelle de Pline*, Liv. XXXV, London.

296 — . 1978. *Naturkunde*, XXXV, ed. and trans. R. König and G. Winkler.

297 PLOMMER, W. H. 1973. *Vitruvius and Later Roman Building Manuals*.

298 POLLITT, J. J. 1972. *Art and Experience in Classic Greece*.

299 PROFI, S., PERDIKATSIS, B. and FILIPPAKIS, S. E. 1977. 'X-Ray analysis of Greek Bronze-Age Pigments from Thera (Santorini)', *Studies in Conservation*, XXII.

300 PROFI, S., WEIER, L. and FILIPPAKIS, S. E. 1974. 'X-Ray analysis of Greek Bronze-Age Pigments from Mycenae', *Studies in Conservation*, XIX.

301 —, —, —. 1976. 'X-Ray analysis of Greek Bronze-Age Pigments from Knossos', *Studies in Conservation*, XXI.

302 RAMER, B. 1979. 'The technology, examination and conservation of the Fayum Portraits in the Petrie Museum', *Studies in Conservation*, XXIV.

303 REQUENO, V. 1787. *Saggi sul ristabilimento dell'antica arte de'greci e romani pittori*, 2 vols, 2nd edn, Parma.

304 RICHTER, G. M. 1937. *Giorgione da Castelfranco*.

305 RIDOLFI, C. 1914. *Le Meraviglie dell'arte* (1648), 2 vols, ed. D. Fr. von Hadeln.

306 ROOD, O. 1879. *Modern Chromatics* (Ger. edn, *Die Moderne Farbenlehre* 1880).

307 ROSE, V. 1875. 'Aristoteles de Lapidibus und Arnoldus Saxo', *Zeitschrift für deutsches Altertum*, N. F, VI.

308 ROSKILL, M. 1968. *Dolce's 'Aretino' and Venetian Art Theory of the Cinquecento*.

309 RUBIN, J. 1975. 'New documents on the Méditateurs: Baron Gérard, Mantegna and French Romanticism c. 1800', *Burlington Magazine*, CXVIII.

310 RUMPF, A. 1947. 'Classical and Post-Classical Greek Painting', *Journal of Hellenic Studies*, LXVII.

311 — . 1962. 'Zum Alexander Mosaik', *Mitteilungen des deutschen Archäologischen Instituts (Athenische Abteilung)*, LXXVII.

312 RUSSELL, R. A. and WINTERBOTTOM, M. (eds). 1972. *Ancient Literary Criticism*.

313 SANDRART, J. VON. 1675. *L'Academia Todesca della Architectura & Pittura oder Teutsche Academie der Edlen Bau, Bild und Mahlerey Künste*, Nuremberg and Frankfurt.

314 — . 1683. *Academia Nobilissimae Artis Pictoriae*, Nuremberg and Frankfurt.

315 SAVOT, L. 1609. *Nova, seu Verius Nova-antiqua de Causis Colorum Sententia*, Paris.

316 SCALIGER, J. C. 1601. *De Subtilitate ad Hieronymum Cardanum* (1576), Frankfurt.

317 SCARMILIONIUS, V. A. 1601. *De Coloribus*, Marburg.

318 SCHARF, A. 1950. *Filippino Lippi*.

319 SCHEFFERUS, J. 1669. *Graphice, id est de Arte Pingendi*, Nuremberg.

320 SCHEFOLD, K. 1963. 'The choice of colour in Ancient Art', *Palette*, XIII, 2.

321 — . 1966. 'The significance of colour in Greek vase painting', *Palette*, XXII, 2.

322 SCHEIBLER, I. 1974. 'Die "Vier Farben" der griechischen Malerei', *Antike Kunst*, XVII.

323 — . 1978. 'Zum Koloritstil der griechischen Malerei', *Pantheon*, XXXVI.

324 SCHIFFERMÜLLER, I. 1772. *Versuch eines Farbensystems* (1771).

325 SCHMID, H. 1926. *Enkaustik und Fresko auf antiker Grundlage*.

326 SEZNEC, J. 1953. *The Survival of the Pagan Gods*.

327 SHORE, A. F. 1972. *Portrait Painting from Roman Egypt*.

328 SMET, A. J. 1968. *Alexandre d'Aphrodisias: commentaire sur les Météores d'Aristote: traduction de Guillaume de Moerbeke*.

329 SOLMSEN, F. 1960. *Aristotle's System of the Physical World*.

330 SONNENBURG, H. VON and PREUSSER, F. 1979. 'Rubens' Bildaufbau und Technik, II: Farbe und Auftragstechnik', *Mitteilungen des Doerner-Instituts*, III.

331 SPEZIALI, P. 1953. 'Leonardo da Vinci et la Divina Proportione di Luca Pacioli', *Bibliothèque d'humanisme et de renaissance*, XV.

332 STOUT, G. L. 1932. 'The restoration of a Fayum Portrait', *Technical Studies in the Field of Fine Arts*, I.

333 TERTULLIAN. 1961. *De Spectaculis*, ed. E. Castorina.

334 THEODORIC OF FREIBERG. 1914. *De Iride*, ed. J. Würschmidt (*Beiträge zur Geschichte und Philosophie des Mittelalters*, XII).

335 THOMPSON, D. V. JR (ed.). 1926. '*Liber de Coloribus*', *Speculum*, I.

336 — . 1934/5. 'Medieval color-making: Tractatus qualiter quilibet artificialis color fieri potest, from Paris B. N. MS Latin 6749ᵇ', *Isis*, XXII.

337 TIETZE-CONRAT, E. 1944. 'Titian as a Letter-Writer', *Art Bulletin*, XXVI.

338 TODD, R. B. 1976. *Alexander of Aphrodisias on Stoic Physics*.

339 UCCELLI, A. 1940. *I Libri di meccanica di Leonardo da Vinci*.

340 VASARI, G. 1878–85. *Le Vite*, 9 vols, ed. G. Milanesi.

341 — . 1962–6. *Le Vite*, 8 vols (Club del Libro).

342 VECKENSTEDT, E. 1888. *Geschichte der griechischen Farbenlehre*.

343 VITRUVIUS. 1521. *De Architectura*, ed. C. Cesariano, Como.

344 VOSSIUS, G. J. 1650. *De Quatuor Artibus Popularibus*, Amsterdam.

345 WAAL, H. VAN DER. 1967. 'The "Linea Summae Tenuitatis" of Apelles: Pliny's phrase and its Interpreters', *Zeitschrift für Aesthetik und Allgemeine Kunstwissenschaft*, XII.

346 WALTER-KARYDI, H. 1986. 'Prinzipien der archaischen Farbgebung' in *Studien zur klassischen Archäologie. Festschrift zum 60. Geburtstag von Friedrich Hiller*.

347 WEBB, D. 1760. *An Inquiry into the Beauties of Painting*, London.

348 WEITZMANN, K. 1976. *The Monastery of Saint Catherine at Mount Sinai, the Icons*, I.

349 WETHEY, H. 1969–75. *The Paintings of Titian*, 3 vols.

350 WILLIAM OF AUVERGNE. 1674. *Opera*, 2 vols. Orléans.

351 WIND, E. 1969. *Giorgione's 'Tempesta'*.

352 WOLFSON, H. A. 1970. *The Philosophy of the Church Fathers*, 3rd edn.

353 WUTTKE, D. 1967. 'Unbekannte Celtis-Epigramme zum Lobe Dürers', *Zeitschrift für Kunstgeschichte*, XXX.

354 YOUNG. D. 1964. 'The Greeks' colour sense', *Review of the Society for Hellenic Travel*, I, v.

355 ZIEGLER, J. C. 1852. *Traité de la couleur et de la lumière*.

3 Light from the East

356 AALEN, S. 1951. *Die Begriffe Licht und Finsternis im alten Testament, im Spätjudentum, und im Rabbinismus*.

357 ABEL, F. M. 1931. 'Gaza au VIᶜ siècle d'après le rheteur Choricus', *Revue biblique*, XL.

358 ACOCELLA, N. 1963. 'La Basilica Cassinense di Desiderio in un carme di Alfano da Salerno', *Napoli Nobilissima*, III.

359 AETHELWULF. 1967. *De Abbatibus*, ed. A. Campbell.

360 ALESSANDRI, L. and PENACCHI, F. 1914. 'I più antichi inventari della sacristia del sacro convento di Assisi (1338–1433)', *Archivum Franciscanum Historicum*, VII.

361 ALEXANDER OF APHRODISIAS. 1901. *In Librum de Sensu Commentarium*, ed. P. Wendland.

362 ALEXANDER, P. J. 1958. *The Patriarch Nicephorus*.

363 ALEXANDER, S. M. 1964/5. 'Medieval recipes describing the use of metal in MSS', *Marsyas*, XII.

364 ALHAZEN. 1989. *Optics*, 2 vols, trans. A. I. Sabra.

365 ANASTOS, M. 1955. 'The argument for Iconoclasm in the Council of 754', *Late Classical and Medieval Studies in Honor of A. M. Friend, Jr*, ed. K. Weitzmann.

366 ANDALORO, M. 1983. 'I mosaici di Cefalù dopo il restauro' in *III Colloquio internazionale sul mosaico antico, 1980*, I.

367 ANDREESCU, I. 1976. 'Torcello III: La chronologie relative des mosaïques pariétales', *Dumbarton Oaks Papers*, XXX.

368 ASTORRI, G. 1934. 'Nuove osservazioni sulla tecnica dei mosaici romani della Basilica di S. Maria Maggiore', *Rivista di archeologia cristiana*, XI.

369 AVICENNA (IBN SINA). 1956. *De Anima (Psychologie d'Ibn Sina d'après son oeuvre Aš Šifa)*, 2 vols, ed. J. Bakoš.

370 BARRAL Y ALTET, X. 1985. *Les mosaïques de pavement médiévales de Venise, Murano, Torcello*.

371 — (ed.). 1986. *Artistes, artisans et production artistique au moyen âge*, I, *Les Hommes*.

372 — . 1987. 'Poésie et iconographie: un pavement du XIIᶜ siècle décrit par Baudri de Bourgueil', *Dumbarton Oaks Papers*, XLI.

373 BATTISCOMBE, C. F. (ed.). 1956. *The Relics of St Cuthbert*.

374 BAUDRI OF BOURGUEIL. 1979. *Carmina*, ed. K. Hilbert.

375 BAUER, H. 1911. 'Die Psychologie Alhazens au Grund von Alhazens Optik', *Beiträge zur Geschichte der Philosophie des Mittelalters*, X, 5.

376 BEATUS OF GERONA. 1930. *In Apocalypsin Libri Duodecim*, ed. H. A. Sanders.

377 BECK, I. 1970. 'The first mosaics of the Capella Palatina in Palermo', *Byzantion*, XL.

378 BELTING, H., MANGO, C. and MOURIKI, D. 1978. *The Mosaics and Frescoes of St Mary Pammakaristos (Fetiye Camii) at Istanbul*.

379 BIEBER, M. and RODENWALT, G. 1911. 'Die Mosaiken des Dioskurides von Samos', *Jahrbuch der Kaiserlichen deutschen Archäologischen Instituts*, XXVI.

380 BLÜMNER, H. 1891. 'Die Farbenbezeichnungen bei den römischen Dichtern', *Berliner Studien für Classische Philologie und Archäologie*, XIII.

381 BOVINI, G. 1954. 'Origine e tecnica del mosaico parietale paleocristiana', *Felix Ravenna*, 3rd series XIV.

382 —. 1957. 'Note sulla successione delle antiche fasi di lavoro nella decorazione musiva del Battistero degli Ariani', *Felix Ravenna* LXXV.

383 —. 1964a. *Storia e architettura degli edifici paleocristiani di culto di Ravenna.*

384 —. 1964b. 'Il mosaico absidiale di S. Stefano Rotondo a Roma', *Corsi d'arte Ravennata e Bizantina*. XI.

385 —. 1966. 'Antichi rifacimenti nei mosaici di S. Apollinare Nuovo', *Corsi d'arte Ravennata e Bizantina*, XIII.

386 —. 1970. *Antichità cristiane di Milano.*

387 BRAUN, J. 1907. *Die liturgische Gewandung im Occident und Orient.*

388 BREHIER, L. 1945. 'Les mosaïques à fond d'azur', *Études byzantines*, III.

389 BRENK, B. 1971. 'Early gold mosaics in Christian art', *Palette*, XXXVIII.

390 BRUNEAU, P. 1972. *Les Mosaïques de Delos.*

391 —. 1984. 'Les mosaïstes antiques avaient-ils des cahiers de modèles?', *Revue archéologique*, II.

392 BRUYNE, L. DE. 1957. 'La décoration des baptistères paléo-chrétiens' in *Actes du Ve congrès international d'archéologie chrétienne, 1954.*

393 BRYER, A. and HERRIN, J. (eds). 1977. *Iconoclasm.*

394 BULTMANN, P. 1821. *Scholia antiqua in Homeri Odysseam.*

395 CAIGER-SMITH, A. 1985. *Lustre Pottery. Technique, Tradition and Innovation in Islam and the Western World.*

396 CALABI-LIMENTANI, I. 1958. *Studi sulla società romana: il lavoro artistico.*

397 CAPIZZI, C. 1964. *PANTOKRATOR: Saggio d'esegesi letterario-iconografica.*

398 CARANDINI, A. 1961/2. *Richerche sullo stile e la cronologia dei mosaici della Villa di Piazza Armerina* (Seminario di Archeologia e Storia dell'Arte Greca e Romana dell'Università di Roma: *Studi Miscellanei*, VIII).

399 CLAVIJO. 1928. *Embassy to Tamerlane, 1403–1406*, trans. G. le Strange.

400 CONSTANTINE VII PORPHYROGENITOS. 1935–40. *Le Livre des Cérémonies*, 4 vols, ed. A. Vogt.

401 CONTI, A. 1988. *Storia del restauro*, 2nd edn.

402 CORMACK, R. S. 1969. 'The mosaic decoration of S. Demetrios, Thessaloniki', *Annual of the British School in Athens*, LXIV.

403 — and HAWKINS, E. J. W. 1977. 'The mosaics of St Sophia at Istanbul: the South-West Vestibule and Ramp', *Dumbarton Oaks Papers* XXXI.

404 DAUPHIN, C. 1978. 'Byzantine pattern-books: a re-examination of the problem', *Art History*, I.

405 DAVIS-WEYER, C. 1971. *Early Medieval Art, 300–1150.*

406 DEICHMANN, F. W. II, 1974. *Ravenna: Hauptstadt des spätantiken Abendlandes.*

407 DELVOYE, C. 1969. 'Les Tissus Byzantines', *Corsi d'arte Ravennata e Bizantina*, XVI.

408 DEMUS, O. 1945. 'The ciborium mosaics of Parinzo', *Burlington Magazine*, LXXXVII.

409 —. 1949. *The Mosaics of Norman Sicily.*

410 —. 1960. *The Church of S. Marco in Venice: History, Architecture, Sculpture.*

411 —. 1984. *The Mosaics of S. Marco in Venice.*

412 *Dictionnaire d'archéologie chrétienne et liturgie*, XII, 1935.

413 DIEHL, C. 1910. *Manuel d'art byzantin.*

414 DIEHL, E. (ed.). 1963. *Inscriptiones Latinae Christianae Veteres* (1925).

415 DIONYSIUS OF FOURNA. 1974. *The painter's Manual*, trans. P. Hetherington.

416 DIX, G. 1945. *The Shape of the Liturgy.*

417 DÖLGER, F. 1918. 'Die Sonne der Gerechtigkeit und der Schwarze', *Liturgiegeschichtliche Forschungen*, II.

418 —. 1925. 'Sol Salutis', ibid., IV–V.

419 —. 1936. 'Lumen Christi: Untersuchungen zum abendlichen Licht-Segen in Antike und Christentum', *Antike und Christentum*, V.

420 DOWNEY, G. 1959. 'Ekphrasis' in *Reallexikon für Antike und Christentum*, IV.

421 DYGGVE, E. 1962. 'Sui mosaici pavimentali', *Stucchi e mosaici alto medioevali* (Atti dell'ottavo congresso di studi sull'arte dell'alto medioevo), I.

422 EBERSOLT, J. 1923. *Les Arts somptuaires de Byzance.*

423 EDDIUS. 1927. *Life of Bishop Wilfrid*, ed. B. Colgrave.

424 EGERIA. 1960. *Itinerarium Egeriae*, ed. O. Prinz.

425 —. 1971. *Travels*, trans. J. Wilkinson.

426 ETTINGHAUSEN, R. 1962. *Arab Painting.*

427 EVANS, M. W. 1980. 'The Geometry of the Mind', *Architectural Association Quarterly*, XII, 4.

428 FAKHRY, M. 1970. *A History of Islamic Philosophy.*

429 FALKE, O. VON. 1921. *Kunstgeschichte der Seidenweberei.*

430 FIORENTINI RONCUZZI, I. 1971. *Arte e tecnologia nel mosaico.*

431 FISCHER, W. 1965. *Farb- und Formenbezeichnungen in der Sprache der altarabischen Dichtung.*

432 FORLATI, F. 1949. 'La tecnica dei primi mosaici Marciani', *Arte Veneta*, III.

433 FORSYTH, G. H. and Weitzmann, K. 1965. *The Monastery of St Catherine at Mount Sinai.*

434 FROLOW, A. 1945. 'Deux églises byzantines', *Études byzantines*, III.

435 —. 1951. 'La mosaïque murale byzantine', *Byzantino-Slavica*, XII.

436 GALAVARIS, G. 1969. *The Illustrations of the Liturgical Homilies of Gregory Nazianzenus.*

437 GAUTHIER, M.-M. 1972. *Émaux du moyen-âge occidental.*

438 GEORGE, W. S. 1912. *The Church of Saint Eirene at Constantinople.*

439 GOLDSCHMIDT, R. C. 1940. *Paulinus' Churches at Nola.*

440 *Gospel of Philip*. 1963. Ed. W. C. Till.

441 GOUSSET, M. T. and STIRNEMANN, P. 1990. 'Indications de couleur dans les manuscrits médiévaux' in *Pigments et colorants de l'antiquité et du moyen âge: Teinture, peinture, enluminure: études historiques et physico-chimiques* (Colloque International du Centre National de la Recherche Scientifique).

442 GRABAR, A. 1955. 'The Virgin in a mandorla of light', *Late Classical and Medieval Studies in Honor of A. M. Friend, Jr*, ed. K. Weitzmann.

443 —. 1957. *L'Iconoclasme byzantine: Dossier archéologique.*

444 —. 1971. 'La verrerie d'art byzantin au moyen-âge', *Monuments Piot*, LVII.

445 GRABAR, O. 1964. 'Islamic art and Byzantium', *Dumbarton Oaks Papers*, XVIII.

446 —. 1973. *The Formation of Islamic Art.*

447 *Greek Anthology*. 1969. trans. W. K. Paton, I (1916).

448 GÜNTER, R. 1968. *Wand, Fenster und Licht in der Trierer Palastaula und in spätantiken Bauten.*

449 HAAS, A. E. 1907. 'Antike Lichttheorien', *Archive für Geschichte der Philosophie*, XX.

450 HAEBERLEIN, F. 1939. 'Grundzüge einer nachantiken Farbikonographie', *Römisches Jahrbuch für Kunstgeschichte*, III.

451 HAWKINS, E. J. W. 1968. 'Further observations on the narthex mosaic in St Sophia in Istanbul', *Dumbarton Oaks Papers*, XXII.

452 HEMPEL, J. 1960. 'Die Lichtsymbolik im alten Testament', *Studium Generale*, XIII.

453 HENDERSON, G. 1987. *From Durrow to Kells: The Insular Gospel-books 650–800.*

454 HESS, T. B. and Ashbery, J. 1969. *Light, from Aten to Laser* (Art News Annual, XXXV).

455 IBN JOBAÏR. 1949–65. *Voyages*, 4 vols, trans. M. Gaudefroy-Demombynes.

456 ISIDORE OF SEVILLE. 1960. *Traité de la Nature*, ed. J. Fontaine.

457 ITTEN, J. 1961. *Art of Color.*

458 IVANKA, I. VON. 1959. 'Dunkelheit, mystische' in *Reallexikon für Antike und Christentum*, IV.

459 JAMES, L. and WEBB, R. 1991. 'To understand ultimate things and enter secret places: ekphrasis and art in Byzantium', *Art History*, XIV.

460 JOB OF EDESSA. 1935. *Book of Treasures*, ed. and trans. A. Mingana.

461 JOLY, D. 1965. 'Quelques aspects de la mosaïque pariétale au 1er siècle de notre ère. D'après trois documents pompéiens' in *La Mosaïque gréco-romaine: Colloques interationaux, Paris 1963.*

462 KÄHLER, H. 1967. *Hagia Sophia.*

463 KANTOROWICZ, E. 1963. 'Oriens Augusti – Lever du Roi', *Dumbarton Oaks Papers*, XVII.

464 KARAGEORGHIS, V. 1969. *The Ancient Civilisation of Cyprus.*

465 KARPP, H. 1966. *Die frühchristlichen und mittelalterlichen Mosaiken in Santa Maria Maggiore zu Rom.*

466 KENDRICK, T. D. et al. 1960. *Codex Lindisfarnensis*, 2 vols.

467 KHATCHATRIAN. A. 1962. *Les Baptistères paléochrétiens.*

468 KHITROWO, B. DE. 1889. *Itineraires russes en Orient.*

469 KIRSCHBAUM, E. 1940. 'L'angelo rosso e l'angelo purchino', *Rivista di archeologia cristiana*, XVII.

470 KITZINGER, E. 1960. *The Mosaics of Monreale.*

471 —. 1963. 'The hellenistic heritage in Byzantine art', *Dumbarton Oaks Papers*, XVII.

472 —. 1977. *Byzantine Art in the Making.*

473 KLEIN, P. K. 1976. *Der ältere Beatus-Kodex Vitr. 14ĉ1 der Biblioteca Nacional zu Madrid. Studien zu Beatus – Illustration und der Spanischen Buchmalerei des 10 Jh.*

474 KLEINBAUER, W. E. 1972. 'The iconography and the date of the mosaics of the Rotunda of Hagios Georgios, Thessaloniki', *Viator*, III.

475 KOCH, J. 1956/7. 'Augustinischer und Dionysischer Neu-Platonismus und das Mittelalter', *Kant-Studien*, XLVIII.

476 KOLDEWEY, R. 1884. 'Das Bad von Alexandria-Troas', *Athenische Mitteilungen*, IX.

477 KONDAKOFF, N. 1924. 'Les costumes orientaux à la cour byzantine', *Byzantin*, I.

478 KOSTOF, S. K. 1965. *The Orthodox Baptistry of Ravenna.*

479 LAFONTAINE-DOSOGNE, J. 1979. 'L'évolution du programme décoratif des églises de 1071 à 1261', *Actes du XVe congrès international d'études byzantines, 1976*, I.

480 LANGE, G. 1969. *Bild und Wort: die katechetischen Funktionen des Bildes in der griechischen Theologie des 6. bis 9. Jahrhunderts.*

481 LAVAGNE, H. 1977/8. 'Histoire de la mosaïque.I, Les mosaïstes antiques', *Annuaire de l'École pratique des hautes études*, IVe sect.

482 —. 1983. '"Luxuria inaudita": Marcus Aemilius Scaurus et la naissance de la mosaïque murale', in *Mosaïque: recueil d'hommages à Henri Stern.*

483 LAZAREV, V. 1966. *Old Russian Paintings and Mosaics.*

484 —. 1967. *Storia della Pittura Bizantina.*

485 LEJEUNE, A. 1948. *Euclide et Ptolémée: deux stades de l'optique géométrique grècque.*

486 LEMBERG, M. and SCHMEDDING, B. 1973. *Abegg-Stiftung Bern in Riggisberg*, II, *Textilien.*

487 LEVI, D. 1947. *Antioch Mosaic Pavements*, 2 vols.

488 LOGVIN, H. 1971. *Kiev's Hagia Sophia.*

489 LUBECK, K. 1912. 'Die liturgische Gewandung der Griechen', *Theologie und Glaube*, IV.

490 LUGLI, G. 1928. 'Studi topografichi intorno alle antichi ville suburbane – VI. Villa Adriana', *Bulletino della Commissione Archeologica Communale di Roma*, LV.

491 McGUCKIN, J. A. 1986. *The Transfiguration of Christ in Scripture and Tradition.*

492 MacMULLEN, R. 1964. 'Some pictures in Ammianus Marcellinus', *Art Bulletin*, XLVI.

493 McNALLY, R. E. 1970. 'The Three Holy Kings in Early Irish Latin writing' in P. Granfield and J. A. Jungmann (eds), *Kyriakon: Festschrift Johannes Quasten*, II.

494 MACRIDES, R. and MAGDALINO, P. 1988. 'The architecture of Ekphrasis: construction and context of Paul the Silentiary's ekphrasis of Hagia Sophia', *Byzantine and Modern Greek Studies*, XII.

495 MAGUIRE, H. 1974. 'Truth and Convention in Byzantine descriptions of works of art', *Dumbarton Oaks Papers*, XXVIII.

496 —. 1987. *Earth and Ocean: the Terrestrial World in Byzantine Art.*

497 MAIER, J.-L. 1964. *Le Baptistère de Naples et ses mosaïques.*

498 MAINSTONE, R. 1988. *Hagia Sophia Architecture, Structure and Liturgy of Justinan's Great Church.*

499 MAKSIMOVIČ, I. 1964. 'Iconography and Programme of the Mosaics at Poreč', *Receuils des travaux de l'Institut d'études byzantines (Mélanges G. Ostrogorsky, II)*.
500 MANGO, C. 1962. *The Mosaics of St Sophia at Istanbul*.
501 —. 1972. *The Art of the Byzantine Empire 312–1453*.
502 — and HAWKINS, F. J. W. 1965. 'The apse mosaics of St Sophia at Istanbul', *Dumbarton Oaks Papers*, XIX.
503 — and PARKER, J. 1960. 'A twelfth-century description of St Sophia', *Dumbarton Oaks Papers*, XIV.
504 MARTINELLI, P. A. 1969. 'Il costume femminile nei mosaici ravennati', *Corsi d'arte Ravennata e Bizantina*, XVI.
505 MATHEW, G. 1975. 'The aesthetic theories of Gregory of Nyssa' in G. Robertson and G. D. S. Henderson (eds), *Studies in Memory of David Talbot Rice*.
506 MATHEWS, T. F. 1971. *The Early Churches of Constantinople: Architecture and Liturgy*.
507 MATTHIAE, G. 1969/70. 'I mosaici di Grottaferrata', *Rendiconti pontificia archaeologia*, XLII.
508 MEDICO, H. E. DEL. 1943. 'Les mosaïques de Germigny-des-Près', *Monuments Piot*, XXXIX.
509 MEGAW, A. H. S. 1963. 'Notes on recent work of the Byzantine Institute in Istanbul', *Dumbarton Oaks Papers*, XVII.
510 — and HAWKINS, E. J. W. 1977. *The Church of the Panagia Kanakaria at Lythrankomi in Cyprus: its Mosaics and Frescoes*.
511 MENENDEZ Y PELAYO, M. 1910. *Historia de las Ideas Esteticas en España*, II.
512 MENTRÉ, M. 1983. 'Espace et couleur dans les Beatus du Xe siècle', *Cahiers de Saint-Michel de Cuxa*, XIV, August.
513 —. 1984. *La Peinture mozarabique*.
514 MESARITES, N. 1957. 'Description of the Church of the Holy Apostles' (ed. G. Downey), *Transactions of the American Philosophical Society*, N.S., XLVII.
515 METHODIUS OF OLYMPOS 1958. *The Banquet of the Twelve Virgins*, ed. and trans. H. Musurillo.
516 MEYENDORFF, J. 1964. 'Byzantine views of Islam', *Dumbarton Oaks Papers*, XVIII.
517 MICHELIS, P. A. 1952. 'Neo-Platonic philosophy and Byzantine art', *Journal of Aesthetics and Art Criticism*, XI.
518 —. 1955. *An Aesthetic Approach to Byzantine Art*.
519 —. 1963. 'L'ésthetique d'Hagia-Sophia', *Corsi d'arte Ravennata e Bizantina*, X.
520 —. 1964. 'Comments on Gervase Mathew's *Byzantine Aesthetics*', *British Journal of Aesthetics*, IV.
521 MIELSCH, H. 1985. *Buntmarmore aus Rom im Antikenmuseum Berlin*.
522 MOURIKI, D. 1985. *The Mosaics of Nea Moni on Chios*.
523 MUGLER, C. 1964. *Dictionnaire historique de la terminologie optique des grecs*.
524 MÜLLER-CHRISTENSEN, S. 1960. *Das Grab des Papstes Clemens II im Dom zu Bamberg*.
525 MUNDÓ, A. M. and SANCHEZ MARIANA, M. 1976. *El Commentario de Beato al Apocalypsis. Catalogo de los Codices*.
526 MÜNTZ, E. and FROTHINGHAM. A. L. 1883. *Il Tesoro della Basilica di S. Pietro*.
527 MURARO, M. 1961. 'The statutes of the Venetian *Arti* and the Mosaics of the

Mascoli Chapel', *Art Bulletin*, XLIII.
528 NICHOLSON, R. A. 1914. *The Mystics of Islam*.
529 NONNOS. 1962. *Dionysiaca*, II, trans. W. H. D. Rouse.
530 NORDHAGEN, P. J. 1965. 'The mosaics of John VII', *Acta Instituti Romani Norvegiae*, II.
531 —. 1983. 'The penetration of Byzantine mosaic technique into Italy in the sixth century A.D.', *III Colloquio Internazionale sul Mosaico Antico, 1980*.
532 OAKESHOTT, W. 1967. *The Mosaics of Rome*.
533 L'ORANGE, H. P. 1974/5. 'L'adorazione della luce nell'arte tardo-antica ed alto-medioevale', *Atti della Pontifica Accademia Romana di Archeologia*, Ser. 3, XLVII.
534 ORLANDOS, A. 1963. *Paragoritissa tis Artis* (with Fr. resumé).
535 PALMER, A. 1988. 'The inauguration anthem of Hagia Sophia at Edessa: a new edition and translation with historical and architectural notes and a comparison with a contemporary Constantinopolitan Kontakion', *Byzantine and Modern Greek Studies*, XII.
536 PASTOUREAU, M. 1983. 'Formes et couleurs du désordre: le jaune avec le vert', *Mediévales*, IV (repr. in M. Pastoureau, *Figures et couleurs 1986*).
537 —. [1989]. 'Rouge, jaune et gaucher: notes sur l'iconographie médiévale de Judas' in *Couleurs, images, symbols*.
538 PELAKANIDIS, S. 1963. *Gli affreschi Paleocristiani ed i più antichi mosaici Parietalè di Salonicco*.
539 PERLER, O. 1953. *Die Mosaiken der Juliergruft im Vatikan* (Freiberger Universitätsreden N.F. XVI).
540 PHOTIUS. 1958. *The Homilies*, ed. and trans. C. Mango.
541 —. 1959–77. *Bibliothèque*, 8 vols, ed. and trans. R. Henry.
542 PRANDI, A. 1952. 'Pietro Cavallini in S. Maria in Trastevere', *Rivista dell'Istituto Nazionale d'Archeologia e dell'Arte*, I.
543 PSELLUS, M. 1953. *Chronographia*, trans. E. R. A. Sewter.
544 PSEUDO-ARISTOTLE. 1912. *Das Steinbuch des Aristoteles*, ed. J. Ruska.
545 PSEUDO-DIONYSIUS. 1987. *The Complete Works*, trans. C. Luibheid.
546 PTOLEMY. 1956. *Optics*, ed. A. Lejeune.
547 PUECH, H. C. 1938. 'La ténèbre mystique chez le Pseudo-Denys', *Études Carmelitaines*, XXIII, ii.
548 REALI, G. (ed.). 1858. *Sul Modo di tagliare ed applicare il musaico* (?c. 1415).
549 *Reallexikon zur deutschen Kunst-Geschichte*, VIII, 1981.
550 REITER, G. 1962. *Die Griechischen Bezeichnungen der Farben Weiss, Grau und Braun*.
551 RICHTER, J. P. 1897. *Quellen der Byzantinischen Kunstgeschichte*.
552 ROBERTSON, C. H. 1965. 'Greek Mosaics', *Journal of Hellenic Studies*, LXXXV.
553 ROGAN, I. 1976. 'Quelques fresques charactéristiques des églises byzantines du Magne', *Actes du XVe congrès internationale d'études byzantines* (in the press).
554 ROSENTHAL, F. 1975. *The Classicial Heritage of Islam*.
555 RUNCIMAN, S. 1975. *Byzantine Style and Civilisation*.
556 RÜTH, U. M. 1977. *Die Farbgebung in der Byzantinischen Wandmalerei der

spätpaläologischen Epoche (1341–1453)*, Ph.D. thesis, Bonn.
557 SABBE, E. 1935. 'L'importation des tissus d'orient en Europe occidentale au haut moyen-âge', *Revue belge de philologie et d'histoire*, XIV, 2.
558 SACOPOULO, M. 1975. *La Theotokos à la Mandorle de Lythrankomi*.
559 SAHAS, D. J. 1986. *Icon and Logos: Sources in Eighth-Century Iconoclasm*.
560 SAUER, J. 1924. *Symbolik des Kirchengebäudes*.
561 SCANLON, G. T. 1968. 'Fustat and the Islamic art of Egypt', *Archaeology*, XXI.
562 SCHAPIRO, M. 1977. *Romanesque Art: Selected Papers*.
563 —. 1979. *Late Antique, Early Christian and Mediaeval Art: Selected Papers*.
564 SCHELLER, R. W. 1963. *A Survey of Mediaeval Model Books*.
565 SCHOLEM, G. 1974. 'Farben und ihre Symbolik in der jüdischen Überlieferung und Mystik', *Eranos Yearbook XLI, 1972*.
566 SCHÖNE, W. 1979. *Über das Licht in der Malerei*, 5th repr.
567 SCIARETTA, V. 1966. *Il Battistero di Albenga*.
568 SERJEANT, R. B. 1972. *Islamic Textiles: Materials for a History up to the Mongol Conquest*.
569 SMALLEY, B. 1952. *The Study of the Bible in the Middle Ages*, 2nd edn.
570 SMITH, A. M. 1983. 'Witelonis Perspectivae Liber Quintus: Book V of Witelo's Perspectiva', *Studia Copernicana*, XXIII.
571 —. 1988. 'The psychology of visual perception in Ptolemy's Optics', *Isis*, LXXIX.
572 SPATHARAKIS, I. 1976. *The Portrait in Byzantine Illuminated Manuscripts*.
573 SPECIALE, L. 1990. 'Indicazioni di colori in un disegno cassinese dell' XI secolo' in *Pigments et colorants de l'Antiquité et du moyen-âge: Teinture, peinture, enluminure: études historiques et physico-chimiques (Colloque International du Centre National de la Recherche Scientifique)*.
574 SPEISER, J. M. 1984. *Thessalonique et ses monuments du IVe au VIe siècle*.
575 STEENBOCK, F. 1965. *Der Kirchliche Prachteinband im frühen Mittelalter*.
576 STERN, H. 1957. 'Le décor des pavements et des cuves dans les baptistères paléochrétiens', *Actes du Ve Congrès international d'archéologie chrétienne, 1954*.
577 —. 1958. 'Les mosaïques de l'eglise de Sainte Constance à Rome' *Dumbarton Oaks Papers*, XII.
578 SUDA. 1935. *Lexikon*, 5 vols, ed. A. Adler.
579 SVENNUNG, J. 1941. *Compositiones Lucenses: Studien zum Inhalt, zur Textkritik und Sprache*.
580 SYMEONIS MONACHUS. 1882–5. *Opera Omnia*, ed. T. Arnold (Rolls Series).
581 TACHAU, K. H. 1988. *Vision and Certitude in the Age of Ockham*.
582 TALBOT-RICE, D. (ed.). 1968. *The Church of Hagia Sophia at Trebizond*.
583 THEOPHILUS. 1961. *De Diversis Artibus*, ed. C. R. Dodwell.
584 THEOPHRASTUS. 1965. *De Lapidibus*, ed. D. E. Eichholz.
585 TILL, W. C. 1959. 'Die Farbenbezeichnungen im Koptischen', *Analecta Biblica: Oriens Antiquus*, XII.
586 TOMAŠEVIĆ, G. C. 1973. *Heraclea Lyncestis*.

587 *Topographie Chrétienne*, II. 1970. Ed. and trans. W. Wolska-Corms.
588 TORP, H. 1963. *Mosaikkene i St Georg-rotunden*.
589 TSCHAN, F. J. II, 1951. *Saint Bernward of Hildesheim*.
590 UNDERWOOD, P. A. 1959. 'The evidence of restorations to the sanctuary mosaics of the Church of the Dormition at Nicaea', *Dumbarton Oaks papers*, XIII.
591 — and HAWKINS, E. J. W. 1961. 'The mosaics of Hagia Sophia at Istanbul. The portrait of the Emperor Alexander', *Dumbarton Oaks Papers*, XV.
592 URSO VON SALERNO. 1976. *De Commixtionibus Elementorum Libellus*, ed. W. Stürner.
593 VOLBEHR, T. 1906. 'Die Neidfarbe gelb', *Zeitschrift für Aesthetik*, I.
594 VOPEL, H. 1899. *Die altchristlichen Goldgläser*.
595 WAAL, A. DE. 1888. 'Figürliche Darstellungen auf Teppichen und Vorhängen in Römischen Kirchen bis zur Mitte des IX Jh. nach dem Liber Pontificalis', *Römische Quartalschrift*, II.
596 WACKERNAGEL, W. 1872. 'Die Farben – und Blumen – sprache des Mittelalters' in *Kleinen Schriften*, 2 vols.
597 WAETZOLDT, S. 1964. *Die Kopien des 17. Jahrhunderts nach Mosaiken und Wandmalereien in Rom*.
598 WALLACE-HADRILL, D. S. 1968. *The Greek Patristic View of Nature*.
599 WEITZMANN, K. 1971. *Studies in Classical and Byzantine Manuscript Illumination*.
600 —, LOERKE, W. C., KITZINGER, E. and BUCHTAL, H. 1975. *The Place of Book Illumination in Byzantine Art*.
601 WENZEL, M. 1987. 'Deciphering the Cotton Genesis miniatures: preliminary observations concerning the use of colour', *British Library Journal*, XIII.
602 WERCKMEISTER, O. K. 1965. 'Islamische Formen in spanischen Miniaturen des 10 Jh. und das Problem der mozarabischen Buchmalerei', *Settimane di Studio del Centro italiano di studi sull'alto medioevo*, XII.
603 WIEDEMANN, E. 1908. 'Ueber die Entstehung der Farben nach Nasir al Dîn al Tûsî', *Jahrbuch für Photographie und Reproduktionstechnik*, XXII.
604 WILLIAMS, J. 1977. *Early Spanish Manuscript Illumination*.
605 WILSON, R. J. A. 1983. *Piazza Armerina*.
606 WINFIELD, D. C. 1968. 'Middle and later Byzantine wall painting methods', *Dumbarton Oaks Papers*, XXII.
607 WINTER. H. 1954. 'The optical researches of Ibn al-Haitham', *Centaurus*, III.
608 WULFF, O. 1929/30. 'Das Raumerlebnis des Naos in Spiegel der Ekphrasis', *Byzantinische Zeitschrift*, XXX.
609 YOUNG, S. H. 1976. 'Relations between Byzantine mosaic and fresco decoration', *Jahrbuch der österreichischen Byzantinistik*, XXV.
610 ZOVATTO, P. L. 1963. *Mosaici paleocristiani delle Venezie*.
611 —. 1968. *Il Mausoleo di Galla Placida: Architettura e Decorazione*.

4 A Dionysian Aesthetic

612 *Ad faciendum emallum*. 1846. Ed. D. Way, *Archaeological Journal*, III.
613 ALAIN DE LILLE. 1955. *Anticlaudianus*.

614 ALBERTUS MAGNUS. 1967. *The Book of Minerals*, ed. D. Wyckoff.

615 —. 1968. *De Anima*, ed. C. Stroick (*Opera Omnia* VII, i).

616 —. 1972. *Super Dionysium De Divinis Nominibus*, ed. P. Simon (*Opera Omnia* XXXVII, i).

617 ALESSANDRI, L. and PENACCHI, F. 1914. 'I più antichi inventari della sacristia del sacre convento di Assisi, 1338–1433', *Archivum Franciscanum Historicum*, VII.

618 ALESSIO, F. 1965. 'La filosofia e le "artes mechanicae" nel secolo XII', *Studi Medievali*, 3 ser., VI.

619 AL-RAZI. 1912. *Secreta Secretorum*, ed. J. Ruska.

620 ANTONIO DA PISA. 1976. *Trattato sulla fabbricazione delle vetrate artistiche*, ed. S. Pezzella.

621 AQUINAS, ST THOMAS. 1950. *In Librum Beati Dionysii De Divinis Nominibus Expositio*, ed. C. Pera.

622 ARNOLDUS SAXO. 1905. *De Finibus Rerum Naturalium*, ed. E. Stange.

623 ARRHENIUS, B. 1985. *Merovingian Garnet Jewellery*.

624 BARB, A. A. 1969. 'Lapis adamas: der Blutstein' in J. Bibauw (ed.), *Hommages à Marcel Renard*.

625 BARTHOLOMEUS ANGELICUS. c. 1230. *De Proprietatibus Rerum*.

626 BARTHOLOMEUS OF BOLOGNA. 1932. *Tractatus de Luce*, ed. I. Squadrani, *Antonianum*, VII.

627 BECKSMANN, R. 1967. *Die architektonische Rahmung des Hochgotischen Bildfensters: Untersuchungen zur oberrheinischen Glasmalerei von 1250 bis 1350.*

628 BELTING, H. 1977. *Die Oberkirche von San Francesco in Assisi.*

629 BETTEMBOURG, J. M. 1977. 'Problèmes de la conservation des vitraux de la façade occidentale de la Cathédrale de Chartres', *Les Monuments historiques de la France.*

630 BEZBORODOV, M. A. 1975. *Chemie und Technologie der antiken und mittelalterlichen Gläser.*

631 BIALOSTOCKI, J. 1967. 'Ars Auro Prior', *Mélanges de littérature comparée et de philologie offerts à M. Brahmer.*

632 BIERWALTES, W. 1977. '"Negati Affirmatio", or the world as metaphor. A foundation for mediaeval aesthetics from the writings of John Scotus Eriugena', *Dionysius*, I.

633 BIGI, V. C. 1961. 'La dottrina della luce in S. Bonaventura', *Divus Thomas*, LXIV.

634 BIHL, P. M. 1941. 'Statuta Generalia Ordinis', *Archivum Franciscanum Historicum*, XXXIV.

635 BISCHOFF, B. 1984. *Anecdota Novissima. Texte des Vierten bis sechzehnten Jahrhunderts (Quellen und Untersuchungen zur Lateinischen Philologie des Mittelalters, VII).*

636 BOETHIUS. 1906. *In Isagogen Porphyrii Commenta*, ed. S. Brandt.

637 BONAVENTURE, ST. 1882–1902. *Opera*, 10 vols.

638 BONNER, G. 1968. *Saint Bede in the Tradition of Western Apocalyptic Commentary* (Jarrow Lecture 1966).

639 BORSOOK, E. 1980. *The Mural Painters of Tuscany*, 2nd edn.

640 BOTTARI, S. 1967. 'Per la cultura di Oderisi da Gubbio e di Franco Bolognese' in *Dante e Bologna nei Tempi di Dante* Facoltà di Lettere e Filosofia dell'Università di Bologna.

641 BOUCHON, C., BRISAC, C., LANTIER, E. and ZALUSKA, Y. 1979. 'La "Belle Verrière" de Chartres', *Revue de l'art*, XLVI.

642 BRANDI, C. 1959. *Il Restauro della "Maestà" di Duccio.*

643 BRAYLEY, E. W. and BRITTON, J. 1836. *The History of the Ancient Palace and late Houses of Parliament at Westminster.*

644 BRENK, B. 1975. *Die frühchristlichen Mosaiken in S. Maria Maggiore zu Rom.*

645 BRIEGER, P. 1967. *The Trinity College Apocalypse.*

646 —, MEISS, M. and SINGLETON, C. 1969. *Illuminated Manuscripts of the Divine Comedy.*

647 BROOKE, R. B. 1959. *Early Franciscan Government.*

648 BROWN, E. A. R. and COTHREN, M. W. 1986. 'The twelfth-century Crusading Window of the Abbey of St Denis', *Journal of the Warburg and Courtauld Institutes*, XLIX.

649 BROWN, K. R. 1979. 'The mosaics of San Vitale: evidence for the attribution of some Early Byzantine jewellery to Court workshops', *Gesta*, XVIII.

650 BRUYNE, E. DE. 1946. *Études d'esthetique médiévale*, 3 vols.

651 CAHN, W. 1979. *Masterpieces: Chapters in the History of an Idea.*

652 CHRÉTIEN DE TROYES. 1987. *Erec et Énide*, ed. and trans. C. W. Carroll.

653 CHRISTE, Y. (ed.) 1979. *L'Apocalypse de Jean.*

654 — and JAMES, M. R. 1981. *Apocalypse de Jean. Fac-Simile du Manuscrit Douce 180.*

655 CIOTTI, A. 1960. 'Alano e Dante', *Convivium*, XXVIII.

656 CLAUSSEN, P. C. 1978. 'Goldschmiede des Mittelalters', *Zeitschrift des deutschen Vereins für Kunstwissenschaft*, XXXII.

657 COLISH, M. L. 1968. 'A twelfth-century Problem', *Apollo*, LXXXVIII.

658 CONANT, K. J. 1975. 'Édifices marquants du temps de Pierre le Vénérable et Pierre Abelard' in *Pierre Abélard, Pierre le Vénérable, les courants philosophiques, littéraires et artistiques en occident au milieu du XIIe siècle* (Cluny, 1972).

659 CONTI, A. 1981. *La Miniatura bolognese: scuole e botteghe, 1270–1340.*

660 COOMARASWAMY, A. K. 1935. 'Medieval Aesthetic I: Dionysius the Pseudo-Areopagite and Ulrich Engelberti of Strasbourg', *Art Bulletin*, XVII.

661 —. 1938. 'Medieval Aesthetic II: St Thomas Aquinas on Dionysius and a note on the relation of beauty to truth', *Art Bulletin* XX.

662 CRAMP, R. 1968. 'Glass finds from the Anglo-Saxon Monastery of Monkwearmouth and Jarrow' in R. J. Charleston, W. Evans, A. E. Werner (eds), *Studies in Glass History and Design.*

663 —. 1970. 'Decorated window-glass from Monkwearmouth', *Antiquaries Journal*, L.

664 CROSBY, S. McK. 1966. 'An international workshop in the twelfth century', *Journal of World History*, X.

665 — and HAYWARD, J., LITTLE, C. T. and WIXOM, W. D. 1981. *The Royal Abbey of Saint-Denis in the Time of Abbot Suger*, New York, Metropolitan Museum of Art.

666 DEICHMANN, F. 1958. *Frühchristlichen Bauten und Mosaiken von Ravenna.*

667 DELISLE, L. 1884. *Inventaire des manuscrits de la Bibliothèque Nationale: Fonds de Cluni.*

668 *Dictionnaire de spiritualité.* 1953–. Ed. C. Baumgartner (14 vols so far).

669 DRACHENBERG, E., MAERCKER, K.-J. and SCHMIDT, C. 1976. *Die mittelalterliche Glasmalerei in den Ordenskirchen und im Angermuseum zu Erfurt* (Corpus Vitrearum Medii Aevi-DDR, I, i).

670 DUBY, G. 1971. *La Société au XIe et XIIe siècles dans la region Maçonnaise.*

671 EASTWOOD, B. S. 1966. 'Robert Grosseteste's theory of the rainbow: a chapter in the history of non-experimental science', *Archives Internationales d'Histoire des Sciences*, XIX.

672 —. 1967. 'Grosseteste's "quantitative" law of refraction', *Journal of the History of Ideas*, XXVIII.

673 ECO, U. 1988. *Art and Beauty in the Middle Ages.*

674 EHRLE, F. 1885. 'Zur Geschichte des Schatzes, der Bibliothek und des Archivs der Päpste im 14 Jh.', *Archiv für Literatur- und Kirchengeschichte des Mittelalters*, I.

675 ENGELBERTI, Ulrich. 1925. *De Pulchro* (ed. M. Grabmann), *Sitzungsberichte der Bayrischen Akademie der Wissenschaften: Philos., Philol. und Hist. Klasse*, V Abt.

676 ENGELS, I. I. 1937. *Zur Problematik der Mittelalterlichen Glasmalerei.*

677 ENGEN, J. VAN. 1980. 'Theophilus Presbyter and Rupert of Deutz: the manual arts and Benedictine theology in the early twelfth century', *Viator*, XI.

678 *English Romanesque Art*, 1066–1200. 1984. London, Hayward Gallery, exh. cat.

679 ERIUGENA, JOHANNIS SCOTUS. 1968–81. *Periphyseon (De Divisione Naturae)*, 3 vols, ed. I. P. Sheldon-Williams.

680 ESMEIJER, A. C. 1978. *Divina Quaternitas.*

681 EULER, W. 1967. *Die Architekturdarstellung in der Arena-Kapelle. Ihre Bedeutung für das Bild Giottos.*

682 EVANS, J. 1922. *Magical Jewels of the Middle Ages and the Renaissance.*

683 FALK, F. 1975. *Edelsteinschliff und Fassungsform.*

684 FALLANI, G. 1971a. *Dante e la cultura figurativa medioevale.*

685 —. 1971b. 'Ricerca sui protagonisti della miniatura dugentesca', *Studi danteschi*, XLVIII.

686 —. 1973. 'Postilla su Oderisi e Franco', *Studi danteschi*, L.

687 *Les Fastes du Gothique.* 1981/2. Paris, Grand Palais, exh. cat.

688 FAVATI, G. (ed.) 1965. *Il 'Voyage de Charlemagne en Orient'.*

689 FORMIGÉ, J. 1960. *L'Abbaye royale de Saint-Denis: recherches nouvelles.*

690 *Franse Kerkramen.* 1973/4. Amsterdam, Rijksmuseum, exh. cat.

691 FRISCH, T. G. 1971. *Gothic Art 1140–c. 1450.*

692 FRODL-KRAFT, E. 1970. *Die Glasmalerei.*

693 GALLO, R. 1967. *Il Tesoro di San Marco e la sua storia.*

694 GANZENMÜLLER, W. 1956. *Beiträge zur Geschichte der Chemie und der Alchimie.*

695 GARDNER, J. 1973. 'Pope Nicholas IV and the decoration of Santa Maria Maggiore', *Zeitschrift für Kunstgeschichte*, XXXVI.

696 GARIN, E. 1965. *Scienza e vita civile nel rinascimento italiano.*

697 GÄTJE, H. 1967. 'Zur Farbenlehre in der muslimische Philosophie', *Der Islam*, XLIII.

698 GAUTHIER, M.-M. 1981. 'Émaux gothiques', *Revue de l'art*, LI.

699 GEILMAN, W. 1962. 'Beiträge zur Kenntnis alter Gläser VII: Kobalt als Färbungsmittel', *Glastechnische Berichte*, XXXV.

700 GERSON, P. L. (ed.). 1986. *Abbot Suger and St Denis.*

701 GILBERT, C. (ed.). 1970. *Renaissance Art.*

702 GIOVANNONI, G. 1908. 'Opere dei Vasselletti marmorari romani', *L'Arte*, XI.

703 GLASER, H. 1965. 'Wilhelm von Saint-Denis: ein Humanist aus der Umgebung des Abt Suger und die Krise seiner Abtei von 1151 bis 1153', *Historisches Jahrbuch*, LXXXV.

704 GLASS, D. F. 1980. *Studies on Cosmatesque Pavements.*

705 GMELIN. 1961. *Handbuch der Anorganischen Chemie: Ergänzungsband, Kobalt.*

706 GOWEN, R. P. 1976. 'The Shrine of the Virgin in Tournai, I: Its restoration and state of conservation', *Aachener Kunstblätter*, XLVII.

707 GRABAR, A. and NORDENFALK, C. 1957. *Le Haut Moyen Âge.*

708 GRINNELL, R. 1946. 'Iconography and philosophy in the Crucifixion window at Poitiers', *Art Bulletin*, XXXVIII.

709 GRODECKI, L. 1949. 'Le vitrail et l'architecture au XIIe et au XIIIe siècle', *Gazette des Beaux-Arts*, XXXVI.

710 —. 1951. 'Les vitraux de la Cathédrale de Poitiers', *Congrès archéologique de France*, CIX.

711 —. 1953. 'Un vitrail demembré de la Cathédrale de Soissons', *Gazette des Beaux-Arts*, XLII.

712 —. 1961a. 'Les vitraux allégoriques de Saint-Denis', *Art de France*, I.

713 —. 1961b. 'Les vitraux de la Cathédrale du Mans', *Congrès archéologique de France*, CXIX.

714 —. 1961c. 'Les vitraux de Saint-Denis: l'enfance du Christ' in M. Meiss (ed.), *De Artibus Opuscula XL: Essays in Honor of Erwin Panofsky.*

715 —. 1975. *La Sainte Chapelle*, 2nd edn.

716 —. 1976. *Les vitraux de Saint-Denis: histoire et restitution* (Corpus Vitrearum Medii Aevi-France: *Études*, I).

717 —. 1977. *Le Vitrail roman.*

718 —. 1986. *Le Moyen Âge retrouvé, de l'an mil à l'an 1200.*

719 HAHNLOSER, H. (ed.). 1965–71. *Il Tesoro di San Marco*, 2 vols.

720 HAMEL, C. DE. 1986. *A History of Illuminated Manuscripts.*

721 HANKE, W. 1962. *Kunst und Geist, das philosophischen Gedankengut der Schrift "De Diversis Artibus" des Priesters und Monachus Theophilus*, Ph.D. thesis Bonn University.

722 HARDEN, A. R. 1960. 'The carbuncle in mediaeval literature', *Romance Notes*, II.

723 HARDEN, D. B. 1969. 'Mediaeval glass in the West', *Eighth International Congress on Glass, 1968.*

724 HÉLIOT, P. 1968. 'Les origines et les debuts de l'abside vitrée (XIe–XIIIe siècles)', *Wallraf-Richartz Jahrbuch*, XXX.

725 HERRAD OF HOHENBOURG. 1979. *Hortus Deliciarum*, 2 vols, ed. R. Green, M. Evans, B. Bischoff and L. Curschmann.

726 HEYD, W. 1936. *Histoire du commerce du Levant au moyen-âge.*

727 HILLS, P. 1987. *The Light of Early Italian Painting.*

728 HOBERG, H. 1944. *Die Inventare des Päpstlichen Schatzes in Avignon.*

729 HOFMANN, K. 1968. 'Sugers "Anagogisches" Fenster in St Denis', *Wallraf-Richartz Jahrbuch,* XXX.

730 HOLMES, U. 1934. 'Medieval Gem Stones', *Speculum,* IX.

731 HUBERT, J. 1949. 'L'"Escrain" dit de Charlemagne au Trésor de Saint-Denis', *Cahiers archéologiques,* IV.

732 HUDECZEK, M. 1944. 'De lumine et coloribus (secundum S. Albertum Magnum)', *Angelicum,* XXI.

733 HUTTON, E. 1950. *The Cosmati.*

734 IHM, C. 1960. *Die Programme der Christliche Apsismalerei.*

735 JAYNE, S. 1963. *John Colet and Marsilio Ficino.*

736 JOHNSON, J. R. 1964. *The Radiance of Chartres.*

737 KIDSON, P. 1987. 'Panofsky, Suger and St Denis', *Journal of the Warburg and Courtauld Institutes,* L.

738 KLESSE, B. 1967. *Seidenstoffe in der Italienischen malerei des 14 Jh.*

739 KREMPEL, U. 1971. 'Das Remaklus Retabel in Stavelot und seine künstlerischen Nachfolge', *Münchener Jahrbuch der Bildende Kunst,* XXII.

740 LAFOND, J. 1968. 'Decouverte de vitraux historiés du moyen âge à Constantinople, *Cahiers archéologiques,* XVIII.

741 LAVIN, M. A. 1981. 'The joy of the Bridegroom's friend: smiling faces in Fra Lippo Lippi, Raphael and Leonardo' in M. Barasch and L. Freeman Sandler (eds), *Art the Ape of Nature: Studies in Honor of H. W. Janson.*

742 LECOY DA LA MARCHE, A. 1867. *Oeuvres complètes de Suger.*

743 LEHMANN-BROCKHAUS, O. 1938. *Schriftquellen zur Kunstgeschichte ses 11. und 12. Jh. für Deutschland, Lothringen und Italien.*

744 — . 1955–60. *Lateinische Schriftquellen zur Kunst in England, Wales und Schottland,* 5 vols.

745 *Liber Pontificalis.* 1886–1957. Ed. L. Duchesne, 3 vols.

746 LICHTENBERG, H. 1931. *Die Architekturdarstellungen in der mittelhochdeutschen Dichtung.*

747 LIGHTBOWN, R. 1978. *Secular Goldsmith's Work in Mediaeval France.*

748 LILLICH, M. P. 1970. 'The band-window: a theory of origin and development', *Gesta,* IX.

749 LINDBERG, D. C. 1968/9. 'The cause of refraction in mediaeval optics', *British Journal for the History of Science,* IV.

750 — . 1983. *Studies in the History of Medieval Optics.*

751 — . 1986. 'The genesis of Kepler's Theory of Light: light metaphysics from Plotinus to Kepler', *Osiris,* N.S. II.

752 LIPINSKY, A. 1962. 'La simbologia delle gemme', *Atti del i congresso nazionale di studi danteschi.*

753 LISKAR, E. (ed.). 1986. *Europäische Kunst um 1300 (Akten des XXV Internationalen Kongresses für Kunstgeschichte, Wien 1983),* VI.

754 LYDGATE, J. 1891. *Temple of Glas,* ed. J. Schick.

755 McGINNIS, H. 1971. 'Cast shadows in the Passion Cycle at S. Francesco, Assisi: a note', *Gazette des Beaux-Arts,* LXXVII.

756 MALAGUZZI VALERI, F. 1896. 'La miniatura a Bologna dal XIII al XV secolo', *Archivio storico italiano,* XVIII.

757 *Mappae Clavicula.* 1974. Ed. C. S. Smith and J. G. Hawthorne, *Transactions of the American Philosophical Society,* LXIV, Pt 4.

758 MARCHINI, G. 1973. *Le Vetrate dell'Umbria* (Corpus Vitriarum Medii Aevi-Italia, I).

759 MARTÈNE, E. and DURAND, U. 1717. *Thesaurus Novus Anecdotorum,* 5 vols, Paris.

760 MARTINDALE, A. 1972. *The Rise of the Artist in the Middle Ages and Early Renaissance.*

761 — . 1988. *Simone Martini: Complete Edition.*

762 MATTHIAE, G. 1967. *Mosaici medioevale delle chiese di Roma.*

763 MAY, F. L. 1957. *Silk Textiles of Spain: Eight to Fifteenth Century.*

764 MÉNARD, P. 1969. *Le Rire et le sourire dans le roman courtois en France au moyen-âge, 1150–1250.*

765 MIDDELDORF, U. (intro.). 1980. *Il Tesoro della Basilica di San Francesco ad Assisi.*

766 MILANESI, G. 1854–6. *Documenti sulla storia dell'arte senese,* 3 vols.

767 MOLINIER, E. XLVI, 1885; XLVII, 1886. 'Inventaire de Trésor du Saint Siège sous Boniface VIII (1295)', *Bibliothèque de l'École des Chartes.*

768 MONTESQUIOU-FEZENSAC, B. DE. 1973. *Le Trésor de Saint-Denis: Inventaire de 1634.*

769 *Monumenta Germaniae Historica Scriptores Rerum Germanicarum,* N.S. XII. 1960. Ed. H. F. Haefelde.

770 MORE, SIR THOMAS. 1551. *Utopia,* trans. R. Robinson.

771 MORGAN, N. J. 1983. *The Mediaeval Painted Glass of Lincoln Cathedral.*

772 MORTET, V. 1911. *Recueil de textes relatifs à l'histoire de l'architecture . . . en France, XIe–XIIe siècles.*

773 NIETO ALCAIDE, V. 1978. *La Luz, Simbolo y Sistema Visual (El Espacio y la Luz en el Arte Gotico y del Renacimiento).*

774 NORDSTRÖM, C.-O. 1953. *Ravenna Studien.*

775 NORDSTRÖM. F. 1955. 'Peterborough, Lincoln and the Science of Robert Grosseteste: a Study in thirteenth-century architecture and iconography', *Art Bulletin,* XXXVII.

776 OIDTMANN, H. 1929. *Die Rheinische Glasmalereien vom 12 bis zum 16 Jahrhundert.*

777 OMAN, C. 1958. *The Gloucester Candlestick.*

778 ONASCH, K. 1962. *Das Licht in der Ikonenmalerei Andrej Rublevs* (Berliner Byzantinische Arbeiten, XXVIII).

779 ORDERIC VITALIS. II, 1969. *Ecclesiastical History,* ed. M. Chibnall.

780 OURSEL, R. 1958/9. 'Pierre le Vénérable, Suger et la lumière gothique', *Annales de l'Académie de Maçon,* XLIV.

781 OVITT, G., Jr 1983. 'The Status of the mechanical arts in medieval classifications of learning', *Viator,* XIV.

782 PANOFSKY, E. 1944. Notes on a controversial passage in Suger's *De Consecratione Ecclesiae Sancti Dionysii', Gazette des Beaux-Arts,* XXVI.

783 — . 1979. *Abbot Suger on the Abbey Church of St Denis and its Art Treasures,* 2nd edn.

784 PASSERA, E. 1921. 'Le cognizioni oftalmologiche di Dante', *Archivio di storia della scienze,* III.

785 PECHAM, J. 1970. *Perspectiva Communis,* in D. C. Lindberg (ed.), *John Pecham and the Science of Optics.*

786 PETER THE VENERABLE. 1967. *Letters,* 2 vols, ed. G. Constable.

787 PLOSS, E. 1960. 'Die Fachsprache der deutschen Maler im spätmittelalter', *Zeitschrift für deutschen Philologie,* LXXIX.

788 PSELLUS, M. 1980. *De Lapidum Virtutibus,* ed. and trans. M. Galigani.

789 PSEUDO-DIONYSIUS. 1950. *Dionysiaca,* 2 vols, ed. P. Chevallier.

790 RADULPHUS PHISICUS. 1962. *De nobilitate domni Sugerii abbatis et operibus eius,* ed. R. B. C. Huyghens, *Studi Medievali,* 3 ser., III.

791 *Roman de Perceforest.* 1951. ed. J. Lods.

792 ROSAND, D. (ed.). 1984. *Interpretazioni veneziane: studi di storia dell'arte in onore di Michelangelo Muraro.*

793 ROUSE, M. A. and R. H. 1971. 'The texts called *Lumen Animae', Archivum Fratrum Praedicatorum,* XLI.

794 RUDOLPH, C. 1990. *Artistic Change at St Denis: Abbot Suger's Program and the Early Twelfth-century Controversy over Art.*

795 RUMPF, K. 1961. *Kobalt (Gmelins Handbuch der Anorganischen Chemie: Ergänzungsband).*

796 SALZMAN, L. F. 1926/7. 'The glazing of St Stephen's Chapel, Westminster, 1351–2', *Journal of the British Society of Master Glass Painters,* I, II.

797 SCHLAUCH, M. 1932. 'The palace of Hugon of Constantinople', *Speculum,* VII.

798 SCHLOSSER, J. VON. 1986. *Quellenbuch zur Kunstgeschichte des abendländischen Mittelalters.*

799 SCHMID, H. R. 1975. *Lux Incorporata: zur ontologischen Begründung einer Systematik des farbigen Aufbaus in der Malerei.*

800 SCHÖNE, W. 1957. 'Studien zur Oberkirche von Assisi', in B. Hackelsberger, F. Himmel-Leber and M. Meier (eds), *Festschrift Kurt Bauch.*

801 SCHROEDER, B. 1972. *Kleinere deutsche Gedichte des XI und XII Jahrhunderts,* 2 vols.

802 SEXTUS AMARCUS. 1969. *Sermones,* ed. K. Manitius (*Monumenta Germaniae Historica: Deutsche Geschichtsquellen des Mittelalters*).

803 SIMONELLI, M. 1967. 'Allegoria e simbolo dal *Convivio* alla *Commedia* sullo sfondo della cultura bolognese' in *Dante e Bologna nei tempi di Dante,* Facoltà di Lettere e Filosofia dell'Università di Bologna.

804 SIMSON, O. VON. 1982. 'Opere superante materiam: zur Bedeutung der Sainte-Chapelle zu Paris', *Mélanges Jacques Stiennon.*

805 — . 1988. *The Gothic Cathedral,* 3rd edn.

806 SIRAT, C. 1968. 'Les pierres précieuses et leurs prix au XVe siècle en Italie, d'après un manuscrit hebreu', *Annales Economies, Sociétés, Civilisations.*

807 SÖHRING, O. 1900. 'Werke bildender Kunst in alt-französischen Epen', *Romanische Forschungen,* XII.

808 SOLINUS. 1958. *Collecteana Rerum Memorabilium,* ed. T. Mommsen, 2nd edn.

809 SOWERS, R. 1966. 'On the blues of Chartres', *Art Bulletin,* XLVIII.

810 STERNAGEL, P. 1966. *Die Artes Mechanicae im Mittelalter.*

811 STRATFORD, N. 1984. 'Three English Romanesque enamelled ciboria', *Burlington Magazine,* CXXVI.

812 STUDER, P. and EVANS, J. 1924. *Anglo-Norman Lapidaries.*

813 TATARKIEWICZ, W. 1970–74. *History of Aesthetics,* 3 vols.

814 THOMAS OF CANTIMPRÉ. 1973. *Liber de Natura Rerum,* ed. H. Boese.

815 TINTORI, L. and MEISS, M. 1967. *The Painting of the Life of St Francis at Assisi,* 2nd edn.

816 TOULMIN, R. M. 1971. 'L'ornamento nella pittura di Giotto, con particolare referimento alla Capella degli Scrovegni' in *Giotto e il suo tempo,* Rome.

817 TRAUBE, L. (ed.). III, 1896. *Monumenta Germaniae Historica, Poeti Latini Aevi Carolini.*

818 TREVISANO, M. 1961. 'De doctrina lucis apud S. Bonaventurae', *Scriptorium Victoriense,* VIII.

819 TROWBRIDGE, M. L. 1928. *Philological Studies in Ancient Glass.*

820 VERDIER, P. [c. 1974] 'Réflexions sur l'ésthetique de Suger: à propos de quelques passages du De Administratione', *Études de civilisation médiévale (Mélanges E.-R. Labaude).*

821 VERDON, T. and FRONT, W. (eds). 1984. *Monasticism and the Arts.*

822 VIARD, J. (ed.). 1927. *Les Grandes Chroniques de France.*

823 VINCENT OF BEAUVAIS. 1624. *Speculum Maius: Speculum Doctrinale,* 4 vols, Douai.

824 VLOBERG, M. 1936. *La Vierge et l'enfant dans l'art français,* II (*Le Sourire de la Vierge-Mère*).

825 VOSS, J. 1972. *Das Mittelalter im historischen Denken Frankreichs.*

826 WALLACE, W. A. 1959. *The Scientific Methodology of Theodoric of Freiberg.*

827 WALSINGHAM, T. I, 1867. *Gesta Abbatum Monasterii Sancti Albani.*

828 WATTENBACH, W. 1896. *Das Schriftwesen im Mittelalter,* 3rd edn.

829 WEISE, G. 1939. *Die geistige Welt der Gotik.*

830 WEISWEILER, H. 1952. 'Sakrament als Symbol und Teilhabe: der Einfluss des Ps-Dionysios auf die allgemeine Sakramentlehre Hugos von St Viktor', *Recherches de théologie ancienne et moderne,* XIX.

831 WENK. K. 1885. 'Uber päpstliche Schatzverzeichnisse des 13. und 14. Jahrhunderts und ein Verzeichniss der päpstlichen Bibliothek vom Jahre 1311', *Mitteilungen des Instituts für österreichische Geschichtsforschung,* VI.

832 WENZEL, H. 1949. 'Glasmaler und Maler im Mittelalter', *Zeitschrift für Kunstwissenschaft,* III.

833 — . 1952. 'Die ältesten Farbfenster in der Oberkirche von S. Francesco zu Assisi und die deutsche Glasmalerei des XIII Jh', *Wallraf-Richartz Jahrbuch,* XIV.

834 WHITE, J. 1981. 'Cimabue and Assisi: working methods and art-historical consequences', *Art History,* IV.

835 WHITE, L., Jr. 1964. 'Theophilus Redivivus', *Technology and Culture,* V.

836 WHITNEY, E. 1990. 'Paradise restored: the mechanical arts from Antiquity through the thirteenth century', *Transactions of the American Philosophical Society,* LXXX, Pt I.

837 ZACCARIA, G. 1963. 'Diario storico della Basilica e Sacro Convento di San Francesco in Assisi', *Miscellanea Francescana,* LXIII.

838 ZAKIN, H. J. 1974. 'French

Cistercian grisaille glass', *Gesta*, XIII.

839 ZIOLKOWSKI, T. 1961. 'Der Karfunkelstein', *Euphorion*, LV.

5 Colour-Language, Colour-Symbols

840 AMES-LEWIS, F. 1979. 'Early Medicean Devices', *Journal of the Warburg and Courtauld Institutes*, XLII.

841 ANTONINUS. 1959. *Summa Major* (1740), 4 vols.

842 ARGOTE DE MOLINA, G. 1957. *Nobleza de Andalucia* (1579).

843 AZCONA, T. DE 1972. *Fundacion y Construccion de San Telmo de San Sebastian*.

844 BACH, A. (ed.). 1934. *Das Rheinische marienlob: Eine deutsche Dichtung des 13. Jahrhundert*.

845 BAEUMKER, C. 1908. *Witelo: ein Philosoph und Naturforscher des XIII Jh*.

846 BARKER, J. R. V. 1986. *The Tournament in England, 1100–1400*.

847 BARLOW, H. B. and MOLLON, J. D. (eds). 1982. *The Senses*.

848 BARTSCH, K. 1863. 'Das Spiel von den sieben Farben', *Germania*, VIII.

849 BAXANDALL, M. 1986. *Giotto and the Orators*, 2nd edn.

850 BENTLEY, J. H. 1988. *Politics and Culture in Renaissance Naples*.

851 BERCHEM, E., FREIHERR VON, GALBREATH, D. L. and HUPP, O. 1939. *Beiträge zur Geschichte der Heraldik*.

852 BERLIN, B. and KAY, P. 1969. *Basic Color Terms*.

853 BLONSKY, M. (ed.). 1985. *On Signs*.

854 BOLTON, R. 1978. 'Black, white and red all over. The riddle of color term salience', *Ethnology*, XVII.

855 BONET, HONORÉ. 1949. *The Tree of Battles*, ed. and trans. G. W. Coopland.

856 BORNSTEIN, M. 1975. 'Qualities of color-vision in infancy', *Journal of Experimental Child Psychology*, XIX.

857 BORSOOK, E. 1966. *Ambrogio Lorenzetti*.

858 BOULY DE LESDAIN, L. 1897. 'Les plus anciennes armoiries françaises (1127–1300)', *Archives héraldiques suisses*, XI.

859 BOUTON, V. (ed.). III, 1884. *Wapenboek, ou Armorial de 1334 à 1372*.

860 BRAULT, G. J. 1972. *Early Blazon: Heraldic Terminology in the 12th and 13th Centuries with Special Reference to Arthurian Literature*.

861 —. 1973. *Eight 13th. century Rolls of Arms in French and Anglo-Norman Blazon*.

862 BRERETON, G. E. and FERRIER, J. M. 1981. *Le Menagier de Paris*.

863 BRÜCKNER, W. 1982. 'Farbe als Zeichen. Kulturtradition im Alltag', *Zeitschrift für Volkskunde*, LXXVIII.

864 BURCHARD, J. 1884. *Diarium*, 3 vols, ed. L. Thuasne.

865 CAMPBELL, L. and STEER, F. 1988. *A Catalogue of the Manuscripts in the College of Arms*, I.

866 CARUS-WILSON, E. 1953. 'La guède française en Angleterre: un grand commerce du moyen-âge', *Revue du Nord*, XXXV.

867 CHAPANIS, A. 1965. 'Color names for color space', *American Scientist*, LIII.

868 CHRISTINE DE PISAN. 1937. *The Book of Fayttes of Armes and of Chivalrye*, ed. A. T. P. Byles.

869 CHYDENIUS, J. 1960. *The Theory of Medieval Symbolism*.

870 CIAN, V. 1894. 'Del significato dei colori e dei fiori nel Rinascimento Italiano', *Gazetta Letteraria*, 13–14.

871 —. 1951. *Un Illustre Nunzio Ponteficio, Baldassare Castiglione*.

872 COULTON, G. G. 1953. *Art of the Reformation*, 2nd edn.

873 CENTRE UNIVERSITAIRE DES ÉTUDES ET DE RECHERCHES MÉDIÉVALES D'AIX. 1988. *Les Couleurs au moyen âge*.

874 DEAN, R. J. 1967. 'An early treatise on heraldry in Anglo-Norman' in V. T. Holmes (ed.), *Romance Studies in Memory of E. Billings Ham*.

875 DELORT, R. 1978. *Le Commerce des fourrures en occident à la fin du moyen âge*.

876 DENNYS, R. 1975. *The Heraldic Imagination*.

877 DIDRECK OF BERN. 1924. *Die Geschichte Thidreks von Bern*, trans. F. Erichsen.

878 —. 1951. *Saga*, ed. G. Jonsson.

879 DOUET D'ARCQ, L. 1858. 'Un Traité du blason du XVᶜ siècle', *Revue Archéologique*, XV.

880 DRONKE, P. 1974. 'Tradition and Innovation in mediaeval western colour-imagery', *Eranos Yearbook*, XLI, 1972.

881 DURANDUS OF MENDE. 1859. *Rationale Divinorum Officiorum*, ed. V. d'Avino.

882 EVANS, J. 1952. *Dress in Mediaeval France*.

883 EVANS, M. 1982. 'An illustrated fragment of Peraldus's *Summa* of Vice', *Journal of the Warburg and Courtauld Institutes*, XLV.

884 EVANS, R. M. 1948. *Introduction to Color*.

885 EVELYN, J. 1906. *Sculptura* (1662), ed. C. F. Bell.

886 FARAL, E. 1924. *Les Arts poétiques du XIIᵉ et du XIIIᵉ siècle*.

887 FERNANDEZ ARENAS, J. (ed.). 1982. *Renacimiento y Baroco en España*.

888 FITTON BROWN, A. D. 1962. 'Black wine', *Classical Review*, N.S., XIII.

889 FLURY-LEMBERG, M. and STOLLEIS, K. (eds). 1981. *Documenta Textilia: Festschrift für S. Müller Christiansen*.

890 FRANCESCO DA BARBERINO. 1875. *Del Reggimento e de costumi delle donne*.

891 GANZ, P. 1899. *Geschichte der heraldischen Kunst in der Schweiz*.

892 GERVAIS DU BUS. 1914/19. *Le Roman de Fauvel*, ed. A. Langfors.

893 GILBERT, C. 1959. 'The Archbishop on the painters of Florence', *Art Bulletin*, XLI.

894 GODDARD, E. R. 1927. *Women's Costume in French Texts of the 11th and 12th Centuries*.

895 GRAS, P. 1951. 'Aux origines de l'héraldique: la décoration des boucliers au début du XIIᶜ siècle d'après la bible de Citeaux', *Bibliothèque de l'École des Chartes*, CIX.

896 GUNDERSHEIMER, W. 1972. *Art and Life at the Court of Ercole I d'Este*.

897 —. 1973. *Ferrara: the Style of Renaissance Despotism*.

898 HADAMER VON DER LABER. 1850. *Die Jagd der Minne*, ed. J. A. Schmeller.

899 HARTE, N. B. and PONTING, K. G. (eds). 1983. *Cloth and Clothing in Mediaeval Europe*.

900 HAUPT, G. 1941. *Die Farbensymbolik in der Sakralen Kunst des abendländischen Mittelalters*.

901 HAYE, SIR GILBERT. 1901. *Prose Works*, ed. J. H. Stevenson.

902 HERING-MITGAU, M. et al. (eds). 1980. *Von Farbe und Farben: Albert Knoepffli zum 70. Geburtstag*.

903 HERNE, G. 1954. *Die Slavischen Farbenbenennungen* (Publications de l'Institut Slave d'Upsal, IX).

904 HILL, P. M. 1972. *Die Farbwörter der russischen und bulgarischen Schriftsprache*.

905 HOEPFFNER, E. 1923. 'Pers en ancien français', *Romania*, XLIX.

906 HUMBERT DE SUPERVILLE, D. P. G. 1827. *Essai sur les signes inconditionelles dans les arts*.

907 HUMPHREY, C. 1960. 'Heraldry in School Manuals of the Middle Ages', *Coat of Arms*, VI.

908 HUMPHREY SMITH, C. R. 1956. 'Purpure', *Coat of Arms*, IV.

909 HUNTER BLAIR, C. H. (ed.). 1930. *A Visitation of the North of England, c. 1480–1500* (Surtees Society, CXLIV).

910 HUON DE MERI. 1976. *Le Tourneiment Antichrist*, ed. M. D. O. Bender.

911 JONES, E. J. (ed.). 1943. *Mediaeval Heraldry*.

912 KEEN, M. 1984. *Chivalry*.

913 KÖHALMI, K. U. 1966. 'Die Farbbezeichnungen der Pferde in den Mandschu-Tungusischen Sprachen', *Acta Orientalia Academiae Scientiarum Hungaricae*, XIX.

914 KOUWER, B. 1949. *Colors and their Character: a Psychological Study*.

915 KURELLA, A. and STRAUSS, I. 1983. 'Lapis lazuli und natürliches Ultramarin', *Maltechnik/Restauro*, LXXXIX.

916 KUSCHEL, R. and MONBERG, T. 1974. '"We don't talk much about colour here": a study of colour semantics on Bellona Island', *Man*, IX.

917 LASSBERG, J. M.-C., FREIHERR VON. (ed.). 1820/5. *Lieder-Saal*, 4 vols.

918 LATINI, BRUNETTO. IV, 1883. *Il Tesoro*, trans. B. Giamboni and ed. L. Gaiter 1878–1883.

919 LEHMANN, P. W. and K. L. 1973. *Samothracean Reflections*.

920 LEWIS, S. 1987. *The Art of Matthew Paris in the 'Chronica Majora'*.

921 LONDON, H. S. 1967. 'Rolls of Arms, Henry III', *Aspilogia*, II.

922 LUCY, J. A. and SCHWEDER, R. A. 1979. 'Whorf and his critics: linguistic and nonlinguistic influences on color naming', *American Anthropologist*, LXXXI.

923 MCNEILL, N. B. 1972. 'Colour and colour terminology', *Journal of Linguistics*, VIII.

924 MANN, M. 1923. 'La couleur perse en ancien français et chez Dante', *Romania*, XLIX.

925 MAXWELL-STUART, P. G. 1981. *Studies in Greek Colour Terminology II, Karopos*.

926 MEIER, C. 1974. 'Das Problem der Qualitätsallegorese', *Frühmittelalterliche Studien*, VIII.

927 MEIER, H. 1963. 'Ein dunkles Farbwort' in H. M. and H. Schommodau (eds), *Wort und Text: Frestschrift für Fritz Schalk*.

928 MELIS, F. I, 1962. *Aspetti della vita economica medioevale*.

929 MENESTRIER, C. F. 1661. *L'Art du blason justifié*, Lyon.

930 MERRIN, C. B., CATLIN, J. and ROSCH, E. 1975. 'Development of the Structure of Color Categories', *Developmental Psychology*, II.

931 MOLLON, J. D. and SHARPE, L. T. (eds). 1983. *Colour Vision, Physiology and Psychophysics*.

932 OPPENHEIM, P. 1931. *Das Mönchskleid im christlichen Altertum*.

933 ORIBASIUS. 1851–76. *Oeuvres*, 6 vols, ed. U. C. Bussemaker and C. V. Daremberg.

934 —. I, 1940. *Oribasius Latinus*, ed. H. Mørland.

935 PASTOUREAU, M. 1982. *L'Hermine et le sinople: études d'héraldique médiévale*.

936 —. 1983. *Armoriale des chevaliers de la table ronde*.

937 —. 1986. *Figures et couleurs: études sur la symbolique et la sensibilité médiévales*.

938 —. 1989a. *Couleurs, images, symboles: études d'histoire et d'anthropologie*.

939 —. 1989b. 'L'Église et la couleur des origines à la Réforme', *Bibliothèque de l'École des Chartes*, CXLVII.

940 PETER OF POITIERS. 1938. *Allegoriae super Tabarnaculum Moysi*, ed. P. S. Moore and J. A. Corbett.

941 POERCK, G. DE. 1951. *La Draperie médiévale en Flandre et en Artois*.

942 PORTAL, F. 1979. *Des Couleurs symboliques dans l'antiquité, le moyen-âge et les temps modernes* (1837).

943 PRINET, M. 1922. 'Le langage héraldique dans le "Tournement Antichrist"', *Bibliothèque de l'Ecole des Chartes*, LXXXIII.

944 PÜCKLER-MUSKAU, H. 1831–6. *Briefe eines Verstorbenen*, 4 vols.

945 RABELAIS, F. 1966. *Gargantua*, 6th edn, ed. J. Plattard.

946 RADLOFF, W. 1871. 'Die Haustiere der Kirgisen', *Zeitschrift für Ethnologie*, III.

947 REEVES, M. and HIRSCH-REICH, B. 1972. *The 'Figurae' of Joachim of Flora*.

948 ROQUE, G. 1990. 'Couleur et mouvement' in R. Bellour (ed.), *Cinéma et peinture: approches*.

949 SAHLINS, M. 1976. 'Colors and cultures', *Semiotica*, XVI.

950 SALAZAR DE MENDOZA, P. 1618. *Origen de las Dignidades Seglares de Castilla y Leon*, Toledo.

951 SCHWYZER, E. 1929. 'Germanisches und ungedeutetes in Byzantinischen Pferdenamen', *Zeitschrift für deutsches Altertum*, LXVI.

952 SELTMAN, C. T. 1924. *Athens: Its History and Coinage before the Persian Invasion*.

953 SEYLER, G. A. 1889. *Geschichte der Heraldik*, repr. 1970.

954 SICILY HERALD. 1860. *Le Blason des couleurs en armes, livrees et divises*, ed. H. Cocheris.

955 —. 1867. *Parties inédites de l'oeuvre de Sicile Héraut d'Alphonse V*, ed. P. Roland.

956 SILVESTRE, H. 1954. 'Le MS Bruxellensis 10147–58 (s. XII–XIII) et son "Compendium Artis Picturae"', *Bulletin de la Commission Royale d'Histoire*, CXIX.

957 SKINNER, Q. 1986. 'Ambrogio Lorenzetti: the artist as political philosopher', *Proceedings of the British Academy*, LXXII.

958 SOURIAU, P. 1895. 'Le symbolisme des couleurs', *La Revue de Paris*, II, ii (15 April).

959 SQUIBB, G. D. 1959. *The High Court of Chivalry*.

960 STAFFORD, B. 1972. 'Medusa, or the Physiognomy of the earth: Humbert de Superville's Aesthetics', *Journal of the Warburg and Courtauld Institutes*, XXV.

961 STEIGER, A. 1958. 'Altromanische Pferdenamen', *Etymologica: Walther von Wartburg zum Siebzigsten Geburtstag*.

962 SUCHENWIRT, PETER. 1827. *Werke*, ed. A. Primisser.

963 SUNDBERG, H. 1985. 'Horse-trading contracts in early seventeenth-century Novgorod: colour adjectives and other vocabulary in horse-descriptions', *Scando-Slavica*, XXXI.

964 THORNDYKE, L. 1960. 'Other texts on colors', *Ambix*, VIII.

965 TOYNBEE, P. 1902. *Dante Studies*.

966 TREMLETT, T. D. (ed.). 1967. 'The Matthew Paris Shields', *Aspilogia*, II.

967 UPTON, NICHOLAS. 1654. *De Studio Militari*, ed. Sir E. Bysshe.

968 VALLIER, D. 1979. 'Le problème du vert dans le système perceptif', *Semiotica*, XXVI.

969 VESPASIANO DA BISTICCI. 1963. *Renaissance Princes Popes and Prelates: the Vespasiano Memoirs*, trans. W. George and E. Waters, 2 vols.

970 VRIES, J. DE. 1965. 'Rood-Wit-Zwart' (1942) in *Kleine Schriften*.

971 VULSON DE LA COLOMBIÈRE, M. 1639. *Recueil de Plusiers Pièces et Figures d'Armoire ... avec un Discours des fondements du Blason et une Nouvelle Méthode de Cognoistre les Metaulx et Couleurs sur la Taille Douce*, Paris.

972 WACKERNAGEL, W. 1872. 'Die Farben- und Blumen-sprache des Mittelalters' in *Kleinere Schriften*, I.

973 WAGNER, A. 1956. *Heralds and Heraldry in the Middle Ages*, 2nd edn.

974 WAGNER, M. L. 1916/17. 'Das Fortleben einiger lateinischer bzw. vulgärlateinischer Pferdenamen in Romanischen, insbesondere im Sardischen und Korsischen', *Glotta*, VIII.

975 WASSERMAN, G. S. 1978. *Color Vision: an Historical Introduction*.

976 WATTENWYL, A. VON AND ZOLLINGER, H. 1981. 'Color naming by art students and science students', *Semiotica*, XXXV.

977 WECKERLIN, J. W. 1905. *Le Drap 'escarlate' au moyen âge*.

978 WEISE, O. 1878. 'Die Farbenbezeichnungen der Indogermanen', *Bezzenbergers Beiträge zur Kunde der Indogermanischen Sprachen*, II.

979 WICKHAM LEGG, J. 1882. 'Notes on the history of the liturgical colours', *Transactions of the St Paul's Ecclesiological Society*, I, iii.

980 ZINGERLE, J. V. 1864. 'Farbenvergleiche im Mittelalter', *Germania*, IX.

6 Unweaving the Rainbow

981 ABRAMS, M. H. 1958. *The Mirror and the Lamp*.

982 ADLER, W. 1982. *Landscapes (Corpus Rubenianum Ludwig Burchard* XVIII, I).

983 ALLTHORPE-GUYTON, M. 1977. *John Thirtle: Drawings in Norwich Castle Museum*.

984 AUSTIN, H. D. 1929. 'Dante Notes XI: the rainbow colours', *Modern Language Notes*, XLIV.

985 BALDINUCCI, F. V, 1728. *Notizie de' professori del disegno da Cimabue in qua*, Florence.

986 BARATHA IYER, K. (ed.). 1947. *Art and Thought*.

987 BARBARO, D. 1568. *Della Perspettiva*, Venice.

988 BARBIER, C. P. 1959a. *William Gilpin*, London, Kenwood, exh. cat.

989 —. 1959b. *Samuel Rogers and William Gilpin*.

990 —. 1963. *William Gilpin*.

991 BARKER, A. II, 1989. *Greek Musical Writings*.

992 BAROCCHI, P. 1960–62. *Trattati d'arte del cinquecento*, 3 vols.

993 BARRY, J. 1783. *An Account of a Series of Pictures in the Great Room of the Society of Arts ...*

994 BAUDISSEN, K. GRAF VON. 1924. *G. A. Wallis*.

995 BEARE, A. C. 1963. 'Color-name as a function of wavelength', *American Journal of Psychology*, LXXVI.

996 BECKETT, R. B. (ed.). IV, 1966. *John Constable's Correspondence*.

997 BEHLING, L. 1968. 'Neue Forschungen zu Grünewalds Stuppacher Maria', *Pantheon*, XXVI.

998 BELL, C. F. 1901. *The Exhibited Works of J. M. W. Turner*.

999 BIERHAUS-RÖDIGER, E. 1978. *Carl Rottmann 1797–1850: Monographie und Kritischer Werkkatalog*.

1000 BLUNT, A. 1938. 'Blake's "Ancient of Days"', *Journal of the Warburg and Courtauld Institutes*, II.

1001 BOETHIUS, A. M. S. 1989. *Fundamentals of Music*, trans. C. M. Bower.

1002 BOIGEY, M. 1923. *La Science des couleurs et l'art du peintre*.

1003 BOLL, F. 1918. *Antike Beobachtungen farbiger Sterne* (Abhandlungen der königliche Bayerische Akademie der Wissenschaften, Philosophische, Philologische und Historische Klasse, XXX, I).

1004 BONACINA, L. C. W. 1937. 'John Constable's centenary; his position as a painter of weather', *Journal of the Royal Meteorological Society*, LXIII.

1005 —. 1938. 'Turner's portrayal of weather', ibid., LXIV.

1006 BÖRSCH-SUPAN, H. and JÄHNIG, K. W. 1973. *Caspar David Friedrich, Gemälde, Druckgraphik und bildmässige Zeichnungen*.

1007 BOTTARI, G. I, 1882. *Raccolta di lettere sulla pittura*, 2nd edn.

1008 BOULTON, S. 1984. 'Church under a cloud: Constable and Salisbury', *Turner Studies*, III, 3.

1009 BOYER, C. B. 1959. *The Rainbow: from Myth to Mathematics*.

1010 BRUCIOLI, A. 1537–8. 'Del Arco Celeste' in *Dialoghi di Antonio Brucioli della naturale philosophia*, 4 vols, Venice.

1011 BUTLIN, M. 1962. *Samuel Palmer's Sketchbook of 1824*.

1012 — and JOLL, E. 1984. *The Paintings of J. M. W. Turner*, 2nd edn.

1013 CARLI, E. 1960. *Il Pintoricchio*.

1014 —. 1974. *Il Sodoma a Sant'Anna in Caprena*.

1015 CARUS, C. G. 1835. *Reise durch Deutschland, Italien und die Schweitz im Jahre 1828*, 2 vols.

1016 —. 1948. *Goethe* (1842), ed. W.-E. Peuckert.

1017 CASTIGLIONE, B. 1946. *Il Libro del Cortegiano*, ed. V. Cian.

1018 COPLEY, J. S. 1914. *Letter and Papers of John Singleton Copley and Henry Pelham*.

1019 CORNELIUS A LAPIDE. 1865. *Commentaria in Scripturam Sacram*, 24 vols.

1020 COUNCIL OF EUROPE. 1959. *The Romantic Movement*, London, exh. cat.

1021 CROMBIE, A. C. 1961. *Robert Grosseteste and the Origins of Modern Science*.

1022 CROPPER, E. 1984. *The Ideal of Painting: Pietro Testa's Düsseldorf Notebook*.

1023 DARWIN, E. 1806. *Poetical Works*, 3 vols.

1024 DAYES, E. 1805, *Works*, ed. E. W. Brayley.

1025 DECKER, H. 1957. *Carl Rottmann*.

1026 DELACROIX, E. 1980. *Journal*, 2nd edn, ed. A. Joubin.

1027 DEPERTHES, J.-B. 1822. *Histoire de l'Art du paysage*.

1028 DIMMICK, F. L. and HUBBARD, M. R. 1939. 'The spectral location of psychologically unique yellow, green and blue', *American Journal of Psychology*, LII.

1029 DUHEM, P. 1906–13. *Léonard de Vinci*, 3 vols.

1030 EGGENBERGER, C. 1973. 'Ein spätantike Virgil-Handschrift: Die Miniaturen des Vergilius Romanus (Cod. Vat. Lat. 3867)', *Sandoz-Bulletin*, XXIX.

1031 ENGLEFIELD, SIR H. C. 1802. 'An account of two haloes, with parhelia', *Journal of the Royal Institution*, II.

1032 ERFFA, H. VON and STALEY, A. 1986. *The Paintings of Benjamin West*.

1033 FARINGTON, J. 1978–84. *The Diary of Joseph Farington*, ed. K. Garlick, A. Macintyre and K. Cave.

1034 FEMMEL, G. (ed.). 1958–73. *Corpus der Goethezeichnungen*.

1035 FIELD, G. 1845. *Chromatics* (1817), 2nd edn.

1036 FINBERG, A. J. 1909. *Complete Inventory of Drawings in the Turner Bequest*, 2 vols.

1037 FORSTER-HAHN, F. 1967. 'The source of true taste. Benjamin West's instructions to a young painter for his studies in Italy', *Journal of the Warburg and Courtauld Institutes*, XXX.

1038 FRANCASTEL, P. 1957. *Du Cubisme à l'art abstrait: les cahiers de Robert Delaunay*.

1039 FRIEDRICH, C. D. 1968. *Briefe und Bekenntnisse*, ed. S. Hinz.

1040 *Caspar David Friedrich*. 1974. Hamburg, Kunsthalle, exh. cat.

1041 GAGE, J. 1971. 'Blake's *Newton*', *Journal of the Warburg and Courtauld Institutes*, XXXIV.

1042 —. 1980a. *Collected Correspondence of J. M. W. Turner*.

1043 —. 1980b *Goethe on Art*.

1044 —. 1987. *J. M. W. Turner: 'A Wonderful Range of Mind'*.

1045 —. 1989. *George Field and his Circle from Romanticism to the Pre-Raphaelite Brotherhood*, Cambridge, Fitzwilliam Museum.

1046 GALT, J. 1820. *The Life of Benjamin West*, 2 vols.

1047 GALTON, S. 1799. 'Experiments on colours', *Monthly Magazine*, VIII, August.

1048 GARIN, E. 1950. *L'Umanesimo italiano*.

1049 GILBERT, C. 1952. 'Subject and Non-Subject in Italian Renaissance Pictures', *Art Bulletin*, XXXIV.

1050 GILBERT, O. 1907. *Die Meteorologischen Theorien des griechischen Altertums*.

1051 GLÜCK, G. 1945. *Die Landschaften von Peter Paul Rubens*.

1052 GOETHE, J. W. VON. 1953. *Farbenlehre*, ed. H. Wohlbold.

1053 Gombrich, E. H. 1966. 'Renaissance artistic theory and the development of Landscape Painting' in *Norm and Form: Studies in the Art of the Renaissance*.

1054 GRANZIANI, R. 1972. 'The "Rainbow Portrait" of Queen Elizabeth I and its religious symbolism', *Journal of the Warburg and Courtauld Institutes*, XXXV.

1055 GREENE, D. J. 1953. 'Smart, Berkeley, the scientists and the poets', *Journal of the History of Ideas*, XIV.

1056 GREENLER, R. 1980. *Rainbows, Haloes and Glories*.

1057 GRIGSON, G. 1960. *Samuel Palmer's Valley of Vision*.

1058 GROTE, L. 1938. *Die Brüder Olivier*.

1059 HAYDON, B. R. 1876. *Correspondence and Table-Talk*, 2 vols, ed. F. W. Haydon.

1060 —. 1960–3. *Diary*, 5 vols, ed. W. B. Pope.

1061 HAYTER, C. 1815. *An Introduction to Perspective*.

1062 HELLMANN, G. 1904. *Neudrücke von Schriften und Karten über Meteorologie und Erdmagnetismus*, XV: *Denkmäler mittelalterliche Meteorologie*.

1063 HENDERSON, G. 1962. 'Late Antique influences in some illustrations of Genesis', *Journal of the Warburg and Courtauld Institutes*, XXV.

1064 HOGARTH, W. 1955. *The Analysis of Beauty* (1753), ed. J. Burke.

1065 HOWARD, H. 1848. *A Course of Lectures on Painting*, ed. F. Howard.

1066 HUNT, W. Holman. 1905. *Pre-Raphaelitism and the Pre-Raphaelite Brotherhood*, 2 vols.

1067 HUSSEY, C. 1927. *The Picturesque*.

1068 JAFFÉ, E. 1905. *Josef Anton Koch*.

1069 JOHNSON, L. 1963. *Delacroix*.

1070 —. 1981–9. *The Paintings of Eugène Delacroix: A Critical Catalogue*, 6 vols.

1071 JUNIUS, F. 1638. *The Painting of the Ancients*, London.

1072 KAWERAU, G. and WIEGAND, T. 1930. *Die Paläste der Hochburg (Altertümer von Pergamon*, V).

1073 KITSON, S. D. 1937. *The Life of John Sell Cotman*.

1074 KLEE, P. 1964. *The Thinking Eye* (1961), 2nd edn, ed. J. Spiller.

1075 LEONARDO DA VINCI. 1721. *A Treatise on Painting*, London.

1076 —. 1956. *Treatise on Painting*, 2 vols, ed. and trans. A. P. McMahon.

1077 LESLIE, C. R. 1860. *Autobiographical Recollections*, 2 vols, ed. T. Taylor (facsimile repr. 1978).

1078 —. 1951. *Memoirs of the Life of John Constable*, ed. J. Mayne.

1079 LÉVI-STRAUSS, C. 1970. *The Raw and the Cooked* (1964).

1080 LOPRESTI, L. 1921. 'Pietro Testa incisore e pittore', *L'Arte*, XXIV.

1081 MACLEAN, J. 1965. 'De kleurentheorie der Arabieren' and 'De kleurentheorie in West-Europa van ca. 600–1200', *Scientiarum Historia*, VII.

1082 MALIN, D. and MURDIN, P. 1984. *Colours of the Stars*.

1083 MANDER, K. VAN. 1973. *Den Grondt der edel vry Schilder-Const*, ed. and trans. H. Miedema.

1084 MANDOWSKY, E. 1939. *Ricerche intorno all'iconologia di Cesare Ripa*.

1085 MANWARING, E. W. 1925. *Italian Landscape in Eighteenth-Century England*.

1086 MARLE, R. VAN. 1923–38. *The Development of the Italian Schools of Painting*, 19 vols.

1087 MENZEL, W. 1842. 'Die Mythen des Regenbogens' in *Mythologische Forschungen und Sammlungen*.

1088 MERKEV, G. S. 1967. 'The rainbow mosaic at Pergamon and Aristotelian color theory', *American Journal of Archaeology*, LXXI.

1089 MEYER, H. B. 1961. 'Zur Symbolik frühmittelalterlicher Majestasbilder', *Das Münster*, XIV.

1090 MILLAIS, J. G. 1899. *Life and Letters of Sir J. F. Millais*, 2 vols.

1091 MIQUEL, P. 1962. *Paul Huet*.

1092 *Musée de Montpellier: La Galerie Bruyas.* 1876.

1093 MUSPER, T. 1935. 'Das Reiseskizzenbuch von J. A. Koch aus dem Jahre 1791', *Jahrbuch der preussischen Kunstsammlungen*, LVI.

1094 NANAVUTTY, P. 1952. 'Blake and Emblem Literature', *Journal of the Warburg and Courtauld Institutes*, XV.

1095 NEWTON, SIR I. 1730. *Opticks* (1704), 4th edn (repr. 1952).

1096 NOVALIS (FRIEDRICH VON HARDENBERG). 1956. *Die Christenheit oder Europa* (1799), ed. W. Rehm.

1097 NUSSENSVEIG, H. M. 1977. 'The theory of the rainbow', *Scientific American*, CCXXXVI, April.

1098 OVERBECK, F. 1843. *Account of the Picture representing Religion Glorified by the Fine Arts.*

1099 PALLUCCHINI, R. (ed.). 1978. *Tiziano e il manierismo europeo.*

1100 PALMER, A. H. 1892. *Life and Letters of Samuel Palmer.*

1101 PARADIN, C. 1557. *Devises héroiques*, Lyon (facsimile repr. 1971).

1102 PARKHURST, C. 1961. 'Aguilonius' Optics and Rubens' Colour', *Nederlands Kunst-Historisch Jaarboek*, XII.

1103 PARRIS, L. and FLEMING-WILLIAMS, I. 1991. *Constable*, London, Tate Gallery.

1104 PICCOLOMINI, A. S. 1960. *Memoirs of a Renaissance Pope*, ed. L. C. Gabel.

1105 PICINELLO, D. P. 1687. *Mundus Symbolicus.* Cologne.

1106 PILES, R. DE 1743. *The Principles of Painting*, London.

1107 [POTT, J. H.]. 1782. *An Essay on Landscape Painting*, London.

1108 PRESSLY, W. 1981. *The Life and Art of James Barry.*

1109 PRICE, U. 1810. *Essays on the Picturesque*, 3 vols (facsimile repr. 1971).

1110 PRIESTLEY, J. 1772. *History and Present State of Discoveries relating to Vision, Light and Colours*, 2 vols, London.

1111 RAEBER, W. 1979. *Caspar Wolf, 1735–1783. Sein Leben und sein Werk.*

1112 RAEHLMANN. E. 1902. *Farbsehen und Malerei.*

1113 REDDING, C. 1858. *Fifty Years' Recollections*, 3 vols.

1114 *Regenbögen für eine bessere Welt.* 1977. Stuttgart, Württemburgischer Kunstverein, exh. cat.

1115 REHFUES, P. J. 1804–10. *Briefe aus Italien*, 4 vols.

1116 REYNOLDS, G. 1961. *Catalogue of the Constable Collection in the Victoria and Albert Museum.*

1117 —. 1984. *The Later Paintings and Drawings of John Constable.*

1118 RICHTER, J. P. 1970. *The Literary Works of Leonardo da Vinci*, 2 vols, 3rd edn.

1119 RIPA, C. 1611. *Iconologia*, Padua.

1120 ROETHEL, H. K. and BENJAMIN, J. K. 1982. *Kandinsky: Catalogue Raisonné of the Oil Paintings*, I, 1900–1915.

1121 ROGERS, S. 1956. *Italian Journal*, ed. J. Hale.

1122 RÖSCH, S. 1960. 'Der Regenbogen in der Malerei', *Studium Generale*, XIII.

1123 ROSENBERG, J. 1928. *Jakob van Ruisdael.*

1124 ROSENTHAL, E. 1972. *The Illuminations of the Vergilius Romanus.*

1125 ROSSETTI, D. G. 1895. *Family Letters*, ed. W. M. Rossetti, 2 vols.

1126 RUBENS, P. P. 1887–1909. *Correspondence*, 6 vols, ed. M. Rooses.

1127 RUNGE, P.O .1840/1. *Hinterlassene Schriften*, 2 vols, ed. D. Runge, (facsimile repr. 1965).

1128 —. 1959. *Farbenkugel*, ed. J. Hebing.

1129 RUSKIN, J. 1900–12. *The Works*, 39 vols, ed. A. Cook and E. T. Wedderburn.

1130 SAND, G. 1896. *Impressions et Souvenirs* (1873) 2nd edn.

1131 SCHINKEL, K. F. III, 1863. *Aus Schinkels Nachlass*, ed. A. von Wolzogen.

1132 SCHUCHARDT, C. 1848–9. *Goethes Kunstsammlungen*, 3 parts.

1133 SCHWEIZER, P.D. 1982. 'John Constable, rainbow science and English color theory', *Art Bulletin*, LXIV.

1134 SEIBOLD, U. 1990. 'Meteorology in Turner's paintings', *Interdisciplinary Science Reviews*, XV.

1135 SHIRLEY, A. 1930. *The Published Mezzotints of David Lucas after John Constable.*

1136 —. 1949. *The Rainbow: a Portrait of John Constable.*

1137 SMITH, J. 1829–42. *Catalogue Raisonné of the Works of the Most Eminent Dutch Painters*, 9 vols.

1138 SMITH, J. T. 1920. *Nollekens and his Times*, 2 vols, ed. W. Whitten.

1139 SMITH, P. 1990. 'Seurat the natural scientist', *Apollo*, CXXXIII.

1140 SOLMI, E. 1976. *Scritti Vinciani.*

1141 SOWERBY, J. 1809. *A New Elucidation of Colours, Original, Prismatic and Material, showing their Coincidence in Three Primitives, Yellow, Red and Blue.*

1142 STORNAJOLO, C. 1908. 'Le miniature della Topografia Cristiana di Cosma Indicopleuste, Cod. Vat. Gr. 699' in *Codices e Vaticanis Selecti*, X.

1143 SUTHERLAND-HARRIS, A. 1967. 'Notes on the chronology and death of Pietro Testa', *Paragone*, CCXIII.

1144 SUTTON, P. (ed.). 1987. *Masters of Seventeenth-Century Dutch Landscape Painting.*

1145 SYNDOW, E. VON 1921. 'K. F. Schinkel als Landschaftsmaler', *Monatshefte für Kunstwissenschaft.*

1146 TEYSSÈDRE, B. 1963. 'Le Cabinet du Duc de Richelieu décrit par Roger de Piles', *Gazette des Beaux-Arts*, LXII.

1147 THIEL, R. 1933. *Luther.*

1148 THORNES, J. 1979. 'Constable's clouds', *Burlington Magazine*, CXXI.

1149 TRAEGER, J. 1975. *Philipp Otto Runge und sein Werk: Monographie und kritischer Katalog.*

1150 VALENCIENNES, P. H. de. 1800. *Eléméns de perspective pratique*, (facsimile repr. 1973).

1151 —. 1956/7. *P. H. de Valenciennes*, Toulouse, Musée Dupuy.

1152 VALLA, G. 1501. *De Expetendis et fugiendis Rebus*, Venice.

1153 WAETZOLDT, W. 1909. 'Das theoretische und praktische Problem der Farbenbenennung', *Zeitschrift für Aesthetik und allgemeine Kunstwissenschaft*, IV.

1154 WEIXLGÄRTNER, A. 1962. *Grünewald.*

1155 WESTPHAL, H. 1910. 'Unmittelbare Bestimmung der Urfarben', *Zeitschrift für Sinnespsychologie (II Abteilung: Zeitschrift für Psychologie und Physiologie der Sinneserscheinungen)*, XLIV.

1156 WILSON, P. W. 1927. *The Greville Diary*, 2 vols.

1157 YOUNG, M. 1800. 'On the number of primitive colorific rays in solar light', *Journal of Natural Philosophy, Chemistry and the Arts*, IV.

1158 ZIFF, J. 1982. 'Turner's first poetic quotations: an examination of intentions', *Turner Studies*, II.

7 *Disegno* versus *Colore*

1159 ABELARD, PETER, 1927. *Glossae super Peri Ermeneias*, ed. B. Geyer.

1160 AGOSTINI, A. 1954. *Le Prospettive e le ombre nelle opere di Leonardo da Vinci.*

1161 ALBERTI, LEON BATTISTA. 1960–73. *Opere volgari*, 3 vols, ed. C. Grayson.

1162 ALESSIO PIEMONTESE. 1975 and 1977. *The Secretes of the Reverende Master Alexis of Piemont* (1555 and 1563).

1163 AMES-LEWIS, F. 1979. 'Filippo Lippi and Flanders', *Zeitschrift für Kunstgeschichte*, XLII.

1164 —. 1981. *Drawing in Early Renaissance Italy.*

1165 ASSUNTO, R. 1961. *La Critica d'arte nel pensiero medievale.*

1166 —. 1963. *Die Theorie des Schönen im Mittelalter.*

1167 BACHMANN, K.-W., OELLERMANN, E. and TAUBERT, J. 1970. 'The conservation and technique of the Herlin Altarpiece', *Studies in Conservation*, XV.

1168 BARASCH, M. 1978. *Light and Color in the Italian Renaissance Theory of Art.*

1169 BARLOW, H. B. and MOLLON, J. D. (eds). 1982. *The Senses.*

1170 BAROCCHI, P. (ed.). 1960–62. *Trattati d'Arte del cinquecento*, 3 vols.

1171 BAUER, L. 1978. '"Quanto si disegna, si dipinge ancora". Some observations on the development of the oil sketch', *Storia dell'Arte*, XXXII.

1172 BAXANDALL, M. 1980. *The Limewood Sculptors of Renaissance Germany.*

1173 —. 1988. *Painting and Experience in Fifteenth-Century Italy*, 2nd edn.

1174 BECK, J. 1988. 'The final layer: "l'ultima mano" on Michelangelo's Sistine ceiling', *Art Bulletin*, LXX.

1175 BELLORI, G. P. 1976. *Le Vite de'pittori, scultori ed architetti moderni*, ed. E. Borea.

1176 BENSI, P. 1980. 'Gli arnesi dell'arte. I Gesuati di San Giusto alle Mura e la pittura del Rinascimento a Firenze', *Studi di Storia dell'Arte*, III.

1177 BERGDOLT, K. 1988. *Der dritte Kommentar Lorenzo Ghibertis: Naturwissenschaften und Medezin in der Kunsttheorie der Frührenaissance.*

1178 BERTI, L. and FOGGI, R. 1989. *Masaccio: catalogo completo.*

1179 BLUNT, A. and CROFT-MURRAY, E. 1957. *Venetian Drawings of the XVII and XVIII Centuries at Windsor Castle.*

1180 BODENHAUSEN, E. VON. 1905. *Gerard David und seine Schule.*

1181 BOLOGNA, F. 1955. *Opere d'arte nel salernitano dal XII al XVIII secolo.*

1182 BOMFORD, D., ROY, A. and SMITH, A. 1986. 'The techniques of Dieric Bouts: two paintings contrasted', *National Gallery Technical Bulletin*, X.

1183 BORA G. 1987. *Due Tavole Leonardesche.*

1184 BORNSTEIN, M. 1975. 'Qualities of color vision in infancy', *Journal of Experimental Child Psychology*, XIX.

1185 BORSOOK, E. 1971. 'Documents for Filippo Strozzi's Chapel in S. Maria Novella and other related papers', *Burlington Magazine*, CXII.

1186 — and SUPERBI GIOFFREDI, F. (eds). 1986. *Tecnica e Stile.*

1187 BOSCOVITS, M. 1973. 'Cennino Cennini: pittore non-conformista', *Mitteilungen des Kunsthistorischen Instituts in Florenz*, XVII.

1188 BOWRON, E. P. 1974. 'Oil and tempera mediums in early Italian paintings: a view from the laboratory', *Apollo*, C.

1189 BRACHERT, T. 1970. 'A distinctive aspect in the painting technique of the "Ginevra de' Benci" and of Leonardo's early works', *Washington, National Gallery of Art: Report and Studies in the History of Art 1969.*

1190 —. 1974. 'Radiographische Untersuchungen am Verkündigungsbild von Monte Oliveto', *Maltechnik/Restauro*, LXXX.

1191 —. 1977. 'Die beiden Felsgrottenmadonnen von Leonardo da Vinci', *Maltechnik*, LXXXIII.

1192 BRESC-BAUTIER, G. 1979. *Artistes, patriciens et confréries. Production et consommation de l'oeuvre d'art à Palerme et en Sicile 1348–1460.*

1193 BROMELLE, N. 1959/60. 'St George and the Dragon', *The Museums Journal*, LIX.

1194 — and SMITH, P. (eds.) 1976. *Conservation and Restoration of Pictorial Art.*

1195 BRUGNOLI, P. (ed.). 1974. *Maestri di pittura veronese.*

1196 BUZZEGOLI, E. 1987. 'Michelangelo as a colourist: revealed in the conservation of the Doni Tondo', *Apollo*, CXXVI.

1197 CADOGAN, J. K. 1983. 'Linen drapery studies by Verocchio, Leonardo and Ghirlandaio', *Zeitschrift für Kunstgeschichte*, XLIV.

1198 CAMERON, A. 1981. 'The Virgin's Robe: an episode in the history of early seventh-century Constantinople', in *Continuity and Change in Sixth-Century Byzantium.*

1199 CANOVA, G. M. 1972. 'Riflessioni su Jacopo Bellini e sul libro dei disegni del Louvre', *Arte Veneta*, XXVI.

1200 CARON, L. 1988. 'The use of color by Rosso Fiorentino', *Sixteenth Century Journal*, XIX, 3.

1201 CENNINI, CENNINO. 1933. *The Craftsman's Handbook*, ed. and trans. D. V. Thompson.

1202 CHAMBERS, D. S. 1970. *Patrons and Artists in the Italian Renaissance.*

1203 CHASTEL, A. ET AL. 1986. *La Capella Sistina, I: Primi restauri, la scoperta del colore.*

1204 CHRISTIANSEN, K. 1982. *Gentile da Fabriano.*

1205 COHEN, J. and GORDON, D. A. 1949. 'The Prevost-Fechner-Benham subjective colors', *Psychological Bulletin.*

1206 COLE, B. 1977. *Agnolo Gaddi.*

1207 CONRAD-MARTIUS, H. 1929. 'Farben: ein Kapitel aus der Realontologie', *Festschrift für Edmund Husserl (Ergänzungsband zum Jahrbuch für philosophische und phänomenologische Forschung).*

1208 CONTI, A. 1986. *Michelangelo e la pittura a fresco. Tecnica e conservazione della volta Sistina.*

1209 COREMANS, P. 1950. 'Technische inleiding tot de studie van de Vlaamse Primitieven', *Gentse Bijdragen tot de Kunstgeschiednis*, XII.

1210 DEGENHART, B. and SCHMITT, A. IV, 1968. *Corpus der italienischen Zeichnungen 1300–1450*, Teil I.

1211 DELBOURGO, S., RIOUX, J. P. and MARTIN, E. 1975. 'L'analyse des peintures du "Studiolo" d'Isabelle d'Este. II: Étude analytique de la matière picturale', *Annales du laboratoire des musées de France.*

1212 EMILIANI, A. 1975. *Mostra di Federico Barocci*, Bologna, Museo Civico.

1213 EQUICOLA, M. 1525. *Libro de Natura de Amor*, Venice.
1214 FANTI, M. 1979. 'Le postille carraccesche alle "Vite" del Vasari: il testo originale', *Il Carrobbio*, V.
1215 FARAGO, C. J. 1991. 'Leonardo's color and chiaroscuro reconsidered: the visual force of painted images', *Art Bulletin*, LXXIII.
1216 FILARETE (A. AVERLINO). 1972. *Trattato di architettura* (1461/2–4), 2 vols, ed. A. M. Finoli and L. Grassi.
1217 FILIPCZAK, Z. Z. 1977. 'New light on Mona Lisa: Leonardo's optical knowledge and his choice of lighting', *Art Bulletin*, LIX.
1218 FIORILLI, C. 1920. 'I dipintori a Firenze nell'arte dei Medici, Speciali e Merciai', *Archivio Storico Italiano*, LXXVIII, ii.
1219 *Firenze e La Toscana dei medici nell'Europa del cinquecento: il primato del Disegno*. 1980. Florence.
1220 FOLENA, G. 1951. 'Chiaroscuro leonardesco', *Lingua Nostra*, XII.
1221 FORTUNA, A. M. 1957. *Andrea del Castagno*.
1222 GAGE, J. 1972. 'Ghiberti's *Third Commentary* and its background', *Apollo*, XCV.
1223 GARGIOLLI, G. (ed.). 1868. *L'Arte della seta in Firenze: trattato del XV secolo*.
1224 GARIN, E. 1982. *La Disputà delle arti nel quattrocento*, 2nd edn.
1225 GARRISON, E. 1949. *Italian Romanesque Panel Painting*.
1226 GETTENS, R. J., FELLER, R. L. and CHASE, W. T. 1972. 'Vermilion and Cinnabar', *Studies in Conservation*, XVII.
1227 GIBBONS, F. 1968. *Dosso and Battista Dossi*.
1228 GLASSER, H. 1977. *Artists' Contracts of the Early Renaissance*.
1229 GOFFIN, R. 1986. *Piety and Patronage in Renaissance Venice*.
1230 GOLZIO, V. 1971. *Raffaello nei Documenti*, 2nd edn.
1231 GOULD, C. 1947. 'Leonardo da Vinci's notes on the colour of rivers and mountains', *Burlington Magazine*, LXXXIX.
1232 GRANGE, A. DE LA and CLOQUET, L. 1888. 'Études sur l'art à Tournai', *Mémoires de la Societé Historique et Littéraire de Tournai*, XXI.
1233 *Gray is the Color*. 1973/4. Houston, Texas, Rice Museum, exh. cat.
1234 GUARESCHI, I. 1907. 'Industria dei colori a Venezia' in *Storia della chimica. VI: sui colori degli antichi: Pt. II: dal secolo XV al secolo XIX*, (Supplimento Annuale alla *Enciclopedia di Chimica*, XXIII).
1235 GUASTI, C. (ed.). 1877. *Lettere di una gentildonna fiorentina del secolo XV*.
1236 HAGOPIAN VAN BUREN, A. 1986. 'Thoughts, old and new, on the sources of early Netherlandish painting', *Simiolus*, XVI.
1237 HALL, M. B. (ed.). 1987. *Color and Technique in Renaissance Painting: Italy and the North*.
1238 HAPSBURG, G. VON 1965. *Die Rundfenster des Lorenzo Ghiberti*, Ph.D. thesis, Fribourg University.
1239 HARDING, E., BRAHAM, A., WYLD, M. and BURNSTOCK, A. 1989. 'The restoration of the Leonardo Cartoon', *National Gallery Technical Bulletin*, XIII.
1240 HARTHAN, J. 1977. *Books of Hours*.
1241 HENNEKE, E. and SCHNEEMELCHER, W. 1959–64. *Neutestamentliche Apokryphen*, 2 vols.
1242 HERALD, J. 1981. *Renaissance Dress in Italy, 1400–1500*.
1243 HOURS, M. 1954. 'Études analytiques des tableaux de Léonard de Vinci au laboratoire du Musée du Louvre' in *Leonardo saggi e ricerche*.
1244 —. 1962. 'À propos de l'examen au laboratoire de "La Vierge aux Rochers" et du "Saint-Jean Baptiste" de Léonard', *Raccolta Vinciana*, XIX.
1245 JAFFÉ, M. and GROEN, K. 1987. 'Titian's "Tarquin and Lucretia" in the Fitzwilliam', *Burlington Magazine*, CXXIX.
1246 JOHNSON, M. and PACKARD, E. 1971. 'Methods used for the identification of binding media in Italian paintings of the fifteenth and sixteenth centuries', *Studies in Conservation*, XVI.
1247 KEMP, M. 1981. *Leonardo da Vinci: the Marvellous Works of Nature and Man*.
1248 KRAMER, H. and MATSCHOSS, O. (eds). 1963. *Farben in Kultur und Leben*.
1249 KRISTELLER, P. 1901. *Andrea Mantegna*, ed. S. A. Strong.
1250 LADIS, A. 1982. *Taddeo Gaddi*.
1251 LANGTON DOUGLAS, F. 1902. *Fra Angelico*, 2nd edn.
1252 LAVIN, M. A. 1956. 'Colour study in Barocci's drawing', *Burlington Magazine*, XCVIII.
1253 LOTTO, LORENZO. 1969. *Il Libro di spese diversi*, ed. P. Zampetti.
1254 MALTESE, C. 1976. 'Colore, luce e movimento nello spazio Albertiano', *Commentari*, N.S., XXVII.
1255 —. 1982. 'Il colore per Leonardo dalla pittura alla scienza' in *Leonardo e l'etá della ragione: Atti del Convegno*, Milan.
1256 —. 1983. 'Leonardo e la teoria dei colori', *Römisches Jahrbuch für Kunstgeschichte*, XX.
1257 MANCINELLI, F. 1983. 'The technique of Michelangelo as a painter. A note on the cleaning of the first lunettes in the Sistine Chapel', *Apollo*, CXVII.
1258 —. 1988. 'La technique de Michel-Ange et les problèmes de la Chapelle Sixtine: la *Création d'Ève* et le *Peché Originel*', *Revue de l'Art*, LXXXI.
1259 MANZONI, L. 1904. *Statuti e matricole dell'arte dei pittori della città di Firenze, Perugia, Siena*.
1260 MARAZZA, A. 1954. 'Gli studi di L. Reti sulla chimica di Leonardo' in *Leonardo saggi e ricerche*.
1261 MARIÀS, F. and BUSTAMENTE, A. 1981. *Las Ideas artisticas de El Greco*.
1262 MASSING, A. and CHRISTIE, N. 1988. '*The Hunt in the Forest* by Paolo Uccello', *Hamilton Kerr Institute Bulletin*, I.
1263 MATTEINI, M. and MOLES, A. 1979. 'A preliminary investigation of the unusual technique of Leonardo's mural "Last Supper"', *Studies in Conservation*, XXIV.
1264 MAURER, E. 1982. 'Zum Koloriti von Pontormos *Deposizione*' in *15 Aufsätze zur Geschichte der Malerei*.
1265 MAZZEI, SER LAPO. 1880. *Lettere di un Notaro a un mercante*, 2 vols, ed. C. Guasti.
1266 MEDER, J. 1923. *Die handzeichnung*, 2nd edn.
1267 MEISS, M. 1941. 'A documented altarpiece by Piero della Francesca', *Art Bulletin*, XXIII.
1268 MICHEL, F. 1852–4. *Recherches sur le commerce, la fabrication et l'usage des étoffes de soie, d'or et d'argent*.
1269 MIDDELDORF, U. 1955. 'L'Angelico e la scultura', *Rinascimento*, VI.
1270 MILANESI, G. 1872. 'Documenti inediti riguardanti Leonardo da Vinci', *Archivio Storico Italiano*, ser. III, XVI.
1271 MOLLON, J. D. 1989. '"Tho she kneel'd in that Place where they grew ...". The uses and origins of primate colour vision', *Journal of Experimental Biology*, CXLVI.
1272 NERI DI BICCI. 1976. *Le Ricordanze*, ed. B. Santi.
1273 NEWTON, S. M. 1988. *The Dress of the Venetians 1495–1525*.
1274 NILGEN, U. 1981. 'Maria Regina: ein politischer Kultbildtypus', *Römisches Jahrbuch für Kunstgeschichte*, XIX.
1275 NIXDORFF, H. and MÜLLER, H. 1983. *Weisse Westen- Rote Roben: von der Farbordnung des Mittelalters zum individuellen Farbgeschmack*, Berlin, Staatliche Museen preussischer Kulturbesitz.
1276 PEDRETTI, C. 1957. 'Storia della Gioconda' in *Studi Vinciani*.
1277 —. 1968. 'Le note di pittura di Leonardo da Vinci nei manoscritti inediti a Madrid', *Lettura Vinciana*, VIII.
1278 PÉRIER D'IETEREN, C. 1985. *Colyn de Coter et la technique picturale des peintres flamandes du XVe siècle*.
1279 PHILIPPOT, P. 1966. 'Les grisailles et les "degrés de réalité" de l'image dans la peinture flamande des XVe et XVIe siècles', *Bulletin des Musées Royaux des Beaux-Arts de Belgique*, XV, iv.
1280 PICCOLPASSO, C. 1934. *The Three Books of the Potter's Art* (1548), trans. B. Rackham and A. van de Put.
1281 PILLSBURY, E. 1978. 'The oil studies of Federico Barocci', *Apollo*, CVIII.
1282 PINO, PAOLO. 1954. *Dialogo di pittura* (1548), ed. E. Camesasca.
1283 PLESTERS, J. 1980. 'Tintoretto's paintings in the National Gallery, II: Materials and Techniques', *National Gallery Technical Bulletin*, IV.
1284 POGGI, G., BAROCCHI, P. and RISTORI, R. I, 1965. *Il Carteggio di Michelangelo*, 5 vols, 1965–83.
1285 POPE-HENNESSY, J. 1939. *Sassetta*.
1286 RATLIF, F. 1976. 'On the psycho-physiological bases of universal color terms', *Proceedings of the American Philosophical Society*, CXX.
1287 REBORA, G. 1970. *Un Manuale di tintoria del quattrocento*.
1288 RISTORO D'AREZZO. 1976. *La Composizione del mondo colle sue cascioni*, ed. A. Morino.
1289 ROLLAND, P. 1932. 'Une sculpture encore existante polychromée par Robert Campin', *Revue Belge d'Archéologie et d'Histoire de l'Art*, II.
1290 ROSENAUER, A. 1965. 'Zum Stil der frühen Werke Domenico Ghirlandaios', *Wiener Jahrbuch für Kunstgeschichte*, XXII.
1291 ROSIŃSKA, G. 1986. *Fifteenth-century Optics between Mediaeval and Modern Science* (*Studia Copernicana*, XXIV; Polish with Eng. summary).
1292 RUBIN, P. 1991. 'The art of color in Florentine painting of the early sixteenth century: Rosso Fiorentino and Jacopo Pontormo', *Art Histoy*, XIV.
1293 RUCCELLAI, G. 1960. *Zibaldone*, ed. A. Perosa.
1294 RUDA, J. 1984. 'Flemish painting and the early Renaissance in Florence: questions of influence', *Zeitschrift für Kunstgeschichte*, XLVIII.
1295 RUHEMANN, H. 1955. 'The cleaning and restoration of the Glasgow Giorgione', *Burlington Magazine*, XCVII.
1296 SANPAOLESI, P. 1954. 'I dipinti di Leonardo agli Uffizi' in *Leonardo saggi e ricerche*.
1297 SERRA, A. DEL. 1985. 'A conversation on painting techniques', *Burlington Magazine*, CXXVII.
1298 SHEARMAN, J. 1962. 'Leonardo's Colour and Chiaroscuro', *Zeitschrift für Kunstgeschichte*, XXV.
1299 —. 1965. *Andrea del Sarto*, 2 vols.
1300 —. 1987. 'Raphael's clouds, and Correggio's' in M. S. Hamoud and M. L. Strocchi (eds), *Studi su Raffaello*, 2 vols.
1301 SIMONELLI, M. P. 1972. 'On Alberti's treatises and their chronological relationship', *Yearbook of Italian Studies*, 1971.
1302 SJÖBLOM, A. 1928. *Die koloristische Entwicklung in der niederländischen Malerei des XV und XVI Jahrhunderts*.
1303 SMITH, M. T. 1957/9. 'The use of grisaille in Lenten observance', *Marsyas*, VIII.
1304 SPIES, O. 1937. 'Al-Kindi's Treatise on the cause of the blue colour of the sky', *Journal of the Bombay Branch of the Royal Asiatic Society*, N.S., XIII.
1305 SRUTKOVA-ODELL, V. 1978. 'L'Alberti e le nuove teorie estetiche del Mantegna', *Commentari*, N.S., XXIX.
1306 STEINBERG, R.M. 1977. *Fra Girolamo Savonarola, Florentine Art and Renaissance Historiography*.
1307 TANTILLO, A. M. 1972. 'Restauri alla Farnesina', *Bolletino d'Arte*, LVII.
1308 TAUBERT, J. 1978. *Farbige Skulpturen: Bedeutung, Fassung, Restaurierung*.
1309 THOMAS OF CELANO. 1904. *Vita Prima S. Francescii Assisiensis*, ed. H. G. Rosedale.
1310 THOMPSON, D. V., JR. 1933. 'Artificial vermilion in the Middle Ages', *Technical Studies in the Field of Fine Arts*, II.
1311 *Il Tondo Doni di Michelangelo e il suo restauro* (*Gli Uffizi, Studi e Richerche*, 2). 1985. Florence, Uffizi.
1312 TRAVERS NEWTON, H. 1983. 'Leonardo da Vinci as a mural painter: some observations on his materials and working methods', *Arte Lombarda*, LXVI.
1313 UCCELLI, G. B. 1865. *Il Convento di S. Giusto alle Mura e i Gesuati*.
1314 UHDE-BERNAYS, H. (ed.). 1960. *Künstlerbriefe über Kunst*.
1315 VASARI, G. 1903. *The Life of Leonardo da Vinci*, trans. H. Horne.
1316 —. 1960. *Vasari on Technique*, ed. G. B. Brown, 2nd edn.
1317 VELTMAN, K. 1986. *Studies on Leonardo da Vinci I: Visual Perspective and the Visual Dimensions of Science and Art*.
1318 VERBRAEKEN, R. 1979. *Clair-Obscur – histoire d'un mot*.
1319 VESCOVINI, G. F. 1965. 'Contributo per la storia della fortuna di Alhazen in Italia: il volgarizzamento del MS Vat. 4595 e il "Commentario Terzo" del Ghiberti', *Rinascimento*, ser. II, V.
1320 —. 1980. 'Il problema delle fonti ottiche medievali del *Commentario Terzo* di Lorenzo Ghiberti' in *Lorenzo Ghiberti e il suo tempo* (*Atti del Convegno Internazionale di Studi 1978*) II.
1321 WEALE, R. A. 1974. *Theories of Light and Colour in Relation to the History of Painting*, Ph.D. thesis, London University.
1322 WHITE, J. 1979. *Duccio: Tuscan Art and the Mediaeval Workshop*.
1323 WITELO. 1572. *Perspectiva* in F. Risner (ed.), *Opticae Thesaurus*, Basle.

1324 WOHL, H. 1980. *The Paintings of Domenico Veneziano.*
1325 WOLFTHAL, D. 1989. *The Beginnings of Netherlandish Canvas Painting, 1400–1530.*
1326 WRIGHT, J. 1980. 'Antonello da Messina: the origins of his style and technique', *Art History*, III.
1327 WYLD, M. and PLESTERS, J. 1977. 'Some panels from Sassetta's Sansepolcro Altarpiece', *National Gallery Technical Bulletin*, I.
1328 ZILOTY, A. 1947. *La Découverte de Jean van Eyck et l'évolution du procédé de la peinture à l'huile du moyen-âge à nos jours*, 2nd edn.
1329 ZUBOV, V. 1958. 'Léon Battista Alberti et les auteurs du moyen âge', *Medieval and Renaissance Studies*, IV.
1330 —. 1960. 'Leon Battista Alberti e Leonardo da Vinci', *Raccolta Vinciana*, XVIII.
1331 —. 1968. *Leonardo da Vinci.*

8 The Peacock's Tail

1332 ALLENDE-SALAZAR, J. 1925. 'Don Felipe de Guevara, coleccionista y escritor de arte del siglo XVI', *Archivo Español de Arte y Arqueologia*, I.
1333 ARETINO, PIETRO. 1539. *I Quattro libri la humanità di Christo*, Venice.
1334 BACON, R. 1859. *Opus Tertium*, ed. J. S. BREWER.
1335 —. 1912. *Opus Tertium*, ed. A. G. Little.
1336 BEDAUX, J. B. 1986. 'The reality of symbols: the question of disguised symbolism in Jan van Eyck's *Arnolfini Portrait*', *Simiolus*, XVI.
1337 BONI, B. 1954. 'Leonardo da Vinci e l'alchimia', *Chimica*, XXX (IX).
1338 BONO, P. DA FERRARA. 1976. *Preziosa Margarita Novella*, ed. C. Crisciani.
1339 [BOTTARI, G.]. 1772. *Dialoghi sopra le tre arti del disegno* (1754), 2nd edn, Naples.
1340 BUDDENSIEG, T. and WINNER, M. (eds). 1968. *Minuscula Discipulorum.*
1341 CALVESI, M. 1962. '*La Tempesta* di Giorgione come ritrovamento di Mosé', *Commentari*, XIII.
1342 —. 1969. 'A Noir (Melancholia I)', *Storia dell'Arte*, IV.
1343 CARBONELLI, G. 1925. *Sulle fonti storiche della chimia e dell'alchimia in Italia.*
1344 COMPTON, S. 1985. *Chagall*, London, Royal Academy, exh. cat.
1345 CONDIVI, A. 1964. *Vita di Michelangelo Buonarotti*, (1553), ed. E. S. Barelli.
1346 COTRUGLI, B. 1602. *Della Mercatura e del mercante perfetto* (1458), Brescia.
1347 CRISCIANI, C. 1973. 'The conception of alchemy as expressed in the "Pretiosa Margarita Novella" of Petrus Bonus of Ferrara', *Ambix*, XX.
1348 CROSLAND, M. P. 1962. *Historical Studies in the Language of Chemistry.*
1349 DAHNENS, E. 1980. *Van Eyck.*
1350 DOBBS, B. J. T. 1975. *The Foundations of Newton's Alchemy, or The Hunting of The Greene Lyon.*
1351 EAMON, W. 1980. 'New light on Robert Boyle and the discovery of color indicators', *Ambix*, XXVII.
1352 ETTLINGER, L. D. 1965. *The Sistine Chapel before Michelangelo.*
1353 FAGIOLO DELL'ARCO, M. 1970. *Il Parmigianino: saggio sull'Ermetismo nel cinquecento.*

1354 FORBES, R. J. 1961. 'Alchemy, dye and colour', *CIBA Review*.
1355 FREEDBERG, S. J. 1950. *Parmigianino.*
1356 GOLDING, J. 1973. *Marcel Duchamp: the Bride Stripped Bare by her Batchelors Even.*
1357 HALLEUX, R. (ed. and trans.). I, 1981. *Les Alchimistes grecs.*
1358 HARTLAUB, G. F. 1953. 'Zu den Bildmotiven des Giorgione', *Zeitschrift des deutschen Vereins für Kunstwissenschaft*, VII.
1359 HIND, A. M. 1910. *Catalogue of Early Italian Engraving in the British Museum.*
1360 HOLMYARD, E. J. 1957. *Alchemy.*
1361 HOPKINS, A. J. 1927. 'Transmutation by colour' in J. Ruska (ed.), *Studien zur Geschichte der Chemie: Festgabe E. O. von Lippmann.*
1362 —. 1938. 'A study of the kerotakis process as given by Zosimus and later alchemical writers', *Isis*, XXIX.
1363 HORNE, H. 1908. *Sandro Botticelli.*
1364 HORST, R. W. 1953. 'Dürers "Melencholia I": ein Beitrag zum Melencholia-Problem', *Forschungen zur Kustgeschichte und Christlichen Archäologie.*
1365 JORET, C. 1892. *La Rose dans l'antiquité et au moyen-âge.*
1366 JUNG, C. G. 1953. *Psychology and Alchemy.*
1367 —. 1963. *Mysterium Coniunctionis.*
1368 KIBRE, P. 1942. 'Alchemical writings ascribed to Albertus Magnus', *Speculum*, XVII.
1369 KIRSOP, W. 1961. 'The legend of Bernard Palissy', *Ambix*, IX.
1370 KRISTELLER, P.O. 1907. *Giulio Campagnola.*
1371 *Liber Claritatis Totius Alkimicae Artis*. 1925/7. Ed. E. Darmstaedter, *Archaeion*, VI–IX.
1372 LUTHER, H. M. 1973. 'A history of the psychological interpretation of alchemy', *Ambix*, XX.
1373 MARTELS, Z. R. W. M. VON (ed.). 1990. *Alchemy Revisited.*
1374 MEIER, C. 1972. 'Die Bedeutung der Farben im Werk Hildegards von Bingen', *Frühmittelalterliche Studien*, VI.
1375 MESNIL, J. 1938. *Botticelli.*
1376 MONFASANI, J. 1983. 'A description of the Sistine Chapel under Pope Sixtus IV', *Artibus & Historiae*, VII.
1377 NEWMAN, W. 1989. 'Technology and alchemical debate in the late Middle Ages', *Isis*, LXXX.
1378 NURMI, M. K. 1957. *Blake's Marriage of Heaven and Hell: a Critical Study.*
1379 OBRIST, B. 1983. *Les Débuts de l'imagerie alchimique, XIVᵉ–XVᵉ siècles.*
1380 OHLY, F. 1977. 'Die Geburt der Perle aus dem Blitz' in *Schriften zur Mittelalterlichen Bedeutungsforschung.*
1381 OTTONELLI, G. D. and BERRETTINI, P. 1973. *Trattato della pittura e scultura: uso et abuso loro* (1652), ed. V. Casale.
1382 PANOFSKY, E. 1966. *Early Netherlandish Painting*, 2 vols.
1383 PAVANELLO, G. 1905. *Un Maestro del quattrocento (Giovanni Aurelio Augurello).*
1384 PEDRETTI, C. 1977. *Commentary on the Literary Works of Leonardo da Vinci*, 2 vols.
1385 PFISTER, R. 1935. 'Teinture et alchimie dans l'orient hellenistique', *Seminarium Kondakovium*, VII.
1386 PLOSS, E. 1962. *Ein Buch von Alten Farben.*
1387 —, ROOSEN-RUNGE, H.,

SCHIPPERGES, H. and BUNTZ, H. 1970. *Alchimia: Ideologie und Technologie.*
1388 PSEUDO-AQUINAS. 1977. *Von der Multiplikation*, ed. D. Goltz, J. Telle and H.J. Vermeer, *Sudhoffs Archiv*, Beiheft 19.
1389 PURTLE, C. J. 1982. *The Marian Paintings of Jan van Eyck.*
1390 READ, J. 1939. *Prelude to Chemistry*, 2nd edn.
1391 —. 1952. 'Alchemy and Art', *Proceedings of the Royal Institution of Great Britain*, XXXV.
1392 RETI, L. 1952. 'Leonardo e l'alchimia' and 'Le arti chimiche di Leonardo da Vinci', *La Chimica e l'Industria*, XXXIV.
1393 REUSNER, H. (FRANCISCUS EPIMETHEUS). 1588. *Pandora: Das ist die edelst Gab Gottes . . .*, Basle.
1394 REYNOLDS, C. D. (ed.). 1983. *Texts and Transmission.*
1395 RICHTER, I. A. 1952. *Selections from the Notebooks of Leonardo da Vinci.*
1396 SABRA, A. I. 1967. *Theories of Light from Descartes to Newton.*
1397 SARAN, B. 1972. 'Der Technologe und Farbchemiker "Matthias Grünewald"', *Maltechnik*, VII.
1398 SARTON, G. 1954. 'Ancient Alchemy and Abstract Art', *Journal of the History of Medicine*, IX.
1399 SCHABAKER, P. 1972. 'De matrimonio ad morganaticum contracto: Jan van Eyck's "Arnolfini" portrait reconsidered', *Art Quarterly*, XXV.
1400 SCHECKENBURGER-BROSCHEK, A. 1982. *Die Altdeutsche Malerei.*
1401 SIMEON OF COLOGNE. 1918. *Speculum Alchimiae Minus*, ch. VI: *De omnibus coloribus accidentibus in opere*, ed. K. Sudhoff, *Archiv für die Geschichte der Naturwissenschaften und der Technik*, IX.
1402 STEINMANN, E. 1901–05. *Die Sixtinische Kapelle*, 5 vols.
1403 STUMPEL, J. 1988. 'On grounds and backgrounds: some remarks about composition in Renaissance painting', *Simiolus*, XVIII.
1404 SZULAKOWSKA, U. 1986. 'The Tree of Aristotle: Images of the Philosophers' Stone and their transference in alchemy from the fifteenth to the twentieth century', *Ambix*, XXXIII.
1405 TIECK, L. 1798. *Franz Sternbalds Wanderungen*, Berlin.
1406 TIETZE, H. and TIETZE-CONRAT, E. 1970. *The Drawings of the Venetian Painters in the 15th and 16th Centuries.*
1407 TUCHMAN, M. (ed.). 1986. *The Spiritual in Art: Abstract Painting 1890–1985*, Los Angeles County Museum of Art, exh. cat.
1408 VASARI, G. III, 1971; IV, 1976; VII, 1965. *Le Vite*, ed. R. Bettarini and P. Barocchi.
1409 WEISE, G. 1957. 'Manieristische und frühbaroke Elemente in den religiösen Schriften des Pietro Aretino', *Bibliothèque d'Humanisme et de Renaissance*, XIX.
1410 ZETZNER, E. (ed.). 1659. *Theatrum Chemicum*, 6 vols.
1411 ZÜLCH, W. K. 1938. *Der historische Grünewald: Matthis Gothardt-Neithardt.*

9 Colour under Control

1412 AGRICOLA, R. 1967. *De Inventione Dialectica* (1523), facsimile repr.
1413 AGUILONIUS, F. 1613. *Opticorum Libri Sex*, Antwerp.
1414 ALGAROTTI, F. 1969. *Newtonianismo per le Dame* (1737) in E. Bonora (ed.),

Illuministi Italiani, 2 vols.
1415 ALLAN, M. 1964. *The Tradescants: their Plants, Gardens and Museum.*
1416 ANQUETIN, L. 1970. *De l'Art.*
1417 AQUINAS, ST THOMAS. 1952. *Meteorologicorum*, ed. R. M. Spiazzi.
1418 ARBER, A. 1940. 'The colouring of sixteenth-century herbals', *Nature*, CXLV.
1419 ARGÜELLES, J. A. 1972. *Charles Henry and the Formation of a Psycho-Physical Aesthetic.*
1420 *Artists, Writers, Politics. Camille Pissarro and his Friends.* 1980. Oxford, Ashmolean Museum, exh. cat.
1421 *Avicenna Latinus: Liber de Anima seu Sextus de Naturalibus.* 1972. Ed. S. van Riet.
1422 BADT, K. 1965. *Eugène Delacroix: Werke und Ideale.*
1423 —. 1969. *Die Kunst des Nicholas Poussin.*
1424 BAILLY-HERZBERG, J. 1980–. *Correspondance de Camille Pissarro*, 4 vols.
1425 BARROW, I. 1860. *Lectiones Opticae* (1669) in *The Mathematical Works*, ed. W. Whewell (Eng. trans., *Optical Lectures*, ed. A. G. Bennett and D. F. Edgar, 1987).
1426 BÄTSCHMANN, O. 1990. *Nicholas Poussin: The Dialectics of Painting.*
1427 BAUMGART, F. 1955. *Caravaggio: Kunst und Wirklichkeit.*
1428 BELL, J. 1983. *Color and Theory in Seicento Art: Zaccolini's "Prospettiva del Colore" and the Heritage of Leonardo*, Ph.D. thesis, Brown University.
1429 —. 1985. 'The Life and Works of Matteo Zaccolini', *Regnum Dei*, XLI.
1430 BELLORI, G. 1976. *Le Vite* (1672), ed. E. Borea.
1431 BERGER, E. IV, 1901. *Beiträge zur Entwicklungsgeschichte der Maltechnik.*
1432 BERNINI, G.-P. 1982. *Giovanni Lanfranco.*
1433 BESSIS, H. 1971. 'L'Inventaire d'après décès d'Eugène Delacroix', *Bulletin de la Societé de l'Histoire de l'Art Français 1969.*
1434 BEZOLD, WILHELM VON. 1876. *The Theory of Color in its Relation to Art and Art-Industry.*
1435 BISTORT, G. 1912. *Il Magistrato alle pompe nella republica di Venezia.*
1436 BLANC, C. 1867. *Grammaire des arts du dessin.*
1437 —. 1876. *Les Artistes de mon temps.*
1438 —. 1882. *Grammaire des arts décoratifs*, 2nd edn.
1439 BOMBE, W. 1928. *Nachlass-Inventare des Angelo da Uzzano und des Lodovico di Gino Capponi.*
1440 BOMFORD, D., BROWN, C. and ROY, A. 1988. *Art in the Making: Rembrandt*, London, National Gallery, exh. cat.
1441 BRENNER, E. 1680. *Nomenclatura et Species Colorum*, Stockholm.
1442 BROUDE, N. 1970. 'Realism, popular science and the re-shaping of Macchia Romanticism, 1862–1886', *Art Bulletin*, LII.
1443 — (ed.). 1978. *Seurat in Perspective.*
1444 BROWN, R. F. 1950. 'Impressionist technique: Pissarro's optical mixture', *Magazine of Art*, January.
1445 BROWNE, SIR T. 1658. *Cyrus-Garden, or the Quincunx Mistically Considered*, London.
1446 BRÜCKE, E. 1866. *Physiologie der Farben* (Fr. version, *Des Couleurs au point de vue physique, physiologique, artistique et industriel*, 1866).

1447 —. 1878. *Principes Scientifiques des Beaux-Arts*.

1448 BUONANNI, F. 1681. *Ricreatione dell'occhio e della mente nell'observation delle chiocciole*, Rome.

1449 BUTLER, M. H. 1982/3. 'An investigation of the techniques and materials used by Jan Steen', *Philadelphia Museum of Art Bulletin*, LXXVIII.

1450 CALLEN, A. 1982. *Techniques of the Impressionists*.

1451 CAMP, M. DU. 1962. *Souvenirs Littéraires*.

1452 CAMPANELLA, T. 1956. *Opere di Giordano Bruno e di Tomasso Campanella*, ed. A. Guzzo and R. Amerio.

1453 *Il Cavaliere d'Arpino*. 1973. Rome, Palazzo Venezia, exh. cat.

1454 CHALCIDIUS. 1963. *Platonis Timaeus interprete Chalcidio*, ed. J. Wrobel.

1455 CHANDLER, A. R. 1934. *Beauty and Human Nature*.

1456 CHARLETON, W. 1677. *Exercitationes de Differentiis & Nominibus Animalium*, Oxford.

1457 CHEVREUL, M. E. 1864. *Des Couleurs et de leurs applications aux arts industrielles*.

1458 —. 1879. 'Complément des études sur la vision des couleurs', *Mémoires de l'Académie des Sciences*, 2e sér., XLI.

1459 —. 1969. *De la Loi du contraste simultané* (2nd edn 1889).

1460 COHEN, I. B. (ed.). 1958. *Isaac Newton's Papers and Letters on Natural Philosophy*.

1461 COMINALE, C. 1754. *Anti-Newtonianismi Pars Prima, in qua Newtoni de Coloribus Systema ex Propriis Principiis Geometrice Evertitur*, Naples.

1462 CONISBEE, P. 1979. 'Pre-Romantic plein-air painting', *Art History*, II.

1463 COREMANS, P. 1965. 'L'autoportrait de Rembrandt à la Staatsgalerie de Stuttgart', *Jahrbuch der Staatliche Kunstsammlungen in Baden-Württemberg*, II.

1464 — and THISSEN, J. 1962. 'Composition et structure des couches originales' in 'La Descente de Croix de Rubens. Étude préalable au traitement', *Bulletin de l'Institut Royal du Patrimoine Artistique*, V.

1465 CROPPER, E. 1980. 'Poussin and Leonardo: the evidence of the Zaccolini MSS', *Art Bulletin*, LXII.

1466 DAGOGNET, F. 1970. *Le Catalogue de la vie*.

1467 DANCE, S. P. 1966. *Shell-Collecting: an Illustrated History*.

1468 DARMON, A. 1985. *Les Corps immatérielles. Esprits et images dans l'oeuvre de Marin Cureau de la Chambre*.

1469 DARWIN, E. 1796. *Zoonomia*, 2 vols, 2nd edn, London.

1470 DARWIN, R. W. 1785. 'On the ocular spectra of light and colours', *Philosophical Transactions of the Royal Society*, LXXVI.

1471 DELACROIX, E. 1935–8. *Correspondance générale*, 5 vols, ed. A. Joubin.

1472 DELBOURGO, S. and PETIT, J. 1960. 'Application de l'analyse microscopique et chimique à quelques tableaux de Poussin', *Bulletin du Laboratoire du Musée du Louvre*, V.

1473 [DIGBY, SIR K.]. 1658. *Two Treatises: in the one of which, the Nature of Bodies . . . is looked into . . .* (1644), 2nd edn.

1474 DITTMANN, L. 1987. *Farbgestaltung und Farbtheorie in der abendländischen Malerei*.

1475 DORRA, H. and REWALD, J. 1959. *Seurat*.

1476 DULON, G. and DUVIVIER, C. 1991. *Louis Hayet. 1864–1940*.

1477 ENGASS, R. 1964. *The Painting of Baciccio: Giovanni Battista Gaulli, 1639–1709*.

1478 *The European Face of Isaac Newton*. 1973/4. Cambridge, Fitzwilliam Museum, exh. cat.

1479 FELLER, R. L. 1973. 'Rubens's *The Gerbier Family*: technical examination of the pigments and paint layers', Washington, National Gallery of Art, *Studies in the History of Art*.

1480 — and STENIUS, A. 1970. 'On the color space of Sigfrid Forsius 1611', *Color Engineering*, VIII, 3.

1481 FÉNÉON, F. 1970. *Oeuvres plus que complètes*, 2 vols, ed. J. Halperin.

1482 FORBES, J. D. 1849. 'Hints towards a classification of colours', *Philosophical Magazine*, 3rd ser., XXXIV.

1483 FORSIUS, S. A. 1952. *Physica*, ed. J. Nordström, *Uppsala Universitäts Årsskrift*, X.

1484 FORSTER, T. 1823. *Researches about Atmospheric Phenomena*, 3rd edn.

1485 FRIEDMAN, J. M. 1978. *Color Printing in England, 1486–1870*, New Haven, Yale Center for British Art.

1486 FROENTJES, W. 1969. 'Schilderde Rembrandt op goud?', *Oud Holland*, LXXXIV.

1487 GAGE, J. 1969. 'A note on Rembrandt's "Meeste ende die natureelste Beweechgelickheijt"', *Burlington Magazine*, CXI.

1488 —. 1983. 'Newton and painting' in M. Pollock (ed.), *Common Denominators in Art and Science*.

1489 —. 1984. 'Colour and its history', *Interdisciplinary Science Reviews*, IX.

1490 —. 1986. 'Jacob Christoph Le Blon', *Print Quarterly*, III.

1491 —. 1987. 'The *technique* of Seurat: a reappraisal', *Art Bulletin*, LXIX.

1492 GEFFROY, G. 1922. *Claude Monet*.

1493 GLISSON, FRANCIS. 1677. *Tractatus de Ventriculo et Intestinis*, London.

1494 GOCLENIUS, R. (THE ELDER). 1613. *Lexicon Philosophicum*, (facsimile repr. 1964).

1495 GODWIN, J. 1979. *Robert Fludd: Hermetic Philosopher and Surveyor of Two Worlds*.

1496 GONCOURT, E. and J. DE 1948. *French XVIII Century Painters*, trans. R. Ironside.

1497 GOWING, L. 1974. 'Nature and the ideal in the art of Claude', *Art Quarterly*, XXXVII.

1498 GREAVES, J. and JOHNSON, M. 1974. 'Technical studies relating to the attribution of Caravaggio's *The Conversion of the Magdalene* in the Detroit Institute of Arts', *Bulletin of the American Institute for Conservation*, XIV, 2.

1499 GROEN, K. 1977. 'Technical aspects of Rembrandt's earliest paintings: microscopical observations and the analysis of paint samples', *Oud Holland*, XCI.

1500 GUERLAC, H. 1971. 'An Augustan monument: the *Opticks* of Sir Isaac Newton' in P. Hughes and D. Williams (eds), *The Varied Pattern: Studies in the Eighteenth Century*.

1501 GUÉROULT, G. 1882. 'Formes, couleurs, mouvements', *Gazette des Beaux-Arts*, 2e pér., XXV.

1502 HALPERIN, J. U. 1988. *Felix Fénéon, Aesthete and Anarchist in Fin-de Siècle Paris*.

1503 *Frans Hals*. 1989. Washington, National Gallery.

1504 HARLEY, R. D. 1982. *Artists' Pigments, c. 1600–1835*, 2nd edn.

1505 HARRIS, J. 1708–10. *Lexicon Technicum, or, An Universal English Dictionary of Arts and Sciences*, 2 vols, London.

1506 HASKELL, F. 1967. 'The apotheosis of Newton in art', *Texas Quarterly*, X.

1507 HAUKE, C. DE and BRAME, P. 1961. *Seurat et son oeuvre*, 2 vols.

1508 HAYTER, J. 1826. *A New Practical Treatise on the Three Primitive Colours*.

1509 HELD, J. 1979. 'Rubens and Aguilonius: new points of contact', *Art Bulletin*, LXI.

1510 HELMHOLZ, H. VON. 1867. *Optique physiologique*.

1511 —. 1900. 'On the relation of optics to painting' in *Popular Lectures on Scientific Subjects*, II, trans. E. Atkinson.

1512 HERBERT, R. L. 1962. *Barbizon Revisited*.

1513 —. 1970. 'Seurat's theories', in J. Sutter (ed.), *The Neo-Impressionists*.

1514 —, CACHIN, F., DISTEL, A., STEIN, S. A. and TINTEROW, G. 1991. *Georges Seurat, 1859–1891*, New York, Metropolitan Museum of Art.

1515 HIBBARD, H. 1983. *Caravaggio*.

1516 HILER, H. 1969. *Notes on the Technique of Painting*, rev. edn.

1517 HOMER, W. I. 1970. *Seurat and the Science of Painting*, 2nd edn.

1518 HOOGSTRATEN, S. VAN. 1678. *Inleyding tot de hooge Schoole der Schilderkonst*, Rotterdam (facsimile repr. 1969).

1519 HOOKE, R. 1961. *Micrographia* (1665).

1520 HOWELL, J. B. 1982. 'Eugène Delacroix and color: practice, theory and legend', *Athanor* (Florida State University), II.

1521 IMDAHL, M. 1987. *Farbe: Kunsttheoretische Reflexionen aus Frankreich*.

1522 JAEGER, W. 1976. *Die Illustrationen des Peter Paul Rubens zum Lehrbuch der Optik des Franciscus Aguilonius*.

1523 JAFFÉ, M. 1971. 'Rubens and optics: some fresh evidence', *Journal of the Warburg and Courtauld Institutes*, XXXIV.

1524 JAMIN, J. 1857. 'L'Optique de la peinture', *Revue des Deux Mondes*, XXVII, 2e pér., VII.

1525 JOHNSON, L. 1965. 'Two sources of oriental motifs copied by Delacroix', *Gazette des Beaux-Arts*, 6e pér., LXV.

1526 —. 1978. 'Towards Delacroix's oriental sources', *Burlington Magazine*, CXX.

1527 JUDSON, J. R. and VAN DE VELDE, C. 1978. *Book Illustrations and Title-Pages* (*Corpus Rubenianum Ludwig Burchard*, XXI).

1528 KAUFMANN, T. DA C. 1975. 'The perspective of shadows: the history of the theory of shadow projection', *Journal of the Warburg and Courtauld Institutes*, XXXVIII.

1529 KEMP, M. 1990. *The Science of Art: Optical Themes in Western Art from Brunelleschi to Seurat*.

1530 KEPLER, J. 1980. *Les Fondements de l'optique moderne: paralipomènes à Vitellion, (1604)*, trans. C. Chevalley.

1531 KIRCHER, A. 1646. *Ars Magis Lucis et Umbrae*, Rome.

1532 KLERK, E. A. DE. 1982. 'De Teechen-Const, een 17de eeuws Nederlands traktaatje', *Oud Holland*, XCVI.

1533 KUEHNI, R. G. 1981. 'What the educated person knew about color A.D. 1700', *Color Research and Application*, VI.

1534 KÜHN, H. 1968. 'A study of the pigments and the grounds used by Jan Vermeer', Washington, National Gallery of Art, *Report and Studies in The History of Art*, II.

1535 —. 1976. 'Untersuchungen zu den Pigmenten und Malgründen Rembrandts, durchgeführt an den Gemälden der Staatlichen Kunstsammlungen Kassel', *Maltechnick/Restauro*, LXXXII.

1536 —. 1977. 'Untersuchungen zu den Pigmenten und Malgründen Rembrandts, durchgeführt an den Gemälden der Staatlichen Kunstsammlungen Dresden', *Maltechnik/Restauro*, LXXXIII.

1537 KUTSCHERA-WOBORSKY, O. 1919. 'Ein kunsttheoretische Thesenblatt Carlo Marattas und seine ästhetische Anschauungen', *Mitteilungen der Gesellschaft für vervielfältigende Kunst*.

1538 LACOUTURE, C. 1890. *Répertoire chromatique*.

1539 LAIRESSE, G. DE. 1778. *The Art of Painting* (1738), 2nd edn, London.

1540 LAMBERT, J. H. 1760. *Photometria, sive de Mensura et Gradibus Luminis, Colorum et Umbrae*, Augsburg.

1541 LAMBERT, S. 1987. *The Image Multiplied: Five Centuries of Printed Reproductions of Paintings and Drawings*.

1542 LAUGEL, A. 1869. *L'Optique et les arts*.

1543 LE BLON, J. C. [1725]. *Coloritto; or the Harmony of Colouring in Painting reduced to Mechanical Practice, under Easy Precepts, and Infallible Rules* [London].

1544 LEE, A. 1987. 'Seurat and Science', *Art History*, X.

1545 LERSCH, T. 1984. 'Von der Entomologie zur Kunsttheorie', *De Arte et Libris: Festschrift Erasmus 1934–1984*.

1546 LILIEN, O. 1985. *Jacob Christophe Le Blon, 1667–1741. Inventor of Three and Four-Colour Printing*.

1547 LINNAEUS (KARL VON LINNÉ). 1938. *Critica Botanica* (1737), trans. A. Hort and M. L. Green.

1548 LOCKE, J. 1975. *An Essay Concerning Human Understanding* (4th edn 1700), ed. P. H. Nidditch.

1549 MACADAM, D. L. (ed.). 1970. *Sources of Color Science*.

1550 MCKIM SMITH, G., ANDERSON-BERGDOLL, G. and NEWMAN, R. 1988. *Examining Velasquez*.

1551 MAHON, D. 1947. *Studies in Seicento Art and Theory*.

1552 MALVASIA, C. 1841. *Felsina Pittrice* (1678), 2 vols, 2nd edn.

1553 MANCINI, G. 1956. *Considerazioni sulla Pittura*, 2 vols, ed. A. Marucchi.

1554 MARCUSSEN, M. 1979. 'Duranty et les Impressionistes, II', *Hafnia*, VI.

1555 MAREK, J. 1969. 'Newton's report ("New Theory about Light and Colours") and its relation to results of his predecessors', *Physis*, XI.

1556 MATSCHE, F. 1984. 'Delacroix als Deckenmaler', *Zeitschrift für Kunstgeschichte*, XLVII, 2.

1557 MATTHAEI, R. 1962. 'Complementäre Farben: zur Geschichte und Kritik eines Begriffes', *Neue Hefte zur Morphologie*, IV.

1558 MAXWELL, J. CLERK. I, 1990. *The*

Scientific Papers of James Clerk Maxwell, ed. P. M. Harman.
1559 MAYERNE, THEODORE TURQUET DE. n.d. *Le Manuscrit de Turquet de Mayerne*, ed. C. Versini and N. Faidutti.
1560 MEYERSON, I. (ed.). 1957. *Problèmes de la couleur*.
1561 MINERVINO, F. 1972. *L'Opera completa di Seurat*.
1562 MOLIÈRE (JEAN BAPTISTE POQUELIN). X, 1949. *Oeuvres complètes*, ed. G. Michaut.
1563 MURDOCH, R. T. 1958. 'Newton and the French Muse', *Journal of the History of Ideas*, XIX.
1564 NICOLSON, M. H. 1946. *Newton Demands the Muse: Newton's "Opticks" and the Eighteenth-Century Poets*.
1565 PACE, C. 1981. *Félibien's Life of Poussin*.
1566 PADGHAM, C. A. and SAUNDERS, J. E. 1975. *The Perception of Light and Colour*.
1567 PARKHURST, C. and FELLER, R. L. 1982. 'Who invented the color-wheel?', *Color Research and Application*, VII.
1568 PIPONNIER, F. 1970. *Costume et vie sociale. La Cour d'Anjou, XIVᵉ–XVᵉ siècle*.
1569 PIRON, A. 1865. *Delacroix, sa vie et ses oeuvres*.
1570 *Pissarro*. 1981. Paris, Grand Palais, exh. cat.
1571 PLANET, LOUIS DE. 1928. *Souvenirs*, ed. A. Joubin, *Bulletin de la Société de l'Histoire de l'Art Français*, II.
1572 PLESTERS, J. 1968. 'Tintoretto's paintings in the National Gallery, II: Materials and Techniques', *National Gallery Technical Bulletin*, IV.
1573 —. 1983. '"Samson and Delilah": Rubens and the art and craft of painting on panel', *National Gallery Technical Bulletin*, VII.
1574 —. 1987. 'The materials and techniques of the "Peepshow" in relation to Hoogstraten's book', *National Gallery Technical Bulletin*, XI.
1575 — and MAHON, D. 1965. 'The dossier of a picture: Nicholas Poussin's "Rebecca al Pozzo"', *Apollo*, LXXXI.
1576 POIRIER, M. 1979. 'Pietro da Cortona e il dibattito disegno-colore', *Prospettiva*, XVI.
1577 POLLACK, O. II, 1931. *Die Kunsttätigkeit unter Urban VIII*.
1578 PRINS, J. 1987. 'Kepler, Hobbes and Mediaeval Optics', *Philosophia Naturalis*, XXIV.
1579 REES-JONES, S. 1960. 'Notes on radiographs of five paintings by Poussin', *Burlington Magazine*, CII.
1580 REGNIER, J.-D. 1865. *De la lumière et da la couleur chez les grands maîtres anciens*.
1581 REHFUS-DECHÊNE, B. 1982. *Farbengebung und Farbenlehre in der deutschen Malerei um 1800*.
1582 REPTON, H. 1803. *Observations on the Theory and Practice of Landscape Gardening*.
1583 RESTOUT, J. 1863. *Essai sur les principes de la peinture*, ed. A.-R. R. de Formigny de la Lande (Caen).
1584 REUTERSVÄRD, O. 1950. 'The Violettomania of the Impressionists', *Journal of Aesthetics and Art Criticism*, IX.
1585 REY, R. 1931. *La Renaissance du sentiment classique*.
1586 ROSENFELD, M. N. 1981. *Largillière and the eighteenth-century French Portrait*, Montreal, Museum of Fine Arts.
1587 ROSENTHAL, D. A. 1977. 'A Mughal portrait copied by Delacroix', *Burlington Magazine*, CXIX.

1588 ROSENTHAL, L. 1914. *Du Romantisme au réalisme*.
1589 ROSETTI, G. 1969. *The Plictho of Giovanventura Rosetti*, ed. and trans. S. M. Edelstein and H. C. Borghetty.
1590 RÖTTGEN, H. 1964. 'Giuseppe Cesari, die Contarini-Kapelle und Caravaggio', *Zeitschrift für Kunstgeschichte*, XXVII.
1591 —. 1965. 'Die Stellung der Contarini-Kapelle in Caravaggios Werk', *Zeitschrift für Kunstgeschichte*, XXVIII.
1592 RUMFORD, B. THOMPSON, COUNT. 1802. *Philosophical Papers*, I.
1593 RUSSELL, J. 1965. *Seurat*.
1594 RZEPIŃSKA, M. 1986. 'Tenebrism in Baroque painting and its ideological background', *Artibus & Historiae*, VII.
1595 SANDRART, J. VON. 1925. *Academie der Bau-Bild- und Mahlerey-Künste* (1675), ed. A. R. Peltzer.
1596 SCHEUCHZER, J. J. I, 1731. *Physica Sacra*, Augsburg and Ulm.
1597 SCOPOLI, G. A. 1763. *Entomologia Carnioloca*, Vienna.
1598 SCOTT, M. 1981. *The History of Dress Series: Late Gothic Europe, 1400–1500*.
1599 SEIDLER, L. 1875. *Erinnerungen und Leben*, ed. H. Uhde.
1600 SÉRULLAZ, M. 1963. *Les Peintures murales de Delacroix*.
1601 SEYMOUR, C. 1964. 'Dark chamber and light-filled room. Vermeer and the camera obscura', *Art Bulletin*, XLVI.
1602 SHAPIRO, A. E. 1980. 'The evolving structure of Newton's theory of white light and color', *Isis*, LXXI.
1603 —. I, 1984. *The Optical Papers of Isaac Newton*.
1604 SHAW, P. 1755. *Chemical Lectures*.
1605 SHEON, A. 1971. 'French art and science in the mid-nineteenth century: some points of contact', *Art Quarterly*, XXXIV/4.
1606 SHERMAN, P. D. 1981. *Colour Vision in the Nineteenth Century: The Young-Helmholtz-Maxwell Theory*.
1607 SIGNAC, P. 1964. *D'Eugène Delacroix au néo-impressionnisme* (1899), ed. F. Cachin.
1608 SILVESTRE, T. 1926. *Les Artistes français*, 2 vols, 2nd edn.
1609 SOEHNER, H. 1955. 'Velasquez und Italien', *Zeitschrift für Kunstgeschichte*, XVIII.
1610 SONNENBURG, H. VON 1970. 'The technique and conservation of a portrait', *Metropolitan Museum Bulletin*, XXXI.
1611 —. 1976. 'Maltechnische Gesichtspunkte zur Rembrandtforschung', *Maltechnik/Restauro*, LXXXII, 1.
1612 SPEAR, R. 1982. *Domenichino*.
1613 SPECTOR, J. 1967. *The Murals of Eugène Delacroix at Saint-Sulpice*.
1614 SPEZZAFERRO, L. 1971. 'La cultura di Cardinale dal Monte e il primo tempo del Caravaggio', *Storia dell'Arte*, IX, 10.
1615 SPINNER, K. H. 1971. 'Helldunkel un Zeitlichkeit. Caravaggio, Ribera, Zurbaran, de la Tour, Rembrandt', *Zeitschrift für Kunstgeschichte*, XXXIV.
1616 SPRAT, T. 1959. *History of the Royal Society* (1667).
1617 SUTTER, D. 1880. 'Les phénomènes de la vision', *L'Art*, XX.
1618 SYMES, P. 1821. *Werner's Nomenclature of Colours, adapted to Zoology, Botany, Chemistry, Mineralogy, Anatomy and the Arts*, 2nd edn.
1619 TAYLOR, BROOK. 1719. *New*

Principles of Linear Perspective . . . 2nd edn, London.
1620 TEYSSÈDRE, B. 1965. *Roger de Piles et les débats sur le coloris au siècle de Louis XIV*.
1621 THEOPHILUS. 1963. *On Divers Arts*, trans. J. G. Hawthorne and C. S. Smith.
1622 THOMPSON, D. 1985. *Seurat*.
1623 TORRITI, C. 1973. *Ristauri nelle Marche*.
1624 TURNBULL, G. 1740. *A Treatise on Ancient Painting*, London.
1625 TURNER, N. 1971. 'Ferrante Carlo's *Descrittione della Cupola di S. Andrea della Valle depinta da Cavalier Gios. Lanfranchi* (1627/8): a source for Bellori's descriptive method', *Storia dell'Arte*, XII.
1626 VAN GOGH, V. 1958. *Collected Letters*, 3 vols.
1627 VELIZ, Z. 1981. 'A painter's technique: Zurbaran's *The Holy House of Nazareth*', *Bulletin of the Cleveland Museum of Art*, LXVIII.
1628 —. 1986. *Artists' Techniques in Golden Age Spain*.
1629 VENTURI, G. B. 1801. *Indagine fisica sui colori*, 2nd edn.
1630 VÉRON, E. 1879. *Aesthetics*.
1631 VOLLARD, A. 1938. *En Écoutant Cézanne, Degas, Renoir*.
1632 VOSSIUS, I. 1662. *De Lucis Natura et Proprietate*, Amsterdam.
1633 VRIES, A. B. DE, TOTH-UBBENS, M. and FRONTJES, W. 1978. *Rembrandt in the Mauritshuis*.
1634 WAGNER, W. 1967. *Die Geschichte der Akademie der Bildenden Künste in Wien*.
1635 WALLER, R. 1686. 'A catalogue of simple and mixt colours', *Philosophical Transactions of the Royal Society*, XVI.
1636 WATELET, M. and LEVESQUE, M. I, 1792. *Dictionnaire des Arts de Peinture*, Paris, 5 vols.
1637 WEALE, R. A. 1972. 'The tragedy of pointillism', *Palette*, XL.
1638 WESTFALL, R. S. 1962. 'The development of Newton's theory of colours', *Isis*, LIII.
1639 —. 1962/5. 'Isaac Newton's coloured circles twixt two contiguous glasses', *Archive for the History of Exact Sciences*, II.
1640 WETERING, E. VAN DE. 1977. 'The young Rembrandt at work', *Oud Holland*, XCI.
1641 —, GROEN, C. M. and MOSK, J. A. 1976. 'Summary report of the results of the technical examination of Rembrandt's *Night Watch*', *Bulletin van het Rijksmuseum*, LXXXIV.
1642 WILLIAMS, W. 1787. *An Essay on the Mechanic of Oil Colours*, Bath.
1643 ZAHN, J. 1658. *Oculus Artificialis Teledioptricus . . . Würzburg*.
1644 ZIGGELAAR, A. 1983. *François d'Aguilón S. J. Scientist and Architect*.

10 The Palette

1645 ARMENINI, G. B. 1988. *De' Veri Precetti della Pittura* (1587), ed. M. Gorreri (Eng. trans. E. J. Olszewski, 1977).
1646 AYRES, J. 1985. *The Artist's Craft*.
1647 BATE, J. 1977. *The Mysteries of Nature and Art* (1663).
1648 BATICLE, J., GEORGEL, P. and WILLK-BROCARD, N. 1976. *Technique de la Peinture – l'atelier* (Musée du Louvre, Les Dossiers du Département des Peintures).
1649 BAZIN, G., HOURS, M., PETIT, J. and RUDEL, J. 1958. 'Une palette du XIVᶜ

siècle decouverte sur un panneau du Musée du Louvre', *Bulletin du Laboratoire du Musée de Louvre*, III.
1650 BEAL, M. 1984. *A Study of Richard Symonds: his Italian Notebooks and their Relevance to Seventeenth-Century Painting Techniques*.
1651 BEHRENDS, R. and KOBER, K.-M. 1973. *The Artist and his Studio*.
1652 BELLONY-REWALD, A. and PEPPIATT, M. 1983. *Imagination's Chamber: Artists and their Studios*.
1653 BON, J.-B., MARQUIS BOUTARD. 1826. *Dictionnaire des arts du dessin*.
1654 BONAFOUX, P. 1985. *Portraits of the Artist*.
1655 BOUVIER, P. L. 1828. *Manuel des jeunes artistes et amateurs en peinture*, (1827), Ger. trans. *Vollständige Anweisung zur Oehlermalerei für Künstler und Kunstfreunde*.
1656 BOYLE-TURNER, C. 1983. *Paul Sérusier*.
1657 BRUYN, J. DE, HAAK, B., VAN THIEL, J. and van de WETERING, E. 1982. *A Corpus of Rembrandt Paintings*, I, 1625–31.
1658 CAREY, W. 1809. *Letter to Ixxx Axxxxx A Connoisseur in London*, Manchester.
1659 *Chardin*. 1979. Paris, Grand Palais, exh. cat.
1660 CONSTABLE, W. G. 1954. *Richard Wilson*.
1661 COOPER, H. A. 1982. *John Trumbull: the Hand and Spirit of a Painter*, New Haven, Yale University Art Gallery, exh. cat.
1662 CORRI, A. 1983. 'Gainsborough's early career: new documents and two portraits', *Burlington Magazine*, CXXV.
1663 DELACROIX, E. 1923. *Oeuvres Littéraires*.
1664 —. 1950. *Journal*, 3 vols, ed. A. Joubin.
1665 *Le Dossier d'un tableau: Saint Luc peignant la Vièrge de Martin van Heemskerk*. 1974. Rennes, Musée des Beaux-Arts, exh. cat.
1666 *Encyclopédie Française – Arts et Littératures*, XVI, 1935.
1667 ERPEL, F. 1964. *Van Gogh: the Self Portraits*.
1668 *Fantin-Latour*. 1982. Paris, Grand Palais, exh. cat.
1669 FÉLIBIEN, A. 1725. *Entretiens sur les vies et les ouvrages de plus excellens peintres anciens et modernes* (1666–88) (facsimile repr. 1967).
1670 GAUTIER, H. 1708. *L'Art de laver, ou la nouvelle manière de peindre sur le papier* (1687), 2nd edn.
1671 *The Genius of Venice*. 1983/4. London, Royal Academy, exh. cat.
1672 GIGOUX, J. 1885. *Causeries sur les artistes de mon temps*.
1673 GIMPEL, R. 1927. 'At Giverny with Claude Monet', *Art in America*, XV.
1674 GOODING, D., PINCH, T. and SCHAFFER, S. 1989. *The Uses of Experiment: Studies in The Natural Sciences*.
1675 GUICHETEAU, M. 1976. *Paul Sérusier*.
1676 HAESERTS, P. 1957. *James Ensor*.
1677 HARLEY, R. D. 1971. 'Oil-colour containers; development work by artists and colourmen in the nineteenth century', *Annals of Science*, XXVII.
1678 HAVEL, M. 1979. *La Technique du tableau*, 2nd edn.
1679 *Herbst des Mittelalters*. 1970. Cologne, Kunsthalle, exh. cat.

1680 HOPPNER, J. 1908. *Essays on Art*, ed. F. Rutter.
1681 HOUSE, J. 1986. *Monet: Nature into Art*.
1682 HUET, R. P. (ed.). 1911. *Paul Huet*.
1683 HUNDERTPFUND, L. 1849. *The Art of Painting restored to its Simplest and Surest Principles*.
1684 JACKSON-STOPS, G. 1985. *The Treasure House of Britain*, Washington, National Gallery.
1685 KANDINSKY, W. I, 1980. *Die gesammelte Schriften*, ed. H. Roethel and J. Hahl-Koch.
1686 —. 1982. *Complete Writings on Art*, 2 vols, ed. and trans. K. Lindsay and P. Vergo.
1687 KAUFMANN, R. C. 1974. 'The photo-archive of color palettes', *Yale University Library Gazette*, XLIX.
1688 KIRBY TALLEY, M. 1981. *Portrait Painting in England: Studies in the Technical Literature before 1700*.
1689 — and K. Groen. 1975. 'Thomas Bardwell and his Practice of Painting', *Studies in Conservation*, XX.
1690 KLEE, F. 1962. *Paul Klee: his Life and Work in Documents*.
1691 KLEE, P. 1957. *Diaries*, ed. F. Klee.
1692 KÜHN, H. 1977. 'Farbmaterial und technischer Aufbau der Gemälde von Niklaus Manuel', *Maltechnik*, LXXXIII.
1693 LABORDE, COMTE DE 1851. *Les Ducs de Bourgogne: études sur les lettres, les arts et l'industrie pendant le XVe siècle*, Pt II, vol. II.
1694 LANDSEER, T. (ed.). 1978. *Life and Letters of William Bewick (Artist)* (1871), 2 vols.
1695 LANE, C. W. and STEINITZ, K. 1942. 'Palette Index', *Art News*, XLI.
1696 LAUGIER, M.-A. 1972. *Manière de bien juger des ouvrages de peinture* (1771).
1697 LEVITINE, G. 1978. *The Dawn of Bohemianism*.
1698 LOWENTHAL, A. 1986. *Joachim Wtewael and Dutch Mannerism*.
1699 McCOLL, D. S. 1902. *Nineteenth-Century Art*.
1700 McCOUBREY, J. 1964. 'The revival of Chardin in French still-life painting', *Art Bulletin*, XLVI.
1701 *Manners and Morals: Hogarth and British Painting, 1700–1760*. 1987. London, Tate Gallery, exh. cat.
1702 MATISSE, H. 1972. *Écrits et propos sur l'art*, ed. D. Fourcade.
1703 MATHIEU, P.-L. 1977. *Gustave Moreau: Complete Edition of the Finished Paintings, Watercolours and Drawings*.
1704 MIEDEMA, H. 1987. 'Over kwaliteitsvoorschriften in het St. Lukasgilde; over doodverf', *Oud Holland*, CI.
1705 MOFFETT, C. S. 1986. *The New Painting: Impressionism 1874–1886*.
1706 MOREAU-VAUTHIER, C. 1923. *Comment on peint aujourd'hui*.
1707 MORLEY FLETCHER, C. 1936. *Colour-Control. The Organisation and Control of the Artist's Palette*.
1708 MORSE, C. R. 1923. 'Matisse's Palette', *Art Digest*, VII.
1709 OUDRY, J.-B. 1861. 'Discours sur la pratique de la peinture', *Cabinet de l'amateur*, N.S.
1710 PENNELL, E. R. and J. 1908. *The Life of James McNeill Whistler*.
1711 PERIER D'IETEREN, C. 1985. *Colÿn de Coter*.
1712 PICART, Y. 1987. *La Vie et l'oeuvre de Jean-Baptiste Corneille*.
1713 [PILES, ROGER DE] 1684. *Les*

Premiers élémens de la peinture pratique (facsimile edn 1973).
1714 PIOT, R. 1931. *Les Palettes de Delacroix*.
1715 POSNER, A. 1971. *Annibale Carracci: A Study of the Reform of Italian Painting around 1590*.
1716 *Prag um 1600*. 1988. Essen, Villa Hügel, exh. cat.
1717 PUY DE GREZ, B. DU. 1700. *Traité sur la peinture pour en apprendre la théorie et se perfectionner dans la pratique*, Paris.
1718 REDON, O. 1979. *À Soi-même: Journal 1867–1915*.
1719 REWALD, J. 1973. *The History of Impressionism*, 4th edn.
1720 —. 1978. *Post-Impressionism from Van Gogh to Gauguin*, 2nd edn.
1721 RICHARDSON, E. P., HINDLE, B. and MILLER, C. B. 1982. *Charles Willson Peale and his World*.
1722 ROBERT, K. (G. MEUSNIER) 1891. *Traité pratique de la peinture à huile (paysage)*, 5th edn.
1723 ROUART, D. 1945. *Degas à la recherche de sa technique*.
1724 SCHMID, F. 1948. *The Practice of Painting*.
1725 SÉRUSIER, P. 1950. *ABC de la Peinture*, 3rd edn.
1726 SHIFF, R. 1984. *Cézanne and the End of Impressionism*.
1727 SIMSON, O. VON 1968. *Il Ciclo di Maria de' Medici*.
1728 SLIVE, S. 1970–74. *Frans Hals*, 3 vols.
1729 SMITH, P. 1991. 'Was Seurat's art Wagnerian? And what if it was?', *Apollo*, CXXXIV.
1730 STOUT, G. L. 1933. 'A study of the method in a Flemish painting', *Technical Studies in the Field of Fine Arts*, I.
1731 SUMOWSKI, G. I, 1983. *Gemälde der Rembrandt-Schüler*.
1732 THÉNOT, J.-P. 1847. *Des Règles de la peinture à l'huile*.
1733 VENZMER, E. 1967. *J. B. Oudry: Farbige Gemäldewiedergaben*.
1734 VIBERT, J.-G. 1892. *La Science de la peinture* (1891), 1902 (repr. 1981), Eng. trans., from the 8th edn.
1735 —. 1895/6. *The Delights of Art*, *Century Magazine*, XXIX.
1736 VOLLARD, A. 1959. *Souvenirs d'un marchand de tableaux*, 3rd edn.
1737 WATKINS, N. 1984. *Matisse*.
1738 WELSH-OVCHAROV, B. 1976. *Vincent van Gogh: his Paris Period, 1886–1888*.
1739 WHITLEY, W. T. 1968. *Artists and their Friends in England*.
1740 WILLIAMS, H. W. 1937. 'Romney's Palette', *Technical Studies in the Field of Fine Arts*, VI.

11 Colours of the Mind

1741 ALLESCH, G. J. VON. 1925. 'Die ästhetische Erscheinungsweise der Farben', *Psychologische Studien*, VI.
1742 AMRINE, F., ZUCKER, F. J. and WHEELER, H. 1987. *Goethe and the Sciences: a Reappraisal*.
1743 ANDERSON, M. 1979. *Colour-Healing: Cromotherapy and how it Works*.
1744 *Archivi del Futurismo*. 1958. Ed. M. Drudi Gambillo and T. Fiori, 2 vols.
1745 *Archivi del Divisionismo*. 1968. Ed. T. Fiori.
1746 ARIOTTI, P. E. 1973. 'A little-known early seventeenth-century treatise on vision: Benedetto Castelli's 'Discorso sopra la Vista', *Annals of Science*, XXX.

1747 *Ausstellung deutscher Kunst aus der Zeit von 1775–1875*. 1906. Berlin.
1748 AUTRET, J. 1965. *Ruskin and the French before Marcel Proust*.
1749 BADT, K. 1943. 'Cézanne's watercolour technique', *Burlington Magazine*, LXXXIII.
1750 BÄHR, J. K. 1860. *Der dynamische Kreis*.
1751 BALL, V. K. 1965. 'The aesthetics of color: a review of fifty years' experimentation', *Journal of Aesthetics and Art Criticism*, XXIII.
1752 BARR, A. 1974. *Matisse: his Art and his Public* (1951).
1753 BARRON, S. and TUCHMAN, M. (eds). 1980. *The Avant-Garde in Russia, 1910–1930: a New Perspective*.
1754 BARRON-COHEN, S., WYKE, M. A. and BINNIE, C. 1987. 'Hearing words and seeing colours: an experimental investigation of a case of synaesthesia', *Perception*, XVI.
1755 BAXANDALL, M. 1985. *Patterns of Intention: on the Historical Explanation of Pictures*.
1756 BECK, J. 1972. *Surface Color Perception*.
1757 BELAIEW-EXEMPLARSKY, S. 1925. 'Über die sogenannten "hervortretenden Farben" ' *Zeitschrift für Psychologie*, XCVI.
1758 BERGER, E. 1911. 'Goethes Farbenlehre und die modernen Theorien', *Die Kunst*, XXIII.
1759 BERNARD, E. 1934. 'Louis Anquetin', *Gazette des Beaux-Arts*, XL.
1760 BERNARDIN DE SAINT-PIERRE, J. H. 1818. *Oeuvres complètes*, 12 vols.
1761 BEUCKEN, J. DE. 1955. *Un Portrait de Cézanne*.
1762 BEUTHER, F. 1833. *Ueber Licht und Farbe, die prismatischen Farben und die Newton'sche Farbenlehre*, Weimar.
1763 BINET, A. 1892. 'Le problème de l'audition colorée', *Revue des Deux Mondes*, CXIII.
1764 BLANKERT, A. ET AL. 1980. *Gods, Saints and Heroes: Dutch Painting in the Age of Rembrandt*, Washington, National Gallery.
1765 BOCK, C. C. 1981. *Henri Matisse and Neo-Impressionism, 1898–1908*.
1766 BOMFORD, D. ET AL. 1990. *Art in the Making: Impressionism*, London, National Gallery.
1767 BORING, E. G. 1942. *Sensation and Perception in the History of Experimental Psychology*.
1768 BORNSTEIN, M. H. 1976. 'Name codes and color memory', *American Journal of Psychology*, LXXXIX.
1769 BORSCH, R. 1941. *Schopenhauer: sein Leben in Selbstzeugnissen, Briefen und Berichte*.
1770 BOUILLON, J.-P. 1970. 'Une visite de Félix Bracquemond à Gaston La Touche', *Gazette des Beaux-Arts*, LXXV.
1771 BOYER D'AGEN. 1909. *Ingres d'après une correspondance inédite*.
1772 BRACQUEMOND, F. 1885. *Du Dessin et de la couleur*.
1773 BRASS, A. 1906. *Untersuchungen über das Licht und die Farben*, I Teil (no more published).
1774 BRATRANEK, F. T. 1874. *Goethes naturwissenschaftliche Correspondenz*, 2 vols.
1775 BRIGANTI, G. ET AL. 1987. *Gli Amori degli Dei: nuovi indagini sulla Galleria Farnese*.
1776 BRISSOT DE WARVILLE, J. P. 1877. *Mémories*, ed. M. de Lescure.

1777 BROUWER, J. W. ET AL. 1974. *Anton van Rappard*.
1778 BRÜCKE, E. 1852. 'Über die Farben, welche trübe Medien im auffallenden und durchfallenden Lichte zeigen', *Sitzungsberichte der Wiener Akademie der Wissenschaften (Mathematische-Naturwissenschaftliche Klasse)* IX.
1779 BRÜES, E. 1961. 'Die Schriften des Francesco Milizia', *Jahrbuch für Ästhetik und allgemeine Kunstwissenschaft*, VI.
1780 BURNET, J. 1845. *Practical Hints on Composition in Painting* (1822), 6th edn.
1781 BURWICK, F. 1986. *The Damnation of Newton: Goethe's Color Theory and Romantic Reception*.
1782 CAMESASCA, E. 1966. *Artisti in bottega*.
1783 CARTIER, J. A. 1963. 'Gustave Moreau, Professeur à l'École des Beaux-Arts', *Gazette des Beaux-Arts*, LXI.
1784 CASSAGNE, A. 1886. *Traité d'aquarelle* (1875), 2nd edn.
1785 CASTEL, L.-B. 1740. *Projet d'une nouvelle optique des couleurs fondée sur les observations et uniquement relative à la peinture, à la teinture et aux autres arts coloristes*, *Mémoires pour l'histoire des sciences et des beaux-arts (Journal de Trévoux)*, April 1739.
1786 CÉZANNE, P. 1976. *Letters*, ed. J. Rewald, 4th edn.
1787 CHASSÉ, C. 1969. *The Nabis and their Period*.
1788 CHU, P. ten-DOESSCHATE. 1982. 'Lecoq de Boisbaudran and memory drawing: a teaching course between idealism and naturalism' in G. P. Weisberg (ed.), *The European Realist Tradition*.
1789 COHN, J. 1894. 'Experimentelle Untersuchungen über die Gefühlsbetonung der Farbenhelligkeiten und ihre Combinationen', *Philosophische Studien*, X.
1790 CONISBEE, P. 1986. *Chardin*.
1791 COOKE, D. 1987. *Collected Works of Velimir Khlebnikov*.
1792 COOPER, D. 1983. *Paul Gauguin: 45 Lettres à Vincent, Théo et Jo Van Gogh*.
1793 CORNILL, A. 1864. *Johann David Passavant*, 2 vols.
1794 COURTHION, P. 1950. *Courbet raconté par lui-même et par ses amis*, 2 vols.
1795 COWART, J. ET AL. 1977. *Henri Matisse Paper Cut-outs*.
1796 —. 1990. *Matisse in Morocco: the Paintings and Drawings, 1912–13*.
1797 CRAIG, W. M. 1821. *A Course of Lectures on Drawing, Painting and Engraving*.
1798 CRONE, R. 1978. 'Zum Suprematismus — Kasimir Malevič, Velemir Chlebnikov und Nicolai Lobačevski', *Wallraf-Richartz Jahrbuch*, XL.
1799 DAMISCH, H. 1982. 'La Géometrie de la couleur' in C. de Pedretti (ed.), *Cézanne, ou la peinture en jeu* (Colloque d'Aix).
1800 DAMMANN, O. 1930. 'Goethe und C. F. Schlosser', *Jahrbuch der Goethe-Gesellschaft*, XVI.
1801 DÉAL, J.-N. 1827. *Nouvel essai sur la lumière et les couleurs ... ouvrage utile aux opticiens et aux peintres ...* (1823), 2nd edn.
1802 DELABORDE, H. 1984. *Notes et pensées de J. A. D. Ingres*.
1803 DERAIN, A. 1955. *Lettres à Vlaminck*.
1804 DEWHURST, W. 1911. 'What is Impressionism?' *Contemporary Review*, XCIX.

1805 DIDEROT, D. and d'ALEMBERT, J. 1751–65. *Encyclopédie*, 17 vols, 2nd edn.

1806 DORAN, M. (ed.). 1978. *Conversations avec Cézanne.*

1807 DUCK, M. J. 1988. 'Newton and Goethe on colour: physical and physiological considerations', *Annals of Science*, XLV.

1808 ELDERFIELD, J. 1978. *Matisse in the Collection of the Museum of Modern Art.*

1809 EYSENCK, H. J. 1941. 'A critical and experimental study of color preferences', *American Journal of Psychology*, LIV.

1810 FAIVRE, E. 1862. *Oeuvres scientifiques de Goethe.*

1811 FELLER, R. L. (ed.). I, 1986. *Artists' Pigments: a Handbook of their History and Characteristics.*

1812 FÉRÉ, C. 1887. *Sensation et mouvement.*

1813 FINEBERG, J. 1979. '*Les Tendances nouvelles*, the Union Internationale des Beaux-Arts, des Lettres, des Sciences et de l'Industrie and Kandinsky', *Art History*, II.

1814 —. 1984. *Kandinsky in Paris, 1906–7.*

1815 FIORILLO, J. D. II, 1800. *Geschichte der zeichnende Künste.*

1816 FLAM, J. 1986. *Matisse: the Man and his Art, 1869–1918.*

1817 FLETCHER, E. (ed.). 1901. *Conversations of James Northcote with James Ward.*

1818 FORICHON, F. 1916. *La Couleur: manuel du coloriste.*

1819 FRANKL, G. R. J. 1975. 'How Cézanne saw and used colour' (1951) in J. Wechsler (ed.), *Cézanne in Perspective.*

1820 FRIEDLÄNDER, S. 1916. 'Nochmals Polarität', *Der Sturm*, VI.

1821 —. 1917/18. 'Das Prisma und Goethes Farbenlehre', *Der Sturm*, VIII.

1822 GAGE, J. 1979. 'Runge, Goethe and the *Farbenkugel*' in H. Hohl (ed.), *Runge Fragen und Antworten.*

1823 —. 1984. 'Turner's annotated books: Goethe's Theory of Colours', *Turner Studies*, IV, 2.

1824 GAUGUIN, P. 1974. *Oviri: écrits d'un sauvage*, ed. D. Guérin.

1825 —. I, 1984. *Correspondance*, ed. V. Merlhès.

1826 *Gauguin.* 1989. Paris, Grand Palais, exh. cat.

1827 GELLER, H. 1961. *C. L. Kaaz: Landschafts-Maler und Freund Goethes, 1773–1810.*

1828 GÉROME-MAËSSE (ALEXIS MÉRODACK-JEANNEAU). 1907. 'L'audition colorée', *Les Tendances nouvelles.*

1829 *Gilberts Annalen der Physik,* XXXIX, 1811.

1830 GIRAUD, V. 1902. *Essai sur Taine.*

1831 GIRAUDY, D. 1971. 'Correspondance Matisse–Camoin', *Revue de l'Art*, XLI.

1832 GOETHE, J. W. VON. 1800. 'Neue Art die Mahlerey zu lernen', *Propyläen* III (repr. 1965).

1833 —. 1840. *Theory of Colours* (1810), trans. C. L. Eastlake.

1834 —. 1919. *Goethes Briefwechsel mit Heinrich Meyer*, ed. M. Hecker (Schriften der Goethe-Gesellschaft XXXIV).

1835 —. 1949. *Goethes Werke: Gedenkausgabe*, ed. E. Beutler, 24 vols.

1836 —. 1971. *Goethe's Colour Theory*, ed. R. Matthaei.

1837 *Goethe, Kirchner, Wiegers: de Invloed van Goethes Kleurenleer.* 1985. Groningen Museum, 2nd edn.

1838 GÖGELEIN, C. 1972. *Zu Goethes Begriff von Wissenschaft auf dem Wege der methodik seiner Farbstudien.*

1839 GOLDSTEIN, K. 1942. 'Some experimental observations concerning the influence of colors on the functions of the organism', *Occupational Therapy and Rehabilitation*, XXI.

1840 GORDON, D. E. 1968. *Ernst Ludwig Kirchner.*

1841 GRANGER, G. W. 1952. 'Objectivity of colour preferences', *Nature*, CLXX.

1842 HAMILTON, G. H. 1984. 'The dying of the light: the late work of Degas, Monet and Cézanne' in J. Rewald and F. Weitzenhoffer (eds), *Aspects of Monet: A Symposium on the Artist's Life and Times.*

1843 HANFSTAENGL, E. 1974. *Wassily Kandinsky, Zeichnungen und Aquarelle. Katalog der Sammlung in der städtischen Galerie im Lenbachhaus, München.*

1844 HARMS, E. 1963. 'My association with Kandinsky', *American Artist*, XXVII.

1845 HEGEL, G. W. VON. VI–IX, 1927. *Sämmtliche Werke*, 26 vols, ed. H. Glockner (1935–75).

1846 —. 1970. *Philosophy of Nature*, ed. and trans. M. J. Petry.

1847 HEIMENDAHL, E. 1961. *Licht und Farbe: Ordnung und Funktion der Farbwelt.*

1848 HEISS, R. 1960. 'Über psychische Farbwirkungen', *Studium Generale*, XIII.

1849 HELMHOLTZ, H. VON. 1901. 'Recent progress in the theory of vision', in *Popular Lectures on Scientific Subjects*, I.

1850 HERBIN, A. 1949. *L'Art non-figuratif-non-objectif.*

1851 HERING, E. 1878. *Die Lehre vom Lichtsinne.*

1852 HESS, W. 1981. *Das Problem der Farbe in den Selbstzeugnissen der Maler von Cézanne bis Mondrian*, 2nd edn.

1853 HOUSE, J. 1986. *Monet: Nature into Art.*

1854 HOWAT, R. D. 1938. *Elements of Chromo-Therapy.*

1855 HOWITT, M. 1886. *Friedrich Overbeck*, 2 vols.

1856 HUBSCHER, A. (ed.). 1960. *Arthur Schopenhauer: Mensch und Philosoph.*

1857 INGRAMS, R. 1970. 'Bachaumont: a Parisian connoisseur of the 18th century', *Gazette des Beaux-Arts*, 6ᵉ sér., LXXV.

1858 JABLONSKI, W. 1930. 'Zum Einfluss der Goetheschen Farbenlehre auf die physiologische und psychologische Optik der Folgezeit', *Archiv für die Geschichte der Mathematik, der Naturwissenschaft und der Technik*, XIII.

1859 JAEGER, W. 1979. 'Goethes Untersuchungen an Farbenblinden', *Heidelberger Jahrbücher*, XXIII.

1860 JACKOBSON, R. 1968. *Child Language, Aphasia and Phonological Universals.*

1861 — and HALLE, M. 1975. *Fundamentals of Language*, 2nd edn.

1862 KAISER, P. K. 1984. 'Physiological response to colour: a critical review', *Color Research and Application*, IX.

1863 KANDINSKY, W. 1984. *Cours du Bauhaus*, ed. P. Sers.

1864 KANE, E. 1983. 'Marie Bracquemond: the artist time forgot', *Apollo*, CXVII.

1865 KAUFFMANN, G. III, 1955–7. 'Studien zum grossen Malerbuch des Gérard de Lairesse', *Jahrbuch für Aesthetik und allgemeine Kunstwissenschaft.*

1866 KLINKOWSTRÖM, A. VON. 1877. *F. A. von Klinkowström und seine Nachkommen.*

1867 KLINKOWSTRÖM, F. VON 1815. 'Über das Wesen der Malerey', *Friedensblätter* II (repr. 1970).

1868 KODERA, T. 1990. *Vincent van Gogh: Christianity versus Nature.*

1869 KRUTA, V. (ed.). 1968. *Básmík & Vědec. Johann Wolfgang Goethe/Jan Evangelista Purkyně.*

1870 *Künstler der Brücke.* 1980. Saarbrücken, Moderne Galerie des Saarland-Museums, exh. cat.

1871 LABORDE, H. 1984. *Notes et pensées de J. A. D. Ingres* (repr. from *Ingres: sa Vie, Ses Travaux, sa Doctrine*, 1870).

1872 LAKOWSKI, R. and MELHUISH, P. 1973. 'Objective analysis of the Lüscher Colour Test', International Colour Association, *Colour 73.*

1873 LANDSBERGER, F. 1931. *Die Kunst der Goethezeit.*

1874 LANKHEIT, K. (ed.). 1974. *The Blaue Reiter Almanac* (1912).

1875 LAUGUI, E. 1947. 'Vincent van Gogh: la technique', *Les Arts Plastiques*, I.

1876 LODDER, C. 1983. *Russian Constructivism.*

1877 LONDON, P. 1984. *In Pursuit of Perfection: the art of J. A. D. Ingres.*

1878 McMANUS, I., JONES, A. C. and COTTRELL, J. 1981. 'The aesthetics of colour', *Perception*, X.

1879 MACKE, W. (ed.). 1964. *August Macke–Franz Marc, Briefwechsel.*

1880 MAHLING, F. 1926. 'Das Problem der "audition colorée"', *Archiv für die gesamte Psychologie*, LVII.

1881 MAIURI, A. 1953. *Roman Painting.*

1882 MALKOWSKY, G. 1899. 'Goethes Farbenlehre und die moderne Malerei', *Moderne Kunst*, XIII.

1883 MANDELKOW, R. K. 1980. *Goethe in Deutschland: Rezeptionsgeschichte eines Klassikers, I, 1773–1918.*

1884 MANTZ, K. 1957. 'Die Farbensprache der expressionistische Lyrik', *Deutsche Vierteljahrschrift für Litteraturwissenschaft und Geistesgeschichte*, XXXI.

1885 MARIANI, V. 1930. *Storia della Scenografia Italiana.*

1886 MARKS, L. E. 1978. *The Unity of the Senses.*

1887 MATILE, H. 1979. *Die Farbenlehre Philipp Otto Runges*, 2nd edn.

1888 MATISSE, H. 1976. 'Autres Propos de Henri Matisse', ed. D. Fourcade, *Macula*, I.

1889 —. 1978. *Matisse on Art*, ed. J. Flam.

1890 MELZER, F. 1978. 'Color as cognition in Symbolist verse', *Critical Inquiry*, V.

1891 MEYER, H. 1799. 'Über Lehranstalten zu Gunsten der bildenden Künste', *Propyläen*, III, ii (repr. 1965).

1892 MILIZIA, F. 1781. *Dell'Arte di vedere nelle Belle Arti del disegno*, Venice (facsimile repr. 1983).

1893 MOFFITT, J. F. 1985. '"Fighting Forms: the Fate of the Animals": the occultist origins of Franz Marc's "Farbentheorie"', *Artibus & Historiae*, XII.

1894 MONGE, G. 1789. 'Mémoire sur quelques phénomènes de la vison', *Annales de Chimie*, III.

1895 —. 1820. *Géométrie descriptive* (1795), 4th edn (repr. 1922).

1896 MONTAUBAN. 1980. *Ingres et son Influence* (Actes du Colloque International).

1897 MORGAN, M. J. 1977. *Molyneux' Question: Vision, Touch and the Philosophy of Perception.*

1898 MÖSENDER, K. 1981. *Philipp Otto Runge und Jakob Böhme.*

1899 MÖTEKAT, H. 1961. 'Variations in Blue', *Yearbook of Comparative and General Literature*, X.

1900 MOTTEZ, V. 1911. *Le Livre de l'art ou Traite de la peinture par Cennino Cennini* (1858), 2nd edn (repr. 1978).

1901 MÜLLER, J. 1826. *Zur vergleichenden Physiologie des Gesichtsinnes.*

1902 —. 1840. *Handbuch der Physiologie des Menschen*, 2 vols, 3rd edn.

1903 MÜLLER-FREIENFELS, R. 1907. 'Zur Theorie der Gefühlstöne der Farbenempfindungen', *Zeitschrift für Psychologie*, XLVI.

1904 NAEF, H. 1964. 'Ingres und die Familie Hittorff', *Pantheon*, XXII.

1905 NIELSEN, K. 'Another kind of light: the work of T. J. Seebeck and his collaboration with Goethe, I', 1989. *Historical Studies in the Physical and Biological Sciences*, XX.

1906 NOCHLIN, L. 1966. *Impressionism and Post-Impressionism, 1874–1904.*

1907 ORTON, F. 1971. 'Vincent's interest in Japanese Prints', *Vincent*, III.

1908 OUDRY, J.-B. 1844. 'Réflexions sur la manière d'étudier la couleur en comparent les objects les unes avec les autres', *Le Cabinet de l'Amateur*, III.

1909 PADRTA, J. 1979. 'Malévitch et Khlebnikov' in J.-C. Marcadé (ed.), *Malévitch: Actes du Colloque International.*

1910 PASTORE, N. 1971. *Selective History of Theories of Visual Perception, 1650–1950.*

1911 —. 1973. 'Helmholtz's Popular Lectures on Vision', *Journal of the History of the Behavioural Sciences*, IX.

1912 —. 1974. 'Re-evaluation of Boring on Kantian influence: nineteenth-century nativism, gestalt psychology, and Helmholtz', *Journal of the History of the Behavioural Sciences*, X.

1913 —. 1978. 'Helmholtz on the projection or transference of sensation' in P. K. Machamer and R. G. Turnbull (eds), *Perception: Interrelationships in the History of Philosophy and Science.*

1914 PERNETY, A. J. 1757. *Dictionnaire Portatif de Peinture; Sculpture et Gravure*, Paris.

1915 PERRY, L. C. 1927. 'Reminiscences of Claude Monet from 1889–1909', *American Magazine of Art*, XVIII.

1916 PETRINI, P. 1807. 'Richerche sulla produzione de colori immaginari nelle ombre', *Memorie della Società Italiana delle Scienze*, XIII, pt II.

1917 —. 1815. *De i colori accidentali della luce, ossia della generazione de i colori ne' vari accidenti d'ombra e di luce*, Pistoia.

1918 —. 1821–2. 'Sulla pittura degli Antichi', *Antologia*, II, III, IV (1821); V, VI, VII (1822), (repr. together 1873).

1919 PETRY, M. J. (ed.). 1987. *Hegel und die Naturwissenschaften.*

1920 PICKFORD, R. W. 1971. 'The Lüscher Test', *Occupational Psychology*, XLV.

1921 PILES, R. DE. 1708. *Cours de Peinture par Principes*, Paris (repr. 1989).

1922 PLATEAU, J. 1878. 'Bibliographie analytique des principeaux phénomènes subjectifs de la vision, depuis les temps anciens jusqu'à la fin du XVIIIᵉ siècle', *Mémoires de l'Académie Royale Belge*, XLIII.

1923 *Post-Impressionism: Cross Currents in European Painting.* 1979/80. London, Royal Academy, exh. cat.

1924 PURKINJE, J. E. 1918. *Beobachtungen und Versuche zur Physiologie der Sinne*, II, 1825. (*Opera Omnia* I).

1925 Pyne, J. B. 1846. 'Letters on Landscape, VI', *The Art Union*, VIII.
1926 Reff, T. 1960. 'Reproductions and books in Cézanne's studio', *Gazette des Beaux-Arts*, LVI.
1927 Rewald. J. 1978. *Post-Impressionism: from van Gogh to Gaugin.*
1928 —. 1985. *Studies in Impressionism.*
1929 —. 1986. *Cézanne: a Biography.*
1930 Ribe, N. M. 1985. 'Goethe's critique of Newton: a reconsideration', *Studies in the History and Philosophy of Science*, XVI.
1931 Richter, M. 1938. *Das Schrifttum über Goethes Farbenlehre.*
1932 Ringbom, S. 1970. *The Sounding Cosmos.*
1933 Roethel, H. K. and Benjamin, J. K. I, 1982. *Kandinsky: Catalogue Raisonné of the Oil Paintings.*
1934 Roskill, M. 1970. *Van Gogh, Gauguin and the Impressionist Circle.*
1935 Rubin, W. (ed.). 1977. *Cézanne: the Late Works.*
1936 Runge, P. O. 1940. *Philipp Otto Runges Briefwechsel mit Goethe*, ed. H. Freiherr von Maltzahn (Schriften der Goethe-Gesellschaft LI).
1937 Ruppert, B. 1958. *Goethes Bibliothek: Katalog.*
1938 Ruskin, J. 1857. *The Elements of Drawing* (repr. 1971).
1939 —. 1906. *Pre-Raphaelitism* (1851) (Everyman edn).
1940 Scheffler, K. 1901. 'Notizen über die Farbe', *Dekorative Kunst*, IV.
1941 Scheidig, W. 1958. *Goethes Preisaufgaben für bildende Künstler* (Schriften der Goethe-Gesellschaft LVII).
1942 Schelling, F. W. I. III, 1959. *Werke*, ed. M. Schröter, III (Ergänzungsband).
1943 Schenk zu Schweinsberg, Eberhard, Freiherrn. 1930. *G. M. Kraus* (Schriften der Goethe-Gesellschaft XLIII).
1944 Scherer, C. 1936. *Zum Briefwechsel zwischen Goethe und Johannes Müller.*
1945 Schlegel, A. W. I, 1962. *Kritische Schriften und Briefe.*
1946 Schmidt, J. H. 1932. 'Zur Farbenlehre Goethes', *Zeitschrift für Kunstgeschichte*, I.
1947 Schmidt, P. 1965. *Goethes Farbensymbolik.*
1948 Schopenhauer, A. 1816. *Über das Sehn und die Farben.*
1949 —. 1851. *Parerga und Paralipomena.*
1950 Scott, I. 1971. *The Lüscher Colour Test.*
1951 Segal, A. 1925. *Lichtprobleme der bildende Kunst.*
1952 Sepper, D. L. 1988. *Goethe contra Newton: Polemics and the Project for a New Science of Colour.*
1953 Serio, G. F., Indorato, L. and Nastali, P. 1983. 'Light colors and the rainbow in Giovanni Battista Hodierna (1597–1660)', *Annali dell' Instituto e Museo di Storia della Scienza di Firenze*, VIII.
1954 Severini, G. 1958. 'La peinture d'avant-garde-II' (1917) in M. Drudi Gambillo and T. Fiori (eds), *Archivi del Futurismo*, I.
1955 Shiff, R. 1978a. 'The end of Impressionism: a study in theories of artistic expression', *Art Quarterly*, N.S., I.
1956 —. 1978b. 'Seeing Cézanne', *Critical Inquiry*, IV.
1957 Stafford, B. M. 1979. *Symbol and Myth: Humbert de Superville's Essay on Absolute Signs in Art.*

1958 Starkie, E. 1961. *Arthur Rimbaud* (1938).
1959 Stefănescu-Goangă, F. 1912. 'Experimentelle Untersuchungen zur Gefühlsbetonung der Farben', *Psychologische Studien*, VII (1911).
1960 Steig, R. 1902. 'Zu Otto Runges Leben und Schriften', *Euphorion*, IX.
1961 Stierlin, H. (ed.). 1981. *The Art of Karl Gerstner.*
1962 Strauss, E. 1983. *Koloritgeschichtliche Untersuchungen zur Malerei seit Giotto*, ed. L. Dittmann, 2nd edn.
1963 Suarez de Mendoza, F. 1890. *L'Audition colorée: étude sur les sensations secondaires physiologiques et particulièrement sur les pseudo-sensations de couleurs associées aux perceptions objectives des sons.*
1964 Sutter, D. 1858. *Philosophie des Beaux-Arts appliquée à la peinture.*
1965 Taine, H. 1870. *De l'Intelligence*, 2 vols, 2nd edn.
1966 Trapp, F. A. 1971. *The Attainment of Delacroix.*
1967 Trevor-Roper, P. 1988. *The World through Blunted Sight*, 2nd edn.
1968 Uitert, E. van 1966–7. 'De toon van Vincent van Gogh: opvattingen over kleur en zijn Hollandse periode', *Simiolus*, II (with English summary).
1969 Vallée, L. L. 1821. *Traité de la science du dessin.*
1970 Vallier, D. 1975. 'Malévitch et le modèle linguistique en peinture', *Critique* XXXI.
1971 *Van Gogh à Paris.* 1988. Paris, Musée d'Orsay, exh. cat.
1972 *Claude Joseph Vernet, 1714–1789.* 1976. Greater London Council.
1973 Watkins, N. 1984. *Matisse.*
1974 Wells, G. A. 1967–8. 'Goethe's scientific methods and aims in the light of his studies in physical optics', *Publications of the English Goethe Society*, XXXVIII.
1975 —. 1971. 'Goethe's qualitative optics', *Journal of the History of Ideas*, XXXII.
1976 Wildenstein, D. 1979. *Claude Monet: Biographie et Catalogue Raisonné*, 4 vols.
1977 Wundt, W. 1902–3. *Grundzüge der Physiologischen Psychologie* (1874), 5th edn, 3 vols.
1978 [Young, T.] 1814. 'Zur Farbenlehre. On the doctrine of colours. By Goethe', *Quarterly Review*, X.
1979 Zastrau, A. (ed.). 1961. *Goethe Handbuch.*
1980 Ziegler, J.-C. 1850. *Études céramiques.*
1981 Zweite, A. (ed.). 1982. *Kandinsky und München: Begegnungen und Wandlungen.*

12 The Substance of Colour

1982 Algarotti, F. 1764. *An Essay on Painting*, London.
1983 Amory, M. B. 1882. *The Domestic and Artistic Life of John Singleton Copley.*
1984 Armenini, G. B. 1820. *De'Veri precetti della pittura . . . con note di Stefano Ticozzi.*
1985 Averroes. 1949. *Averrois Cordubensis Compendia Librorum Aristotelis qui Parva Naturalia Vocantur*, ed. A. L. Shields.
1986 Bancroft, E. 1813. *Experimental Researches concerning the Philosophy of Permanent Colours.*
1987 Beal, M. 1984. 'Richard Symonds in Italy: his meeting with Nicholas

Poussin', *Burlington Magazine*, CXXVI.
1988 Bennett, J. A. 1984. *The Celebrated Phenomena of Colours*, Cambridge, Whipple Museum of the History of Science.
1989 Bernard, E. 1908. 'Julien Tanguy', *Mercure de France*, LXXVI.
1990 Berthollet, C. L. and A. B. 1824. *Elements of the Art of Dying*, 2 vols, trans. A. Ure, 2nd edn.
1991 Bie, C. de 1971. *Het Gulden Cabinet van de Edel Vry Schilderconst* (1661) ed. G. Lemmens.
1992 Bowlt, J. (ed. and trans.) 1976. *Russian Art of the Avant-Garde: Theory and Criticism 1902–1934.*
1993 Brett, D. 1986. 'The aesthetical science: George Field and the "Science of Beauty"', *Art History*, IX.
1994 Brisseau de Mirbel, C. F. 1815. *Élémens de Physiologie végétale et de botanique*, 2 vols.
1995 Buck, R. D. 1973. 'Rubens's *The Gerbier Family*: examination and treatment', *Studies in the History of Art* (Washington, National Gallery).
1996 Butler, M. 1973. 'Pigments and Techniques in the Cézanne painting "Chestnut Trees" (Minneapolis Institute of Arts)', *Bulletin of the American Institute for Conservation of Artistic Works*, XIII.
1997 Cachin, F. 1971. *Signac.*
1998 Cadorin, P., Veillon, M. and Mühlethaler, B. 1987. 'Décoloration dans la couche picturale de certains tableaux de Vincent van Gogh et de Paul Gauguin' in K. Grimstad (ed.), *International Council of Museums Committee for Conservation: 8th Triennial Meeting, Sydney, Australia*, Preprints, I.
1999 Callen, A. 1991. 'Impressionist techniques and the politics of spontaneity', *Art History*, XIV.
2000 Chaptal, J. A. 1807. *Chimie appliquée aux arts*, 4 vols.
2001 Daval, J.-L. 1985. *Oil Painting.*
2002 Doesburg, T. van 1923. 'Von der neuen Aesthetik zur materiellen Verwirklichung', *De Stijl*, VI (repr. 1968).
2003 Dossie, R. 1764. *The Handmaid to the Arts* (1758), 2 vols, 2nd edn, London.
2004 Dowley, F. H. 1965. 'Carlo Maratti, Carlo Fontana and the Baptismal Chapel in St Peter's', *Art Bulletin*, XLVII.
2005 Ephrussi, C. 1891. 'S-J. Rochard', *Gazette des Beaux-Arts*, 3ᶜ pér. VI.
2006 Faraday, M. 1971. *Selected Correspondence*, 2 vols, ed. L. Pearce Williams.
2007 Fiedler, I. 1984. 'Materials used in Seurat's *La Grande Jatte* including color changes and notes on the evolution of the artist's palette', *American Institute of Conservation of Historical and Artistic Works*, Preprints.
2008 —. 1989. 'A technical evaluation of the *Grande Jatte*', The Art Institute of Chicago, *Museum Studies*, XIV.
2009 Field, G. 1841. *Chromotography*, (1835), 2nd edn.
2010 —. 1845. *Chromatics* (1817), 2nd edn.
2011 —. 1846. *TRITOGENIA, or, a Brief Outline of the Universal System* (1816; *The Pamphleteer*, IX, 1817), 2nd edn.
2012 Fielding, T. H. 1839. *Painting in Oil.*
2013 Fletcher, J. 1979. 'Marco Boschini and Paolo del Sera – collectors and connoisseurs of Venice', *Apollo*, CX.
2014 Gage, J. 1964. 'Magilphs and

Mysteries', *Apollo*, LXXX.
2015 —. 1986. 'Jacob Christoph Le Blon', *Print Quarterly*, III.
2016 —. 1987. *J. M. W. Turner: 'A wonderful range of mind'.*
2017 —. 1989. *George Field and his Circle, from Romanticism to the Pre-Raphaelite Brotherhood*, Cambridge, Fitzwilliam Museum.
2018 Gautier d'Agoty, J. 1753. *Observations sur l'histoire naturelle, sur la physique et sur la peinture*, pt VIII.
2019 Goethe, J. W. von. 1871. 'Aufsätze über bildende Kunst', *Jahrbücher für Kunstwissenschaft*, IV.
2020 Goldwater, R. and Treves, M. 1976. *Artists on Art from the 14th Century to the 20th Century.*
2021 Goupil, F. A. A. 1858. *Manuel complet et simplifié de al peinture à l'huile.*
2022 Gowing, L. 1988. *Paul Cézanne: the Basel Sketchbooks*, New York, Museum of Modern Art.
2023 Grégoire, G. ·c. 1812. *Théorie des couleurs, contenant explication de la Table des Couleurs.*
2024 Hackney, S. 1990. 'Texture and application: preserving the evidence in oil paintings' in *Appearance, Opinion, Change: Evaluating the Look of Paintings*, Preprints of the United Kingdom Institute of Conservation/Association of Art Historians Conference.
2025 Hamilton, J. 1738. *Stereography*, 2 vols.
2026 Harris, M. *c.* 1776. *The Natural System of Colours* (repr. 1963).
2027 Herbert, R. L. 1962. *Seurat's Drawings.*
2028 House, J. 1985. 'Renoir's worlds' in *Renoir*, London, Arts Council of Great Britain.
2029 Jones, E. H. 1977. *Monet Unveiled: a New Look at Boston's Paintings.*
2030 Jones, T. 1946–8. *Memoirs*, ed. A. P. Oppé, *Walpole Society*, XXXII.
2031 Kockaert, L. 1979. 'Note on the green and brown glazes of old paintings', *Studies in Conservation*, XXIV.
2032 Kühn, H. 1969. *Die Pigmente in den Gemälden der Schack-Galerie* (App. to E. Ruhmer et al., *Schack-Galerie*, II).
2033 —. 1982. 'Die Technik der Farbenherstellung in der Neuzeit', *Maltechnik*, LXXXVIII.
2034 Lˣˣˣ, M. de. *c.* 1829. *Manuel du peintre en miniature, à la gouache et à l'aquarelle . . .*
2035 Lamarck, J.-B. 1797. 'Sur l'état de combinaison des principes dans les différentes molécules essentielles des composées . . .' in *Mémoires de physique et d'histoire naturelle*, Paris.
2036 Latreille, P. A. 1802. *Histoire naturelle générale et particulière des crustaces et des insectes*, 14 vols, Paris.
2037 Lemaistre, A. 1889. *L'École des Beaux-Arts.*
2038 Maheux, A. F. 1988. *Degas Pastels*, Ottawa, National Gallery of Canada.
2039 Malone, E. 1797. *The Works of Sir Joshua Reynolds* (2nd edn, 1798).
2040 Martin, W. 1901. 'Een "Kunsthandel" in een Klappermans-wachthuis', *Oud Holland*, XIX.
2041 Massoul, C. de. 1797. *A Treatise on the Art of Painting and Composition of Colours*, London.
2042 Mérimée, J.-F.-L. 1830. *De la peinture à l'huile* (repr. 1981).
2043 Merrifield, M. P. 1844. *A Treatise on Painting written by Cennino Cennini in the year 1437.*

2044 MOTTEZ, V. 1911. *Cennino Cennini: Le Livre de l'Art* (1858), 2nd edn (repr. 1978).

2045 NAKOV, A. B. and PÉTRIS, M. (eds). 1972. *Le Dernier tableau*.

2046 OWEN, F. and BROWN, D. B. 1988. *Collector of Genius: A Life of Sir George Beaumont*.

2047 OZENFANT, A. 1968. *Mémoires 1886–1962*.

2048 *Paintings by Renoir*. 1973. Chicago Art Institute, exh. cat.

2049 PENNY, N. (ed.). 1986. *Reynolds*, London, Royal Academy, exh. cat.

2050 PFANNENSCHMIDT, A. L. and SCHULZ, E. R. 1792. *Essai sur la manière de mélanger et composer toutes les couleurs au moyen du bleu, du jaune et du rouge*, 2nd edn, Lausanne.

2051 PINET, G. 1913. *Léonor Mérimée, Peintre (1757–1836)*.

2052 PRACHE, A. 1966. 'Souvenirs d'Artur Guéniot', *Gazette des Beaux-Arts*, VIe pér. LXVII.

2053 PUTTFARKEN, T. 1985. *Roger de Piles' Theory of Art*.

2054 RECOUVREUR, A. 1890. *Grammaire du peintre*.

2055 REFF, T. 1971. 'The technical aspects of Degas' Art', *Metropolitan Museum Journal*, IV.

2056 — and SHOEMAKER, I. H. 1989. *Paul Cézanne: Two Sketchbooks*, Philadelphia Museum of Art.

2057 RENOIR, J. 1962. *Renoir my Father*.

2058 REWALD, J. 1951. *Carnets de Cézanne*.

2059 —. 1973. *History of Impressionism*, revised edn.

2060 RIGAUD, S. F. D. 1984. *Facts and Recollections of the XVIIIe Century in a Memoir of John Francis Rigaud Esq. R.A.* (1854), ed. W. Pressly, *Walpole Society*, L.

2061 ROBERTSON, E. (ed.). 1897. *Letters and Papers of Andrew Robertson*.

2062 SANDBY, W. 1892. *Thomas and Paul Sandby*.

2063 SAUVAIRE, N. 1978. *Le Rôle de la famille Haro, marchand de couleurs, dans l'oeuvre de Delacroix* (Maîtrise, Histoire de l'Art, Université de Paris IV).

2064 SHELDRAKE, T. 1798. 'Dissertation on Painting in Oil', *Transaction of the Society of Arts*, XVI.

2065 SULLY, T. 1965. *Hints to Young Painters* (1873), ed. F. Birren.

2066 TABARANT, A. 1923. 'Couleurs', *Bulletin de la vie artistique*, IV.

2067 TERNOIS, D. 1956. 'Livres de comptes de Madame Ingres', *Gazette des Beaux-Arts*, VIe pér. XLVIII.

2068 THORNBURY, W. 1877. *The Life of J. M. W. Turner, R.A.* 2nd edn.

2069 TRÉVISE, Duc de. 1927. 'Le pèlerinage à Giverny', *Revue de l'art ancien et moderne* (Jan/Feb.).

2070 VENTURI, L. 1939. *Les Archives de l'Impressionisme*, 2 vols.

2071 WAINEWRIGHT, T. G. 1880. *Essays and Criticism*, ed. W. C. Hazlitt.

2072 WINGLER, H. 1975. *The Bauhaus*, 3rd edn.

13 The Sound of Colour

2073 AGEE, W. 1965. *Synchromism and Color Principles in American Painting*.

2074 ANSCHÜTZ, G. 1926. 'Untersuchungen über komplexe musikalische Synopsie', *Archiv für die gesamte Psychologie*, LIV.

2075 APOLLONIO, U. 1973. *Futurist Manifestos*.

2076 ARNHEIM, R. 1974. *Art and Visual Perception (The New Version)*.

2077 BABLET, D. 1965. *Esthétique générale du décor de théâtre de 1870 à 1914*.

2078 BADT, K. 1981. *Paolo Veronese*.

2079 BALJEU, J. 1974. *Theo van Doesburg*.

2080 BARKER, A. 1984. *Greek Musical Writings, I, The Musician and his Art*.

2081 BESANT, A. and LEADBEATER, C. W. 1961. *Thought Forms* (1901).

2082 BIERNSON, G. 1972. 'Why did Newton see Indigo in the spectrum?', *American Journal of Physics*, XL.

2083 BISHOP, B. 1893. *A Souvenir of the Colour Organ, with some suggestions in Regard to the Soul of the Rainbow and the Harmony of Light*.

2084 BLOTKAMP, C. et al. 1986. *De Stijl, The Formative years, 1917–1922*.

2085 BOODT, A. B. de 1609. *Gemmarum et Lapidum Historia*, Hanau.

2086 BORNSTEIN, M. H. 1975. 'On light and the aesthetics of color: Lumia kinetic art', *Leonardo*, VII.

2087 BOSSI, G. 1821. 'Saggi di ricerche intorno l'armonia cromatica naturale ed artificiale', *Memorie dell'Imperiale Regia Istituto del Regno Lombardo-Veneto, 1814, 1815*, II.

2088 BRACHERT, T. 1971. 'A musical canon of proportion in Leonardo's *Last Supper*', *Art Bulletin*, LIII.

2089 BRAGDON, C. 1918. *Architecture and Democracy*.

2090 BREWSTER, Sir D. 1819. *Treatise on the Kaleidoscope*.

2091 BRYENNIUS, MANUEL. 1970. *Harmonics*, ed. and trans. G. H. Jonker.

2092 BUJIĆ, B. 1988. *Music in European Thought, 1851–1912*.

2093 CARDANO, G. 1570. *Opus Novum de Proportionibus Liber V*, Basle.

2094 CASTEL, L. B. 1722. [Review of] J. P. Rameau, *Traité d'harmonie, Journal de Trévoux*, October–November.

2095 —. 1723. [Review of] Sir I. Newton, *Traité d'optique, Mémoires de Trévoux*, August.

2096 —. 1725. 'Lettre a M. D[ecourt]', *Mercure de France*, November.

2097 —. 1726. 'Difficultés sur le clavecin oculaire avec leur réponses' *Mercure de France*, March.

2098 —. 1728. [Review of] J. P. Rameau, *Nouveau système de musique théorique*, *Journal de Trévoux*, March.

2099 —. 1735. 'Nouvelles expériences d'optique & d'acoustique, Pt. II–IV', *Mémoires de Trévoux*, August–October.

2100 —. 1737. [Review of] J. C. Le Blon, *Coloritto, Mémoires de Trévoux*, August.

2101 —. 1739. 'Project d'une nouvelle optique des couleurs, fondée sur les observations, et uniquement relative à la peinture, à la teinture, et aux autres arts coloristes', *Mémoires de Trévoux*, April.

2102 —. 1740. *L'Optique des Couleurs*.

2103 CASWELL, A. B. 1980. 'The Pythagoreanism of Arcimboldo', *Journal of Aesthetics and Art Criticism*, XXXIX.

2104 CHENEY, S. 1932. *A Primer of Modern Art* (1924), 7th edn.

2105 CHEVREUL, M. E. 1879. 'Complément d'études sur la vision des couleurs', *Mémoires de l'Académie des Sciences*, XLI.

2106 CLICHTOVE, JOSSE. 1510. *Philosophiae Naturalis Paraphrasis*, Paris.

2107 COHEN, H. F. 1984. *Quantifying Music: the Science of Music in the First Stage of the Scientific Revolution, 1580–1650*.

2108 COMOTTI, G. 1989. *Music in Greek and Roman Culture*.

2109 CRAWFORD, J. C. 1974. 'Die Glückliche Hand: Schoenberg's Gesamtkunstwerk', *Musical Quarterly*, LX.

2110 CROCKER, R. L. 1962. 'Discant, Counterpoint and Harmony', *Journal of the American Musicological Society*, XV.

2111 —. 1963. 'Pythagorean mathematics and music', *Journal of Aesthetics and Art Criticism*, XXII.

2112 CURJEL, H. 1975. *Experiment Krolloper, 1927–1931*.

2113 DAVIS, J. W. 1979. Letter in *Leonardo*, XII.

2114 DEHNOW, F. 1919. 'Hörbare Farben', *Allgemeine Musik-Zeitung*, XLVI.

2115 DEROUET, C. and BOISSEL, J. 1985. *Oeuvres de Vassily Kandinsky (1866–1944)*.

2116 DICKREITER, M. 1973. *Der Musiktheoretiker Johannes Kepler*.

2117 DIDEROT, D. 1965. *Oeuvres Esthétiques*, ed. P. Vernière.

2118 DISERTORI, B. 1978. 'Il Domenichino pittore, trascrittore di musiche e musicologo' in *La Musica nei Quadri Antichi*.

2119 DOESBURG, N. van 1971. 'Some memoirs of Mondrian', *Studio International*, CLXXXII.

2120 ERDMAN-MACKE, E. 1962. *Erinnerungen an August Macke*.

2121 ERHARDT-SIEBOLD, E. von. 1931–2. 'Some inventions of the Pre-Romantic period and their influence upon literature', *Englische Studien*, LXVI.

2122 ERNST, M. 1944. 'As Ernst remembers Mondrian', *Knickerbocker Weekly*, 14 February.

2123 EVANS, R. J. W. 1973. *Rudolf II and his World*.

2124 FARMER, H. G. 1926. *The Influence of Music: from Arabic Sources* (Lecture to the Musical Association).

2125 FECHNER, G. T. II, 1898. *Vorschule der Aesthetik* (1876–7), 2nd edn.

2126 FERRIS, J. 1959. 'The evolution of Rameau's harmonic theories', *Journal of Musical Theory*, III.

2127 FIELD, G. 1820. *Aesthetics, or the Analogy of the Sensible Sciences Indicated, with an Appendix on Light and Colors (The Pamphleteer*, XVII).

2128 FISCHER, O. 1907. 'Über Verbindung von Farbe und Klang. Ein literar-psychologische Untersuchung', *Zeitschrift für Aesthetick*, II.

2129 GAFFURIO, F. 1518. *De Harmonia Musicorum Instrumentorum Opus*, Milan (repr. 1972).

2130 GALILEI, V. 1602. *Dialogo della Musica Antica e della Moderna* (1581), Florence.

2131 GARNER, W. 1978. 'The relationship between colour and music', *Leonardo*, XI.

2132 GEIGER, B. 1954. *I Dipinti Ghiribizzosi di Giuseppe Arcimboldi*.

2133 GEVAERT, F. 1875. *Histoire et Théorie de la Musique dans l'Antiquité*, 2 vols.

2134 GILBERT, B. 1966. 'The reflected-light compositions of Ludwig Hirschfeld-Mack', *Form* (Cambridge), II.

2135 GODWIN, J. (ed.). 1986. *Music, Mysticism and Magic: a Sourcebook*.

2136 GOETHE, J. W. von. 1907. *Goethe im Gespräch*, ed. F. Diebel and F. Gundelfinger, 3rd. edn.

2137 —. 1962. *Schriften zur Kunst* (dtv Gesamtausgabe 33), 2 vols.

2138 GOLDINE, N. 1964. 'Henri Bate,

chanoine et chantre de la Cathédrale Saint Lambert à Liège et théoricien de la musique', *Revue Belge de Musicologie*, XVIII.

2139 GOLDSCHMIDT, R. H. 1927/8. 'Postulat der Farbwandelspiele', *Sitzungsbericht der Heidelberger Akademie der Wissenschaften, Philosophische-Historische Klasse*, XVIII.

2140 GÖLLER, G. 1959. 'Vincenz von Beauvais und sein Musiktraktat in Speculum Doctrinale', *Kölner Beiträge zur Musik-Forschung*, XV.

2141 GOLLEK, R. 1980. *Franz Marc 1880–1916*, Munich, Städtische Galerie im Lenbachhaus.

2142 GREENEWALT, M. H. 1918. 'Light: fine art the sixth', *Transactions of the Illuminating Engineers' Society*, XIII/7, 10 October.

2143 —. 1946. *Nourathar: the Fine Art of Light Color Playing*.

2144 GROTE, L. (ed.). 1959. *Erinnerungen an Paul Klee*.

2145 GUEST, I. 1948. 'Babbage's ballet', *Ballet*, V.

2146 GUYOT, E. G. 1769. 'Musique oculaire' in *Nouvelles Recréations physiques et mathématiques*, III.

2147 HAHL-KOCH, J. 1984. *Arnold Schoenberg–Wassily Kandisky. Letters, Pictures and Documents*.

2148 *Der Hang zum Gesamtkunstwerk*. 1983. Zurich, Knsthaus, exh. cat.

2149 HARTLEY, D. 1749. *Observations on Man*, 2 vols.

2150 HAWKINS, Sir J. 1853. *A General History of the Science and Practice of Music* (1776), 2nd edn (repr. 1963).

2151 HESS, H. 1961. *Lyonel Feininger*.

2152 HOLTZMAN, H. and JAMES, M. (eds). 1987. *The New Art – The New Life: the Collected Writings of Piet Mondrian*.

2153 HUTCHINS, J. IV, 1815. *The History and Antiquities of Dorset*, 2nd edn.

2154 HURAY, P. le and DAY, J. 1981. *Music and Aesthetics in the 18th and early 19th centuries*.

2155 HUSSEY, G. 1756. J. W. 'Mr Giles Hussey's System of Colours (1756)', *Monthy Magazine*, December 1799.

2156 ITTEN, J. 1961. *Kunst der Farbe* (Eng. version 1962).

2157 *Johannes Itten: Künstler und Lehrer*. 1984. Berne, Kunstmuseum, exh. cat.

2158 *Johannes Itten*. 1980. Münster, Westfälisches Landesmuseum, exh. cat.

2159 JAMESON, D. D. 1844. *Colour-Music*.

2160 JONES, T. DOUGLAS 1972. *The Art of Light and Color*.

2161 KAGAN, A. 1983. *Paul Klee: Art and Music*.

2162 KANDINSKY, N. 1976. *Kandinsky und Ich*.

2163 KAUFMANN, T. DA C. 1989. *The School of Prague: Painting at the Court of Rudolph II*.

2164 KEMP, M. 1970. 'Ingres, Delacroix and Paganini: exposition and improvisation in the creative process', *L'Arte* N.S., III.

2165 KEPLER, J. XIV, 1969. *Gesammelte Werke*, ed. M. Caspar.

2166 KLEE, P. 1973. *Notebooks II: the Nature of Nature*, ed. J. Spiller.

2167 —. 1976. *Schriften, Rezensionen und Aufsätze*, ed. C. Geelhaar.

2168 *Klee et la musique*. 1985/6. Paris, Centre Georges Pompidou, exh. cat.

2169 KLEIN, A. B. 1937. *Coloured Light: an Art Medium*.

2170 KOENIGSBERGER, D. 1979.

Renaissance Man and Creative Thinking: a History of Concepts of Harmony, 1400–1700.

2171 KOLLERITSCH, O. (ed.). 1980. *Alexander Skrjabin.*

2172 LANKHEIT, K. (ed.). 1974. *The Blue Rider Almanac.*

2173 —. (ed.). 1983. *Wassily Kandinsky–Franz Marc Briefwechsel.*

2174 LÁSZLÓ, A. 1925a. *Die Farblichtmusik.*

2175 —. 1925b. 'Die Farblichtmusik', *Die Musik*, XVII/9, June, II.

2176 LEVIN, G. 1978. *Synchromism and American Color Abstraction 1910–1925.*

2177 LIPPMAN, E. A. 1963. 'Hellenic conceptions of harmony', *Journal of the American Musicological Society*, XVI.

2178 LOCKE, J. 1975. *Essay on Human Understanding* (1690), ed. P. H. Nidditch.

2179 LOWINSKY, E. E. 1966. 'Music of the Renaissance as viewed by Renaissance musicians' in B. O'Kelley (ed.), *The Renaissance Image of Man and the World.*

2180 MACADAM, D. L. 1986. Letter in *Color Research and Application*, XI.

2181 MACGREGOR, A. A. 1961. *Percyval Tudor Hart.*

2182 MCKINNON, J. (ed.). 1987. *Music in Early Christian Literature.*

2183 MCLAREN, K. 1985. 'Newton's Indigo', *Color Research and Application*, X.

2184 —. 1986. Letters in *Colour Research and Application.*

2185 MACLEAN, K. 1936. *John Locke and English Literature in the Eighteenth Century.*

2186 MACROBIUS. 1952. *Commentary on the Dream of Scipio*, ed. and trans. W. H. Stahl.

2187 MANIATES, M. R. 1979. *Mannerism in Italian Music and Culture, 1530–1630.*

2188 MARKS, L. 1975. 'On colored-hearing synaesthesia: cross-modal translations of sensory dimensions', *Psychological Bulletin*, 82.

2189 MASON, W. 1958/9. 'Father Castel and his color clavecin', *Journal of Aesthetics and Art Criticism*, XVII.

2190 MATON, 1797. *Observations relative chiefly to the Natural History, Picturesque Scenery and Antiquities of the Western Counties of England*, 2 vols.

2191 MAUR, K. VON. 1979. *Oskar Schlemmer, Monographie und Oeuvrekatalog*, 2 vols.

2192 —. 1985. *Vom Klang der Bilder. Die Musik in der Kunst des 20 Jh.*

2193 MERSENNE, M. 1636/7. *Harmonie Universelle*, 2 vols, Paris.

2194 MIZLER, L. 1743. *Musikalische Bibliothek.*

2195 MOHOLY-NAGY, L. 1922. 'Produktion–Reproduktion', *De Stijl*, V. no. 7.

2196 MOTTE-HABER, H. DE LA. 1990. *Musik und bildende Kunst: von der Tonmalerei zur Klangskulptur.*

2197 MRAS, G. 1963. '*Ut pictura musica*: a study of Delacroix's *Paragone*', *Art Bulletin*, XLV.

2198 MYERS, C. S. 1915. 'Two cases of synaesthesia', *British Journal of Psychology*, VII.

2199 NAJOK, D. 1972. *Drei anonyme griechische Traktate über die Musik.*

2199a NEWTON, SIR I. 1959–. *Correspondence*, ed. H. W. Turnbull, J. F. Scott and A. R. Hall.

2200 O'KONOR, L. 1971. *Viking Eggeling 1880–1925.*

2201 OLLESON, E. (ed.). 1980. *Modern Musical Scholarship.*

2202 ONIANS, J. 1984. 'On how to listen to High Renaissance art', *Art History*, VII.

2203 OSTWALD, W. 1931–3. *Colour Science*, 2 vols.

2204 PALISCA, C. V. 1985. *Humanism in Italian Renaissance Musical Thought.*

2205 PEČMAN, R. (ed.). 1970. *Mannerism and Music of the Sixteenth and Seventeenth Centuries* (Colloquium Musica Bohemica et Europea Brno).

2206 PILES, R. DE. 1715. *Abrégé de la Vie des Peintres* (Engl. version 1970).

2207 PLATEAU, J. 1849. 'Ueber eine neue sonderbare Anwendung des Verweilens der Eindrücke auf die Netzhaut', *Annalen der Physik und Chemie*, LXXVIII.

2208 PLUMMER, H. C. 1915. 'Color-Music', *Scientific American*, CXII.

2209 POPPER, F. 1967. *Naissance de l'Art Cinétique* (Engl. version 1970).

2210 RAMEAU, J.-P. 1967–72. *Complete Theoretical Writings*, ed. E. R. Jacobi, 6 vols.

2211 RAUPP, H.-J. 1978. 'Musik im Atelier: Darstellungen musizierender Künstler in der niederländischen Malerei des 17 Jh.', *Oud Holland*, XCII.

2212 REMIGIUS OF AUXERRE. 1965. *Commentum in Martianum Capellam*, ed. C. E. Lutz, 2 vols.

2213 REYNOLDS, SIR J. 1975. *Discourses on Art*, ed. R. Wark.

2214 ROCHAS, A. DE. 1885. 'L'Audition colorée', *La Nature*, I.

2215 ROSENFELD, S. 1981. *Georgian Scene Painters and Scene Painting.*

2216 ROTZLER, W. (ed.). 1972. *Johannes Itten: Werke und Schriften.*

2217 ROUGE, J. 1949. 'Goethe et l'essai sur la peinture de Diderot', *Études Germaniques*, IV.

2218 RUDOLF OF ST TROND. 1911. *Quaestiones in Musica*, ed. R. Steglich.

2219 RUMFORD, B. THOMPSON, COUNT. 1794. 'An account of some experiments upon coloured shadows', *Philosophical Transactions of the Royal Society.*

2220 SARGANT-FLORENCE, M. 1940. *Colour Co-ordination.*

2221 SCHIER, D. S. 1941. *L. B. Castel, Anti-Newtonian Scientist.*

2222 SCHLEMMER, O. 1972. *Letters and Diaries*, ed. T. Schlemmer.

2223 SCHLOEZER, B. DE. 1987. *Scriabin: Artist and Mystic* (1923).

2224 SCHMOLL, GEN. EISENWERTH, J. A. 1974. 'Hommage à Bach: ein Thema der bildenden Kunst des 20 Jh.' in *Convivium Musicorum: Festschrift Wolfgang Boetticher*, ed. H. Hüschen and D.-R. Moser.

2225 SCHOENBERG, A. 1966. *Harmonielehre* (1911), ed. J. Rufer.

2226 SÉRUSIER, P. 1950. *ABC de la Peinture*, 3rd edn.

2227 SHAPIRO, A. 1979/80. 'Newton's "achromatic" dispersion law: theoretical background and experimental evidence', *Archive for History of Exact Sciences*, XXI, 2.

2228 SMITH, R. 1749. *Harmonics, or the Philosophy of Musical Sounds.*

2229 SORABJI, R. 1972. 'Aristotle, mathematics and colour', *Classical Quarterly*, N.S., XXII.

2230 STEIN, D. M. 1971. *Thomas Wilfred: Lumia. A Retrospective Exhibition*, Washington, Corcoran Gallery of Art, exh. cat.

2231 STEIN, S. 1983. 'Kandinsky and abstract stage-composition: practice and theory, 1909–1912', *Art Journal*, XLIII.

2232 STILLINGFLEET, B. 1771. *The Principles and Power of Harmony.*

2233 TEYSSÈDRE, B. 1967. 'Peinture et Musique: la notion d'harmonie des couleurs au XVIIᵉ siècle français', in *Stil und Überlieferung in der Kunst des Abendlandes*: (Akten des XXI Internationalen Kongresses für Kunstgeschichte, Bonn, 1964), III.

2234 *Tiziano a Venezia; Convegno Internazionale di Studi.* 1976. Venice.

2235 *Towards a New Art: Essays on the Background to Abstract Art, 1910–1920.* 1980. London, Tate Gallery.

2236 TRISKA, E.-M. 1979. 'Die Quadratbilder Paul Klees' in Cologne, Kunsthalle, *Paul Klee: Das Werk der Jahre 1919–1933.*

2237 TROY, N. 1983. *The De Stijl Environment.*

2238 —. 1984. 'Figures of the dance in De Stijl', *Art Bulletin*, LXVI.

2239 TUDOR HART. P. 1918a. 'The analogy of sound and colour', *Cambridge Magazine*, VII, March 2.

2240 —. 1918b. 'A new view of colour', *Cambridge Magazine*, VII, February 23.

2241 VAUGHAN, G. 1984. 'Maurice Denis and the sense of music', *Oxford Art Journal*, VII.

2242 VERDONE, M. 1967. 'Ginna e Corra: cinema e letteratura del Futurismo', *Bianco e Nero*, XXVIII, October–December.

2243 VRIESEN, G. 1957. *August Macke.*

2244 WAGNER, D. (ed.). 1983. *The Seven Liberal Arts in the Middle Ages.*

2245 WASHTON-LONG, R. C. 1980. *Kandinsky: the Development of an Abstract Style.*

2246 WEDDINGEN, E. 1984. 'Jacopo Tintoretto und die Musik', *Artibus & Historiae*, X.

2247 WELLEK, A. 1935. 'Farbharmonie und Farbenklavier: ihre Entstehungsgeschichte im 18 Jh.', *Archiv für die gesamte Psychologie*, XCIV.

2248 —. 1963. *Musikpsychologie und Musikästhetik.*

2249 WHITFIELD, T. W. A. and SLATTER, P. E. 1978. 'Colour harmony: an evaluation', *British Journal of Aesthetics*, XVII.

2250 WILFRED, T. 1947. 'Light and the Artist', *Journal of Aesthetics and Art Criticism*, V.

2251 —. 1948. 'Composing in the art of Lumia', *Journal of Aesthetics and Art Criticism*, VII.

2252 WINTERNITZ, E. 1982. *Leonardo da Vinci as a Musician.*

2253 WITTKOWER, R. 1962. *Architectural Principles in the Age of Humanism.*

2254 WRIGHT, W. H. 1923. *The Future of Painting.*

2255 WÜRTENBERGER, F. 1979. *Malerei und Musik: die Geschichte des Verhaltens zweier Künste zueinander.*

2256 ZARLINO, GIOSEFFO. 1573. *Institutioni Harmoniche*, 2nd edn (repr. 1966).

2257 —. 1588. *Sopplimenti Musicali* (repr. 1966).

2258 ZILCZER, J. 1987. '"Color-Music": synaesthesia and nineteenth-century sources for abstract art', *Artibus & Historiae*, XVI.

14 Colour without Theory

2259 *Abstraction: Towards a New Art. Painting 1910–1920.* 1980. London, Tate Gallery.

2260 ADLER, B. (ed.). 1921. *Utopia: Dokumente der Wirklichkeit.*

2261 ALBERS, J. 1963. *Interaction of Color* (rev. paperback edn 1975).

2262 —. 1967. 'My course at the Hochschule für Gestaltung at Ulm' (1954), *Form*, IV.

2263 *Josef Albers: the American Years. 1965/6.* Washington, Gallery of Modern Art, exh. cat.

2264 *Josef Albers: a Retrospective. 1988.* New York, Guggenheim Museum, exh. cat.

2265 ALBRECHT, H. J. 1974. *Farbe als Sprache: Robert Delaunay, Josef Albers, Richard Paul Lohse.*

2266 BAIRD, G. 1969. 'Former members of the Bauhaus talk to George Baird about their memories of the School', *The Listener*, LXXXI.

2267 BAJKAY, E. 1984. 'A Hungarian founder of the Dutch Constructivists', *Acta Historiae Artium Academia Scientiarum Hungaricae*, XXX, 3–4.

2268 BARNES, S. J. 1989. *The Rothko Chapel: an Act of Faith.*

2269 BERLIN, BAUHAUS ARCHIV-MUSEUM. 1981. *Sammlungskatalog.*

2270 BIEMA, C. VAN 1930. *Farben und Formen als lebendige Kräfte.*

2271 BLAVATSKY, H. P. 1888. *The Secret Doctrine: the Synthesis of Science, Religion and Philosophy*, 2 vols, 2nd edn.

2272 BLOTKAMP, C. 1975–6. Book review in *Simiolus*, VIII.

2273 — ET AL. 1982. *De Beginjaren van De Stijl.*

2274 BOWLT, J. 1973/4. Concepts of color and the Soviet avant-garde', *The Structurist*, 13/14.

2275 BROWN, T. M. 1958. *The Work of Gerrit Rietveld, Architect.*

2276 BUCKBERROUGH, S. A. 1979. 'The simultaneous content of Robert Delaunay's Windows', *Arts Magazine*, September.

2277 —. 1982. *Robert Delaunay: the discovery of Simultaneity.*

2278 CAMPBELL, J. 1978. *The German Werkbund.*

2279 CARMEAN, E. A., JR. 1979. *Mondrian: the Diamond Compositions*, Washington, National Gallery of Art.

2280 CAUSSY, F. 1904. 'Psychologie de l'Impressionisme', *Mercure de France*, December.

2281 CLEARWATER, B. 1984. *Mark Rothko: Works on Paper.*

2282 COHEN, A. A. 1975. *Sonia Delaunay.*

2283 —. 1984. *Herbert Bayer: the Complete Works.*

2284 COHN, M. B. (ed.). 1988. *Mark Rothko's Harvard Murals* (Center for Conservation and Technical Studies, Harvard University Art Museums).

2285 *Colour Since Matisse. 1985.* Edinburgh International Festival, exh. cat.

2286 COUWENBERGH, P. and DIEU, J. 1983. 'Les oeuvres algébriques de 1930–1935: de l'unité vers l'infinité', *ICSAC Cahier*, I.

2287 CRANMER, D. 1987a. 'Painting materials and techniques of Mark Rothko: consequences of an unorthodox approach' in *Mark Rothko 1903–70*, London, Tate Gallery.

2288 —. 1987b. 'Ephemeral paintings on "permanent view": the accelerated ageing of Mark Rothko's paintings', ICOM Committee for Conservation, 8th Triennial Meeting, Sydney, *Preprints* I.

2289 CRAVEN, D. 1990. 'Abstract Expressionism, Automatism and the age

of Automation', *Art History*, XIII.
2290 DE KOONING, E. 1950. 'Albers paints a picture', *Art News*, XLIX, November.
2291 DELAUNAY, R. 1957. *Du Cubisme à l'Art Abstrait*, ed. P. Francastel.
2292 DELAUNAY, S. 1956. 'Collages de Sonia et de Robert Delaunay', *XXᵉ Siècle*, January.
2293 *Robert Delaunay*. 1976. Baden-Baden, Staatliche Kunsthalle, exh. cat.
2294 *Robert et Sonia Delaunay*. 1985. Paris, Musée de'Art Moderne de la Ville de Paris, exh. cat.
2295 *Sonia Delaunay: a Retrospective*. 1980. Buffalo, Albright-Knox Art Gallery, exh. cat.
2296 DOESBURG, T. VAN. 1969. *Principles of Neo-Plastic Art* (1925), based on *Grondbegrippen van de nieuwe beeldende Kunst* (1919), ed. S. V. Barbieri, C. Boekrad, J. Leering, 1983.
2297 DOIG, A. 1986. *Theo van Doesburg: Painting into Architecture, Theory into Practice*.
2298 DUBERMANN, M. 1972. *Black Mountain: an Exploration in Community*.
2299 ELDERFIELD, J. 1986. *Morris Louis*.
2300 ERFFA, H. VON. 1943. 'The Bauhaus before 1922', *College Art Journal*, III.
2301 EX, S. and HOEK, E. 1985. *Vilmos Huszár, Schilder en Ontwerper 1884–1960*.
2302 FAGIOLO DELL'ARCO, M. 1970. *Futurballa*.
2303 FARMER, J. D. and WEISS, G. 1971. *Concepts of the Bauhaus: the Busch-Reisinger Museum Collection*.
2304 FIEDLER, K. 1926. 'Das Schwarz-Weiss Problem', *Neue Psychologische Studien*, II.
2305 FIELD, G. 1850. *Rudiments of the Painter's Art; or a Grammar of Colouring*.
2306 FRIEDMAN, M. (ed.). 1982. *De Stijl: 1917–1931, Visions of Utopia*.
2307 FUCHS, W. 1923. 'Experimentelle Untersuchungen über das simultane Hintereinandersehen auf derselben Sehrichtung', *Zeitschrift für Psychologie*, XCI (Eng. trans. 'On Transparency' in W. D. Ellis (ed.), *A Source-Book of Gestalt Psychology*, 1950).
2308 FULLER, B. 1978. 'Josef Albers (1888–1976)', *Leonardo*, XI.
2309 GASSNER, H. and GILLEN, E. 1979. *Zwischen Revolutionskunst und Sozialistischem Realismus*.
2310 GIBSON, A. 1990. 'Abstract Expressionism's evasion of language' in D. and C. Shapiro, *Abstract Expressionism: a Critical Record*.
2311 GOMRINGER, E. 1968. *Josef Albers*.
2312 GROHMANN, W. 1958. *Wassily Kandinsky, Leben und Werk*.
2313 GUICHARD, E. 1882. *Grammar of Colour*.
2314 HAHN, P. (ed.). 1985. *Bauhaus Berlin*.
2315 HARRIS, M. E. 1987. *The Arts at Black Mountain College*.
2316 *Jacoba van Heemskerk 1976–1923; eine expressionistische Künstlerin*. 1983/4. The Hague, Gemeentemuseum.
2317 HENRY, C. n.d. 'La lumière, la couleur, la forme', *L'Esprit Nouveau*, 6–9.

2318 HERBERT, R. L. 1968. *Neo-Impressionism*, New York, Guggenheim Museum.
2319 HERZOGENRATH, W. 1979/80. 'Josef Albers und der "Vorkurs" am Bauhaus, 1919–1933' *Wallraf-Richartz Jahrbuch*, XLI.
2320 HIRSCHFELD-MACK, L. 1963. *The Bauhaus*.
2321 HOBBS, R. C. and LEVIN, G. 1981. *Abstract Expressionism: the Formative Years*.
2322 HOELZEL, A. 1919. 'Zur Farbe', *Das Gelbe Blatt*, I.
2323 HOFMANNSTHAL, H. VON. 1951. *Prosa*, II.
2324 HOLLOWAY, J. H. and WEIL, J. A. 1970. 'A conversation with Josef Albers', *Leonardo*, III.
2325 ISAACS, R. R. I, 1983. *Walter Gropius: der Mensch und sein Werk*.
2326 ITTEN, J. 1964. *Design and Form: the Basic Course at the Bauhaus*.
2327 JAMESON, D. and HURVICH, L. 1975. 'From contrast to assimilation: In art and in the eye', *Leonardo*, VIII.
2328 JOHNSON, E. H. 1982. *American Artists on Art from 1940 to 1980*.
2329 JUNGHANNS, K. 1982. *Der deutsche Werkbund: sein erstes Jahrzehnt*.
2330 *Kandinsky: Russian and Bauhaus Years, 1915–1933*. New York, Guggenheim Museum, exh. cat.
2331 *Wassily Kandinsky: Die erste sowejetische Retrospektive*. 1989. Frankfurt, Schirn Kunsthalle, exh. cat.
2332 KERBER, B. 1970. 'Streifenbilder. Zur Unterscheidung ähnlicher Phänomene', *Wallraf-Richartz Jahrbuch*, XXXII.
2333 KLEE, P. 1979a. *Beiträge zur bildnerische Formlehre*, ed. J. Glaesemer.
2334 —. 1979b. *Briefe an die Familie*, ed. F. Klee.
2335 *Yves Klein*. 1983. Paris, Centre Georges Pompidou, exh. cat.
2336 *Franz Kline: the Colour Abstractions*. 1979. Washington, Phillips Collection, exh. cat.
2337 KNIGHT, V. (ed.). 1988. *Patrick Heron*.
2338 KUPKA, F. 1989. *La Création dans les arts plastiques* (1923), ed. and trans. E. Abrams.
2339 LEE, A. 1981. 'A critical account of some of Josef Albers' concepts of color', *Leonardo*, XIV.
2340 LISLE, L. 1986. *Portrait of an Artist: a Biography of Georgia O'Keeffe*, 2nd edn.
2341 LISTA, G. 1982. *Balla*.
2342 LODDER, C. 1983. *Russian Constructivism*.
2343 MANCUSI-UNGARO, C. 1990. 'The Rothko Chapel: treatment of the Black-Form, Triptychs' in J. S. Mills and P. Smith. *Cleaning, Retouching and Coatings* (IIC Preprints of the Brussels Congress).
2344 MALÉVITCH, K. 1977. *Le Miroir suprématiste*, trans. J.-C. Marcadé.
2345 MARTIN, M. 1968. *Futurist Art and Theory*.
2346 MILESI, A. 1907. [Review of] G. Previati, *Principi scientifici del*

divisionismo in Les Tendances nouvelles, XXIX.
2347 MOFFETT, K. 1977. *Kenneth Noland*.
2348 MUCHE, G. 1965. *Blickpunkt*.
2349 MUNSELL, A. 1905. *A Color Notation*.
2350 NEUMANN, E. 1970. *Bauhaus and Bauhaus People*.
2351 NICKERSON, D. 1976. 'History of the Munsell Color System, Company and Foundation', II, *Color Research and Application*, I.
2352 O'CONNER, F. V. and THAW, E. V. (eds). 1978. *Jackson Pollock: a Catalogue Raisonné*, 4 vols.
2353 OPPLER, E. C. 1976. *Fauvism Re-Examined*.
2354 OSTWALD, W. 1904. *Malerbriefe* (Eng. edn, *Letters to a Painter on the Theory and Practice of Painting*, trans. H. W. Morse, Boston, 1907).
2355 —. 1917. 'Beiträge zur Farbenlehre', *Abhandlungen der mathematische-physikalische Klasse der sächsischen Gesellschaft der Naturwissenschaften*, XXXIV.
2356 —. 1922. *Die Harmonie der Formen*.
2357 —. 1969. *The Color Primer*, ed. F. Birren.
2358 —. 1926–7. *Lebenslinien*, 3 vols.
2359 OZENFANT, A. and JEANNERET, C. E. 1918. *Après le Cubisme*.
2360 PACHECO, F. 1956. *Arte de la Pintura*, 2 vols, ed. F. Sanchez Canton.
2361 *Paintings by Josef Albers*. 1978. New Haven, Yale University Art Gallery, exh. cat.
2362 PARRIS, N. G. 1979. *Adolf Hoelzel's Structural and Color Theory and its Relationship to the Development of the Basic Course at the Bauhaus*, Ph.D. thesis, University of Pennsylvania.
2363 PETITPIERRE, P. 1957. *Aus der Malklasse von Paul Klee*.
2364 POLING, C. V. 1973. *Color Theories of the Bauhaus Artists*, Ph.D. thesis, Columbia University.
2365 —. 1976. *Bauhaus Color*, Atlanta, High Museum of Art.
2366 —. 1982. *Kandinsky-Unterricht am Bauhaus* (Engl. trans. 1987).
2367 POLUNIN, V. 1927. *The Continental Method of Scene Painting*.
2368 PREVIATI, G. 1929. *Principi scientifici del Divisionismo* 1906, 2nd edn. (Fr. trans. 1910).
2369 REYNES, G. 1981. 'Chevreul interviewé par Nadar (1886)', *Gazette des Beaux-Arts*, XCVIII.
2370 ROQUE, G. 1983. '"... d'un espace limité à un univers illimité"', *ICSAC Cahier*, I.
2371 ROSE, B. *c.* 1972 *Frankenthaler*.
2372 ROWELL, M. 1975. *František Kupka: a Retrospective*, New York, Guggenheim Museum.
2373 RUBIN, W. 1970. *Frank Stella*.
2374 RUDENSTINE, A. 1981. *Russian Avant-Garde Art: the George Costakis Collection*.
2375 SCHEFFLER, K. 1901. 'Notizen über die Farbe', *Dekorative Kunst*, IV.
2376 SCHLEMMER, O. 1927. 'Bühne', *Bauhaus* no. 3.

2377 SCHLEMMER, T. (ed.). 1972. *The Letters and Diaries of Oskar Schlemmer*.
2378 SCHMIDT, P. F. 1919. 'Werkbund Krisis', *Cicerone*, XI.
2379 SCHOENMAEKERS, M. H. J. 1913. *Mensch en Natuur: een mystische Levensbeschouwing*.
2380 —. 1915. *Het Nieuwe Wereldbeeld*.
2381 SCHREYER, L. 1929. 'Anmerkungen zu Goethes Farbenlehre', *Bühne und Welt*, XXXI, i.
2382 SCHUMANN, F. 1900. 'Beiträge zur Analyse der Gesichtswahrnehmungen', *Zeitschrift für Psychologie und Physiologie der Sinnesorgane*, XXIII.
2383 SCHURÉ, E. 1912. *The Great Initiates* (1889), 2 vols.
2384 SEIDLITZ, W. VON. 1900. *Über Farbengebung*.
2385 SERWER, J. D. 1987. *Gene Davis: a Memorial Exhibition*, Washington, National Museum of American Art.
2386 SEVERINI, G. 1921. *Du Cubisme au Classicisme*.
2387 SOUPAULT, P. 1963. 'Quand j'étais l'élève de Kandinsky', *Jardin des Arts*, CIII.
2388 SPATE, V. 1979. *Orphism: the Evolution of non-Figurative Painting in Paris, 1910–14*.
2389 STELLA, F. 1986. *Working Space*.
2390 *Gunta Stölzl, Weberei am Bauhaus und aus eigener Werkstatt*. 1987. Berlin, Bauhaus Archiv-Museum, exh. cat.
2391 TORBRUEGGE, M. K. 1974. 'Goethe's theory of color and practising artists', *Germanic Review*, XLIX.
2392 TUCKER, M. 1971. *The Structure of Color*, New York, Whitney Museum.
2393 *Bart van der Leck 1876–1958*. 1980. Paris, Institut Néerlandais, exh. cat.
2394 VANTONGERLOO, G. 1924. *L'Art et son avenir*.
2395 VELDE, H. VAN DE. 1902. *Kunstgewerblichen Laienpredigten*.
2396 —. 1962. *Geschichte meines Lebens*.
2397 VENZMER, W. 1982. *Adolf Hoelzel – Leben und Werk, Monographie und Werkverzeichnis*.
2398 VRIESEN, G. and IMDAHL, M. 1967. *Robert Delaunay – Licht und Farbe*.
2399 *The Washington Color Painters*. 1965/6. Washington, Gallery of Modern Art, exh. cat.
2400 WEBER, N. F. 1984. *The Drawings of Josef Albers*.
2401 WELLIVER, N. 1966. 'Albers on Albers', *Art News*, LXIV.
2402 WELSH, R. P. and JOOSTEN, J. 1969. *Two Mondrian Sketchbooks, 1912–14*.
2403 WHITFORD, F. 1984. *Bauhaus*.
2404 WICK, R. 1982. *Bauhaus Pädagogik*.
2405 WILK, C. 1981. *Marcel Breuer: Furniture and Interiors*.
2406 WINGLER, H. M. (ed.). 1977. *Kunstschulreform 1900–1933*.
2407 WINTER, G. 1984. 'Durchblick oder Vision. Zur Genese des modernen Bildbegriffs am Beispiel von R. Delaunays "Fenster-Bildern"', *Pantheon*, XLII.
2408 WRIGHT, W. D. 1981. 'The nature of blackness in art and visual perception', *Leonardo*, XIV.

LIST OF ILLUSTRATIONS

Shield of Faith from Peraldus, *Summa de Vitiis*, *c.*1240/55. MS Harley 3244, folio 28, British Library, London.

53 Funeral effigy of Geoffrey Plantagenet, 1151/60. Enamel, 63 × 33 ($24\frac{7}{8}$ × 13). Musée Tessé, Le Mans. Photo Musées du Mans.

54 Attributed to Byrtferth of Ramsey, *The four-fold system of Macrocosm and Microcosm*, *c.*1080–90. MS St John's College 17, folio 7v. The President and Fellows of St John's College, Oxford.

55 Joachim of Flora, *The Holy Trinity*, from *Liber Figurarum*, twelfth century. MS CCC. 255 A, folio 7v. Courtesy of the President and Fellows of Corpus Christi College, Oxford. Photo Bodleian Library, Oxford.

56 Ambrogio Lorenzetti, *Maestà* (detail), *c.*1335. Oil on canvas. Palazzo Communale, Massa Marittima. Photo Scala.

57 D.P.G. Humbert de Superville, *Synoptic Table*, 1827. From Humbert de Superville, *Essai sur les Signes inconditionnels dans l'Art*, Leyden 1827–32.

58 George Field, Armorial bookplate. From Field, *Chromatics*, London 1817. Photo Fitzwilliam Museum, Cambridge.

59 The Story of Noah, from Aelfric, *Paraphrase of the Pentateuch and Joshua*, Anglo-Saxon, second quarter of eleventh century. Vellum, 32.8 × 21.7 ($12\frac{7}{8}$ × $8\frac{1}{2}$). MS Cotton Claudius B.IV, folio 16v. British Library, London.

60 *Allegory of Judgment*, from Cesare Ripa, *Iconologia*, Padua 1611.

61 Rainbow in the story of Noah, from Hartmann Schedel, *Weltchronik* (*The Nuremberg Chronicle*), Nuremberg 1493.

62 Pietro Testa, *Triumph of Painting on Parnassus* (detail), early 1640s. Engraving, second state, 47.6 × 72.5 ($18\frac{3}{4}$ × $28\frac{1}{2}$). Collection Bertarelli, Castello Sforzesco, Milan.

63 *The formation of the rainbow*, from J.J. Scheuchzer, *Physica Sacra*, Augsburg and Ulm 1 1731.

64 *God's Covenant with Noah*, from the *Vienna Genesis*, sixth century. ? Syria. Cod. Theol. Graec. 31, page 5. Österreichische Nationalbibliothek, Vienna.

65 *Noah's Ark*, from a *Book of Hours*, Normandy, *c.*1430/50. MS Auct D Inf 2.11 folio 59v. Bodleian Library, Oxford.

66 Matthias Grünewald, *Stuppach Madonna*, 1517/19. Oil on canvas on pine, 185 × 150 ($72\frac{7}{8}$ × 59). St Maria, Stuppach. Photo Kapellenpflege 'Stuppacher Madonna', Stuppach.

67 Peter Paul Rubens, *Rainbow Landscape*, 1636/8. Oil on oak panel, 135.6 × 235 ($53\frac{3}{8}$ × $92\frac{1}{2}$). The Wallace Collection, London.

68 Jacob van Ruisdael, *The Jewish Cemetery* (detail), 1670s. Oil on canvas, 42 × 89 (56 × 74). The Detroit Institute of Arts.

69 Angelika Kauffmann, *Self-portrait as 'Painting'*, *c.*1780. Oil on canvas, 132 × 149.8 (52 × 59). Royal Academy of Arts, London.

70 After Johann Wolfgang von Goethe, *Mountain Landscape with Rainbow*, 1826. Coloured copper engraving, 4.7 × 10.7 ($1\frac{7}{8}$ × $4\frac{1}{4}$). Goethe-und-Schiller Archiv, Weimar. Photo Stiftung Weimarer Klassik.

71 John Glover (1767–1849), *A Rainbow*. Watercolour, 24 × 60 ($9\frac{1}{2}$ × $23\frac{5}{8}$). British Museum, London.

72 John Constable, *London from Hampstead, with a double rainbow*, inscribed 'between 6 & 7 o'clock Evening June 1831'. Watercolour, 19.6 × 32.2 ($7\frac{3}{4}$ × $12\frac{3}{4}$). British Museum, London.

73, J.M.W. Turner, *Durham Cathedral*
74 with a Rainbow, 1801. Watercolour, each 17.4 × 12.3 ($6\frac{7}{8}$ × $4\frac{7}{8}$). The Turner Collection, Tate Gallery, London.

75 Andy Goldsworthy, *Rainbow Splash, River Wharf, Yorkshire, October 1980*. Courtesy of the artist.

76 Matthew Paris, *Parhelia seen in 1233* from *Chronica Majora*. MS 16, folio 83v, Corpus Christi College, Cambridge. Reproduced by permission of the Master and Fellows of Corpus Christi College, Cambridge. Photo Courtauld Institute of Art, University of London.

77 John Sell Cotman, *Parhelion at Hunstanton*, 6 July 1815. Sepia drawing, 28.5 × 19 ($11\frac{1}{4}$ × $7\frac{1}{2}$). Leeds City Art Galleries. Photo Courtauld Institute of Art, University of London.

78 Caspar David Friedrich, *Landscape with Lunar Rainbow*, 1808. Oil on canvas, 70 × 102.5 ($27\frac{1}{2}$ × $40\frac{3}{8}$). Folkwang Museum, Essen.

79 Sir Thomas Lawrence, *Benjamin West PRA*, *c.*1821. Oil on canvas, 268.3 × 176.8 ($105\frac{5}{8}$ × $69\frac{5}{8}$). Tate Gallery, London.

80 Philipp Otto Runge, *Day*, 1803. Pen and wash, 71.7 × 48 ($28\frac{1}{4}$ × 19). Drawing for the series *Times of Day*. Kunsthalle, Hamburg.

81 Carl Gustav Carus, *Allegory on the death of Goethe*, after 1832. Oil on canvas, 40 × 56 ($15\frac{3}{4}$ × 22). Goethe Museum, Frankfurt.

82 David Lucas after John Constable, *Salisbury Cathedral from the Meadows, The Rainbow*, *c.*1835. Mezzotint, 55.1 × 69.2 ($21\frac{5}{8}$ × $27\frac{1}{4}$). Private collection.

83 John Constable, *Diagram of the formation of colours in drops of water*, *c.*1833. Pen and pencil, 16.2 × 19.7 ($6\frac{3}{8}$ × $7\frac{3}{4}$). Private collection.

84 Karl Friedrich Schinkel, *Medieval Town on a River*, 1815. Oil on canvas, 94 × 140 (37 × $55\frac{1}{8}$). Nationalgalerie, Staatliche Museen Preussischer Kulturbesitz, Berlin.

85 J.M.W. Turner, *Buttermere Lake with part of Cromackwater, Cumberland, a shower*, 1798. Oil on canvas, 88.9 × 119.4 (35 × 47). The Turner Collection, Tate Gallery, London.

86 Franz Marc, *Blue Horses with Rainbow*, 1913. Watercolour, gouache and pencil on paper, 16.2 × 25.7 ($6\frac{3}{8}$ × $10\frac{1}{8}$). Collection, The Museum of Modern Art, New York. John S. Newberry Collection.

87 Fra Bartolommeo, *Pala della Signoria*, *c.*1512. Monochrome on wood, 444 × 305 ($174\frac{3}{4}$ × 120). Museo di San Marco, Florence. Photo Alinari.

88 Fra Angelico, *The Annunciation*, *c.*1434. Oil on canvas, 150 × 180 (59 × $70\frac{7}{8}$). Museo Diocesano, Cortona. Photo Scala.

89 Attributed to Benedetto di Bindo, *Madonna of Humility* and *St Jerome translating the Gospel of John*, diptych, *c.*1400. Oil on wood, 29.2 × 41.9 ($11\frac{1}{2}$ × $16\frac{1}{2}$). Philadelphia Museum of Art, John G. Johnson Collection.

90 Stefano di Giovanni, called Sassetta, *St Francis renouncing his heritage*, 1437/44. Panel from an altarpiece, tempera on wood, *c.*87.6 × 52.7 ($34\frac{1}{2}$ × $20\frac{3}{4}$). National Gallery, London

91 Jan van Eyck, *The Virgin with Chancellor Rolin* (detail), *c.*1437. Oil on wood. Musée du Louvre, Paris. Photo Réunion des musées nationaux.

92 Andrea Mantegna, *Parnassus* (detail), Apollo and the Nine Muses, *c.*1497. Oil on canvas. Musée du Louvre, Paris. Photo Réunion des musées nationaux.

93 Leonardo da Vinci, *Ginevra de' Benci*, *c.*1474. Oil on wood, 38.8 × 36.7 ($15\frac{1}{4}$ × $14\frac{1}{2}$). National Gallery of Art, Washington. Ailsa Mellon Bruce Fund.

94 Michelangelo, lunette with *Eleazar* (detail), *c.*1510. Sistine Chapel, Vatican Palaces. Photo Vatican Museums.

95 Federico Barocci, *Il Perdono di Assisi*, 1574/6. Oil on canvas, 410 × 220 ($161\frac{3}{8}$ × $86\frac{5}{8}$). S.Francesco, Urbino. Photo Scala.

96 Workshop of Taddeo Gaddi, *Presentation of the Virgin*, after 1330. Silverpoint with white heightening and colours on paper, 36.4 × 28.3 ($14\frac{3}{8}$ × $11\frac{1}{8}$). Musée du Louvre, Paris. Photo Réunion des musées nationaux.

97 Leonardo da Vinci, *Adoration of the Magi*, *c.*1481. Oil on wood, 243.8 × 246.4 (96 × 97). Uffizi Gallery, Florence. Photo Alinari.

98 Leonardo da Vinci, *The Madonna and Child with Cat*, *c.*1478. Pen, ink and wash, 33.5 × 24.1 ($13\frac{1}{4}$ × $9\frac{1}{2}$). British Museum, London.

99 Mariotto Albertinelli, *The Annunciation*, 1510. Oil on canvas, 325 × 230 ($127\frac{7}{8}$ × $90\frac{1}{2}$). Accademia, Florence. Photo Alinari.

100 Federico Barocci, study for head of St Francis in *Il Perdono di Assisi* (pl. 95). Coloured pastels, 34.5 × 26.8 ($13\frac{1}{2}$ × $10\frac{1}{2}$). National Gallery of Scotland, Edinburgh.

101 The Peacock, from Gregory the Great, *Moralia in Job*, written and illuminated by the monk Florentius, 945. Biblioteca Nacional, Madrid. Photo Mas.

102 Cosimo Rosselli, *The Giving of the Law and the Adoration of the Golden Calf* (detail). Fresco, *c.*1481. Sistine Chapel, Vatican Palaces. Photo Vatican Museums.

103 Matthias Grünewald, *The Resurrection* from the Isenheim Altar (detail), *c.*1515. Oil on panel. Musée Unterlinden, Colmar. Photo Max Seidel.

104 Martin Schaffner, *The Heavenly Universe*, 1533. Wooden painted table-top, 108.5 × 111.7 ($42\frac{3}{4}$ × $46\frac{1}{4}$) Hessisches Museum, Kassel

105 *The White Rose*, manuscript, *c.*1550. From H. Reusner (ed.) *Pandora: Das ist die edelst Gab Gottes*, Basel, 1582. MS L IV 1, p66. Universitätsbibliothek, Basel.

106 Jan van Eyck, *Giovanni Arnolfini and Giovanna Cenami (The Arnolfini Marriage)*, 1434. Oil on oak, 81.8 × 59.7 ($32\frac{1}{4}$ × $23\frac{1}{2}$). National Gallery, London.

107 Francesco Mazzuoli called Parmigianino, *The Madonna of the Rose*, 1528/30. Oil on oak, 109 × 88.5 ($42\frac{7}{8}$ × $34\frac{7}{8}$). Gemäldegalerie Alte Meister, Dresden. Photo Deutsche Fotothek, Dresden.

108 Giulio Campagnola, *Landscape with Two Men*, *c.*1510. Pen and brown ink, 134 × 258 ($52\frac{3}{4}$ × $101\frac{1}{2}$). Musée du Louvre, Paris. Photo Réunion des musées nationaux.

109 Francesco Mazzuoli called Parmigianino, *Woman seated on the ground (St Thais?)*. Etching, 13 × 11.2 ($5\frac{1}{8}$ × $4\frac{3}{8}$). British Museum, London.

110 William Blake, *A Memorable Fancy*, from Blake, *The Marriage of Heaven and Hell*, 1790–3. Relief etching,

181 Paolo Veronese, *The Marriage at Cana* (detail), 1563. Oil on canvas. Musée du Louvre, Paris. Photo Réunion des musées nationaux.

182 Gioseffo Zarlino, Table of harmonic proportions from Zarlino, *Istituni Harmoniche*, Venice 1573.

183 François d'Aguilon, Colour scale from d'Aguilon, *Opticorum Libri Sex*, Book I, Antwerp 1613.

184 Marin Cureau de la Chambre, Table of musical harmony of colours, from Cureau de la Chambre, *Nouvelles Observations et Conjectures sur l'Iris*, Paris 1650.

185 René Descartes, Circle of major and minor tones, from Descartes, *Compendium Musicae*, Utrecht 1650.

186 G.G. Guyot, *Musique Oculaire*, 1769 from Guyot, *Nouvelles Recreations physiques et metaphysiques*, Vol. III, Paris 1769. By permission of the Houghton Library, Harvard University, Cambridge, MA.

187 Francis Webb, *Panharmonicon* (detail), London 1815.

188 Attributed to Paul Bril (1554–1626), *Artist playing a lute*. Oil on canvas, 70.8 × 77.1 ($27\frac{7}{8} × 30\frac{3}{8}$). Museum of Art, Rhode Island School of Design, Providence, RI. Museum appropriation. Photo Cathy Carver.

189 Paul Klee, *Ad Parnassum*, 1932. Oil on canvas, 100 × 126 ($39\frac{3}{8} × 49\frac{5}{8}$). Verein der Freunde, Kunstmuseum, Bern.

190 Paul Klee, Exercises in mirror-reversal in coloured grids, c.1922. Paul-Klee-Stiftung, Kunstmuseum, Bern.

191 Piet Mondrian, *Victory Boogie-Woogie*, 1943/4. Oil on canvas, 126 × 126 ($49\frac{5}{8} × 49\frac{5}{8}$). Private collection.

192 Wassily Kandinsky, *Composition VI*, 1913. Oil on canvas, 195 × 300 ($76\frac{3}{4} × 118\frac{1}{8}$). Hermitage Museum, St Petersburg.

193 Morgan Russell, *Creavit Deus Hominem (Synchromy No. 3: Color Counterpoint)*, 1914. Oil on canvas mounted on cardboard, 30.2 × 26 ($11\frac{7}{8} × 10\frac{1}{4}$). Collection, The Museum of Modern Art, New York. Given anonymously.

194 Theo van Doesburg, *Ragtime (Composition in Greys)*, 1918. Oil on canvas, 95 × 58.5 ($37\frac{3}{8} × 23$). Peggy Guggenheim Collection, Venice.

195 Scriabin, score for the *Prometheus Symphony*, page 1.

196 Performance of Scriabin's *Prometheus Symphony*, from *Scientific American*, April 1915.

197 Mary Hallock Greenewalt, design for *A Light-Color Play Console*, 1927. From Greenewalt, *Nourathar: The Fine Art of Color-Light Playing*, Philadelphia, 1946.

198 *Thomas Wilfred rehearsing a composition*, from A.B. Klein, *Coloured Light: an Art Medium*, London 1937.

199 Gerrit Rietveld, *Red-Blue Chair*. Reconstruction. Black-stained frame, lacquered seat and back, 88 × 65.5 × 83 ($34\frac{5}{8} × 25\frac{3}{4} × 32\frac{5}{8}$). Cassina SpA.

200 Georges Vantongerloo, *Triptiech (Triptych)*, 1921. Oil on wood, middle panel 12.5 × 11 ($4\frac{7}{8} × 4\frac{3}{8}$), side panels 11 × 6.5 ($4\frac{3}{8} × 2\frac{1}{2}$). Private collection, The Netherlands.

201 Mondrian, *Composition C*, 1920. Oil on canvas, 60.3 × 51 ($23\frac{3}{4} × 24$). Collection, The Museum of Modern Art, New York. Acquired through the Lillie P. Bliss Bequest.

202 Illustration of 'film color', from Josef Albers, *Die Wechselbeziehungen der Farbe* (Interaction of Color), (XVII–1), Starnberg 1973.

203 *Advancing and Retiring Colors*, from Emily C. Noyes Vanderpoel, *Color Problems. A Practical Manual for the Lay Student of Color*, New York 1902.

204 *Goethe-triangle*, Barry Schactman and Rackstraw Downes after Carry van Biema, from Josef Albers, *Die Wechselbeziehungen der Farbe* (Interaction of Color), XXIV–1, Starnberg 1973.

205 Wilhelm Ostwald, *Section through the colour-solid*, from Josef Albers, *Die Wechselbeziehungen der Farbe* (Interaction of Color), XXIV–2, Starnberg 1973.

206 Josef Albers, *Homage to the Square*, 1950. Oil on masonite panel, unframed 52.3 × 52 ($20\frac{5}{8} × 20\frac{1}{2}$). Yale University Art Gallery, Gift of Anni Albers and the Josef Albers Foundation, Inc.

207 Giacomo Balla, *Iridescent Interpenetrations No. 13*, 1912. Tempera on canvas, 84 × 72 ($33 × 28\frac{3}{8}$). Galleria Civica d'Arte Moderna, Turin.

208 Robert Delaunay, *Sun, Moon, Simultané I*, 1913. Oil on canvas, 64 × 100 ($22\frac{1}{2} × 48\frac{3}{8}$). Stedelijk Museum, Amsterdam.

209 Sonia Delaunay, Patchwork coverlet, 1911. 100 × 81 ($39\frac{3}{8} × 31\frac{7}{8}$). Musée d'Art Moderne, Paris.

210 Helen Frankenthaler, *Mountains and Sea*, 1952. Oil on canvas, 220 × 297.8 ($86\frac{5}{8} × 117\frac{1}{4}$). Collection of the artist on loan to the National Gallery of Art, Washington DC.

211 Morris Louis, *Golden Age*, 1959. Acrylic on canvas, 230 × 378 ($90\frac{1}{2} × 148\frac{7}{8}$). Photograph reproduced by kind permission of the Trustees of the Ulster Museum.

212 Mark Rothko, *Orange Yellow Orange*, 1969. Oil on paper mounted on linen, 123.2 × 102.9 ($48\frac{1}{2} × 40\frac{1}{2}$). Photo Marlborough Gallery Inc., New York. © 1992 Kate Rothko-Prizel & Christopher Rothko/ARS, New York.

213 Kenneth Noland, *2–1964*, 1964. Acrylic on canvas, 172.7 × 172. ($68 × 68$). Kasmin Ltd.

214 Gene Davis, *Limelight/Sounds of Grass*, 1960. Magna on canvas, 234.9 × 226.6 ($92\frac{1}{2} × 89\frac{1}{4}$). Courtesy of the Estate of Gene Davis.

215 Vilmos Huszár, *Composition*, 1918. Technique, dimensions and whereabouts unknown.

216 Alfred Arndt, questionnaire for the Wallpainting workshop, Bauhaus, 1923. Bauhaus-Archiv, Berlin.

217 Johannes Itten, *Forms and Colours*. From Itten, *The Art of Color*, New York 1961.

218 Timetable for the Preliminary Course (detail), Bauhaus, Weimar, c.1924. Thuringian State Archive, Weimar.

219 Frantisek Kupka, version of Newton's wheel, c.1910. From Kupka, *Tvorení V Umení Výtvarném (Creation in the Plastic Arts)*, Prague, 1923.

220 Paul Klee, *Suspended Fruit*, 1921. Watercolour and pencil on textured paper, mounted on green wove paper on cardboard, 24.8 × 15.2 ($9\frac{3}{4} × 6$). The Metropolitan Museum of Art, The Berggruen Klee Collection, 1984.

221 Josef Albers, The 'Goethe Triangle' divided into 'expressive colour combinations', from Albers *Interaction of Color*, London and New Haven 1963.

222 Frank Stella at work in his studio, New York. Photo M. Knoedler and Co. Inc., New York.

INDEX

Pantokrator 45, 48, 70, 276 n.103
Panziera, Ugo 117
papier de Gauguin 205
Paracelsus 140
Paradise, rivers of 40, 74, *20*
paragone 228–9
Parament of Narbonne 117
parhelia 93, 105, *76, 77*
Paris, Matthew 82, 83, 108, 274 n.90, *43, 76*
Parmigianino 149, 284 n.66, *107, 109*
Passavant, J.D. 203
pastels 135, 138, 296 n.69, *100*
Pasteur, Louis 214
patronage 15, 129, 131, 144, 156, 287 n.41, 288 n.44
Paul the Silentiary 39, 46, 47, 48, 275 n.45
Paulinus of Nola 57, 69
Pausanius 271 n.45, 276 n.93
Peale, Charles Willson 187
Pecham, John 133, 282 n.103, 284 n.27
Peiresc, Nicholas Claude Fabri de 95
Pèlerinage de Charlemagne 278 n.41
Pepusch, J.C. 232
Peraldus 52
Peripatetics (*see also* Theophrastus) 31, 108, 227
    On Audible Things 296 n.3
Perkin, Sir William, 221
Pernety, A.-J. 292 n.74
Perrot, Catherine 291 n.24
Persian fashion 61–2, 277 n.156
perspective, single-point 58, 118, 119, 228
Perugino, Pietro 143–4
Peter of Poitiers 83
Peter of St Omer (Audemar) 280 n.45
Peter the Venerable 84
Petra-Sancta, P. Silvestre de 91
Petrini, Pietro 191
Petronius 15, 30
Petty, Sir William 154
Pfannenschmidt, A.L. 216, 221
Pforr, Franz 204
Pheidias 271 col.3 n.5, *4*
Philander, Georges 35, 274 n.92
Phillips, Thomas 274 n.114
Philo of Alexandria 14, 63
Philostratus 15, 25, 26, 48, 117
Photius 44, 48, 276 nn.115, 136
photography, black and white 9, 117, 291 n.61
photometer 222
Picasso, Pablo 63, 268, 277 n.171
Piccolpasso, Cipriano 285 n.131
Picturesque movement 105
Piero di Cosimo 143
Pietro da Cortona 149
Pietro della Francesca 120, *129*
PIGMENTS (*see also* colours)
    29, 30, 31, 35, 129, 131, 133, 136, 137, 139, 150, 167, 168, 178, 187, 188, Ch.12 *passim*, 213, 214, 215, 221–4, 271 nn.44, 49, 273 n.70, 284 nn.65, 66, 68, 70, 285 nn.130, 131, 286 n.2, 287 nn.71, 21, 291 nn.71, 78, 302 n.154, *103, 115, 117, 139, 150, 151, 178*
    'Antwerp blue' 295 n.2
    atramentum 29, 30, 35, 167
    azurite 35, 129, 131, 167, 168
    bice 288 n.60
    brown-pink 216
    cadmiums 223, 224, 293 n.98
    chrome-yellow 296 n.66
    chrysocolla 273 n.41
    cinnabar *see* vermilion
    cobalt blue 38, 215, 224, 291 n.71
    cobalt glass 291 n.24
    copper-green 172, 286 n.80
    crimson 26, 129, 130, 284 n.62
    giallorino 35, 167, 223, 284 n.70
    indigo 12, 73, 90, 167, 216, 232, 259,
272 n.66
    lapis-lazuli *see* ultramarine
    lead-white 134, 137, *99, 191*
    lemon-yellow 295 n.35
    madder-lake 137, 169, 215, 221, 291 n.71, 295 nn.35, 47, 296 n.64
    miltos (red ochre) 30
    minium (red lead) 30, 77, 172
    Naples yellow 188, 223, 224, 295 n.47, 296 nn.64, 68, 69
    Prussian blue 169, 213, 216, 221, 295 nn.2, 14, 296 n.83
    rubrica 30
    schitgeel 167, 169–70
    sinopis 29, 30, 35, 82
    synthetic and industrial 9, 134, 137, 139, 150, 152, 206, 214, 215, 216, 221, 222–4, 267–8, 274 n.87, 286 n.2, 287 n.80, 295 nn.15, *178, 210, 211, 213, 222*
    ultramarine 9, 35, 73, 82, 129, 130, 131, 141, 144, 149, 166, 167, 168, 178, 215, 216, 221, 278 n.41, 280 n.34, 284 n.66, 288 nn.41, 44, 295 nn.35, 47, 296 n.64, *89, 115, 117,* French 291 n.71, 302 n.158
    Van Dyke brown 291 n.87
    vermilion 30, 31, 129, 130, 131, 139, 150, 152, 168, 169, 216, 223, 273, n.40, 286 nn.2, 3, 287 n.80, *103, 115*
    vert émeraude (viridian) 223, 224
    zinc yellow 295 n.18, *178*
Pino, Paolo 131, 132, 137, 230, 273 n.80
Pinturicchio, Bernardino 94, 131, 144, 201, 282 n.72
Piper, John 9
Pissarro, Camille 176, 187, 211, 224, 283 n.173, 291 n.71, 294 n.154, 296 n.66, *146*
PLACES AND MONUMENTS
Aegina, Temple of Aphaia 26
Albenga, Baptistry 45, *25*
Amsterdam, Moderne Kunstkring 248
Aquileia, Cathedral 40, 57
Arezzo, S.Francesco 120
Arta, Paragoritissa 45, 275 n.38
Assisi, S.Francesco 7, 61, 76–7, *46*
Athens:
    Kerameikos 26
    Parthenon 11, *4*
    Temple of Ilissus 271 col.2 n.3
Augsburg, Cathedral 70
Baia, Temple of Diana 275 n.57
Berlin, Jahrhundertsausstellung 208
Boscotrecase 16
Bottrup 264
Budakshan (Afghanistan) 131
Caen, St Nicholas 278 n.33
Cambridge, King's College Chapel 81
Chartres 69, 278 n.12
Chios, Nea Moni 41, 58, 59, 60, 61
Chiusi 25
Constantinople:
    Christ in Chora (Karije Djami) 27, 42, 47, 48, 60, *27, 55*
    Great Palace 48, 57
    Holy Apostles 59
    Pammacaristos (Fetiye Djami) 45
    Sta Eirene 41, 43, 48
    St George of Mangana 57
    Sta Sophia 39, 41, 43, 44, 45, 46, 47, 57, 130, 275 nn.41, 67, 276 n.79, *29*
    Virgin of Pharos (Palatine Chapel) 44, 276 n.115
Damascus, Great Mosque 64
Daphni 45, 58, 60, 275 n.27, *39*
Delos, House of the Masks 41
Delphi, Siphnian Treasury 16
el-Fayum 31, *8*
Epidauros, Asclepion 16
Euganean Hills 149

Florence:
    Orsanmichele 286 n.26
    S.Croce 9, 120, 156, 279 n.103, 283 n.8
    S.Lorenzo *87*
    Sta Maria del Carmine, Brancacci Chapel 284 n.20
    Sta Maria Novella, Strozzi Chapel 131
    S.Miniato al Monte 132
Gaza:
    St Sergius 40
    St Stephen 39
Gerasa, St John the Baptist 40
Germigny-des-Prés 275 n.41
Ghumdan (Yemen), Palace, 277 n.185
Grado, Sta Eufemia 57, *38*
Halicarnassus, Mausoleum 11
Harvard University, Rothko murals 267
Hawara 31, 273 n.30
Heraclea Lyncestis (Bitola) 40, 42
Herculaneum 16, 36, 40, 41, 272 n.9, 273 n.28, 274 n.105
Hosios Loukas 45, 58, 275 n.27
Istanbul (*see also* Constantinople)
    Pera Palace Hotel 46
Jarrow 278 n.33
Jerusalem:
    Church of the Holy Sepulchre 57, 58
    Church of the Resurrection 57
    Dome of the Rock 64
Karaburun 272 n.15
Kastoria, Moni Mavriotissa 61
Kazanlak 29
Kiev, Sta Sophia 45, 48, 276 n.117
Kizilbel 30
Knossos 11, 15, 30
Lefkadia 29
Le Mans, Cathedral 278 n.33
Lincoln, Cathedral 74
London:
    The British School 215
    Crystal Palace 221
    Society of Arts 213
Milan:
    Ambrosian Basilica 41
    S.Lorenzo, Chapel of S.Aquilino 275 n.37
Mistra, Church of the Hodegetria 276 n.123
Monboso, Mount 133
Monkwearmouth 278 n.33
Monreale, Cathedral 41, 46
Morgantina 16
Murnau 105, 283 n.173
Mycenae 11, 30
Naples, Baptistry 45
Nerezi 60
Nola, Basilica of St Felix 69
Orvieto, Cathedral 284 n.64
Olympia, Temple of Zeus 271 n.45
Padua, Scrovegni Chapel 283 nn.3, 7
Paestum, Tomb of the Diver 30, *5*
Palermo 61, 129
    Palatine Chapel 39–40, 41, 276 n.76, *21*
    Stanza del Re Ruggero 44
Palestrina, Temple of Fortune 40, 57, *20*
Paris:
    Bernheim Jeune 189
    Church of St Vincent 57
    Delacroix Museum, Place Furstenberg 174, 186
    Ecole des Beaux-Arts 187, 210, 211, 214, 221
    Ecole Polytechnique 215
    Exposition des Arts Décoratifs 246
    Galerie Georges Petit 189
    Louvre, Salle d'Apollon 174, 189, *128*

Palais Bourbon 173, 186, 290 n.57
Palais du Luxembourg 173–4
Sainte-Chapelle 281 n.98
Saint-Denis du Saint-Sacrément 174
Sorbonne, Laboratory of the Physiology of Sensations 259
Val-de-Grace 165
Pergamon 16, 93
Piazza Armerina 40, 57, 62
Poitiers, Cathedral 70, 278 n.33
Pompeii 15, 16, 26, 30, 31, 40, 41, 43, 273 n.28, *14*
Ponte Aven 206, 293 n.91
Poreč 41, 45, 275 n.61
Prousa 276 n.123
Ravenna:
    Arian Baptistry 40, 45
    Basilica Ursiana 48
    'Mausoleum' of Galla Placida 41, 46, 276 n.108, *30*
    Monastery of St Andrew the Apostle 46
    S.Apollinare in Classe 46, 275 n.26
    S.Apollinare Nuovo 43, 48, 61, 275 n.37, 276 n.139, *40*
    S.Vitale 45, 46, 48, 61, 73
Rheims, Cathedral 78
Rome:
    Chapel of John VII 48
    Farnesina 288 n.45
    Gesù 165, *113, 121*
    Lupercal Chapel 45
    S.Agostino, Chapel of SS.Agostino and Guglielmo, 165
    S.Andrea della Valle, 165, 178, *112*
    SS.Cosmas and Damian 40, 45, 46, *32*
    S.Clemente 45
    Sta Costanza 40, 41, 284 n.18, *26*
    Sta Francesca Romana 45
    S.Ignazio 165
    St John Lateran 276 n.86, 278 n.33
    S.Lorenzo fuori le Mura 41
    S.Luigi dei Francesi, Contarelli Chapel 156, 165
    Sta Maria Maggiore 43, 48, 73, 275 nn.37, 41, 276 n.76, *42*
    Sta Maria del Popolo, Cerasi Chapel 156
    Sta Maria in Trastevere 276 n.123, 278 n.33
    S.Pancrazio 275 n.61
    St Peter's 62
        Mausoleum of the Julii 40
    Sta Prassede, Chapel of S.Zeno 42, 275 n.37, *28*
    Sta Pudenziana 41
    Sta Sabina 39
    S.Stefano Rotondo 276 n.107
    Vatican, Sistine Chapel 143–4, 149, *94, 102*
St Denis, Abbey Church 69–73, 278 n.23, *41, 45*
Saqqâra 30, 7
Schaffhausen, Rhine Falls 105
Selinunte, Temple of Empedocles *11*
Sens, Cathedral of St Etienne 78, *48*
Serra Orlando 16
Sfax, Museum 276 n.86
Siena:
    Cathedral 69
    Piccolomini Library 131, 201
Sinai, Monastery of St Catherine 31, 41, 43, 60, *33*
La Skhirra, Baptistry 276 n.86
Soganli, Sta Barbara 276 n.123
Soissons, Cathedral 278 n.24
Staro Nagoričane 48, 58
Strasbourg, Café Aubette 300 n.47
Stuppach, Parish Church *66*
Tarquinia 15
Terni, falls at 105